To the many teachers, principals, counselors, psychologists, nurses, and other educational professionals who cherish every child in their care.

Seventh Edition

Child Development and Education

Teresa M. McDevitt
University of Northern Colorado, Emerita

Jeanne Ellis Ormrod
University of Northern Colorado, Emerita

Pearson

Director and Publisher: Kevin M. Davis
Content Producer: Janelle Rogers
Sr. Development Editor: Alicia Reilly
Media Producer: Lauren Carlson
Portfolio Management Assistant: Maria Feliberty
Executive Field Marketing Manager: Krista Clark
Executive Product Marketing Manager: Christopher Barry
Procurement Specialist: Carol Melville
Full Service Project Management: Pearson CSC, Kathy Smith
Cover Designer: Pearson CSC
Cover Image: © GettyImages/GlobalStock
Composition: Pearson CSC
Printer/Binder: LSC Communications
Cover Printer: LSC Communications
Text Font: Palatino LT Pro

Library of Congress Cataloging-in-Publication Data
Names: McDevitt, Teresa M., author. | Ormrod, Jeanne Ellis, author.
Title: Child development and education / Teresa M. McDevitt, University of Northern Colorado, Emerita, Jeanne Ellis Ormrod, University of Northern Colorado, Emerita.
Description: Seventh Edition. | Hoboken, NJ : Pearson, [2019] | Includes bibliographical references and indexes.
Identifiers: LCCN 2018049761 | ISBN 9780134806778 | ISBN 0134806778
Subjects: LCSH: Child development. | Adolescent psychology. | Educational psychology.
Classification: LCC LB1115 .M263 2019 | DDC 305.231--dc23
LC record available at https://lccn.loc.gov/2018049761

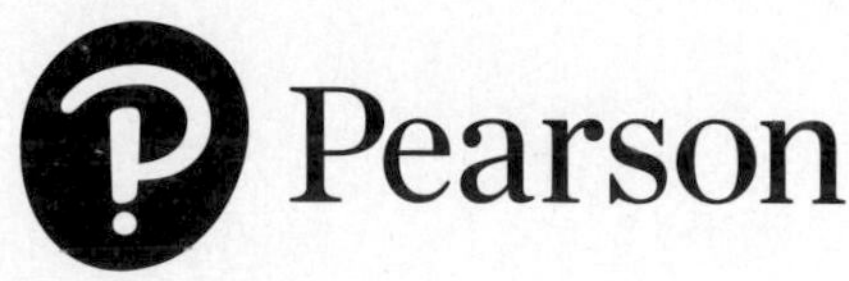

ISBN 10: 0-13-480677-8
ISBN 13: 978-0-13-480677-8

About the Authors

Teresa M. McDevitt (left) is a psychologist with specializations in child development and educational psychology. She received a Ph.D. and M.A. in child development from Stanford University's Psychological Studies in Education program, an Ed.S. in educational evaluation from Stanford University, and a B.A. in psychology from the University of California, Santa Cruz. Now Professor Emerita of Psychological Sciences at the University of Northern Colorado, she served the University of Northern Colorado since 1985 in a variety of capacities—in teaching courses in child psychology, human development, educational psychology, program evaluation, and research methods; advisement of graduate students; administration and university governance; and research and grant writing. Her research focuses on child development, families, and teacher education. She has published articles in *Child Development, Learning and Individual Differences, Child Study Journal, Merrill-Palmer Quarterly, Youth and Society,* and *Science Education,* among others. She has gained practical experiences with children, including by raising two children with her husband and working as an early childhood teacher of toddlers and preschool children, early childhood special education teacher, and volunteer in school and community settings. Teresa enjoys spending time with her husband, their sons and their beloved partners, and, when she has the chance, traveling internationally with her family.

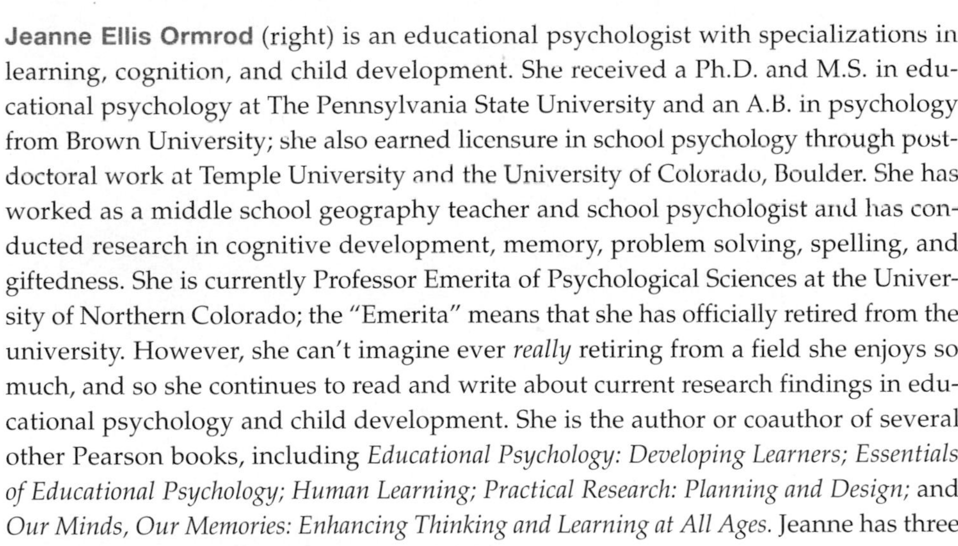

Jeanne Ellis Ormrod (right) is an educational psychologist with specializations in learning, cognition, and child development. She received a Ph.D. and M.S. in educational psychology at The Pennsylvania State University and an A.B. in psychology from Brown University; she also earned licensure in school psychology through postdoctoral work at Temple University and the University of Colorado, Boulder. She has worked as a middle school geography teacher and school psychologist and has conducted research in cognitive development, memory, problem solving, spelling, and giftedness. She is currently Professor Emerita of Psychological Sciences at the University of Northern Colorado; the "Emerita" means that she has officially retired from the university. However, she can't imagine ever *really* retiring from a field she enjoys so much, and so she continues to read and write about current research findings in educational psychology and child development. She is the author or coauthor of several other Pearson books, including *Educational Psychology: Developing Learners; Essentials of Educational Psychology; Human Learning; Practical Research: Planning and Design;* and *Our Minds, Our Memories: Enhancing Thinking and Learning at All Ages.* Jeanne has three grown children and three young grandchildren.

Preface

As psychologists and teacher educators, we have taught child and adolescent development for many years. Our primary intention has been to help students translate developmental concepts into practical implications in their own teaching. In past years, the child development textbooks available to our students were thorough in their descriptions of theory and research but limited in concrete suggestions for working with infants, children, and adolescents. With this book, now in its seventh edition, we bridge the gap between theory and practice. We draw from innumerable theoretical concepts; research studies conducted around the world; and our own experiences as parents, teachers, psychologists, and researchers to identify strategies for promoting young people's physical, cognitive, and social-emotional growth. As in the previous editions, this book focuses on childhood and the adolescent years and derives applications that are primarily educational in focus.

Several features of the book make it different from other textbooks about child and adolescent development. In particular, the book

- Continually relates abstract theories to educational practices in schools
- Not only describes but also *demonstrates* developmental phenomena
- Guides observations of children
- Facilitates analysis of what children say, do, and create
- Offers concrete strategies for effective teaching of, and working with, children
- Fosters a thorough understanding of children's growth from infancy to late adolescence within the domains of physical, social-emotional, and cognitive development.

In the next few pages, we explain and illustrate how the book helps readers learn how to:

- Apply developmental insights in their work with children
- Refine their observations, assessments, and decisions
- Appreciate and accommodate children's upbringing
- Take a strategic approach to learning concepts in child development.

Concepts and the multitude of exercises are organized within sections devoted to specific learning objectives. For each objective, readers can engage with several exercises that solidify conceptual understandings and practical knowledge. Readers can review children's artwork and essays, observe children's actions and statements in video clips, and check their comprehension at the end of each section, with explanations immediately accessible to confirm expectations and correct misconceptions.

Seventh Edition

A primary goal for the seventh edition was to deepen readers' ability to employ a developmentally informed manner with children. That has been our goal since the first edition, yet our motivation intensified with the rising tide of research on strategies for nurturing children's academic skills and resilience. There is so much to share! We also realized that telling the developmental story effectively required thoughtful attention to pedagogy. We knew from our teaching and reading that fostering conceptual change requires accurate information; repeated exposure to abstract, difficult, and counterintuitive ideas, a safe environment for trying out new knowledge; and feedback. We doubled our efforts to present concepts clearly, and we improved exercises by clarifying dimensions of a high-quality education. We hope that the resulting presentation is effective in promoting accomplishments in readers.

Focus on Development-Enhancing Education in the New Edition

In the seventh edition, we became more explicit about the whole and parts of developmentally informed instruction. To give our readers a coherent perspective on the field of child development, we distilled separate insights into a single notion. The insights came from investigations into developmentally appropriate practice, culturally responsive education, developmental systems perspectives, resilience, positive psychology, psychopathology and mental health, cognitive science, and youth-asset frameworks. Previously, these and other frameworks articulated single aspects of a high-quality education, yet collectively, they were fragmented. For the seventh edition, these frameworks were integrated into the powerful theme of a *development-enhancing education*.

Development-enhancing education refers to schooling that is warm, individualized, age appropriate, health promoting, culturally inclusive, and academically challenging. When teachers and other school professionals emulate these qualities, children thrive academically *and* developmentally. Educators need not choose between a strong education and attention to holistic childhood. With the right training, practice, and dispositions, educators can do both, and the result is a more vibrant learning environment for children. To help readers learn about development-enhancing education and its implications, we created several opportunities for exposure and practice:

1. In Chapter 1, the theme is introduced in text and its properties are illustrated in Table 1.2. Educators who provide children with a development-enhancing education exhibit five qualities: compassion, age-appropriate instruction, cultural inclusivity, attunement with individual needs, and encouragement of children's initiative.

Table 1.2 Properties of a Development-Enhancing Education

QUALITIES	EXAMPLES OF INDICATORS
Is compassionate with children	• Expresses interest, concern, and positive emotions when interacting with children • Over time establishes warm and secure relationships with children • Warmly invites children's contributions during class, validates their knowledge, and gently nudges them toward more advanced understandings
Harmonizes lessons, interactions, classroom procedures, and other services with children's age-related abilities	• Sets instructional objectives that are within the grasp of children • Selects academic concepts that are relevant, understandable, and consequential for children • Facilitates positive peer relationships in age-appropriate groups, classroom rules, and guidance on friendships
Is inclusive of the cultures, identities, and demographic backgrounds of the children, families, and communities being served	• Speaks to a classroom of children in a way that is inclusive and compatible with their cultural traditions • Shows sensitivity to the identities that children develop depending on their gender, race, ethnicity, religion, and national origin • Addresses the assets and hardships children experience in their communities
Is attentive to children's individual needs	• Designs instruction such that children of varying ability levels can achieve reasonable progress • Adapts instructional objectives, the format of the lesson, and assessment strategies for children for whom the lesson is not an optimally challenging exercise • Provides coaching for children who have trouble coping with transitions between subjects, dealing with anger or frustration, and attentional demands of school
Is encouraging of children's initiative during lessons, interactions, and decision making	• Arranges for children to share their knowledge at the beginning of a lesson, actively process information during the lesson, and demonstrate new knowledge at its conclusion • Allows children to make meaningful choices in curricular matters, for example, in which of several books to read or topics to examine in an essay • Engages children in active exploration of topics, for instance, by exploring a local habitat, acting out a scene in a play, and making predictions and analyzing data

2. The new *MyLab Education Application Exercise—Identify Development-Enhancing Education* asks readers to review videorecordings of lessons and interactions with children and determine which of the five qualities are present in the interactions recorded in the video. The same rubric is used in each exercise.

MyLab Education Application Exercise 6.1
Identify Development-Enhancing Education
In this video a fourth-grade science teacher scaffolds his students' scientific thinking.

3. New MyLab Education Application Exercises—*Detect Developmental Levels* and *Meet Individual Needs*—concentrate on two specific qualities of Development-Enhancing Education: age appropriateness and individualization. The *Detect Developmental Levels* exercises give learners practice in identifying age-appropriated tasks and curriculum. The *Meet Individual Needs* exercises help learners recognize and address variations in childrens' understandings and experiences.

MyLab Education Application Exercise 8.2
Detect Developmental Levels
How do children of different ages define freedom?

4. The *Development in Culture* features foster readers' sensitivity to the traditions and values children inherit from their cultures, another essential feature of a development-enhancing education.

Development In Culture

Playing Around

From the perspective of cultural learning, play is a productive medium through which children voluntarily socialize themselves into their community's traditions (Boyette, 2016; F. P. Hughes, 2010).

To some degree, lessons in cultural practices change as children grow. Early on, adults guide the direction of play. Mothers, fathers, and other adults invite infants to join games of peekaboo, pat-a-cake, and other good-humored exchanges that vary from one cultural group to the next. One psychologist, Heidi Keller, found distinct patterns in infant play in mothers and infants from urban German middle-class families and rural Cameroonian Nso families (H. Keller, 2003). German mothers tended to spend a considerable amount of time interacting verbally with their infants—talking with them and encouraging themselves—developing verbal skills and playing with objects in German families and staying physically close to mothers and exercising new motor skills in Nso families.

Children continue to integrate familiar cultural routines into play as they grow. In societies that encourage serious chores in children, children pretend to be adult laborers (F. P. Hughes, 2010). In Botswana, men herd oxen, and boys regularly play the "cow game." Taking on complementary roles, some boys pretend to be oxen yoked with twine, and others act as drivers who control them (Bock & Johnson, 2004). Girls pretend to pummel grain with reeds, sticks, dirt, and imaginary mortars (Bock & Johnson, 2004). In industrialized cultures that separate children from the daily work of adults, children are apt to include fantasy figures that they have seen on television and in video games (F. P. Hughes, 2010; Lehrer & Petrakos, 2011). Not every culture values or encourages pretend play, and in some groups children play creatively with objects and with one another without taking on defined roles (Farver & Shin, 1997; F. P. Hughes, 2010; Smilansky, 1968).

In middle childhood and after, youngsters participate in structured games. Children in many societies play competitive games, wherein participants follow prescribed rules and vie to be the winner (Bonta, 1997; F. P. Hughes, 2010). In hunting societies, children play games of physical dexterity, including foot races and contests of tracking and spear-throwing, pursuits that allow for practice of valuable motor skills. In nomadic groups, children play games whose outcomes are determined by chance, perhaps preparing them for largely uncontrollable environmental conditions, as their parents must do to survive.

PLAYTIME. These boys enjoy a morning swim at a lake in Sri Lanka. While sharing a fun pastime, they are acquiring cultural knowledge about friendship and leisure time.

5. In addition to formulating recommendations for teachers and other professionals throughout the text, we provide *Development-Enhancing Education* features with concrete techniques for facilitating children's development. To help readers move from research to practice, each strategy is followed by examples of a professional implementing it in a classroom or other setting. You will find the *Development-Enhancing Education* illustrations in every chapter.

Development-Enhancing Education

Scaffolding Children's Performance on Challenging Tasks

Ask questions that get children thinking about a task.

- A middle school teacher asks her students a series of questions as they prepare to deliver a persuasive speech: *What are the main points you want to make? Who will make them? What kind of objections and counterarguments can you anticipate? How will you respond to them?* (Early Adolescence)
- As students in a high school science class begin to plan their experiments for an upcoming science fair, their teacher encourages them to separate and control variables with the following questions: *What do I think causes the phenomenon I am studying? What other possible variables might influence it? How can I be sure which variables are influencing the results I obtain?* (Late Adolescence)

When learners are unfamiliar with a task, provide explicit guidance and give frequent feedback.

- A preschool teacher watches children attempt to write their names. With a girl who writes the sequence backward, the teacher puts a green dot under the first letter and tells her to start with it. With a boy who forgets a few letters, the teacher highlights missing letters with a color pen. With another boy, the teacher writes the letters he cannot remember and asks has him to add the letters he knows. (Early Childhood)
- When an outdoor educator takes 12-year-olds on their first camping trip, he has the children work in pairs to pitch their tents. Although he has previously shown the children how to put up a tent, this is the first time they've actually done it themselves, and so he provides a sequence of pictures with instructions for each step. In addition, he circulates among campsites and provides assistance as necessary. (Early Adolescence)

Teach children how to talk themselves through a complex procedure.

- A school psychologist teaches children with cognitive disabilities to classify shapes by asking themselves questions (e.g., Does the object have three or more sides? Is it round?). The children begin to ask themselves these questions and learn to classify shapes more accurately. (Middle Childhood)
- A physical education teacher shows beginning tennis players how to use self-instructions to remember correct form when swinging the racket:
    1. Say *ball* to remind yourself to look at the ball.
    2. Say *bounce* to remind yourself to follow the ball with your eyes as it approaches you.
    3. Say *hit* to remind yourself to focus on contacting the ball with the racket.
    4. Say *ready* to get yourself into position for the next ball to come your way. (Early Adolescence)

Divide a complex assignment into several smaller, simpler tasks, and ask children to complete each in small groups.

- A fourth-grade teacher has his students create a school newspaper with news articles, a schedule of upcoming events, a couple of political cartoons, and classified advertisements. Several students work together to create each feature, with students assuming distinct roles (e.g., fact finder, writer, editor) and occasionally switching parts. (Middle Childhood)
- A film analysis teacher asks high school students to divide up their assignments into manageable parts and then share the results. After the class watches *Citizen Kane*,

Content Changes in the New Edition

More than 800 new citations are included with this edition, reflecting the many important discoveries that have been made in recent years. Every chapter includes updates that create a cutting-edge perspective on children's growth. With up-to-date knowledge, readers will be better prepared to meet the needs of children from many walks of life. Selected examples from each of the chapters include:

- **Chapter 1.** Added coverage of holistic perspective on childhood; development-enhancing education; educational equality and equity.
- **Chapter 2.** New material on measurement of stress; developmental dimensions with assessments, including progressions in children's vocabulary, physical coordination, and reasoning skills; children's understanding of the broad implications of achieving at a certain level on standardized achievement tests.
- **Chapter 3.** Reorganized sections of the chapter to allow for more foundational treatment of ethnicity and race, implicit bias, discrimination, prejudice, and educators' roles in ameliorating these problems; added strategies for reducing bias and addressing disparities; expanded coverage on the effects of divorce on children, school programs for children undergoing family transitions, parents raising children with special needs, and foster care.
- **Chapter 4.** Expanded coverage of transactions among genes, the environment, and the child (co-action, passive-gene environment, evocative reactions, active gene-environment relations); added evidence-based strategies for children with particular genetic conditions; material on universal design, educational needs of pregnant adolescents, and the learning capacity of the human fetus.
- **Chapter 5.** Added coverage of self-regulation of eating, sleep, and executive functions in the brain; food allergies; critical functions of sleep; brain connectivity; explicit age-related changes in brain during childhood; assistive devices and mobile applications for children with delayed motor skills; transgender youth.
- **Chapter 6.** In Piaget's theory, expanded section on association between assimilation and accommodation, discouragement of rushing children through childhood, and appreciating the legacy while accepting the need for revisions. In Vygotsky's theory, expanded section on digital literacy as a cognitive tool; age-related issues with computer use; strategies for cultivating digital literacy; universal design and meeting the needs of children with diverse learning needs.
- **Chapter 7.** Added new material on non-cognitive factors in the operations of cognitive processes, emotional needs and goals, and informational processing framework, stress and self-regulation, mindfulness, training and working memory, strategies for children with attention disorders, educational techniques recognizing variations in background knowledge.
- **Chapter 8.** Clarified basic features of intelligence, such as why children's abilities change with age while their IQ scores do not. Included new material on emotional intelligence (evidence for and against); school-based interventions for fostering children's emotional understanding and regulation; factors other than cognitive brainpower that affect performance on intelligence tests; relationships between intelligence and academic achievement; applications for children who are gifted and talented and peers with intellectual disabilities; neurological basis of intelligence; and Kagan Test of Intelligence.
- **Chapter 9.** Expanded sections on instrumental functions of neurological bases of language; working memory and prior knowledge in listening comprehension; strategies for helping children listen, attend, follow verbal instructions, draw inferences from what they hear, and develop metalinguistic insights. Elaborated on

diversity of language needs with attention to children growing up in low-income backgrounds; connections between bilingualism and metalinguistic awareness, ethnic dialects and formal English, and nonverbal learning disorders.

- **Chapter 10.** Expanded on the value of learning developmental changes in academic areas. Included digital applications for scaffolding steps and orchestration of cognitive processes for reading and writing. Added recommendations related to metacognition in mathematics and science.
- **Chapter 11.** Added educational applications for children with insecure attachments, applications for fostering healthy emotional development in children, and recommendations for fostering empathy in children. Provided an explanation of applications from the medical model, special education model, and three-tier models for intervention.
- **Chapter 12.** Added coverage of young people's communication on social networking sites and effects on self-perceptions and cyberbullying; characteristics and needs of gender nonconforming and transgender youth; challenges to self-esteem during adolescence; no-tease zones for disabilities; contexts in which children with autism might not understand the perspectives of other people; and neurological research on autism.
- **Chapter 13.** Added discussions of educational relevance of self-regulation; cultural contexts of self-regulation; effects of toxic stress on concentration and self-control; and how to strengthen self-regulation in children who have faced multiple significant hardships. Expanded discussions of achievement goals and cultural research; goal achievement theory; recent evidence regarding occasional benefits of performance approach goals; cultural dynamics of performance-avoidance goals; growth and fixed mindsets and interventions.
- **Chapter 14.** For moral development, expanded coverage of young children's emotional intuitions about morality, infants' reactions to unequal distribution of goods, neurological basis of morality, and contributions of theories to current understanding of moral development. For prosocial development and aggression, added discussions of animal maltreatment and other indicators of problems in adjustment, moral disengagement and aggressive tendencies, bystanders during bullying, and three-tier intervention model for addressing aggressive tendencies.
- **Chapter 15.** For peers, added strategies for helping children get along with classmates; a discussion of the benefits of friendships across ethnic lines; section on youth subcultures and descriptions of Hip Hop, Goths, Pro-Ana, and gangs. For schools, provided an introduction of Eccles's notion of stage-school fit; Pianta's theory of classroom processes. For society, discussed advantages and risks with social networking and video gaming; self-management skills with digital media.

MyLab Education

One of the most visible changes in the seventh edition, also one of the most significant, is the expansion of the digital learning and assessment resources embedded in the eText and the inclusion of MyLab Education in the text. MyLab Education is an online homework, tutorial, and assessment program designed to work with the text to engage learners and to improve learning. Within its structured environment, learners see key concepts demonstrated through real classroom video footage, practice what they learn, test their understanding, and receive feedback to guide their learning and to ensure their mastery of key learning outcomes. Designed to bring learners more directly into the world of K–12 classrooms and to help them see the real and powerful impact of child development concepts covered in this book, the online resources in MyLab Education with the Enhanced eText include:

- **Video Examples.** About four to seven times per chapter, an embedded video provides an illustration of a child development principle or concept in action. These video examples most often show students and teachers working in classrooms. Sometimes they show students or teachers describing their thinking or experiences.
- **Self-Checks.** In each chapter, self-check quizzes help assess how well learners have mastered the content. The self-checks are made up of self-grading multiple-choice items that not only provide feedback on whether questions are answered correctly or incorrectly, but also provide rationales for both correct and incorrect answers.
- **Application Exercises.** These exercises give learners opportunities to practice applying the content and strategies from the chapters. The questions in these exercises are usually constructed-response. Once learners provide their own answers to the questions, they receive feedback in the form of model answers written by experts.
- **Practice for Your Licensure Exam features.** Every chapter ends with an exercise that gives learners an opportunity to answer multiple-choice and constructed-response questions similar to those that appear on many teacher licensure tests. As with the other exercises in MyLab Education, Practice for Your Licensure Exam exercises provide feedback.

Supplementary Materials

The following supplements are available to help instructors organize, manage, and enliven their courses and to enhance students' learning and development as teachers.

Online Instructor's Manual

Available to instructors for download at www.pearsonhighered.com/educator is an *Instructor's Manual* with suggestions for learning activities, supplementary lectures, group activities, and class discussions. These have been carefully selected to provide opportunities to support, enrich, and expand on what students read in the textbook.

Online PowerPoint® Slides

PowerPoint slides are available to instructors for download on www.pearsonhighered.com/educator. These slides include key concept summarizations and other graphic aids to help students understand, organize, and remember core concepts and ideas.

Online Test Bank

The *Test Bank* that accompanies this text contains both multiple-choice and essay questions. Some items (lower-level questions) simply ask students to identify or explain concepts and principles they have learned. But many others (higher-level questions) ask students to apply those same concepts and principles to specific classroom situations—that is, to actual student behaviors and teaching strategies. The lower-level questions assess basic knowledge of development and its implications in educational settings. But ultimately it is the higher-level questions that can best assess students' ability to use principles of child and adolescent development in their own teaching practice.

TestGen

TestGen is a powerful test generator available exclusively from Pearson Education publishers. You install TestGen on your personal computer (Windows or Macintosh) and create your own tests for classroom testing and for other specialized delivery options, such as over a local area network or on the web. A test bank, which is also called a Test

Item File (TIF), typically contains a large set of test items, organized by chapter and ready for your use in creating a test, based on the associated textbook material. Assessments—including equations, graphs, and scientific notation—may be created for both print and testing online. The tests can be downloaded in the following formats:

TestGen Testbank file—PC

TestGen Testbank file—MAC

TestGen Testbank—Blackboard 9 TIF

TestGen Testbank—Blackboard CE/Vista (WebCT) TIF

Angel Test Bank (zip)

D2L Test Bank (zip)

Moodle Test Bank

Sakai Test Bank (zip)

Acknowledgments

Although we are listed as the sole authors of this textbook, in fact many individuals have contributed in significant ways to its content and form. Our editor, Kevin Davis, recognized the need for an applied child development book and nudged us to write one. Kevin has been the captain of our ship throughout all seven editions, charting our journey and alerting us when we drifted off course. We thank Kevin for his continuing encouragement, support, insight, vision, and high standards.

We have been equally fortunate to work with a series of expert development editors: Julie Peters (on the first and second editions), Autumn Benson (on the third edition), Christie Robb (fourth edition), Linda Bishop (early planning and fifth edition), Gail Gottfried (sixth edition), and Alicia Reilly (seventh edition). It was a special treat to work with Alicia on the current edition given her expertise as an editor and especially, her talents with keeping progress moving in a supportive and relaxed manner. Julie, Autumn, Christie, Linda, Gail, and Alicia have seen us through the day-to-day challenges of writing the book—for instance, offering creative ideas for improving the manuscript, locating artifacts to illustrate key concepts, pushing us to condense when we were unnecessarily wordy, insisting that certain concepts be clarified, overseeing the quality of the book's increasingly sophisticated online resources, being a willing ear whenever we needed to vent our frustrations, and, in general, coordinating our writing efforts until books went into production. We thank Julie, Autumn, Christie, Linda, Gail, and Alicia for their advice, support, and good humor, and also for their willingness to drop whatever else they were doing to come to our assistance at critical times—even on subsequent editions of the book!

Others at Pearson Education and Pearson/CSC have been key players in bringing the book to fruition. Kathy Smith worked diligently to keep the manuscript focused, concise, and clear. Kathy Smith, Janelle Rogers, and Lauren Carlson guided the manuscript through the production process; without a complaint, they let us continue to tweak the book in innumerable small ways even as production deadlines loomed dangerously close.

We are also deeply indebted to the children, teachers, and other adults who appear in the videos that are included in the book. Recordings of children's images and actions allow us to better understand and address the needs of children generally. We greatly appreciate the assistance of Janelle Rogers and Alicia Reilly, who helped us sort through possible videos, and the many professionals who applied arranged environments and conducted interviews in which children could be themselves and relay their thoughts and feelings. Thanks to Jayne Downey, Stuart Garry, Jason Cole, Greg Pierson, Keli Cotner, Dana Snyder, Kelle Nolke, Stacey Blank, Tara Kaysen, Addie Lopez, Laura Sether, Lisa Blank, and many others for their creative and technical assistance. We also appreciate the work of Adam Jordan, who prepared content material for supplementary materials.

Children, Adolescents, Teachers, and Other Professionals Equally important contributors to the book were the many young people and practitioners who provided the work samples, written reflections, photographs, other artifacts, and verbal responses that appear throughout the 15 chapters and other resources for the book. The work of the following young people and adults contributed immeasurably to the depth and richness of our discussions:

Davis Alcorn
Jacob Alcorn
Curtis Alexander
Kyle Alexander
David Alkire
Geoff Alkire
Brenda Bagazuma
Andrew Belcher
Katie Belcher
Kayla Blank
Madison Blank
Brent Bonner
Diamond Bonner
Ricco Branch
Marsalis Bush
Eric Campos
Leif Carlson
Zoe Clifton
Wendy Cochran
Jenna Dargy
Noah Davis
Shea Davis
Mayra de la Garza
Brandon Doherty
Daniel Erdman
Rachel Foster
Tina Ormrod Fox
Eddie Garcia
Palet Garcia
Veronica Garcia
James Garrett III
Amaryth Gass
Andrew Gass
Tony Gass
Dana Gogolin
Ivy Gogolin
Kenton Groissaint
Acadia Gurney
Amanda Hackett
Jared Hale
Cody Havens
Tyler Hensley
Elisabet Deyanira Hernandez
Lauryn Hickman
Sam Hickman
William Hill
Brandon Jackson
Rachel Johnson
Jordan Kemme
Marianne Kies
Sarah Luffel
Jessica Lumbrano
Dave Magnacca
Joan Magnacca
Maria Magnacca
Krista Marrufo
Steven Merrick
Margaret Mohr
Tchuen-Yi Murry
Mike Newcomb
Malanie Nunez
Dustin O'Mara
Alex Ormrod
Jeff Ormrod
Shir-Lisa Owens
Isiah Payan
Isabelle Peters
Michelle Pollman
Laura Prieto-Velasco
Cooper Remignanti
Ian Rhoades
Talia Rockland
Oscar Rodriguez
Elizabeth Romero
Corey Ross
Katie Ross
Trisha Ross
Amber Rossetti
Bianca Sanchez
Daniela Sanchez
Corwin Sether
Alex Sheehan
Connor Sheehan
Aftyn Siemer
Karma Marie Smith
Alex Snow
Sam Snow
Connor Stephens
Megan Lee Stephens
Joe Sweeney
Emma Thompson
Grace Tober
Sarah Toon
David Torres
Joseph Torres
Samuel Torres
Madison Tupper
Danielle Welch
Brady Williamson
Carolyn Wilson
John Wilson
Joey Wolf
Lindsey Woollard
Anna Young

To ensure that we included children's work from a wide variety of geographic locations and backgrounds, we contacted organizations north and south, east and west to obtain work samples that would reflect ethnic, cultural, and economic diversity. We want to thank several individuals for their assistance and coordination efforts: Don Burger at Pacific Resources for Education and Learning (PREL), Michelle Gabor of the Salesian Boys' and Girls' Club, Rita Hocog Inos of the Commonwealth of the Northern Mariana Islands Public School System, Bettie Lake of the Phoenix Elementary School District, Heidi Schork and members of the Boston Youth Clean-Up Corps (BYCC), Ann Shump of the Oyster River School District, and Chelsie Hess and Laura Pool from Eyestone Elementary School in Fort Collins, Colorado. Furthermore we thank the many professionals—a child welfare case worker, a neurologist, a public health educator, and many others—who were so helpful to our efforts to identify artifacts, anecdotes, dialogues, and strategies to illustrate developmental concepts; key among them were Janet Alcorn, Rosenna Bakari, Trish Belcher, Paula Case, Michael Gee, Jennifer Glynn, Evie Greene, Diana Haddad, Betsy Higginbotham, Betsy Hopkins, Dinah Jackson, Jesse Jensen, Mike McDevitt, Erin Miguel, Michele Minichiello, Andrew Moore, Dan Moulis, Tina Ormrod Fox, Annemarie Palincsar, Kellee Patterson, Elizabeth Peña, Jrene Rahm, Nancy Rapport, Lori Reinsvold, Gwen Ross, Karen Scates, Cindy Schutter, Karen Setterlin, Jean Slater, Julie Spencer, Nan Stein, Pat Tonneman, Peggy Torres, Sally Tossey, Pat Vreeland, and Cathy Zocchi.

Colleagues and Reviewers In addition, we received considerable encouragement, assistance, and support from our professional colleagues. Developmental scholars, educational psychologists, and teacher educators at numerous institutions around the country have offered insightful reviews of one or more chapters. We are especially indebted to the following reviewers for this edition:

Nurun N. Begum, East Stroudsburg University
Laura Dinehart, Florida International University
Debolina Ghosh, University of Florida
Nicola Montelongo, Texas A&M–Commerce
Kathleen Moritz Rudasill, University of Nebraska–Lincoln

We continue to appreciate the guidance of reviewers for earlier editions of the book. These individuals helped guide our early efforts:

Karen Abrams, Keene State College
Daisuke Akiba, Queens College
Jan Allen, University of Tennessee
Lynley Anderman, University of Kentucky
Patricia Ashton, University of Florida
David E. Balk, Kansas State University
Thomas M. Batsis, Loyola Marymount University
Brigid Beaubien, Eastern Michigan University
Jennifer Betters-Bubon, University of Wisconsin–Madison
Doris Bergen, Miami University
Irene Bersola-Nguyen, California State University–Sacramento
Gary Bingham, Georgia State University
Donna M. Burns, The College of St. Rose
Jean Clark, University of South Alabama
John Corey Steele, Loyola University Chicago
Heather Davis, University of Florida
Teresa K. DeBacker, University of Oklahoma
Michael Cunningham, Tulane University
Heather Davis, North Carolina State University
Tami Dean, Illinois State University
Deborah K. Deemer, University of Northern Iowa
Karen Drill, University of Illinois at Chicago
Eric Durbrow, The Pennsylvania State University
William Fabricius, Arizona State University
Daniel Fasko, Morehead State University
Suzanne Fegley, University of Pennsylvania
Kathleen Fite, Texas State University
Hema Ganapathy-Coleman, Indiana State University
Connie Gassner, Ivy Tech Community College
Sherryl Browne Graves, Hunter College
William Gray, University of Toledo
Michael Green, University of North Carolina–Charlotte
Glenda Griffin, Texas A&M University
Deborah Grubb, Morehead State University
Linda L. Haynes, University of South Alabama
Melissa Heston, University of Northern Iowa
James E. Johnson, The Pennsylvania State University
Ithel Jones, Florida State University
Joyce Juntune, Texas A&M University
Michael Keefer, University of Missouri–St. Louis
Judith Kieff, University of New Orleans
Nancy Knapp, University of Georgia
Jennie Lee-Kim, University of Maryland
Carol A. Marchel, Winthrop University
Mary McLellan, Northern Arizona University
Sharon McNeely, Northeastern Illinois University
Kenneth Merrell, University of Iowa
Nanci Monaco, Buffalo State College
Marilyn K. Moore, Illinois State University
Tamera Murdock, University of Missouri–Kansas City
Bridget Murray, Indiana State University
Kathy Nakagawa, Arizona State University
Virginia Navarro, University of Missouri–St. Louis
Terry Nourie, Illinois State University

Larry Nucci, University of Illinois–Chicago
Elizabeth Pemberton, University of Delaware
Lisa Pescara-Kovach, University of Toledo
Debra S. Pierce, Ivy Tech Community
Jennifer Parkhurst, Duke University
Sherrill Richarz, Washington State University
Kent Rittschof, Georgia Southern University
Valerie Roderick, Arizona State University
Linda Rogers, Kent State University
Richard Ryan, University of Rochester
Candy Skelton, Texas A&M University–Corpus Christi
Sue Spitzer, California State University, San Bernardino
Benjamin Stephens, Clemson University
Julia Torquati, University of Nebraska–Lincoln
Bruce Tuckman, The Ohio State University
Rob Weisskirch, California State University–Monterey Bay
Kathryn Wentzel, University of Maryland–College Park
Andrew R. Whitehead, East Stroudsburg University of Pennsylvania
Allan Wigfield, University of Maryland–College Park
Thomas D. Yawkey, The Pennsylvania State University

Increasingly, we have heard from colleagues at other institutions who have taken the time to let us know what they think about the book and how it might be improved. We are grateful for such very helpful feedback. In addition, staff and administrators at the University of Northern Colorado—especially staff at the Michener Library and Mark Alcorn, Carolyn Edwards, Helen Reed, Eugene Sheehan, Nancy Sileo, and Robbyn Wacker—unselfishly provided advice, resources, and time.

Our Families Finally, our families have been supportive and patient over the extended period we have been preoccupied with reading, researching, writing, and editing. Our children gave of themselves in anecdotes, artwork, and diversions from our work. Our husbands picked up the slack around the house and gave us frequent emotional boosts and comic relief. Much love and many thanks to Eugene, Connor, and Alex (from Teresa) and to Richard, Tina, Alex, and Jeff (from Jeanne).

T.M.M.
J.E.O.

Brief Contents

Contents

Special Features

The Only Comprehensive Child Development Text Written Specifically for Educators

Development-Enhancing Education

Observation Guidelines

The Difference Between Reading About Development and Seeing It In Diverse Settings

Case Studies

Developmental Trends

Basic Developmental Issues

Development in Culture

Chapter One

Introduction to Child Development

Monkey Business Images/Shutterstock

Learning Objectives

1.1 Describe the field of child development including its origins, focus, and basic issues.

1.2 Identify major characteristics and educational implications of the five developmental periods.

1.3 Differentiate among the seven major theoretical perspectives of child development in terms of their underlying principles and educational implications.

1.4 Formulate educational practices that foster children's age-related development and academic achievement.

CASE STUDY

Tonya

At any given moment, in almost every classroom, at least one child is having difficulty with the demands of school. The struggling child may be delayed in academic skills or could be inattentive to classroom rules or be rejected by peers. Mary Renck Jalongo remembers one little girl, Tonya, who faced each of these problems during her first-grade year (Jalongo, Isenberg, & Gerbracht, 1995).

Fortunately for Tonya, Mary was knowledgeable about children's development. Mary realized that Tonya, like every child, had positive qualities and, with the right support, could surmount her challenges. To determine how best to help Tonya, Mary considered Tonya's age, abilities, and circumstances. Academically, Tonya was delayed. She had been retained in kindergarten and was not catching up with her peers. Physically, Tonya received inadequate nutrition and was often hungry. Socially, Tonya had few friends. She had previously badgered classmates into giving her their snacks and prized possessions, and when they refused, she pilfered items from their desks.

Mary knew that Tonya did not receive the loving attention she needed. Tonya's mother was sick with lupus, then at a debilitating stage, and was not able to work or attend school functions. Mary's principal was unsympathetic and thought that harsh punishment—no recess for a month—was an appropriate response to Tonya's thefts.

Mary understood that Tonya was able to grow, change, and help solve some of her own problems. When Mary asked Tonya why she took other children's snacks, she answered simply that she was hungry. When asked if she ate breakfast, Tonya replied that she had not because she needed to take care of her younger brother. After Mary invited her to think about possible solutions, Tonya volunteered that she and her brother might be able to get breakfast at their aunt's house. After their discussion, Tonya followed through with this solution, walking with her brother to their aunt's house for an early morning meal.

Mary also realized that Tonya had the ability to repair relationships with her peers. After obtaining Tonya's promise that she would stop taking other children's things, Mary stood by Tonya's side and announced to the class that Tonya had agreed to stop taking her classmates' belongings. Afterward, Tonya earned the acceptance of the other children and began to concentrate on her schoolwork. She caught up with peers and ultimately blossomed into a healthy, well-adjusted young woman (M. R. Jalongo, personal communication, June 12, 2007).

- What knowledge of child development did Mary reveal in her support of Tonya?
- What kind of impact did Mary Jalongo have on Tonya's life?

Outline

Mary realized that Tonya could grow and change if given sensitive, loving care. By encouraging Tonya and her brother to eat breakfast with their aunt, Mary helped fulfill Tonya's physical needs and paved the way for closer ties to extended family. By repairing Tonya's damaged reputation with her peers, Mary helped Tonya earn their acceptance. Feeling comfortable physically and secure emotionally, Tonya became better prepared to tackle academic tasks and develop a healthy sense of who she was and how she fit into the world around her. Thanks, in part, to Mary's thoughtful intercession, Tonya would ultimately thrive.

We know that you, too, want to educate children in the most effective ways possible. Our primary goal with this book is to help you support the healthy development of all children in your care. We pursue this goal with two approaches. First, we ask you to learn how children think, feel, and act at various ages. Becoming sensitive to children's age-related characteristics is an important part of your preparation as a skilled educator. Second, we ask you to apply what you learn about child development to help all children succeed. We do so by explaining and showing you practical techniques for nurturing children.

The Study of Child Development

1.1 Describe the field of child development including its origins, focus, and basic issues.

The field of **child development** seeks to identify and explain changes in the physical, cognitive, and social-emotional development of children. Child development theory covers the early part of the human life span—beginning with the union of sperm and ovum at conception and extending through prenatal growth, birth, infancy, childhood, and adolescence.

Origins of the Field

For thousands of years, and probably since the dawn of humanity, people wondered how and why children grow as they do. In the last few centuries, these musings took form as philosophical positions. For example, the British philosopher, educator, and physician **John Locke** (1632–1704) suggested that human beings are born as blank slates. Locke saw children as empty vessels who were eager to learn, especially through their senses (Overton & Molenaar, 2015). According to Locke, parents met children's needs by instilling good habits and encouraging virtue and rationality.

Another influential philosopher, **Jean-Jacques Rousseau** (1712–1778), was born in Geneva, Switzerland and became well known in France for his political theories. Rousseau believed that children were inherently good actors in the natural world who were capable of making decisions (Elkind, 2012). From Rousseau's perspective, a sound education allowed children to explore their surroundings and develop critical thinking abilities. Parents were to lead by example and wait a while to introduce society's expectations. Pressuring children to grow up too quickly would distort their natural intuitions. Adults were to let children be children.

By the late 1800s and early 1900s, philosophical arguments promoted a desire for evidence. Biologists, psychologists, anthropologists, and educators began to study children, sometimes documenting growth in their own offspring (Charlesworth, 1994). From these observations, the field of child development emerged. Also foundational to the new field was a concern for the welfare of children, especially those from economically disadvantaged backgrounds (Hulbert, 1999). Scholars realized that they had a responsibility to use scientific information to improve children's lives, particularly when adversity was significant.

As data accumulated, investigators were able to evaluate the philosopher's ideas against the evidence. Developmental scientists agreed with Locke that infants are eager to learn yet disagreed that their minds were ever empty. Clever research methods showed that infants are capable of perceiving the visual properties of objects, the structure of language, and the existence of emotions. Scholars likewise determined that Rousseau's respect for children's curiosity was well justified, yet his discounting of adult guidance was not. Researchers from a range of disciplines found that parents, teachers, and other caring adults play an integral role in children's learning and adjustment.

After decades of research, developmental growth is now understood to be the result of an active interplay of factors. This complexity warrants multiple frameworks, each explaining one or more changes the child undergoes. In this book, we draw primarily from the disciplines of psychology, biology, sociology, and anthropology, and the applied fields of early intervention, education, child and family studies, juvenile justice, counseling, social work, and medicine. We emphasize research that has practical implications for children at school.

Essential Features of Development

Developmental scientists have identified three defining features of development. First, developmental changes are *progressive*: Children gradually become capable and responsible, even though they sometimes revert to lesser forms, as when a 4-year-old girl who has learned to talk through disagreements occasionally regresses when angry, to hitting classmates. Second, developmental changes are *persistent*: Once a new ability is introduced, it typically remains in the child's repertoire of skills, as occurs with walking and talking. Finally, developmental changes are *cumulative*: A new ability builds on the previous ones, as when a toddler shifts from speaking one word to uttering two-word combinations and later to speaking in complex sentences.

The progressive, persistent, and cumulative changes of childhood are themselves the result of four factors. Contributors to the developmental journey include the following:

- *Existing conditions.* The characteristics of the child's brain, body, and psychological states allow for new possibilities.
- *Nature.* The child's genetic inheritance enables and directs certain kinds of growth.
- *Nurture.* The child's physical environment, nutrition, interpersonal relationships, and the broader setting in which he or she interacts invite particular kinds of responses and initiative, meet the body's needs, and fulfill other conditions for growth.
- *The child's activity.* The child's choices and behaviors influence the emergence of new and changing states.

As you will discover in your reading, development includes certain changes that occur in almost everyone as well as others that are common in a fewer number, sometimes only in those who share a characteristic, such as having a particular gene or experiencing homelessness. Thus, at times, we talk about developments that nearly everyone undergoes, such as acquiring mature language skills or becoming increasingly considerate of other people's feelings, and in other situations, we emphasize diversity, as when some children respond to academic struggles by seeking support from teachers and others withdraw from school (M. B. Spencer, 2006).

Three Domains of Development

The study of child development is organized into three domains. **Physical development** is concerned with biological changes in the body. It includes genetics, growth in the womb, the sequences of childbirth, brain development, acquisition of motor skills, and behaviors that promote and impede health. **Cognitive development** refers to age-related transformations in reasoning, concepts, memory, language, and intellectual skills—changes that are cultivated by involvement in families, schools, and communities. **Social-emotional development** includes the many modifications that occur in emotions, self-concept, motivation, social relationships, and moral reasoning and behavior—advancements that depend, in large part, on interactions with other people.

Preparing for Your Licensure Examination

Your teaching test might ask you to identify the kinds of growth that occur in the cognitive, social-emotional, and physical domains.

Although the three domains appear to be independent, they are, in fact, closely intertwined. Getting physical exercise fosters mental concentration, learning a second language facilitates new friendships, and, as occurred with Tonya, feeling emotionally supported by a teacher motivates learning at school. When educators respect the entirety of psychological functions, they are taking a **holistic perspective on child development**. Wise educators realize that the child is greater than the sum of his or her separate parts, and although it often makes sense to focus in on a single skill, for example, reading comprehension, the child's welfare depends on simultaneous consideration of each of the domains.

Effects of Context on Development

All areas of development depend on the **contexts** of children's lives—on their experiences in families, schools, neighborhoods, community organizations, cultural and ethnic groups, and society at large. Child development research has shown that some sort of family or presence of one or more affectionate parent figures is necessary for optimal development. Schools, too, play a significant role, not only by cultivating cognitive skills but also by supplying teachers and classmates as social partners. In neighborhoods, children gain access to peers and recreation and, in society, media, social services, banks, clinics, libraries, courts, and houses of worship. As a member of one or more **cultures**—long-standing groups with defined values, traditions, and symbol systems—children engage in daily activities with familiarity and purpose.

Becoming aware of children's upbringing, as Mary did in the introductory case study, is a necessary step for understanding the knowledge, skills, and needs students bring to school. When children face serious problems, perhaps malnutrition, death in the family, or exposure to community violence, concerned educators often find it helpful to seek out informed colleagues who can help them determine how to reassure children, find appropriate referrals, reach out to the family, and ameliorate threats to safety.

The dynamics of children's development are also worthy of your attention. Gaining an appreciation for three dimensions of development will enhance your ability to foster growth in the heterogeneous collection of children you serve. First, experts in child development wonder how genetic and environmental factors combine during development. Second, they speculate about which developmental paths are true for everyone and which others are unique to individuals and those who share certain characteristics. Third, they debate about the developmental changes that reflect major transformations or, alternatively, are the result of a series of gradual trends. Let's look closely at these three issues, which are referred to as questions of (a) nature and nurture, (b) universality and diversity, and (c) qualitative and quantitative change.

Nature and Nurture

In the study of development, **nature** refers to the inherited characteristics that influence growth. **Nurture** consists of the environmental conditions that affect the progression of changes. Nature and nurture are partners in growth.

Nature contributes to both common traits and individual differences in children. Some genes (the basic units of heredity) appear in virtually everyone. Almost all infants are born with a capacity to learn to walk, understand language, imitate others, use simple tools, and draw inferences about how other people view the world. Other characteristics, including stature, eye color, and facial appearance, are strongly determined by heredity and cause variations among children. Similarly, children's **temperaments**—their characteristic ways of responding to emotional events, novel stimuli, and impulses—are likewise affected by their individual genetic makeup (J. R. Gagne & Saudino, 2016; Rothbart & Bates, 2006; Z. Wang & Deater-Deckard, 2013). Similarly, being slow or quick to learn at school and from everyday experiences has a partial genetic basis (Petrill et al., 2004; Plomin & Deary, 2015).

Heredity is powerful, but it has limits. For one thing, the child's stage of growth affects which genes come into play. Whereas some hereditary instructions, such as the chromosomes that determine sex, exert an influence from the beginning, other instructions emerge only gradually through the process of **maturation**, the genetically guided changes that occur over the course of development. For example, puberty begins when the pituitary gland in the brain senses it is time to release certain hormones, the excretion of which initiates sexual maturation.

Children's experiences affect all aspects of their being, from the health of their bodies to the curiosity of their minds. *Nurture* affects children's development through multiple channels: physiologically through nutrition, activity, affection, light, stress, pollutants, and contagious illness; intellectually through informal experiences and academic instruction; and socially through exposure to role models and interaction in interpersonal relationships. However, nurture faces definite limits. Even the best environments cannot overpower every defective gene. And, unfortunately, healthy environments are not always available. Abuse, neglect, poor nutrition, and racism are just a few threats that some children encounter.

Decades ago, theorists saw nature and nurture as rival factors. Numerous early theorists believed that biological factors are ultimately responsible for growth. Other theorists assumed that children become whatever the environment shapes them to be. Neither extreme position has stood the test of time. Present-day theorists appreciate that nature and nurture intermesh dynamically in the lives of active children. Consider the following principles of how nature and nurture interact.

The developmental process constrains growth. Genes and environment alone are not sufficient to explain the complex sequence of events in brain and body. The developmental process, as guided by existing structures, channels future growth and learning (Champagne, 2009; Sabbagh, Koenig, & Kuhlmeier, 2016; Stiles, 2008). During prenatal development new cells specialize and move to strategic locations depending on signals they receive from nearby cells. In the globular hands that first emerge during prenatal development, cells at the top of budding extensions respond to certain chemicals by duplicating and taking on specified properties. Precursors to fingers sprout, elongate, and differentiate into the elegant digits that will later permit drawing, keyboarding, and fastening buttons. This same principle applies to learning. Children acquire new knowledge based on what they already know and can do. Preferences in the brain at birth direct attention to certain kinds of phenomena, such as looking at facial expressions and listening to speech.

The relative effects of heredity and environment differ across distinct areas of development. Some abilities are strongly influenced by genetically controlled systems in the brain. Distinguishing among various speech sounds and using appropriate grammatical structures occur without formal training and under a wide range of environmental conditions (Archer & Curtin, 2011; Gallistel, Brown, Carey, Gelman, & Keil, 1991). In contrast, abilities in traditional school subject areas (e.g., reading, geography, and music) rely heavily on instruction (Bruer, 1999; R. K. Olson, Keenan, Byrne, & Samuelsson, 2014).

Inherited tendencies make children more or less responsive to particular environmental influences. Because of their unique genetic makeup, some children are deeply affected by certain stimuli, whereas others are less affected (Rutter, 1997; Zhang, Cao, Wang, Ji, & Cao, 2016). For example, some children are born exceptionally sensitive to the quality of caregiving and, when exposed to abuse and other adverse life events, become highly aggressive themselves, whereas children without this vulnerability tend not to be seriously affected by similar exposures (Hygen et al., 2015). A few other children are inclined by their genetic heritage to be shy and inhibited and, when they have few social experiences outside the family, to be nervous around strangers. However, if adults arrange for them to make friends, these otherwise reserved children are apt to become socially outgoing (Arcus, 1991; Kagan & Fox, 2006).

Some genes exert effects only under certain conditions. Some children are born with particular genes that put them at risk for developing psychological problems. A specific chemical, serotonin, is produced in the brain and influences a person's mood. Some people have a short form of a gene (known as 5-HTT), with the result that their brain struggles to recycle serotonin, and consequently to maintain positive emotions. Individuals with this particular form of the gene are at risk for being chronically sad and irritable. Yet the short form of this gene does not typically culminate in full-blown depression unless the individual was maltreated during childhood (Caspi et al., 2003).

Certain hereditary characteristics develop more fully in nurturing settings than in impoverished environments. Children raised by parents who are warm, involved, and sensitive are generally able to develop skills and qualities that are compatible with their heredity profiles. Children who grow up with adequate nutrition, a warm and stimulating home environment, and challenging educational experiences are able to make many of their own choices, and heredity affects how quickly and thoroughly they acquire new skills. When children receive little human contact or grow up in coercive families, they cannot make choices that would allow certain genetic tendencies to emerge (A. B. Miller et al., 2018; D. C. Rowe, Almeida, & Jacobson, 1999; Venables & Raine, 2016).

Timing of environmental exposure matters. When children are changing rapidly, they are especially prone to influence. Early in a mother's pregnancy, her use of certain drugs can damage the offspring's quickly growing organs and limbs. Just prior to birth, exposure to the same drugs may adversely affect the baby's brain, which at that point is forming neurological connections for learning. For a few years after birth, the brain continues to develop rapidly and remains vulnerable to harmful substances.

Just as certain substances need to be avoided during particular phases of growth, particular kinds of stimulation must be provided for a few abilities to be activated (C. Blakemore, 1976; Hubel & Wiesel, 1965; Niechwiej-Szwedo, Chin, Wolfe, Popovich, & Staines, 2016). When a certain stimulation is required for a physiological structure to become activated, a *critical period* is said to take place. For example, at birth, specified regions of the brain are tentatively reserved for processing visual patterns—lines, shapes, contours, depth, and so forth. Virtually all infants encounter adequate stimulation to preserve these brain circuits. However, when cataracts are present at birth and not removed for a few years, or when the child's vision is obstructed for some other reason, areas of the brain that would otherwise develop visual functions permanently redirect themselves for other purposes.

With many other abilities, the brain is receptive to stimulation at one point yet capable of benefiting from it later as well. Developmental theorists use the term **sensitive period** to refer to the rather lengthy time frame of heightened receptivity to environmental experience (Curley & Champagne, 2016). Sensitive periods appear to be more common than critical periods, reflecting nature's fortunate practice of giving children second chances to learn important skills. For example, during early childhood, children are predisposed to tune in to the sounds, structure, and meaning of language. They are essentially hungry to process verbal information and easily build neurological foundations for language from the input they encounter. When there are delays, educators can realistically expect to make meaningful progress by arranging for missing experiences.

Children's actions partly determine resources accessible to them. In addition to being affected by nature and nurture, children's growth is influenced by their own behaviors. Youngsters make many choices, seek out information, and, over time, refine their knowledge and beliefs. Children often request information ("What does *cooperate* mean, Mommy?") and experiences ("Ignacio, can I play on your computer?"). Children even create environments that intensify their genetic tendencies. Those with irritable dispositions might pick fights, thereby creating a more aggressive climate in which to interact.

As children get older, they become increasingly able to seek information and experiences that suit their natural tendencies. Imagine that Marissa has an inherited talent for verbal processing. As a young child, Marissa depends on her parents to read to her. As she grows older, Marissa chooses her own books and reads by herself. Marissa's experience would suggest that certain genetic tendencies become more powerful as children grow older—an expectation that is consistent with genetic research (Scarr & McCartney, 1983; Trzaskowski, Yang, Visscher, & Plomin, 2014).

Universality and Diversity

Developmental changes that occur in just about everyone reflect **universality**. Unless significant disabilities are present, all young children learn to sit, walk, and run, almost invariably in that order. Other developmental changes are highly individual or differ between groups—for example, between boys and girls or among members of different cultures. These variations reflect **diversity** and remind us of the many healthy manifestations and a few maladaptive pathways that are found in children's growth.

Theorists differ in their beliefs regarding the extent to which developmental accomplishments are universal among human beings or unique to individuals and groups. Some scholars emphasize that shared genes and maturational processes contribute to universality (e.g., A. Gesell, 1928). They point out that despite widely varying environments, virtually all human beings acquire basic motor skills, proficiency in language, and the ability to inhibit immediate impulses. Certain consistencies in children's environments provide an additional route to universality. In all corners of the world, children observe objects falling down rather than up and people getting angry when someone intentionally harms them. From these everyday observations, children acquire an intuitive sense of physics and psychology. Similarly, children just about everywhere participate in household chores that prepare them for adult roles.

Other scholars are impressed by diversity in child development. They point out that nature permits variations in genes affecting facial features, physical characteristics, temperament, and intellectual abilities. Many of the diversity-oriented theorists view the environment (nurture) as weighing heavily in development. They propose that factors as global as the historical era of one's upbringing and as personal as one's relationships with family and friends generate individuality (Baltes, Lindenberger, & Staudinger, 2006; Flouri & Sarmadi, 2016). Another source of diversity is culture: Children differ in the competencies they acquire based on the particular languages, tools, activities, and values they encounter (Griedler & Shields, 2008; Paradise & Robles, 2016; Rogoff, 2003).

Earlier we mentioned that the relative influences of nature and nurture vary from one area to the next. The same pattern is true with universality and diversity. Development tends to be similar in some aspects of physical development, such as the order of early motor skills and sequences in which puberty unfolds. In other areas, including many aspects of cognitive and social-emotional development, diversity is prevalent. In fact, there is always *some* diversity, even in physical development. Obviously, children vary in height, weight, and skin color, and a few are born with physical disabilities, start puberty comparatively early or late, or become seriously injured.

If you consider children you know, you will probably see instances of universality, but just as often you are likely to notice divergences in developmental pathways. Gaining an appreciation for both commonalities and exceptions will help you meet everyone's needs. As a second-grade teacher, you may find that most of your students enjoy listening quietly to a few pages of a favorite book. Aware of unique needs in your class, you arrange for one boy to sit near you as you read, two English language learners to listen to the story prerecorded in their native language, and a girl who has an intellectual ability to page through a homemade picture book of the story.

MyLab Education Application Exercise 1.1
Meet Individual Needs

What kinds of diversity does a sixth-grade mathematics teacher accommodate in her instruction?

Qualitative and Quantitative Change

Sometimes development reflects dramatic changes in the underlying structure of a characteristic. These major reorganizations are called **qualitative changes**. When children learn to run, they propel their bodies forward in a way that is distinctly different from walking—they are not simply moving faster. When they begin to talk in two-word sentences rather than with single words, they are, for the first time, using a rudimentary form of grammar. And when they shift from obeying a teacher because they do not want to be punished to following classroom rules because it is the right thing to do, they are transforming the way they think about morality. With a qualitative change, there is a metamorphosis, such that the organism takes existing states and converts them into entirely new forms. Just as a tadpole is transformed into a frog, a caterpillar into a butterfly, and a seed into a plant, the infant turns into an adult through a series of dynamic restructurings.

In comparison to the overhaul that occurs with qualitative change, other developments are gradual progressions, or *trends*, with many small additions. These incremental progressions in behavior, physical states, and learning are called **quantitative changes**. For example, children gradually grow taller and learn more and more about such diverse realms as the animal kingdom and society's rules for showing courtesy.

MyLab Education Application Exercise 1.2
Meet Individual Needs

Which of 12-year-old James's changes seem to be quantitative in form? Which others are qualitative?

As you are learning, both qualitative and quantitative changes contribute to the child's development, yet scholars have been especially fascinated with the former. Theorists who emphasize *qualitative* changes often use the term **stage** to refer to a period of development characterized by an exact way of behaving or thinking. According to a **stage theory** of development, individuals progress through a series of stages that are qualitatively different from one another.[1] Some stage theories specify movement through *hierarchical* levels. In hierarchical models, each stage is seen as providing the essential foundation for modifications that follow.

After observing children in a wide variety of thought-provoking situations, the eminent psychologist **Jean Piaget** (1896–1980) proposed a stage theory in children's logical reasoning. His observations led him to conclude that as infants, children interact with the world primarily through trial-and-error exploration. As infants mouth a rubber ball and watch it roll, they discover its properties. As children mature, they symbolically represent concepts and make mental predictions about objects and actions. They know from experience that the ball will bounce on the wooden floor. Later they begin to derive logical inferences, perhaps concluding that the ball is made out of a pliable substance. And once they reach adolescence, they become capable of thinking systematically about abstract ideas—for instance, in conceiving of unseen physical forces (e.g., *momentum, gravity*).

Another famous stage theorist, **Erik Erikson** (1902–1994), focused on major challenges that individuals face at different points in their lives. During their infancy and early childhood, youngsters learn first to trust others and then to act self-sufficiently. Adolescents reflect on their identities as boys or girls, as members of particular ethnic groups, and as individuals with defined interests and goals. In Erikson's theory, people do not fully replace earlier developments with new modes of thinking (Kohlberg, Levine, & Hewer, 1983). Instead, earlier struggles persist—and sometimes intrude—into new challenges. Thus, a young adult who has failed to develop a clear identity may be confused about the role to play in a romantic relationship (J. Kroger, 2003).

Historically, stage theories emphasized *universal* stages: All children were thought to go through the same cycle of changes, with slight variations in timing because of dissimilarities in environmental support. Piaget was a strong believer in universal progressions in children's thinking. However, research has not entirely confirmed that young people proceed through general stages one at a time or that they always move in the same direction (e.g., Ceci & Roazzi, 1994; Giammarco, 2016). A 9-year-old girl may easily plan ahead while playing chess (her hobby) but strain to design a complex essay (an unfamiliar activity). Nor do stage progressions always appear to be universal across cultures and educational settings (e.g., Arnold, 2015; S.-C. Li, 2007; Seiffge-Krenke, 2016).

[1]Note that developmental scholars have a more precise meaning for the term *stage* than is communicated by the same word in everyday speech. Parents often make comments like "He's at the *terrible twos stage*." Such comments reflect the idea that children are behaving typically for their age group. When developmental scientists say a child is in a certain stage, they additionally assume that the child is undergoing a series of age-related transformations that represent a qualitative overhaul to one or more aspects of thinking or behavior.

Youngsters raised in different cultures learn to think in discrete ways. Given these and other research findings, few contemporary developmental theorists endorse strict versions of stage theories (Parke, Ornstein, Rieser, & Zahn-Waxler, 1994).

Today theorists accept that both quantitative and qualitative forms of change occur in children's lives. Evidence indicates that children grow gradually in the developmental domains; quantitative changes are well accepted as a fundamental type of growth. Data also suggest that qualitative changes exist—not as inevitable, universal, and hierarchical patterns but, rather, as dynamic and occasionally individual states of thinking that evolve with exploration. It is obvious that the actions of adolescents differ from those of 2-year-old children! Fifteen-year-olds are not simply taller and more knowledgeable; they go about their day-to-day living in qualitatively different ways. Maturation-based developments, such as the brain's increases in memory capacity, plus ever-expanding knowledge, permit both gradual and occasionally dramatic changes in thinking and behaving (A. R. Cassidy, 2016; Morra, Gobbo, Marini, & Sheese, 2008).

Applying Lessons from Basic Issues in Child Development

As you read this book, you will find that the three developmental issues of nature and nurture, universality and diversity, and qualitative and quantitative change surface periodically and are highlighted in the Basic Developmental Issues tables. The first of these tables, "Illustrations in the Three Domains," provides examples of how the dimensions are reflected in the domains of physical, cognitive, and social-emotional development. The themes also have several implications for your work with children:

- **Accept the powerful influences of nature and nurture.** A child's fate is never sealed—it always depends on care from adults, peer relationships, and the child's own efforts. Again and again, nurture matters. As does nature. How children respond to guidance depends, in part, on their genetic inheritance. An important implication is that when

BASIC DEVELOPMENTAL ISSUES
Illustrations in the Three Domains

ISSUE	PHYSICAL DEVELOPMENT	COGNITIVE DEVELOPMENT	SOCIAL-EMOTIONAL DEVELOPMENT
Nature and Nurture	Nature guides the order and timing in which parts of the brain and body form. Genetic factors contribute to individual characteristics, such as a tendency toward thinness or susceptibility to diabetes. All growth depends on nurture. Nutrition, physical activity, and protection from excessive stress promote health and motor skills (Chapters 4 and 5).	Intelligence, learning, and language are affected by genetically guided brain maturation. Many contemporary theorists emphasize environmental influences, including informal learning experiences, adult modeling and mentoring, family relationships, and formal schooling (Chapters 3, 6, 7, 8, 9, and 10).	The basic capacity to form attachments with other people is made possible by genes and altered by social experience. Environmental influences are strong in self-esteem and motivation. Becoming especially aggressive, empathic, shy, or socially outgoing occurs due to the combined influences of nature and nurture (Chapters 11, 12, 13, and 14).
Universality and Diversity	The order in which key physical features emerge (e.g., gender-specific characteristics during puberty) is similar. Diversity is evident in the ages at which children accomplish motor milestones (e.g., becoming able to sit, stand, and walk), as well as in their general state of physical health (Chapter 5).	The basic components of language (e.g., an ability to combine words using grammatical rules) and thinking (e.g., the mechanisms for interpreting new information through the lens of existing understandings) are nearly universal. Diversity appears in memory capacity and the effectiveness of academic learning (Chapters 6, 7, 8, and 9).	The need for peer affiliation represents a universal aspect of development. The benefits of friendship are the same across children in the same general age. There are individual differences in the kinds of social groups that young people form and the degree to which they accept one another as desirable companions (Chapter 15).
Qualitative and Quantitative Change	Some aspects of physical development (e.g., transformations in body parts during prenatal development) unfold as qualitative changes. Much of the time, physical development occurs gradually as a result of many small changes (e.g., young children slowly grow taller (Chapters 4 and 5).	Children's logical reasoning skills show qualitative change; for instance, children develop sophisticated ways of solving problems that integrate and restructure previous methods. Quantitative change occurs as children gradually gain knowledge of academic subjects (Chapters 6, 7, and 10).	With social experience, children's understanding of morality undergoes qualitative change. In a quantitative manner, children gradually come to understand how other people's minds work and discover how others' perspectives differ from their own (Chapters 12 and 14).

children show unusual talents, you can offer an extra challenge. And when children's natural inclinations become stumbling blocks, you can provide new kinds of support.

• **Become familiar with developmental trends and typical variations.** Children's customary ways of learning determine the instructional goals and methods educators can reasonably pursue. An elementary teacher familiar with Piaget's theory knows that children have difficulty with abstract ideas and therefore arranges many concrete, hands-on experiences. Unique patterns in developmental pathways—the timing, appearance, and form of changes—must also be accommodated. By becoming acquainted with diversity among children, you can deepen your understanding of how to accommodate breadth in learning requirements.

• **Look for both quantitative and qualitative changes in children's characteristics.** Much of children's learning is done quantitatively. Children soak up facts and skills incrementally, sometimes rapidly. You can support such learning by providing children with rich and varied resources. Qualitative features of learning likewise merit consideration. Think about the dramatically different kinds of care that infants, preschoolers, elementary school children, middle school students, and high school students need. Students crave environments that fit their age-related needs for affection, autonomy, exploration, and intellectual challenge (Eccles & Roeser, 2009); Symonds & Hargreaves, 2016).

Summary

The field of child development examines how human beings change beginning in conception and throughout prenatal development, infancy, childhood, and adolescence. Each child's journey is guided by four factors: nature, nurture, existing conditions in the brain and body, and personal activity. Developmental theorists focus on progressions in the three domains—physical, cognitive, and social-emotional arenas—and look at how a variety of contexts affect growth in these areas and in overall adjustment.

Developmental theorists wrestle with three basic issues related to children's development. First, they wonder about the degree to which development is influenced by both nature (heredity) and nurture (environment). Second, they speculate about the extent to which developmental paths are universal (true for everyone) or diverse (unique to individuals and groups). And finally, they debate which types of changes are qualitative (involving major transformations) or quantitative (reflecting gradual trends) in form. Clearly, development is influenced by nature and nurture, certain aspects of development are universal and others reflect diversity, and the course of development is characterized at various times by qualitative and quantitative changes.

Now that you have been introduced to the basic features of child development, you are ready to check your knowledge of essential concepts. In the summary for each major section, you will see a *self-check* exercise. Click on the self-check icon to find out how well you understand major concepts.

MyLab Education Self-Check 1.1

Developmental Periods

1.2 Identify major characteristics and educational implications of the five developmental periods.

Children learn and grow every day. Many changes are imperceptible until the journey is separated into meaningful chunks. Thus, we make the task of exploring child development manageable by dividing the years into specific periods. In our discussions of changes, we consider five periods: infancy (birth–2 years), early childhood (2–6 years), middle childhood (6–10 years), early adolescence (10–14 years), and late adolescence (14–18 years). Here we give an overview of children in each period, identify typical abilities, and derive implications for teachers and other practitioners. As we proceed, we refer to video clips that illustrate environments designed for each age group.

MyLab Education
Video Example 1.1

Find Developmental Meaning *How is the environment designed such that infants are enticed to explore their surroundings?* Notice that a mirror attracts attention, colorful toys beg to be touched, mobiles over cribs encourage inspection, and a tunnel invites peekaboo games. Falling would pose little threat because furniture has been crafted with soft, rounded edges.

Infancy (Birth–2 Years)

A newborn is completely dependent on others. But a baby is equipped with an arsenal of skills that elicit comfort and stimulation (e.g., a distinctive cry, physical reflexes, an interest in human faces, and a brain alert to novelty and sameness). In a matter of weeks, the baby smiles broadly during good-humored exchanges with familiar caregivers. As caregivers respond warmly and consistently, attachments grow.

A sense of security nourishes the desire to learn. Babies want to know everything: what car keys taste like, what family members do in the kitchen, and what happens to a bowl of peas as it drops to the floor. Emotional reactions, such as a fear of heights and uneasiness in the presence of strangers, provoke withdrawal. Infants' facility with language builds on interests in concrete experiences (e.g., saying "dog" for the neighbor's pet and "mah" when asking Daddy for *more* bits of banana). Curiosity fuels babies' drive to exercise physical skills. They reach, crawl, and climb to get to attractive objects. The urge to explore coincides with a budding sense of mastery. Infants gain confidence by using their bodies to exert effects on people and things—watching Mom laugh after gurgling, noticing the imprint of a ball after chewing on it, and making a clatter by pounding on kitchen pots. Infants love to push buttons, hammer toys, pound boxes, and perform other actions with obvious effects.

Caregivers who work effectively with infants realize that each baby is unique, develops at his or her own rate, and is hungry for loving interaction. Skilled caregivers treat infants individually, providing tender, loving care with each (Chazan-Cohen, Jerald, & Stark, 2001; Y. Kim, 2016; S. L. Recchia & Shin, 2012). They prioritize time to respond warmly to infants' bids for attention, tend to their physical needs, and share their attention to objects and events, for example, while paging through a storybook together. Knowledgeable caregivers design the environment to allow infants to explore surroundings safely.

Early Childhood (2–6 Years)

Early childhood is a time for creativity and fantasy. Preschool-aged children see life as a forum for invention, imagination, and drama. Language and communication skills develop rapidly. The cautious movements of infancy give way to fluid rolling, tumbling, running, and skipping. Preschoolers are endearing, trusting, and affectionate creatures who sometimes need help coping with sporadic aggressive and self-centered impulses.

Effective teachers channel young children's natural energy with gentle guidance. Teachers respect children's desire to try on new roles, and they realize that children learn a great deal from play (Hirsh-Pasek, Golinkoff, Berk, & Singer, 2009; Lillard et al., 2013). Environments for young children are designed to encourage active and purposeful learning (National Association for the Education of Young Children [NAEYC], 1997, 2009). Relationships with teachers continue to be important, and highly qualified teachers know how to offer guidance in a low-key manner that allows children to exercise increasing levels of self-control (Hatfield, Burchinal, Pianta, & Sideris, 2016).

MyLab Education
Video Example 1.2

Find Developmental Meaning *How does this preschool encourage active learning?* Notice that the preschool allows children to draw and paint, climb, hide, and search. Tables and chairs make it possible to sit and talk during mealtimes and group activities. A dramatic play area encourages imagination. Elsewhere in the room, children look at books and take turns on a computer. Outdoors, children can scoot on vehicles, ride bicycles, and play in the sand.

Middle Childhood (6–10 Years)

Children continue to play during the elementary years and now are also capable of learning from formal instruction (Bergen & Fromberg, 2009; S. G. Paris, Yeung, Wong, & Luo, 2012).[2] Many children in industrialized societies learn to read and write, follow the rules of familiar games, and operate digital technologies for a range of purposes, including education, communication, and entertainment.

[2] Many children retain qualities typical of early childhood, including an interest in pretend play, until age 8 or older, which has led the NAEYC to classify children from birth until age 8 as "young children" (NAEYC, 1997). We have used age 6 as the cutoff between early and middle childhood. Although age 6 is somewhat arbitrary, it marks the typical age for first grade, during which time schools introduce an academic curriculum. We also wanted to distinguish middle childhood from the early adolescent years, as some youngsters (girls in particular) begin the first phases of puberty as early as age 8 or 9.

In the elementary school years, children internalize admonishments they have previously heard (e.g., "Don't play near the river"; "Watch your fingers near the stove"). They gain a sense of what is expected of them, and most are inclined to live up to their responsibilities, for example, by looking after younger siblings after school. Motor skills improve, and many children become proficient in athletic skills.

Serious commitments to peers, especially to playmates of the same age and gender, occur during middle childhood. Friendships are valued by elementary school students, who learn much from spending time together and getting into—and out of—scuffles. Children compare themselves to others and wonder why they stick out in certain ways. Why am I the slowest reader in my class? Am I good enough to be picked for the baseball team? Why am I so short?

Students of this age do their best thinking when familiar with a topic. Teachers nurture students' skills with instruction that is tailored to their existing understandings and includes tools for guiding mental procedures (e.g., graph paper, a computer application, and a worksheet that reminds them of specific sections to include in their essay; Association for Childhood Education International, 2009; National Board for Professional Teaching Standards, 2001).

MyLab Education
Video Example 1.3

Find Developmental Meaning *How does this elementary school support academic learning?* Notice that maps are visible in several places, suggesting the importance of geography. Frequently used words are posted on cabinets for children to consult while writing. Small objects can be manipulated, counted, and classified according to shape. Books, a computer, chalkboards, and other resources extend learning. Tables and chairs permit group work, and sofas allow relaxation while reading.

Early Adolescence (10–14 Years)

In early adolescence, a youngster enters a dramatic transition, that of moving from a child's to an adult's body. Physical growth follows a series of steps that span several years and culminate in reproductive maturity. The physical changes of puberty are accompanied by equally dramatic reorganizations in learning and relating to parents, teachers, and peers.

Although the physical changes of puberty are orderly and predictable, many boys and girls experience them as disconcerting transitions. Young adolescents sometimes look and feel awkward. Hormonal changes can lead to mood swings. Diversity is present in every developmental phase, and individual differences are especially obvious during early adolescence, especially in the wide range of ages at which puberty begins. Thus, not all young adolescents start puberty during the 10- to 14-year-old age range. Some, girls especially, begin puberty before age 10. Others, boys in particular, begin puberty after age 14.

Interpersonal connections also change. Relationships with parents are renegotiated, with adolescents pushing for greater autonomy and parents insisting on more accountability. The young person's sense of self intensifies. Adolescents become introspective and worry about how their peers perceive them. Peers become a sounding board through which adolescents obtain assurance that their appearance, abilities, and behavior are acceptable. Adolescents also begin to think in a far-reaching, logical, and abstract manner, with interests broadening well beyond family and peer groups (Anderman, 2012). Energized and idealistic, adolescents challenge the existing order, wondering why schools, governments, and the earth's ecosystem cannot be improved overnight.

MyLab Education
Video Example 1.4

Find Developmental Meaning *How does this middle school help young adolescents meet their personal needs and feel that they belong?* In this video, there is a code of conduct that reminds adolescents to treat themselves, others, and the environment with respect; a small room set aside for private conversations; and classrooms decorated with students' artwork, papers, and a diorama.

Middle school educators recommend that every student be assigned an adviser who keeps an eye on his or her academic and personal welfare (Association for Middle Level Education, 2011). Warm and unwavering adviser–student relationships help young adolescents weather rapid developmental changes. Flexible instructional methods, multiple opportunities for mastering challenging skills, and ample time for learning engender achievement. Breadth in the curriculum and choices in elective classes accommodate adolescents' need for autonomy (Anderman, 2012).

Late Adolescence (14–18 Years)

As teenagers continue to mature, they lose some of the gawky, uneven features of early adolescence and blossom into attractive young adults. With an intensified desire to make their own decisions, young people find acceptance in peer groups, where they can experiment with adult roles. Most adolescents continue to savor ties with trusted adults and preserve fundamental values championed at home and school, such as the importance of a good education and the need to be honest and fair.

Late adolescence can be a confusing time because of an abundance of mixed messages. Teenagers may be encouraged by parents to abstain from sexual activity all the while encountering provocative sexual images in the media. Similarly, adults urge healthy eating habits, yet junk food is everywhere—in vending machines, at the convenience store, and often in kitchen cabinets at home. Temptations to try alcohol, drugs, sex, and violence abound.

Older adolescents need behind-the-scenes support from adults. Schools that offer personalized services to adolescents—for example, those that ensure that the aspirations, strengths, and limitations of individual students are known by at least one teacher or other school staff member—help to meet their needs (Mero & Hartzman, 2012; National Association of Secondary School Principals, 2004). Adults focus in on the full spectrum of needs by students, for example, in keeping track of their assignments, asking for help when struggling, and gaining a sense of ownership over schoolwork (S. A. Rutledge & Cannata, 2016).

MyLab Education
Video Example 1.5

Find Developmental Meaning *How does this high school facilitate personal growth?* Notice furniture being arranged so that students face one another and no one is anonymous, statements of responsibility are posted on a wall, and a mural captures a wide range of interests, including music, drama, and athletics.

You can see a summary of physical, cognitive, and social-emotional characteristics during each of the five periods in the following Developmental Trends table, "Accomplishments and Diversity at Different Age Levels." Notice that these different age levels have distinct implications for teachers and other practitioners.

DEVELOPMENTAL TRENDS
Accomplishments and Diversity at Different Age Levels

AGE	WHAT YOU MIGHT OBSERVE	DIVERSITY	IMPLICATIONS
Infancy (Birth–2 Years)	**Physical Development** • Rolling over, sitting, crawling, standing, and walking • Emerging ability to reach, grab, manipulate, and release objects • Rudimentary self-feeding by end of infancy **Cognitive Development** • Ability to distinguish among different faces in first months • Rapid growth in communication through gestures, facial expressions, mutual eye contact, babbling, and one-word and two-word sentences • Ability to imitate simple gestures, progressing to more complicated patterns • Growing ability to remember people and things out of sight **Social-Emotional Development** • Formation of close bonds with affectionate caregivers • Use of words to label needs and desires • Playing side by side with peers and interacting at times • Increasing awareness of ownership and boundaries of self ("Me!" "Mine!") • Developing sense of personal will ("No!")	• Variation occurs in age when, and manner in which, babies develop motor skills. • Self-help skills appear later in families that encourage reliance on adults. • Children's temperaments affect their exploration of environment. • Infants receiving restricted nutrition may lack alertness and energy. • Presence of dangers in environment may lead families to limit exploration. • Some young children learn two or three languages. • The ability to pretend is displayed early by some infants and later by others. • Depending on customs, a child may be encouraged or discouraged from eye contact with an elder. • Children who have little contact with peers may appear tentative, curious, or aggressive. • Some children are encouraged by families to share possessions, and others are asked to respect individual property rights.	• Provide a safe and sensory-rich environment that allows exploration of surroundings and objects. • Gently hold infants, and attentively care for physical needs. • Respond sensitively to each infant's style in approaching or resisting new people, objects, and events. • Encourage but do not rush infants to acquire new motor skills. • Learn what families want for children and provide culturally sensitive care. • Recognize that children's early images of themselves are influenced by adults' unconscious messages (e.g., "I enjoy holding you" or "I'm too sad to deal with your needs"). • Speak to infants regularly and enrich their language development. • Communicate regularly with families about infants' daily moods and activities, including how much and what they ate and drank and how well they played and slept.

DEVELOPMENTAL TRENDS (Continued)

AGE	WHAT YOU MIGHT OBSERVE	DIVERSITY	IMPLICATIONS
Early Childhood (2–6 Years)	**Physical Development** • Ability to run and skip, throw a ball, build block towers, and cut with scissors • Growing competence in self-care and personal hygiene **Cognitive Development** • Dramatic play and fantasy • Ability to draw simple figures • Basic knowledge of colors, letters, and numbers • Recounting of familiar stories and events **Social-Emotional Development** • Developing understanding of gender and ethnicity • Emerging abilities to defer immediate gratification, share toys, and take turns • Rudimentary appreciation that other people have their own desires, beliefs, and ideas • Some demonstration of sympathy for people in distress	• Children begin to coordinate separate movements (e.g., hopping and skipping). • Individual differences in fine motor and gross motor proficiencies are substantial. • Some have had few prior experiences with age-mates; others have been with peers since infancy. • Family and cultural backgrounds influence skills at entry of school. • Some children have had a lot of experience listening to storybooks, whereas others have been read to rarely. • Many children at this age have difficulty following rules, standing quietly in line, and waiting for their turns in a group.	• Provide sensory-rich materials that invite exploration (e.g., a water table, sandbox, textured toys). • Arrange a variety of fine-motor and gross-motor activities (e.g., assembling puzzles, coloring, building with blocks, dancing). • Encourage children to engage in fantasy play by arranging props and dedicated areas for play. • Read to children regularly to promote vocabulary and literacy skills. • Engage children in games that allow them to distinguish speech sounds, identify letters, and count objects. • Say expectations so that children learn to follow rules. • Communicate regularly with families about children's progress.
Middle Childhood (6–10 Years)	**Physical Development** • Mastery of complex movements, as in skateboarding, playing basketball, and riding a bicycle • Steady growth in height and weight • Participation in organized sports **Cognitive Development** • Mastery of basic skills in reading, writing, and mathematics • Ability to reason logically about concrete objects and events **Social-Emotional Development** • Growing awareness of how one's personal and social abilities compare with those of peers • Desire to spend time with age-mates, especially friends of same gender • Increasing responsibility for household chores • Adherence to rules of games and respect for fairness	• Children who perceive they are doing poorly academically may have less motivation to achieve. • Some children are unable to sit quietly for the duration of a classroom lesson. • Individual differences are evident in children's academic performance. • Some children develop gregarious personalities whereas others become shy and reserved. • A few children show unacceptable levels of aggression. • Some children are given a lot of responsibility at home, and others are not. • Some children have tutoring, music lessons, or sports after school, and others play with peers or siblings or entertain themselves.	• Use cooperative groups, individualized assignments, and choices in activities to accommodate variations in knowledge. • Address minor weaknesses in basic skills (e.g., in reading, writing, and mathematics) to enable success and prevent serious delays. • Provide moderately challenging tasks that inspire children to learn new skills and study hard. • Teach children how to deal with anger, disappointment, and frustration. • Foster friendship skills and the social inclusion of children who are rejected or neglected by classmates. • Prohibit bullying and enforce codes of conduct.
Early Adolescence (10–14 Years)	**Physical Development** • Onset of puberty (e.g., with breast budding in girls and testicle enlargement in boys) • Significant growth spurt • Increased appetite • Staying up later at night and feeling tired during day **Cognitive Development** • Emerging capacity to think and reason about abstract ideas • Preliminary exposure to advanced academic concepts and skills **Social-Emotional Development** • Increasing interest in peer relationships • Self-consciousness about appearance • Emerging sexual interest • Challenges to parents and teachers over rules • Occasional moodiness and rashness	• Young adolescents exhibit variability in age at which they begin puberty. • Academic problems become more pronounced during adolescence. • Students who encounter frequent failure typically become less engaged at school. • Adolescents seek peers with compatible values and inclinations to recognize their accomplishments. • Some young adolescents begin to engage in risky activities (e.g., unprotected sex, cigarette smoking, and use of drugs and alcohol). • A few adolescents begin to exhibit signs of low self-esteem, depression, anxiety, or aggression.	• Suggest and demonstrate effective study strategies for difficult assignments. • Give struggling adolescents the extra academic support they need to be successful. • Provide a regular time and place where adolescents may talk with you (e.g., offer your classroom or office as a place where students can eat lunch). • Encourage adolescents to take initiative in clubs and recreation centers. • Impose appropriate consequences when adolescents break rules. • Reassure adolescents about normal range of ages in going through puberty.

(Continued)

DEVELOPMENTAL TRENDS (Continued)			
AGE	**WHAT YOU MIGHT OBSERVE**	**DIVERSITY**	**IMPLICATIONS**
Late Adolescence (14–18 Years)	**Physical Development** • Progress toward sexual maturity and adult height • For some teens, development of a regular exercise program • Gravitation toward independent eating habits (e.g., becoming a vegetarian, consuming junk food) **Cognitive Development** • In-depth study of certain academic areas • Consideration of career tracks and job prospects **Social-Emotional Development** • Dating • Increasing independence (e.g., driving a car, making own choices with free time) • Frequent questioning of rules and societal norms • Increasing commitment to personal values, career prospects, and ethnic affiliations	• Older adolescents aspire to widely differing career tracks (e.g., some hope to go to college, others anticipate employment after high school, and still others make no plans whatsoever). • Some teens participate in extracurricular activities; those who do are more likely to graduate. • Some adolescents affiliate with peers who take part in deviant activities. • Some teens become sexually active, and a few become parents. • Teenagers' neighborhoods offer differing opportunities and temptations. • Some adolescents are keenly aware of prejudice toward themselves and their family.	• Communicate affection and respect for adolescents. • Allow choices in academic subjects and assignments and hold adolescents to high standards for performance. • Provide the assistance that low-achieving students need to be successful. • Teach young people how to manage their time in completing multistep projects. • Help adolescents explore a variety of vocational and career paths and options for higher education. • Encourage involvement in extracurricular activities. • Arrange opportunities for adolescents to participate in meaningful volunteer projects.

Summary

Infancy (birth–2 years) is a remarkable time for the rapid emergence of essential human traits, including emotional bonds with other people, language, and mobility. Early childhood (2–6 years) is an era of imaginative play, rapid language development, advancing motor skills, and expanding social skills. During middle childhood (6–10 years), children tackle the abilities that they need to participate effectively in adult society; they also develop friendships and internalize many of society's rules and prohibitions. In early adolescence (10–14 years), youngsters are preoccupied with the changes of puberty and their appearance; at the same time, they are thinking in increasingly abstract and logical ways. Late adolescence (14–18 years) is a period of intensive interaction with peers, growing independence from adults, and a desire to make their own decisions, many of which are sound but some of which lead to risky behaviors.

MyLab Education Self-Check 1.2

Theories of Child Development

1.3 Differentiate among the seven major theoretical perspectives of child development in terms of their underlying principles and educational implications.

Now that you have considered the dramatic changes that occur over childhood, you are ready to review explanations for growth. Over the years, scholars have created developmental **theories** to explain how and why children grow and change. Numerous theories have been proposed, with seven approaches being especially important historically. We examine these major theories and their practical implications here and then refer to them selectively in later chapters, in conjunction with other specific frameworks, as each becomes pertinent to an aspect of children's lives.

Biological Theories

Biological theories examine how a child's brain and body contribute to survival, growth, and learning. Some structures, such as the placenta, an organ that forms in the mother's uterus and delivers oxygen and nutrients to the fetus, are crucial for a time (Hernández

Blasi & Bjorklund, 2003). Other emerging characteristics are thought to prepare the child for the future, as the preschool child's fantasies of becoming a firefighter or hairdresser help him or her anticipate responsible roles in later life (Bjorklund, 1997).

Initial biological theories emphasized the *maturation* of the body, perceptual abilities, and motor skills (A. Gesell, 1928). Early theorists compiled detailed charts of the average ages at which children learn to sit, crawl, reach for objects, and so forth. According to this view, children walk when they are physiologically ready, and puberty begins when a biological clock triggers the release of relevant hormones. These scholars also realized that maturational states make children especially receptive to certain stimuli during designated periods, as occurs when infants eagerly attend to patterns in visual displays and speech.

Child specialists who take a biological perspective have emphasized how important it is to observe children's spontaneous activities. Italian physician and educator **Maria Montessori** (1870–1952) noticed that infants are perceptive of order in the physical world and that preschool-aged children eagerly soak up details in language (Montessori, 1936/1966, 1949). In the many Montessori schools now in existence in North America and Western Europe, teachers study children's natural tendencies and provide stimulating materials that entice children to use their up-and-coming perceptual and cognitive abilities.

Montessori appreciated that nature and nurture were intertwined during development. Some other early biological theorists did not take as balanced a perspective (Dalton, 2005). In fact, a limitation of many early biological scientists was that they largely overlooked the effects of children's experiences. Today, biological theorists appreciate that genes are flexible instructions that give rise to a range of possible outcomes depending on the child's circumstances (Carnell, Kim, & Pryor, 2012; Cicchetti, McGowan, & Roth, 2015; Gottlieb, Wahlsten, & Lickliter, 2006).

Three key principles that a practitioner can take away from biological theories are that (a) maturational levels impose limits on abilities and interests, (b) age-related motivations serve valuable functions in prompting exploration, and (c) individual children are born with unique dispositions that interact with experience to influence learning. Remaining aware that abilities are limited by maturation will help you encourage but not rush children. Similarly, if you realize that children are predisposed to be physically active, you will understand that they need regular play in safely equipped yards. And if you accept that each child has a one-of-a-kind profile of genes, you will strive to design flexible instructional plans that allow everyone to be successful.

Behaviorism and Social Learning Theories

Whereas early biological theorists saw heredity (nature) as the principal driving force behind development, advocates of behaviorism proposed that developmental change is largely due to environmental influences (nurture). Conducting research with humans and other species (e.g., dogs, rats, pigeons), behaviorists showed that habits emerge for an organism in a particular environment. As a proponent of **behaviorism**, American psychologist **B. F. Skinner** (1904–1990) suggested that children actively "work" for rewards, such as food, praise, or physical contact, and avoid actions that lead to punishment (Skinner, 1953, 1957). Other behavioral theorists have revealed how children learn emotional responses to certain stimuli (e.g., a fear of dogs) based on experience (e.g., having been bitten by a dog).

A limitation of behaviorism is that it focuses almost exclusively on actions and gives little consideration to internal thought processes. Contemporary behavioral scholars do have an interest in mental processes. Canadian American psychologist **Albert Bandura** proposed a **social learning theory** that credited children with learning a great deal by observing what other people did. His theory helps us understand a toddler pretending to mow the lawn after seeing a parent do it, elementary school children trying out new soccer kicks they saw at a local match, and middle and high school students adopting the slang they hear from friends. Bandura came to appreciate that children reproduced behaviors that allowed them to achieve certain goals or standards. Over several decades, Bandura gave increasing credit to children's thought processes, especially their beliefs about what they personally could accomplish; accordingly, his

MyLab Education
Video Example 1.6
Find Developmental Meaning *What would a theorist with a behavioral or social-learning perspective notice about this lesson?* The teacher encourages the boy to attain a standard of accuracy and reinforces him when he achieves it. The boy appears happy when he accomplishes his goal and enthusiastic about the next round of learning challenges.

most recent frameworks are called *social cognitive theory* and *self-efficacy theory* (Bandura, 2012a; Schunk, 2012).

Numerous practical applications have been derived from behaviorism, social learning theory, social cognitive theory, and self-efficacy theory, and you will encounter many of them as you study child development. Let's look at three overarching principles. First, environmental stimuli, such as rewards and punishments, affect children's actions and feelings. Mary Jalongo, in the opening case study, chose not to follow the advice of her principal to punish Tonya harshly because doing so would do more harm than good. Second, children's actions are affected by behavior around them. Children often imitate others' actions, whether those behaviors are desirable (e.g., the hoop shots of a famous basketball player) or disagreeable (e.g., a teacher's condescending actions toward the school custodian). Finally, children's confidence in their ability to achieve certain standards is based largely on their past experiences on similar tasks. Thus, adults can point out the results of children's hard work and encourage them to set realistic goals for future improvements.

Psychodynamic Theories

Psychodynamic theories focus on the interactions between a person's internal conflicts and the demands of the environment. These frameworks assert that early experiences play a critical role in later behavior. They typically focus on social and personality development and, often, on abnormal development.

The most famous psychodynamic theorist, **Sigmund Freud** (1856–1939), was an Austrian physician who argued that young children continually find themselves torn by sexual and aggressive impulses, on one hand, and desires to gain approval from parents and others in society, on the other (Freud, 1905, 1910/1965, 1923/1960). Freud proposed that children progress through a series of qualitatively distinct stages, in ideal cases learning to channel impulses in socially appropriate ways. Another psychodynamic theorist, Erik Erikson, who was born in Germany and moved to the United States, suggested that people grow as a result of resolving their own internal struggles. Compared to Freud, Erikson focused less on sexual and aggressive impulses and more on desires to feel competent and confident in one's values, commitments, and direction in life (Erikson, 1963).

Psychodynamic perspectives have made a lasting contribution by highlighting the significance of children's social-emotional experiences. Several psychodynamic ideas remain convincing today: Early social relationships influence children's sense of security; children defend themselves from criticism, neglect, and traumatic events; concerted efforts are needed to dislodge children from unhealthy paths; and young people wrestle with age-related issues during certain phases of life (Josephson, 2013; Ludwig-Körner, 2012; Mukherjee, Datta, Sanyal, Dogra, & Das, 2016).

A significant weakness of psychodynamic theories has been the difficulty in evaluating their claims with research data. For one thing, it is difficult to verify the internal conflicts a particular person might have, in part because these struggles are hidden from self-awareness. If we ourselves are not consciously aware of our mental and emotional dynamics, we would not be able to talk accurately about these feelings with another person. In addition, generalizations cannot be made from his interviews with troubled adults—individuals whose childhoods do not necessarily reflect typical experiences. Critics also point out that desires to restrain sexual urges (in Freud's theory) and define one's personal identity (in Erikson's theory) may be central motives for some people but not others. Finally, research has refuted several ideas central to psychoanalytical perspectives. Although Freud recommended that children perform mildly aggressive acts as a way to release inborn aggressive tendencies, research indicates that encouraging such acts can actually *increase* aggressive behavior (Mallick & McCandless, 1966; C. E. Smith, Fischer, & Watson, 2009).

Despite these problems, psychodynamic theories remind educators of two things. First, children often have mixed and confusing emotions. Adults can help children by teaching them to express their feelings in ways that both honestly reflect their experience and are acceptable to other people. Second, children who have gotten off to a rough start in family relationships need extra support at school, usually in the form of explanations of getting along with others and occasionally with more intensive interventions and counseling.

Cognitive-Developmental Theories

Cognitive-developmental theories emphasize thinking processes and how they change, qualitatively, over time. According to these views, children play an active role in their own development: They seek out new and interesting experiences, think over what they see and hear, and reconcile any discrepancies between new information and what they previously believed to be true. Through reflection, children's reasoning becomes increasingly logical, comprehensive, and abstract.

The earliest and best-known cognitive-developmental theorist was Swiss scientist Jean Piaget. With a career that spanned decades and spawned thousands of research studies around the world, Piaget focused primarily on children's cognitive development (Piaget, 1928, 1929, 1952a, 1952b). Using detailed observations, in-depth interviews, and ingenious experimental tasks, Piaget investigated the nature of children's logical thinking about such topics as numbers, physical causality, and psychological processes. Another prominent cognitive-developmental theorist, American psychologist **Lawrence Kohlberg** (1927–1987), is known for his extensive research on children's moral reasoning (Kohlberg, 1963, 1984).

Piaget, Kohlberg, and their colleagues have suggested that taking a developmental perspective means looking sympathetically at children and understanding the logic of their thinking. Although adultlike reasoning may be the eventual, desired outcome for young people, cognitive-developmental theorists believe that it is a mistake to hurry children beyond their current capacities—that one cannot *make* a child think in ways beyond his or her current stage. These experts also believe that adults who push children beyond their present abilities instill stress and derail learning.

Many cognitive-developmental ideas are well regarded by contemporary scholars. Present-day experts recognize that children's thinking reflects a reasonable attempt to make sense of puzzling information. Nevertheless, not all tenets of cognitive-developmental theories are accepted. A central reservation is that performance rarely reflects the clear-cut stages expected by cognitive-developmental scholars. Instead, children move back and forth between more and less advanced ways of thinking. As we mentioned earlier, children are sometimes able to reason at a high level with certain topics while simultaneously being incapable of advanced reasoning in other areas.

Perhaps the most important principle that emerges from cognitive-developmental theories is that teachers need to understand children *as children*. To facilitate children's learning, educators must listen closely to children's conversations, permit them to explore their environment, observe their actions, and gently probe their ideas. Only when adults appreciate the integrity of children's thinking can they hope to nurture it.

Cognitive Process Theories

Cognitive process theories focus on basic thinking processes. Central issues are how children interpret and remember what they see and hear and how these processes change with growth and experience. Cognitive process researchers conduct detailed analyses of what children think and do. Investigators have studied eye movements of children while scanning pictures, the length of time it takes them to read text, and their strategies in completing puzzles. Detailed models of how children attend to information, find meaning in it, and use it in a range of settings guide the analyses.

Research by American psychologist **Robert Siegler** illustrates the cognitive process approach. Siegler has found that children spontaneously use several different strategies when first learning to complete tasks in arithmetic. In solving the problem "2 + 4 = ?" children may count on their fingers, starting with the first number and then counting on from there ("two . . . then three, four, five, six—six altogether") or simply recall the number fact ("2 + 4 = 6") from memory. The same versatility is present as children begin to tackle such tasks as telling time, spelling, and reading. This general tactic of trying out a few solutions is productive in identifying which methods work most effectively on particular kinds of problems (Siegler, 2006, 2016; van der Ven, Boom, Kroesbergen, & Leseman, 2012).

Cognitive process theories now dominate research in cognitive development. A key contribution has been the production of painstakingly detailed descriptions of thinking. As a result of peering into previously hidden mental processes, scholars have generated a wealth of concrete, research-tested instructional applications. These frameworks offer implications for keeping children's attention, guiding their elaboration of new information, using limited memory capabilities, and challenging misconceptions in academic topics (L. A. Barker, 2016; Mayer, 2012). Yet critics suggest that there is a price to pay for taking a myopic view of learning. Cognitive process researchers can easily overlook the larger issue of *why* children think as they do. These approaches often neglect social-emotional factors and the contexts of children's lives, factors that other theories treat as significant.

Sociocultural Theories

Cognitive developmental and cognitive process theorists focus on how intellectual skills develop in an individual. By and large, both have paid little attention to the roles played by the broader settings in which individuals live. **Sociocultural theories**, on the other hand, concentrate on the impact of *social systems* (e.g., families, teacher–child relationships, and community agencies) and *cultural* traditions (e.g., customs with print, household chores, and memory aids). These conceptual frameworks portray development as the process of children becoming full participants in the society into which they were born.

Russian psychologist and educator **Lev Vygotsky** (1896–1934) is the pioneering figure recognized with advancing our knowledge of how children's minds are shaped by everyday social experiences. Having studied the learning of both children and adults, Vygotsky concluded that people grow intellectually by taking part in routine activities and gradually assuming higher levels of responsibility for their completion (Vygotsky, 1962, 1978). Vygotsky believed that guidance with tools, such as using as a protractor in mathematics, and mental prompts, such as using a memory strategy to learn the names of planets, foster cognitive growth. Because different cultures impart their own tried and tested ways of performing daily tasks, children's thoughts and behaviors develop in culturally specific ways.

The last few decades have seen an expansion into research conducted from a sociocultural perspective (Barnyak & McNelly, 2016; Göncü & Gauvain, 2012; Salomo & Liszkowski, 2013; H. T. Zimmerman & McClain, 2016). This evidence is often well received by teachers because it focuses on children in real settings and has clear implications for supporting learning. Depending on their society, children may learn to weave, hunt, raise crops, care for livestock, look after younger children, worship in a religious community, barter and trade, read and write, program computers, or acquire a combination of these or other skills. Teachers can reach out to heads of family to learn about home traditions, livelihoods, and the family's leisure pastimes.

Another strong suit of sociocultural theories is that they show just how differently separate cultural groups are in teaching children intellectual abilities. From their families and communities, children learn cultural ways of telling stories, asking questions, respecting authority figures, and solving problems. Knowledge of these ways can help teachers make children feel welcome in the classroom. Children can be encouraged to apply knowledge learned at home while at school and to learn to use academic tools, including mental strategies, that enable them to master complex projects.

As with any theoretical approach, sociocultural theories have limitations. Vygotsky and his heirs have described children's thinking with less precision than have investigators from cognitive process perspectives. In some cases, sociocultural theorists have taken for granted that children learn important skills simply by taking part in an activity, whereas in reality, some children merely go through the motions without becoming accountable for their share of task completion.

Developmental Systems Theories

Developmental systems theories address the multiple factors that converge during development. Seen through this theoretical lens, the child's body is an active, living *system*, an organized assembly of parts that grow together and collectively draw from resources in the multilayered and interacting environments of family, community, and society.

Proponents of developmental systems frameworks reject the premise that a child's growth ever occurs as the result of only nature *or* nurture. Instead, developmental outcomes, such as gaining a proficiency in language, always emerge because of a combination of conditions—having a healthy brain, receiving adequate nutrition, being immersed in a family, and engaging in conversations with others. With so many factors at play in a developmental system, it is not always a straightforward matter to portray the dynamic exchanges that allow for growth.

Two types of transactions have garnered attention by scholars. First, biologically oriented systems theorists examine how genes in the child's body interact with experience in guiding the maturation of physical structures. For example, a child who receives loving care from parents and other caregivers typically develops a brain with robust capacities for empathy, self-control, and goal-directed behavior. In comparison, a child who encounters stressful events, unaccompanied by reassurance, is at risk for developing a brain with weak layouts for these capacities (DeSocio, 2015; Gershoff, 2016).

The second type of transaction involves the child's participation in social groups and institutions (Baltes et al., 2006; N. N. Merrill & Fivush, 2016; Zaff, Donlan, Pufall Jones, & Lin, 2015). The most widely known developmental systems theorist, **Urie Bronfenbrenner** (1917–2005), was a native of Russia and immigrant to the United States at age 6. Bronfenbrenner focused on the child's experiences in interacting in groups and demonstrated that a given characteristic, such as being born premature, had dramatically different outcomes depending on such factors as the mother's socioeconomic status and the child's access to a high-quality education. In his *bioecological model* of human development, Bronfenbrenner described the influences of the child's own characteristics (including genes and maturational level, reflecting the *bio* in the theory's name) and the people, institutions, and prevailing cultural practices (the *ecology* of growth).

Bronfenbrenner found close family members with whom children interact every day to be of utmost importance (Bronfenbrenner & Morris, 2006). In the best of circumstances, parents and other caregivers form close bonds with children, meet their emotional needs, and arrange for them to take on grown-up responsibilities. Bronfenbrenner also noticed that children have influential relationships with people outside the family. Teachers, peers, and neighbors regularly support children and, in some cases, compensate for delayed skills and disadvantages at home or in the community (Criss, Pettit, Bates, Dodge, & Lapp, 1992; Crosnoe & Elder, 2004; Youn, 2016). In our introductory case study, Mary Jalongo played an important role for Tonya by expressing confidence in her and by taking a few practical steps toward meeting her needs.

Other institutions, such as the workplace, involve parents, who bring home the customs, resources, frustrations, and coping skills that they acquire on the job (Bronfenbrenner, 1979, 2005; Fusarelli, 2015). Parents who work reasonable hours and have decent wages and positive relationships with coworkers generally have adequate income and energy to care for children. Those who don't may find it difficult to provide sufficient food and comfortable housing and, in a few situations, are under such pressure themselves that they struggle to meet children's basic needs.

As is the case with the sociocultural framework, the bioecological model underscores the importance of culture. A culture shows children what proper behavior is—for example, how they should respect adults and interact with peers at school. Children also infer from treatment in their community whether they are members of a valued group or, alternatively, part of a persecuted one (E. McGee & Spencer, 2015; M. Spencer et al., 2012; M. B. Spencer, 2006). As a result of personal, familial, and cultural influences, all children have protective factors—perhaps strong family relationships or close ties with neighbors—as well as risk factors—possibly economic poverty or racism in the community—that together affect their adjustment.

Preparing for Your Licensure Examination

Your teaching test might ask you about the basic ideas of B. F. Skinner, Jean Piaget, Erik Erikson, Lev Vygotsky, Urie Bronfenbrenner, and other key developmental theorists.

FIGURE 1.1 The child participates in an interactive, multilayered, and changing environment.

The bioecological framework was developed by Urie Bronfenbrenner and has been since elaborated by other theorists (e.g., M. B. Spencer et al., 2012; M. B. Spencer, 2006).

As powerful as other people are in children's lives, children themselves partly determine the way they are treated (see Figure 1.1). A boy who is quiet and reflective elicits a different style of instruction than does another who is disruptive and inattentive. Connections among the separate settings in which the child develops are also influential. When parents and teachers develop frank and courteous relationships, they are likely to magnify each other's encouragement. When parent–teacher relationships are conflicted, the adults may blame one another for the child's limitations, with the result that no one teaches the missing skills. Because children and others are constantly changing, relationships evolve over time.

The power of the developmental system framework is its ability to capture it all—nature, nurture, and the child's developmental level, activity, and personal characteristics. Any of these factors can provoke change, and growth is sufficiently embedded in relationships and institutions that educators are urged to find out about the child's family, community, and culture. Children's own interpretations of their personal circumstances are important; thus, developmental systems theorists recommend keeping in tune with children's interpretations as well (M. B. Spencer, 2006).

MyLab Education
Video Example 1.7

Find Developmental Meaning *How would Piagetian and Vygotskian theorists interpret this lesson?* A Piagetian theorist might notice that the students were interested in water quality, the specimens they collected, and the hands-on investigation. A Vygotskian theorist might notice that the teacher provided detailed instructions about the investigation and gave students access to the necessary tools to complete their work.

Ironically, the integrative character of this framework generates a weakness. It is difficult to make predictions about any single factor (e.g., a child's chronic health condition) because that feature is inextricably intertwined with other elements (e.g., the family's income level). Thus, growing up in a certain culture and having unique personal characteristics (e.g., perhaps an exceptional talent or disability) are hints rather than reliable indicators of the child's needs. The child remains open to change, and adults who are mindful of the child's ecology can build on its resources and offset any trouble spots.

Taking a Strategic Approach to Theory

Table 1.1 summarizes the seven theoretical perspectives. With so many theories, the question arises, "Which one is right?" The answer is that, to some extent, they all are. Each perspective provides unique insights that no other approach offers, acting as a lens for bringing certain phenomena into sharp focus and leaving other patterns blurry or out of the picture.

Table 1.1 Theories of Child Development

THEORIES	RESEARCH ILLUSTRATIONS	BASIC DEVELOPMENTAL ISSUES	EXAMPLES OF THEORISTS[a]
Biological theories	Investigators focus on genetic factors, physiological structures, maturational sequences, and individual differences in health and everyday habits. In one investigation, adolescents who slept relatively little and reported interrupted sleep exhibited reduced activity in the part of the brain that handles positive emotions and sensations of feeling rewarded (S. M. Holm et al., 2009).	*Nature and nurture*: Genes guide the emergence of characteristics that enhance survival and reproduction. Adequate nutrients, supportive relationships, and exploration are essential for growth. *Universality and diversity*: Most children form bonds with caregivers and develop brain structures for learning about language, numbers, and people's feelings. Diversity in appearance and motor coordination arise because of variations in genes and experience. *Qualitative and quantitative change*: Qualitative changes occur during periods of heightened responsiveness to input in the environment. In other respects the child grows gradually through quantitative changes.	Charles Darwin Arnold Gesell Maria Montessori Konrad Lorenz John Bowlby Mary Ainsworth Sandra Scarr Robert Plomin David Bjorklund Michael Tomasello Susan Gelman Elizabeth Spelke Renée Baillargeon Melvin Konner
Behaviorism and social learning theories	In one investigation a group of girls with cystic fibrosis were more likely to engage in health-promoting exercise when they were given small, immediate rewards (e.g., special snacks) and allowed to earn points that could be exchanged for other prizes (e.g., playing a game with parents; Bernard, Cohen, & Moffet, 2009).	*Nature and nurture*: Emphasis is on nurture. Children change their behavior based on the rewards and punishments they experience and the goals and confidence they have. *Universality and diversity*: All children work for rewards. Preferences for specific incentives are individual, and because environments vary in responses to children's actions, diversity is expected. *Qualitative and quantitative change*: Children increase the frequency of behaviors that prove reinforcing and allow for goal achievement.	B. F. Skinner John B. Watson Ivan Pavlov Sidney Bijou Donald Baer Albert Bandura Dale Schunk Barry Zimmerman
Psychodynamic theories	In an investigation in which divorced parents and their children were studied over a 10-year period, researchers detected sibling rivalries that were based, in part, on unconscious allegiances to one parent (Wallerstein & Lewis, 2007).	*Nature and nurture*: Sexual and aggressive urges are considered inborn. Family and society affect how children express urges, trust others, and perceive themselves. *Universality and diversity*: Most children struggle with impulses to act in a ways not approved by families. Relationships vary as do coping skills. *Qualitative and quantitative change*: Through a series of stages, children learn to resolve mixed feelings and gain a sense of identity.	Sigmund Freud Anna Freud Erik Erikson Donald Winnicott Joan Berzoff Tom Billington
Cognitive-developmental theories	One researcher found that young children focused on their own concrete views of an event, whereas older children were able to think about how several individuals could see an single event from different points of view (Selman, 1980).	*Nature and nurture*: Children are motivated to make sense of their world (nature). Access to a complex environment is vital to development (nurture). *Universality and diversity*: Similar milestones occur in sequence. Variations across students are prevalent at the highest stages. *Qualitative and quantitative change*: The essence of reasoning undergoes reorganization. Quantitative additions occur within stages.	Jean Piaget Bärbel Inhelder Lawrence Kohlberg John Flavell David Elkind Robbie Case Juan Pascual-Leone Kurt Fischer Sergio Morra Camilia Gobbo
Cognitive process theories	In one study 7-year-old Dutch children who were learning one-digit multiplication problems used a variety of strategies: counting on their fingers, drawing items and counting them, using repeated addition (e.g., $5 \times 7 = 7 + 7 + 7 + 7 + 7$), trying short-cuts (for 6×4, starting with $4 + 4 + 4 = 12$ and adding $12 + 12$ to get 24), and retrieving answers from memory (van der Ven et al., 2012).	*Nature and nurture*: Children are born with capacities to perceive, interpret, and remember information; these abilities are refined with experience. *Universality and diversity*: The desire to make sense of the world is universal. Diversity is due to unique experiences and personal talents. *Qualitative and quantitative change*: The methods by which children perceive, interpret, and remember information are transformed qualitatively (e.g., inventing new rules for solving arithmetic problems) and quantitatively (e.g., becoming proficient with a strategy).	David Klahr Deanna Kuhn Robert Siegler Ann L. Brown Henry Wellman Susan Gelman John Flavell Robbie Case Alison Gopnik Erik Thiessen

(*continued*)

Table 1.1 Theories of Child Development *(continued)*

THEORIES	RESEARCH ILLUSTRATIONS	BASIC DEVELOPMENTAL ISSUES	EXAMPLES OF THEORISTS[a]
Ssociocultural theories	In one study children's ability to plan ahead in accomplishing informal activities (such as deciding what to eat for breakfast and do after school) improved over the elementary years and depended on cultural experiences (Gauvain & Perez, 2005).	*Nature and nurture*: Emphasis is on nurture. Children become familiar with tools during daily activities. The capacity for acquiring cultural traditions is made possible by genetically-guided abilities. *Universality and diversity*: Virtually all children acquire language, values, and practical skills by participating in everyday activities. Variations occur in the tools, customs, and ideas children learn. *Qualitative and quantitative change*: Initially, a child looks to an older child or adult for help on a task and later tries out procedures independently. As quantitative advancements, children gradually become more knowledgeable about cultural information and traditions.	Lev Vygotsky A. R. Luria James Wertsch Barbara Rogoff Patricia Greenfield Mary Gauvain Jerome Bruner Michael Cole Alex Kozulin Jose Medina Virginia Martinez
Developmental systems theories	In one study a wide range of factors were associated with hours children slept, including children's own activities (excessive television viewing was associated with little sleep), family functioning (eating meals together on weekdays was associated with long sleep), and demographic factors (older African American children slept fewer hours than did children from other groups; Adam, Snell, & Pendry, 2007).	*Nature and nurture*: Multiple factors in the child (nature) and outside the child (nurture) interweave in development. The child's own activity also affects growth. *Universality and diversity*: Developmental changes occur in everyone from conception to death. Some changes are common, whereas others are unique and linked to historical events, family relationships, and personal circumstances. *Qualitative and quantitative change*: Most change is quantitative, but shifts occur that result in entirely new ways of behaving. A baby swats awkwardly at a rattle with her hand and later picks it up with in a proficient finger grip.	Urie Bronfenbrenner Arnold Sameroff Margaret Beale Spencer Suzanne Fegley Richard Lerner Kurt Fischer Esther Thelen Gilbert Gottlieb Paul Baltes Theodore Wachs

[a]Several theorists have contributed to two or more theoretical perspectives.

As you read future chapters, you will see references to the seven major theories as well as to additional, more narrowly defined theoretical frameworks that home in on a particular capacity, such as morality or language acquisition. These latter frameworks are similar to the seven broad theories we have discussed in that they examine the trajectory of and contributors to growth, yet they do so with a narrower focus.

Any well-regarded developmental theory—big or small—explains a portion of a child's growth while omitting other parts. Hence, a good theory is neither right nor wrong but, rather, a more or less useful tool in understanding development. As you work with children, you may find that certain theories help you make sense of a situation. A student who appears unable to remember instructions may prompt you to apply the cognitive process perspective, whereas another young person who is chronically off task may prod you to consult the behavioral learning framework.

Developmental Systems Prompt 1.1

As you learn about children, watch for the influences of family, culture, and community on their growth.

Whichever theory you apply to a classroom situation, it's important to keep in mind that children's upbringing affects all areas of their growth. For example, when applying a cognitive process framework to children's comprehension of speech, you may find it instructive to consider not only intellectual processes but also cultural traditions. A boy who looks away when confused may have learned at home to listen quietly and not ask questions. Thus, we encourage you to get in the habit of pausing every now and then, and think about how connections among customs at home, at school, and in the community collectively interact with children's abilities, interests, self-perceptions, and genetic profiles. As you have learned, developmental systems theories are productive tools for revealing the interaction of factors. We invite you to watch for *Developmental Systems Prompts* as you read, margin notes that scaffold your ability to recognize the implications of complexity in the child's life.

Summary

Developmental theorists have proposed a variety of explanations as to how and why children change over time. These explanations are classified into seven theoretical frameworks: biological, behaviorism and social learning, psychodynamic, cognitive-developmental, cognitive process, sociocultural, and developmental systems perspectives. The seven frameworks focus on different elements of development and place greater or lesser importance on nature versus nurture, universality versus diversity, and qualitative versus quantitative change. Teachers and other practitioners may find that one or more of these frameworks, along with more specific theories, are relevant to their work. A lot can be learned about specific aspects of growth by looking through the lens of a single theoretical framework, yet it can also be useful to periodically broaden their mind-set to a range of factors, including the child's genetic profile, resources in the environment, and any personal hardships, that are likely to affect developmental change.

MyLab Education Self-Check 1.3

From Theory to Practice

1.4 Formulate educational practices that foster children's age-related development and academic achievement.

The field of child development offers practical information for those who teach, guide, and support children in other ways. Yet it is up to educators and other practitioners to do the hard work of translating general developmental knowledge into actual practice with children. At the heart of this translation process is compassion for children. Children are nurtured most effectively when adults understand how children commonly progress toward maturity and adjust to individual needs and cultural backgrounds. A part of this translation process is encouragement of children's initiative, such that children take action, make choices, and reflect on their knowledge.

Teachers, counselors, nurses, and family advocates apply similar sensitivities in their services for children. Exactly how professionals embody these qualities depends on the populations they serve and the specific goals they pursue. In educational environments, teachers and other school professionals have the opportunity to integrate this knowledge while delivering a high-quality education for all students in their care. When educators provide exemplary instruction *and* respond sensitively to children's current states and trajectories of growth, they are providing children with a **development-enhancing education**. In Table 1-2, you can see qualities of schooling that that fosters children's academic achievement while also nurturing their physical, cognitive, and social-emotional well-being.

By studying the developmental pathways of students, you set the groundwork for effective instruction. By further empathizing with students' unique personalities, talents, disabilities, and cultural knowledge, you amplify your positive impact on children. In delivering a strong education that reflects concern for personal needs, you stand to truly make a difference in their lives. The feature on pages 27 to 28, "Development-Enhancing Education with Infants, Children, and Adolescents," provides illustrations of educators guiding young people of various ages while responding perceptively to their cultural and individual needs.

MyLab Education Application Exercise 1.3
Identify Development-Enhancing Education

Evaluate a kindergarten teacher's lesson on sinking and floating from the perspective of development-enhancing education. In the Identify Development-Enhancing Education exercises, you can practice looking for compassion, age-appropriate instruction, cultural inclusion, attunement with individual needs, and encouragement of children's initiative..

MyLab Education Application Exercise 1.4
Identify Development-Enhancing Education

Examine a high school lesson from the perspective of development-enhancing education.

Applying Knowledge of Child Development

Providing all children with a development-enhancing education is an ambitious goal but one you can aspire to throughout your career. Let's look at 10 specific objectives that can help you get started:

- **Respect children.** One of the joys of being an educator is having daily exposure to the curiosity, imagination, empathy, and enthusiasm of children. Developmentally responsive educators realize that these wonderful qualities serve as catalysts for learning. It is up to adults to recognize children's distinctive ways of learning, encourage their expression, and gradually scaffold children toward greater self-control, consideration of others, and depth of knowledge.

Table 1.2 Properties of a Development-Enhancing Education

QUALITIES	EXAMPLES OF INDICATORS
Is compassionate with children	• Expresses interest, concern, and positive emotions when interacting with children • Over time establishes warm and secure relationships with children • Warmly invites children's contributions during class, validates their knowledge, and gently nudges them toward more advanced understandings
Harmonizes lessons, interactions, classroom procedures, and other services with children's age-related abilities	• Sets instructional objectives that are within the grasp of children • Selects academic concepts that are relevant, understandable, and consequential for children • Facilitates positive peer relationships in age-appropriate groups, classroom rules, and guidance on friendships
Is inclusive of the cultures, identities, and demographic backgrounds of the children, families, and communities being served	• Speaks to a classroom of children in a way that is inclusive and compatible with their cultural traditions • Shows sensitivity to the identities that children develop depending on their gender, race, ethnicity, religion, and national origin • Addresses the assets and hardships children experience in their communities
Is attentive to children's individual needs	• Designs instruction such that children of varying ability levels can achieve reasonable progress • Adapts instructional objectives, the format of the lesson, and assessment strategies for children for whom the lesson is not an optimally challenging exercise • Provides coaching for children who have trouble coping with transitions between subjects, dealing with anger or frustration, and attentional demands of school
Is encouraging of children's initiative during lessons, interactions, and decision making	• Arranges for children to share their knowledge at the beginning of a lesson, actively process information during the lesson, and demonstrate new knowledge at its conclusion • Allows children to make meaningful choices in curricular matters, for example, in which of several books to read or topics to examine in an essay • Engages children in active exploration of topics, for instance, by exploring a local habitat, acting out a scene in a play, and making predictions and analyzing data

Development-Enhancing Education

Development-Enhancing Education with Infants, Children, and Adolescents

Infancy

Set up a safe and interesting environment for exploration.

- A caregiver in an infant center designs her environment so that babies and toddlers can safely crawl, walk, and climb both inside and on the playground. A quiet corner is reserved for small infants not yet able to move around. Various materials are carefully arranged to be within reach. Duplicates of popular toys are available.

Arrange clean and quiet areas for meeting physical needs.

- A teacher in an early intervention program sets up the environment so that he can help toddlers with diapering, using the toilet, and washing their hands in a hygienic area. He talks to children while feeding, diapering, and toileting, explaining what's happening and encouraging small steps toward self-care.

Provide culturally sensitive care, and support families' home languages.

- A teacher who is bilingual cares for a few toddlers who speak Spanish at home. The teacher speaks mainly in Spanish to the children but also rotates through stories and songs in English and Spanish and includes labels in the two languages on toys and supplies.

Early Childhood

Provide reassurance to children who have difficulty separating from their families.

- A child care provider establishes a routine for the morning. After children say good-bye to their parents, they stand at the window with their teacher, wave to parents walking to their cars, and find an activity to join.

Create a classroom environment that permits children to explore their surroundings.

- A preschool teacher makes several centers available to children during free-choice time. The stations include areas for playing with blocks, completing puzzles, doing arts and crafts, engaging in dramatic play, and listening to recordings of books.

Introduce children to the joys of literature.

- A preschool teacher reads to children at least once each day. She chooses books with entertaining stories and vivid illustrations that capture children's attention.

Middle Childhood

Encourage family members to actively participate in their children's education.

- A religious educator invites parents and other family members to contribute in some small way to one of the classes. Parents assist with organizing musical performances, baking cookies, and hands-on help during lessons.

Ensure that all students acquire basic academic skills.

- A second-grade teacher individualizes reading instruction for her students based on their skill levels. She works on letter identification and letter–sound correspondence with some, comprehension of simple stories with others, and selection of books with students who are already reading independently.

Give children the guidance they need to develop positive relationships with peers.

- When two children are quarreling, their teacher asks them to take turns telling their sides and then generates a few ways they might settle the dispute.

Early Adolescence

Design a challenging curriculum that incorporates knowledge from several content areas.

- A middle school teacher designs a unit on "war and conflict," integrating writing skills and concepts from social studies. He encourages students to bring in newspaper clippings about current events and compare the circumstances to events in history.

Assign every young adolescent an adviser who looks after his or her welfare.

- During homeroom with her advisees, a seventh-grade teacher makes sure that each student is keeping up with assignments. She encourages her advisees to let her know their concerns about course work, school, and classmates.

Show sensitivity to youngsters who are undergoing the physical changes of puberty.

- A sports coach makes sure that adolescents have privacy when they dress and shower after team practice.

(Continued)

Development-Enhancing Education *(Continued)*

Late Adolescence

Expect students to meet high standards for achievement, and give them the support they need to meet those standards.

- An English composition teacher posts a list of major steps involved in writing—planning, drafting, writing, editing, and revising—and asks his students to use these steps in preparing their essays. He then monitors students' drafts and gives feedback to guide revisions.

Encourage adolescents to give back to their communities.

- A high school requires all students to participate in 50 hours of volunteer work or service learning in their town. Students follow a protocol for setting up the internship and reflecting on their learning afterwards in written reports.

Educate adolescents about the academic requirements of jobs and colleges.

- A high school guidance counselor posts vacant positions in the area, listing the work experience and educational requirements for each.

MyLab Education
Artifact Example 1.1

Find Developmental Meaning *How does 11-year-old Melanie portray her teacher, Mrs. Lorenzo?* Children draw teachers they like as Melanie did, caring for children, bandaging injured knees, sharing treats at snack time, providing private help with a worksheet, etc.

MyLab Education
Content Extension 1.1

Learn about the kinds of concerns with children that various kinds of professionals have.

- **Develop warm relationships.** Teacher–student relationships emerge over time. Affectionate relationships with teachers promote children's emotional adjustment, engagement in lessons, academic achievement, and inclusion with peers (Gagnon, Huelsman, Kidder-Ashley, & Ballard, 2009; Pham & Murray, 2016; K. M. White, 2016). Support from teachers is especially advantageous when things go awry in a student's life. When children experience disruption in the family, rejection by peers, or other upsetting situations, having a good relationship with a teacher facilitates coping (Elledge et al., 2016). You can see how 11-year-old Melanie portrays the warmth of her teacher, Mrs. Lorenzo, in Artifact Example 1.1.

- **When planning the curriculum, consider age-related abilities.** In many aspects of learning, children at a certain age exhibit similar abilities. Suggesting mathematical development, an infant might notice that one pile of blocks has more than another, a preschool child count 10 plastic teddy bears, a second grader perform basic numerical calculations, and a high school student understand quadratic equations (Berthold & Renkl, 2009; M. Carr, 2012; Ebersbach, 2016). By matching the demands of the curriculum to children's evolving levels of understanding, adults maximize children's learning. A 3-year-old child could be encouraged to march to a lively song but would not be asked to explain its historical themes.

- **Gently nudge children forward.** To communicate effectively with students, adults must meet children *where they are*, at their current levels of functioning. But to promote development, adults must also introduce tasks of increasing complexity. Adults can guide children in pursuing learning objectives that are within reach, given a little hard work and modest levels of guidance. A school counselor, for instance, may guide a reserved girl on how to gain acceptance by peers, suggesting that she smile, stand close to a group of classmates, and say something relevant to their conversation. Children may initially need reminders when trying new behaviors but eventually try them on their own. Other basic strategies for extending children's abilities depend on the specific duties that professionals have, as you can read about in a For Further Exploration feature.

- **Balance choice with guidance.** During each age level, children need to make some decisions on their own while, in other situations, they need direction from adults. An infant's choices are quite simple—choosing whether to return an eye gaze with an adult, which toys to play with, and whether to crawl one direction or another. In the preschool years, teachers sometimes introduce academic concepts during play yet allow plenty of latitude in the roles children take (Weisberg, Hirsh-Pasek, & Golinkoff, 2013). With older students, teachers often give students choices in how they demonstrate knowledge—for example, in writing essays, preparing posters, or designing graphic presentations (Hagay & Baram-Tsabari, 2015; Patall, Cooper, & Wynn, 2010).

Development in Culture

Development-Enhancing Education in Japan

Teachers in Japan share many beliefs with American teachers about appropriate care of young children. Japanese teachers take a holistic view and value children's physical, social-emotional, and cognitive growth. Like American teachers, they endorse such practices as giving children outdoor play, fostering cooperation among peers, engaging in realistic tasks from their everyday world, and encouraging the success of *all* children (Hegde, Sugita, Crane-Mitchell, & Averett, 2014; Nakayasu, 2016).

How Japanese teachers express their sensitivity to children is somewhat unique. In Japan, teachers achieve attunement with children by carefully observing and anticipating their needs. Teachers interpret subtle facial cues and situational factors that reveal children's motivations (Rothbaum, Nagaoka, & Ponte, 2006). A Japanese preschool teacher who observes a worried preschooler staring intently at a juice box would not wait for the child to ask for help but would discretely demonstrate how to put the straw into the box and sip the juice. Japanese teachers value empathy and emotional closeness and believe that they should help children *before* children verbalize their concerns (Rothbaum et al., 2006).

Japanese teachers also demonstrate compassion while encouraging children to get along with peers. They ask children to respond sympathetically and inclusively when classmates appear isolated (Hayashi, Karasawa, & Tobin, 2009). Teachers may unobtrusively ease a shy child into a group of children playing together—for example, by asking the child to join a pretend tea party in the housekeeping area of the classroom. Because preschool class sizes are large in Japan, children have many occasions to solve conflicts on their own, teach one another rules of etiquette, and assist peers in distress (Hayashi et al., 2009). When arguments between children escalate, teachers do not confront children directly but rather tactfully show or explain proper behavior (Peak, 2001; Tobin, Wu, & Davidson, 1989).

Sourcenext/Alamy Stock Photo

I CAN HELP. Many Japanese teachers anticipate children's needs before children express them.

With older students, Japanese teachers tend to express their affection by communicating high expectations and providing engaging activities. In Japan, all children are considered capable but not necessarily equally motivated (Ansalone, 2006). As a result, teachers often remind children to work diligently. When individual differences in achievement levels become obvious, exceptionally skilled students are invited to tutor less proficient peers.

- **Reflect on children's upbringing.** To some degree, methods of *development-enhancing education* are culturally defined. Therefore, you will serve children from unfamiliar cultures most effectively if you find out about their traditions, remain sensitive to any signs of confusion or discomfort at school, and make the effort to explain why rules are the way they are. You can read about how adults in one society express compassion to children in the Development in Culture feature "Development-Enhancing Education in Japan."

- **Make a commitment to supporting every child in your care.** As you are finding in your reading, helping all children achieve requires professional insight. Many teachers and other school personnel strive for **educational equality**, the motivation to provide all students with the same high standard of education. Yet not every student succeeds with instruction that is well designed yet does not accommodate personal needs. Thus, some educators additionally aspire toward **educational equity**, the notion that all children deserve to be provided with a high-quality education that meets their individual needs.

- **Capitalize on each child's strengths.** Individual children have their own talents and assets. A child who is particularly curious about the physical world may, as an infant, carefully observe patterns of light; at later ages, become an industrious builder of blocks; and, eventually, a bioengineer who designs lifesaving medical equipment. Adults can sustain the child's curiosity by encouraging exploration and arranging instructive experiences. Finding a child's strengths is particularly important when he or she acts out or has obvious trouble learning. Special talents can become access points for future learning, especially when the lesson is reduced in complexity (Fenton & McFarland-Piazza, 2014).

- **Offset adversity.** When children have had more than their share of hardships, you can address their needs while conveying optimism. Children who have faced serious problems (e.g., abuse, neglect, or parents' substance abuse) gather strength when teachers form a caring relationship with them, communicate high expectations for achievement, and allow them a voice in their education (Roffey, 2016).

- **Integrate cultural customs into lessons.** By learning about the cultures of children in your care, you gain a basis for making activities meaningful. When you invite children to share information about their hobbies or family origins, you validate the importance of these aspects of their lives. As you plan instruction, you can address individual interests or experiences, perhaps a fascination with sports, familiarity with another culture, living with a seriously ill grandparent, having a passion for music, or having moved from another state or country.

Strengthening the Commitment

You will learn a lot about child development from this book and from observations of children, informal conversations with them, analyses of their work, and discussions with experienced professionals. But you cannot learn all there is about children from one college course or a year in a school classroom. As you move through your career, you will find yourself stumped every now and then as children struggle despite your best efforts. Continued access to the field of child development can help you address dilemmas as they come up and stay abreast with new research. Following are three things to consider:

- **Continue to take courses in child development.** Additional course work is one sure way of keeping up to date on (a) the latest scientific results on child development and (b) evidence on the effects of certain practices with young people. Such course work has been shown to enhance teachers' understanding of children's development and effective use of instructional strategies (Algozzine et al., 2011; Buettner, Hur, Jeon, & Andrews, 2016; Darling-Hammond & Bransford, 2005; T. M. McDevitt, Jobes, Sheehan, & Cochran, 2010).

- **Reach out to colleagues who share your commitments.** Working together, you and like-minded teachers can keep each other focused on your goal of a high-quality education, one in which individuals are given the chance to progress academically and develop along a healthy trajectory. You can remind one another to select age-appropriate curricula, use engaging instructional methods, establish safe and inclusive classroom environments, maintain uniformly high expectations, and facilitate warm relationships with children (Early et al., 2007).

- **Stay abreast with new insights from developmental scientists and educators.** Many professional organizations hold regular meetings at which you can hear researchers and practitioners exchange ideas. Such meetings enable everyone to learn about the latest research findings and instructional methods. School district offices regularly invite experts to inform educators about teaching, learning, and maintaining school policies and procedures that encourage active learning. As you listen to these presentations, take a holistic perspective, thinking about how new methods align with the full range of children's physical, cognitive, and social-emotional states and pathways of change.

Summary

Care of youngsters is enriched with an understanding of typical developmental pathways and their many variations. As a future educator, counselor, nurse, or other type of professional, you can identify and capitalize on individual children's strengths and nudge them toward increasing responsibility. Through ongoing education, conversations with colleagues, and participation in professional organizations, you can keep up-to-date on advancements in child development and maintain an optimistic outlook on your ability to serve children.

MyLab Education Self-Check 1.4

Practicing For Your Licensure Examination

Many teaching tests require students to apply what they have learned about child development to brief vignettes and multiple-choice questions. You can practice for your licensure examination by reading the following case study and answering a series of questions.

Latisha

Latisha, who is 13 years old, lives in a housing project in an inner-city neighborhood in Chicago. An adult asks her to describe her life and family, her hopes and fears, and her plans for the future. She responds as follows:

> My mother works at the hospital, serving food. She's worked there for 11 years, but she's been moved to different departments. I don't know what my dad does because he don't live with me. My mother's boyfriend lives with us. He's like my stepfather.
>
> In my spare time I just like be at home, look at TV, or clean up, or do my homework, or play basketball, or talk on the phone. My three wishes would be to have a younger brother and sister, a car of my own, and not get killed before I'm 20 years old.
>
> I be afraid of guns and rats. My mother she has a gun, her boyfriend has one for protection. I have shot one before and it's like a scary feeling. My uncle taught me. He took us in the country and he had targets we had to like shoot at. He showed us how to load and cock it and pull the trigger. When I pulled the trigger at first I feel happy because I learned how to shoot a gun, but afterward I didn't like it too much because I don't want to accidentally shoot nobody. I wouldn't want to shoot nobody. But it's good that I know how to shoot one just in case something happened and I have to use it.
>
> Where I live it's a quiet neighborhood. If the gangs don't bother me or threaten me, or do anything to my family, I'm OK. If somebody say hi to me, I'll say hi to them as long as they don't threaten me. . . . I got two cousins who are in gangs. One is in jail because he killed somebody. My other cousin, he stayed cool. He ain't around. He don't be over there with the gang bangers. He mostly over on the west side with his grandfather, so I don't hardly see him. . . . I got friends in gangs. Some of them seven, eight years old that's too young to be in a gang. . . . They be gang banging because they have no one to turn to. . . . If a girl join a gang it's worser than if a boy join a gang because to be a girl you should have more sense. A boy they want to be hanging on to their friends. Their friends say gangs are cool, so they join.
>
> The school I go to now is more funner than the school I just came from. We switch classes and we have 40 minutes for lunch. The Board of Education say that we can't wear gym shoes no more. They say it distracts other people from learning, it's because of the shoe strings and gang colors.
>
> My teachers are good except two. My music and art teacher she's old and it seems like she shouldn't be there teaching. It seem like she should be retired and be at home, or traveling or something like that. And my history teacher, yuk! He's a stubborn old goat. He's stubborn with everybody.
>
> When I finish school I want to be a doctor. At first I wanted to be a lawyer, but after I went to the hospital I said now I want to help people, and cure people, so I decided to be a doctor. (J. Williams & Williamson, 1992, pp. 11–12)[a]

Constructed-Response Question

1. How do the contexts in which Latisha is growing up affect her development? Describe at least three elements of Latisha's environment that seem to influence her.

Multiple-Choice Questions

2. Which of the following theoretical accounts of Latisha's characteristics would most likely focus on the active role that Latisha plays in her own development and the stagelike changes that may periodically take place in her thinking?

   a. A biological theory
   b. A behaviorist or social learning theory
   c. A psychodynamic theory
   d. A cognitive-developmental theory

3. Which of the following theoretical accounts of Latisha's characteristics would most likely explain her characteristics as being the outcome of her personal activity and the numerous factors interacting inside her and in her multilayered social environment?

   a. A cognitive-process theory
   b. A sociocultural theory
   c. A developmental systems theory
   d. A biological theory

[a] "Case Study: Latisha" by J. Williams and K. Williamson, from "I Wouldn't Want to Shoot Nobody: The Out-of-School Curriculum as Described by Urban Students" from ACTION IN TEACHER EDUCATION, Volume 14, No. 2, pp.11–12, 1992. Copyright © 1992 by J. Williams and K. Williamson. Reprinted with permission of Action in Teacher Education, published by the Association of Teacher Educators, Manassas Park, VA.

MyLab Education Licensure Practice 1.1

Key Concepts

child development (p. 3)
physical development (p. 4)
cognitive development (p. 4)
social-emotional development (p. 4)
holistic perspective on child development (p. 4)
context (p. 5)
culture (p. 5)
nature (p. 5)
nurture (p. 5)
temperament (p. 5)
maturation (p. 5)
sensitive period (p. 7)
universality (p. 7)
diversity (p. 7)
qualitative change (p. 8)
quantitative change (p. 9)
stage (p. 9)
stage theory (p. 9)
theory (p. 16)
biological theory (p. 16)
behaviorism (p. 17)
social learning theory (p. 17)
psychodynamic theory (p. 18)
cognitive-developmental theory (p. 19)
cognitive process theory (p. 19)
sociocultural theory (p. 20)
developmental systems theory (p. 21)
development-enhancing education (p. 25)
educational equality (p. 29)
educational equity (p. 29)

Chapter Two

Research and Assessment

Ariel Skelley/DigitalVision/Getty Images

Learning Objectives

2.1 Explain how knowledge of child development derives from the scientific method, in which critical thinking is used, ethical standards are maintained, and children and families provide information about their lives.

2.2 Describe the data-collection techniques and research designs used in the field of child development and the ways that educators can apply developmental research results in their schools and classrooms.

2.3 Explain how educators can use assessments at school to guide children in a developmentally appropriate manner.

CASE STUDY

Jack's Research

Jack Reston, an elementary school principal, had recently joined a district committee charged with reducing student absenteeism. He realized that data from children and families could inform the work of his committee. He carefully considered a productive direction for an investigation. Looking back, he wrote,

> I began by asking three questions:
>
> 1. What student characteristics are associated with student absenteeism?
> 2. What are some longitudinal effects of student absenteeism?
> 3. What are some effective strategies to prevent student absenteeism?
>
> I reviewed current studies, literature, local and national profiles, written surveys, and interviews. I found that absenteeism was highly associated with dropping out of school, academic failure, and delinquency. I learned what students and parents in our school believed about the relationship between school and absenteeism. I concluded that I really did not understand the belief systems of families at risk for poor attendance in school. I conducted a massive survey of students and parents within a four-day period of time. Surveys gathered data concerning such things as respectfulness of students, safety in school, conflict management, discipline, school rules, self-esteem, and academics. In addition, the survey gathered data on mobility rates, volunteerism, and levels of education in parents. The identity of the families surveyed was kept unknown. . . .
>
> Student teachers from a nearby university and local educators with experience in action research interviewed selected students and parents. The interviews were conducted over the telephone or face-to-face. (Reston, 2007, pp. 141–142)[a]

After collecting and analyzing his data, Jack realized that, by and large, his students were not motivated by such extrinsic rewards as prizes or certificates. He also concluded that students did not perceive the rules to be fair or effectively enforced by the school. By reflecting on these observations and the relatively low achievement of students, Jack realized that he needed to change his policies and style of interacting with students:

> This information led to major changes in our approach to improving attendance in our school. First, we stopped spending large sums of money for rewards and drawings. Although these are nice things for students, they are ineffective in dealing with the problem of poor attendance. Second, we recognized punitive measures were having little effect on attendance. This led us to the belief that students succeeding in school were more likely to attend school regularly.
>
> We began a concentrated effort to improve the success of students at school both academically and emotionally. This included the use of student/parent/teacher/principal contracts, daily planners for students, individual conferences between the student and the principal every 14 days to review grades and behaviors, better assessments to locate students having academic problems, improved instructional techniques and alignment of curriculum, and more concentrated efforts to improve the self-esteem of students . . . .
>
> Based on these findings, I worked with teachers and parents to develop quick responses that unite the student, parent, educator, and community in a preventive effort to minimize absenteeism. (Reston, 2007, p. 142)[a]

- How did Jack ensure that his research was of high quality?
- What ethical practices did Jack use as he conducted his research?

[a]Excerpts from "Reflecting on Admission Criteria" by J. Reston. In *Action Research: A Guide for the Teacher Researcher* (3rd ed., pp. 141–142), by G. E. Mills, 2007, Upper Saddle River, NJ: Merrill/Prentice Hall. Reprinted with permission of the author.

Jack Reston understood that in order to reduce students' absenteeism, he would first need to determine why students were skipping school. To answer this question and find out what would make school more inviting for students, he learned what he could from other experts, collected all sorts of information, and analyzed responses with an open mind. The integrity of Jack's research derived from his critical thinking, in which he questioned his own assumptions and waited to form conclusions until he examined all the data and talked through interpretations with stakeholders. He also followed ethical practices by protecting the confidentiality of participants' individual responses and engaging all members of the community in a search for solutions. In the end Jack's research was key to strengthening educators' relationships with students, improving their assessments, and prompting them to scaffold students' organizational skills.

Outline

Principles of Research

2.1 Explain how knowledge of child development derives from the scientific method, in which critical thinking is used, ethical standards are maintained, and children and families provide information about their lives.

To contribute to knowledge of child development, researchers must follow three basic principles. First and foremost, they must obey a strict ethical code. Second, they must follow the steps of the scientific method. Finally, they must select children and adolescents who can provide needed information. We examine each of these principles in turn.

Ethical Protection of Children

A paramount concern for scholars of child development is that they conduct research in an ethical manner, in particular, that they are honest and respectful of the rights of children (American Psychological Association, 2002; Ruhe et al., 2016; Society for Research in Child Development, 2007). To protect children's rights, developmental scientists aspire to these codes of conduct:

- *Do no harm.* Researchers prioritize the welfare of children over their own desires for information. They avoid procedures that cause children stress, embarrassment, or pain.
- *Get approval from authorities.* Before collecting data from children, researchers prepare a proposal of the kinds of data children will provide, any risks and benefits children might encounter, procedures for reducing harm to minimal levels, and measures for advising children and families about the research. They then seek approval for their proposed study from authorities at their university, school district, or other organization.
- *Obtain consent from participants and their families.* Also before collecting data, researchers explain to parents and children what the study entails in time and involvement and ask parents for written permission for children to take part in the research. Children are asked to give their assent orally or in writing, depending on their age. If permission is unnecessary because researchers will not intrude into children's customary activities (e.g., researchers want to observe children's spontaneous play at the park), appropriate institutional authorities review the study and do not require consent.
- *Preserve children's privacy.* Investigators usually describe group trends in their results. When they single out a particular child, they use a fictitious name and withhold identifying information.
- *Be honest.* Children expect adults to be honest. Researchers do not exploit or undermine this assumption. Thus, deception with children is almost always avoided. Exceptions are evaluated by authorities and generally require an explanation to children afterward and efforts to regain their trust.
- *Communicate openly.* After children provide the data that will be used in the investigation, researchers respond to any questions from children and parents. When investigators write up their results, they often send families a brief description of their findings. Investigators share the results with other scholars and, if appropriate, with the public.

The Scientific Method

The **scientific method** is a powerful strategy for acquiring and refining insights about children because it requires researchers to think critically about the data they collect and the conclusions they draw. For developmental scholars, the scientific method includes these general steps:

1. *Pose a question.* Researchers clearly state the question they want to answer. When they are able to make predictions about the outcomes of their study, they state hypotheses.
2. *Design an investigation.* Once the question is clear, researchers must figure out the kinds of information that will help answer it and, if applicable, test hypotheses. With specific methods in mind, they obtain guidance on ethical dimensions.
3. *Collect data.* Researchers recruit children and gather information using carefully defined procedures.
4. *Analyze the data.* Researchers organize the data, categorize children's responses, look for themes, and, when appropriate, perform statistical tests. After making sense of the data, they draw conclusions relevant to their research question.
5. *Share the results.* Researchers write up the study's purpose, methods, results, and conclusions and present the paper at a conference, submit it to a journal, or both. Scientific peers evaluate the investigation on its merits, identify any flawed arguments, and build on conclusions they find convincing. Provocative results may lead the original investigator or colleagues to start the cycle again with a new question or hypothesis.

This give-and-take among scientists leads to progress. What makes the scientific method especially powerful is that well-tested assertions are an impetus to theoretical advancement. Ideas about growth that are contradicted with data should be revised, and interventions that fail to generate positive outcomes must be reconsidered. This is not to say that scholars always generate clear results, interpret their results realistically, or give up on favorite hypotheses in the face of contradictory results. Yet the fundamental commitment of scientists to correct their conclusions based on new evidence distinguishes developmental knowledge from everyday beliefs about children.

Research Participants

In most developmental research, investigators wish to make broad claims about children at a certain age or background. To make their work efficient, researchers limit attention to a manageable number of children. They first define a population and then select a subgroup, or **sample**, of that population. The sample provides a reasonable basis for making conclusions about the larger population, which it presumably resembles but is more cost-effective to examine. For example, imagine that a team of psychologists wants to know what adolescents in public high schools in San Francisco, California, think about desirable careers. With the help of administrators in San Francisco schools, the researchers obtain a list of homeroom teachers and randomly select 10% of these teachers. Next, the researchers ask the selected teachers to distribute letters, consent forms, and surveys. If the return rate of materials from students and parents is high, investigators can be reasonably confident that their *sample* of adolescents is representative of the larger *population* of adolescents in San Francisco. If, instead, a good number of potential participants decide not to join the study, or they drop out before data collection is completed, the resulting sample may be so small that the results cannot be said to represent trends in the population.

In other kinds of studies, generalizing to a large population is not the goal. For instance, a team of scholars may study one child or a small group of children intensively. These researchers hope to analyze children's experiences in enough depth that they can draw accurate conclusions about the experiences of *these children*—not about all children. In this kind of investigation, researchers recruit children who have characteristics of interest (for example, being from a certain cultural group) and then follow them closely. In their reports, the investigators would conscientiously describe the experiences of these children while protecting their anonymity and not presuming that their experiences apply to others with similar circumstances.

Regardless of whether investigators want to obtain a large representative sample or a small number of children for in-depth analysis, they must consider the role that children's backgrounds play in their conclusions. Historically, children from middle-income, white European American backgrounds were overrepresented in research, whereas children of color and those who were learning English as a second language and growing up in low-income communities were underrepresented (M. H. Bornstein, Jager, & Putnick, 2013; García Coll et al., 1996). Fortunately, many developmental researchers now recruit participants more inclusively, such as those from diverse ethnic and economic backgrounds and from families whose members are migrant, homeless, or incarcerated (Di Santo, Timmons & Pelletier, 2016; Joseph-Salisbury, 2016; Tasca, Mulvey, & Rodriguez, 2016). These outreach efforts are currently enriching our knowledge of diversity in children's personal assets and daily challenges. In writing this book, we have made special efforts to include research with diverse samples of children, and we encourage you to watch for information about the characteristics of research participants when you read reports yourself. When the backgrounds of participants differ significantly from those of children in your care, you will want to be especially cautious in accepting the conclusions.

Summary

Research with children needs to be guided by strong ethical standards, the scientific method, and access to children and families who are able and willing to provide data. The manner in which researchers integrate these principles into their investigations depends largely on the particular methods they use. The field of child development advances through the collective efforts of scientists in conducting original research studies and in the sifting, critiquing, and analyzing of patterns in the data and their relevance to theory.

MyLab Education Self-Check 2.1

Methods of Research

2.2 Describe the data-collection techniques and research designs used in the field of child development and the ways that educators can apply developmental research results in their schools and classrooms.

Investigators convert general principles of research into specific methods. Each investigation, with its theoretical foundation, research questions, and arrangements in collecting data, has advantages and disadvantages. The limitations of one study can be offset by the strengths of another investigation on the same topic, and the general conclusions about the domains of child development take all these considerations into account.

In your career as an educational professional, you will encounter claims in the media and occasionally from colleagues and parents about the latest research about children. Some of these will be well founded, and others will not be. Because not all such research is sound, some claims are based on opinions and not facts, and even well-conducted investigations can be misinterpreted, having a basic awareness of the values and shortcomings of research has become a necessary skill set for school professionals. To interpret developmental research critically, you will need to become familiar with common data-collection techniques and research designs.

Data-Collection Techniques

Researchers gather data using four kinds of techniques: self-reports, assessments, physiological measures, and observations of behavior. Each of these methods offers a unique window into the minds and habits of children.

MyLab Education
Video Example 2.1

Find Developmental Meaning *How does an interviewer encourage Claudia to explain her classification of seashells?* In this video an interviewer gently but persistently asks 12-year-old Claudia why she grouped seashells precisely as she did. Notice that Claudia initially describes her reasoning in a fairly general way, but after several questions, she elaborates on her reasoning.

Self-Reports

Researchers often ask children to explain their beliefs, attitudes, hopes, and frustrations. In fact, some of the most informative research data come in the form of youngsters' statements about themselves—that is, in the form of **self-reports**. Self-reports take two primary forms: interviews and questionnaires.

During **interviews**, researchers ask questions of children to explore their reasoning. Interviewers who succeed in making children feel safe and comfortable can learn a lot. They may sit beside children on the floor, reassure children that whatever they tell them is fine, and invite children to talk about themselves. Interviewers often start with general questions before asking for specific information.

Investigators typically conduct interviews through face-to-face conversations, which allow them to communicate directly with children. Researchers occasionally interview young people over the telephone, reducing costs of travel and involving participants who might avoid a face-to-face interview. For example, one group of researchers interviewed 14- to 16-year-old adolescents over the phone and found that they reported being able to purchase alcohol by showing fake driver's licenses or getting drink from others, behaviors they might not have revealed in face-to-face interactions (M.-J. Chen, Gruenewald, & Remer, 2009).

Developmental researchers use **questionnaires** when they need to gather responses from a large number of participants. When young people complete questionnaires, they typically read questions or statements and choose from defined options that best express their feelings, attitudes, or actions. In studies of motivation, researchers have often asked adolescents to indicate whether they want to learn as much as possible in school or, alternatively, just want to avoid failing there. From such responses, researchers have learned that both motivations exist, are sometimes even more complicated, and affect the courses they select in high school and the levels of achievement they attain (Crosnoe & Huston, 2007; Witkow & Fuligni, 2007).

Questions are asked on paper or through a digital format such as an online survey (S. M. Flanagan, Greenfield, Coad, & Neilson, 2015; Langhaug, Cheung, Pascoe, Hayes, & Cowan, 2009). Researchers have tried other technologies as well, including beepers or pagers that emit signals at regular intervals throughout the day to remind adolescents to record their experiences in notebooks or respond to a text message on their mobile phone (Hedin, 2014; Larson & Richards, 1994; K. T. Phillips, Phillips, Lalonde, & Prince, 2018).

Self-reports have complementary advantages and disadvantages. Valuable insights can emerge when researchers ask children about their views, probe their understandings in a thorough yet sensitive fashion, and confirm children's statements with other types of data. However, interviews are time-consuming and highly dependent on the interviewer's skill. Questionnaires are an efficient means to collect data yet exceed many children's reading abilities, do not allow researchers to probe, and provide no mechanism for children to express confusion or mixed feelings. In addition, when researchers are unaware of children's thinking about a topic, they may unintentionally create response options that are out of sync with children's actual views. Computers and other technologies lend efficiency to the research but are costly and depend on youngsters' familiarity with the equipment.

Another limitation of interviews and questionnaires is **social desirability**, the tendency of children to give answers that will be perceived favorably by others. For instance, adolescents may underestimate their use of illicit drugs or number of sexual partners if they perceive that the researchers view these behaviors negatively. Researchers can reduce the effects of social desirability by establishing rapport with participants, advising them that they are not being judged, letting them know that their responses will be kept confidential, and encouraging their honesty. Such tactics improve the likelihood that self-reports provide accurate glimpses into the thoughts and actions of youngsters.

Perhaps the most serious concern about self-reports is that children are not always consciously aware of their own knowledge, motivations, or behavior. The problems are most serious with young children, who do not have the verbal abilities to articulate the impressions they have. Fortunately, other kinds of data are available to supplement self-reports.

Assessments

Assessments are samples of things children say or create that reveal their knowledge, abilities, and other characteristics. A **test** is an important kind of assessment, an instrument designed to assess children's knowledge, abilities, or skills in the same manner from one individual to the next. Some tests use paper and pencil, whereas others do not, but all typically yield a result in the form of a number (e.g., a score on an intelligence test) or category (e.g., "alert" or "proficient").

Tests are frequently used to gauge the effectiveness of educational programs. In an intervention for children from low-income families, participants regularly completed tests of cognitive ability from ages 3 months to 12 years and again at ages 21 and 30 years (F. Campbell et al., 2014; F. A. Campbell, Ramey, Pungello, Sparling, & Miller-Johnson, 2002). Scores indicated that individuals who participated in a full-time high-quality child-care program as infants not only exhibited larger cognitive gains in the first few years of life but also had higher reading and math scores at age 21, compared to individuals who did not participate in the program. A second intervention, beginning at age 5 and lasting for 3 years, was less effective. These tests lead many scholars to conclude that comprehensive interventions are most effective when initiated at a young age.

MyLab Education
Video Example 2.2

Find Developmental Meaning *What does this assessment reveal about Alicia's understanding of proverbs?* It appears that Alicia can look beneath common expressions and comprehend their underlying meanings. Whether she infers the meaning of the expression, uses strong reasoning skills, or has previously encountered explanations for these sayings cannot be concluded from the assessment.

Other assessments that are not strictly tests include judgments of children's interests and moods and a wide array of behaviors and artifacts. For example, investigators might collect children's artwork, examine their essays, record children's efficiency in navigating through a maze, or analyze their understanding of commonly used verbal expressions. Some assessments involve spoken language—not the in-depth interviews described earlier but brief question-and-answer exchanges that reveal the child's knowledge, as in the assessment of 14-year-old Alicia's understanding of proverbs:

Interviewer: What does it mean when someone says, "Better to light a candle than to curse the darkness"?
Alicia: Well, it means, probably, that you're actually getting somewhere than just complaining about it and not doing anything about it.
Interviewer: What does it mean when someone says, "An ant may well destroy a dam"?
Alicia: I think it probably means that even though they're really small, they can still change things.

An advantage of assessments is that they provide clues to children's thinking. Assessments tell us only so much, however. They do not tell us how children developed the relevant skills and understandings or how deeply they know them. Nor can single assessments tell us how children might advance in their abilities if given particular kinds of instruction. Accordingly, researchers sometimes administer several assessments, perhaps before, during, and after instruction. We will return to assessments later in this chapter as a tool teachers use to guide children's learning.

Physiological Measures

To learn about children's physical, cognitive, and social-emotional development, researchers often turn to **physiological measures**, systematic appraisals of conditions in the body, including heart rate, hormone levels, bone growth, brain activity, eye movements, body weight, and lung capacity. Physiological measures yield important information about children's well-being. They allow us to monitor health with indicators of cardiovascular fitness, obesity, malnutrition, and growth processes. Adequate nutrition, weight and height trajectories, and access to vaccines are of concern to doctors and nurses working throughout childhood. Additional issues with sexual health, adequate sleep, and abstinence from drugs are a priority for health professionals serving adolescents. Physiological tests have been especially influential in recent years in persuading community health experts and educators to provide extra reassurance and support in coping skills for children who are living through traumatizing experiences, such as a disruption in the family, a parent's substance abuse, and mental health problems in a parent (M.-K. Lei, Beach, & Simons, 2018; Zalewski, Lengua, Thompson, & Kiff, 2016).

Physiological measures also uncover information about infants' cognitive development. Infants cannot use words to tell what they know, but they do reveal a lot from their behavior and physiological reactions. For example, when infants are shown the same object or pattern repeatedly, they grow accustomed to it and lose interest. This

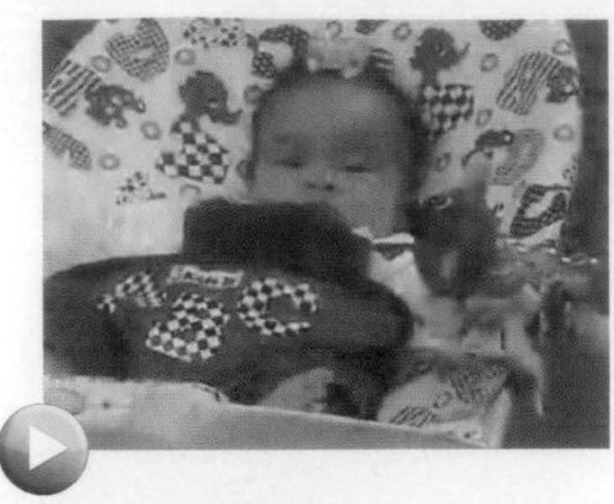

MyLab Education
Video Example 2.3

Find Developmental Meaning *What clues do you find in the video suggesting that the baby habituates to the rattle?* Notice that the baby is initially interested in the rattle, visually scanning it for a few seconds. After growing accustomed to it, she looks away. The pattern of first being engrossed with a stimulus and then getting bored with it is called habituation.

tendency, called **habituation**, can be assessed through changes in eye gaze, heart rate, and sucking. Researchers have learned a great deal about infants' attention, perception, and memory by exploiting infants' tendency to respond differently to familiar and unfamiliar stimuli. Studies in habituation have shown that infants perceive depth from visual cues and discriminate among particular consonants and vowels, the number and size of objects, and types of movements (Cantrell, Boyer, Cordes, & Smith, 2015; Fais, Kajikawa, Shigeaki, & Werker, 2009; Kavšek, 2013).

Other technologies have improved our understanding of children's brain development. We have learned of fascinating developmental patterns through animal research, analyses of brains of individuals who died during childhood, and new technologies that are implemented with living children. An example of the last of these methods is magnetic resonance imaging (MRI), which measures the varying magnetic densities of different parts of the brain (Botellero et al., 2016). You can see an example of MRI scans of a child's brain in Figure 2.1. Scan results can provide dramatic evidence when implemented in a developmental design. One team of investigators examined MRIs of the brains of healthy individuals from age 7 to age 30 and found that, compared to the children's brains, adults' brains showed fewer but stronger connections in areas of the brain that support judgment, restraint, and the ability to plan for the future (Sowell, Delis, Stiles, & Jernigan, 2001).

An advantage of physiological measures is that they give precise indications of how children's bodies and brains are functioning. A disadvantage is that the meaning of the data they yield is not always clear. The fact that infants perceive contrasts among various perceptual stimuli (e.g., between two and three items) does not necessarily indicate that they are consciously aware of these patterns (e.g., by counting the number in each set and then comparing the totals) or that they can act on their perceptions in any meaningful way. Another limitation is that many physiological tests cannot be administered frequently because they cause discomfort (e.g., some brain-scan procedures are noisy) or may be harmful if done too often (as is the case with X-rays).

Observations

Researchers conduct **observations** when they carefully watch the behavior of youngsters. Observations offer rich portraits of children's lives, particularly when they take place over an extended time and are supplemented with interviews, tests, and other data.

Researchers who conduct observations generally keep a detailed record of meaningful events in a particular setting, perhaps the family home, a classroom, or a neighborhood playground. The following notes describe interactions between a father and his 5-year-old daughter, Anna:

11:05 a.m.	Anna looks at her father, who is sitting on the couch reading the newspaper: "Wanna play Legos, Dad?" Dad says, "Sure," and puts down the paper and gets on the floor. Anna pushes a pile of Legos toward Dad and says, "Here. You can build the factory with the volcanoes."
11:06 a.m.	Dad looks puzzled and says, "What factory?" Anna laughs and says, "The one where they make molten steel, silly!" Dad says, "Oh, I forgot," and picks up a gray Lego and fits a red one to it. (Pellegrini, 1996, p. 22)

FIGURE 2.1 MRI of a child's brain.

Medical experts can tell from MRIs and other brain scans which areas of the brain are operational and how particular areas (e.g.,those registering visual sensations, verbal interpretations, or inhibition of impulsive behavior) connect up with separate regions specializing in different psychological or physiological functions).

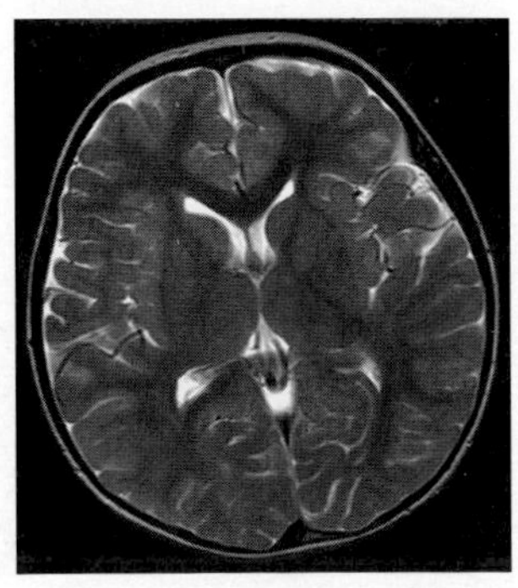

Steven Needell/Science Source

Although observers hope to describe events as faithfully as possible, they must make decisions about what to record and what to ignore. The observer who writes about Anna and her father focuses on the pair's negotiations over what to play and what to pretend. Other events, such as Anna dropping toys or her father scratching his head, would receive less attention.

Researchers frequently use observations to document characteristics and behaviors (e.g., hairstyles, dress codes, bullying behaviors) that young people display in public settings. Observations are also helpful in identifying actions that individuals may be unaware of or unable to articulate (e.g., the types of questions adults direct toward boys vs. girls or young children's ability to explain why they like to play in sand) and behaviors that violate social rules (e.g., temper tantrums, petty thefts).

The contribution of observations rests in their ability to tell us what children actually *do*—not what children *say* they do or what parents report about children's actions. Observations have their weaknesses, however. For one thing, the presence of an observer might change the actions under investigation. Children may misbehave or, alternatively, stay on task more than usual. Some young people become self-conscious or even anxious in the company of a stranger. To minimize these reactions, researchers often spend considerable time in a setting before collecting data. That way, children grow accustomed to the researchers and eventually carry on as they normally would.

Another weakness of observations is that researchers' expectations can influence their conclusions. An observer who perceives children as hostile may categorize an interaction between two boys as "hitting," whereas an observer who perceives children as friendly may see the same scuffle as "energetic play." Researchers handle this problem by spending as much time as possible in the setting, carefully defining the events and behaviors they observe, and discussing their observations with other observers. Finally, some actions, such as extreme temper tantrums in third-grade classrooms, would require a lengthy and expensive period for trained observers to obtain an adequate record and therefore are not studied often.

Integrity in Data Collection

Regardless of exactly how scholars collect their information, they continually ask themselves how they know their data-collection methods are of high quality. The specific terms for quality vary somewhat with the type of investigation. In studies with relatively large samples and statistical analyses, researchers typically are concerned with **validity**, the extent to which data-collection methods actually assess what the researchers intend to measure. To address validity, investigators must show that they are examining the essential parts of a well-defined domain. For instance, researchers who see mathematical ability as being comprised of computational proficiencies (adding, subtracting, multiplying, dividing) *and* problem-solving skills (making sense of situations by determining underlying mathematical patterns) would make a point to include *both* types of competencies in their assessments.

To protect the validity of their measurements, researchers must also rule out the influence of irrelevant traits. For instance, do scores on a test of mathematical ability reflect children's knowledge of a particular culture—for instance, are there too many questions about American sports? Are children expected by test developers to answer questions rapidly even though they have been socialized to be cautious and introspective? Does a test of scientific reasoning assess children's desire to please the experimenter as much as it assesses finesse in thinking skills? Only when researchers can say no to such questions are they reassured that their methods are valid.

The validity of data can also be enhanced by the researcher's consideration of children's energy and mindset during the research activities. Skilled investigators recognize that children must be rested and attentive during experimental tasks. Investigators also recognize that young people bring their own expectations and agendas to interactions with adults. Some participants (adolescents especially) may give responses to shock a researcher or in some other way undermine the research effort. Others may tell a researcher what they think he or she wants to hear (recall the concept of *social desirability*). Youngsters may understand words and phrases differently than researchers do. Probing sensitively, searching for confirmation through a variety of sources, and reassuring children that they are not being judged are strategies investigators use to improve the validity of data.

Researchers must also ask whether their data-collection techniques are yielding consistent, dependable results—in other words, whether their methods have **reliability**. Data are reliable when the same result is obtained in a variety of circumstances. In general, reliability is lower when unwanted influences (usually temporary in nature) affect the results. Children inevitably may be more or less rested, attentive, cooperative, honest, or articulate, depending on their circumstances. Their performance can also be influenced by characteristics of the researcher (e.g., gender, educational background, ethnic origin, appearance) and conditions in the research setting (e.g., how quiet the room is, how instructions are worded, and what kinds of incentives are given for participation).

Preparing for Your Licensure Examination

Your teaching test might ask you to identify the characteristics of valid and reliable measurements.

Sometimes an instrument itself influences the reliability of scores, as can occur when two forms of an assessment yield dissimilar conclusions about children. This could happen if one form is more difficult or if two researchers interpret the same responses differently. When researchers are making subjective judgments (e.g., about the sophistication of children's artistic skills), they must establish clear standards or run the risk of making idiosyncratic decisions.

In studies with small sample sizes in which investigators aim to portray the experiences of children with sensitivity and insight, different terms for the integrity of data collection, analysis, and interpretation are used. Scholars might suggest that they have tried to produce *trustworthy* or *credible* results by spending a long time observing children, reflecting on their own biases, asking participating children for their interpretations of events, getting input from colleagues, and corroborating the results with other information—perhaps children's interview responses, their behavior, comments from teachers and parents, and the assignments they complete at school.

Research Designs

The *research design* translates the research question into the concrete details of an investigation. The design specifies the procedures and schedule of data collection and strategies for analyzing the records that are obtained. In child development research the design typically focuses on plans to document: (a) the effects of new interventions on children, (b) the elements of children's development that occur together, (c) the particular aspects of children's behavior that change with time and those others that stay the same, or (d) the nature of children's experiences in carrying out routines in familiar groups. In Table 2.1, you can see the kinds of questions researchers attempt to answer in these four designs.

Identification of Causal Effects

In an **experimental study**, the investigator manipulates one aspect of the environment and measures its impact on children. Experiments typically involve an intervention, or *treatment*. Participants are divided into two or more groups, with the separate groups receiving different treatments or perhaps with one group (a **control group**) receiving either no treatment or a presumably less effective one. Following the treatment(s), the investigator looks for differences between the groups' performances.

In a true experimental design, participants are assigned to groups on a *random* basis; they have essentially no choice in the treatment (or absence of treatment) that they receive.[1] Random assignment increases the likelihood that any differences in

Table 2.1 Types of Developmental Designs

TYPE OF DESIGN	FOCUS	EXAMPLE
Experimental studies	Identifying causal effects in interventions	What are the effects of a counseling treatment on children's aggression?
Correlational studies	Documenting associations	What is the correlation between the number of hours per week children view aggressive television and the number of their aggressive acts at school?
Developmental studies	Revealing developmental change and stability	What is the association between children's exposure to a punitive style of parenting and their later aggressiveness?
Naturalistic studies	Describing children's daily experiences and perspectives	How do children justify having committed violent acts?

[1]Ethical considerations may lead researchers to give members of the control group an alternative treatment—something of value that will not compromise the experimental comparison. For example, in an investigation into the effects of a new tutoring program for delayed readers, identified children who do not participate in the program might receive a collection of children's books, extra help in mathematics, or another resource. In other circumstances researchers make the experimental treatment available to children in the control group *after* the study has been completed.

individuals (perhaps in the motivations or personalities of group members) are evenly distributed between groups. With the exception of administering a particular treatment, the experimenter makes all conditions of the experience identical or very similar for all groups. The researcher thus tries to ensure that the only major difference between or among groups is the experimental treatment itself. For example, during a monthlong experiment with third-graders, the treatment group receives a new science unit whereas the control group receives the regular science unit. The treatment and control lessons are each taught by equivalently knowledgeable, experienced, and enthusiastic teachers; both groups of children participate in science instruction for the same period. Therefore, any differences in the children's subsequent scientific understandings are almost certainly the result of differences in the curricula.

In many situations experiments are impossible, impractical, or unethical. When random assignment is not a viable strategy, researchers may conduct a **quasi-experimental study**, in which they administer one or more experimental treatments to existing groups (e.g., classrooms or schools; D. T. Campbell & Stanley, 1963). Because researchers cannot make sure that the groups are similar in every respect, the possibility exists that some other variable (e.g., presence of gangs at one school but not the other) may account for differences in performance at the end of the treatment.

An illustration of a quasi-experimental design is found in an investigation examining the effectiveness of different treatments for aggression with 904 elementary and junior high students in Israel (Shechtman & Ifargan, 2009). Three classrooms at a single grade level in each of 13 schools were randomly assigned to one of three 4-monthlong treatments. A counseling group informed children about aggression and coached them in controlling these urges. Students who participated in an in-class intervention read literature and took part in activities fostering empathy for classmates and emphasizing the inappropriateness of aggression. Students who participated in a control group took part in their regular classes. This study is considered a quasi-experiment because the children as individuals were not randomly assigned to treatments—rather, they were members of a particular classroom and shared the same treatment (or no treatment) with their classmates. Before and after the 4-month period, students rated their own behavior on a 7-point scale in terms of how typical various aggressive behaviors were of them (with 1 being *is not characteristic of me at all* and 7 being *is very characteristic of me*). Among the key findings were that children who had been previously identified by teachers as being especially aggressive rated themselves as significantly less aggressive after participating in either the counseling or in-class intervention group, whereas children in the control group did not, as you can see in the following data:

Average Scores on Levels of Aggression Before and After Treatment[2]

TYPE OF AGGRESSION	COUNSELING GROUP		IN-CLASS INTERVENTION		CONTROL GROUP	
	Before	After	Before	After	Before	After
Verbal aggression	4.49	4.06	4.45	3.90	4.23	4.37
Physical aggression	4.09	3.28	4.28	3.28	4.04	3.89

Another variant on experiments is the single-subject design, in which a child's behavior is studied intensively as interventions are introduced and removed. For example, investigators might look at the effects of a certain strategy, such as temporarily removing children from interaction with peers, after they have acted aggressively. The investigators would keep a careful chart of the occurrences of the target behavior before

[2]The averages in this table are means, which, if you are familiar with statistics, you will realize are calculated by adding all scores in a group and dividing by the number of individuals in that group. In a followup calculation, a judgment would be made as to whether the groups are statistically different by examining the magnitude of the difference between the means of the groups relative to the variation (or spread among scores) among the groups.

the intervention, note its frequency immediately after the intervention, and record the behavior after the intervention is removed and then reinstated (C. Wilson, Robertson, Herlong, & Haynes, 1979). If the frequency of the behavior of concern ebbs and flows consistently with the presence and absence of the intervention, the investigators can be reasonably confident that the intervention is having an effect.

True experiments are unique among research designs in the degree to which outside influences are regulated and therefore eliminated as possible explanations for results. For this reason, experiments are the method of choice when a researcher wants to identify cause-and-effect relationships. Another strength of experiments is that their rigorous procedures allow additional researchers to replicate the conditions of the study. A common drawback, however, is that to ensure adequate control of procedures, researchers regularly conduct their interventions in artificial settings, with many restrictions, which are considerably different from conditions in the real world. Because it is impossible in many situations to conduct true experiments, many quasi-experiments and single-design studies are carried out and generate tentative conclusions about causality.

Documentation of Associations

In an investigation examining associations, a researcher collects information on one factor and sees if it is related to another. Recall that in our introductory case study Jack worried about the absenteeism of his students. Imagine that he wondered whether there was a positive association between days in attendance and standardized tests scores. In Figure 2.2a, you can see the type of graph Jack might have calculated. In this hypothetical illustration, as students' days in attendance increase, their test scores rise; conversely, those with poor attendance tend to score at low levels. Of course, such an association would need to be interpreted carefully because there has been no intervention. It stands to reason that attendance promotes academic performance, yet it is possible that students who struggle academically choose to skip school because of the frustration they experience.

In other circumstances, negative associations are detected. Recall that Jack found that students needed direction with their study skills. Suppose he wanted to look into the connection between undisciplined study behaviors and achievement. He could create a simple checklist of 20 things students with disorganized study habits tend to do—forget to turn in homework, daydream in class, wait to start a demanding assignment until the night before it is due, study while simultaneously monitoring a cell phone, and so on. He could then ask students to complete the checklist, add their grade point average (GPA), and assure them that their responses would be anonymous. The total number of disorganized behaviors students reported could be plotted against their GPA. Figure 2.2b shows that in this imaginary illustration, the more disorganized behaviors the students reported, the lower their academic achievement was.

FIGURE 2.2 Positive and negative associations

(a) Positive association between students' attendance and achievement

(b) Negative association between students' disorganized study habits and grades

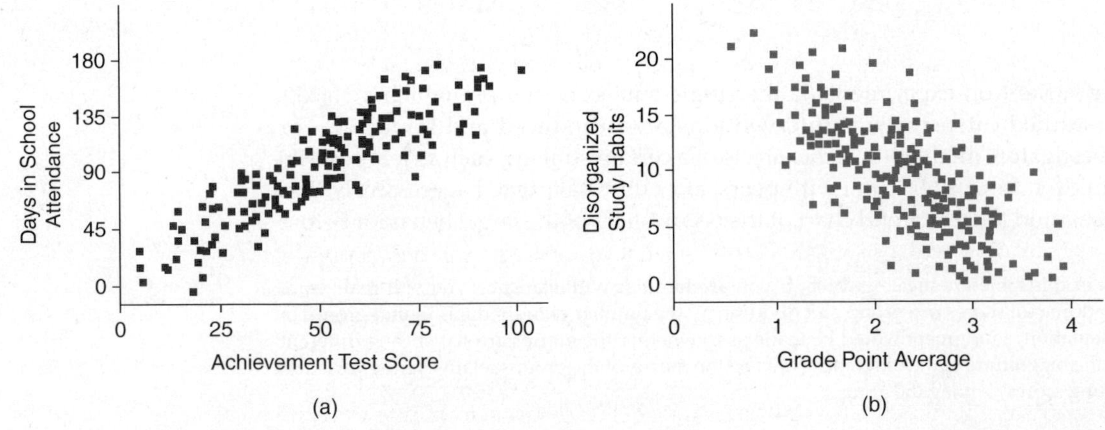

Associations are often measured with a statistic known as the *correlation coefficient*, a number that measures the extent to which two variables are related to each other and is typically between −1 and +1. The sign of the coefficient (+ or −) tells us about the direction of the relationship, positive or negative. The size of the coefficient tells us how strong the relationship is. A coefficient that is close to either +1 or − 1 (e.g., +.89 or −.76) indicates a strong link between the variables, whereas coefficients that are close to zero (e.g., +.15 or −.22) indicate a weak connection. Coefficients in the middle range (e.g., those in the .40s and .50s, whether positive or negative) indicate moderate associations.

In a **correlational study**, investigators look for naturally occurring associations among existing characteristics, behaviors, or other factors. In a study with ninety 10- to 11-year-old girls in a rural community in the northwestern part of the United States, the number of hours girls watched physically aggressive programs on television was associated with the levels of aggression in them as seen by teachers. Viewing a lot of aggressive content on television was associated with rates of verbal aggression (e.g., calling children names, with a coefficient of +.38), physical aggression (e.g., hitting or kicking peers, with a coefficient of +.25), and relational aggression (e.g., spreading rumors or gossiping about classmates, in a coefficient of +.21; Linder & Gentile, 2009). Because these data are correlational and not experimental, they do not give definitive clues as to what factors might have led girls exposed to high levels of violence to become aggressive. Although televised aggression might have provoked aggression in the girls, other conditions, such as troubled relationships at home, may have prompted the girls to watch television *and* become aggressive at school. Note also that the associations are weak, suggesting that additional factors accounted for girls' antagonism with classmates.

Correlational studies have the advantages of being relatively inexpensive to conduct and permitting the analysis of several relationships. The disadvantage is that cause-and-effect relationships cannot be determined from correlational data alone, a serious problem when it comes to interpretation. Nevertheless, correlational studies provide fascinating clues that can be examined further with other kinds of studies.

Documentation of Developmental Change and Stability

Some designs, known as *developmental studies*, examine how children grow, change, or stay the same as they grow. One approach is a **cross-sectional study**, in which a researcher compares individuals at two or more age levels at the same point in time. In a study with first- and third-grade boys, Coie, Dodge, Terry, and Wright (1991) found that first-graders were more likely to be targets of aggression than were third-graders.

Another option for examining developmental stability and change is the **longitudinal study**, in which a researcher examines one group of children over a lengthy period, often for several years and sometimes for decades. Longitudinal studies allow us to see changes in a characteristic when the same measurement is taken on repeated occasions. They also allow us to examine factors in children's early years that forecast their later adjustment. An example of a longitudinal study is Eron's (1987) investigation into factors related to aggressive behavior. Eron collected data at three points in time, first when the participants were in third grade, a second time 10 years later, and a third time 12 years after that. Factors evident when the participants were children, including parents' punitive style of discipline, the children's own preferences for watching violent television shows, and the children's lack of a guilty conscience in hurting others, were associated with their aggressiveness and criminal behavior 10 and 22 years later.

To strengthen inferences that can be made about child development, researchers have adapted developmental designs. A few have tried *microgenetic methods*, which you might think of as brief but thorough longitudinal designs. Researchers implementing these methods may study children's responses closely after training or while learning a new task over a few hours, days, or weeks (Siegler, 2006; Vygotsky, 1978). Other variations include a combination of cross-sectional and longitudinal designs. A *cohort-sequential design* replicates a longitudinal study with new *cohorts*—that is, with one or more additional groups of people born in certain subsequent years. Suhr (1999) conducted a cohort-sequential study to examine children's scores in mathematics, reading recognition, and reading comprehension. Scores had been collected every 2 years for children who were born in 1980, 1981, 1982, and 1983. Suhr found that growth in skills was rapid between ages 5 and 10 and slowed down after age 10. Because the design included children from four different birth years, Suhr could be reasonably confident that the spurt of learning that occurred between 5 and 10 years was an accurate result and not an anomaly of just one group.

As you have learned, the strengths and limitations of developmental studies are to some degree design-specific. Cross-sectional studies offer an efficient snapshot of how characteristics or behaviors differ with age, but these age differences can be attributed to a variety of factors, including maturation, schooling, and general changes in society. Longitudinal studies allow prediction of later characteristics based on earlier qualities but are expensive, time-consuming, and of questionable relevance to unstudied populations. The hybrid projects that combine features of cross-sectional and longitudinal designs, for example, the microgenetic and cohort-sequential designs mentioned earlier, have definite advantages, but they are expensive to carry out and create demands for continued involvement in waves of data collection that participants would rather avoid.

Descriptions of Children's Everyday Experiences

In a *naturalistic study*, researchers examine children's experiences in families, peer groups, schools, clubs, and elsewhere. In this type of investigation, researchers try not to prejudge children's ideas and instead listen carefully to what children say. In a recent study with adolescents from low-income families who were attending middle schools in an urban community, interviewers asked students to talk about how they might respond to particular conflicts (Farrell et al., 2008). Adolescents regularly described their emotional responses (e.g., "If they just keep on coming and coming . . . I lose my temper"; Farrell et al., 2008, p. 402) and personal goals (e.g., "I want to be able to stay on a good record like I got. I don't want to stay in fights and stuff. Because that's the way that you won't get in college and you won't get a good job"; Farrell et al., 2008, p. 403). The themes that are found in a naturalistic investigation are not necessarily those that are expected by the researchers, and a sense of discovery is a regular benefit of this kind of work.

In some naturalistic studies, known as **ethnographies**, scholars look at the everyday rules of behavior, beliefs, social structures, and other cultural patterns of an entire group of people—perhaps a community, a classroom, or a family. Researchers who conduct ethnographies typically spend many months and occasionally even a year or more collecting detailed notes in an ordinary setting, getting to know the people who congregate there and what customs mean to them (Mears, 2013; Wolcott, 1999).

In another type of naturalistic investigation, a researcher conducts a **case study**, wherein a single person's or a small group's experiences are documented in depth. (Research case studies are not to be confused with the case studies that begin the chapters in this book, which are more limited in scope.) Other naturalistic designs take the form of **grounded theory studies**, in which researchers typically collect in-depth data on a particular topic and use those data to develop a theory about the situation (Corbin & Strauss, 2008). For example, a researcher might ask young children to describe and draw pictures of playgrounds in an attempt to capture children's perspectives on play and physical activity (Hyvönen & Kangas, 2007; Noonan, Boddy, Fairclough, & Knowles, 2016).

The results of naturalistic studies usually appear as verbal assertions, often with quotations from research participants, drawings, photographs, excerpts from essays, and descriptions of the settings in which participants interacted. Reports are less reliant on statistical tests than is the case with the three other designs we've examined.[3] As an example, two researchers conducted interviews with 17 adolescent boys living in a residential treatment center or a halfway home and summarized the kinds of justifications the boys gave for their aggression (V. A. Lopez & Emmer, 2002). Using a grounded theory approach, the researchers asked the boys about their violent crimes and identified two motives. In "vigilante crimes," the boys used physical aggression to avenge another person's actual or perceived wrongful act. Sixteen-year-old Tax used a vigilante motivation in trying to protect his cousin:

[3]Naturalistic studies are sometimes called *qualitative studies* because their analyses draw heavily on verbal interpretations. Of course, many qualitative studies do report numerical results, including the number of children who articulate a particular theme.

> We had went over there to go use the phone and I went to go use the restroom. And when I came out, they had beat him [cousin] down, and hit him with a brick in his head, and cracked his skull open. So I got into a fight with one of them. I hit him with a lock and broke his jaw. He had to get three stitches in his head. (V. A. Lopez & Emmer, 2002, p. 35)

In "honor crimes," the boys used violence to protect themselves or their gang. Seventeen-year-old Muppet gave this explanation for his participation in a drive-by shooting:

> Around my birthday me and a bunch of my cousins [fellow gang members] found out about B [name of rival gang] named A who was talking shit and had jumped one of my cousins so we found out where he [rival gang member] lived and we went by and shot up his trailer house. We don't like Bs [members of rival gang] to begin with. (V. A. Lopez & Emmer, 2002, p. 37)

A key strength of naturalistic studies is their sensitivity to children's own views of everyday events and relationships. In the study we just examined, young people interpreted their aggressive acts as reasonable ways to preserve their identities, protect their kin, and solve conflicts. This kind of research also makes it possible to capture the nuances of children's involvement in complex environments. Thus, naturalistic studies can be informative windows into complex developmental systems because they inevitably speak to the power of the environment. Whether it comes to children's knowledge of science, the qualities of their friendships, or the uses to which they put digital technologies, the settings in which children grow are instrumental in learning. Naturalistic studies have limitations, however. They are difficult and time-consuming to carry out, usually require extensive data collection, and produce results that fail to disentangle causes and effects in children's lives.

In the description of investigations in this section, we included several studies focusing on one topic, children's aggression. We learned that conscientiously planned interventions can diminish aggression in children, that watching violence on television is associated with children's own fighting, that punitive child rearing by parents is connected with aggressiveness later in life, and that violent youth see their aggressive acts as justified. Each of the designs we've examined affords valuable insights, and together they give us a more complete picture.

Developmental Systems Prompt 2.1

As you read research about children, consider circumstances not examined in the study that could affect well-being. See if you can identify one or more unexamined variables, for example, cultural values and traditions, that might affect children's learning and adjustment.

Becoming a Thoughtful Consumer of Research

As you examine research studies, you will want to get in the habit of critically reading methods, results, and conclusions. If you ask a few simple questions of the investigations, you can begin to distinguish studies that are worthy of your consideration from those that are not.

As an illustration, imagine that a group of elementary teachers wants to improve children's ability to get along at school. In their initial conversations, the teachers decide that what they most want to do is increase the frequency of kind, respectful, and cooperative behaviors toward one another and school staff. A committee is appointed to study the matter and, in particular, to look at the success of existing programs. The committee addresses the following questions.

What Is the Purpose of the Research?

The committee wants to find research into effective programs that foster respectful and cooperative behaviors. With the help of a librarian, the committee identifies promising electronic databases and keywords (e.g., *character education, moral education, prosocial behavior*) to include in its search. It soon finds articles examining three widely used programs: the Ethics Curriculum for Children (Leming, 2000), the Positive Action program (Flay & Allred, 2003), and Caring School Community (Solomon, Watson, Delucchi, Schaps, & Battistich, 1988). They also review an Internet site that compares the effectiveness of these and similar programs (Institute of Education Sciences, 2006). The committee focuses on investigations into the three programs.

MyLab Education

Content Extension 2.1

Read about the research properties of three interventions in character education.

Developmental Systems Prompt 2.2

While searching educational interventions, try to find a few investigations with children who are similar to students in your care—at least in terms of age, culture, and income level. Some educational programs work effectively with children from certain backgrounds and not others because of distinctions in personal strengths, relationships, resources, and risk factors.

Who Participated in the Investigations?

The committee notes that all three investigations had fairly large samples. The projects drew from different parts of the country, families with varying income levels, and a range of ethnicities. However, none of the samples is as diverse as the population at the committee's own school, which includes many children from immigrant families, English language learners, and diverse ethnic backgrounds.

What Are the Designs of the Studies?

Each of the investigations used a quasi-experimental design. Because participants were not randomly assigned to treatment and control groups, the committee cannot know for sure whether any group differences in outcomes were due to program content, pre-existing differences between groups, or some other factor. However, there were certain procedures in the comparisons that lend some credibility to the experimental programs likely having certain effects.

What Information Is Presented about the Integrity of the Data?

The strength of the data varied across the three studies. The evaluation of the Ethics Curriculum for Children depended on participating teachers' ratings of students' behaviors; in making their ratings, the teachers may have been affected by *observer bias*—that is, they may have seen what they *expected* to see in students. The evaluation of Positive Action involved school records of disciplinary referrals, suspensions, and absentee rates. Absenteeism has probably been recorded accurately, but administrators' disciplinary actions might have been influenced by personal biases toward or against particular students, their rapport with students, or their professional skills. If biases were stronger in the experimental than the control groups, or vice versa, the results could be compromised. The investigators examining the Caring School Community program appeared to have been especially thoughtful about the quality of their data in that observers examined children without knowing which program they participated in, thereby reducing bias in interpretations.

Are the Studies Published in Reputable Journals?

Most journals use the process of sending manuscripts out to specialists in the field to comment on strengths, limitations, and suitability for publication. The committee determines that each of the three articles was published in a reputable journal that accepts only articles that have been favorably reviewed by experts in the field.

Do the Analyses Suggest Significant Results in Areas of Concern?

Results were not consistently favorable in the Ethics Curriculum for Children study. Results were generally promising for the Positive Action and Caring School Community programs. The committee finds additional support for the Positive Action and Caring School Community programs in the other documentation it examines (Battistich, 2003; Institute of Education Sciences, 2006). After considerable discussion, the committee decides that the outcomes for the Positive Action program are only tangentially related to the goals of fostering cooperative and helping behaviors. The educators conclude that the Caring School Community yielded results that are most closely aligned with their own goals for children. While making recommendations to their colleagues, the committee members suggest that they cautiously examine the program's results with children at their school given that the sample in the research is different from their own student body.

As you read research articles and reports, you can ask yourself questions similar to the ones the committee addressed. You will find that it takes practice to determine the strong and weak points of data-collection techniques and research designs. With experience, you will begin to distinguish dependable information about child development from untrustworthy sources and false conclusions..

Summary

Developmental researchers use a collection of methods in collecting data, including interviews and questionnaires, tests and other assessment tasks, physiological measures, and observations. For a type of data to be credible, it must be shown to be an accurate measure of the characteristics or behaviors being studied (a matter of *validity*) and minimally influenced by temporary, irrelevant factors (an element of *reliability*). Research designs are available that allow conclusions about cause-and-effect relationships, find associations among two or more variables, trace age trends over time, and observe children in natural environments. To make the most of developmental investigations, you must judge whether the conclusions are warranted and applicable to your own work with young people.

MyLab Education Self-Check 2.2

Assessments at School

2.3 Explain how educators can use assessments at school to guide children in a developmentally appropriate manner.

In addition to helping you understand how children develop, the field of child development offers you tools for assessing children's learning and well-being at school. In the remaining sections, we elaborate on educational assessments that identify children's abilities and needs.

Assessments in the Classroom

In education, assessments are used to evaluate what a child knows, understands, feels, and does. Teachers create tests, worksheets, essays, and other methods to assess children's academic learning, and they arrange for oral presentations, musical recitals, athletic contests, and other activities for children to show what they can do. In the best of all worlds, assessments signal to children that they have accomplished important standards and can upgrade their skills in a few key areas (Souchal et al., 2014; van den Berg, Harskamp, & Suhre, 2016). However, assessments are not always interpreted so positively. Children sometimes feel that tests expose their failures and inadequacies (Kousholt, 2016). To accentuate the positive functions of assessments, consider the following recommendations:

- **Informally assess children's abilities prior to instruction.** Assessments at the beginning of a lesson or unit of study can provide valuable information about readiness for instruction. A third-grade child who does not understand place value in mathematics will likely not add up two three-digit numbers, and a ninth-grade student lacking basic composition skills will not easily write a business letter. Asking students to perform a few relevant tasks the week before a unit begins is one way to judge the general proficiency of the class and individual needs that must be accommodated to make the schoolwork meaningful.

- **Advise children of the standards they will be working toward.** From a very early age, children are able to direct their behavior toward simple standards for tidiness, obedience, kindness, fairness, and cooperation (J. Kagan, 2008; Rakoczy, Kaufmann, & Lohse, 2016). When they go to school, children learn how the teacher defines expectations for how to comport themselves. Written rules and guidelines can be helpful, especially when children are new to the environment or first trying out complicated tasks. Teachers use *checklists* when they wish to evaluate the degree to which children's behaviors or work products reflect a set of characteristics. Figure 2.3 shows a checklist that a teacher might use to evaluate a student's oral presentation. Another tool is the **rubric**, in which a teacher communicates levels of performance on ideal features of an academic task. If you have shared the rubric ahead of time (and we encourage you to do so), children will be better able to guide their learning and understand your feedback (E. J. Lee & Lee, 2009; Shelton et al., 2016; Stiggins, 2007). In Figure 2.4, you can see a rubric for a third-grade writing assignment.

FIGURE 2.3 Checklist for evaluating an oral presentation.

From Gronlund's Writing Instructional Objectives for Teaching and Assessment (8th ed., pp. 86–87), by Norman E. Gronlund and Susan M. Brookhart, 2009, Upper Saddle River, NJ: Pearson Education. Copyright 2009 by Pearson Education. Reprinted with permission.

Directions: On the space in front of each item, place a plus sign (+) if the performance is satisfactory; place a minus sign (–) if the performance is unsatisfactory.

____ 1. States the topic at the beginning of the report.
____ 2. Speaks clearly and loudly enough to be heard.
____ 3. Uses language appropriate for the report.
____ 4. Uses correct grammar.
____ 5. Speaks at a satisfactory rate.
____ 6. Looks at the class members when speaking.
____ 7. Uses natural movements and appears relaxed.
____ 8. Presents the material in an organized manner.
____ 9. Holds the interest of the class.

• **Give feedback that guides students' learning.** Children are more likely to learn when they receive explicit feedback about their accomplishments and flaws (e.g., "You gave an excellent presentation on fish in our local streams. You hit the major points and did a nice job saying them in your own words. Remember that the assignment also requires you to think of some practical implications from the topic. If you're having trouble thinking up examples, I can help you."). Specific comments can advise children as to what they are doing well and how they might improve.

FIGURE 2.4 Rubric for stories by third-grade students

Student ____________________ Name of Story ______________________________

Element	**Needs to Work on Element** (0 points)	**Meets Expectations** (1 point)	**Exceeds Expectations** (2 points)
Organization	The paper does not make sense.	Most of the sentences seem relevant to the story and are placed in a reasonable order.	All of the sentences in the paper are about the story and unfold in a logical order.
Content	The paper includes few details that help the reader visualize the story.	A few of the paragraphs include details about the story.	Every paragraph includes details that communicate rich information about the story.
Language Usage	It is difficult to read the paper because of numerous errors in punctuation and spelling.	Most but not all beginning capitals and ending punctuation is correct. Only a few words are misspelled.	Beginning capitals and ending punctuation are all correct. No words are misspelled.
Story Elements	Setting, characters, story problem, and resolution are not clearly described.	Some story elements are clearly described and others are not.	Setting, characters, story problem, and resolution are all clearly described.
Legibility	It is difficult to decipher the words in the story due to sloppy handwriting.	Most but not all of the story is neatly written.	The entire story is legible and carefully written.
Style	The story does not include varied language or any interesting phrases.	The story includes a few colorful images and attempts at a unique and interesting style.	The story uses attention-grabbing mechanisms, creative dialogue, and varied language.

- **Remember that validity and reliability apply to all assessments.** Never over-interpret any single test score, observation, or artifact. For example, imagine that a 6-year-old draws a self-portrait with a frowning face, as one of Teresa's sons once did. The boy's teacher concluded that he was unhappy and had low self-esteem, but nothing could have been further from the truth: He was (and continues to be) a happy, self-confident individual. Perhaps on that single occasion he was simply having a bad day or was annoyed with the teacher who asked him to draw the picture.

- **Be aware of the advantages and limitations of specific assessments.** Paper-and-pencil and digital tests are often efficient ways for determining what children have learned. However, appraisals of children that rely exclusively on single formats, such as written expression, paint a lopsided picture. Children who have limited literacy skills (perhaps because they have a learning disability or only recently began to learn English) are likely to perform poorly on a test in spite of relevant knowledge. Most tests, by their very nature, can tell us little if anything about children's self-confidence, motor skills, ability to work well with others, or expertise at using equipment.

- **Look at multiple sources of information.** Because no single source of data has absolute validity, teachers and other school personnel often look for corroborating evidence when a decision must be made about a child's progress. Multiple kinds of information are useful when classrooms of children perform differently than expected. A high school teacher who notices low scores on a test may realize there are other explanations besides students not studying. Did the students not have the prerequisite understandings, were they inattentive the day of testing, or did they struggle for other reasons? Could they demonstrate concepts more easily with a drawing or graph? To gather additional information, the teacher could talk with the students, perhaps individually, or ask them to write about what they understood and were confused about in the subject.

Preparing for Your Licensure Examination

Your teaching test might ask you if it is advisable to make a decision based on a single test score.

- **Watch for bias in assessments.** Children often interpret test questions differently than do adult examiners. As an example, one team of researchers analyzed the science scores of a culturally and linguistically diverse group of elementary children (Luykx et al., 2007). Many of the children misinterpreted questions because of their cultural and language backgrounds. Several of the Spanish-speaking children confused the abbreviations of F and C (intended to stand for Fahrenheit and Celsius) with the Spanish words *frío* and *caliente*, and a few Haitian children misconstrued an item that asked how long they would be able to play between 4 p.m. and a 6 p.m. dinner, probably because they typically would have had their own main meal (which they called "dinner") earlier in the day. This assessment seems to have been biased against children who did not speak English or had different everyday experiences than did the test developers. An assessment is tainted with **cultural bias** when it offends or unfairly penalizes some individuals because of their ethnicity, gender, socioeconomic status, or cultural background. When examining children's responses, consider how children's errors may arise because of a language difference or distinct cultural perspective. If you suspect a cultural bias, you will need to obtain additional information about children's abilities.

- **Ask children to interpret their own performance.** Children regularly take notes, write essays, and create projects that hint at their understandings. Yet it is not always clear what children mean from what they write. A teacher can ask children about their work. A case in point can be seen in Artifact Example 2.1, in which 14-year-old Connor shares his U.S. history notes. Rather than assuming Connor understands the abstract concepts, his teacher might ask him to explain *popular sovereignty* and *social contract*, technical terms that he might only partially grasp.

B. Declaration of independence
1. written in 1776 By thomas Jefferson and presented to the Second Continental congress For Approval
(2) Declaration gives reasons why the U.S. wished to repel against the British
(3) the declaration presents some Basic ideals the US Adopted
A. Popular Sovereignity - Belief that people choose there own government.
B. Natural rights - All people have a certain right that noone could take Away (life, Liberty, Happiness)
C. Social Contract - In order to Be safe people needed to Form govt's, But the people should Be able to choose the goverment
4. the declaration officially created the united States.

MyLab Education
Artifact Example 2.1

Find Developmental Meaning *How does 14-year-old Connor understand abstract concepts in history?* A teacher examining 14-year-old Connor's history notes might conclude that Connor has been exposed to key doctrines in U.S. history. To determine what Connor understands about these concepts, the teacher would need to ask him to explain these ideas in his own words.

MyLab Education
Video Example 2.4

Find Developmental Meaning *How does this sixth-grade teacher prepare her students for a statewide achievement test in mathematics?* Notice how she prepares her students to answer extended-response items in mathematics, a format that they will encounter on the test. She reminds them of standards and gives them practice in solving a mathematical problem, applying a specific concept, and explaining steps in their work.

• **Help children prepare for, and make sense of, standardized tests.** Standardized **achievement tests** are assessments developed by test companies to measure consistently how well students have learned academic subjects. Periodic snapshots of students' scores on standardized tests can be informative, as when a school district finds that its students aced the language arts test but performed poorly on mathematics items. Educators may wonder whether students' low scores in mathematics were due to an ineffective curriculum, a mismatch between what students learned and what they were tested on, a cultural bias in the test, or distracting conditions on the day of the tests. An inspection of the items and discussions with students might illuminate reasons for the low performance.

• **Teach children how to take standardized tests.** Part of what tests measure, beyond the obvious academic concepts, is what children know about taking tests. To prepare students for this kind of assessment, educators can provide practice in taking tests with a similar layout, which might include multiple-choice items and other structured-response formats. You can also show children how to use their time efficiently and stick with the correct format (e.g., practicing on the computer or bubbling in answer sheets). Many students are unaccustomed to answering questions for which they have only partial information and can benefit by the teacher reasoning aloud, eliminating alternatives, and coaching students through a few items.

• **Interpret the results of standardized tests cautiously.** A critical implication of single assessments not having perfect validity and reliability is that major decisions about children, such as whether they are promoted to the next grade or allowed to graduate from high school, should *never* be made on the basis of a single test score (American Educational Research Association, 2000; Elliott, Kurz, & Neergaard, 2012). Standardized tests have other limitations that we've discussed, including being incomplete and biased reflections of skills students have acquired.

• **Reassure young people about standardized tests.** Some students have not received adequate help in rebounding from a history of poor performance. As a result, they may enter the test feeling disinterested, discouraged, or even humiliated (Kearns, 2016; Wasserberg & Rottman, 2016). Others may be well prepared for an assessment yet agonize over it because a low score, however unlikely, has negative consequences, such as not being able to play on the basketball team. One high school student in Texas described his concerns with the Texas Assessment of Knowledge and Skills (TAKS):

> In general, like, school is easy, but the TAKS test . . . make you feel like if you don't pass it you're like, "Why am I going to school?" . . . I have friends who doesn't pass the TAKS and they don't even want to come because they're not going to graduate, 'cause the tests. So they feel like, "oh, I spent my whole, my three, my four years here for nothing . . . ." They want to drop out. (Heilig, 2011, p. 2658)

Obviously, students who believe that they have no real option besides dropping out of school need immediate access to school resources, including counseling, tutoring, and career planning. Other students need support with anxiety when taking high-stakes tests, and a few perfectionists need to be reminded to strive high yet set realistic expectations for performance.

• **Educate the public about limitations in what standardized tests can tell us.** Some parents, policy makers, and members of the local community misconstrue children's standardized test scores as objective reflections of what students have learned. These scores offer a glimpse into what children know yet also reflect children's motivations, prior achievement, and test-taking savvy. The test itself affects scores based on how closely it is aligned with the school's curriculum and any cultural biases or technical flaws. Just as tests are not perfect indications of what students have learned, nor are they unequivocal signs of how well teachers have taught. Many other factors besides teaching effectiveness (including students' prior achievement and the properties of tests) affect students' performance.

• **Stay focused on children's needs.** In all the commotion over standardized tests, teachers may find it easier to remain levelheaded if they pause regularly to concentrate on children's needs. One research team identified three priorities of teachers that helped them contend with testing pressures: (1) focusing on their faith in students' abilities and individualizing instruction as necessary; (2) teaching in a culturally sensitive fashion, such that teachers and students regularly share how and what they have learned at home and in their community; and (3) showing students how the concepts and skills they are learning help them achieve important tasks rather than being merely a way to pass a test (Elish-Piper, Matthews, & Risko, 2013, p. 12).

- **Apply your knowledge of age-related abilities when designing assessments.** Assessments must match children's age-related abilities because children in each developmental period express their understandings somewhat differently. Young children can sometimes draw pictures of their understandings, say, the life cycle of a frog, that would be difficult for them to articulate orally or in writing (N. Chang, 2012). As frequent children grow older, they become increasingly proficient in putting ideas into words, although it remains a frequent challenge to express complicated understandings in writing.

MyLab Education Application Exercise 2.1
Detect Developmental Levels
In this video notice how assessments of intellectual abilities vary by age of the children. Note that pointing and moving objects can reveal knowledge in infants, whereas adolescents are able to use words and define abstract terms.

Listening to What Children Say and Watching What They Do

In addition to assessing children's learning, educators can gain insight into children's experiences through careful listening and observation. When adults establish warm and affectionate relationships with children, they set the stage for children behaving naturally and speaking their minds. It is becoming increasingly clear that teachers who have good rapport with children are able to help them make friends, develop self-control, feel comfortable at school, and facilitate their academic motivation and achievement (Graziano, Garb, Ros, Hart, & Garcia, 2016; McCormick, O'Connor, Cappella, & McClowry, 2013; Ruzek et al., 2016). While working on their relationships with children, teachers, counselors, and other school professionals can monitor mood, comfort, and overall adjustment and determine which individuals need extra reassurance. In this section, we suggest actions teachers can take to obtain valuable information from what children say and do.

Listening to What Children Say

From a young age, children are motivated to tell adults what makes them feel relaxed, interested, or happy on the one hand, or angry, bored, or sad, on the other. It is up to adults to set aside the time, put youngsters at ease, and let them speak their minds. Here's how you can gain access to children's perspectives:

- **Let children know you care.** The surest way into a child's heart is to express affection sincerely and dependably. Continual reassurance is important, particularly for children who have not developed secure relationships with parents. Greeting children with affection, smiling at them, keeping promises, staying tactful, and letting them know that you respect them are ways to earn trust over time. When you have earned students' confidence, they are more likely to articulate what's on their mind.

MyLab Education
Video Example 2.5

Find Developmental Meaning *How does a first-grade teacher encourage students to share perceptions of goldfish?* Note how she arranges for food, plants, and a tunnel to be placed in the fish bowls, prompting the children to observe effects on the fish. She reassures the children, commenting on their work and validating their observations.

- **Develop your interviewing skills.** Too often, conversations between adults and children are short, ask-a-question-and-get-an-answer exchanges. Lengthier dialogues can be far more informative. Getting children to talk takes experience, but there are a few specific things you can do (D. Fisher & Frey, 2007; Graue & Walsh, 1998; Koekoek, Knoppers, & Stegeman, 2009). First of all, you can try a combination of open-ended questions ("How was your day?") and closed-ended questions ("Did you watch TV when you went home from school?"). Also, include some general requests for information that are not in question form ("Tell me more about that.") Try not to ask a long series of questions so that your probing does not seem like an inquisition. Make sure you pause after asking a question to give children plenty of time to formulate their thoughts. When possible, allow children to carry on with an activity, for example, drawing a picture, building blocks, playing with puppets, or eating a snack, as they talk with you (Driessnack & Gallo, 2013; C. Green, 2012).

- **Listen intently to children's perspectives.** It is all too easy to misread students. For example, although educators sometimes interpret young adolescents as disrespectful and defiant, many young people want to achieve in school. In a study with sixth-graders in the Philadelphia public schools (B. L. Wilson & Corbett, 2001), young adolescents appeared to share many priorities and goals with teachers they cared about. The students stated that they wanted teachers to push them to complete assignments (even when they resisted), to maintain order (even when they misbehaved), and to teach them difficult material (even when they struggled). Despite having a desire to succeed, the students were unaware of what it took to do well when subjects became challenging, and they were naive about skills needed for success in college. From these results, we realize that teachers need to explain and reexplain demanding concepts, teach study skills, and prepare adolescents for the reality of college.

- **Develop classroom practices inviting self-expression.** Certain routines support children in speaking up and sharing their ideas. Some teachers use the Think–Pair–Share discussion strategy, in which they stop midway through a lesson, ask children to think about a particular question or issue, pair children to discuss their responses, and then invite them to share ideas with the rest of the class (Alanís, 2013; Lyman, 1981). Other teachers use the Whip Around technique, a structured activity at the end of a lesson. They pose a question, ask children to write their responses on a piece of paper, and then "whip around" the group, asking everyone for brief responses (D. Fisher & Frey, 2007). These techniques foster self-expression in children when everyone is encouraged to participate and no one is ridiculed for what he or she says.

Observing Children

By carefully watching children as they study and interact with others, you can learn a lot about their interests, values, and abilities. Here are some suggestions for deepening your observation skills:

- **Observe how children respond in different settings.** On a daily basis, teachers and other practitioners see children moving in and out of the classroom, cafeteria, and playground. When you are able to make observations across separate settings, you gain deeper insights into the needs of children. For example, a child who appears happy and carefree on the playground but fearful and tense in the classroom may need tutoring or other assistance to become academically successful.

- **Notice children's nonverbal behaviors.** Careful observation of children's postures, actions, and emotional expressions can yield valuable clues about their preferences and abilities. An infant caregiver may learn that one 18-month-old toddler slows down, pulls at his ear, and seeks comfort when he's sleepy, whereas another child speeds up, squirms, and becomes irritable when ready for a nap. During an interview with a teenage boy, a school counselor might notice that he seems withdrawn and discouraged. In response, the counselor inquires sympathetically about how things are going for him at home and school.

Preparing for Your Licensure Examination

Your teaching test might ask you what you can infer from children's hand gestures, eye gaze, facial expressions, and tone of speech.

OBSERVATION GUIDELINES

Learning from What Children Say and Do

CHARACTERISTIC	LOOK FOR	EXAMPLE	IMPLICATION
What Children Say	• Verbal expressions of likes and dislikes • Thoughtful questions about a topic (probably indicates high engagement and motivation) • Previously answered questions (might stem from inattentiveness or lack of understanding) • Complaints about difficulty with an assignment (might indicate low motivation, lack of confidence, or overloaded schedule)	In a whining tone, Danielle asks, "Do we really have to include three arguments in our persuasive essays? I can only come up with one!"	Read between the lines in the questions children ask and the comments they make. Consider what their statements might reveal about their knowledge, skills, motivation, and self-confidence.
What Children Do	• Exploration of the environment through manipulation of objects, focused attention, and verbal comments about what they are noticing (may indicate inquisitiveness about situations) • Preferred activities during free time (may show children's foremost desires and interests) • Interest in people, including initiating interactions and responding to others' social gestures (may reflect comfort in social situations) • Quiet self-absorption (may demonstrate either thoughtful self-reflection or sadness) • Facial expressions (reflecting enjoyment, excitement, boredom, sadness, confusion, anger, or frustration) • Tenseness of limbs (might signify either intense concentration or excessive anxiety) • Slouching in seat (might indicate fatigue or resistance to an activity)	Whenever his teacher engages the class in a discussion of controversial issues, James eagerly participates. When she goes over the previous night's homework, however, he crosses his arms, droops low in his seat, pulls his hat low over his eyes, and says nothing.	Provide a safe environment with interesting objects for active exploration. Periodically make changes to the environment that offer new options for examination. Get to know individual children's preferences for activities. Use children's body language as a rough gauge of interest, and modify activities that fail to engage children's attention. Speak confidentially with children who appear sad or angry.

• **Consider children's developmental states.** When you sense an unmet need in a child, you can analyze his or her circumstances with your knowledge of child development. The Observation Guidelines table, "Learning from What Children Say and Do," suggests some general things to look for as you interact with young people.

• **Distinguish what you see from what it might mean.** Never be content with a single interpretation of an unusual behavior no matter how obvious that explanation might seem. Always consider multiple reasons for what you see, and resist the temptation to settle on one of them as "correct" until you've had a chance to eliminate other possibilities. It is not possible to be entirely objective, but you can try periodically to reflect on your reactions to events. One strategy is to keep separate records of what you see and how you make sense of the experience. Here are some notes from a student teacher, Ana, who recorded her observations in a "Notetaking" column and her interpretations in a "Notemaking" one:

Notetaking	Notemaking
A child is working at the computer. There are fourteen students working at their desks. Six students are working with another teacher (aide) in the back of the room. It is an English reading/writing group she is working with—speaking only in English. I see a mother working with one child only and she is helping the student with something in English. There is a baby in a carriage nearby the mother. I hear classical music playing very lightly. I can only hear the music every once in a while when the classroom is really quiet. I stand up and move around the room to see what the children at their desks are working on. They are writing scary stories. The baby makes a funny noise with her lips and everyone in the class laughs and stares for a few seconds, even the teacher.	The class seems to be really self-directed . . . . I am not used to seeing students split up into different groups for Spanish and English readers because in my class they are Spanish readers, but it is really good for me to see this because it happens in a lot of upper grade settings, and I will be working in an upper grade bilingual setting next placement. I really like the idea of putting on music during work times. I know that when I hear classical music it really helps me to relax and calm down, as well as focus. I think that it has the same effect on the students in this class. I'm noticing more and more that I really cherish the laughter in a classroom when it comes from a sincere topic or source. It is also nice to see the students and the teacher laughing . . . . (C. Frank, 1999, pp. 11–12)[4]

[4]From *Ethnographic Eyes: A Teacher's Guide to Classroom Observation* (pp. 11–12), by Carolyn Frank, 1999, Portsmouth, NH: Heinemann.

Trying to notice order in children's activities without jumping to conclusions can help you become a perceptive observer. As you begin to record your observations, you will likely notice the actions that make you happy, nervous, proud, and irritated. You can also learn about your own priorities as a teacher, as Ana may have done when rereading her "Notemaking" comments.

• **Try out different kinds of observations.** The types of observations you conduct will depend on what you hope to gain from watching children. *Running records* are narrative summaries of a child's activities during a single period (Nicolson & Shipstead, 2002).[5] Running records provide teachers and other professionals with opportunities to focus on one child. In Figure 2.5 you can see an excerpt from a running record prepared by a language specialist of a child with a hearing impairment. After thinking about the running record, the language specialist concluded that Taki understood some aspects of spoken language as she followed directions. However, Taki needed help when completing the Listening Lotto game, and the language specialist might look further into Taki's hearing ability.

Anecdotal records are descriptions of brief incidents observed by teachers and other professionals (McClain, Schmertzing, & Schmertzing, 2012; Nicolson & Shipstead, 2002; Paley, 2007). An anecdotal record is typically made when an adult notices something a child does or says that is developmentally significant. Anecdotal records are made of specific accomplishments, patterns in social interaction, ways of thinking, a concern, or a child's **developmental milestone**, a major physical, cognitive, or social-emotional skill that is age-related and unfolds as part of a predictable sequence of accomplishments. Examples include the baby's first steps, the appearance of pretend play, or a new ability to follow three-part instructions. Anecdotal records tend to be much briefer than running records and may be written up later in the day. Teachers often gather these notes about children and share them with family members

FIGURE 2.5 Running record for Taki during Listening Lotto.

Specialists in child development often list a child's age in years and additional months, separating the two numbers by a semicolon. Taki's age of 5 years and 1 month is indicated as "5;1."

From Through the Looking Glass: Observations in the Early Childhood Classroom (3rd ed., pp. 118–119), by S. Nicolson and S. G. Shipstead, 2002, Upper Saddle River, NJ: Merrill/Prentice Hall. Copyright 2002 by Pearson Education. Reprinted with permission.

Center/Age Level: Center for Speech and Language/3- to 6-Year-Olds

Date:	7/17	Time:	10:20–10:26 AM
Observer:	Naoki	Child/Age:	Taki/5;1
		Teacher:	Camille

	Comments
Taki is seated on the floor with Kyle (4;8) and Camille, the teacher, in a corner of the classroom; both children have their backs to the center of the room. Taki sits with her right leg tucked under her bottom and her left leg bent with her foot flat on the floor. The Listening Lotto card is in front of her on the floor, and she holds a bunch of red plastic markers in her right hand. Camille begins the tape.	10:20 No intro of game.
The first sound is of a baby crying. Taki looks up at Camille, who says, "What's that?" Taki looks at Kyle, who has already placed his marker on the crying baby. Camille says, "That's a baby crying," and points to the picture on Taki's card. Taki places the marker with her left hand as the next sound, beating drums, begins.	Hearing aid working.
Taki looks at Kyle as the drumming continues. Camille points to the picture of the drums on Taki's card, and Taki places her marker.	Understands process.
The next sound is of a toilet flushing. Taki looks at Kyle and points to the drums. Kyle says, "Good, Taki. We heard drums banging." Taki smiles. Camille says, "Do you hear the toilet flushing?" as she points to the correct picture. Taki places her marker and repositions herself to sit cross-legged. She continues to hold the markers in her right hand and place them with her left. . . .	10:22 Kyle supportive of Taki.

Conclusions: Taki's receptive language was on display when she followed the teacher's directions in Listening Lotto (put markers on the appropriate spots), but she did not demonstrate success on her own. Her fine motor control was in evidence as she adeptly handled small markers.

[5]The term *running records* is also used by literacy specialists to refer to a structured technique for detecting accuracy and errors in a child's oral reading of a written passage.

during conferences. Seven-year-old Matthew's teacher made this anecdotal record of his insights:

> While discussing *In a Dark, Dark Room and Other Scary Stories* by Alvin Schwartz, Matthew thoughtfully shared, "Do you know what kind of scary things I like best? Things that are halfway between real and imaginary." I started to ask, "I wonder what . . . " Matthew quickly replied, "Examples would be aliens, shadows, and dreams coming true."[6] (Nicolson & Shipstead, 2002, p. 139)

One means of recording observations is not necessarily better than another. Instead, each observational system has a distinct purpose. As you gain experience in observing youngsters, you are likely to find that your own understanding of children grows when you try several observational methods and supplement them by listening to what children say.

Conducting Action Research

Teachers sometimes conduct systematic studies of children's experiences in school and then revise their instruction based on what they learn. In our introductory case study, Jack Reston conducted research in order to evaluate and improve absenteeism policies. Such practically focused investigations, known as **action research** studies, are time consuming but shed light on educational processes that require an adjustment. Examples include assessing the effectiveness of a new teaching technique, gathering information about adolescents' opinions on a schoolwide issue, sharing impressions of classroom dynamics with students and families, and conducting an in-depth case study of individual children (Cochran-Smith & Lytle, 1993; Fleischer, 2016; G. E. Mills, 2007). You can see illustrations of methods for gathering information at school in the Development-Enhancing Education feature "Getting a Flavor for Conducting Action Research."

Development-Enhancing Education

Getting a Flavor for Conducting Action Research

Keep a journal of your observations and reflections.

- A kindergarten teacher regularly makes notes of the centers that children visit when they have a free choice, using the information to make adjustments in unpopular areas. (Early Childhood)
- A high school English teacher keeps a daily log of students' comments about the novels they are reading. The teacher reassigns novels that provoke the most interest the following year and replaces books that do not engage students. (Late Adolescence)

Talk with your colleagues about what you are noticing.

- A middle school teacher observes that a new student who has been homeless comes to class late without a notebook or pen and appears distracted. The teacher wonders about the family's financial resources and speaks privately with the principal to see if the school can secure school supplies and a backpack for the young man. (Early Adolescence)
- A school counselor notices that a group of low-achieving girls are excited about their work in a community service club. She asks colleagues for their ideas on how they might capitalize on the girls' involvement in blood drives, senior visits, and animal shelter work at school. (Late Adolescence)

Invite children and families to contribute to your inquiry.

- A teacher in an infant room hears parents complain that their employers do not grant them time off to care for sick children. She asks three parents who have been most vocal to help her look into family leave rights and regulations. (Infancy)
- A high school principal notices that numerous students have been referred to her this year for physical aggression. She asks a school improvement team of teachers, school counselors, parents, and students to examine possible reasons for the increase in violence and come up with possible solutions. (Late Adolescence)

(continued)

[6]From *Through the Looking Glass: Observations in the Early Childhood Classroom* (3rd ed., p. 139), by S. Nicolson and S. G. Shipstead, 2002, Upper Saddle River, NJ: Merrill/Prentice Hall. Copyright 2002 by Pearson Education. Reprinted with permission.

Inquire into the circumstances of children who appear sad, inattentive, or disengaged at school.

- A preschool teacher is concerned about a 3-year-old girl who has recently appeared upset at school. During free play, the young girl quietly and repeatedly puts a doll in a box and places the box under a toy crib. The teacher talks with the girl's mother at the end of the day and learns that the mother, who had been a full 5 months along in her pregnancy, recently had a miscarriage. Her 3-year-old daughter knew about the pregnancy and was upset about the family's loss. The teacher expresses her sympathy to the mother and suggests that the little girl seems to be coping through play but might want to talk about their family loss. (Early Childhood)
- A middle school teacher observes that a few students sit in the back of the room and appear to be mentally "tuned out." She talks privately with the students, learns about their backgrounds and interests, and tries out new strategies that might capture their attention. (Early Adolescence)

Enlist the assistance of children or families.

- An elementary teacher wonders what her children are thinking about during independent learning time. She asks the children to interview one another and take notes on each other's answers. In analyzing the children's responses, the teacher realizes that only some of the children are using the time effectively. (Middle Childhood)
- A career counselor would like to help high school students explore career interests and gain employment experience. She enlists the help of adolescents to survey local businesses about possible opportunities for after-school jobs and internships. (Late Adolescence)

To make action research a feasible endeavor in the midst of an educator's busy day, it is helpful to divide it up into the following steps:

1. *Identify an area of focus.* The teacher-researcher begins with a practical problem at school and gathers preliminary information that might shed light on the situation. Usually this involves perusing the research literature for investigations into similar problems and perhaps searching the Internet and talking with colleagues. He or she develops a research plan that addresses a question and specifies data-collection techniques, the design, and so forth. At this point, the teacher seeks guidance from supervisors and experts in research ethics.
2. *Collect data.* The teacher-researcher collects data relevant to the question, perhaps in the form of questionnaires, interviews, observations, achievement tests, journals, portfolios, or existing records (e.g., school attendance patterns, rates of referral for discipline problems, hours spent on school projects). Many times the teacher-researcher uses two or more sources to address the question from different angles.
3. *Analyze and interpret the data.* The teacher-researcher looks for patterns in the data. Sometimes the analysis involves computing simple statistics (e.g., percentages, averages, correlation coefficients). At other times it involves a non-numerical inspection of the data. In either case, the teacher-researcher looks for relevance in the data to the original question.
4. *Develop an action plan.* The final step distinguishes action research from more traditional research: The teacher-researcher uses the information collected to formulate a new strategy—for instance, a change in instructional techniques, advising practices, home visiting schedules, or school policies. In many cases, the teacher will go on to study the outcome of the new strategy.

A good example of action research is a case study conducted by Michele Sims (1993). Initially concerned with why intelligent middle school students struggle to comprehend classroom material, Sims began to focus on one of her students, a quiet boy named Ricardo. She talked with Ricardo, had conversations with other teachers and university faculty, wrote her ideas in her journal, and made notes of Ricardo's work. The more she learned, the better she understood who Ricardo was as an individual and how she could foster his learning. She also became increasingly aware of how often she and her fellow teachers overlooked the needs of quiet students:

> We made assumptions that the quiet students weren't in as much need. My colleague phrased it well when she said, "In our minds we'd say to ourselves—'that child will be all right until we get back to him.'" But we both wanted desperately for these children to do more than just survive. (Sims, 1993, p. 288)

Action research serves many positive functions. It can solve problems, broaden perspectives on adults' relationships with children, clarify children's understandings of and attitudes toward learning particular academic topics, and foster a community spirit among adults (Buck, Cook, Quigley, Prince, & Lucas, 2014; Chant, 2009; Noffke, 1997). It can be especially informative about the characteristics of children from unfamiliar cultures, which you can learn about in the Development in Culture feature "Using Action Research to Learn About Children and Families."

Development in Culture

Using Action Research to Learn About Children and Families

Misunderstandings occasionally arise in people from different cultures, including teachers and children from dissimilar backgrounds. For example, some teachers wonder why children from immigrant families do not learn English quickly, actively participate in lessons, or achieve at advanced levels, whereas children may be puzzled as to why their teachers seem insensitive and strange (Rothstein-Fisch, Trumbull, & Garcia, 2009).

Such a clash of cultures is not inevitable. Teachers can gain an appreciation for children's traditions by observing children at school and encouraging them to talk and write about their cultural origins. However, everyday observations and assessments are not always enough. When teachers' initial efforts prove insufficient, teachers can turn to action research as a way to delve into children's customs and frames of mind.

Action research that has three elements can be especially effective in fostering teachers' cultural sensitivity. First, teachers can acquire new understandings about children by remaining open to using entirely new ways of interpretation. Tiffany, an experienced elementary teacher, conducted research in her second-grade classroom of ethnically diverse children from low-income families, the majority of whom were Mexican American (Riemer & Blasi, 2008). Tiffany had previously mandated which classroom centers individual children could visit during the day but wondered how the children would respond if they were able to make some of their own decisions. The children surprised her with their maturity:

> I began to notice that they were taking control of their learning. They researched and learned what they wanted to learn about, they worked with other students that they or I would normally not group them with, and they even created their own organizational tool to keep track of the centers they visited. They gave themselves choices between working on research projects, preparing presentations of the research collected, and/or visiting centers . . . . I gave them more independence and therefore, they did not need me as much. They also relied more on one another . . . . I have had increased awareness as to what my students are truly capable of, owning their education. (Riemer & Blasi, 2008, p. 58)

Second, teachers may increase their understanding of children when given time to reflect on their own values and biases. One kindergarten teacher joined a research team of university faculty and teacher colleagues who were hoping to learn more about the needs of students and their immigrant Latino families (Rothstein-Fisch et al., 2009). As a result of her introspection and discussions with colleagues, she realized that these parents had a valid perspective that was different from her own:

> It was a revelation that the parents weren't wrong, just different, because it never felt right to me to think they were wrong. But deep down I thought they were wrong and I knew that was racist and that was eluding me (Rothstein-Fisch et al., 2009, p. 477).

After conducting her research, the teacher and her colleagues began to open up to families in new ways, talking informally with parents as they dropped off and picked up their children, taking photographs of families at open houses, experimenting with formats for conferences, and building on families' desires for a relaxed atmosphere during school meetings.

Finally, teachers can learn a lot by spending time with children and their families (Lahman, 2008). Bernie, a sophomore preparing to teach, conducted an in-depth observational study of Amish children in Ohio (Glasgow, 1994). Early in her research Bernie was judgmental, confessing that she thought of the Amish as "a simple, unsophisticated people with very naive ideas about the ways

Ira Berger/Alamy Stock Photo

GAINING INSIGHT. Teachers and other practitioners can learn a great deal about children's cultural beliefs and traditions by reflecting on their own values, remaining open to new interpretations of children's abilities, and spending time with children in their community.

(continued)

of our world" (Glasgow, 1994, p. 43). She noticed a sense of peacefulness in their lives but also believed that "the Amish culture stifles personal growth, intellectual advancement, and creativity" (Glasgow, 1994, p. 43). As she spent more time in the Amish community, Bernie became increasingly attuned to cultural traditions and values, gaining permission from an Amish elder to visit a one-room schoolhouse and take careful field notes about what she saw. With increasing contact with people in the Amish culture, Bernie came to appreciate the integrity of their customs. At the end of her observations, she planned to explore new ways to reach Amish children in her future classrooms.

By being open to new interpretations, reflecting on their own biases and values, and collecting data over an extended time, teachers and other practitioners can acquire a thoughtful understanding of children and families from different cultures. This heightened sensitivity can pay enormous dividends in relationships between teachers and children.

Regardless of your specific techniques in collecting data from children, you must protect their welfare. Consider the following guidelines:

- **Be sensitive to children's perspectives.** Children are apt to notice any unusual attention you give them. When Michele Sims was collecting data about Ricardo, she made the following observation:

> I'm making a conscious effort to collect as much of Ricardo's work as possible. It's difficult. I think this shift in the kind of attention I'm paying to him has him somewhat rattled. I sense he has mixed feelings about this. He seems to enjoy the conversations we have, but when it comes to collecting his work, he may feel that he's being put under a microscope. Maybe he's become quite accustomed to a type of invisibility. (Sims, 1993, p. 285)

When data collection makes children feel so self-conscious that their performance is impaired, a teacher-researcher must seriously consider whether the value of the information collected outweighs possible detrimental effects. Otherwise, teachers' good intentions can actually put children at a disadvantage.

- **Be tentative in your conclusions.** Careless observations of children can do more harm than good. For instance, a teacher might wrongly infer that children have poor comprehension skills because they scored at low levels on a reading test, even though they had, in fact, been distracted by a fire alarm during the test's administration. Acting on a false perception, the teacher might attempt to remediate children's alleged weaknesses. Therefore, you should try not to put too much weight on any single piece of information. Instead, you can look for consistent trends across a range of data sources—possibly written essays, test scores, projects, and informal observations of performance. Finally, when sharing your perceptions of children's abilities with parents, acknowledge that these are your *interpretations*, based on the data you available, rather than irrefutable facts. In Artifact Example 2.2, you can practice restraint in drawing conclusions about 6-year-old Alex's writing abilities.

I went
to davis's
house
Alex

MyLab Education
Artifact Example 2.2

Find Developmental Meaning *What does 6-year-old Alex know about punctuation?* Note that although there are two obvious violations to punctuation (failure to capitalize proper name "Davis" and absence of a period at the end of the sentence, after "house"), do not automatically conclude that Alex has not acquired basic rules of punctuation. Alex may be emulating the informal style of sending a text message, in which periods are not commonly used, or copying a note from his older brother about his whereabouts.

- **Administer and interpret tests only if you have adequate training.** Many instruments, especially psychological assessments, physiological measures, and intelligence tests, must be administered and interpreted only by individuals trained in their use. In untrained hands tests can yield erroneous conclusions. For example, a teacher who interprets an intelligence test without guidance from a school psychologist or other professional might wrongly conclude that the child is not capable of benefiting from classroom instruction. The test result is only one imperfect indication of the child's potential and, without interpretation from specialized professionals, says little itself about the kinds of instructional modifications that might be helpful to the child.

- **Maintain confidentiality.** When teachers have obtained the necessary permissions and clearances, they are permitted to share general results with colleagues. Some teachers also make their findings known to an audience beyond the walls of their institution; for instance, they may make presentations at conferences or write journal articles describing what they have learned. However, they must not broadcast research findings in ways that violate the confidentiality of children's responses. Children would naturally feel betrayed if teachers were to disclose their identity and the responses that they as individuals have made. Teachers must likewise protect data from examination by onlookers: It would be unwise to leave a notebook containing records of individual children on a table where other children would have access to them.

- **Keep your supervisor informed of your research initiatives.** Principals and other supervisors can advise teachers, counselors, and other practitioners on how to protect the rights of children and families. School leaders can inform you of regulations in your district or community and procedures for getting your research plan approved. They can also give you a fresh set of eyes in interpreting results and generating implications for changes in practice.

Summary

Teachers, school nurses, mental health providers, and caregivers gather data about children as a means of improving services. Educators can learn a great deal from their conversations with youngsters, analyses of students' assignments, and everyday observations of their behavior. Systematic action research can also provide useful information, from which teachers address a specific question and strive to improve their ability to meet children's needs. As with other kinds of investigations, research carried out by teachers and other practitioners must be conducted with concern for ethics and the integrity of the data.

MyLab Education Self-Check 2.3

Practicing For Your Licensure Examination

Many teaching tests require students to apply what they have learned about child development to brief vignettes and multiple-choice questions. You can practice for your licensure examination by reading the following case study and answering a series of questions.

The Study Skills Class

As a last-minute teaching assignment, Deborah South took on a study skills class of 20 low-achieving and seemingly unmotivated eighth graders. Later she described a problem she encountered and her attempt to understand it through action research (South, 2007):

> My task was to somehow take these students and miraculously make them motivated, achieving students. I was trained in a study skills program before the term started and thought that I was prepared . . . .
>
> Within a week, I sensed we were in trouble. My 20 students often showed up with no supplies. Their behavior was atrocious. They called each other names, threw various items around the room, and walked around the classroom when they felt like it . . . .
>
> Given this situation, I decided to do some reading about how other teachers motivate unmotivated students and to formulate some ideas about the variables that contribute to a student's success in school. Variables I investigated included adult approval, peer influence, and success in such subjects as math, science, language arts, and social studies, as well as self-esteem and students' views of their academic abilities.
>
> I collected the majority of the data through surveys, interviews, and report card/attendance records in an effort to answer the following questions:
>
> - How does attendance affect student performance?
> - How are students influenced by their friends in completing schoolwork?
> - How do adults (parents, teachers) affect the success of students?
> - What levels of self-esteem do these students have?
>
> As a result of this investigation, I learned many things. For example, for this group of students attendance does not appear to be a factor—with the exception of one student, their school attendance was regular. Not surprisingly, peer groups did affect student performance. Seventy-three percent of my students reported that their friends never encouraged doing homework or putting any effort into homework.
>
> Another surprising result was the lack of impact of a teacher's approval on student achievement. Ninety-four percent of my students indicated that they never or seldom do their homework to receive teacher approval. Alternatively, 57 percent indicated that they often or always do their homework so that their families will be proud of them.
>
> One of the most interesting findings of this study was the realization that most of my students misbehave

out of frustration at their own lack of abilities. They are not being obnoxious to gain attention but to divert attention from the fact that they do not know how to complete the assigned work.

When I looked at report cards and compared grades over three quarters, I noticed a trend. Between the first and second quarter, student performance had increased. That is, most students were doing better than they had during the first quarter. Between the second and third quarters, however, grades dropped dramatically. I tried to determine why that drop would occur, and the only common experience shared by these 20 students was the fact that they had been moved into my class at the beginning of the third quarter.

When I presented my project to the action research class during our end-of-term "celebration," I was convinced that the "cause" of the students' unmotivated behavior was my teaching . . . . This conclusion, however, was not readily accepted by my critical friends and colleagues . . . who urged me to consider other interpretations of the data. (pp. 1–2)[a]

Constructed-Response Question

1. Describe one potential strength and limitation for each method Deborah used.

Multiple-Choice Questions

2. What kind of research did Deborah conduct?

   a. Action research
   b. An experimental study
   c. A correlational study
   d. A cross-sectional study

3. Deborah tentatively concluded that her own teaching led to the dramatic drop in grades from the second quarter to the third. Is her conclusion justified?

   a. Yes, Deborah's conclusion is justified because she collected several different kinds of data.
   b. Yes, Deborah's conclusion is justified because she is in the best position to understand her students.
   c. No, Deborah's conclusion is not fully justified because without an experimental design, multiple reasons for the change in students' behavior are possible.
   d. No, Deborah's conclusion is not fully justified because teachers are not able to collect data of any merit.

[a]From "What Motivates Unmotivated Students?" by D. South. In *Action Research: A Guide for the Teacher Researcher* (3rd ed., pp. 1–2), by G. E. Mills, 2007, Upper Saddle River, NJ: Merrill/Prentice Hall. Reprinted with permission of the author.

MyLab Education Licensure Practice 2.1

Key Concepts

scientific method (p. 36)
sample (p. 36)
self-report (p. 38)
interview (p. 38)
questionnaire (p. 38)
social desirability (p. 38)
assessment (p. 39)
test (p. 39)
physiological measure (p. 39)
habituation (p. 40)
observation (p. 40)
validity (p. 41)
reliability (p. 41)
experimental study (p. 42)
control group (p. 42)
quasi-experimental study (p. 43)
correlational study (p. 45)
cross-sectional study (p. 45)
longitudinal study (p. 45)
ethnography (p. 46)
case study (p. 46)
grounded theory study (p. 46)
rubric (p. 49)
cultural bias (p. 51)
standardized achievement test (p. 52)
developmental milestone (p. 56)
action research (p. 57)

Chapter Three
Family, Culture, and Society

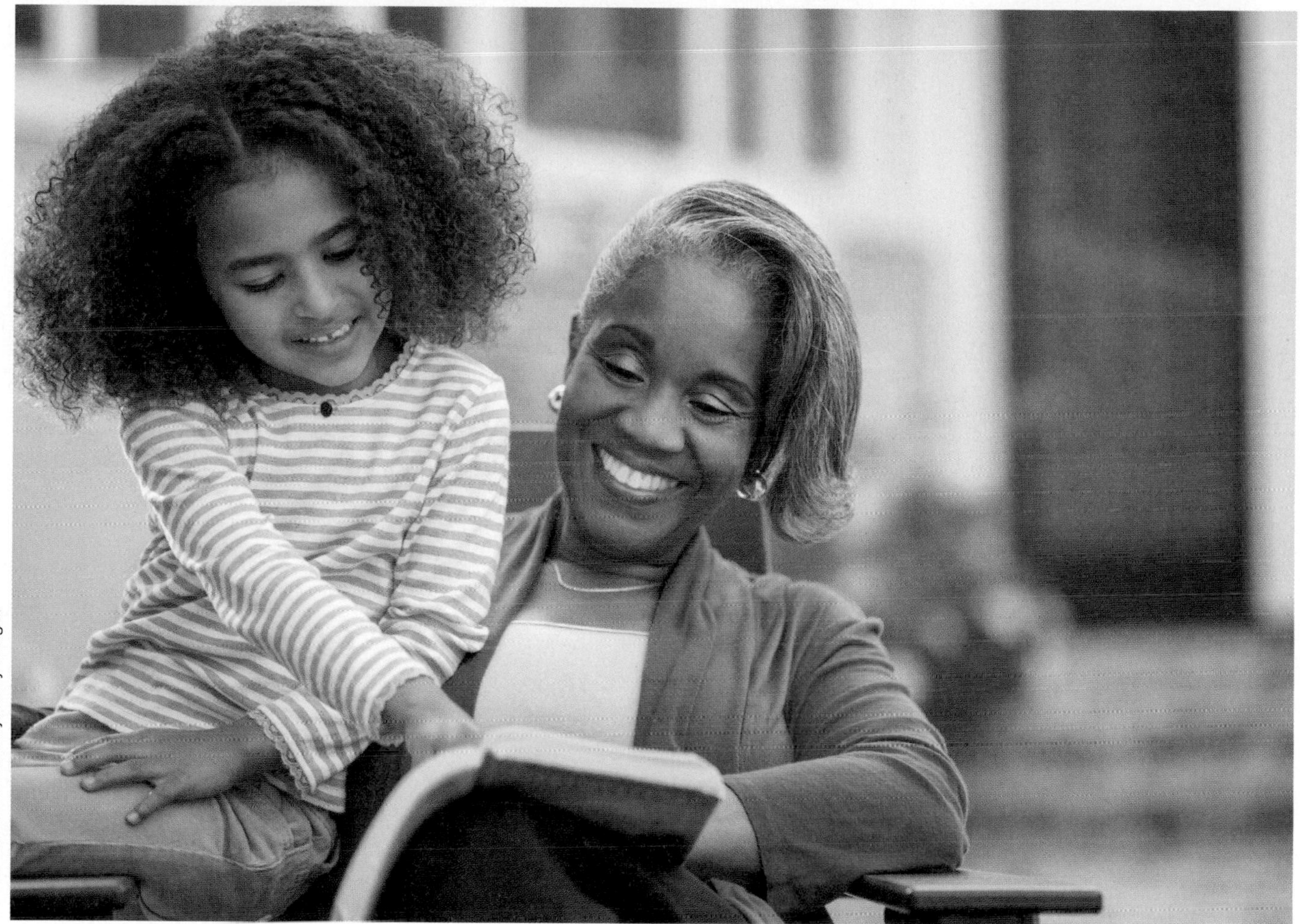
Dennis Lane/Photolibrary/Getty Images

Learning Objectives

3.1 Identify the primary roles that family, culture, and society play in a child's development.

3.2 Describe common types of family structures and their implications for educators.

3.3 Define key elements of family interaction and educational partnerships with families.

3.4 Portray the experiences of children in families whose unique circumstances merit accommodation at school.

CASE STUDY

Cedric and Barbara Jennings

Cedric Lavar Jennings and his mother Barbara are a close-knit family of two. One night during Cedric's senior year, he and his mother go to his high school to pick up his first-semester grades report. Knowing that he is one of the top students—perhaps *the* top student—in his physics class, Cedric is shocked to discover a B for his semester's work. He's furious because, as he tells his mother, other students cheated on class examinations, all the while he completed the tests honestly. At first Barbara isn't overly concerned, but as Ron Suskind reports in *A Hope in the Unseen* (1998), when Cedric asks what *they* will do, she soon realizes that he needs her to act as the vigilant protector she has always been. Cedric spurs her on.

The two of them go in search of Cedric's physics teacher, Mr. Momen. After finding him, Cedric complains that Mr. Momen allows rampant cheating when leaving the room. Although Mr. Momen doubts Cedric and defends himself, Barbara stands firm, insisting that her son would not lie about something so important. Mr. Momen eventually agrees to give Cedric a retest over the semester's material.

Afterward, Barbara advises her son that he *must* get an A. Cedric studies hard for the test, earns a perfect score, and ultimately receives an A for the semester. He brings home the test for her to examine, and as she looks at it, it dawns on her that their relationship is changing, that she will no longer be able to stand at his side when he goes to college. Cedric realizes that he is now ready to advocate for himself. He points to the test score and suggests that the paper certifies Barbara's accomplishments—as a mother.

- Why could Cedric assume that his mother would help him at school?
- What qualities might Cedric have learned from his mother?

As a child, Cedric had found his mother to be a loving caregiver. Having grown accustomed to her responsive care, Cedric could now safely assume that she would back him up when he needed her. Like Cedric, most children depend on their families for love and reassurance, food and shelter, oversight and guidance. In this chapter, you will learn that the family's care has profound effects on children, as does culture and society. From Barbara, Cedric learned to work hard, act with integrity, and confront injustice. Having benefited from his mother's support, and having learned to make good choices on his own, Cedric was ready to enter the world as a productive young man.

Cradles of Child Development

3.1 Identify the primary roles that family, culture, and society play in a child's development.

A happy and healthy childhood depends on loving relationships in the family, regular exposure to the traditions of a culture, and access to a rich array of institutions in society. As children participate in close relationships and social customs, they learn who they are, how they are expected to behave, and where they fit in society.

Family

A **family** consists of two or more people who live together and are related by such enduring factors as birth, marriage, adoption, or long-term mutual commitment. Families with children usually have one or two adults (most often the parents) who serve as heads of family. Heads of family exercise authority over children, take responsibility for their welfare, and interact affectionately with them over a period of years, if not decades.

Every child needs at least one adult devoted to his or her health, education, and welfare (Bronfenbrenner, 2001). Typically, heads of family have the necessary dedication to meet the child's many needs. Caring for offspring ideally begins before birth, when prospective parents shield themselves from toxins that might be detrimental to a developing baby. After birth, sensitive care makes it possible for infants to form close bonds with parents, explore the world, and develop harmonious relationships with people outside the family (Ainsworth, 1963, 1973; Behrens, Haltigan, & Bahm, 2016; Bowlby, 1969/1982).

As the child grows, the family must feed, clothe, and attend to basic needs. Just as important, family members are key figures in the **socialization** of children. By encouraging certain behaviors and beliefs (and *dis*couraging others), parents and other heads of family help children learn to act and think in ways society deems appropriate. Heads of family model proper ways of behaving in various situations, reward certain behaviors and punish others, arrange for children to participate in worthwhile pastimes and discourage unproductive pursuits, and advise children how to cope with emotional feelings (S. R. Beach et al., 2016; Gauvain & Parke, 2010; Kehoe, Havighurst, & Harley, 2014).

Despite the family's powerful influences on children, no family is an island. Relationships, values, traditions, cultural symbols, and threats in the outside world permeate parents' childrearing goals and actions. Thus, to understand the family's role in child development, it is helpful to first consider the influences that culture and society have on the family. After explaining these two concepts, we examine families in greater detail.

OUTLINE

Culture

A culture is defined as the values, traditions, and symbol systems of a long-standing social group. Culture gives meaning to children's everyday activities and makes events predictable. An intellectual dimension is present as well in in that every cultural group prepares children to use mental tools (e.g., alphabets, musical notations, calculators) and understand literature, art, dance, music, scientific thought, and other creative works.

The effects of culture are especially evident in contrasts in behavior between separate groups. Different cultures exhibit variations in mealtime habits (what and with whom they eat), division of responsibility (who goes out to work and who looks after the children), and social practices (how children and marital partners interact). Cultural groups also encourage children's education in distinct ways. For instance, one mother volunteers at school by helping out at a school carnival and reading to small groups of children whereas another mother helps her own children at home doing homework, having learned that respect is to be shown to teachers by *not* interfering with their work (García Coll & Marks, 2009).

Cultural beliefs, although not as obvious as behaviors, are an equally important part of a group's heritage. Core beliefs vary among societies. For example, **individualistic cultures** encourage independence, self-assertion, competition, and expression of personal needs (Greenfield & Quiroz, 2013; Louie, Wang, Fung, & Lau, 2015; Markus & Hamedani, 2007). Many families from the United States and Western Europe raise their children in an individualistic manner. Core ideas in **collectivistic cultures** are that people should be honorable and cooperative, obedient to authority figures, and invested in the accomplishments of the group rather than in personal achievements. Many families in Asia, Africa, and South America raise their children in a collectivistic manner.

The two bookends of culture—behaviors and beliefs—are closely related. Common practices are grounded in beliefs about what is true, healthy, appropriate, and rational (Kitayama, Duffy, & Uchida, 2007). Adults within a culture justify their typical ways of raising children by asserting familiar values. As an example, consider how families defend children's sleeping practices. Many European American parents have children sleep alone in their own rooms and explain that this practice ensures nighttime privacy for adults and fosters independence in children. Other parents, particularly those in certain Asian and Caribbean cultures, sleep beside children and say that co-sleeping arrangements foster intimacy and solidarity in the family (S. Li et al., 2009; Luijk et al., 2013; Shweder et al., 1998).

Developmental Systems Prompt 3.1

As you become familiar with children, watch for the knowledge they have acquired in their family, culture, and society that can be connected to the curriculum.

Developmental Systems Prompt 3.2

Children adapt cultural customs to their personal needs. As you interact with children, notice the cultural themes that pervade their stories, play, hobbies, and leisure activities.

Such incongruities between cultures do not negate shared human qualities. Ultimately, we are more similar than we are different. Parents around the world see value in treating young children with sensitivity and responding affectionately as needs arise (Mesman et al., 2016). Many cultural groups share aspirations in achieving academically and treating others respectfully. Hence, within a single classroom, children from separate cultures share fundamental values and behaviors even though on the surface they appear quite different (Greenfield & Quiroz, 2013).

Moreover, dissimilarities *between* groups are often eclipsed by prominent individual differences *within* groups. In a classroom children may adhere to individualistic principles in their own ways, with one student winning the spelling bee, another achieving advanced levels in computer games, and a third raising record levels of money for a local charity (Gauvain, 2009). Furthermore, a group's strong commitment to a worldview does not prevent its members from endorsing beliefs emphasized in other value systems. Plenty of Western parents encourage children to assert their personal rights (an individualistic orientation) and live by a code of honor (a collectivistic orientation). Likewise, numerous non-Western parents socialize children to be mindful of the family's needs while pursuing their private wishes. The Observation Guidelines table "Identifying Cultural Practices and Beliefs" describes characteristics that teachers and other school personnel can accommodate.

OBSERVATION GUIDELINES

Identifying Cultural Practices and Beliefs

CHARACTERISTIC	LOOK FOR	EXAMPLE	IMPLICATION
Individualism	• *Independence*, assertiveness, and self-reliance • *Eagerness to pursue individual assignments* and tasks • *Willingness to compete* against others • *Pride in personal accomplishments*	When given the choice of doing a project by herself or with a partner, Melissa decides to work alone. She is thrilled when she earns a third-place ribbon in a statewide competition.	Provide time for independent work, and accommodate children's individual levels of achievement so that everyone can be successful. Give feedback about individual accomplishments in private rather than in front of peers.
Collectivism	• *Willingness to depend on others* • *Emphasis on group accomplishments* over individual achievements • *Preference for cooperation* over competition • *Concern about bringing honor* to family • *Strong sense of loyalty* to family	Tsusha is a talented and hard-working seventh grader. She is conscientious in bringing home her graded assignments to show her parents but appears uncomfortable when praised in front of classmates.	Emphasize group progress over individual achievement. Implement cooperative learning activities, arranging for students in each group to take on complementary roles (e.g., task master, note keeper, and resource finder). Rotate roles among children over time.
Behavior toward Authority Figures	• *Looking down* in the presence of an authority figure versus looking him or her in the eye • *Observing an adult quietly* versus asking questions when one doesn't understand • *Suspicion of authority figures* versus expectations that the adult has the child's bests interests at heart	A Native American child named Jimmy never says a word to his teacher. He appears frightened when his teacher looks him in the eye and greets him each morning. One day, the teacher looks in another direction and says, "Hello, Jimmy" as he enters the classroom. "Why hello Miss Jacobs," he responds enthusiastically (Gilliland, 1988, p. 26).	Recognize that different cultures show respect for authority figures in their own ways; don't misinterpret lack of eye contact or nonresponse as an indication of disrespect. When students perceive you as an adversary, reach out to them and find a time to express concern for their well-being and ask how you can help.
Values and Expectations	• *Hopes for high achievement* in traditional academic areas • *Values for achievement* out of personal pride or for bringing honor to family • *Expectations for excellence* in culture-specific activities, such as art, storytelling, or dance • *Enjoyment in retelling or making up stories* or preference for factual accounts	Clarence is a very bright young man but exhibits ambivalence about showing his knowledge in front of peers. He often earns high marks in papers he writes, but he rarely participates in class discussions and does not show his knowledge on tests.	Show how academic subjects relate to skills gained at home. Acknowledge achievement in nonacademic as well as academic pursuits. Communicate confidence in the potential of youngsters and encourage hard work and good study habits. Invite children to bring music and artwork from home to school for use in school assignments.

CHARACTERISTIC	LOOK FOR	EXAMPLE	IMPLICATION
Conceptions of Time	• *Concern for punctuality* and conscientious commitment to meet assignment deadlines • *Relaxed feelings about specific times* and schedules • *Planning for the future* as opposed to living in the present	Lucy and her parents are diligent about going to parent–teacher conferences but often arrive well after their scheduled time.	Encourage punctuality in order to enhance children's long-term success. At the same time, recognize that not all children are concerned about clock time. Advise parents that they can help you by being punctual for meetings, conferences, and recitals.

Sources: Banks and Banks (1995); Basso (1984); Duncheon and Tierney (2013); García (1994); Garrison (1989); Gilliland (1988); C. A. Grant and Gomez (2001); Heath (1983); Losey (1995); Maschinot (2008); N. L. Norton (2014); McAlpine and Taylor (1993); L. S. Miller (1995); Oyserman and Lee (2007); Raval (2013); N. Reid (1989); Shweder et al. (1998); M. B. Spencer (2006); Stoicovy, Fee, and Fee (2012); Tharp (1994); Torres-Guzmán (1998); Trawick-Smith (2010); Yamamoto and Sonnenschein (2016).

Although we have implied that children are raised within a single culture, the fact is that many children become acquainted with more than one culture. Parents may socialize children to develop an allegiance to their ancestral roots, to their new society, or to a combination of cultures. An immigrant child who was born in Riyadh, Saudi Arabia, and currently residing in Toronto, Canada, may learn to identify him- or herself as a Saudi Arabian, a Saudi immigrant, a Canadian, a Muslim, or a Canadian Muslim, depending on circumstances. As they grow, children develop complex cultural identities and draw on customs from the one or more societies in which they have been immersed over time (Acevedo-Polakovich et al., 2014; García Coll & Marks, 2009; Gonzales-Backen, 2013; Graham, 2016).

Society

Whereas a culture makes life meaningful, a society provides amenities and contact with other people. Children and their families are members of a **society**, the relatively large and enduring collection of people who live in the same region and share government services, economic markets, legal systems, and medical care. A single society may be composed of several cultural groups and individuals who differ by ethnicity, race, and income levels.

Community

Beginning in children's first years, the **community**, the local neighborhood and surrounding areas, creates a bridge from the family to the outside world. Children are apt to make friends close to home, school, and in other nearby settings such as parks, recreation centers, and houses of worship. As they grow older, youngsters continue to spend spare time in activities that are reasonably close by even as they venture farther from home. Local settings afford children different exposure depending on their age and abilities, as you can see in a comparison of two children's drawings of their cities in Artifact Example 3.1.

Local neighborhoods vary in characteristics. Some have nicely furnished schools and safe spaces. These resources are assets for children, as are the relationships they have with friends and neighbors and the fun recreational activities made possible there. In economically disadvantaged neighborhoods, youngsters have peers who model delinquent activities and schools that are not safe or well furnished (Duncan, 2013; Leventhal, Dupéré, & Brooks-Gunn, 2009). When neighbors commit crimes and prey on youth, young people are at increased risk for low achievement, bullying, destroying property, cheating and telling lies, and school misbehaviors. (Eamon & Mulder, 2005; K. Lee & Ludington, 2016). Fortunately, not all low-income neighborhoods are hazardous for children. Many parents in economically disadvantaged regions band together to watch out for one another's children.

The community, with its jobs, libraries, courts, merchants, and clinics, affects parents directly. Parents obtain salaries, benefits, groceries, health care, and services from agencies, which together affect their ability to meet children's needs. The social environment also affects parents' care of children. Ideally but not universally, heads of household have friends who step in to supervise children, offer advice on parenting strategies, and provide emotional support (Algood, Harris, & Hong, 2013; Bronfenbrenner, 2005). When a young person faces one or more serious challenges, perhaps a significant disability, economic poverty, or a parent's mental illness, affectionate contact with neighbors, coaches, and others in the community can be enormously important.

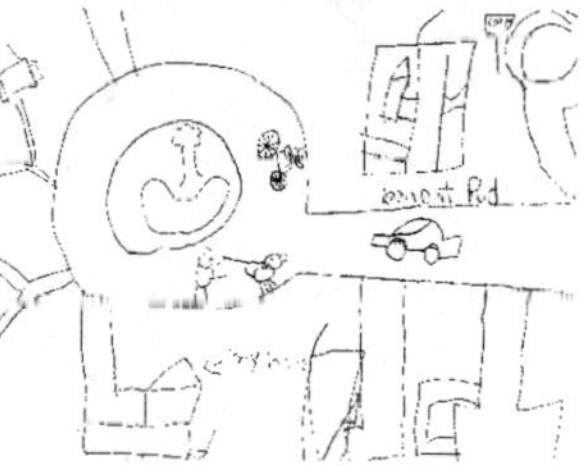

Jamie, age 7

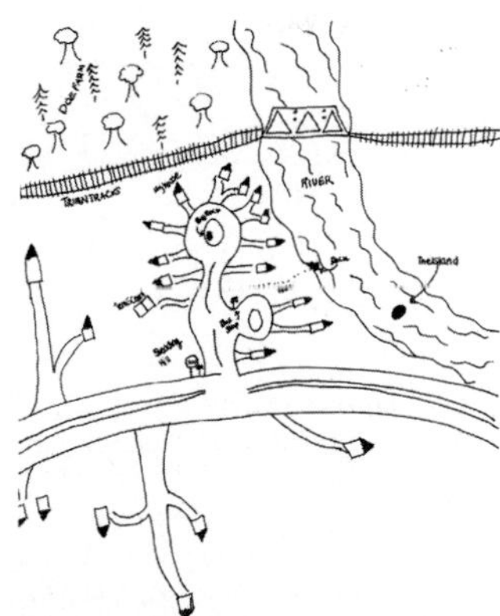

Heather, age 15

MyLab Education
Artifact Example 3.1

Find Developmental Meaning *How do 7-year-old Jamie and his 15-year-old sister Heather represent their neighborhood?* Notice that both children draw the cul-de-sac, but Heather includes the more distant areas—the river, railroad tracks, and surrounding neighborhoods.

MyLab Education
Video Example 3.1

Find Developmental Meaning *What does Brendan say about recreational opportunities in his neighborhood?* Brendan talks about his friendly neighbors and the enjoyable things he gets to take part in with them.

Ethnicity and Race

A child's **ethnicity** refers to the collection of people with whom he or she identifies as having a common heritage, tribe, geographical origin, language, religious faith, or combination of these characteristics. A child's **race** refers to the group of people with whom he or she has shared physical features such as skin color, eye shape, hair texture, and facial bone structure. Children from a single race (e.g., Asians) have, by definition, subtle physical features in common but may or may not share an ethnic or cultural heritage. Ethnicity affects children by exposing them to traditions and beliefs and giving them a sense of kinship with individuals from similar backgrounds. Race is influential because it is a salient characteristic that others notice and use to make judgments about a person's ability and motivation.

Ethnicity has a complex connection to culture. Typically, an ethnic group includes people from several different cultural roots. For example, people who are *Hispanic* tend to speak Spanish or Portuguese (or are descended from individuals who spoke these languages) and originate from one of several regions (e.g., Spain, Portugal, Mexico, Central and South American countries, and Spanish-speaking Caribbean nations). As a result of dispersed ancestries, individual Hispanics share a few common values but follow many distinct cultural practices (C. B. Fisher, Jackson, & Villarruel, 1998; García & Jensen, 2007). In addition, people who are Hispanic can come from any racial group. The implication of this heterogeneity is that knowing a child comes from a Hispanic American background gives only a rough idea as to what his or her cultural practices and beliefs might be.

Millions of people around the world travel from one region to another for a range of reasons. Migrants seek education, business opportunities, an escape from poverty, reunification with family, and refuge from oppression, persecution, and violence. In certain countries, for example, the United States, the United Kingdom, Spain, and the United Arab Emirates, newcomers are creating an increasingly multicultural and ethnically diverse society in their new homeland (Inkpen, 2014). Variations in birth rates contribute to certain groups growing more rapidly than others. As you can see in Table 3.1, the population in the United States is becoming more varied in ethnic and racial backgrounds.

A growing number of children are *multiethnic* or *multiracial*, in which their ancestry includes more than a single ethnic or racial group. A girl whose mother has both African American and Native American heritages and whose father emigrated from Spain will be exposed to several family traditions. Multiethnic and multiracial children may affiliate with two or more distinct groups and selectively carry out traditions depending on

Table 3.1 Percentages of U.S. Children in Racial and Ethnic Groups

	ESTIMATES FOR YEAR		PROJECTIONS FOR YEAR			
RACE AND ETHNICITY	2000	2010	2020	2030	2040	2050
American Indian and Alaska Native	1.0	0.9	0.8	0.8	0.7	0.7
Asian	3.5	4.4	5.2	6.0	6.8	7.4
Black	14.8	14.1	13.5	13.4	13.2	13.1
Native Hawaiian and Other Pacific Islander	0.2	0.2	0.2	0.2	0.2	0.2
White	61.2	53.7	49.8	46.6	42.5	38.8
Hispanic	17.2	23.2	25.7	27.2	29.8	31.9
Two or More Races	2.2	3.7	4.7	5.8	6.8	7.9

Note: Figures are for U.S. children 17 years and under. Accumulated percentages may not equal 100 due to rounding error. Children whose parents identified them as Hispanic are counted in this table as being Hispanic regardless of any race or races they might also have selected.

Source: Forum on Child and Family Statistics (2016a).

the context (e.g., speaking English at school and Spanish at home; Dunham & Olson, 2016; Henriksen & Paladino, 2009; Kennedy & Romo, 2013). Children with more than one heritage tend to become flexible in navigating through different cultural environments but occasionally confront pejorative comments about their blended heritage.

Disparities in Society

It is an unfortunate fact that not all children have access to a high-quality education, a safe environment, and encouragement for pursuing their dreams. One reason for these discrepancies is that children and families are treated differently according to their ethnicity, race, religion, sexual orientation, and national origin. Such a distinction arises because people generally view others who are similar to themselves positively and those who are different less favorably (Balliet, Wu, & De Dreu, 2014; Tajfel, 2010). Historically this preference has led to groups in power giving preferential resources to others from comparable backgrounds. In extreme cases, negative feelings toward "outsiders" have provoked tragic injustices, including segregation, slavery, and genocide.

The widespread inequities that exist in society are deeply ingrained. Nevertheless, schools can be beacons of hope for achieving equity and inclusion. Many educators work tirelessly to provide the entire student body with a high-quality education. These dedicated professionals also tackle biases that students and adults, even they themselves, bring to school (P. Clark & Zygmunt, 2014). Let's examine key issues that egalitarian educators consider.

Unconscious biases are at the heart of inequities. Many, probably most, professionals realize that having a prejudice, and acting on it, are wrong. Yet compelling evidence conducted over several decades indicates that practitioners around the world (including teachers) harbor negative impressions of others yet are not aware of these perspectives. **Implicit bias** refers to the relatively unconscious judgments people make about individuals with a particular racial affiliation or other characteristic (Greenwald, McGhee, & Schwartz, 1998; Staats, 2016). Having implicit biases makes discriminatory behavior more likely. For example, teachers in the United States dole out discipline more severely—on average—to African American students than to European American students for the *same offences* (e.g., using a cell phone during a lesson or talking back to a teacher; Horner, Fireman, & Wang, 2010). U.S. teachers also expect lower academic achievement for African American students, even when the students' history of performance has been similar (McKown & Weinstein, 2002). As we will soon explain, these unconscious biases can be tempered, and when they do persist, they do not inevitably deteriorate into preferential and intolerant behaviors (Capatosto, 2015; Staats, 2016).

Stereotypes, prejudice, and discrimination are harmful to children. **Stereotypes** exist when people notice a salient characteristic a person has, such as race, and make erroneous assumptions. Stereotypes are prevalent in society and are problematic at school because they affect educators' and classmates' expectations about, and behavior toward, children. For example, if a teacher were to have a stereotype that children of color are less capable than children from European American backgrounds, he or she might offer the former children less encouragement than the latter. Children easily absorb stereotypes and become anxious when asked to perform in areas in which their abilities are underestimated (Alter, Aronson, Darley, Rodriguez, & Ruble, 2010; Wasserberg, 2014).

Stereotypes encompass a host of negative attributes (e.g., being "stingy," "lazy," or "promiscuous"). These perceptions predispose people to exhibit negative attitudes, feelings, and behaviors—that is, **prejudice**—to the group in question. Stereotypes and prejudice in and of themselves do not cause a person to treat others unfairly, but they are known to serve as a justification for **discrimination**, the unfair treatment of people sharing a certain characteristic, such as race or ethnicity.

Children are targets of discrimination when they are excluded from opportunities made available to their peers (e.g., being exceptionally bright but not receiving special services like other gifted and talented children). Bigotry toward children is clearly unfair and can be illegal depending on a society's legal standards. Children are also affected by discrimination to family members, for example, when qualified parents are not selected for jobs, do not receive optimal mortgage rates for new homes, and are wrongly accused of crimes they did not commit (Gassman-Pines, 2015; Hou, Kim, Hazen, & Benner, 2016).

Lack of awareness of children's knowledge and skills can contribute to disparities. Educators and other practitioners do not always realize the know-how students have developed at home. Classrooms in the United States tend to be dominated by the traditions of European American backgrounds, and students from different backgrounds may bring talents and family assets that are not noticed or appreciated. For example, some African American families have infused traditions of spirituality, storytelling, resistance to oppression, and close extended family networks into their child rearing, characteristics that are not always recognized at school (Elmore & Gaylord-Harden, 2013; Jarrett, Bahar, & Kersh, 2016; Vereen, Hill, & Butler, 2013).

Addressing Children's Formative Experiences

Children enter school having had foundational experiences in their family, culture, and society. The Basic Developmental Issues table "Considering Family, Culture, and Society" describes the growth-promoting ways in which nature and nurture, universality and diversity, and qualitative and quantitative change are manifested.

Children also face certain hazards. Dealing with a few small problems—perhaps having a learning disability, being exposed to a parent's mental illness, and growing up in a community with a high unemployment rate—can prompt the young person to stretch and grow, for example, by becoming more responsible at home and developing strong coping skills. In comparison, being exposed to numerous serious threats is overwhelming. Skilled and dedicated teachers consider both the advantages and disadvantages that students face and try to see every child in a positive light. Following are proactive responses to children's formative experiences in a diverse society:

BASIC DEVELOPMENTAL ISSUES
Considering Family, Culture, and Society

ISSUE	FAMILY	CULTURE	SOCIETY
Nature and Nurture	At a child's conception, parents pass on genes for basic human traits (e.g., for language) and individual characteristics (such as dispositions to be healthy or frail) (nature). Families care for children, serve as role models, and encourage participation in shared routines (nurture).	The general capacity for culture has evolved over millions of years and is inscribed in the human genetic code. Cultural traditions nurture children by giving meaning, purpose, and predictability to interpersonal relationships, activities, and tool use.	Human beings are a social species with a natural inclination to congregate in groups. When a community has friendly neighbors, decent housing, accessible playmates, safe playgrounds, and reasonably well-paying jobs, there are beneficial influences on development.
Universality and Diversity	Children universally need an adult to advocate for their welfare; heads of family usually serve in this role. Families differ in membership and styles of expressing affection and authority.	Children need (and almost always have) opportunities to participate in cultural activities. Diversity occurs in beliefs about children's capabilities and practices in household maintenance.	Communities universally create a link to the outside world for children. Communities vary in population density, jobs, parks, libraries, and access to fresh food and medical care.
Qualitative and Quantitative Change	Some changes in family roles occur in a trend-like fashion, as when children slowly master steps in preparing a meal (e.g., washing the vegetables, buttering the bread, and grilling the meat). Other changes produce entirely new ways of thinking and behaving, as when an 8-year-old boy is asked to look after his 4-year-old sister for the first time.	Some cultures institute abrupt qualitative changes; for instance, certain rituals signify passage from childhood to adulthood and are accompanied by major changes in roles. Other cultures view development as a series of small, gradual steps; for instance, children are gradually given more independence in completing chores.	Children's experiences show a few qualitative changes. Getting a driver's license or parttime job allows for entirely new choices in transportation, pastimes, and purchases. Many changes are incremental, as when children gradually learn about a city's neighborhoods through walks and bus rides.

• **Look within.** As you have learned, people are inclined to have sub-conscious preferences for certain characteristics—racial categories, ethnicities, types of physique, and so forth. These partialities are not always amenable to conscious inspection. Virtually no one wants to be prejudiced; hence, people who believe there are differences among racial groups in intelligence or other characteristics are likely to justify their perceptions with their own experience. Since most of us have one or more biases that we may not be aware of, it behooves us to admit that that it is possible for a preconception to lead us to treat some children better than others. Admitting that biases might exist is a first step toward mitigating them (P. Clark & Zygmunt, 2014; M. B. Spencer et al., 2012). You might ask yourself:

- What might I believe yet be unable to articulate about children of different races and ethnicities?
- Is it possible that I have distinct expectations for children's learning based on these characteristics?
- In my one-on-one interactions with children, is it possible I am perpetuating racial and ethnic stereotypes?
- Is the curriculum of equivalent benefit to *all* children?

Curbing biases is not something that is fully achieved after a few soul-searching questions. Rather, it is a lifelong challenge. You can help to avoid any preferential or prejudicial action by going out of your way to search for children's assets and give them chances to achieve their goals.

Developmental Systems Prompt 3.3

From a developmental systems perspective, the presence or absence of a single factor, including advocacy from a teacher, can change the trajectory of growth. As you learn about the formative experiences of a child who is struggling at school, consider the transformational role you can play.

• **Reflect on your childhood.** Reminiscing about your upbringing, privileges, and experiences with unfamiliar groups can sensitize you to your personal values and biases (Tilley & Taylor, 2013; H. Wang & Olson, 2009). What have you learned about caring for family members? Being a good person? Serving your community? Achieving in school and in a job? With a clearer recognition of the ideals and traditions that you have come to take for granted, you are ready to learn about others. By immersing yourself in others' community events, reading biographies of prominent figures, and studying reports about a culture's history, you can enhance your sensitivity to the heritage of children.

Preparing for Your Licensure Examination

Your teaching test might ask you to identify strategies for integrating children's cultural knowledge, traditions, and values into lessons and routines.

• **Watch for the cultural knowledge that children bring to school.** All children possess what Puerto Rican American psychologist **Luis Moll** calls *funds of knowledge*, the understandings and traditions that are essential for completing key activities in a household and local community (Moll, Amanti, Neff, & González, 2005). Examples include knowledge needed to prepare family meals, celebrate traditions at home, take part in hobbies, get along with others in the community, and so on. Such personal knowledge defines how children see the world and determines ways in which relationships are to be carried out. If you observe young children's play, you may observe them acting out jobs and housekeeping functions that they see at home (H. Hedges, 2015). Older children may appreciate when teachers integrate information about the family's livelihoods into academic lessons.

• **Validate children's funds of knowledge.** Practitioners increase their effectiveness with youngsters by tailoring their instruction, interactions, and services to children's cultural backgrounds and personal experiences (Chesworth, 2016; Howard, 2007; G. M. Rodriguez, 2013). In an elementary school in Canada, children who were Punjabi Sikh interviewed their grandparents and prepared picture books about family upbringings (Marshall & Toohey, 2010). A secondary school teacher arranged for students in Grades 8 and 9 to use clay animation to tell about their lives (Henderson & Zipin, 2010). Children also learn a lot from materials that show how different groups solve similar problems in different ways, as 9-year-old Dana reveals in her school notes in Artifact Example 3.2. The following are illustrations of how teachers can uncover multicultural traditions for children:

- In history, look at wars and other major events from more than one perspective (e.g., the Spanish perspective of the Spanish–American War and Native American groups' views of pioneers' westward migration in North America).
- In social studies, examine discrimination and oppression.

MyLab Education
Artifact Example 3.2

Find Developmental Meaning *How did nine-year-old Dana see the purpose and source of light in two societies?* In her drawing, Dana appears to show that an urban society and the Maasai tribe in eastern Africa share the need for supplementary light at night. The origins of light in the two societies are different, street lights and electricity in one, fireflies and the moon in the other. Art by Dana.

We get our light from streetlights
The Masai get their light from the moon, fireflies and stars.

- In mathematics, use numerical problems that refer to traditional legends and calendars from different eras and societies.
- In literature, present the work of minority authors and poets.
- In art, consider creations and techniques by artists from around the world.
- In music, teach songs from many cultures and nations.
- In physical education, teach games or folk dances from other countries and cultures. (Averill et al., 2009; Boutte & McCormick, 1992; McMillan, 2013; NCSS Task Force on Ethnic Studies Curriculum Guidelines, 1992; N. L. Norton, 2014; Sleeter & Grant, 1999)

• **Foster respect for diverse groups.** When talking about cultural practices, teachers can emphasize the merits of these customs for the groups involved. Ingredients of meals in a subsistence society, immigration patterns around the world, and dances in traditional cultures can all be understood by learning about the history, customs, and living conditions of those involved. Teachers can select materials that represent groups in a positive light—for instance, by choosing books and movies that portray people from varying ethnic backgrounds as legitimate participants in society rather than as exotic "curiosities" who live in a separate world. Educators should avoid (or at least comment critically on) materials that portray members of minority groups in a simplistic, romanticized, exaggerated, or otherwise stereotypical fashion (Banks, 1994; Boutte & McCormick, 1992; Pang, 2007). You can see some illustrations of adults validating distinct backgrounds in the Development and Practice feature "Supporting Children in Their Cultural Knowledge."

Development-Enhancing Education

Supporting Children in Their Cultural Knowledge

Establish connections with local communities.

- An elementary school in a Mexican American community in Chicago reaches out to families by inviting children, parents, and teachers to take part in Mexican Folklorico dance classes (Olmedo, 2009). The school includes both Mexican and American flags on an outdoor mural and celebrates the holidays of both nations. (Middle Childhood)
- A high school teacher encourages adolescents to take part in community service projects. The students may choose from a wide range of possibilities, including neighborhood cleanups, story time with preschoolers at the library, and volunteer work at a food bank. (Late Adolescence)

Learn about the funds of knowledge children are exposed to at home.

- A preschool teacher invites families to describe how they use plants as ingredients in health remedies and meals (Riojas-Cortez, Huerta, Flores, Perez, & Clark, 2008). The families' strategies for using plants are integrated into science lessons, and the families are invited to take part. (Early Childhood)
- A small team of educators visits the family of fourth-grader Jacobo (Genzuk, 1999). The team learns that Jacobo's father is a skilled hydraulics mechanic and that Jacobo himself is interested in mechanics. His teacher asks Jacobo

Development-Enhancing Education (continued)

to create an automotive journal that can be used as a resource in the classroom. Jacobo enthusiastically writes in his journal and shares it with others in the class. (Middle Childhood)

Endorse children's home knowledge in the classroom.

- An infant caregiver purchases tunes of lullabies in Spanish and Mandarin Chinese, the two languages that are most often spoken by the immigrant families she serves. She encourages the babies to clap their hands and sway with the music. (Infancy)
- A teacher asks her second-grade children to bring in lyrics from rap songs. She screens out those that are offensive and selects a few. The children perform the selected songs and analyze their literal and figurative meanings, rhyme scheme, and principles of alliteration (Ladson-Billings, 1995). (Middle Childhood)

Adapt to the cultural beliefs and practices of children.

- A Japanese family has recently placed their 8-month-old son in part-time child care. The baby is accustomed to his mother hand-feeding him. His new caregiver holds him during mealtime and offers him small pieces of food. (Infancy)
- A third-grade teacher notices that only a few of the children are willing to answer her questions about domesticated animals, even though it is clear from individual conversations that most have pets. She discovers that bringing attention to oneself is not appropriate in the children's culture and modifies her style to allow for group responses. (Middle Childhood)

Use materials that represent all ethnic groups in a competent light.

- An elementary school librarian examines history books in the school's collection for the manner in which various cultural groups are represented. The librarian orders a few additional books to balance the treatment of groups that have been excluded or misrepresented in the compendium. (Middle Childhood)
- A middle school history teacher peruses a textbook to make sure that it portrays all ethnicities in a nonstereotypical manner. He supplements the book with readings that highlight important roles played by members of various groups throughout history. (Early Adolescence)

Expose youngsters to successful models from various ethnic backgrounds.

- A kindergarten teacher in an ethnically diverse school collaborates with a third-grade teacher in the building to establish a reading program. The older children come to kindergarten once a week to read to their younger buddies. Older children gain experience in reading aloud, and younger children enjoy the stories and attention. (Early Childhood)
- A middle school teacher invites several successful professionals from different ethnicities to tell her class about their jobs. When some youngsters seem interested in particular careers, she arranges for them to spend time with professionals at their workplaces. (Early Adolescence)

Be neutral, inclusive, and respectful regarding children's religious practices.

- A preschool teacher encourages children in her class to bring in decorations and other materials showing how they celebrate holidays during the winter months. Children bring in decorations related to Christmas, Ramadan, Kwanzaa, Hanukkah, and the winter solstice. The teacher passes around the materials and explains that children in her class celebrate many different holidays. (Early Childhood)
- A social studies middle school teacher asks students to select a figure in history who struggled against religious discrimination. After the students conduct individual investigations, they take part in a class discussion and learn about the wide range of religious groups that have experienced persecution. (Early Adolescence)

• **Balance your attention to risks and protective factors.** In a theoretical extension to the bioecological model, American psychologist **Margaret Beale Spencer** and her colleagues have examined *risks* in children's environments, conditions that increase vulnerability to problematic outcomes (e.g., dropping out of school, being incarcerated, becoming an adolescent parent) and *protective factors*, conditions that help children deal with hardships, mitigate their harm, and catalyze positive growth (Cicchetti, Spencer, & Swanson, 2013; McGee & Spencer, 2015; M. B. Spencer, 2006; M. B. Spencer & Spencer, 2014). Risk factors include economic poverty, unstable family conditions, restrictive gender stereotypes, racial discrimination, and underfunded schools. Protective factors include being intelligent, affectionate, good-humored, and physically attractive, having involved families, and living in a close-knit community.

• **Accept that what you do (and fail to do) can perpetuate inequities.** Although very few professionals intentionally discriminate against young people based on their ethnicity or skin color, their actions can perpetuate disparities (Howard, 2007; McGrady & Reynolds, 2013). For instance, some teachers rarely modify instruction for students with diverse needs; instead, they present instruction in a take-it-or-leave-it manner. Clearly, teaching children from diverse backgrounds requires more than giving lip service to cultural diversity; it requires a genuine commitment to modifying materials and interactions so that children can achieve their full academic potential (Bakari, 2000).

• **Recognize the variation that exists within groups and across individuals.** It is human nature to see cultural groups as uniform entities. The reality is that any given group (e.g., children whose parents are Native Americans or Polynesian) is usually heterogeneous. For example, immigrant parents hold beliefs about education that vary depending on country of origin and personal experience—some might be seasonal migrant workers and others diplomats, foreign-born university students, or political asylum seekers (Kağitçibaşi, 2007). And, of course, children have varied interests, skills, and views that transcend their group's typical patterns. Teachers can get to know children as individuals by asking them about their hopes for the future, preferences for free time, interests at school, responsibilities at home, and prior experiences related to academic areas (Hogg, 2011; Villegas & Lucas, 2007).

• **Confront inequities.** Educators regularly take the stand that inequities will *not* be tolerated at school. To profess its commitment to fairness and justice, one school district displays a statement of its "Equity Vision":

> Roseville Area Schools is committed to ensuring an equitable and respectful educational experience for every student, family, and staff member, regardless of race, gender, sexual orientation, socioeconomic status, ability, home or first language, religion, national origin, or age. (Howard, 2007, p. 20)

Of course, children and families want to see such words backed up with fair, respectful, and compassionate deeds. Teachers and other school professionals must confront practices that favor one group or another, for example, in assigning inexperienced teachers to work with students who need the most help, communicating low expectations to students from ethnic minority backgrounds, or showing preferences for students from one ethnicity over another when selecting recipients for awards (Villegas & Lucas, 2007).

Summary

Family, culture, and society create foundations for child development. These contexts teach children who they are as human beings, how they should relate to others, and what they can aspire to become as adults. Families exert powerful influences on children through the bonds they form, the advocacy they provide, and the socialization they carry out. Children grow up in one or more cultures that guide their foremost values and activities. Increasingly children are exposed to two or more distinct cultures and may develop allegiances to, and practices from, more than one of these civilizations. The society in which children grow is influential by providing playmates, neighbors whom children see coming and going, access to institutions, and treatment based on their race, ethnicity, and personal characteristics. Educators can help children by learning about their backgrounds, building on their strengths, reducing the damaging effects of risk factors, becoming self-reflective about their own biases, and ensuring that giving all children a high-quality education.

MyLab Education Self-Check 3.1

Family Membership

3.2 Describe common types of family structures and their implications for educators.

Now that you understand the profound influences culture and society have on children, you are ready to delve into the heart and center of children's lives—their family. The family offers children close emotional ties and takes on responsibility for raising them. This responsibility involves helping children acquire important skills, find a place in society, and interpret cultural traditions.

To understand the partnerships educators can form with families, it is important to learn about who is in the family and how they interact. Let's start with family membership. A child's **family structure** refers to the makeup of the family—those individuals who live in the family home, including the one or more adults who care for the child and any siblings. Consider these statistics on family structures of American children:

- 64.7% live with two married parents.
- 4.5% live with two unmarried parents.
- 23.1% live with their mother only.
- 3.7% live with their father only.
- 3.9% live without a parent in their household and instead reside in some other living arrangement, such as with grandparents, other relatives, or foster parents (Forum on Child and Family Statistics, 2016b).

Of course, many family conditions defy these cut-and-dried categories. At any given time, a child may be adjusting to one or more family changes, perhaps the addition of a new stepparent, the marriage of previously unmarried parents, or the coming or going of a parent's unmarried (*cohabiting*) partner. A child may live with one parent yet stay in contact with the second parent, in accordance with custody arrangements or informal agreements.

What matters most to children is not who is in their family but, rather, that they are loved. Five-year-old Alex, who was adopted, portrays family unity in his drawing in Artifact Example 3.3. Regardless of family type, children eagerly soak up affection from responsive adults and siblings. Nevertheless, family membership can affect children's needs at school. Although you would never want to pigeonhole a child based on his or her family type, you can learn to anticipate the general assets and challenges that tend to occur in particular family situations.

MyLab Education
Artifact Example 3.3

Find Developmental Meaning *How does 5-year-old Alex portray his family?* Notice how Alex arranges his family as a unit, with everyone holding hands. Nearby are the family house and goldfish. Art by Alex.

Mothers and Fathers

When a mother and a father are present in the home, children often form close bonds with both parents (Kochanska & Kim, 2013; M. E. Lamb, Chuang, & Cabrera, 2005). Having two adults in the home magnifies the affection children receive and allows one parent to compensate when the other one is unable (Gaumon, Paquette, Cyr, Émond-Nakamura, & St-André, 2016; Meteyer & Perry-Jenkins, 2009). In large part, because of the emotional and financial resources that tend to be present in two-parent families, children living with a mother and a father achieve at higher levels in school and show fewer behavior problems than is the case with children in other kinds of families (Magnuson & Berger, 2009).

Being in a two-parent family also exposes children to two approaches to parenting. Mothers generally care for children's physical needs (e.g., feeding, bathing, scheduling doctors' appointments), watch over children, and display affection (Belsky, Gilstrap, & Rovine, 1984; L. Craig & Powell, 2013; Phares, Fields, & Kamboukos, 2009). As children grow, relationships with mothers tend to be more intimate than those with fathers, and mothers are more likely to encourage children to open up about personal matters (Harach & Kuczynski, 2005; Smetana, Metzger, Gettman, & Campione-Barr, 2006).

Fathers, in contrast, are more playful and instrumental in guiding children to get along with people outside the family and prepare for future challenges in life (M. E. Lamb et al., 2005; Musick, Meier, & Flood, 2016; Parke & Buriel, 2006). Obviously, fathers are not simply playmates; most spend substantial amounts of time caring for their children and are quite competent in feeding, bathing, and in other ways nurturing children (Jeynes, 2016; M. E. Lamb, Frodi, Hwang, Frodi, & Steinberg, 1982; Mackey, 2001). In many societies fathers become more involved as children grow older, especially in disciplining, encouraging self-reliance, and modeling subtle masculine qualities, such as being a dependable provider for the family (Munroe & Munroe, 1992; Pruett & Pruett, 2009).

In addition to having two caregivers, two-parent families show children how to carry out adult relationships. A man and a woman have much to work out on a daily basis as an intimate couple and as **coparents**, partners in raising their children (Feinberg, Kan, & Goslin, 2009; Tavassolie, Dudding, Madigan, Thorvardarson, & Winsler, 2016). Many parents air their differences constructively and search for solutions that are mutually beneficial, giving children valuable lessons in conflict resolution (Cummings & Merrilees, 2010; J. P. McHale & Rasmussen, 1998). Children gain in another way from their parents' healthy relationships. Emotionally close couples are inclined to shower affection on their children (Holland & McElwain, 2013; Ward & Spitze, 1998).

The lessons other children encounter are different. Some children frequently overhear heated arguments. Loud and bitter exchanges frighten children and are poor standards for communication. When parents' disputes are intense and protracted, young children tend to become upset and blame themselves, and older children feel insecure (Goeke-Morey, Papp, & Cummings, 2013; Ruhland, Hardman, Becher, & Marczak, 2016). Arguments put parents in a foul mood, which can quickly spill over into harsh interactions with children (S. G. O'Leary & Vidair, 2005; Yoo, Popp, & Robinson, 2014). As a result, intense marital conflict is associated with assorted problems in youngsters, including depression, anxiety, aggression, and difficulties in personal relationships (Bornovalov et al., 2014; Brock & Kochanska, 2016; Feinberg, Kan, & Hetherington, 2007; Koss et al., 2013).

An increasing number of unmarried couples have children together. As with the children of married couples, the offspring of unmarried couples are likely to receive loving care. Cohabiting families are becoming increasingly common, and many children in these families are well adjusted (W. D. Manning, 2015; Parent, Jones, Forehand, Cuellar, & Shoulberg, 2013; C. J. Patterson & Hastings, 2007). Nevertheless, compared to married parents, *cohabiting parents* are (on average) younger; less educated, wealthy, and affectionate; and less satisfied with their relationships with partners and more apt to break up with them (Aronson & Huston, 2004; Klausi & Owen, 2009; Kotila & Kamp Dush, 2012; W. D. Manning, 2015). As is the case in any family structure, the adjustment of children with unmarried parents ultimately depends on their individual characteristics, the relationships they have with their parents, and the support coming from the extended family.

Divorced Parents

Once an infrequent occurrence, divorce is now commonplace in many corners of the world. In the United States more than 4 to 5 in 10 marriages end in divorce, and approximately half of American children are affected by this family transition (American Psychological Association, 2016; M. M. Stevenson, Braver, Ellman, & Votruba, 2013). Divorce rates are similarly high in Australia and Europe (Mahony, Walsh, Lunn, & Petriwskyj, 2015).

For children, the divorce of parents is not a single event but a series of occurrences, each requiring adjustment. News of a divorce can come as a blow to children, even though they may have previously witnessed parents' strained communication, emotional distance, or intense arguments. Immediately after being told about the separation, children are likely to receive less attention due to parents' own preoccupation with the changes (Kaslow, 2000). Custodial parents—one or both parents who look after the children in their homes—may struggle to complete all the tasks involved in maintaining an organized household, including shopping, cooking, cleaning, paying bills, and monitoring children's activities (Wallerstein & Kelly, 1980). Financial setbacks can complicate everyone's adjustment. Parents who previously owned a house may have to sell it, and so, on top of everything else, children must move to new (and inevitably smaller) quarters farther away from friends (W. G. Austin, 2012; J. B. Kelly, 2007; Schramm et al., 2013).

As coparents establish separate households, children learn how their parents will get along (or not) and what role each parent will now play for them. One parent may withdraw from the children and eventually invest, both emotionally and financially, in a new life and perhaps a new family. Thus, one possible consequence of divorce is children losing contact from one of their parents, usually the father (J. B. Kelly, 2007; M. M. Stevenson et al., 2013). Fortunately, this trend is by no means universal. Many fathers actively seek joint custody arrangements after a divorce (R. A. Thompson, 1994b; M. M. Stevenson et al., 2013).

Children struggle with these multiple changes. Divorce is especially troubling for young children, who may erroneously believe that their own naughty behavior caused the family's breakup (Fausel, 1986; Lansford, 2009). Older children usually respond reasonably well, even though they may initially find their parents' divorce quite upsetting (Hetherington, Bridges, & Insabella, 1998). Given time and support, many youngsters ultimately accept the permanence of their parents' divorce (Kulik & Kasa, 2014; Lansford, 2009; M. M. Stevenson et al., 2013). Nevertheless, depression and aggression problems can occur and persist for some young people (J. M. Weaver & Schofield, 2015).

Adjustment to divorce is facilitated by several factors. Coparents and other adults assist children by maintaining affectionate relationships with their sons and daughters, enforcing rules consistently, listening sympathetically to their concerns, and encouraging their continued contact with friends, nonresident parents, and extended family members (Hetherington & Clingempeel, 1992; S. Holt, 2016; J. M. Weaver & Schofield, 2015). Children who are intelligent and have good coping skills, for example, in talking with a friend when upset rather than letting anxiety escalate, are more likely to adjust favorably after the breakup (Pedro-Carroll, 2005; Schaan & Vögele, 2016; J. M. Weaver & Schofield, 2015). Children are also able to adapt effectively when coparents establish reasonably productive relationships, agree on expectations and disciplinary measures, keep a lid on their own disputes, and seek counseling when children are deeply troubled by the breakup (Hetherington, Cox, & Cox, 1978; Regev & Ehrenberg, 2012; M. M. Stevenson et al., 2013).

Single Parents

About 23% of American children grow up with a single parent, one who has no coparent in the home (Forum on Child and Family Statistics, 2016c). Most single parents are divorced or have never been married, but a few are widowed or separated, and some have a spouse who is temporarily absent (U.S. Census Bureau, 2013a). The vast majority are women. Some single mothers, particularly older unmarried mothers who are highly educated, are well able to provide adequate food, shelter, and opportunities for their children, whereas others, especially those who are young and uneducated, are apt to have limited financial resources (C. J. Patterson & Hastings, 2007; M. Wen, 2008).

Single parents carry out the tasks of parenting with the realization that much responsibility falls on their shoulders (Beckert, Strom, Strom, Darre, & Weed, 2008). This realization often leads them to prioritize their children's needs. Perhaps because of this focus, many single-parent families function extremely well, particularly when they have a reasonable standard of living and stable network of family and friends (W.-C. Chen, 2016; Fennimore, 2013; C. J. Patterson & Hastings, 2007). In fact, the simple structure of single-parent families has advantages: Children may be shielded from intense conflict between parents, observe strong coping skills in their custodial parent, and enjoy the intimacy of a small family.

Despite their varied circumstances, single-parent families are apt to share certain challenges. Single parents, mothers and fathers alike, often express reservations about their ability to "do it all"—juggle children, home, and work responsibilities (Beckert et al., 2008; R. A. Thompson, 1994b). Unless they have the support of extended family

Mom is Wow

She is great at hide-and-seek
She takes me to look at an antique
I get to see her three times a week

Mom is Wow

She helped teach me multiplication
She encourages my imagination
She is involved when it comes to participation

Mom is Wow

She's a great stepmom, I guarantee
She lets us watch Disney TV
She is an important part of the family tree

Mom is Wow

No matter what, she is never late
If I have a question, she will demonstrate
When it comes to stepmoms, she's great

Mom is Wow

MyLab Education
Artifact Example 3.4

Find Developmental Meaning *How does 9-year-old Shea describe her stepmother?* In her fourth-grade class, Shea wrote a Mother's Day poem for her stepmother, Ann, using the "Mom is Wow" structure the teacher provided. Notice that Shea portrays Ann as a kind and reliable caregiver who enriches her life, helps her learn productive skills, and shares leisure time with her.

members, neighbors, and friends, single parents may have difficulty in remaining affectionate and patient and offering children the rich range of roles, activities, and relationships known to maximize positive developmental outcomes (Daryanani, Hamilton, Abramson, & Alloy, 2016; Garbarino & Abramowitz, 1992; Miljkovitch, Danet, & Bernier, 2012; Sitnick, Masyn, Ontai, & Conger, 2016). It can be particularly challenging for single parents when they themselves are sick, disabled, or responsible for infirm family members. Fortunately, many single parents are well aware of their personal limitations and reach out to others for assistance.

Parents and Stepparents

Many divorced parents eventually remarry. When they do, they and their children become members of a **stepfamily**, a single-parent family that is expanded to include a new adult and any children in his or her custody.[1] Approximately 6% of children in two-parent families live with a biological or adoptive parent and a stepparent (Federal Interagency Forum on Child and Family Statistics, 2013b).

As is true for all family structures, children in stepfamilies are exposed to advantages and challenges. A new adult may bring additional income to the family and help with household duties. Children have a chance to forge relationships with a new parent figure and, sometimes, with new brothers and sisters. Yet children may feel that they must now share their parent's time with the new spouse. They may believe, too, that the new stepparent is interfering with a possible reunion of the divorced parents and that by showing affection to the stepparent, they are betraying the nonresident parent (R. Berger, 2000; Bigner, 2006; Schrodt, 2016). A feeling that the original family has been torn apart is likely to occur when there is strained communication between the original parents. The son or daughter may feel forced to declare loyalty to one parent or the other, a dynamic that can undermine the integration of the stepparent into the new family structure.

For a stepfamily to blend successfully, it must establish its own identity. Whereas a couple without children can initially focus on one another, a newly married parent and stepparent must attend to the needs of the children as well as to their own relationship. Having entered the marriage with habits of their own, the man and the woman must decide how to spend money, divide household chores, prepare and serve meals, and celebrate holidays. Initially the stepparent is apt to defer to the biological parent when the child needs to be disciplined, but the couple must eventually agree on rules and discipline (Pettigrew, 2013).

Most children in stepfamilies ultimately adjust well to their new family situation (E. R. Anderson & Greene, 2013; R. Berger, 2000). The child's mental health (e.g., having been generally well-adjusted or anxious and depressed) and relationship with the first parents (e.g., feeling close, conflicted, or aloof with them) are important factors in relationships with new parent figures (V. King, Amato, & Lindstrom, 2015). In many (probably most) instances, stepparents soon become important parts of children's lives.

Extended Family

Many children have strong ties with relatives. In the United States, about 6% of all children live with at least one grandparent (U.S. Census Bureau, 2013b). Grandparents often become primary guardians when a child's parents are young and economically poor, neglectful, imprisoned, deployed in the military, incapacitated by illness or substance

[1]Stepfamilies are also known as *reconstituted, repartnered, remarried,* and *blended families.*

abuse, or have died (Berrick & Hernandez, 2016; Bertera & Crewe, 2013; Dolan, Casanueva, Smith, & Bradley, 2009; O. W. Edwards & Taub, 2009).

Typically, kin caregivers are older, less well-off financially, and less educated than the general population (Berrick & Hernandez, 2016). Custodial grandparents sometimes worry that they do not have adequate energy and funds to raise a second generation of children, yet their mature outlook and parenting experience often lead them to be competent caregivers, especially when offered support from other family members, teachers, and other professionals (C. B. Cox, 2000; Y. R. Green & Gray, 2013; Letiecq, Bailey, & Dahlen, 2008). For some children, other extended family members assume central roles. Aunts, uncles, and cousins regularly step forward to raise children when they are the only viable parent figure (Milardo, 2010; Sear & Mace, 2008). Occasionally, older siblings may become primary caregivers when they are mature enough.

Given the varied and sometimes tragic circumstances in which kin take over the responsibility of raising children, sensitive outreach from educators is likely to be appreciated. Kin parents may face a range of challenges and are likely to shift over time in the particular roles they take on with children, perhaps beginning in a temporary and informal responsibility and progressing through foster care and adoption. Teachers and other school professionals can help by listening intently to parent figures, assuring them with updates about the child's accomplishments, sharing perspectives of any special needs the child may have, and advising the families about resources in the school and community (Berrick & Hernandez, 2016).

MyLab Education
Video Example 3.2

Find Developmental Meaning *Who is in 6-year-old Joey's family?* Joey's family picture includes himself, his grandfather, his grandmother, and his younger brother. Joey fishes and plays baseball with his grandfather, golfs with his uncle, and plays with his dog. Joey appreciates this attention and takes pride in helping his younger brother play video games.

Adoptive Parents

Two out of every 100 children in the United States are adopted (Federal Interagency Forum on Child and Family Statistics, 2013c). Adoption is almost always a positive arrangement for children, especially when the new parents have thoughtfully chosen to expand their family and embrace children's individual qualities. Adoption is invariably a blessing for adoptive parents and siblings as well, as these individuals find themselves with a new child to love. A journal entry from newly adoptive brother Connor, shown in Artifact Example 3.5, show that within a few days children learn about the likes and dislikes of their new siblings.

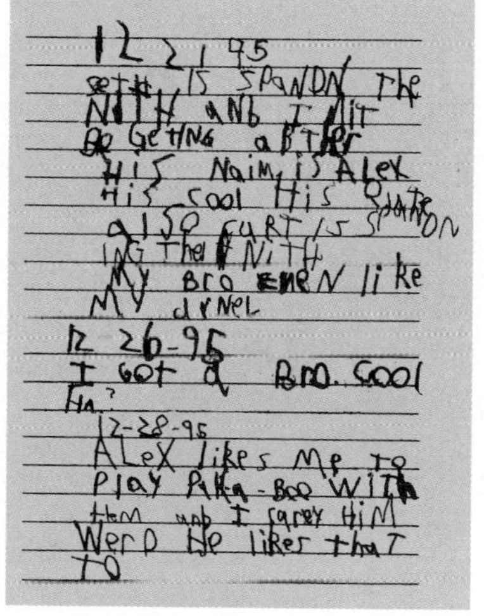

MyLab Education
Artifact Example 3.5

Find Developmental Meaning *How does 7-year-old Connor express his excitement about becoming a big brother?* Eight-month-old Alex is placed in Connor's family on December 20, originally in a foster arrangement, and by December 28, Connor is aware of some of Alex's likes, such as playing peekaboo.

The past few decades have seen several changes in adoption policies. One growing practice is *open adoption*, in which the birth mother (perhaps in consultation with her own parents, the birth father, and agency counselors) chooses the adoptive family. Adoptive families often gain access to medical records through open adoption, and adopted children may have a chance to meet their birth parents someday. In *international adoption*, families in one country adopt children orphaned or relinquished in another country. The number of international adoptions by U.S. parents has decreased in the last 10 years, due primarily to reductions in available children (U.S. Department of Health and Human Services Administration for Children and Families, 2018). Nevertheless, numerous countries continue to allow native children to be adopted by families abroad. In 2017, large numbers adopted by U.S. families came from China (1905), Ethiopia (313), South Korea (276), India (221), Haiti (227), the Ukraine (215), Colombia (181), and Nigeria (176) (U.S. Bureau of Consular Affairs, 2018). In a third trend, many adoption agencies are increasingly flexible in evaluating potential adoptive parents; the result is a growing number who are single, older, gay, lesbian, from lower-income groups, and from a different racial background than the adopted child (Bigner, 2006; Logan, 2013).

Although adopted children are at slightly greater risk for emotional, behavioral, and academic problems compared to children reared by biological parents, most adopted children grow up to be well-adjusted individuals (Agnich, Schueths, James, & Klibert, 2016; Christoffersen, 2012; Freeark, 2006; J. Palacios & Sánchez-Sandoval, 2005). Adopted children seem to cope best when family members talk openly about the adoption and provide the same love and nurturance that they would offer biological offspring (Bigner, 2006; Brodzinsky, 2006).

Children who are adopted after infancy and early childhood occasionally have physical or mental disabilities due to preexisting conditions or poor care earlier in life (Follan & McNamara, 2014; Julian, 2013; Rutter, 2005). In extreme cases children were abused or neglected or had several different placements before being adopted and later have trouble in forming secure relationships with new family members. Elementary school students who have spent their infancy and early childhood in neglectful or unstable homes sometimes exhibit problems paying attention in class, relating to peers, and forming secure attachments to adults. Teachers can use resources at their school to address these needs, including collaboration with school counselors and psychologists (F. S. Baker, 2013).

Adolescent Parents

Adolescent mothers are likely to find the responsibility of caring for their infants to be overwhelming, especially when they are unaware of infants' physical, cognitive, and social characteristics and their typical progressions (Borkowski et al., 2002; Lee Smith, Gilmer, Salge, Dickerson, & Wilson, 2013; McHugh, Kvernland, & Palusci, 2015). Teenage mothers who are anxious and unrealistic about child development are apt to be inattentive, inconsistent, and critical with their young children. The unhappy result is that their children face risks for delayed language development and lower-than-average academic achievement (Borkowski et al., 2002; Lefever, Nicholson, & Noria, 2007). Nevertheless, adolescent mothers can learn to be competent caregivers, and educators can improve the odds for young mothers and their offspring by motivating them to complete high school, learn about child development, and take advantage of local programs that support new mothers (Jahromi, Guimond, Umaña-Taylor, Updegraff, & Toomey, 2014; Lee Smith et al., 2013; Robbers, 2008).

Much less is known about adolescent fathers, but they also face challenges. Before the birth of the baby, adolescent fathers may encounter disapproval from others. They may struggle to maintain a good relationship with their pregnant girlfriend and worry about their ability to fulfill the responsibilities of raising a child (T. T. Williams, Mance, Caldwell, & Antonucci, 2012). After the baby is born, teenage fathers may find that their fears were well founded, as the relationship with the baby's mother is likely to become strained and their search for well-paying jobs unsuccessful (T. T. Williams et al., 2012). Young mothers and fathers alike can benefit from support from their own families and from professionals who understand their pressures. Educators can offer practical advice in staying involved with their children and accepting the importance of their own age-typical tasks, such as developing an identity of who they are, what they stand for, and where they are going in life (A. Lewin et al., 2015).

Gay and Lesbian Parents

Growing numbers of children live with gay or lesbian parents. In the United States, approximately one in five male couples and one in three female couples are raising children from adoption, donor insemination, a previous marriage, or other arrangements (H. Bos, 2013; R. H. Farr, 2016; R. H. Farr & Patterson, 2013). Children who have gay or lesbian parents have many assets, including being as intelligent and well adjusted as children from other kinds of family (Crowl, Ahn, & Baker, 2008; Golombok et al., 2014; C. J. Patterson, 2009). They are also inclined to become tolerant and open-minded adults who respect diversity in its many forms (Goldberg, 2007; Telingator, 2013).

Prejudice and discrimination are challenges that gay and lesbian parents and their children face. Children of homosexual parents may encounter peers teasing their parents but are usually able to cope with this prejudice without too much problem (C. J. Patterson, 2009). Unfortunately, some children are persistently bullied because of their parents' sexual orientation, and they sometimes shield their parents from the derogatory remarks so as not to trouble them (Telingator, 2013). Because of concerns about stigmatization, gay and lesbian parents may be reluctant to share their sexual orientation with teachers and other personnel at school. The children themselves are apt to be cautious in whom they confide. When they do "come out" about having gay parents, children often feel relieved to be able to share this part of themselves (M. G. Welsh, 2011, p. 63).

Although being shunned by others can be troubling to parents and children, both parties generally cope effectively, especially when there are close and loving relationships within the family (C. J. Patterson, 2009; Telingator, 2013; M. G. Welsh, 2011). Experts suggest that an inclusive school climate and a curriculum that is openly accepting of gay, lesbian, bisexual, and transgender (GLBT) individuals helps not only students themselves who are GLBT but also the children of GLBT parents (Byard, Kosciw, & Bartkiewicz, 2013; J. E. Hart, Mourot, & Aros, 2012). Teachers and school leaders can also ask how coparents wish to be addressed, make a point to invite the child's entire family to school events, and include multiple spaces on school forms for all guardians.

Foster Parents

In *foster care*, children are placed with families in a legal but temporary arrangement, often due to their birth parents' neglect, maltreatment, or substance abuse (P. A. Fisher, Kim, & Pears, 2009; J. Smith, Boone, Gourdine, & Brown, 2013). Many children in foster care must survive the ordeal of being separated from birth parents, whose care may have been insensitive, unstable, and unreliable, yet they nevertheless cultivated a sense of family connection, the disruption of which requires adjustment (Mehta, Baker, & Chong, 2013). Court officials generally try to keep siblings together, although unified arrangements are not always possible, as when the family size is large or sibling relationships have become abusive or destructive (Summers, Gatowski, & Dobbin, 2012).

Foster parents face significant challenges. They must build a trusting relationship with a child who could be a victim of abuse and currently exhibits emotional and behavioral problems (M. E. Cox, Orme, & Rhoades, 2003; Orme & Buehler, 2001). Foster parents receive minimal financial support from the state and must deal with numerous social service agencies. Fortunately, many foster parents take in children for the right reasons—because they themselves grew up in foster care or are committed to caring for children who have faced difficult conditions (Barber & Delfabbro, 2004).

Many children in foster care grow attached to their new families but nevertheless long to return to their birth families (Mehta et al., 2013; Samuels, 2009a). In fact, the majority of children in foster care are reunited with birth families within the first year (U.S. Department of Health and Human Services, 2007). Some birth parents are unable or unwilling to resume duties as parents, and their children are kept in foster care or eventually adopted, on average at about 6 or 7 years of age, often by their foster parents and sometimes by other adults who decide to adopt older children (U.S. Department of Health and Human Services, 2007). Unfortunately, because of heavy caseloads in agencies, crowded court dockets, and a common preference for newborn infants, foster children are sometimes shuffled among several temporary arrangements before being placed into permanent homes (McKenzie, 1993). Such a transitory existence is particularly detrimental when children have already faced serious problems, including neglect, abuse, or exposure to drugs and violence.

Despite their adversities, many children in foster care show resilience. A good number form healthy relationships with foster parents, do well in school, develop friendships with peers, go on to college, and grow up as productive adults with good jobs and stable relationships (L. Jones, 2012; Kufeldt, Simard, & Vachon, 2003; G. Schofield & Beek, 2009; Strolin-Goltzman, Woodhouse, Suter, & Werrbach, 2016). Foster parents who have specialized training from social workers are especially likely to be effective in nurturing children toward good developmental outcomes (P. A. Fisher et al., 2009).

Teachers and other school professionals can promote this hardiness. Becoming aware of children's individual needs is an important first step. Children may have missed a lot of school due to their family's eviction, homelessness, or substance abuse, and teachers can help children acquire missing academic skills. Movements between schools require the transfer of the child's records, immediate enrollment, and reassurance. Extra efforts to put the child at ease at school, acquaint him or her with the routines of the classroom, and encourage academic progress are essential. Mental health services may be necessary, as the child might withdraw in depression or lash out at others in frustration. The child may also need to leave school occasionally because of court-mandated meetings with social workers, visits with birth parents, and medical appointments. School personnel can excuse the absences without penalty and assist the child in making up schoolwork.

Teachers, social workers, and others with expertise serving children who have had an unstable family life can also reach out to foster parents. Foster parents invariably need support themselves in providing children, especially those who are deeply troubled, with a secure and loving home (Crum, 2010). Experts can instill an understanding in foster parents of persevering with steadfast love, familiar routines, and firm and consistent discipline. Children in foster care have relatively high rates of special educational needs, making it important for educators and foster parents to exchange perspectives on children's individual strengths, limitations, and preferences within the academic learning (Neiheiser, 2015).

Accommodating Family Diversity and Transitions

Most school professionals place a high value on being inclusive and respectful of children and their families. Following are some tactics educators use to champion for children in a wide range of family circumstances:

- **When organizing activities, make them inclusive to children from varied backgrounds.** School assignments and extracurricular activities sometimes involve one or more family members. With a little creativity, teachers can broaden activities so that they accommodate diverse family structures. Recall the Mother's Day poem Shea wrote to her stepmother (p. 78). Shea's teacher gave her enough time to write two poems, one for her mother and one for her stepmother.

- **Foster a climate of acceptance for diverse family structures.** As you have learned, children occasionally tease classmates from nontraditional families. At the preschool and elementary levels, teachers can counteract intolerant attitudes by reading stories about children in different family structures and expressing the view that loving families are formed in many ways. Obviously, it is crucial to express intolerance for rude remarks about others' families. In the secondary grades, adolescents tend to be more accepting of diverse family structures; nevertheless, at this age level as well, teachers should keep an ear open for, and emphatically discourage, any derogatory comments about a classmate's family.

- **Include mothers, fathers, custodial grandparents, and other heads of family at school.** By equalizing communications to children's coparents, teachers validate the incredibly influential roles that various parent figures play. It is also important to acknowledge the presence of other heads of family, such as grandparents serving as guardians. And whenever possible, extended family members should be welcome at school open houses, plays, and concerts.

- **Be supportive when children undergo a major family transition.** Divorce, remarriage, the departure of a parent's nonmarital partner, the death of a family member, or movement from one foster family to another can change a child's life dramatically. In each case one or more caregivers may become unavailable, and other new relationships begin (Adam, 2004; Dush, 2013). Adjustment to family transitions takes time, and practitioners should be prepared to offer long-term support. Adults can help children express their feelings, accept that they are not being abandoned and did not cause the family change, distinguish events that they can and cannot control, consider benefits to being in the new family structure, and develop friendships with peers and compassionate relationships with teachers (Pedro-Carroll, 2005; Pedro-Carroll & Velderman, 2016; Recker, Clark, & Foote, 2008). Educators can also remain attentive to behavioral changes children may exhibit during bouts of intense stress, such as being unusually combative on the playground or sad, lonely, and inattentive during classroom lessons. Under such circumstances, children may need ample reassurance, gentle reminders of classroom rules, and lots of affection.

- **Remain patient while children are figuring out how to adjust to new family structures.** Many youngsters must adapt to moving back and forth between two houses (Smart, Neale, & Wade, 2001). In such circumstances teachers can express sympathy for any distress or frustration and also encourage the child to come up with a plan for adjusting to the transitions and keeping track of belongings (including homework) during moves between residences. Teachers can also ask for the child's schedule in moving between households so that they are aware where the child is and whom to call in the event of an emergency.

• **Let children say what they want to say.** Children often prefer to keep family matters to themselves. They may feel that teachers and counselors are snooping into their personal lives by asking questions about their family life. It is desirable, therefore, for adults to lend a sympathetic ear without being too inquisitive. When children bring up family issues, you can help them generate options for dealing with their problems, such as compiling a portfolio of schoolwork when getting ready to move to a new school.

• **Anticipate children's needs based on what you know about their families.** A student with a grandparent living with the family may be able to come to school meetings when the single mother is away on business trips. A child whose family has recently moved needs information about the school day and procedures for gathering supplies, getting in line for lunch, getting settled after recess, and so on. Another child with a chronically sick parent may need help in getting to school on time; perhaps a classmate's parent would be willing to drive the child to and from school.

• **Extend an extra hand to students living in foster care.** A number of children in foster care are emotionally burdened yet have trouble asking for assistance. Some have profound social needs and engage in behaviors that upset even experienced professionals. Others desperately miss their birth parents and any brothers and sisters staying with other families. Because of such serious challenges, children in foster care may need lots of support in coping with feelings of loss and upheaval. Predictable routines at school can be therapeutic when family transitions are traumatic, especially when teachers take time to express their concern, communicate expectations, and advise children of services. Teachers can also offer practical help with homework and assignments when children miss school because of attending court hearings or moving between residences.

• **Advocate for evidence-based programs for children during difficult family transitions.** Affectionate relationships with teachers and other staff can be enormously helpful to children during family changes. Familiar routines and support from good friends can also be comforting. Yet sometimes the emotions run so strong that they exceed children's coping, and intensive support is needed. Programs designed by psychologists, counselors, and other mental health professionals have been designed and implemented for children at school. Such programs can help children cope during stressful family changes and prevent serious behavioral and emotional problems from emerging (E. M. Abel, Chung-Canine, & Broussard, 2013; Angacian et al., 2015). Not all programs have been shown to be effective, and teachers and other school professionals will want to examine reports on the efficacy of interventions they are considering. Programs that have had a positive impact on children include individual counseling and interventions in small groups that enhance children's emotional expression and problem solving in social settings.

Summary

Families come in many forms, including those with two parents, single parents, stepparents, adoptive parents, kin heads of household, adolescent parents, gay and lesbian parents, and foster parents. Many youngsters experience one or more changes in family structure (e.g., as a result of divorce, remarriage, or death of a parent) at some point during their childhood. Particular family structures have unique benefits and challenges for children, but ultimately the quality of family relationships exceeds family membership in significance. Teachers are advised to be inclusive of children and their families by welcoming everyone, reassuring children during family transitions, discouraging discriminatory remarks, and respecting children's privacy.

MyLab Education Self-Check 3.2

Family Interaction

3.3 Define key elements of family interaction and educational partnerships with families.

How parents raise their children has profound effects on children's adjustment. By virtue of their personalities and activities, children influence parents and other family members in return. In this section we examine the mutually influential interchanges in the family. We also examine educational strategies for establishing productive relationships with families.

Families' Influences on Children

As agents of socialization, parents and other heads of family convey affection and transmit expectations for mature behavior. They also encourage children to participate in everyday routines and become involved in their education.

Parenting Styles

The foundation of parenting is love. Parents communicate affection by responding sensitively to children's initiatives, comforting them when distressed, and celebrating their accomplishments. A second vital element of parenting is discipline. Children have strong wills of their own but lack foresight and self-restraint. Parents teach children to rein in their impulses, anticipate the outcomes of their actions, follow rules, and make amends for wrongdoings. Parents use a variety of techniques for disciplining children, including reasoning, scolding, withdrawing affection, removing privileges, imposing restrictions, and, in some families, spanking children. A reasonable balance between affection and discipline fosters children's self-regulation, the ability to direct and control personal actions, thinking, and emotions (Maccoby, 2007; L. A. Newland, 2015; K. E. Williams, Ciarrochi, & Heaven, 2012).

Most parents around the world manage to find acceptable, balanced ways to share their love and wield authority over their children (R. H. Bradley, Corwyn, McAdoo, & Coll, 2001; Rohner & Rohner, 1981; Scarr, 1992). Yet parents vary in the ways in which they express affection and implement discipline; that is, they develop individual **parenting styles**. Research on parenting styles was pioneered in the 1960s by American psychologist **Diana Baumrind** and has been subsequently refined by Baumrind and her colleagues (Baumrind, 1967, 1971, 1980, 1989, 1991, 2013).

Substantial evidence indicates that parenting that combines affection with firm discipline helps children become mature, competent, confident, cheerful, independent, considerate, and committed to academic achievement (Baumrind, 2013; Dornbusch, Ritter, Leiderman, Roberts, & Fraleigh, 1987; Lamborn, Mounts, Steinberg, & Dornbusch, 1991; Pinquart, 2016; Simons-Morton & Chen, 2009). Parents who use this approach, called an **authoritative parenting style**, foster children's healthy development and sense of autonomy with valuable guidance tailored to abilities (Baumrind, 2013; Gauvain, Perez, & Beebe, 2013; Grolnick & Pomerantz, 2009; Uji, Sakamoto, Adachi, & Kitamura, 2014).

In a different approach, known as the **authoritarian parenting style**, parents demand immediate compliance but withhold affection, give very few reasons for requests ("Clean your room because I told you to—and I mean *now*!") and allow little chance for negotiation. Like authoritative parenting, authoritarian parenting includes direction for children's behavior, but authori*tative* parents guide children with warmth and flexibility, whereas authori*tarian* parents are harsh and rigid. Children of consistently authoritarian parents tend to be withdrawn, mistrusting, and unhappy; they are apt to have low self-esteem, little self-reliance, and poor social skills; and they have a greater-than-average tendency to act aggressively (Baumrind, 2013; Braza et al., 2015; Coopersmith, 1967; Gauvain et al., 2013; Lamborn et al., 1991). Authoritarian parents offer structure for the children but fail to support their sense of autonomy (Grolnick & Pomerantz, 2009).

In a third pattern, parents exert *little control* over children, and children generally suffer from this lack of direction. Parents who use a **permissive parenting style** appear to care about their children but relinquish important decisions to children (even fairly young ones)—allowing them to decide when to go to bed, what chores (if any) to do around the house, and what curfews to abide by (e.g., "Okay. Stay up later, but try to get *some* sleep tonight."). Children in such families are typically immature, impulsive, demanding, dependent on parents, and, not surprisingly, disobedient when parents ask them to do something they do not want to do. These children also tend to have difficulty in school, are aggressive with peers, and engage in delinquent acts as adolescents (C. Christopher, Saunders, Jacobvitz, Burton, & Hazen, 2013; Lamborn et al., 1991; Pulkkinen, 1982; J. Tucker, Ellickson, & Klein, 2008). Apparently, these generally warm family environments do not adequately compensate for their lack of guidance.

A few parents are not only permissive but also indifferent to children. When using a fourth pattern, the **uninvolved parenting style**,[2] parents make few demands and respond to children in an uncaring and even rejecting manner. Children of uninvolved parents frequently exhibit serious difficulties, including problems with school achievement, emotional control, tolerance for frustration, aggression, and delinquency (Kawabata, Alink, Tseng, Van IJzendoorn, & Crick, 2011; Lamborn et al., 1991; Rothrauff, Cooney, & An, 2009; Simons, Robertson, & Downs, 1989). These children receive neither adequate affection nor the supervision they need to develop essential skills.

Evidence indicates that children fare best when parents use an authoritative style. But there are qualifications to this conclusion. For one thing, parents are not fully consistent from one situation to the next. Instead, they adjust their tactics depending on their moods, children's misbehaviors, and the demands of the situation (Grusec & Davidov, 2007; Solem, 2013). For instance, in the morning, a father may reason with his 4-year-old son about bringing a jacket, advising him of the weather but allowing him to make the final decision. Yet in the afternoon, when the boy ventures into a busy street, his father forcefully removes him from harm's way. Thus, rather than being the adult's only method of caregiving, parenting style is more accurately thought of as a parent's preferred techniques for expressing affection and controlling behavior.

The associations that exist between parenting styles and children's skills result largely from the actions of parents in fostering or inhibiting of certain kinds of competencies. Nevertheless, children are partly responsible for the dynamics. For one thing, children influence the way they are treated. Through their temperaments and actions, children elicit certain reactions from parents. Parents generally reason with compliant children and use harsh discipline with easily angered children (K. E. Anderson, Lytton, & Romney, 1986; Kochanska & Kim, 2013; A. S. Morris, Cui, & Steinberg, 2013). In addition, the discipline that parents use affects individual children differently. Children whose temperaments predispose them to be irritable, when raised by harsh parents, are likely to develop high levels of aggression and oppositional behavior (Kochanska & Kim, 2013). In comparison, children who are agreeable cope more easily with severe and punitive parents.

Children are influential in another way. How children themselves make sense of parents' actions and gestures affects their overall adjustment. Children view discipline as being legitimate (if not always welcome) to the degree that parents have previously been involved, affectionate, and respectful of their needs (Grusec & Davidov, 2007; Maccoby, 2007; C. R. Martinez & Forgatch, 2001). Through a variety of tactics, parents demonstrate their concern and persuade children that they are imposing restrictions for children's own good. As a result, children usually accept parents' authority, even though they sporadically—and sometimes recurrently—haggle over limitations (Hoffman, 1994). In comparison, when parents come across as demeaning, cruel, or hostile, children may comply with parents' demands only when parents are present to enforce them.

The effects of parenting styles are also mediated by practices and values in the family's community (Baumrind, 2013; Chao, 1994; Deater-Deckard, Dodge, Bates, & Pettit, 1996; Steinberg, Lamborn, Darling, Mounts, & Dornbusch, 1994; Yu, Cheah, & Calvin, 2016). Although authoritative parenting is broadly associated with good developmental outcomes, some aspects of authoritarian parenting are productive in certain settings. In collectivistic cultures, including some East Asian and Middle Eastern societies, demands for immediate compliance are associated with parental warmth and

[2]Some scholars use the term *disengaged* or *rejecting-neglecting* for uninvolved parenting (Baumrind, 2013).

acceptance—not rejection—and generate healthy outcomes in children (Chao, 1994, 2000; Rudy & Grusec, 2006). This positive result is probably due to children's perceptions that their strict parents are helping them meet the obligations of society.

Other aspects of families' lives can make the authori*tative* style ineffective or difficult to use. When families live in dangerous neighborhoods, parents protect children in some situations by issuing stern commands (Baumrind, 2013; Hale-Benson, 1986; G. Nicholas, 2016). In other circumstances, parents are strict not because they are preparing children to survive in hazardous environments but, rather, because economic stresses provoke them to be short-tempered (Bronfenbrenner, Alvarez, & Henderson, 1984; L. F. Katz & Gottman, 1991; Ricketts & Anderson, 2008). Unless they receive substantial support, these parents may find it difficult to reason calmly or enforce rules consistently.

Daily Activities

When children are ready to make strides in caring for themselves or interacting with others, parents teach them specific skills, for example, how to tie their shoes, brush their teeth, and greet relatives. **Guided participation**, in which a child engages in everyday adult tasks and routines, typically with considerable supervision, is another method by which parents support children's learning. Parents include children in such activities as cooking, completing errands, worshipping, gardening, and volunteering in the community. As they learn, children are allowed to take on progressively higher levels of responsibility for planning and carrying out tasks (Gauvain et al., 2013; Perez & Gauvain, 2009; Rogoff, 2003; Vedder-Weiss, 2016).

The activities parents arrange, both inside and outside the home, affect children's academic learning, expectations about school, and knowledge of work-related skills. Many parents read to children, talk to them about schoolwork, and expose children to books, art, music, computer technology, and scientific and mathematical thinking (Carolan, 2016; Eccles, 2007; Farver, Xu, Lonigan, & Eppe, 2013; Hess & Holloway, 1984). Children also observe parents exhibiting skills that come in handy in employment, as when a parent balances expenses on a spreadsheet, builds a cabinet, or analyzes evidence for or against a certain conclusion (Denmark & Harden, 2012; González, Moll, & Amanti, 2005; Koppman, 2016).

Parents also exert important effects through their involvement in children's schooling. When children begin school, parents advise them on how to behave, what goals to strive for, and how hard to try. As children progress through the grade levels, heads of family may discuss school activities with children, assist with homework, and give feedback about in-class projects. At school, they may volunteer in the classroom, participate in parent advisory groups, join fund-raising projects, and confer with teachers about children's progress. Students whose parents are involved at school generally achieve at higher levels than those whose parents are not, perhaps because involved parents convey a high value for education, communicate effectively with teachers, foster children's positive feelings about school, and learn how they can help children at home (Crosnoe, 2009; Eccles, 2007; D. F. Perkins et al., 2016; T. T. Williams & Sánchez, 2013).

Although the family's participation in schooling is usually constructive, there are exceptions. Some parents become overinvolved, intrusively direct homework or even do it for their children, or put excessive pressure on the child to achieve (Moroni, Dumont, Trautwein, Niggli, & Baeriswyl, 2015; Silinskas, Niemi, Lerkkanen, & Nurmi, 2013; E. T. Tan & Goldberg, 2009). Furthermore, not every parent finds it easy to help out at school or sees their presence there as welcome. Parents in some cultures believe that they should offer tangible assistance at home and *not* interfere at school (García Coll & Marks, 2009). These families may set aside a quiet place at home for schoolwork and monitor children's academic progress without ever meeting teachers or attending school events.

Employment and Child Care

The majority of children in the United States have parents who are employed, a pattern that holds true in many other nations as well (U.S. Department of Labor, 2013). Among U.S. families with children, 87.8% have at least one working parent. In single-mother families, 67.1% of women are employed; in single-father families, 81.6% of men are employed. In two-parent families, 59% have both parents working.

A parent's employment influences children in several ways. Jobs give the family income, occupy parents' schedules, and, in some cases, provide sick leave and health insurance. Parents are apt to tell their children about their duties at work and to advise them as to what they have to look forward to—or might wish to avoid—in their future careers. Long hours on the job can mean that parents have little remaining time for relaxing with children, checking homework, and cooking nutritious meals (K. W. Bauer, Hearst, Escoto, Berge, & Neumark-Sztainer, 2012; Cooklin et al., 2016; Samad, Reaburn, & Di Milia, 2015).

Employment is also significant in that others typically care for children when parents are working. From middle childhood and on, schools fulfill this function for some of the day. Yet many children are cared for by extended family, neighbors, or employed caregivers for 10 to 40 hours per week or more, depending on their age. Caregivers provide oversight in activities that can be either developmentally attuned or incongruent with children's emerging needs, interests, and motivations (Hartman, Warash, Curtis, & Day Hirst, 2016; Pelatti, Dynia, Logan, Justice, & Kaderavek, 2016).

Children's Influences on Families

You have learned that parents are powerful forces in children's development through expressions of love, enforcement of discipline, and inclusion in enriching activities. Yet as children comply with parents' guidance, they also express their own desires, often quite emphatically, as Cedric did when prodding his mother into action in our chapter-opening case study.

Developmental Systems Prompt 3.4

Watch for recurring exchanges between parents and children in which they communicate in a familiar manner. Occasions to observe reciprocal effects include greetings and departures, mealtime conversations, bedtime routines, games, and of arguments.

Children's Effects on Parents

As you found when reading about parenting styles, socialization involves *reciprocal influences*, whereby children and parents simultaneously affect one another from the beginning of life (R. Q. Bell, 1988). Babies demand comfort by crying, but they also coo, chatter, and lure their parents into contact in a most disarming manner. A father intent on sweeping the kitchen floor will find it hard to resist the antics of his 6-month-old daughter who wriggles, chatters, and smiles at him.

Reciprocal influences continue as children grow. Preschoolers frequently play games with parents that incorporate imitation and turn taking (Kohlberg, 1969). In everyday interactions, children respond to parents in much the same way as they have been treated. Children also develop desires, skills, and viewpoints outside the family and bring them home, in turn influencing the actions of parents. They may ask parents to bring them certain places, play ball, read a book, and buy them treats, clothing, and toys (Chaudhary & Gupta, 2012). With growth the child exercises new kinds of requests. For example, young people sometimes ask parents about their perspectives on controversial issues and occasionally express outlandish views themselves so as to provoke parents' explanations (M. McDevitt & Kiousis, 2015; M. McDevitt & Ostrowski, 2009).

MyLab Education
Artifact Example 3.6

Find Developmental Meaning *What does 10-year-old Samuel appreciate about his mother?* Notice how Samuel expresses gratitude for his mother's all-encompassing care.

Reciprocal influences are similarly evident in emotional expressions. Children know their parents' trigger points and what brings them pleasure. When parents treat their children warmly, the children usually respond with affectionate gestures, as you can see in 6-year-old Alex's note to his bereaved father in Artifact Example 3.7. In contrast, when parents establish a negative climate, children may learn to challenge, accuse, and ridicule their parents. In some families, parents and children intensify demands as they interact, as shown in this interchange:

Mother: I told you to clean your room. This is a *disaster*.
Daughter: Get outta *my* room!
Mother: *(raises her voice)* You clean up that mess or you're grounded! *(stamps her foot)*
Daughter: Hah! You can't make me!
Mother: For a month! *(shouting now)*
Daughter: You stink! *(stomps out of her room and marches to the front door)*
Mother: For two months! *(shouting louder)*
Daughter: As if you'd notice I was gone! *(slams door)*

During this exchange, things go from bad to worse: The daughter is blatantly disobedient, the mother escalates her demands, and both mother and daughter explode.

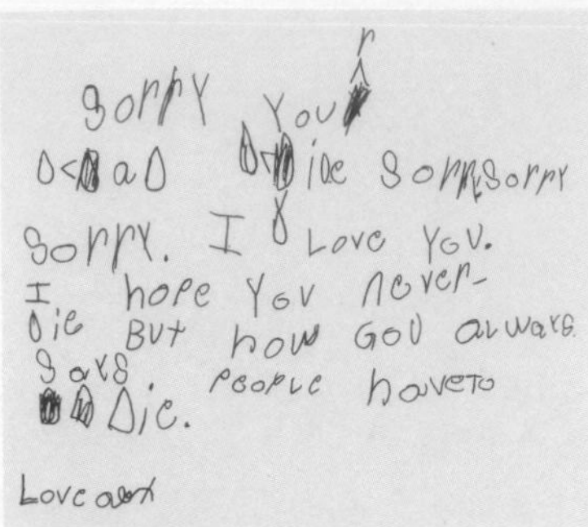

MyLab Education
Artifact Example 3.7

Find Developmental Meaning *How does 6-year-old Alex comfort his father the day Alex's grandfather (his father's father) died?* Alex consoles his father by telling him that he is sorry. The implication that his father will eventually die strikes Alex, and he helps them both cope by making the loss of a parent seem normal.

Such exchanges are common in troubled families (Brody et al., 2014; Lunkenheimer, Lichtwarck-Aschoff, Hollenstein, Kemp, & Granic, 2016; G. R. Patterson & Reid, 1970). When negative interactions become ingrained as habits, it is difficult for family members to ease up on their ultimatums. However, both parents and children *can* grow and change, especially when the family participates in counseling (Bugental, 2009; Shayne & Miltenberger, 2013).

The Presence of Siblings

Many, perhaps most, children have at least one sibling, although family size varies around the world (ChildTrends, 2014). In many parts of the world, the average number of children hovers around two, suggesting that growing up with one or more siblings is a common occurrence. For example, on average there are 2.6 children born to mothers in Malaysia, 2.7 in Saudi Arabia, 2.4 in South Africa, 1.9 in the United States, and 1.9 in the United Kingdom. In several African countries, fertility rates are much higher—in Uganda, mothers have an average of 6.1 children and in the Democratic Republic of the Congo, 5.7. Mothers in Taiwan and Singapore have an average of only 1.1 and 1.3 children respectively, indicating that only a minority of children there have a sibling.

Having a brother or sister, or being one of multiple offspring, shapes children's daily experiences. Siblings influence the interactions children have in the family, for example, what children talk about during family meals and how they spend free time after school. Growing up with one or more siblings decreases one-on-one time with parents, but it also generates the possibility of gaining additional support within the family. Close sibling relationships can supplement parent–child bonds, especially during such difficult transitions as divorce (Ehrenberg, Regev, Lazinski, Behrman, & Zimmerman, 2014; K. Jacobs & Sillars, 2012; Seibert & Kerns, 2009). Other influences by siblings depend on the relative ages of children. In Western society, older siblings often look after young children when parents do brief errands. In many other societies, older children are the primary caregivers for younger brothers and sisters for a significant part of the day, serving as role models, tutors, and playmates (Hafford, 2010; Weisner & Gallimore, 1977).

Sibling relationships also allow for practice of social skills. During early and middle childhood, children spend more time with siblings than with parents or peers (J. Dunn, 2007). The relationships that evolve among siblings are often warm and familiar but can be marked with competition over limited resources, including parents' attention. These contests motivate children to take a sibling's perspective, either to better assist or outsmart the other child (Recchia & Howe, 2009; J. S. Tucker & Kazura, 2013). Occasionally rivalry becomes downright combative over outwardly trivial issues (such as who gets to select first from a full plate of freshly baked cookies: "*Lemme* go first!" "No, it's *my* turn!"). Resentment can brew if one child feels slighted by a parent (G. H. Brody, Stoneman, & McCoy, 1994; J. Dunn, 2007). Long-term conflict among brothers and sisters portend later difficulties in adjustment and may reflect a need to learn new ways for expressing feelings and resolving interpersonal differences (Pike & Oliver, 2016).

Parents treat individual children within the family somewhat differently depending on each child's characteristics, their prior experience in caring for children, and whatever is going on in their lives at the time. The intellectual and social experiences of children depend partly on *birth order*—that is, on whether children were born first, second, or later down the line. Older siblings have a slight advantage academically, perhaps because of the exclusive time they have had with their parents before siblings came along (Chiu, 2007; Härkönen, 2014; Zajonc & Mullally, 1997). Yet younger siblings reap their own rewards, developing strong interpersonal skills, probably as a result of asserting their positions with older siblings and listening attentively to their social tips (J. Dunn, 1984; N. Miller & Maruyama, 1976; N. Palacios, Kibler, Yoder, Baird, & Bergey, 2016; B. C. Wright & Mahfoud, 2012).

Of course, not all children have siblings, and only children are by no means deprived of an essential relationship. On average, only children[3] perform well in school, enjoy strong relationships with their parents, and have good mental health, possibly because in close attention from parents, they are coached in coping skills (Falbo & Polit, 1986; Riordan, Morris, Hattie, & Stark, 2012). Some evidence suggests that children without siblings are not as skilled in making and keeping friends as are peers with siblings;

[3]Only children are sometimes called "singletons."

however, this social disadvantage, if it really exists, is probably minor and likely to be eliminated with positive peer experiences (D. B. Downey, Condron, & Yucel, 2015).

Forming Partnerships with Families

Parents and teachers have much in common. They both take on tough responsibilities that demand long hours, unwavering devotion, and flexible methods. When teachers and families communicate effectively (as Barbara and Mr. Momen eventually did in our opening case study, with help from Cedric), they are likely to magnify their positive effects on students. Based on the work of experts in family involvement, we offer the following recommendations on forming constructive partnerships with families (J. L. Epstein, 2001; J. L. Epstein, Galindo, & Sheldon, 2011; Hutchins, Greenfield, Epstein, Sanders, & Galindo, 2012; Mac Iver, Epstein, Sheldon, & Fonseca, 2015; Núñez et al., 2015; Willemse, Vloeberghs, de Bruïne, & Van Eynde, 2016):

- **Make schools family-friendly.** One of the best things you can do to establish effective relationships with families is to set up an environment that is conducive to interactions among parents, teachers, students, and siblings in the school building. Teachers, psychologists, and other personnel sometimes devote a room for families to drop in and have a cup of coffee; occasionally they provide babysitters for special events at the school and arrange for transportation for families that are not otherwise able to visit. With a family-friendly environment, parents and other family members are more inclined to attend school events.

- **Communicate with each primary caregiver.** As you have learned, families come in many forms. Thus, an important first step is to determine who the guardians are and whether other family members care for children on a regular basis. When two parents are actively involved in a child's life—whether they live in the same household or not—teachers should try to get to know both. A good first step when meeting parents and guardians is to ask them how they like to be addressed and keep a record of these preferences ("Señora Torres, thank you for coming to Davey's conference"; "Good afternoon, Jillian"). As you get to know caregivers, you will learn how they guide their children and what you can do together to address their challenges.

MyLab Education
Video Example 3.3
Find Developmental Meaning *How did 14-year-old Ryan's parents guide, encourage, and advocate for him during his school years?* Note references to John's coaching, Mary's supervision of homework, and their encouragement of Ryan's participation in theater and extracurricular activities.

- **Accommodate family transitions.** Families undergoing significant transitions usually appreciate being kept in the loop. For example, a teacher might encourage a third-grade boy to send photographs of an exemplary diorama to his father, who is deployed abroad on a military assignment. Children also need support under special family circumstances. For instance, a teacher might help a fourth-grade girl make up homework after spending a couple of days out of town to visit her incarcerated mother.

- **Include brothers and sisters.** Teachers can validate children's close-knit relationships with siblings, especially when children face a loss or challenge. In times of family crisis (e.g., with the death of a grandparent or a parent's imprisonment), children may appreciate contact with siblings, perhaps on the playground, in the lunchroom, or in the nurse's office. Educators can welcome brothers and sisters during school events by reserving a room and making durable toys and child-friendly snacks available. During parent–teacher conferences, teachers can refrain from making comparisons between students and their siblings.

- **Put heads of family at ease.** Most parents want to be heard rather than just "talked at," yet some are anxious, distrustful, or reluctant to voice their perspectives (Hoover-Dempsey & Sandler, 1997; M. Janssen, Bakker, Bosman, Rosenberg, & Leseman, 2012). Educators can look for signs of discomfort, use friendly body language, comment optimistically about children's abilities, display a sense of humor, treat parents as authorities about children's needs, and assure parents that they should feel free to call when they have questions or concerns.

- **Ask heads of family about their goals, concerns, and strategies for supporting children.** During conversations with families, teachers can invite parents to talk about their philosophies of parenting and priorities for children. Some teachers invite parents to come to the classroom to talk about their ancestors and cultures, which can be a good way to honor students and their family heritage (Kersey & Masterson, 2009).

MyLab Education
Content Extension 3.1
Read how parents and teachers develop divergent beliefs about children.

To understand your adolescent, you need to consider . . .
. . . the child's basic individuality.
. . . what is expected of anyone of his or her particular age level.
. . . what environment your child finds himself or herself in.

Eleven-year-olds can be . . .
egocentric,
energetic,
always "loving" or "hating";

as well as . . .
not as cooperative or accepting as in the past
more angry than in the past
inattentive
hungry all the time
more interested in the clothes they wear (but not in cleaning them!)
uncertain
more apt to cry
fearful
rebellious
very interested and involved in family activities

MyLab Education
Artifact Example 3.8

Find Developmental Meaning *How does teacher Erin Miguel help parents to understand their children?* In this flyer, Erin describes young adolescents' physical, cognitive, and social-emotional characteristics, thereby helping parents to interpret the occasionally perplexing behavior of young people of this age.

• **Advise parents about children's age-related assets and challenges.** Being familiar with children of a particular age level, teachers have special insights into developmental needs. For example, teachers realize that infants regularly protest separation from parents at the child-care center, young children exhibit oppositional behavior when frustrated, elementary school children worry when they don't read as well as peers, and so on. Teachers can help parents understand age-related characteristics and constructive ways to address them. In Artifact Example 3.8, teacher Erin Miguel normalizes middle school students' developmental qualities. You can find a list of typical concerns of parents and ways teachers might address them in the Developmental Trends table "Family Concerns for Children of Different Ages."

• **Remember that parents are apt to view their children's behavior as a reflection of their own competence.** Parents typically feel proud when their children are successful in school and get along well with friends. Conversely, they may respond to children's academic difficulties or behavior problems with embarrassment, shame, anger, or denial. Teachers are more likely to have productive discussions with parents if they avoid placing blame for students' struggles and instead propose that students, parents, and teachers work as a team to identify solutions. Whenever possible, teachers and other practitioners should share at least one favorable comment about a child each time they contact his or her parent (Kersey & Masterson, 2009).

• **Respect cultural differences.** When conferring with parents about children's achievement and classroom behaviors, educators should keep in mind that people from different cultures inevitably have distinct ideas about how children should be educated and disciplined. For example, some immigrant Chinese parents respect the instruction of teachers yet also tutor their children at home to ensure children achieve the high standards of their homeland (Wong-Lo & Bai, 2013). As educators talk with family members, they can tell them about their own instructional strategies and find out about how parents help at home.

• **Build positive relationships with families of all ethnic backgrounds.** Children and parents from ethnic minority groups are less likely to enjoy close relationships with teachers than are children and parents from European American backgrounds (J. Hughes & Kwok, 2007). Weak or conflicted ties are particularly likely to occur when teachers are unaware of families' cultural perspectives and communication styles. Knowing that good parent–teacher and teacher–child relationships are beneficial for *all* children, teachers can make extra efforts to reach out to individuals with backgrounds different from their own. Written notes to families about the school schedule, curriculum, and activities can be a good way to set a tone of respect for parents' role in children's education. Invitations to visit the school, attend parent–teacher–student conferences, and advise the teacher of any concerns are also desirable.

• **Accommodate language and literacy differences.** Many immigrant parents are not yet fluent in the dominant languages of their new society. When parents speak a language other than English, educators can invite a bilingual interpreter to meetings. Educators should also have newsletters and other written messages translated whenever it is reasonable to do so.

• **Invite families to join in school activities.** Many family members have special talents (such as woodworking, calligraphy, and storytelling) that they would happily demonstrate at school. Likewise, bilingual parents are likely to wish to step forward, if needed, to translate school materials for others (Finders & Lewis, 1994). To arrange for your classroom

DEVELOPMENTAL TRENDS

Family Concerns for Children of Different Ages

AGE	TOPICS	DIVERSITY	IMPLICATIONS
Infancy (Birth–2 Years)	**Physical Development** • Ensuring safety by instituting precautions such as placing gates on stairs • Meeting physical needs (e.g., feeding on baby's schedule, diapering when soiled, and easing into sleep schedule that conforms to adults' patterns) • Giving proper nutrition to match physiological needs and pace of growth **Cognitive Development** • Responding enthusiastically to smiling and babbling • Encouraging infants to take turns in conversations and join simple games • Providing appropriate sensory stimulation **Social-Emotional Development** • Abiding by infants' preferences (e.g., after noticing interest in vehicles, sharing picture books with trucks) • Arranging for responsive caregivers during parents' work • Affirming infants' feelings • Responding sympathetically to cries	• Some parents promote independence by encouraging infants to try self-help actions, such as picking up bits of food and feeding themselves; others prefer to do these things for infants. • Nap time depends on parents' ideas about sleeping practices. • Some parents verbalize frequently to infants; others focus on nonverbal gestures. • Some parents leave infants only for brief periods with familiar relatives. Others are comfortable with employed caregivers. • Concerns depend partly on the temperament and health of infants. When infants are difficult to soothe or are sick, parents may be worried.	• Complete daily records of physical care so parents are aware of how their infants' needs are met and the kind of day they have had. • Talk with parents about the developmental milestones you notice in infants. For example, tell parents when you see a new tooth breaking through the gums. • Post a chart of typical developmental milestones (e.g., rolling over, sitting up, uttering first words) so that parents can watch for emerging skills. Select a chart that emphasizes variation in ages of milestones. • Invite parents to share concerns about their infants, and offer reassurance and, if appropriate, a description of how the family doctor could help.
Early Childhood (2–6 Years)	**Physical Development** • Ensuring basic safety by protecting children from street traffic, household chemicals, water sources • Helping children with self-care routines (e.g., dressing, brushing teeth) • Finding appropriate outlets for physical energy **Cognitive Development** • Answering children's incessant questions • Channeling curiosity into constructive activities • Reading stories and talking about words and letters • Preparing for transition to formal schooling **Social-Emotional Development** • Curbing temper tantrums • Promoting sharing with siblings and peers • Addressing conflicts and aggressive behavior • Forming relationships with teachers	• Some parents are reluctant to leave young children in the care of others. • Low-income families have little or no discretionary income to purchase books. • Some kindergartners and first graders have little or no prior experiences with other children. • Some parents arrange for intellectually challenging activities and forget the value of play. • Some parents over-emphasize one aspect of development (e.g., social-emotional development) over other areas.	• Suggest approaches to teaching young children self-care habits, social skills, and impulse control. • Keep parents informed about children's progress in academic and social skills. • Make books available for parents to check out and use at home. • When parents are concerned about accelerating children's cognitive development, explain the need for balance between stimulation and relaxation. • Advise parents of the value of addressing the full spectrum of children's needs.
Middle Childhood (6–10 Years)	**Physical Development** • Fostering healthy eating habits • Encouraging use of safety equipment (e.g., seat belts in car, helmets for cycling) • Establishing exercise routines and limiting television and electronic games **Cognitive Development** • Deciding which school to enroll children • Teaching good study habits (e.g., setting goals and checking on progress in assignments) • Promoting mastery of basic academic skills • Getting involved at school or encouraging homework **Social-Emotional Development** • Promoting responsibility for getting up on time, doing homework, turning in assignments, etc. • Monitoring interactions with siblings and playmates • Instilling moral values (e.g., honesty)	• Some parents are under stress from pressures at work. • Some neighborhoods have few playgrounds or safe places for children to play. • Children's special talents and interests influence their choices of leisure activities. • Some children look after themselves after school, and they may or may not use this time wisely. • Some parents may worry that children are not receiving a sufficiently high-quality education. • Some parents whose children have disabilities worry that children's needs are not met at school.	• Distribute literature about safety measures from pediatricians, police departments, and fire stations. • Provide resource materials focusing on children's development and needs. • Encourage parents' involvement in school activities, homework, and parent–teacher groups. • Suggest programs (e.g., soccer leagues, scout organizations) providing after-school recreation and chances to exercise skills. • Advise parents of how any academic delays can be reduced with tutoring, homework, and other individualized services.

(continued)

DEVELOPMENTAL TRENDS (Continued)

AGE	TOPICS	DIVERSITY	IMPLICATIONS
Early Adolescence (10–14 Years)	**Physical Development** • Adjusting to early stages of puberty • Encouraging physical fitness • Affording new clothing during periods of rapid growth **Cognitive Development** • Supporting expectations for advanced academic performance • Fostering young adolescents' talents and interests **Social-Emotional Development** • Showing self-consciousness about appearance • Accommodating requests for more leisure time with peers • Dealing with increased conflict and requests for autonomy • Protecting young people from exploitation on the Internet • Discouraging bullying and reassuring children hurt by humiliating remarks from peers	• Adolescents differ in the age at which they begin puberty. • Some youngsters have little access to recreation. • Some parents have difficulty allowing their adolescents greater independence. • Overt parent–teenager conflicts are rare in some cultures, especially those emphasizing respect for elders. • Some peer groups encourage unproductive behaviors. • Some students need extra reassurance while transitioning into middle school. • Some parents worry about adolescents using video games and social media rather than doing homework.	• Inform parents about athletic and social programs in the community. • To avoid overload for students, create a coordinated homework program (e.g., math assignments on Monday and Wednesday; writing on Tuesday; others on Thursday). Post due dates on the school's website so that parents can help monitor assignments. • Share with parents your expectations for independence and responsibility in young adolescents. • Advise parents of typical developmental characteristics at this age.
Late Adolescence (14–18 Years)	**Physical Development** • Keeping track of teenagers' whereabouts • Encouraging students to get enough sleep • Worrying about inexperienced and risky driving • Concern about possible alcohol and drug use **Cognitive Development** • Encouraging youth to persist with challenging assignments • Marveling at adolescents' expanding capacity for logical thinking • Educating adolescents about college and future employment requirements **Social-Emotional Development** • Stewing over loss of control over teenagers' activities • Finding a balance between supervision and allowing independence	• Alcohol and drugs are available in most communities, but their use is more prevalent in some families than others. • Some parents refuse to believe that their adolescents could be involved in risky activities, even when faced with convincing evidence. • Families differ in their knowledge of, and experiences with, higher education, vocational training, and the world of work. • Parents differ in the extent to which they encourage teenagers' employment.	• Advise parents of extracurricular activities and recreation centers for youth. • Share information about part-time job vacancies, internships, and community service openings. • Provide information about possible careers and educational opportunities after high school; advise students of numerous options, including part-time and full-time vocational programs, community colleges, and 4-year colleges and universities.

Sources: Blustein, Carter, and McMillan (2016); Borgen and Hiebert (2014); V. Davis (2012); Gallo, Hadley, Angst, Knafl, and Smith (2008); Guttman (2013); A. Kirby, Edwards, and Hughes (2008); Kong et al. (2013); Kutner, Olson, Warner, and Hertzog (2008); Maccoby (1984); Montemayor (1982); Mortimer, Shanahan, and Ryu (1994); Murray (2016); Nesteruk, Marks, and Garrison (2009); Paikoff and Brooks-Gunn (1991); Pipher (1994); Ren and Pope Edwards (2016); Warton and Goodnow (1991); and Youniss (1983).

to reap the advantages of these gifts and resources, you can ask families at the beginning of the year about their interests in sharing expertise at school.

• **Accommodate schedules when asking for help.** Encouraging parents to attend meetings or help at school is most likely to be effective when teachers recognize potential obstacles. Some parents have exhausting work schedules, inadequate child care, and difficulty communicating in English. Thus, invitations must be sincere and include a variety of things that could be done during the day, in the evening, or over the weekend.

• **Visit families in their homes and in the community.** Home visits are a relatively common way of supporting parents' efforts at home, especially in families with young children (Gomby, Culross, & Behrman, 1999; S. Smith, 2013; Whyte & Karabon, 2016). Home visiting programs typically focus on getting to know parents, seeing children's routines, and informing teachers about the values and knowledge cultivated at home. To make these visits maximally effective, educators can present themselves as friendly and nonjudgmental, share a small gift of school supplies, begin the conversation with compliments about the child, ask about the child's chores and hobbies, and offer practical suggestions for the age. Some experts recommend bringing a colleague if possible. When home visits are not feasible, teachers can learn more about the backgrounds of families by reaching out to them by phone or getting involved in community festivals and meetings of local groups.

MyLab Education
Video Example 3.4

Find Developmental Meaning *How might the third-grade students taught by this teacher progress academically as a result of her conversations with their parents?* The teacher expresses enthusiasm for students' mathematical learning and advises the mother about the skills they are learning and what she can do to promote them.

• **Advise parents of activities children can do at home that strengthen learning at school.** In general, families that are actively involved in their children's education have children who are academically and socially competent (Toldson & Lemmons, 2013). To help parents choose activities at home that deepen learning, teachers can offer developmentally supportive guidance. With young children, teachers can encourage regular conversations with children; reading children's books to them; teaching them basic concepts such as shapes, colors, numbers, and the alphabet; and taking them on visits to zoos, farms, museums, concerts, and theatrical performances (Clair, Jackson, & Zweiback, 2012). Parents can support older children's studies by setting aside quiet areas for reading and doing schoolwork, limiting television and electronic games, and expressing interest in their academic skills. Given that school involvement tends to decline during adolescence, you can advise parents about how they might show an interest in their sons' and daughters' schoolwork and extracurricular activities (Benner, Boyle, & Sadler, 2016; J. L. Epstein, 1996; Roderick & Camburn, 1999).

• **Validate parents' role in children's learning.** Parents may avoid school events when they feel discomfort about visiting school or have been raised in a cultural tradition of showing respect to teachers by not invading their territory. Yet many parents work tirelessly at home to back up their children's education. Some have left their native country to ensure decent opportunities for their children, and others do everything they can to teach children relevant skills. In newsletters and informal conversations during parents' pick up and drop off of children, teachers can let parents know that they see the skills children have learned at home (S. W. Nelson & Guerra, 2009). To keep parents informed, teachers might also post a link to videotapes of children's work at school or share photographs of their children in a play or other events (Kersey & Masterson, 2009).

• **Inform parents of services available to them.** Parents in distress are sometimes unaware of free and low-cost community services for which they are eligible. Teachers and other professionals can advise them of potentially helpful services, such as outlets for family recreation. A variety of parent education programs, such as those teaching parents how to maintain their composure when provoked by children, have proven effective in improving parents' behaviors (Knerr, Gardner, & Cluver, 2013).

• **Use a variety of communication formats.** Families appreciate hearing about children's accomplishments, and they deserve to know when children's behaviors interfere with their learning. Likewise, teachers can learn a lot about a child's needs from talking with family members. Here are a few helpful forms of communication:

- *Meetings.* Most schools schedule parent–teacher–student conferences one or more times a year. These meetings are an excellent forum for celebrating children's successes and identifying areas that need additional attention. For example, at a conference it may be mutually agreed that the teacher will find new assignments that better match the child's needs, the child will keep track of due dates for homework, and the family will reserve a quiet place at home for the child to do homework uninterrupted.
- *Written communications.* Educators can fill out structured forms to inform parents how children are doing. Forms that specify activities and leave space for individual comments can be especially informative. A growing number of mobile applications also allow teachers to send home notes to parents (Sharnoff, 2014). Paper newsletters can communicate about school events, resources, and policies.
- *Telephone conversations.* Telephone calls are useful for introductions and for addressing issues that require immediate attention. Teachers might call parents to express concern when a student's behavior deteriorates unexpectedly, and they might also call to express their excitement about an important step forward. Parents, too, should feel free to call teachers. Keep in mind that many parents are at work throughout the school day; hence, it is often helpful for teachers to take calls at home during the early evening hours.

Summer Tips for Children and Parents

Early June means the end of the school year, and with it, a lot of kids without much to do. Summer should be relaxing and a fun time for kids, but at the same time they still need to keep their minds and bodies active. The following Tips for Parents will help you plan fun summer activities for your kids.

Keep Their Minds Active

Summer shouldn't mean taking a break from learning, especially when it comes to reading. Studies show that most students experience a loss of reading skills over the summer months, but children who continue to read actually gain skills. During the summer, parents can help children sustain (and even bolster) reading skills, strengthen their vocabulary, and reinforce the benefits of reading for enjoyment.

- Read aloud together with your child every day. Make it fun by reading outdoors. For younger children, be sure to practice letter–sound correspondence, do lots of rhyming and clapping out of syllables, and explore the relationships between oral language and print.
- Set a good example! Keep lots of reading material around the house. Turn off the TV and have family reading time.
- Let kids choose what they want to read. Every so often, read the same book your child is reading and discuss it together.
- Buy books on tape or check them out at the library.
- Visit the library regularly with your children.
- Set a reading goal with your child, such as reading five books, with a reward at completion.

Keep Their Bodies Active

The American Academy of Pediatrics (AAP) warns that more than 2 hours a day in front of the TV leads to increased obesity and lowered academic achievement. The AAP recommends no more than 1 to 2 hours a day of screen time (TV, video games, computer).

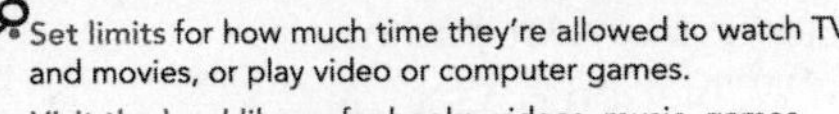

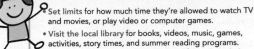

- Set limits for how much time they're allowed to watch TV and movies, or play video or computer games.
- Visit the local library for books, videos, music, games, activities, story times, and summer reading programs. For tips and ideas, visit the American Library Association, www.ala.org.
- Sports: Have the kids join a team. If that's not possible, encourage them to play basketball, soccer, baseball, badminton, volleyball, or croquet in the yard or with friends who live nearby.
- Outdoor fun: Tree climbing, jumping rope, camping in the backyard, bike riding, sidewalk chalk, building forts out of cardboard boxes, playing with pets, swimming, jumping on a trampoline, or running through the sprinkler are all great outdoor activities. Check out Family Education's Outdoor Activities, http://fun.familyeducation.com/play/outdoor-activities/33394.html, for tons of great ideas for kids 6 to 10 years old.
- Projects: Encourage children to undertake a project, such as planting a vegetable or flower garden, writing a book or journal, painting a series of paintings on a theme, planning and performing a play, making a movie with a camcorder, etc.
- Learn a new sport or musical instrument, study geology or geography with field trips, or study astronomy and stargazing.
- Arts and crafts activities: Visit Creative Kids at Home's Summer Activities, www.creativekidsathome.com/summerkidsactivities2.html, for fun ideas.
- Start a collection: Kids can collect bugs, rocks, dried plants or flowers, books, or found objects.
- Help children plan, advertise, and run a small summer business, such as babysitting; lawn mowing; pet sitting; or selling baked goodies, crafts, or jewelry they've made; or have them start plants from seeds and sell them. Read the Money Instructor's Child Business Tips, http://content.moneyinstructor.com/664/kids-starting-business.html.
- Volunteer: Kids learn a lot from helping others. They can help an elderly neighbor, coach a younger team, be a teen volunteer at the local hospital, or organize a charity event such as car wash, barbecue, or mothers' luncheon. Teens can visit Do Something, www.dosomething.org/volunteer, for volunteer opportunities near them.
- Summer camp: Have children go to an accredited camp for a week or two for a change of scenery and good fun. Visit the American Camp Association, www.acacamps.org/, for accredited camps in your area.
- Planned outings: Visit the zoo, museum, planetarium, beach, park, or swimming pool, or go camping or hiking, stargazing, or fishing.
- Cooking: Have children plan, shop, and prepare for a family dinner each week. They can visit the award-winning kids cooking website Spatulatta, www.spatulatta.com/, for measuring instructions, safety tips, recipes, and more.
- Community events: Check your local paper or visit your library to find out about fairs, festivals, and other community events to do as a family.
- Board games: Encourage children to make games exciting by having neighborhood chess tournaments, for example. Or have a family game night.
- Chores: OK, doing chores is rarely fun, but it's important for kids to take part in the family's chores. They learn responsibility, and feel proud that they can contribute. Require that kids clean up after themselves, and have them help out with laundry or watering the garden. Reward them for a job well done.

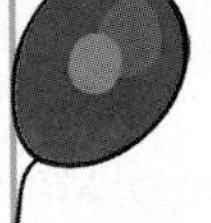

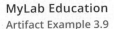

MyLab Education

Artifact Example 3.9

Find Developmental Meaning *What kinds of options do two elementary school counselors advise parents to arrange for their children over the summer?* Notice the wide range of activities, including things that can be done at home, outside, in the neighborhood, and in community recreation centers.

Courtesy of Laura Pool and Chelsie Hess, Fort Collins, Colorado.

- *E-mail and websites.* Increasingly, educators find that they can maintain regular contact with parents electronically—for instance, by sending e-mail messages and creating web pages that list events, policies, and assignments (D. Johnson, 2013; S. Mitchell, Foulger, & Wetzel, 2009). Parents can also be encouraged to send e-mails to teachers and complete brief forms online. Such electronic communication can be used only when families have easy access to computer technology and the Internet.
- *Parent discussion groups.* In some instances, teachers, counselors, and principals may want to assemble a group of parents to discuss mutual concerns. School leaders might want to use a discussion group as a sounding board for evaluating possible school improvement plans. Or, a school counselor might convene a committee to plan such events as a career night or Black History Month concert (J. Bryan & Henry, 2008).

None of the strategies described will, in and of itself, guarantee a successful working relationship with heads of families. Meetings with parents occur somewhat infrequently. Written communication is unrealistic for parents who have limited literacy skills. Some families do not want to be visited at home. And, of course, not everyone has a cell phone or e-mail account. Despite difficulties with staying in touch, effective teachers and other practitioners do their best to form and maintain productive partnerships with families (e.g., see the Development-Enhancing Education feature "Making Schools Family Friendly").

Development-Enhancing Education

Making Schools Family Friendly

Learn about families.

- An elementary teacher hosts a Family Welcome Night at the beginning of the school year and asks parents to complete a questionnaire (available in English and a few other common languages) about children's interests, abilities, and hobbies (Kersey & Masterson, 2009). (Middle Childhood)
- A high school adviser calls parents at the beginning of the school year. The adviser asks the parents about any special needs, gives parents his cell phone number and e-mail address, and encourages their contact with questions or concerns. (Late Adolescence)

Help children and their families feel that they are appreciated members of the school.

- A caregiver of toddlers provides storage boxes ("cubbies") for each child. Each box is adorned with photographs of the child and his or her family. Children point to their parents and other family members throughout the day. (Early Childhood)
- A middle school principal sets up a school improvement team of a few teachers, the school counselor, a group of parents, and a couple of students. The principal treats the team with utmost respect and sends everyone letters of appreciation for their time and efforts. (Early Adolescence)

Recognize the significance of families in children's lives.

- A music teacher asks students to bring in the lyrics from a favorite family song. She posts the words of the songs on a bulletin board labeled "My Family and Me." (Middle Childhood)
- A middle school social studies teacher invites parents and other family members to come to class and describe their jobs and memories of ancestors. (Young Adolescence)

Acknowledge the strengths of family backgrounds.

- An elementary teacher asks a community leader to come to class and talk about the cultural traditions of immigrant families. (Middle Childhood)
- When planning a lesson on the history of farming in Colorado, a middle school social studies teacher encourages families to send in photographs of the farm tools they use while planting and harvesting crops. (Early Adolescence)

Use a variety of formats to communicate with parents.

- A fourth-grade teacher works with the children in his class to produce a monthly newsletter for parents. Two versions of the newsletter are created, one in English and one in Spanish. (Middle Childhood)
- A high school drama teacher takes photographs of individual students during play practice and sends home the images with e-mail messages. (Late Adolescence)

Acknowledge children's strengths, even when communicating about shortcomings.

- An elementary teacher is concerned about a child's disruptive behavior in class. In a phone call to the girl's parents, the teacher asks for the parents' insights, "I appreciate your daughter's energy and sociability. I'm

(*continued*)

Development-Enhancing Education (continued)

impressed with her leadership on her soccer team! During lessons at school, she can get distracted. I'd like to work with you to find a way to increase her time on task" (Christenson, Palan, & Scullin, 2009, p. 11). (Middle Childhood)

- A high school counselor talks on the phone with parents of a student. She describes several areas in which the student has made considerable progress but also asks for advice about strategies that might help him become more agreeable with peers. (Late Adolescence)

Be sensitive to parents' concerns.

- A 3-year-old girl's parents are concerned with her speech. They mention to her teacher that she says "sool" for "school" and "hairpane" for "airplane." The teacher reassures the parents that such mispronunciations are common in young children and also advises the parents that a speech therapist is available at the district office if they want an expert opinion. (Early Childhood)
- A school counselor talks with worried parents of a 16-year-old girl who has begun smoking and possibly experimenting with drugs. Thinking about the girl's interest in photography, the counselor informs the parents about an after-school photography club with the hope that companionship with academically oriented peers will get the student back on track. (Late Adolescence)

Encourage parents and guardians to get involved with school activities.

- An infant caregiver asks for volunteers to give their input into decisions about programs for children, such as how to staff a new room when enrollment grows or the kind of outdoor play space that makes the most sense given toddlers' needs and the budget of the center (J. Daniel, 2009). (Infancy)
- A high school principal sends home a book of "coupons" printed with assorted activities that parents might assist with at school (e.g., tutoring in the classroom, baking goodies for an open house, serving on the parent advisory group). She supplements the book with a letter expressing her hope that all parents who have time will return at least one coupon. (Late Adolescence)

Summary

Parents influence children's development by forming relationships with them, showing affection, disciplining children, engaging children in activities, and becoming involved in their education. Children influence their families, in turn, by virtue of their temperaments, interests, and abilities. Children also influence one another as siblings, yet having a sibling is not vital to healthy development. Effective partnerships between educators and families are grounded in mutual respect and ongoing communication. Toward these ends, teachers can validate the contributions of families, diversify their methods of communication (e.g., parent–teacher–student conferences, newsletters, e-mail, and the telephone), and encourage parents to become—and stay—actively involved in their children's education.

MyLab Education Self-Check 3.3

Diversity in Family Life

3.4 Portray the experiences of children in families whose unique circumstances merit accommodation at school.

We have seen that several factors within the family affect the child's development—family membership, transitions in families, styles of caregiving, everyday home activities, sibling relationships, and interactions with society. Six additional characteristics in the family are worthwhile for educators to learn about because of their effects on family life and the needs children. In this final section, we examine families in which a child has special educational needs, a parent is in the military, the family has emigrated from another country, a parent is incarcerated, a parent maltreats his or her children, and the family lives in economic poverty.

Families Raising a Child Who Has Special Educational Needs

In many industrialized nations, children with disabilities and other significant exceptionalities (including extraordinary gifts and talents) are entitled to receive services that optimize their personal and academic success. In the United States, parents are asked to partner with a classroom teacher, a special education teacher, a school district representative, and other specialists in developing an **Individualized Education Plan** (IEP). The IEP identifies the child's current intellectual and social abilities, outlines academic goals for the year, and determines desired activities and accommodations that will help him or her succeed. When the student turns 16, he or she may participate in the IEP meetings and sometime does so at a younger age if requested by the parents.

Given the value of family involvement in children's education, it makes sense that parents of children with special educational needs would participate in educational decisions at school. Historically, parents have been strong advocates for including children with disabilities in the regular classroom and for having individual needs be addressed. Having cared for their children since birth, parents invariably understand their children best, and they may know as much or more than classroom teachers about educational modifications and medical treatments that have proven effective for individuals with the same conditions (Ray, Prewitt-Kinder, & George, 2009; V. Tucker & Schwartz, 2013).

Before reaching out to parents with a child with special needs, it makes sense to imagine their daily life. Parents, of course, love their child and experience many expected joys in family interactions. Yet having a child with significant developmental delays has its distressing moments because of extra caregiving challenges and the difficulty in obtaining accurate information. Some conditions, such as Down syndrome, a genetic disorder that causes health problems and difficulties in learning, are well understood and usually obvious at birth. Other conditions take time to be identified. Regardless of when parents first hear of their child's diagnosis, they will soon learn that there is wide variation in abilities among individuals who share the condition. Parents may worry as they come to grips with the obstacles their children face, especially when pathways to adult independence are unclear. Other stressors occur, such as dealing with demeaning remarks about their children, confronting the reality of the disability, and finding sufficient energy to meet their children's needs while being employed and managing the household (Kalek, 2014).

Teachers ought to remember that the process of developing an educational plan for a child with special needs is an unfamiliar endeavor for most parents. The regulations surrounding the IEP are complicated. The meeting in which parents join educators and specialists to prepare the IEP can be intimidating. Obstacles to communication can be especially serious when parents have a first language or cultural background that is different than that of the educators (T. G. Mueller, 2014). Teachers who try to get to know families before the formal meetings, arrange for a translator or other facilitator for the parents at the meetings, and pause periodically during discussions to allow parents to pose questions and make observations, can help parents relax and express their views (T. G. Mueller, 2014). When parents are being asked to have the child practice certain skills at home, educators can encourage follow through with concrete examples, demonstrations, and explanations (Lo, Correa, Anderson, & Swart, 2014). Outside the formal meetings, ongoing communication about the child's adjustment is important.

Military Families

In the United States, approximately 1.2 million children have one or more parents in military service, and 2 million children have lived through a parent's deployment, in which the parent is assigned to a remote location, often overseas, in order to accomplish a military mission (De Pedro et al., 2011; Ohye, Rauch, & Bostic, 2012). Having an enlisted parent is a source of pride for many children, a feeling that is often validated at school through such initiatives as honoring wounded warriors and sending care packages to troops separated from their loved ones. Yet interruptions punctuate the family's life. For children, being raised by a military parent often requires one or more moves to a new base, each of which requires adjustments to new schools, peer groups, and communities. Teachers and counselors can help the child by suggesting ways to stay in touch and making sure families have appropriate records, including report cards, test scores, grading scales, curriculum, and verification of the child's extracurricular activities, community service hours, academic recognitions, and individual accommodations (Military Child Education Coalition, 2013). After the move, new teachers can learn as much as possible about the child's education history, introduce the child to the class, and identify a buddy to accompany him or her around the building for a couple of days.

In the situation of a parent's deployment and the family staying home, additional services may be necessary. Children with a deployed parent face numerous challenges—separation from the parent, concern about his or her welfare, reactions to anxiety in the at-home parent, and distress if the military parent returns with a significant injury or trauma (Lester et al., 2016; De Pedro et al., 2011). Children who encounter these problems are vulnerable to mental health problems, behavioral disorders, and academic delays. Young children, given their rudimentary coping skills, regularly become overwhelmed by such separations. Older children can more easily understand the purposes of their parent's work and the time frame for the deployment. In fact, adolescents may take on extra household chores and support the at-home parent and younger siblings (Huebner & Mancini, 2005). Educators can communicate their ongoing concern to children and address heightened stress with compassion and visits with a school counselor.

Immigrant Families

Children whose parents enter one society after growing up a different country enrich schools with their knowledge of multiple languages, cultural values, and pastimes. To support them, educators can learn about the families' origins, any hardships the children have undergone, and the many factors that support their welfare, including the family's value for education, loyalty to one another, and sense of belonging in the community (Pieloch, McCullough, & Marks, 2016).

It is also valuable for educators to consider the migratory journey children and their parents have taken and adaptations they have made in the new community. As immigrants participate in new customs and take on the values of their adopted culture, **acculturation** occurs. Acculturation takes four different forms:

- **Assimilation.** Some individuals totally embrace the values and customs of the new culture, giving up their original identity in the process. Assimilation is typically a gradual process that occurs over several generations and occurs when immigrants feel accepted by the host society.[4]
- **Separation.** Sometimes people move to a new culture without taking on any of their new community's cultural practices. Complete rejection of a new culture may occur when individuals have little need to interact in the new culture or have been segregated to isolated regions.
- **Selective adoption.** Sometimes immigrants acquire some customs from the new culture while retaining other customs from their homeland. For example, families begin to celebrate a few holidays of their new culture while continuing to observe other traditions from their country of origin. Children are likely to adopt the host society's customs when parents encourage them to embrace their new community's traditions and when they feel accepted there.
- **Bicultural orientation.** Some people retain their original culture yet also acquire beliefs and master practices of their new culture, and they readily adjust behaviors to fit the particular contexts in which they find themselves. A bicultural orientation is promoted when the new society is tolerant of diversity. (Delgado-Gaitan, 1994; Mana, Orr, & Mana, 2009; E. Yoon et al., 2013; J. Yu et al., 2016.)

[4]Developmental scholars use the term *assimilation* in two separate ways. In Piaget's theory *cognitive assimilation* refers to a process of learning. In studies of immigration, *cultural assimilation* is a gradual progression by which settlers take on customs and beliefs of their adopted society, giving up their original cultural patterns in the process.

In previous decades, total assimilation was considered by many people in the United States to be the optimal situation for immigrants. The route to success was presumed to be a "melting pot" in which people of different backgrounds become increasingly similar. Nowadays researchers have discovered that when young immigrants give up their family's cultural values and traditions, they are at greater risk for developing conflicts with their parents, achieving at lower levels in school, and engaging in such risky behaviors as consuming alcohol and drugs, having unprotected sex, and engaging in criminal activities (Hwang, 2006; K. M. Roche, Ghazarian, & Fernandez-Esquer, 2012; Roosa et al., 2009; Ying & Han, 2007).

The idea that societies with large immigrant populations are melting pots is giving way to the idea that civilizations can be more productively thought of as a "mosaics" of cultural and ethnic pieces that all legitimately contribute to the greater good of society (C. B. Fisher et al., 1998). Consistent with this view, many immigrant children and their families adjust successfully when they learn about their new culture while also retaining other aspects of their original culture—that is, when they show a pattern of either *selective adoption* or *bicultural orientation* (Rutland et al., 2012; Upegui-Hernández, 2012; J. Yu et al., 2016). You can read more about children from different countries in the Development in Culture feature "Children in Immigrant Families."

One common challenge children in immigrant families encounter is that their abilities and motivations are regularly misunderstood. Unless educators come from a similar background or make an effort to learn about children's upbringing, they may be unaware of the skills and traditions that children bring to school (C. Brown & Chu, 2012; Olmedo, 2009; Riojas-Cortez et al., 2008; Soutullo, Smith-Bonahue, Sanders-Smith, & Navia, 2016). Refugee children, whose families have experienced traumatic events prior to and during the move (e.g., war, family separation, rape, unsafe living conditions, and discrimination), have special needs that can be addressed with compassion from teachers, counseling, and integration into a friendly peer environment at school (Pieloch et al., 2016).

Families with an Incarcerated Parent

With increased drug use and mandatory sentencing laws, growing numbers of parents are separated from their children by imprisonment (Alleyne, 2006; B. J. Myers, Smarsh, Amlund-Hagen, & Kennon, 1999). Fathers are more frequently incarcerated than mothers, yet children are more deeply affected by mothers' detention because mothers are typically the primary caregiver (B. J. Myers et al., 1999; Newell, 2012). In the case of an incarcerated father, the child would usually live with the mother, whereas under the circumstance of an incarcerated mother, the child is apt to move in with a grandparent, aunt, or other relative (Kjellstrand, Cearley, Eddy, Foney, & Martinez, 2012; Mackintosh, Myers, & Kennon, 2006).

Children who have a parent in prison face substantial risks. Those who witness their parent's arrest are apt to find the confrontation disturbing (Dallaire & Wilson, 2010; B. J. Myers et al., 1999). Even if the child is not present during the arrest, he or she is likely to be devastated by the sudden departure. After the arrest, the child may feel anxious about the separation and challenges in adjusting to a new caregiver and household. When the arrest, verdict, sentencing, and incarceration become public knowledge, the child may feel ashamed; if the family's circumstances are kept a secret, he or she is apt to feel alone and isolated (Gust, 2012; Newell, 2012; E. B. Nichols, Loper, & Meyer, 2016). Incarceration adds to existing hardships, including economic poverty, exposure to community violence, family stress, and impaired caregiving emanating from a parent's mental illness, alcoholism, or drug abuse (D. Johnston, 2012, B. J. Myers et al., 1999; Newell, 2012). Thus, it appears that the separation, stigma, and other risks associated with the parent's incarceration undermine the child's already-troubled family life. Under these profoundly difficult conditions, it is not surprising that children of incarcerated parents sometimes develop emotional problems, academic delays, and adjustment difficulties at school (Kjellstrand et al., 2012; E. B. Nichols et al., 2016).

Development in Culture

Children in Immigrant Families

Individual children in immigrant families have a few similar experiences. They go to school, make friends, learn about two or more cultures, and master increasingly difficult concepts and skills. Often they learn a second language and adjust to discrepant expectations at home and in the host community. Yet children from immigrant families are by no means fully alike. They have quite different experiences depending on their personal characteristics and the circumstances of their family's immigration, their parents' jobs and income, and their ethnicity's standing in the adoptive society (Akiba & García Coll, 2003; Glick & Bates, 2010; Hernandez, Denton, & Macartney, 2010; Shen, Kim, & Wang, 2016; T. Urdan, 2012).

Such similarities and differences are evident among children from immigrant families in Providence, Rhode Island (García Coll & Marks, 2009). Many of the immigrant families there had moved from Cambodia, the Dominican Republic, or Portugal. Children from these three cultural groups had somewhat comparable experiences in that they grew up in low-income families, had parents with high expectations for their education, and achieved at relatively high levels at school. Yet the three groups also varied in beliefs and customs. Cambodian, Dominican, and Portuguese American children ate the foods of their ancestors, celebrated holidays compatible with their separate heritages, and worshipped in their own churches or temples. Within each group, individual children developed unique habits and self-perceptions.

Families from Cambodia had moved to the United States to escape war, starvation, and persecution. Two parents with approximately 4 years of formal education were typical heads of Cambodian American families. Parents spoke Khmer to their children and were somewhat segregated from their new society. Teachers perceived Cambodian American parents to be uninvolved because the parents rarely came to school. However, from the parents' perspective, parents are supposed defer to teachers' authority and not interfere with instruction. Teachers saw these children as attentive, conscientious, and socially skilled.

Families from the Dominican Republic had usually moved to the United States for economic opportunities and a safe environment for their children. Single-parent and two-parent families were common in Dominican immigrants. Families remained closely connected with extended family members back on the island, traveling back and forth between Providence and the Dominican Republic for birthdays, weddings, funerals, and family crises; likewise, Dominican relatives often came to visit families in Providence. A strong network of Dominicans in the United States eased the adaptation of new immigrants and enriched children with role models, festivals, and other cultural resources. With their typically dark skin, Dominican American youngsters were perceived to be black by others, yet the Dominican American children generally identified with their Dominican heritage and not as African Americans. The children tended to do well in school but frequently received lower grades as they grew older, and they had relatively high rates of absenteeism from school.

Families from Portugal tended to enter long-standing communities of Portuguese Americans. Recently, immigrating Portuguese families had moved to the United States for economic opportunities. Most families had two parents in the home. Members of the Portuguese American community not only celebrated their cultural heritage but also moved in and out of the mainstream society with ease, in part because their white, European American facial features resembled the appearance of local residents. Established Portuguese sports clubs and religious societies welcomed new immigrants, and numerous Portuguese Americans had penetrated positions of authority as police officers, political officials, and teachers. Two parents with little formal education were the typical heads of family.

Children in each of these three immigrant cultures generally coped well, drew on rich traditions from family culture, and took advantage of opportunities in the new land. In other respects, the children were unique. They developed personally distinct ways of expressing themselves and combining the various cultural practices in which they were immersed.

Robert Nickelsberg/Getty Images

ALIKE, DIFFERENT, AND UNIQUE. Immigrant children face not only some similar developmental tasks but also different experiences and family circumstances.

As you might expect, the developmental level of the child affects his or her adjustment to the incarceration. Young children find a parent's incarceration especially upsetting if they witness the parent being arrested, have previously observed the parent committing a crime, are worried about the parent's wrongdoing, and have previously developed only rudimentary coping skills (D. Johnston, 1995; B. J. Myers et al., 1999). Older children face cumulative stresses if the parent has been imprisoned several times. Resulting emotional difficulties are manifested in nightmares, restlessness, aggression, and other problems. During adolescence, the young person is at risk for being lured into joining gangs, stealing, disengaging from school, failing classes, and consuming drugs or alcohol (Gust, 2012; D. Johnston, 2012; E. B. Nichols et al., 2016). Some adolescents with incarcerated parents believe that going to prison is an inevitable part of growing up.

Fortunately, many children with incarcerated parents have protective factors that help to offset these risks. Examples include the child's own intelligence and interests, a high-quality relationship and continued contact with the incarcerated parent, ongoing support from new caregivers, a strong alliance between the incarcerated parent and the new caregivers, support from faith-based groups, and services in the community (Loper, Phillips, Nichols, & Dallaire, 2013; Mackintosh et al., 2006; Newell, 2012).

Community organizations and prisons have tried to make children's visits to parents easier by arranging transportation and child-friendly rooms in the prison for family get-togethers (D. Johnston, 2012; B. J. Myers et al., 1999). Educational instruction for pregnant prisoners and preschool programs for young children have aided both parents and children. After-school programs for older children have included peer support, academic lessons, and recreational activities shown to promote children's academic skills and decrease their behavior problems. Training in job skills, career planning, and cultivation of entrepreneurial abilities have fostered adolescents' knowledge of business, self-confidence, and employment experience.

Maltreatment in Families

Unfortunately, not all families provide nurturing environments for children. **Child maltreatment** is the most serious outcome of an unhealthy family environment and takes four major forms (Benbenishty & Schmid, 2013; Centers for Disease Control and Prevention [CDC], 2009b; English, 1998). *Neglect* occurs when caregivers fail to provide food, clothing, shelter, health care, or affection and do not adequately supervise children's activities (the *uninvolved* parents we described earlier would be considered neglectful when they are truly disengaged from their children). Caregivers engage in *physical abuse* when they intentionally cause physical harm to children, perhaps by kicking, biting, shaking, or punching them. If spanking causes serious bruises or other injuries, it, too, is considered physical abuse. Caregivers engage in *sexual abuse* when they seek sexual gratification from children through such acts as genital contact or pornographic photography. Caregivers engage in *emotional abuse* when they consistently ignore, isolate, reject, denigrate, or terrorize children or when they corrupt them by encouraging substance use or criminal activity. Sadly, some parents submit children to more than one form of abuse.

Approximately one in seven U.S. children has been maltreated by a family member or other caregiver (CDC, 2013; Finkelhor, Ormrod, Turner, & Hamby, 2005). The occurrence of maltreatment seems to be related to characteristics of both the adult and the child. Adults who maltreat children suffer from such serious psychological problems as depression, anxiety, and substance abuse (Ayoub, 2006; E. M. Douglas, 2017; Esser et al., 2016). Many have little contact with extended family or friends, are economically disadvantaged, move around a lot, were maltreated themselves as children, have large families to care for, abuse alcohol and drugs, and believe that physical punishment is justified by religious or cultural beliefs. Some abusive parents are naive about children's development and become angry when children fail to meet their unrealistic expectations.

Within a single family, one child may be maltreated and others not, although some parents, such as those with a substance abuse problem, are uniformly neglectful and harsh with all of their children. Children most likely to be maltreated are those who are very young (premature infants are especially at risk); have disabilities; and are irritable, aggressive, or exceedingly noncompliant (Ayoub, 2006; Barth, 2009).

Tragically, children can suffer long-term consequences from being neglected or assaulted by family members (CDC, 2013; E. M. Douglas, 2017). Children who have been maltreated are at risk for becoming aggressive, withdrawn, and depressed; for viewing themselves negatively; and for developing maladaptive ways of dealing with stress and interacting with other people. These children are also at risk for physical problems and even death.

Occasionally, children reveal the anguish of their abuse with a teacher. Generally, children will do this only when they feel safe. Such a conversation is best responded to with empathic concern. The teacher's role is to listen and support, and later to follow up with authorities, not to try to verify or delve into the details of the abuse (Collin-Vézina, 2013). In fact, asking leading questions (e.g., about whether a parent touched the child's private parts when the child did not mention being touched) can jeopardize a later prosecution because of the possibility that these questions plant false memories (Otgaar, Verschuere, Meijer, & van Oorsouw, 2012). Whoever is told about abuse will want to express concern, emphasize that it is not the child's fault, and advise him or her that a plan will be developed to get help (Collin-Vézina, 2013).

In many societies, educators must, by law, contact proper authorities (e.g., the school principal or Child Protective Services) when they suspect child abuse or neglect, regardless of whether the child has described the abuse to them. Two helpful resources are the National Child Hotline (1-800-4-A-CHILD®, or 1-800-422-4453)[5] and the Internet website for Childhelp USA®, childhelpusa.org. When a concern is expressed to Child Protective Services, the authorities may be able to verify the maltreatment and provide the family with counseling, parent education, housing assistance, substance treatment, home visits, and referrals for other services. Interventions must balance the safety of the child with the family's right to preservation (Fluke, Corwin, Hollinshead, & Maher, 2016). Unfortunately, reports to Child Protective Services do not always lead to immediate services because of lack of sufficient evidence and high caseloads that prevent prompt attention to individual families (Larner, Stevenson, & Behrman, 1998; Wolock, Sherman, Feldman, & Metzger, 2001).

As they wait for intervention, maltreated children desperately need stable, caring relationships with adults outside the family. Teachers can help by expressing their confidence in children's abilities, building on such protective factors as individual talents, and providing a sense of normalcy during upheaval in the family (Bernard & Popard Newell, 2013; Phasha, 2008). Sadly, many maltreated children have acquired negative social behaviors that elicit rejection from other adults, and possibly for this reason are at risk for developing low-quality relationships with teachers (Pianta, Hamre, & Stuhlman, 2003). Teachers are advised to make special efforts that address children's reactions to maltreatment (e.g., inattentiveness, disruptive behavior, or withdrawal from activities). When an investigation is underway, continued sensitivity is essential because children must adjust to disruptions in family structure (e.g., a child might be placed with a foster family) or family climate (e.g., a mother might become depressed when she learns she could lose custody of her children). After Child Protective Services intervenes, the child must adjust to new family conditions.

Sensitive educators watch for things they can do to support children who have been maltreated. Before and after parents have received interventions through Child Protective Services, their children may exhibit signs of distress, such as by becoming anxious, irritable, sad, inattentive, or aggressive. Referrals within the school system for counseling may prove helpful, and in the classroom, warm relationships with teachers are invaluable. Of course, identifying and meeting the needs of children who have been maltreated take practice, as does accommodation of other family characteristics. The Observation Guidelines table "Identifying Family Conditions" lists family membership and other characteristics that teachers can take into consideration.

Family Income and Economic Poverty

A child's experience in a community is strongly affected by the family's personal and financial resources. This idea is captured in the notion of the family's **socioeconomic status (SES)**, that is, its standing in the community based on income level, the prestige of parents' jobs, and parents' levels of education. A family's socioeconomic status—whether high SES,

[5]The National Child Abuse Hotline receives calls from the United States, U.S. Territories, and Canada. Many other countries have similar organizations.

OBSERVATION GUIDELINES
Identifying Family Conditions

CHARACTERISTIC	LOOK FOR	EXAMPLE	IMPLICATION
Family Membership	• *Single versus multiple caregivers* • *Presence or absence of siblings* • *Extended family members* living in the home • *Nonrelatives* living in the home • *Children's relationships* with other family members	Alexis's chronic kidney disease causes periodic bouts of pain and fatigue. During flare-ups, she finds comfort in being with her older sister. Teachers arrange for the girls to be together at lunch when Alexis is feeling poorly.	Accept all heads of family as valued, legitimate caregivers of children. Invite extended family members to school functions. Give youngsters time to be with siblings in times of personal crisis.
Cultural Background	• *Language(s)* spoken at home • *Routines* in eating, bathing, sleeping, and carrying out chores • *Loyalty* to and sense of responsibility for other family members • *Attitudes* toward cooperation and competition • *Communication styles* (whether they make eye contact and ask questions)	Carlos is reserved in class. He follows instructions and clearly wants to do well in school. However, he rarely asks for his teacher's help. Instead, he often asks his cousin (a classmate) for assistance.	Remember that most children and parents value academic achievement, despite what their behaviors may make you think. Try to determine children's preferred ways of interacting and communicating. Consider how families' cultural knowledge and skills can enrich the classroom. Invite families to share their traditions and talents at school.
Family Livelihood	• *Family business* (e.g., running a farm or cottage industry) that requires children's involvement • *Parental unemployment* or job turnover • *Older children and adolescents with part-time jobs* (e.g., grocery store work, paper routes)	April completes several chores on the family farm before going to school each morning. She keeps records of the weight and health of three calves born last year. She constructs charts to show their progress as a project for her science class.	Take outside work commitments into account when assigning homework. For example, give students at least 2 days to complete short assignments and a week for longer ones.
Parenting Styles	• *Parents' warmth or coldness* toward children • *Parents' expectations* for children's behavior • *Parents' willingness to discuss issues* and negotiate solutions with children • *Parents' disciplinary techniques* • *Effects of children's temperaments* on parents' discipline • *Children's interpretations* of parents' motives in using discipline • *Cultural values* that affect discipline • *Dangers and opportunities* in the community that influence parenting methods	At a parent–teacher conference, Julia's parents express their exasperation about getting Julia to do her homework: "We've tried everything—reasoning with her, giving ultimatums, offering extra privileges for good grades, punishing her for bad grades—but nothing works. She'd rather hang out with her friends every night."	Realize that most parents have children's best interests at heart when they discipline children. Recognize that parents adapt their parenting styles to children's temperaments. With all children, communicate high expectations, show sensitivity to children's needs, and give reasons for requests. Explain rules and your rationale for the particular disciplinary methods you use because children may be accustomed to entirely different techniques at home.
Transitions and Disruptions	• *Change in family membership* (e.g., as a result of death, divorce, or remarriage) • *Residential mobility* due to parents finding new jobs, being deployed in the military, or being incarcerated • *Physical or mental illness*, alcoholism, or substance abuse • *Economic poverty* and its associated deprivations • *Stress* in the family affecting parents' responsiveness	Justin has had trouble concentrating since his parents' divorce, and he now shows little enthusiasm for classroom activities. He has moved to a new neighborhood and has yet to make new friends there.	Show compassion for children undergoing a family transition. Listen patiently if children want to talk. Realize that some families quickly return to healthy functioning after a change, but others remain in turmoil for lengthy periods. Seek the assistance of a counselor when children have a serious or prolonged difficulty with changes.
Maltreatment	• *Frequent injuries* attributed to "accidents" • *Age-inappropriate sexual knowledge* or behavior • *Extreme negative emotions*, perhaps withdrawal, anxiety, or depression • *Excessive aggression and hostility* (e.g., with name calling and hitting) • *Untreated medical or dental needs* • *Chronic hunger* • *Poor hygiene* • *Lack of warm clothing in cold weather*	Johnny often has bruises on his arms and legs, which his mother says are the result of a "blood problem." He recently broke his collarbone, and soon after that he had a black eye. "I fell down the stairs," he explained, and refused to say more.	Immediately report signs of possible maltreatment to a school counselor or principal. Contact Child Protective Services for advice about additional courses of action that are warranted.

middle SES, or low SES—gives us a sense of how much flexibility family members have in where they live and what they buy, how much influence they have in political decision making, and what educational opportunities they can offer children.

Children from high- and middle-SES families enjoy material comforts and usually go to well-equipped schools with teachers who are experienced and highly prepared in the subjects they teach. Children are typically encouraged by parents to learn productive skills in after-school activities, for example, in soccer leagues, music lessons, and ballet classes. Families also socialize children to cooperate in structured teams and negotiate with authority figures (Lareau, 2003). Advantaged parents converse regularly with young children, expose them to sophisticated vocabulary, and foster their reasoning skills. Yet sometimes well-to-do parents pressure children to succeed, and their children may have insufficient time to relax and play. Despite attending good schools and living in safe neighborhoods, children are at risk for emotional problems and substance abuse when parents put unrealistic demands on them and fail to stay involved in their day-to-day activities (Luthar & Latendresse, 2005; Weissbourd, 2011).

Children from low-income families have fewer material resources yet definite advantages. In many low-income families, children receive substantial emotional support, are allowed discretion in how they spend their free time, and gain experience in managing their freedom (Lareau, 2003). Even so, children from low-income families are not always prepared for the academic demands of school and thus benefit from having teachers who cultivate their unique talents while helping them fill in the gaps in foundational knowledge.

Children Living in Economic Poverty

Some families do not merely scrape by with limited means. They go without. Families in economic poverty have so little in financial resources that their ability to nurture children is compromised (Dawson-McClure et al., 2014; G. W. Evans & Kim, 2007). Approximately 21% of U.S. children live in poverty (Forum on Child and Family Statistics, 2016d).

Children living in poverty face serious challenges. Typical problems include the following:

- *Corrosive physical environment.* Compared to their well-to-do peers, children in economically disadvantaged families are more likely to be exposed to factory pollution, toxic waste dumps, tainted drinking water, allergens that trigger asthma, and excessive noise.
- *Inadequate housing and material goods.* Many children live in tight quarters, perhaps sharing one or two rooms with several other family members. Some children have no place to live at all, except, perhaps, the family car or a homeless shelter. Children from homeless families are sometimes reluctant to go to school because they lack bathing facilities and presentable clothing. Even the most basic school supplies are beyond the family's reach.
- *Inadequate nutrition and health care.* Some children are poorly fed and have little access to adequate health care; as a result, they may suffer from malnutrition and other chronic health problems.
- *Increased probability of disabling conditions.* Children who live in poverty are more likely to have physical, mental, or social-emotional disabilities. Low-income families do not always have an adequate support network to address these disabilities.
- *Gaps in background knowledge.* Teachers assume that children have had certain kinds of experiences before they begin school—for instance, that they have been read to, have seen many kinds of animals at farms or zoos, and have had many occasions to explore the physical environment. Some children who live in extreme poverty miss out on these foundational experiences.
- *Emotional stress.* Many poor families live in chronically stressful conditions, constantly worrying about where their next meal is coming from, how to find transportation from one place to another, how to pay for electricity to heat or cool the home, where to find clothes for growing children, and how long the landlord will wait before evicting them for not paying rent. Low-income parents who are under

constant stress struggle in remaining calm with their children, and children easily absorb parents' anxieties. Exposure to serious hardships over an extended time when unaccompanied by adequate reassurance from familiar adults can culminate in the child's **toxic stress**. Toxic stress is a prolonged physiological reaction that leaves the child in a state of unremitting worry; it triggers stress-related conditions later in life, including heart disease, depression, and substance abuse. Toxic stress also undermines the health of certain structures of the brain, especially those that support learning, memory, attention, and coping skills.

- *Lower-quality schools.* Schools in low-income neighborhoods are often poorly funded and equipped, and they have high teacher turnover rates. Unfortunately, some teachers in these schools have low expectations for students, offer an undemanding curriculum, assign little homework, and set low standards for performance.
- *Exposure to neighbors who are indifferent and callous.* Children in low-income families are likely to have neighbors who are struggling themselves. Living in nerve-wracking adversity, people are at risk for losing hope and self-control and as a result may use drugs, commit violent acts on family members and others, and exploit children or try to recruit them into criminal activity.
- *Public misconceptions.* People from economically advantaged backgrounds often have mixed feelings about low-SES families: They may feel pity yet simultaneously believe that people who are poor are responsible for their misfortunes because of laziness, promiscuity, or overdependence on social welfare programs.

(L. M. Berger, Paxson, & Waldfogel, 2009; Berliner, 2009; G. W. Evans & Kim, 2007; G. W. Evans & Schamberg, 2009; K. Fong, 2016; A. S. Garner et al., 2012; Gershoff, Aber, & Raver, 2005; Graff, 2014; Linver, Brooks-Gunn, & Kohen, 2002; McLoyd, 1998a; Murnane, 2007; Payne, DeVol, & Smith, 2006; Schmeer & Yoon, 2016; Willingham, 2012)

Preparing for Your Licensure Examination

Your teaching test might ask you about the kinds of challenges experienced by children in low-income families.

Some students find the challenges of poverty so overwhelming that they engage in behaviors—dropping out of school, abusing drugs and alcohol, participating in criminal activities—that create further problems. However, many other students actively confront their many hardships (Abelev, 2009; Felner & DeVries, 2013; Kim-Cohen, Moffitt, Caspi, & Taylor, 2004). These youngsters show **resilience**, the ability to thrive despite adverse environmental conditions. Let's examine strategies educators use to nurture resilience in low-income youngsters.

Working with Children and Families Living in Economic Poverty

Adults who want to make a difference in children's lives are especially likely to do so in schools serving low-SES populations. But to be effective, teachers and other school personnel must fully commit to their jobs, think creatively about how they can make the most of limited resources, show a contagious enthusiasm for learning, and work with families and other members of the community (L. W. Anderson & Pellicer, 1998; S. Griffin & Green, 2012; E. H. Ogden & Germinario, 1988). Experts offer these recommendations for working with children from low-income families:

- **Invest in children's strengths.** Youngsters may become discouraged when teachers concentrate on their weaknesses. In contrast, focusing on what's *right* with children can generate optimism, excitement, and a definite commitment to learning. It doesn't take long to figure out children's strengths when you are intentionally looking for them. Many children of low-income immigrant families have two parents at home who support them, are physically healthy, and have extended families concerned with their welfare (Shields & Behrman, 2004). Young children from low-income families are apt to be curious, eager to acquire language and literacy skills, and receptive to forming close relationships with teachers (Maier, Vitiello, & Greenfield, 2012). Adolescents who work part-time to help their families make ends meet have a sense of purpose and a good understanding of the world of work (Schilling, 2008). Children of single working parents may know far more than peers do about cooking, cleaning, and taking care of younger siblings (Whiting & Edwards, 1988).

- **Foster a sense of community.** Children from low-income backgrounds benefit from teachers' efforts to form personal relationships with them and build a **sense of community**—a collection of shared beliefs that individuals in the group (e.g., a class or school) have common goals, respect one another's efforts, and believe that everyone makes an important contribution (L. W. Anderson & Pellicer, 1998; Edelstein, 2015; M. Watson & Battistich, 2006). Teachers can assign chores on a rotating basis, use cooperative learning activities, involve students in cross-grade tutoring, and encourage everyone's participation in extracurricular activities (J. Downey, 2000). Because youngsters feel more connected to their community when, in some small way, they give something back, educators can also sponsor community service projects. Children might conduct a neighborhood cleanup, volunteer in a nursing home, serve as readers at the local library, or raise funds to benefit community causes (Ladson-Billings, 1994).

- **Convey clear expectations for behavior.** For all children, and especially for those who have had more than their share of hardships, knowing what's expected is important. Hence adults need to describe their expectations in clear, concrete terms (J. Downey, 2000; Reinke, Herman, & Stormont, 2013). When finishing lunch in the cafeteria, children might be asked to "empty the napkins and leftovers into the trash bin, put the trays and dishes on the counter, and go quietly outside." When working in cooperative groups, young people might be reminded that "everyone needs to participate in discussions and contribute to the project."

- **Establish a warm, predictable, and safe environment.** Children who face harsh and adverse circumstances, especially over a long time, above all else need to feel safe and loved. Teachers can establish pleasant routines, such as greeting them with affection first thing in the morning and saying good-bye to them personally, by name, in the afternoon. Adults can also show their affection for children by encouraging them to pursue their interests and providing individualized feedback on their learning progress (C. Howes, Fuligni, Hong, Huang, & Lara-Cinisomo, 2013). When children manifest exceptionally high levels of stress, for example, by biting their fingernails, sucking their fingers, clinging to adults, having daytime toileting accidents, complaining of headaches and stomach pains, developing rashes, and being withdrawn or acting out, they need extra support from adults.

- **Acquaint children with resources in their community.** Students who have not had the opportunity to see institutions in their society can learn a lot from brief visits. Teachers can take their classes on field trips to a zoo, museum, post office, fire station, and so forth and thereby create new knowledge for children to build on in academic lessons. When field trips are too expensive or logistically impractical, an alternative is to bring the community to children—perhaps by having a representative of the local zoo bring some of the zoo's smaller residents or by asking a police officer to come describe the many public services that the police department provides.

- **Encourage children to get involved in extracurricular activities.** Participation in sports and after-school activities appears instrumental in exposing children to worthwhile skills and discouraging such problematic behaviors as drug use, thefts, and violence (Landsman, 2014; McLoyd et al., 2009). Teachers can inspire young people to get involved in fun and rewarding activities while advising them of community resources that could offset any expenses required for participation. The timing of events is also an issue for some students in immigrant families, who may be reluctant to spend too much time away from their parents; organized activities right after school might work for them (Simpkins, Delgado, Price, Quach, & Starbuck, 2013).

- **Communicate high expectations for children's success.** Some children from low-SES backgrounds do not expect much of their own academic skills. Yet teachers can communicate a can-do attitude, urge students to challenge themselves, and provide support for reaching personal goals. Offering tutoring sessions for challenging classroom material, finding low-cost academic enrichment programs available during the summer, helping adolescents fill out applications for college scholarships, and arranging for them to take college admission tests are just a few examples of useful assistance (Kunjufu, 2006).

- **Give homeless children school supplies and help them adjust at school.** Children who are homeless reside in a range of settings, for example, motels, campgrounds, temporary shelters, cars, parks, abandoned buildings, and bus stations. Educators who work with children of homeless families can first of all help them in finding needed learning materials. Teachers, principals, and school counselors might provide a notebook, clipboard, or other portable "desk" on which children can do their homework at the temporary residence; ask civic organizations to donate school supplies; meet with parents at the shelter if desired by the family; and pair homeless children with classmates who can demonstrate school procedures (Bowman & Popp, 2013; Pawlas, 1994). Educators can make another valuable contribution for children whose families plan to move by keeping a portfolio of children's assignments and sending it to the new school.

In the United States, homeless children have the right to a free and appropriate public education under the McKinney–Vento Act. Teachers and other school personnel must determine children's individual needs, clues of which may surface during conversations with children about their previous educational experiences (e.g., whether they had a teacher who worked with them individually or in small groups outside the regular classroom, perhaps indicating a customized intervention; Bowman & Popp, 2013). Tutoring can be arranged with help from school psychologists, special education teachers, and other personnel. A school counselor may address difficulties in adjustment, and a nurse might be able to arrange for showering facilities, clothing, and medical care. Discretion is essential with these services because homeless children are apt to feel uncomfortable in discussing their personal and family situations.

- **Be a mentor.** Young people from low-income families often benefit from assistance in navigating through difficulties at school. A trusted teacher, counselor, or coach can show children how to express their needs in educational environments. Particularly when youngsters encounter serious obstacles in their schooling, for example, failing subjects, missing school, or becoming a teenage parent, mentors can suggest practical ways to overcome difficulties (Abelev, 2009; Curtin, Schweitzer, Tuxbury, & D'Aoust, 2016; Schilling, 2008).

- **Advocate for improvement of schools.** Teachers and other practitioners can join community groups that are striving to improve schools. Various initiatives have been productive, including efforts to work within existing school systems and others that focus on charter or alternative schools with high expectations for family involvement (Fruchter, 2007; Kunjufu, 2006).

Summary

Six characteristics of families influence children's needs at school. When parents are raising a child with a significant special educational need, they are likely to have multiple stressors yet, in the process of coping with difficult experiences, may become strong and informed advocates for their children's education. Children growing up in military families take pride in their parents' heroic actions yet find it challenging to cope with the family's moves, a parent's absence during deployment, and a parent's adjustment to traumatic events after being reunited with the family. Children whose families have immigrated from another country enjoy the riches of multiple cultures while deciding which customs they will follow and dealing with the unique features of their family, in some situations growing up in a low-income setting or surviving persecution or warfare in the homeland. When a parent is incarcerated, the child has a number of upsetting events to cope with—the parent's sudden departure, the stigma attached to their parent's imprisonment, and possible residential moves. Maltreatment of children by families comes in several forms and is inherently harmful to the child's welfare yet can moderated to some degree by caring practitioners. Finally, children growing up in low-income families have definite strengths as well as potentially debilitating hardships that can be addressed, in part, through the thoughtful intercessions of teachers who nurture children's strengths, maintain reliable classroom routines, offer affection, and make adjustments for missing skills. Educators can build on children's experiences in various kinds of families and help economically disadvantaged children by providing support and resources and recognizing children's personal strengths.

MyLab Education Self-Check 3.4

Practicing For Your Licensure Examination

Many teaching tests require students to use what they have learned about child development in responses to brief vignettes and multiple-choice questions. You can practice for your licensure examination by reading the following case study and answering a series of questions.

Four-Year-Old Sons

A common behavior displayed by preschoolers is asking a lot of *why* questions. *Why are carrots orange? Why does Daddy have a beard? Why do I have to go to bed now?*

In a study about the lives of women, Belenky and her colleagues interviewed several mothers (Belenky, Bond, & Weinstock, 1997). The authors found distinct perspectives on how mothers viewed questions by their children. Elizabeth describes her son Charles as being disrespectful in questioning her authority. For example, when Elizabeth tells Charles not to touch a dead bug, he questions her about why the insect is dead and why he shouldn't touch it. She believes his frequent questions reflect his intention to anger her by not listening respectfully or accepting her statements.

In contrast, Joyce describes her son Peter as having an insatiable curiosity. She believes that his frequent questions are a natural outgrowth of his need to analyze the world around him. She sees his responses to her requests as a natural outgrowth of his mental reflection. She admires and appreciates her son's questions because she believes that he sees dimensions to things that she misses, and his questions help her to think through what they are doing together.

Constructed-Response Question

1. How do the two mothers interpret their sons' questions? How might they have developed their different orientations to children's queries?

Multiple-Choice Questions

2. How might a teacher form a partnership with each of these mothers?

   a. A teacher could let the mothers know how happy she is to have the boys in her class and see if either mother has any concerns to discuss.

   b. A teacher could advise the mothers about how she addresses typical characteristics of children this age, including their natural curiosity and frequent question asking.

   c. A teacher could use a variety of formats to inform the mothers of the preschool curriculum, policies, and events by sending home newsletters about classroom activities and getting these reports translated if possible for families who speak another language.

   d. A teacher could try all of the strategies listed above.

3. Should a teacher be concerned that Elizabeth is maltreating her son?

   a. No, because emotional abuse, which Elizabeth is exhibiting, does not reach the threshold for maltreatment.

   b. No, because although Elizabeth expresses frustration with her son's frequent questioning, she does not say anything that indicates she is harming her son physically or emotionally.

   c. Yes, Elizabeth's dislike of her son's questioning is proof that she is physically maltreating him.

   d. Yes, because impatience with a child's questioning is an indication of emotional maltreatment.

MyLab Education Licensure Practice 3.1

Key Concepts

family (p. 64)
socialization (p. 65)
individualistic culture (p. 65)
collectivistic culture (p. 65)
society (p. 67)
community (p. 67)
ethnicity (p. 68)
race (p. 68)
stereotype (p. 69)
prejudice (p. 69)
discrimination (p. 69)
implicit bias (p. 69)
family structure (p. 75)
coparents (p. 76)
stepfamily (p. 78)
parenting style (p. 84)
authoritative parenting style (p. 84)
authoritarian parenting style (p. 84)
permissive parenting style (p. 84)
uninvolved parenting style (p. 85)
guided participation (p. 86)
individualized education plan (p. 97)
acculturation (p. 98)
assimilation (p. 98)
separation (p. 98)
selective adoption (p. 98)
bicultural orientation (p. 98)
child maltreatment (p. 101)
socioeconomic status (SES) (p. 102)
toxic stress (p. 105)
resilience (p. 105)
sense of community (p. 105)

Chapter Four

Biological Beginnings

Ariel Skelley/Blend Images/Alamy Stock Photo

Learning Objectives

4.1 Explain how genes and environmental experiences are mutually influential during development, and describe how teachers can customize educational strategies according to children's unique genetic profiles.

4.2 Characterize the phases of prenatal growth and the qualities of effective practices for protecting rapidly growing offspring and their expectant parents.

Outline

4.3 Describe the multistage birth process, the period right after birth, and professional practices that support newborn infants and their parents.

CASE STUDY

Maria

Joan and Dave longed for a baby. Time and again they were disappointed when a conception did not occur. Months turned to years, and the couple gradually accepted that their future would be childless. Joan and Dave invested in their marriage, faith, jobs, service to the community, and precious time with family and friends. Their lives were full and meaningful.

Joan E. Magnacca

One day they were astonished to find that they were expecting a baby. Disbelief gave way to excitement as medical tests, morning sickness, and a little bump protruding from Joan's abdomen convinced the couple of the reality of their growing child. Midway through her pregnancy, Joan's doctor advised the prospective parents that because of Joan's age (39) and the presence of an irregular feature in the ultrasound scan, they had an elevated risk for having a baby with a birth defect. Although apprehensive about their baby's condition, Joan and Dave decided to avoid any intrusive medical tests. Instead, they resolved to love their baby.

And love her they did. Joan and Dave adored baby Maria. At birth, Maria was beautiful, healthy, and snuggly. She relaxed in their arms, was happily comforted when distressed, and eased into a sleep schedule that quickly resembled their own. Being informed about her medical status did throw a wrinkle into the family's adjustment, however. The new parents were advised that Maria had Down syndrome.

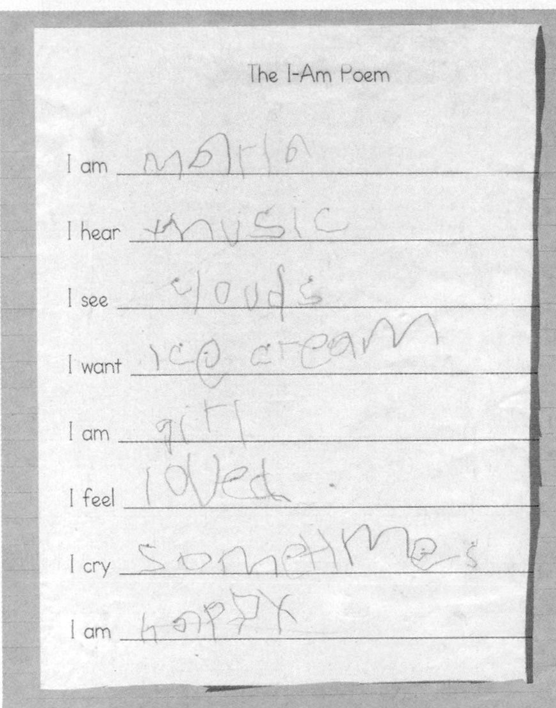

MyLab Education
Artifact Example 4.1

Find Developmental Meaning *Maria at age 11 filled in the blanks in an I-Am Poem. What can you infer about Maria's abilities from this artifact?* By writing that she hears music, sees clouds, wants ice cream, is a girl, feels loved, cries sometimes, and is happy, Maria shows that she can comprehend simple written stems, has self-insight into her internal states, and can transcribe her experiences into legible words.

In the years ahead, Dave and Joan were to learn a great deal about Down syndrome. Just as important, they were to learn about Maria's individuality and appreciate her radiant, buoyant, and demonstrative personality. The new parents cared for Maria at home during her infancy. They tended to her needs, showered her with affection, enjoyed her antics, read to her, and encouraged her mastery of the developmental milestones of sitting, crawling, walking, and eating independently. At 18 months, Maria entered an early childhood intervention center and received numerous services that effectively nurtured her understanding of language and her speech, cognition, and desire to explore the world. She thrived.

The move to kindergarten was unexpectedly difficult. Her teacher was an experienced educator in a private school who agreed to include Maria in her classroom. It turned out that the teacher was unfamiliar with the needs of children with special needs and accommodations for helping them reach their potential. Maria had a special knack for sensing how people judged her, and with this teacher she felt unaccepted, a perception that was difficult for her to articulate to her parents. Fortunately, Joan and Dave were perceptive themselves and became increasingly concerned about the tension over school they perceived in Maria.

One day, as they approached school, Maria protested, "No. No. *No!!!*" It was a turning point for Joan and Dave, who quickly moved Maria to a new school, where she was sincerely welcomed, accepted, and loved. Again she would flourish. Maria bonded with her teachers and several classmates, including both typical students and others classified as having special needs. Maria divided her school day among lessons with a special education teacher, other specialists, and her regular classroom teacher. Shifts between the settings were seamless, especially when the different educators were able to communicate regularly. There were a few occasions when Joan had to remind the school that Maria could be—and therefore *should be*—included in more activities in the regular classroom—in classroom photographs, for example, and particular lessons that could be easily adapted to Maria's abilities. Fortunately, the principal and teachers were receptive to making these revisions.

Maria progressed well during the elementary school years. She worked hard. She learned to read and write, studied spelling lists, and absorbed important concepts. She made and kept friends. She swam, rode horses, and enjoyed roller coasters. Although Maria struggled with certain things—forming letters, following multistep instructions, and grasping abstract ideas—customized goals and strategies allowed her to succeed. You can see an assignment that Maria completed, saying some things she liked to do, in Artifact Example 4.1.

Now she is ready for the next major transition: entry into middle school. There will be significant challenges ahead, not the least of which are adjusting to a new building, facing a different schedule of classes, coping with intensified academic demands, and adjusting to adolescence. Yet continued advocacy from Joan and Dave, a principal who has reached out to the family, long-standing friends who will accompany her to the new school, and, of course, Maria's own cheerful self and good health—are assets that will ease the transition.

- How did Maria's parents contribute to her well-being?
- How did Maria's biological characteristics influence her development?

Maria had a happy childhood in large part because her parents, Joan and Dave, loved her, recognized her individuality, and advocated for her rights. Maria contributed to her own positive growth with an affectionate and joyful personality, a willingness to work hard, and a capacity for friendship. Teachers, principals, and other specialists provided invaluable support, successfully nurturing her abilities and confidence. Of course, natural biological processes were also an essential part of Maria's growth. Nine months of healthy prenatal development, modestly deterred by the chromosomal condition of Down syndrome, culminated in the birth of a beloved child.

In this chapter we show that genetic foundations, prenatal growth, and childbirth reflect extraordinary symphonies of developmental processes, each orchestrated by a harmonious blend of nature and nurture. We find that there are many things prospective parents and caring professionals can do to give children healthy beginnings.

Genetic Foundations

4.1 Explain how genes and environmental experiences are mutually influential during development, and describe how teachers can customize educational strategies according to children's unique genetic profiles.

Like Maria, every child has a unique profile of hereditary instructions that support his or her life, growth, human traits, and individuality. These guidelines are contained in the child's **genes**, the basic units of heredity.

Structure of Genes

Each gene tells the body to create one or more proteins or regulate the operations of other genes. Proteins produced by genes create life-sustaining reactions that, with adequate nutrition and a favorable environment, build the foundation for a healthy child. Some proteins guide the production of new cells (e.g., elastic skin cells or message-sending brain cells). Other proteins tell the body to increase in size, fight infection, repair damage, or carry chemical signals elsewhere in the body. And a few, as we have said, activate or inhibit other genes.

The 21,000 to 25,000 or so genes that exist in the human body are laid out in an orderly way on rodlike structures called **chromosomes** (Pennisi, 2012; U.S. Department of Energy Office of Science, 2008). Chromosomes are organized into 23 distinct pairs that are easily seen with a high-powered microscope (Figure 4.1). These 46 chromosomes reside in the center of virtually every cell in the body. One chromosome in each pair is inherited from the mother, the other from the father.

FIGURE 4.1 One person's chromosomes.

Photograph of human chromosomes, which have been extracted from a human cell, colored, and magnified. (Courtesy of Jane Ades, National Human Genome Research Institute (NHGRI))

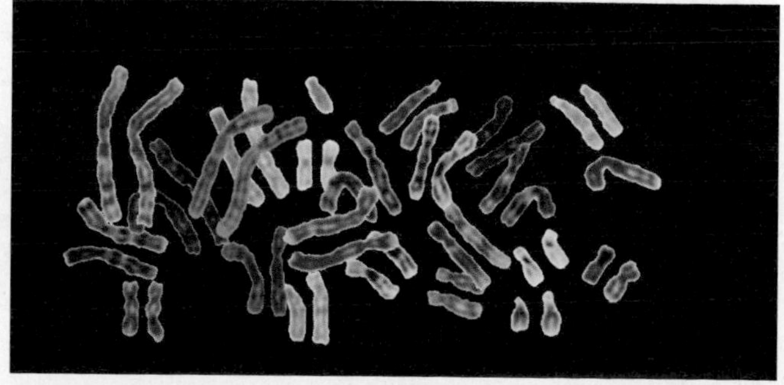

Genes are made up of deoxyribonucleic acid, or **DNA**. A DNA molecule is structured like a ladder that has been twisted many times into a spiral staircase (see Figure 4-2). Pairs of chemical substances compose each step on the staircase, with each gene being composed of a series of these steps. Location on the staircase helps scientists determine the identity of particular genes. Above and below genes on the ladder are other instructions that tell genes when they should turn on and off and do other things that scientists have yet to discover. The hierarchical relationships among cells, chromosomes, genes, and DNA molecules are represented in Figure 4.2.

Operation of Genes

Most genes are identical—or at least very similar—across children. Among these universal genes are those that make it possible for children to develop fundamental human abilities, such as communicating with language, walking and running, and forming social relationships. The remaining genes vary among children. Variable genes predispose individual children to be relatively tall or short, heavy or thin, active or sedentary, eager to learn new things or content to rely on existing knowledge, emotionally agreeable or combative, and healthy or vulnerable to disease. Remarkably, universal and individual genes blend together in their effects, with all children having human eyes, a nose, and a mouth, as directed by universal genes, yet the form of each varying slightly, according to individual genes, such that each child becomes distinctive.

FIGURE 4.2 Relationships among genetic structures within the body.

The body contains billions of cells, most of which contain 46 chromosomes. Each chromosome contains thousands of genes. Genes are long sequences of DNA that assemble proteins and regulate other genes. Proteins are released and affect activities in the cell and, depending on location in the body, health, and maturational stage.

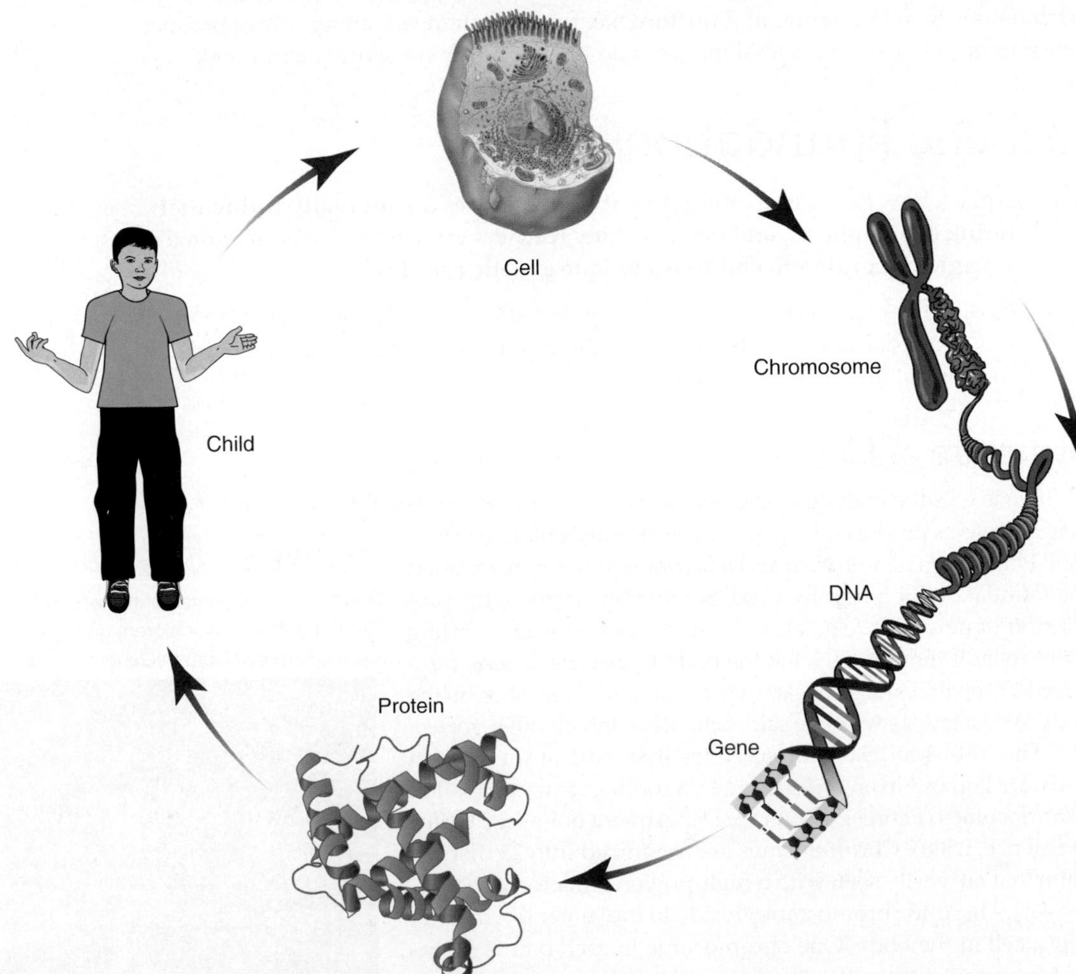

Both universal and variable genes initiate chains of events in the body. Genes directly affect the operations of individual cells present in the child's organs, brain, and other physiological systems. These structures and processes, in turn, affect the child's behavior, relationships, and learning. Thus, genes are powerful, but they are *not* simple recipes or blueprints for traits. Rather, the proteins that originate from genetic instructions are released into the child's cells, and their effects depend partly (largely, in some cases) on the child's health and activity. To illustrate, an 8-year-old boy genetically predisposed to asthma may rarely have respiratory flare-ups because his family gives him proper medical care and shields him from the hair and dander of dogs, his personal trigger for wheezing and coughing.

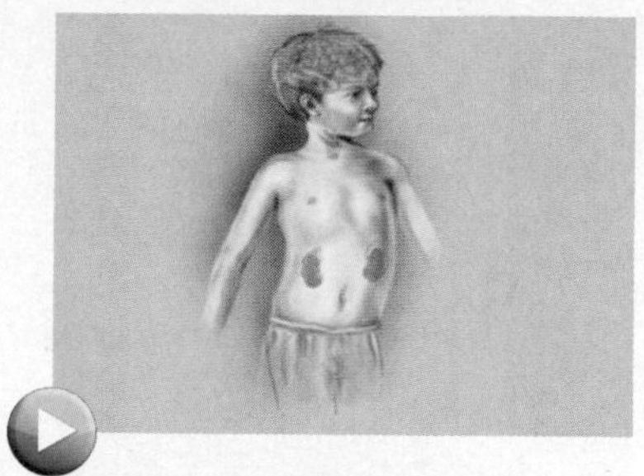

MyLab Education
Video Explanation 4.1
This video shows the effects of hormones on children's bodies.

The causal chain also operates in reverse, with the environment affecting genetic expression. The environment provides opportunities for learning and exposure to nutrition and toxins, these factors affect the body, and the health and operations of physical systems activate (or suppress) certain genes. For example, a 1-year-old boy who has been exposed to high levels of lead may not be able to fully express genes that otherwise would have permitted good motor skills and insatiable learning.

Developmental stage and still other factors affect genetic expression. In fact, only a subset of genes is active in a cell at any given moment. Responding to the body's health, maturational state, and chemicals circulating within the body, cells activate a limited collection of genes. Other genes within the cell remain dormant until it is their turn to be called into action. Hormones are chemical messengers that flow through the bloodstream and generate reactions in cells that have matching receptors. A child is born with genes for sexual maturation, but the body waits to release relevant hormones until adolescence. The delay in the action of genes also explains why some diseases and mental health conditions appear seemingly out of nowhere. Genes that make people vulnerable to certain conditions remain silent until maturational states and environmental circumstances elicit them.

The Role of Genes in Forming a Child

As you have learned, genes work by generating proteins within cells and regulating the activation of other genes. This work begins even before a person's first cell is formed. In a cascade of events, reproductive cells are formed and become ready to unite as a new organism.

Normal human cells contain 46 chromosomes. As an important exception, male and female reproductive cells, called **gametes**, have only 23 chromosomes each—one from each chromosome pair. Gametes, which take the form of *sperm* in men and *ova* in women, are created in a process called **meiosis** (see Figure 4.3).

Meiosis

In the process of creating new reproductive cells, the 46 chromosomes within a male or female *germ cell* (a precursor to a gamete) pair up into 23 matched sets. The germ cell duplicates each chromosome, and pairs of chromosomes line up side by side. Next, segments of genetic material are exchanged between each pair. This *crossing-over* of genetic material shuffles genes between paired chromosomes generating new hereditary combinations that do not exist in either parent's chromosomes.

After crossing-over takes place, the pairs of duplicated chromosomes separate, and the cell divides into two new germ cells with half from each pair. Chance determines which of the duplicated chromosomes from each of the 23 pairs moves to one or the other of the two new cells. This phase thus provides a second route to genetic individuality. During the first cell division, one of the two new female germ cells gets the bulk of the cell matter and is strong and healthy whereas the second, smaller cell disintegrates. Both new male germ cells are viable.

A second cell division takes place, and the duplicated chromosomes separate. Each new cell receives one of the duplicate chromosomes from each pair. The resulting male germ cells are ready to mature and become male gametes (sperm). The female germ cells undergo this second division only after being fertilized by sperm. When the female cell divides, once again, only one of the two new cells, a female gamete (an ovum), is viable. The process of meiosis thus produces one ovum and four sperm.[1]

[1]Sperm are produced continuously throughout a male's reproductive years. In girls, up to 2 million germ cells are present at birth. Many subsequently decay, and only about 40,000 remain at the beginning of adolescence. About 400 ova will be released over the woman's lifetime.

FIGURE 4.3 Formation of reproductive cells.

Meiosis is the process of forming sperm (left) and ova (right) in these steps: (A) development of precursor cells begins at puberty in boys and prenatally in girls (only one of the 23 pairs of chromosomes is shown for sperm and ova); (B) the precursor cells duplicate their chromosomes; (C) pairs of duplicated chromosomes unite and exchange pieces during a process called crossing over; (D) pairs of chromosomes separate, with each from the pair going to one of two offspring cells; and (E) offspring cells divide in two again, with each double-sided chromosome separating into two single-strand chromosomes (in sperm, four cells are potentially viable, whereas only one of the four ova will be). After meiosis and during fertilization, (F) the sperm enters the ovum, and (G) the two cells intermingle each of the 23 sets of single-strand chromosomes and unite as a single-celled zygote with 23 pairs of double-strand chromosomes.

Based on information in K. L. Moore, Persaud, and Torchia (2013) and Sadler (2010).

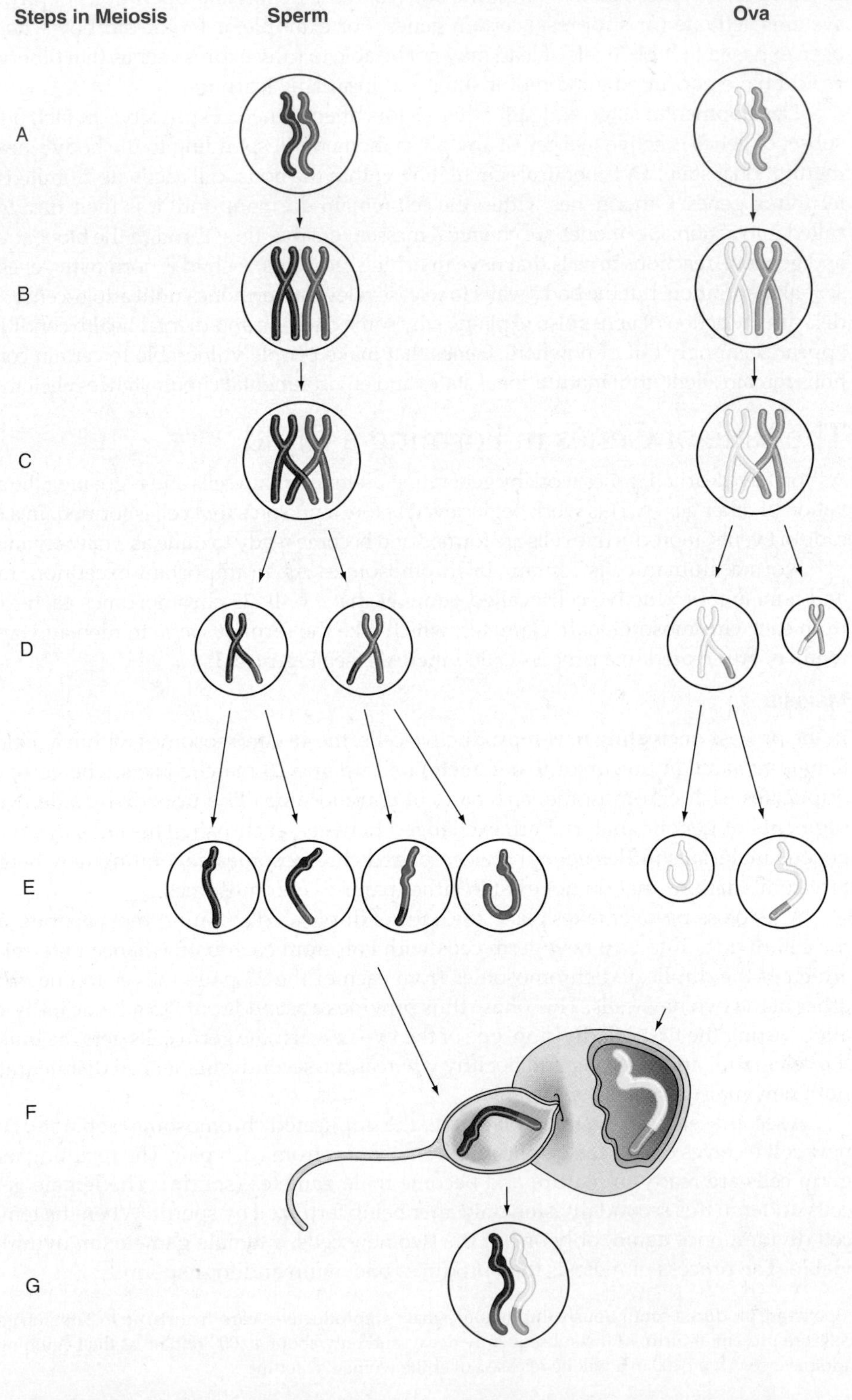

The multiple steps of meiosis shown in Figure 4.3 ensure that most traits are preserved across generations while a few entirely new traits are created. Children share some features with both of their parents because they inherit half of their chromosomes from each parent. Children are unlike their parents (and siblings) in other respects because parts of chromosomes change slightly during meiosis.[2] Furthermore, a single gene transmitted from parent to child (and shared by both) can operate differently in the two family members because other genes (not shared by both) intensify or weaken its effects.

Fertilization

When one sperm and an ovum unite at conception, the 23 chromosomes from each parent come together and form a new being (the **zygote**) with 46 chromosomes. The 23rd chromosome pair determines the gender of the individual: Two *X chromosomes* (one each from the mother and the father) produce a female, and a combination of an *X chromosome* and a *Y chromosome* (from the mother and the father, respectively) produces a male. After that first human cell is formed, its development depends on the health of its genes and the well-being of the mother.

Occasionally, more than one zygote is formed. A zygote splits into two separate cell clusters, resulting in two offspring instead of one. *Identical*, or **monozygotic twins**, come from the same fertilized egg and so have the same genes. At other times, two ova simultaneously unite with two sperm cells, again resulting in two offspring. These **dizygotic twins**, also known as *fraternal* twins, are as similar to one another as ordinary siblings. They share some genetic traits but not others.

Because monozygotic and dizygotic twins differ in the degree to which they have overlapping genes, researchers have compared them extensively. Twin studies permit rough estimates of the relative impact of heredity and environment on human characteristics. Considerable data indicate that monozygotic twins are more similar to one another than is the case with dizygotic twins in their tendencies to learn new concepts and become cooperative or aggressive (Ganiban, Ulbricht, Saudino, Reiss, & Neiderhiser, 2011; Knafo & Plomin, 2006; Lester et al., 2016). Even so, "identical" twins are *not* indistinguishable in all psychological characteristics or even in their physical features—an indication that environment, experience, children's own choices, and random factors affect development.

The Expression of Genetic Traits

Shortly after the zygote is formed, it begins to grow through cell divisions in an operation called **mitosis**. The new organism adds cells through a duplication process that typically preserves the original 46 chromosomes. During mitosis, the spiral staircase of DNA straightens itself up and splits down the middle, and each half re-creates the original structure. After two exact copies of the chromosome have been formed, one version from each pair moves to opposite sides of the cell, with the two sides gradually splitting apart into new cells. This process of mitosis continues throughout the life span and permits both growth and replacement of worn-out cells.

When new cells are formed, they take on the particular properties of nearby cells and find their way to a location in the body. New cells take on a productive role, such as sending signals within the brain, expanding a muscle or bone, circulating oxygen in the bloodstream, helping with digestion, or taking on another specialty according to nearby circumstances. The many shared genes that children have contribute to the common order in which children grow and refine body parts and motor skills. Integrating with these universal physical progressions are small tweaks in the grand design, courtesy of genes that take different forms. Let's look at common human genes and the discrepancies that occur in genetic instructions.

Shared Human Traits

Unvarying human genes, carried by all parents, are transmitted to every child. These genes contribute to universal sequences we see in developing structures of the body.

[2]For any given parent, each event of meiosis begins with the exact same chromosomes. The process of meiosis tweaks the structure of chromosomes slightly; no two meiotic events alter chromosomes in precisely the same way.

They guide the way that layers of cells grow together in prenatal beings and create cavities around which the brain, organs, and lungs form. New cells know how to specialize and where to move based on the signals they receive from nearby cells and the pathways that have already formed in tissues. Simple evolves into complex, as when global blobs differentiate into hands and fingers.

Human body parts—for example, a complex brain capable of creating new knowledge, hands and fingers adept with a paintbrush and keyboard, and ears and related brain networks receptive to processing language, emotional tone, and music—form because human genes act in concert with developmental processes. Early in prenatal development, the rudimentary ball of cells cleaves into separate tissues for the nervous system, skin, lungs, gut, muscles and connective tissues. Body parts become increasingly mature, with different structures taking on specialized functions, such as digesting food, detoxifying chemicals, sensing patterns in the world, and distributing oxygen.

After birth, universal maturational influences are seen in *critical periods*, age ranges during which time specific environmental exposure is necessary for normal development. For the duration of a critical period, the child is primed to develop a specific ability, provided that certain conditions are present. For example, children are receptive to language input during infancy and early childhood. Those who are deprived of language in the first few years of life require intervention if they are to acquire a first language later in life. Similarly, to develop normal vision, children must be given a chance to distinguish objects that are close and far from themselves. Individuals whose lenses are cloudy during infancy because of cataracts could become permanently incapable of perceiving deviations in distance (Wiesel & Hubel, 1965). Children almost always gain exposure to the stimuli they need for normal development, and when they do not, interventions are sometimes effective in activating the relevant skill. Recently, scientists have begun to investigate substances that might reinstate communication among nerve cells set aside by nature for these abilities (M. Davis et al., 2015; Gao et al., 2014).

Individual Traits

Whereas universal genes guide structures of the human brain and body through the same general format, other genes take two or more forms, generating dissimilarities in children's appearance, health, personalities, and learning abilities. Genes that differ are transmitted through systematic patterns of inheritance as well as by less common mechanisms and biological errors.

Some individual characteristics occur as a result of one gene taking priority over its partner. When the two sets of 23 chromosomes match up during conception, the corresponding genes inherited from each parent also pair up. Each gene pair related to a particular physical characteristic includes two forms of the protein-coding instructions—two **alleles**. Sometimes the two genes in an allele pair give the same instructions ("Have dark hair!" "Have dark hair!"). At other times they give very different instructions ("Have dark hair!" "Have blond hair!"). When two genes give different instructions, one gene is more influential than its counterpart. A **dominant gene** manifests its characteristic, in a sense overriding the instructions of a **recessive gene** with which it is paired. A recessive gene influences growth and development primarily when its partner is also recessive. For example, genes for dark hair are dominant, and those for blond hair are recessive. Thus, a child with a dark-hair gene and a blond-hair gene will have dark hair, as will a child with two dark-hair genes. Only when two blond-hair genes are paired together will a child have blond hair.

When two genes in an allele pair disagree, one gene doesn't always dominate completely. Sometimes one gene simply has a stronger influence than its partner, a phenomenon known as **codominance**. *Sickle cell disease*, a blood disorder, is an example. The disease develops in its full-blown form only when a person has two (recessive) alleles for it. Nevertheless, when an individual has one recessive allele for sickle cell disease and one healthy allele, he or she may experience temporary, mild symptoms when short of oxygen, only occasionally develop more serious health problems, and have greater-than-average resistance to malaria (Aneni, Hamer, & Gill, 2013; Jorde, Carey, & Bamshad, 2010).

Individual differences also emerge when many genes add separate small effects to a complex characteristic. In **polygenic inheritance** children inherit a wide range of genes that each contribute to a dimension, such as height and weight. Of course, height and weight are also affected by nutrition, exercise, sleep, stress, and exposure to toxins. With a **multifactorial trait**, many genes work together with environmental factors in the manifestation of a characteristic. Height and weight are multifactorial traits, as are susceptibilities to diabetes, epilepsy, obesity, gastrointestinal disorders, and cancer (J. W. Ball, Bindler, & Cowen, 2010; Dibbens, Heron, & Mulley, 2007; Marques, Oliveira, Pereira, & Outeiro, 2011; A. Smith & Weber, 2016).

Developmental Systems Prompt 4.1

Children who have the same genetic anomaly (such as Down syndrome) differ in such major characteristics as intelligence, attesting to the complexity and malleability of genetic expression. When you learn about a particular disorder, find out about typical characteristics of the condition as well as variations among affected children.

Co-Action by Heredity and Environment

Genes and environmental exposure blend together in complex processes called **co-action**. Co-action occurs in three primary ways. First, with *direct effects* the environment enables genetic expression, providing conditions necessary for survival and a unique physical, cultural, and familial environment that together enable the child's growth and initiative. Children are apt to achieve their full genetic potential when they participate in progressively challenging activities and obtain nutritious meals, affection from caregivers, encouragement to act with self-control, opportunities for physical activity, and protection from toxins (Aboud & Yousafzai, 2015; Brant et al., 2009; W. Johnson, Deary, & Iacono, 2009; Lopez Boo, 2016; Rutter, 2014). Under ideal circumstances, children grow to their maximum height, stay healthy, get along with other people, and acquire important cultural skills. When nutrition and attention are inadequate, and when children are exposed to lead and other toxins, physical and psychological growth can be stunted.

Evidence for direct effects is found in children's temperament and intelligence. People have genetic predispositions to various temperaments—for example, in becoming more or less cheerful, outgoing, moody, anxious, and aggressive (P. T. Davies, Cicchetti, Hentges, & Sturge-Apple, 2013; Glahn & Burdick, 2011; Rothbart, Posner, & Kieras, 2006). Yet direct effects do not occur without being intensified or reduced by the environment, For example, a child's emerging personality depends to some degree on child-rearing experiences (Lemery-Chalfant, Kao, Swann, & Goldsmith, 2013; Plomin, Owen, & McGuffin, 1994). Parents may encourage their children to play with other children or alternatively they may restrict children's social exposure. Thus, we're not born wild or shy; instead, we're born with certain tendencies that our environments may or may not promote. The same principle holds with children's intellectual talents. Virtually all children obtain ample complexity in their child rearing to develop strong abilities, yet some children receive more enrichment than others and, as a result, achieve a comparatively large vocabulary, effective memory strategies, and sophisticated reasoning skills (Plomin, DeFries, Knopik, & Neiderhiser, 2016).

Second, *gene–environment interactions* occur when certain environments affect children selectively, based on the particular genes they have. For example, some children grow up in a harsh and abusive family setting but do not exhibit problematic behaviors themselves, possibly because they have healthy genes for regulating their mood. Children who are maltreated and lacking in healthy genes are prone to **antisocial behavior**, actions they intentionally perform to hurt others and show their defiance. One gene, monoamine oxidase A (MAOA), which exists on the arm of an X chromosome, appears to be especially important. Most children have a long sequence of DNA in their MAOA gene, but a few have short versions. Those with long versions are able to maintain good brain chemistry; those with the short version are susceptible to depression and aggression. Among children who have been abused or neglected by their parents, those with the short version of MAOA are far more likely to develop negative outcomes than are those with the longer form of the gene (Caspi et al., 2002; Kim-Cohen et al., 2006).

Third, in *gene–environment alignment*, the child's family and other agents in the environment offer personalized training according to the child's genetically empowered talents and dispositions. There are three specific methods by which the child's setting converges with his or her genetic tendencies (Kovas, Tikhomirova, Selita, Tosto, & Malykh, 2016; Plomin, DeFries, & Loehlin, 1977):

- In a *passive gene–environment correlation,* the parent passes on genes that foster a particular talent or disposition. The parent, by virtue of his or her own interests and inclinations, engages the child in experiences that nurture relevant characteristics. A mathematically gifted mother may have a young son who is developing efficient brain circuits for processing numerical patterns and learns a lot from doing number puzzles.
- In an *evocative reaction,* the child develops an appearance, style of behavior, or other characteristic that affects how other people respond to him or her. A little boy with a contagious smile and sunny personality is likely to rouse warm regard from parents and teachers. Conversely, a little girl who is irritable and combative tends to provoke punitive and coercive responses from adults.
- In an *active gene–environment correlation,* the child has inherited a characteristic that affects his or her initiative in various situations. As children grow, they become progressively capable of altering their surroundings to achieve their needs. A girl with an exceptional talent in music may request clarinet lessons and join the high school band. This process is called **niche construction** and is thought to become increasingly prevalent during middle childhood and adolescence (E. G. Flynn, Laland, Kendal, & Kendal, 2013; Saltz & Nuzhdin, 2014; T. Ward & Durrant, 2011).

It should now be clear that genes do not dictate appearance, behavior, or even cell functioning in any simple way. Genes operate in concert with one another; are affected by nutrition, stress, and other environmental agents and experiences; and are galvanized by hormones, physiological circumstances, and children's own behavior. Furthermore, individual genes are apt to influence development during particular age ranges. Occasionally, characteristics emerge that *seem* to come "from nowhere," having been dormant for many years before being brought into play.

Problems in Genetic Instructions

Sometimes errors occur in genetic instructions, with resulting exceptionalities in one or more areas of growth (see Table 4.1). There are five primary ways by which genes create risks for the child's health.

Chromosomal Abnormality. A child with a *chromosomal abnormality* has an extra chromosome, a missing one, or a wrongly formed chromosome. Because each chromosome holds thousands of genes, a child with a chromosomal abnormality has many affected characteristics, causing major physical and cognitive problems. Chromosomal abnormalities occur when chromosomes divide unevenly during meiosis. Errors can also occur *after* meiosis, if the zygote's cells divide unevenly, such that the zygote has some cells with normal chromosomes and others with abnormal chromosomes. Chromosomal abnormalities are triggered by a variety of factors, including a parent's exposure to viruses, radiation, toxins, or drugs.

Chromosomal abnormalities occur in about 1 in 150 births (March of Dimes, 2013). One abnormality, the presence of an extra 21st chromosome or piece of one, causes *Down syndrome.* Children with Down syndrome show delays in mental growth and are susceptible to heart defects and other health problems. You can watch a Video Explanation about the special medical needs of children with Down syndrome. The severity of disabilities caused by Down syndrome and many other chromosomal abnormalities varies from one affected child to the next. Children with Down syndrome have many personal strengths, as you learned from Maria in our opening case study. Educational strategies and medical treatments have improved considerably in recent years, such that life expectancy has increased to nearly 60 years. A growing number of young people with Down syndrome are earning their high school diplomas, attending college, holding down jobs, and living independently (Prows et al., 2013).

MyLab Education
Video Explanation 4.2
This video discusses the characteristics of children with Down syndrome.

Single-Gene Defects. A child occasionally inherits an error on one of his genes from one or both parents. Children can have an error on a dominant gene on one of the 22 paired chromosomes, a recessive defect on both chromosomes in one of the 22 matched pairs, or an anomaly on a recessive gene on the single X chromosome for boys or a problem on a gene on both X chromosomes for girls. Resulting physical problems tend to be

Table 4.1 Prevalent Chromosomal and Genetic Disorders in Children

DISORDER	INCIDENCE	CHARACTERISTICS
Chromosomal Abnormalities		
Down syndrome	1 per 700 births	Children with an extra 21st chromosome or part of one develop distinctively shaped eyes, a protruding tongue, thick lips, flat nose, short neck, wide gaps between toes, short fingers, risk for heart problems and hearing loss, intellectual disability, good visual discrimination, and delays in speech.
Klinefelter syndrome	1 per 500–1,000 boys	Boys have one Y chromosome and two or more X chromosomes and tend to have long legs, modest breast tissue, and lower-than-average verbal ability. Diagnosis may not occur until adolescence when testes fail to enlarge.
Turner syndrome	1 per 2,500–5,000 girls	Girls have one X chromosome. Affected girls have broad chests, webbed necks, short stature, health problems, normal verbal ability but lower-than-average visual and spatial abilities, and difficulty in making friends.
Prader-Willi syndrome	1 per 10,000–25,000 births	Children are missing a segment of chromosome 15 from the father and tend to become obese, have an intellectual disability, develop small hands and feet, become short in stature, and exhibit maladaptive behaviors such as throwing temper tantrums, picking at their skin, eating excessively, and consuming unappealing substances (e.g., dirt).
Angelman syndrome	1 per 10,000–30,000 births	A deletion of a segment on chromosome 15 is inherited from the mother and causes children to develop an intellectual disability and small head and to exhibit seizures, jerky movements, and unusual, recurrent bouts of laughter not associated with happiness.
Single-Gene Defects		
Neurofibromatosis	Mild form occurs in 1 per 2,500–4,000 births; severe form occurs in 1 per 40,000–50,000 births	Children develop tumors in the central nervous system and may exhibit learning disabilities or a significant intellectual disability. Most individuals experience only minor symptoms, such as having colored, elevated spots on their skin.
Huntington disease (HD)	3–7 per 100,000 births	Children develop a disorder of the central nervous system typically by age 35 to 45, sometimes much earlier or later. A protein destroys brain cells, causing irritability, clumsiness, depression, and forgetfulness, and eventually may result in loss of motor control, slurred speech, and mental disturbances.
Phenylketonuria (PKU)	1 per 15,000 births, with rates highest in people of Celtic origin (e.g., from Ireland and Scotland)	Children are at risk for developing an intellectual disability, eczema, seizures, motor problems, aggression, self-mutilation, and impulsivity. Children's livers cannot produce an enzyme necessary for breaking down phenylalanine (an amino acid), which accumulates and becomes toxic to the brain.
Sickle cell disease	1 per 500–600 children of African lineage; rates are also elevated in Mediterranean descendants	Beginning age 1 or 2 children develop blood cells that are rigid and can't pass through small blood vessels and may experience pain, stroke, infection, tissue damage, and fatigue.
Cystic fibrosis (CF)	1 per 3,300 children from European backgrounds and 1 per 9,500 children from Hispanic backgrounds	Children develop glands that produce thick, sticky mucus that creates serious problems with breathing and digestion. Usually beginning in infancy, children exhibit persistent coughing, wheezing, pneumonia, and a big appetite with little weight gain. Many individuals with CF now live well into their 40s.
Tay-Sachs disease	1 per 2,500–3,600 children among Ashkenazi Jews (of Eastern European ancestry)	Children develop a fatal, degenerative condition of the central nervous system because they lack an enzyme required to break down a fatty substance in brain cells. At about 6 months of age, children decelerate in growth, lose vision, and develop an abnormal startle response and convulsions. Children develop an intellectual disability, lose the ability to move, and die by age 3 or 4.
Thalassemia (Cooley's anemia)	1 in 800–2,500 individuals of Greek or Italian descent in the United States; rates are lower in other groups	Children develop blood cells that do not transmit oxygen effectively and as a result become pale, fatigued, and irritable within their first 2 years of life and may also develop feeding problems, diarrhea, enlargement of the spleen and heart, infection, and unusual facial features and bone structures and may die by early adulthood.

(continued)

Table 4.1 Prevalent Chromosomal and Genetic Disorders in Children (*Continued*)

DISORDER	INCIDENCE	CHARACTERISTICS
Duchenne muscular dystrophy	1 per 3,000–4,000 boys	Boys develop a progressive muscular weakness because of the absence of a protein needed by muscle cells. Between ages 2 and 5, they stumble and walk on their toes. Between 8 and 14 they may stop walking and eventually die from respiratory and cardiac problems.

Sources: Austeng et al. (2013); J. W. Ball et al. (2010); Blachford (2002); Burns, Brady, Dunn, and Starr (2000); Cody and Kamphaus (1999); Dykens and Cassidy (1999); Hazlett, Gaspar De Alba, and Hooper (2011); Jorde et al. (2010); Lepage, Dunkin, Hong, and Reiss (2013); Massimini (2000); J. L. Miller, Lynn, Shuster, and Driscoll (2013); S. Mills and Black (2014); K. L. Moore et al. (2013); Nilsson and Bradford (1999); M. P. Powell and Schulte (1999); Prows, Hopkin, Barnoy, and Van Riper (2013); Riehle-Colarusso and Oster (2016); J. T. Smith (1999); Waisbren and Antshel (2013); and Wynbrandt and Ludman (2000).

more contained than the encompassing disorders caused by chromosomal abnormalities. Nonetheless, some single-gene defects are quite serious. The usual pattern of inheritance is that children who inherit a dominant-gene defect show the problem. Those who inherit a recessive-gene defect show the problem only if both genes in the allele pair are defective (transmission is slightly different in X-chromosome-linked defects).

A few conditions are mild or severe depending on the particular sequence of chemical compounds on the gene. An example is *fragile X syndrome*, which results from a genetic defect on the X chromosome. When this defect is small and limited, people who carry the problem gene are able to produce some of the necessary protein and as a result show no symptoms or only mild learning disabilities. The defect can intensify as it is passed from one generation to the next and lead to full-blown fragile X syndrome (Narayanan & Warren, 2006). Children with this condition develop severe learning disabilities, emotional problems, communication limitations, and intellectual disabilities (Hagerman & Lampe, 1999; McDuffie, Thurman, Channell, & Abbeduto, 2017; Rague, Caravella, Tonnsen, Klusek, & Roberts, 2018). Children tend to have prominent ears, long faces, double-jointed thumbs, and flat feet, and they are prone to sinus and ear infections. They also tend to be socially anxious, sensitive to touch and noise, and inclined to avoid eye contact and repeat certain activities over and over (e.g., spinning objects, waving their arms, and saying a particular phrase). The problems girls with fragile X syndrome face are generally less serious than those of boys because girls have a second X chromosome that is usually healthy enough to produce the missing protein.

Mitochondrial Errors. The DNA we have examined thus far resides in the center, called the *nucleus*, of the cell. There is another specialized type of DNA that exists in the center and in the periphery of the cell and is responsible for breaking down fat, proteins, and carbohydrates and in creating energy, maintaining organ function (e.g., in the nervous systems, gastrointestinal tract, and heart), and cleaning up toxic substances in the body. Mitochondrial DNA is passed on from the mother and exists in nearly all cells in the body. Because mitochondrial DNA fulfills so many purposes, malformations can trigger brain seizures, developmental delays, migraine headaches, muscle weakness, exercise intolerance, visual impairment, hearing loss, autism, and diabetes mellitus (Distelmaier et al., 2015; Goh, Dong, Zhang, DiMauro, & Peterson, 2014; Langwinska-Wosko, Skowronska, Kmiec, & Czlonkowska, 2016; Marin & Saneto, 2016; Miyauchi et al., 2018).

Multifactorial Problems. We have explained that many complex physical and psychological traits are the result of a cluster of separate genes interacting with substances and experiences that originate in the environment. A range of physical problems occur because of a multifactorial process. *Spina bifida* (in which the spinal cord is malformed) and *cleft palate* (in which a split develops in the roof of the mouth) are examples of such conditions, which tend to run in some families but do not typically follow simple patterns of genetic transmission. Instead, affected children have gen es that make them susceptible to particular risks, such as their mother's vitamin deficiency (especially, the shortage of folic acid, a B vitamin), illness, or medications such as anticonvulsant drugs taken by their mother while pregnant (J. W. Ball et al., 2010; K. L. Moore et al., 2013; Wallingford, Niswander, Shaw, & Finnell, 2013). Although such conditions are permanent, the child can lead a happy and productive life. In cases in which the child has multiple disabilities and exceptionalities, each of the conditions needs to be considered.

Epigenetic Changes. A child's DNA does not change over the life span, but the activity of genes can change. **Epigenetic changes** refer to long-lasting modifications on switches that turn genes on and off. Changes to the activation of genes are generated by a wide range of circumstances, including those related to nutrition, exercise, sleep, stress, caregiving, and exposure to toxins. The effects can be strong and accumulate across the life span. Earlier we used maltreatment as an illustration of interactive effects between genes and environment. Stressful early childhood experiences, including family maltreatment, also reveal epigenetic effects. When children are neglected or abused by parents, they undergo epigenetic changes in the immune system, for example, in turning off receptors in the brain and blood cells that respond to stress hormones. With a muted ability to sense stress, the body stops putting a brake on anxious reactions. The child remains in constant worry, which puts him or her at risk for risk for runaway inflammatory processes and depression, alcohol and drug abuse, diabetes, heart disease, and high-risk behaviors (G. H. Brody, Yu, & Beach, 2016; Cicchetti, Hetzel, Rogosch, Handley, & Toth, 2016; D. Mehta et al., 2013; Naumova et al., 2016; Romens, McDonald, Svaren, & Pollak, 2015).

MyLab Education
Video Example 4.1

Find Developmental Meaning *How did Abigail's parents learn to meet her needs?* Notice the expectations that Abigail's parents adjusted as she grew.

Acknowledging Nature and Nurture in Children's Lives

Genetics may appear far removed from the responsibilities of teachers. Yet one reality of working in a busy classroom is finding that children learn and react differently, variations that exist in part because of heredity. At the same time, evidence of strong environmental influences inspires optimism in our ability to make a difference for children. We offer the following recommendations:

- **Celebrate the natural variation that exists in a classroom.** Teachers who value a multitude of physical characteristics, personality types, and talents are apt to put youngsters at ease. Children who are tall and short, chubby and thin, coordinated and clumsy, shy and outgoing, and calm and irritable all have a rightful place in the hearts of adults who educate them. Thus, the first step in accommodating children's genetic profiles is to keep an open mind about the wondrous diversity that exists among children.

- **Learn about serious genetic problems affecting children in your care.** All children benefit from individualized care, but those with chromosomal abnormalities, single-gene defects, and other genetic conditions can require carefully designed interventions to achieve their potential. Finding out about the genetic condition is important, as is an assessment of the child's potential. Given what you have learned about genetic foundations, you will realize that general information about a genetic condition alone does not reliably predict the child's future because what's in store depends on the child's other genes, family relationships, health, activity, and other factors.

- **Be mindful of your own reactions to challenging characteristics.** Evidence suggests that parents adapt their caregiving styles to individual children's temperaments (Deater-Deckard, 2009; Pener-Tessler et al., 2013). Those with mild temperaments and good self-control elicit calm reactions from parents, whereas others who are irritable are likely to push parents' buttons. This same reactivity may also occur with adults outside the family as they also are likely to respond to children's congeniality or prickliness. Consequently, teachers and other professionals must try to remain calm when interacting with oppositional children (Keogh, 2003; Rudasill, Pössel, Winkeljohn Black, & Niehaus, 2014).

- **Modify instruction to meet the needs of children with certain conditions.** Some techniques have broad relevance to children with numerous different genetic conditions. For example, children with several distinct genetic disorders have trouble paying attention and thus benefit from strategies that strengthen their concentration (C. Reilly, 2012). In other respects genetic conditions can be sufficiently distinct to require their own treatment plans. Children with *Prader-Willi syndrome* are obsessed with food and eating. With these students, special educators may need to restrict access to between-meal snacks at school and ensure physical activity (C. Reilly, 2012). With children who have one of the *autism spectrum disorders*, a group of disabilities in

Preparing for Your Licensure Examination

Your teaching test might ask you about the educational rights of students with exceptional learning needs.

language, communication, repetitive behaviors, and delays in cognitive skills, experts advise interventions that promote joint attention, social skills, and academic proficiencies (Blumberg et al., 2016; C. Bond et al., 2016). When you take on school responsibilities, you may participate in an *Individualized Education Plan* (IEP), a process by which the classroom teacher, other professionals, and parents determine the child's abilities, academic goals for the year, accommodations for helping him or her succeed, and methods for assessing progress. This process is used in the United States, and similar arrangements are implemented in other countries.

MyLab Education Self-Check 4.1

MyLab Education Application Exercise 4.1
Meet Individual Needs

Practice identifying the needs of Star, a girl whose genetic disorder affects her learning.

- **Adjust the curriculum.** In **universal design**, teachers compare the needs of individual learners with the demands of the curriculum and make three kinds of adjustments (T. E. Hall, Meyer, & Rose, 2012). First, teachers present concepts through multiple means of representation, including definitions of vocabulary, written summaries of main ideas, pictures and diagrams, and audio- or video-recorded documentaries and stories. Second, teachers ask children to conduct an activity that demonstrates their knowledge, for example, in writing an essay about characters in a story, providing a verbal explanation for patterns in a graph, or giving an oral presentation on a topic. Third, teachers engage children with choices, such as presenting a variety of nonfiction books from which to select, encouraging students to make meaningful connections to personal interests, and assigning active roles in small group discussions. Universal design is a valuable framework because of its explicit accommodations of a range of learning needs such that *all* children become able to achieve high academic standards.

- **Notice which individuals struggle.** There is an extended window of time for most types of learning, but we cannot leave it to chance that delayed children will catch up on their own. Basic intellectual, social, and emotional skills affect many aspects of life, making it important to offer extra guidance when progress in any of these domains is unusually slow. Furthermore, without appropriate intervention, children who straggle behind peers may come to doubt their capability for learning, leading to even more serious problems, such as dropping out of school. Children with special needs will typically be assigned to a team of experts whom the classroom teacher can consult on learning goals and strategies.

MyLab Education Application Exercise 4.2
Identify Development-Enhancing Education

In this video several educational professionals talk about their goals and services for Star, a girl with a genetic disorder.

- **Customize interventions based on genetic tendencies.** When educators and other practitioners are sensitive to individual children's talents, temperaments, and deficits, they alter their guidance to accommodate these characteristics. Adults do not ignore or overpower children's heredity; instead, they recognize and work with it. For example, children who are predisposed to be distractible or irritable can, with guidance, acquire productive ways of staying on task and dealing with frustration (Beauchaine et al., 2013; Reiss, 2005; A. E. West & Weinstein, 2012).

- **Encourage children to make growth-promoting choices.** Especially as they grow older, youngsters actively seek out experiences that allow them to exercise their natural tendencies. Adults can present options for cultivating youngsters' talents and remediating any pronounced weaknesses. For instance, a socially outgoing boy with an excessive amount of energy and little self-control often interrupts lessons. His teachers may give him opportunities to express his opinion as well as remind him on other occasions to give others a chance to speak.

Summary

All children have genetic instructions that guide their development beginning at fertilization, through prenatal development, and after birth and into old age. Most of the genes that children inherit are shared with others, giving them a common human heritage. Additional genes contribute to children's individuality in appearance, health, and behavior. Shared and individual genes exert their effects on children through interactive processes in cells and throughout the systems of the body. Children's health, physiological processes, and experiences partly determine genetic expression. Teachers and other professionals can keep in mind that all children have genetically based characteristics that make certain kinds of relationships, behaviors, and accomplishments relatively easy or difficult. A variety of genetic abnormalities and conditions must be considered by practitioners if children are to achieve their potential. In most characteristics, such as height and weight, susceptibility to health problems, and temperament and personality, many separate genes each contribute a small amount to their manifestation. Children's intelligence, health, personality, and other personal features are also strongly affected by relationships, nutrition, experience, and additional factors in the environment. Thus, teachers and other caregivers often address genetically mediated traits and express their confidence in children's natural tendencies and capacity to achieve high personal standards.

Prenatal Development

4.2 Characterize the phases of prenatal growth and the qualities of effective practices for protecting rapidly growing offspring and their expectant parents.

After the union of sperm and ovum, the organism grows, one step at a time, with pregnancy typically lasting around 280 days or 40 weeks after the first day of the mother's last menstrual cycle. During **prenatal development**, the period of growth between fertilization and birth, a simple, single cell is transformed, step by step, into a complex human being. During this remarkable interlude, the developing organism is nurtured within the mother's uterus, a cushioned home that provides nutrition, expels waste, and allows space for movement, exposure to flavors in the mother's diet, and muffled sounds of her voice.

Phases of Prenatal Growth

The developing baby-to-be must accomplish several important tasks, including growing new cells, moving through the mother's body, settling into the interior wall of the mother's uterus, forming and refining basic body structures, and activating rudimentary learning abilities. Following *fertilization*, the offspring accomplishes these tasks over the periods of the *zygote*, *embryo*, and *fetus* (see Figure 4.4).

Development of the Zygote

During the middle of a woman's menstrual cycle, an *ovum* (female gamete) emerges from one of her two *ovaries*. The ovum enters the adjacent *fallopian tube*, a narrow

FIGURE 4.4 Miracles of prenatal growth.

Human prenatal development begins at fertilization (top left) and then progresses through the periods of the zygote (top right), embryo (bottom left), and fetus (bottom right).

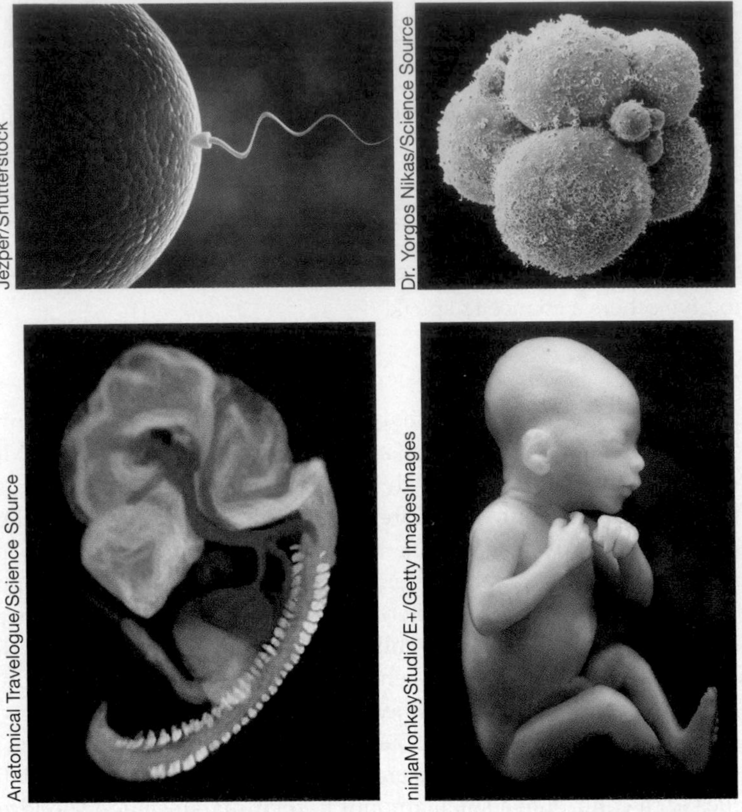

and curved pipe that connects the ovary to the uterus. The ovum is guided toward the uterus by pliant fringes in the fallopian tube. When a man ejaculates during sexual intercourse, he releases 200 to 600 million sperm into the woman's vagina, with about 200 finding their way into the uterus and all the way through the fallopian tube (K. L. Moore et al., 2013). When fertilization takes place, a single sperm attaches to, and enters, the ovum (Figure 4.5). The ovum cooperates by rearranging its exterior layers so that no other sperm can enter. The ovum and sperm combine their chromosomes, and the *zygote*, a new being, is formed.

The zygote creates additional cells as it travels downward through the fallopian tube and toward the uterus. Mitosis begins while the zygote is still moving. The first cell separates into two cells, these two cells divide to make four cells, four split into eight, and by the time the zygote has 16 cells, it is entering the uterus. Cells align themselves as the exterior lining of a sphere. Now about a week old, the zygote attaches itself to the inside wall of the uterus. The zygote separates into two parts, one a tiny being that will develop further into an embryo, and the other the *placenta*, the spongy structure in the uterus that provides nourishment. Cells begin to specialize and merge with other similar cells to form distinct structures, such as the nervous system and brain. The implanted zygote releases hormones, telling the ovaries that a conception has occurred and that menstruation should be prevented. In 2 short weeks, the new offspring has initiated its own growth, taken a journey, and found a hospitable home.

Development of the Embryo

The period of the **embryo** extends from 2 through 8 weeks after fertilization. Tasks of the embryonic period are to instigate life-support systems and form basic body structures. The placenta becomes larger, stronger, and more elaborate as it goes about its job of supplying food, liquid, and oxygen; removing wastes; and secreting hormones that sustain the pregnancy. An *umbilical cord* forms and connects the embryo to the placenta.

FIGURE 4.5 Fertilization and the zygote.

(a) Sperm are deposited in the vagina and make their way into the uterus and Fallopian tubes. One sperm enters the ovum and releases its chromosomes; *fertilization* occurs. (b) The fertilized egg (1), now called the *zygote*, begins its journey in the fallopian tube as it (2) fuses its two sets of chromosomes into one nucleus. About 30 hours after fertilization, the organism starts to grow through cell division (3), first slowly and then rapidly until the zygote resembles a ball of tiny cells (4, 5, and 6). Cells adhere to one another, leaving room for a fluid-filled cavity that provides space for growth, extension outward for emerging appendages, and formation of the placenta. The zygote enters the uterus (7) and implants in the uterine wall (8) where, conditions permitting, it will grow for 9 months and be born.

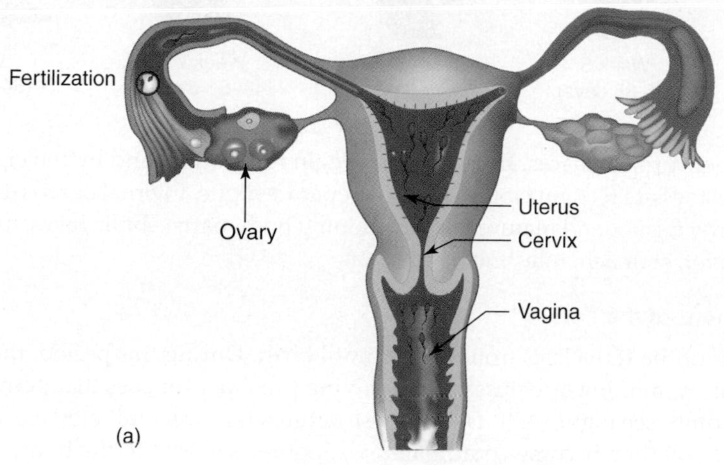

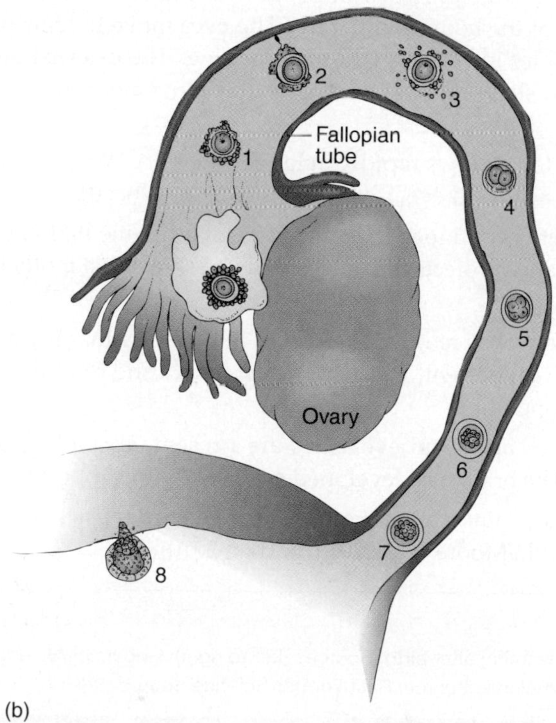

The embryo itself undergoes rapid structural transformation and enlargement. During prenatal development, growth occurs from top to bottom (head first, feet last) and from inside to outside (torso before limbs, arms and legs before hands and feet). Consistent with these trends, the head and heart are among the first structures to develop (see Figure 4.6). The growth of the neural tube that will give rise to the brain and spinal cord is under way. Neurons—the cells that form connections in the brain—emerge and

FIGURE 4.6 Development of the embryo.

In 4 short weeks, the prenatal being is transformed from a simple structure into a formation that is recognizably human.

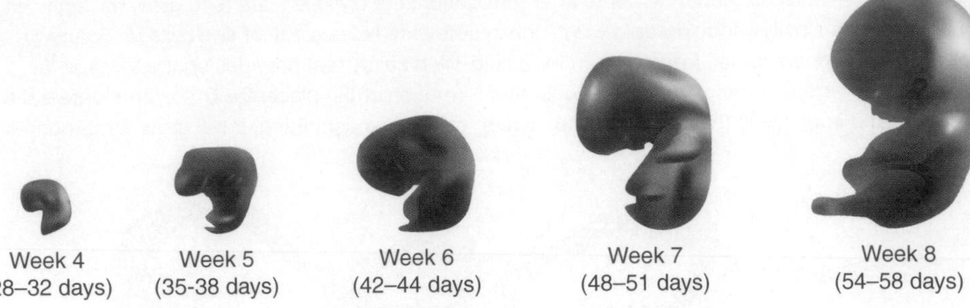

move to their proper places. Buds of limbs begin to develop, and by the eighth week, fingers and toes are recognizably distinct as separate digits. Internal organs differentiate out of nearby tissues and mature into functioning body parts—brain, eyes, lungs, heart, kidneys, liver, stomach, intestines, and so on.

Development of the Fetus

The period of the **fetus** lasts from week 9 until birth. During this period, the offspring grows rapidly, refining structures and receiving finishing touches that permit life outside the womb (see Figure 4.7). The many structures that were initiated earlier are now expanded, and they become coordinated with other systems in the body. The fetus's body is elaborated through a series of changes:

- *Third month*—the head is large in comparison to the rest of the body and now allows other parts of the body to catch up. The eyes move to their proper places, and the fetus becomes increasingly human looking. The external genitalia grow. The fetus begins to show reflexes and muscular movement. A few mothers feel these movements.
- *Fourth month*—the fetus grows rapidly in length (height). Weight increases slowly. Hair grows on the head and eyebrows. Eye movements occur.
- *Fifth month*—the fetus continues to increase in length. Fine hair covers the body, and a greasy substance protects the fetus's delicate skin. Most mothers can feel the fetus's movement by now.
- *Sixth month*—the fetus has red, wrinkled skin and a body that is lean but gaining weight. Fingernails are present. The respiratory system and central nervous system synchronize their operations.
- *Seventh month*—eyes open and eyelashes are present. Toenails grow. The body begins to fill out. The brain has developed sufficiently to support breathing.
- *Eighth month*—skin is pink and smooth. Fat grows under the skin. The testes (in males) descend. (K. L. Moore et al., 2013; Sadler, 2010)

FIGURE 4.7 Development of the fetus.

During the period from 9 to 36 weeks, the fetus prepares for life and learning after birth. Sources (left to right): Dopamine/Science Source; Claude Edelmann/Science Source; Neil Bromhal/Photo Researchers/Science Source; Petit Format/Science Source

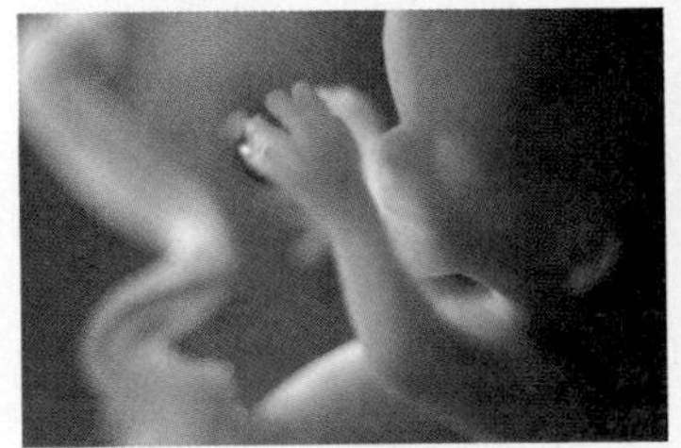

9–12 weeks

13–18 weeks

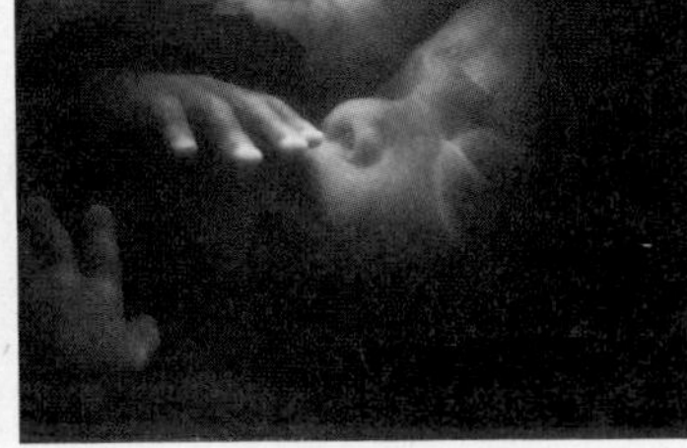

19–24 weeks

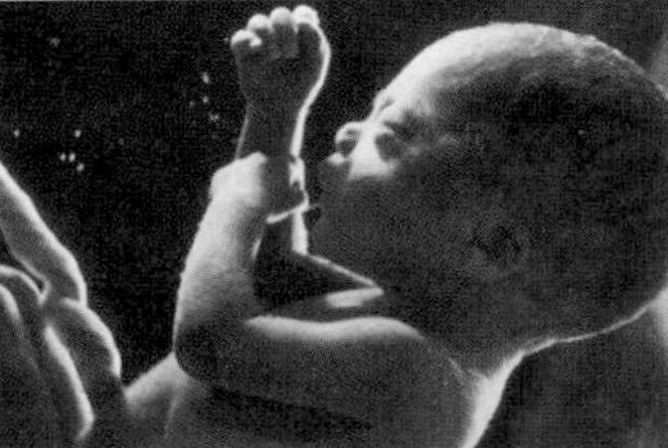

25–36 weeks

During the final weeks of prenatal development, the fetus finishes its basic body structures and puts on weight, steadily as birth approaches. On average, the fetus at 6 months of prenatal growth weighs approximately 1 pound 13 ounces; at 7 months, 2 pounds 14 ounces; at 8 months, 4 pounds 10 ounces; and at 9 months, 2 weeks (full term), 7 pounds 8 ounces (K. L. Moore et al., 2013). These last few weeks of weight gain dramatically increase the chances of an infant's survival. In fact, infants rarely survive when they are born before 5½ months of prenatal growth or at weights of less than 1 pound 6 ounces.

The miraculous changes that occur during prenatal development result from a combination of factors. Cells grow, divide, and take on particular purposes depending on where they emerge in the brain and body, the structures that already exist there, and the chemical signals they encounter. With proper nutrition, protection from harmful substances, and healthy genes, the brain and the body gain the amazing physiological and neurological structures that allow human beings to talk, sing and dance, empathize with others, play the guitar, climb trees, and walk and run.

Activity is an important part of the fetus's growth, especially in the later stages of prenatal development. Initial movements are of the whole body, with the tiny fetus tumbling around in the womb. Movements gradually become smoother, smaller, and coordinated, for example, as the fetus opens its lips and puts its hand inside its mouth (Hepper, 2015). In the several weeks before birth, the baby responds to light, react to sounds, and even learns. In the womb, babies grow accustomed to recurrent flavors in their mother's diet, showing a preference after birth for familiar scents and tastes in breast milk. In investigations that have systematically exposed offspring to patterns in speech and music prenatally (e.g., by having mothers read certain stories aloud while resting), infants show that they recognize passages after birth, recollections that are detected by changes in their heart rate (Hepper, 2015).

As you have seen, the formation of a human life is the outcome of many changes. Growth is carefully managed by nature, constantly drawing from nurture. In spectacular feats of coordination, new cells extend body parts and allow structures to become increasingly defined—for example, with simple paddles turning into elongated arms, arms adding hands, and hands sprouting fingers. Genetic expression and prenatal development show wonderful balances between nature and nurture, universality and diversity, and qualitative and quantitative change, as you can read more about in the Basic Developmental Issues table "Biological Beginnings."

BASIC DEVELOPMENTAL ISSUES
Biological Beginnings

ISSUE	GENETIC FOUNDATIONS	PRENATAL DEVELOPMENT
Nature and Nurture	Nature forms sperm and ova and fuses them as a new organism with a unique genetic makeup. Nurture is evident in environmental effects on parents' chromosomes, as when radiation destroys reproductive cells. During prenatal development, nature and nurture work in concert: Particular genes are activated according to the organism's maturation and health.	Nature and nurture are closely intertwined during prenatal development. The effects of nature are evident in ordered changes to body parts and in the formation and operation of supporting physical structures, such as the placenta. The effects of nurture are seen in nutrition, protection from harmful substances, and the mother's stress management.
Universality and Diversity	The vast majority of children are born with 46 chromosomes. Most genes are uniform instructions across children for building bodies and brains. Some genes vary systematically across children and permit individual differences in height, weight, physical appearance, motor skills, health, intellectual abilities, and temperament. Errors in chromosomes and genes are another source of diversity.	In healthy organisms, phases of the zygote, embryo, and fetus occur universally and culminate in a birth after approximately 9 months. Diversity occurs because of variations in mothers' health, the genetic vulnerability of the fetus, the efficiency with which physical structures in the womb sustain life, and exposure to or protection from harmful substances.
Qualitative and Quantitative Change	Qualitative changes are made possible by the careful sequence with which particular genes are triggered. At appropriate times, selected genes spring into action and create qualitative changes in the child's body, including the makeover of puberty. As genes direct the body to mature, they also permit quantitative changes, including steady increases in height and weight.	Future baby undergoes qualitative transformations. As a zygote it travels through the fallopian tube, produces cells, and burrows into the uterus. As an embryo it forms basic structures of the body. As a fetus it refines body parts and activates breathing and reflexes. Quantitative changes are evident in production of new cells in brain and body throughout prenatal development and prior to birth.

Medical Care

Prospective parents invariably hope for healthy children. To enhance their chances of giving birth to strong, well-formed infants, prospective mothers and fathers can look after themselves and follow medical advice.

Preparing for Pregnancy

A woman can increase her chances of having a healthy infant by caring for herself *before* becoming pregnant. Physicians, midwives, and nurses may suggest to a woman hoping to conceive that she watch her diet, take approved vitamin supplements, exercise moderately, and avoid alcohol and drugs. Medical experts will review her prescriptions and over-the-counter medicines because some are harmful to embryos and fetuses. For example, the acne medication Isotretinoin appears to cause serious malformations in offspring (M. R. Davidson, London, & Ladewig, 2008; Organization of Teratology Information Specialists [OTIS], 2013a). Medical personnel may also address existing health problems that can become complicated during a pregnancy, such as hypertension or diabetes. Finally, physicians and nurses may discuss any concerns related to the woman's age. Pregnant women younger than 17 sometimes have poor nutrition and give birth to infants with low birth weight. Advanced age in mothers and fathers (35 or older for mothers, 40 or older for fathers) is associated with slightly elevated risks for genetic problems, and older mothers are at minor risk for complications during the pregnancy and for giving birth to a baby with a physical malformation (M. R. Davidson et al., 2008; D. Vaughan, Cleary, & Murphy, 2014).

The responsibility for avoiding toxic substances must not rest entirely on mothers-to-be. Prospective fathers, too, should take precautions in the days, weeks, and months before conceiving a child. Evidence is growing that men's exposure to mercury, lead, alcohol, cigarettes, and other substances is associated with miscarriage (spontaneous loss of the offspring), low birth weight, and birth defects in their offspring (Engeland et al., 2013; Sadler, 2010). The expectant father's prior exposure to toxic substances is also associated with birth defects in offspring (Desrosiers et al., 2012).

A man and a woman concerned about conceiving a child with significant problems may consult a genetic counselor. The genetic counselor examines the couple's medical records and those of siblings, parents, and other biological relatives. Diagnostic tests may be conducted, including an analysis of potential parents' chromosomes. Genetic counselors inform the couple of medical facts, inheritance patterns, risks for having a child with a birth defect, and ways to deal with risks. Counselors may recommend that prenatal diagnostic tests be conducted during a pregnancy and refer parents for counseling should they want it.

Avoiding Harmful Substances

During prenatal development, some babies-to-be are unfortunately exposed to harmful chemicals, or **teratogens**. Examples of teratogens include many prescription and nonprescription drugs; alcohol; infectious agents such as rubella, syphilis, and human immunodeficiency virus (HIV); and dangerous environmental chemicals, including lead and polychlorinated biphenyls.

Prenatal development includes a series of *sensitive periods* for forming physical structures. Body parts are especially vulnerable when they are first emerging, growing speedily, and laying the foundation for more refined extensions. Thus, the timing of exposure to teratogens partly determines their impact. A newly formed *zygote* has not yet begun to form separate body parts and tends not to sustain structural defects when exposed to teratogens. Occasionally, exposure to teratogens can cause death of the zygote, yet perhaps more often, a few cells will die or become damaged, with these cells being replaced with healthy cells (K. L. Moore et al., 2013). For the *embryo*, damage can be serious. The principal parts of the body, including the limbs and the internal organs, are formed during this phase, and exposure to drugs, alcohol, and other teratogens can cause major problems. Limbs are particularly sensitive to harm 24 to 36 days after conception. During this early phase of pregnancy, women may not yet know they are pregnant. As a general rule, the *fetus* is less susceptible to serious structural damage, although there are many exceptions: Notably, the brain continues to grow until (and after) birth, and as a result, it is susceptible to damage late in pregnancy and during infancy.

The genetic makeup of both mother and baby moderates the effects of teratogens. For example, phenytoin is an anticonvulsant medication prescribed for some people who have epilepsy. Between 5% and 10% of children exposed to phenytoin as embryos develop a small brain, an intellectual disability, wide spaces between eyes, a short nose, and other distinctive facial features (K. L. Moore & Persaud, 2008). About a third of exposed embryos show minor congenital problems, and approximately half are unaffected. Presumably, genetic factors are at least partly responsible for these different outcomes.

The amount of exposure is also influential. The greater the exposure, the more severe and widespread the effects. Clearly, women who are pregnant must exercise caution in the food and substances they ingest and the toxins they are exposed to in the environment. In fact, this need for caution extends to all women who are sexually active and capable of being pregnant. Here are some examples of particular teratogens and their potential effects on offspring:

- *Alcohol*—women who drink alcohol excessively during pregnancy are prone to have infants with *fetal alcohol syndrome.* Cells in the brain are disrupted, physical development is delayed, facial abnormalities occur, intellectual disabilities are common, and children become impulsive and exhibit other behavioral problems. In less severe cases, children may develop learning disabilities and minor physical problems.
- *Nicotine*—women who smoke cigarettes are in danger of giving birth to small, lightweight babies and (less often) to losing their offspring through miscarriage.
- *Marijuana*—women who smoke marijuana regularly during pregnancy are at risk for giving birth to infants with low birth weight and attention problems.
- *Cocaine*—women using cocaine during pregnancy are likely to have a miscarriage, give birth prematurely, and have babies with low birth weight, small head size, lethargy, and irritability.
- *Methamphetamines*—babies exposed to methamphetamines may be born early, small, and light and have risks for problems in respiration, hearing, seeing, and learning.
- *Organic mercury*—pregnant women who ingest high levels of mercury from diets rich in fish are at risk for offspring with abnormal brains, intellectual disabilities, attention problems, and motor disabilities.
- *Rubella*—pregnant women who become infected with the virus rubella (also known as German or three-day measles) early in their pregnancy may give birth to children with cataracts, heart problems, and deafness.
- *Toxoplasmosis*—toxoplasmosis is an infection contracted by exposure to a parasite found in cat feces and undercooked infected meat. Infants who have been exposed prenatally to this condition may develop such problems as abnormal growth of the brain, heart, kidneys, or other internal organs, and they may have trouble seeing and hearing.
- *Herpes simplex*—pregnant women with the herpes simplex virus are vulnerable to having a miscarriage or giving birth prematurely to infants with physical problems.
- *HIV infection and AIDS*—unless treated medically, pregnant women with the HIV virus are in jeopardy of passing on the condition to their children, and children who become infected may show delays in motor skills, language, and cognitive development and ultimately develop more serious health impairments (Boucher et al., 2014; Buka, Cannon, Torrey, Yolken, & the Collaborative Study Group on the Perinatal Origins of Severe Psychiatric Disorders, 2008; M. R. Davidson et al., 2008; Gupta, Gupta, & Shirasaka, 2016; N. H. Hunt et al., 2017; K. S. Montgomery et al., 2008; OTIS, 2013b, 2013c, 2013d; Slotkin, 2008; C. B. Smith, Battin, Francis, & Jacobson, 2007; Tzilos, Hess, Kao, & Zlotnick, 2013).

Maternal anxiety can create problems for the fetus. Pregnant women who experience high levels of stress may develop complications and give birth to infants with low birth weight and short-tempered dispositions and later difficulties in focusing attention and dealing with negative emotions (Bekkhus, Rutter, Barker, & Borge, 2011; Guardino & Dunkel Schetter, 2014; Huizink, Mulder, & Buitelaar, 2004; Y. Lin et al., 2017; Wakeel, Wisk, Gee, Chao, & Witt, 2013; Zhang et al., 2018). Of course, most women experience some stress during their pregnancy, and mild emotional strain is probably harmless and may even help stimulate growth of the fetus's brain (DiPietro, 2004).

Implementing Medical Procedures

Several medical procedures are available for checking on the health of prenatal offspring. With requests from parents for diagnostic information, medical personnel schedule the tests for periods of pregnancy that yield accurate results.

Some permit only noninvasive tests, which do not involve probes or needles being inserted into the uterus. Examples of noninvasive tests include maternal blood samples and assessment of the relative size and structure of particular parts of the fetus's body from an ultrasound scan. The mother's age is also considered to identify risks for chromosomal abnormalities such as Down syndrome, spina bifida, and defects in the abdominal wall.

The *ultrasound examination* (also known as ultrasonography) has become a routine part of obstetric care for pregnant women in many countries. Ultrasound devices emit high-frequency sound waves that bounce off tissues in the fetus, typically after 6 to 7 weeks of prenatal development. The apparatus is passed over the woman's abdomen or inserted in her vagina. Echoes from the waves are converted into two-dimensional images and displayed on a television monitor, providing an image similar to Figure 4.8. Ultrasound examinations provide good estimates of the age of the fetus, detect multiple fetuses, and reveal major abnormalities. Ultrasounds are also used as anatomical guides during the implementation of other prenatal tests. No long-term risks to the fetus from an ultrasound test have been found, although the procedure is recommended only if necessary (American Pregnancy Association, 2013a). Images also confirm the reality of the pregnancy for expectant parents, as one father reported:

> Yes, when (she) got pregnant I didn't really understand it. But after we had the ultrasound I did.... It was the most exciting thing I have done as far as the baby is concerned. It was more exciting than when I heard that we were going to have a baby. (Ekelin, Crang-Svalenius, & Dykes, 2004, p. 337)

FIGURE 4.8 Image of fetus in an ultrasound scan.

The ultrasound image reveals information about the health of the baby for nurses and doctors and the reality of the developing offspring for parents. Source: Dr. Najeeb Layyous/Science Source

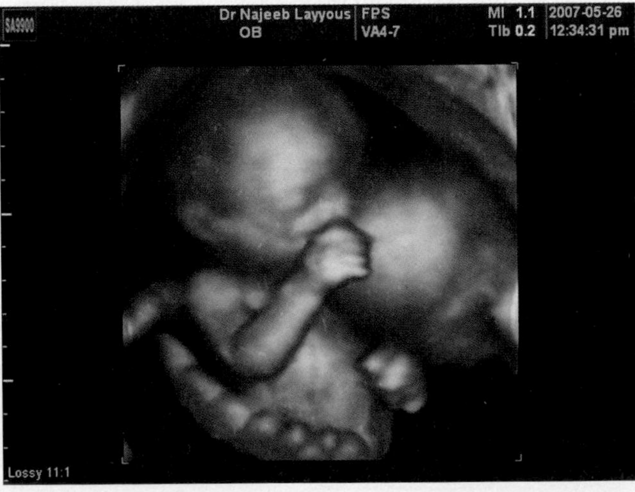

Several other prenatal diagnostic techniques are available but generally avoided except by women with high-risk pregnancies. *Chorionic villus sampling* (CVS) is an invasive diagnostic procedure performed between 10 and 12 weeks after conception (London, Ladewig, Ball, & Bindler, 2007). A needle is inserted into the woman's abdomen, or a tube is guided through her cervix, and tiny amounts of chorionic villi (blood vessels that grow on the membrane surrounding the developing fetus) are collected. Abnormalities detected by CVS include chromosomal abnormalities, X-chromosome-linked disorders such as Tay-Sachs disease, and some diseases of the blood, for example, sickle cell disease. Results are typically available within a few days. The procedure entails a small risk for damage to an arm or leg of the embryo or fetus, and miscarriage is possible but rare (Sadler, 2010).

Amniocentesis is an invasive diagnostic procedure usually performed between 14 and 20 weeks after conception. A needle is inserted into the woman's abdomen to draw a small amount of fluid from the uterus. The fluid is analyzed for high concentrations of a fetal protein present with *neural tube defects* and other anatomical problems. Fetal cells floating in the amniotic fluid are analyzed for possible chromosomal abnormalities. Other problems detected by amniocentesis are biochemical defects, prenatal infections, gene defects, chromosomal errors, and blood diseases. Results from cell cultures usually take 2 to 4 weeks to analyze. Risks associated with amniocentesis are trauma to the fetus, infection, and miscarriage (fetal loss rates are less than 1%; Sadler, 2010).

Medical researchers are now working on diagnostic tests that are not invasive and can instead be conducted with a simple blood test from the mother. Fetal cells are cast off and circulate in the mother outside the uterus and thus can be detected in the mother's bloodstream. Noninvasive blood tests can identify chromosomal and genetic defects in the fetus (Benn, 2016). Other tests are performed only as certain conditions are suspected. In consultation with the mother, a physician may use a *fetoscope*, an instrument with a tiny camera and light, to examine the fetus for defective limbs or other deformities. Corrective surgery is performed in rare circumstances.

When couples learn that their offspring has a chromosomal abnormality or other serious defect, they may be shocked initially and subsequently ask for support from counselors, medical personnel, and family and friends (Lalor, Begley, & Galavan, 2009; S. Thompson et al., 2015). Depending on their values and circumstances, some couples choose to terminate the pregnancy, concerned that they will not be able to care adequately for a child with special needs. Other couples want practical tips and emotional support in preparing for the birth of a child with a disability, believing in the fetus's right to life and their ability to care for the child.

When Adolescents Have Babies

Adolescent girls who find that they are pregnant must come to grips with the reality of their condition. Pregnant teenagers may worry about giving birth, having a child, finding financial resources to raise the child, getting along with or separating from their boyfriend, and breaking the news about the condition to parents and others (Hodgkinson, Beers, Southammakosane, & Lewin, 2014). These pressures can be overwhelming and trigger **anxiety**, an emotional ailment characterized by worry and apprehension, and **depression**, an ongoing condition characterized by sadness, discouragement, hopelessness, and, in children, irritability. Some pregnant girls decide to terminate the pregnancy, and others have miscarriages, in which they lose the embryo or fetus because of genetic abnormalities or their own drug use, illness, infection, or trauma (S. R. Wheeler & Austin, 2001).

In addition to confronting the parenting challenges that await them, pregnant teens ideally obtain medical care and persist with their education. The reality is that making prenatal visits is tough without insurance and transportation. Navigating the social climate at school can also be an ordeal when news of the pregnancy spreads. Prospective mothers must contend with unusual attention and disapproval from classmates and educators. Other students may make rude remarks about their sexuality or appearance. Required time for prenatal care, childbirth, and parenting the newborn baby can make it difficult to make up missed schoolwork. Because of these and other struggles, adolescent mothers are at risk for dropping out of school (Steinka-Fry, Wilson, & Tanner-Smith, 2013).

Educators and other practitioners can encourage pregnant teens to continue their education. In certain countries, pregnant students have educational rights that need to be respected. In the United States, Title IX of the Education Amendments of 1972 formalizes the rights of pregnant adolescent girls to attend regular courses; continue in extracurricular activities, such as sports or band; and be protected from harassment about the pregnancy (U.S. Department of Education Office of Civil Rights, 2013). Schools cannot discriminate against students after they have their baby; nor can they insist on parenting classes.

Supporting Parents, Protecting Babies

If you work with prospective parents, you may be able to advise them about how to protect their future child. Here are some tactics to take, should the opportunity arise:

- **Encourage women to evaluate their health *before* becoming pregnant.** Women who are planning a pregnancy or who are capable of becoming pregnant can consult with a physician, nurse, or midwife. Those who take over-the-counter or prescription medications can learn about risks to a pregnancy and alternative ways of managing chronic conditions. Expectant mothers can watch their diet carefully and, if medically warranted, take prenatal supplements. Those who have a sexually transmitted disease will be treated, which will prevent harm to the offspring. Others who have contracted an illness that is dangerous to an embryo or fetus, such as rubella, malaria, or the Zika virus, need to be monitored closely.

- **Remind sexually active students to take care of themselves.** Women may be several weeks along (or longer) in a pregnancy before they become aware of it. Consequently, young women who might be pregnant should watch their diet and restrict their exposure to teratogens, including alcohol, drugs, and certain prescriptions. Young men can be advised that they, too, put future children at risk by exposing themselves to harmful substances prior to the pregnancy.

- **Urge pregnant women to seek medical care.** Educators can help pregnant women overcome obstacles to seeing nurse practitioner, physician's assistant, or doctor. Logistically, accessing prenatal care can be challenging because of limitations with transportation, knowledge about medical risks, and health insurance. Prenatal care is valuable in detecting and treating problematic conditions in mothers and offspring. For example, pregnant women with HIV can be treated with antiretroviral therapy, helping control the infection and, in many cases, preventing transmission to offspring. Under the guidance of a doctor, some pregnant women begin or adjust an exercise program, which can help them maintain stamina, prepare for birth, and ease up on stress. Getting enough sleep is an important goal for pregnant women, even though it is difficult, especially when mothers have other children, jobs, and household responsibilities.

- **Sensitize prospective mothers to the growth within.** Unlike many developmental accomplishments, for instance, learning to talk, walk, and ride a bicycle, most aspects of prenatal development cannot be observed directly. Nevertheless, scientific evidence and the mother's firsthand experience provide benchmarks as to what is happening to baby-to-be. The Developmental Trends table "Phases of Prenatal Growth" provides a synopsis of the key progressions.

- **Use well-researched strategies when reaching out to young women.** Outreach can be effective if the right channels of communication are used. Public health officials who have talked with pregnant women have found that effective strategies include toll-free hotline numbers, radio spots, posters in visible locations, and materials in the language spoken by expectant mothers (P. A. Doyle et al., 2006; Kentoffio, Berkowitz, Atlas, Oo, & Percac-Lima, 2016; Torres, Smithwick, Luchok, & Rodman-Rice, 2012). When women come in for their first prenatal visit, health care professionals can try to make the experience pleasant and informative. In one program targeting women who were young and uninsured, participants met four times with a registered nurse and

DEVELOPMENTAL TRENDS
Phases of Prenatal Growth

PHASE OF PRENATAL GROWTH	WHAT YOU MIGHT OBSERVE	DIVERSITY	IMPLICATIONS
Zygote (Fertilization until 2 Weeks after)	• The zygote begins to develop at fertilization with the fusing of the sperm and ovum. The offspring's first cell divides into two cells, two divide into four, four into eight, and so forth. The zygote is a ball of cells as it travels down the fallopian tube and into the uterus. • Indications of pregnancy are not typically noticeable to the prospective mother.	• Couples vary in their chances of having a child. • Some children are conceived with the assistance of reproductive technologies. • Large numbers of zygotes perish because errors in chromosomes cause serious malformations. • Hormonal factors in the mother can trigger loss of a zygote.	• Encourage prospective parents to plan for pregnancy by taking stock of their health and, if they have concerns about genetic problems, seeing a genetic counselor. • Advocate that prospective parents follow the physician's recommendations regarding medications, over-the-counter drugs, and vitamins. • Advise sexually active women to avoid alcohol and drugs.
Embryo (2–8 Weeks after Fertilization)	• Body parts and organs form rapidly. At the end of the period, the little being has a head structure and limbs that are recognizably human. • The prospective mother may notice that her menstrual cycle is late. She may experience nausea, food aversions, sensitivities to smells, fatigue, abdominal swelling, tender breasts, and moodiness.	• The embryo is susceptible to damage from toxic substances. The extent of harm done by teratogens depends on the timing and duration of exposure, dose, and the genetic vulnerability of the embryo and mother. • Miscarriage is fairly common during this period. • Mothers differ in their feelings about the pregnancy.	• Encourage a prospective mother to see a medical practitioner if she believes she might be pregnant. • Encourage pregnant women to shield themselves from potentially harmful substances. Tell them about the impact of teratogens on developing offspring. • Address any unmet psychological conditions.
Fetus (9 Weeks after Fertilization until Birth)	• Organs and body parts continue to grow and mature. • The mother can feel the fetus moving, lightly at first and vigorously with time. • The mother's abdomen swells, and she gains weight. A bump is evident about four months along. • In the weeks before the anticipated date of delivery, moving around and sleeping can be difficult.	• Many pregnant women feel strong and healthy during the final months of pregnancy, but some experience nausea and fatigue. • A few women develop serious health problems in the later months of pregnancy, such as unstable blood sugar levels or high blood pressure. • Fetuses vary in their movements, growth rates, birth weights, and readiness for survival at birth.	• Encourage pregnant women to eat well, exercise moderately, and gain a reasonable amount of weight. • Listen to prospective mothers and fathers about their hopes, fears, and expectations for the baby. • Advocate for abstinence from alcohol, drugs, and cigarettes. • Encourage pregnant women to manage their stress. • Inform pregnant women of nearby childbirth classes.

Sources: Browne, O'Brien, Taylor, Bowman, and Davis (2014); Harden et al. (2014); K. L. Moore et al. (2013); B. A. Ward (2017).

wrote out their goals, attended childbirth classes, and received books, a car seat, maternity clothes, and a few other materials (Kapka, 2013). These young women had healthier babies than did women with similar risks who did not participate in the program.

• **Advise pregnant women about nutritional requirements and relevant programs.** All expectant mothers need balanced diets. Yet some women may not remember to eat well, and others cannot afford to do so. With encouragement, expectant mothers can set goals for eating wholesome meals, and, if they need it, registering with community agencies. For example, the U.S. Special Supplemental Nutrition Program for Women, Infants, and Children offers supplemental foods with nutrients that are generally lacking in the diets of low-income populations yet vital for healthy prenatal development (e.g., protein, iron, folic acid, calcium, and vitamins A and C).

• **Urge pregnant women to stay clear of teratogens.** Smokers can be encouraged to reduce the number of cigarettes they smoke or, better, quit smoking altogether. Twenty-year-old Veronica, first-time mother and smoker since the age of 13, was concerned that her smoking would harm her baby and decided to phase out cigarette smoking one cigarette at a time until the fourth month of her pregnancy, when she quit altogether, and commented, "I have done what I can, now the rest is up to God" (Nichter et al., 2007, p. 754).

Expectant women who drink alcohol or take drugs can be confronted with the permanent damage these substances can cause in children. Obviously, pregnant women who are physiologically dependent on alcohol or drugs need immediate professional help. For their own sake and that of their offspring, women who continue to abuse substances after the birth need professional treatment that addresses the addiction, other mental health issues, and parenting skills (J. A. Bailey et al., 2013; J. V. Brown, Bakeman, Coles, Platzman, & Lynch, 2004; Slesnick, Feng, Brakenhoff, & Brigham, 2014).

- **Ask pregnant women how they are doing.** Many expectant mothers have experiences they want to share. They may worry about birth defects, labor and delivery, and the costs of raising a child. Or they may want to communicate excitement about the sensation of the fetus stirring within. Pregnant women almost always appreciate sympathetic listeners who let them talk about their hopes, concerns, and uncertainties.

- **Ask fathers to talk about their experiences.** Prospective fathers gain just as much as mothers from having a sensitive listener with whom to share their worries and hopes. Many fathers are mystified with the physical changes their pregnant wives and girlfriends are undergoing. Some feel excluded from the pregnancy. Although they had an obvious hand in creating the new being, they may believe they are not needed in further development (Genesoni & Tallandini, 2009; R. Grand, 2016). Of course, fathers can play an enormously important role in supporting expectant mothers.

- **Advise new parents about how to care for offspring exposed to teratogens.** Children born to mothers who have taken harmful substances during pregnancy sometimes exhibit intellectual delays during infancy. Many affected children catch up when they receive responsive, predictable, and developmentally appropriate care. For example, many children who have been exposed to cocaine and other teratogens develop proficient language, communication, and interpersonal skills when they receive sympathetic and high-quality care from parents, foster families, and other caregivers (J. V. Brown et al., 2004; Tsantefski, Parkes, Tidyman, & Campion, 2013). Special educational services are an integral part of academic and social learning for numerous teratogen-exposed children. In the case of substance-abusing mothers, treatment is generally a necessary first step to becoming a responsible parent.

MyLab Education
Content Extension 4.1
Learn how you can work effectively with children who have learning delays as a result of prenatal alcohol exposure.

- **Help pregnant adolescent girls address the multiple challenges in their lives.** Pregnant teenage girls have typical age-related needs. Many are motivated to form a personal identity, find a place in their complex social world, and assert their autonomy. On top of these age-related tasks, pregnant teens must cope with the transformations of pregnancy, the experience of childbirth, and the need to determine who will care for the baby and pay for his or her many expenses. At school, teachers and other professionals can encourage prospective mothers to remain involved with extracurricular activities and school events, maintain progress toward graduation, and develop fully as young women. Among other things, adolescent mothers may benefit from tutoring, parent education, medical care, and counseling.

Summary

At fertilization, the new offspring inherits a unique genetic makeup that guides the lifelong process of growing, changing, and interacting with the environment. Development begins when the *zygote*, a one-celled being, divides multiple times and becomes a ball of cells that burrows into the uterus. From weeks 2 through 8, the *embryo* grows rapidly, forming structures needed to sustain future growth. Between week 9 and birth, the *fetus* continues to grow quickly, now receiving the finishing touches on body and brain and becoming sufficiently heavy and strong to live in the outside world. Professionals can support healthy prenatal growth by informing prospective parents (and all sexually active individuals) about the damaging effects of teratogens, the desirability of evaluating health and medical regimens before or early on in a pregnancy, and the value of stress management, a healthful diet, sensible exercise, and ongoing medical care. Pregnant women, generally, and teenager mothers, in particular, can benefit from medical appraisals that address nutritional needs, chronic conditions, and exposure to substances that are harmful to an embryo or fetus. Support for the young mother's academic progress in high school, career goals, and other areas of growth is worthwhile.

MyLab Education Self-Check 4.2

Birth of the Baby

4.3 Describe the multistage birth process, the period right after birth, and professional practices that support newborn infants and their parents.

Childbirth is a complex series of events. The steps that precede the new arrival are affected by the health of mother and baby, the relationships the mother has with family and friends, her preferences for managing labor and delivery, and her cultural traditions and beliefs.

In many societies, childbirth is a natural process, unaccompanied by drugs or medical procedures. Numerous women in Western societies long for a completely natural childbirth yet frequently follow medical practices that ease discomfort and protect their baby from complications. Women who choose to take medication and permit one or more procedures typically have good outcomes. In some cases, medical interventions save the life of mother or baby. However, in a few other cases women are pressured into medical procedures that are probably unnecessary and, in some cases, potentially harmful to them or the offspring (Janssen et al., 2009).

In Western and non-Western societies alike, a clash often arises between traditional customs and the standards of practice for modern medicine. As you can see in the Development in Culture feature "Having Babies in Nepal," numerous contemporary health providers invite women to select from the best features of traditional methods and medical techniques.

Developmental Systems Prompt 4.2

Childbirth is affected by biological processes and the mother's choices, experience, and traditions, and by the practices of those attending the momentous occasion. When you have the privilege of attending a labor and delivery, be receptive to the mother's hopes, expectations, and unique needs.

Development in Culture

Having Babies in Nepal

Nepal is a small developing country nestled between China and India. Three rivers and a rough mountainous terrain make it difficult for the Nepalese to grow crops and travel between villages. Harsh conditions have given rise to a hardy people, most of whom are Hindu or Buddhist and advocate for loyalty to family, respect for elders, nonviolence, and commitment to meditation (Rolls & Chamberlain, 2004).

Sex roles are clearly demarcated in Nepalese culture, especially in sparsely populated regions. In rural areas, women collect water, prepare meals, wash clothes, and aspire to live by ethics of modesty, obedience, and self-sacrifice. Men make the major decisions for the family, carry out strenuous agricultural tasks, and trade with other men in the village. Marriages typically take place between young women in their teens and young men in their early 20s. Newly married couples eagerly await their first child and commonly have three or more additional offspring.

Nepalese women are expected to remain self-sufficient during pregnancy and childbirth. Prenatal development is presumed to involve natural processes that progress with divine help (Matsuyama & Moji, 2008). Medical care was not historically available in the rural areas, nor could women easily travel to hospitals. In recent years, more and more clinics have been built yet are not always used as women do not want to be examined by unfamiliar doctors, nurses, or midwives. When pregnant women decide that they need help, they generally ask mothers-in-law for practical advice and traditional healers for assistance in banishing evil spirits (Justice, 1984; Regmi & Madison, 2009). When expectant mothers and fathers are educated about the need for prenatal care, they are more likely to obtain medical attention (Joshi, Torvaldsen, Hodgson, & Hayen, 2014). 1234

Most Nepalese women are robust. They work throughout their pregnancies, have smooth deliveries, and resume household toils soon after their babies are born. More than 9 out of 10 deliveries occur at home or in a cowshed (Regmi & Madison, 2009). Nepalese women typically give birth without medication while kneeling, squatting, or standing (Carla, 2003). They regularly take herbal remedies to ease recovery after the birth.

(Continued)

A BLESSING. Many Nepalese women have their first child during their teenage years, welcome the baby as a divine blessing, and bear the discomforts of pregnancy and childbirth without complaint.

But not every Nepalese woman has an easy time with pregnancy or birth. Occasional serious problems, including poor nutrition and health complications, go untreated, and as a result, the mortality rate of Nepalese pregnant mothers is high—539 deaths per 100,000 live births (Kulkarni, Christian, LeClerq, & Khatry, 2009; Matsuyama & Moji, 2008). Almost one in 20 infants dies during childbirth or before their first birthday because of inadequate nutrition, impure water, prolonged exposure to the cold, and the contraction of infectious diseases (Central Intelligence Agency, 2010; Justice, 1984).

In recent decades, international agencies and local authorities have tried to prevent and treat medical problems of Nepalese women. Medical personnel have had mixed success, in part because their interventions have failed to address barriers in local conditions and have been seen as incompatible with cultural practices. In one program young women trained as midwives came primarily from the urban areas and were shunned in the villages because of the widespread belief that young women should not travel on their own or work side by side men (Justice, 1984). Some women have avoided going to hospitals because of the reputation of medical staff in discouraging local childbirth traditions, including delivery postures that incorporate mobility (Carla, 2003; Regmi & Madison, 2009).

Health initiatives have begun to accommodate the traditions of Nepalese culture while offering mothers the benefits of modern medicine. A few programs are educating mothers-in-law about maternal health, prenatal care, and danger signs during pregnancy and labor (Regmi & Madison, 2009). Many health care workers are now showing respect for cultural traditions, encouraging women to make their own choices, and implementing intrusive medical procedures only when there are obvious risks (Barker, Bird, Pradhan, & Shakya, 2007; Safe Motherhood Network Federation, 2010).

Preparation for Birth

The birth of a child unleashes a range of feelings in parents—excitement, fear, pain, fatigue, and joy. The events of birth are managed best when families prepare ahead of time, obtain adequate care, and hold reasonable expectations about the baby's abilities.

Other than sharing a few common concerns, parents are highly individual in their feelings about pregnancy and birth. One first-time mother may be eager to have her baby but worried about changes to her life, new financial pressures, and her lack of experience with children. Another prospective mother has plenty of support from her family and takes the momentous physical changes in stride. Such feelings, along with any concerns about controlling pain, can influence the actual birth experience (Guszkowska, 2014; W. A. Hall et al., 2009; Matvienko-Sikar, Lee, Murphy, & Murphy, 2016; Soet, Brack, & Dilorio, 2003). Excessive levels of stress prolong the early stages of labor, raise the mother's blood pressure, and decrease oxygen to the baby. Parents can reduce anxiety by getting organized for the baby, reaching out to loved ones, practicing relaxation exercises, and preparing other children in the family for the new arrival.

Health care providers and family educators give useful information and needed reassurance. They might teach relaxation techniques; offer tips for posture, movement, and exercise; and persuade women to eliminate potentially risky behaviors. In Western societies, *prepared childbirth classes* are common. These programs typically include the following elements:

- Information about changes in, and nutritional needs of, the prospective baby
- Preparation for the baby's arrival, including arranging for the baby at home and deciding about breastfeeding or bottle feeding

- Relaxation and breathing techniques that encourage the mother to stay focused, manage pain, reduce fear, and use muscles effectively during of labor.
- Support from a spouse, friend, or family member throughout labor and delivery. Labor coaches remind the mother to use breathing techniques, massage her and talk softly to her, and encourage her to stay focused.
- Education about the mechanics of delivery, positions during labor and delivery, and pain medications and medical interventions (American Pregnancy Association, 2013b; Dick-Read, 1944; Jaddoe, 2009; Lamaze, 1958).

The pregnant woman and her partner, if she has one, may decide ahead of time where the birth will take place and who will attend to it. Hospitals offer the latest technology, well-trained medical staff, arrangements for insurance coverage, and pain medication, but they have definite disadvantages. Some parents perceive hospitals as using unnecessary treatments and as creating an impersonal climate that separates rather than unites family members during the important occasion. Hospitals have responded to concerns about the lack of family orientation by creating birthing rooms that are attractive, comfortable, and large enough to accommodate several family members. Community birth centers are homelike, inexpensive, and welcoming of extended contact with the newborn; however, they are less appropriate for women with high-risk deliveries, those who need emergency care, or those do not have adequate insurance to cover costs. Home settings offer a comforting environment, allow family members to participate, are inexpensive, and give extended contact with the newborn. They have disadvantages similar to those of community birth centers and in many cases offer no pain medication, few emergency procedures, and minimal access to trained birth attendants (Brintworth & Sandall, 2013; Cheyney, Burcher, & Vedam, 2014; Symon, Winter, Inkster, & Donnan, 2009).

In North America, physicians most often deliver babies. Other common attendants include certified *midwives* who may or may not be trained as nurses. Midwives typically assume responsibility for advising the mother on prenatal care, delivery, and recovery after the birth. Increasingly mothers also turn to *doulas*, attendants at the birth who do not provide medical care but do offer emotional and physical support. Doulas help the mother develop a birth plan ahead of time and then stay by a mother's side throughout the childbirth, guiding her in breathing techniques, massaging her back, and coaching her through the process (Deitrick & Draves, 2008; Devereaux & Sullivan, 2013; Hye-Kyung, 2014).

In addition to seeking conventional medical treatment, many women avail themselves of *complementary therapies* during pregnancy and childbirth. Complementary therapies supplement standard medicine and offer advantages for health and relaxation (J. Byrne, Hauck, Fisher, Bayes, & Schutze, 2014; M. R. Davidson et al., 2008; Fontaine, 2011; K. L. Madden, Turnbull, Cyna, Adelson, & Wilkinson, 2013). In other cases, women use *alternative therapies*, healing practices that are tried *instead* of conventional treatments. As complementary therapies or in lieu of conventional medical procedures, numerous women obtain *acupuncture*, a traditional Chinese treatment in which thin stainless-steel needles stimulate precise locations on the body so as to relieve pain and promote wellness; *biofeedback*, a method for controlling muscle tension; or *self-hypnosis*, a state of relaxation and receptivity to suggestions about reducing distress. Many women derive a sense of well-being from *prayer*, during which they address (silently or vocally) the divine being of their faith, or from *meditation*, a quiet transcendent state during which the mind is still and peaceful. Other common complementary and alternative therapies include *massage therapy*, relaxing manipulation of the body's soft tissues to reduce tension and promote comfort; *hatha yoga*, an Eastern practice of gentle exercises and breathing techniques; and use of herbs and essential oils.

Complementary and alternative therapies offer the advantages of being relatively low in cost, emphasizing wellness, and being noninvasive. Unfortunately, childbirth risks can appear suddenly and do not always respond to natural therapies. In rare situations medical procedures are needed to save the life of the mother or infant.

The Birth Process

Amazingly, medical researchers are still not able to pinpoint the cascade of events that trigger a woman's labor. Currently, experts believe that a combination of factors precipitates the contractions, including hormonal changes in the mother's uterus and placenta and substances released by the baby's brain and lungs (L. Dixon, Skinner, & Foureur, 2013a). Some evidence indicates that up until the time of labor, a couple of genes suppress contractions with help from the hormone progesterone. These genes lose the ability to prevent contractions when progesterone wanes; according to this explanation, the hormone oxytocin then unleashes contractions (Zakar & Mesiano, 2013).

Typically, the mother's uterus begins preparations for birth 38 to 40 weeks into the pregnancy. Here is the incredible sequence of events that constitutes the birth process in a typical vaginal delivery:

- As the pregnancy advances, the mother experiences *Braxton Hicks contractions*. These irregular contractions exercise the mother's uterine muscles without causing the cervix to open.
- In most cases, the baby settles in a head-downward position, which facilitates its passage through the birth canal. When babies are in breech position (situated to come out buttocks or legs first) or in a sideways position (a shoulder would likely come out first), the mother is monitored closely and often undergoes a *cesarean delivery*, a surgical procedure in which the baby is removed after an incision is made in the mother's abdomen and uterine wall.
- A few events may occur in the days immediately before labor. The mother may experience a descent of the baby into the pelvis, feel a rush of energy, lose 1 to 4 pounds as her hormonal balance changes, and notice vaginal secretions. Sleep becomes difficult. Health providers may coach mothers in using relaxation techniques and reassure them that sleep disturbances prior to labor rarely interfere with its progression.
- Contractions widen the cervix opening and mark the beginning of childbirth, which progresses through four stages (Figure 4.9a–d). These stages are significant to midwives and medical personnel but are not necessarily experienced as distinct periods by mothers, with the exception of the baby's arrival, of course.

FIGURE 4.9 Stages of a typical birth.

In the first stage of labor, the mother's cervix dilates (a). After numerous contractions the cervix opens completely, the baby's head moves down the vagina, and the second stage of labor begins (b). The second stage continues with the mother pushing with each contraction, the baby moving down the vagina, the baby's head appearing, and, gradually, the rest of the body emerging (c). The third stage of labor is the delivery of the placenta (d).

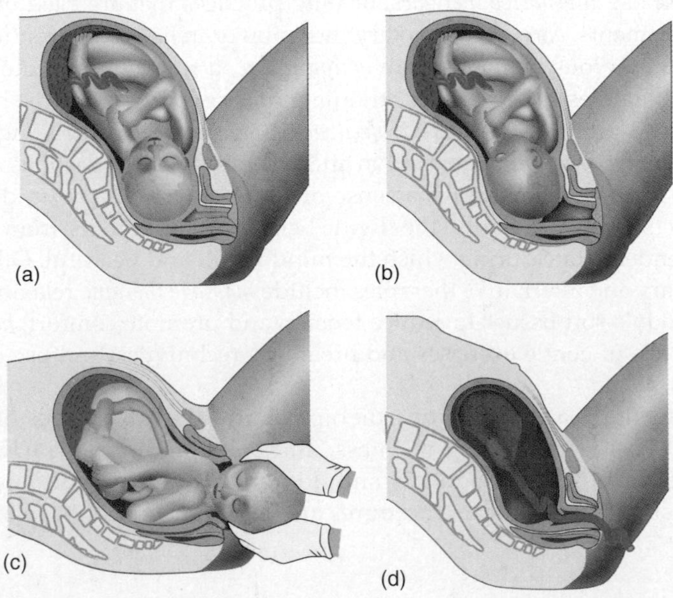

- In the *first stage of labor*, the mother experiences regular contractions. These contractions last until the cervix is dilated to about 10 centimeters (approximately 4 inches). Mothers feel pain during contractions, especially in their pelvis and back. This first stage typically takes about 12 to 16 hours for mothers who are having their first baby and 6 to 8 hours for mothers who have previously delivered one or more babies. Medical personnel keep track of the cervix opening and monitor the fetal heartbeat. They may offer pain medication and encourage the mother to walk around. At the beginning of the first stage of labor, contractions are spaced widely apart (e.g., every 15 to 30 minutes) and are mild to moderate in intensity. When the cervix dilates to 3 centimeters, an "active" phase begins and lasts until full dilation. Contractions become stronger and longer (they last 30 to 60 seconds) and occur every 2 to 3 minutes.

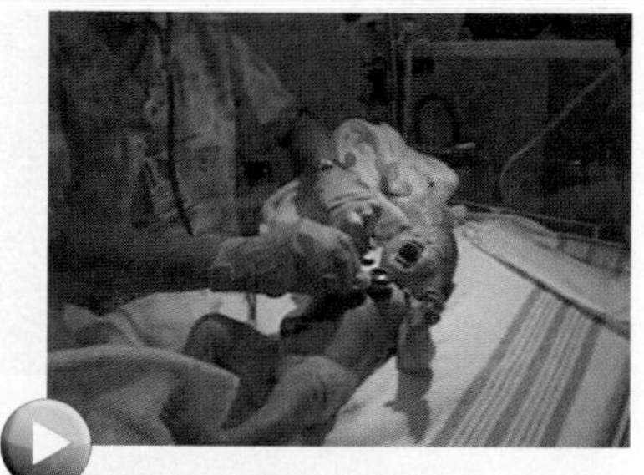

MyLab Education
Video Example 4.2

Find Developmental Meaning *How is the health of the newborn infant assessed in the first moments after birth?* Note the time intervals between the test's administrations and the methods for recording breathing effort, heart rate, muscle tone, reflexes, and skin color.

- In the *second stage of labor*, the cervix is fully dilated, the baby proceeds down the birth canal, and he or she is born. This stage may take about half an hour, but in first pregnancies it often lasts up to 2 hours. Contractions come often and hard. They appear every other minute and last for a minute at a time. Mothers must push hard to help move the baby down and out. Medical personnel continue to keep tabs on the fetal heartbeat. The doctor may use forceps or call for a cesarean delivery if uterine contractions slow down or the baby does not move quickly enough. Too fast is not good because the pressure might tear the mother's tissues or the baby's head. The doctor or midwife may place a hand on the part of the baby coming out and ease it out methodically. Medical personnel may also help rotate the baby's head so that it can get around the mother's pelvic bones. As the head comes out, the doctor or midwife checks to make sure the umbilical cord is not wrapped around the head, and if it is, the cord is removed. The nose and mouth are cleansed of fluids. The mother ejects the baby's shoulders and body. The baby is gently wiped dry, and after the blood has drained from the umbilical cord into the baby's body, the cord is clamped and cut. The baby is born! The baby is placed on the mother, and the father or other coach may take a turn holding him or her. Oftentimes the baby is alert and looks around the room—a stunning and memorable event for the mother, the father, or other partner and accompanying friends and family.
- In the *third stage of labor*, the placenta and fetal membranes (collectively known as the *afterbirth*) are expelled from the uterus (see Figure 4.9d). Usually, this process happens without assistance, although medical personnel watch to make sure it happens. The mother is checked to see if lacerations have occurred and if medical treatment is needed.
- In the *fourth stage of labor*, 1 to 4 hours after birth, the mother's body begins to readjust after the exertion. Having lost some blood, the mother may experience a slight decrease in blood pressure, shake and feel chilled, and want to drink water and get something to eat. (M. R. Davidson et al., 2008; Demarest & Charon, 1996; L. Dixon, Skinner, & Foureur, 2013b; Sherwen, Scoloveno, & Weingarten, 1999). From start to finish, it takes about 14 hours to birth the baby, less in later pregnancies.

Medical Interventions

Medical personnel, midwives, and the mother's partner can do many things to facilitate labor and delivery and comfort the mother. Following are examples of procedures used in many Western societies:

- Physicians may *induce labor* that is, start it artificially—with medications (e.g., Pitocin, a form of oxytocin, a hormone that stimulates contractions). Candidates for an induced labor include women past their due dates and those with diabetes or pregnancy-induced hypertension.
- Midwives, doulas, partners, and medical staff may address the mother's pain with methods that do not require medication. Some mothers are assisted by a warm whirlpool bath, visual images of the cervix opening, music, hypnosis, biofeedback, and massage. You can see a setting for a water birth in Figure 4.10.

FIGURE 4.10 Water birth.

This new mother delivered her baby in relaxing warm tub with help from a midwife.

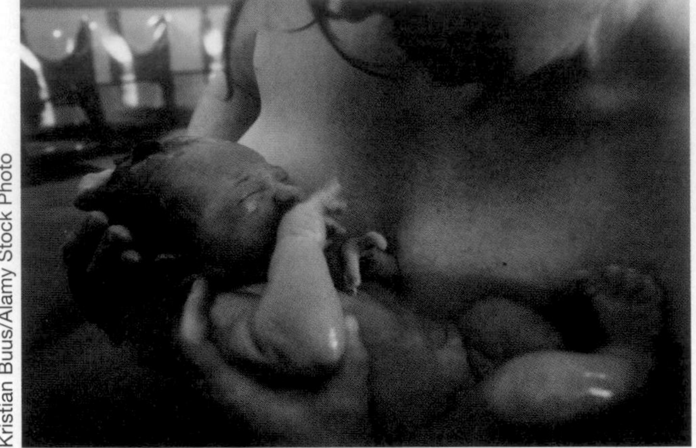

Kristian Buus/Alamy Stock Photo

- Physicians sometimes offer *analgesics*, medicines that reduce pain without loss of consciousness. Medications injected into the mother's spine (such as *epidural analgesia*) are a common method of relief. Generally, these medications are not offered early in labor, because they may slow progress, but also not too late, because physicians want the medicine to be metabolized by mother and baby prior to birth. Some analgesic medications can increase the need for other medical interventions, such as use of forceps and cesarean deliveries, and they may reduce breathing in the newborn.
- Physicians may offer *anesthetics* to women in active labor if extreme pressure must be applied (such as occurs with forceps) or when a cesarean delivery must be performed. Anesthetics cause loss of sensation and in some cases lead to loss of consciousness.
- Women sometimes take *opioids* (also known as narcotics), medicines that reduce the sensation of pain by changing the way it is perceived by the brain. Opioids have several disadvantages, including limited effectiveness in reducing pain, occasional side effects such as nausea and drowsiness, and tendency to adversely affect the baby's breathing and sucking.
- Slightly more than 30% of babies born in the United States are delivered through cesarean surgery, a rate that experts suggest is higher than it should be (B. E. Hamilton, Martin, & Ventura, 2011). Cesarean deliveries are performed when the physician believes the safety of the mother, child, or both is at stake. Examples of conditions that might lead to a cesarean delivery are fetal distress, health problems of the mother, failure to progress in labor, infections in the birth canal, and presence of multiple babies. The birth can take less than an hour, including removing the placenta and suturing the incisions. The mother will usually remain awake and will have a regional anesthetic that numbs them in the abdomen and legs so that they cannot feel the pain of the surgery.

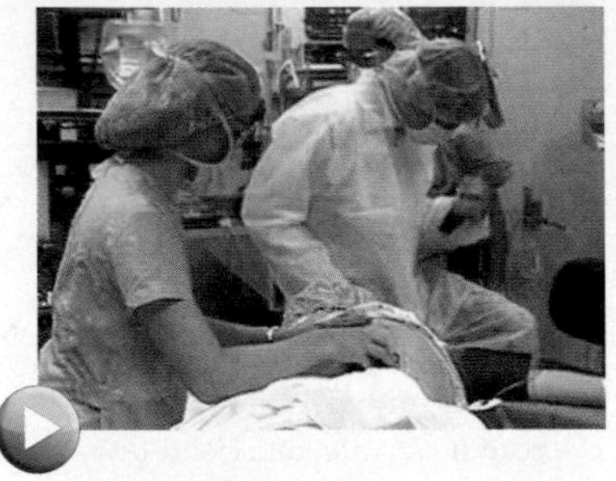

MyLab Education
Video Example 4.3

Find Developmental Meaning *This video shows a cesarean delivery.* Learn how a cesarean surgery differs from a vaginal delivery in time for the process, prevalence among births, and selection factors.

Regardless of the medical treatments mothers receive, they and their families invariably appreciate consideration of their needs and preferences. Nurses, midwives, doulas, and other attendants offer sympathetic reassurance to women in pain. Depending on their cultural traditions, mothers will also appreciate support from their husbands, other partners, friends, or close family members during labor and delivery.

Many medical personnel and attendants consciously try to accommodate women's cultural practices. For example, some Latino families prefer to stay at home during the early stages of labor, and when they arrive at the hospital, may want to pray together (Callister, Corbett, Reed, Tomao, & Thornton, 2010; Champion, 2013; Spector, 2004). The hospital staff show respect for prayer, meditation, and devotion by not interrupting them. Muslim women might become distressed if unfamiliar male doctors and nurses see them uncovered; thus, medical personnel take measures to ensure that mothers are covered and accompanied by other women during examinations (Abushaikha & Massah, 2013; Rassin, Klug, Nathanzon, Kan, & Silner, 2009). Chinese mothers may wish to follow cultural traditions of eating traditional foods, drinking tea, and asking for extra blankets to stay warm (Callister, Eads, & See Yeung, 2011). When they can, nurses adapt to these wishes. Women from a few cultural groups (e.g., some Native Americans and the Hmong from Laos) may ask to take the placenta home for burial in alignment with their religious beliefs, and medical personnel who understand the cultural practice will help them make these arrangements (M. R. Davidson et al., 2008; Fadiman, 1997).

Babies at Risk

Some babies are born before they are able to cope with the demands of life outside the womb. Two categories of babies require special care:

- *Babies born early*—A baby is considered full term at 38 weeks. The **premature infant** is born before the end of 37 weeks after conception (Sherwen et al., 1999). Premature labor may be precipitated by several factors, including infection, presence of two or more babies, abnormalities in the fetus, death of the fetus, abnormalities in the womb, and serious disease in the mother. Extremely early babies (born after only 32 or fewer weeks of prenatal growth) face serious risk factors, including higher-than-usual rates of death during infancy. After birth, premature infants are at risk for health problems, including breathing problems, anemia, brain hemorrhages, feeding problems, and temperature instability.
- *Babies born small for date*—Some infants are small and light given the amount of time they have had to develop in the mother's uterus. These babies are at risk for many problems, including neurological deficiencies, structural problems in body parts, breathing difficulties, vision limitations, and other serious health problems (Charkaluk et al., 2012; Sadler, 2010). Small babies may have chromosomal or genetic abnormalities or may have been exposed to harmful substances or received inadequate nutrition during their prenatal development.

Developmental Care for Babies at Risk

Babies born especially early or small may not have the physical maturity to breathe independently, regulate their temperature, or suck adequately to meet nutritional needs. Despite these challenges, babies can often survive with access to life-sustaining devices and medicines. Physicians and nurses create a therapeutic atmosphere that is nurturing and developmentally appropriate. The following guidelines are recommended for a fragile infant:

- Reduce the infant's exposure to light and noise.
- Regulate the amount of handling of the infant by medical staff.
- Position the baby to increase circulation.
- Encourage parents to participate in the care of the infant.
- Inform parents about the infant's needs.
- Arrange diapering, bathing, and changing of clothes so that interruptions are minimized.
- Encourage mothers and fathers to cuddle with the infant and carry him or her often and for long periods.
- Swaddle the baby in a blanket or with arms bent and hands placed near the mouth to permit sucking on fingers or hands.
- Provide skin-to-skin contact and massage the baby.
- Educate parents about the infant's condition and methods for caring for him or her (Beijers, Cillessen, & Zijlmans, 2016; L. F. Brown, Pridham, & Brown, 2014; L.-L. Chen, Su, Su, Lin, & Kuo, 2008; T. Field, 2001; E. C. Hall, Kronborg, Aagaard, & Brinchmann, 2013; Helth & Jarden, 2013; Sherwen et al., 1999).

When fragile babies become strong enough to leave the hospital and go home with their families, they may need specialized treatments. Their families may also benefit from support because these babies are not easily soothed. If parents of premature and health-impaired infants learn to fulfill infants' needs confidently and tenderly, however, these infants generally calm down and develop healthy responses to distress (J. M. Young, Howell, & Hauser-Cram, 2005).

The developmental journeys of most premature and sick newborn infants are *not* destined to be rocky ones. In fact, many early and small infants go on to catch up with peers in their motor, intellectual, and communication skills, particularly when families, educators, and other professionals meet their special needs (de Wit, Sas, Wit, & Cutfield, 2013; Sheffield, Stromswold, & Molnar, 2005). Some premature children have intellectual delays or persisting medical problems, such as visual problems or asthma, and they benefit from appropriate medical care, advocacy from families, and educational services that help them progress academically and socially. As they grow older, children may require continued services, such as speech therapy and other individualized interventions. Without sensitive care and, if needed, intervention, some premature and low-birth-weight infants continue to face later difficulties in coping with negative emotions and in learning at school (Hack et al., 2012; Nomura, Fifer, & Brooks-Gunn, 2005; Shenkin, Starr, & Deary, 2004).

Enhancing Parents' Sensitivity to Newborn Infants

To give infants a healthy start on life, parents and other caregivers must recognize infants' abilities, interests, and styles of self-expression. Family educators and other professionals can support infants indirectly—yet powerfully—when they teach family members how to observe their infants closely and respond sympathetically to infants' individual needs. To get a sense of how you might enhance caregivers' awareness of these needs, see the examples in the Development and Practice feature "Being Sensitive with Newborn Infants." Also consider these recommendations:

Development-Enhancing Education

Being Sensitive with Newborn Infants

Carefully observe the sensory abilities of newborn infants.

- A pediatric nurse watches a newborn infant scanning her parents' faces. The nurse explains that infants can see some shapes and patterns, are especially attracted to human faces, and rapidly gain visual acuity in their first few months. (Infancy)
- A doctor notices a 3-day-old infant turn his head after his mother begins speaking. The doctor comments softly to the baby in front of the mother, "Oh, you hear your mother talking, don't you, young man?" (Infancy)

Point out the physiological states of newborn infants.

- A family educator talks with parents about their newborn infants, commenting that infants commonly sleep for long cycles but usually have brief periods each day when they are receptive to quiet interaction. (Infancy)
- A child-care director watches the gaze of a newborn infant as her parents tour the child-care center. "Hello, little one," says the director. "You are taking it all in now, aren't you?" (Infancy)

Notice the kinds of stimuli that attract infants' attention.

- A mother watches her newborn infant while he is awake and alert. She notices that her son intently inspects her face and certain other stimuli, such as the edges of the bassinet. (Infancy)
- A 2-week-old infant stares at his father's face while sucking on the bottle. His father smiles back at him. (Infancy)

Encourage parents to watch for infants' preferences in being soothed.

- A pediatrician asks a new mother how she is getting along with her baby. When the mother reports that the baby cries a lot, the doctor asks her how the baby likes to be comforted. The doctor explains that most infants find it soothing to be held tenderly but that some relax while riding in a car or stroller. The doctor suggests that the mother keep informal records of the infant's fussy times and the kinds of care that prove calming. (Infancy)
- A visiting nurse asks a new mother and her partner about the infant's frequent crying. The parents express their frustration and listen appreciatively when the nurse demonstrates several ways for calming the baby. (Infancy)

Model sensitive care for new parents.

- A family educator shows a new father how to hold the baby, change her diaper, and interact quietly and sensitively with her. (Infancy)
- A grandmother demonstrates to her daughter how to bathe her newborn son. Grandmother carefully tests the temperature of the water in the kitchen sink and assembles all the bathing supplies before immersing him in a few inches of warm, sudsy water and gently patting his skin with a clean cloth. (Infancy)

Tailor care to the needs of fragile infants.

- A hospital offers lifesaving care to fragile infants and attends to their sensory abilities and psychological needs by reducing light, noise, and unnecessary medical procedures and by massaging the infants a few times each day. (Infancy)
- In the neonatal intensive care unit of the hospital, mothers and fathers are invited to hold their premature infants for a couple of hours every day in a practice known as Kangaroo Care. One parent lies down on a bed and holds the infant on his or her bare chest. The baby's head is placed to one side to facilitate hearing of the parent's heartbeat. A blanket is then placed over the baby, and the parent is encouraged to relax and allow the baby to do the same. (Infancy)

• Reassure new mothers that they will be able to find the energy to care for their babies. Many new mothers return home from the hospital feeling tired, sore, and overwhelmed by the demands of an infant, as reflected in these comments:

- "I guess I expected that our lives would change dramatically the moment we walked in the door with him … which they did!"
- "It's hard, and sometimes I don't want the responsibility."
- "I felt very much like I didn't know what to do!"
- "Some people are giving too much advice." (George, 2005, pp. 253–254)

These accounts reveal a need for adjustment. Although mothers and fathers may want information about infants and their care, they are best able to act on this information when they have caught up on rest and feel supported by friends, family, and health care professionals.

• Share what you know about infants' sensory and perceptual abilities. Infants learn a lot about the world from external stimulation. **Sensation** refers to the infant's detection of a stimulus; for example, a newborn may sense a father's stroking movements on her hand. Infants sense many things that they don't necessarily focus on or think about. When infants do attend to and interpret a sensation, **perception** takes place, such as when a 6-month-old baby watches a moving image and perceives it to be his father. At birth, many newborns look intently at the faces of parents and others, giving people the impression that they are learning from the beginning of life. In fact, babies have been learning since before birth. Before birth, they are sensing flavors, light, touch, and sounds. What newborns actually *perceive* cannot be determined with certainty, but researchers have established that newborns are able to *sense basic* patterns and associations. The majority of infants see well-defined contrasts and shapes, such as large black-and-white designs on checkerboards, and vision improves as the various parts of the eye connect up with brain structures that interpret stimuli.

During the first year of life, vision matures (D. L. Mayer & Dobson, 1982; Perone & Spencer, 2014; Ricci et al., 2010; van Hof-van Duin & Mohn, 1986). Infants can see best from a distance of about 6 to 12 inches, quickly develop a preference for looking at faces, and explore the visual properties of objects. Yet the sense of hearing is more advanced at birth than is vision. Recall that late in prenatal development, fetuses begin to hear and recognize their mothers' voices after birth. Typically developing infants are born with the ability to experience touch, taste, and smell. Sensory and perceptual abilities continue to develop after infancy, and these abilities will, of course, make critical contributions to an expanding knowledge of the world.

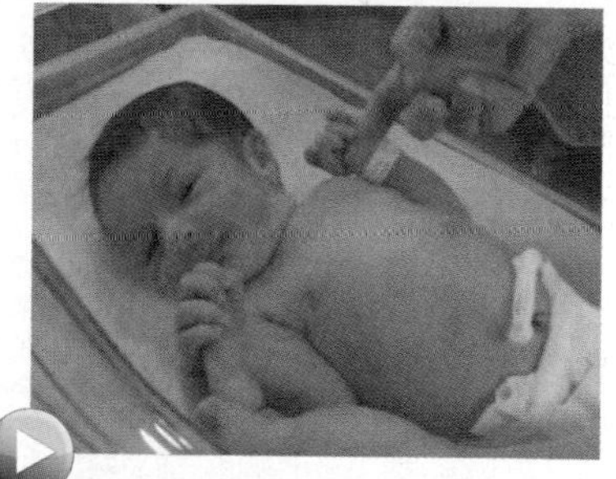

MyLab Education
Video Example 4.4

Find Developmental Meaning *This video shows the reflexes of newborn infants.* Learn information about the functions of reflexes and changes in appearance over time.

• Point out the physiological states of newborn infants. Unless they have previously had a child or been around newborn infants, parents may be surprised at how their infants act, how long they sleep, and how they respond to stimuli. Infants may appear to grimace, twitch, and jerk in unfamiliar ways, sleeping and waking at odd intervals. Family educators and medical personnel can educate parents by explaining the nature of infants' **states of arousal**, the physiological conditions of sleepiness and wakefulness that they experience throughout the day. Infant practitioners can also point out **reflexes**, those automatic motor responses to stimuli. One example of a reflex is an infant blinking his eyes when his father moves him close to a bright light. Take a look at the Observation Guidelines table "Indicators of Health in Newborn Infants" for descriptions of physical states you can share with parents.

• Encourage families to watch infants' responses to stimuli. Infants give off clues about what they like and dislike, find interesting, and experience as pleasant or painful. It may take a while for caregivers to decipher infants' signals and the circumstances that elicit them. When infants are drowsy, asleep, or agitated, they do not show curiosity. When they are rested, comfortable, and awake, they may scan the visual environment, intently study the properties of a mobile, and smile at soft vocalizations from a parent. By observing the textures, tastes, sounds, and visual properties that attract infants' sustained attention, parents and other caregivers can guess about things that interest infants—perhaps that the blanket feels soft, the juice tastes sweet, the melody is pleasing, and the rubber duck is attractive.

OBSERVATION GUIDELINES

Indicators of Health in Newborn Infants

CHARACTERISTIC	LOOK FOR	EXAMPLE	IMPLICATION
Adjustment after Birth	• First breaths are taken within a half-minute after birth (the doctor may suction fluid from mouth and throat). • Attempts to nurse at breast occur shortly after birth. Baby may lose a few ounces of weight during first few days. • First urination and bowel movements occur within first 2 days. • In some babies, elongated head after birth that gradually regains round appearance; skin may be scratched and contain discolored spots that disappear in a few days.	Immediately after birth, Trinisha begins crying. Her head is misshapen, and she has some blotchy spots on her skin. Her mother places Trinisha on her chest, and the baby quiets down, opens her eyes, and scans the room.	Before birth, encourage parents to arrange for age-appropriate medical care for their newborn babies. After birth, reassure parents about the appearance of their infant.
States of Arousal	• *Quiet sleep:* The infant lies still with closed eyelids and relaxed facial muscles. • *Active sleep:* Although the infant is sleeping, eyes may open and shut and move from side to side, facial expressions change and breathing is irregular. • *Drowsiness:* The infant's eyelids may open and close without focus, and breathing is regular and rapid. • *Quiet alert:* The infant is awake, calm, happy, and engaged with the world. • *Active waking:* The infant wriggles in bursts of vigorous movements, breathes in an irregular tempo, has flushed skin, and may moan or grunt. • *Crying:* The infant cries and thrashes and has a flushed and distressed face.	In the first few days after birth, Kyle spends most of his time sleeping. Some sleep appears peaceful, and at other times he appears to be dreaming. When Kyle is awake, he sometimes looks intently at people and objects close by. Occasionally he appears agitated, and these episodes often escalate into loud and persistent crying.	Help parents notice infants' distinct states of arousal. Encourage them to develop a sensitive style in responding to infants' distress. Advise parents that when infants are in the quiet, alert state, it is a good time to interact calmly.
Reflexes	• *Rooting:* When touched near the corner of the mouth, infant turns toward the stimulus, as if in search of nipple. • *Sucking:* When nipple or finger touches the infant's mouth, he or she begins to suck it. • *Swallowing:* Liquids are transferred from mouth to stomach with muscles in throat. • *Grasping:* Infant grasps onto finger or other small object placed in his or her hand. • *Moro reflex:* When startled, infant stretches arms outward and brings them together in hugging motion. • *Babinski reflex:* When the inner side of infant's foot is rubbed from heel to toe, the big toe moves upward and other toes fan inward toward bottom of foot. • *Stepping:* When baby is held upright under arms with feet touching hard surface, legs take rhythmic steps. • *Tonic neck reflex:* If infant is lying on his or her back and head is moved toward one side, the arm on that side extends out and away from the body, and other side is flexed close to head with clenched fist in fencing position.	Little Josefina lies on her back on a blanket as her mother washes the dishes. When her mother accidentally drops and breaks a dish, Josefina appears alarmed, extends her arms, and seems to be grasping for something in midair.	Gently demonstrate infants' reflexes. Family members, including the baby's siblings, may begin to use the finger grasping reflex as a way to interact with the baby. Explain that reflexes indicate that the infant's brain and body are operating as they should.

Sources: Adamović, Sovilj, Ribarić-Jankes, Ljubić, and Antonović (2013); Adolph and Berger (2011); Jadcherla, Gupta, Stoner, Fernandez, and Shaker (2007); Shevell (2009); C. W. Snow and McGaha (2003); and Wolff (1966).

• **Discuss the kinds of stimulation infants might find soothing.** Babies have distinct preferences for being comforted. Different babies relax to varying sensations—listening to the rumble of the clothes dryer, nursing at Mother's breast, sleeping on Father's chest, or going for a ride in the car. Mothers and fathers who have not yet found the antidote to fussy periods may be grateful for suggestions about a range of soothing techniques.

- **Model sensitive interactions with infants.** Not all caregivers know how to interact in a gentle, reassuring manner with infants. Practitioners can show parents and other caregivers how to slow their pace, hold the baby gently but firmly, speak quietly, and watch for signs that the baby is ready to interact (e.g., when the baby looks into caregivers' faces) or is distressed by the interaction (e.g., the baby looks away).

- **Show parents how to care for the baby.** First-time parents may appreciate hands-on tips for administering to the needs of a new baby. Unless they have seen a baby being bathed, nursed, fed a bottle, diapered, or carried, new parents may not know how to perform these caretaking functions.

- **Offer early and continued support to parents of fragile infants.** Infants who are at risk for one reason or another—for example, those who are premature or have serious disabilities—require special types of attention. Infants might cry often, be difficult to console, or need an intensive medical treatment. Some infants with health problems may be sluggish and solicit little interaction. In such cases family members may have practical questions about optimal care for their children and benefit from parent education.

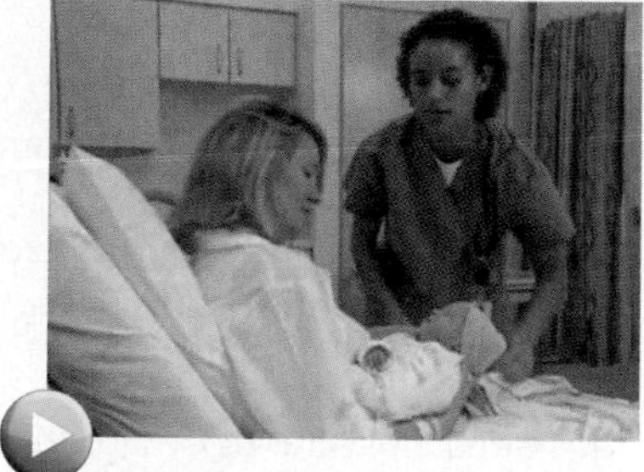

MyLab Education
Video Example 4.5

Find Developmental Meaning *How does a nurse encourage a new mother to breastfeed her baby?* Notice the practical advice the nurse gives.

Summary

The birth of the baby is an exciting and sometimes nerve-wracking event for parents, who can reduce their stress by preparing for childbirth. Birth is a multistage process that is grounded in culture and often assisted by family members and doctors, nurses, midwives, and doulas. The health and medical needs of newborn infants depend on their birth weight, size, prior exposure to teratogens, and genetic vulnerabilities. Family educators and other professionals can help parents develop realistic expectations about their newborn infants and respond sensitively to their physical and psychological needs. Learning about the infant's physiological states and reflexes, and the kinds of cuddling and vocalizations that elicit relief and comfort, are foundations for sensitive caregiving.

Practicing For Your Licensure Examinaton

Many teaching tests require students to use what they have learned about child development in responses to brief vignettes and multiple-choice questions. You can practice for your licensure examination by reading the following case study and answering a series of questions.

Nadia's Horses

Nadia, an English child of Ukrainian immigrants, was identified as being autistic at age 6 (Selfe, 1977). As we explained earlier in this chapter, children with autism typically have difficulty learning to speak and comprehending language. They generally withdraw from eye contact and other kinds of social interaction, do not understand social gestures or participate in pretend games, repeat particular actions incessantly (e.g., repeatedly turning the pages of a book), and resist changes in routine. Nadia exhibited each of these challenges.

By age 3, Nadia had spoken only 10 words, which she uttered rarely. Her language did not progress much further in the following years, and she found it especially difficult to learn abstract and superordinate concepts (e.g., "furniture"; Selfe, 1995). Nadia was clumsy, showed no concern for physical danger, and displayed regular temper tantrums. Yet like a small minority of other children with autism (Treffert & Wallace, 2002; Winner, 2000), Nadia was an exceptionally talented artist. After noticing her unusual artistic ability, Nadia's parents and a psychologist gave her paper and pens. Nadia drew several times a week, reproducing pictures she had studied days before in children's books, newspapers, or other printed material. Nadia's drawings were not only realistic but also creative representations of images she had seen—she occasionally reversed the orientation, changed the size, or constructed a composite of several images. As you examine two of her drawings, answer the following questions.

Constructed-Response Question

1. How might you as a teacher support Nadia's interest in drawing horses?

Multiple-Choice Questions

2. Which of the following statements most effectively represents how *nature* played a complex role in Nadia's abilities?

a. Nadia's amazing ability to represent the contours of moving animals; realistic details in their faces, legs, and hooves; and depth and perspective may have had some genetic basis.
b. Nadia's genes may have contributed to her autism.
c. Nada's genes may have contributed to her delayed language ability.
d. Genetic factors may have played a role in Nadia's artistic ability, autism, and language delays.

3. If Nadia had an Individualized Education Program (IEP), who would contribute to the plan, and what would it contain?

a. Nadia's psychologist would prepare the IEP given that he or she would have the necessary expertise to determine Nadia's needs; the IEP would contain educational goals and strategies.
b. Nadia's parents would advise her teacher and specialists about what they want Nadia to achieve. The teacher and specialists would convert the parents' wishes into educational jargon that would be acceptable to district officials. The IEP would contain educational goals and strategies.
c. Nadia's teacher would prepare the draft of the IEP, with Nadia's parents and specialists subsequently having the right to veto separate sections. The IEP includes motivational aspirations for career goals for the student to achieve after completing school.
d. Nadia's parents, teacher, other specialists, and perhaps Nadia herself would participate in the IEP meeting. The IEP would include educational goals and strategies for achieving these goals based on Nadia's abilities and experiences.

MyLab Education Self-Check 4.3

MyLab Education Licensure Practice 4.1
Assessing Children
Practice assessing the needs of a child with a genetic disorder.

Artwork by Nadia. Horse; age 3½ years (left). Horse and rider; age 5½ years (below). Originally published in Selfe, Lorna (1977). *Nadia: A Case of Extraordinary Drawing Ability in an Autistic Child*. London, England: Academic Press. Used with permission of Lorna Selfe.

Key Concepts

gene (p. 111)
chromosome (p. 111)
DNA (p. 112)
gamete (p. 113)
meiosis (p. 113)
zygote (p. 115)
monozygotic twins (p. 115)
dizygotic twins (p. 115)
mitosis (p. 115)
alleles (p. 116)
dominant gene (p. 116)
recessive gene (p. 116)
codominance (p. 116)
polygenic inheritance (p. 117)
multifactorial trait (p. 117)
co-action (p. 117)
antisocial behavior (p. 117)
niche construction (p. 118)
epigenetic changes (p. 121)
universal design (p. 122)
prenatal development (p. 123)
embryo (p. 124)
fetus (p. 126)
teratogen (p. 128)
depression (p. 131)
anxiety (p. 131)
premature infant (p. 141)
sensation (p. 143)
perception (p. 143)
state of arousal (p. 143)
reflex (p. 143)

Chapter Five
Physical Development

FatCamera/E+

Learning Objectives

5.1 Outline principles of physical development and the primary characteristics of children during each of the five developmental periods.

5.2 Summarize basic issues related to children's physical health and explain how educators can assist children in acquiring health-promoting habits and avoiding health-compromising behaviors.

5.3 Identify the brain's basic structures and developmental processes and derive implications for educating children.

CASE STUDY

Project Coach

Sam Intrator and Donald Siegel, professors in exercise and sports science, have devoted their careers to getting children actively involved in high-quality athletic programs. For Sam and Donald, helping children develop proficiency in sports is not an end in and of itself but rather a means to foster children's health, confidence, academic achievement, and communication skills (Intrator & Siegel, 2008, 2014).

As one of their initiatives, Sam and Donald reviewed children's involvement in sports in Springfield, Massachusetts, an economically distressed city with numerous adolescents who were not exercising, achieving in school, or protecting themselves from a pregnancy. Young people had few prospects to immerse themselves in sports, were not accustomed to exercising, and did not have adults who could supervise their leagues. Few parents were able to serve as coaches. No one stepped forward to volunteer.

The situation seemed bleak to Sam and Donald until one day, in a conversation with Jimmy, the parks and recreation director, they came up with a creative solution: Ask teenagers in the community to work as coaches. The teenagers could benefit from the leadership training, and the children would finally have a sports league. Jimmy was enthusiastic about the idea, and Project Coach was launched.

As a training program, adolescents were recruited into an after-school program that taught them rules of sports, methods of coaching, and benefits of becoming a leader. The adolescent coaches acquired other advantages as well. They found themselves on a productive path for their own future and saw their reputations restored as responsible citizens, rather than, as formerly, "problems to be managed" (Intrator & Siegel, 2008, p. 22). They learned how to solve dilemmas, communicate clearly, and give effective feedback to children.

The elementary children who participated loved the program. With teen leaders now trained, elementary children had a chance to play soccer and other sports. They had somewhere to go after school. And they had adolescent mentors expressing interest in their welfare. Having proven successful for both coaches and children, Project Coach drew interest from the local community, where it took roots and expanded (Intrator & Siegel, 2014). Academic tutoring was incorporated into the program, and in a recent report, 100 percent of teen coaches graduated from high school, compared to the city's rate of only 69 percent (Smith College Jandon Center for Community Engagement, 2018).

- What kinds of physical needs did the children in Springfield have?
- How did the sports league affect children and their mentors?

As children develop, they undergo physical changes. They learn to crawl, walk, run, and play sports. They grow taller and stronger. They become increasingly proficient at handling small objects.

At each step along the way, physical development draws on good nutrition, ample physical activity, and adequate rest and sleep. Teachers and other practitioners who care for children must consider these physical needs as they guide children. Protecting them from harm is also necessary. For some children, hazards come in the form of junk food. Others cope with chronic illnesses or injuries. Many lack opportunities to exercise. Adolescents confront temptations with drugs and alcohol. In the case of young people in Springfield, they were inactive, bored, and careless.

Fortunately, Sam and Donald believed in the power of youth. They realized that the children could become physically fit and that local adolescents were part of the solution. New sports leagues allowed elementary school children to rehearse athletic skills, forge friendships, and have fun. Adolescent coaches gained lessons in leadership as well as positive outlets for their time.

As the Springfield youth demonstrate, health depends on conditions at home, at school, and in the community. In this chapter, we examine age-related changes in physical development, brain growth, and the many strategies adults can implement to foster young people's physical well-being.

Physical Development

5.1 Outline principles of physical development and the primary characteristics of children during each of the five developmental periods.

Principles of growth underlie children's physical development. One modification after another transforms the newborn infant, cradled in a parent's arms, into a walking toddler, an active child, an exploring adolescent, and eventually, an independent adult.

Outline

Principles of Growth

The changes that occur during physical development are methodical. Patterns of growth follow these regularities:

Each part of the body has its own rate of growth. Genes tell particular parts of the body to grow quickly during specific time periods. As a result, the relative proportions of different body parts change over childhood (see Figure 5.1). Early in development heads are closer to adult size than are torsos, which are more advanced than arms and legs. In the upper limbs, the hand approaches adult size sooner than the forearm does; the forearm approaches adult size before the upper arm does. Likewise, in the lower limbs, the foot is more advanced than the calf, which is more mature than the thigh. You can see systematic changes in one boy's development in photographs taken between age one and seventeen (see Figure 5.2).

Internally, separate systems also grow at different rates (London, Ladewig, Ball, Bindler, & Cowen, 2011; J. M. Tanner, 1990). The lymphoid system (e.g., tonsils, adenoids, lymph nodes, and the lining of the small intestines) grows rapidly throughout childhood and then slows in adolescence. Lymphoid organs help children resist infection, which is

FIGURE 5.1 Physical development.

Children and adolescents grow taller and heavier as they develop, and the relative proportions of their body parts change as well.

FIGURE 5.2 Young man under construction.

This boy is wearing the same T-shirt in photographs taken at ages 1, 5, 9, 13, and 17. Notice that the boy's head is proportionally large during his first couple of years, after which time the torso and limbs accelerate in size. With time the boy grows taller, his arms and legs get longer, his face shifts from round to angular, and his hair color darkens.

particularly important during the early and middle childhood years when children are exposed to many contagious illnesses for the first time. Following a different trajectory, reproductive organs expand slowly until adolescence, at which time they undergo a substantial burst of growth.

The outcome of separate systems growing at distinct rates is the body as a whole increasing in size, albeit with its parts progressing unevenly. Typical growth curves for height and weight reveal rapid increases during the first 2 years, slow but steady growth during early and middle childhood, an explosive spurt during adolescence, and a leveling off to mature levels in early adulthood (Hamill et al., 1979). Patterns of growth are similar for boys and girls, although girls, on average, have their adolescent growth spurts a year and a half earlier, and boys end up taller and heavier.

FIGURE 5.3 Growing apart.

The separate fingers on a child's hand start out similar looking but become increasingly distinct.

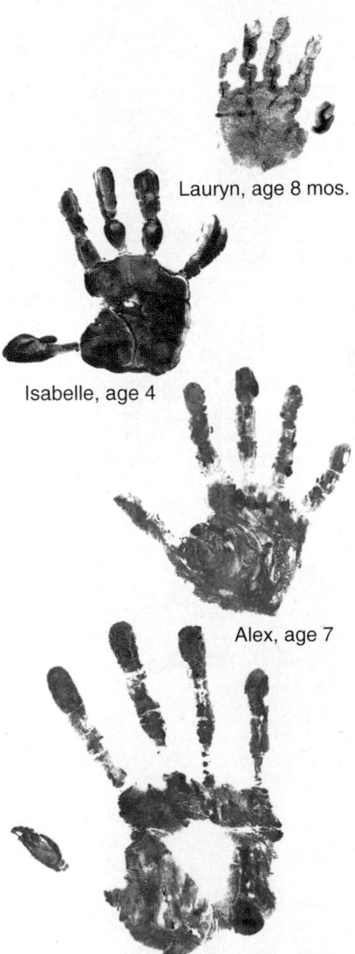

Functioning becomes increasingly differentiated. Every cell in a person's body (with the exception of sperm and ova) contains the same genetic instructions. As cells grow, they take on specific functions, some aiding with digestion, others transporting oxygen, still others transmitting signals, and so on. Individual cells "listen" to only a subset of the many instructions they have available. This progressive shift from having the *potential* to become many things to actually carrying out a specialized function is known as **differentiation**.

Differentiation characterizes many aspects of development. During prenatal development, the arms first protrude as tiny shoots, which gradually become longer buds, sprout globular hands, and eventually differentiate into fingers. After birth, fingers continue to elongate and become distinct. In Figure 5.3, you can see differentiation in the hand over the childhood years. Motor skills, too, become increasingly specialized: They first appear as rough, unsteady actions but gradually evolve into precise, controlled motions. Likewise, the human brain becomes increasingly differentiated in that separate areas become proficient in processing particular functions.

Functioning becomes increasingly integrated. Differentiating body parts begin to work together. Their coordinated efforts are known as **integration** (J. M. Tanner, 1990). The various parts of the eye coordinate their mechanical movements to permit vision. The mouth, stomach, liver, pancreas, and intestines play complementary roles in the digestion of food. The respiratory system and circulatory system work together in taking in oxygen and distributing it throughout the body and expelling carbon dioxide. You will learn later in this chapter that separate parts of the brain actively share information in marvelous feats of coordination.

Each child follows an individual growth curve. Children's bodies pursue predetermined heights—not as specific as 4′9″ or 6′2″, but with definite ball-park targets nevertheless. Height and weight show rapid growth during infancy, a slower rate of growth in middle childhood, and a spurt during adolescence. In individual children, growth curves, with height or weight plotted against age, are especially revealing when things go awry. Circumstances such as serious illness or poor nutrition may briefly halt height increases. Yet when health and adequate nutrition are restored, children grow rapidly again. Before you know it, they're back on track—back to where we might have expected them to be, given their age and original rate of growth.

Sadly, exceptions to this self-correcting tendency occur when severe malnutrition begins early in life and extends for a long time. Thus, children who have been seriously undernourished during their prenatal phase end up shorter than they would have been otherwise; occasionally, they also develop brain damage, mental and behavioral deficiencies, motor problems, and such chronic health conditions as diabetes and asthma (Rees, Harding, & Inder, 2006; Roseboom, de Rooij, & Painter, 2006; Salti & Ghattas, 2016; Tooley, Makhoul, & Fisher, 2016; M.-Q. Xu et al., 2009). For malnourished children who gain access to good nutrition later on, the difficulties may diminish, but some health challenges are likely to persist.

MyLab Education
Video Example 5.1

Find Developmental Meaning
What kind of motor abilities does 7-month-old Madison exhibit during play? She scoots up on her knees, stands and balances with support, tries to mouth a ball, holds up her head while resting on her belly, sits and reaches for a book, and crawls toward her father.

Physical development is characterized by both quantitative and qualitative changes. Quantitative changes are perhaps most obvious. Children continually eat, of course, and in most cases, they gain weight steadily. Motor skills result from numerous gradual advancements, as when a young girl slowly improves in manual dexterity and eventually ties her shoes independently. Qualitative changes occur as well (see Figure 5.4). As they grow from infants to toddlers to preschoolers, children walk more quickly and undergo qualitative transformations in posture, center of gravity, and rhythm (Gallahue & Ozmun, 1998; C. Hyde & Wilson, 2011).

Children's bodies function as dynamic systems. As you have learned, parts of the body develop over time, as do connections among these parts, and with time and activity, motor skills emerge and change. To illustrate, infants apply considerable effort in coordinating muscles in their arms and hands to reach objects. Having moved their limbs reflexively during the prenatal period, infants move intentionally and by 3½ to 4 months of age, they reach for objects, first shakily (Thelen & Smith, 2006). After some small improvements, infants exhibit temporary *declines* in speed, directness, and smoothness of reaching, as if they must figure out how to address changes in muscle tone or deal with another new factor.

Children gradually discover how to offset personal limitations while coordinating their body parts. Infants who make vigorous movements in their first few months of life must learn to control their arms in order to make contact with objects. In contrast, infants who generate few and slow movements have a different set of problems to solve: They must learn how to exert muscle tone while holding arms stiffly and extending them forward. With considerable practice, and typically before 14 months of age, most infants can reach easily and quickly (Gottwald et al., 2017). The act of reaching, like so many motor skills, shows individual differences in pathways to proficiency.

Developmental Systems Prompt 5.1

Children's health-related habits are acquired in familiar settings in which parents, siblings, teachers, and classmates model relevant behaviors. When possible, ask community leaders about typical family meals, popular sports, and leisure activities in the region to learn about the prevailing context for children's health.

Children's health is affected by the people in their lives and the resources they share. During family interaction, children learn to like certain foods and dislike others, follow an energetic or inactive lifestyle, and take or avoid physical risks (Berge, MacLehose, Larson, Laska, & Neumark-Sztainer, 2016; Kwon, Janz, Letuchy, Burns, & Levy, 2016). Parents' jobs affect children's health by generating resources for food, housing, and medical insurance (Gnanasekaran et al., 2016; Y. R. Harris & Graham, 2007). Peers instigate outdoor play and, as they grow older, gather at fast-food restaurants, in the park, at the

FIGURE 5.4 Qualitative changes in walking.

In walking, children progress from (A) having difficulty maintaining balance and using short steps in flat-footed contact, to (B) a smoother pattern, where arms are lower and heel-toe contact occurs, to (C) a relaxed gait with spontaneous arm swing (Gallahue & Ozmun, 1998).

Initial Motor Activity	Practiced Motor Activity	Mature Motor Activity
A	B	C

MyLab Education
Video Example 5.2

Find Developmental Meaning

What kind of motor abilities does 16-month-old Corwin exhibit? Corwin uses a range of motor skills to achieve his personal intentions. He pushes himself up from seated position and stands, maneuvers around a toy while walking quickly toward his mother, and waddles with arms held high in good balance and searches under pillows. Corwin dislodges a pillow and retrieves a toy, sits, crawls, and lunges into the pillow.

gym, or on a street corner. School personnel restrict or encourage children's physical activity and provide wholesome or nonnutritious meals on the lunch line. Neighbors are overweight, of healthy body type, or underweight and demonstrate particular pastimes, perhaps playing catch in the park, walking from one errand to the next, or sitting all day watching television and playing video games.

Growth During the Developmental Periods

Each age level presents unique physical needs and opportunities. We now describe the developmental periods in terms of physical characteristics and health-related issues.

Infancy (Birth–Age 2)

Infancy is a period of rapid growth. A baby typically doubles in weight within the first six months and triples by the end of the first year (Centers for Disease Control & Prevention [CDC], 2009a, 2009b). Before the umbilical cord is cut, the first reflex, *breathing*, begins, providing oxygen and removing carbon dioxide. Blinking and a few other reflexes occur and operate throughout life. Additional reflexes, such as automatically grasping small objects placed in hands, last only a few months. With maturation and learning, the infant skillfully coordinates sucking, breathing, and swallowing, allowing for consumption of milk and eventually solid foods.

As infants grow older, they move their body in a sequence of predictable ways. Motor skills emerge in a particular order, following *cephalocaudal* and *proximodistal* trends (W. J. Robbins, Brody, Hogan, Jackson, & Green, 1928). The **cephalocaudal trend** refers to the vertical order of emerging skills, proceeding from the head downward. Infants first learn to control their heads, then shoulders and trunk, and later their legs. The **proximodistal trend** refers to the inside-to-outside pattern in which growth progresses outward from the spine. Infants first learn to control their arms, then their hands, and, finally, their fingers. In the first 12 to 18 months, infants hold up their heads, roll over, reach for objects, sit, crawl, and take first steps. In the second year, they walk with increasing coordination.

Preparing for Your Licensure Examination

Your teaching test might ask you about major milestones in physical development.

Because infants cannot use words to communicate needs, practitioners must observe them carefully and also ask families about sleeping, eating, drinking, diapering, and comforting preferences. We offer ideas of what to look for in the Observation Guidelines table "Assessing Physical Development in Infancy."

MyLab Education
Video Example 5.3

Find Developmental Meaning

What motor skills do Acadia and Cody exhibit while playing in the park? Children run, climb a jungle gym, scoot around the top, and descend; step onto a balancing bar and teeter on it while moving toward the stairs, climbing up step by step, holding onto the handrails, and ascending to the top platform; and slide down the slide, all the while carrying out a conversation.

Early Childhood (Ages 2–6)

Dramatic changes occur in gross motor and fine motor skills during early childhood. **Gross motor skills** (e.g., walking, running, hopping, tumbling, jumping, climbing, and swinging) permit movement throughout the environment. **Fine motor skills** (e.g., drawing, writing, cutting with scissors, and manipulating small objects) involve controlled and precise movements, primarily with the hands.

During the preschool years, gross motor skills become smoother and better coordinated as a result of several factors—practice, maturation of arms and legs, and increases in muscular control. Optimism, determination, and pleasure in using new skills also contribute to the learning process. When Teresa's son Alex was 4, he repeatedly asked his parents to throw him a baseball as he stood poised with a bat. Not at all deterred by an abysmal batting average (about 0.05), Alex would frequently exclaim, "I almost got it!" His efforts paid off, as he gradually did learn to track the ball and coordinate his swing with its path.

A lot of chatter, fantasy, and joy accompany gross motor movements in early childhood. Often young children infuse pretend roles into physical play. They become superheroes and villains, cowboys and cowgirls, and astronauts and aliens.

Children also make major strides in fine motor skills. They dress and undress themselves and eat with utensils. They build blocks, put small pieces of puzzles together, and string beads. Some children spend considerable time drawing and cutting, forming creative shapes (e.g., by combining circles and lines to represent human beings), and mimicking adults' cursive writing with wavy lines or connected loops (Braswell & Callanan, 2003; Kellogg, 1967).

OBSERVATION GUIDELINES
Assessing Physical Development in Infancy

CHARACTERISTIC	LOOK FOR	EXAMPLE	IMPLICATION
Eating Habits	• *Ability to communicate hunger* by crying, reaching, and uttering a few words • *Developing ability to suck, swallow, and chew* • *Ability to enjoy and digest food* without abdominal upset • *Cultural and individual differences* in how families feed infants	Wendy Sue is a listless eater who doesn't seem as interested in food as are the other infants. The caregiver tells her supervisor she is concerned, and the two decide to talk with Wendy Sue's parents.	Talk with parents to learn about infant's individual health needs. Ask parents for their thoughts on infant's preferences for drinking, eating, and sleeping.
Mobility	• *Coordination of looking and touching* • *Emerging ability to move* toward objects • *Temperamental factors* that affect speed and frequency of movements • *Physical challenges*, including hearing and visual impairments, that affect exploration • *Temporary disruptions* in exploration, as when separating from parents in the morning	Due to neurological damage during birth, Daniel's left arm and leg are less strong than his right. His teacher notices that he seldom moves around the center. During a home visit, the teacher sees that Daniel's crawling is lopsided yet energetic. The teacher realizes that Daniel needs to feel secure before being able to explore in the center.	Set up the environment so infants find it safe, predictable, attractive, and interesting. Help individual children find challenges in the environment that match their interests.
Resting Patterns	• *Typical moods and behavior* prior to nap • *Families' expectations* for sleeping arrangements • *Difficulty falling asleep* • *Evidence that families understand risk* for sudden infant death syndrome (SIDS)	Angie cries a lot when falling asleep, in part because she naps on her stomach at home. Her teacher explains to her parents that he places babies on their backs to reduce the risk of SIDS. He rubs Angie's head as she adjusts to her new sleeping position.	Talk to parents about risk factors for SIDS (see upcoming section on "Rest and Sleep"). Explain why babies should be placed on their backs rather than abdomens when falling asleep.
Health Issues	• *Possible symptoms of infections*, such as irritability, fever, and respiratory difficulty • *Suspicious injuries and unusual behaviors* consistent with abuse • *Symptoms of prenatal drug exposure*, including irritability, feeding problems, and imbalance • *Physical disabilities* requiring accommodation	A teacher enjoys having 18-month-old Michael in her care. Michael has cerebral palsy, making it difficult for him to scoot around. His teacher encourages him to move toward favorite objects. When he has a fever, she calls his mother or father, as she would with any child.	Remain alert to signs of illness and infection in children. Contact family members when infants have a fever or show other unusual symptoms. With children who have physical disabilities, look for adaptive devices, such as special cups for toddlers with motor difficulties.

Early childhood educators notice pronounced individual differences in children's fine motor skills. Some children can tie their shoes by age 4 whereas others cannot do so until age 7 or later. In general, girls find certain fine motor activities (e.g., cursive handwriting) easier than do boys, although many young girls have limited dexterity, and plenty of boys find it easy and pleasurable to write, draw, and cut with scissors. Children born with certain disorders (e.g., Turner syndrome, Williams syndrome, or autism) and those exposed to alcohol during prenatal development show delays in writing with a pencil, typing on a keyboard, and tying their shoes (Berencsi, Gombos, & Kovács, 2016; Provost, Lopez, & Heimerl, 2007; Starke, Wikland, & Möller, 2003). Development of fine motor skills is constrained by the child's current neurological capacity; therefore, progress can be facilitated with fun activities. In Artifact Example 5.1, you can see 3½-year-old Isabelle's creations in writing, drawing, and cutting. Teachers might also arrange for children to make clay figures, color with crayons, string beads, trace felt letters, cut with scissors, crumple paper into small balls, and so on (Case-Smith, 1996; Maraj & Bonertz, 2007). Teachers can demonstrate certain hand grips yet allow children to use the kind of firm grasp that they are prepared for developmentally.

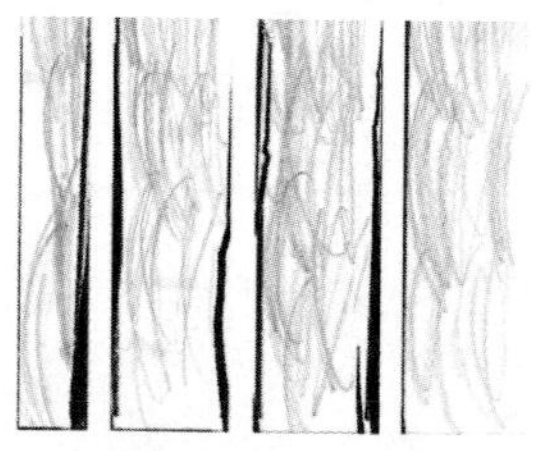

MyLab Education
Artifact Example 5.1

Find Developmental Meaning *What kind of literacy and fine motor skills did 3½-year-old Isabelle reveal in her artwork and name?* Isabelle is learning to write and spell her name, having included two *E*s and two *L*s, and mixing the order of these letters. In the artwork at right, she practiced her cutting and corrected her work in the third rectangle from the left. She appears to have traced a shape above her name and shows emerging control of colored pencils with her rectangles.

Preparing for Your Licensure Examination

Your teaching test might ask you about individual differences in age of achieving physical milestones, such as coloring with crayons, riding a two-wheel bicycle without training wheels, and entering puberty.

Until children with delayed fine motor skills start to catch up, they may benefit from academic activities that do not require these skills. Because many literacy and mathematics lessons require the handling of small objects (e.g., with tracing felt letters and counting small plastic bears), children with significant impediments in dexterity may miss out on educational benefits unless educators allow mastery through other formats (Cameron, Cottone, Murrah, & Grissmer, 2016; Palsbo, Marr, Streng, Bay, & Norblad, 2011). For example, children can learn to trace large letters and count shapes on the screen of a mobile device.

Middle Childhood (Ages 6–10)

Over the course of middle childhood, youngsters typically exhibit slow but steady gains in height and weight. Their bodies grow larger without undergoing major alterations in basic structures. As a result, proportions of separate body parts change less than in infancy or early childhood. With these slow, continuous gains come a few losses: Children lose their 20 primary ("baby") teeth, one by one, which are replaced by permanent teeth that at first appear oversized in the small mouths of 6-, 7-, and 8-year-olds. Girls mature somewhat more quickly than do boys, erupting permanent teeth sooner and progressing earlier toward skeletal maturity.

In middle childhood, children improve steadily in physical capabilities, becoming capable of refined fine motor skills. Their drawings, supported by physiological maturation and cognitive expansions, are more detailed, and their handwriting becomes smaller, smoother, and more consistent.

MyLab Education Application Exercise 5.1
Detect Developmental Levels

This exercise demonstrates the developmental progression in hand grips by comparing three children, Corwin (16 months), Zoe (4 years old), and Elena (9 years old). Notice differences in fluidity and control in children's movements.

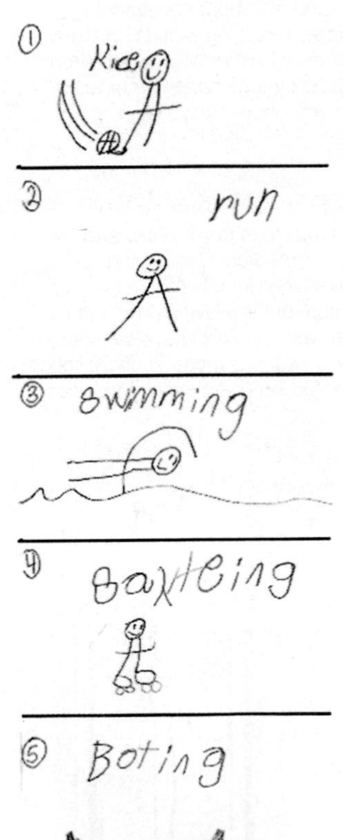

MyLab Education
Artifact Example 5.2

Find Developmental Meaning
What does 6-year-old Alex show he likes to do in this assignment? All of the activities Alex selected are movements. His favorite activities are kicking, running, swimming, skating, and boating. Many children of this age find athletic activities to be enjoyable.

Children in this age range also begin to tackle such fine motor activities as sewing, model building, and arts-and-crafts projects. Many gross motor skills, once uncertain, are now executed smoothly. Children put running to use in games and sports and intensify their speed and coordination in kicking, catching, and dribbling. Physical activity remains highly enjoyable for many children, as is reflected in Artifact Example 5.2. Sports also provide an entrée for children to interact and strengthen friendships (Cameron et al., 2016).

As children proceed through middle childhood, they become more sensitive about their physical appearance. In a variety of cultures, a person's physical attractiveness is connected with his or her self-esteem (Harter, 1999). Although many children exaggerate their physical flaws, the reality is that appearance *is* influential in social relationships (Raustorp & Lindwall, 2015). Peers and adults find attractive children more intelligent, believable, and fun than less attractive children (Bascandziev & Harris, 2016; Liechty, Clarke, Birky, Harrison, & STRONG Kids Team, 2016). Children occasionally tease one another based on their physical features, and educators must, of course, prohibit rude remarks and keep their own reactions in check.

Healthy physical growth happens naturally but not automatically. Teachers and other practitioners can support children's healthy physical development. In the Development-Enhancing Education feature "Accommodating the Physical Needs of Children," we give examples of strategies for addressing children's physical needs.

Development-Enhancing Education

Accommodating the Physical Needs of Children

Meet the requirements of individuals rather than expect everyone to conform to a universal schedule.

- A caregiver keeps a schedule of times each infant wants to be fed. That way, she can plan her feeding rotations and give every baby as much attention as possible. (Infancy)
- A child-care director asks for volunteers from a local senior group to drop in during the early afternoon when most infants want to be held before falling asleep. The director encourages the seniors to partner with the same couple of infants each visit. (Infancy)

Integrate physical needs into the curriculum.

- An infant caregiver understands the importance of meeting physical requirements in ways that deepen relationships. She uses one-to-one activities, such as diaper changing, as occasions to interact. (Infancy)
- A preschool teacher involves children in the preparation of healthful midmorning snacks by asking them to place crackers and apple slices on plates, serve peers, and sponge down the table. (Early Childhood)

Make sure the environment is safe for exploration.

- After a new carpet is installed in his classroom, a few children complain of headaches. Their teacher wonders if the recently applied adhesive is to blame and asks the director to evaluate the situation. Meanwhile, activities are conducted outdoors and in other rooms. (Early Childhood)
- The principal of a new elementary school consults with the playground inspector to examine specifications for secure anchoring in the ground, accessibility for children in wheelchairs, and a cushioning surface for reducing injuries. (Middle Childhood)

Provide frequent opportunities for children to engage in physical activity.

- A preschool teacher schedules "Music and Marching" for midmorning, "Outdoor Time" before lunch, and a nature walk after nap time. (Early Childhood)
- Elementary school teachers organize a walking club in which students stroll around the grounds three times a week recording steps with pedometers (Satcher, 2010). (Middle Childhood)

Plan activities that help children develop fine motor skills.

- A teacher introduces spoons and bowls when toddlers show an interest in feeding themselves with utensils. (Infancy)
- An after-school caregiver invites children to make mosaics of vehicles. The children glue a variety of small objects (e.g., beads, sequins, beans, colored rice) onto line drawings of cars, trains, boats, airplanes, and bicycles. (Middle Childhood)

Design physical activities so that students with widely differing skills can participate.

- During an outdoor play session, a teacher provides balls of varying sizes so that individual children at a range of proficiency levels can throw and catch balls. (Early Childhood)
- During a unit on tennis, a physical education teacher has children practice the forehand stroke with tennis rackets. First, she asks them to practice bouncing and then hitting the ball against the wall of the gymnasium. When they master basic skills, she asks them to see how many times they can hit the ball against the wall. When they reach five successive hits, she suggests they shift the height of the ball from waist high to shoulder high (Logsdon, Alleman, Straits, Belka, & Clark, 1997). (Middle Childhood)

Add physical activity into selected academic lessons.

- When teaching about molecules and temperature, a second-grade teacher asks children to stand in a cluster in an open area of the classroom. To show children how molecules behave when something is cold, she asks them to move slowly and stay close together. To show heat, she has them spread farther apart and move more quickly. (Middle Childhood)
- A preschool teacher reads *Alphabet Under Construction* by D. Fleming (2002) and then takes the children for a walk to examine the architecture of local buildings (Bredekamp, 2011). (Early Childhood)

Give children time to rest.

- After a full-day kindergarten class has been playing outside, their teacher offers a snack of apple slices, crackers, and milk. Afterward, the children gather around him on the floor while he reads a story. (Early Childhood)
- A third-grade teacher arranges for children to read books quietly after returning from lunch. (Middle Childhood)

Respect children's self-care.

- A teacher shows toddlers how to wash their hands after toileting and before eating. The teacher stands by the children and helps them rub their hands together with soap and water and then rinse. (Infancy)
- In an after-school program, a teacher allows the children to go to the restroom whenever they need to. He asks children to hang a clothespin with their name on an "out rope" when they leave the room and then return the pin to the "in rope" when they get back. (Middle Childhood)

MyLab Education
Video Example 5.4

Find Developmental Meaning
What aspects of Kyle and Curtis's basketball game suggest that it might be familiar and fun for them? Notice that the boys seem to be accustomed to playing basketball together. They appear happy and relaxed, pass the ball back and forth with ease, use mutually understood names for moves, and smile.

Early Adolescence (Ages 10–14)

The most obvious physical change in early adolescence is the beginning of **puberty**. Ushered in by a cascade of hormones, puberty entails a series of biological developments that lead to reproductive maturity. Puberty is accompanied by a **growth spurt**, a rapid increase in height and weight. The release of hormones has other repercussions as well, including increases in bone density, facial oil production (often manifested as acne), and sweat secretions (Styne, 2003).

Girls typically progress through puberty before boys do. Puberty begins in girls sometime between ages 8 and 13 (on average, at age 10). It starts with a growth spurt, budding of the breasts, and emergence of pubic hair. These changes are typically gradual; however, first menstruation, **menarche**, is an unprecedented event that can be either exciting or frightening depending on a girl's preparation. The first menstrual period occurs late in puberty, usually between 9 and 15 years of age. Nature apparently delays menstruation, and with it the possibility of conception, until girls are close to adult height and strong enough to bear a child.

For boys, puberty starts between 9 and 14 years (on average, at 11½ years), when the testes enlarge and the scrotum changes in texture and color. A year or so later, the penis grows larger, and pubic hair appears; the growth spurt begins soon after. At about 13 to 14 years, boys have their first ejaculation, the **spermarche**, often while sleeping. Boys seem to receive less information about this milestone than girls do about menstruation, and little is known about boys' feelings about it. Later developments for boys include the growth of facial hair, the deepening of the voice, and eventually the attainment of adult height.

In addition to developing different reproductive organs, boys and girls become increasingly distinct in height and muscle mass. On average, boys end up taller than girls. Boys also have a longer period of steady prepubescent growth, and they add a bit more height during their growth spurt. With the onset of puberty, boys also gain more muscle mass than girls, courtesy of the male hormone *testosterone*. The course of puberty for boys and girls is depicted in Figure 5.5.

Variations exist in age of puberty. Heredity, nutrition, exercise, and stress influence the age of onset (Mustanski, Viken, Kaprio, Pulkkinen, & Rose, 2004; Parent, Franssen, Fudvoye, Gérard, & Bourguignon, 2015). Some adolescents are pleased to see first signs of puberty, whereas others are not at all happy with their changing bodies. They may believe they are too thin, fat, flabby, or unattractive or are developing too quickly or slowly.

FIGURE 5.5 Maturational sequences of puberty.
Girls start puberty a little before boys, on average, whereas boys typically end up a little taller.

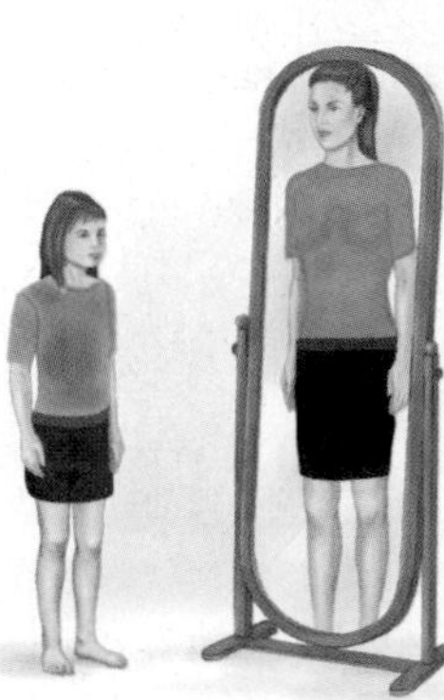

IN GIRLS

Initial elevation of breasts and beginning of growth spurt (typically between 8 and 13 years; on average, at 10 years)

Appearance of pubic hair (sometimes occurs before elevation of breasts)

Increase in size of uterus, vagina, labia, and clitoris

Further development of breasts

Peak of growth spurt

Menarche, or onset of menstrual cycle (typically between 9 and 15 years)

Completion of height gain (about two years after menarche), breast development, and pubic hair growth

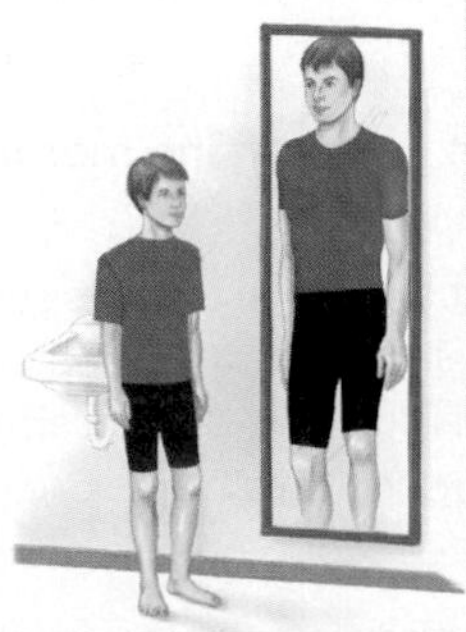

IN BOYS

Enlargement of the testes and changes in texture and color of scrotum (typically between 9 and 14 years; on average, at 11½ years)

Increase in penis size and appearance of pubic hair

Beginning of growth spurt (on average, at 12½ years)

Spermarche, or first ejaculation

Peak of growth spurt, accompanied by more rapid penis growth

Appearance of facial hair

Deepening voice, as size of larynx and length of vocal cords increase

Completion of penis growth, height gain, and pubic hair growth

Youngsters who begin puberty early, girls especially, are often dissatisfied with their bodies and vulnerable to anxiety, eating disorders, precocious sexual activity, and substance abuse disorders (K. Hedges & Korchmaros, 2016; Zehr, Culbert, Sisk, & Klump, 2007). Children entering puberty later than peers are apt to be self-conscious and worried that something is wrong with them (Lindfors et al., 2007). Adjustments for early and late developers depend on the full spectrum of strengths, resources, and risks in their lives. Those who have weak coping skills are especially likely to find untimely puberty stressful (J. Hamilton et al., 2014).

School personnel can help youngsters adjust to puberty by being a source of steadfast support. In the Development-Enhancing Education feature "Accommodating the Physical Needs of Adolescents," we give specific examples of strategies for accommodating puberty and its diversity.

Whenever it begins, puberty has far-reaching effects on the young person. Hormones that are released during puberty intensify activity in areas of the brain that process rewards, emotions, and social reasoning about why people act as they do (Peper & Dahl, 2013). Puberty loosens restraints on problematic behaviors, in part, because brain changes accentuate the pleasure adolescents feel when taking risks, especially in the presence of peers. In many cultures the onset of puberty is associated with experimentation with alcohol, drugs, and cigarettes and the misbehaviors of lying, shoplifting, and stealing (R. Carter, Jaccard, Silverman, & Pina, 2009; S. M. Kogan et al., 2015; S. M. Martino, Ellickson, Klein, McCaffrey, & Edelen, 2008). We explore adolescents' risk behavior and its implications later in this chapter.

Late Adolescence (Ages 14–18)

On average at about age 15 for girls and 17 for boys, the growth spurt ends and sexual maturity is attained. By this age level many young people have shed the gawky appearance of younger adolescence, now presenting as attractive young adults, comfortable in their own skin and balanced in the relative sizes of their separate body parts Those who eat well and exercise are apt to enjoy a peak in fitness, strength, and flexibility.

Development-Enhancing Education

Accommodating the Physical Needs of Adolescents

Anticipate concerns adolescents have about developing normally.

- A middle school basketball coach gives students plenty of time to shower in stalls that have curtains for privacy. (Early Adolescence)
- A high school teacher advising the Yearbook Club asks student photographers to take pictures of boys and girls from different ethnicities and of varying heights, weights, and appearances so as to emphasize diversity in appearance in the student population. (Late Adolescence)

Be sensitive to adolescents' feelings about early or late maturation.

- A middle school's health curriculum describes the sequences of puberty in boys and girls. It also stresses that the timing of these changes varies widely from one person to the next. (Early Adolescence)
- During an advising session, a high school teacher asks a late-developing freshman boy about his goals for the year. The adviser admits that his primary goal at the same age was to grow a few inches, which makes the boy smile. (Early Adolescence)

Keep in mind that menstruation, which is often accompanied by discomfort, can first happen at unexpected times.

- An eighth-grade girl comes into class obviously upset, and her best friend approaches the teacher to explain that the two of them need to go to the nurse's office. The teacher realizes what has probably happened and gives them permission to go. (Early Adolescence)
- A high school nurse allows girls to rest on a sofa in her office when they have menstrual cramps. (Late Adolescence)

Make sure adolescents understand what sexual harassment is, and do not tolerate it.

- A middle school includes a sexual harassment policy in its student handbook. Homeroom teachers explain the policy at the beginning of the school year and require signatures from students and parents acknowledging they have read it. (Early Adolescence)
- When a high school junior teases a classmate about her "big rack," his teacher takes him aside and explains that his comment not only constitutes sexual harassment (and so violates school policy) but also makes the girl feel embarrassed. The boy admits that he spoke without thinking and, after class, tells the girl he's sorry. (Late Adolescence)

Table 5.1 Percentages of U.S. Students in Grades 9–12 Who Reported Engaging in Risky Behaviors

RISKY BEHAVIOR	GIRLS	BOYS
Substance use		
Alcohol (in last 30 days)	33.5	32.2
Tobacco (in last 30 days)	27.7	34.9
Marijuana (in last 30 days)	20.1	23.2
Cocaine (in lifetime)	3.8	6.3
Inhalants (in lifetime)	6.6	7.2
Heroin (in lifetime)	1.2	2.7
Methamphetamine (in lifetime)	2.3	3.6
Ecstasy (MDMA; in lifetime)	3.9	6.0
Hallucinogenic drugs (e.g., LSD, mescaline, or angel dust; in lifetime)	4.6	8.0
Steroids without prescription (in lifetime)	2.7	4.0
Prescription drugs without prescription (in lifetime)	15.6	17.8
Sexual behaviors		
Had sexual intercourse (in lifetime)	39.3	43.2
Sexually active (had intercourse in past 3 months)	29.8	30.3
No method of birth control during last intercourse (among sexually active adolescents)	15.2	12.2
Alcohol or drug use at last sexual intercourse (among sexually active adolescents)	16.4	24.6
Had four or more sexual partners (in lifetime)	8.8	14.1
Behaviors that contribute to unintentional injuries		
Rarely or never wore seat belts in car	4.9	7.2
Rarely or never wore helmet on bicycle (in those who rode bike in last year)	80.1	82.4
Rode with a driver who drank alcohol (in last 30 days)	20.2	19.6
Drove car after drinking alcohol (in last 30 days)	6.0	9.5
Texted or sent email while driving a car or other vehicle (in last 30 days)	40.4	42.4
Weapon use		
Carried a weapon (e.g., knife, club, gun; in last 30 days)	7.5	24.3
Carried a gun (in last 30 days)	1.6	8.7

Sources: CDC (2016).

With sexual maturation comes a motivation to enter close relationships with hugging, kissing, and, for many teens, intimate contact (Baams, Dubas, Overbeek, & Van Aken, 2015; DeLamater & MacCorquodale, 1979).

In some teens, the motivation to engage in dangerous behaviors, which began during early adolescence, intensifies during the high school years. In fact, numerous young people engage in one or more behaviors that could undermine their long-term physical health. Table 5.1 (above) presents the prevalence of risky behaviors in American high school students. Given their significance, we examine several of these behaviors in more detail in an upcoming section.

The Developmental Trends table "Physical Development at Different Age Levels" summarizes the key characteristics of each age group and provides implications for teachers and other professionals. In the next section, we examine young people's activities that contribute to good health and, conversely, those that undermine it.

DEVELOPMENTAL TRENDS
Physical Development at Different Age Levels

AGE	WHAT YOU MIGHT OBSERVE	DIVERSITY	IMPLICATIONS
Infancy (Birth–2 Years)	• Emergence of reflexes • Rapid growth and weight gain • Ability to move around, first by squirming; then rolling, crawling, creeping, and scooting; and finally, by walking • Beginning to coordinate hand movements with vision • Increasing self-help skills in feeding, dressing, washing, toileting, and grooming	• Children vary in timing of rolling over, crawling, and sitting up depending on genetic and cultural factors. • Parents provide infants varying amounts of time on the floor for exploration. • Eye–hand coordination develops earlier or later depending on genetic makeup and practice with visually guided movements. • Motor skills emerge somewhat later in infants with low birthweight.	• Celebrate each child's patterns of growth. • Watch for exceptional delays that might require intervention. • Encourage movements of squirming, rolling, scooting, crawling, and walking. • Don't push infants to reach milestones. Encourage each phase of development and allow infants to attempt new skills when ready.
Early Childhood (2–6 Years)	• Elongating of face, arms, and legs • Boundless energy for running, hopping, tumbling, climbing, and swinging • Occasional collisions while learning to coordinate movements • Awkward pencil grip (child might use fist to hold pencil at age two and pincer grip with three fingers around five) • Transition away from afternoon nap, initially marked by fussiness in the afternoon	• Individual children differ considerably in the ages at which they master motor skills. • On average, boys are more active than girls, but girls are somewhat healthier. • Some home environments (e.g., small apartments) limit vigorous physical activity; others have hazardous conditions (e.g., lead paint, toxic fumes). • Children with intellectual disabilities may have delayed motor skills.	• Provide frequent opportunities to play outside or (in inclement weather) in a large indoor space. • Intersperse vigorous physical exercise with rest and quiet time. • Encourage use of fine motor skills with finger painting, puzzles, clay, blocks, and crafts. • When children cannot trace letters or count small objects, provide assistive devices or mobile applications that support early literacy and numeracy.
Middle Childhood (6–10 Years)	• Steady gains in height and weight • Loss and replacement of primary teeth with occasional chewing on objects to relieve gum tenderness • Refinement and consolidation of gross motor skills in play activities • Participation in organized sports • Increasing fluency in writing and other activities requiring fine motor skills	• Variations in weight and height are apparent. • Some children show exceptional athletic talents and interests. • Gender differences appear in preferences for certain sports. • Some neighborhoods lack safe play areas. • Some children continue to be delayed in fine motor skills. • Some children prioritize video games over outdoor pursuits.	• Integrate physical movement into selected academic activities. • Provide daily opportunities for play. • Teach children the basics of sports, and encourage them to participate in athletic programs. • Encourage practice with fine motor skills, and don't penalize children whose fine motor precision is delayed.
Early Adolescence (10–14 Years)	• Periods of rapid growth in height • Changes in body shape • Large appetite • Beginning of puberty • Secondary sex characteristics • Self-consciousness about physical changes • Occasional risk-taking behavior	• Onset of puberty varies over several years. • Puberty typically occurs earlier in girls than boys. • Adolescents differ in strength, endurance, physical activity, and talent for sports. • Boys are generally stronger and more confident in sports than are girls.	• Be a role model for exercising and eating well. • Arrange for privacy while changing clothes and showering. • Explain what sexual harassment is, and do not tolerate it. • Arrange after-school clubs for fun activities. • Supervise adolescents and restrict their access to risky activities.
Late Adolescence (14–18 Years)	• In girls, attainment of mature height • In boys, ongoing increases in stature • Ravenous appetites • Sexual arousal and intimate sexual activity • Some risky behaviors (e.g., drinking alcohol, taking drugs, having unprotected sex, driving while impaired, revealing personal information on Internet) • Adolescents are less likely than younger children to get regular medical care.	• Gender differences in physical abilities increase; boys more often join organized sports programs. • Some teens limit risky behaviors after previously compromising their health. • Eating disorders may appear, especially in girls. • Adolescents use drugs and alcohol based largely on access, personality, peer norms, and parent behaviors. • Some adolescents prioritize Internet use over physical activity.	• Provide adolescents with the facts about sexual intercourse. • Encourage abstinence when adolescents are not sexually active. • When adolescents are sexually active, advise them to use protective measures and restrict numbers of partners. • Encourage young people to form worthwhile goals for their future. • Reduce adolescents' exposure to potentially risky situations. • Enforce policies on sexual harassment.

Sources: Bredekamp (2011); Flensborg-Madsen and Mortensen (2017); Gallahue and Ozmun (1998); Kretsch, Mendle, Cance, and Harden (2016); Moreno, Jelenchick, and Christakis (2013); Potvin, Snider, Prelock, Kehayia, and Wood-Dauphinee (2013); V. F. Reyna and Farley (2006); Steinberg (2007); J. M. Tanner (1990); and C. Wood (2007).

Summary

The body is a dynamic system that changes and matures during interaction with people. Over time, physiological functioning becomes increasingly *differentiated* (e.g., cells take on discrete roles depending on maturational state and location in the body) and *integrated* (e.g., separate body parts work closely together). Children's bodies basically aim for general targets in size and height, trajectories that can be temporarily disrupted by mild illnesses or nutritional inadequacies. Enduring health problems can be more disruptive to growth. Assuming healthy genes and conditions, predictable changes occur in physical functioning. In infancy, survival mechanisms, such as reflexes, are introduced, and motor skills compel exploration. Early childhood is marked by vigorous physical activity and the acquisition of purposeful motor skills. Middle childhood is a time of consolidation, when children's growth continues but the rate decelerates, and children put motor skills to purposeful use. Puberty marks the onset of adolescence and extends over several years' time. Adult height, sexual maturation, and a typically more mature outlook on personal health are attained in late adolescence.

MyLab Education Self-Check 5.1

Health and Well-Being

5.2 Summarize basic issues related to children's physical health and explain how educators can assist children in acquiring health promoting habits and avoiding health-compromising behaviors.

Educators foster children's health when they provide good choices for snacks, meals, and physical activity. Of course, children are faced with other options outside of school, and as they grow into their adolescent years, they are faced with temptations that can undermine their health. To help young people strengthen their desire and ability to keep themselves healthy, teachers, counselors, and school leaders focus on **self-regulation**, the processes by which people direct their own actions, learning, and emotions according to acquired standards. Self-regulation appears in many areas of childhood, for example, in emotional development in tempering the expression of anger and frustration, in behavioral self-control in resisting distractions, and in academic learning in breaking up difficult assignments and methodically finishing each part. In the context of physical development, self-regulation applies to lifelong habits that safeguard one's health.

In the following sections, we look at children's eating habits, physical activity, rest and sleep, and health-compromising behaviors. We also identify strategies that adults can use to encourage healthful lifestyles. Periodically we return to the concept of self-regulation because of its utility in helping children develop habits of self-care.

Eating Habits

Children's diet affects all aspects of their well-being. In many but unfortunately not all circumstances, the nutrition children consume is sufficient to enable growth, energy, and the ability to learn and remember.

At birth, breastfeeding is the preferred source of nutrition because breast milk is rich in vitamins, provides antibodies against illness, nourishes the growing brain, is easier to digest than infant formulas, and offers long-term protection against obesity and cardiovascular disease (London et al., 2011; Lutter & Lutter, 2012; Zalewski et al., 2017). Of course, some mothers cannot easily breastfeed, others do not want to, and a few (e.g., mothers who carry the human immunodeficiency virus [HIV] or are undergoing certain treatments) do not because infections and medications would be passed to the baby. As an alternative, many families select one of the iron-fortified formulas that have been commercially prepared from cow's milk or soybeans to match infants' digestive abilities and requirements for protein, calories, vitamins, and minerals. Specialized formulas are available for infants with food allergies and intolerances. Infant caregivers generally try to support families' preferences and suggest medically advisable strategies, for example, introducing nutritious soft cereals and fruits at about 4 to 6 months and avoiding hard foods that infants cannot chew or swallow.

As children grow, they develop habits and preferences during meals at home and with family. For some children, mealtime is a chance to refuel, enjoy cultural customs, and talk about the day. When parents have few financial resources or are far from markets with fresh produce, meals can be unhealthy. When children are underfed or given primarily nonnutritious foods, consequences become serious. Anemia (iron deficiency) is a common nutritional problem and contributor to delays and behavioral disturbances (Domellöf & Szymlek-Gay, 2012; Killip, Bennett, & Chambers, 2007; S. P. Walker et al., 2007). Developing a preference for meals that are high in fat, sugar, and salt contributes to obesity and other long-term medical problems (S. O. Hughes et al., 2016; A. Miller et al., 2016).

FIGURE 5.6 Healthy Meals at School.

The USDA presents guidelines for meals and beverages at school that offer children essential nutrition and hydration without excessive calories. *Reprinted from the USDA (2012).* The school day just got healthier. *USDA Center for Nutrition Policy and Promotion 10 Tips Education Series. Retrieved from* www.choosemyplate.gov/food-groups/downloads/TenTips/DGTipsheet21SchoolDayJustGotHealthier.pdf

10 tips
Nutrition Education Series

the School Day just got Healthier

United States Department of Agriculture

Nearly 32 million children receive meals throughout the school day. These meals are based on nutrition standards from the U.S. Department of Agriculture. New nutrition standards for schools increase access to healthy food and encourage kids to make smart choices. Schools are working to make meals more nutritious, keep all students hunger-free, and help children maintain or reach a healthy weight.

1 healthier school meals for your children
Your children benefit from healthier meals that include more whole grains, fruits and vegetables, low-fat dairy products, lower sodium foods, and less saturated fat. Talk to your child about the changes in the meals served at school.

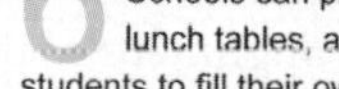

2 more fruits and vegetables every day
Kids have fruits and vegetables at school every day. A variety of vegetables are served througout the week including red, orange, and dark-green vegetables.

3 more whole-grain foods
Half of all grains offered are whole-grain-rich foods such as whole-grain pasta, brown rice, and oatmeal. Some foods are made by replacing half the refined-grain (white) flour with whole-grain flour.

4 both low-fat milk (1%) and fat-free milk varieties are offered
Children get the same calcium and other nutrients, but with fewer calories and less saturated fat by drinking low-fat (1%) or fat-free milk. For children who can't drink milk due to allergies or lactose intolerance, schools can offer milk substitutes, such as calcium-fortified soy beverages.

5 less saturated fat and salt
A variety of foods are offered to reduce the salt and saturated fat in school meals. Main dishes may include beans, peas, nuts, tofu, or seafood as well as lean meats or poultry. Ingredients and foods contain less salt (sodium).

6 more water
Schools can provide water pitchers and cups on lunch tables, a water fountain, or a faucet that allows students to fill their own bottles or cups with drinking water. Water is available where meals are served.

7 new portion sizes
School meals meet children's calorie needs, based on their age. While some portions may be smaller, kids still get the nutrition they need to keep them growing and active.

8 stronger local wellness programs
New policies offer opportunities for parents and communities to create wellness programs that address local needs. Talk with your principal, teachers, school board, parent-teacher association, and others to create a strong wellness program in your community.

9 MyPlate can help kids make better food choices
Show children how to make healthy food choices at school by using MyPlate. Visit ChooseMyPlate.gov for tips and resources.

10 resources for parents
School meal programs can provide much of what children need for health and growth. But for many parents, buying healthy foods at home is a challenge. Learn more about healthy school meals and other nutrition assistance programs at www.fns.usda.gov.

Go to www.ChooseMyPlate.gov for more information.

DG TipSheet No. 21
August 2012
USDA is an equal opportunity provider and employer.

What, exactly, *should* children be eating? The U.S. Department of Agriculture recommends that half a person's plate be covered with fruits and vegetables, and that water and nonfat or one percent milk be offered as beverages instead of sugary drinks and whole milk (U.S. Department of Agriculture [USDA] Center for Nutrition Policy and Promotion, 2013). According to this model, a 10-year-old boy who is 51 inches tall (4 feet 3 inches) and 71 pounds in weight would consume about 1,800 calories per day and eat 6 ounces of grains (at least half of which are whole grains), 2½ cups of vegetables, 1½ cups of fruits, 3 cups of milk, and 5 ounces of meats, beans, or other low-fat proteins. A few small snacks (e.g., cookies and potato chips) are considered acceptable as long as children are physically active and obtain needed nutrition. There are many opportunities for schools to encourage this kind of healthy diet, as you can see in Figure 5.6.

Most children between ages 2 and 17 do *not* meet the dietary requirements established by the USDA (USDA, 2013). The diets of young American children (between 2 and 5 years of age) generally include adequate amounts of fruit, milk, and meat but insufficient servings of dark green vegetables, beans, and whole grains. Children also eat far too much "bad" stuff—the fatty, sugary, and salty foods. Older children also become less inclined to eat breakfast, resulting in difficulty concentrating at school (CDC, 2005a).

How might adults encourage children to eat more of the good stuff and less of the bad stuff? The self-regulatory processes we introduced earlier—setting goals, keeping track of their relevant behaviors, and evaluating what they can do to improve—are good targets for improvement. The National Health Education Standards identifies relevant behaviors that could be fostered at school (CDC, 2013a). One of the standards is that "Students will demonstrate the ability to use goal-setting skills to enhance health." First-grade children might meet this standard by setting goals to increase their consumption of fresh fruits and vegetables. In a middle school program, students learn about the human body, the importance of good nutrition, the value of physical activity, and the harmfulness of junk food (Contento Koch, Lee, Sauberli, & Calabrese-Barton, 2007). In one intervention, young students set goals for healthier eating and subsequently decreased their consumption of sweetened beverages, fast food, and packaged snacks. Older students might conduct a comprehensive analysis of their own diets, set goals for improvement, maintain a monthlong chart of the foods and beverages they consume and evaluate the alignment of their diet with their goals.

Overweight Youth

In part because of increasing reliance on processed foods and a sedentary lifestyle, a staggering number of children have become overweight during the last few decades. Children are considered *overweight* when their body mass index (BMI), a measure of weight in relation to height, is at or above the 85th percentile for children of the same age and sex (CDC, 2013b). Obviously, there is significant variation among overweight students. Children are considered **obese** if their BMI is at or above the 95th percentile for someone of the same age and gender. Approximately 17% of children in the United States between ages 2 and 17 are obese (CDC, 2013c). Comparably high rates occur in many other countries as well. In fact, obesity is now considered a global health crisis (Y. Wang & Lim, 2012; World Health Organization, 2000).

Obesity is a concern because it is associated with serious health risks in childhood, including asthma. Even deadlier problems occur in adolescence and early in adulthood, for example, diabetes, elevated blood pressure, and high cholesterol (CDC, 2013d; Jelalian, Wember, Bungeroth, & Birmaher, 2007; Mehl et al., 2017). Obesity also has detrimental social consequences. Sadly, some peers torment overweight classmates, calling them names and excluding them from social activities.

Obesity has complex origins. For some obese children, weight problems may have a genetic basis, but environmental experiences, especially the family's lack of access to affordable fresh food and customs in eating high-fat meals, are also causes (Berger-Jenkins et al., 2017; H. Thomas, 2006). Acquiring an appetite for unhealthy foods, eating too much and too often, sitting for long periods in front of televisions and computers, and spending little time in physical activity all contribute to obesity in children. Interventions in clinics, dietary counseling, setting goals for optimal calorie levels, and tracking progress toward goals can culminate in weight loss in obese children (Lochrie et al., 2013).

Increasingly, educators are realizing that schools are an important setting for tackling children's weight problems. Schools regularly provide breakfast to children whose families cannot easily afford it. Not only does breakfast provide essential nutrients and energy, allowing children to concentrate on schoolwork, it also increases the chances that children eat more healthily at other meals during the day (Affenito et al., 2013). Many educators are making sure that water is available for drinking (rather than carbonated sodas), adjusting cafeteria menus, and replacing the sweet, salty, and fatty snacks in vending machines with more nutritious items (Cluss, Fee, Culyba, Bhat, & Owen, 2014; Fetro, Givens, & Carroll, 2009; Lumeng, 2006).

A more controversial program has been for schools to issue BMI report cards to children. Intended to help children and families keep track of children's weight, BMI report cards can embarrass children and are not always accompanied by chances for physical activity at school or a climate that warmly accepts all body shapes and sizes (Nihiser et al., 2009). At this point, it is not clear that the BMI reports prevent or reduce obesity in children (CDC, 2015a).

Eating Disorders

Whereas some young people eat too much, others eat too little and develop eating disorders that threaten their health. People with **anorexia nervosa** eat hardly anything. In contrast, people with **bulimia** eat voraciously, especially fattening foods, and then purge their bodies by taking laxatives and forcing themselves to vomit. Unfortunately, extreme weight control methods, such as drastically reducing calories, taking diet pills or laxatives, and vomiting, are fairly widespread among adolescents. Approximately 10% of high school girls and 4% of boys in the United States are anorexic (S. B. Austin et al., 2008; Stice, Marte, & Rohde, 2013).

Individuals with eating disorders often have a distorted body image (believing they are "fat" when they appear dangerously thin to others). They may exercise compulsively to lose additional weight. In addition to jeopardizing health, eating disorders tend to slow down the bodily changes of puberty (London et al., 2011). Moreover, the malnutrition that accompanies anorexia can, in extreme cases, cause heart failure. Tragically, anorexia is associated with thoughts related to, and attempts at, suicide.

Many experts believe that society's obsession with thinness is partly to blame for anorexia nervosa and bulimia (Ahern & Hetherington, 2006). Images of attractiveness in the media are unrealistic for most young people. Those individuals who are extremely dissatisfied with their bodies are at risk for developing an eating disorder (A. S. Hartmann, Greenberg, & Wilhelm, 2013; Stice, Gau, Rohde, & Shaw, 2017). Psychological factors, some of which may be partly inherited, come into play. Individuals with eating disorders are apt to ruminate over their problems and to be lonely, depressed, and anxious, and some have been maltreated or abuse illicit substances (Brietzke, Moreira, Toniolo, & Lafer, 2011; Dominé, Berchtold, Akré, Michaud, & Suris, 2009; Manuel & Wade, 2013; M. Seidel et al., 2016).

Educators can watch symptoms of increasing thinness, complaints of being "too fat," unusual eating habits, lengthy exercise routines, lack of energy, and cognitive impairments (which might be from malnutrition). The psychological problems young people with eating disorders are apt to suffer, such as anxiety, sometimes become apparent to educators through the young person's rapid breathing, sweaty palms, worried facial expressions, and complaints of headaches and nausea. Given their disorders in body image, students do not necessarily see themselves unhealthy or in need of treatment. In fact, a large percentage of students with eating disorders are *not* slender; some eat a lot, purge regularly, and appear normal to others.

Fortunately, many young people with eating disorders respond favorably to intensive and long-term intervention from specialists (Abbate-Daga, Marzola, Amianto, & Fassino, 2016). When students return to school, they are likely to require special assistance, perhaps reduced workload as they regain their strength, counseling at school, and tutoring on academic material they missed during absences (National Eating Disorder Toolkit, 2017). Of course, each student with an eating disorder is unique. Adults can listen sympathetically to young people who choose to tell them about their own experiences.

MyLab Education Application Exercise 5.2
Meet Individual Needs

In this video a young woman describes her experience with anorexia nervosa. How did it make her feel to avoid eating?

Promoting Good Nutrition

We end this section with thoughts about what teachers and other practitioners can do to encourage good nutrition:

- **Make children's health a priority.** Health advisory councils can be established at school to promote children's physical welfare. A team of teachers, parents, community members, and students can make recommendations for cafeteria menus, guidelines for birthday celebrations, and opportunities for physical activity (e.g., minutes per week in physical activity, time for recess, and movement in academic lessons; CDC, 2011; Hager et al., 2016).

- **Offer nourishing food at school.** Teachers and other school personnel can advocate for healthful foods and drinks on the cafeteria line, in vending machines at school, at concession stands at school events, and at meetings with families (Azzam, 2009/2010; Budd & Volpe, 2006; CDC, 2011). When children are permitted to bring snacks, teachers can send home guidelines for appropriate items (e.g., carrot sticks, pretzels, and granola bars). As a fourth-grader, Teresa's son Alex was advised that chocolate (a passion for him) was *not* a good idea for a midmorning snack. He began to bring other snacks instead, such as granola bars, and as you might suspect, he was happy to find granola bars sprinkled with chocolate chips!

- **Provide between-meal snacks for young children.** Crackers, healthy cookies, and fruit and vegetable slices can invigorate active preschoolers. Young children burn through calories and need to be refueled. Depending on their metabolism, older children benefit from munchies as well, especially when they contain needed fiber and missing nutrition. Snacks are particularly important for children who are growing rapidly without adequate meals at home.

- **Encourage children to try new foods.** Children who have grown accustomed to processed food may initially resist fresh food. Young children may not try a new food until they have seen it multiple times, sometimes not until 10 to 15 presentations (Blissett & Fogel, 2013; Zero to Three: National Center for Infants, Toddlers, and Families [Zero to Three], 2010). Strategies that successfully encourage culinary exploration include offering new foods next to preferred foods; using such healthy dips as yogurt, hummus, ketchup, and low-fat salad dressings alongside vegetables and fruits; and enlisting the involvement of children in preparation of the meal (Zero to Three, 2010). Educators in the Baltimore City public schools included a piece of fresh fruit in every lunch as part of a program called "No thank you bites," in which children try small portions of a new fruit, vegetable, or entrée item; ask for more if they like it or say, "No thank you" and move down the cafeteria line (Geraci, 2009/2010). Another strategy of Baltimore schools has been to open an organic farm that produces fresh food and allows students to work there, instilling an interest in the crops they grow together. What is *not* effective is to restrict the child's preferred food, for example, chocolate chip cookies, until he or she eats a portion of an alternative substance, for example, broccoli. Children who are controlled in this manner may very well eat broccoli in order to gain access to cookies but typically will not select broccoli unless accompanied by an incentive (Blissett & Fogel, 2013).

- **Educate children about good and bad food.** Children can learn about nutrients that are essential for health, the ideal amounts of certain foods, and the consequences of eating excessive calories and too many sweet, salty, and fatty foods. Many activities, including electronic games, activity sheets, videos, and songs, are available through the USDA's ChooseMyPlate.Gov programs (choosemyplate.gov/kids/ParentsEducators.html).

MyLab Education Application Exercise 5.3
Identify Development-Enhancing Education
Examine a preschool teacher's introduction to the health benefits of fruits and vegetables.

• **Ask children to set goals and monitor progress in eating well.** Children can evaluate their diets based on recommended servings in basic food groups. In Artifact Example 5.3, 8-year-old Charlotte realizes she has been consuming too many sugary snacks. After analyzing their diets, young people can set specific goals (e.g., substituting salty snacks with an apple or yogurt) and chart their progress toward these goals (Lochrie et al., 2013; Schinke, Moncher, & Singer, 1994).

• **Make referrals when you suspect students have eating disorders.** Youngsters with eating disorders urgently need medical intervention. If you suspect a student has an eating disorder, you will want to contact your principal, school counselor, or nurse. Even after beginning medical care, children may require services at school to help them cope with the trials and tribulations of being in an academically challenging, complex social environment.

• **Follow up when you suspect serious nutritional problems.** Malnutrition can occur as a result of many factors. When low income is the cause, practitioners can help families obtain free or reduced-cost lunches at school. When parental neglect or mental illness might be involved, teachers can report their suspicions to principals, counselors, or school nurses and find the best approach for protecting children and supporting families.

• **Respect the feelings of students.** Youngsters who struggle with obesity or eating disorders are often distressed when others make unflattering comments on their appearance. Unfortunately, rude remarks are made, as recalled by these overweight adolescents: "'Kids make fun of me, they say, 'You fat ugly cow, you make a whale look small,' 'In the gym, they laugh and talk behind my back'" (M. J. Smith & Perkins, 2008, p. 392). Adults must insist that classrooms and after-school programs are "no-tease zones" about weight.

• **Attend to serious food allergies.** Food allergies are relatively common and can be a health threat at school when conditions are serious and allergens are present. In the United States, approximately one in thirteen children has a food allergy (Food Allergy Research & Education, 2017). Of these children, about 17% have had an allergic reaction at school, some of whom have not previously been diagnosed with the problem. There are several things that teachers, nurses, and other school staff can do to protect children. Many schools have a food allergy management program, in which school nurses invite parents to advise them of children's allergies (e.g., peanuts, milk, eggs, wheat, or shellfish), symptoms (e.g., hives, eczema, swelling of throat or mouth, or vomiting), and treatments (e.g., an antihistamine, asthma inhaler, or epinephrine auto-injector; Food Allergy Research & Education, 2017). Educators can keep a list of children in the classroom with food allergies, ask children to wash hands before and after eating, avoid known allergens in classroom projects, and for especially sensitive children, arrange allergy-friendly areas in the cafeteria.

I think I have ate to many sweets on Sunday. I had 1 to many things from the dairy gropp. I had the right amount of meat, but not anof vegetables, I had only one vegetble. You wone't belve this, I had no fruits at all! I realy need to eat more fruits and veget bles. If I ate two more things from bread grocp I would have had anof.

MyLab Education
Artifact Example 5.3

Find Developmental Meaning
How does Charlotte (age 8) evaluate her weekend diet? Charlotte understood that she should draw from certain food groups, some of which were easier for her to sample or avoid than others. She realized that she needed to reduce sugary snacks and increase servings of fruit and vegetables. Setting goals and keeping progress with their diet can help children develop wholesome eating habits.

Physical Activity

Infants and toddlers are highly motivated to learn new physical skills. As they wiggle, squirm, reach, and grasp, they improve their motor abilities. For preschool children, physical activity is so enjoyable—and increasingly controllable—that children become even more active. A common type of physical activity in early and middle childhood is **rough-and-tumble play**, or good-natured mock "fighting" (Harvey, 2011; A. P. Humphreys & Smith, 1987; Pellegrini, 2006; Veiga et al., 2017). Young children often derive considerable pleasure from roughhousing, find it a healthy release from intellectually demanding tasks, and defend it as just "playing" or "messing around." Teachers can set reasonable rules that reduce the chances of injury while still allowing children to run and shout. Less vigorous movements are a regular part of the indoor schedule, with teachers inviting children to move between stations, march during music time, and squirm while listening to stories.

After the preschool years, there is a decline in physical activity, even though children continue to need to move their bodies regularly. In elementary school and beyond, children need to move periodically throughout the day to be able to concentrate. In many schools, children are given a chance to move within the classroom in ways that solidify academic understandings, for example, in navigating around the school building while learning how to use a compass (Mavilidi, Okely, Chandler, & Paas, 2016). Even with periodic movement within the classroom, children concentrate better when allowed to unwind outdoors or in large open spaces indoors. When children in kindergarten through fourth grade are given recess, they are generally better able to focus their attention on academic work (CDC, 2010; Cook-Cottone, Tribole, & Tylka, 2013; Pellegrini & Bjorklund, 1997; Pellegrini & Bohn, 2005).

Physical education provides children with training in motor skills, sports, and health practices. When it incorporates vigorous exercise and motivates young people to maintain an active lifestyle, it generates benefits in bone health, muscular development, mood, and overall fitness (CDC, 2015b). The trick, of course, is to make exercise enjoyable at school. In a national study with U.S. high school students, just over half of students in Grades 9 through 12 derived pleasure from their physical education classes (Brener et al., 2013). Movement and sports can become more fun and effective when guidelines for high-quality physical education are followed. Experts recommend daily physical education in kindergarten through 12th grade; a curriculum that is based in national standards with carefully sequenced skills (from easy and low intensity to difficult and strenuous); encouragement for children to set personal goals and evaluate progress; and adaptive devices such as oversized bats and balls that facilitate movement of children with disabilities (CDC, 2011).

Sports and Athletic Activities

In the chapter's opening case study, a group of adolescents were trained as coaches, creating an outlet for their exercise and that of local elementary school children. Organized sports offer the means for enhancing physical strength, endurance, and agility. Sports can promote social development by fostering communication, cooperation, and leadership skills. Particularly when parents and coaches encourage children to try hard and work together as a team, children tend to enjoy sports and see themselves as competent athletes (Ullrich-French & Smith, 2006).

Organized sports have a downside when adults promote unhealthy competition, put excessive pressure on children to perform well, and encourage athletically talented children at the expense of their less gifted teammates. Well-meaning coaches can rob children of their intrinsic enjoyment of sports and, when they fail to implement safety procedures, put children at risk for injury (Holt, Tink, Mandigo, & Fox, 2008; R. E. Smith & Smoll, 1997; N. Waters, 2013). Yet with proper training, coaches can not only train athletic skills but also contribute significantly to young people's well-being (Vella, Gardner, & Liddle, 2016).

Many children do *not* like team sports but nevertheless want to exercise. A few are drawn to such individual athletic activities as running, skateboarding, snowboarding, and mountain biking. Although not necessarily part of teams, youngsters who engage in individual sports often spend time with peers while exercising. Personal athletic pursuits have the advantages of requiring initiative and at least moderate levels of physical activity but, when unsupervised, the disadvantage of incurring risk for injury.

Encouraging Physical Activity

Physical activity is an essential part of every child's day. Here are some strategies educators can follow to promote movement and sports:

- **Be "pro-ACTIVE."** Teachers can incorporate physical movement into several activities. As we have summarized, regular breaks that include physical activity can increase attention during cognitively demanding tasks. A 15- to 20-minute break for children can make a big difference to children's concentration. Teachers can also resist the temptation to punish children by eliminating recess because movement is essential to all children, especially those who are boisterous (Blad, 2015). For 11-year-old Grace, recess is a fun time at school, as you can see in Artifact Example 5.4.

MyLab Education
Artifact Example 5.4

Find Developmental Meaning
What values does 11-year-old Grace perceive in recess? Grace shows that recess allows for spontaneous play, social interaction, physical activity, and pleasure in free movement. From a developmental perspective, recess benefits children across the domains of physical well-being, cognition, and social-emotional welfare.

- **Encourage physical activity during recess.** In general, boys tend to be more active than girls (A. M. Woods, Graber, & Daum, 2012). Boys typically play ball games, often in large groups, whereas girls spend time jumping rope and sitting together talking in small groups (Blatchford, Baines, & Pellegrini, 2003). Allowing children to make their own choices is an important feature of recess, although adult supervisors may wish to encourage both boys and girls to join games and activities that require moderate levels of physical activity (C. A. Howe, Freedson, Alhassan, Feldman, & Osganian, 2012).

MyLab Education Application Exercise 5.4
Identify Development Enhancing Education

Practice assessing the developmental qualities of recess in a group of second- and third-grade children.

- **Provide safe equipment for physical activity.** Open space, playground equipment, balls, and other athletic props encourage physical exercise. Equipment should be chosen carefully to allow children to experiment safely, ideally minimizing times when adults have to say no to movement (Bronson, 2000). Equipment and exercise facilities should also be properly designed to fit children's body sizes and abilities (Frost, Shin, & Jacobs, 1998; Nolte, Krüger, Els, & Nolte, 2013). Educators often provide jungle gyms, sandboxes, slides, swings, towers, tunnels, and other equipment, yet simple outdoor spaces for jumping, skipping, and chasing also give children valuable venues for exercise (Brunelle, Herrington, Coghlan, & Brussoni, 2016).

- **Make exercise enjoyable.** By the time they reach high school, many young people have had unpleasant experiences with physical workouts and, as a result, associate exercise with regimentation, discomfort, failure, embarrassment, competitiveness, boredom, and injury (Rowland, 1990). Some students live sedentary lives, sitting most of the time at school and home. Furthermore, many adolescents do not have physically active role models. These are significant obstacles, yet educators can promote children's physical activity when they capitalize on children's interests (e.g., in karate), pleasure in physical self-expression (e.g., through dance), and camaraderie during group activities (e.g., exercising together in an aerobics class; W. C. Taylor, Beech, & Cummings, 1998).

- **Plan physical activities with diversity in mind.** Not everyone can be a skilled quarterback, baseball pitcher, or dancer. But nearly all children can find enjoyment in exercise of some form. Offering a range of activities, from dance to volleyball, and modifying them for children with special needs can maximize the number of students who participate. A child who is unusually short might look to such activities as soccer, cycling, or gymnastics because they do not require exceptional height (Rudlin, 1993). Another child in a wheelchair might go up to bat in a softball game and then have a classmate run the bases for her.

• **Provide high-quality athletic opportunities for boys and girls.** Ensuring that children are not discriminated against in their athletic opportunities based on gender is a worthwhile goal for educators. According to Title IX of the U.S. Educational Amendments of 1972, schools that receive federal funds must give boys and girls the same chances to participate in athletic programs and, in fact, in all aspects of academic life. Boys and girls must receive comparable quality in coaching, practice, locker facilities, and publicity for their athletic accomplishments. This same principle of equal opportunity applies to young people who have a **transgender identity**, in which they see themselves as having a gender that is different from that assigned at birth (i.e., a child born as a boy who has a self-identity as a girl and a child born as a girl who has a self-identity as a boy; U.S. Department of Justice and U.S. Department of Education, 2016).

• **Focus on self-improvement rather than competition with peers.** Focusing on personal improvement is, for most children, far more motivating than attending to relative standing with peers. Dwelling too much on competition leads children to believe that physical ability is largely a matter of "natural talent," when in fact physical skills require practice (Ames, 1984; R. W. Proctor & Dutta, 1995). Thus, adults can direct children to focus on progress they are making as individuals (e.g., "Wow, Libby, you have become one fine kicker this week"). Adults can also encourage children to record their own accomplishments on worksheets and examine trends over time.

Your Name: Connor Your Age: 15 Adult Supervising: MOM

Record of Physical Activity

	Activity 1: Sit ups		Activity 2: Push ups		Activity 3: up-downs	
Day 1-5: Exercise	How many did you do?	How did it feel?	How many did you do?	How did it feel?	How many did you do?	How did it feel?
1	37	Good	26	Hard to keep back straight.	21	Hard to keep balance
2	22	Stomach sore from yesterday. Sore	30	easy	25	Harder
3	26	Stomach is better OK	22	Sore	23	Sore
4	15	Hurt really bad!	20	Sore	25	Hard
5	30	tried to beat #1 but to sore to	31	Beat It	25	use a lot of energy
Day 6: Reflect	What parts of your body did you use? Stomach muscels! What did you do to prevent injury? Stopped when It hurt.		What parts of your body did you use? Upper Body. What did you do to prevent injury? Tried to keep Balance		What parts of your body did you use? A Full body work out What did you do to prevent injury? Stopped when I needed to	

MyLab Education Application Exercise 5.5 Meet Individual Needs

Practice assessing a record of scaffolded exercise completed by Connor, a 15-year-old student, who was supervised by his mother.

• **Make sure that children don't overdo it.** Becoming fanatical about exercise can create medical problems for children. The soft and spongy parts of bones in growing children are susceptible to injury from repeated use (R. H. Gross, 2004; S. Jenny & Armstrong, 2013; Micheli, 1995). Weight-training machines are almost always designed for adult-sized bodies, amplifying chances for injury. Overuse injuries are frequently seen in distance running, competitive swimming, and gymnastics. Medical experts recommend that children are discouraged from concentrating solely on one sport before adolescence, never asked to "work through" stress fractures, and monitored by a physician for effects of intensive training (e.g., delays in sexual maturation; American Academy of Pediatrics [AAP] Committee on Sports Medicine and Fitness, 2000).

Rest and Sleep

Rest and sleep are essential to health. During sleep, the body gains the energy needed to strengthen the immune system, remove toxins from the brain, release growth hormones, and instill a feeling of being rested. Sleep also helps with consolidating new memories by moving the information to an area in the brain designed for long-term storage. Sleep is also important to children's self-regulation. When children have slept well and long, they are better able to express their emotions constructively, relax after stressful circumstances, and act cautiously rather than recklessly (Grigg-Damberger, 2017).

Prenatal Development

Fetuses cycle between wakeful periods and sleep. Most of their time is spent asleep, when they rotate among three states—active sleep, which is similar to a dream state; quiet sleep, in which there is little movement; and a less organized condition of indeterminate sleep (Yiallourou, Wallace, Miller, & Horne, 2016). During active sleep, the fetus squirms and twitches, and these sensations activate the center of the brain that registers feelings of pressure and touch (Grigg-Damberger, 2017).

Infancy

Newborn babies spend a long time sleeping—16 to 18 hours a day (Wolff, 1966). Gradually, infants develop wake–sleep cycles that correspond closely to adults' rhythms (St. James-Roberts & Plewis, 1996). They begin to sleep through the night when they are ready, depending in part on their own biological rhythms. Teresa recalls that her sons were oblivious to a pediatrician's guideline that they should be able to sleep through the night by 10 weeks of age and 10 pounds in weight. Sleeping habits are also affected by cultural practices, suggesting that there is no single "best" way to put babies to sleep (Shweder et al., 1998).

Although there may be no best way, there is one *wrong* way to put babies to sleep. Medical experts advise caregivers *not* to place babies on their stomachs for sleeping because this position puts babies at risk for **sudden infant death syndrome (SIDS)**, a loss of life that occurs (usually during sleep) in infants without an apparent medical cause. SIDS is a leading cause of death among infants from 1 month through 1 year in age (AAP Task Force on Infant Sleep Position and Sudden Infant Death Syndrome, 2000). During the period that SIDS is most common (between 2 and 4 months), infants' brains are developing neurological circuits for controlling arousal, breathing, and heart rate. Minor abnormalities in these areas may prove fatal if infants are under physical stress, for example, if they have a respiratory infection, are overheated with excessive clothing or blankets, or have an obstructed airway with faces nestled into the mattress (Kinney, 2009; Rohde et al., 2013; F. M. Sullivan & Barlow, 2001).

Infant caregivers need to be aware of current advice not only for reducing the risk of SIDS but also for preventing suffocation generally. Recommendations include placing babies on their backs (faceup) to sleep, refraining from smoking nearby, keeping babies at a comfortable temperature, using a firm mattress, and avoiding soft surfaces and loose bedding (Task Force on Sudden Infant Death Syndrome, 2011; T. C. S. Ward & Balfour, 2016). Room-sharing, but not bed-sharing, is considered ideal by medical experts because of the increased chance for SIDS when infants sleep in the same bed with parents. Some parents use a cot that attaches safely to the side of the parents' bed.

Early Childhood through Adolescence

Time spent sleeping decreases steadily over the course of childhood. Within a 24-hour period, 1- to 2-year-olds typically need 11 to 14 hours of sleep; 3- to 5-year-olds, 10 to 13 hours; 6- to 12-year-olds, 9 to 12 hours; and 13- to 18-year-olds, 8 to 10 hours (AAP, 2016). These are general recommendations, of course. The number of hours of sleep children of a particular age need to feel rested varies among individuals.

Occasional sleep problems occur. Nightmares are widespread between ages 3 and 6, and children may ask adults to help them battle the demons of the night. Pronounced sleep disturbances (e.g., waking repeatedly during the night) can happen because of serious health problems, excessive stress, use of street drugs, and side effects from prescribed medications. Repeated nightmares are common among children who have experienced abuse or traumatic incidents or witnessed domestic violence (Durand, 1998; Insana, Foley, Montgomery-Downs, Kolko, & McNeil, 2014). Also, some children with certain disabilities (e.g., cerebral palsy, severe visual impairment, autism, and psychiatric disorders) have difficulty sleeping (Durand, 1998; Mannion, Leader, & Healy, 2013; Silvestri & Aricò, 2017).

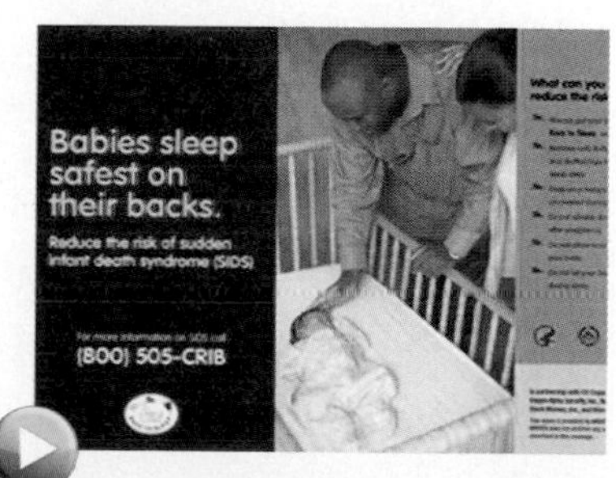

MyLab Education
Video Explanation 5.1
How can adults reduce risks of sudden infant death syndrome (SIDS)?

Especially as they grow older, children get insufficient sleep because of poor sleep habits. Adolescents in particular are at risk for *sleep deprivation*, a state of being tired after not sleeping sufficiently and as a result having difficulty in reasoning, learning, and remembering. Although they require less sleep than they did in their earlier years, adolescents are still growing rapidly, and their brains and bodies require sleep and rest (Bei et al., 2013; Blake et al., 2016). Yet out-of-school obligations—extracurricular activities, part-time jobs, social engagements, homework assignments, and the ubiquitous World Wide Web—can keep teenagers up until the wee hours of the morning. When young people lose sleep, they are likely to become short-tempered and impatient. Depending on their age, sleep-deprived youngsters may also become aggressive and depressed, have trouble concentrating, perform at low levels academically, and engage in high-risk behaviors (Bruni & Angriman, 2017; R. E. Dahl & Lewin, 2002; Perkinson-Gloor, Lemola, & Grob, 2013).

Accommodating Children's Needs for Sleep

Educators often have youngsters in their classrooms who do not sleep well, including some who are truly sleep deprived. With this situation in mind, we offer the following suggestions:

- **When appropriate, provide time for sleep during the day.** Infants and toddlers *must* sleep during the day. It is a common custom, and most certainly good practice, to include an optional naptime in the schedule of preschoolers who attend school in the afternoon. Young children typically give up their afternoon nap sometime between ages 2 and 5, but for quite some time after that, they need to recharge their batteries in the afternoon with quiet and restful activities (e.g., listening to stories or music). A few older children and adolescents—for instance, youngsters with brain injuries or other chronic health conditions—may need an hour or two of sleep as well, perhaps on a couch in the school nurse's office (Lewandowski & Rieger, 2009; Ormrod & McGuire, 2007).

- **Communicate with families about the importance of sleep.** Teachers and other practitioners can speak tactfully with family members when they think chronic fatigue is causing a child's difficulty in concentrating, maintaining good spirits, and resisting aggressive impulses. The topic of sleep can also be addressed in tips to parents in school newsletters with such recommendations as turning off the television and computer an hour or two before bedtime and enforcing reasonable bedtimes.

- **Encourage youngsters to make steady progress on lengthy assignments.** At the high school level, adolescents may have several hours of homework each night. Add to this workload extracurricular events, social activities, family commitments, and part-time jobs, and you get adolescents who are seriously overstretched. When assigning major projects, teachers can encourage regular progress by giving interim deadlines for the various *parts* of the assignment.

- **Schedule school events with reasonable ending times.** Athletic practices, plays and musical performances, club meetings, and other school events can be planned with definite starting and ending times that allow students to wrap up commitments early enough to get home at sensible hours (Bergin & Bergin, 2009/2010). Occasionally, school dances and special events may extend far into the night (and into the morning), but late-night activities should be the exception rather than the rule.

- **Deliberate over the starting time for high school.** Some high schools delay the start of morning classes to allow students to sleep in an extra hour or so (M. Barnes et al., 2016; Bergin & Bergin, 2009/2010). Such schedule revisions have been well received, especially by adolescents, who generally sleep more rather than staying up later at night (M. Short et al., 2013; Wolfson & Carskadon, 2005). However, the implications of schedule changes for families and school personnel must also be considered during discussions.

- **Recognize that sleep problems can be a sign of illness or emotional stress.** Words of acknowledgment and kindness ("You look tired today, Darragh. Did you sleep all right last night?") may give tired children permission to share their troubles and, as a result, take the first step toward resolving them. With seriously disturbed children, guidance from a counselor or psychologist is likely to be necessary.

As you have seen, advances that occur in physical development take many forms and depend on several factors, including maturational processes, adequate nutrition, physical activity, and sleep. In the Basic Developmental Issues table "Physical Development," we summarize how growth shows nature and nurture, universality and diversity, and qualitative and quantitative change. Because good health comes not only from acquiring health-promoting habits but also from avoiding negative substances, we now focus on the important topic of health-compromising behaviors.

BASIC DEVELOPMENTAL ISSUES
Physical Development

ISSUE	PHYSICAL GROWTH	MOTOR SKILLS	HEALTH AND ACTIVITY
Nature and Nurture	Genetic instructions guide the changes that occur as bodies grow larger and provide targets for mature appearance, height, and weight. Normal progressions depend on adequate nutrition, movement, affection, sleep, and protection from toxic substances.	Nature sets boundaries on the motor skills a child can execute. A 6-month-old cannot run, and a 10-year-old cannot clear 15 feet in the standing high jump. Nurture allows children to maximize their athletic achievements within existing constraints.	Nature influences children's individual activity level and susceptibility to illness. Nurture affects children's access to nutrition and daily activities. Children learn habits related to eating and exercising from parents, peers, teachers, coaches, and others in their community.
Universality and Diversity	Children tend to show similar sequences in physical development (e.g., in the emergence of male and female characteristics during puberty) across a range of circumstances. The rate of development differs from one child to the next as a result of genetic factors, personal choices, family stresses, and cultural variations.	Motor skills often develop in a similar sequence. Children can, on average, pick up crumbs at age 1, scribble with a crayon at age 2, and build a tower 10 blocks high at age 4 (Sheridan, 1975). Diversity is present in the exact ages at which children master motor skills, due to differences in genes and environmental support.	All children need good nutrition, plenty of rest, and a moderate amount of physical activity. Diversity exists in the kinds of meals that children obtain at home, in opportunities for exercise, and in access to medical care. Children also vary in their susceptibility to illness, physical disabilities, and need for accommodations at school.
Qualitative and Quantitative Change	Many advancements result from quantitative changes (e.g., gradual increases in limb length and strength). Qualitative changes are implicated in the differential growth that happens in organs in early life and in the changes of puberty during adolescence.	As a general rule, children must practice motor skills for a long time before they can execute them smoothly. Some motor skills, such as throwing a ball, are transformed qualitatively, such that new styles emerge and replace previous ones.	During middle childhood, children gradually gain control over what they eat and how they spend their leisure time (a quantitative change). Reorganizations in thinking about danger and acting on impulses occur during adolescence.

Health-Compromising Behaviors

Especially as they grow older and gain independence from direct supervision, students face many choices and temptations. With freedom comes an element of danger. Here we look at three health-compromising behaviors: cigarette smoking, alcohol and drug use, and unprotected sexual activity.

Cigarette Smoking

Every year, more adolescents begin to smoke cigarettes (see Table 5.1 on p. 158). Unfortunately, teens often continue to use tobacco when they become adults. Because the health risks are so well publicized, it is difficult to understand why adolescents choose to smoke. Undoubtedly, "image" is a factor. Teens may smoke cigarettes to look older, rebel, and affiliate with certain peer groups. Advertising plays a role as well. The majority of teen smokers choose from only a few cigarette brands, perhaps because of the youthful, sophisticated, and fun-loving images that tobacco companies project in their advertising. Regardless of the reasons adolescents start smoking, those who make it a habit are at risk for becoming dependent on nicotine and developing health problems they might otherwise avoid (Do & Galván, 2016).

Alcohol and Drug Use

Alcohol and drugs are among the most serious threats to adolescents' health. While under the influence of these substances, adolescents become vulnerable to engaging in unprotected sexual activity, driving impaired, assaulting others, and committing crimes. Those who are intravenous drug users sometimes share needles, putting themselves at risk of contracting hepatitis C and HIV (described later in the chapter), and other infections (J. L. Evans, Hahn, Lum, Stein, & Page, 2009; Klevens, Jones, Ward, Holtzman, & Kann, 2016). Occasionally a large dosage of a particular drug leads to permanent brain damage or even death. Figure 5.7 describes common substances abused by adolescents.

FIGURE 5.7 Substances abused by adolescents.

- *Alcohol* depresses the central nervous system, incites a feeling of elation, and impairs coordination, perception, speech, and judgment; inebriated drinkers may talk incoherently and walk with a staggered gait. Teens who drink heavily are more likely to have car accidents and commit rape than those who do not.
- *Methylene dioxymethamphetamine* (MDMA, or "ecstasy") gives users a sense of euphoria and exuberance, sensory enhancements and distortions, and feelings of being at peace with the world and emotionally close to others. The feeling of euphoria often leads users to ignore bodily distress signals, such as muscle cramping and dehydration; more serious effects include convulsions, impaired heart function, and death. It is often available at dance clubs ("raves"), where its effects are intensified with music and flashing lights.
- *Inhalants* are attractive to many adolescents because they cause an immediate "high" and are readily available in the form of such household substances as glue, paint thinner, aerosol paint cans, and nail polish remover. These dangerous substances can cause loss of sensation, brain damage, and death.
- *Marijuana* not only delays reaction time, modifies perception, and instills a mild feeling of bliss, but it can also heighten fears and anxieties and impair thinking. Teens who smoke marijuana may have red eyes, dry mouths, mood changes, and loss of interest in friends and hobbies, and they may exhibit impaired driving.
- *Synthetic cannabinoids* are laboratory-produced mind-altering chemicals that are sprayed on shredded plants for smoking or vaporized and inhaled. Although marketed as being safe, synthetic cannabinoids have powerful effects on the brain and can become addictive and life-threatening.
- *Methamphetamine* ("speed") is a stimulant that gives users a sense of energy, alertness, confidence, and well-being. Overdoses are possible, addiction frequently results, and changes to the brain and heart can occur. People who use speed regularly combat psychiatric problems, such as becoming violent and confused and believing that "everyone is out to get me."
- *Cocaine* (including *crack*, a particularly potent form) overstimulates neurons in the brain and gives users a brief sense of energy and euphoria; it can also cause tremors, convulsions, vomiting, respiratory problems, overheating, strokes, and heart failure. Cocaine users may be energetic, talkative, argumentative, and boastful; longtime users may appear anxious and depressed. Crack users are prone to violence and crime.
- *Bath salts (designer cathinones)* are synthetic stimulants contained in a white powder that is typically snorted. The salts can cause heart beat racing (and sometimes heart attacks), dizziness, paranoia, seizures, delusions, and suicidal thoughts.
- *Rohypnol* is a central nervous depressant that causes muscle relaxation, a sense of euphoria, impaired judgment, amnesia, and slow breathing (which in extreme cases can culminate in death). It has been called the "rape drug" because it has been placed in alcoholic drinks of unsuspecting women to render them defenseless during a sexual assault.
- *Prescription medications* are used improperly by a growing number of adolescents because of their pleasurable effects on the body. Painkillers, such as OxyContin and Vicodin, are potentially addictive narcotics that reduce sensations of discomfort and increase feelings of relaxation and pleasure. Stimulants such as Adderall and Ritalin that treat attention and hyperactivity disorders are sometimes sold to adolescents who want to get "high." Anabolic steroids, another type of medication for which there is an illicit market among teenagers, increase muscle development, but regular users experience unwanted side effects (e.g., in boys, shrinking testicles and breast development; in girls, growth of facial hair and menstrual changes; in both, liver damage and high blood pressure).

Sources: DanceSafe (2000a, 2000b); E. W. Gunderson, Kirkpatrick, Willing, and Holstege (2013); L. D. Johnston, O'Malley, Bachman, and Schulenberg (2007); Kulberg (1986); National Institute on Drug Abuse (2010a, 2010b, 2010c, 2010d, 2010e, 2010f, 2010g, 2010h, 2015, 2017); Neinstein (2004); Patnode et al. (2014); M. E. Patrick et al. (2016); P. Stevens and Smith (2013); J. M. Taylor (1994); U.S. Department of Justice Drug Enforcement Administration (2011).

Given the hazards of alcohol and drugs, why do adolescents use them? For some, it's a matter of curiosity: After hearing about alcohol and drugs, not only from their peers but also from adults and the media, teens may want to experience the effects firsthand. For others, trying alcohol and drugs is an impulsive event with little forethought. Many adolescents who use drugs or alcohol have parents who abuse drugs themselves, fail to monitor their sons' and daughters' whereabouts, and do little to promote teens' willingness to abide by society's rules or pursue long-term goals (Branstetter & Furman, 2013; Jessor & Jessor, 1977; P. Wu, Liu, & Fan, 2010). Drug and alcohol use is more typical when people in the local community are tolerant of such behavior (Curcio, Knott, & Mak, 2015). Peer-group norms and behaviors are yet another factor affecting adolescents' substance use (M. H. Lai et al., 2013; P. Wu et al., 2010).

Regardless of initial reasons for trying alcohol and drugs, continued use often creates serious problems. If these substances give adolescents pleasure, satisfy a desire for thrills, alleviate anxiety, or deaden feelings of pain and depression, they may start to use substances regularly (Conner, Hellemann, Ritchie, & Noble, 2010; R. C. Palmer et al., 2013).

Unfortunately, some users eventually develop an **addiction** to, or dependence on, drugs or alcohol. Their brains grow accustomed to the substance and need increasing quantities to produce the desired effect. When they try to stop, addicts have intense cravings and unpleasant reactions (M. A. Lindberg & Zeid, 2017).

Unsafe Sexual Activity

Learning about sexuality is an important part of coming of age, and many adolescents become sexually active during the secondary school years. On average, 4 in every 10 high school students in the United States report having had sexual intercourse (CDC, 2016; see Table 5.1). About one in 10 students have had four or more sexual partners, and more than one in 10 who are sexually active did not use any precautions during last intercourse. From the perspective of physical health, early sexual activity is problematic because it can lead to infections, pregnancy, or both.

Sexually Transmitted Infections. Sexually transmitted infections (STIs) vary in long-term effects. Syphilis, gonorrhea, and chlamydia can be treated with antibiotics, but affected teens do not always seek prompt medical help. Without treatment, serious problems can occur, including infertility and sterility, heart problems, and birth defects in future offspring. Genital herpes has no known cure, but medication can alleviate the severity of symptoms. Undoubtedly the most life-threatening STI is acquired immune deficiency syndrome (AIDS), a medical condition in which the immune system is weakened, permitting severe infections, pneumonias, and cancers to invade the body. AIDS is caused by HIV, which can be transmitted through body fluids (e.g., blood and semen) during a single contact. HIV is spread through contact with infected fluids, most often through sexual contact and intravenous drug injections with contaminated needles (U.S. Department of Health and Human Services, 2015).

Pregnancy. Pregnancy rates in U.S. adolescents have decreased during the past few decades in large part due to increased use of condoms and other contraceptive methods (L. Lindberg, Santelli, & Desai, 2016). Nevertheless, numerous pregnancies occur in teens, some of which end in miscarriage or abortion and others of which go full term. The current rate is 11 births per 1,000 girls ages 15 to 17 in the United States (Forum on Child and Family Statistics, 2016). Girls who become teenage mothers are apt to come from low-income families, have weak academic performance, believe they have few career options, be prone to depression, achieve status with the birth of the baby, and yearn for an emotional connection (Coley & Chase-Lansdale, 1998; C. Y. Huang, Costeines, Ayala, & Kaufman, 2014; Mistry et al., 2016).

Addressing Health-Compromising Behaviors

Schools and community organizations can do a great deal to reduce physical risk. We offer a few thoughts on support:

- **Provide healthy options for free time.** Children are less likely to engage in health-compromising behaviors when they have better things to do with their time. In our chapter-opening case study, a new program afforded productive activities for both children and their adolescent coaches. Community leaders can choose from numerous kinds of after-school programs and community athletic leagues depending on resources and the preferences of local youth.

- **Prevent problems.** It is much easier to teach adolescents to resist cigarettes, alcohol, and drugs than it is to treat their dependence on these substances. Schools are important sites for prevention because they serve so many young people (Allara et al., 2015; Hale, Fitzgerald-Yau, & Viner, 2014; Pokhrel et al., 2013). Effective programs take advantage of the protective factors that young people have, for example, strong family ties can be leveraged with newsletters about drug prevention (Bukstein & Deas, 2010; National Institute on Drug Abuse, 2003). Activities can foster children's self-control, emotional awareness, communication skills, social problem solving, and academic achievement. In middle, junior high, and high school, successful programs address drug-resistance skills, antidrug attitudes, and commitments for avoiding drugs and

Developmental Systems Prompt 5.2

Health-compromising behaviors emerge in response to temptations, family practices, community norms, and the young person's personality and coping skills. As you work with young people who are at risk for partaking in risky behaviors, consider their individual assets, challenges, and circumstances for growing up.

alcohol. Repeated exposure to the same antidrug messages across multiple settings, for example, at school and home, in faith-based organizations, and in the media, can be especially effective.

• **Discourage drug and alcohol use in all settings.** The kinds of programs educators implement are determined largely by their duties and the needs of youngsters with whom they work. Coaches and other staff members in the Forest Hills School District in Cincinnati, Ohio, designed a productive drug prevention program (see Figure 5.8). Participation was encouraged by school coaches, principals, other school staff, team captains, parents, and the adolescents themselves (U.S. Drug Enforcement Administration, 2002). Coaches spoke openly about substance use. Peer pressure was enlisted. When athletes did break the rules, they were given defined consequences in a way that communicated hope that they would try harder next time.

• **Encourage adolescents to protect themselves.** Approaches to preventing adolescent pregnancy and transmission of STIs can be contentious. Parents may object to the school's distribution of condoms and advocacy of "safe sex." (And, of course, at the present time condom use is no guarantee of protection against either infection or pregnancy.) Evidence suggests, however, that having condoms accessible at school moderately increases condom use by students who are already sexually active (and so offers some protection against infection and pregnancy) and does not increase overall rates of sexual activity (Alan Guttmacher Institute, 2001; Fonner, Armstrong, Kennedy, O'Reilly, & Sweat, 2014). Programs that encourage sexual abstinence are a less controversial

FIGURE 5.8 Team Up drug prevention materials from high school athletic coaches.

From Team Up: A Drug Prevention Manual for High School Athletic Coaches, *by the U.S. Drug Enforcement Administration, 2002, Washington, DC: U.S. Department of Justice Drug Enforcement Administration.*

Student's Pledge

As a participant in the ______________ High School Athletic Program, I agree to abide by all training rules regarding the use of alcohol, tobacco, and other drugs. Chemical dependency is a progressive but treatable disease, characterized by continued drinking or other drug use in spite of recurring problems resulting from that use. Therefore, I accept and pledge to abide by the training rules listed in the athletic handbook and others established by my coach.

To demonstrate my support, I pledge to:

1. Support my fellow students by setting an example and abstaining from the use of alcohol, tobacco, and other drugs.
2. Not enable my fellow students who use these substances. I will not cover up for them or lie for them if any rules are broken. I will hold my teammates responsible and accountable for their actions.
3. Seek information and assistance in dealing with my own or my fellow students' problems.
4. Be honest and open with my parents about my feelings, needs, and problems.
5. Be honest and open with my coach and other school personnel when the best interests of my fellow students are being jeopardized.

Student ________________________ Date ______________

**PARENTS: We ask that you co-sign this pledge to show your support.

Sample Letter from Coach to Parent about a Drug or Alcohol Violation

Dear Parent:

Your daughter ______________ has violated the ______________ High School extra-curricular activities code of conduct. She voluntarily came forward on Thursday afternoon and admitted her violation of the code, specifically, drinking alcohol. The code is attached.

We respect her honesty and integrity and hope you do as well. Admitting a mistake such as this is very difficult for her. Not only does she have to deal with authorities such as us, she must face you, her parents, as well as her peers—which is probably the most difficult. We understand that no one is perfect and that people do make mistakes. Our code, and the resulting consequences of violating the code, is a nationally recognized model and is designed to encourage this type of self-reporting where the student can seek help and shelter from guilt without harsh initial penalties. She has admitted to making a mistake and is willing to work to alleviate the negative effects of the mistake.

As you can see in the enclosed code, we require that your daughter complete 10 hours of drug and alcohol in-service education and counseling. In addition, she must sit out 10 practice days of competition. She is still part of the team and must attend practices and competition; she is just not allowed to compete or participate in games for 10 days.

We hope you understand and support our effort to provide a healthy athletic program for the students. If you have any questions, please call either one of us at the high school.

Sincerely,

alternative and are found to discourage sexual intercourse in the short run; however, they are relatively ineffective over the long run (Paik, Sanchagrin, & Heimer, 2016; Raghupathy, Klein, & Card, 2013). Some programs encourage both abstinence and use of contraception, and it appears that young people easily grasp the merits of these two strategies for different situations (D. Kirby & Laris, 2009; L. Lindberg & Maddow-Zimet, 2012). All things considered, young people seem to benefit from sex education that is comprehensive, includes information about risks and methods of protection, and portrays sexuality as a healthy part of human development.

- **Get help for young people who have become addicted to drugs or alcohol.** Teachers and other practitioners can share suspicions with parents and counselors about drug or alcohol use. Various kinds of treatment, including medication (that differs by the target of addiction, age of the young person, and presence of other mental health conditions), family-based approaches (with therapy for the entire family), and cognitive-behavioral programs (that set targets and monitor progress) have proven effective (National Institute on Drug Abuse, 2014; Pokhrel et al., 2013). Some adolescents go through treatment voluntarily, whereas others are required by families and court orders to participate. Relapses in drug and alcohol use are common and signify the need for additional intervention.

The four areas we've discussed in this section—eating habits, physical activity, sleep, and health-compromising behaviors—all have major effects on youngsters' physical development. In the Observation Guidelines table "Assessing Children's Health Behaviors and Characteristics," we identify attributes of good and poor health. Obviously, practitioners should not provide treatment for which they are untrained, but they can help young people acquire habits of self-care.

Special Physical Needs

Some children have long-term physical conditions that affect school performance, friendships, and leisure activities. Here we look at chronic medical conditions, serious injuries, and physical disabilities. We then identify strategies for accommodating these conditions.

Preparing for Your Licensure Examination

Your teaching test might ask you about exceptionalities in physical development.

Chronic Medical Conditions

All children get sick now and then, but some have ongoing, long-term conditions because of genetic legacies (e.g., cystic fibrosis), environmentally contracted illnesses (e.g., AIDS), or an interaction between the two (e.g., some forms of asthma and cancer). As many as one or two in 10 children have a chronic condition that causes them noticeable limitations in strength, vitality, relaxation, or alertness (Nabors, Little, Akin-Little, & Iobst, 2008).

MyLab Education
Content Extension 5.1
Read how children of various ages cope with chronic illness.

Teachers and other school professionals come face-to-face with children's health flare-ups and lapses in self-care. For instance, a fourth-grade girl with diabetes needs to monitor her blood sugar levels and take appropriate follow-up action. She may need to leave the classroom and make one or more trips to the nurse's office every day. Yet children with chronic conditions are not always reliable in assessing their own symptoms and sometimes forget to take prescribed medications (Bal et al., 2016; D. J. Bearison, 1998; N. M. Clark, Gong, & Kaciroti, 2014). Accordingly, school nurses will typically ask parents about health conditions at the beginning of the year so that a designated team at school is aware of potential symptoms, warning signs, and the child's regimen of self-care.

In addition to learning about illnesses, educators can watch for cultural practices families follow with their children. Children with Type 1 diabetes who were growing up in Minnesota with parents who had immigrated from Somalia were well cared for by their parents but had trouble managing their condition because their diet was rich in carbohydrates (Sunni et al., 2015). An implication of this situation is that the diet charts had to be expanded for these children to include typical Somali foods so that they could be monitored along with American meals and snacks.

Finally, educators can support chronically ill children in their peer relationships. Children with a lot of school absences have a hard time staying in touch with classmates.

OBSERVATION GUIDELINES
Assessing Children's Health Behaviors and Characteristics

CHARACTERISTIC	LOOK FOR	EXAMPLE	IMPLICATION
Eating Habits	• *Frequent consumption* of junk food (e.g., candy, chips, sodas, fast food) • *Unusual heaviness or thinness,* especially when these characteristics become more pronounced over time • *Lack of energy,* possibly due to poor nutrition • *Reluctance to eat* at lunchtime	Melissa is a good student, an avid runner, and a member of the student council. She is exceptionally thin, eats only a couple of pieces of celery at lunch, and wears baggy clothes that hide her figure. Her school counselor suspects an eating disorder and contacts Melissa's parents to share the suspicion.	Observe what children eat and drink during the school day. Seek free or reduced-cost breakfasts and lunches for children from low-income families. Consult with parents and specialists when eating habits seem to be seriously detrimental to children's health.
Physical Activity	• *Improvements in gross motor skills* (e.g., running, skipping, jumping) • *Restlessness, lethargy, or inattention* during lengthy seatwork (possibly reflecting a need for a break) • *Overexertion* (increasing the risk of injury)	Before beginning a soccer scrimmage, a coach asks children to run up and down the grounds, accelerating and decelerating while taking turns kicking a ball. She then has them practice evading another player. Only then does she begin a game (Logsdon et al., 1997).	Incorporate regular physical activity into the daily schedule. Choose tasks and activities that are enjoyable and allow for a range of skill levels. Make sure youngsters have mastered prerequisite skills and are warmed up before introducing more challenging moves.
Rest and Sleep	• *Listlessness* and lack of energy • *Inability to concentrate* • *Irritability* and overreaction to frustration • *Lashing out to peers* when frustrated, and other signs of poor self-control • *Sleeping in class*	A teacher in an all-day kindergarten notices that some of his students become cranky during the last half-hour of school, and so typically reserves this time for storybook reading and other quiet activities.	Provide regular opportunities for rest. When a youngster seems unusually tired day after day, talk with him or her (and perhaps with parents) about how lack of sleep can affect attention and behavior. Together seek possible solutions.
Health-Compromising Behaviors	• *Smell of cigarettes* on clothing • *Physiological symptoms of drug use,* possibly red eyes, dilated pupils, tremors, respiratory problems, slurred pronunciation, fast talking, incoherence, poor coordination, impaired decision making, mood changes, or unusual energy • *Change in personality and friends* • *Rapid weight gain* and a tendency to wear increasingly baggy clothes (in girls who might be pregnant) • *Conversations about sexual activities*	A school counselor notices a dramatic change in James's personality. Whereas he used to be eager to engage in conversation, he now begins to "zone out" during counseling sessions. He slumps in his chair, looks out the window, and speaks unintelligibly. The counselor asks James if he is using drugs, which he denies. The counselor advises James's parents about her fears and mentions a range of treatment options in the community.	Prevent health-compromising behaviors by providing opportunities to be successful, academically and socially. Educate young people about the dangers of substance abuse and unprotected sexual activity; teach behaviors for resisting temptations, tailoring instruction to age and cultural background. Enforce alcohol and drug policies on school grounds and in extracurricular activities. Arrange productive leisure activities. Consult with a nurse or counselor when you worry that a youngster is pregnant or abusing drugs.

Some sick children feel so "different" that they are hesitant to approach peers (Alison, Negley, & Sibthorp, 2013; M. Jackson, 2013; A. Turnbull, Turnbull, & Wehmeyer, 2010). They may blame their physical condition (perhaps accurately, perhaps not) for any problems they have with friendships (Kapp-Simon & Simon, 1991). In some cases, peers may avoid a student with a chronic illness because of naive notions about contagion. For instance, preschoolers sometimes believe that people contract cancer by being in the same room as someone else with that condition (Bibace & Walsh, 1981; M. Jackson, 2013).

MyLab Education
Video Explanation 5.2
How do different cultures view children's illness?

Serious Injuries and Health Hazards

Injuries represent another problem affecting children. Young children are at risk for ingesting poisons, drowning in pools, falling from heights, and getting burned from the stove. As children get older, their increasing independence makes them susceptible to different kinds of injuries. In the United States, injuries from firearms, motor vehicle crashes, unintentional drowning or poisoning, and suicide are the primary causes of death during the adolescent years (CDC, 2013e).

Although some injuries heal quickly, others have long-term effects that must be accommodated at school. **Traumatic brain injuries (TBIs)** are hits or jolts to the head that alter brain functioning; TBIs range from mild concussions to severe wounds. Children sustain TBIs from playground falls, bicycle mishaps, skiing and motor vehicle accidents, sports injuries, assaults, and other harrowing events (CDC, 2013f; Ilie et al., 2015; McKinlay et al., 2008). Depending on location in the brain and the severity of the wound, TBIs can have temporary or lasting effects. Children with mild concussions experience a brief loss of consciousness or sense of being disoriented and may have memory lapses for events immediately before or after the accident. Youngsters frequently have headaches, nausea, and trouble concentrating for several months after the injury. Depending on symptoms, a teacher might minimize distractions in the classroom, allow extra time for completing assignments, or adjust expectations for performance in the first few weeks (Gioia, 2016; A. Turnbull et al., 2010). Children who have had a serious brain injury may exhibit difficulties in learning, controlling emotions, speaking, walking, and seeing or hearing. Therapy and modifications to the curriculum may be necessary.

Many childhood injuries are avoidable, of course, and schools can play a key role in educating children about preventive measures. Teachers can advise children to use seat belts while riding in motor vehicles and wear helmets while cycling, snowboarding, and skating (CDC, 2013g; Klassen, MacKay, Moher, Walker, & Jones, 2000). Coaches can instruct athletes on how to reduce risks for head injuries, recognize signs of concussions, and get help after a possible TBI (CDC, 2010). After an injury, an athlete needs ample time to recover before returning to practice and should be reminded to take precautions in avoiding future collisions.

Physical Disabilities

Children with physical disabilities, such as cerebral palsy, muscular dystrophy, and blindness, have the same essential physical needs as other children, namely, a good diet, regular exercise, and adequate rest and sleep (Einarsson, Jóhannsson, Daly, & Arngrímsson, 2016). Because exercise is central to health, adults must find ways to adapt physical activities to sensory and physical conditions, such that successful movement becomes possible. For example, a teacher can assist students who have visual impairments by guiding their bodies into correct positions and inserting bells or other noisemakers inside playground balls (Poel, 2007). For a student who likes baseball but lacks strength and endurance, a teacher might allow another student to run around the bases after a hit (Pangrazi & Beighle, 2010). For students with hearing impairments, teachers need to ask parents whether any assistive devices, such as hearing aids and cochlear implants, should be removed during vigorous physical activity.

Preparing for Your Licensure Examination

Your teaching test might ask you about accommodations that allow children with physical disabilities to participate in sports.

Promoting Physical Well-Being in All Children

As you are learning, children with chronic illnesses, serious injuries, and physical disabilities often require individualized accommodations for health protection. Several guidelines apply to *all* children but especially to those with special physical needs:

- **Seek guidance from parents and specialized organizations about accommodations that help children stay in sports.** Parents and guardians often have helpful suggestions for encouraging children's exercise. Professional organizations—most are easily found on the Internet—offer a wealth of ideas about adapting instruction and equipment for children with chronic conditions and disabilities. Two broadly focused organizations are the American Alliance for Health, Physical Education, Recreation and Dance and the National Consortium for Physical Education and Recreation for Individuals with Disabilities. Specific disabilities are the focus of other organizations, such as the American Athletic Association for the Deaf and the U.S. Association for Blind Athletes.

- **Encourage children to monitor their health.** Children gradually learn to cope with the everyday demands of chronic health conditions, but they may need reminders about following procedures (e.g., to test blood glucose levels if they have diabetes), go to the nurse's office at appropriate times (e.g., to take medicines), and look after their recurring physical needs (e.g., to eat nutritious snacks and use the toilet regularly).

- **Encourage children and their families to take protective measures.** Caregivers and teachers can teach young children safety precautions, such as how to handle dangerous situations, for example, how to make an emergency phone call or respond when they are lost or approached by a stranger, are touched inappropriately, or come across a gun (Brenick, Shattuck, Donlan, Duh, & Zurbriggen, 2014; S. O'Neill, Fleer, Agbenyega, Ozanne-Smith, & Urlichs, 2013; M. C. Roberts, Brown, Boles, & Mashunkashey, 2004). At school, teachers and other staff can explain (and enforce) safety rules for using playground equipment and distribute safety brochures on seat belts, bicycle helmets, and precautions with fire and smoke.

- **Design environments to minimize injuries.** Careful attention to equipment can reduce children's injuries (M. C. Roberts et al., 2004). An infant caregiver can purchase cribs with slats close together to prevent babies' heads from getting stuck between them. He or she can also examine toys for choking hazards, set the temperature of water heaters below scalding, and confirm that the refrigerator door will not lock from the inside. A principal can ensure that a playground has no sharp edges; that the ground's surface has soft, cushioning materials; and that smoke detectors are installed properly and checked regularly for live batteries.

- **Know what to do in a health emergency.** Some children have conditions that could result in life-threatening situations. A child with diabetes could go into insulin shock, a child with asthma might have trouble breathing, and a child with epilepsy could have a serious seizure at school. When teachers learn that a child has a chronic health condition, they can consult with parents to find out how to respond in emergencies.

- **Educate children about physical disabilities.** Children are more likely to show kindness to a peer with a physical impairment if they understand the nature of the disability. Children should know, for example, that cancer cannot be spread by breathing the same air and that epileptic seizures, although frightening, are only temporary. Keep in mind, however, that a teacher should talk about a child's physical condition *only* if he or she and the parents have given permission to do so (Shapiro & Manz, 2004).

- **Keep lines of communication open with children who are hospitalized or homebound.** Sometimes children's health conditions keep them out of school for a lengthy time. In such circumstances, children can participate in classroom lessons, activities, and social events by telephone or a voice-conferencing system such as Skype or FaceTime. When children cannot regularly communicate, they may appreciate correspondence and photographs from classmates and other important people in their lives.

- **Teach social skills to children who find themselves excluded from friendship groups.** School absences and the stresses of a chronic condition (and occasional overprotection from parents) can put a strain on children's peer relationships. Teachers can keep an eye out for the inclusion of children with chronic illnesses who are reentering school after repeated or lengthy absences. Teachers can also coach sick children to try particular social skills, such as listening sympathetically and gaining entry into an existing group of children (Kapp-Simon & Simon, 1991).

- **Address any problems in learning that accompany children's illnesses.** Depending on their conditions and the medicines they take, children with chronic illnesses may develop problems with attention and organization (Shapiro & Manz, 2004). Teachers can encourage children to stay focused and teach them how to organize their work. Teachers can also arrange for hospitalized children to make up missed work when they have regained their strength.

- **Use appropriate precautions when caring for children.** Educators can teach children basic safety precautions, such as sneezing into their own elbow, staying away from a friend's bloody knee, and washing hands after using the toilet. Adults also must take precautions. The use of appropriate barrier precautions for blood (e.g., latex gloves) is advisable when helping children with open wounds. Experts also direct caregivers to wash their hands after changing diapers and wiping noses (AAP Committee on Pediatric AIDS and Committee on Infectious Diseases, 1999).

Summary

Health depends on eating habits, physical activity, and rest and sleep. Children can benefit from overtures by adults that affirm health protection and discourage problematic behaviors. Some children exhibit behavior that jeopardizes their physical well-being (e.g., with eating disorders, overreliance on sedentary activities, and lack of sleep). In adolescence, additional health-compromising behaviors may emerge with cigarette smoking, alcohol and drug use, and unprotected sexual activity. Prevention can be emphasized at school and supplemented with individualized treatment, counseling, and other services when young people who put themselves in harm's way. Youngsters with chronic illness, serious injuries, and physical disabilities often benefit from modifications in instruction, equipment, and the physical environment. Ultimately, educators should strive to include all children in physical activity.

MyLab Education Self-Check 5.2

Brain Development

5.3 Identify the brain's basic structures and developmental processes and derive implications for educating children.

Now that you have a foundation in children's physical development, you are ready to learn about the maturation of the brain, the extraordinary human organ that senses information in the environment, guides movement, regulates other systems in the body, and allows for language, thinking, and creativity. The brain follows the general patterns of physical development we introduced earlier, for example, with parts of the brain maturing at different rates and the separate parts connecting up over time.

How is this amazing organ structured? Altogether, the mature brain is made up of trillions of cells, the two primary kinds being *neurons* and *glia*. One hundred billion **neurons** transmit information to other neurons (Naegele & Lombroso, 2001; R. W. Williams & Herrup, 1988). Each neuron has a long, armlike **axon** that sends chemicals on to other neurons. Partner neurons absorb the chemicals that axons release down their branchlike extensions called **dendrites** (Figure 5.9). An axon from one neuron and dendrites from other neurons come close together in junctions called **synapses**. When any neuron is stimulated to a certain degree by a chemical, it either "fires," generating an electrical impulse that triggers the release of its own substance (culminating in the stimulation and subsequent firing of adjacent neurons), or it is inhibited from firing, depending on the amount and type of chemicals emitted by neighbors.

Most neurons have thousands of synapses, making a great deal of cross-communication possible. Groups of neurons grow together as communities that specialize in certain functions. Following the principle that there is strength in numbers, these communities, called *circuits* or *networks*, are laid out in side-by-side wires that reach out to other groups of neurons. The result is that important processes in the brain (such as feeling emotions, paying attention, understanding language, and learning new ideas) are supported by robust structures.

Intermingling with neurons are a trillion or more **glial cells**. Glial cells perform numerous functions (Figure 5.10). *Oligodendrocytes* coat the

FIGURE 5.9 Neurons

The neuron at left (in salmon color) is receiving information from cells at far left (only one's blue dendrites are shown) and will subsequently fire and incite neurons at right to fire in a chain of activity. Arrows show the direction of messages being sent.

Based on Carlson, N. R. (2014). *Foundations of behavioral neuroscience* (9th ed.). Boston, MA: Pearson.

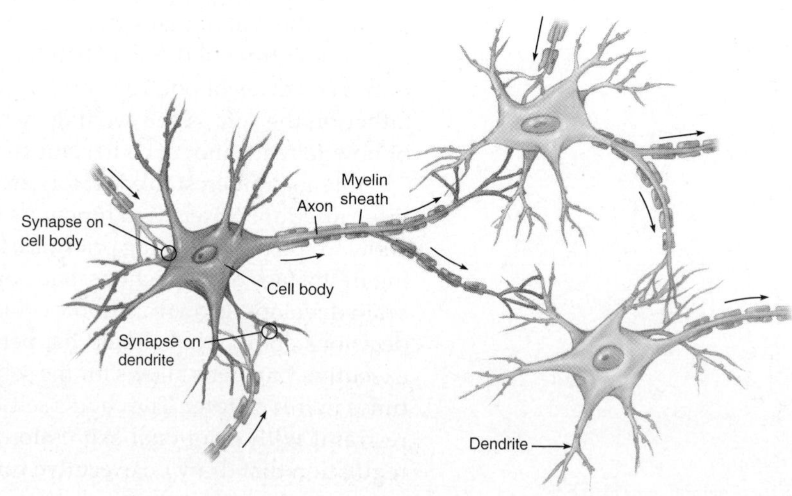

FIGURE 5.10 Glial cells come in several distinct forms.

Oligodendrocytes insulate neurons and increase efficiency in firing. *Microglia* rid the brain of infectious and damaged material. *Astrocytes* play numerous roles, including communicating with one another and nourishing and regulating neurons.

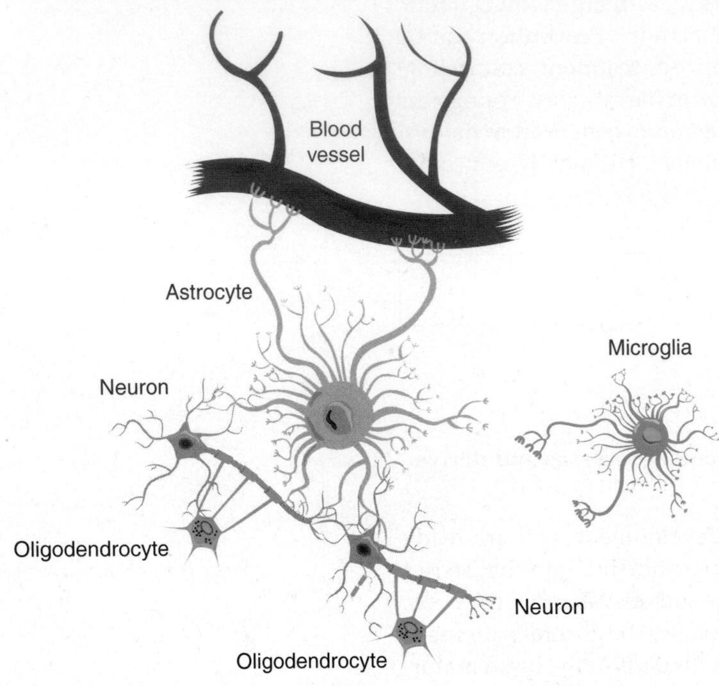

axons of neurons with insulating myelin, speeding up electrical signals. *Microglia* rid the brain of damaged neurons, bacteria, and viruses. **Astrocytes** are glial cells that regulate blood flow to the brain, bring nutrients to neurons, metabolize chemicals released by neurons, communicate with other astrocytes and with neurons, help integrate information in the brain, and guide the growth of synapses and axons (Fields, 2009; Reemst, Noctor, Lucassen, & Hol, 2016; X. Tong, Shigetomi, Looger, & Khakh, 2013; Volterra, Liaudet, & Savtchouk, 2014).

Structures and Functions

Neurons and glial cells organize themselves into networks, as you have read, and these bundles of neurons communicate with other bundles of neurons. Networks form in hierarchies, with small bundles being part of medium-sized circuits, which, in turn, are part of broader regions. From a macro perspective, the brain develops into three major sections: the hindbrain, midbrain, and forebrain (Figure 5.11). Each of these sections has identifiable functions:

- The **hindbrain** controls basic processes that sustain survival, including breathing, blood pressure, sleep, arousal, balance, and movement (thank your hindbrain for your slow, methodical breathing as you sleep blissfully at night).
- The **midbrain** connects the hindbrain to the forebrain and acts as a relay station between the two; for instance, it sends messages to the forebrain about priorities for attention ("Hello! Alarm clock ringing! Time to rise!").
- The **forebrain** produces complex thinking, emotional responses, and the forces of motivation ("Ugh! I can sleep another 10 minutes if I skip breakfast. No . . . I better get up.").

Each of the three parts is critical to human survival. The hindbrain and the midbrain ensure basic physiological processes. The forebrain is of special relevance to educators because it allows children to learn concepts of all kinds. The forebrain contains the **cortex**, a wrinkled cap that rests on the midbrain and hindbrain. Physiologically, the cortex is extremely convoluted. Fibers of neurons repeatedly fold in on themselves. This arrangement permits a huge capacity for storing and transmitting information throughout the brain. Memories are stored, interpretations are made, and goals are established. It is also the seat of many personality traits, such as being enthusiastic and sociable or quiet and introverted, and of habitual ways of responding to events and novel information. The cortex of one 10-year-old girl would control the way she snuggles up to her father on the sofa in the evening, her exuberant style with friends, her understanding of how to read, and, of course, much more.

Of major interest to educators are specialized operations in the cortex called **executive functions**. Executive functions refer to those deliberate thinking processes that allow for planning, setting priorities, focusing attention, juggling multiple tasks, persisting in the face of distractions, and solving problems when obstacles arise. It is as if the brain develops its own air-traffic controller system for filtering information and making decisions about what should happen, when, in what order. Neurological support for executive functions allows for the self-regulatory processes we have referred to several times in this chapter. The child's self-control in the classroom, sustained concentration, restraint with emotional expression, and resistance to temptations are types of self-regulation that draw on executive functions.

FIGURE 5.11 Structure of the human brain.

The human brain is an intricate organ with three main parts: the hindbrain, midbrain, and forebrain.
Based on Carlson, N. R. (2014). *Foundations of behavioral neuroscience* (9th ed.). Boston, MA: Pearson.

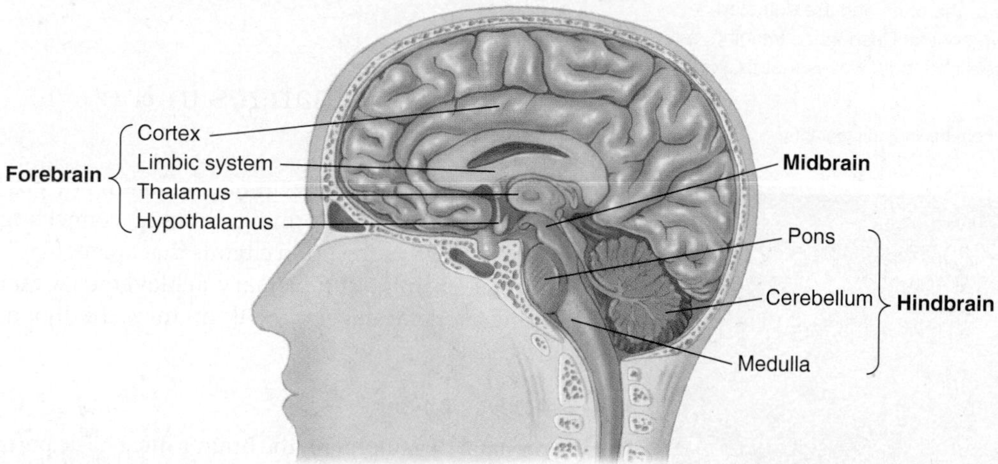

Specialization and Communication

Consistent with the principle of differentiation, various parts of the cortex take on their own psychological processes. The cortex consists of relatively large regions (called *lobes*) that are wired together in support of particular functions, including decision making and planning (front), understanding and producing language (sides), and visual processing (rear). In addition, the cortex is divided into two halves, or *hemispheres*. In right-handed individuals, the **left hemisphere** controls the right side of the body, and the **right hemisphere** manages the left side. In most people the left hemisphere dominates in *analysis*, breaking up information into constituent parts and extracting order in a sequence of events, as occurs with talking, understanding speech, reading, writing, mathematical problem solving, and computer programming (N. R. Carlson, 2014; Pinel & Dehaene, 2009). It is usually the right hemisphere that excels in *synthesis*, pulling together information (especially nonlinguistic information) into a coherent whole, as when we recognize faces; detect geometrical patterns; read body language; and appreciate musical melodies, humor, and emotions (N. R. Carlson, 2014; Gainotti, 2007). Left-handed individuals often have reversed patterns, with the right hemisphere dominant in analysis and the left hemisphere involved in synthesis (Toga & Thompson, 2003). A few individuals (particularly those who use both hands equally well) blend psychological functions within hemispheres in unique configurations (Biduła & Króliczak, 2015; Sheehan & Smith, 1986).

Consistent with the principle of integration, the two hemispheres are in constant communication, trading information through a thick bundle of neurons. For example, the right hemisphere processes a complex emotion, the mixed feelings people experience at a high school graduation, while the left hemisphere searches for the right words to communicate these feelings. Thus, it is not accurate to say that a child is a "right-brained" or "left-brained" thinker, as is sometimes done by well-meaning educators. Continual cross-talk between the hemispheres means that a child who is strong in a particular mode of representation, such as spatial or verbal reasoning, not only develops representations that are facile with that particular talent but also blends input from various parts of the brain.

Accompanying the continuous contact between the hemispheres is pervasive communication within and across separate parts of the cortex. Ideas, sensations, memories, and feelings are all integrated into a person's conscious experience. Supplementing these circuits are connections *between* the cortex and other parts of the brain. As an illustration, basic "energizing" activities that reside outside the cortex (e.g., certain aspects

FIGURE 5.12 Neural networks.

This image shows active networks of neurons in a person's brain. The perspective is as if the person is looking to left and you are seeing the cortex from the inside and upwards. Pathways of neurons of each color transmit signals to other regions of the brain and are detected by High-Definition Fiber Tractography Magnetic Resonance Imaging, a procedure generated by a magnetic field and radio waves that tracks operations of neurons.

Source: Healthy adult human brain viewed from behind, tractography' by Henrietta Howells, NatBrainLab.

of attention, emotion, and motivation) regularly interact with reflective "intellectual" processes in the cortex. Children who feel alert and happy readily grasp a classroom lesson, whereas children who are sleepy or distracted do not. In Figure 5.12, you can see a diagram of connections that exist in the brain.

Developmental Changes in the Brain

The magnificent intricacy of the human brain is made possible by a lengthy course of forming, refining, connecting its parts, and strengthening brain circuits that are regularly used. Here we examine the primary achievements that occur during prenatal development, infancy, childhood, and adolescence.

Prenatal Development

During prenatal development, the brain's most basic parts are formed. The brain begins as a tiny tube approximately 25 days after conception, as illustrated in Figure 5.13. This seemingly simple tube grows longer in places and folds inward to form pockets (Tierney & Nelson, 2009). Three bulges appear early on and become the forebrain, the midbrain, and the hindbrain. Soon the brain takes on more complex features, with the forebrain cleaving down the middle and specializing into the left and right hemispheres (Stephan, Fink, & Marshall, 2007). Before the brain can develop any further, it must become a factory for neurons. Beginning in the fifth week, neurons reproduce in the inner portion of the tube. Production peaks between the third and fourth prenatal months, when several hundred thousand new neurons are generated *each minute* (C. A. Nelson, Thomas, & de Haan, 2006). The vast majority of neurons that will ever be used by a person are formed during the first 7 months of prenatal development (Rakic, 1995).[1]

Once formed, neurons move, or *migrate*, to specific brain locations where they will do their work. Some young neurons push old cells outward, creating brain structures underneath the cortex. Others actively seek out their destination, climbing up polelike glial cells, and once arriving, forming the cortex. When in place, neurons send out axons, which grow together as teams, reaching toward other groups of neurons (their targets) that attract them with certain chemicals. As axons get close to neighboring neurons, they generate branches that become the dendrites, which, in turn, form synapses with other cells. The target cells do their part, forming small receptors with dendrites at the point of the synapse. Only about half of neurons ultimately make contact with other cells. Those that do, survive; the others atrophy and die. Nature's tendency to overproduce neurons and eliminate those that fail to connect ensures that the brain invests in connections that actually work (M. Diamond & Hopson, 1998; P. R. Huttenlocher, 1990).

In the months before birth, the brain forms circuits for breathing, sucking, swallowing, crying, forming simple associations, and learning about people and the physical world. If all goes well, the infant is born with capacities to survive, interact, move, and learn. Yet not all prenatal beings have ideal conditions for growth, and those that are exposed to alcohol and drugs, viruses, and other toxins may deviate from typical pathways, for example, growing too few neurons or sending them off into the wrong direction. Thus, the prenatal phase is a *sensitive period* for the brain, a time of rapid growth in foundational structures that can be derailed with biochemical

[1]Some new neurons are formed later in development, including during the adult years, in a structure of the brain that forms memories (C. A. Nelson et al., 2006). Astrocytes continue to duplicate throughout life.

substances in the mother's womb, injury, and radiation. Consequently, nurses, doctors, midwives, and educators who advocate for a pregnant woman's self-care, access to proper nutrition, and avoidance of harmful influences may contribute to the offspring's healthy start.

Infancy and Early Childhood

At birth and for a couple of days afterward, astrocytes and other glial cells continue to proliferate and find their places near neurons. Neurons reach out to one another in countless new connections (synapses), a phenomenon known as **synaptogenesis**. In the first few years of life, so many new synapses appear that their number far exceeds adult levels (Goddings & Giedd, 2014; C. A. Nelson et al., 2006). Following this fantastic proliferation of synapses, frequently used connections become stronger, and rarely used connections wither away in a process known as **synaptic pruning**. Particular regions of the brain take their turns growing and shedding synapses (P. R. Huttenlocher, 1990; Muftuler et al., 2012). Psychologists speculate that by generating more synapses than will ever be needed, human beings can adapt their psychological processes to a wide variety of conditions. Synaptic pruning, then, is Mother Nature's way of customizing a brain to work efficiently with actual circumstances.

Early brain development is also marked by **myelination**, a process in which glial cells grow around the axons of neurons to form a fatty coating (*myelin*) that insulates axons and enables rapid firing by neurons. Just as synaptic proliferation and pruning proceed in order through particular areas of the brain, myelination rotates through regions of the brain in a predictable order (Yakovlev & Lecours, 1967). It begins during the prenatal period, with the coating of neurons involved in basic survival skills. During infancy, myelination takes place on neurons in the sensory areas of the brain, followed by those involved in motor skills in childhood, and eventually (well into adolescence) with those responsible for complex thinking processes, judgment, planning, and self-control (M. Diamond & Hopson, 1998; C. A. Nelson et al., 2006; Sanchez et al., 2012).

FIGURE 5.13 Prenatal brain growth.

During the first few months, the basic structures appear (for 25 and 50 days, the relative sizes have been increased to show detail in forms). During the middle months of prenatal development, basic structures are refined. In the final weeks prior to birth, the cortex folds in and out of itself, allowing for learning.

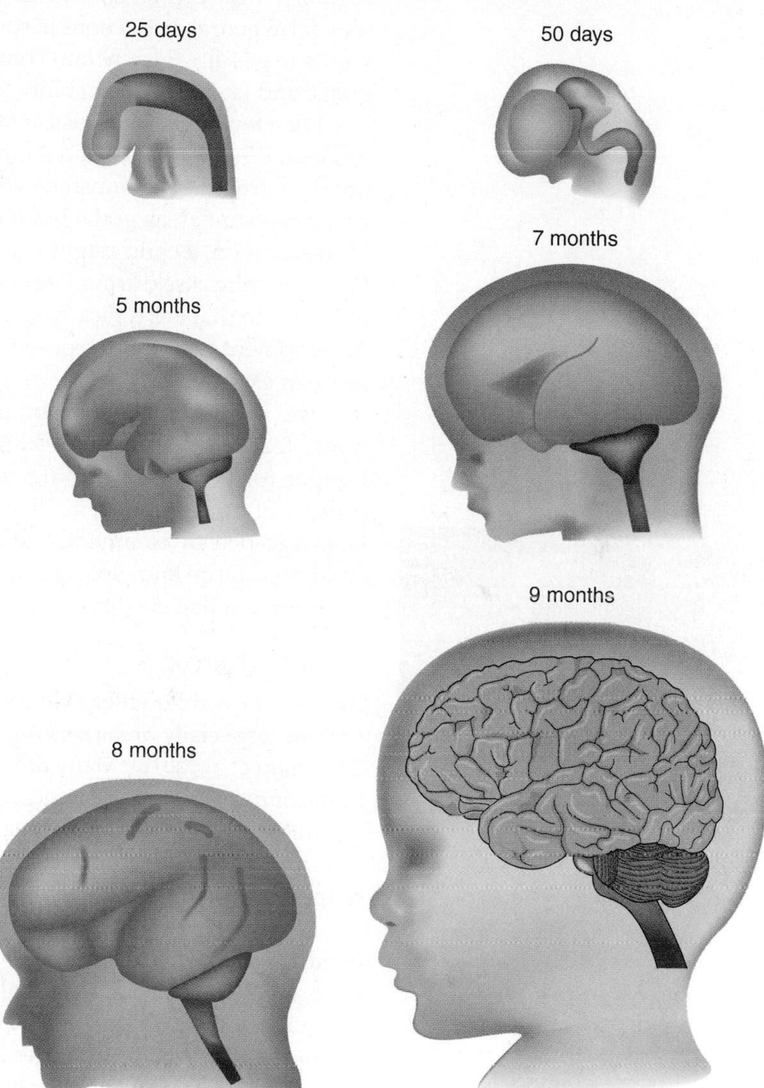

Given that myelination concentrates on sensory areas during infancy, it makes sense that small children learn by seeing, feeling, hearing, touching, and tasting. The infant brain is devoted to exploring the world and identifying its underlying forms, designs, and configurations. American psychologist **Alison Gopnik** has studied the amazing abilities of infants to form inferences and generalizations from what they perceive around them (A. Gopnik, 2009a, 2009b, 2009c; C. M. Walker, Bridgers, & Gopnik, 2016; R. Wu, Gopnik, Richardson, & Kirkham, 2011). Infants recognize such things as toys being colorful, shiny, and made of hard substances; one object launching another; their native language being composed of ordered sounds (e.g., *p* and *t* often occur together within English words, as in *Peter*, but not in direct succession, as in *Pteer*).

During infancy and early childhood, regularities in perceptions are memorialized as circuits in the brain. Groups of neurons that fire together reinforce one another, merging into bundles that operate together when faced with similar stimuli. The budding circuits essentially obligate the infant to spot features consistent with patterns he or she has previously noticed. The brain's tendency to convert initial observations into networks that constrain future learning has been described as making *neural commitments* (Kuhl, 2007; Kuhl, Conboy, Padden, Nelson, & Pruitt, 2005; Partanen et al., 2013). For example, when infants regularly hear certain sounds in their native language (e.g., the sound *ba* in English), they form neural distinctions in sounds (e.g, *ba* vs. *ga*), aiding them in hearing full-blown words (e.g., *ba*ll). Such neural commitments help young children learn their native language and later *limit* their ability to learn a second language with different sounds.

For a few human abilities, infancy and early childhood are *sensitive periods* in development. When young children miss out on fundamental experiences with language, do not have trusting relationships with caregivers, or miss out on normal sensory experiences, relevant areas in the brain do not develop normally. Depending on the severity of deprivation, a child might later develop these capacities but not as easily as would have been the case during infancy and, in some circumstances, not as fully. Networks in the brain that are typically reserved for certain capacities yet are not prompted into development will be repurposed to represent other processes that help the child make sense of experiences.

The rapid growth of the brain during early childhood offers educational implications. Teachers and staff working with young children can accommodate children's hunger for affection, learning, and spontaneous play. Educators cannot control all aspects of young children's lives, but they can provide loving care, a sensory- and language-rich environment, and attention to substantial developmental delays. Young children acquire knowledge most effectively when immersed in a reasonably complex environment that encourages their initiative.

MyLab Education
Video Example 5.5

Find Developmental Meaning
What kind of memory capacity does 6-year-old Brent reveal? Brent has an intuitive understanding of the kind of information that is easy to remember—material that is simple or that he learned recently or practiced. He is optimistic about words he can remember and shows a good capacity, which will expand for him as a result of practice, guidance, and neurological maturation.

Middle Childhood

By the time a child enters kindergarten, his or her brain is basically mature in certain regions, especially areas serving sensory and perceptual processes (Fusaro & Nelson, 2009; Taki et al., 2013). Many others, including networks supporting memory and emotion, continue to reach out and connect with other circuits. A progression in linking up separate neurological centers makes it possible for a child to deepen his or her understanding of familiar concepts (e.g., the defining features of animals, the characteristics of the self, and qualities of a friend).

Synaptic pruning of weak connections becomes a major force of change during childhood. Yet even as unused synapses are being pruned back, new ones continue to be formed with learning, especially in the cortex (National Research Council, 1999; Taki et al., 2013). The process of myelination also continues, protecting neurons and speeding up the transmission of messages (Yakovlev & Lecours, 1967). This practice of solidifying existing neurological circuits allows children to reinforce perceptions of regularities in the environment. Also during this period children become increasingly proficient in their native tongue, acquiring sophisticated words and grammatical structures.

Another important outcome of neurological maturation at this age is an expanding capacity to hold several ideas in mind (Solé-Padullés et al., 2016). The ability to juggle multiple ideas remains under development well into adolescence and afterward. Usually, children in the elementary grades have a fairly limited attention span and cannot easily plan for the future. They are responsive to support, however, suggesting that the circuits or executive functions are being laid and benefit from practice.

Elementary school teachers and other practitioners can accommodate the strengths and limitations of children's brains. Teachers can ask children to identify patterns in subject matter, for example, the changing seasons, tidal movements, holidays, artistic designs, musical rhythms, and historical events. School professionals can also help children to exercise their fragile executive skills. They might post a calendar, offer reminders, set interim goals for complex tasks, and encourage them to keep track of progress on projects. Teachers, counselors, and psychologists can scaffold children's preliminary efforts in regulating emotions by talking with them about their feelings and modeling productive ways to convey anger, disappointment, and sadness. Finally, children of this age continue to acquire expertise in language through conversation, literature, poetry, and immersion in second languages.

Preparing for Your Licensure Examination

Your teaching test might ask you about strategies for supporting children's organizational skills (e.g., by asking them to set goals, manage time, and assemble learning materials in preparation for a lesson). These organizational skills are important self-regulatory processes and build on executive functions.

Adolescence

The cortex continues to change in important ways during adolescence (Aoki, Romeo, & Smith, 2017; Casey, Giedd, & Thomas, 2000; Sowell, Delis, Stiles, & Jernigan, 2001). Synaptic pruning and myelination occur in parts of the brain devoted to complex thought processes. As a result of numerous long-term changes, adults' brains are more efficient than children's in their connections (through synapses) and insulation (through myelination).

Given the significant transformations that brains are going through in the teenage years, young people are able to look beyond the surface of things. The capacity to consider multiple ideas simultaneously allows for comparisons among different facets of concepts and culminates in abstract thinking. Yet as adolescents are developing high-brow intellectual abilities, they also are gaining a taste for adventure (Alarcón, Cservenka, & Nagel, 2017; Carlisi, Pavletic, & Ernst, 2013; Steinberg, 2007). Many previously compliant youngsters suddenly violate basic rules, perhaps stealing, taking drugs, or driving recklessly.

How is it that adolescents can act intelligently one minute and rashly the next? The answer seems to lie in a temporary imbalance that occurs in the adolescent brain. During this period, circuits in the brain devoted to enjoying immediate rewards (e.g., laughing uproariously with friends at a classmate's expense) mature before circuits for avoiding adverse consequences (e.g., realizing that the classmate might overhear the remarks and telling friends to stop). Gradually, neurological systems for curbing impulsive behavior catch up to the impetus to indulge immediate desires and make it easier for young people to control their impulses.

Of course, precisely how youth respond to impetuous feelings depends a great deal on the expectations of adults and the conduct of friends. Some societies tolerate testing of limits whereas others discourage or redirect this behavior. Amish people, a peaceful, traditional Christian sect in rural areas of Pennsylvania, Ohio, Indiana, other areas in the United States, and Ontario, Canada, allow a period of "Rumspringa," a time when adolescents engage in such misbehavior as wearing nontraditional clothing, driving automobiles instead of horse-drawn vehicles, drinking alcohol, and engaging in premarital sex (Cates & Weber, 2012; Stevick, 2014). At the end of this period, Amish youth are encouraged to resume traditional ways, get baptized, and marry. Many other societies ask young people to profess their commitment to adult roles after education and exploration, as you can learn about in the Development in Culture feature "Initiation Ceremonies."

The complex neurological changes of adolescence have implications for teachers and other professionals. Adults can foster abstract thinking by providing opportunities to test hypotheses in science, analyze characters' motivations in literature, and identify conflicting perspectives in history. They can similarly encourage adolescents to polish skills in areas of personal interest, perhaps computer programming, religious studies, or film production. Given the penchant for impetuous behavior at this age, adults must also try to shield young people from harm by restricting their access to hazardous activities. Adolescents are generally able to appraise the risks of dangerous behaviors (e.g., drinking and driving, having unprotected sex), but they easily lose good judgment when overwhelmed by immediate social pressures (Carlisi et al., 2013; V. F. Reyna & Farley, 2006; Somerville, Jones, & Casey, 2010; Steinberg, 2007, 2015). As a result, efforts to educate adolescents about the consequences of risk-taking behaviors are only modestly effective unless paired with mechanisms that limit temptations. Thus, adults can educate adolescents about problems with underage drinking but also make it not only illegal but also expensive and inconvenient for them to obtain alcoholic beverages. Similarly, giving adolescents chances to engage in fun and supervised after-school programs can be far more effective in reducing risky behaviors than simply telling them about the risks of unprotected sex, drugs, and alcohol.

Irregularities in Brain Development

In some cases, children's brains have unusual networks or distorted structures, malformations that can interfere with learning and behavior. Too many or too few cells form, connections among cells are laid out in unusual ways, or neurons become unusually slow or quick to fire (Alwadei et al., 2016; Kumar, Arya, & Agarwal, 2017; C. A. Nelson et al., 2006). These neurological conditions affect children's ability to pay attention, learn efficiently, control impulses, relate to other people, and deal with negative emotions.

A neurological disorder that begins in childhood takes a particular developmental course depending on the underlying genetic condition or environmental cause.

Development in Culture

Initiation Ceremonies

To help young people remain committed to a productive life, some societies arrange for *initiation ceremonies*, rites of passage in which boys and girls are shepherded through an educational process and afterward accepted as men and women. In Latin American cultures, a 15-year-old girl may take part in a *Quinceañera* celebration after publically affirming her religious faith. A 13-year-old Jewish boy may become a *Bar Mitzvah* and a 12-year-old girl a *Bat Mitzvah* after reading from the Torah during a religious ceremony. Many Christian youth take part in *Confirmation* ceremonies, during which time they profess their faith and become full members of their religious community.

Penny Tweedie/Alamy Stock Photo

COMING OF AGE. Initiation ceremonies prepare adolescent boys and girls for adult roles. These Aboriginal boys in Arnhem Land, Australia, are heading into the bush with elders to celebrate their manhood.

In nonindustrialized societies, initiation ceremonies prepare girls for womanhood and boys for manhood (H. Montgomery, 2009). In the Tswapong culture of Botswana, a girl who has had her first menstrual period is designated a "mothei" and secluded to a hut for 7 days. The mothei is ushered through several intense rituals, including observing village women dancing, being smeared with python dung and swatted on the back, eating special food, and listening to women recite codes of conduct (Werbner, 2009). The mothei is seen as undergoing the transformation from child to adult.

Many boys in nonindustrialized societies also take part in initiation ceremonies, often in groups (Lancy, 2008; Schlegel & Barry, 1980). For instance, the Tapirapé, an indigenous tribe in the Amazon rain forest of Brazil, bring young adolescent boys into the "takana," a men's club that socializes the boys for manhood (Wagley, 1977). Boys stay in the takana for several months—some for up to a year—and learn about such masculine traditions as making bows and arrows. When the boys are considered mature and ready to find a spouse, they undergo another ceremony, in which they dance for a full day and night and are then considered men.

Children mentally prepare for their personal transformation, having observed older siblings and cousins go through the process. The road to adulthood is not always an easy one, but guidance from adults in the form of initiation ceremonies can ease the transition by offering education and signaling the mature status to others.

Children who are *autistic* are apt to be born with brains that are smaller than usual (N. R. Carlson, 2014). After birth until about age 2, their brains grow more rapidly than is typical and then slow down such that by adolescence their brains are only minimally larger than average. Specific regions involved in the interpretation of verbal and social stimuli grow especially rapidly to begin with and then more slowly than usual. Also significant is that the connections can be different from those in the brains of nonautistic children, for example, with more links within certain centers of the brain and less cross-talk with areas across the cortex (Mevel, Fransson, & Bölte, 2015).

Children with *Down syndrome* are born with brains that are lighter than usual and have a cortex that is less convoluted than normal; therefore, they have a slightly diminished capacity for interconnections among neurons (N. R. Carlson, 2014; N. R. Lee et al., 2016). Children with Down syndrome also have small frontal lobes, regions that support executive functions, and a less advanced superior gyrus, which is crucial for language comprehension. With three rather than the customary two copies of the 21st chromosome, children's bodies produce a larger than average amount of a specific protein that directs movement of young neurons to their final locations. With too much of the protein, cells developing into neurons are impelled to migrate before a sufficient number have grown (Dierssen, 2012).

Schizophrenia, a serious psychiatric disorder that affects one in 100 people, often surfaces during late adolescence or early adulthood (Anjum, Gait, Cullen, & White, 2010; N. R. Carlson, 2014). Individuals with schizophrenia display thought disorders (e.g., irrational ideas and disorganized thinking), hallucinations (e.g., "hearing" non-existent voices), delusions (e.g., worrying that "everyone is out to get me"), and social withdrawal (e.g., avoiding eye contact or conversation with others). Genes, viral infections and malnutrition during prenatal development, childbirth complications, and stressful environments seem to share responsibility. Possibly, certain people are born with genes that make them vulnerable to this condition, and then, after being exposed prenatally to extreme maternal stress, teratogens, or traumatic events, develop symptoms. The causes of schizophrenia are not fully understood, although young people with this condition have distinct neurological characteristics, such as unusually high or low levels of certain transmitters in certain parts of the brain (J. J. Weinstein et al., 2017). Fortunately, medication often quells troublesome symptoms.

Applications of Research on Brain Development

We have considered needs that arise because of neurological trends and exceptionalities. Let's look at applications more systematically.

• **Nurture the skills that brains are eager to acquire.** When there is a *sensitive period* in development, the child's brain is essentially primed to develop a capacity but can only do so when certain stimulation is provided, and other exposures are avoided. As you have learned, the brain grows quickly during infancy and early childhood and requires reasonably good nutrition, varied experiences, and nurturing relationships with caregivers. When small children do not receive high-quality care, structures in their brain develop weaknesses, as for example, when a young child is neglected and develops a brain that is hypersensitive to fear and struggles to learn new information (Lyons-Ruth, Pechtel, Yoon, Anderson, & Teicher, 2016). When older students are not guided in resisting rash impulses, they may not easily gain pathways for these capacities (Piekarski et al., 2017).

• **Help children who have been abused to form warm, trusting, and stable relationships.** Children develop expectations, written into their neurological circuits, about relationships (e.g., whether caregivers are affectionate or rejecting), emotions (e.g., whether anger dissipates or explodes into a turbulent outburst), and themselves (e.g., whether they are intrinsically worthy people or not; W. A. Cunningham & Zelazo, 2010; S. Hart, 2011; Siegel, 2001). When children have had many negative lessons early in life, it is up to caring adults to show that new kinds of relationships, emotional expressions, and self-perceptions are possible. Professional interventions are sometimes necessary when children have been subjected to repeatedly harsh or neglectful treatment.

• **Pay attention to the initiative that children of a particular age display.** During infancy and early childhood, much of the motivation for learning emanates from children themselves. Instead of learning best with flash cards, teacher-directed lessons, or television programs, young children acquire knowledge most effectively when immersed in a reasonably complex environment and allowed to play, explore, and communicate with others. In fact, because neurological changes in certain areas do not take place until middle childhood or later, young children are typically not able to benefit from educational experiences that require the inhibition of spontaneous responses. Sustained attention comes later, when elementary school children develop more mature executive functions and can now implement systematic cognitive skills.

• **Be optimistic that children can learn essential skills throughout childhood.** Certainly, early stimulation *is* necessary for normal development, especially for visual processing and depth perception. Yet varied experiences around the world provide enough stimulation for normal development in visual areas of the brain (Bruer, 1999; Greenough, Black, & Wallace, 1987; C. Harris, 2011). Equally important during this period (for other areas of the brain) is access to loving caregivers, chances to explore the environment, and exposure to language. As they grow, children benefit from such "brain-friendly" experiences as carefully designed instruction, exposure to rich cultural contexts (visits to museums, libraries, and the like), and teachers' warm relationships with them.

• **Consider the connections that exist among cognitive processes, emotional experiences, and bodily sensations.** Although educators often prioritize children's cognitive abilities over their social-emotional and physical needs, the reality is that children's thoughts trigger emotions, which in turn play out as sensations in the body (Immordino-Yang & Damasio, 2007). A group of third-graders may become distressed as they listen to a teacher's description about a recent famine, with their faces tensing, fists clenching, and bodies fidgeting. Noticing their reaction, the teacher might talk about her own feelings, reassure them about the productive actions officials are taking in response to the tragedy, and solicit children's ideas about how they, as a class, might address the problem.

- **Accommodate the needs of children with neurological delays and disabilities.** Individualizing instruction is especially important for children who have neurological conditions that hinder learning. Children with difficulty in paying attention or distinguishing among various sounds of speech often profit from intensive training in related processes (T. A. Keller & Just, 2009; H. E. Kirk, Gray, Ellis, Taffe, & Cornish, 2016; Simos et al., 2007). Similarly, children who have trouble performing basic numerical, verbal, or visual skills may have brain networks that do not easily process relevant information but can be strengthened with intervention (Abitbol Avtzon, 2013; Posner & Rothbart, 2007). Some children with genetic problems or were exposed to alcohol, cocaine, and other drugs during prenatal development strain to process particular kinds of information. They may need assistance in understanding abstract ideas (e.g., a teacher's request to be "responsible"), inhibiting inappropriate responses (e.g., hitting bothersome peers), and generalizing rules to multiple settings (e.g., "keep your hands to yourself" applies to the playground as well as to the classroom). Ultimately, adults must remember that, with proper guidance, most children with exceptional brain networks can lead fulfilling lives.

- **Guide children in sustaining attention and regulating impulses.** As they grow, children typically acquire skills related to self-regulation. These abilities are fostered by maturation in the prefrontal cortex and also by the support they receive at home, in school, and in other settings. Yet not all children receive adequate support for self-control, and others develop genetically guided networks that predispose them to be tense and combative (Eisenberg, 2006). By the time children enter school, major individual differences are obvious in children's self-regulatory abilities. Some children are able to deal productively with disappointment, distraction, and frustration, whereas others cannot easily restrain themselves (Blair, 2002). Children who lack self-regulatory skills need the same loving, sensitive care as do other children, but they also need extra guidance in waiting patiently in line, keeping their hands to themselves, and expressing their emotions in culturally appropriate ways.

Summary

The human brain is an intricate organ that regulates physiological functions (e.g., heart rate), sensations of pleasure and pain, motor skills and coordination, emotional responses, and intellectual processes. The brain consists of millions of interconnected circuits of neurons and glial cells, which collectively make up the distinct parts of the brain. The various parts connect up with time and allow for coordination of such multifaceted capacities as executive functions.

During prenatal development, neurons form and migrate to places where they will do their work. During infancy, brain cells connect up, others whither away, and the brain as a whole concentrates on perceptual learning, exploration of the environment, first relationships, and language and communication. During early and middle childhood, the brain protects those connections that are used often and lets the others fade; particular refinements solidify language skills and complex learning processes. During adolescence, the brain makes new interests and passions possible, sparks impetuous behavior, and grows in areas that will play key roles in forethought and judgment.

MyLab Education Self-Check 5.3

Practicing For Your Licensure Examination

Many teaching tests require students to use what they have learned about child development in responses to brief vignettes and multiple-choice questions. You can practice for your licensure examination by reading the case study and answering the questions. After you submit responses to all the questions, you'll receive instant feedback.

My Health by Nick

When Nick was 18 and getting ready to head to college, he agreed to describe his health during childhood and address his eating and sleeping habits, sports and exercise, major illnesses and injuries, and experiences with drugs, alcohol, and sex. Here is his essay:

My Health

by Nick

I've been fortunate to be healthy most of my life. I was born an average-sized baby, about seven pounds. At about a year and a half, I had pneumonia. I don't remember it but my Mom told me I had to take antibiotics and breathe through a nebulizer. After treatments, I used to run around the house bumping into walls until the jitteriness wore off.

I wasn't sick very much after that, in fact I got perfect attendance awards at school for a couple of years. During my senior year in high school I had the flu for 10 days. It was bad. I couldn't walk, I had a fever, and every bone in my body hurt. I felt weak for a couple of weeks but made a full recovery.

I love sports. I played soccer in preschool and then focused on football and basketball. It was so much fun to run around the field and court with my friends. Coaches told me I was talented and agile. I continued to play football and basketball through the beginning of middle school and then stopped. I was slow to get my growth spurt and got tired of being knocked down by bigger players. In high school I went to the gym and worked out instead and took up snowboarding.

I never broke an arm or a leg but did have a minor head injury at my 12th birthday party. We rented a local gymnastic center and my friends and I had fun running and jumping on the trampolines. At one point the manager turned off the lights. I ran full speed into a lateral pole and blacked out. I saw stars and bled from my forehead. I was disoriented and kept trying to wash off the blood even when it dried up, or so I have been told. I don't remember much except that my Dad tried to make a joke of it and took my photograph and my Mom freaked out. For a couple of weeks afterwards I was very tired and had a headache every day. My Mom made me go to the doctor, and he gave me some kind of brain test and I passed it. I haven't had a concussion again, and don't want another one, either.

I finally started catching up in height with my friends during my junior year. Before then, I felt like something was wrong with me because I was so short and delayed. I used to worry about it. My doctor told me I was normal. I didn't believe him until I started going through puberty. Puberty was okay but I was hungry and tired all the time. There never seemed to be enough food in the house. My parents cooked weird stuff like fish and vegetarian lasagna. I prefer plain hamburgers and spaghetti and meatballs. At lunch I went out with my friends and usually we would order two-dollar cheese quesadillas, sometimes a burger and fries. I ate a lot of snacks as well—trail mix, chips, apples, Pop-Tarts, and cookies mainly. I'm now tall, thin, and muscular. I'd like to gain some weight.

In high school I started staying up late, playing video games, and hanging out with friends on the Internet. It was always hard to get enough sleep. On school days I woke feeling like I was drugged. It was a struggle to climb out of bed.

Speaking of feeling drugged, I tried marijuana during my junior year and liked it. I also drank alcohol a few times with friends. I am going to college next week and am looking forward to the freedom and the parties. But I've decided I won't smoke marijuana anymore. I don't think it's wrong but I don't want to be excluded from certain jobs in the future. I never tried the other drugs, like ecstasy, that I heard some kids talking about. Really, why would anyone purposefully kill brain cells?

I have a girlfriend but we haven't had sex yet. I'm in no hurry really. I want to wait until it's the right time. I know that sex can mess up your emotions and I don't need that right now. I know I should use a condom when the time comes.

I hope I can stay healthy in college. I will play Ultimate Frisbee, work out at the gym, and snowboard when I can. I have a meal plan, which should be good and keep me well fed. I know I have to be careful at college parties. My brother says you always have to have a DD (designated driver). My Dad showed me how you can walk around at a party with an empty beer can so no one pressures you to have another drink. My Mom says I should count the number of drinks I have so I keep track.

I will have a roommate, and we'll have to agree on a lights-out time. I'm not ready to give up video games at night but know I can get carried away when playing them. I guess I'll figure that out.

Constructed-Response Question

1. What did Nick do during his childhood to stay healthy? What kind of risks has he taken with his health? What challenges lie ahead for him as he enters college?

Multiple-Choice Questions

2. Nick engaged in some risky behaviors, and he has shown restraint. Why do adolescents partake in potentially hazardous activities?

   a. Adolescents engage in risky behaviors because they like to experiment with new things.

   b. Adolescents engage in risky behaviors because their brains now have a heightened sensitivity to rewards and pleasure in interacting with peers, whereas the areas of the brains that inhibit impulses have not advanced sufficiently to exert strong control.

   c. Adolescents engage in risky behaviors because they do not understand the dangerous consequences that can result from such actions.

   d. Both *a* and *b* are reasons that adolescents engage in risky behaviors.

3. Nick was behind his peers in the age at which he began puberty. How does the timing of puberty affect the psychological development of boys and girls?

   a. The timing of puberty is entirely the result of existing distress in children's lives, with high levels of anxiety precipitating or delaying the onset of puberty, such that distress is the cause, rather than the effect, of an early or late puberty.

   b. Young people who are exceptionally early or late in their sexual maturation are inevitably maladjusted due to the stress involved.

   c. It is the changes of puberty, not the timing, that influence adolescents.

   d. Boys and girls who have an early or late puberty are apt to be self-conscious but their level of distress depends on their coping skills and the resources and risks in their lives.

MyLab Education Licensure Practice 5.1

Key Concepts

differentiation (p. 150)
integration (p. 150)
cephalocaudal trend (p. 152)
proximodistal trend (p. 152)
gross motor skills (p. 152)
fine motor skills (p. 152)
puberty (p. 156)
growth spurt (p. 156)
menarche (p. 156)
spermarche (p. 156)
self-regulation (p. 160)
obesity (p. 162)
anorexia nervosa (p. 163)
bulimia (p. 163)
rough-and-tumble play (p. 166)
transgender identity (p. 168)
sudden infant death syndrome (SIDS) (p. 169)
addiction (p. 173)
traumatic brain injury (TBI) (p. 176)
neuron (p. 179)
axon (p. 179)
dendrite (p. 179)
synapse (p. 179)
glial cell (p. 179)
astrocyte (p. 180)
hindbrain (p. 180)
midbrain (p. 180)
forebrain (p. 180)
cortex (p. 180)
executive functions (p. 180)
left hemisphere (p. 181)
right hemisphere (p. 181)
synaptogenesis (p. 183)
synaptic pruning (p. 183)
myelination (p. 183)
schizophrenia (p. 186)

Chapter Six

Cognitive Development: Piaget and Vygotsky

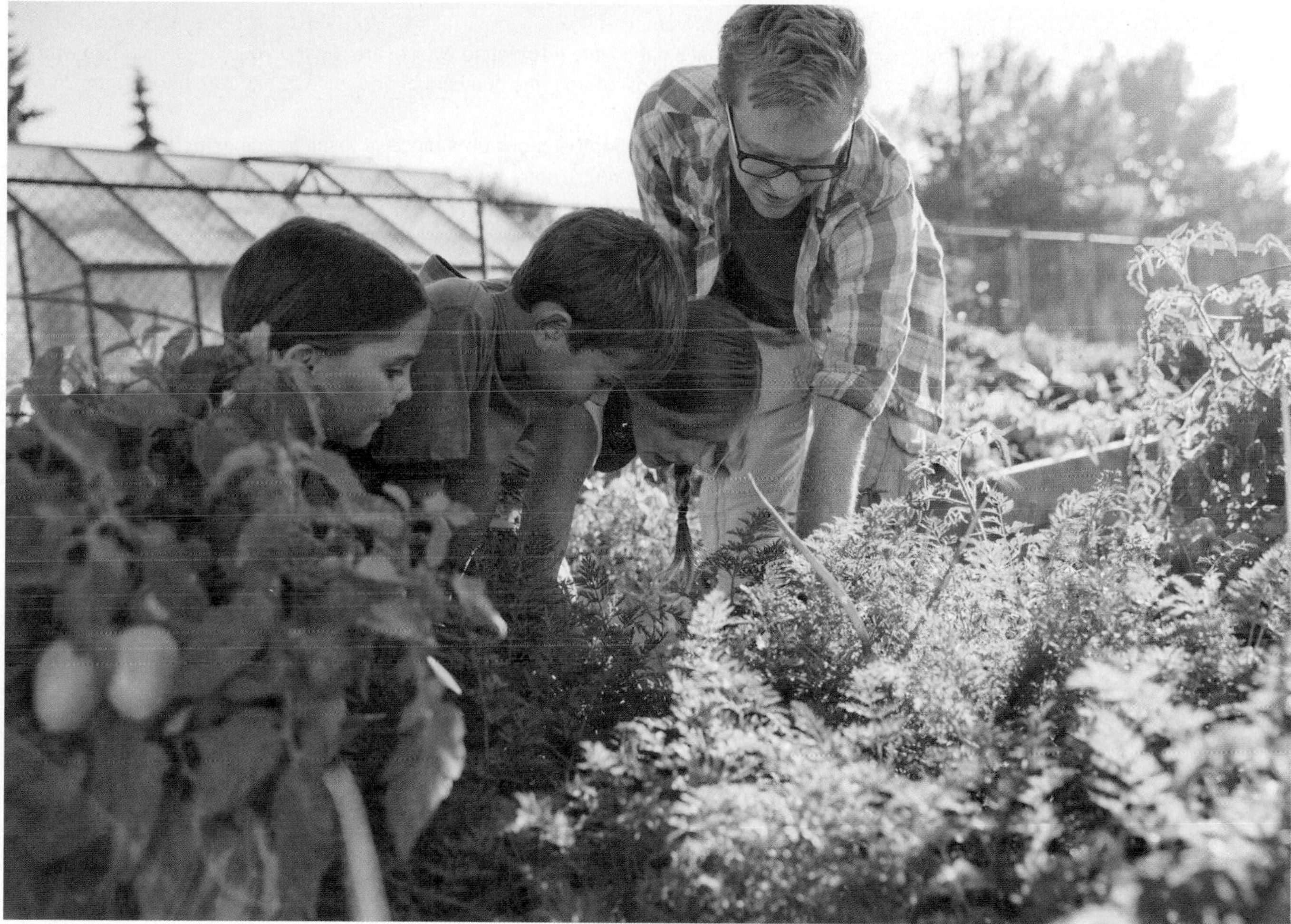

Hero Images Inc./Alamy Stock Photo

Learning Objectives

6.1 Describe Piaget's theory of cognitive development in terms of its seven principles, four stages, legacy into present day, and implications for fostering children's learning.

6.2 Explain Vygotsky's theory, including its nine key principles, modern applications, and ideas for promoting children's learning.

6.3 Outline similarities and differences between Piaget's and Vygotsky's views on cognitive development and appropriate educational practice.

CASE STUDY

Museum Visit

Four-year-old Billy is fascinated by dinosaurs. He and his mother have read many children's books about dinosaurs, and he has developed knowledge about these creatures and the geological periods in which they lived. As Billy and his mother visit a dinosaur exhibit at a natural history museum, they have the following conversation:

Mother: This is a real dinosaur rib bone. Where are your ribs? Where are your ribs? No that's your wrist. Very close.

Billy: Oh, yeah, right here.

Mother: Yeah, that's right. Here. Protecting your heart . . . and your lungs. And this was one from a dinosaur from the Jurassic period, also found from our country. In a place called Utah.

Mother: And this one . . . [Mother picks up a piece of fossilized dinosaur feces, known as *coprolite*] Oh! You're not . . . guess what that is. Look at it and guess what that is.

Billy: Um, what?

Mother: Guess. What's it look like?

Billy: His gum? What? Mom!

Mother: It's dinosaur poop.

Billy: Ooooo! (laughs)

Mother: That's real dinosaur poop.

Billy: I touched it! (laughs)

Mother: It's so old that it doesn't smell anymore. It turned to rock. It's not mushy like poop. It's like a rock. And that's from the Cretaceous period but we don't know what dinosaur made it. And this was also found in our country in Colorado. I think that's pretty funny.

Billy: What's this?

Mother: So this one . . . . Oh, that's called . . . that's a stone that dinosaurs . . . remember in your animal book it says something about how sometimes chickens eat stones to help them digest—it helps them mush up their food in their tummy?

Billy: Yeah.

Mother: Well, dinosaurs ate stones to mush up their food in their tummy and this was one of the stones that they ate. They're so big, that to them this was a little stone. Right? And that also comes from Colorado. (Dialogue is from Crowley & Jacobs, 2002, p. 346; "Billy" is a pseudonym.)[a]

- What knowledge does Billy have that can help him understand what he sees in the dinosaur exhibit?
- What does Mother do to help Billy make sense of the exhibit?

Thanks to the many books that 4-year-old Billy and his mother have read together, Billy knows a lot about dinosaurs. He understands that the words *Jurassic* and *Cretaceous* refer to earlier times and knows that some animals have stones in their stomachs to aid digestion. Mother helps him connect what he sees to his prior knowledge—not only about geological periods and stomach stones but also about commonplace concepts such as ribs and "poop." Yet Billy, like all children, is not simply a "sponge" who passively soaks up information. Instead, his cognitive development is, in large part, the result of his *own active efforts* to make sense of his world.

In this chapter, we consider the classic developmental theories of Jean Piaget and Lev Vygotsky, both of whom studied children's active learning. The notion that

[a]Excerpt from *Learning Conversations in Museums* by Kevin Crowley. Copyright © 2002 by Kevin Crowley. Reprinted with permission.

children create knowledge, rather than passively absorb it, is known as **constructivism**. Formulated in the first half of the 20th century, these two theories have provided much of the foundation for our current understanding of how children think. Between them, the frameworks tell us a great deal about how children make sense of everyday events, both on their own and in collaboration with adults and peers. As you will find out, the two theories also have much to say about how parents, teachers, and other adults can help children learn effectively.

Outline

Piaget's Theory

6.1 Describe Piaget's theory of cognitive development in terms of its seven principles, four stages, legacy into present day, and implications for fostering children's learning.

Jean Piaget (1896–1980) was formally trained as a biologist. He also had interests in philosophy and psychology and was especially fascinated with the nature of children's knowledge and its changes with development. In the 1920s he began observing children's everyday actions and listening to their reasoning. In his laboratory in Geneva, Switzerland, Piaget pioneered the **clinical method**, a procedure by which an adult presents a task or problem and asks a child a series of questions about it, tailoring subsequent questions to the child's responses. Drawing from his observations and interviews, Piaget came up with a theory of cognitive development that has transformed scientific knowledge of how children think and learn (e.g., Piaget, 1928, 1952b, 1959, 1985).

Key Ideas in Piaget's Theory

Central to Piaget's theory are seven principles.

Children are energetic learners. In the chapter-opening case study, Billy is eager to make sense of the fossils he sees in the natural history museum. Piaget proposed that children are naturally curious about their world and persistently ask for answers to their questions (e.g., Piaget, 1952b). They often tinker around with objects and observe the effects. We authors think back to the days when our children were in high chairs, experimenting with their food (pushing, squishing, dropping, and throwing it) as readily as they would eat it. As they grew older, they spent hours in the sandbox, shaping hills and valleys and pushing toy trucks through hidden passageways. According to Piaget, such exploration—the nature of which changes with age—is the engine for intellectual growth.

Contemporary theorists share Piaget's view that much of the motivation for learning comes from within. Children are understood to be driven by an insatiable curiosity as to how the world works; we watch them poke and prod at things to see what reactions they get. Similarly, children are intrigued with other people and watch them carry out daily activities (R. Brooks & Meltzoff, 2014; S. Engel, 2015; Hunnius & Bekkering, 2010; K. Nelson, 1996a).

MyLab Education
Video Example 6.1

Find Developmental Meaning
What evidence is there that 2-year-old Maddie is acting out of curiosity?
Maddie explores a toy's properties by feeling and tasting it, flattening it and watching it spring back. Her spontaneous actions, without directions or praise, suggest that she acts primarily out of personal interest.

Children organize what they learn into cohesive understandings. Children don't interpret observations as a collection of unrelated facts. Instead, they pull separate experiences together into an integrated view of how the world operates. For instance, by observing that food, toys, and other objects always fall down (never up), children construct a basic understanding of gravity. As they interact with family pets, visit zoos, look at picture books, and observe creatures around them, they develop an understanding of animal life.

In Piaget's terminology, the things that children learn and can do are organized as **schemes**, sets of similar actions or thoughts that they use repeatedly in response to the environment. Initially, children's schemes are largely behavioral in nature, but over time they become increasingly mental and, eventually, abstract (Inhelder & Piaget, 1958; Piaget, 1952b, 1954). An infant has a behavioral scheme for putting things in her mouth, an action that she uses in dealing with a variety of objects, including her thumb, toys, and blanket. A 7-year-old has a relatively concrete scheme for identifying snakes, one that includes their long, thin bodies; a slithery nature; and the absence of legs.

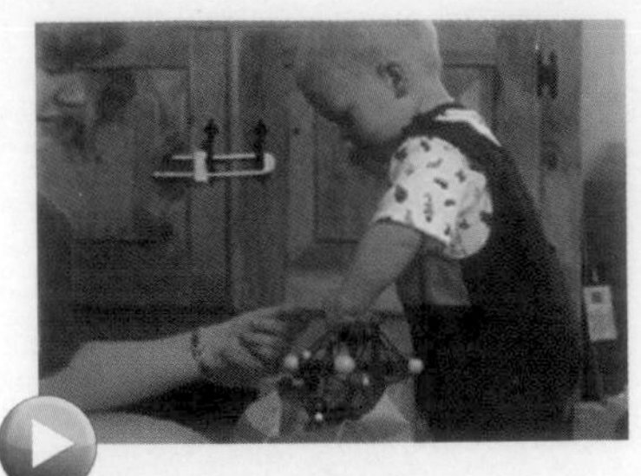

MyLab Education
Video Example 6.2
Find Developmental Meaning
What scheme does Corwin use during playtime with his mother? Notice that Corwin repeatedly uses a "putting-in" and "taking-out" scheme with a toy and a bag.

As a 13-year-old, Jeanne's daughter Tina had her own opinion about what constitutes fashion, a mental scheme that allowed her to classify articles of clothing at the mall as being either "totally awesome" or "really stupid."

Piaget proposed that children use newly acquired schemes over and over. In the process of repeating their schemes, children refine and combine them. Eventually, they integrate schemes into broader systems of mental processes called **operations**. This integration allows children to think in progressively advanced ways. For example, a little boy integrates his schemes for ordering blocks by size with his habit of forming tall towers into the new activity of placing the largest blocks on the bottom and building upward with smaller and smaller blocks.

Children adapt to new information. Children are continually exposed to unfamiliar objects, ideas, scenes, events, people, animals, sounds, tastes, smells, and appearances. These experiences spur children to expand their knowledge, change their ideas, and refine their skills. As a result, children become better at achieving their goals in a complex environment. According to Piaget, *adaptation* occurs as a result of two complementary processes: assimilation and accommodation (Piaget, 1954). **Assimilation** entails responding (physically or mentally) to an unknown object or event in a way that is consistent with existing schemes.[1] Basically, the child filters novel experiences through the lens of current schemes and operations. Thus, you can think of assimilation as absorbing new information into a concept or skill without changing its essence. An infant assimilates a ball into her putting-things-in-the-mouth scheme, a 7-year-old assumes a new slithery creature is a snake, and a teenage boy assumes that other students are as attentive to his new haircut as he is.

Yet children must adjust existing schemes and operations at least a little in order to respond to a new object or event. Thus, **accommodation** is likely to occur. Children either modify an existing scheme to account for the properties of a new object or event or else form an entirely new scheme to deal with it. An infant may have to open her mouth wider than usual to accommodate a teddy bear's paw. A 7-year-old may find a long animal with a snakelike body that cannot possibly be a snake because it has four legs. After making inquiries, he will develop a new scheme—*salamander*—for this creature. And the teenager will find out that many of his classmates have not noticed the new haircut.

Assimilation and accommodation work hand in hand. Children interpret each new event in the context of their existing knowledge (assimilation), and when the encounter does not fit with current understandings, they may modify their ideas (accommodation). In the chapter-opening case study, Billy initially thinks that the piece of coprolite is a large wad of dinosaur gum—that is, he mistakenly assimilates the object into his "chewing gum" scheme. But with his mother's help, he creates a new scheme, "fossilized dinosaur poop," that more accurately accounts for what he is seeing. Later Mother helps Billy assimilate a large stone into a "stones-that-help-digestion" concept he has previously acquired. In the process, however, he must also modify this scheme so that it applies not only to chickens but also to dinosaurs.

On occasion one of the two adaptive responses dominates over the other. Piaget noticed that during play, children actively impose their existing ideas on the world (in other words, they *assimilate*). When a little boy is pretending to talk with Grandma, he picks up a small block and pretends it is a mobile phone; in so doing he assimilates the block to his image of the phone. Assimilation is also at work when children distort new information to fit what they perceive to be the case. When a girl believes that the world is flat and is exposed to information about the world being a sphere, she visualizes a flat round pancake. Children *accommodate* when they imitate patterns they have previously witnessed, for example, the businesslike demeanor of an airline pilot or the doting style of a grandfather. When children memorize a poem without understanding it, they are also accommodating because they are reproducing the information without making connections to what they already know.

[1]Note that Piaget's concept of assimilation is quite different from the process of cultural assimilation described in Chapter 3.

The process of equilibration generates increasingly advanced thinking. Piaget proposed that children are sometimes in a state of **equilibrium**: They comfortably address new situations using their existing schemes and operations. But equilibrium doesn't last indefinitely. Children regularly encounter circumstances that challenge their present abilities. These circumstances create **disequilibrium**, a sort of mental "discomfort" that spurs children to try to deal with the situation at hand. By replacing or reorganizing certain schemes, children are better able to address the situation, and so they can return to equilibrium. This dynamic of moving from equilibrium to disequilibrium and back to equilibrium again is known as **equilibration** (e.g., Inhelder & Piaget, 1958). The end result is a more integrated, inclusive, and stable scheme and operations than children had previously. Thus, the equilibration process gradually leads to increasingly organized and complex concepts and mental skills.

Developmental Systems Prompt 6.1

Piaget testified to the informative lessons a child receives during exploration of the environment, especially when a situation challenges his or her expectations. Watch for occasions in which children are puzzled and motivated to find an explanation for a situation.

As you might suspect, there are connections among equilibration, assimilation, and accommodation. Disequilibrium is experienced as mental unrest and prompts either assimilation or accommodation (or both), processes that restore mental harmony. As children encounter an unfamiliar situation, they typically try to assimilate it, but when they recognize that the new information is incongruent with what they already know, they may accommodate to the external reality. It is significant that in Piaget's framework, children themselves are largely responsible for mental growth through self-directed attempts to figure out how the world works. Adults cannot hurry mental growth without causing stress in the child.

The processes of assimilation, accommodation, and equilibration make sense but were not explained in any detail by Piaget (e.g., Karmiloff-Smith, 2012; Keating, 2012; Klahr, 1982). Contemporary developmental scientists have looked further into these processes and confirmed that children's new ideas emerge out of earlier ones and become modified as children are exposed to additional information. Developmentally speaking, more advanced knowledge, skills, and cognitive processes don't appear out of thin air—they emerge out of children's quest for understanding, existing ideas, discontent with personal knowledge, and creative thinking processes.

Interaction in the physical environment drives cognitive development. Piaget was persuasive that children need to touch things around them and pursue their own questions. By exploring and manipulating the world around them—by conducting many little "experiments" with objects and noticing their effects—children learn about the physical world. As they explore, they ask themselves such questions as "What does the jar of beans sound like when I shake it?" "Does the funny star-shaped toy fit into the round hole?" and "Is a coiled rope the same length as another rope stretched out on the ground?"

Interaction with other people is also crucial. Piaget suggested that children learn a great deal from interacting with their fellow human beings. As you will discover shortly, preschoolers occasionally have difficulty seeing the world from others' perspectives. By conversing, exchanging ideas, and arguing, they gradually come to realize that individuals often see things differently and that their own view of the world is not necessarily completely accurate. Likewise, older children begin to recognize logical inconsistencies in what they say and do when someone else points out discrepancies.

Children think in qualitatively distinct ways at different age levels. Piaget proposed that as a result of brain maturation, environmental experiences, and children's natural desire to make sense of their world, cognitive abilities undergo qualitative change. He described youngsters' cognitive abilities as falling into four general stages (Piaget, 1971). Thinking begins during infancy with reflections on sensations, reflexes, and movements. Thereafter, abilities are constructed out of preceding thought. Thus, the four stages are *hierarchical*—each one depends on its predecessors—and so children progress through them in a predictable order. Piaget also assumed that these stages are *universal* in that they were present in all children around the world.

As you will discover later in the chapter, many psychologists question the notion that cognitive development is as universally stage-like as Piaget suggested. Nevertheless, Piaget's stages provide insights into different age levels, and so we look closely at them.

Piaget's Stages of Cognitive Development

Piaget's four stages are summarized in Table 6.1. The ages of onset for all but the sensorimotor stage are *averages*: Some children show characteristics associated with a particular stage a little earlier; others, a bit later. At any given time, some children will be in *transition* from one stage to the next, displaying characteristics of two adjacent stages at the same time. Furthermore, children don't always take advantage of their advanced cognitive abilities, and so they show considerable variability in sophistication of thinking across activities (Piaget, 1960b). Figure 6.1 depicts the transitional and flexible nature of progress through stages.

Table 6.1 Acquisitions during Piaget's Four Stages

STAGE	AVERAGE AGE OF ONSET	DESCRIPTION	EXAMPLES OF ACQUISITIONS
Sensorimotor Stage	Begins at birth	Schemes are based largely on behaviors and perceptions. Especially in the early part of the stage, children cannot think about things that are not immediately in front of them and instead focus on what they are doing and seeing at the moment.	• *Trial-and-error experimentation:* Exploration of objects to determine their properties • *Goal-directed behavior:* Intentional actions to bring about desired result • *Object permanence:* Realization that objects continue to exist when removed from view • *Symbolic thought:* Mental representation of physical objects and events (*symbols*)
Preoperational Stage	Appears at about age 2	Thanks in part to rapidly emerging symbolic abilities, children can now think and talk about things beyond their immediate experience. However, they do not yet reason in logical, adult-like ways.	• *Language:* Rapid expansion of vocabulary and grammar • *Extensive pretend play:* Enactment of scenarios with plots and complementary roles (e.g., mommy and daddy, hunter and prey, hero and villain) • *Intuitive thought:* Some logical thinking based on "hunches" and "intuition" rather than logical principles
Concrete Operational Stage	Appears at about age 6 or 7	Adult-like logic appears but is limited to reasoning about concrete, real-life situations.	• *Distinction between own and another's perspective:* Recognition that personal thoughts and feelings may be different from those of others • *Class inclusion:* Ability to classify objects as belonging to two or more categories simultaneously • *Conservation:* Realization that an amount stays the same if nothing is added or taken away, regardless of change in appearance
Formal Operational Stage	Appears at about age 11 or 12	Logical reasoning processes are applied to abstract ideas as well as concrete situations. New capabilities allow for advanced reasoning in science and mathematics.	• *Reasoning about abstract, hypothetical, and contrary-to-fact ideas:* Ability to draw conclusions about situations that cannot be directly perceived • *Separation and control of variables:* Ability to test hypotheses by manipulating one variable at a time while holding others constant • *Proportional reasoning:* Understanding of fractions, percentages, decimals, and ratios • *Idealism:* Ability to envision alternatives to social practices (with little regard for what is realistically possible)

Sensorimotor Stage (beginning at birth)

Piaget believed that in the first month of life, infants' behaviors are little more than biologically built-in responses to stimuli—that is, they are *reflexes* (e.g., sucking on a nipple)—that keep them alive. In the second month infants begin to exhibit voluntary behaviors that they repeat over and over, reflecting the development of perception- and behavior-based *sensorimotor schemes*. Initially, such behaviors focus

FIGURE 6.1 Emerging and continuing abilities.

As children grow, they develop increasingly mature reasoning skills while holding onto traces from previous stages.

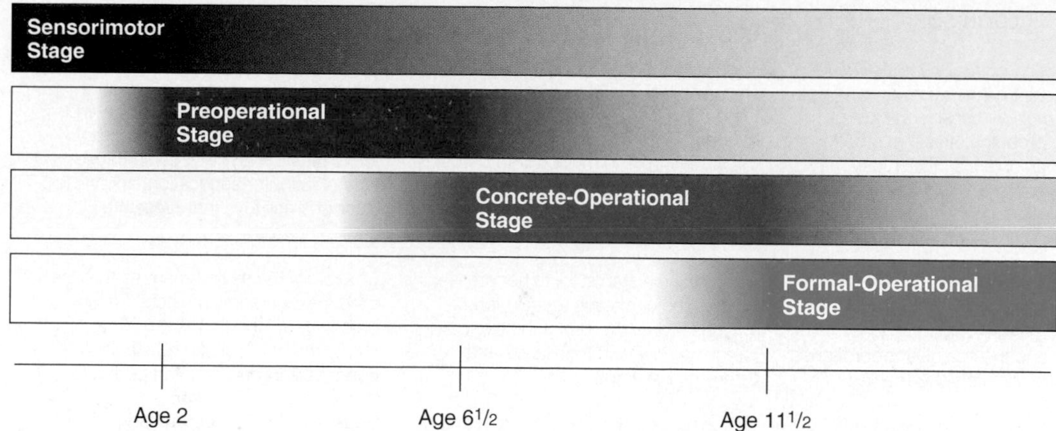

almost exclusively on infants' own bodies (e.g., putting a fist in one's mouth), but eventually they involve nearby objects as well. For much of the first year, Piaget suggested, infants' behavior is largely spontaneous.

Late in the first year, after having repeatedly observed that certain actions lead to specific consequences, infants develop knowledge of cause-and-effect relationships. At this point, they begin to engage in **goal-directed behavior**: They behave in ways that they know will bring about desired results. An infant who pulls a blanket to retrieve a small object lying on it shows goal-directed behavior. At about the same time, infants acquire **object permanence**, an understanding that physical objects continue to exist even when out of sight.

Piaget believed that for much of the sensorimotor period, children's thinking is restricted to objects in the immediate environment—that is, to the here and now. But in the latter half of the second year, young children develop **symbolic thought**, the ability to represent objects and events as internal, mental entities, or *symbols* (Piaget, 1962). They may "experiment" with objects in their minds, first predicting what will happen if they do something to an object—say, if they give a toy car a hard push toward the edge of a tabletop—and then put their plan into action. They may also recall and imitate behaviors they have seen other people exhibit—for instance, "talking" on a toy mobile phone or "driving" with a toy steering wheel.

The acquisitions of the sensorimotor stage are basic building blocks that later cognitive development extends. The Observation Guidelines table "Assessing Cognitive Advancements in Infants and Toddlers" presents some of the behaviors you might look for in small learners.

MyLab Education
Video Example 6.3

Find Developmental Meaning
Which aspects of 7-month-old Madison's behavior suggest spontaneity? Madison attends to nearby toys and books rather than reaching for items out of range.

OBSERVATION GUIDELINES
Assessing Cognitive Advancements in Infants and Toddlers

CHARACTERISTIC	LOOK FOR	EXAMPLE	IMPLICATION
Repetition of Gratifying Actions	• *Repetition of actions involving the child's own body* • *Replication of actions on objects*, for example, persistently banging toy on floor • *Evidence that the child repeats an action* because he or she notices and enjoys the effects	Myra waves her arms, stops, and waves her arms again, repeating the sequence several times. She then utters a sound ("Gah!") and repeats it ("Gahhh! Gahhhhhh" Gah!"), as if she enjoys listening to her own voice.	Provide a variety of visual, auditory, and tactile stimuli. Play "This little piggy" with an infant's toes, hang a mobile safely over the crib, and provide age-appropriate objects (e.g., rattles, plastic cups, balls). Be patient when infants repeat seemingly "pointless" actions (e.g., dropping favorite objects).

(continued)

OBSERVATION GUIDELINES

Assessing Cognitive Advancements in Infants and Toddlers (continued)

CHARACTERISTIC	LOOK FOR	EXAMPLE	IMPLICATION
Exploration of Objects	• *Apparent curiosity about the effects* that different behaviors have on objects • *Use of multiple behaviors* (feeling, poking, dropping, shaking, etc.) to explore an object's properties • *Use of several sensory modalities* during play (e.g., seeing, listening, feeling, and tasting)	Paco reaches for his caregiver's large, shiny earring. The caregiver removes the earring and holds its sharp fasteners between her fingers while Paco touches the silver loop and multicolored beads that hang from it.	Provide objects that infants can explore using multiple senses, making sure they are free of toxic substances and lack sharp edges and loose cords. Avoid plastic bags that could cause strangulation or suffocation, and steer clear of small toys that present a choking hazard.
Experimentation	• *Creativity and flexibility* in behaviors for discovering how things work • *Specific problems* that the child tackles and the particular approaches he or she uses to solve them	Jillian drags a step stool to her dresser so that she can reach toys on top of it. One by one, she drops the toys, watching how each one lands and listening to its impact.	Childproof the environment so that the child's experiments are safe. Provide objects that lend themselves to a sequence of actions (e.g., stacking cups, building blocks, and pulling toys).
Imitation and Pretending	• *Imitation of actions modeled by another person* • *Imitation of actions when the model is no longer present* • *Use of one object to stand for another*	Darius holds a doll and sings to it in the same way his mother sings to him. He combs the doll's hair with a spoon and uses an empty plastic vitamin bottle to feed the doll.	Engage children in reciprocal, imitative games (e.g., peekaboo, hide-and-seek). Provide props that encourage pretend play (miniature shopping carts, plastic carpentry tools, dolls, etc.).

MyLab Education
Video Example 6.4

Find Developmental Meaning
How do Corwin's actions reveal object permanence? Corwin looks for the toy elephant in the location he saw his mother hide it moments earlier.

Preoperational Stage (beginning at about age 2)

The ability to represent objects and events mentally (i.e., with symbolic thought) gradually gives children a more elaborate worldview. The words in children's rapidly increasing vocabularies provide labels for mental schemes and serve as symbols for objects and events that are out of sight. Children can now recall and verbalize past events, and they can compare and categorize their memories (e.g., into times they were happy or sad), allowing for a conceptual basis to their perceptions the world.

The emergence of symbolic thought is reflected not only in rapidly expanding language but also in the changing nature of children's play. Preschoolers often engage in make-believe, using realistic objects or reasonable substitutes as props to supplement their imagination. Piaget proposed that such pretend play enables children to practice newly acquired symbolic schemes and become familiar with the various roles others take on.

Despite far-reaching advances in symbolism, young children's thinking is limited by weak perspective taking. Piaget described young children as exhibiting **egocentrism**, the inability to view situations from another person's perspective.[2] You may observe preschoolers playing games together without ever checking to see if they are following the same rules. Or maybe you have noticed young children say things without considering the perspective of the listener—for instance, by leaving out critical details as they tell a story. Here we see one reason why, in Piaget's view, social interaction is so important. By getting repeated feedback from other people, children learn that their thoughts are unique to them and must be expressed systematically, with due consideration to what listeners already understand.

A second limitation preschoolers exhibit is making off-the-cuff judgments without taking all relevant factors into account. Preoperational thinking, especially during the preschool years, is illogical (from an adult's point of view). Following is an example of reasoning that characterizes preoperational thought:

> We show 4-year-old Lucy the three glasses at the top of Figure 6.2. Glasses A and B are identical in size and shape and contain an equal amount of water. We ask Lucy if the two glasses of water contain the same amount, and she replies confidently that they do. We then pour the water in Glass B into Glass C. We ask her if the two glasses of water (A and C) still have the same amount. "No," Lucy replies. She points to Glass A and says, "That glass has more because it's taller."

[2] Consistent with common practice in representing Piaget's work, we use the term *egocentrism* to refer to the egocentric thinking that characterizes preoperational thought. Piaget actually talked about different forms of egocentrism at *each* of the four stages of development. For instance, he described egocentrism in the formal operations stage as involving an inability to distinguish one's own logical conclusions from the constraints of the real world. Adolescents' idealism about social issues is one manifestation of formal operational egocentrism.

FIGURE 6.2 Conservation of liquid.

in the top picture, Glasses A and B contain the same amount of liquid. In the bottom picture, do Glasses A and C contain the same amount of water after water in Glass B is poured into Glass C?

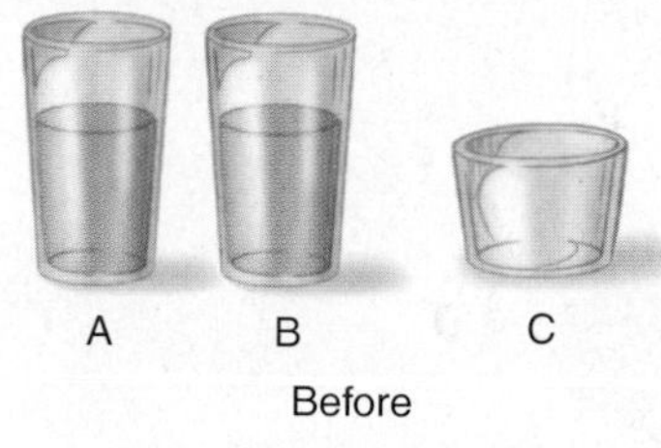

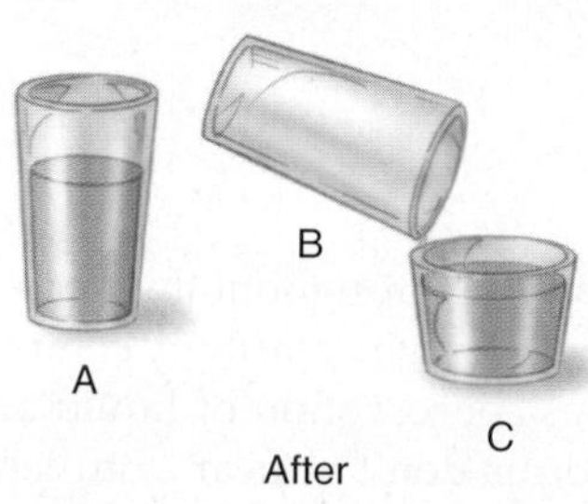

Piaget used this task to assess a logical thought process known as **conservation**, the recognition that an amount must stay the same if nothing is added or taken away, despite any changes in shape or arrangement. Lucy's response reveals that she is not yet capable of *conservation of liquid*: The differently shaped glasses lead her to believe that the actual amount of water has changed. Similarly, in a *conservation of number* task, a child engaging in preoperational thought might say that a row of five pennies spread far apart has more than a row of five pennies spaced close together, even though she has previously counted the pennies in both rows and found them to have the same number. Young children often confuse changes in appearance with changes in amount, possibly because children of this age depend more on perception than on logic.

Another ability that young children find challenging is **class inclusion**, the recognition that an object can belong both to a particular category and to one of its subcategories simultaneously. Preschool-aged children demonstrate lack of class inclusion in response to questions such as "Are there more brown beads or more wooden beads?" in a situation where there are 10 brown beads and 2 white beads and all beads are made of wood (Piaget, 1952a). They may insist that there are more brown beads whereas in reality there are more wooden beads.

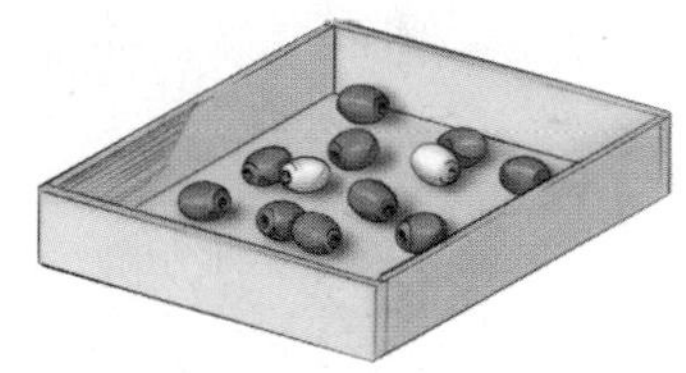

Sometime around age 4 or 5 children show early signs of thinking more logically than they did previously. For example, they occasionally draw correct conclusions about conservation problems (e.g., the water glasses task) and class inclusion problems (e.g., the wooden beads task). But they base their reasoning on intuition rather than on any conscious awareness of underlying logical principles, and so they cannot yet explain *why* their conclusions are correct.

Concrete Operational Stage (beginning at about age 6 or 7)

In the early primary grades, children become capable of thinking about various perspectives on a situation. For example, children now know that other people have perceptions and feelings different from their own. Accordingly, they realize that their own views reflect personal opinion rather than reality, and so they may ask for validation of their ideas ("What do you think?" "Did I get it right?").

Children in the concrete operations stage show many forms of logical thought, and they can readily explain their reasoning. They can now classify objects into two categories simultaneously, making it easier for them to solve class inclusion problems. And they are capable of conservation: They readily understand that if nothing is added or taken away, the amount stays the same despite changes in appearance. They can say with confidence that juice poured from a short, wide glass into a tall, thin glass hasn't changed in amount: "Just because this is skinny doesn't mean it's . . . this one is just wider, this one is skinnier, but they have the same amount of juice."

MyLab Education
Video Explanation 6.1
How do children of various ages demonstrate conservation?

FIGURE 6.3 Conservation of weight.
Balls A and B initially weigh the same. When Ball B is flattened into a pancake shape, how does its weight now compare with that of Ball A?

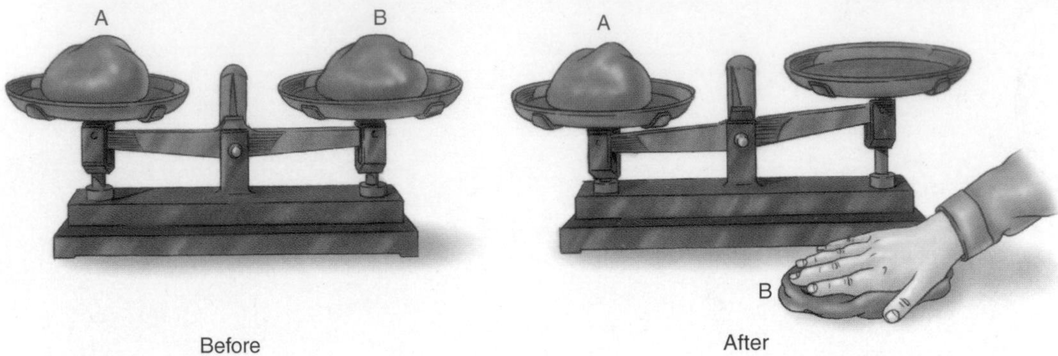

Preparing for Your Licensure Examination

Your teaching test might ask you about the major advancements that children achieve in their thinking during Piaget's four stages.

Children continue to develop logical thinking capabilities throughout the elementary school years. Over time they become capable of dealing with increasingly complex conservation tasks. Some forms of conservation, such as conservation of liquid and conservation of number, appear at age 6 or 7. Other forms don't appear until later. Consider the task involving *conservation of weight,* depicted in Figure 6.3. Using a balance scale, an adult shows a child that two balls of clay have the same weight. One ball is removed from the scale and smashed into a pancake shape. The child is then asked if the pancake weighs the same as, or more or less of, the un-smashed ball. Children typically do not achieve conservation of weight—that is, they don't realize that the flattened pancake weighs the same as the round ball—until age 9 or 10 (Piaget, 1970).

Although children in concrete operations show many signs of logical thinking, their cognitive development is not yet complete. In particular, they have trouble reasoning about abstract or hypothetical ideas (hence the term *concrete* operations stage). In language, this weakness may be reflected as an inability to interpret the underlying, nonliteral meanings of proverbs. In mathematics, it may be reflected in confusion over *pi* (π), *infinity*, and *negative number*. And in social studies, it may limit children's comprehension of such abstract notions as *democracy, communism,* and *human rights.*

Formal Operational Stage (beginning at about age 11 or 12)

Piaget concluded that sometime around puberty children become capable of thinking about things that have little or no basis in reality. They can think logically about abstract concepts, hypothetical ideas, and statements that contradict what they know to be true. Also emerging are scientific reasoning abilities that enable children to identify cause-and-effect relationships in physical phenomena. As an example, consider the following task:

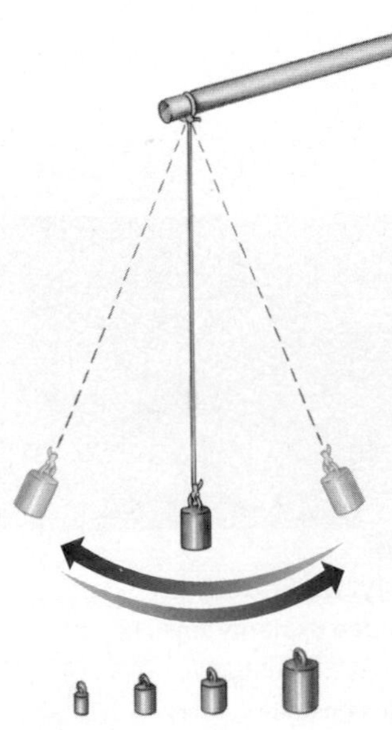

> An object suspended by a rope or string—a pendulum—swings indefinitely at a constant rate. Some pendulums swing back and forth very quickly, whereas others swing more slowly. Design an experiment that can help you determine what factor or factors affect a pendulum's oscillation rate.

To solve this problem successfully, you must first *formulate hypotheses* about possible variables affecting a pendulum's swing. You might consider (a) the weight of a suspended object, (b) the length of the string that holds the object, (c) the force with which the object is pushed, and (d) the height from which the object is initially released. You must then *separate and control variables*, testing one factor at a time while holding all others constant. To test the hypothesis that weight makes a difference, you should try different weights while keeping constant the length of the string, the force with which you push each weight, and the height from which you release it. Similarly, if you hypothesize that the length of the string is critical, you should vary the length of the string while continuing to use the same weight and starting the pendulum in motion with constant force. If young people carefully separate and control variables, their observations should lead them to conclude that only *length* affects a pendulum's oscillation rate.

Once formal operational thinking appears, advanced verbal and mathematical problem-solving procedures are possible. Adolescents become able to see beyond literal interpretations of such proverbs as "A rolling stone gathers no moss" and "An ant may well destroy a dam." Adolescents also become better able to understand such concepts as *negative number* and *infinity* because they can now comprehend that numbers can be below zero and two parallel lines will never touch even if they go on forever. Furthermore, they can understand the nature of proportions (e.g., fractions, ratios, decimals) and correctly use them when working on mathematical problems. And they gain an appreciation for contrary-to-fact ideas.

The emerging capacity to think about hypothetical and contrary-to-fact ideas allows adolescents to envision how the world might be different from, and possibly better than, the way it is now. Thus, they may be idealistic about social, political, spiritual, and ethical issues—climate change, world hunger, animal rights, religious conversion, and so on. Sometimes they offer recommendations for change that seem logical but aren't practical in today's world. For example, they may argue that racism would disappear overnight if people would just "love one another." Piaget suggested that adolescent idealism reflects an inability to separate personal abstractions from practical considerations and the perspectives of others. Through experience adolescents temper their optimism with realism about what is possible in a given time frame, under certain constraints, and with limited resources.

Current Perspectives Related to Piaget's Theory

Piaget's theory has sparked a great deal of research about children's cognitive development. In general, this research supports Piaget's observations of the *sequence* with which abilities emerge. Initial thinking originates in sensations and perceptions, is soon enriched with purposeful explorations with objects, and then symbolic representations. As children grow intellectually, they integrate principles of logic into their thinking, first in everyday situations and later when imagining the future and other abstract topics (Borst, Poirel, Pineau, Cassotti, & Houdé, 2013; Flavell, Miller, & Miller, 2002; Morra, Gobbo, Marini, & Sheese, 2008; C. M Walker & Lombrozo, 2016).

Capabilities of Different Age Groups

Using different research methods than those available to Piaget, present-day researchers have found that infants are more competent than portrayed in his descriptions of the sensorimotor stages. When Piaget studied the development of object permanence, he focused largely on whether infants reached for an object that was no longer in view. Contemporary researchers examine subtler cues, such as how long infants look at an object or how their heart rates change as they watch it. Such innovative techniques reveal that infants show preliminary signs of object permanence as early as 2 to 6 months old and gradually learn to reach toward hidden objects (Baillargeon, 2004; Bremner, Slater, & Johnson, 2015; Cacchione, 2013; Dineva & Schöner, 2018).

Modern-day developmental scholars similarly find unexpected competence in preschoolers and elementary school children. To reveal these capabilities, scholars have made experiments less artificial and placed fewer demands on children's memory than was characteristic of Piaget's tasks. When tasks are modified in these ways, young children are often capable of conservation and class inclusion (Bjorklund & Causey, 2018; M. Donaldson, 1978; R. Gelman & Baillargeon, 1983; Rule, 2007). In addition, young children find it easier to reason effectively when they are able to think about the issues at hand without being incited into habitual ways of responding. For example, when asked to compare numbers of items in a subcategory (e.g., brown beads) to those in a category (e.g., beads), children may easily assume that the requested comparison is between the two subcategory groups (e.g., brown and white beads; Borst et al., 2013). Indicators from everyday life also suggest that children are far less egocentric than Piaget thought. Although young children may have trouble telling intricate stories to others, their difficulty has more to do with telling events in order than it does with failing to take the perspective of listeners. When the communication task is

MyLab Education
Content Extension 6.1
Read how four theoretical perspectives explain the weaknesses of young children's speech in adapting to listeners' needs.

familiar, as when young children interact with their baby brothers and sisters, they often use advanced skills, for example, maintaining their siblings' attention by altering tone and simplifying vocabulary (Shatz & Gelman, 1973).

Many elementary school students—and occasionally even 4-year-olds—show an ability to think abstractly, logically, and hypothetically about unobserved events (S. Carey, 1985; Markovits, Brisson, de Chantal, & St-Onge, 2016; Schulz, Goodman, Tenenbaum, & Jenkins, 2008; Winkler-Rhoades, Carey, & Spelke, 2013). Even kindergarteners and first- and second-graders can understand simple ratios and proportions (e.g., fractions such as ½, ⅓, and ¼) if they can see relevant sections in everyday objects (Empson, 1999; Tobias & Andreasen, 2013). Older elementary students can understand ratios when presented with such familiar circumstances as people in a restaurant. Knowing that for every 12 customers, 4 are children, students can extrapolate that if there are 20 children, there must be 60 people. Similarly, elementary students often control variables in science when the task is broken up and they are given hints about the importance of controlling all variables except the one they are testing (Danner & Day, 1977; Lazonder & Kamp, 2012; Strand-Cary & Klahr, 2008).

Yet Piaget probably *overestimated* what adolescents can do. Formal operations emerge much more gradually than Piaget suggested, and youngsters fail to use these skills as regularly as Piaget had us believe (Bjorklund & Causey, 2018; Kuhn, Pease, & Wirkala, 2009; Pascarella & Terenzini, 1991). Even adults have numerous biases in their reasoning, being prone to believe what someone told them rather than employ methodical solutions (Kahneman, 2016; Toplak, West, & Stanovich, 2017). Adults also look for evidence that confirms their existing beliefs, and they ignore evidence that contradicts these assumptions. When finding out about personally significant events, such as a sister getting divorced, grown-ups are apt to conclude that they had had a hunch about the situation, even when they really had not. They also generally overestimate how much control they have over a situation and give themselves too much credit for a group's accomplishments.

Thus, although Piaget realized that formal operations are not always used by adolescents and adults, he seems to have exaggerated the role these functions play in human life. In fact, some theorists suggest that formal operational reasoning is not really the final stage of cognitive development. Several experts in human development have proposed that adults progress to a fifth stage of envisioning multiple approaches to an important issue, each of which is valid from a particular perspective, the integration of which generates the most constructive response (Galupo, Cartwright, & Savage, 2010; Sinnott, Hilton, Wood, Spanos, & Topel, 2016; C. T. Wynn, 2015).

Effects of Experience

Piaget acknowledged that as children gain new thinking abilities, they might apply skills in one area and not another (Piaget, 1941). It is becoming increasingly apparent that for people of all ages, reasoning in a particular situation depends on relevant understandings (Bjorklund & Causey, 2018; Croker & Buchanan, 2011; Seiver, Gopnik, & Goodman, 2013). It appears that what young people learn, with support, is how to think systematically about particular topics rather than how to use all-purpose rules of logic.

As an illustration of how prior knowledge affects formal operational thinking, consider the fishing pond shown in Figure 6.4. In a study by Pulos and Linn (1981), 13-year-olds were shown a similar picture and told, "These four children go fishing every week, and one child, Herb, always catches the most fish. The other children wonder why." If you look at the picture, it is obvious that Herb is different from the other children in several ways, including the bait he uses, the length of his fishing rod, and his location at the pond. Children who had fished frequently identified variables more effectively than they did for the pendulum problem described earlier, whereas the reverse was true for children without fishing experience. In the following conversation, two adolescents consider potentially influential factors in Figure 6.4.

FIGURE 6.4 Gone fishing.

What are some possible reasons why Herb is catching more fish than are the others?

Based on descriptions in Pulos and Linn (1981).

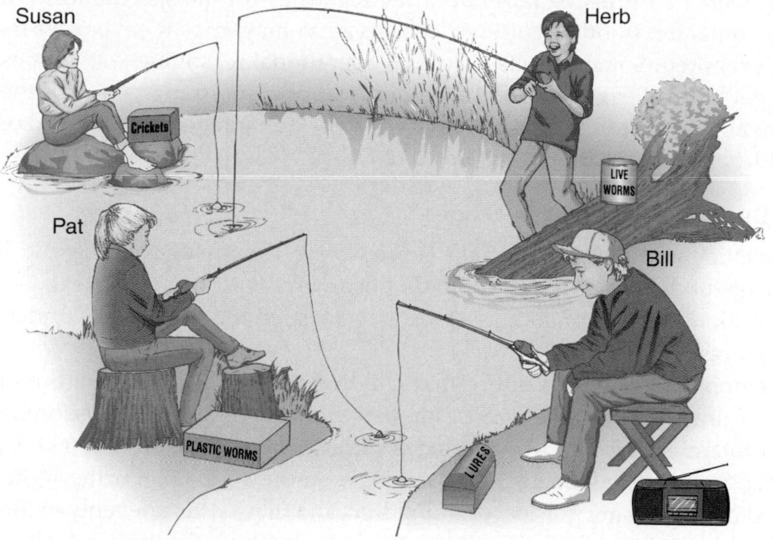

Kent: He has live . . . live worms, I think. Fish like live worms more, I guess 'cause they're live and they'd rather have that than the lures, plastic worms . . . . Because he might be more patient or that might be a good side of the place. Maybe since Bill has a boombox thing [referring to the radio], I don't think they would really like that because . . . and he doesn't really have anything that's extra . . . . But he's the standing one. I don't get that. But Bill, that could scare the fish away to Herb because he's closer . . . .

Alicia: Because of the spot he's standing in, probably . . . . I don't know anything about fishing. Oh, OK! He actually has live worms for bait. The other girl's using saltine crackers [she misreads *crickets*] . . . . She's using plastic worms, he's using lures, and she's using crackers and he's actually using live worms. So obviously the fish like the live worms the best.

MyLab Education
Video Example 6.5

Find Developmental Meaning

How do 10-year-old Kent and 14-year-old Alicia interpret influential factors in fishing? Note a connection between experience in fishing and identification of multiple conditions conducive to catching fish.

Experience at school promotes advanced reasoning. In academic settings, students learn to weigh evidence, see things from more than a single perspective, and consider the merits of various kinds of arguments. In childhood, attending school is associated with mastery of concrete and formal operational tasks (Adhikari, 2016; Artman & Cahan, 1993; Sophian, 2013). The same effects with education occur during the adult years. You may be happy to learn that taking college courses in a particular subject (in child development, perhaps?) leads to improvements in reasoning skills in that area (U. Diamond, Bartolo, Badin, & Shatkin, 2017; Lehman & Nisbett, 1990; Maruši, & Sliško, 2012; T. M. McDevitt, Jobes, Sheehan, & Cochran, 2010).

Effects of Culture

Piaget acknowledged that children grow intellectually as they reflect on exchanges with other people and handling objects in the environment. He further recognized that cultural variations in intellectual opportunities lead to differences across children's skills (Piaget, 1972). Yet many contemporary theorists conclude that Piaget did not understand just how powerfully culture shapes children's minds or how strongly his theory favors scientific reasoning as the pinnacle of human accomplishment (H. Keller, 2011; Maynard, 2008).

Considerable research indicates that culture exerts a more prominent role in the later stages than it does with the earlier ones. Infants in all known societies learn a lot by exploring their physical environment, almost regardless of culture, and young children in the preschool years universally learn to express their ideas with language and intuitive logic. In comparison, concrete and formal operational abilities are far more responsive to cultural experiences. For example, Mexican children whose families make pottery for a living seem to acquire conservation skills earlier than Piaget found to be true for Swiss children (Price-Williams, Gordon, & Ramirez, 1969). Apparently, creating pottery requires children to make frequent judgments about needed quantities of clay and water—judgments that must be fairly accurate regardless of the specific form of the clay or water container. In other cultures, conservation may appear several years later than Piaget proposed. Some aspects of formal operational reasoning—at least as measured by Piaget and colleagues—do not generally appear in young people if the relevant skills are not cultivated at school or shown to be advantageous in everyday life (Fahrmeier, 1978; H. Keller, 2011; Maynard, 2008).

Does Cognitive Development Occur in Stages?

In light of all the evidence, does it still make sense to talk about stages of cognitive development? Piaget understood that children do not always reason at their peak, yet he did not see deviations in performance as a reason to question the existence of underlying logical structures (Piaget, 1941).

Today's developmental scholars doubt that children operate in one structure of thought at a given time. Instead, they conclude that children adapt their reasoning according to their interests, prior knowledge, experience, and task at hand (Borst et al., 2013; K. W. Fischer, Stein, & Heikkinen, 2009; Halford & Andrews, 2006). Furthermore, many developmental changes are gradual or individual, and they occur unevenly in different areas of thinking, such as calculating an algebra formula versus figuring out why a classmate is angry. Virtually no one disputes Piaget's legacy in helping adults understand how children think, yet few scholars today accept all of Piaget's explanations for growth.

Key Ideas in Neo-Piagetian Theories

Neo-Piagetian theorists share Piaget's belief that children's skills and understandings change qualitatively over time. Unlike Piaget, however, they have been able to show how children's abilities vary across domains and change as a result of brain maturation. Following are several principles that are central to neo-Piagetian approaches.

Cognitive development is constrained by neurologically-based information-processing mechanisms. Neo-Piagetian theorists have echoed Piaget's belief that cognitive development depends on brain maturation. One particularly important capacity that develops in the brain is **working memory**, the part of the human memory system in which people hold ideas and actively think about information. Addition of two numbers might take three units of working memory—one for each of the two numbers and a third for the process of addition. Comparisons of proportions would typically be more taxing of working memory, because two units are used for each of two numbers, for example, ⅖ and ⅜, and a fifth unit make judgments about the relative sizes of the fractions. Neo-Piagetian theorists propose that a gradual expansion in working memory capacity allows for increasingly advanced reasoning, mathematical thinking, social perception, and language skills (Blain-Brière, Bouchard, Bigras, & Cadoret, 2014; Case, 1985; Dauvier, Bailleux, & Perret, 2014; Davidse, de Jong, Bus, Huijbregts, & Swaab, 2011; Morra, 2015; Pascual-Leone, 2013).

Children acquire new knowledge through both intentional and unintentional learning processes. Many contemporary psychologists conclude that children learn some things with little or no conscious awareness. Consider this question about household pets: "On average, which are larger, cats or dogs?" Even if you've never intentionally thought about this issue, you can easily answer "dogs" because of the many characteristics (including size) you've learned to associate with both species. Children unconsciously learn about patterns around them and can reflect on these if asked. Beginning in the first year or two of life, children increasingly reflect on their experiences and deliberately solve the many little problems that come their way each day (Case & Okamoto, 1996; Pascual-Leone, 1970). Thus, children become progressively more intentional in their learning while also continuing to absorb information about patterns in their environment (Case, 1985; Weinert, 2009; Yim & Rudoy, 2013).

Children acquire cognitive structures within particular domains of thought. Neo-Piagetian theorists reject Piaget's proposal that children develop general-purpose mental operations for a broad range of tasks. Instead, they suggest, children acquire specific concepts and thinking skills that influence reasoning in particular areas. Hence, children think differently when trying to comprehend a story than when trying to figure out a mathematical problem.

Canadian psychologist **Robbie Case** (1944–2000) and his colleagues have proposed that integrated networks of thoughts and skills within certain areas, called **central conceptual structures**, form the basis of children's reasoning (Case, 1991; Case & Okamoto, 1996; S. Griffin, 2009). A central conceptual structure related to *number* underlies children's ability to reason about and manipulate mathematical quantities. This structure reflects a unified understanding of how numbers, counting, addition, and subtraction are interrelated. A central conceptual structure related to *spatial relationships* underlies children's performance in such areas as drawing, construction and use of maps, replication of geometric patterns, and psychomotor activities (e.g., writing in cursive, hitting a ball with a racket). This structure enables children to align objects in space according to one or more reference points (e.g., the x- and y-axes used in graphing). A central conceptual structure related to *social thought* underlies children's analysis of interpersonal relationships, knowledge of common patterns in human interaction, and comprehension of motivations in short stories. This structure includes children's general beliefs about human beings' thoughts, desires, and behaviors. Case has found evidence indicating that the three conceptual structures develop in a wide variety of contexts (Case & Okamoto, 1996).

Cognitive growth capitalizes on subtle distinctions within the newborn brain. Swiss scientist **Annette Karmiloff-Smith** (2012, 2013) agrees with her esteemed mentor, Jean Piaget, that children develop cognitive abilities as they interact with the world. Unlike Piaget, however, Karmiloff-Smith views changes in children's understandings as arising out of additional factors besides assimilation and accommodation. Karmiloff-Smith argues that tiny features in the brain exist at birth and evolve with experience into sophisticated networks for learning. When a baby is born, slight variations exist in different regions of the brain, with certain localities being more facile than others in processing particular kinds of information—language, spatial ability, facial expressions, mathematics, and so on. These circumscribed regions are transformed from being marginally advantaged in dealing with particular stimuli into supercenters of specialized processing. Thus, although Piaget's processes of assimilation and accommodation are factors in learning, dedicated neurological mechanisms, which are progressively constrained by experience, are now understood to guide development (D'Souza & Karmiloff-Smith, 2017).

Advances in cognitive performance are enabled by expansions in executive functions. Research on brain development has shown that maturation of *executive functions*, neurologically based abilities for purposeful thinking processes, facilitate advancements in memory, planning, decision making, and reasoning. Recent evidence indicates that young people become increasingly able to focus their attention, resist counterproductive urges, and use strategies effectively (Keating, 2012). Neo-Piagetians have integrated these results into frameworks of cognitive development, for example, by showing that children exhibit conservation and class inclusion only after learning to inhibit such automatic responses as reacting to misleading perceptual information (Borst et al., 2013).

Miniature stages occur within certain areas of expertise. Although neo-Piagetian theorists reject Piaget's notion that a single series of global stages characterizes cognitive development, they speculate that cognitive development within a specific content domain may have a stagelike character (e.g., K. W. Fischer & Immordino-Yang, 2002; G. Young, 2012). Children's entry into a particular stage is marked by the acquisition of new abilities, which children practice and gradually master over time. Eventually, they integrate these abilities into more complex structures that result in a transition into a higher stage.

Even in a particular subject area, however, cognitive development is not necessarily a simple sequence of stages like climbing rungs on a ladder. In some circumstances development might be better characterized as progression along "multiple strands" of skills that interconnect, consolidate, and separate in a weblike fashion (K. W. Fischer, 2008; K. W. Fischer & Immordino-Yang, 2002; Mascolo & Fischer, 2015; Mascolo, van Geert, Steenbeek, & Fischer, 2016). From this perspective, children acquire more advanced levels of competence in a particular area through any of several pathways. For instance, as they become proficient in reading, children gradually develop word-decoding skills, comprehension abilities, and so on and draw on these assorted skills when reading a book. Individual children vary in their competence with particular skills and the speed with which they learn to coordinate them.

Applying the Ideas of Piaget and His Followers

Educators who have taken Piaget's theory to heart respect the natural curiosity of children, give them opportunities to make choices, and appeal to their interests. Adults who are inspired by Piaget and his advocates have tried these specific strategies:

Preparing for Your Licensure Examination

Your teaching test might ask you about Piaget's contributions to educational practice.

- **Indulge children's curiosity.** A major tenet of Piaget's theory is that children are naturally curious learners. When allowed to explore on their own, children tinker around with objects in a manner that allows them to form conjectures and test hypotheses about how things work (C. Cook, Goodman, & Schulz, 2011; Yardley, 2014). They push buttons, pull levers, shake toys, knock down towers, interact on the Internet, and take a political stand. In the process, they notice patterns, alter their ideas, and formulate new questions. Children also spontaneously classify objects with similar attributes together. Teachers can remark on what the children seem to be trying to do ("Very nice . . . Are you watching how quickly the balls slide down the ramp?"). And when it is not possible to answer a child's question immediately or arrange for them to pursue a particular topic during the lesson, teachers can validate the interest and provide a later option for pursuing it (e.g., "What a wonderful question, Marcie! Let's see if we can explore that issue in science class"; Engel, 2011).

- **Let children play.** In infancy and early childhood, and to some degree in middle childhood and adolescence as well, play is an active forum for learning. To facilitate play, teachers can provide interesting materials and allow a period or two of free choice during the day. At the preschool level, children might have access to a puzzle area, science corner, reading center, and pretend area with such alternating themes as fire station, science laboratory, and doctor's office. With older children, teachers can arrange for daily recess. Children can also enjoy brief periods of exploration at the beginning of a lesson, as with making imaginative designs in pattern blocks before a structured geometry lesson. Similarly, children can be invited to play around with concepts, words, and ideas, much like scientists, artists, and other experts do when inventing and creating. The performing arts in particular—drama, music, and dance—can engender a sense of playful discovery when children express themselves freely with new techniques.

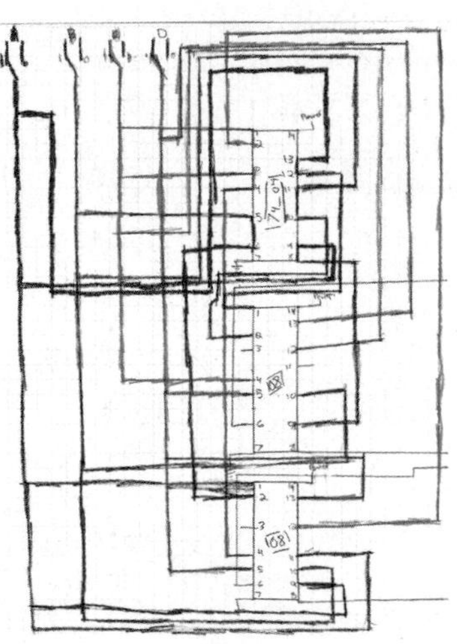

MyLab Education
Artifact Example 6.1

Find Developmental Meaning *What kind of reasoning did 15-year-old Habtom use as he designed and tested his circuit board?* From a Piagetian perspective, Habtom exercised formal reasoning as he formulated hypotheses about the operations in his configuration and systematically tested them.

- **Provide opportunities for experimentation with physical objects.** An important part of every child's learning involves exploration in the physical environment, including the sandbox, classroom, library, marine ecosystem, and beyond (H. P. Ginsburg, Cannon, Eisenband, & Pappas, 2006; Gurholt & Sanderud, 2016; Haywood-Bird, 2017; B. Y. White & Frederiksen, 1998; Winkler-Roades et al., 2013). In infancy, this might involve access to mobiles, rattles, stacking cups, pull toys, and other objects with visual and auditory appeal. At the preschool level, it might involve playing with water, sand, wooden blocks, and age-appropriate manipulative toys. During the elementary school years, hands-on exploration might entail working with clay, clustering objects with similar properties, and building stick structures. Despite their increased capability for abstract thought, adolescents also benefit from opportunities to manipulate concrete materials—perhaps equipment in a science laboratory, food and cooking utensils, and woodworking tools. Such activities allow teens to tie their emerging abstract ideas to the physical world, as 15-year-old Habtom did with a circuit board in Artifact Example 6.1.

A limitation of hands-on activities is that children sometimes misinterpret what they observe, either learning the wrong thing or confirming existing misconceptions (Fitzsimmons, Leddy, Johnson, Biggam, & Locke, 2013; Legare, Gelman, & Wellman, 2010; Schauble, 1990). Consider the case of Barry, an 11th-grader whose physics class was studying the idea that an object's mass and weight do *not*, in and of themselves, affect the speed at which the object falls. Students were asked to build an egg container for studying the effects of weight on falling speed. Convinced that heavier objects fall faster, Barry added several nails to his egg's container. Yet when he dropped it, classmates recorded its fall at 1.49 seconds, a time very similar to that for other students' lighter containers. Rather than concluding that weight did not matter, Barry decided that his classmates were not accurately timing the drops (Hynd, 1998).

At the elementary and secondary levels, misconceptions that arise from spontaneous explorations can be addressed. Teachers can plan lessons that combine exploration with guidance, for instance, by gently challenging the feasibility of children's beliefs, showing how a scientific model better explains a situation, and introducing new concepts that apply in the events just witnessed (K. K. Cook, Bush, & Karp, 2016; R. G. Fuller, Campbell, Dykstra, & Stevens, 2009; I. Hardy, Jonen, Möller, & Stern, 2006; D. T. Hickey, 1997; C. C. Howe, Devine, & Taylor, 2013; Lillard et al., 2013). The Development-Enhancing Education feature "Facilitating Discovery Learning" illustrates methods for arranging exploration that prompts scientific interpretations.

Development-Enhancing Education

Facilitating Discovery Learning

Activate students' prerequisite knowledge for understanding new explanations.

- A first-grade teacher asks students what they already know about air (e.g., people breathe it, wind is air that moves). After finding that students have an awareness that air has substance, she engages her class in an experiment in which a glass containing crumpled paper is turned upside down and immersed in a bowl of water. The teacher eventually removes the glass from the water and asks students why the paper towel didn't get wet. (Middle Childhood)
- Before asking students to build a simulated volcano, a high school science teacher introduces types of magma and defines important terms such as *cinder cone*, *lava dome*, *caldera*, and *flood basalt*. (Late Adolescence)

MyLab Education
Video Example 6.6

Find Developmental Meaning *How does the teacher prepare children for a hands-on lesson?* In this video the teacher activates children's relevant ideas prior to the experiment.

Show puzzling results to create disequilibrium.

- A middle school science teacher shows her class two glasses of water. In one glass an egg floats at the water's surface. In the other glass an egg rests on the bottom. The students give a simple explanation for the difference: One egg has more air inside and so must be lighter. But then the teacher switches the eggs into opposite glasses. The egg that the students believe to be "heavier" now floats, and the "lighter" egg sinks to the bottom. The students are surprised and demand to know what is going on. (Ordinarily, water is less dense than an egg, so an egg placed in it will quickly sink. But in this demonstration, one glass contains salt water—a mixture denser than an egg and capable of keeping it afloat.) (Early Adolescence)
- A high school social studies teacher asks students to decide whether adolescents in the past 60 years can be better characterized as conforming or rebellious. The teacher distributes two sets of readings that support each of the conclusions and asks students to examine the evidence, determine why there might be a discrepancy in viewpoints, and ultimately justify a position. (Late Adolescence)

Structure lessons so that students proceed logically toward discoveries you want them to make.

- Most of the students in a third-grade science class believe that some very small things (e.g., a tiny piece of Styrofoam, a single lentil bean) are so light that they have no weight. Their teacher asks them to weigh a pile of 25 lentil beans on a balance scale, and the students discover that the beans together weigh approximately 1 gram. In class discussion, the students agree that if 25 beans have weight, a single bean must also have weight. The teacher then asks them to use math to estimate the weight of a single bean. (Middle Childhood)
- Students in a high school chemistry class bring in samples of household water and then analyze the amount of chemicals in the fluids. After it is determined that the fluids contain harmful levels of acid, the teacher asks the students to brainstorm ways that their community can reduce acid rain. (Late Adolescence)

(continued)

Development-Enhancing Education (continued)

Help students relate their findings to an academic discipline.

- A teacher distributes slices of five kinds of apples—Granny Smith, Golden Yellow, Red Delicious, Fuji, and McIntosh—for purposes of taste testing. The teacher asks children to indicate their first preference for apples, and together they aggregate the results into a graph, identifying the most and least favorite apples. Afterward, the teacher shows the class other examples of graphs and explains the uses of diagrams. (Middle Childhood)
- After students in a social studies class have collected data on average incomes in counties within their state, their teacher asks, "How can we interpret these data in economic terms?" (Late Adolescence)

Sources: Blevins (2010; apple chart example); Center for History and New Media (2006; teenage conformists and rebels example); de Jong and van Joolingen (1998); Frederiksen (1984); Hardy et al. (2006); D. T. Hickey (1997); Lillard et al. (2013); R. E. Mayer (2004); Palmer (1965; egg example); Purpura, Baroody, Eiland, and Reid (2016); C. L. Smith (2007; Styrofoam example); Smithsonian National Museum of Natural History (2010; volcano example); Water Educational Training Science Project (2002; acid rain example).

In probing youngsters' reasoning, teachers and other practitioners need not stick to traditional Piagetian tasks. On the contrary, Piaget's clinical method is applicable to a wide range of topics—children's understandings of friendship, the animal kingdom, forms of government, phases of the moon, symbolism of maps, and so forth (e.g., Arias Pablopulos, 2016; diSessa, 2007; Ginsburg, 2009; Sinclaire-Harding, Miserez, Arcidiacono, & Perret-Clermont, 2013). Typically, an adult would begin a clinical interview by asking a child to explain a natural process, such as how mountains are formed, or to make a prediction about the effects of an intervention, for example, what would happen if water in a stout beaker is poured into a tall, thin glass (S. J. Mayer, 2005). After the child responds, the adult asks for more information using the child's vocabulary (e.g., if the child says that mountains are formed by God shoveling dirt into piles, the adult might ask where God gets the dirt or how many shovels full of dirt he [or she] uses). When the adult is familiar with this age and follows the young person's lead during the conversation, the clinical method can reveal perspectives that are dramatically different from his or her views. You can consider other indicators of children's reasoning in the Observation Guidelines table, "Assessing Piagetian Reasoning in Children and Adolescents."

OBSERVATION GUIDELINES
Assessing Piagetian Reasoning in Children and Adolescents

CHARACTERISTIC	LOOK FOR	EXAMPLE	IMPLICATION
Concrete Thought	• *Heavy reliance on concrete objects* to understand concepts • *Difficulty understanding abstract ideas*	Tobey solves arithmetic word problems more easily when he can draw pictures of them.	Use concrete objects, drawings, and other realistic illustrations of abstract situations, concepts, and problems.
Abstract Thought	• *Ability to understand strictly verbal explanations* of abstract concepts • *Ability to reason about hypothetical or contrary-to-fact situations*	Elsa can imagine how two parallel lines might go on forever without ever coming together.	When working with adolescents, occasionally use verbal explanations (e.g., short lectures) to present information, and assess students' understanding regularly.
Idealism	• *Optimistic notions* about how the world should be • *Difficulty taking other people's needs and perspectives into account* when offering ideas for change • *Inability to adjust ideals* in light of what realistically can be accomplished	Martin advocates a system of government in which all citizens voluntarily contribute their earnings to a common "pool" and then withdraw money only as they need it.	Engage adolescents in discussions about challenging political and social issues.
Scientific Reasoning Skills	• *Formulating multiple hypotheses* for a particular phenomenon • *Separation and control of variables*	Serena proposes three possible explanations for a result she has obtained in her physics lab.	Have students conduct simple experiments in which they control variables (e.g., measuring growth of plants after keeping sunlight constant and comparing different amounts of water).
Mathematical Reasoning Skills	• *Understanding abstract mathematical symbols* (e.g., π, the variable *x* in algebraic equations) • *Understanding proportions* in mathematical problem solving	Giorgio uses a 1:240 scale when drawing a floor plan of his school building.	Initially, introduce abstract mathematical tasks with simple examples (e.g., when introducing proportions, use fractions such as ⅓ and ¼). Progress to more complex examples when youngsters are ready.

• **Keep Piaget's stages in mind when planning activities, but don't take them literally.** As you have learned, Piaget's four stages are not fully accurate descriptions of children's capabilities, but they provide a rough idea as to kinds of reasoning at various age levels (Bjorklund & Causey, 2018; Crain, 2011; Kuhn, 1997; Lefmann & Combs-Orme, 2013). Thus, infant caregivers should remember that repetitive behaviors, even those that make a mess or cause inconvenience (dropping food, throwing toys), are an important means for mastering basic motor skills and learning about cause-and-effect relationships. Preschool teachers should not be surprised to hear young children arguing that a candy bar broken into four pieces has more candy than a similar, unbroken bar (a belief that reflects lack of conservation). Elementary school teachers should recognize that their students might have trouble with proportions (e.g., fractions, decimals) and such abstract concepts as *time* in astronomy and *negative number* in mathematics (B. Adams, 2008; Kaufmann, 2008; A. A. Stephens et al. 2013; Tourniaire & Pulos, 1985). With high school students, educators can expect to hear passionate arguments that reflect idealistic notions about how schools, cities, and society should operate.

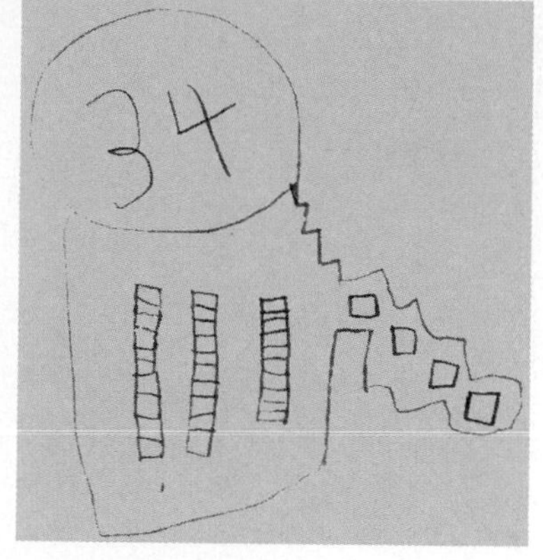

MyLab Education
Artifact Example 6.2

Find Developmental Meaning
How does third-grade student Noah symbolize place value? Eight-year-old Noah demonstrates that the number 34 is equal to the combination of three rows of ten squares and four single ones. This kind of exercise helps children conceptualize place value in concrete terms.

Piaget's stages also provide implications for strategies that are apt to be effective in teaching children of different age levels. For instance, given the intangible nature of historical time, elementary teachers planning history lessons should probably limit talk about specific dates in favor of active investigations into people's motivations, conflicts, and accomplishments (Barton & Levstik, 1996; K. Greene, 2014; Levstik, 2008; Santoli, Vitulli, & Giles, 2015). Especially in the elementary grades (and to a lesser degree in middle and high school), instructors should find ways to make abstract ideas more concrete. As one example, a third-grade teacher, realizing that the abstract concept of *place value* might be difficult, showed her students how to depict two-digit numbers with blocks, using 10-block rows for the tens column and single blocks for the ones column. You can see Noah's rendition of place value in Artifact Example 6.2.

• **Present situations children cannot easily explain.** Events that conflict with youngsters' current understandings create disequilibrium that motivates reevaluation of beliefs (Cañada, González-Gómez, Airado-Rodríguez, Niño, & Acedo, 2017; Hadjiachilleos et al., 2013; Vosniadou, 2009). If students believe that "light objects float and heavy objects sink" or that "wood floats and metal sinks," a teacher might present a common counterexample: a metal battleship (floating, of course) that weighs many tons. Yet after being shown compelling information that conflicts with their present ideas, children sometimes discount it. To instill an open mind, teachers can encourage children's interest in the topic, ask them to talk and write about their observations, and be very clear about how a scientific explanation accounts for the data.

• **Use familiar content when asking children to reason.** Earlier we presented evidence to indicate that young people display more advanced reasoning skills when they work with topics they know well. With such evidence in mind, teachers and other practitioners might ask young people to do the following:

- Conserve liquid within the context of a juice-sharing task.
- Separate and control variables within the context of a familiar activity (perhaps designing two paper airplanes, one with long wings and the other with short wings, or comparing the time it takes for raw and refined sugars to dissolve in boiling water).
- Consider abstract ideas about subject matter in a concrete fashion (e.g., introducing the concepts of *inertia* and *momentum* to explain such everyday experiences as throwing a ball and driving quickly around a sharp curve).

• **Assess children's learning needs.** Neo-Piagetians have made a good case for the value in determining the challenges that children face in their assignments. A teacher might find that children have a preestablished idea about a task (e.g., mistakenly assuming that the arithmetic problem 4 + __ = 7 requires them to add the two numbers, writing "11" as the answer). Some children have an inadequate memory capacity for completing a task (e.g., remembering only a few steps in a teacher's lengthy verbal instructions). Others misinterpret the requirements of a problem (e.g., not realizing that "=" in mathematics means "make the same") or fail to check their work (e.g., submitting the wrong answer on a long-division problem because of careless errors in subtraction

(S. S. Brown, Gutiérrez, & Alibali, 2016; Case, 1980; Morra et al., 2008; A. A. Stephens et al., 2013). After identifying children's shortcomings, teachers can instruct children in missing skills, address their misconceptions, repeat instructions as necessary, and alleviate memory load with handouts or wall charts showing steps in an assignment.

• **Plan activities that prompt perspective-taking.** As noted earlier, Piaget proposed that interaction with peers teaches children that others view the world very differently than they themselves do. Interactions with age-mates that generate differences of opinion—situations that create **sociocognitive conflict**—can cause disequilibrium and spur children to reevaluate their current perspective about an issue. Interactions with peers may help promote cognitive growth because of the following:

- Peers speak at a level that children can understand.
- Whereas children often accept an adult's ideas without argument, they are more willing to disagree with their peers.
- Disagreements with peers incite children to consider why others think as they do. (Damon, 1984; De Lisi & Golbeck, 1999; C. Howe, 2009; Hsin & Snow, 2017; Murphy & Alexander, 2008; Rubin, Bowker, & Kennedy, 2009; A. G. Young, Alibali, & Kalish, 2012).

When sharing their views with one another, however, children are sometimes confronted with misinformation (Good, McCaslin, & Reys, 1992; Gooding & Metz, 2011). In such circumstances, teachers can point out that they have heard several different explanations and follow through with a deeper analysis of the evidence. On other occasions, children persist with their original ideas, and teachers face the challenge of guiding them toward scientifically, mathematically, and otherwise academically advanced understandings. For conceptual change to happen, it generally needs to be voluntary; if the teacher insists that children parrot the "right answer," children will likely memorize the information and not update existing competing ideas.

Although children learn a great deal from their interactions with others, cognitive development is, in Piaget's theory, ultimately an individual enterprise. By assimilating information with present ideas and accommodating to new experiences, children develop increasingly advanced and integrated schemes over time. Thus, Piaget's perspective depicts children as doing most of the mental "work" themselves. In contrast, Lev Vygotsky's theory, which we soon introduce, places more of the responsibility on adults.

Summary

Piaget portrayed children as active and motivated learners who, through numerous interactions in their physical and social environments, construct an increasingly complex understanding of the world around them. He proposed that children's thinking progresses through four stages: (a) the sensorimotor stage, when cognitive functioning is based primarily on behaviors and perceptions; (b) the preoperational stage, when symbolic thought and language become prevalent yet reasoning remains "illogical" by adult standards; (c) the concrete operations stage, when logical reasoning capabilities emerge but are limited to tangible objects and events; and (d) the formal operations stage, when thinking about abstract, hypothetical, and contrary-to-fact ideas becomes possible.

Developmental researchers have found that Piaget probably underestimated the capabilities of infants, preschoolers, and elementary school children and overestimated the capabilities of adolescents. Furthermore, children's reasoning on particular tasks depends heavily on their prior knowledge, experience, and formal schooling relative to those tasks. Contemporary developmental scholars doubt that cognitive development is consistently characterized with general stages. Some neo-Piagetians propose that children acquire specific concepts and thinking skills within particular domains, abilities that sometimes change in a stagelike manner. Virtually all present-day theorists acknowledge the value of Piaget's research methods, his portrayal of cognitive development as a constructive process, and his delineation of qualitative changes in cognitive development.

MyLab Education Self-Check 6.1

Vygotsky's Theory

6.2 Explain Vygotsky's theory, including its nine key principles, modern applications, and ideas for promoting children's learning.

Whereas Piaget had a background in biology and philosophy, Russian psychologist **Lev Vygotsky** (1896–1934) had training in law, history, philosophy, literature, and education. Vygotsky was deeply influenced by Karl Marx's proposal that historical changes in society have a significant impact on how people think and behave. And like Marx's colleague Friedrich Engels, Vygotsky saw much value in *tools* moving a society forward (Gredler & Shields, 2008; Vygotsky, 1997e). According to Vygotsky, numerous tools influence thinking, many of which are tangible, for example, paper, writing utensils, stories, and books. In many societies today, computers and handheld devices facilitate communication, entertainment, and work. In Vygotsky's theory, *cognitive* entities—concepts, theories, problem-solving strategies, memory techniques, and scientific methods for investigating hypotheses and reasoning about observations—are also influential tools.

Vygotsky believed that adults in any society intentionally foster children's learning. Parents, teachers, and other grown-ups engage children in meaningful and challenging activities, show them how to use tools known to facilitate performance, and help them make sense of experience. Because Vygotsky emphasized the importance of adult guidance in promoting cognitive advancements—and more generally because he stressed the influence of *social* and *cultural* factors—his perspective is known as a *sociocultural theory*.

With the assistance of his students, Vygotsky conducted numerous studies on children's thinking from the 1920s until his early death from tuberculosis in 1934. He typically described his findings in general terms, saving the details of technical reports for a small number of research psychologists working in Russia at the time (Kozulin, 1986). Although his own research was limited, Vygotsky's followers have been persuaded by the integrity of science that Vygotsky espoused. According to Vygotsky, research with children should have a coherent theoretical foundation instead of being based in a hodgepodge of ideas. He argued that scholars must focus on essential mental processes rather than on isolated responses and document developmental changes in mental processes rather than take isolated snapshots of children's thinking (Gredler & Shields, 2008; Vygotsky, 1987a, 1997a, 1997d).

FIGURE 6.5 Learning how to use memory aids.

Vygotsky showed two sets of cards to children, inviting them to think of a possible connection between each word and the picture with which it was paired. Some children were coached in forming an association between items in a pair. For example, a child might imagine a connection between candles and trees by picturing trees next to a tall building lit up with candles. Other children acted as they normally would without guidance. Afterward, cards with words were removed and the children were asked to recall as many words as possible from just the pictures.

Based on information in Vygotsky (1997c).

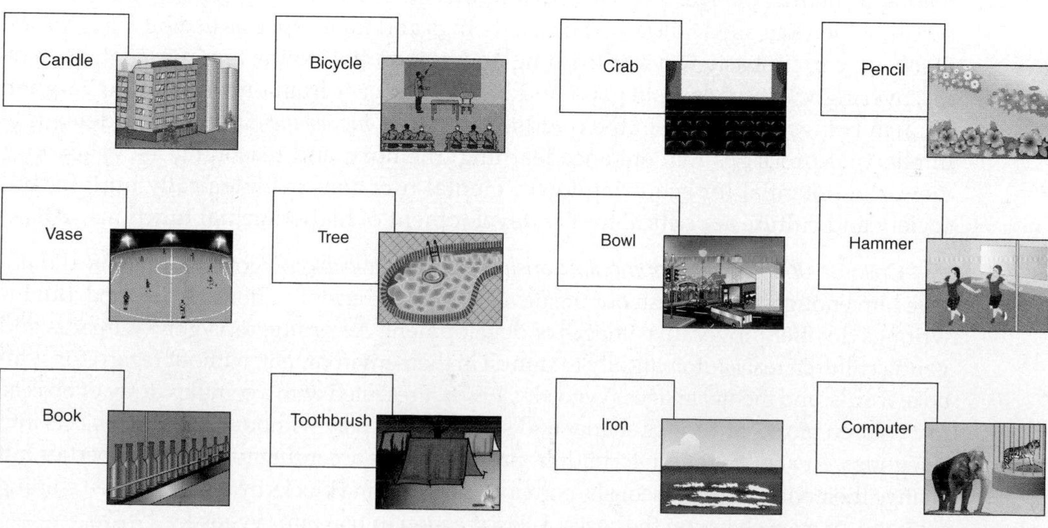

In their investigations, Vygotsky and his collaborators gave primary attention to how children improve in their use of cultural materials, especially when assisted by others. In Figure 6.5 you can see the types of materials Vygotsky included in his research. Interested in how children use external stimuli to augment basic memory processes, Vygotsky told children he would show them a long list of words that would be impossible to remember without help. He encouraged children to form associations between words and pictures on cards, the latter of which could be used as cues for retrieval. For young children, the pictures did not help and in some cases were distracting, but older children were generally able to use the pictures effectively. An older child might associate the word "crab" with the picture of a theater by connecting the two together in an image: "The crab is looking at the stones on the bottom, it is beautiful, for him it is a theater" (Vygotsky, 1997c, p. 181). Later, the child would easily remember the word *crab* when shown a picture of the theater.

In his book *Thought and Language*, Vygotsky explained that his approach to studying children's cognitive development was radically different from frameworks by Piaget and other psychologists of his era. Rather than determine the kinds of tasks children could successfully perform *on their own* (as Piaget did), Vygotsky often examined activities that children could complete *only with adult assistance*. For example, he described two hypothetical children who could, without help, do things that a typical 8-year-old might be able to do. He would give each child progressively more difficult tasks and offer a little help, perhaps asking a leading question or suggesting a first step. With such assistance, both children could typically tackle more difficult tasks than they could handle on their own. However, the *range* of tasks the children could complete with assistance might be quite different, with one child "stretching" his or her abilities to succeed at typical 12-year-old-level tasks and the other succeeding only at 9-year-old-level tasks (Vygotsky, 1934/1986, p. 187).

Western psychologists were largely unfamiliar with Vygotsky's work until the last few decades of the 20th century, when his major writings were translated from Russian into English (e.g., Vygotsky, 1934/1986, 1978, 1997b). Although Vygotsky's premature death meant he did not have the chance to develop his theory fully, his views remain evident today in discussions about learning.

Key Ideas in Vygotsky's Theory

Vygotsky acknowledged that biological factors play a role in development. For example, he understood that brain development allows children to use complicated tools. He also realized that children bring inherited characteristics to learning (Vygotsky, 1997b). Some children find it easier than others to acquire cultural skills based partly on genetic advantages in learning. However, Vygotsky's primary focus was on the role of nurture, and especially on the ways in which a child's social and cultural environments foster cognitive growth. Following are central ideas in Vygotsky's theory.

Some cognitive processes are seen in people and non-human animals; others are unique to human beings. Vygotsky distinguished between two kinds of mental processes, which he called *functions*. Human beings and many species exhibit *lower mental functions*: certain basic ways of learning and responding to the environment, such as discovering what foods taste good and how best to get from one location to another. Human beings are unique in their additional use of *higher mental functions*: deliberate intellectual processes that enhance learning, memory, and reasoning. In Vygotsky's view, the potential for acquiring lower mental functions is biologically built in, but society and culture are critical for the development of higher mental functions.

Children undergo developmental transitions in their thinking. Vygotsky's short life did not give him enough time to flesh out the developmental transformations he detected, but his writings do offer provocative images of development. According to Vygotsky, infants and young children react automatically to stimuli in their environment, without regard for symbols, words, and mental images (Vygotsky, 1997f). Presented with a complex array of objects, say, colored blocks of various shapes and sizes, infants play without clustering objects into categories. At about age 3 or 4, children classify objects according to simple properties but change their criteria spontaneously, perhaps first grouping blocks by color and then shifting to shape, or even changing the basis of classification midstream (Vygotsky, 1987a).

During middle childhood, a major transformation occurs, during which time children think and remember with the help of rules, concepts, and symbols. Given a piece of paper but no writing implement, and asked to remember a number, they might tear the sheets into the same number of pieces or create shapes that resemble the number. Shown a shape and told it is a "square," they can identify other squares. In adolescence, young people are able to group and remember ideas through mental connections. One of Vygotsky's colleagues found that an adolescent could remember the words *beach, hail*, and *dress* by creating associations among the elements with the sentence, "A lady walked on the beach; it began to hail and ruined her dress" (Leont'ev, 1959, p. 94). As young people learn to make such mental associations, they become capable of purposeful thinking, remembering, and regulating mental activities. As a result, they are able to take full advantage of their society's rich heritage in science, mathematics, art, history, and other intellectual fields of study.

In their interactions with children, adults convey how to interpret events and circumstances. Adults regularly explain the meaning of objects, events, and, more generally, human experience. As they do so, they actually *transform* the situations children encounter. This process of helping children make sense of experiences in culturally appropriate ways is known as **mediation**. Meanings are conveyed through a variety of mechanisms—language, mathematical symbols, art, music, and so on. In the "Museum Visit" case at the beginning of the chapter, Mother helps 4-year-old Billy make sense of several dinosaur artifacts. She points out how dinosaur ribs and human ribs serve the same function ("Protecting your heart . . . and your lungs"). She relates some of the artifacts to scientific concepts that Billy already knows (*Jurassic, Cretaceous* eras). And she substitutes everyday language ("dinosaur poop") for an unfamiliar scientific term (*coprolite*).

Developmental Systems Prompt 6.2

Vygotsky proposed that guidance from adults is essential for children to master cultural symbols, strategies, and tools. Make sure that children are familiar with foundational concepts (e.g., a story structure in literature or a number line in mathematics) when delving into a lesson in that discipline.

Informal conversations are a common method by which adults pass along culturally appropriate ways of interpreting situations. But no less important in Vygotsky's eyes is formal education, where teachers systematically impart the ideas, concepts, and terminology used in academic fields. Although Vygotsky, like Piaget, saw value in allowing children to make discoveries on their own, he gave greater attention to the significance of adults passing along the technologies and discoveries of previous generations (Vygotsky, 1934/1986).

Every culture passes along tools that make daily living more efficient. Not only do adults teach children ways of interpreting experience; they also instruct them about specific tools that can help them tackle challenges. Some tools, such as shovels, sewing machines, and computers, are physical objects. Others, such as writing systems, maps, and spreadsheets, are partly physical and partly symbolic. Still others, such as using mental arithmetic to estimate the cost of purchases at a store, are entirely mental. In Vygotsky's view, mastering tools that are partly or entirely symbolic—**cognitive tools**—greatly enhances learning.

Different cultures pass along different tools. Thus, Vygotsky's theory leads us to expect greater diversity in children than Piaget's theory does. For instance, recall a point made earlier in the chapter: Children acquire conservation skills at a younger age if conservation of clay is important for their family's pottery business. Similarly, children are more likely to acquire map-reading skills if maps (perhaps of roads, subway systems, and shopping centers) are a part of their experience (I. Hemmer et al., 2013; Liben & Myers, 2007; Yuan, Uttal, & Gentner, 2017). Likewise, children are more apt to have a keen sense of time if clocks and calendars synchronize their activities (H. Forman, 2015; Graesch, 2009; K. Nelson, 1996a). In the opening case study, Billy has some understanding of distant time periods, drawing on what he has learned from geology in books, museum visits, and discussions with his mother.

Thought and language become increasingly interdependent. One very important cognitive tool is language. For us as adults, thought and language are closely interconnected. We often think by using the specific words that our language provides. When we think about household pets, our thoughts contain such words as *dog* and *cat*. We usually express our thoughts when we converse with others. In other words, we "speak our minds." In comparison, Vygotsky proposed that thought and language are separate abilities for infants and young toddlers. In the early years, thinking occurs independently of language, and when language appears, it is first used primarily as a means of communication and not as a mechanism for facilitating thinking. Sometime around age 2, thought and language start to become intertwined. Children begin to think in words and express these thoughts out loud.

FIGURE 6.6 Weaving of thought, social experience, and language into a capacity for self-regulation.

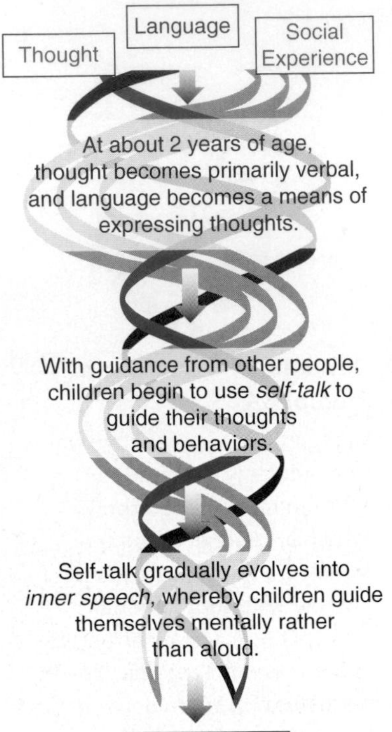

In infancy, thought is nonverbal in nature, and language is used primarily as a means of communication.
Thought
Language
Social Experience
At about 2 years of age, thought becomes primarily verbal, and language becomes a means of expressing thoughts.
With guidance from other people, children begin to use *self-talk* to guide their thoughts and behaviors.
Self-talk gradually evolves into *inner speech*, whereby children guide themselves mentally rather than aloud.
Self-Regulation

When thought and language first merge, children often talk to themselves, a phenomenon known as **self-talk** (you may also see the term *private speech*). Vygotsky suggested that self-talk serves an important function in cognitive development. By talking to themselves, children learn to guide their own behaviors through complex maneuvers in much the same way that adults previously guided them. Self-talk eventually evolves into **inner speech**, in which children "talk" to themselves mentally rather than aloud (Figure 6.6). They continue to direct themselves verbally through tasks and activities, but others can no longer hear them do it (Vygotsky, 1934/1986).

Recent research has supported Vygotsky's views regarding the functions and progression of self-talk and inner speech. The frequency of children's audible self-talk decreases during the preschool and early elementary years, but this decrease is at first accompanied by an increase in whispered mumbling and silent lip movements, presumably reflecting a transition to inner speech (Bivens & Berk, 1990; Ostad, 2013; J. Sawyer, 2017; Winsler & Naglieri, 2003). Self-talk increases when children are performing more difficult tasks and helps them regulate their behavior by staying focused on certain steps ("First select puzzle pieces with straight edges . . . second place these in matching slots.") and standards ("Too messy. No smudges."; Abdul Aziz, Fletcher, & Bayliss, 2017; Berk, 1994; J. Sawyer, 2017; Vygotsky, 1934/1986).

Complex mental processes begin as social activities and gradually evolve into mental processes. Vygotsky proposed that complex strategies, including the use of cognitive tools, have their roots in social interaction. As children discuss objects and events with adults and other knowledgeable individuals, they gradually incorporate words, concepts, symbols, and strategies into their ways of thinking. The process through which social activities evolve into internal mental activities is called **internalization**. The progression from self-talk to inner speech just described illustrates this process: Over time, children gradually internalize adults' directions so that they are eventually giving *themselves* directions.

Not all mental processes emerge as children interact with adults, however. Some develop as children interact with peers. For example, children frequently argue with one another about a variety of matters—how best to carry out an activity, what games to play, who did what to whom, and so on. According to Vygotsky, childhood arguments help children discover that there are several ways to view the same situation. Eventually, he suggested, children internalize the "arguing" process and develop the ability to look at a situation from several different angles on their own.

Each child acquires a culture's tools in his or her own terms. Recall that Vygotsky was a constructivist. He believed that children do not necessarily internalize *exactly* what they see and hear in a social context. Rather, they often transform ideas, strategies, and other cognitive resources to make these tools uniquely their own. You may sometimes see the term **appropriation** to refer to this process of internalizing but also selectively implementing some skills rather than others and adapting the strategies of one's culture for personal use. Furthermore, children do not necessarily learn all cultural pastimes easily or enthusiastically. Instead, individual children approach educational activities using their own motivations, prior understandings, and creative learning processes.

Children can perform more challenging tasks when assisted by advanced helpers. Vygotsky distinguished between two kinds of abilities that children are apt to have at any particular point in their development. A child's *actual developmental level* is the upper limit of tasks that he or she can perform independently, without help from anyone else. A child's *level of potential development* is the upper limit of tasks that he or she can perform with the assistance of a more competent individual. To get a true sense of children's cognitive development, Vygotsky suggested, teachers should assess children's capabilities both when performing alone *and* when performing with assistance.

As we noted earlier, Vygotsky found that children typically accomplish more difficult things in collaboration with adults than they can do on their own. With the assistance of a parent or teacher, young people may be able to grasp more complex prose than they comprehend independently. They can play more difficult piano pieces when an adult helps them locate some of the notes on the keyboard or provides suggestions about which fingers to use. And they can be coached to develop such basic arithmetic skills as addition, subtraction, multiplication, and division and such intricate explanations as how the honeybee hive collects nectar (Danish, Saleh, Andrade, & Bryan, 2017; A. L. Petitto, 1985).

FIGURE 6.7 In the zone.

Tasks within a child's zone of proximal development are optimal for promoting cognitive advancements.

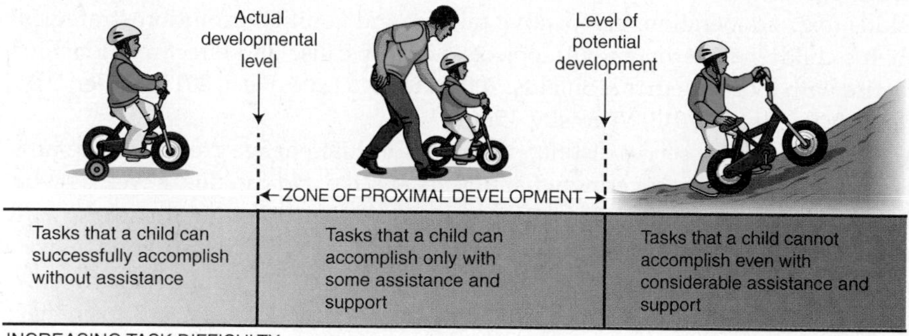

Challenging tasks promote maximum cognitive growth. The range of tasks that children cannot perform independently yet *can* perform with guidance from adults or, in some cases, from peers or older children who are skilled in performing an activity, is, in Vygotsky's terminology, the **zone of proximal development, or ZPD** (see Figure 6.7 above). In his strategic use of terms, Vygotsky is telling us that children's ability to benefit from subtle guidance from an adult indicates that an ability is in formation: "proximal development" means that a new facility is emerging. A toddler who is listing numbers from one to twenty may falter after ten and listen as the parent says "eleven [pause], twelve [pause], thirteen. . . . " Vygotsky's use of the term *zone* was deliberate, suggesting that children can be learning a few relevant facts and skills during shared time with an adult.

Vygotsky proposed that children learn little from performing tasks they can already do independently. Instead, they develop primarily by attempting tasks they can accomplish only with modest guidance from a more competent individual—that is, when they attempt tasks within their zone of proximal development. In a nutshell, it is the shared challenges in life, not the easy or independent successes, that promote cognitive development.

Whereas moderately difficult tasks are educational for children, tasks that they cannot do even with considerable assistance are of no benefit whatsoever. For example, it is pointless to ask a typical kindergartner to solve for x in an algebraic equation. A child's ZPD therefore sets a limit on what he or she is capable of learning. The ZPD changes as the child has more experiences and the adult reduces the level of guidance. As some tasks are mastered, other, more complex ones appear on the horizon.

As you might expect, ZPDs vary considerably among children. Whereas some children may, with assistance, be able to "reach" several years above their actual (independent) developmental level, others may be able to handle tasks that are only slightly more difficult than what they can currently do on their own. Vygotsky paid special attention to the needs of children with disabilities and suggested that educators identify equipment, materials, and guidance that would allow every child to succeed on meaningful tasks (Vygotsky, 1987b). A boy who is visually impaired may read a story in Braille, and a girl with a significant intellectual disability might be reminded by a poster in the restroom to use the toilet, flush, and wash her hands with soap and water.

MyLab Education
Video Example 6.7
Find Developmental Meaning
How does this preschool teacher identify and enter children's zone of proximal development? The teacher draws children's attention to a simple color pattern in a row of toy trucks. She knows from past experience that children of this age are capable of noticing this design, and by letting the children guess the next color in the series, she gains clues as to who needs help.

Play allows children to stretch themselves cognitively. During play, children pretend to take on adult roles, such as being a restaurant manager, server, and cook, and they practice a variety of adultlike behaviors, for example, assembling the necessary materials for a restaurant, creating menus, keeping track of customers' orders, and tallying final bills. In real life, this scenario would be impossible. Very few young children have the cooking, reading, writing, mathematical, or organizational skills necessary to run a restaurant. Yet the element of make-believe brings these tasks within children's reach (e.g., Lillard, 1993). In Vygotsky's words,

> In play a child always behaves beyond his average age, above his daily behavior; in play it is as though he were a head taller than himself. (Vygotsky, 1978, p. 102)

Many contemporary psychologists share Vygotsky's and Piaget's belief that play provides an arena for practicing skills needed later in life. Not only does play promote social skills (e.g., cooperation, perspective taking, and conflict resolution strategies); it also helps children experiment with objects, identify cause-and-effect relationships, and practice with tools (Gredler & Shields, 2008; Hedegaard & Fleer, 2013; Sikder, 2017; Sutherland & Friedman, 2013; Vygotsky, 1966).

To some degree, play serves distinct purposes for different age groups. For infants, one primary outcome is discovering what objects are like and can do, as well as what people can do *to* and *with* the objects. Through such discoveries, infants learn many properties of the physical world—which objects bounce, feel mushy, taste good, make a loud noise, and fit together (Gopnik, 2009b; Morris, 1977; R. Wu, Gopnik, Richardson, & Kirkham, 2011). Through social games, including peekaboo, pat-a-cake, and exchanges of sounds, infants practice imitation, learn the rhythms of interpersonal exchange, and acquire rudimentary skills in cooperation and turn-taking (Bigelow & Best, 2013; Bruner & Sherwood, 1976; Flavell et al., 2002; Håkstad, Obstfelder, & Øberg, 2017; Powers & Trevarthen, 2009).

When play takes on an element of make-believe around age 2, children begin to substitute one object for another in imaginary actions—for instance, "eating" pretend food with an invented fork (Markova & Legerstee, 2012; Pederson, Rook-Green, & Elder, 1981). Vygotsky suggested that imagination helps children distinguish between objects and their symbolic representations. In play, children respond to an internal representation (e.g., to the concept of *fork*) more than to the immediate appearance of the actual object (Bodrova & Leong, 1996; S. M. Carlson, White, & Davis-Unger, 2014; Osório, Meins, Martins, Martins, & Soares, 2012). In the preschool years, children expand their pretend play into elaborate scenarios—sometimes called **sociodramatic play**—in which they practice such complementary roles as parent and child, waiter and customer, or villain and superhero. When young children play together in make-believe roles, they learn to conform to cultural standards and fit in with playmates' perspectives. While pretending to be boyfriend and girlfriend, for example, they may learn that they are expected to hold hands and express affection with terms of endearment.

As children reach school age, role-playing activities gradually diminish, and other forms of play take their place. Elementary school children spend time with friends constructing things from cardboard boxes or Legos, playing cards and board games, and engaging in team sports. Many of these activities continue into adolescence. While they are adhering to rules in games, youngsters learn to plan ahead, think before they act, cooperate and compromise, solve problems, and engage in self-restraint—skills critical for successful participation in the adult world (E. Baines & Blatchford, 2011; Bierman & Torres, 2016; Christie & Johnsen, 1983; Hromek & Roffey, 2009; Sutton-Smith, 1979).

Play, then, is hardly a waste of time. It is a valuable training ground for the adult world. Perhaps for this reason it is seen in children worldwide. In the Development in Culture feature "Playing Around," you can learn how playing alone and with others helps children gain proficiency in cultural practices.

Current Perspectives Related to Vygotsky's Theory

As you have learned, Vygotsky's descriptions of developmental processes were imprecise. Despite this weakness, many contemporary theorists and practitioners have found his theory to be insightful. Advocates have taken Vygotsky's notions in several different directions that typically address the social construction of meaning, scaffolding, participation in adult activities, and acquisition of teaching skills.

Social Construction of Meaning

Contemporary psychologists have elaborated on Vygotsky's proposal that adults help children attach meaning to objects and events. They point out that an adult (e.g., a parent or a teacher) often helps a child make better sense of the world through joint discussion of mutual experiences (Crowley & Jacobs, 2002; Feuerstein & Falik, 2010;

Development In Culture

Playing Around

From the perspective of cultural learning, play is a productive medium through which children voluntarily socialize themselves into their community's traditions (Boyette, 2016; F. P. Hughes, 2010).

To some degree, lessons in cultural practices change as children grow. Early on, adults guide the direction of play. Mothers, fathers, and other adults invite infants to join games of peekaboo, pat-a-cake, and other good-humored exchanges that vary from one cultural group to the next. One psychologist, Heidi Keller, found distinct patterns in infant play in mothers and infants from urban German middle-class families and rural Cameroonian Nso families (H. Keller, 2003). German mothers tended to spend a considerable amount of time interacting verbally with their infants—talking with them and encouraging their eye contact and play with toys. In comparison, Nso mothers attended to the physical needs of their infants by breastfeeding, soothing, and providing close body contact. The Nso mothers gently jiggled and tugged at infants' limbs. As infants from both groups were enjoying social interaction, they were simultaneously obtaining guidance in conducting themselves—developing verbal skills and playing with objects in German families and staying physically close to mothers and exercising new motor skills in Nso families.

(C) Chromix Imaging/Alamy

PLAYTIME. These boys enjoy a morning swim at a lake in Sri Lanka. While sharing a fun pastime, they are acquiring cultural knowledge about friendship and leisure time.

Children continue to integrate familiar cultural routines into play as they grow. In societies that encourage serious chores in children, children pretend to be adult laborers (F. P. Hughes, 2010). In Botswana, men herd oxen, and boys regularly play the "cow game." Taking on complementary roles, some boys pretend to be oxen yoked with twine, and others act as drivers who control them (Bock & Johnson, 2004). Girls pretend to pummel grain with reeds, sticks, dirt, and imaginary mortars (Bock & Johnson, 2004). In industrialized cultures that separate children from the daily work of adults, children are apt to include fantasy figures that they have seen on television and in video games (F. P. Hughes, 2010; Lehrer & Petrakos, 2011). Not every culture values or encourages pretend play, and in some groups children play creatively with objects and with one another without taking on defined roles (Farver & Shin, 1997; F. P. Hughes, 2010; Smilansky, 1968).

In middle childhood and after, youngsters participate in structured games. Children in many societies play competitive games, wherein participants follow prescribed rules and vie to be the winner (Bonta, 1997; F. P. Hughes, 2010). In hunting societies, children play games of physical dexterity, including foot races and contests of tracking and spear-throwing, pursuits that allow for practice of valuable motor skills. In nomadic groups, children play games whose outcomes are determined by chance, perhaps preparing them for largely uncontrollable environmental conditions, as their parents must do to survive. In cultures that are technologically advanced, children play games that require some degree of strategy (e.g., computer games), advancing their facility with complex systems (S. Elliott & Elliott, 2014). In societies that do not encourage competition, children may play cooperative games, tell one another stories, and copy adult roles (Bonta, 1997; Boyette, 2016; F. P. Hughes, 2010).

Kozulin et al., 2010; Mahn & John-Steiner, 2013). Such an interaction, sometimes called a **mediated learning experience**, encourages the child to think about the event in a culturally relevant way by attaching labels to it, recognizing underlying principles, drawing certain conclusions, and so on. In this kind of a conversation, the adult must consider the prior knowledge of the child and tailor the discussion accordingly, as Billy's mother does in the chapter-opening case study (Newson & Newson, 1975).

In addition to co-constructing meaning with adults, children often talk among themselves to understand their experiences. With siblings and friends, children share fantasies and troubleshoot how to play a game or make sense of someone's confusing behavior (Palacios,

Kibler, Yoder, Baird, & Bergey, 2016). School is another obvious place where children toss around ideas about a particular issue and reach consensus about how best to interpret a topic. Children also acquire misconceptions from well-meaning peers who convincingly tout a false explanation, making it worthwhile for teachers to interject other considerations into the discussion.

Scaffolding

Theorists have given considerable thought to the kinds of assistance that help children accomplish challenging tasks. The term **scaffolding** is often used to describe the guidance provided by adults and experienced peers who help children perform tasks in their ZPD. To understand this concept, think of the scaffolding used in the construction of a new building. The *scaffold* is an external structure that supports workers (e.g., with a place where they can stand) until the building itself is strong enough to carry their weight. As the building gains strength and stability, the scaffold becomes less necessary and is gradually removed.

In much the same way, an adult guiding a child through a new task provides a scaffold to early efforts. Scaffolding can take a variety of forms. Here are a few of the many possibilities:

MyLab Education
Video Example 6.8

Find Developmental Meaning
How does a teacher scaffold a child's puzzle completion? The teacher advises a boy to examine the layout, find pieces with straight edges at the periphery, and search for pieces that belong in the center.

- Demonstrate proper performance on a task in a way that children can easily imitate.
- Divide a complex task into several smaller, simpler duties.
- Provide a structure or set of guidelines for how the task should be accomplished.
- Provide a calculator, computer software (word processing program, spreadsheet, etc.), or other technology to make some aspects of the task easier.
- Ask questions that get children thinking in appropriate ways.
- Keep children's attention focused on relevant dimensions.
- Give frequent feedback about how children are progressing (Andre, Durksen, & Volman, 2017; Bodrova & Leong, 2009; A. Collins, 2006; Gallimore & Tharp, 1992; Pentimonti & Justice, 2010; Rogoff, 1990; Smit, van Eerde, & Bakker, 2013; Torres-Guzmán, 2011; Weisberg, Hirsh-Pasek, Golinkoff, Kittredge, & Klahr, 2016; D. Wood, Bruner, & Ross, 1976).

In order for scaffolding to work, it must be customized to children's skills. As they become more adept at performing an activity, assistance is gradually phased out so that they eventually accomplish it on their own. As you might expect, learning to offer just the right level of support takes practice.

MyLab Education Application Exercise 6.1
Identify Development-Enhancing Education

In this video a fourth-grade science teacher scaffolds his students' scientific thinking.

Participation in Adult Activities

Virtually all cultures allow—and, in fact, usually require—children to be involved in adult activities. Yet children's early experiences are often at the fringe of the action. As children acquire greater competence, they gradually take a more central role in the activity until, eventually, they are full-fledged participants (Lave & Wenger, 1991; Rogoff et al., 2007).

In most cases children's early involvement in adult activities is scaffolded through what is sometimes called **guided participation** (Bhatia & Ebooks, 2014; Rogoff, 2003). When taking a nature walk together, a mother may show her son how to find a description of a flowering plant in a field guide (Zimmerman, & McClain, 2016). When our own children were preschoolers, we authors often enticed them to help bake cookies, asking them to measure, pour, and mix ingredients as we stood close by and offered suggestions. When they got older, we took them to the office and had them press the buttons in the elevator, check our mailboxes, open envelopes, and deliver documents to the department secretary, all the while keeping a close eye on what they were doing and instructing them when necessary. In later years, we gave them increasing responsibility. By the time they were in high school, they were baking their own pastries and sometimes running errands for the family.

Parents are not the only ones who engage children in responsible activities. Schools sometimes invite students to be members of decision-making committees, and parent–teacher organizations ask students to help with fund-raising efforts. Girl Scout troops introduce girls to salesmanship, accounting, and other adult business practices during annual cookie drives (Rogoff, 2003; Rogoff, Topping, Baker-Sennett, & Lacasa, 2002). And many local newspapers take on high school students as cub reporters, movie reviewers, and editorial writers.

In some instances, adults work with children in formal or informal **apprenticeships**, one-on-one relationships in which adults teach young people new skills, guide their initial efforts, and present increasingly difficult tasks as proficiency improves. Many cultures use apprenticeships as a way of gradually introducing children to particular skills and trades in the adult community—perhaps weaving, tailoring, playing a musical instrument, or trying out the responsibilities of a new job (D. A. Davis & Davis, 2012; D. J. Elliott, 1995; D. Horn, 2016; Lave & Wenger, 1991; Tsethlikai & Rogoff, 2013).

In apprenticeships, children learn not only useful actions but also the language of the skill or trade (Lave & Wenger, 1991). When master weavers teach apprentices their craft, they might use such terms as *warp*, *weft*, *shuttle*, and *harness* to focus attention on a particular aspect of the process. Similarly, when teachers guide students through scientific experiments, they use words like *hypothesis*, *evidence*, and *theory* to help students evaluate their procedures and results (Perkins, 1992). Children may also be exposed to how adults think about a task—a situation known as a **cognitive apprenticeship**. For instance, an adult and a child might work together to sew a patchwork quilt, collect water samples in fieldwork, or make a cogent argument for a letter to a newspaper. In the process of talking about various aspects of the task, the adult is likely to verbalize the best approaches and benchmarks to watch for during the activity (Bodrow & Magalashvili, 2009; Bouta & Retalis, 2013; A. Collins, 2006; Papathomas & Kuhn, 2017).

Acquisition of Teaching Skills

When learning new techniques from more experienced members of the community, children observe the teaching process. They subsequently teach younger children basic skills (Gauvain, 2001; N. Howe, Recchia, Della Porta, & Funamoto, 2012). For instance, children in The Gambia help siblings learn new clapping games by giving verbal directions and moving younger children's hands into the appropriate positions (Koops, 2010). Many older children have an intuitive sense of instructional formats that appeal to younger children and may use local materials, for example, seeds, sticks, stones, and familiar songs and stories, when imparting such fundamental skills as counting objects (Mweru & Murungi, 2013).

With age and experience, children become increasingly adept at teaching others what they themselves have learned. In a study in rural Mexico (Maynard, 2002), Mayan children were observed as they worked with younger siblings in preparing food and washing clothes. The children's earliest form of "instruction" (perhaps around age 4 or 5) was simply to let a younger brother or sister join in and help. At age 6 or 7, children tended to be directive and controlling, giving commands and taking over if something wasn't done correctly. By the time they were 8, they were proficient teachers, using a combination of demonstrations, explanations, physical guidance, and feedback to scaffold their siblings' efforts. When children help others, the "teachers" often benefit as much, or nearly as much, as the "students" (Bowman-Perrott et al., 2013; Howe, Porta, Recchia, & Ross, 2016; Karcher, 2009; Webb & Palincsar, 1996).

Applying the Ideas of Vygotsky and His Followers

Vygotsky's work and the advances it has spawned have numerous implications for teaching. Educators taking a Vygotskian perspective guide children in taking on increasing levels of responsibility for culturally important endeavors.

Preparing for Your Licensure Examination

Your teaching test might ask you about Vygotsky's contributions to educational practice.

• **Help children acquire the cognitive tools they need to succeed with academic disciplines.** Obviously, children in an industrialized society need to learn to read, write, and do arithmetic. Children can become better musicians when they read music and understand what *keys*, *chords*, and *thirds* are. In the disciplines of science, mathematics, and social studies, our culture passes along other key concepts (e.g., *molecule, negative number, democracy*), symbols (e.g., H_2O, π, x^3), and visual displays (e.g., graphs, maps) that facilitate interpretation of advanced material.

• **Use group learning activities to help children internalize cognitive strategies.** Contemporary researchers have found that, as Vygotsky suggested, children often internalize—and so eventually use independently—the complex thinking processes they first use in social interaction (e.g., Andriessen, 2006; Murphy, 2007). We find an example in **reciprocal teaching**, a model of reading instruction that has had great success in enhancing reading comprehension skills (A. L. Brown & Palincsar, 1987; Y. Law, 2014; S. Lee & Tsai, 2017; Mandel, Osana, & Venkatesh, 2013; Palincsar & Brown, 1984). This approach is designed to foster four effective reading strategies:

- *Summarizing:* Identifying the main ideas of a reading passage
- *Questioning:* Asking oneself questions to check comprehension of ideas
- *Clarifying:* Taking steps to better understand a confusing point
- *Predicting:* Anticipating what points an author is apt to make in later sentences or paragraphs

MyLab Education
Video Explanation 6.2
How does reciprocal teaching unfold in high school classrooms?

In this approach, a teacher and several students meet in a group to read a piece of text, occasionally stopping to discuss it aloud. Initially, the teacher leads the discussion, asking questions about the text to promote summarizing, questioning, clarifying, and predicting. He or she gradually turns this "teaching" role over to a few students, who for a short time take charge of the discussion and ask one another the same kinds of questions the teacher modeled. Eventually, the students can read and discuss a text almost independently of the teacher, making sense of it together and checking one another for comprehension.

Reciprocal teaching has been used successfully with learners, ranging from first-graders to college students. In many cases students become far more effective readers and transfer their new reading strategies to other subject areas (A. L. Brown & Palincsar, 1987; Mandel et al., 2013; Palincsar & Brown, 1984, 1989; Stricklin, 2011).

MyLab Education
Artifact Example 6.3
Find Developmental Meaning *How did 4-year-old Hannah's teacher scaffold the little girl's familiarity with numbers?* In this simple worksheet, the preschool teacher used dots that Hannah could connect into numerals and small circles that Hannah could count to determine numbers of items.

• **Provide tangible reminders about what children should be doing while learning.** Teachers can ask preschool children to draw a picture or write simple notes about their plans during a free-choice activity. A 4-year-old boy draws a picture of himself building blocks with a friend. He brings his picture to the block area and guides his play according to his plan (Bodrova, Leong, & Akhutina, 2011). Similarly, three first-grade children enter the science center, with each child taking a picture of an ear, lips, and pencil to remind themselves to be a listener, speaker, or recorder when completing the assignment. Their teacher reminds them to follow their plan when they drift away from it.

• **Scaffold performance on challenging tasks.** For optimal learning, teachers and other adults need to present assignments that a child can perform successfully only with assistance—that is, tasks within the child's ZPD. Although it is not always practical to assess and accommodate every child's ZPD, teachers can offer assignments that are moderately challenging for most students and make a range of scaffolds available, the selection of which depends on skill levels. In Artifact Example 6.3, you can examine numerals formed by a young child by connecting up the dots. The Development-Enhancing Education feature "Scaffolding Children's Performance on Challenging Tasks" presents additional examples.

Development-Enhancing Education

Scaffolding Children's Performance on Challenging Tasks

Ask questions that get children thinking about a task.

- A middle school teacher asks her students a series of questions as they prepare to deliver a persuasive speech: *What are the main points you want to make? Who in your team will make them? What kind of objections and counterarguments can you anticipate? How will you respond to them?* (Early Adolescence)
- As students in a high school science class begin to plan their experiments for an upcoming science fair, their teacher encourages them to separate and control variables with the following questions: *What do I think causes the phenomenon I am studying? What other variables might influence it? How can I be sure which variables are influencing the results I obtain?* (Late Adolescence)

When learners are unfamiliar with a task, provide explicit guidance and feedback.

- A preschool teacher watches children attempt to write their names. With a girl who writes the sequence backward, the teacher puts a green dot under the first letter and tells her to start with it. With a boy who forgets a few letters, the teacher highlights missing letters with a color pen. With another boy, the teacher writes the letters he cannot remember and asks has him to add the letters he knows. (Early Childhood)
- When an outdoor educator takes 12-year-olds on their first camping trip, he has the children work in pairs to pitch their tents. Although he has previously shown the children how to put up a tent, this is the first time they've actually done it themselves, and so he provides a sequence of pictures with instructions for each step. In addition, he circulates among campsites and provides assistance as necessary. (Early Adolescence)

Provide a calculator, computer software, worksheet, or other material that reduces the difficulty of a task while still allowing children to tackle relevant steps.

- Children in a third-grade class have mastered basic addition, subtraction, and multiplication facts. They are now applying their knowledge of arithmetic to determine how much money they would need to purchase a list of recreational items from a mail-order catalog. Because the list is long and includes varying quantities of each item, their teacher gives them calculators to do the necessary multiplication and addition. (Middle Childhood)
- A high school history teacher distributes a worksheet with a partially completed table of cultural inventions from ancient African and Middle Eastern societies. A few cells contain summaries that serve as models for notes students can take as they read their book. (Late Adolescence)

Teach children how to talk themselves through a complex procedure.

- A school psychologist teaches children with cognitive disabilities to classify shapes by asking themselves questions (e.g., Does the object have three or more sides? Is it round?). The children begin to ask themselves these questions and learn to classify shapes more accurately. (Middle Childhood)
- A physical education teacher shows beginning tennis players how to use self-instructions to remember correct form when swinging the racket:
  1. Say *ball* to remind yourself to look at the ball.
  2. Say *bounce* to remind yourself to follow the ball with your eyes as it approaches you.
  3. Say *hit* to remind yourself to focus on contacting the ball with the racket.
  4. Say *ready* to get yourself into position for the next ball to come your way. (Early Adolescence)

Divide a complex assignment into several smaller tasks, and ask children to complete each in small groups.

- A fourth-grade teacher has his students create a school newspaper with news articles, a schedule of upcoming events, a couple of story cartoons, and classified advertisements. Several students work together to create each feature, with students assuming distinct roles (e.g., fact finder, writer, editor) and occasionally switching parts. (Middle Childhood)
- A film analysis teacher asks high school students to divide up their assignments into manageable parts and then share the results. After the class watches *Citizen Kane*, the teacher gives poster paper to groups of students. One group pieces together flashbacks of the life of Charles Foster Kane, another reads the screenplay, a third group examines the movie's filmmaking innovations, and a fourth group looks into the reception the movie originally received. (Late Adolescence)

Gradually withdraw guidance as children become proficient.

- A preschool teacher has 2- and 3-year-olds take turns distributing crackers, fruit, and napkins at snack time, and she asks them to bring their dishes and trash to the kitchen after finished eating. Initially, she shows them how to carry trays so that they don't spill. As the year progresses, reminders are less necessary, although she must occasionally say, "I think two of you have forgotten to bring

(*continued*)

Development-Enhancing Education

Scaffolding Children's Performance on Challenging Tasks (continued)

your cups to the kitchen. I'm missing the ones with Big Bird and Cookie Monster." (Early Childhood)

- In an after-school service club, a teacher facilitates discussion and eventually encourages students to find a worthwhile program for their community. As the adolescents narrow the field of programs they might implement, the teacher is silent, allowing students to review the advantages and limitations of each. (Late Adolescence)

Sources: Benko (2012); Bodrova and Leong (2009; kindergarten writing example); Gallimore and Tharp (1992); Helibronner (2013); Kirshner (2008; persuasive speech example); Lajoie and Derry (1993); Meichenbaum (1985); Rosenshine and Meister (1992); D. Wood, Bruner, and Ross (1976); Ziegler (1987; tennis example).

One powerful strategy, teaching children how to talk themselves through a complex new procedure, makes use of Vygotsky's concept of *self-talk* to enable children to create their *own* scaffolding. Children can learn how to follow five steps, as you see in Figure 6.8 (Meichenbaum, 1977, 1985).

In this sequence, the adult initially serves as a model both for the behavior itself and for the process of self-guidance. Responsibility for performing the task is soon turned over to the child. Eventually, responsibility for guiding performance is assumed by the child as well.

FIGURE 6.8 Self-talk.

In a five-step process, the child shifts from needing adult assistance to completing the task independently.

	TASK PERFORMANCE	TASK INSTRUCTIONS
Step 1	The adult performs the task, modeling it for the child.	The adult verbalizes instructions.
Step 2	The child performs the task.	The adult verbalizes instructions.
Step 3	The child performs the task.	The child repeats the instructions aloud.
Step 4	The child performs the task.	The child whispers the instructions.
Step 5	The child performs the task.	The child thinks silently about the instructions.

- **Assess abilities under a variety of conditions.** To foster children's cognitive development, educators need to determine under what conditions the children are most likely to accomplish assignments successfully. Can children finish an assignment entirely on their own? If not, can they do it in collaboration with one or two peers? Can they do it if they have some adult guidance and support? By addressing such questions, teachers can get a better sense of the tasks that are in each child's ZPD and the kinds of assistance that will be helpful to children individually and to the class as a whole (Bodrova & Leong, 2009; Haywood & Lidz, 2007; Mahn & John-Steiner, 2013).

- **Provide opportunities to engage in authentic activities.** As you have learned, children's participation in realistic activities plays a critical role in their cognitive development. However, children spend much of their day at school, removed from cultural routines involved in running a household, performing the duties of a job, worshipping, and interacting in other institutions of society. A reasonable alternative is **authentic activities**—classroom projects that closely resemble typical adult activities. Following are examples:

- Participating in a debate
- Designing an electrical circuit
- Conducting an experiment
- Creating and distributing a class newsletter
- Organizing a volunteer campaign to address a community need
- Performing in a concert
- Planning a personal budget
- Conversing in a foreign language
- Creating a museum display
- Developing a home page on the Internet
- Filming and editing a video

By placing classroom activities in real-world contexts, teachers can enhance a variety of skills in students, including their mastery of classroom subject matter and ability to work effectively in groups (Asatryan, 2016; A. Collins, Brown, & Newman, 1989; Silva, Lopes, & Silva, 2013). For instance, students may show greater improvement in writing skills when they practice composing essays and letters for real people, rather than completing short, artificial exercises (Curwood, Magnificio, & Lammers, 2013; Nail, 2007). Likewise, they may gain a more complete understanding of how to interpret maps when they construct their own rather than simply interpret maps in workbook exercises (Gregg & Leinhardt, 1994a).

MyLab Education Application Exercise 6.2
Identify Development-Enhancing Education
Watch a high school English teacher coach her students through an authentic project.

• **Promote digital access and literacy.** Computers are now an important tool for children to learn in most societies. Before considering how to teach children how to use computers, issues of access need to be considered. Children in low-income families are less likely to have computers and Internet at home than are children in families with higher incomes (K. K. Mills, 2010). This imbalance is a concern because familiarity with digital technologies is increasingly foundational to academic learning, personal expression, and career readiness. School districts have responded to this disparity in a variety of ways, including loaning digital tablets to children, boosting signal strength at the school to reach nearby neighborhoods, and sending wireless hotspots home for children and their families to use (Ark, 2017).

Having addressed issues of access to the best of their abilities, educators can integrate digital technologies into ongoing instruction. It is increasingly clear that becoming technologically savvy entails a lot more than pushing buttons, moving the cursor, surfing the World Wide Web, and keyboarding words. It involves strategic use of electronic information to achieve personal goals. Explicit instruction in **digital literacy**, the ability to retrieve, interpret, evaluate, create, and communicate information from interactive technologies, helps children take full advantage of available resources (American Library Association, 2011). Thus, educators can advise children that some websites provide reliable information and others do not, and it is worthwhile to compare perspectives on the Internet with reports known to be credible. Professionals can also provide children with programs for creating video clips and designing simple web pages, fostering their ability to take an active role in the digital world. Finally, teachers and other school staff can protect students by screening out potentially harmful websites on the school's network, encouraging caution with disclosing personal information on social media sites, and advising students on how to recognize and avoid the lure of predators.

As with any instructional method, electronic devices need to implemented in such a way that existing knowledge and skills are accommodated. Age-related abilities specifically need to be considered as computer devices are employed. Although parents may make smartphones and tablets available to their infants, psychologists and medical experts recommend that exposure should be limited. Infants' needs are better met through interaction, sensory experiences, and hands-on exploration (Reid Chassiakos, Radesky, Christakis, Moreno, & Cross, 2016). Preschool children can learn letters, numbers, and other basic concepts from interactive computer programs, and these lessons are strengthened when adults talk with children about what they are learning. Beginning in elementary school and extending through high school years, interactive technologies offer a tremendous store of information, occasions for practice with academic skills, and a forum for creative expression. However, overuse, bullying, and risks in cyberspace necessitate adult guidance (Reid Chassiakos et al., 2016).

• **Differentiate instruction for children with special needs.** Vygotsky believed that children with special needs are not inevitably delayed in their development, especially when well-designed devices are available (Vygotsky, 1987b). A certain number of cultural tools, for example, Braille, lip reading, and sign language, facilitate communication for children with sensory impairments (Mahn & John-Steiner, 2013). Other adjustments promote learning, including diversity in the presentation of concepts (e.g., using more visual images than is customary), types of instruction (e.g., increasing scaffolding of steps of a task), and pace and repetition (e.g., offering more practice than is necessary with other learners; Bøttcher & Dammeyer, 2012).

It had been Vygotsky's hope that a science of special education would emerge that catalogued instructional devices and techniques for helping children compensate for visual impairments, intellectual disabilities, and other handicaps (Vygotsky, 1987b). In keeping with this goal, a recent educational framework, *universal design for learning*, has been developed by Anne Meyer, David Rose, and David Gordon (2014) to meet a wide range of learning needs. Meyer and colleagues have identified tactics for differentiation within three instructional domains:

- *Motivating students with engaging activities* (e.g., by promoting high expectations, focusing on personal progress, and teaching selected lessons in small-group activities)
- *Enriching students' knowledge of the material* (e.g., by starting with reminders of what students already know, emphasizing patterns and themes, teaching vocabulary, and diversifying the formats of materials, as by providing fiction in bound books and on tape)
- *Guiding students' strategic learning* (e.g., by teaching them to set goals and monitor their progress, giving them feedback on how well they are doing, and providing relevant tools)

In the universal design framework, breadth in instructional procedures is intended to benefit a broad array of intellectual profiles, variations that can be made in almost every classroom. A strength of this instructional model is that it recognizes the uniqueness of every student and the necessity for a heterogeneous collection of educational technologies (C. C. Lee & Picanco, 2013; Rao, Smith, & Lowrey, 2017).

• **Scaffold children's play.** Many developmental theorists advocate for the inclusion of play in the curriculum, especially during the preschool and early elementary years. Play allows for conversation, fantasy, self-control, emotional expression, and relaxation. Following are several suggestions for promoting young children's play:

- Reserve a separate corner in the classroom as a play center. Furnish the play area with realistic toys (e.g., dolls with a range of ethnicities, dress-up clothes, dishes, pots and pans, wallets and purses, keys, toy cell phones) that suggest certain functions, as well as more versatile objects (e.g., Legos, wooden blocks, cardboard boxes) that encourage open-ended fantasy. Rotate theme-related materials in alignment with topics in the curriculum (perhaps a doctor's office, hair salon, fire station, or veterinarian hospital).
- Read a story to children (e.g., *Diary of a Worm* by Doreen Cronin, 2003) and then supply props (e.g., plastic worms, toy birds, paper, and crayons) for children to act it out.
- Expose children to in-depth information about a topic, for instance, by reading to them, inviting speakers (e.g., a paleontologist when teaching about dinosaurs), showing videos, and supplying relevant props for the play area (e.g., plastic bones, shovels, brushes).
- Take a secondary role in children's pretend play. Help children integrate information they have been learning (e.g., the job of an emergency responder) by spending a little time in the play center and temporarily taking on a part (e.g., a distressed victim asking for help from a 911 operator).
- Occasionally ask children to set a goal for their play, such as running a shop together. When conflicts escalate, remind children of their goal and suggest how to compromise ("It sounds as if you both want to be the cashier. Your shop needs a cashier *and* a stocker. I wonder if you might trade off in these jobs.").
- Provide enough toys and equipment to minimize potential conflicts, but keep them limited enough that children can practice sharing.
- Exercise sensitivity in responding to children's individual needs. A young boy who is shy may appreciate reassurance about joining high-spirited peers, whereas a girl who is fascinated with wheels, gears, and pulleys can be shown a new construction toy (Bodrova & Leong, 2009; Bredekamp, 2011; R. C. Fowler, 2017; Frost, Shin, & Jacobs, 1998; J. Jung & Recchia, 2013; Leong & Bodrova, 2012; S. L. Massey, 2013; Moreno, Shwayder, & Friedman, 2017).

By observing children during play, teachers gain insights into the abilities and skills that individual children are acquiring. Examples of things to look for are presented in the Observation Guidelines table "Observing the Cognitive Aspects of Young Children's Play." In a Meet Individual Needs Video, you can observe a teacher's guidance with children building a tower together.

MyLab Education Application Exercise 6.3
Meet Individual Needs

In this video a preschool teacher scaffolds the ability of children to contribute to a joint building project.

Summary

Vygotsky suggested that human beings are different from other species in their acquisition of complex mental processes. In his view, adults promote children's cognitive development by articulating meanings for objects and events, introducing the tangible and cognitive tools of their society, and assisting them with challenging tasks. Social activities are often precursors to, and form the basis of, complex mental processes: Children initially use new skills in the course of interacting with adults or peers and slowly internalize skills for their own use.

Contemporary theorists have extended Vygotsky's theory in several directions. Some suggest that adults can help children benefit from their experiences through the joint construction of meanings, guided participation, and cognitive apprenticeships. Others recommend that adults engage children in authentic, adultlike tasks, initially providing enough scaffolding such that youngsters can accomplish tasks successfully and gradually withdrawing support as proficiency increases.

MyLab Education Self-Check 6.2

OBSERVATION GUIDELINES

Observing the Cognitive Aspects of Young Children's Play

CHARACTERISTIC	LOOK FOR	EXAMPLE	IMPLICATION
Exploratory Play with Objects	• *Interest in exploring objects* in the environment • *Ability to handle objects adeptly* • *Use of multiple senses* in exploratory play	When Tyler sees a new toy guitar in the playroom, he picks it up, inspects all sides, and turns the crank (not enough to elicit any musical notes). After Tyler leaves it to play with something else, Sarah picks up the guitar, sniffs it, puts the crank in her mouth, and begins to suck and chew it.	Provide a wide variety of objects for infants and toddlers to explore, making sure that they are safe, clean, and nontoxic. Recognize that children may use these things in unexpected ways (and not necessarily how their manufacturers intended) and will typically move quickly from one object to another.
Group Play	• *Extent to which children play* with one another • *Extent to which children cooperate* during play	LaMarr and Matthew are playing with trucks in the sandbox, but each boy seems to be in his own little world.	Give children opportunities to play together, and provide toys that encourage cooperation.
Use of Symbolic Thought and Imagination	• *Degree to which children use an object* to stand for another • *Imaginary objects* incorporated into play	Julia tells her friend she is going to the grocery store, opens an imaginary car door, sits on a chair inside her "car," steers her pretend steering wheel, and says, "Beep, beep" as she blows her "horn."	When equipping a play area, include objects (e.g., wooden blocks, cardboard boxes) that children can use for a variety of purposes.
Role Taking	• *Children's use of language* (e.g., tone of voice and specific phrases) *and behaviors* (e.g., mannerisms, characteristic actions) to perform a particular role or job • *Extent to which children coordinate multiple roles* within a complex play scenario	Mark and Alisa are playing doctor. Alisa brings her teddy bear to Mark's "office" and politely says, "Good morning, Doctor. My baby has a sore throat." Mark holds a Popsicle stick against the bear's mouth and instructs the "baby" to say "Aaahhh."	Provide toys and equipment associated with particular roles (e.g., toy medical kit, cooking utensils, play money).

Comparing Piagetian and Vygotskian Perspectives

6.3 Outline similarities and differences between Piaget's and Vygotsky's views on cognitive development and appropriate educational practice.

Together, Piaget's and Vygotsky's theories give us a deeper understanding of cognitive development than either theory does on its own. For educators who wish to meet children's individual, cultural, and age-related needs, it helps to understand both the differences and similarities between these two prominent perspectives.

Common Themes

If we look beyond the very different vocabulary Piaget and Vygotsky used to describe the phenomena they observed, we notice four themes that their theories share: constructive processes, readiness, challenge, and social interaction. Each of these themes has important implications for education.

Constructive Processes in Learning

Neither Piaget's nor Vygotsky's theory depicts cognitive development as a process of simply "absorbing" one's experiences. Rather, both frameworks portray the acquisition of new knowledge and skills as an energetic and constructive process. In Piaget's view, children increasingly organize their thoughts as schemes and, later, as operations that apply to a wide variety of circumstances. In Vygotsky's view, children gradually internalize—in their own creative and idiosyncratic ways—the interpretations and cognitive tools they encounter and use in social contexts.

MyLab Education
Artifact Example 6.4

Find Developmental Meaning
How does 6-year-old Laura's drawing reveal both Piagetian and Vygotskian concepts? Compatible with Piaget's ideas, Laura assimilates fish to her ideas about underwater mammals, in which air is expelled as bubbles. Compatible with Vygotsky's ideas, Laura has acquired skill in drawing with writing implements, valuable tools for creative expression.

These two perspectives on constructivism are complementary. Piaget's theory focuses largely on how children construct knowledge *on their own*; his perspective is sometimes labeled **individual constructivism**. In contrast, the ideas of Vygotsky and his followers focus more on how children construct meanings in collaboration with adults and peers, processes sometimes called **social constructivism**. Without a doubt, children acquire increasingly sophisticated thinking processes through *both* their own individual efforts and joint meaning-making efforts with others. In Artifact Example 6.4, you can see that 6-year-old Laura's drawing of how fish breathe can be interpreted from both Piagetian and Vygotskian perspectives.

Readiness

Both Piaget and Vygotsky suggested that at any point in time a child is cognitively ready for some experiences and not others. Both theorists acknowledged that brain maturation places limits on what children can do at various points in development. Piaget proposed that children recognize new objects and events only when they can assimilate the information into existing schemes, and they can think logically about new problems only if they have constructed the relevant logical operations. Vygotsky, meanwhile, portrayed children's readiness for tasks as comprising an ever-changing zone of proximal development. As children master skills and abilities, other, slightly more advanced ones emerge and are refined with adult support.

For Piaget and Vygotsky, children are always prepared to learn *something*. For Piaget, they are continually ready to learn based on their current structures and ample curiosity about the world. For Vygotsky, children are ready to learn concepts and skills used by people in their home and community, especially in tasks that children can accomplish with a smidgen of help.

Challenge

We see the importance of challenge most clearly in Vygotsky's concept of the zone of proximal development: Children benefit most from tasks that they can perform only with the assistance of more competent individuals. Yet challenge, albeit of a somewhat different sort, also lies at the heart of Piaget's theory: Children develop more sophisticated knowledge and thought processes when they encounter phenomena they cannot adequately understand using existing knowledge—in other words, phenomena that create disequilibrium.

Importance of Social Interaction

In Piaget's eyes, the people in a child's life can present information and arguments that create disequilibrium and, as a result, foster greater perspective taking and logical thinking processes. For instance, when young children disagree with one another, they realize that different people have discrepant yet equally valid viewpoints, and they gradually shed the egocentrism that characterizes preoperational thought. In Vygotsky's view, social interactions provide the very foundation for thought processes. Children internalize processes they use when conversing with others until ultimately, they use these processes independently. Tasks within the ZPD can, by definition, be accomplished only when others assist in children's efforts.

The four qualities in which there is theoretical agreement produce a coherent picture of children's reasoning with implications for education. The Developmental Trends table "Thinking and Reasoning Skills at Different Age Levels" draws on both perspectives in defining the logical characteristics of youngsters.

Differences between the Two Theories

The core beliefs that Piaget and Vygotsky pronounced have stood the test of time. Identifying how children think and implementing dynamic, challenging lessons are without a doubt worthwhile endeavors. Yet it is also important to recognize that the two scholars held opposing views on significant matters. In the Basic Developmental Issues table "Contrasting Piaget and Vygotsky" on page 229, we compare the two perspectives in terms of nature and nurture, universality and diversity, and qualitative and quantitative change. Here we concentrate on differences in convictions about the role of language and environment in cognitive growth.

Theoretical Differences

Following are four questions that capture distinctions between Piaget's and Vygotsky's theories.

To what extent is language essential for cognitive development? According to Piaget, language provides verbal labels for many of the concepts that children have already developed. It is also the primary means through which children interact with others, and language helps children transform particular experiences (e.g., snuggling with Fido) into formal symbols (e.g., "petting" a "dog"). Yet in Piaget's view, much of cognitive development occurs independently of language.

For Vygotsky, language is critical for cognitive development. Children's thought processes are internalized versions of social interactions that are largely verbal in nature. Through two language-based phenomena—self-talk and inner speech—children guide their actions in ways that others have previously guided them. In their conversations with adults, children learn the meanings that their culture imposes on events.

The truth of the matter probably lies somewhere between Piaget's and Vygotsky's perspectives. Piaget clearly underestimated the importance of language: Children acquire more complex understandings not only through their own interactions with the world but also (as Vygotsky suggested) by learning how others interpret these occurrences. On the other hand, Vygotsky overstated the case for language. Some concepts emerge *before* children have verbal labels to attach to them (R. Brooks & Meltzoff, 2014; Gopnik, 2009b; Halford & Andrews, 2006; Yermolayeva & Rakison, 2014). Furthermore, verbal exchanges may be less important for cognitive development in some cultures than in others. For instance, adults in some rural communities in Guatemala and India place heavy emphasis on gestures and demonstrations, rather than on verbal instructions, to teach and guide children (Rogoff, Mistry, Göncü, & Mosier, 1993).

What kinds of experiences promote development? Piaget maintained that children's independent, self-motivated explorations of the physical world form the basis for many developing schemes, and children often create schemes with little guidance from others.

DEVELOPMENTAL TRENDS

Thinking and Reasoning Skills at Different Age Levels

AGE	WHAT YOU MIGHT OBSERVE	DIVERSITY	IMPLICATIONS
Infancy (Birth–2 Years)	• Exploratory actions in the environment becoming increasingly complex, flexible, and intentional over time • Growing awareness of simple cause-and-effect relationships • Emergence of ability to represent the world mentally (e.g., as revealed in daily conversations and make-believe play)	• Temperamental differences (e.g., the extent to which infants are adventuresome vs. timid) influence exploratory behavior. • In some cultures, adults encourage infants to focus more on people than on the environment, in which case infants are less inclined to explore physical surroundings.	• Set up a safe, age-appropriate environment for exploration. • Provide objects that stimulate the senses with things that babies can look at, listen to, feel, and smell. • Suggest age-appropriate toys and activities that parents can provide at home.
Early Childhood (2–6 Years)	• Rapidly developing language skills • Reasoning that is, by adult standards, illogical • Limited perspective-taking ability • Frequent self-talk • Sociodramatic play • Capacity for learning tangible and mental tools	• Shyness may limit children's willingness to talk with others and engage in sociodramatic play. • Adult-like logic is more common when children have accurate information (e.g., about cause-and-effect relationships). • Children learn to interpret events in culture-specific ways.	• Provide numerous opportunities for children to interact with one another during play. • Introduce children to a variety of real-world situations through picture books and field trips. • Talk with children about their interpretations of events. • Expose children to basic tools, for example, paper and writing utensils, the alphabet, and numerals.
Middle Childhood (6–10 Years)	• Conservation, class inclusion, and other forms of adultlike logic • Limited ability to reason about abstract or hypothetical ideas • Emergence of group games and team sports that involve coordination of multiple perspectives • Ability to participate to some degree in many adult activities	• Development of logical thinking skills is affected by the ubiquity of those skills in a child's culture. • Formal operational reasoning may occasionally appear in simple tasks and in familiar contexts, especially in 9- and 10-year-olds. • Roles for involvement in adult activities vary by culture.	• Use concrete objects to illustrate concepts. • Supplement verbal explanations with concrete examples, pictures, and hands-on activities. • Allow time for organized play activities. • Integrate tools into activities, such as the scientific method in a laboratory assignment and spreadsheets and databases in a mathematical lesson.
Early Adolescence (10–14 Years)	• Increasing ability to reason about abstract ideas • Emerging scientific reasoning (e.g., formulating and testing hypotheses, separating and controlling variables) • Increasing ability to reason about mathematical proportions • Some idealism about political and social issues, often without taking realistic constraints into consideration • Increasing ability to engage in adult tasks	• Adolescents can think more abstractly on topics for which they have considerable knowledge. • Adolescents are more likely to separate and control variables in familiar situations. • Formal operational reasoning skills are affected by their utility in the culture. • Adolescents' idealistic notions may reflect religious, cultural, or socioeconomic backgrounds.	• Present abstract concepts central to academic disciplines, but tie them to concrete examples. • Help students engage in scientific investigations with familiar objects and concepts. • Assign math problems that require use of simple fractions, ratios, or decimals. • While demonstrating how to perform a new task, talk about how to *think* through the steps. • Scaffold challenging assignments with interim steps.
Late Adolescence (14–18 Years)	• Abstract thought and scientific reasoning skills becoming prevalent, especially in familiar topics • Idealistic notions tempered by realistic considerations • Ability to perform many realistic tasks in mature manner • Intensified desire to interact with peers provides a chance to reflect on social groups	• Abstract thinking is more common in some content areas (e.g., mathematics, science) than in others (e.g., history, geography). • Formal operational reasoning skills are less likely to appear in cultures that don't enlist these skills. • Teenagers' proficiency in adult tasks varies considerably from individual to individual and from task to task.	• Study academic disciplines in depth; introduce complex explanations. • Encourage discussions about social, political, and ethical issues; elicit multiple perspectives regarding issues. • Involve adolescents in activities that are similar to tasks they will eventually do as adults. • Provide the minimal guidance adolescents need to complete difficult assignments.

BASIC DEVELOPMENTAL ISSUES
Contrasting Piaget and Vygotsky

ISSUE	PIAGET	VYGOTSKY
Nature and Nurture	Piaget believed that biological maturation probably constrains the rate at which children acquire new thinking capabilities. However, his focus was on how interactions with both the physical environment (e.g., handling concrete objects) and the social environment (e.g., discussing issues with peers) promote cognitive development.	Vygotsky acknowledged that children's inherited traits and talents affect the ways in which they interpret the environment. But his theory primarily addresses the environmental conditions (e.g., engagement in challenging activities, guidance from more competent individuals, exposure to cultural interpretations) that influence cognitive growth.
Universality and Diversity	In Piaget's view, children make similar advancements in their logical reasoning capabilities despite the particular environment in which they grow up. Individual children differ slightly in the ages at which they acquire new abilities.	From Vygotsky's perspective, the specific cognitive abilities that children acquire depend on the cultural contexts in which they are raised and the specific activities in which they are encouraged to participate.
Qualitative and Quantitative Change	Piaget proposed that children's logical reasoning skills progress through four qualitatively distinct stages. Any particular reasoning capability continues to improve in a gradual (quantitative) fashion throughout the stage. The child slowly learns how to generalize a logical skill (e.g., conservation) to a wide range of areas (e.g., volume, weight, and liquid).	Vygotsky acknowledged that children undergo qualitative changes in their thinking. Much of his theory points to gradual and presumably quantitative improvements in skills. At any moment in time, qualitative changes are at work in a particular task, in which a child shifts from inability to mentored performance to independence.

In contrast, Vygotsky argued for activities that are facilitated and interpreted by more competent individuals. The distinction, then, is primarily one of self-exploration versus guided study. Children almost certainly need both kinds of experiences: opportunities to manipulate and experiment with physical phenomena and chances to draw on the wisdom of others (Brainerd, 2003; Karpov & Haywood, 1998; Silcock, 2013).

What kinds of social interactions are most valuable? Both theorists saw value in interacting with people of all ages. However, Piaget emphasized the benefits of interactions with peers (who could create conflict and disequilibrium), whereas Vygotsky placed greater importance on interactions with adults and to some degree older children (who could support performance on challenging tasks and introduce mature interpretations).

Some contemporary theorists have proposed that interactions with peers and adults play different roles in children's cognitive development (Damon, 1984; S. A. Gelman, Ware, Manczak, & Graham, 2013; Hartup, 2009; Rogoff, 1991). When children's development requires that they abandon old perspectives in favor of new, more complex ones (e.g., regarding their understanding of why they must follow classroom rules or the purposes of friendship in a person's life), the conflict that often occurs among age-mates can be optimal for bringing about change. But when children's development instead requires that they learn general knowledge and new skills (e.g., on how to operate a microscope), the thoughtful, patient guidance of an informed adult may be more beneficial.

How influential is culture? Although Piaget acknowledged that separate cultural groups foster different ways of thinking, he gave only modest attention to culture as a factor in development (Chapman, 1988). In Vygotsky's view, culture is of paramount importance in determining thinking skills. Vygotsky was more on target here. Earlier in the chapter we presented evidence to indicate that children's reasoning skills do not necessarily appear at the same ages in different parts of the world. In fact, some reasoning skills (especially those involving formal operational thought) rarely appear unless a child's culture cultivates them.

Teachers and other practitioners must keep in mind, however, that there isn't necessarily a single "best" or "right" way for a culture to promote cognitive development (Rogoff, 2003). Despite diverse instructional practices around the world, at a foundational level virtually all societies have developed strategies for helping children acquire the knowledge and skills they need to be successful participants in their community.

Educational Differences

Divergences between Piaget's and Vygotsky's core ideas are manifested in their respective applications. Piaget believed that educators should honor the direction of children's curiosity and allow them flexibility in exploring the physical world. Vygotsky professed that educators ought to guide children with cultural tools. In Table 6.2, you can see

Table 6.2 Teachers with Piagetian and Vygotskian Perspectives

OPPORTUNITY FOR LEARNING	PIAGETIAN PERSPECTIVE	VYGOTSKIAN PERSPECTIVE
A second-grade class takes a field trip to see hands-on exhibits at an aquarium. As the children walk around exhibits, the teacher recalls her plans for interacting with the children.	Miss Sánchez takes children to the hands-on tide pool, advises them of rules for touching marine life, encourages them to learn about the animals, and listens intently to their conversations. She asks the parent chaperones to enforce safety rules but to otherwise allow children to explore freely. Miss Sánchez endorses Piaget's notion that children learn a great deal based on their own curiosity.	Mr. Avraham reminds the children of the words they recently learned: *camouflage*, *hide*, *enemy*, and *disguise*. He distributes pencils and sheets of paper and asks parent chaperones to encourage children to draw pictures of animals that are camouflaged near sand, rocks, coral, and seaweed. Mr. Avraham accepts Vygotsky's ideas that children learn a lot from cultural tools and educational support from adults.
Five-year-old Berlinda sits at a table completing a puzzle with imprints of pieces. She frowns as she stares at the shapes of outlines in the tray. After a few unsuccessful attempts at inserting pieces, she grows frustrated and tosses puzzle pieces onto the floor. She returns later in the day and inspects the puzzle.	Mr. Moses concludes that Berlinda is motivated to complete puzzles. Over the next few days, he continues to make puzzles available in the classroom. He notices that Berlinda continues to select puzzles during free time and systematically improves in her skill. Mr. Moses applies Piaget's ideas that adults need to be sympathetic observers of children's initiatives and arrange for the experiences children find intriguing.	Ms. de la Cruz shows Berlinda how to start with pieces that have straight edges on the periphery and then fill in other pieces. She then encourages Berlinda to try a few pieces by herself. When Berlinda struggles, Ms. de la Cruz gently directs the girl's attention to a shape in the inlaid outline, and together they search for its match. Ms. de la Cruz applies Vygotsky's ideas that adults should offer judicious help on worthwhile tasks.
A group of 3- and 4-year-old children sit side by side in the sandbox, moving their vehicles this way and that and building tunnels and towers. Elliott says, "I'm going to the rocky quarry." Roz says, "My castle is getting bigger."	Mrs. Dean smiles at the children, interpreting their language as being benignly self-centered, a charming quality that will fade as they move into concrete operations. Mrs. Dean agrees with Piaget's conclusion that children's speech is often egocentric during the preschool years.	Mr. Sidorov interprets the speech of children as externalized thought that helps guide their activities. He shares Vygotsky's view that children gradually emit less audible speech while continuing to talk themselves through difficult tasks.

how teachers firmly committed to either a Piagetian or Vygotskian perspective might respond differently to similar situations.

Which theory do you prefer—and why? Are you like Piaget, inclined to search for universal, stagelike changes across the lifespan, or are you more like Vygotsky, watching for children's increasingly advanced thinking given mentorship and tool use? Whichever way you lean, keep in mind that complementary insights can be gained from *both* perspectives. For example, after focusing on students' ability to form testable hypotheses, an interest of Piaget, you might switch your perspective to how scientific reasoning has been modeled at home and mentored in earlier grades, a concern of Vygotsky.

MyLab Education
Video Example 6.9

Find Developmental Meaning
How might Piagetian and Vygotskian theorists interpret Ms. Swartz's geometry lesson? A Piagetian theorist would infer that folding paper into congruent halves and discussing the concepts with peers would nurture an understanding of triangles. From a Vygotskian perspective, students acquire facility with cognitive tools in geometry through the teacher's instruction and available resources (i.e., paper folding exercise, displays on the board, and records of observations).

Summary

Constructive processes, readiness, challenge, and social interaction are central to the theories of both Piaget and Vygotsky. However, the two perspectives differ in the role of language in cognitive development, the relative value of free exploration versus guided activities, the comparative importance of interactions with peers versus adults, and the influence of culture. The two theories also offer somewhat different educational applications, especially with regard to scaffolding of challenging tasks.

MyLab Education Self-Check 6.3

Practicing For Your Licensure Examination

Many teaching tests require students to use what they have learned about child development in responses to brief vignettes and multiple-choice questions. You can practice for your licensure examination by reading the following case study and answering a series of questions.

Adolescent Scientists

Scott Sowell has just introduced the concept of *pendulum* in his seventh-grade science class. When he asks his students to identify variables that might influence the frequency with which a pendulum swings, they suggest three possibilities: the amount of weight at the bottom, the length of the pendulum, and the "angle" from which the weight is initially dropped.

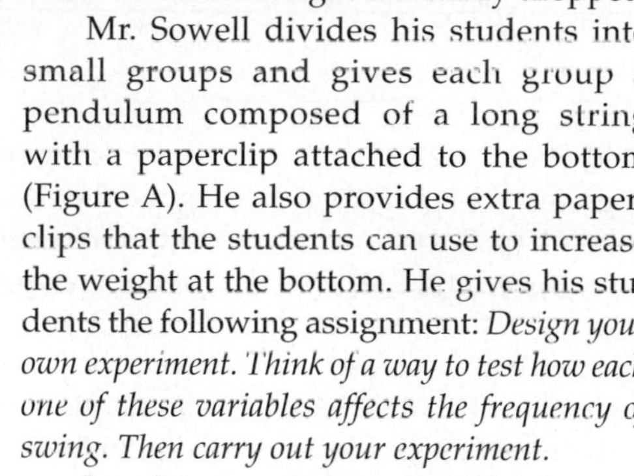

Figure A

Mr. Sowell divides his students into small groups and gives each group a pendulum composed of a long string with a paperclip attached to the bottom (Figure A). He also provides extra paperclips that the students can use to increase the weight at the bottom. He gives his students the following assignment: *Design your own experiment. Think of a way to test how each one of these variables affects the frequency of swing. Then carry out your experiment.*

Jon, Marina, Paige, and Wensley are coming to grips with their task as Mr. Sowell approaches their table.

Marina: We'll time the frequency as the seconds and the . . . um . . . what? [She looks questioningly at Mr. Sowell.]

Mr. S.: The frequency is the number of swings within a certain time limit.

The group agrees to count the number of swings during a 15-second period. After Jon determines the current length of the string, Wensley positions the pendulum 25 degrees from vertical. When Jon says "Go" and starts a stopwatch, Wensley releases the pendulum. Marina counts the number of swings until, 15 seconds later, Jon says "Stop." Jon records the data from the first experiment: length = 49 cm, weight = 1 paper clip, angle = 25°, frequency = 22.

The group shortens the string and adds a second paper clip onto the bottom of the first clip. The students repeat their experiment and record their data: length = 36 cm, weight = 2 paper clips, angle = 45°, frequency = 25.

Wensley: What does the weight do to it?

Marina: We found out that the shorter it is and the heavier it is, the faster it goes.

Mr. Sowell joins the group and reviews its results from the first two tests.

Mr. S.: What did you change between Test 1 and Test 2?

Marina: Number of paper clips.

Mr. S.: OK, so you changed the weight. What else did you change?

Wensley: The length.

Marina: And the angle.

Mr. S.: OK, so you changed all three between the two tests. So what caused the higher frequency?

Wensley: The length.

Marina: No, I think it was the weight.

Jon: I think the weight.

Paige: The length.

Mr. S.: Why can't you look at your data and decide? [The students look at him blankly.] Take a look at the two tests. The first one had one paper clip, and the second had two. The first test had one length, and the second test had a shorter length. Why can't you come to a conclusion by looking at the two frequencies?

Marina: All of the variables changed.

Mr. Sowell nods in agreement and then moves on to another group. The four students decide to change only the weight for the next test, so they add a third paper clip to the bottom of the second. Their pendulum now looks like Figure B. They continue to perform experiments but are careful to change only one variable at a time, or so they think. In reality, each time the group adds another paper clip, the pendulum grows longer. Mr. Sowell visits the students once again.

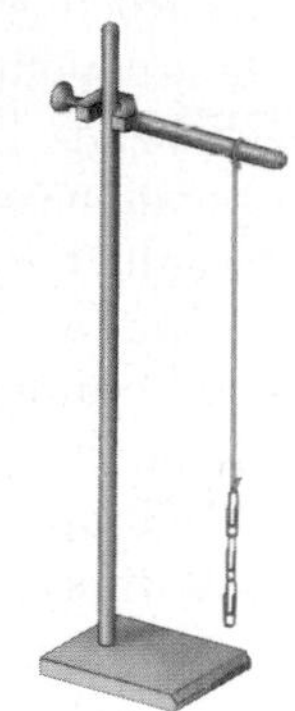

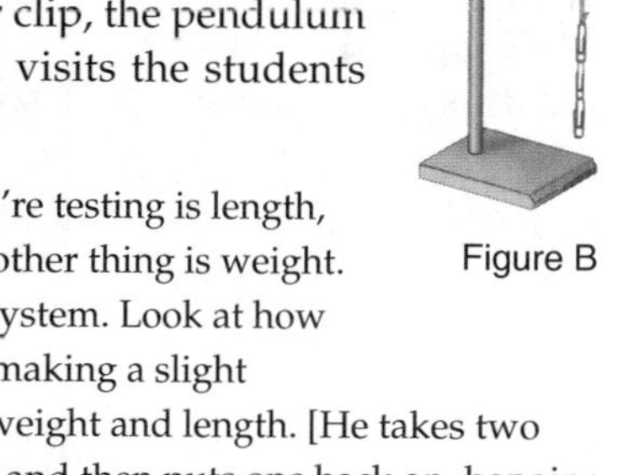

Figure B

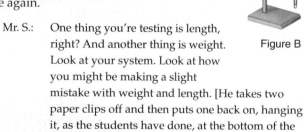

Mr. S.: One thing you're testing is length, right? And another thing is weight. Look at your system. Look at how you might be making a slight mistake with weight and length. [He takes two paper clips off and then puts one back on, hanging it, as the students have done, at the bottom of the first paper clip.]

Marina: It's heavier *and* longer.

Mr. S.: Can you think of a way to redesign your experiments so that you're changing only weight? How can you do things differently so that your pendulum doesn't get longer when you add paper clips?

Jon: Hang the second paper clip from the bottom of the string instead of from the first paper clip.

When Mr. Sowell leaves, the students add another paper clip to the pendulum, making sure that the overall length of the pendulum stays the same. They perform another test and find that the pendulum's frequency is identical to what they obtained in the preceding test. Ignoring what she has just seen, Marina concludes, "So if it's heavier, the frequency is higher."

Constructed-Response Question

1. In what ways does Mr. Sowell scaffold students' efforts during the lab activity?

Multiple-Choice Questions

2. In which one of Piaget's stages is students' reasoning most representative?
   a. The sensorimotor stage, because students are focusing on the sensory properties of objects and using proficient motor skills in manipulating them
   b. The preoperational stage, because students use language proficiently yet do not engage in a systematic analysis of the effects of separate factors
   c. The concrete operations stage, because students are systematic in inspecting the objects but not yet able to separate and control variables in their experimentation
   d. The formal operations stage, because students are displaying the pinnacle of advanced human reasoning

3. Given current perspectives on Piaget's theory, how might a teacher help students to separate and control variables?
   a. Teachers might simply wait a few years until the students mature.
   b. Teachers ought to lecture students on the merits of scientific reasoning.
   c. Teachers could give students practice in pouring liquids to and from containers of various sizes and asking students if the volume remains the same.
   d. Teachers can give students practice in separating and controlling variables, for example, by growing sunflowers under varying conditions or charting their progress in a particular athletic skill with different training regimens.

MyLab Education Licensure Practice. 6.1

Key Concepts

Chapter Seven
Cognitive Development: Cognitive Processes

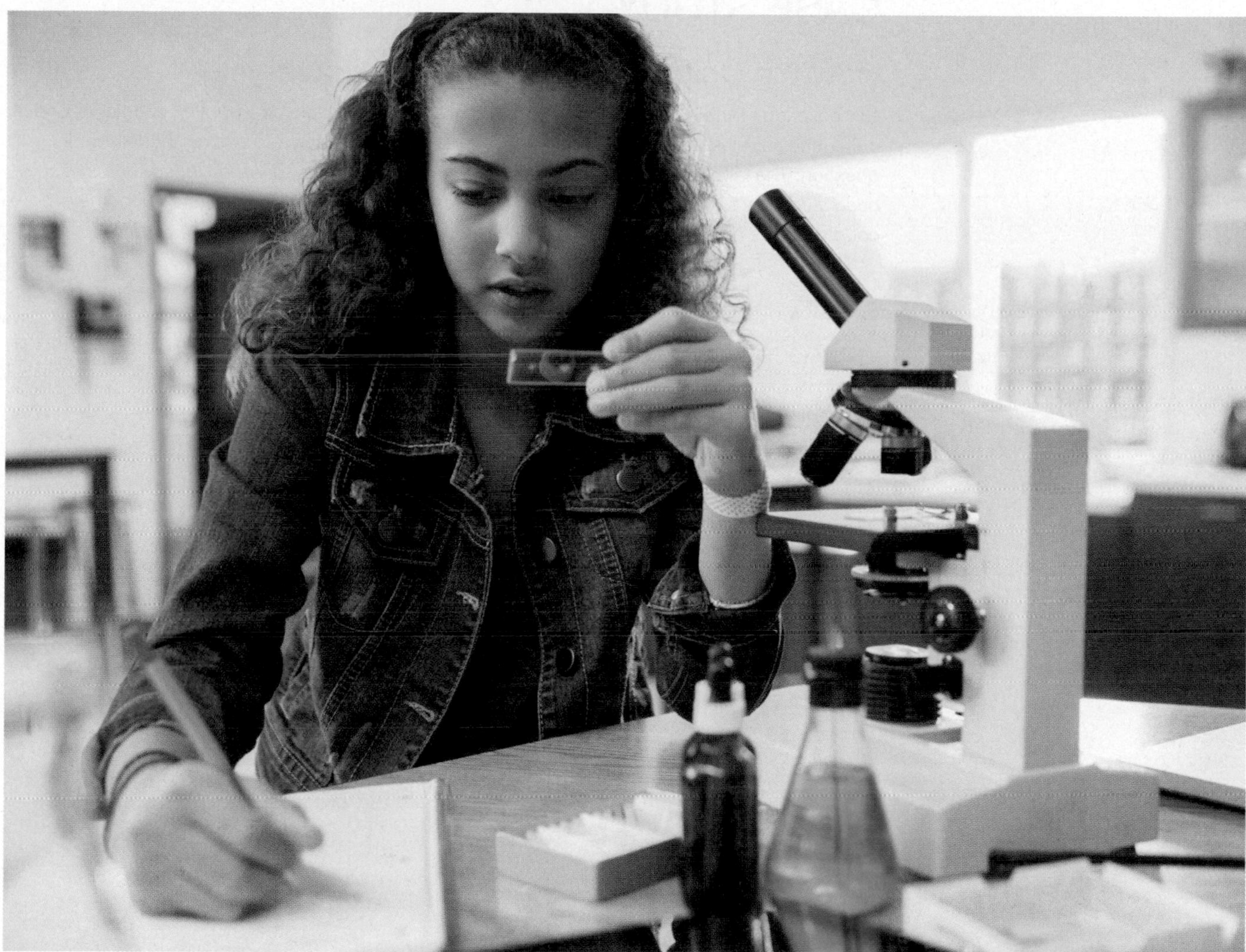

Hero Images/Getty Images

Learning Objectives

7.1 Describe children's basic cognitive processes, their difficulties in regulating attention, and educational approaches that deploy their intellectual resources purposefully.

7.2 Trace the development of children's metacognition and cognitive strategies along with educational methods that facilitate their growth.

7.3 Explain how children construct integrated belief systems about particular topics and what teachers can do to address children's personal theories.

7.4 Synthesize knowledge of children's development using insights from information processing, personal theory construction, and noncognitive human functions.

CASE STUDY

How the United States Became a Country

Our colleague Dinah Jackson worked for many years in the Colorado public schools. At one point, she asked students in Grades 2 through 8 to write essays addressing the following question: *The land we live on has been here for a very long time, but the United States has been a country for only a little more than 200 years. How did the United States become a country?* Here are some of their responses:

Second-grader:

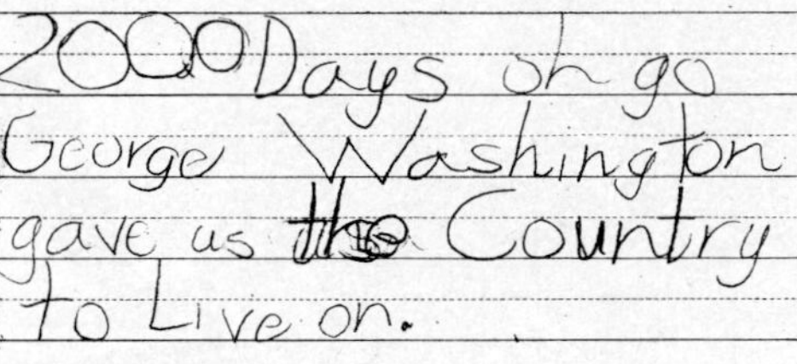

2000 Days ago George Washington gave us the Country to Live on.

Third-grader:

The pilgrims came over in 17 hundred, when they came over they bilt houses. The Idians tihout they were mean. Then they came fraends and tot them stuff. Then winter came and alot died. Then some had babies. So thats how we got here.

Sixth-grader:

The U.S.A. became a country by some of the British wanting to be under a different rule than of the kings. So, they sailed to the "new world" and became a new country. The only problem was that the kings from Britin still ruled the "new world". Then they had the revolutionary war. They bet Britin and became an independent country.

Eighth-grader:

We became a country through different processes. Technology around the world finally caught up with the British. There were boats to travel with, navigating tools, and the hearts of men had a desire to expand. Many men had gone on expeditions across the sea. A very famous journey was that of Christopher Columbus. He discovered this land that we live. More and more people poured in, expecting instant wealth, freedom, and a right to share their opinions. Some immigrants were satisfied, others were displeased. Problems in other countries forced people to move on to this New World, such as potato famins and no freedom of religions. Stories that drifted through people grew about this country. Stories of golden roads and free land coaxed other families who were living in the slums. Unfortunately, there were slums in America. The people helped this country grow in industry, cultures, religions, and government. Inventions and books were now better than the Europeans. Dime-novels were invented, and the young people could read about heroes of this time. May the curiosity and eagerness of the children continue

- What do the four compositions suggest about developmental changes in children's knowledge of written language?
- What do the responses indicate about growth in knowledge about American history?

Certainly, the older children know *more* about the mechanics of writing and American history. But if you look closely at what the children have written, differences in the *quality* of children's writing and knowledge of history are evident as well. Whereas the third-grader describes the nation's history as a list of seemingly unrelated facts, the sixth- and eighth-graders have pulled what they have learned into an integrated whole that hangs together. In addition, the younger children's descriptions reflect concrete understandings (e.g., the country was a gift from George Washington, the Pilgrims came over and built houses). In contrast, the eighth-grader uses abstract concepts (e.g., technological progress, freedom of religion, and optimistic expectations for wealth) to explain immigration to the new land.

In this chapter, our focus is on contemporary research on children's thinking. As you will discover, today's developmental scientists build on the work of Piaget and Vygotsky. Like these prominent figures, present-day theorists assume that children actively make sense of their worlds. In contrast to the methods of developmental pioneers Piaget and Vygotsky, modern theorists use precise research procedures, search for changes in children's knowledge and skills, and document the efficiency of mental processes.

Outline

Basic Cognitive Processes

7.1 Describe children's basic cognitive processes, their difficulties in regulating attention, and educational approaches that deploy their intellectual resources purposefully.

Do children become better able to control their attention as they grow older? Do they remember things more effectively? How does knowledge develop with age? How do changes in the brain enable improvements in learning?

Researchers in cognitive science are intrigued by these questions. **Cognitive science** is an interdisciplinary field that examines how information is represented and processed in the human mind. Especially popular within this field has been **information processing theory**, a family of perspectives that address how humans mentally acquire, interpret, and remember information. The information processing framework emerged in the late 1950s and early 1960s and evolved in the decades that followed. Early information processing theorists drew parallels between how people think and computers operate. As a result, computer terms are sometimes used to describe thought processes, as with people *storing* (i.e., putting) symbolic information in memory and *retrieving* (i.e., finding) it when they need it at a later time. Initial frameworks portrayed these processes in simple ways, for example, as when a child is exposed to a new fact and later recalls it. More recent analyses reveal creativity in thinking. Many contemporary information processing perspectives have a *constructivist* flavor similar to Piaget's and Vygotsky's theories, in which children are credited with creating their own original ideas (Newcombe, 2013). As an example, consider the second-grader's explanation in the opening case study:

> 2000 Days oh go George Washington gave us the Country to Live on.

Almost certainly, no one has told her that the United States was a gift from George Washington. Instead, she uses something she has learned—that Washington was a key figure in the country's early history—to construct what is, to her, a logical explanation of her country's origins. Not knowing how to spell *ago*, she uses two words she does know (*oh* and *go*) to construct a reasonable (albeit incorrect) spelling. Following in the footsteps of Piaget and Vygotsky, cognitive scientists would notice the second-grader's original blend of ideas.

Cognitive science represents a collection of frameworks, rather than a single theory, that together examine the wide range of changes in cognitive development. *Neuroscientists* tell us about the networks of cells that are activated during mental processes. Experts in *artificial intelligence* study computer simulations of human intelligence, such as the processes involved in visual perception, speech recognition, and decision making. *Psychologists* have learned a lot about how the memory system works, for example, how a certain smell might trigger a memory, and they increasingly uncover the influences of emotions and motivation on cognitive processes. *Linguists* have examined the conventions of grammar that govern speech without children's conscious awareness. In this chapter, we pull from these and other fields as we examine three types of abilities: basic cognitive processes, strategic learning procedures, and personal theories.

Preparing for Your Licensure Examination

Your teaching test might ask you to identify key elements of basic cognitive processes.

Key Ideas in Cognitive Process Theories

The information processing framework portrays thinking as an exchange of information with the environment combined with flowing sensations and ideas between and among separate mental storage systems. Figure 7.1 presents the human information processing system, adapted from its original contents with two additions, the conscious oversight of mental processes by a watchful self (the central executive) and the acknowledgement of noncognitive factors that affect thinking. Information processing theorists subscribe to several points:

Input from the environment provides the raw material for learning and remembering. Human beings encounter stimulation through the senses (e.g., by seeing, hearing, or touching) and translate that raw input into more meaningful information. The first part of this process, detecting stimuli in the environment, is *sensation*. The second part, interpreting those stimuli, is *perception*. Even the simplest interpretation of an environmental event takes mental processing. Many theorists believe that human memory includes a mechanism that allows people to remember raw sensory data for a very short time (perhaps 2 to 3 seconds for auditory information and less than a second for visual information). This mechanism goes by a variety of names, but we'll refer to it as the **sensory register**.

In addition to the sensory register, human memory includes two other storage mechanisms: working memory *and long-term memory.* Working memory is that part of the human memory system in which people actively hold and think about information. It is in working memory that children solve a problem or make sense of what they are reading. Working memory can keep information for only a very short time (probably less than a minute), so it is sometimes called *short-term memory*.[1] Working memory appears to have a limited capacity—only a small amount of "space" in which people can hold and think about events or ideas. As an illustration, try computing the following division problem in your head:

59)49,383

Did you find yourself having trouble remembering some parts of the problem while you were dealing with other parts? Did you ever arrive at the correct answer of 837? Most people cannot solve a multistep division problem like this unless they write it on

FIGURE 7.1 The human information processing system.

Model based on the frameworks of R. C. Atkinson and Shiffrin (1968), Baddeley (1981), and Neisser (1976) and updated with recognition of the power of self-regulatory processes and noncognitive factors, including the child's interests, motivation, emotions, and stress reactions.

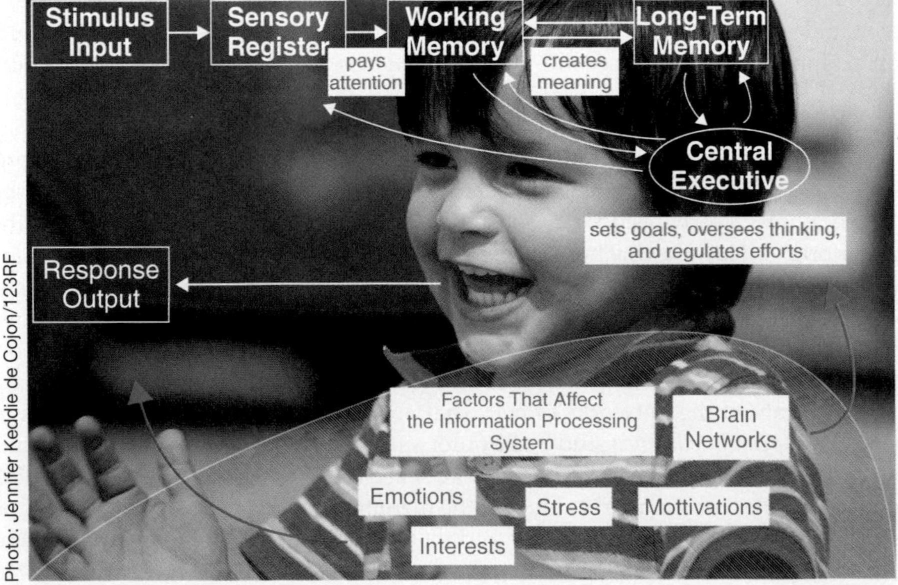

[1]In everyday language, people often use the term short-term memory to refer to memory that lasts for a few days or weeks. Based on the research, information processing theorists characterize working memory as lasting less than a minute.

paper or use a calculator. For most of us, there simply isn't "room" in working memory to hold all the numbers in mind while solving the problem.

Long-term memory is the component of the information processing system that allows human beings to save the things they've learned from experience. It might include such knowledge as where cookies can be found in the kitchen and how much 2 and 2 together equal, as well as such skills as how to ride a bicycle and use a microscope. Things in long-term memory don't necessarily last forever, but they do last for a lengthy period, especially if revisited occasionally. Long-term memory appears to have an unlimited capacity, "holding" as much information as a person could possibly need in the future. To think about information previously stored in long-term memory, people must retrieve and reflect on it in working memory. Although people's capacity to keep information in long-term memory may be boundless, their ability to *think about* what they've stored is limited to whatever they can hold in working memory at any one time.

MyLab Education
Video Example 7.1

Find Developmental Meaning *How does 10-year-old David express his understanding of the effects of attention?* David remembers only 3 of the 12 words that the interviewer reads to him. He attributes his limited recall to a lapse in attention: "My brain was turned off right now."

Attention is essential to the learning process. Information processing theorists suggest that attention is the primary process through which information moves from the sensory register to working memory. When children pay attention to something, such as a teacher's words, it means they are focusing on that stimulus and ignoring other things—children outside on the playground, a classmate sneezing, and colorful pictures on a newly decorated bulletin board. The teacher's explanation cannot move into a child's working memory unless he or she has paid attention to it.

Special cognitive processes are involved in moving information from working memory to long-term memory. Whereas attention is instrumental in moving information from the sensory register to working memory, more complex processes are needed if people are to remember information for longer than a minute or so. Occasionally simply repeating information over and over (*rehearsing* it) is sufficient for its long-term storage. More often, effective storage requires making connections between new information and the ideas that already exist in long-term memory. For instance, people might use their existing knowledge either to *organize* or expand (i.e., *elaborate*) on newly acquired information.

Cognitive development involves gradual changes in, and a few qualitative transformations to, the information processing system. Many information processing theorists reject Piaget's global stages. Instead, they propose that children's cognitive abilities develop primarily as ongoing *trends*. Children slowly but surely develop efficient mental processes. For example, maturation in the brain allows children to keep a larger number of ideas in mind at any given moment. An expanding memory capacity allows children to compare and integrate statements as they listen, consider an additional factor or two in a science experiment, calculate complicated mathematical formulas, and attend to multiple steps in a teacher's instructions. With a larger working memory, children also become better able to notice inconsistencies, synthesize information, and understand complicated verbal information. Qualitative transformations happen when a mental resource (e.g., working memory capacity) expands to such an extent that an entirely new learning strategy becomes possible.

Children learn to control cognitive processes. As children pursue their goals, they must adjust their attention, emotions, and behavior (Schunk & Zimmerman, 2013). Some sort of internal "supervisor" helps to ensure that learning and memory work effectively. This component, sometimes called the **central executive**, oversees the flow of information in the memory system and focuses children on achieving their goals. *Executive functions* refer to deliberate thinking processes that allow for planning, setting priorities, focusing attention, juggling multiple tasks, persisting in the face of distractions, and solving problems when obstacles arise. Seven-year-old Joey practices executive functions as he keeps his eyes on the teacher and resists temptations to pass notes with a friend.

Children's motivations, emotions, and stress affect their intellectual processes. Noncognitive characteristics were not included in the original information processing model yet are increasingly found to influence thinking, attention, and self-control. As teachers know, enthusiasm, indifference, and other states reflecting interest affect learning. A high school girl who is bored in class daydreams about an upcoming concert, absorbing little algebra; a middle school boy who has been ridiculed by a classmate ignores the literacy lesson and instead contemplates how he can retaliate (S. A. Graham, San Juan, & Khu, 2017; Jäggi &

Kliewer, 2016; D. H. Lee & Anderson, 2017). Excessive levels of **stress**, the physiological responses to being worried, tense, and pressured, hinder executive functions. Children who feel anxious due to multiple hardships, perhaps coping with a father moving out of the house, witnessing violence in the community, and being bullied at school, are apt to struggle with concentration (C. Blair, Ursache, Greenberg, Vernon-Feagans, & Family Life Project Investigators, 2015; Blitz, Anderson, & Saastamoinen, 2016; Koziol, Budding, & Hale, 2013; R. Thompson, 2014; Wimmer, Bellingrath, & von Stockhausen, 2016).

The components of the information processing system, and their interactions, change with maturation and experience. In the following sections, we look at their development and that of reasoning skills, a primary method by which children make sense of the world.

Sensation and Perception

The foundations of sensory and perceptual abilities emerge during prenatal development, infancy, and early childhood. Researchers have reached the following conclusions about these developments:

Some sensory and perceptual capabilities are present at birth, and others emerge within the first few months of life. Even newborns can sense and discriminate among different sights, sounds, tastes, and smells (Turati, Gava, Valenza, & Ghirardi, 2013; Winberg, 2005). The ability to perceive—that is, to *interpret*—this sensory information appears quite early as well. For example, newborns have some ability to determine the direction from which a sound originates (Morrongiello, Fenwick, Hillier, & Chance, 1994). At birth, visual acuity is about 20/600, which means that infants can see an image from 20 feet as well as an adult with average eyesight sees at 600 feet. This acuity may not seem very good, but infants can do a great deal with their limited eyesight (Courage & Adams, 1990). When they are only a few days old, they learn to recognize the contours of their mother's face (Colombo, Brez, & Curtindale, 2013; de Heering et al., 2008; T. Field, Woodson, Greenberg, & Cohen, 1982; Werker, Maurer, & Yoshida, 2010). Vision develops rapidly, and by 6 months of age, acuity is close to 20/20 (Sokol, 1978).

From birth or soon afterward, infants are sensitive to the convergence of sensory cues across different modalities (Colombo et al., 2013). Infants prefer to watch videos of a ball bouncing and a face speaking that are synchronized with sounds of the bounce and voice, respectively, over distorted recordings (Colombo et al., 2013; Streri, Coulon, & Guellaï, 2013). In the second half year of life, infants can even tell the difference between dancers who do and do not move in coordination to music (Hannon, Schachner, & Nave-Blodgett, 2017).

Infants show consistent preferences for certain types of stimuli, especially social ones. Within 3 days of birth, they recognize their mother's voice and suck vigorously on a synthetic nipple if doing so turns on a recording of her speaking (DeCasper & Fifer, 1980). In the first month, infants prefer to inspect spatial configurations that look like faces, with large shapes resembling eyes at the top (Werker et al., 2010). This early inclination to focus on social stimuli is advantageous for infants, who must attend to people if they are to acquire interpersonal skills, language, and cultural traditions (Colombo et al., 2013; Lucion et al., 2017).

FIGURE 7.2 Visual cliff.

By refusing to crawl onto the "deep" side of this glass-covered table, infants demonstrate a fear of heights.

Mark Richard/PhotoEditInc.com

Perceptual development is a blend of maturation and experience. We find a clear illustration of the integration of nature and nurture in *depth perception*, the ability to perceive distances between objects in three-dimensional space. To determine when infants acquire depth perception, researchers sometimes use a *visual cliff*, a large glass table with a patterned cloth close beneath the glass on one side and, on the other, the same pattern on the floor, farther from the glass (see Figure 7.2). In a classic study (E. J. Gibson & Walk, 1960), infants age 6 to 14 months were placed on a narrow platform between the "shallow" and "deep" sides of a visual cliff. Mothers stood at one end of the table and actively coaxed their babies to crawl toward them, across the glass. Although most infants willingly crawled off the platform to the "shallow" side, very few ventured onto the "deep" side, suggesting a perception of depth.

The level of maturation largely defines what is possible with depth perception. Visual acuity must be suitably developed to enable infants to perceive edges, inclines, and the relative distances between objects. Animals that walk almost immediately after birth (e.g., chicks, lambs, baby goats) show avoidance of the deep side of a visual cliff within the first days of life (E. J. Gibson & Walk, 1960), suggesting a neurological basis for fear of heights in the animal kingdom. But learning also is involved. Infants who have had experience with self-locomotion, either through crawling or using a walker (a framed seat with wheels attached to the base),[2] show greater fear of drop-offs than infants without this motor experience (Bertenthal, Campos, & Kermoian, 1994; A. Dahl et al., 2013).

The coordination of nature and nurture is also apparent in the perceptual preferences of small children. Genes guide the formation of a child's brain to be receptive to certain kinds of perceptual information, such as faces, voices, and a warm, gentle touch. Experience fine-tunes the brain such that perceptual abilities help the child get along in the world. In this manner, infants look intently at all faces from birth, quickly come to recognize the appearance of beloved caregivers, and gradually distinguish among faces of individuals outside the family (Altvater-Mackensen, Jessen, & Grossmann, 2017; Colombo et al., 2013; Werker et al., 2010).

Attention

As with developments in perception, age-related changes in attention are due, in part, to brain maturation. The brain has three primary attention networks that emerge and interconnect with development (Breckenridge, Braddick, & Atkinson, 2013; Casagrande et al., 2012; Posner, 2004; Posner & Rothbart, 2013):

- An *orienting system* develops in the first year of life and allows children to direct mental energies to interesting objects and events. This system is at work when a child looks at one thing at a time, for example, by visually tracking a cat running after a bird, and then, after seeing the cat take a nap, shifting focus to flowers in the yard.
- An *arousal system* permits children to maintain focused alertness when thinking about something. The arousal system operates when children exhibit increasingly long periods of sustained attention while exploring toys, conversing with others, and listening to explanations.
- The *executive control system*, which takes many years to mature, lets children plan ahead, keep goals in mind, and disregard irrelevant stimuli. This system makes it possible for children to stay focused during a lesson and follow classroom rules.

Preparing for Your Licensure Examination

Your teaching test may ask you about developmental changes in attention.

The maturation of these three attention systems contributes to the following developmental trends.

Children's attention is affected by stimulus characteristics and, later, by familiarity. Like all human beings, infants quickly turn their attention to new, unusual, and intense stimuli—for instance, by orienting to a flash of light, loud noise, or sudden movement. Once children have gained some knowledge about their everyday world, familiarity comes into play. Infants are motivated to examine objects and events that are moderately different, but not too dissimilar, from those they have previously experienced, such as Daddy's face after shaving his beard (J. Atkinson & Braddick, 2013; McCall, Kennedy, & Applebaum, 1977).

MyLab Education
Video Example 7.2

Find Developmental Meaning *How does 16-month-old Corwin demonstrate interest in a new toy?* Notice Corwin's rapt attention as he turns the sphere around and about.

With age, distractibility decreases and sustained attention increases. Children as young as 6 months exhibit focused attention for brief periods when captivated by an object or event (J. Atkinson & Braddick, 2013; J. E. Richards & Turner, 2001). Yet by and large, young children's attention moves quickly from one thing to another

[2]Traditional walkers are now considered unsafe by medical experts (Conners, Veenema, Kavanagh, Ricci, & Callahan, 2002).

(Ruff & Lawson, 1990). As children move through the elementary school years, they become better able to sustain their attention on a particular task despite distractions (Merrill & Conners, 2013; Ruff & Lawson, 1990).

Attention becomes increasingly purposeful. By the time children are 3 or 4 months old, they show an ability to anticipate where a moving object will soon appear and focus their attention accordingly (Haith, Hazan, & Goodman, 1988; Reznick, 2009). In the preschool years, they intentionally attend to information if they want to remember it, and their ability to concentrate improves during the elementary and middle school years (Hagen & Stanovich, 1977; Kar & Srinivasan, 2013; F. C. Lewis, Reeve, Kelly, & Johnson, 2017). Indeed, much of children's learning becomes a function of what they *want* to remember.

MyLab Education
Video Example 7.3

Find Developmental Meaning *What aspects of the interaction between Corwin and his mother suggest joint attention?* Notice that Corwin climbs voluntarily into his mother's lap and they look together at a book that is familiar to them both. Mother pauses occasionally to ask questions, and Corwin readily responds.

Shared attention develops within social relationships. For two people to communicate, they must rely on shared understandings. Each member of the pair has an awareness of what the other person sees, knows, thinks, and feels. Such mutual understanding is first seen in shared attention and is known as **intersubjectivity**. The beginnings of this ability are seen between 2 and 6 months of age, when infants and their caregivers focus on one another through eye contact, exchanges of smiles, and give-and-take in vocalizations (Adamson & McArthur, 1995; Kokkinaki, Vasdekis, Koufaki, & Trevarthen, 2017; Legerstee, 2013).

Sometime around 9 or 10 months of age, intersubjectivity takes the form of **joint attention**. At this point, an infant and caregiver can simultaneously focus on a single object, possibly a book, ball, or puppy, with both individuals monitoring each other's attention and coordinating their behaviors toward the target (Deák, Triesch, Krasno, de Barbaro, & Robledo, 2013; Salley et al., 2016; Trevarthen & Hubley, 1978). Young children gather information about the identity, names, and characteristics of objects during joint attention. When an adult uses an unfamiliar word, a toddler is apt to look at the speaker's face and follow his or her line of vision to an object. In this way, children learn many new object labels (Kwisthout, Vogt, Haselager, & Dijkstra, 2008; Salley, Panneton, & Colombo, 2013).

At age 1, infants engage in **social referencing**, the act of looking at someone else for clues about how to respond to and feel about an object, person, animal, or event (Feinman, 1992; Schmitow & Stenberg, 2013; Stenberg, 2017). Children are most likely to engage in social referencing when they encounter a new and uncertain situation. In one study (Klinnert, 1984), 1- and $1\frac{1}{2}$-year-old infants were shown three new toys to which their mothers had been instructed to respond with a happy, fearful, or neutral expression. Upon seeing each new toy, most infants looked at their mother and chose actions consistent with her response. They typically moved toward the toy if Mom showed pleasure but moved away from it if she showed fear.

MyLab Education
Content Extension 7.1

Read about the role of attention and other cognitive processes in children's social learning.

Working Memory and the Central Executive

Working memory and the central executive are closely connected and jointly responsible for what children pay attention to, how they think about information, and how well they remember things. Three developmental trends in these capacities enable children to handle increasingly complex cognitive tasks.

Processing speed increases. As youngsters move through childhood, they execute cognitive processes more quickly and efficiently (Fry & Hale, 1996; Jarrold, 2017; Kail, McBride-Chang, Ferrer, Cho, & Shu, 2013). Some of the increased speed is because of genetically driven insulation of brain neurons, a developmental progression that allows for faster firing of impulses. Experience is involved as well. By practicing certain mental and physical tasks, children undergo **automatization** of relevant processes. Children learn to perform repeated tasks rapidly and with little or no conscious effort. Once thoughts and actions become automatized, they take up very little "space" in working memory, enabling children to think about other things, including more challenging elements of the task. Consider the benefits of automatizing reading. When children first begin to read, they devote considerable mental effort to identifying the words on a page—for instance, figuring out what the letters *f-r-i-e-n-d* spell—and may recall little about the *meaning* of what they've read. But with increasing exposure to reading materials, word identification becomes automatic, such that children immediately recognize many words. At this point, they can focus their efforts on understanding what they're reading.

The capacity of working memory expands with age. One common way of measuring working memory is to ask people to remember a sequence of unrelated items, perhaps a series of digits or unrelated objects or words. Toddlers remember more items than infants, older children remember more items than younger children and adolescents remember even more. Much of this increase in working memory capacity is due to cognitive processes becoming faster and more efficient (Cowan, 2014). Basic maturational processes in the brain, including insulation around neurons, the withering away of unused neurons, and increased connections among separate regions in the brain, contribute to the speed of processing and maximization of working memory capacity (Downes, Bathelt, & De Haan, 2017; Luna, 2009; Myatchin & Lagae, 2013).

The central executive increasingly takes charge of cognitive processes. Thanks in large part to ongoing maturation of the brain, youngsters gain increasing control of their cognitive processes (Korkman, Lahti-Nuuttila, Laasonen, Kemp, & Holdnack, 2013; Nigg, 2017; Zelazo, Müller, Frye, & Marcovitch, 2003). With such control comes new and improved abilities. Youngsters become better able to plan and direct actions toward certain standards. They also improve in their ability to inhibit inappropriate thoughts and behaviors. And they begin to reflect on their thinking, as we'll see in our discussion of *metacognition* later in the chapter. Self-control of one's thinking takes extended practice, and the central executive is still a "work in progress" until well into adulthood.

Long-Term Memory

Some content in long-term memory is virtually universal. Children around the globe learn that people have two legs but cats and dogs have four. Other understandings depend on unique experiences. In the children's compositions in the opening case study, we see the vantage point of early European colonization rather than one of invasion and resistance, the latter of which might occur with children living in certain Native American communities.

While memory is expanding in its contents, its operations are changing in an age-related manner. The following trends in long-term memory have been documented.

The capacity to remember information in long-term memory appears early and improves with age. Before birth, children have simple abilities to learn and remember experiences. For instance, infants develop some initial taste preferences based on flavors they were exposed to prenatally in the amniotic fluid (as a result of their mother's diet; Mennella, Jagnow, & Beauchamp, 2001). Similarly, encounters with their mother's speech, muffled in the womb, help infants recognize their mother's voice after birth (Kisilevsky et al., 2009; Partanen et al., 2013).

As babies grow, their long-term memory is exercised in new ways. When a ribbon connected to a mobile is tied to a 2-month-old baby's foot, the baby easily learns that kicking makes the mobile move and remembers the connection over a period of several days—even longer if given an occasional reminder (Rovee-Collier, 1999). At 6 months, infants can also recall and imitate actions they saw 24 hours earlier, and their ability to remember the movements increases in the months that follow. By the time children reach their second birthday, they are able to retain a complex sequence of actions for a year or more (P. J. Bauer, DeBoer, & Lukowski, 2007). Such advancements in long-term memory ability occur in part, because of brain maturation (Friedrich & Friederici, 2017; Fujioka, Mourad, & Trainor, 2011; Lavenex & Banta Lavenex, 2013).

Children initially develop memories without conscious awareness and gradually become reflective about what they are learning. Early memories are, by and large, acquired through an *implicit memory* process—infants are not aware that they are learning information, and they cannot, of course, articulate their memories in words (Lloyd & Newcombe, 2009). Implicit memories are evident in infants' responses to parents versus unfamiliar adults, preferences for some foods above others, and selection of a favorite blanket when tired. As they grow, children cannot necessarily recall these memories in any detail. In fact, children typically have little, if any, *conscious* recall of things that happened during their first 2 years—a phenomenon known as **infantile amnesia**. For much of the preschool period, recall of past events continues to be sketchy. Several explanations for infantile amnesia have been offered, including the immaturity of brain structures and the absence of reminders later in life that would trigger recollections from infancy (Lavenex & Banta Lavenex, 2013; Madsen, & Kim, 2016; H. L. Williams & Conway, 2009). The condition of infantile amnesia is slowly overcome as the brain matures and forms memories as images and symbols and connects them up with an emerging sense of self.

Of course, the fact that children cannot recall their earliest experiences does not mean that these memories serve no function in life. On the contrary, first experiences are the foundation for long-term knowledge (Hayne & Simcock, 2009; Madsen & Kim, 2016). Rudimentary bonds with parents teach children about trustworthiness. Regularities in the physical world let children anticipate the texture and properties of water, sand, wood, and plastic. Exposure to language and storybooks entice children to participate in conversation and consume literature. Thus, the early years of life yield images, information, and habits that guide children's behavior and expectations for the future.

Children's awareness of past events improves dramatically when people engage them in discussions about shared experiences (M. L. Howe, Courage, & Rooksby, 2009; Langley, Coffman, & Ornstein, 2017; K. Nelson, 1996b). It appears that talking about events enables children to store memories in a language-based form, making circumstances easier to recall. Initially, parents do most of the work, reminiscing, asking questions, and prompting recall, but by the time children are 3 years old, they are active participants in conversations about the past (Fivush, 2009). By the end of the preschool years, young children can typically give detailed narratives of important events, for example, what they did on their last birthday. These memories converge into an **autobiographical self**, a mental "history" of important events in a person's life. The autobiographical self continues to change with development, adding details during middle childhood and coherence to life events in adolescence (Y. Chen, McAnally, & Reese, 2013; E. Reese et al., 2017). The manner in which adults interpret events for a child depends partly on cultural traditions, as you can read about in the Development in Culture feature "Memory."

Development in Culture

Memory

Across a wide range of circumstances, children develop common memory characteristics, including an increasingly efficient working memory capacity and an expanding knowledge base. Coexisting with these common trends are cultural variations in memory.

Communities immerse children in routines that affect the *content* of their memories. At the kitchen table, on city streets, and in the classroom, children form images and recollections of how institutions operate. Distinct *methods* of remembering are also acquired during familiar exchanges. Children easily learn and remember meaningful patterns in songs, stories, dances, woodcarvings, and games (Gaunt, 2006; Kearins, 1981; Rogoff, 2003). In technologically advanced societies, children are taught to use memory strategies for learning and retrieving abstract information (e.g., state capitals, types of rocks and minerals, and kinds of national governments) (Bjorklund, Dukes, & Brown, 2009). Children may be encouraged to listen for the main point, take notes during lectures, and use memory tricks.

Cultural experiences also influence children's autobiographical memory. As children reminisce with their parents and other adults, they learn customs for sharing life stories (Q. Wang, 2013). Children who are regularly asked to talk about personal experiences are apt to recall early memories. The Māori, an indigenous people of New Zealand, speak in great detail with children about such significant experiences as the occasion of their birth (E. Reese, Hayne, & MacDonald, 2008). Children cannot recall their own births but these discussions prompt Maori children to conjure up past events. The earliest memories of Māori adults date back to $2\frac{1}{2}$ years on average whereas other cultures exhibit later ages for first memories—typically at about $3\frac{1}{2}$ to 4 years (E. Reese et al., 2008).

The focus of adults' questions affects the content of children's memories. Many mothers in European American families prompt children with questions about how events unfolded, why people acted as they did , and what emotions they seemed to feel at the time (Fivush, 2009; M. L. Howe, Courage, & Rooksby, 2009; Q. Wang, 2009).

Parents in several other cultures do not request details about their feelings and motivations and instead concentrate on other features of events. Many parents from Chinese families regularly ask their children to think about moral lessons and shared experiences with family members (Fivush, 2009; M. L. Howe et al., 2009; Q. Wang, 2006). For example, they ask children to think through why they were restricted from certain things, such as watching television, and punished for others, such as taking cookies from the jar without permission.

In large part by talking with parents about past experiences, young children create a personal history. These conversations convey all sorts of cultural principles, such as the value of accomplishments or moral codes. Generally, parents who ask young children to elaborate on past experiences foster the ability to narrate aspects of life experiences that are meaningful in their society (Fivush, 2009; Salmon & Reese, 2016).

Conversations about shared events are apt to occur during periods of mutual focus, as when parents sit down and play with their children, toss a ball back and forth, or prepare a meal together. Preliminary evidence in Israel indicates that professional caregivers can play a role in children's development of an autobiographical self (Aviezer, Sher-Censor, & Stein-Lahad, 2017). During relaxed routines, such as meals or rest time, teachers and caregivers might occasionally ask about memories that are significant to children. In addition, teachers can recognize children's early experiences in assignments, for example, with a social studies lesson to write an autobiography or prepare a photographic essay on hobbies or milestones in life.

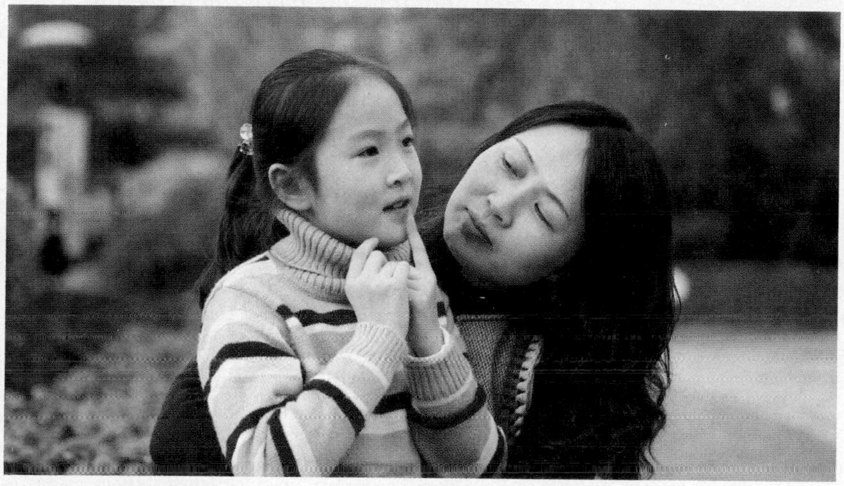

Mamahoohooba/Fotolia

DO YOU REMEMBER WHEN . . . ? As this girl talks with her mother about an event they experienced together, she strengthens images of events in her childhood.

The amount of knowledge stored in long-term memory increases many times over. This trend is an expected one, and the four essays in the opening case study illustrate it clearly. Yet the obviousness of children becoming better informed does not diminish the significance of this development. Long-term memory provides the **knowledge base** from which children draw as they respond to new situations. As their awareness of facts, beliefs, customs, and experiences grows, children interpret new events with greater accuracy, sophistication, and maturity. A deeper knowledge base thus allows for increasing efficiency in learning new information. Artifact Example 7.1 allows you to compare the maps that three children drew of their hometown. An inspection of these maps reveals age-related advancements in knowledge about the community (Forbes, Ormrod, Bernardi, Taylor, & Jackson, 1999; Liben, 2009).

On average, older children learn new information and skills more easily than do younger children. A key reason is that older children have more knowledge that they can use to make sense of new information (Kail, 1990). When the tables are turned—when young children know more about a particular topic than older children or adults do—the younger ones are often the more effective learners (Chi, 1978; Löffler, von der Linden, & Schneider, 2016; H. Waters & Waters, 2010). In one classic study, elementary and middle school children who were expert chess players better remembered where chess pieces were located on a chess board than did college-educated adults who were relative novices at chess (Chi, 1978).

Children's realizations about the world become better integrated. Children begin categorizing their experiences as early as 3 or 4 months of age (more about this point

First Grader

Third Grader

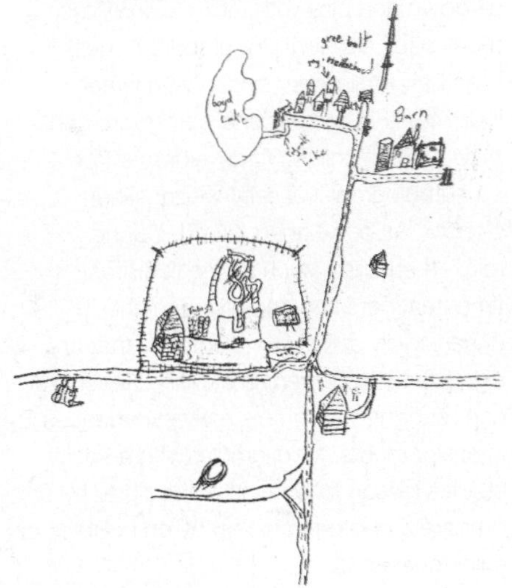

Seventh Grader

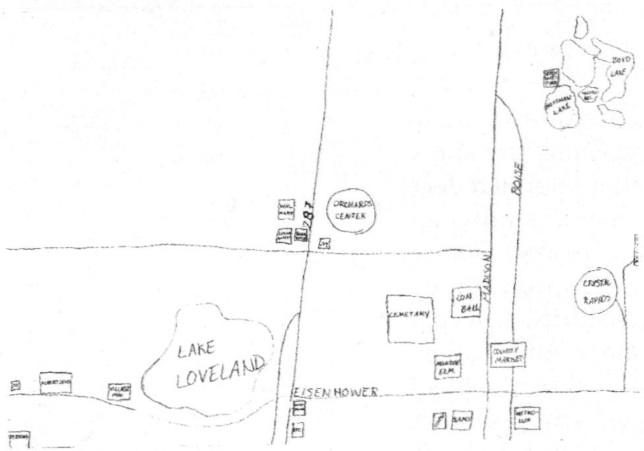

MyLab Education
Artifact Example 7.1

Find Developmental Meaning *How do these maps reflect a developmental progression in knowledge of the shared hometown of Loveland, Colorado?* The first-grader's map (top) includes only a few features that she knows well (her house and school, nearby mountains). The third-grader's map (middle) shows several characteristics of his neighborhood and their proximity to one another. The seventh-grader's map (bottom) encompasses town landmarks and their relative locations on major streets and makes greater use of symbols—single lines for roads, squares for buildings, and distinctive letter *M*s that indicate McDonald's restaurants.

later). Even so, much of what young children know about the world consists of separate facts that other people have told them or they have figured out with curiosity, exploration, and simple observations (C. M. Walker, Lombrozo, Williams, Rafferty, & Gopnik, 2017). In contrast, older children's knowledge includes many associations between and among perceptions and ideas (Bjorklund, 1987; Darling, Parker, Goodall, Havelka, & Allen, 2014; M. Schneider & Hardy, 2013; M. C. Wimmer & Howe, 2009). This developmental change is undoubtedly a reason why older children can think more logically and draw inferences more readily: They have a more cohesive understanding of the world around them.

As an example, let's return to the essays in the opening case study. Notice how the third-grader presents a chronological list of events without any attempt at tying them together:

> *The Idiuns thout they were mean. Then they came friends, and tot them stuff. Then winter came, and alot died. Then some had babies.*

In contrast, the eighth-grader identifies and implies cause-and-effect relationships among events:

> *More and more people poured in, expecting instant wealth, freedom, and a right to share their opinions. Some immigrants were satisfied, others were displeased. Problems in other countries forced people to move on to this New World, such as potato famins and no freedom of religions. Stories that drifted through people grew about this country. Stories of golden roads and free land coaxed other families who were living in the slums.*

Children organize elements of their experience into knowledge structures called schemas and scripts. **Schemas** are tightly integrated ideas about specific objects or situations.[3] You might have a schema for what a typical horse looks like (e.g., it's a certain height, and it has a mane and an elongated head) and another schema for what a typical office contains (it probably has a desk, computer, and bookshelves). **Scripts** encompass knowledge about the predictable sequence of events related to particular activities. You may have a script related to how weddings typically proceed, and even many 3-year-olds can tell you what usually happens when they go to McDonald's for a meal (K. Nelson, 1997). Schemas and scripts help children make sense of experience and anticipate future events (Zampini, Suttora, D'Odorico, & Zanchi, 2013). Templates for negative behaviors are acquired as well, such as when a child sees his mother regularly become intoxicated and belligerent with others (Huesmann et al., 2017).

[3] From an information processing perspective, schemas are similar, but not identical, to Piaget's schemes. From an information processing perspective, schemas are organized mental representations of a phenomenon. In Piaget's theory, a scheme is an organized group of similar actions or thoughts that are used repeatedly in response to something in the environment.

Schemas and scripts change with development (Flavell, Miller, & Miller, 2002; Hudson & Mayhew, 2009). To begin with, these representations are pre-verbal. Toddlers can act out typical scenarios (scripts) with toys long before they are able to describe what they are doing (P. J. Bauer & Dow, 1994). As children get older, their mental structures are less tied to physical actions and perceptual qualities and become more detailed, organized, and flexible as representations (M. Schwartz & Shaul, 2013). Whereas a boy in preschool has a simple script for ordering and eating at a fast-food restaurant, when he enters kindergarten, he expands his script to include a drive-through option, variations in routines at different restaurants, and a few other steps, including paying the bill and getting napkins ahead of time and using the restroom afterward.

Preparing for Your Licensure Examination

Your teaching test may ask you how children use organized networks of ideas to represent their knowledge.

Reasoning

From an information processing perspective, many developmental changes occur in **reasoning**, the ability to think logically and weigh evidence soundly when drawing conclusions. Here we look at three trends in children's analysis of information.

Logical thinking improves with age. The initial manifestations of logical thinking appear in infancy and are related to perceptions of physical events. Long before their first birthday children can perceive a cause-and-effect relationship in a sequence of events. When 6-month-olds see one object hit another and watch the second object move immediately at impact, they seem to understand that the first object has essentially "launched" the second one (L. B. Cohen & Cashon, 2006; Schlottmann, Ray, & Surian, 2012).

By preschool age, children can draw logical inferences from verbal information. For instance, they draw conclusions about events depicted in children's stories (M. Donaldson, 1978; R. Gelman & Baillargeon, 1983; McKie, Butty, & Green, 2012). However, preschoolers and elementary school children do not always draw *correct* inferences, and they have difficulty distinguishing between what *must* be true versus what *might* be true given the evidence before them (Galotti, Komatsu, & Voelz, 1997; Pillow, 2002). Reasoning ability varies widely from one young person to another, and it is often influenced by the circumstances of the situation as well as by personal motives, beliefs, and biases (Goswami, 2011; Kail, 2013; Kuhn & Franklin, 2006; Steegen & De Neys, 2012).

Toward the end of infancy, symbols are incorporated into reasoning. In Piaget's influential theory of cognitive development, the content of infants' schemes is primarily sensorimotor—that is, based on perceptions and behaviors. Near the end of the sensorimotor stage (at about 18 months, Piaget suggested), children begin to think in terms of **symbols**, mental entities (e.g., words) that do not strictly reflect the perceptual and behavioral qualities of the objects or events they represent (e.g., a "ball" is called by different names in different languages). Such symbolic thought enables children to infer characteristics they haven't directly observed. When a 3-year-old who is familiar with common household pets hears her father use the word *cat*, she might easily visualize a small animal that has pointy ears and whiskers, walks on four legs, and purrs.

Piaget was probably correct in stating that sensorimotor images of objects and events precede symbolic representations. In fact, the shift from one to the other is quite gradual. A great deal of learning occurs before children are able to use symbols. Infants notice all sorts of regularities in the world before they can put observations into words. Infants detect regularities in the probabilities of certain events (e.g., if shown a box full mainly with red ping-pong balls and just a couple of white balls, 6- to 12-month-old infants appear surprised and look longer when an adult extracts mostly white balls; F. Xu & Kushnir, 2013). Little by little, children become conscious of their observations. Long before children reach school age, they begin to use such symbols as words, numbers, pictures, and miniature models to represent real-life objects and events (DeLoache, 2011; K. Nelson, 1996a; Tsubota & Chen, 2012). Yet when children begin elementary school, they struggle with some of the symbols they encounter. For example, elementary school teachers often use blocks and other concrete objects to represent numbers or mathematical operations, but not all kindergartners and first-graders make the connection between these objects and the intended concepts (DeLoache, Miller, & Rosengren, 1997). As children grow older, they use symbols to think, remember, and solve problems more frequently and with greater expertise. Eventually, their symbolic abilities allow them to transcend everyday realities, think about what could or should happen in the future, and develop abstract understandings about their physical and social worlds (Bandura, 2006; Kuhn, 2009; Vallotton & Ayoub, 2010).

Gestures sometimes foreshadow advancements in reasoning. As children make the transition to more mature forms of reasoning—for example, on traditional Piagetian tasks or mathematical problems—they often show reasoning in their gestures before they show it in their speech (Cooperrider & Goldin-Meadow, 2017; Goldin-Meadow, 2006; Pine, Lufkin, Kirk, & Messer, 2007). Gestures provide a way for children to "experiment" (cognitively) with new ideas. Gestures may also alleviate the strain on working memory as children wrestle with more complex ways of thinking (Goldin-Meadow, 2006; G. O'Neill & Miller, 2013).

Facilitating Basic Cognitive Processes

There is a great deal that teachers and other practitioners can do to foster and accommodate children's mental resources. Our discussion of information processing theories leads to several implications:

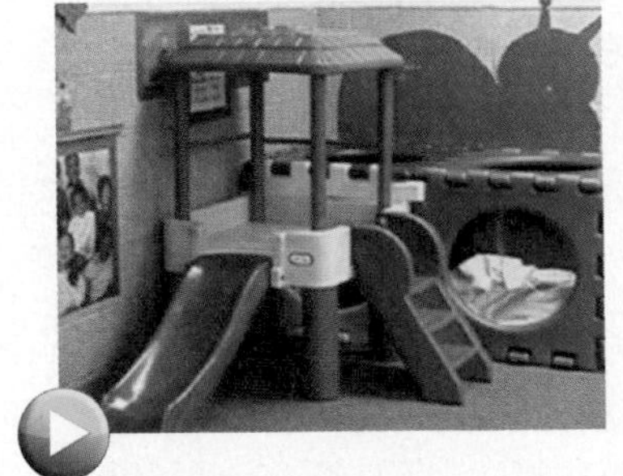

MyLab Education
Video Example 7.4

Find Developmental Meaning *How does this setting encourage exploration of stimulating objects?* The classroom allows babies to pull down interesting toys from accessible shelves. Mirrors encourage self-inspections while enjoying tummy time. Attractive decals give sitting infants shapes and colors to scan. Infants can listen to stories and relax in the arms of adults in rocking chairs. Soft ramps, cushions, and standing toys encourage crawling, tumbling, and stretching tall to see vistas from up high. Mobiles in cribs provide visual stimulation, and stacking toys challenge infants to place rings in order of size.

- **Provide a variety of sensory experiences for infants and young children.** In the first years of life, children learn many things about the world through direct contact—by looking, listening, feeling, tasting, smelling, and sensing the convergence of sensory cues. Experiences required for perceptual development are *not* those that involve intense, nonstop stimulation. Instead, needed arrangements are ones that children encounter in any reasonably nurturing setting—everyday contact with the expressive faces and voices of caregivers, a loving touch, a warm bath, cheerful music, and a variety of objects—maybe toys, boxes, and pots and pans from the kitchen. Thus, adults can offer an interesting environment but should not overdo it. The Development-Enhancing Education feature "Providing Appropriate Stimulation for Infants and Young Children" offers several suggestions for structuring materials and settings for small children.

- **Regularly engage infants in social exchange.** In infants' early months, social interaction may involve the caregiver making eye contact, smiling and vocalizing, extending a finger to be grabbed, and shifting the infant's position when distressed. Later it includes jointly looking at, manipulating, experimenting with, and talking about objects. Such activities, simple though they may be, foster the shared attention that is vital for language and social-emotional development. (Hobson, 2004; K. Nelson, 2005; Øberg, Blanchard, & Obstfelder, 2014; R. A. Thompson & Virmani, 2010).

- **Watch for and address problems with perception.** By the time they enter preschool, most, but not all, children will have been previously screened by a pediatrician or nurse for delays in seeing and hearing or unusual sensitivities to tastes, smells, sights, or tactile sensations (Council on Early Childhood, & Council on School Health, 2016; Rine & Wiener-Vacher, 2013; Turnbull, Turnbull, & Wehmeyer, 2010). Yet not every child with a perceptual impairment will have been identified, and teachers who suspect a limitation will want to reach out to specialists at the school about possible assessments for identifying needs for intervention. Educators themselves can do a lot for children who have been identified as having sensory and perceptual limitations. A teacher might relocate a girl who complains about the noises of a fan to a quieter part of the classroom. A school psychologist might refer a boy with delayed language to an audiologist. A special education teacher might ask a girl with tactile sensitivities if she can tolerate messy hands during a cooking lesson.

Development-Enhancing Education

Providing Appropriate Stimulation for Infants and Young Children

Give children choice in sensory experiences.

- A home caregiver offers a variety of simple toys for infants to explore. She places several items within reach and respects infants' occasional rejection of one thing or another. (Infancy)
- A preschool teacher makes available sensory materials that children observe, touch, smell, and handle. The teacher includes jars that contain various scents (e.g., herbs, vanilla, and orange slices), boxes with small objects (e.g., rice, beans, and coarse salt) for shaking, and a water table with plastic funnels, cups, and pouring toys. (Early Childhood)

Allow children periods of calm.

- A teacher in an infant center realizes that his room is busy and noisy. Knowing that too much stimulation can be unsettling, he monitors the sights, sounds, textures, and smells that are present at any one time. He tones down the environment a bit when introducing a new child to the center and during afternoon naptime. (Infancy)
- A preschool teacher includes a brief rest period after snack time to allow children to recharge their batteries. Children who need to sleep lie down on mats, while non-nappers complete puzzles or participate in other quiet activities. (Early Childhood)

Avoid the "better baby" trap.

- A child-care provider attends a workshop on brain development, where several presenters make a pitch for products that are supposedly conducive to superior intellectual growth. Fortunately, she realizes that children benefit from a wide variety of toys and that an intensive "sensory stimulation" approach is *not* in children's best interest. She warns parents of the disadvantages of putting too much pressure on children to acquire academic skills. (Infancy)
- A toddler teacher designs his curriculum carefully, exposing children to a wide range of developmentally appropriate objects, including blocks, dolls, trucks, durable books, and coloring materials. When parents ask about his plans to "multiply the intelligence" of children, he explains that he cultivates their intelligence through a carefully selected curriculum that fosters curiosity and a budding sense of self, language development, and knowledge of the world. (Infancy)

Recognize that a child's temperament and cultural experiences help determine the optimal level of stimulation.

- A teacher in a child-care center has noticed that a few of the toddlers in her group respond to sensory overload by getting excited and animated, whereas others fuss, go to sleep, or in some other way indicate that they have had enough. Although she prefers a quiet, peaceful room, one of her coworkers enjoys lively salsa music and often plays it while the children are awake. The two teachers compare notes about how children respond to quiet versus busy environments. (Infancy)
- A kindergarten teacher observes that children vary in how they respond to discussions during story time. Some children are animated and spontaneous in their comments, whereas others remain quiet. The teacher realizes that the silent children may have learned customs at home for showing respect to adults. The teacher makes a point to ask non-vocal children about their thoughts at the end of the lesson. (Early Childhood)

- **Talk with young children about their experiences.** Children begin to talk about their experiences almost as soon as they speak, and by age 2 they do it fairly often (van den Broek, Bauer, & Bourg, 1997). Caregivers can join in: Talking with children about shared experiences enhances children's memories of what they are seeing and doing and helps children interpret their experiences in culturally meaningful ways (Fivush, 2009; Ota & Austin, 2013). Educators can invite older children to talk about instances in which they felt different from other people, had a turning point in their lives, or felt a conviction to make a change in their health, friendships, or career direction.

- **Highlight important information for children.** As we've seen, attention is a critical factor in learning. Yet many children, young ones especially, are easily distracted by extraneous sights and sounds. Even highly motivated high school students can't keep their minds on a single task indefinitely. Several strategies for helping children focus their attention are presented in the Development-Enhancing Education feature "Getting and Keeping Children's Attention."

Development-Enhancing Education

Getting and Keeping Children's Attention

Capture children's interest with bright colors, intriguing sounds, and objects that invite exploration.

- A music teacher provides several instruments (e.g., a xylophone, toy guitar, and set of drums) for children to explore. The teacher also allows the children to take turns playing on a piano keyboard. (Middle Childhood)
- A fourth-grade teacher takes his class on a trip to a local pond to create small biospheres. Children fill their jars with water, mud, and algae. During the following weeks, the children observe changes in the color of water, growth of plants, and appearance of snails. (Middle Childhood)

Minimize loud noises and other distractions when working with children who are easily diverted from task completion.

- A school psychologist is administering a battery of tests to an easily distracted 7-year-old boy suspected of having a learning disability. Before the testing session, the psychologist puts away the Russian nesting dolls that decorate her office shelves. She also removes the testing materials, putting items in front of the boy only when it is time to use them. (Middle Childhood)
- When administering a test at the end of a term, a high school mathematics teacher closes the classroom door, answers questions individually in a hushed voice, and reminds students to remain quiet while waiting for others to finish. (Late Adolescence)

Present stimulating activities in which students *want* to pay attention.

- In a unit on nutrition, a high school biology teacher has students determine the nutritional value of menu items at a popular local fast-food restaurant. (Late Adolescence)
- In a photo-editing class, high school students are excited to be asked to help with the yearbook. Students design page spreads, crop photos, and apply special effects on images. (Late Adolescence)

Get students physically involved in lessons.

- A middle school history teacher plans a special event late in the school year when students will "go back in time" to the American Civil War. In preparation for the occasion, the students spend several weeks learning about the Battle of Gettysburg, researching typical dress and meals of that era, gathering appropriate clothing and equipment, and preparing snacks and lunches. On the day of the "battle," students assume the roles of Union and Confederate soldiers, government officials, merchants, housewives, and doctors and nurses. (Early Adolescence)
- In an earth science class, students go outside to examine the relationships among ecological systems: a hydrosphere (e.g., pond), a biosphere (e.g., tree), and a geosphere (e.g., floodplain). The teacher gives students a worksheet and asks them to draw the different systems and speculate about their interdependencies. (Late Adolescence)

Incorporate a variety of activities into the schedule.

- After explaining how to calculate the area of a square and rectangle, a fourth-grade teacher has her students calculate area in word problems. She then breaks the class into groups. Each group is given a tape measure and calculator and asked to determine the area of the classroom floor, excluding those parts of the floor covered by cabinets. To complete the task, the students must divide the room into several smaller rectangles, compute the area of each rectangle separately, and add the figures together. (Middle Childhood)
- In a high school drama class, a teacher introduces students to forms of comedy. Students watch and critique a brief recording of a stand-up comedian and then read a couple of pages from a comedic play. Students end the lesson by forming teams and performing brief improvisational skits about awkward high school moments. (Late Adolescence)

Provide breaks during sedentary activities.

- To provide practice with the alphabet, a kindergarten teacher occasionally has students make letters with their bodies: one child standing with arms extended up and out to make a *Y*, two children bending over and joining hands to form an *M*, and so on. (Early Childhood)
- After a class discussion about a book they are reading together, a middle school literacy teacher allows students to move quietly around the room as they plan the key ideas that they will elaborate on in written reports. (Early Adolescence)

- **Relate new concepts to what children already know.** People of all ages learn information more effectively when they can relate it to what they already know. Yet children don't always make meaningful connections on their own. For instance, they may not realize that subtraction is simply the reverse of addition or that Shakespeare's *Romeo and Juliet* is in some ways similar to modern-day ethnic clashes. By pointing out such connections, adults can foster an integrated knowledge base (Ormrod, 2014; K. L. Roberts, 2013; Vosniadou, 2009).

- **Give children practice with basic skills.** Some skills are so fundamental that children must learn to execute them with little effort. To write well, children should be able to form letters and words without having to stop and think about how to make an uppercase *G* or spell the word *friend*. And to solve mathematical word problems, they should have such number facts as "2 + 4 = 6" and "5 × 9 = 45" on the tips of their tongues. Typically, children automatize basic skills by using or practicing them (J. C. Anderson, 1983; Ruitenberg, Abrahamse, & Verwey, 2013; W. Schneider & Shiffrin, 1977). This is definitely *not* to say that teachers should fill each day with endless drill and practice. Automatization can occur just as readily when the basics are embedded in interesting activities—counting crops in the school garden, calculating profits in the school snack bar, or writing birthday wishes to the parent of a classmate who is deployed abroad on military assignment.

- **Adjust to limitations in working memory.** Although it might be tempting to train working memory, interventions that do so do not typically improve academic achievement (Sala & Gobet, 2017). Rather than try to increase working memory itself, teachers may find it more effective to help children make the most of their concentration, for example, by pacing instructions slowly. Educators might also write down complex directions on a chalkboard or ask children to write them on paper or mobile devices. Because individual differences in working memory capacity are sizable, it behooves teachers to monitor everyone's comprehension of steps in complex tasks (Cowan, 2014). Teachers who determine that students cannot achieve a complicated objective because of low working memory can provide calculators or audio recordings of a written passage, give practice ahead of time, or assign another task in which higher order learning objectives are possible with fewer demands on basic skills.

- **Don't sway children's answers when it's important to obtain their accurate recollections.** Because young children are impressionable, what adults say to them can influence their memories. Imagine that a man identified as "Sam Stone" briefly visits a preschool classroom. He comments on the story the teacher is reading to the children, strolls around the perimeter of the room, waves good-bye, and leaves. Later another adult asks, "When Sam Stone got that bear dirty, did he do it on purpose or was it an accident?" and "Was Sam Stone happy or sad that he got the bear dirty?" When asked such questions, children may recall that Sam soiled a teddy bear, even though he had never touched a stuffed animal during his visit (Leichtman & Ceci, 1995, p. 571). Susceptibility to leading questions is more common in 3- and 4-year-olds than in 5- and 6-year-olds.

As you might expect, police officers and attorneys working with young children thought to be victims or witnesses of a crime must try not to bias recollections. Rather than asking pointed questions about who did what, professionals are advised to follow strict protocols, for example, by first establishing rapport and then asking children to tell them what happened (J. Anderson et al., 2010). Teachers can show restraint when talking with young children about injuries on the playground—not jumping to conclusions and instead talking with students and asking general questions before specific follow-up questions.

- **When assessing what children are ready to learn, consider not only what they say but how they act and what they create.** Imagine a 6-year-old says that a tall, thin glass has more water than a short, wide dish because of the height difference between the two containers. At the same time, she gestures that the tall container has a smaller diameter than the short one. Such discrepancies in what children say and do suggest preparation for growth—for instance, a readiness for acquiring conservation of liquid (Goldin-Meadow, 1997; Goldin-Meadow, Shield, Lenzen, Herzig, & Padden, 2012). In some instances, adults might assess children's current knowledge by asking them to draw rather than describe what they have learned. As you can see in Artifact Example 7.2, 8-year-old Noah understands sequences in plant germination and growth.

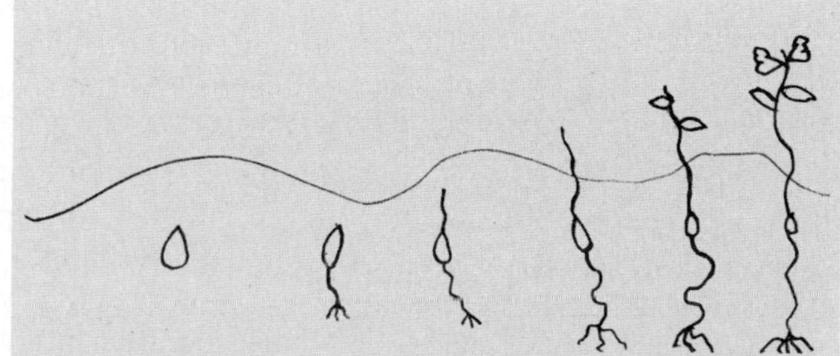

MyLab Education
Artifact Example 7.2

Find Developmental Meaning *What does eight-year-old Noah understand about plant growth?* Noah draws a seed becoming a plant. His picture reveals understandings that roots typically go down before a stalk grows up and that leaves gradually increase in size and number.

- **Use classroom tests to solidify children's learning.** Considerable research indicates that taking tests can help children remember material (Agarwal, Finley, Rose, & Roediger, 2017; Roediger, McDermott, & McDaniel, 2011). The act of retrieving information makes it more likely that children will recall it in the future and apply it to new situations. Although it can be time-intensive for teachers to develop and grade tests, there are simple things teachers can do, for example, asking students clear-cut questions and using a computer program that has assessments at the end of each lesson (J. Jia et al., 2013). Because self-testing also improves memory, students may be shown how to ask themselves pertinent questions while studying (M. Smith, Roediger, & Karpicke, 2013).

- **Tailor the difficulty of lessons to knowledge levels.** Adapting instruction to children's understandings is one of the most important accommodations a teacher can make. This does not mean that a teacher provides a different lesson for each child; instead, he or she can use a combination of whole-group instruction, small-group work, peer tutoring, individual instruction, guidance from special educators, or other adaptations (de Neve & Devos, 2017; Duquette, 2016).

MyLab Education Application Exercise 7.1
Meet Individual Needs

In this video a fifth-grade teacher, Amy De La Riva, uses customized assignments to address variations in students' knowledge of polygons and tessellations.

Exceptionalities in Information Processing

Every child learns in his or her own way. Yet the information processing capabilities of some children are sufficiently different from those of peers that they require specially adapted instructional practices and materials. Here we consider two kinds of exceptionalities in information processing: learning disabilities and attention-deficit hyperactivity disorder.

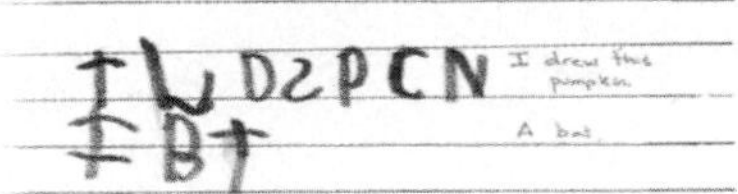

MyLab Education
Artifact Example 7.3

Find Developmental Meaning A few days before Halloween, Nathan, age 7, created the writing sample shown here. His first-grade teacher recorded what he intended to say: "I drew this pumpkin" and "A bat." Nathan correctly captured some of the sounds he was trying to spell: the *d* in *drew*, the *s* in *this*, and the *b* and *t* in *bat*. He omitted several other consonants and all vowel sounds except the initial *I*. It is possible that Nathan has difficulty hearing sounds in spoken words and matching them with letters, however, one writing sample is not definitive evidence of this disability.

Learning Disabilities

A **learning disability** is a significant ongoing difficulty with one or more cognitive processes that cannot be attributed to a sensory impairment, general intellectual disability, emotional or behavioral disorder, or lack of instruction. This difficulty interferes with academic achievement to such a degree that special educational services are warranted (E. K. Anderson, 2013; Sotelo-Dynega, Flanagan, & Alfonso, 2011).

Many learning disabilities have a biological basis. For example, some children have minor abnormalities in brain structures devoted to concentration, making them vulnerable to distraction (Ashkenazi, Black, Abrams, Hoeft, & Menon, 2013; Kovas, Haworth, Dale, & Plomin, 2007; Xia, Hancock, & Hoeft, 2017). Other children have weak circuits for the sounds and scripts of language. In Artifact Example 7.3, you can see the difficulties Nathan has in representing sounds with letters, a problem that is common in young elementary children with reading disabilities.

Children with learning disabilities are a diverse group, having a wide range of talents, cognitive limitations, and personalities. Some children easily gain proficiency in mathematics but have significant problems in reading, whereas others show the reverse pattern. Other children have trouble expressing their thoughts in language, interpreting visual information, spelling words, typing and forming letters, or performing in still other domains. Many have exceptional talents as well.

Children with learning disabilities also have certain characteristics in common. They are apt to have trouble with executive functions—focusing attention, concentrating on learning goals, inhibiting inappropriate actions, and so on (de Weerdt, Desoete, &

Roeyers, 2013; Potocki, Sanchez, Ecalle, & Magnan, 2017; Semrud-Clikeman, Fine, & Bledsoe, 2013). With few effective strategies at their disposal, children may take a rather "passive" approach to schoolwork—for instance, staring blankly at a textbook instead of actively thinking about what the words mean (M. T. Brownell, Mellard, & Deshler, 1993; Meltzer & Krishnan, 2007). Some children have less working memory capacity than their age-mates do, making it difficult for them to engage in multiple cognitive processes simultaneously or to remember long instructions (H. L. Swanson & Jerman, 2006; Toffalini, Giofrè, & Cornoldi, 2017; Wesley & Bickel, 2013).

Preparing for Your Licensure Examination

Your teaching test may ask you about the needs of children with learning disabilities and attention disorders.

As students with learning disabilities reach the secondary grades, the school curriculum becomes increasingly challenging, textbooks are written in a more sophisticated language, and teachers expect greater independence. Unless they have considerable scaffolding in study skills, high school students with learning disabilities are likely to become discouraged. Perhaps for this reason, adolescents with learning disabilities are often among those students most at risk for dropping out of school (Barga, 1996; L. Gonzalez, 2011). A few suffer from low self-esteem and emotional problems, due at least partly to frustration with repeated academic failure (Al-Yagon, 2012; Horowitz, Darling-Hammond, & Bransford, 2005; Majorano, Brondino, Morelli, & Maes, 2017). The potential of these students motivates educators to provide early and continuous intervention.

Attention-Deficit Hyperactivity Disorder

Children with **attention-deficit hyperactivity disorder (ADHD)** have either or both of the following characteristics:

- *Inattention*—Children are easily distracted by either external stimuli or their own thoughts. They may daydream, have trouble listening to and following directions, or give up easily when working on difficult tasks.
- *Hyperactivity and impulsivity*—Children have an excess amount of energy. They may be fidgety, move around at inappropriate times, talk constantly, or have difficulty working or playing quietly. They may show impulsive behaviors, for example, blurting out answers, interrupting others, making careless mistakes, and acting without thinking about potential ramifications (American Psychiatric Association DSM-5 Task Force, 2013).

For a person to be classified as having ADHD, he or she needs to have exhibited symptoms in a few settings before the age of 12. A weakness with executive functions, especially in the inhibition of inappropriate thoughts and actions, may be at the heart of ADHD (Denckla, 2007; Langberg, Dvorsky, & Evans, 2013). Limitations in reward mechanisms in the brain, especially favoring immediate over delayed rewards, appear to share responsibility (Carmona et al., 2009; Silvetti, Wiersema, Sonuga-Barke, & Verguts, 2013; van Hulst et al., 2017).

In large part, because of their inattentiveness, hyperactivity, and impulsivity, children identified as having ADHD have difficulties with academic learning, interpersonal skills, and classroom behavior (Barkley, 1998; B. A. White, Jarrett, & Ollendick, 2013). Problems can escalate if not addressed effectively early in childhood. Adolescents with ADHD have greater difficulty than peers in meeting challenges in the teenage years—the physical changes of puberty, complex classroom assignments, and expectations for responsible behavior. Compared to peers, young people with ADHD are more prone to use tobacco and alcohol, get in traffic accidents, and drop out of school (Barkley, 1998; Ramos Olazagasti et al., 2013).

Given the pervasive challenges children with ADHD experience—and create—at home and in the classroom, several interventions have been tried. In consultation with parents, physicians often prescribe psychostimulants (e.g., Adderall or Ritalin), which accentuate the operations of dopamine, a neurotransmitter operating in attention centers of the brain (M. D. Rapport, Orban, Kofler, & Friedman, 2013). Stimulants generally reduce inattention and disorderly behavior but can have side effects, and their long-term consequences are unknown. Mental health experts offer training to parents in effective discipline and guidance to children in self-control. This support is given in addition to, or instead of, medication.

As you have learned, both typical progressions and exceptionalities have implications in the classroom. You can see a summary of these characteristics in the Developmental Trends table "Basic Cognitive Processes at Different Ages."

DEVELOPMENTAL TRENDS

Basic Cognitive Processes at Different Ages

AGE	WHAT YOU MIGHT OBSERVE	DIVERSITY	IMPLICATIONS
Infancy (Birth–2 Years)	• Some ability to learn and remember from before birth • Adult-like hearing sensitivity within hours after birth • Improvement in visual acuity during the first year • Preference for moderately complex stimuli • Attention drawn automatically to intense or novel stimuli • By 3 or 4 months, an ability to integrate information into simple categories	• Variations in attention span are related to differences in temperament. • Some infants consistently seek new experiences, whereas others are more comfortable with familiar objects. • Persistent inability to focus on a single object may signal a cognitive disability. • Health, good nutrition, and loving care foster infants' alertness and interest in exploration.	• Change toys and materials regularly to re-capture infants' interests in exploration. • Provide objects that can be categorized (e.g., colored blocks, plastic farm animals). • Allow for differences in interest and exploratory behavior; offer choices of toys and activities. • Comment on things that capture infants' attention, such as music or a new poster.
Early Childhood (2–6 Years)	• Short attention span • Distractibility • Conscious recall of past events • Some understanding and use of symbols • Limited knowledge base with which to interpret new experiences • Growing ability to sustain attention to favorite activities	• Children's prior knowledge differs markedly by cultural and socioeconomic background. • Young children who experience significant stress may find it difficult to concentrate at school. • First signs of ADHD or learning disabilities might include difficulty in rhyming; learning basic literacy tools, such as the alphabet; following simple directions; unusual delays in buttoning and snapping clothes; apparent inability to sit still; and frustration and aggression.	• Change activities fairly often to meet the short attention spans of children. • Reduce unnecessary distractions. • Arrange experiences (field trips to the library, fire department, etc.) that enrich children's knowledge base. • Consult experts when delays in basic skills suggest a possible learning disability. • Enlist the help of parents or community volunteers to facilitate relaxing activities, such as by reading individually to children in a corner of the classroom.
Middle Childhood (6–10 Years)	• Growing ability to focus on important stimuli and ignore irrelevant information • Thought that is increasingly symbolic in nature • Gradual automatizing of basic skills • Exposure to environments beyond the home and family, leading to an expanding knowledge base • Knowledge of academic subject matter consisting of some un-integrated facts, especially in science and social studies	• Many children with learning disabilities or attention disorders have short attention spans. • Trouble learning to read, spell, and acquire basic arithmetic skills is sometimes due to learning disabilities. • Some children with learning disabilities have a smaller working memory capacity than that of their peers. • Mild learning disabilities may not be evident until the upper elementary grades or after, if at all. • Variations in home traditions affect learning and memory skills.	• Intersperse sedentary assignments with physically active events. • Ask children to rehearse basic knowledge and skills (e.g., number facts, word recognition) as part of authentic tasks. • Establish routines to attract children's attention during transitions, for example, with hand signals, music, or a particular phrase. • Ask children to set goals for attention and periodically assess their mental focus during lessons. Recognize and reward concentration.
Early Adolescence (10–14 Years)	• Ability to attend to a single task for an hour or more • A core of automatized skills in reading, writing, and mathematics (e.g., word identification, common word spellings, basic math facts) • Growing (although not necessarily well integrated) knowledge base related to various topics and academic disciplines	• Individual differences in proficiency with basic reading and numerical skills • Many adolescents with learning disabilities have trouble paying attention for a typical class period and may dislike school. • Some adolescents with sensory disabilities (e.g., those with visual impairments) have less-than-average knowledge of the physical world.	• Incorporate variety in learning activities as a way of keeping young adolescents' attention. • Frequently point out how concepts and ideas are related to one another, both within and across content domains. • Provide extra guidance and support for those with diagnosed or suspected information processing difficulties. • Teach and reward use of organization skills with time, materials, and learning tasks.
Late Adolescence (14–18 Years)	• Ability to attend to a single task of personal interest for lengthy periods • Extensive and moderately integrated knowledge in some content domains • Ability to engage in fairly sophisticated symbolic reasoning • Growing ability to think about the future, imaginary situations, and abstract ideas (e.g., leaving a "carbon footprint," the commitment to a "moral compass")	• High school students have choices in course selection, intensifying gaps in knowledge of science, mathematics, and other academic subjects. • Students' attention can vary considerably from one class to another, depending on their intrinsic interest in the subject matter at hand. • Students with disabilities may forget to turn in homework, bring supplies to class, and refer to a calendar with due dates.	• Occasionally give assignments that require focus on a topic for an extended period. • Ask adolescents to think about the "hows" and "whys" of topics. • Visually depict relationships among ideas in maps, webs of concepts, and graphs of relationships. • Scaffold students' use of calendars, adding deadlines for major projects (e.g., a 4-page history essay), and dates for sub-tasks (e.g., the outline, first draft, and revision).

Working with Children Who Have Difficulty in Paying Attention and Processing Information

Some children with learning disabilities, ADHD, or other conditions might stare out the window instead of working on assignments. Others interrupt the lesson, pester a classmate, and get out of their seats at all the wrong times. Yet it is generally a neurological deficit, rather than laziness or rudeness, that causes these problems. In fact, children with cognitive difficulties invariably *want* to learn and behave like their classmates. They just need guidance in doing so. Because they are apt to fall behind in their school work, academic delays must also be addressed. Fortunately, several broad-spectrum tactics can improve learning, attention, and behavior:

- **Examine children's work for clues as to how learning disabilities affect academic progress.** Writing samples, math homework, and other assignments can be a rich source of information about cognitive deficits. A child who solves a subtraction problem this way

$$\begin{array}{r} 85 \\ -29 \\ \hline 64 \end{array}$$

may be applying a reasonable but inappropriate rule to subtraction ("Always subtract the smaller number from the larger one"). A child who reads the sentence *I drove the car* as *I drove the cat* may have trouble in using context clues when deciphering words. Instruction that hones in on these particular "bugs" in thinking can be beneficial to children.

- **Provide extra scaffolding in areas of weakness.** Children with significant delays in foundational subjects, especially reading and mathematics, need personalized instruction. One child needs one-on-one tutoring in basic arithmetic calculations whereas another requires extra practice in recognizing common words. Learning skills may also need to be taught. Such support might take the form of structured note-taking, handouts that list major ideas, memory techniques for recalling information, after-school homework programs, tips in breaking up ambitious projects into manageable steps, and the like (T. Bryan, Burstein, & Bryan, 2001; Meltzer, 2007).

- **Teach children organizational skills.** Children with learning disabilities and attention problems often need assistance in keeping track of assignments, school supplies, and schedules (Abikoff et al., 2013; Bikic, Reichow, McCauley, Ibrahim, & Sukhodolsky, 2017). A teacher might help a fourth-grade boy prepare colored folders labeled for each of his classes. With difficult projects, the teacher might prepare a checklist that allows a student to mark off parts as they are being completed. A monthly calendar can list projects, assignments, and tests. Children can be recognized for consistently using these organizational tools and eventually, for developing and implementing their own.

MyLab Education
Video Example 7.5

Find Developmental Meaning *How does third-grade teacher Sheila Brown maintain the attention of her students?* In this video Ms. Brown captures children's attention in a lesson accompanied by resources (e.g., the SMART Board, manipulatives) that fortify understandings and a worksheet that guides mental processes. She herself has a calm demeanor and uses facial expressions, gestures, questions, and directions that prompt attention. Students' work in small groups contributes to their engagement.

- **Help children stay focused on the task at hand.** Many children with information processing difficulties are easily sidetracked. Adults should minimize distractions, and for those with attention disabilities, consider seating them away from the window, find an uncluttered room for tasks requiring sustained concentration, and pull down window shades when alluring events unfold outside. Important concepts need to be stressed, and instructions should be delivered step by step and accompanied by posters, chalkboard reminders, or individual worksheets that identify parts of the assignment and criteria for success.

- **Provide opportunities to practice learning strategies.** Many children with learning disabilities and attention problems need to learn how to acquire, store, and recall information (M. Montague, Enders, & Dietz, 2011; Turnbull et al., 2010). Teachers can ask students to use learning strategies that regulate these basic processes. They can be taught to formulate a goal when undertaking a task, divide complex activities (e.g., reading a long passage) into easily handled units, and identify key concepts to look for when starting a lesson.

- **Incorporate movement and restful transitions in the schedule.** All children, but especially those with information processing difficulties, need regular opportunities to release pent-up energy through recess, sports, and hands-on activities (Cortese, 2013; Panksepp, 1998). After a period of physical activity, adults might give children a "set-tling-in" time that allows them to calm down gradually (Pellegrini & Horvat, 1995). When children return from lunch, an elementary teacher could read a passage from a relaxing storybook before introducing new concepts. Some children remain fidgety regardless of these measures and may appreciate permission to stand at the back of the classroom or squeeze a pliable ball.

- **Teach children strategies in purposeful learning and self-control.** Children with ADHD are apt to behave most productively when they receive clear expectations and earn rewards for turning in an assignment on time, waiting to speak instead of calling out an answer, helping peers during a group assignment, following lunchroom rules, and bringing supplies to class (Center for Children and Families, 2013). A daily report card can be kept of targeted behaviors and shared with the child and his or her parents. At school, the child might select from an array of rewards, for instance, being a messenger for the office, caring for classroom pets, preparing popcorn, having extra time on the computer, choosing stickers, or eating at a special table. Parents can examine the report card and offer their own rewards, for example, having an extra bedtime story, doing a puzzle together, baking cookies, or enjoying another privilege suggested by the child.

- **Communicate warmth and high expectations.** A child with an attention disorder is most likely to be relaxed and focused when he or she feels welcome in the classroom and liked by the teacher (Hatfield & Williford, 2017; Moore, Russell, Arnell, & Ford, 2017). Recognizing strengths, too, is constructive because a child's assets are the foundation for future progress. For example, a young girl with an attention problem and a love of literature might gradually lengthen her focus while listening to stories.

Summary

Information processing theories focus on how children acquire, interpret, and remember information and how these cognitive processes change with development. Basic sensory and perceptual capabilities exist at birth and develop further with maturation and experience. In general, children are less efficient learners than adults are. They have shorter attention spans, a smaller working memory capacity, and a less integrated knowledge base. Children's limitations in information processing can be addressed by breaking up tasks; arranging activities that are varied and attention-grabbing, including visual displays and verbal reminders; and delivering interesting lessons that incorporate practice in fundamental skills. The information processing capabilities of some children (e.g., those with learning disabilities and those with ADHD) require specially adapted instruction. Although children with such disabilities have diverse abilities and needs, most benefit from explicit instruction in effective cognitive strategies and tailored learning tasks.

MyLab Education Self-Check 7.1

Metacognition and Cognitive Strategies

7.2 Trace the development of children's metacognition and cognitive strategies along with educational methods that facilitate this growth.

In the process of learning and remembering information, children gain insights into how the mind works. The capacity for understanding and controlling mental processes is known as **metacognition**. The related processes that children intentionally use to regulate their own thinking are known as **cognitive strategies**. In this section, we look at development of four elements of metacognition: learning strategies, problem-solving strategies, metacognitive awareness, and self-regulated learning.

Preparing for Your Licensure Examination

Your teaching test may ask you to distinguish metacognition from basic cognitive processes.

Learning Strategies

As you have found, children are able to remember some, but not all, of the information they encounter on a daily basis. It is educationally significant that learning and remembering operate selectively, sometimes yet not always under conscious control. By teaching children to think strategically, with attention to goals and effective mental techniques, educators are likely to enhance achievement at school. Yet guidance in learning strategies must be adjusted to children's readiness.

Toddlers try to remember things when prompted (DeLoache, Cassidy, & Brown, 1985). When asked to remember where a doll has been hidden in their home, they may stare or point at the location where they saw it being placed until they are able to go get it. Preschool children are inclined to verbalize the location (L. A. Henry & Norman, 1996). In everyday life, young children rarely make a point of learning and remembering something. In fact, 4- and 5-year-olds can remember a set of objects more successfully by playing with the objects than by intentionally trying to remember them (L. S. Newman, 1990). Later on, children learn information deliberately, with an intention to remember it later. As they progress through school, students develop an increasing number of *learning strategies*—techniques that they deliberately use to learn or remember information. Three that appear during the school years are rehearsal, organization, and elaboration.

Rehearsal

Imagine you are sitting in your car, leaving shortly to do errands. Before you begin driving, you listen to a message from your partner about items you need at the grocery store ("toilet paper, light bulbs, apples, something for dinner . . . "). Your cell phone is low on battery, and you are not able to write down the items. Do you repeat the items mentally as a way of keeping the list in your working memory? Repetition of information in order to remember it is known as **rehearsal**.

Rehearsal is rare in preschoolers but increases in frequency and effectiveness throughout the elementary school years. By ages 5 to 8, children rehearse information in order to remember it (Bebko, McMorris, Metcalfe, Ricciuti, & Goldstein, 2014; Jarrold & Citroën, 2013). By age 9 or 10, they become more strategic, combining items into a list as they rehearse. If they hear the list "cat, dog, horse," they might say "cat" after the first item; "cat, dog" after the second; and "cat, dog, horse" after the third. Repeating items in a cumulative manner helps children remember items more successfully, at least for a minute or so (Bjorklund, Dukes, et al., 2009; Kunzinger, 1985). Although rehearsal becomes more polished with age and experience, it is actually a relatively *in*effective strategy for remembering information unless, in the process, children also relate it to something they already know (Cermak & Craik, 1979; M. Lehmann & Hasselhorn, 2012).

Organization

Take a minute to study and remember the following 12 words, and then cover them and try to recall as many as you can:

shirt	table	hat
carrot	bed	squash
pants	potato	stool
chair	shoe	bean

In what order did you remember the words? Did you recall them in their original order, or did you rearrange them somehow? If you are like most adults, you grouped the words into three categories—clothing, furniture, and vegetables—and recalled them category by category. In other words, you used **organization** to help you learn and remember the information.

As early as 3 or 4 months old, children begin to organize their experiences into mental categories (Kovack-Lesh, Horst, & Oakes, 2008; Quinn, 2002). After seeing pictures of different breeds of dogs, infants gradually lose interest. Their attention perks up when they see a picture of a cat, suggesting an ability to distinguish cats from dogs long before they

MyLab Education
Video Example 7.6
Find Developmental Meaning *How does 17-year-old Paul reveal flexibility in mental classification?* Notice that Paul considers multiple organizational structures as he sorts seashells.

can label each. Infants' initial categories are based on perceptual similarity (e.g., *balls* are round, *blocks* are cubes), but they also show emerging knowledge of more general categories (e.g., *vehicles, furniture*; Horst, Oakes, & Madole, 2005; Mash, Bornstein, & Banerjee, 2014). By age 2, children may physically pick up objects and sort them by theme or function, perhaps using classifications such as "things for the feet" or "kitchen things" (Cacchione, Schaub, & Rakoczy, 2013; DeLoache & Todd, 1988; Mandler, Fivush, & Reznick, 1987).

As children move through the elementary, middle school, and secondary grades, they become increasingly effective in using organization as a learning strategy (Lucariello, Kyratzis, & Nelson, 1992; Megalakaki & Yazbek, 2013; Pressley & Hilden, 2006; Ware, 2017). They may sort items into categories when they want to remember them. Their organizational strategies become more sophisticated and prevalent, with children incorporating a variety of dimensions and becoming flexible in their organizational schemes.

Elaboration

If we authors tell you that we've both spent many years living in Colorado, you will probably conclude that we either live or have lived in or near the Rocky Mountains. In this situation, you're not only learning the information we told you, you're also learning some information that you yourself supplied. This process of embellishing on new information with existing knowledge is known as **elaboration**. Elaboration usually facilitates learning and memory, sometimes dramatically.

Children elaborate on everyday experiences in preschool and while reading in the elementary years (Fivush, Haden, & Adam, 1995; van der Schoot, Reijntjes, & Lieshout, 2012). They may say, "That pottery looks like Papa's stone bowl," or "I don't think a spider would really try to help a pig." As a strategy that they *purposefully* use to help them learn, however, elaboration appears relatively late in development (usually around puberty) and only gradually increases during the teenage years (Bjorklund, Dukes, et al., 2009; W. Schneider & Pressley, 1989). In fact, this strategy is not a guaranteed outcome by any means. Even in high school, it is primarily students with high academic achievement who use existing knowledge to help them learn and remember new information. Students who are low achievers or have intellectual disabilities are much less likely to use elaboration when they study, and students of all ability levels resort to rehearsal for difficult, hard-to-understand material (J. E. Barnett, 2001; D. L. Butler, Schnellert, & Cleary, 2015; Pressley, 1982; Rosende-Vázquez & Vieiro-Iglesias, 2013). The following interview with 15-year-old "Beth," who earns mostly As in her classes but must work hard to get them, illustrates how infrequently some high school students think to use elaboration as a study strategy:

Adult: Once you have some information that you think you need to know, what types of things do you do so that you will remember it?
Beth: I take notes . . . [pause].
Adult: Is that all you do?
Beth: Usually. Sometimes I make flash cards.
Adult: What types of things do you usually put on flash cards?
Beth: I put words I need to know. Like spelling words. I put dates and what happened then.
Adult: How would you normally study flash cards or your notes?
Beth: My notes, I read them over a few times. Flash cards I look at once and try to remember what's on the other side and what follows it. (interview courtesy of Evie Greene. Used with Permission.)

Notice how Beth emphasizes taking notes and studying flash cards, approaches that typically require little or no elaboration. She does not expand on, consider the implications of, or wonder about the relevance of classroom subject matter for herself or others. The use of flash cards is really just a form of rehearsal.

Why do some students learn to use advanced learning strategies whereas others do not? Instruction is key. When teachers talk about memory (e.g., "What are some good ways to remember that formula? Can you form a picture in your mind?") and encourage memory strategies, children tend to deploy these techniques and achieve at high levels (Moely, Santulli, & Obach, 1995; Okoza, Aluede, & Owens-Sogolo, 2013; P. A. Ornstein, Grammer, & Coffman, 2010). Teachers can also instruct children in use of elaboration strategies by regularly asking children to develop analogies ("What is ________________ like?"), paraphrase the material ("Say it in your own words; what does ________________ mean?"), draw inferences ("What else might be true?"), and compare and contrast ("How is ________________ similar to and different from ________________?"); (Weinstein, Ridley, & Dahl, 1988).

Problem-Solving Strategies

Problem solving involves several steps: analyzing the situation, developing a plan, identifying steps toward resolution, and checking on the results (Bayazit, 2013). Like so many other important capacities in life, problem-solving appears first as a rudimentary ability in infancy and evolves slowly well into adolescence. Imagine that a 12-month-old sees an attractive toy beyond her reach. One end of a string is attached to the toy, and its other end is attached to a cloth closer at hand. Between the cloth and the infant is a foam rubber barrier. The infant puts two and two together, realizing that to accomplish her goal (getting the toy), she has to do several things in sequence. She removes the barrier, pulls the cloth toward her, grabs the string, and reels in the toy—Voila! (Willatts, 1990).

Initially, children engage in a lot of trial-and-error experimentation, typically not grasping the problem or possible solutions until they have tinkered with relevant materials (Boncoddo, Dixon, & Kelley, 2010; Comalli et al., 2016). The abilities to break a problem into two or more steps and enact these steps develops during the preschool and elementary school years (Klahr & Robinson, 1981; M. C. Welsh, 1991). Gradually, children learn to inhibit impulses, generate multiple solutions, and shift attention flexibly while trying to solve a problem (Agostino, Johnson, & Pascual-Leone, 2010; Mehnert et al., 2013; H. L. Swanson, 2011).

By elementary school, children envision several different strategies for dealing with particular problems. With time and practice, they become more adept at applying new tactics efficiently, flexibly, and successfully (P. A. Alexander, Graham, & Harris, 1998; L. P. Flannery & Bers, 2013; Siegler & Alibali, 2005). Some strategies are more successful than others, and because children initially have trouble using the more advanced ones, they often resort to less efficient but dependable "backup" strategies. For example, even after children have learned their basic math facts ($2 + 4 = 6$, $9 - 7 = 2$, etc.), they sometimes resort to counting on their fingers while solving addition and subtraction problems. Eventually, children acquire sufficient familiarity with advanced strategies that they can leave the less efficient ones behind (P. A. Alexander et al., 1998; Kuhn & Pease, 2010; Siegler & Alibali, 2005). Children also use tried-and-true strategies in new contexts. For example, most children learn to add whole numbers in the early elementary grades and then, a few years later, impose the same tactic when adding fractions, mistakenly totaling numerators and denominators (e.g., $\frac{1}{2} + \frac{2}{3} = \frac{3}{5}$; Braithwaite, Tian, & Siegler, 2018). As children acquire a deeper understanding of what it means to add fractions, they come to appreciate why a different technique is necessary.

American psychologist **Robert Siegler** and his colleagues have observed that the rise and fall of thinking strategies resemble *overlapping waves,* as are depicted in Figure 7.3 (Siegler & Alibali, 2005). In areas as diverse as crawling, spelling, and counting, children experiment with a series of techniques, trying each out for a time, and persisting with those that yield successful outcomes (Chetland & Fluck, 2007; Heineman, Middelburg, & Hadders-Algra, 2010; Kwong & Varnhagen, 2005; Young-Suk, Apel, Al Otaiba, Nippold, & Jotte, 2013). Teachers can expect to see overlapping waves of strategies when children tackle the same problem over time and with discretion in how they go about solving it.

Metacognitive Awareness

At the same time children are acquiring learning and problem-solving strategies, they are gaining insight into the nature of thinking. **Metacognitive awareness** includes a

FIGURE 7.3 Strategy development as a progression of overlapping waves.

Children gradually replace simple tactics with more advanced and effective strategies. Here we see how five different methods for dealing with the same task might change in frequency over time.

Based on *Children's Thinking* (4th ed., p. 98), by R. Siegler and M. W. Alibali, 2005, Upper Saddle River, NJ: Prentice Hall. Copyright 2005 by Prentice Hall.

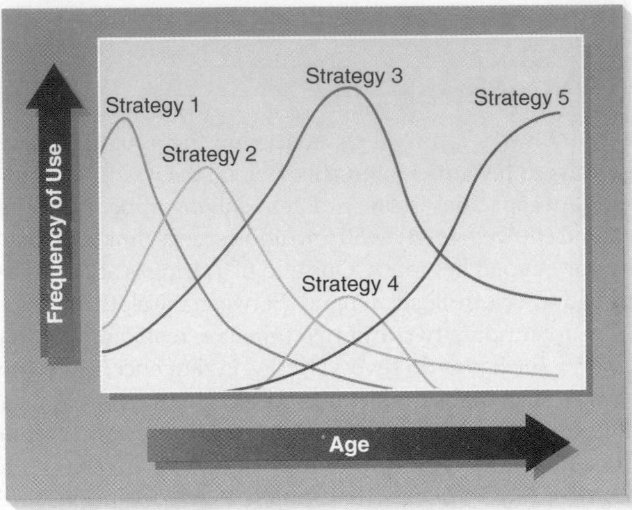

conscious appreciation of thought processes, an understanding of the limits of human memory, and knowledge of the relative effectiveness of various learning strategies.

Awareness of Thought

By the time children are 3 years old, they are aware of thinking as something people do (Flavell, Green, & Flavell, 1995). They may also begin to have a feeling that they know something, can remember certain kinds of information, or are having difficulty understanding a story (K. E. Lyons & Zelazo, 2011). Their initial images of thought are quite simplistic, however. They are likely to say that a person is "thinking" only when he or she appears to be physically engaged in a task or has a puzzled facial expression. They also view thinking as holding information and not as engaging in active processes (Flavell et al., 1995; Wellman, 1990).

It takes several years before children comprehend internal experiences. Although many preschoolers use the words *know*, *remember*, and *forget*, they don't fully grasp these mental states. For instance, 3-year-olds use the term *forget* to mean "not knowing" something, regardless of whether they knew the information at an earlier time (Lyon & Flavell, 1994). When 4- and 5-year-old children are taught a new fact, they may say that they've known it for quite some time (M. Taylor, Esbensen, & Bennett, 1994). During the elementary and secondary school years, young people become better able to reflect on their mental states (Jaswal & Dodson, 2009; K. E. Lyons & Ghetti, 2013; Wellman & Hickling, 1994). This growth is facilitated when adults talk about how they think and remember information themselves and what they do to avoid forgetting important facts (Salmon & Lucas, 2011).

Understanding Memory Limitations

Young children tend to be optimistic about how much they can remember. As they grow older and encounter a wide variety of learning tasks, they discover that some things are especially difficult to learn, and they may not be as capable as they thought (Flavell et al., 2002; Grammer, Purtell, Coffman, & Ornstein, 2011; K. E. Lyons & Ghetti, 2013; Miele, Son, & Metcalfe, 2013). They also realize that their memories are not perfect and they cannot possibly remember everything they see or hear. In one study (Flavell, Friedrichs, & Hoyt, 1970), preschoolers and elementary school children were shown pictures of 1 to 10 objects and asked to predict how many objects they could remember for a short period. The average predictions of each of four age groups and the average number of objects the children actually remembered were as follows:

Age Group	Predicted Number	Actual Number
Preschool	7.2	3.5
Kindergarten	8.0	3.6
Grade 2	6.0	4.4
Grade 4	6.1	5.5

Notice that children in all four age groups predicted that they would remember more objects than they actually did. But the older children were more realistic about the limitations of their memories.

Being overconfident is a mixed blessing for young children. Anticipating that they will easily remember information, young children do not apply extra effort (Destan & Roebers, 2015). Yet their optimism has a distinct benefit. It gives children self-assurance to try new and difficult tasks—challenges that are likely to promote cognitive growth (Bjorklund, Periss, & Causey, 2009).

Knowledge about Learning and Memory

Imagine that it's winter and you live in a cold climate. Just before you go to bed, some friends ask you to go ice skating after school tomorrow. What might you do to make sure you remember to take your ice skates with you in the morning? Older children typically generate more strategies than younger children for remembering the skates. Yet even 5- and 6-year-olds can identify one or more effective strategies—perhaps writing a note to themselves, recording a reminder on a tape recorder, or leaving the skates next to their school bag (Kreutzer, Leonard, & Flavell, 1975).

Not only do children acquire more effective learning strategies (e.g., organization, elaboration) as they grow older, but they also become increasingly aware of which strategies are effective in different situations (S. B. Lovett & Flavell, 1990; J. Metcalfe & Finn, 2013; W. Schneider & Lockl, 2002). Consider the simple idea that when you don't learn something the first time, you need to study it again. This is a strategy that 8-year-olds use, but 6-year-olds do not (Masur, McIntyre, & Flavell, 1973). Similarly, 10th-graders are more aware than 8th-graders of the advantages of using elaboration to learn new information (H. S. Waters, 1982). Even so, many youngsters are relatively uninformed about which learning strategies work most effectively for them in various situations (Joseph, 2010; Kuhn, Garcia-Mila, Zohar, & Andersen, 1995). The following interview with "Amy," a 16-year-old with a history of low school achievement, suggests a lack of exposure to learning strategies:

Adult: What is learning?
Amy: Something you do to get knowledge.
Adult: What is knowledge?
Amy: Any information that I don't know.
Adult: What about the things you already know?
Amy: That doesn't count.
Adult: Doesn't count?
Amy: As knowledge, because I already know it.
Adult: How do you know when you have learned something?
Amy: When I can repeat it, and it is the same as what the teacher said or what I read, and I can remember it forever or a really long time. (interview courtesy of Jennifer Glynn. Used with permission.)

Notice how Amy thinks she has learned something when she can repeat what a teacher or textbook has told her. She says nothing about *understanding* classroom subject matter. And curiously, she thinks of knowledge as things she *doesn't* know.

Self-Regulated Learning

As children gain awareness of their learning and memory processes, they become more capable of **self-regulated learning**—that is, they become more proficient in directing their own learning. Self-regulated learning involves strategies such as these:

- Setting goals for a learning activity
- Planning effective use of study time
- Keeping attention on the subject matter to be learned

- Persisting while studying
- Identifying and using appropriate learning strategies
- Monitoring progress toward learning goals
- Adjusting goals or learning strategies depending on progress
- Evaluating knowledge gained from a learning activity (Boekaerts, 2006; Hessels-Schlatter, Hessels, Godin, & Spillmann-Rojas, 2017; J. Malmberg, Järvenoja, & Järvelä, 2013; Meltzer & Krishnan, 2007; Muis, 2007; S. M. Reis, 2011; B. J. Zimmerman & Schunk, 2004).

Developmental Systems Prompt

Teachers gradually shift responsibility for completion of academic tasks from themselves to children. When scaffolding children's goals, learning strategies, and self-evaluation processes, consider what you know about their experience in setting and pursuing goals.

Rudimentary capacities for self-regulated learning emerge during infancy and early childhood. Young children at times show flashes of self-control, perhaps by ignoring an annoying classmate rather than hitting him, looking at an array of items for a long time when trying to remember the content, or remaining steadfast in building a tower after several pieces tumble (Demetriou, 2000; Kopp, 1982; U. Wagener, 2013). Despite flashes of self-regulation, the constituent skills are a long time in the making. Throughout the school years, students face difficulties in regulating their learning (Bronson, 2000; B. J. Zimmerman & Risemberg, 1997).

With support, students have the capacity to build self-regulatory skills. Some preschool teachers encourage children to make plans for their free time by asking them to verbalize their intentions with a specific activity (perhaps playing with a friend in the housekeeping area or riding a tricycle outside) and later asking them how they did (Bodrova & Leong, 2009; S. Jones, Bub, & Raver, 2013). In the elementary, middle, and secondary grades, teachers can foster self-regulatory learning by asking students to set goals, encouraging them to pursue questions of personal interest, and monitoring their performance (Cano, García, Berbén, & Justicia, 2014; Merritt, Wanless, Rimm-Kaufman, Cameron, & Peugh, 2012; Perels, Merget-Kullmann, Wende, Schmitz, & Buchbinder, 2009; Tracy, Reid, & Graham, 2009; C. Yoon, 2009).

Cultural Roots of Metacognition

Active mental engagement makes a strong contribution to academic learning (J. Lee, 2014). Across many settings, there is a close connection between children's metacognition and their academic achievement (Afflerbach, Cho, Kim, Crassas, & Doyle, 2013; Onyekuru & Njoku, 2015; Roebers, Krebs, & Roderer, 2014; H. L. Swanson, 2001). To make the most of the benefits of metacognitive insights and self-regulatory powers, teachers need to consider the cultural environments in which children are raised.

Developmental Systems Prompt

Learning strategies emerge in part through the child being socialized by parents about how to think about daily activities. Ask parents how children are encouraged to learn new information and skills at home.

From a traditional East Asian perspective, true learning is not a quick-and-easy process. Advanced knowledge comes with diligence, concentration, and perseverance (Dahlin & Watkins, 2000; H. Grant & Dweck, 2001; J. Li & Fischer, 2004; Q. Wang & Pomerantz, 2009). As part of their emphasis on hard work, many East Asian parents and teachers encourage rehearsal and rote memorization as learning strategies (Dahlin & Watkins, 2000; D. Y. F. Ho, 1994; Purdie & Hattie, 1996). Rehearsal is common in cultures that commit oral histories or verbatim passages to memory (Alhaqbani & Riazi, 2012; MacDonald, Uesiliana, & Hayne, 2000; Rogoff et al., 2007).

A commitment to hard work can become a productive bridge to metacognition for children who have not yet acquired active learning methods. For example, children from a traditional East Asian society can be advised of the benefits of active learning methods in reading or mathematics and be given a chance to practice them and reflect on their role in learning (Hansen & Jessop, 2017). In a study in the United Kingdom, Chinese students who were originally unacquainted with purposeful learning strategies saw significant advantages after trying them (C. Simpson, 2017).

From the perspective of many Western cultures, the acquisition of knowledge is more for personal gain. Children learn in order to acquire new skills and abilities. Even though self-directed learning meshes well with Western values, relevant skills are often assumed rather than taught. Teachers at each grade level have many opportunities to motivate children to use self-regulatory strategies. The Developmental Trends table "Cognitive Strategies and Metacognitive Understandings at Different Age Levels" summarizes developmental changes in children's metacognitive understandings and strategies, as well as some of the metacognitive diversity you are likely to see in any age group.

DEVELOPMENTAL TRENDS

Cognitive Strategies and Metacognitive Understandings at Different Age Levels

AGE	WHAT YOU MIGHT OBSERVE	DIVERSITY	IMPLICATIONS
Infancy (Birth–2 Years)	• Use of one object to obtain another (in second year) • Ability to plan a simple sequence of actions to accomplish a goal (appearing at age 1) • Absence of intentional learning strategies but ability to look or point at a location to remember where an object is hidden • Little awareness of thought processes but appreciation that other people have intentions	• Emergence of early problem-solving strategies is dependent on opportunities to experiment with objects. • Trial-and-error exploration is partly a function of temperament and motor abilities. • Health and nutrition influence how vigorously infants explore the environment, attend to language, and initiate interactions with caregivers.	• Model tool use and basic problem-solving strategies. • Pose simple problems for infants and toddlers to solve (e.g., place desired objects slightly out of reach). • Watch for strategies that infants use in mastering language and gaining information about their world, methods that are not necessarily intentional but are adaptive in identifying patterns.
Early Childhood (2–6 Years)	• Beginning use of rehearsal in preschool, with little effect on learning and memory • Occasional organization of concrete objects • Ability to learn simple strategies demonstrated by others • Growing awareness of thought in self and others • Overestimation of how much information one can remember • Emerging intuitive awareness that some things are more difficult to learn than others • At ages 5 and 6, receptivity to thinking about simple strategies in performing concrete tasks	• Children's awareness of mental processes depends on the extent to which adults talk about thinking. • Many young children with autism have little conscious awareness of thought, especially in other people. • Cultural preferences affect opportunities for memorization (e.g., with poetry, scripture, or the alphabet) and interpretation (e.g., being asked about the moral lesson of a fable or the way a toy operates). • Excessive stress can undermine children's purposeful regulation of thinking and behavior.	• Talk about thinking processes (e.g., "I *wonder* if . . . ," "Do you *remember* when . . . ?"). • Model strategies for simple memory tasks (e.g., pinning permission slips on jackets to remind children to get parents' signatures). • Ask children open-ended questions that engage their thinking (e.g., while reading, "What do you think is going to happen to Sam next?"). • Encourage children to ask questions as they perform a task (e.g., ask, "What will happen if I mix red and blue paint?").
Middle Childhood (6–10 Years)	• Use of rehearsal as the predominant learning strategy • Gradual increase in organization as an intentional learning strategy • Emerging ability to reflect on the nature of personal thought processes • Continued overestimation of personal memory capabilities • Capacity for, but underdeveloped state of, self-regulated learning	• Some Chinese and Japanese children rely more heavily on rehearsal than do peers in Western schools; this difference continues into adolescence. • Children with cognitive disabilities struggle to organize material as they learn it. • A few high-achieving children are capable of sustained self-regulated learning.	• Encourage children to repeat and practice the things they need to learn. • Introduce organization as a learning strategy, and ask children to categorize familiar themes and objects. • Ask children to engage in simple self-regulated learning strategies, perhaps setting a goal or evaluating which strategies helped them understand a history document.
Early Adolescence (10–14 Years)	• Emergence of elaboration as an intentional learning strategy • Few and relatively ineffective study strategies (e.g., ineffective note-taking skills) • Increasing flexibility with learning strategies • Belief that knowledge consists of a collection of discrete facts	• Adolescents differ considerably in their use of effective learning strategies. • Some adolescents, including many with cognitive disabilities, have few strategies for engaging in self-regulated learning. • Students may employ learning strategies when mentored by teachers	• Ask questions that encourage adolescents to elaborate on new information. • Teach and demonstrate effective strategies within the context of subject areas. • Assign tasks that require independent learning, but provide structure that guides their efforts.
Late Adolescence (14–18 Years)	• Growing use of elaboration in learning • Awareness of which cognitive strategies are most effective in particular situations • Increasing self-regulatory learning strategies (e.g., setting goals and keeping track of progress) • Emerging realization that knowledge involves understanding of connections among ideas • Willingness to critically evaluate conflicting perspectives on an issue (in some students)	• High-achieving teenagers are likely to use sophisticated learning strategies. • Low-achieving students typically resort to simple and ineffective strategies (e.g., rehearsal). • Many teenagers with cognitive disabilities have insufficient study skills to comprehend typical high school textbooks. • Willingness to critically evaluate others' ideas is, in part, a function of cultural and religious upbringings.	• Require and guide effective learning strategies. • Assign complex tasks, giving the necessary structure for those who do not spontaneously set goals or keep track of interim benchmarks. • Teach specific criteria (e.g., presence of research evidence, logical consistency) by which to evaluate assertions. • Talk about your own metacognitive insights in coming to conclusions, changing your mind, and offsetting memory limitations.

Promoting Metacognition, Self-Regulation, and Use of Strategies

As you have learned, metacognitive insights and active learning strategies can be exceedingly helpful to children. Following are several suggestions for fostering their development:

- **Engage children in discussions about the mind.** As you've seen, even preschoolers have an awareness of the mind. Yet there is plenty of room for growth. Adults can enhance metacognitive knowledge by regularly referring to mental activities—for example, by asking children to put on their "thinking caps," describing someone's mind as "wandering," and encouraging children to explain how they think about completing a difficult puzzle (Grammer, Coffman, & Ornstein, 2013; Wellman & Hickling, 1994). As young people become more introspective in the secondary school years, they are better able to reflect on and describe the kinds of things they do while learning. At earlier points in the chapter, we've presented interviews in which students described their views about thinking and learning. Such interviews can shed light on young people's study strategies that adults can, in turn, address.

MyLab Education Application Exercise 7.2
Detect Developmental Levels

In this video 6-year-old Brent and 16-year-old Hilary try to remember information and reflect on their learning strategies. How do the two students differ in their memories and learning strategies?

- **Demonstrate age-appropriate cognitive strategies.** Adults can foster effective problem-solving strategies by modeling them. Infants as young as 6 to 10 months can overcome obstacles to obtaining an attractive toy if someone shows them how to do it (Z. Chen, Sanchez, & Campbell, 1997; Gerson & Woodward, 2013). Learning strategies, too, can be modeled and taught. Three- to 5-year-olds can be shown how to organize objects into categories as a way of helping them remember items (Augustine, Smith, & Jones, 2011; M. Carr & Schneider, 1991; Lange & Pierce, 1992).

As children encounter ever more challenging learning tasks, simple categorization is not enough. By the time they reach high school, students need to learn—and often must be explicitly taught, such strategies as self-questioning and elaborating on new ideas. Ideally, such instruction should be integrated into lessons about specific academic topics, rather than being delivered generically in its own course (R. E. Mayer, 2010; Pressley, El-Dinary, Marks, Brown, & Stein, 1992). Although there are broadly applicable tactics that cut across different academic areas (e.g., setting objectives for a study session, checking one's work after completion, and developing a plan to distribute study time), many aspects of metacognition are geared toward certain subjects (e.g., summarizing main ideas after reading an expository passage, comparing the answer to a multiplication problem with an estimate in mathematics, and drawing a picture of a new concept during science class).

- **Encourage strategic learning.** The origins of self-regulated learning can be found in infancy, wherein tiny learners try to control their attention and impulses (Hendry, Jones, & Charman, 2016). A baby girl trying to wake the pet dog may try a few gestures—rubbing his back, poking at his face, and pulling his ears—until one of the gestures wakes him. Infants' attempts at pursuing their goals and solving problems are spontaneous. By early childhood and the early elementary years, children are ready for guidance in self-regulation. Adults can encourage children to set goals and show them how to watch for progress. A preschool teacher might show children steps to putting on a jacket and say, "You know when you're ready to go outside when you look down at your jacket and see that it is all closed up."). Later in the elementary and secondary school years, teachers and can scaffold self-regulation by instructing children in more sophisticated learning strategies. For instance, they might provide a form that identifies distinct parts of self-regulation that students can comment on—how they formalized goals, removed distractions from the learning environment, proceeded through the various steps and completed the final project. As children develop increasing proficiency with each self-regulation strategy, the scaffolds can gradually be removed (Meltzer & Krishnan, 2007; Pressley et al., 1992).

Preparing for Your Licensure Examination

Your teaching test may ask you how to foster children's metacognitive knowledge and strategies.

• **Create opportunities for children to evaluate their own learning.** Depending on the lessons offered, students have numerous options to keep tabs on how well they are doing. By engaging in ongoing self-evaluation, they can develop appropriate standards and apply those criteria to their accomplishments—true hallmarks of a self-regulating learner. Self-evaluation can be facilitated in several ways:

- Teach children to ask themselves, and then answer, questions about the topic.
- Have children set specific objectives for each session and then describe how they've met each one.
- Provide criteria that children can use to judge their performance.
- Encourage children to evaluate their performance realistically, and then reinforce them (e.g., with praise or extra-credit points) when their accomplishments match an established standard.
- Have children compile portfolios that include samples of their work, along with a written reflection on the quality of each assignment (M. Carr, 2010; McCaslin & Good, 1996; Nicolaidou, 2013; Paris & Ayres, 1994; Perry, 1998; Pilegard & Fiorella, 2016; S.P. Pratt & Urbanowski, 2016; Rosenshine, Meister, & Chapman, 1996; Schraw, Potenza, & Nebelsick-Gullet, 1993; Tracy et al., 2009; Winne, 1995b).

MyLab Education
Video Example 7.7
Find Developmental Meaning *How does 8-year-old Keenan evaluate her work?* With support from her teacher, Keenan notices her growth in punctuation, capitalization, and use of the dictionary.

• **Comment on the power of strategic learning.** Young people are best able to achieve at high levels when they believe that they can learn and achieve through effort and technique rather than inborn talent. American psychologist **Carol Dweck** has demonstrated the value of children's belief that they can grow intellectually with hard work (Dweck, 2012). Teachers can educate children that the brain changes with experience and grows in capacity like a muscle. Rather than praising children for their intelligence, teachers can draw attention to strategies that generate high achievement—persistence on a task, rereading of difficult materials, and methodical approaches to challenges (Dweck, 2008). With an appreciation for tactics that matter, children are more likely to aspire to adding techniques to their study habits.

• **Teach children how to study.** Homework is a perfect time to exercise self-regulatory skills when teachers have already scaffolded the component skills. A high school advisor might advise students how to prepare a homework plan for the week. A homework-helper tool might include tips for studying, setting reasonable goals for each study session, finding a quiet place to concentrate, breaking up a task into manageable chunks, taking brief breaks, and distributing study sessions over time rather than creating a situation that reinforces cramming the night before a test (S. Carpenter, Cepeda, Rohrer, Kang, & Pashler, 2012; L. Rosen, Mark Carrier, & Cheever, 2013).

Summary

The term *metacognition* encompasses both the knowledge that people have about their own cognitive processes and the intentional strategies they use in learning and remembering. Children's metacognitive knowledge and cognitive strategies improve throughout the school years. When supported by educators, children become more proficient in rehearsal, organization, and elaboration, and they acquire increasingly powerful and effective ways of solving problems and learning new material. With age, they become more aware of the nature of thinking, and they develop strategies for regulating academic performance.

MyLab Education Self-Check 7.2

Personal Theory Construction

7.3 Explain how children construct integrated belief systems about particular topics and what teachers can do to address children's personal theories.

Born with little knowledge of the world, infants rapidly learn while exploring surroundings, interacting with people, and reflecting on observations. This point was made convincingly by Piaget and Vygotsky, historical giants in the field of child development. Yet these two scholars and their disciples stopped short of giving clear explanations as to how exactly children piece together bits of information into creative explanations of circumstances and events. In the intervening decades, cognitive scientists developed ingenious research methods that make principles underlying knowledge growth more transparent.

Thus far in this chapter, you have read about numerous ways that children mentally represent information. Children develop perceptual images, autobiographical memories, symbols, scripts, schemas, and other kinds of ideas. These assorted thoughts are analyzed by children as they search for meaning. Children speculate about causality—for example, about laws of nature and forces in everyday physics—and about people—why others and they themselves act as they do, what their intentions are, and how different people see the same situation in unique ways. Over time, children revise these ideas and combine them into integrated belief systems, or *theories*. This approach to cognitive development is called **theory theory** (Asakura & Inui, 2016; Gopnik & Meltzoff, 1997; Morton, 1980; Musholt, 2017). Let's look at a focus of this framework that has garnered a lot of research—children's ideas about properties of physics.

Children's Theories of the Physical World

Young infants learn quickly about the physical world. By age 3 or 4 months, they show signs of surprise when one solid object passes directly through another one, when an object seems to be suspended in midair, or when an object appears to move immediately from one place to another without traveling through intervening space (Baillargeon, 1994; Bremner, Slater, Mason, Spring, & Johnson, 2016; Newcombe, Sluzenski, & Huttenlocher, 2005; Spelke & Kinzler, 2007). Such findings suggest that young infants know that objects (a) are substantive entities with definite boundaries, (b) fall unless something holds them up, and (c) move in a continuous manner across space.

This early knowledge begs the question of how it is acquired. Some cognitive scientists presume that children are endowed at birth with specialized capacities for registering patterns in physical forces (Fodor, 2000; Spelke & Kinzler, 2007). The idea that a child is born with a brain network already set up to notice regularities in movement life is known as **nativism**. Built-in knowledge about the world offers an advantage, of course—it gives infants a head start in learning about the environment (S. A. Gelman & Kalish, 2006; Spelke, 2000).

Other scholars who espouse theory theory believe that infants construct intuitions out of perceptions of statistical patterns in what they observe (e.g., in objects invariably falling down rather than up, certain sounds occuring together in English words, and people with angry faces lashing out in emotional outbursts). These patterns are registered by specially designed brain networks that easily register regularities in physics, language, and human emotions. The human brain is not considered to be hardwired with knowledge but, instead, is "softly assembled" with neurological networks with proclivities for registering patterns (Gopnik & Wellman, 2012; Thelen & Smith, 2006).

Thus, virtually everyone agrees that the human brain is jump-started with separate areas specialized with neurological structures that excel with particular kinds of information—language grammar, perceptual signals, social-emotional data, and other human functions. Experience then hones the brain's networks. What experts disagree about is how much the brain's initial wiring versus actual experience is necessary for skill development.

Whatever their origins may be, children's first ideas about objects, movement, and physical forces provide a foundation for an elaborate theory about the world. Given that children are creative thinkers, they make sense of incomplete knowledge in novel ways. In the preschool and early elementary years, many of children's ideas are unique fusions of their observations and personal speculations. For instance, young children are apt to believe that natural phenomena have a purpose. Thus, they may believe that pointy rocks exist so that animals can scratch themselves when they have an itch (Kelemen, 1999, 2004; Piaget, 1929). The belief that people play a significant role in physical causes (e.g., in forming mountains, making clouds move, and causing hurricanes) is widespread in the preschool and early elementary years (O. Lee, 1999; Piaget, 1929, 1960a). In Artifact Example 7.4, 4-year-old Isabelle has drawn her idea that lakes are formed by a person pouring water into a large hole.

Some of these misconceptions persist well into adolescence. For example, many high school and college students believe that an object persists in movement only if a force continues to act on it, and they expect an object dropped from a moving train or airplane to fall straight down (diSessa, 1996; diSessa, Gillespie, & Esterly, 2004; M. McCloskey, 1983). In reality, an object continues to move at the same speed in a particular direction unless a force acts to *change* its speed or direction (reflecting the law of inertia). Thus, object dropped from a moving train or plane not only falls but also continues to move forward (reflecting the laws of gravity and inertia).

MyLab Education
Artifact Example 7.4

Find Developmental Meaning *How does 4-year-old Isabelle illustrate the origins of lakes?* When Isabelle is asked "How were lakes made?" she offers an explanation: "You get a bucket and you fill it up with water. You get lots and lots of buckets." She illustrates her theory with the picture shown here.

Several factors contribute to inaccuracies in children's theories (D. B. Clark, 2006; Glynn, Yeany, & Britton, 1991b; Keil, 2012; Vosniadou, 2009). For one, misconceptions result from how things appear to be. From our perspective here on Earth, the sun looks as if it moves around the earth rather than vice versa. Several misconceptions are encouraged by common expressions in language (e.g., the sun "rises" and "sets"). Various cultural mechanisms—fairy tales, television shows, local folklore, occasionally even textbooks—play a role. After cartoon "bad guys" run off the edge of a cliff, they usually remain suspended in air until they realize that there's nothing solid holding them up, and at that point they fall straight down—impossible actions in the real world.

That students hold strongly onto certain misconceptions presents a challenge for educators. Consider that many children in the early elementary grades believe that the earth is flat rather than round. When adults tell them that the earth is actually round, they may interpret that information within the context of what they already "know" and hence think of the earth as being *both* flat and round—in other words, shaped like a pancake (Vosniadou, 2009).

Facilitating Children's Theory Construction

Theory theory and research on children's misconceptions yield several practical implications for parents, teachers, and other adults who work with young people.

- **Welcome children's questions.** Young children ask many *why* and *how* questions: "Why is the sky blue?" "How does a cell phone call know how to connect with another phone?" Such questions often pop up within the context of shared activities with adults (Callanan & Oakes, 1992; Frazier, Gelman, & Wellman, 2009; Siry & Max, 2013). These queries reflect children's genuine desires to make sense of their experiences. Of course, children often need to see for themselves. Astute educators find ways to address children's questions by arranging for them to make focused observations relevant to their questions and by asking them pointed questions that nudge them to revamp their conclusions (Siry & Max, 2013).

• **Before teaching a new topic, determine relevant knowledge.** Adults can more successfully address children's misconceptions when they know what those false impressions are (P. K. Murphy & Alexander, 2008). When beginning a new curriculum unit, teachers might assess students' existing beliefs about the topic, perhaps simply by asking a few informal questions that probe what students know and misunderstand. For instance, when asked if plants need food to survive, children may respond with a variety of ideas, for instance, that plants need to make food for animals, don't have mouths and cannot eat, and use fertilizer as food (Keeley, 2012). Such ideas can help focus lessons on correct mechanisms, such as the biochemical process of photosynthesis, in which food is produced for the plant.

• **When children have misconceptions, steer them toward more accurate understandings.** Even as children encounter scientific perspectives, they do not necessarily relinquish existing misunderstandings. In fact, because early "knowledge" influences the interpretation of subsequent experiences, misconceptions are often quite resistant to change (Kuhn, 2001b; P. K. Murphy & Mason, 2006). Thus, teachers must make a concerted effort to help youngsters revise their assumptions in favor of correct information. In other words, they must help youngsters undergo **conceptual change**. Theorists and researchers have offered several strategies for promoting conceptual change:

- Ask children to articulate their current beliefs in words or drawings.
- While challenging students' misconceptions, show utmost respect for their reasoning.
- Present evidence that children cannot adequately explain with their existing perspectives—in other words, create *disequilibrium*.
- Engage children in discussions of the pros and cons of various explanations for the observed phenomena.
- Explicitly point out differences between children's beliefs and scientific explanations.
- Show how a scientifically accepted explanation of an event or phenomenon makes more sense than naïve beliefs when all the evidence is taken into account.
- Provide children with compelling evidence (e.g., video of the earth from outer space) that contradicts misconceptions they are apt to have (e.g., that the earth is flat).
- Arrange for children to get hands-on experiences that address the underlying presuppositions children have about a topic.
- Have children study a topic for an extended period so that accurate explanations are thoroughly understood rather than learned in a superficial, rote manner.
- Teach a more thorough explanation than is the case with children's intuitive frameworks for a phenomenon, such as moving children from viewing nutrition as simple consumption and excretion to it additionally consisting of extracting nutrients from digested food.
- Share dramatic changes in thinking about a scientific topic (e.g., medicine before and after discoveries of germs, interpretations of earthquakes after advancements in plate tectonics, and the history of astronomical beliefs about movements of stars and planets) (D. B. Clark, 2006; Gripshover & Markman, 2013; P. K. Murphy & Alexander, 2008; P. K. Murphy & Mason, 2006; C. L. Smith, 2007; Vosniadou, 2009).

MyLab Education Application Exercise 7.3
Identify Development-Enhancing Education

In this video Crystal Thayer, a fourth-grade teacher, addresses children's misconceptions about mammals and food webs and guides them toward scientifically accurate understandings.

Summary

Some theorists propose that children gradually construct integrated belief systems (theories) about physical, biological, and social worlds, and mental events. Such integrated conceptual models are not always accurate, however. For example, children's theories may include erroneous beliefs about the solar system and laws of motion. To the extent that children's theories include misconceptions, they may interfere with the ability to acquire more sophisticated understandings. Educators can use strategies known to facilitate conceptual change to overcome these misconceptions.

MyLab Education Self-Check 7.3

An Integrative Account of Cognitive Processes

7.4 Synthesize knowledge of children's development using insights from information processing, personal theory construction, and noncognitive human functions.

The information processing and theory theory frameworks examine children's mental representations in detail. With their advanced research methods, the two frameworks have generated scientific knowledge that extends Piaget's and Vygotsky's theories of cognitive development. Information processing research has made significant inroads into how children process information and how their thinking changes with age, experience, and instruction. Theory theory helps us understand how children develop beliefs that persist in the face of contradictory evidence. The Basic Developmental Issues table "Comparing Theories in Cognitive Science" compares the information processing framework and theory theory with respect to nature and nurture, universality and diversity, and qualitative and quantitative changes.

BASIC DEVELOPMENTAL ISSUES
Comparing Theories in Cognitive Science

ISSUE	INFORMATION PROCESSING	THEORY THEORY
Nature and Nurture	Nature endows children with brain mechanisms that direct and sustain attention, process incoming information and compare it to prior understandings, and retain knowledge and skills. Information processing difficulties can have biological origins. Nevertheless, the focus of the framework is primarily on environmental factors, in particular, on how environmental input is interpreted, stored, integrated, and remembered and on how formal instruction can facilitate learning.	Basic understandings of the physical world—or at least predispositions to divide up and interpret events in particular ways—seem to be in place within the first few weeks or months after birth, and infants' neurological preferences evolve with experience. As children act and interact with their physical and social environments, they construct increasingly elaborate and integrated understandings about physical, social, and mental phenomena.
Universality and Diversity	The components of the information processing system (i.e., the sensory register, working memory, long-term memory, and central executive) are universal. However, some children use their information processing capabilities more effectively than others, especially when instructed to do so. Children's prior knowledge and cognitive strategies influence the degree to which they learn new information.	Several biologically built-in predispositions (e.g., for developing depth perception and being able to distinguish among different human faces) are universal across cultures. Informal experiences, formal schooling, and community practices and beliefs—things that are apt to differ from one culture to the next—lead children to embellish on initial abilities in culturally specific ways.
Qualitative and Quantitative Change	Over the course of development, children develop new learning strategies that are qualitatively different from earlier ones. Improvement in strategies is gradual and mainly quantitative in form. Children select a few of the more powerful strategies when solving problems of a particular kind.	As children gain information about their world, they may add to their theories in a quantitative manner. Under certain conditions, including concerted instruction and new and compelling experiences, children overhaul their theories in a way that reflects a dramatic qualitative change.

The two frameworks have limitations. The theory theory approach has revealed that children act like scientists in forming and revising conjectures about how things work. Yet children do not consciously evaluate every kind of data, nor do they automatically recognize when they have conflicting viewpoints about an issue. Thinking is not as rational as the child-as-scientist model presumes. Investigations into information processing have identified operations in attention, working memory, and knowledge base. Social-emotional factors that influence basic cognitive processes have not been a focus. The information processing perspective illuminates certain aspects of learning (e.g., growth in knowledge, patterns in memory), and the theory theory perspective accounts for children's beliefs about casually rich matters (e.g., what makes objects move and people act as they do). Both frameworks can be enriched with a broadening of factors influencing thinking processes. As we wait for further advancements in cognitive science, we can apply the insights we have achieved (see the Observation Guidelines table "Inferring Cognitive Ideas, Processes, and Metacognition").

OBSERVATION GUIDELINES

Inferring Cognitive Ideas, Processes, and Metacognition

CHARACTERISTIC	LOOK FOR	EXAMPLE	IMPLICATION
Intersubjectivity	• Reciprocal interactions with caregivers • Attempts to coordinate personal actions toward an object with related actions by someone else • Social referencing (i.e., responding to an object or event based on how a trusted adult responds to it)	A teacher at a child care center is frightened when a large dog appears just outside the fenced-in play yard, and she shouts at the dog to go away. Fifteen-month-old Owen observes her reaction and begins to cry.	Regularly engage infants in affectionate and playful interactions (smiles, coos, etc.). Remember that your own reactions communicate messages about the value, appeal, and safety of objects and events.
Attention	• Orienting toward movement, noise, or bright light • Sustained attention to human beings and inanimate objects • Ability to stay on task for an age-appropriate period • On-task behavior when distracting stimuli are present	During story time, a second-grade teacher has been reading Roald Dahl's (1964) *Charlie and the Chocolate Factory*. Most of the children are attentive, but Ben fidgets and soon finds a new form of entertainment: making silly faces at nearby classmates.	Offer interesting lessons that elicit children's engagement. If children have exceptional difficulty staying on task, minimize distractions, teach them strategies for focusing their attention, and give them regular opportunities to release pent-up energy.
Automatization of Basic Skills	• Retrieval of simple facts in a rapid, effortless fashion • Ability to use simple problem-solving strategies quickly and efficiently	Elena easily solves the problem $4/12 = x/36$ because she realizes almost immediately that it is the same as 1/3.	Give children numerous opportunities to use and practice basic facts and skills; whenever possible, do so within the context of interesting and motivating activities.
Learning Strategies	• Use of rehearsal in the elementary grades • Use of more integrative strategies (e.g., organization, elaboration) in the secondary grades • Flexible use of strategies for different learning tasks	Terri studies each new concept in her physics class by repeating the textbook definition aloud three or four times. Later she can barely remember the definitions and is unable to apply the concepts when trying to solve relevant problems.	Show struggling learners that their difficulties may be due to ineffective strategies, and teach them techniques that can help them learn more successfully.
Self-Regulated Learning Capabilities	• Initiative in identifying and seeking out needed information • Intentional efforts to keep attention focused on an assigned task • Establishment of goals for learning • Effective planning and time management	At wrestling practice one day, John tells his coach that he has just read several articles about the pros and cons of using steroids to increase muscle mass. "I'm confused about why experts advise against them," he says. "Can you help me understand their argument?"	When youngsters fail to complete independent assignments in a timely or thorough manner, provide more structure for subsequent tasks. Gradually remove the structure as they become better able to regulate their learning and performance.
Children's Personal Theories about Academic Concepts	• Statements that reveal explanatory models of physical, social, biological, and mental causes • Resistance to accepting new perspectives due to commitment to existing views • Vacillations in beliefs about a topic, such as about phases of the moon	Second-grade children mention a variety of explanations about plant needs and growth. A few believe that plants absorb food directly from the soil or from fertilizer rather than make their own food during photosynthesis.	Before beginning a new unit, ask children a few simple questions about what they already know about the topic. Try to address their misconceptions by providing counter-evidence and showing them how an unfamiliar model is more scientifically accurate, comprehensive, and consistent with the evidence.

The limitation of an implicit assumption in cognitive science that intellectual matters can be represented without consideration for non-cognitive factors stands in contrast to new research. This weakness is a serious concern because children's goals, emotions, motivations, and neurological networks are increasingly recognized as influences on mental processes. In the years ahead, we anticipate that the cognitive science framework will give increasing prominence to factors that are neglected today. Even now, one practical direction has already achieved significant. There is solid evidence that children's abilities to pay attention, stay on task, and persist toward academic goals are undermined by excessive stress. In recognition, many schools have recently introduced the concept of **mindfulness**, a state of quiet calm in which a person focuses on the present moment and personal cognitive, emotional, and physiological conditions (Cook-Cottone, 2017; Kabat-Zinn, 2005).

A growing number of teachers, counselors, and other educators have begun to implement such tactics as breathing exercises, yoga, and meditation. Many of these interventions have been shown to be effective in supporting children's concentration, physical health, and academic achievement, particularly when parents are reassured that these techniques help children concentrate and are not being implemented as part of a religious faith (Butzer et al., 2017; Cheek, Abrams, Lipschitz, Vago, & Nakamura, 2017; de Carvalho, Pinto, & Marôco, 2017; Felver, Celis-de Hoyos, Tezanos, & Singh, 2016; Frank, Kohler, Peal, & Bose, 2017; van de Weijer-Bergsma, Langenberg, Brandsma; Oort, & Bögels, 2014).

Yoga, a practice that involves breathing control, relaxation, and the enactment of physical postures that engender strength and flexibility, has Hindu spiritual origins and ties to Buddhism and other religions (Antony, 2014). Although yoga is taught in Western schools for its benefits to children's well-being and not as a campaign to endorse a religious doctrine, some families have reservations about overreach into children's spiritual development. Parents are sometimes given the option of excluding their children from the activity if they feel that it threatens their religious faith. In Figure 7.4, you can see children doing yoga at school.

FIGURE 7.4 Yoga for Relaxation.

Children practice yoga at school in an intervention designed to increase their strength, flexibility, and concentration.

Hero Images/Getty Images

Additional methods ease children's worry and promote their attention. A few alternatives include warm and predictable classroom routines, affectionate relationships between children and teachers, ongoing counseling, and contemplative practices (e.g., deep breathing and relaxation; Blaustein & Kinniburgh, 2017; A. K. Searle, Miller-Lewis, Sawyer, & Baghurst, 2013; S. L. Shapiro et al., 2015). Minimizing threats to children's well-being, such as bullying or an undiagnosed learning disability, reduces their anxiety, allowing them to relax and profit from applications of cognitive science at school.

Summary

Cognitive science significantly advances our understanding of children's cognitive development. How children attend to, think about, and remember perceptions, facts, and experiences has been the focus of the information processing framework. Children's understandings of physical properties, including naïve ideas about the laws of physics and the nature of living things, are the focus of the theory construction perspective. Both frameworks offer promising applications for educators. Limitations include the narrow array of within the cognitive domain, and a neglect of goals and emotions. Given increasing evidence of the detrimental role of stress in children's self-regulatory learning, educators are advised to ameliorate excessive anxiety in children and enhance their focus on classroom lessons.

MyLab Education Self-Check 7.4

Practicing For Your Licensure Examination

Many teaching tests require students to use what they have learned about child development in responses to brief vignettes and multiple-choice questions. You can practice for your licensure examination by reading the following case study and answering a series of questions.

The Library Project

In the final year of her teacher education program, Jessica Jensen is a teacher intern in four eighth-grade social studies classes. She has recently assigned a monthlong group project that involves considerable library research. Midway through the project, Jessica writes the following entry in her journal:

> Within each group, one student is studying culture of the region, one has religion, one has economy, and one government. The point is for the students to become "experts" on their topic in their region. There are a lot of requirements to this assignment. I'm collecting things as we go along because I think a project this long will be difficult for them to organize . . . ?
>
> So we spent all week in the library. I collected a minimum of two pages of notes yesterday, which will be a small part of their grade. The one thing that surprised me in our work in the library was their lack of skills. They had such difficulty researching, finding the information they needed, deciding what was important, and organizing and taking notes. As they worked, I walked around helping and was shocked. The librarian had already gotten out all of the appropriate resources. Even after they had the books in front of them, most did not know what to do. For instance, if they were assigned "economy," most looked in the index for that particular word. If they didn't find it, they gave up on the book. After realizing this, I had to start the next day with a brief lesson on researching and cross-referencing. I explained how they could look up *commerce, imports, exports,* and how these would all help them. I was also shocked at how poor their note-taking skills were. I saw a few kids copying paragraphs word for word. Almost none of them understood that notes don't need to be in full sentences. So, it was a long week at the library.
>
> Next week is devoted to group work and time to help them work on their rough drafts. With the difficulty they had researching, I can imagine the problems that will arise out of turning their notes into papers. (journal entry courtesy of Jessica Jensen)

Constructed-Response Question

1. Initially, Jessica realizes that her students will need some structure to complete the project successfully. In what ways do she and the librarian structure the assignment for the students?

Multiple-Choice Questions

2. How does the students' prior knowledge influence the effectiveness of their strategies?

   a. Students' lack of knowledge about such terms as *economics* makes it difficult for them to use the index and to cross-reference terms.

   b. Students' limited knowledge about their topic makes it difficult for them to make sense of the material they read.

   c. Students' lack of exposure to the topics they are researching makes it difficult for them to paraphrase and summarize what they've read.

   d. All of the above.

3. Given the information on metacognition in this chapter, how might Jessica teach students about strategy usage?

   a. Jessica needs to realize that due to their age, the eighth-grade students are not yet capable of acquiring learning strategies.

   b. Jessica can model and give students practice in using such strategies as identifying the main point of a passage, paraphrasing the material they read, referring to an index in a book, and keeping notes organized.

   c. None, because with additional reflection, Jessica will come to the conclusion that students already know how to use learning strategies and simply need to be told to try harder.

   d. Jessica should teach students to memorize the assertions of experts and repeat these comments verbatim in their reports.

MyLab Education Licensure Practice 7.1

Key Concepts

cognitive science (p. 235)
information processing theory (p. 235)
sensory register (p. 236)
long-term memory (p. 237)
central executive (p. 237)
stress (p. 238)
intersubjectivity (p. 240)
joint attention (p. 240)
social referencing (p. 240)
automatization (p. 240)
infantile amnesia (p. 242)
autobiographical self (p. 242)
knowledge base (p. 243)
schema (p. 244)
script (p. 244)
reasoning (p. 245)
symbol (p. 245)
learning disability (p. 250)
attention-deficit hyperactivity disorder (ADHD) (p. 251)
metacognition (p. 254)
cognitive strategy (p. 254)
rehearsal (p. 255)
organization (p. 255)
elaboration (p. 256)
metacognitive awareness (p. 258)
self-regulated learning (p. 259)
theory theory (p. 264)
nativism (p. 264)
conceptual change (p. 266)
mindfulness (p. 269)

Chapter Eight
Intelligence

Moodboard/Alamy Stock Photo

Learning Objectives

8.1 Describe human abilities according to well-known theories of intelligence, historical views of these capacities, and practical applications.

8.2 Outline methods for assessing children's intelligence and implications of intelligence testing for children.

8.3 Review evidence of separate and interacting factors contributing to intellectual growth.

8.4 Explain key methods for nurturing the growth of children who are exceptionally low or high in general intelligence.

CASE STUDY

Gina

Seventeen-year-old Gina has always been an enthusiastic learner. As a toddler, she loved to learn the meaning of new words. She talked early and often. As a 4-year-old, Gina asked her mother to identify a few words in a reading primer. She used these words to deduce letter–sound relationships and deciphered additional words on her own. By the time she reached kindergarten, she was reading first- and second-grade storybooks.

In elementary school Gina consistently achieved straight As on her report cards until finally, in sixth grade, she broke the pattern by getting a B in history. Since then, she has earned a few more Bs, but As continue to dominate her record. Her performance has been highest in advanced math courses, where she easily grasps the abstract concepts that many of her classmates find difficult to understand. Now in her senior year in high school, Gina has other talents as well. She won her high school's creative writing contest 2 years in a row. She landed challenging roles in her school's drama productions. And as president of her school's National Honor Society, she exhibits impressive drive while coordinating a peer-tutoring program for struggling students.

Gina's teachers describe her as a "bright" young woman. Her friends affectionately call her a "brainiac." Test results in her school file bear out these appraisals: An intelligence test that she took in junior high school yielded a score of 140, and she recently performed at the 99th percentile on college aptitude tests. This is not to say that Gina is strong in every arena. She shows little artistic ability in her paintings or clay sculptures. Her piano playing is mediocre despite 5 years of weekly lessons. In athletic events she has little stamina, strength, or flexibility. She is shy and unsure of herself at social events. And she hasn't earned an A in history since fifth grade, in large part because her idea of how best to learn history involves simply memorizing people, places, and dates.

- What evidence is there that Gina is intelligent?
- In which abilities does Gina exhibit her strongest talents?
- In which other abilities is Gina apparently less advanced?

Every child is intelligent to a certain degree. Gina's performance reflects exceptional intelligence: She earned high marks in many subjects throughout her school career and scored well on ability tests. Yet intelligence is not a set-in-concrete characteristic that youngsters either have or don't have. Gina has definite talents as well as areas that are a challenge for her, and all of these abilities expand with experience. Her assets are in academic areas that rely on advanced verbal skills, organizational abilities, and mathematical reasoning. Gina also excels at dramatic self-expression. She does not show the same extraordinary potential in history, art, music, athletics, or informal social situations, yet she will certainly advance in these competencies if she puts her mind to it and is assisted in her efforts. Like Gina, every child is poised to make the most of his or her unique abilities if given appropriate support at home, in school, and within the community.

Theories of Intelligence

8.1 Describe human abilities according to well-known theories of intelligence, historical views of these capacities, and practical applications.

Theorists think of intelligence in a range of different ways, yet most agree that it has several qualities:

- It involves a capacity for *learning*. People who are intelligent in particular areas (e.g., verbal reasoning) learn new information and procedures more quickly and easily than people who are less intelligent in those domains.
- It is *adaptive*, in that abilities are used adaptively to meet a person's goals in particular situations.
- It involves the *use of prior knowledge* in analysis of new conditions.
- It reflects the thoughtful coordination of *many distinct mental processes*.
- It *develops* with age, such that specific mental processes and their orchestration become more efficient with experience and maturation.
- It is embedded in *culture*. In different societies, being intelligent might mean reasoning about complex and abstract ideas, getting along with others, acquiring strong moral values, respecting one's elders, or exhibiting coordinated motor skills (Crago, 1988; Greenfield, 1998; H. Keller, 2003; Laboratory of Comparative Human Cognition, 1982; Nisbett, 2009; Sternberg, 2018).

With these qualities in mind, we offer one possible (and intentionally broad) definition of **intelligence**: the ability to apply past knowledge and experiences flexibly and in a culturally appropriate manner while accomplishing challenging new tasks.

Models of Intelligence

Views on intelligence have evolved considerably over the past two centuries. Inquiries into intelligence were initially based on concern for children who were not succeeding with standard educational methods. In the early 1900s, school officials in France asked psychologist **Alfred Binet** (1857–1911) to develop a method for identifying students who would have exceptional difficulty in regular classrooms without special educational services. To accomplish the task, Binet devised a test that measured general knowledge, vocabulary, perception, memory, and abstract thought (Binet & Simon, 1948). He found that students who performed poorly on his test tended to perform poorly in the classroom as well. Binet's test was the earliest version of what we now call an **intelligence test**.

Such down-to-earth interests have since been supplemented with theoretical discussions on intelligence. Scholars have debated whether intelligence is one characteristic that a child has to a greater or lesser degree or, alternatively, if it is a compilation of distinct abilities, each of which represents a strength or weakness for the child. As you will find out, evidence is strong for both positions. Many theorists now conclude that children have more or less of a general ability that permits them to solve novel problems, as well as a collection of specific abilities (e.g., comprehending spoken words or holding a lot of information in memory) that they employ in circumscribed situations.

Another issue that has garnered interest is the extent to which intelligence is inherited or derived from experience. Originally, scholars were impressed with data suggesting genetic origins to intelligence, yet increasingly experts have found strong evidence for the effects of child-rearing, schooling, nutrition, and other environmental factors. Currently, experts in intelligence are optimistic that intelligence can be enhanced with appropriate conditions (Brinch & Galloway, 2012; Dweck, 2009; J. Hayes & Stewart, 2016; Nisbett, 2009). These themes—practical implications, underlying structures, and origins—are addressed to varying degrees in the following five theories of intelligence.

Outline

Spearman's g

In the early 1900s, British psychologist **Charles Spearman** (1863–1945) proposed that intelligence comprises both (a) a single, pervasive reasoning ability (a *general factor*) that is used in a wide range of tasks and (b) a number of narrow abilities (*specific factors*) involved in executing select tasks (Spearman, 1904, 1927). From Spearman's perspective, children's performance in any given situation depends both on how generally bright they are and on any specific skills that the task requires. Measures of various language skills (vocabulary, word recognition, reading comprehension, etc.) are all highly correlated, presumably because they each reflect general intelligence and the same specific factor, verbal ability. A score on language skills will correlate to a lesser extent with a score on mathematical problem solving because the two measures tap into different specific abilities.

The strong correlations that exist among distinct intellectual abilities support the existence of a general factor in intelligence (e.g., N. Brody, 2006). This factor is often known simply as Spearman's **g**. Some contemporary theorists suspect that the ability to process information quickly may be at the heart of *g*. This speculation is supported by substantial correlations between measures of general intelligence and information processing speed (e.g., as measured by rapidly pressing the *M* key every time the number *5* appears on the right side of a computer screen; Demetriou, Mouyi, & Spanoudis, 2008).

Neurological evidence supports a biological basis for general intelligence. Neurons, cells in the brain that transmit signals for images, memories, and thoughts, seem to work especially efficiently in children who are highly intelligent. Smart children tend to have healthy neurons and the accompanying cells that insulate them in the top-front areas of the brain (behind the forehead). In these areas, conscious and effortful thinking are activated. These deliberate processes include planning, sustaining attention, ignoring distractions, anticipating consequences for actions, and making decisions (L. E. Engelhardt et al., 2016; Gläscher et al., 2010; Schubert, Hagemann, & Frischkorn, 2017; van den Heuvel, Stam, Kahn, & Hulshoff Pol, 2009). Compared to less intelligent children, exceptionally bright students have sturdier connections across separate regions in the brain, allowing for easy integration of different kinds of signals (e.g., verbal, emotional, and kinesthetic images) into a coherent representation (e.g., verbal instructions for dancers in a play; Khundrakpam et al., 2017).

Not every psychologist agrees that there is a neurological basis to general intelligence or even that a *g* factor exists in any meaningful way. Some suggest that the evidence for a single general factor can be either strong or weak depending on the specific abilities measured and the particular statistical methods used to analyze the test scores (Neisser, 1998a; Sternberg, 2003a; Sternberg & Grigorenko, 2000). Others argue that the appearance of a general factor is an artifact of test tapping into skills valued in a limited number of societies, especially mainstream cultures of Europe and North America (Gardner, 2006).

Increasingly, experts point out that even if *g* exists, children possess specific abilities that are preferable to address (Mather, 2009; McGrew, 2005). Teachers can arrange for practice after learning about children's specific limitations, such as having trouble identifying sounds and matching them with letters. In comparison, finding out about general intelligence scores provides little direction for instruction unless scores are exceptionally low or high (we address strategies for guiding children with intellectual gifts and disabilities later in this chapter).

Cattell–Horn–Carroll Theory of Cognitive Abilities

The Cattell–Horn–Carroll theory of cognitive abilities is a merger of views that expand on the conjectures of **Raymond Cattell** (1905–1998), a British psychologist who worked in the United States. Extending the ideas of Spearman, Cattell (1963, 1987) had found evidence for two distinctly different components of general intelligence. First, Cattell proposed, children differ in **fluid intelligence**, the ability to acquire knowledge quickly and adapt to new situations effectively. Second, they differ in **crystallized intelligence**, the knowledge and skills accumulated from past experiences, schooling, and culture. These two components may be more or less relevant to different intellectual trials. Fluid intelligence relates more to novel tasks, especially those that require rapid decisions and are largely nonverbal in nature. Crystallized intelligence is more important for familiar tasks, especially those heavily dependent on language and prior knowledge.

According to Cattell, fluid intelligence is largely the result of inherited biological factors, whereas crystallized intelligence depends on fluid intelligence and experience and thus is influenced by both heredity and environment (Cattell, 1980, 1987). Fluid intelligence peaks in late adolescence and begins to decline gradually in adulthood. In contrast, crystallized intelligence continues to increase throughout childhood, adolescence, and most of adulthood (Cattell, 1963).

Recent work has led to refinements in Cattell's abilities. Psychologists John Horn and John Carroll have corroborated the distinction between fluid and crystallized abilities, yet they also found other abilities. Other scholars derived abilities out of fluid and crystallized intelligence, and a new integrative framework emerged, the Cattell–Horn–Carroll (CHC) theory of cognitive abilities (P. L. Ackerman & Lohman, 2006; D. Flanagan, Alfonso, & Reynolds, 2013; Golay & Lecerf, 2011; J. L. Horn, 2008; McGrew, 2005). In the CHC theory, intelligence has three layers, or *strata.* At the top layer (Stratum III) is general intelligence, or *g*. Emerging out of *g* are 10 broad abilities (in Stratum II), including *fluid intelligence* and *crystallized intelligence*, the two abilities originally identified by Cattell, as well as 8 additional broad abilities:

- *Quantitative knowledge* (applying knowledge about mathematical operations)
- *Reading/writing* (performing complex literacy skills)
- *Long-term storage and retrieval* (putting information into memory and remembering it)
- *Short-term memory* (attending to and remembering a small number of items for a short time)[1]
- *Visual-spatial abilities* (generating visual images and identifying patterns in an incomplete visual display)
- *Auditory processing* (analyzing and synthesizing sound elements and auditory patterns)
- *Cognitive processing speed* (performing easy and familiar tasks efficiently)
- *Decision/reaction time* (making decisions quickly about simple stimuli).

Out of these broad abilities, 70 to 100 very specific abilities (Stratum I) are differentiated—reading speed, mechanical knowledge, visual memory, and so on.

MyLab Education
Content Extension 8.1
Read examples of narrow abilities in the Cattell–Horn–Carroll model.

The CHC model has extensive research support. Numerous investigations with large samples have fairly consistently found evidence of the hypothesized structures, including a hierarchy of abilities at the three expected levels (M. Chang, Paulson, Finch, Mcintosh, & Rothlisberg, 2014; Flanagan et al., 2013; Golay & Lecerf, 2011). The model is also generally consistent with research on the brain, data on developmental changes in intelligence, and evidence of hereditary and environmental influences on intelligence (McGrew, 2005).

Another advantage of this model is that it can help teachers identify the abilities called into play during a particular kind of lesson. When individual children show significant delays in one or more abilities, teachers can assign practice or provide supplements (e.g., handouts with steps in the task).

When the needs of a child exceed a teacher's resources, referrals to a school psychologist are in order. Numerous school psychologists suggest that the CHC model can guide services for children who achieve at exceptionally low or advanced levels in one or more broad abilities (Bergeron & Floyd, 2006; Claeys, 2013; Fiorello & Primerano, 2005; Floyd, Bergeron, & Alfonso, 2006; Volker, Lopata, & Cook-Cottone, 2006).

[1]The CHC broad ability of short-term memory is similar to the notion of working memory, which is known to have a limited capacity that increases during childhood.

For example, when one teacher noticed that a sixth-grade girl appeared to be having trouble with short-term memory and basic reading skills, she consulted with a school psychologist who found that most of the girl's abilities were strong (i.e., she had good language skills, vocabulary, long-term memory, and knowledge of letter–sound relationships). Yet she showed difficulty in remembering sequences of spoken words (i.e., a problem with working memory for auditory information), a situation that impaired her performance on many tasks (Fiorello & Primerano, 2005). The psychologist recommended that the girl receive drills in spelling and letter–sound combinations so that these operations could be enacted without major demands on memory. Other recommendations included having her record lessons for later reference, request notes from a classmate, and listen to assigned books on tape.

There are limitations, of course. The CHC model is still evolving, and not in a fully transparent direction. The precise configurations in the three layers vary somewhat from test to test and sample to sample; therefore, the particular abilities described are approximations rather than clear-cut aptitudes (Assis Gomes, de Araújo, Gomes Ferreira, & Golino, 2014; Benson, Kranzler, & Floyd, 2016; Kranzler, Benson, & Floyd, 2016). A final disadvantage is that the theory has been derived primarily from traditional intelligence tests.

MyLab Education Application Exercise 8.1

Meet Individual Needs

Which broad abilities does this preschool teacher tap into during the lesson? How do individual children respond?

Gardner's Multiple Intelligences

American psychologist **Howard Gardner** argues that traditional definitions of intelligence are too narrow (Gardner, 1993, 1995, 2003, 2009, 2011). He concedes that a general factor of intelligence may exist but questions its usefulness in explaining people's performance across situations. In his view, children and adults have at least eight distinctly different abilities, or *multiple intelligences* (MI), which are illustrated in Table 8.1. Three of the intelligences—linguistic, logical-mathematical, and spatial abilities—resemble the kinds of abilities that are tapped by conventional intelligence tests. According to Gardner, the remaining intelligences—musical, bodily-kinesthetic, interpersonal, intrapersonal, and naturalist abilities—are legitimate intellectual domains that have been neglected by test developers. Gardner also speculates that there may be a ninth, "existential" intelligence dedicated to philosophical and spiritual issues (e.g., Who are we? Why do we exist?). Because Gardner is on the fence about whether sufficient data distinguish an existential ability as a separate intelligence, it is not included in Table 8.1 (Gardner, 1999, 2003, 2009). From Gardner's vantage point, it is not as important to agree on a specific number of intelligences as it is to accept that abilities exist as a plurality across domains.

Gardner presents far-reaching evidence to back the existence of multiple intelligences. He describes people who are quite skilled in one area (perhaps in composing music) yet average in other areas. He points out that people who suffer brain damage sometimes lose specific abilities. One person might show deficits primarily in language, whereas another might have difficulty with tasks that require spatial reasoning. Furthermore, Gardner argues that each of the intelligences has its own symbolic operations and has played an important role historically in people's adaptations to their environments. Thus, whereas Spearman's theory and the Cattell–Horn–Carroll model are based heavily on traditional test scores, Gardner and his colleagues claim that other kinds of data (e.g., studies of people with exceptional talents, documentation of people with brain injuries) must be considered in accounts of human abilities (Gardner, 2008, 2009, 2016; Gardner & Moran, 2006).

Table 8.1 Gardner's Multiple Intelligences

TYPE OF INTELLIGENCE[a]	EXAMPLES OF RELEVANT BEHAVIORS
Linguistic Intelligence Ability to use language effectively	• Making persuasive arguments • Writing poetry • Identifying subtle nuances in word meanings
Logical-Mathematical Intelligence Ability to reason logically, especially in mathematics and science	• Solving mathematical problems quickly • Generating mathematical proofs • Formulating and testing hypotheses about observed phenomena[b]
Spatial Intelligence Ability to notice details in visual scenes and imagine and manipulate visual objects in one's mind	• Conjuring up mental images • Drawing a visual likeness of an object • Making fine discriminations among very similar objects
Musical Intelligence Ability to create, comprehend, and appreciate music	• Playing a musical instrument • Composing a musical song or instrumental piece of work • Showing a keen awareness of the underlying structure of music
Bodily-Kinesthetic Intelligence Ability to use one's body skillfully	• Dancing • Playing basketball • Performing pantomime
Interpersonal Intelligence Ability to notice subtle aspects of other people's behaviors	• Correctly perceiving another's mood • Detecting another's underlying intentions and desires • Using knowledge of others to influence their thoughts and behaviors
Intrapersonal Intelligence Awareness of one's own feelings, motives, and desires	• Identifying subtle differences in one's experiences of such similar emotions as sadness and regret • Identifying the motives guiding one's own behavior • Using self-knowledge to relate more effectively with others
Naturalist Intelligence Ability to recognize patterns in nature and differences among natural objects and life-forms	• Identifying members of particular plant or animal species • Classifying natural forms (e.g., rocks, types of mountains) • Applying one's knowledge of nature in farming, landscaping, or animal training

[a]Gardner also suggested the possibility of an existential intelligence dedicated to philosophical and spiritual issues, but he acknowledges that evidence for it is weaker than is the case for the eight intelligences described here.

[b]This example may remind you of Piaget's theory of cognitive development. Many of the abilities that Piaget described fall within the realm of logical-mathematical intelligence.

Sources: J. Chen and Gardner (2012); Gardner (1983, 1993, 1999, 2000, 2009); and Gardner and Hatch (1990).

Gardner and his colleagues have identified several implications for education. One application is to give children choices in how they demonstrate knowledge. Gardner recommends that teachers help children refine their unique profiles of abilities, for example, by implementing computer programs that personalize training. Teachers can vary their instructional modalities, for example, by asking students to show their mastery of mathematics with written formulas (logical-mathematical abilities) on one occasion, self-reflections on learning (intrapersonal abilities) on another, and analyses of data collected from the local ecology (naturalistic abilities) still later. Soliciting a range of abilities increases the chances that the special talents of every child are exercised at some point and that children generally develop well-rounded understandings of subject matter (J. Chen & Gardner, 2012; Gardner, 2009).

Educators around the world have embraced the value of implementing varied instructional methods and giving all children a chance to shine now and again by playing to their personal strengths (Armstrong, 2009; L. Campbell, Campbell, & Dickinson, 1998; Rattanavich, 2013; Rizzo, 2009). In the Development in Culture feature, "Multiple Intelligences in China," you can learn how educators in China have integrated Gardner's theory into their teaching.

In psychological circles, reviews of Gardner's theory are mixed. Some psychologists do not believe that Gardner's evidence is sufficiently convincing to conclude that there are eight or nine distinctly different abilities (N. Brody, 2006; A. R. Jensen, 2007; Sternberg, 2013). Others agree that people have a variety of independent abilities but disagree on which ones exist (D. Flanagan et al., 2013; J. L. Horn & Noll, 1997; Sternberg et al., 2000). Still others reject the idea that abilities in music, body movement,

MyLab Education
Video Example 8.1

Find Developmental Meaning

How does Mr. Tobin help his seventh-grade students to learn about the human body? In this video, Mr. Tobin encourages students to create a song, drawing, or other representation of the circulatory and skeletal systems.

Development in Culture

Multiple Intelligences in China

Three aspects of Howard Gardner's theory of multiple intelligences (MI) have been endorsed by educators around the world. First, integral to Gardner's theory is the idea that each of the eight (or nine, or more) intelligences is developed in unique ways in virtually all cultures (Gardner, 1983). People in varied circumstances see the uses of language, mathematics, spatial images, movement, music, personal insights, interpersonal understandings, and knowledge of nature within their daily lives (Armstrong, 2009; Dixon, Humble, & Chan, 2016). Second, the theory's advocacy for the arts and physical education has been compelling to many educators who believe that joy of learning in a broad range of human endeavors is important (Gardner, 2009). Finally, educators have appreciated Gardner's interest in reaching underserved students with inclusive methods.

Educators in China have been particularly enthusiastic about applying lessons from the theory of MI. In fact, hundreds of thousands of Chinese educators have received training in this framework (J.-Q Chen, 2009; Zhang & Kong, 2012). Chinese educators increasingly recognize that traditional methods of instruction, which have emphasized memorization of basic facts, yield capabilities that are inadequate in a rapidly changing society. For modern Chinese teachers, active learning, respect for individual differences, and innovation make MI theory an ideal framework for nurturing human potential (J.-Q. Chen, 2009; H. H.-P. Cheung, 2009).

The theory's compatibility with cultural ideals in learning has also contributed to its adoption in China. Dating back to the days of Confucius, Chinese culture has admired the plurality of human abilities (J.-Q. Chen, 2009; Shen, 2009). Today, an appreciation for individual differences has helped teachers respond sympathetically to learners who do not perform well on traditional academic tasks. In reflecting on the MI framework, one Chinese teacher said, "Unlike before, when I look at my students now, they are all good students. Everyone has shining points to appreciate" (H. H.-P. Cheung, 2009, p. 45). Another teacher made a similar observation, "I noticed some of my students who did not have high scores in school turned out to be more successful. MI theory shows me the reason. Those students' interpersonal intelligences might be higher. Each of them is unique" (H. H.-P. Cheung, 2009, p. 45).

In the process of absorbing basic tenets of MI theory, Chinese educators have adapted the framework to fit two features of their culture. First, intelligence in young children is considered inseparable from the abilities of their families (J.-Q. Chen, 2009). In other words, intelligence is a property of the family, not a quality of the individual child. Each family has its own profile of intellectual strengths, interests, and skills, and each member of the family complements and supports the intelligence of other members. In this spirit, educators trained in MI theory hold classes in the evening and on weekends for parents. At school, children are encouraged to learn about their parents' values, interests, and child-rearing strategies so as to increase children's receptivity to family lessons.

BLOOMimage/Getty Image

INTELLIGENCE IN THE FAMILY. In China, Gardner's theory of multiple intelligences has drawn attention to the growth of intellectual development within the family.

Second, the cultural ideal of harmony is integrated into interpretations of MI theory. Chinese educators view children's intellectual strengths as balancing their weaknesses. To be effective, teachers must take into account the entire package of abilities and limitations in a child. The notion of harmony also applies to offering an array of lesson formats so that everyone has a chance to succeed (J.-Q. Chen, 2009; Jing, 2013).

Chinese educators wrestle with certain challenges in translating the principles of MI theory to instruction (H. H.-P. Cheung, 2009). Large class sizes make it difficult to individualize innovative instructional methods. Pressures to prepare high school students for college entrance examinations complicate the applications for older adolescents. Finally, some Chinese educators have the misconception that the framework directs them to train every child to a high level of accomplishment in each of the eight or nine intelligences rather than allowing children the freedom to excel with the talents of their choice.

and self-insight are really "intelligence" (Bracken, McCallum, & Shaughnessy, 1999; Sattler, 2001).

Sternberg's Theory of Successful Intelligence

American psychologist **Robert Sternberg** has developed a series of interrelated theories on how people use their cognitive abilities to achieve personal goals. Sternberg sees intelligence as a multifaceted capacity that allows an individual to adapt effectively to the environment (see Figure 8.1). He suggests that people may be more or less intelligent in three abilities (Sternberg, 1985, 2005, 2009). *Analytical intelligence* involves making sense of, analyzing, contrasting, and evaluating the kinds of information seen in academic settings and on intelligence tests. *Creative intelligence* involves imagination, invention, and synthesis of ideas within new situations. *Practical intelligence* involves applying knowledge and skills effectively to everyday problems and social dilemmas. Children blend these three types of intelligence in everyday tasks and gradually recognize their personal strengths in each, use them to personal advantage, and correct or compensate for weaknesses.

These three types of intelligence involve the interplay of three additional factors: (a) the environmental *context* in which the behavior occurs, (b) the way in which one's memory of prior *experience* is brought to bear on a particular task, and (c) the *cognitive processes* required by the task (Sternberg, 1985, 1997, 2003b).

FIGURE 8.1 Sternberg's theory of successful intelligence.

According to Sternberg, a child uses a multifaceted collection of abilities to achieve personal goals.

Successful Intelligence

- Is comprised of analytical, creative, and practical abilities
- Helps a person achieve personal goals
- Requires a balancing among particular abilities
- Draws from memory and engages specific cognitive processes
- Allows a person to adapt, shape, and select environments

Environmental Context. In Sternberg's view adjustment to the environment might take one of three forms: (a) modifying a response to deal successfully with specific conditions, (b) modifying the environment to better fit one's own strengths and needs, or (c) selecting an alternative environment more conducive to success. Thus, a given action may be considered more or less intelligent depending on the demands of the setting. For example, learning to describe events in explicit detail is intelligent in some contexts (e.g., at school), whereas speaking in an informal manner with reference to shared experiences is smart in other settings (e.g., with friends).

MyLab Education
Video Explanation 8.1
In this video, advocates of Multiple Intelligences theory make recommendations for accommodating diversity in abilities.

Prior Experience. Intelligent behavior sometimes involves the ability to deal successfully with a brand-new situation. At other times, it involves the ability to respond to familiar situations rapidly and efficiently. In both cases, a child's prior experiences play a critical role. When children encounter a new task or problem, they must consider the kinds of reactions that have been effective in similar circumstances. When they deal with familiar tasks, the necessary processes can be completed quickly and effortlessly because relevant skills have been previously practiced.

Cognitive Processes. In addition to examining how context and prior experience affect behavior, we must consider how a child thinks about a situation. Sternberg suggests that numerous cognitive processes are involved in intelligent behavior, including interpreting a new situation in productive ways, sustaining concentration on a task, separating important information from irrelevant details, identifying possible problem-solving strategies, finding relationships among seemingly different ideas, and making effective use of external feedback. Different cognitive processes are likely to be relevant to different situations, and so a child may behave more or less "intelligently" depending on specific demands.

Sternberg and his colleagues recommend that teachers diversify the abilities they tap. Although it is not realistic to target the full gamut of abilities in any single lesson, teachers can alter the instructional formats they use across lessons and over time. In a science unit, students might conduct standard experiments on light, write a fantasy story about a light beam traveling around the world, and identify patterns in astronomical data with speed of light (Sternberg, Jarvin, & Grigorenko, 2009). In one investigation, students who took part in a well-balanced curriculum, one that activated analytical, practical, and creative intelligence over the course of the unit, performed at higher levels than did students who received conventional instruction (Sternberg, Torff, & Grigorenko, 1998).

Sternberg's perspective has advanced our understanding intelligence by drawing attention to the cognitive processes that underlie a child's multifaceted abilities. The theory reminds us that a child's ability to behave intelligently varies according to context, his or her goals, and the knowledge required by a task. A fair amount of research supports these ideas. Some evidence indicates that analytical, creative, and practical skills exist and are somewhat independent of one another and from general intelligence (Sternberg, 2009). Other results indicate that measurements of Sternberg's abilities are associated with later academic success, sometimes even more strongly than is the case with conventional intelligence tests (Sternberg, 2018). However, scholars worry that certain aspects of Sternberg's theory (e.g., how different factors work together) are described in such general terms that it is unclear how to test them (Sattler, 2001; Siegler & Alibali, 2005). Other intelligence specialists are not yet convinced that the practical abilities identified in Sternberg's theory are really all that different from general intelligence (N. Brody, 2006; Ekinci, 2014; Gottfredson, 2003).

Distributed Intelligence

Implicit in our discussion so far has been the assumption that intelligent behavior is something that children engage in with little if any help from external resources. But some psychologists point out that youngsters are far more likely to behave intelligently when they have the support of their physical, social, cultural, and digital environments (Hoerr, 2015; Pea, 1993; Perkins, 1995; Sternberg, Grigorenko, & Bridglall, 2007). For example, it's easier for many adolescents to solve for x in the equation

$$\frac{7}{25} = \frac{x}{375}$$

if they have pencil and paper in hand. Similarly, they are more likely to write a convincing essay if they brainstorm their ideas with peers before beginning to compose their notes.

This idea that intelligent behavior depends on physical, social, and cultural support mechanisms is referred to as **distributed intelligence**. Learning specialists **Roy Pea** and **David Perkins** have observed that children can "distribute" their thinking (and therefore think more intelligently) in at least three ways (Pea, 1993; Perkins, 1992, 1995). First, young people use physical objects, especially technology (e.g., calculators, computers), to handle and manipulate large amounts of information. Second, they work with others to explore ideas and solve problems. Third, they represent the situations they encounter with symbolic tools—for instance, the words, diagrams, charts, mathematical equations, and so on—that help them simplify or make better sense of complex topics and problems.

The framework of distributed intelligence has considerable appeal to many educators who recognize that *all* children—not just those who have the advantage of "smart" genes or those whose families foster their academic skills at home—deserve to have their abilities nurtured by teachers and classmates (Barab & Plucker, 2002; Hoerr, 2003). In fact, children often develop more advanced skills when working together, pooling their knowledge, using digital technologies, and tackling realistic problems (C. Alvarez, Salavati, Nussbaum & Milrad, 2013; Greeno, 2007; K. E. Ramey & Uttal, 2017; L. Xu & Clarke, 2012). Theorists have only begun to explore the implications of a "distributed" view of intelligence, however. Much work remains to be done, both in identifying the specific ways in which the environment can support intelligent behavior and in determining the effect such support has.

The five perspectives just presented provide diverging views of human intelligence. Differences with respect to three themes—nature and nurture, universality and diversity, and qualitative and quantitative change—are presented in the Basic Developmental Issues table "Contrasting Theories of Intelligence."

Other Perspectives on Intelligence

Associations between intellectual abilities and school achievement have been a dominant focus in the study of intelligence. A few other approaches are less grounded in this research yet suggestive of other capabilities not measured by existing intelligence tests. These additional competencies have been detected in various cultures, in settings that invite innovation, and situations that are emotionally expressive.

BASIC DEVELOPMENTAL ISSUES
Contrasting Theories of Intelligence

ISSUE	SPEARMAN'S GENERAL FACTOR *(g)*	CATTELL–HORN–CARROLL THEORY OF COGNITIVE ABILITIES	GARDNER'S THEORY OF MULTIPLE INTELLIGENCES	STERNBERG'S THEORY OF SUCCESSFUL INTELLIGENCE	THEORY OF DISTRIBUTED INTELLIGENCE
Nature and Nurture	Spearman did not specifically address the issue of nature versus nurture. Researchers have subsequently found evidence that *g* is related to both heredity and environment.	Proponents of the Cattell-Horn-Carroll model claim that fluid intelligence is determined by genetic factors whereas crystallized intelligence is influenced by both heredity and environment.	Gardner believes that heredity provides a basis for individual differences in assorted intelligences. Culture influences the form of each intelligence, and informal experiences and instruction determine intellectual achievements.	Sternberg emphasizes environmental context (e.g., culture), prior experience, and the person's own goals and choices in particular environments. Thus, his focus is primarily on nurture.	People act more intelligently when they have access to resources. Specific mechanisms for supporting thinking (physical tools, social interaction, and symbolic representations of culture) vary among individuals and settings.
Universality and Diversity	Spearman assumed that the existence of *g* is universal across cultures. People vary both in their general intellectual capacity and in their more specific abilities.	Substantial evidence suggests that the multidimensional structure of abilities is universal. Individual children differ in levels of general intelligence, broad abilities, and specific abilities.	The various intelligences are products of human evolution and are seen worldwide. However, any particular intelligence will manifest itself differently in separate settings and cultures.	Context, experience, and cognitive processes universally affect intelligent behavior. Different cultures place distinct demands on analytical, creative, and practical abilities.	The physical, social, and symbolic support mechanisms at one's disposal vary widely from situation to situation and from one cultural group to another.
Qualitative and Quantitative Change	Spearman derived his theory from various tests of cognitive abilities. Implicit in his tests is the assumption that abilities change quantitatively over time, with gradual increases to specific skill-sets of overall capacities, while individual rankings from low to high in overall intelligence remain fairly stable.	A quantitative increase occurs in fluid analytical abilities in childhood and is followed by a decline in later adulthood (Cattell, 1963). Abilities also change qualitatively, as when a baby first attends to interesting stimuli and later verbalizes these observations.	Growth in intelligences reflects both quantitative and qualitative changes. For example, in logical-mathematical intelligence, children gain skills in increments (quantitatively) but also acquire new (and qualitatively different) abilities.	The effects of prior experiences, more automatized knowledge and skills, and progressively efficient cognitive processes involve quantitative change. The acquisition of new strategies involves qualitative change.	Some resources enhance intelligence quantitatively (e.g., paper and pencil allow more complicated mathematics than mental calculations alone). Other instruction enhances intelligence qualitatively (e.g., enhancing comprehension by asking one another thought-provoking questions).

Cultural Views on Intelligence

Because one indicator of intelligence is being able to adapt to the demands of a society, it stands to reason that the way children apply their intellectual skills will depend on cultural values and practices (Sternberg, 2018). Children acquire cultural views about learning, intelligence, and their own abilities through everyday interactions with parents, siblings, peers, teachers, and others in the community. In Western civilizations, intelligence is a means for analyzing information into categories and propositions, whereas in Eastern cultures people invest their intelligence in perceptions of complexity, contradiction, and social obligation (Nisbett, 2003).

Developmental Systems Prompt

Your impact on children's intellectual abilities depends in part on your awareness of factors inside and outside children that affect learning. For example, when young children have had few opportunities to hear stories at home, you may want to amplify their exposure to stories with objectives in enhancing children's vocabulary, comprehension, knowledge base, and love of literature.

Creativity

Questions on intelligence tests generally have right or wrong answers, unlike dilemmas in real life, whose remedies transcend known facts. How people decide on a career to pursue, compose a story, invent a cure for cancer, and express personal feelings through artwork are complicated endeavors with unknown answers. Attempts at formulating answers require **creativity**, the process of generating novel and worthwhile solutions to goals, needs, and problems.

Traditionally, creativity has been measured by a test that requires people to formulate original solutions to unfamiliar problems, such as by generating as many ways as possible to use a pencil, book, or brick (Goff & Torrance, 2002; Guilford, 1967;

Torrance, 1981). Creativity scores are calculated from the number of different ways of using the item and the number of uniquely original ways (not proposed by others) that a person formulates. Fluency in formulating novel uses for objects is only part of creativity, however. Experts believe that the additional step of taking brainstormed ideas and pruning them down to a limited number of options is a key part of the creative process (Goodwin & Miller, 2013).

When thinking creatively, a person uses existing intellectual processes, such as searching memory, comparing ways of representing a problem, putting ideas together in new ways, and selecting final answers that have been carefully vetted (C. S. Lee & Therriault, 2013). Nevertheless, creativity is not the same as intelligence. The ability to act imaginatively requires talents in applying mental processes fluidly and dynamically. Yet being original is not enough to be considered creative. A creative act achieves a goal or solves a problem in a way that stays within certain parameters, such as using available materials or communicating a particular message. Teams of children in a third-grade classroom are creative when they design different kinds of forts out of existing school materials.

The exercise of inventive abilities changes with development but perhaps not in the manner you might think. Unlike intelligence, creativity does not necessarily increase with development. In fact, children are more creative than adults, and younger children are more creative than older children, suggesting that this capacity *diminishes* as children progress through the school years (Goodwin & Miller, 2013; Land & Jarman, 1992). Part of the decline is due to children learning society's conventions for solving common problems. Instructional strategies may also stifle creativity by emphasizing facts and procedures over free expression.

This age-related decrease is not inevitable. Arts and crafts are a common forum for encouraging free expression, especially during early childhood. Structured lessons in elementary and secondary schools can incorporate options for completing the project (D. Davies et al., 2013; Plucker, Guo, & Dilley, 2018). An elementary teacher might ask children to brainstorm about funny things that farm animals do before selecting an animal to write a story about, and a middle school science teacher could encourage students to come up with several hypotheses before pursuing the implications of one (S. Brookhart, 2013). Building a structurally sound bridge out of toothpicks, writing an essay on how life would be different had the Internet not been invented, and preparing a video discouraging bullying at school are just a few of the many projects that engender creative processes.

Emotional Intelligence

Just as some students have special talents that make it easy for them to solve algebraic equations or explain the meaning of an archaic poem, other students have exceptional abilities with emotions. The former students have intellectual abilities that support their academic success. Do the latter students have emotional capacities that contribute to their well-being? Surely, they do. They have strong insights into why they feel as they do, and they employ effective coping skills when angered, disappointed, sad, or frustrated. They express their feelings honestly and productively and show empathy to people in need.

Given that some children are more skilled than others in expressing and managing their feelings, is it possible that this proficiency is an actual intelligence? The answer is complicated. As with general intelligence, coping with emotions depends on prior knowledge and a certain flexibly in addressing new challenges. As well, the ability to handle emotions has several of the qualities of intelligence we introduced previously. Strong coping skills help a child maintain productive interpersonal relationships, improve with experience, and to some degree are culture-specific. For these reasons, a few developmental experts see the ability to perceive, understand, and regulate affective feelings to be a specialized capacity that deserves to be elevated with the term **emotional intelligence** (Curci, Lanciano, Soleti, Zammuner, & Salovey, 2013; D. Goleman, 1995; Keefer, Holden, & Parker, 2013; Laborde, Lautenbach, Allen, Herbert, & Achtzehn, 2014).

Despite having proponents, emotional intelligence does not seem to have all of the qualities that are expected of an intelligence. For one thing, emotional competencies do not seem to be a coherent ability. Figuring out how to cope with anger requires somewhat different abilities than empathizing with a friend's sorrow after losing a parent in a tragic automobile accident. Nor do emotional skills appear to be completely different from intelligence or personality (N. Brody, 2004; Brouzos, Misailidi, & Hadjimattheou, 2014; Waterhouse, 2006). Finally, whereas intelligence is known to expand with development, the reasoning and skills presumed to be part of emotional intelligence do not as consistently show common developmental progressions (Esnaola, Revuelta, Ros, & Sarasa, 2017).

Regardless of whether emotional capacities are ultimately determined to be an intelligence, the constituent skills contribute to children's well-being. With a foundation in emotional awareness, children can learn to cope with frustration and persevere during learning tasks. In recent years, interventions inspired by the concept of emotional intelligence have become popular in schools and have generated positive effects on children's mental health, peer relationships, and academic achievement (Nathanson, Rivers, Flynn, & Brackett, 2016; R. D. Taylor, Oberle, & Weissberg, 2017). One example of this type of program is RULER, an acronym for *Recognizing* emotions in oneself and others; *Understanding* causes of emotions; *Labeling* distinct emotions, such as regret or pride; *Expressing* feelings productively rather bottling them up or letting them escalate; and *Regulating* feelings by considering how a situation can be looked at from different perspectives (Nathanson et al., 2016). This program has produced improvements in how safe, inclusive, and welcoming the school feels to children and how strongly they perform academically.

Practical Insights from Theories of Intelligence

Although experts disagree about the exact nature of intelligence, sufficient consensus exists for a few applications. Consider these implications:

- **In your instruction, vary demands on specific intellectual abilities.** As you have learned, intelligence is a multifaceted cluster of abilities. Although traditional forms of education emphasize verbal and quantitative skills, students have many other talents, including artistic and musical abilities, creative powers, and athletic skills. As we saw in recommendations by Howard Gardner and Robert Sternberg, lessons, projects, and assessments can elicit a healthy assortment of intellectual abilities. Oftentimes a single project exercises two or more distinct abilities, as you can infer in a drawing by 10-year-old Amaryth in Artifact Example 8.1.

MyLab Education
Artifact Example 8.1

Find Developmental Meaning *Which abilities does 10-year-old Amaryth employ in her sketches of sunflower seeds?* Amaryth seems to have applied Gardner's naturalist intelligence by detecting patterns in the sunflower seeds, spatial intelligence by measuring the insect and sunflower, and linguistic intelligence when describing the stem as "very fuzzy like my arm."

- **Be on the lookout for children's personal strengths and weaknesses.** From the beginning of the school year, teachers gradually notice which children easily grasp concepts across the curriculum, and which others regularly run into trouble, patterns that arise in part due to varying levels of general intelligence. As the year progresses, teachers begin to observe nuances in individual children's proficiencies and struggles with specific abilities. One child may excel at all things mathematical, and another may have trouble keeping lengthy instructions in mind.

- **Document children's abilities.** You can collect work samples that reveal students' strengths and difficulties, perhaps in visual-spatial abilities in geometry, auditory processing while learning to read, or mathematical competencies when calculating numerical equations. When children struggle with one or more of these skills, teachers can provide handouts with written procedures, audiotaped books, or other resources that bolster learning. On the other hand, extraordinary accomplishments indicate the need for new challenges. School psychologists and other specialists are regularly available to offer advice on adapting lessons for children with unusual intellectual profiles. The Observation Guidelines table "Seeing Intelligence in Children's Everyday Behavior" characterizes behaviors that reveal intelligence.

- **Invite children to pool their knowledge.** Although we generally think about talent as an individual matter, the reality is that children often achieve at higher levels in groups

OBSERVATION GUIDELINES
Seeing Intelligence in Children's Everyday Behavior

CHARACTERISTIC	LOOK FOR	EXAMPLE	IMPLICATION
Oral Language Skills	• *Sophisticated vocabulary* • *Colorful speech* • *Creative storytelling* • *Clever jokes and puns*	Jerome entertains his friends with jokes and wild exaggerations about the characteristics and actions of other people.	Look for unusual creativity or advanced language development in children's everyday speech.
General Intelligence	• *Ability to learn new information quickly* • *Exceptional knowledge* about a topic • *Ability to find relationships* among diverse ideas • *Excellent memory* • *Ability to stay focused on task*	Four-year-old Gina teaches herself to read using primers she finds at home. Initially, her mother identifies a few words for her. From these words, she deduces letter–sound correspondences that enable her to decipher other words.	Make note of situations in which a child learns and comprehends new material more quickly than peers. Look for creative analogies, smart wordplay, serious artwork, and other manifestations of intelligence.
Problem-Solving Skills	• *Ability to solve challenging problems* • *Flexibility* in applying previously learned strategies to new kinds of problems • *Ability to improvise* with commonplace materials	A fourth-grade class plans to perform a skit during an upcoming open house. Jeff suggests that they turn their desks to face the side of the classroom and hang a sheet from a light fixture as stage curtain.	Present unusual tasks and problems for which children have no ready-made strategies or solutions.
Cognitive and Metacognitive Strategies	• *Use of sophisticated learning strategies* • *Desire to understand* rather than memorize • *Effective comprehension monitoring* • *Making adjustments to strategies* when struggling to learn	Shannon, a sixth grader, explains that she learned countries on South America's west coast (Colombia, Ecuador, Peru, Chile) by creating the sentence "*C*olin *e*ats *p*eas and *ch*ocolate."	Ask children to describe how they think about things they are trying to learn and remember. Teach powerful strategies, such as setting goals for a study session and checking your work.
Curiosity and Inquisitiveness	• *Voracious appetite for knowledge* • *Tendency to ask a lot of questions* • *Intrinsic motivation* to master challenging subject matter	Alfredo reads every book and article he can find about outer space. He has a particular interest in black holes.	Find out what children like to do in their free time and direct them to relevant resources. Watch for occasions when children seem puzzled and energized to learn more.
Leadership and Social Skills	• *Ability to persuade* and motivate others • *Insightful sensitivity* to other people's feelings • *Ability to mediate disagreements* and facilitate compromises	As a high school student, Gina organizes and directs a peer-tutoring program.	Observe how children interact with their peers at play, in cooperative group work, and during extracurricular activities. Present them with challenging situations that they can talk through and address together.

Sources: Blake and Giannangelo (2012); B. Clark (1997); A. W. Gottfried, Gottfried, Bathurst, and Guerin (1994); Y. Huang, Hsu, Su, and Liu (2014); Maker (1993); Nilsen, Huyder, McAuley, and Liebermann (2017); Perkins (1995); Sousa (2009); Torrance (1995); Turnbull, Turnbull, and Wehmeyer (2010); Winner (1997).

than alone and with access to technologies than without such resources. The theory of distributed intelligences reminds us that children—like adults in the workplace—think more effectively when they can consult with others and use suitable tools.

• **Encourage creativity.** Given the emphasis in most classrooms on core knowledge, children realize that they are expected to learn procedures and concepts as presented by teachers. Yet there are occasions when real creativity enhances learning. Because children may not automatically identify circumstances in which they have freedom of expression, teachers need to signal when novel thinking is welcome. It helps to structure these lessons to be conducive to innovation—for example, by providing an assortment of materials, communicating that achieving a solution may take innumerable forms, and encouraging children to brainstorm ideas at the beginning of the assignment.

• **Learn about talents cultivated in the community.** Spending time in local neighborhoods and city events is a valuable way to learn about respected talents in the culture. Invitations to families to share their aspirations for children at school meetings can be useful. In the classroom, teachers can offer options, such as a selection of historical novels and multiple formats for demonstrating comprehension (e.g., oral presentations, posters, essays, or cartoons).

• **Promote intelligent strategies.** Teachers can promote intelligent behavior by showing children how to use effective study skills (Cornoldi, 2010; Perkins, 1995; Sternberg, 2002). Students from across the general intelligence continuum can benefit from explicit instruction into a range of learning objectives, from doing laundry to inferring motivations of story characters (Barth & Elleman, 2017; K. A. Smith, Shepley, Alexander, & Ayres, 2015). Emotions provide another context for acquiring new strategies. Teachers and other professionals can guide children with relaxation and emotional regulation (Nathanson et al., 2016; R. D. Taylor, Oberle, Durlak, & Weissberg, 2017).

Summary

Intelligence involves effective learning processes and adaptive behaviors in particular settings. Some theorists (e.g., Spearman) believe that intelligence is a single entity (a general factor, or *g*) that influences children's learning and performance across a wide variety of tasks. This belief is reflected in the widespread use of IQ scores as general estimates of academic ability. Other theorists (e.g., Gardner and Sternberg) propose that intelligence consists of a number of somewhat independent abilities that cannot be accurately reflected in a single IQ score. Increasing evidence reveals that children are more likely to behave "intelligently" when they have physical, social, and symbolic support systems to ease their efforts. Emerging views suggest the existence of additional talents, including culture-specific abilities, creative knacks, and emotional sensitivities.

Individual children are intelligent in somewhat distinctive ways. Teachers can capitalize on these unique strengths in lessons, encouraging children to go beyond the requirements of assignments. Adults can also give children social support and the physical and symbolic tools that enhance intelligent thinking and performance. Significant limitations in core abilities can be buttressed with guidance from school psychologists, counselors, and special education teachers.

MyLab Education Self-Check 8.1

Measurement of Intelligence

8.2 Outline methods for assessing children's intelligence and implications of intelligence testing for children.

Although psychologists have not been able to agree on exactly what intelligence is, they have been trying to measure it for more than a century. Most intelligence tests in use today have been developed to do the same thing that Alfred Binet's first test was intended to do: identify children with special needs who would benefit from customized educational services.

Tests of Intelligence

A diagnostic battery of intelligence tests is administered to determine why certain children are showing developmental delays or academic difficulties. In other instances, intelligence tests are used to identify children with exceptionally high abilities who require more in-depth instruction and advanced classwork to nurture their cognitive growth. Intelligence tests typically include a wide variety of questions and problems for children to tackle. By and large, the focus is not on what children have specifically been taught at school but, rather, on what they have learned and deduced from everyday experiences. Four commonly used tests include the following:[2]

[2]You can find descriptions of several widely used tests at http://www.datarecognitioncorp.com/Pages/default.aspx (for Data Recognition Corporation instruments, including TerraNova® Third Edition), www.pearsonassessments.com (for Pearson instruments, including WISC®-V and Bayley Scales of Infant and Toddler Development®, Third Edition) and http://www.hmhco.com/classroom/classroom-solutions/assessment (for HMH Assessments, including Stanford Binet Intelligence Scales, Woodcock Johnson® IV Tests, and Universal Nonverbal Intelligence Test Second Edition.™).

- The *Wechsler Intelligence Scale for Children (WISC-V)* is a widely used test designed for children ages 6 to 16. The test yields index scores in Verbal Comprehension, Visual Spatial, Fluid Reasoning, Working Memory, Processing Speed, and a Full Scale IQ (Wechsler, 2014). Types of items used are illustrated in Figure 8.2.
- The *Stanford-Binet Intelligence Scales* (fifth edition) can be used with children (as young as age 2), adolescents, and adults. The test yields an overall IQ score. Its most recent edition also yields Verbal and Nonverbal IQs and more specific scores in Fluid Reasoning, Knowledge, Working Memory, Visual-Spatial Processing, and Quantitative Reasoning (Roid, 2003; Roid & Pomplun, 2012).
- The *Universal Nonverbal Intelligence Test*, or UNIT, is administered without verbal language for children ages 5 to 17 (S. M. Bell, 2017; Bracken & McCallum, 1998, 2009; McCallum & Bracken, 2012; A. F. Moore, McCallum, & Bracken, 2017). The test administrator communicates with gestures, pantomime, and demonstrations, and the child responds by either pointing or manipulating objects. For example, the child may trace a path through a maze or construct a three-dimensional design using colored cubes.
- The *Cognitive Assessment System* (CAS, second edition) is a multidimensional measure of cognitive processes that have been identified in neurological research (McGill, 2015; Naglieri & Otero, 2012). Items focus on four abilities: *Attention*, involving selective concentration on stimuli while ignoring distractions; *Simultaneous* processes, in which a figure needs to be found within a complex pattern;

FIGURE 8.2 Illustrations of Items on Intelligence Tests.

These questions have a similar format to items on the Wechsler Intelligence Scale for Children®—Fifth Edition. *Copyright © 2014 by NCS Pearson, Inc. Reproduced with permission. All rights reserved.*

Verbal Comprehension

Similarities

- In what way are a lion and a tiger alike?
- In what way are an hour and a week alike?
- In what way are a circle and a triangle alike?

Working Memory

Letter-Number Sequence

[Child listens to letter-number combination and then repeats first numbers in numerical order and letters in alphabetical order.]

- Q-3 [Response: 3-Q]
- M-3-P-6 [Response: 3-6-M-P]
- 5-J-4-A-1-S [Response: 1-4-5-A-J-S]

Fluid Reasoning

Arithmetic

- Sam had three pieces of candy and Joe gave him four more. How many pieces of candy did Sam have altogether?
- Three women divided eighteen golf balls equally among themselves. How many golf balls did each person receive?
- If two buttons cost $0.15, what will be the cost of a dozen buttons?

Visual Spatial

Block Design

[Child looks at a series of designs, such as the one to the right, and re-creates the patterns using blocks that are solid red on two sides, solid white on two sides, and diagonally red and white on the remaining two sides.]

Planning, in which a tactic is to be determined and carried out while solving a novel problem; and *Successive* processes, whereby information needs to be handled in a specific order.

Intelligence Scores

In the early 20th century, psychologists began to calculate scores from intelligence tests by comparing a child's *mental age* (referring to the age-group of students whose performance is most similar to the child's performance) with his or her chronological age (W. Stern, 1949; Terman, 1916). The mathematical formula involved division, and so the resulting score was called an *intelligence quotient*, or **IQ score**.[3] Even though we still use the term *IQ*, intelligence test scores are no longer based on the old formula. Instead, they are determined by comparing a person's performance on the test with the performance of others in the same age-group. Scores near 100 indicate average performance: Children with a score of 100 have performed better than half of their age-mates on the test and not as well as the other half. Scores well below 100 indicate below-average performance on the test, and scores well above 100 indicate above-average performance.

Figure 8.3 shows the percentage of people with scores at different points along the scale (e.g., 12.9% get scores between 100 and 105). Notice how the curve is high in the middle and low at both ends. This shape tells us that many more people obtain scores close to 100 than scores very much higher or lower than 100. If we add up the percentages in different parts of Figure 8.3, we find that approximately two thirds (68%) of individuals in any particular age group score within 15 points of 100 (i.e., between 85 and 115). In contrast, only 2% score as low as 70, and only 2% score as high as 130.[4] Figure 8.3 does not include scores below 70 or above 130. Such scores are possible but relatively rare. You might recall that Gina, in the opening case study, once obtained a score of 140 on an intelligence test. A score of 140 is equivalent to a percentile rank of 99.4. In other words, only 6 people out of every 1,000 would earn a score as high as or higher than Gina's.

Knowing a child's relative standing on an aggregate of varied items is arguably less informative than finding out the particular intellectual domains in which a child excels and struggles (Mather, 2009; Stanovich, 1999). Consider the performance of an elementary student on the scales of the *Cognitive Assessment System* (Naglieri & Conway, 2009). Gary performed below average but still in the normal range on the full-scale CAS, specifically at the 19th percentile, meaning that approximately 8 in 10 children outperformed him (CAS scales are defined on pp. 286–287). What is more illuminating, however, is his uneven performance across the four scales and especially his score on the *Planning* scale. Gary performed better than 55% of peers on the *Attention* scale, 23% on the *Simultaneous* scale, 39% on the *Successive Subtest* scale; but only 5% on the *Planning scale*. After receiving test score results, Gary's teacher focused on the challenges that Gary faced in planning. The teacher moved him to a quiet corner where he was not likely to be distracted and taught him steps in pursuing his goals, for example, in carrying out a task carefully, making sure he wrote digits into the proper column for subtraction problems, and checking his work. With support related to planning and evaluating his performance, Gary improved in his mathematics achievement, more than doubling the number of correct problems.

Preparing for Your Licensure Examination

Your teaching test might ask you about the kinds of information included on intelligence tests.

Validity and Reliability of Intelligence Tests

For tests to inform decisions about services for children, the scores need to be accurate. The *validity* of an intelligence test is the extent to which it actually measures

[3]Alfred Binet himself objected to the use of intelligence quotients, believing that his tests were too imprecise to warrant such scores. Lewis Terman, an American psychologist, was largely responsible for popularizing the term *IQ* (A. Montagu, 1999).

[4]If you have some knowledge of descriptive statistics, you probably recognize Figure 8.3 as a normal distribution. IQ scores are based on a normal distribution with a mean of 100 and, for most tests, a standard deviation of 15.

FIGURE 8.3 Distribution of General Intelligence.
Percentages of IQ scores in different ranges.

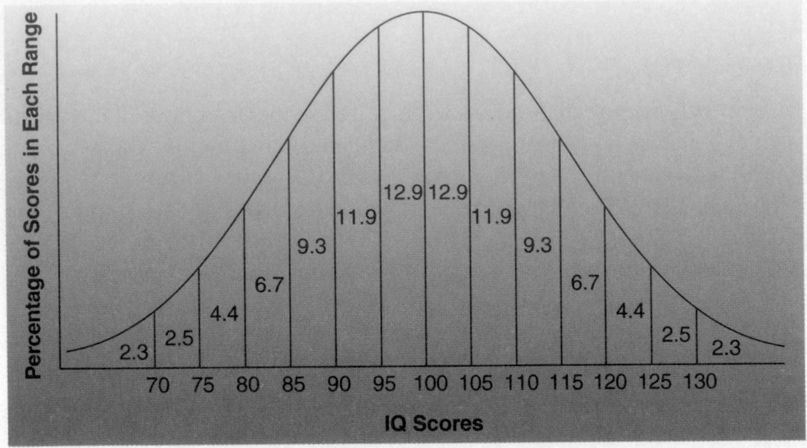

intelligence. The *reliability* of an intelligence test is the extent to which it yields consistent, dependable scores. Both qualities bear on the usefulness of test scores.

For an intelligence test to be valid, its scores should predict success on mentally challenging activities. A primary consideration for validity is how closely IQ scores correlate with school achievement and other demanding endeavors. Many studies indicate that traditional measures of general intelligence, such as WISC-V, Stanford-Binet, and CAS, have validity in this respect. On average, students who earn higher scores on these tests achieve at advanced levels academically and complete more years of education than do their lower scoring peers (N. Brody, 1997; Firkowska-Mankiewicz, 2011; Gygi, Hagmann-von Arx, Schweizer, & Grob, 2017; Naglieri, De Lauder, Goldstein, & Schwebech, 2006). To a lesser degree, intelligence scores in adults predict income and occupation (Baum & Bird, 2010; Firkowska-Mankiewicz, 2011; Furnham & Cheng, 2013; Sternberg, 1996). We have less information about the UNIT, but emerging evidence indicates that it, too, has some validity as a measure of intelligence (N. L. Bell, McConnell, Lassiter, & Matthews, 2013; McCallum & Bracken, 2012).

Another indication of validity is fairness. A test has **cultural bias** when one or more of its items either offend or unfairly penalize people of a particular ethnic background, gender, or socioeconomic status, to the point that the validity of test results is undermined. For example, a test should not emphasize items that refer to Western sports, popular culture, or other content that does not directly assess intelligence. Tests that emphasize such information run the risk of confusing a child who would be able, with different content, to perform the relevant intellectual operations. A lack of familiarity with question format (e.g., multiple-choice items) can also hamper children's performance (Heath, 1989; Neisser et al., 1996). Children for whom English is a second language sometimes perform relatively poorly on tests written in English even though may understand the target concepts (Graves & Nichols, 2016; E. C. Lopez, 1997). Publishers of intelligence tests routinely employ individuals from diverse backgrounds to ensure that test content is fair and appropriate for students of all races and ethnicities (R. L. Linn & Miller, 2005; L. A. Suzuki, Onoue, & Hill, 2013). Nevertheless, tests can be biased in ways that are not always recognized by test developers and the professionals who implement them. Hence, educators should always be cautious about the meaning of scores.

Tests must also be valid indicators of how well children of a certain age can think, reason, and remember information. Thus, there is an expectation that tests are fine-tuned to measure the typical intellectual challenges that children of a certain age are able to tackle. Results confirm this point: Older children generally perform better on ability tasks than do younger children. Consider how three children define the word *freedom*:

Kate (age 8): You want to be free. Or you want to play something . . . and you got caught and they have to keep you like in jail or something like in a game and you want to get free.
Ryan (age 13): It means that you can, like, do stuff that you want.
Paul (age 17): Basically, something that everyone has these days or should have. It's the right to be able to make your own decisions and choose for yourself what you want to do or want to be.

MyLab Education Application Exercise 8.2
Detect Developmental Levels
How do children of different ages define freedom?

Test developers understand that children undergo developmental progress in verbal abilities, reasoning skills, and decision-making acumen, and they make their assessments accordingly age-sensitive. Therefore, age-related growth is not reflected in children's scores, as comparisons are anchored at a particular age level.

To determine the reliability of intelligence tests, researchers look at various reflections of consistency, especially the extent to which the same test yields similar scores on two different occasions. Other indicators of reliability include evidence that different forms of a test yield comparable results and that two different examiners score a child's performance in a similar way. Children's scores on the WISC-V, Stanford-Binet, UNIT, and CAS are highly reliable in these respects. Nevertheless, measures of reliability are based on aggregate data from groups, and an individual child's score can be inconsistent, perhaps because of being ill or distressed on one day of testing but feeling healthy, alert, and motivated the next time the test is administered.

Despite the advances of test developers, no intelligence test has perfect validity or reliability. IQ scores can be *generally* predictive of achievement in a group of children yet misleading for one or more individual children because of discrepancies between the content of the test and children's native language and culture or because of a condition that impairs children's performance, perhaps an illness, distraction, or some other factor. And, of course, there are many things besides intellectual abilities that influence children's academic learning at school. For example, highly intelligent children may lack self-confidence, dislike their teacher, or have trouble paying attention, causing achievement to be far below what would be anticipated from their intellectual capacity.

Preparing for Your Licensure Examination

Your teaching test might ask you about the degree to which intelligence tests are valid and reliable.

Dynamic Assessments

The approaches described so far focus on what children can *currently* do with little or no assistance from anyone else. In contrast, **dynamic assessment** focuses on assessing the ability to learn in new situations, usually with an adult's assistance (Camilleri & Botting, 2013; Feuerstein, 1979; Feuerstein, Feuerstein, & Gross, 1997; Poehner & Infante, 2017). Typically, dynamic assessment involves (a) identifying one or more tasks that children cannot initially do independently, (b) providing in-depth instruction and practice in behaviors and cognitive processes related to the task(s), and then (c) determining the extent to which each child has benefitted from the instruction. Accordingly, dynamic assessment is sometimes called *assessment of learning potential.*

Dynamic assessment is a fairly new approach to measuring intelligence, and psychologists are only beginning to discover its strengths and weaknesses. On the plus side, it often yields more optimistic evaluations of children's abilities than are represented with traditional measures of intelligence (H. L. Swanson & Lussier, 2001; Tzuriel, 2000). In another important advantage, dynamic assessment can provide a wealth of qualitative information about children's approaches to learning, which can be helpful in guiding future instruction (Camilleri & Botting, 2013; Feuerstein, 1979). To illustrate, a boy named Justin was initially able to tell only a very simple story. After a brief period of instruction, Justin articulated complex ideas, expressed varied vocabulary, and used advanced grammar. In studying the boy's responses and records, his intervention team realized that his previous academic delays had probably been due to frequent absences, tardiness, and a weak educational foundation—not to limited intelligence. Accordingly, the team decided that Justin could benefit from instruction that addressed his missing academic skills. In this manner, dynamic assessments can be especially effective in determining the academic concepts and learning strategies that children need to practice (Kazemi & Noroozi, 2017; Lin, 2010; T.-H. Wang, 2010).

Yet disadvantages of dynamic assessment are also apparent. A dynamic assessment often involves considerable training before it can be used properly, and it typically requires a great deal of time to administer (Anastasi & Urbina, 1997; J. Hill, 2015; Tzuriel, 2000). Furthermore, questions have been raised about how best to determine the validity and reliability of dynamic assessment instruments, which have been evaluated as less strong than is the case with traditional measures of intelligence (H. L. Swanson & Lussier, 2001).

Developmental Assessments with Infants and Young Children

Thus far, we have examined common intelligence tests for school-aged children. Now we move to special considerations for examining infants and young children. These young learners are not always able to stay alert, pay attention, and maintain interest in the tasks. Because of such factors, assessments for infants and young children are not highly reliable (Anastasi & Urbina, 1997; L. Ford & Dahinten, 2005; C. E. Snow & Van Hemel, 2008). Yet educators sometimes need to monitor the learning of infants and young children, perhaps to identify significant delays or determine readiness for educational experiences. Developmental assessments are used in these circumstances. Here we briefly describe the nature of tests available for infants, toddlers, and preschoolers.

Assessments with Infants and Toddlers

Infants born in modern hospitals are typically assessed as soon as they are born. At 1 minute and 5 minutes after birth, a doctor or nurse evaluates newborn babies' color, heart rate, reflexes, muscle tone, and breathing, giving each characteristic a rating between 0 and 2. A perfect score on this *Apgar Scale* is 10. Another instrument, the *Neonatal Behavioral Assessment Scale,* assesses alertness and attention, quality of visual and auditory processing, and a variety of reflexes and behaviors in infants from birth until 2 months (Brazelton, 2009; Nugent, 2013).

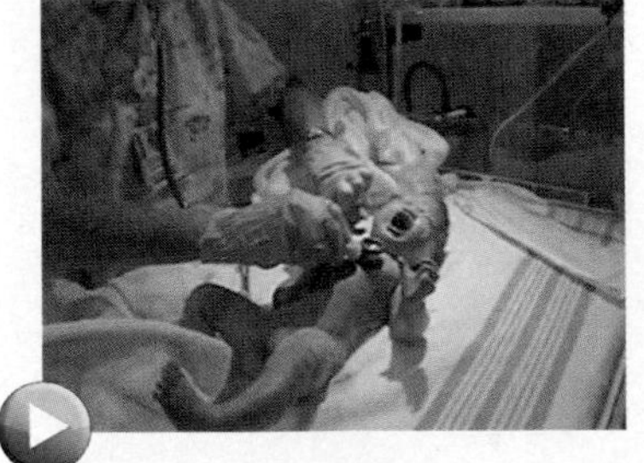

MyLab Education
Video Explanation 8.2
How is the Apgar conducted?

By the time infants are a few months old, they learn rapidly, and the tests must keep up with them. One technique has been to assess infants' ability to notice differences between visual stimuli (e.g., with pictures of faces of a woman and child; Fagan, 2011). In the *Fagan Test of Infant Intelligence,* infants are shown a picture of one object for a brief period, after which a new stimulus is placed beside the original picture. After this sequence is repeated several times, infants are given a score for the relative time they spend looking at novel pictures compared to images they had already seen. Infants with a high novelty preference appear to have become familiar with a broader range of stimuli than is the case with peers. Thus, the Fagan Test seems to tap into the efficiency with which a child's neurological structures enable learning and remembering (Fagan, 2011).

A widely used test for older infants and toddlers is the third edition of the *Bayley Scales of Infant Development* (Bayley, 2006). Designed for children ages 1 month to 3½ years, it includes five scales. Scales for cognitive development (attention, memory, concept formation, etc.), language, and motor skills are assessed through interactions with the child. Two additional scales—for social-emotional functioning and adaptive behavior—are assessed through parent questionnaires.

Ability tests for infants and toddlers are somewhat helpful in diagnosing difficulties in learning and are moderately predictive of later abilities (dos Santos, de Kieviet, Königs, van Elburg, & Oosterlaan, 2013). Yet there are many exceptions. "Bright" babies do not necessarily become the smartest fourth graders, and toddlers who appear slow to learn may catch up to, or even surpass, peers (more about this point in a later discussion of IQ stability).

MyLab Education
Video Example 8.2

Find Developmental Meaning *What are some ways to assess cognitive abilities in toddlers?* In this video, an adult (the boy's mother) conducts activities that are similar to assessments of small children. She asks him to follow simple instructions and identify an object from an array of pictures.

Assessments with Preschoolers

The Stanford-Binet Intelligence Scales, which were introduced previously, can be used for children as young as 2 years. Another commonly used test at this age level is the third edition of the *Wechsler Preschool and Primary Scale of Intelligence,* or WPPSI-IV (M. W. Watkins & Beaujean, 2013; Wechsler, 2012). Suitable for children ages $2\frac{1}{2}$ to $7\frac{1}{2}$ the WPPSI-IV gives an overall IQ, Verbal Comprehension Index, Visual Spatial Index, Working Memory Index, and, for children ages 4 and older, Fluid Reasoning and Processing Speed Indexes.

As measures of intelligence for young children, both the Stanford-Binet and WPPSI-IV correlate with other measures of intelligence and provide reasonable estimates of children's current cognitive functioning. In other words, their scores have some degree of validity and reliability (Roid & Tippin, 2009; Wechsler, 2012). Although young children's IQ scores correlate somewhat with their scores in later years, the correlations are modest at best—no doubt because many young children have high energy levels, short attention spans, and little interest in sitting still for more than a few minutes and because the content of tests for young and older children is different. Thus, measures of IQ obtained in the preschool years cannot be used to make confident predictions about children's academic performance over the long run.

Other tests for preschoolers, known as *school readiness tests,* are designed to determine whether children have acquired the necessary skills for succeeding in formal schooling (e.g., abilities to pay attention; count and perform simple mathematical procedures; and identify letters, colors, and shapes). Although widely used in school districts, these tests have come under fire for two reasons. First, their scores correlate only moderately with children's academic performance even a year or so later (La Paro & Pianta, 2000; Stipek, 2002). Second, by age 5, most children are probably ready for some sort of structured educational program. Rather than determining whether children can adapt to an existing curriculum, it is arguably better to determine how to welcome children who have not yet achieved expected standards, form positive relationships with them, and adapt instructions to their delays and strengths (Lidz, 1991; Panter & Bracken, 2013; Pretti-Frontczak et al., 2016; Stipek, 2002).

Critiques of Intelligence Testing

The study of intelligence is at a crossroads, having shifted from the underlying premise that intelligence is a largely inherited, one-dimensional characteristic to the realization that it is a multifaceted core of abilities, each of which is influenced by experience. In the context of these changes in thinking, several concerns about intelligence testing are compelling:

IQ scores have been interpreted without recognition of their fallibility. Over the years, the use of intelligence tests has been controversial. As recently as the 1970s, IQ scores were frequently used as the sole criterion for identifying children with an intellectual disability. In part as a result of this practice, children from racial and ethnic minority groups were disproportionately represented in special education classes, where their potential for academic achievement was tragically underestimated and ineffectively nurtured.

Clinical and school psychologists, counselors, and other specialists now have sufficient training in assessment to understand that a single IQ score should never warrant a diagnosis of intellectual disability. Decisions about special educational services must always be based on multiple sources of information about the child.

Unfortunately, many other people (including a few teachers) view IQ scores as indisputable records of permanent characteristics. We occasionally hear remarks such as "She has an IQ of such-and-such" spoken in much the same matter-of-fact manner as someone might say "She has brown eyes."

For most children, IQ scores are reasonably accurate reflections of their general learning potential. But for some children, IQ scores are poor summaries of what they can do at present or in the future. Furthermore, the use of IQ scores obscures the differentiated profiles in children's intellectual strengths and fragilities. Thus, teachers and other school professionals must be extremely careful not to put too much stock in any single intelligence score.

Assessment of intelligence emphasizes skills valued in Western culture. The items found on traditional intelligence tests focus on cognitive skills (logical reasoning, abstract thought, etc.) that are valued primarily in middle-class and high-income societies (Sternberg, 2012). Yet measuring the child's awareness of common knowledge in an advantaged background is not a legitimate purpose of intelligence tests. This kind of bias can be harmful to children from other backgrounds because their scores will not be an accurate picture of their potential. Learning disabilities or low general intelligence might be suggested when in reality the student does not speak the language of the test, having recently immigrated to a new community, and is not familiar with references to art, culture, travel, and sports, which are common in a well-to-do bracket and not in low-income families.

Intelligence tests overlook dispositions and metacognitive strategies that are influential in intellectual accomplishments. Most measures of intelligence focus on specific things that a child *can* do (abilities), with little consideration to what a child *wants* to do (motivations) or is *likely* to do (dispositions). Intelligence tests don't evaluate the extent to which children can view a situation from multiple perspectives, examine information critically, regulate learning, or reflect on behavior. Nor do they assess children's self-discipline or changes in strategy after setbacks. Yet such qualities can be just as important as intellectual abilities in achieving success in academic and real-world tasks (Dias & Seabra, 2017; Duckworth & Seligman, 2005; Dweck, 2010; Kuhn, 2001a; Nisbett, 2009; P. A. O'Keefe, 2013; Perkins, 1995).

Many theorists have placed higher priority on measuring intelligence than on developing it. Implicit in the practice of intelligence testing is the assumption that intelligence is a relatively fixed, and largely inherited, ability. Fortunately, some psychologists and educators are now calling for a shift from the assessment of intelligence to its enhancement (Boykin, 1994; Nisbett, 2009; Olszewski-Kubilius, Subotnik, & Worrell, 2017; Sternberg et al., 2000). As theorists and researchers gain a better understanding of intelligence and the environmental factors that promote it, schools can, we hope, adopt a more proactive approach, one in which all children are given the opportunities and resources they need to maximize learning.

Intelligence tests have been used for improper purposes. Existing intelligence tests have been designed primarily to identify individuals who require special educational services, and in this context, if interpreted carefully and supplemented with other evidence, they can be helpful. Yet researchers have used them in other ways as well—for instance, to evaluate the effectiveness of educational programs. Intelligence tests have advantages and disadvantages when used for secondary purposes. For example, if an early childhood intervention was designed to enhance children's general well-being and educational success, then an intelligence test alone would provide an overly narrow glimpse into its effects. Results from such assessments would not illuminate a program's effects on health, self-control, confidence, and interpersonal skills, all characteristics that play an important part in academic achievement.

Educational Implications of Intelligence Testing

Teachers can help children by making recommendations for testing when a learning delay occurs and by providing customized accommodations when test results corroborate a special need. Consider the following advice:

• **Maintain a healthy skepticism about IQ scores.** Intelligence tests can, in many cases, provide a general idea of children's current cognitive functioning. Yet IQ scores are rarely dead-on measures of what children can do. As we have seen, the scores of young children can vary considerably from one testing to the next and are not always accurate predictors of children's future academic success. Furthermore, the scores of children are affected by their background experiences, motivation, and English proficiency. We cannot stress this point enough: IQ scores should *never* be used as the sole criterion in making diagnoses and decisions about children.

• **Foster growth in intellectual abilities.** Children whose test results accurately identify weaknesses often thrive academically when educators communicate confidence in their learning and follow through with customized instruction. In some lessons, individualized guidance allows a child to improve in areas of weakness (e.g., with a young child who has trouble perceiving sounds in words, an adult might use rhymes, clapping exercises, and word games). In others lessons, teachers arrange to leverage strengths (e.g., for a child with strong spatial-visual skills, an adult might present a maze, puzzle, or chart).

• **Explain the value of intelligence testing to parents.** As you have learned, obtaining the outcomes of intelligence test can be advantageous for a child who has been struggling at school. It is not always possible to know why a child is having difficulty from everyday observations. Profiles from intellectual tests are not definitive, as we have repeatedly said, yet their results, when combined with other data, can lead to instructional goals and formats that improve the child's chances of achieving his or her potential. School psychologists and other appropriately trained personnel can answer parents' questions about tests, communicate nuances about what can and cannot be learned from them, put results in the context of other information about the child's abilities, and underscore the significance of other personal characteristics, such as motivation and persistence.

• **When schoolwork reveals difficulties or talents, document children's performance.** By saving artifacts completed by a child, the teacher compiles indications of talents and weaknesses, information that can illuminate intelligence test results. For example, a first-grade girl may exhibit significant delays in drawing, forming letters, and cutting yet be verbally facile in composing stories orally, a few of which were transcribed by the teacher and placed in her record. In her case, an intelligence test might reveal information about advanced verbal skills that was not apparent in most of her assignments due to a neuromuscular delay.

• **Collaborate with colleagues and parents when a child needs special services.** The classroom teacher is a full participant in developing the individualized education program (IEP) for a child. Parents, the student's primary teacher, school psychologists, special education experts, others with knowledge of the child's condition, and often the student him or herself, collaborate in developing individualized goals and instructional strategies. Classroom teachers contribute perspective based on their familiarity with children's schoolwork. Teachers can guide the IEP planning process by describing the academic challenges the child faces on a daily basis, his or her regular achievements, and accommodations that have proven effective thus far.

Preparing for Your Licensure Examination

Your teaching test might ask you about appropriate cautions to follow when interpreting the results of intelligence tests.

Summary

Most intelligence tests have been developed primarily to identify individuals who have special needs (e.g., those who are gifted or have an intellectual disability). Contemporary intelligence tests include a variety of tasks designed to assess what people have learned from experience. Performance on these tests is usually summarized as total IQ scores or as index scores of reasoning, working memory, and other specific abilities. Whatever their form, intelligence scores are generally reported as a comparison between an individual's performance and the results of others of the same age. In some instances, dynamic assessments may be more useful for evaluating children's capabilities in specific areas and for predicting their ability to benefit from certain kinds of instruction. Developmental assessments for infants and young children are often helpful in identifying those who have significant delays; however, these tests should not be used to make long-term predictions about cognitive development.

Historically, intelligence tests were misinterpreted, and today we still need to be cautious in our inferences about children's abilities. Test scores provide a basic idea of the child's current cognitive functioning, provided he or she has understood the instructions, is reasonably motivated, and shares general cultural views with the test's developers. Test results must always be supplemented by additional information about the child's abilities. Educators and other practitioners should remain optimistic about every child's potential for intellectual growth, especially when instructional formats are rich and varied and make necessary accommodations.

MyLab Education Self-Check 8.2

Development of Intelligence

8.3 Review evidence of separate and interacting factors contributing to intellectual growth.

Intelligence follows an age-related course in that children try out new skills (e.g., identification of sounds, comprehension of words, and verbal reasoning) in a particular order and also become increasingly proficient in exploring their interests. Children have unique genetic profiles, and they develop personal habits—playing football, doing crossword puzzles, or reading books—that allow them to exercise emerging talents. They also respond to opportunities, pressures, and risks and are affected by diet and schooling. Let's examine the trends by which intelligence is transformed with age.

Age-Related Growth in Intelligence

As you have learned, children definitely become more "intelligent" as they develop: They know more, think in increasingly complex ways, and solve problems more effectively. However, IQ scores are based not on how much children develop over time but, rather, on how well children perform in comparison with their agemates. By definition, the average IQ score for any age group is 100. This IQ does not increase simply with age. A child would not be expected to advance in an IQ score unless provided outstanding instruction and other facilitating conditions.

IQ scores do change in two important ways over the course of development:

IQ scores in individual students become increasingly stable. As noted previously, performance on infant assessments is not terribly predictive of later intelligence. One reason is that infants' moods and priorities can be at odds with the demands of testing, making the scores somewhat unreliable. A second reason is that the types of items on assessments for young children are different than items on tests for older children and adolescents. The Developmental Trends table "Intelligence at Different Age Levels" specifies common indicators of intelligence during the developmental periods, along with important considerations for fostering intelligence at each age level.

Developmental Systems Prompt

Your impact in promoting children's intellectual abilities derives in part from your awareness of factors inside and outside children that affect these capabilities.

As children progress through the school years, their IQ scores hover within a narrow range, and their relative standing among peers changes less and less (N. Brody, 1992; Neisser et al., 1996; van Soeleln et al., 2011). In the chapter's opening case study, Gina obtained an IQ score of 140 (equivalent to the 99th percentile) in junior high school and performed at a similar level on college aptitude tests several years later. The increasing activation of genes that guide brain growth constrains intellectual skills (Briley & Tucker-Drob, 2013). With maturing abilities and emerging independence, children are better able to select their own activities, and they gravitate toward options that give them just the right amount of intellectual challenge. Thus, a student with a penchant for music might join an after-school band and acquire musical notation, a new ability that sets the stage for further improvements in musical skill.

DEVELOPMENTAL TRENDS

Intelligence at Different Age Levels

AGE	WHAT YOU MIGHT OBSERVE	DIVERSITY	IMPLICATIONS
Infancy (Birth–2 Years)	• Success on test items that require recognition of previously seen objects or names for common things, for example, balls, keys, blocks, and bottle. • Visual preferences and placing like objects together • Distractibility and short attention span • Different responses to familiar adults and strangers • Variability in performance from one assessment to the next • Performance dependent on examiner's ability to establish a positive relationship with infant	• Temperamental differences (e.g., a tendency to be shy or cautious) affect infants' willingness to interact with the examiner. • Compared to full-term infants, infants born prematurely are less physically developed, more easily fatigued, and more prone to obtain low test scores. With responsive care, premature infants gradually develop into healthy, intelligent individuals. • Exposure to drugs or alcohol before birth may adversely affect test performance.	• Create a relaxed tone and comfortable examiner–child interaction before beginning an assessment. • Use results only to identify significant delays requiring immediate intervention; refrain from making long-term predictions about intellectual growth. • Communicate honestly with parents about the child's performance, while also describing the assessment's strengths and weaknesses as a tool for learning about children's abilities.
Early Childhood (2–6 Years)	• Success on test items that involve naming objects, stacking blocks, drawing circles and squares, remembering short lists, and following simple directions • Short attention span, influencing test performance • Variability in test scores from one occasion to the next	• Significant developmental delays in the early years may indicate an intellectual disability. • On average, children from economically disadvantaged families perform at lower levels on measures of cognitive development than do children from middle-income families; however, enriching preschool experiences can narrow the gap.	• Use cognitive assessments primarily to identify significant delays in development; follow up by arranging intervention programs for children with delays. • Provide preschool experiences that foster language skills, knowledge of numbers and counting, and visual-spatial thinking.
Middle Childhood (6–10 Years)	• Success on test items that involve defining concrete words, remembering sentences and short sequences of digits, grasping concrete analogies, recognizing similarities among objects, and identifying absurdities in illogical statements • Some consistency in test scores from one occasion to the next	• For this age range, intelligence tests are heavily verbal in content; thus, proficiency with English can significantly affect test performance. • Children with learning disabilities are apt to perform poorly on some parts of an intelligence test. • Children may perform weakly in situations where the examiner has not established rapport.	• For some lessons, individualize instruction to capitalize on children's learning strengths. • Do *not* assume that poor performance in one domain (e.g., verbal tasks) indicates limited ability in other areas (e.g., quantitative reasoning). • Take children's cultural and linguistic backgrounds into account when interpreting IQ scores.
Early Adolescence (10–14 Years)	• Success on test items that involve defining commonly used abstract words, drawing logical inferences from verbal descriptions, and identifying similarities between opposite concepts • Curiosity, personal interests, ability to synthesize data and criticize assumptions	• Some adolescents may not perceive a high score as personally advantageous and so may not be motivated to perform at their best. • Cultures that stress traditional gender roles may actively discourage girls from achieving in mathematics and science and boys from achieving in literacy.	• Expect considerable diversity in adolescents' ability to master abstract classroom material; individualize instruction accordingly. • Make sure that school enrichment programs include students from all ethnic groups. Do not rely exclusively on IQ scores to identify students as gifted.
Late Adolescence (14–18 Years)	• Success on test items that involve defining infrequently encountered words, distinguishing overlapping abstract words, interpreting proverbs, and breaking down complex geometric figures into component parts • Relative stability in IQ scores • Independence in arranging activities consistent with personal ability levels	• Concerns about appearing "too smart" may continue into the high school years. • Some adolescents may underperform due to the stress of being tested in a subject for which their ethnicity is widely believed to be incapable (see upcoming discussion of stereotype threat on p. 302).	• Provide challenging activities for teenagers who are gifted. • Encourage bright adolescents from lower-income families to pursue a college education, and help them with the logistics of college applications (e.g., applying for financial aid).

Sources: Bayley (2005); Bornstein, Hahn, and Wolke (2013); Brooks-Gunn (2003); Colombo (1993); G. A. Davis and Rimm (1998); D. J. Matthews (2009); L. C. Mayes and Bornstein (1997); McLoyd (1998b); Meisels, Wen, and Beachy-Quick (2010); Mello, Mallett, Andretta, and Worrell (2012); Natarajan et al. (2013); Ogbu (1994); Steele (1997); Terman and Merrill (1972); A. Thomas and Chess (1977); Thorndike, Hagen, and Sattler (1986); Wechsler (2002, 2003).

Despite the growing stability of IQ scores, a degree of change (sometimes as much as 10 to 20 points' worth, and occasionally even more) can be expected over the years. The longer the time interval between two test administrations, the greater the change in IQ we are likely to see, especially when young children are involved (B. S. Bloom, 1964; McCall, 1993; Sattler, 2001). The magnitude and direction of major changes in scores—higher or lower or oscillations up and down—depend on children's access to nutrition, health status, and exposure to stimulating activities, as you will learn about shortly.

IQ scores become increasingly accurate predictors of academic achievement. As IQ scores become more stable with age, their usefulness in predicting classroom performance increases. Yet educators should remember two things about the relationship between IQ and academic achievement. First, intelligence by itself does not *cause* achievement. Intelligence certainly plays an important role in school performance, but many other factors—motivation, quality of instruction, family resources and support, peer-group norms, and so on—are obviously involved. Second, the relationship between IQ scores and achievement is an imperfect one, with many exceptions. For a variety of reasons, some children with high IQ scores do not perform well in the classroom, and other children achieve at higher levels than would be predicted from their IQ scores.

Evidence for Hereditary Influences

Earlier we mentioned that measures of information processing speed correlate with IQ scores. The speed of processing depends on neurological efficiency, which, in turn, is guided by the operations of genes in growing the brain. From this standpoint, we have support for a hereditary basis for intelligence. The fact that children with certain genetic defects (e.g., Down syndrome) have, on average, significantly lower IQ scores than their nondisabled peers provides further proof of heredity's influence (J. Carr, 2012; Keogh & MacMillan, 1996; Rihtman et al., 2010). But perhaps the most convincing evidence comes from twin and adoption studies.

Twin Studies

Numerous studies have compared monozygotic (identical) twins and dizygotic (fraternal) twins to get a sense of how strongly heredity affects IQ. Because monozygotic twins begin as a single fertilized egg, which then separates, their genetic makeup is virtually identical. In contrast, dizygotic twins are conceived as two separate fertilized eggs. Dizygotic twins share about 50% of their genes, with the other 50% being unique to each twin. Most twins of both types are raised together by the same parent(s) in the same home, so they have similar environments.

In one investigation, children were studied over several years to determine how their IQ scores correlated with siblings' scores (E. G. Bishop et al., 2003). If you take a look at the two columns for twins in Table 8.2, you will notice that the correlations for monozygotic twins are consistently higher than the correlations for dizygotic twins, nontwin siblings, and adopted siblings.[5] This pattern has been observed in many other investigations and suggests that intelligence has a sizable genetic basis. In fact, even when twins are raised separately (perhaps because they have been adopted by different parents), they generally have similar IQ scores (T. J. Bouchard & McGue, 1981; J. S. Kaplan, 2012; Plomin & Petrill, 1997; N. L. Segal, 2012). Twin studies also provide evidence for environmental effects, as we will see in a moment.

Adoption Studies

Another way to identify the effects of heredity is to compare adopted children with both their biological and adoptive parents. Adopted children tend to be more similar to their biological parents in genetic makeup yet are raised in an environment that more closely matches the intellectual resources of their adoptive parents. Researchers have found that adopted children's IQ scores are more highly correlated with their biological parents' IQs than with their adoptive parents' IQs. In other words, in a group of people who place their infants up for adoption, those with the highest IQs tend to have offspring who, despite being raised by other people, also have the highest IQs. Furthermore, the IQ correlations between adopted children and their

[5]In our teaching experiences, some college students erroneously interpret the higher correlations as indicating that identical twins are smarter than nontwins. This is not the case. The size of each correlation indicates the *strength of the relationship* between twins' IQs, not the *level* of their intelligence.

Table 8.2 Correlations between IQs of Sibling Pairs Living Together

AGE OF CHILDREN[a]	MONOZYGOTIC TWINS	DIZYGOTIC TWINS	NONTWIN BIOLOGICAL SIBLINGS	ADOPTED SIBLINGS
Age 1	.59	.40	.38	.07
Age 3	.77	.51	.37	.26
Age 7	.76	.40	.47	.04
Age 9	.80	.21	.40	.24

[a]Tests of ability were administered to the same children repeatedly over several years in this longitudinal study.

Source: E. G. Bishop et al. (2003).

biological parents become stronger, and those between the children and their adoptive parents become weaker, as children grow older (T. J. Bouchard, 1997; J. S. Kaplan, 2012; McGue, Bouchard, Iacono, & Lykken, 1993; Plomin, Fulker, Corley, & DeFries, 1997). (We will provide an explanation for an age-related increase in genetic effects a little later.)

Researchers also compare correlations in the IQs of adopted siblings with associations in twins and nonadopted siblings (ordinary biological brothers and sisters). If you look again at Table 8.2, you can see that the correlations for dizygotic twins and nonadopted siblings are generally higher than most of the correlations for adopted siblings. In other words, children who are genetically related resemble one another intellectually more than do children who are unrelated biologically. Although other factors are at work in such associations (which we will soon examine), twin and adoption studies point to a strong genetic component in intelligence (T. J. Bouchard, 1997; N. Brody, 1992; J. S. Kaplan, 2012).

Evidence for Environmental Influences

Considerable evidence indicates that the environment also has a significant impact on intelligence. We find some of this evidence in other analyses in twin and adoption studies. Nutrition, toxic substances, home environment, early intervention, and formal schooling contribute to the environment's impact. Also, a modest but steady increase in intelligence scores over the past several decades—known as the *Flynn effect*, which will be discussed shortly—is probably at least partly attributable to environmental factors.

Twin Studies and Adoption Studies Revisited

Comparing across separate investigations, researchers have found an average correlation of .85 for monozygotic twins reared together and .74 for monozygotic twins reared apart (Devlin, Daniels, & Roeder, 1997; Nisbett, 2009). In other words, twins raised in different homes have less similar IQs than twins reared in the same home. Adoption studies, too, indicate that intelligence is affected by environmental experiences, especially during childhood (Capron & Duyme, 1989; J. S. Kaplan, 2012; Nisbett, 2009).

Consider also that twin and adoption studies do not fully disentangle environmental effects (J. S. Kaplan, 2012; Wahlsten & Gottlieb, 1997). An adopted child has shared a common environment for at least 9 months—the period of prenatal development—with his or her biological mother. Likewise, monozygotic twins who are separated at birth are often placed by adoption agencies in families that are similar in educational backgrounds and income levels. Furthermore, twin studies and adoption studies do not allow researchers to clarify how heredity and environment interact in their effects on intelligence. In genetic studies, interactive effects are included on the "heredity" side of the scoreboard (J. S. Kaplan, 2012; Nisbett, 2009; Turkheimer, 2000).

Other data suggest that environmental effects are stronger than they might first appear because most genes are only expressed when environments are reasonably supportive. Twin studies are generally drawn from middle-income families because these individuals are inclined to participate in longitudinal research (Nisbett, 2009). Genetic effects tend to be stronger in financially stable families than in low-income families, probably because children in advantaged families have the experiences they need to express their full potential whereas children in less well-to-do families do not (T. C. Bates, Lewis, & Weiss, 2013; Turkheimer, Haley, Waldron, D'Onofrio, & Gottesman, 2003). Good conditions in a moderately supportive and challenging environment are essential to the activation and operation of many genes.

Additional evidence corroborates the power of the child's upbringing. In a range of comprehensive studies on genetic contributions to intelligence, there is almost always an indication of strong effects from the environment. Let's look at some specific ways that the environment affects intelligence directly.

Nutrition

Severe malnutrition, either before birth or during the early years of life, can hinder neurological development (Lutter & Lutter, 2012; Protzko, Aronson, & Blair, 2013; Ricciuti, 1993). Attention, memory, abstract reasoning, intelligence, and general school achievement are all affected when diets are poor. Children regularly recover from short periods of poor nourishment (due, perhaps, to war or illness), but the adverse effects of long-term deprivation are apt to be enduring (Lutter & Lutter, 2012; Sigman & Whaley, 1998).

When it is possible, educators and other advocates for children can try to improve the nutrition of children. Medical researchers have provided medically approved food supplements and vitamins to expectant mothers, infants, and young children who would not otherwise have adequate nutrition. When omega-3 fatty acids are given as a supplement to infants and young children who have had a restricted diet, there is a modest increase in children's intelligence, probably because they nurture growing brains (Protzko et al., 2013). Similarly, iron, vitamin B, and other supplements have generated modest improvements in intelligence in children with restricted diets.

Toxic Substances

Toxic substances, or *teratogens*, in prenatal environments—for instance, alcohol, drugs, radiation, and lead—affect neurological development and IQ scores (e.g., Betts, 2013; H. Eriksen et al., 2012; Streissguth, Barr, Sampson, & Bookstein, 1994). Children whose mothers consumed large amounts of alcohol during pregnancy are apt to develop fetal alcohol syndrome, with resulting delays in motor coordination, language, and cognitive skills. Exposure to toxic substances is problematic during infancy and early childhood because the brain continues to grow rapidly and is vulnerable to producing too many or too few of chemicals in the brain that fuel concentration, reflection, and mood change (Roussotte et al., 2011).

Home Environment

Correlational studies indicate that stimulating home environments, in which parents regularly interact with children, read to them and make books and other reading materials available, mentor them with challenging skills, and use complex language, are associated with higher IQ and achievement scores in children (R. H. Bradley & Caldwell, 1984; Hamadani et al., 2014; Keltikangas-Järvinen et al., 2010; Nisbett, 2009; Rindermann & Baumeister, 2015; S. Tong, Baghurst, Vimpani, & McMichael, 2007). These associations may occur because parents impart intellectual skills through their interactions with them, yet another plausible reason is that children share intelligence levels with their parents because of shared intelligence genes, and smart children are inciting their smart parents to provide them with optimal stimulation.

We can be more confident about parents having a causal effect on children's intellectual skills with investigations that have systematically trained parents to use certain interactional styles with children. When the children of these two groups of parents differ in their rates of cognitive growth, we can be reasonably certain that the source of the difference is the variation in training. In fact, numerous interventions have taught parents how to cultivate children's intelligence. Experimental programs have provided parents of young children with puzzles, books, and other educational materials, as well as training in fostering cognitive skills. Programs that have taught parents how to read interactively with their children, ask children open-ended questions, encourage their curiosity, and engage their children in discussions about the past, have generated modest increases in children's intellectual skills (Protzko et al., 2013).

Early Intervention

In the last few decades, many young children who grew up in low-income families in the United States participated in preschools and other childhood centers that were developmentally appropriate and nurturing. Children who took part in the Project Head Start preschool program had short-term IQ gains and other cognitive benefits (Bronfenbrenner, 1999; R. Lee, Zhai, Brooks-Gunn, Han, & Waldfogel, 2013; NICHD Early Child Care Research Network, 2002; Zigler, 2003). The intellectual effects of these programs did not continue indefinitely, however. Unless they received follow-up interventions during the elementary school years, children fell behind peers in cognitive growth (Brooks-Gunn, 2003).

As graduates of the Head Start program entered elementary school, they lost a little of the intellectual glow that came from preschool, yet they went on to exhibit other advantages: They repeated grade levels less often, achieved at higher levels in school, more often attended college, enjoyed greater health, and exhibited less criminal behavior (Garces, Thomas, & Curry, 2002; Ludwig & Miller, 2007; Zigler & Styfco, 2010). Presumably, children in Head Start developed curiosity, motivation, self-control, and such self-regulatory abilities as sustaining attention and curbing impulses. These skills, in turn, helped them learn and persevere at school, in interpersonal relationships, and eventually in employment settings (Fuhs & Day, 2011; A. J. Reynolds, Englund, Ou, Schweinhart, & Campbell, 2010).

Other interventions have incorporated slightly different models of education for young children, for example, starting children in an educational environment as early as six months of age. In general, early childhood interventions have been conducive to cognitive growth when teachers are warm and nurturing and the educational curriculum is age-appropriate and scaffolds learning strategies. Additional assets emerge during the adolescent years, including relatively high achievement, in comparison to persons who grew up in similar neighborhoods and did not receive preschool. Later as adults, the preschool graduates completed more years of formal education and had better earnings, more stable marriages, and better health (W. S. Barnett, 1992; F. A. Campbell et al., 2014; Heckman, 2011; Muennig, Schweinhart, Montie, & Neidell, 2009; A. J. Reynolds et al., 2010; Schweinhart & Weikart, 1993).

Formal Schooling

The very act of attending school leads to small increases in IQ. In Western societies, children who begin their educational careers early and attend school regularly have higher IQ scores than children who do not. When children must start school later than is typical, their IQs are at least 5 points lower for every year of delay. In addition, children's IQ scores decline slightly over the summer months if children are not attending school. Other things being equal, children who drop out of school have lower IQ scores than do children who remain in school, losing an average of 2 to 3 IQ points for every year of high school not completed (Ceci & Williams, 1997; Falch & Sandgren Massih, 2011).

Although not every classroom is intellectually enriching, students who progress through until high school graduation are typically asked at one time or another to think flexibly, reason critically, and generate new ideas. As Vygotsky (1997c) pointed out, schooling provides a systematic means through which children can acquire cultural tools, such as alphabets, mathematical systems, or musical scales. Other intellectual skills result from practice of learning strategies, for example, as when reading a difficult history book, elaborating on the academic concepts by finding relevance of earlier times to present day and thinking about the mindset of the authors and the themes that are regularly present (M. Cole, 2006; Falch & Sandgren Massih, 2011; Nettelbeck & Wilson, 2005).

The Flynn Effect

The last few decades have seen a slow, steady increase in average performance on IQ tests throughout the industrialized world (J. R. Flynn, 1987, 2007; D. F. Marks, 2011; Neisser, 1998b; R. L. Williams, 2013). This trend is commonly known as the **Flynn effect**, named in recognition of James R. Flynn's original observation of generation-wide improvements in intelligence.

Why might children become smarter across generations? Conceivably some genetic factors are having an impact. Recent decreases in numbers of children conceived by first cousins and other close relatives appear to have strengthened the health of the gene pool (Mingroni, 2007). Genetic problems, including certain intellectual disabilities, are more prevalent in children of blood relatives than in those from unrelated parents. Closely related parents share a portion of defective genes that, when not offset by healthier forms, can result in a problem. Yet most theorists believe that the Flynn effect is largely the result of changes in children's environments. Better nutrition, protection from infectious diseases, smaller family sizes, intellectually stimulating home environments, higher quality schooling, and more enriching stimulation (through access to television, the Internet, and reading materials, etc.) are likely all factors (D. D. Baker et al., 2015; Daley, Whaley, Sigman, Espinosa, & Neumann, 2003; Eppig, Fincher, & Thornhill, 2010; Neisser, 1998b; R. L. Williams, 2013).

The Fusion of Nature and Nurture

Intelligence draws from factors inside and outside the child. What is not clear is *how much* power nature and nurture have over intelligence during various periods of life. Although it is impossible to separate the relative effects of heredity and environment, the two categories of factors interact in three ways.

Heredity establishes a range rather than a precise figure. Heredity does not dictate that a child will have a particular IQ score. Instead, it appears to set a range of abilities that a child will eventually develop, with the actual level depending on his or her environmental exposure and experience (Weinberg, 1989). Heredity may also affect how susceptible or resistant a child becomes to particular influences (Rutter, 1997). In the opening case study, Gina learned how to read before she attended school and with only minimal help from her mother. Yet had she not had this help her or grew up malnourished, Gina's intellectual gifts may have failed to blossom as early or fully.

Genetic expression is influenced by environmental conditions. Genes, the basic units of heredity, are not self-contained, independent "carriers" of characteristics but, rather, flexible instructions that respond directly to conditions in the child's body and indirectly to features in the environment. In an extremely impoverished setting—one with inadequate nutrition and little if any stimulation—heredity may have little to say about the extent to which children develop intellectually. In an ideal environment—one in which nutrition, parenting practices, and educational opportunities are optimal and age-appropriate—heredity can have a significant influence on children's intelligence (Ceci, 2003; Turkheimer et al., 2003).

Especially as they get older, children choose their activities. Children actively seek out environmental conditions that match their inherited abilities—a phenomenon known as **niche-picking** (Benbow & Lubinski, 2009; Corrigall & Schellenberg, 2015; Halpern & LaMay, 2000; Scarr & McCartney, 1983; Tucker-Drob & Harden, 2012). Children who, genetically speaking, have the capacity for an exceptional quantitative reasoning ability may enroll in advanced mathematics courses, voluntarily tackle mathematical brainteasers, and in other ways nurture their own inherited talents. Children with average quantitative ability are less likely to take on challenges for exercising mathematical skills. Given the ubiquity of choices children make, especially as they grow older, the relative effects of heredity and environment are difficult to tease apart.

Earlier we mentioned that the IQ correlations between adopted children and their biological parents become stronger over time. We now have a possible explanation for this finding. Children gain increasing independence with growth. Especially as they reach adolescence, they spend less time in their home environment and make more of their own decisions, which are undoubtedly based, in part, on their natural talents and tendencies (McGue et al., 1993; Petrill & Wilkerson, 2000). Similarly, correlations between the IQs of monozygotic twins increase in strength with age and presumably reflect a growing ability to act on genetic tendencies they share (you can see an age-related increase in IQ correlations for monozygotic twins in Table 8.2; Hoekstra, Bartels, & Boomsma, 2007).

Developmental Systems Prompt

Watch for situations in which children grow up in an intellectually restricted environment. When it's possible, expose them to enriching activities in the arts, literature, and science.

Demographic Factors

The intellectually enriching activities that children have to select from is constrained by the environment in which they live. The experiences that children have as boys and girls, as recipients of steady resources or financial insecurity, and as members of ethnic and racial groups, affect learning opportunities. As you will find out, differences in abilities between individuals sharing a personal characteristic (e.g., gender) are small and mostly attributable to variations in resources.

Gender

Apart from a greater frequency of intellectual disabilities in boys, there are few gender differences in general intelligence (Halpern et al., 2007; D. Lai, Tseng, Hou, & Guo, 2012; Neisser et al., 1996). This finding is at least partly a function of how intelligence tests are developed: As a general rule, test constructors eliminate any test items on which one gender performs better than the other.

Small gender differences in a few specific abilities are sometimes found. Girls are often slightly better at verbal tasks in reading and writing (Calvin, Fernandes, Smith, Visscher, & Deary, 2010; Fearrington et al., 2014; Maccoby & Jacklin, 1974). Especially after puberty, boys perform somewhat better on tasks involving visual-spatial thinking (which require people to imagine two- or three-dimensional figures and mentally manipulate them), and adolescents with extremely advanced mathematical abilities are more likely to be male (Calvin et al., 2010; Hegarty & Kozhevnikov, 1999; D. Reilly & Neumann, 2013). In verbal, visual-spatial, and mathematical domains, however, there is typically a great deal of overlap between the sexes.

These gender differences in specific abilities may be partly due to subtle anatomical differences in the brain (Halpern, 2004; D. Reilly & Neumann, 2013). Environmental factors play a role as well. In many Western cultures boys are more likely to have toys that require physical manipulation in space (e.g., blocks, model airplanes, and footballs). In contrast, girls are more likely to have dolls, housekeeping items (e.g., dishes, plastic food), and board games—items that are apt to encourage verbal communication with peers (Auster & Mansbach, 2012; Halpern, 1992; Kotsopoulos, Zambrzycka, & Makosz, 2017; Leaper & Friedman, 2007).

In part because of the push for equitable resources, differences in specific abilities between the sexes have become small (L. C. Ball, Cribbie, & Steele, 2013; Spelke, 2005). For all intents and purposes, educators should expect that boys and girls have similar potential in all subject areas. Nevertheless, boys and girls do not always seek out activities that would expand their abilities. Thus, it is wise to nurture skills not spontaneously exercised by one gender or the other. For example, teachers can encourage visual-spatial skills in girls by encouraging play with blocks and puzzles and mental rotations of objects, and they can foster verbal abilities in boys by providing plenty of options for reading, including nonfiction books that appeal to boys' interests (Heyder, Kessels, & Steinmayr, 2017; Newcombe & Frick, 2010; A. Williams, 2012).

Socioeconomic Status

Intelligence test scores are correlated with socioeconomic status (SES). On average, children from lower SES families earn somewhat lower IQ scores and perform at lower levels in school than do children from middle-SES families (Brooks-Gunn, 2003; Linver, Brooks-Gunn, & Kohen 2002; H. Wong & Edwards, 2013). Children who endure only short-term poverty are apt to fall behind peers in intellectual skills, at least temporarily, and those who grow up in relentlessly impoverished conditions are at risk for consistently weak performance (McLoyd, 1998b).

Several factors contribute to differences in ability between socioeconomic levels (Berliner, 2009; C. Fitzpatrick, McKinnon, Blair, & Willoughby, 2014). Poor nutrition, lack of health care, and greater-than-average exposure to environmental toxins can impede neurological development among children in low-income families. Also, parents who work long hours (especially single parents) have little time to spend with their children and may be unable to find high-quality child care (Marshall, 2004). Excessive hardships can undermine parents' ability to remain emotionally responsive with children, who, in turn, sometimes become overwhelmed, fail to acquire healthy coping skills, and develop weak brain circuits for self-control (R. Grant, Gracy, Goldsmith, Shapiro, & Redlener, 2013; Pilyoung et al., 2013).

We urge you to address the practical difficulties that children face in low-income environments. Educators can provide missing materials (e.g., through community drives to supply calculators, crayons, and backpacks) while also communicating high expectations, forming affectionate relationships with children, implementing a challenging curriculum, and filling in gaps to academic knowledge (M. M. McCormick, O'Connor, & Parham Horn, 2017). Coping with stress, acting with willpower, and persisting in the face of difficulty are among the abilities that children are able to practice at school, with a cascade of benefits to health, concentration, and academic achievement (Spengler, Damian, Martin, Brunner, Lüdtke, & Roberts, 2015).

Ethnicity and Race

Every ethnic, racial, and cultural group has child-rearing practices that nurture the intellectual development of its young people. Yet not every group is given the same opportunities for enrichment by society. Minor variations in intelligence result from differences in resources, privileges, and mentorship. On average, Asian Americans and European Americans slightly outperform African Americans and Hispanic Americans (Ang, Rodgers, & Wänström, 2010; N. Brody, 1992; Neisser et al., 1996; Nisbett et al., 2012).

The primary reason for these small differences in average IQ is that children in African American and Hispanic American families is economic inequality (Brooks-Gunn, Klebanov, & Duncan, 1996; McLoyd, 1998b). As you have been reading, low socioeconomic status can undermine nutrition, access to stimulating toys and books, the academic quality of parents' interactions with children, and teachers' familiarity with children's home knowledge. A second reason is that conventional intelligence tests are, to a degree, afflicted with cultural bias. The content of these tests and the format expected for expressing comprehension are less familiar to children of color than to children from White families, and therefore an underestimation of abilities of non-White children is likely.

Finally, children of color are apt to be aware of, and to react to, other people's perceptions that they lack intelligence. Some children give minimal answers (e.g., "I don't know") as a way of shortening an unsettling testing session (Zigler & Finn-Stevenson, 1992). Others exhibit a phenomenon known as **stereotype threat**: They perform more poorly—unintentionally and perhaps as a result of excessive anxiety—if they believe others with the same personal characteristic, such as race or disability, do not do well on tests of certain abilities (Désert, Préaux, & Jund, 2009; Guyll, Madon, Prieto, & Scherr, 2010; Heerboth & Mason, 2012; Steele, 1997; S. Weber, Appel, & Kronberger, 2015).

An encouraging historical trend is that the IQ scores and other measures of cognitive ability have, in recent years, become increasingly similar among ethnic and racial groups. Such a trend is attributed to more equitable conditions across schools and other institutions (Ceci, Rosenblum, & Kumpf, 1998; Dickens & Flynn, 2001; Nisbett et al., 2012). Nevertheless, it remains a serious concern that not every child has the chance to develop his or her intellectual skills to full potential.

Nurturing the Intelligence of *All* Children

You have learned that children develop specific talents and abilities through the operations of genes, personal activity, instruction at school, guidance at home, and interactions with peers and others outside the family. Most of the environments in which children grow up are sufficiently complex that children are able to exercise a broad range of abilities. We recommend the following strategies for supporting intellectual growth of children in impoverished communities:

• **Back early intervention programs.** Early intervention can be of great value to young children living in low-income neighborhoods, growing up in an unstable family, or having a developmental disability such as a delay in language. Interventions can take the form of regular checkups and nutritional support for pregnant women, stimulating infant care and preschool programs for young children, and education for parents. Interventions are most effective when they start in infancy or early childhood, integrate a variety of services, are staffed with well-prepared teachers, and address children's comprehensive needs across the physical, social, and emotional domains (S. S. Landry et al., 2014; Loeb, Fuller, Kagan, & Carroll, 2004; Shonkoff & Phillips, 2000).

• **Cultivate intellectual abilities throughout the school years.** Research evidence strongly supports the role that schools can play in fostering children's potential throughout the preschool, elementary, middle, and secondary school years (A. Bennett et al., 2007; Nisbett, 2013; Sternberg et al., 2007). In particular, youngsters from economically disadvantaged families are positively affected when teachers foster their curiosity and explicitly teach advanced intellectual abilities. As we suggested earlier, teachers can help fill in any gaps in children's knowledge, make sure children are familiar with basic mathematical concepts and reading processes, and scaffold children's applications in new contexts (A. Bennett et al., 2007).

• **Reassure children about taking tests.** We explained previously that children sometimes feel threatened by an upcoming test if the focus is on them being part of a group whose members are believed to be incapable. As a result, these children may feel anxious and unable to concentrate on problems on the test. Teachers can try to head off this debilitating reaction by conveying their confidence in children's abilities, recasting the situation as a challenge rather than a danger, emphasizing the utility of test results in guiding future learning, and giving children practice with the kinds of items on tests (Alter, Aronson, Darley, Rodriguez, & Ruble, 2010).

Summary

Performance on intelligence tests predicts school achievement to some degree, with IQ scores becoming increasingly stable and having greater predictive power with age. Nevertheless, some children's IQ scores change considerably over time, especially during the early years.

Studies with twins and adopted children indicate that intelligence may be partly an inherited characteristic. Environmental conditions, including nutrition, exposure to toxic substances, home environment, preschool programs, and formal schooling, also appear to have a significant impact on IQ scores. Heredity and environment blend in their effects to the point where it is ultimately impossible to separate these two factors in intellectual development.

MyLab Education Self-Check 8.3

Exceptionalities in Intelligence

8.4 Explain key methods for nurturing the growth of children who are exceptionally low or high in general intelligence.

No matter how we measure intelligence, we find that some children show exceptional talent and others exhibit sizable delays relative to peers. For the most part, educators can accommodate such variability within normal instructional practices. In some circumstances, however, young learners have ability levels so different from those of age-mates that they require special educational services to reach their full potential. We turn now to exceptionalities in intelligence. The two ends of the intelligence continuum are commonly known as *giftedness* and *intellectual disability*.

Children with Gifts and Talents

Gina, first introduced in the opening case study, is an example of someone who is gifted (you may also see the term *gifted and talented*). **Giftedness** is an unusually high ability or aptitude in one or more areas (e.g., mathematics, science, creative writing, art, or music) to the point that special educational services are necessary for a youngster to achieve full potential (C. M. Ackerman & Fifield, 2005; U.S. Department of Education, 1993). Some school districts identify students as gifted primarily on the basis of IQ scores, often using 125 or 130 as a minimum cutoff point. Yet many experts argue that IQ scores should not be the only criterion for selection into special services and that creativity, motivation, and everyday accomplishments should also be considered. Examining multiple indicators, including a portfolio of the child's work, is especially useful in identifying talented individuals from diverse backgrounds who, perhaps because of a language barrier, a lack of confidence, weak academic preparation, or test bias do not score high on intelligence tests (Council for Exceptional Children, 1995; S. Graham, 2009; F. O'Reilly & Matt, 2012).

Students who are gifted are a diverse lot, but many share a few characteristics. Compared to children not identified as gifted, these youngsters process information quickly and remember it easily and use advanced reasoning, metacognitive skills, and learning strategies (K. R. Carter & Ormrod, 1982; K. E. Snyder, Nietfeld, & Linnenbrink-Garcia, 2011). Oftentimes, they have an abundant curiosity, seek out new challenges, express themselves creatively, and master tasks independently (D. A. Greenspan, Solomon, & Gardner, 2004; Rakow, 2012; Winner, 2000). They tend to set extremely high standards for their performance, sometimes to the point of perfectionism (W. D. Parker, 1997; Tsui & Mazzocco, 2007). Most have high self-esteem, good social skills, and above-average emotional adjustment, although a small percentage of gifted children have trouble getting along with others and dealing with criticism (Edmunds & Edmunds, 2005; Garces-Bacsal, 2011; A. E. Gottfried, Fleming, & Gottfried 1994; Sousa, 2009).

As you might expect, giftedness is partly an inherited characteristic, but the environment plays a role as well (B. Clark, 1997; A. W. Gottfried, Gottfried, & Guerin, 2009; Shavinina & Ferrari, 2004). Children who are gifted are prone to be firstborn or only-born children and thus exposed to more attention from parents than is the case with other children. Many have had opportunities to practice exceptional abilities from an early age, long before they are identified as being gifted. And they are more inclined to seek out enriching opportunities—an example of the *niche-picking* phenomenon described earlier.

MyLab Education
Video Example 8.3

Find Developmental Meaning *What types of accommodations did Briana seem to benefit from during her elementary school years?* In the video, Briana explains how teachers at different points in time encouraged her to have fun at school and be productive.

Students who are gifted are similar to their classmates in that they want to feel accepted at school. Yet they may feel that unless they hide their exceptional talents, they do not belong there (J. J. Cross, Bugaj, & Mammadov, 2016; Swiatek, 1998). Some gifted students fear that peers will ridicule them for their high academic abilities, especially in secondary school (Covington, 1992; DeLisle, 1984; J. O'Connor, 2012). Girls are prone to hide their talents, especially if they have been raised in cultures that do not value high achievement in women (G. A. Davis & Rimm, 1998; M. L. Nichols & Ganschow, 1992).

Preparing for Your Licensure Examination

Your teaching test might ask you about strategies for fostering the intellectual skills of children with gifts and creative talents.

Fostering the Development of Children with Gifts and Talents

Gifted students tend to be among our schools' biggest underachievers. When required to progress at the same rate as non-gifted peers, they achieve at levels far short of their capabilities (K. R. Carter, 1991; Rakow, 2012). Many students with special gifts and talents become bored or frustrated when school assignments do not allow them to exercise their unique abilities (Feldhusen, Van Winkle, & Ehle, 1996; Rakow, 2012; Winner, 2000). Some lose interest at school and put in only the minimum effort needed to get by in the classroom. When complex problems are presented, gifted students may appreciate the chance to tackle them. Nine-year-old Elena reveals her desire for challenge in her description of PEAK, a program at her school for students who are gifted:

Adult: What do you like best about school?
Elena: I like PEAK. . . . It's for smart kids who have, like, good ideas for stuff you could do. And so they make it more challenging for you in school. So instead of third-grade math, you get fourth-grade math.

In order to receive special services, students who are exceptionally bright usually need to be assessed by school psychologists. Of course, multiple measures should be employed to ensure that bright students from under-represented backgrounds have an equal shot at receiving services (Cao, Jung, & Lee, 2017). With assessment results in place, teachers, school psychologists, special educators, parents, and sometimes the students themselves can identify the kinds of assignments that they need to accomplish standards that are high yet reachable. General techniques include acceleration (e.g., skipping grades or moving to an advanced class in one or more subjects); pull-out programs, in which students leave the regular classroom for a few hours each week to take part in enrichment activities; participation in an online community with peers having similar interests; enrichment activities within the regular classroom; and magnet schools (VanTassel-Baska & Hubbard, 2016).

MyLab Education
Video Example 8.4

Find Developmental Meaning
How does Elena express her feelings about a challenging curriculum? In this video Elena explains what she likes about a special mathematics program for gifted children.

Subject-specific techniques are also worthwhile. Some gifted students who are passionate about reading teach themselves to read, as Gina did in our opening case study (Brighton, Moon, & Huang, 2015). In mathematics, gifted and talented students may learn best when encouraged to be creative with numerical and geometric patterns (Sheffield, 2017). Talented students with artistic and musical skills may enjoy exercising technical expertise, expressing themselves emotionally, and being inventive in the stories they tell (Haberlin, 2017). Students with extraordinary intelligence may soak up scientific principles and facts and investigate their own questions.

MyLab Education Application Exercise 8.3
Identify Development-Enhancing Education

In this video, kindergarten teacher, Christina Higgins, asks her student, Jacob, about what he has learned during a geology unit. How does the lesson embody principles of a development-enhancing education?

Some children who are gifted are slow to learn core academic skills. Children with exceptional intelligence occasionally have learning disabilities, ADHD, autism, emotional disorders, or physical or sensory challenges (e.g., Hettinger & Knapp, 2001; Lovett & Sparks, 2013). In such situations teachers and other practitioners should address the disabilities as well as giftedness. Several strategies for helping children with exceptional abilities to maximize their potential are illustrated in the Development-Enhancing Education feature "Addressing the Unique Needs of Children with Gifts and Talents."

Children with Intellectual Disabilities

Children with an **intellectual disability** show developmental delays in several areas of life.[6] Two characteristics are evident before the age of 18 in a person diagnosed with an intellectual disability (American Association on Intellectual and Developmental Disabilities, 2013):

- *Significantly below-average general intelligence.* Children with an intellectual disability perform poorly on traditional intelligence tests, with IQ scores being no higher than 70 or 75 (reflecting performance in roughly the bottom 2% of their age group). They learn slowly and perform poorly on school tasks in comparison with age-mates, and they show consistently low achievement in most or all academic areas.

MyLab Education
Video Example 8.5

Find Developmental Meaning
How did Elizabeth come to be seen as being gifted and as having a learning disability? In this video Elizabeth relates the time it took for her parents and teachers to identify her intellectual gifts and learning disabilities and for Elizabeth herself to embrace being different.

[6] Although readers may be more familiar with the term *mental retardation* for the condition of low general intelligence, many advocates for students with special needs prefer the term *intellectual disability* because it has less of a social stigma (American Association on Intellectual and Developmental Disabilities, 2013).

Development-Enhancing Education

Addressing the Unique Needs of Children with Gifts and Talents

Watch for unusual gifts and talents in children.

- A second-grade teacher, Mr. Evans, periodically takes notes on the accomplishments of each student. One student, Abrielle, is bossy and disruptive and a mystery to Mr. Evans. After he reviewed his notes, Mr. Evans realized that several of her characteristics suggested a gifted intellect: She occasionally corrects him and classmates with highly detailed information, displays an advanced sense of humor, wonders aloud why certain rules are necessary, and reads advanced nonfiction books about recent inventions in technology. Mr. Evans talks with her parents about having Abrielle tested to see if she qualifies for the school's gifted and talented program. (Middle Childhood)
- A fifth-grade teacher notices that one of her students has exceptional skill with spatial and mechanical tasks. The boy repairs the class's broken clock, navigates with a homemade map as he rides the bus, completes intricate mazes, and draws plans for robots. Although he achieves only average grades in school, the teacher is impressed with his talents and mentions them to a school psychologist, who will follow up on his eligibility for special services. In the meantime, the teacher introduces him to robotics and machine learning. (Middle Childhood)

Individualize instruction in accordance with students' specific talents.

- With help from the kindergarten teacher, the school librarian provides numerous nonfiction picture books about a variety of topics (e.g., with themes related to animal life, historical figures, astronomy, and airplanes). Children each select one book of interest, examine its illustrations, and draw a few pictures of their own. With assistance from the teacher, they create individual booklets on what they have learned. (Early Childhood)
- Two mathematically gifted junior high school students study calculus with a retired mathematician who volunteers her time three mornings a week. They are preparing a booklet for future students to use when learning about calculus. They save illustrations that are helpful in demonstrating the relevance of concepts and prepare a series of cartoons of these applications (e.g., speed and velocity of a rocket and area under a curve) for future students. Their advisor encourages the students to submit their booklet as a capstone project. (Early Adolescence)

Form study groups of gifted students who have similar abilities and interests.

- A music teacher provides semiweekly practice sessions for a quintet of musically talented 10- and 11-year-olds. As group members polish skills, they enjoy themselves sufficiently that they begin meeting daily on their own. They and their teacher develop a plan they can follow when they encounter a problem with coordination of their roles. (Early Adolescence)
- A high school dramatic arts teacher arranges for students to write a play in their study groups. Several members of the theater club spend the entire weekend scripting the dialogue and perform it enthusiastically for the school. (Late Adolescence)

Teach complex cognitive skills within the context of specific school topics.

- An elementary teacher asks a few children with advanced science interests to conduct a series of experiments. To promote critical thinking, she guides the students in establishing hypotheses and procedures and in evaluating rival explanations during the experiments. (Middle Childhood)
- In an earth science class, a middle school teacher gives students a variety of projects related to weather. For students who have little background on the topic, the teacher provides basic information and asks them to prepare a public service announcement about an upcoming storm (Sousa, 2009). For students who want more difficulty, the teacher asks students to prepare and administer a survey about weather patterns. (Early Adolescence)

Provide opportunities for independent study.

- A second-grade teacher finds educational software through which a mathematically gifted 8-year-old can study decimals, exponents, square roots, and other advanced concepts. (Middle Childhood)
- A high school student who is exceptionally talented in the arts is encouraged by her advisor to offer recommendations about the kind of studios, stages, theatrical supplies, and musical instruments that the school needs to offer support for budding artists. (Late Adolescence)

Encourage students to set high goals for themselves without expecting perfection.

- A middle school literacy teacher encourages students to set increasingly high goals in reading and writing. She gives them their test score results and information on state standards in literacy so that students can select their own short-term goals for bridging the gap between current proficiencies and the standards. (Early Adolescence)
- A high school counselor encourages a gifted student from a low-income, single-parent family to consider going to a prestigious college. He helps the student find sources of financial assistance. (Late Adolescence)

Challenge children to express themselves creatively.

- An elementary teacher encourages children to express their knowledge creatively. The teacher asks children to compose poems, write speeches, detect patterns in mathematics, and design multimedia presentations. (Middle Childhood)

- In a high school lesson on romanticism, a teacher asks students to imagine that Ralph Waldo Emerson is coming to their school. For the assignment, the students write an essay on conditions in their community and speculate on how Emerson might respond to these situations. (Late Adolescence)

Seek outside resources to help students develop their exceptional talents.

- A high school student with an aptitude for learning foreign languages takes a Russian course at a local university. Through her new contacts in the class, she finds correspondence buddies in Russia and talks with them on Skype. (Late Adolescence)
- A high school requires students to complete a series of requirements across their 4 years of study—community service as freshmen, job shadowing as sophomores, an internship as juniors, and a major project during their senior year. In planning each activity, students are encouraged to obtain advice from teachers, parents, and experts in their community. (Late Adolescence)

Sources: Ambrose, Allen, and Huntley (1994); Cao, Jung, and Lee (2017); Feldhusen (1989); Fiedler, Lange, and Winebrenner (1993); Harradine, Coleman, and Winn (2014); Milner and Ford (2007); S. M. Moon, Feldhusen, and Dillon (1994); W. D. Parker (1997); Piirto (1999); Rakow (2012); Smutny, von Fremd, and Artabasy (2009); Spicker (1992); and Sternberg et al. (2009).

- *Deficits in adaptive behavior.* The second characteristic is a deficit in **adaptive behavior**, everyday skills that allow the child to take care of him or herself. To become autonomous, the child needs to master a range of competencies, including conceptual understandings (e.g., about time, number, language, and literacy), social skills (e.g., getting along with others, being responsible, and not being victimized), and practical skills (e.g., involving personal self-care, using public transportation, talking and texting on a mobile phone, and purchasing items with correct change). Children with an intellectual disability exhibit adaptive behaviors typical of individuals much younger than themselves.

Children with intellectual disabilities show impairments in information processing. Some have weak attention and a diminished working memory capacity (Schuchardt, Gebhardt, & Mäehler, 2010; A. Witt & Vinter, 2013). Others have trouble generalizing what they learn to new situations (Dempster & Corkill, 1999). Some find it difficult to understand how other people think and feel, and many need extra guidance in coping effectively with anger, frustration, and embarrassment (Baurain & Nader-Grosbois, 2013). The play activities of children with intellectual disabilities are kinds that would ordinarily be observed in younger children, such as a third-grader intruding into peers' activities, asking inappropriately personal questions, and failing to wait a turn during conversation (F. P. Hughes, 2010; Malone, Stoneham, & Langone, 1995; Matson & Fodstad, 2010). Nevertheless, using a younger mental age when referring to students with intellectual disabilities is imprecise because it captures only cognitive deficits, misses their strengths, and implies that these individuals remain juvenile. In fact, young people with intellectual disabilities gain knowledge from experience, in some cases learn in qualitatively different ways than peers, often identify with age mates, and, during the adolescent years, usually mature physically and sexually.

Intellectual disabilities are often caused by abnormal genetic conditions (e.g., Down syndrome or Fragile X syndrome). Yet heredity is not always to blame. Some instances of intellectual disabilities are due to noninherited biological causes, such as severe malnutrition or substance abuse during the mother's pregnancy (e.g., recall our earlier discussion of fetal alcohol syndrome), oxygen deprivation associated with a difficult birth, or serious conditions such as meningitis or exposure to such environmental toxins as lead (National Dissemination Center for Children with Disabilities, 2013; Streissguth et al., 1994; Wodrich, Tarbox, Balles, & Gorin, 2010).

Fostering the Development of Children with Intellectual Disabilities

The great majority of children with intellectual disabilities attend school, and many of them are capable of learning academic and vocational skills. Yet students with intellectual disabilities usually learn best when activities are divided into concrete steps, with each step practiced several times, and then the entire task executed until proficient. Digital technologies can provide practice on adaptive tasks. Other helpful tactics include orienting the student to lessons and appointments during the day, for example, with a written schedule for nonreaders that shows a mathematics class with a simple formula and lunchtime with a drawing of an apple and sandwich. Keeping instructions brief and including visual aids (e.g., charts, diagrams, and pictures) are worthwhile strategies for many learners with intellectual disabilities. Teachers can also advise students when and where to use new skills. A young person who has learned how to greet his classmates can extend a greeting to a server in the cafeteria and the physical education teacher in the gymnasium.

MyLab Education Application Exercise 8.4

Meet Individual Needs

At Haugland School in Columbus, Ohio, Colin, a secondary school student, is learning practical skills with assistance from a mobile application and his teacher. How did the teacher and mobile application scaffold Colin's emerging skills?

Children with intellectual disabilities are often described as developmentally delayed. Indeed, these children often use immature strategies for learning and relating to others (Goharpey, Crewther, & Crewther, 2013). However, children with intellectual disabilities are not simply "slow" learners. They acquire concepts and skills in distinct ways depending on their disability and personal experience, talents, and limitations. For example, children with Down syndrome tend to have a limited working capacity for orally transmitted information, yet they also typically have a relatively strong visual working memory and acquire sight words fairly easily (Ratz, 2013). Reading requires a complex collection of abilities beyond sight reading, and children with Down syndrome need extra practice in phonological awareness and sounding out words. Of course, every child with Down syndrome is unique and such general patterns needs to be supplemented according to personal circumstances. The Development-Enhancing Education feature "Maximizing Learning in Children with Intellectual Disabilities" illustrates several effective strategies that apply broadly and can be customized to the needs of individual learners.

Preparing for Your Licensure Examination

Your teaching test might ask you about strategies for fostering the academic, social, and life skills of children with intellectual disabilities.

Summary

Children identified as having gifts and talents show exceptional promise in one or more domains. Giftedness may be manifested differently across cultures, but in general, gifted individuals demonstrate rapid learning, advanced reasoning, and sophisticated cognitive strategies. Children with an intellectual disability exhibit low general intellectual functioning and deficits in adaptive behavior. In individual children, either kind of exceptionality may have genetic roots, environmental causes, or both. Children with unusually high or low intelligence grow cognitively when they participate in lessons geared to their unique strengths and weaknesses.

MyLab Education Self-Check 8.4

Development-Enhancing Education

Maximizing Learning in Children with Intellectual Disabilities

Encourage young children to use the strengths they have, and offer instruction in acquiring new knowledge and skills in delayed subjects.

- An 18-month-old boy who has intellectual and physical disabilities has recently begun attending an infant center. His caregiver thinks creatively about how to help him interact in the physical environment. She glues Popsicle sticks to the pages of cardboard books so that he can easily grab them and turn the pages. To help him feel secure in his infant chair, she puts skid-proof material on the seat of the chair and cushions on the sides to keep him upright. (Infancy)
- A preschool teacher encourages 4-year-old Sierra, who is characteristically nonverbal, to articulate her desires. When Sierra points at a cabinet, her teacher anticipates that the little girl wants her favorite ball. The teacher prompts Sierra, "Do you want to play with the ball, Sierra?" Sierra smiles and nods affirmatively. The teacher asks her, "Can you say 'ball,' Sierra?" Sierra says, "Bah." The teacher replies, "Good job, Sierra; you asked for your ball. Let me get it for you now." (Early Childhood)

Introduce new material at a slower pace, and provide opportunities for practice.

- A fourth-grade teacher gives a student only two new addition facts a week, primarily because any more overwhelm him. Every day, the teacher has the student practice writing the new facts and reviews addition facts learned in previous weeks. (Middle Childhood)
- A paraprofessional stands by as 13-year-old Yarah completes a mathematics worksheet with single-digit multiplication problems. Yarah completes the problems and occasionally asks for help. Yarah will work on a similar worksheet tomorrow and also a few days next week to solidify her memory of multiplication facts. (Early Adolescence)

Explain tasks concretely and with explicit attention to required steps.

- An elementary art teacher gives a student explicit training in the steps to take at the end of each painting session: (1) Rinse the paintbrush at the sink, (2) put the brush and watercolor paints on the shelf in the back room, and (3) put the painting on the counter by the window to dry. Initially, the teacher needs to remind the student of every step. With time and practice, the student eventually carries out the process independently. (Middle Childhood)
- In preparation for an internship, a teacher tells students about general requirements of jobs—being on time, following directions, using a quiet voice, and so forth. The teacher asks students to anticipate some potential problems and consider how they might respond—for example, how they will get to work if their parents are unable to drive them. (Late Adolescence)

Give explicit guidance about how to study.

- An elementary teacher tells a student, "When you study a new spelling word, it helps if you repeat the letters out loud while you practice writing the word. Let's try it with *house*. Watch how I repeat the letters—H . . . O . . . U . . . S . . . E—as I write the word. Now you try doing what I just did." (Middle Childhood)
- A high school teacher advises a student how to take a standardized test. The teacher tells the student that it's important to write your name at the top of the first page, fill in the bubbles, check when done to see that all the items have been answered, and do your best without worrying about the result. (Late Adolescence)

Give feedback about specific behaviors rather than about general performance.

- A fourth-grade teacher notices that a student in his class is showing a lot of progress in library skills. He tells the student, "I saw how interested you have been at the library. You returned your two books from last week and checked out three books this week. I can't wait to hear about your new books." (Middle Childhood)
- A vocational educator tells a high school student, "You did a good job in woodshop this week. You followed the instructions correctly and put away the equipment when you were finished with it." (Late Adolescence)

Encourage self-determination.

- An elementary teacher shows a boy how to find a seat during lunchtime. The teacher encourages the boy to find a familiar face from class, ask politely if he can join the others, and listen to the conversation before making a relevant comment. In the future, the boy tries these procedures when entering a scout meeting. (Middle Childhood)
- A life skills instructor shows a high school student how to use her calculator to figure out her total lunch bill. The instructor also gives the student practice in identifying the correct bills and coins to use when paying various amounts. (Late Adolescence)

Sources: K. L. Fletcher and Bray (1996); Patton, Blackbourn, and Fad (1996); Perkins (1995); Shogren, Kennedy, Dowsett, and Little (2014); R. R. Pennington and Koehler (2017); and Turnbull et al. (2010).

Practicing For Your Licensure Examination

Many teaching tests require students to use what they have learned about child development in responses to brief vignettes and multiple-choice questions. You can practice for your licensure examination by reading the following case study and answering a series of questions.

Fresh Vegetables

Twelve-year-old Steven had no known genetic or other organic problems but had been officially labeled as having an intellectual disability (mental retardation) based on his low scores on a series of intelligence tests. His prior schooling had been limited to just part of one year in a first-grade classroom in inner-city Chicago. His mother had kept him home after a bullet grazed his leg while he was walking to school one morning. Fearing for her son's safety, she would not let him outside the apartment after that, not even to play, and certainly not to walk the six blocks to the local elementary school.

When a truant officer finally appeared at the door one evening 5 years later, Steven and his mother quickly packed their bags and moved to a small town in northern Colorado. They found residence with Steven's aunt, who persuaded Steven to go back to school. After considering Steven's intelligence and achievement test scores, the school psychologist recommended that he attend a summer school class for students with special needs.

Steven's summer school teacher soon began to suspect that Steven's main problem might simply be a lack of the background experiences necessary for academic success. One incident, in particular, stands out in her mind. The class had been studying nutrition, and so she had asked her students to bring in some fresh vegetables to make a large salad for their morning snack. Steven brought in a can of green beans. When a classmate objected that the beans weren't fresh, Steven replied, "The hell they ain't! Me and Momma got them off the shelf this morning!"

If Steven didn't know what *fresh* meant, the teacher reasoned, then he might also be lacking many of the other facts and skills on which any academic curriculum is inevitably based. She and the teachers who followed her worked hard to help Steven make up for all those years in Chicago during which he had learned few traditional academic skills. By the time Steven reached high school, he was enrolling in regular classes and maintaining a 3.5 grade point average.

Constructed-Response Question

1. Does Steven really seem to have an intellectual disability? Why or why not?

Multiple-Choice Questions

2. What factors have contributed to Steven's current abilities and intellectual weaknesses?
   a. Steven's intellectual limitations are primarily the result of genetic factors.
   b. Steven's profile of intellectual skills and limitations is exclusively from environmental experiences.
   c. Steven's skills and limitations derive from a blend of genetic and environmental factors.
   d. Steven's intellectual abilities are due to a series of developmental changes, with genetic factors contributing a lot during infancy and environmental experiences being influential in the childhood years.
3. Which of the following statements is the most accurate interpretation of Steven's academic performance?
   a. Steven's limited exposure to school made it unlikely that he would be able to succeed academically without intensive instruction.
   b. Given evidence of Steven's low intelligence, we can expect that he will never succeed in any school subject.
   c. Steven has low general intelligence but may have special abilities in focused areas, for example, a keen sensitivity to other people's needs or advanced coordination in athletics.
   d. If Steven's teacher offered him daily training in taking items similar to those on intelligence tests, his intellectual capacity would increase and allow for rapid improvements in academic achievement.

MyLab Education Licensure Practice 8.1

Key Concepts

intelligence (p. 273)
intelligence test (p. 273)
g (p. 274)
fluid intelligence (p. 274)
crystallized intelligence (p. 274)
distributed intelligence (p. 280)
creativity (p. 281)
emotional intelligence (p. 282)
IQ score (p. 287)
cultural bias (p. 288)
dynamic assessment (p. 289)
Flynn effect (p. 300)
niche-picking (p. 300)
stereotype threat (p. 302)
giftedness (p. 304)
intellectual disability (p. 305)
adaptive behavior (p. 307)

Chapter Nine

Language Development

Erik Isakson/Tetra Images/Alamy Stock Photo

Objectives

9.1 Evaluate the merits and limitations of five theoretical frameworks of language development.

9.2 Trace developmental changes in semantics, syntax, listening abilities, speaking skills, knowledge of pragmatics, and metalinguistic awareness.

9.3 Summarize and apply research on second-language learning.

9.4 Examine diversity and exceptionalities in language abilities.

Outline

CASE STUDY

Mario

As a young boy growing up in rural Vermont, Mario had the good fortune to learn two languages. At home, his parents spoke Spanish almost exclusively, communicating to one another in their shared native tongue and passing along their cultural heritage to their son. Most of Mario's early exposure to English was in the child care centers and preschools he attended off and on from the time he was 2 years old.

When Mario was 5, his dominant language was Spanish, but he was proficient in English as well. After his first 2 months in kindergarten, his teacher wrote the following in a report to Mario's parents:

> [Mario is] extremely sociable. He gets along fine with all the children, and enjoys school. He is quite vocal. He does not seem at all conscious of his speech. His slight accent has had no effect on his relations with the others. Whenever I ask the class a question, he is always one of the ones with his hand up.
>
> His greatest problem seems to be in the give and take of conversation. Since he always has something to say, he often finds it difficult to wait his turn when others are talking. When he talks, there are moments when you can see his little mind thinking through language—for he sometimes has to stop to recall a certain word in English which he might not have at his fingertips. (Fantini, 1985, p. 28)

The "slight accent" in Mario's English led a speech therapist to recommend speech therapy, which Mario's parents declined. In fact, all traces of an accent disappeared from Mario's speech by age 8, and his third-grade teacher was quite surprised to learn that he spoke a language other than English at home.

Standardized tests administered over the years attested to Mario's growing proficiency in English. Before he began kindergarten, his score on a standardized English vocabulary test was at the 29th percentile, reflecting performance that, although a little on the low side, was well within the average range. Later, when he took the California Achievement Test in the fourth, sixth, and eighth grades, he obtained scores at the 80th percentile or higher (and mostly above the 90th percentile) on the reading, writing, and spelling subtests. When Mario spent a semester of fifth grade at a Spanish-speaking school in Bolivia, he earned high marks in Spanish as well, with grades of 5 on a 7-point scale in reading, writing, and language usage.

As Mario grew older, his vocabulary and written language skills developed more rapidly in English than in Spanish, in large part because most of his instruction at school was in English. His father described the situation this way:

> [B]y about fifth grade (age ten), he had entered into realms of experience for which he had no counterpart in Spanish. A clear example was an attempt to prepare for a fifth grade test on the topic of "The Industrial Revolution in England and France." It soon became clear that it was an impossibility to try to constrain the child to review materials read and discussed at school—in English—through Spanish. With this incident, [use of English at home] became a fairly well established procedure when discussing other school topics, including science, mathematics, and the like. (Fantini, 1985, p. 73)[a]

- What language skills did Mario develop?
- How did Mario's experiences in his family and school affect his language?

Learning a new language is a challenging undertaking. To use a language effectively, children must master its four components. First, they acquire **phonology**: They must know how words sound and produce the sequence of sounds that make up any given word. Second, they master **semantics**, the meanings of a large number of words. Third,

[a]Excerpts from "Case Study: Mario" from *Language Acquisition of a Bilingual Child: A Sociological Perspective* by A. E. Fantini.

they gain command of **syntax**, the rules for how words can be legitimately combined to form understandable phrases and sentences. Finally, children learn the **pragmatics** of language, the social conventions that enable effective communication.

Mastering the four components of language is a remarkable achievement for any child. For children like Mario who learn more than one language, the task is even more impressive. Given the multifaceted nature of human language, it is not surprising that Mario needed extra time to acquire basic skills in both English and Spanish. At age 5, he had minor difficulties with English phonology (the kindergarten teacher mentioned a "slight accent"), semantics (his score on a vocabulary test was a tad on the low side), and pragmatics (especially taking turns in conversation). Over the long run, however, Mario's bilingual upbringing did *not* hinder his language development. The accent in his English disappeared by age 8, and test scores in the fourth and fifth grades were well above average.

In this chapter, we explore the monumental achievements of language learning during childhood. We begin our discussion by looking at several theoretical perspectives on how children acquire their first language—that is, their **native language**.

Developmental Systems Prompt

As you read about language development, consider the many factors—neurological foundations, cognitive processes, motor skills, interpersonal interactions, and formal instruction—that facilitate children's expertise with the phonology, semantics, syntax, and pragmatics of their native language.

Theories of Language Development

9.1 Evaluate the merits and limitations of five theoretical frameworks of language development.

By age 3 or 4, most children have acquired enough proficiency in language that they are able to carry on productive conversations with people around them. How they rapidly accomplish these skills is one of the great mysteries of child development. Theorists have attempted to explain how children learn one or more languages. Here we describe an early framework based on modeling and reinforcement plus four contemporary perspectives: nativism, cognitive process theories, sociocultural theories, and functionalism.

Modeling and Reinforcement

The behaviorist B. F. Skinner (1957) noticed that children often repeat what others say. Since Skinner wrote his book on *Verbal Behavior*, many scholars have agreed that observation and imitation of others' speech are involved in the acquisition of language (Arbib, 2005; R. Moore, 2013). Infants copy the specific sounds and general vocal patterns that caregivers emit (Balog, 2010; D. W. Evans & Marsh, 2017; Tronick, Cohn, & Shea, 1986). Likewise, older children repeat other people's words and expressions. When Mario began attending an English-speaking preschool, he came home using such expressions as "Shut up!" and "Don't do dat!" that he had learned from classmates (Fantini, 1985, p. 97).[1]

Skinner (1957) suggested that *reinforcement* also plays a role because parents and other adults sometimes praise or in some other way reward mature language use. In Skinner's view, when infants randomly make speech sounds, adults respond favorably to—and so encourage children to repeat—those sounds used in the local language. As children grow older, Skinner proposed, adults reinforce the use of words, then the use of multiword combinations, and eventually word combinations that are, from an adult's perspective, grammatically correct.

Despite their intuitive appeal, theories of imitation and reinforcement are not fully satisfactory. Children do listen intently to speech and respond more actively when encouraged by adults (Schmelzkopf, Greer, Singer-Dudek, & Du, 2017). Yet the speech of young children includes many phrases (e.g., "Allgone milk") that people around them neither say nor reinforce (R. N. Aslin, 2014; N. Chomsky, 1959). Moreover, parents usually reinforce their children's statements based on what is factually accurate rather than what is grammatically correct (R. Brown & Hanlon, 1970; Byrnes & Wasik, 2009). Thus, when a little boy says, "Two kitties" when there are actually three, his mother

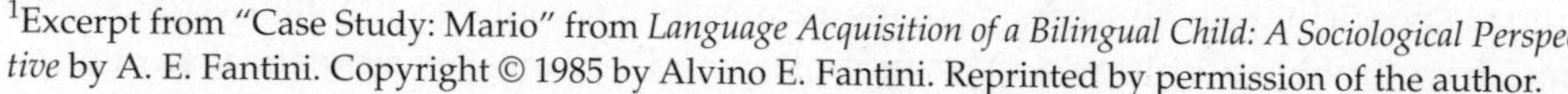
[1]Excerpt from "Case Study: Mario" from *Language Acquisition of a Bilingual Child: A Sociological Perspective* by A. E. Fantini. Copyright © 1985 by Alvino E. Fantini. Reprinted by permission of the author.

might say, "Look, Branson, let's count: One, two, three, kittens. There are *three* kittens. Aren't they lovely?" When parents do attempt to correct children's grammar, they often find children continue to produce grammatically incorrect sentences, as the following dialogue illustrates:

> Child: Nobody don't like me.
> Mother: No, say "nobody likes me."
> Child: Nobody don't like me.
> [Eight repetitions of this dialogue]
> Mother: No, now listen carefully; say "nobody likes me."
> Child: Oh! Nobody don't likes me. (D. McNeill, 1966, p. 68)

Clearly, neither modeling nor reinforcement alone—or even together—is sufficient to explain how children acquire an adultlike form of their native language.

Nativism

In an approach known as **nativism**, theorists have turned to biology to explain language development. One linguist and cognitive scientist, **Noam Chomsky** (1965, 1976, 2006, 2017), proposed that growing children have a biologically built-in mechanism—a **language acquisition device**—that enables them to learn complex aspects of language in a very short time. This mechanism enables certain "prewired" knowledge and skills that make the task of learning far easier than it would be otherwise.

According to Chomsky, children have the basis for a *Universal Grammar*, an abstract set of rules that every language embodies (N. Chomsky, 2006; Guimarães, 2013). The world's many languages have their own rules for how to combine words, yet at a basic level, these rules come from the same general categories and are limited to what the human brain is able to record and process. Based on the anatomy of a child's brain, he or she is able to make sense of simple forms of speech, for example, a *noun* (a word that describes a person, place or thing) and a *verb* (a word that describes an action or state of being). This proficiency is largely unconscious, although children often become aware of parts of speech and grammatical rules as they progress through school.

Despite its credibility, Chomsky's hypothesized *language acquisition device* has not been verified with solid evidence. Even if research ultimately confirms the existence of such an apparatus, questions are likely to remain about how its processes result in language use (Pinker, 1987). In the meantime, many contemporary theorists suspect that multiple mechanisms are at work, some of which code for language specifically and others of which serve as general-purpose capacities that operate in all sorts of cognitive processes, including but not limited to language comprehension. The perspective currently accepted by scholars is that the human brain is uniquely qualified to learn and use language. Milestones in language development are nearly universal and depend on shared brain circuits for noticing regularities in sounds, interpreting verbal meaning, and creating sounds of speech. Virtually all infants, even those who are born deaf and have never heard a human voice, produce speechlike syllables in the first year of life (de Clerck, Pettinato, Verhoeven, & Gillis, 2017; S. Iyer & Oiler, 2008; Lieven & Stoll, 2010; J. L. Locke, 1993). A few months later, they produce one word at a time and later speak in full sentences. When they are exposed to two or more languages—either spoken or manually signed—they likewise produce meaningful words in each language and string them together in interpretable sequences (Crago, Allen, & Hough-Eyamie, 1997; Vohr, Topol, Watson, St. Pierre, & Tucker, 2014).

Thus, although a single mechanism for language acquisition has not been found, a collection of specialized centers in the brain clearly facilitate language learning. The ease with which children acquire two or more languages also attests to the juvenile brain's capacity for making sense of speech. Moreover, the existence of *sensitive periods* for language reveals a biological condition for learning—a state of maturational readiness. Young children achieve mastery of language skills provided that they have certain experiences during a limited period of time. Most young children obtain sufficient verbal stimulation to achieve important language milestones. Children who have had little exposure to speech in the early years, perhaps because of a parent's mental illness or exhaustion, have trouble acquiring a rich vocabulary and advanced grammatical structures.

An exception is when young children who have been deprived of language receive high-quality early interventions rich in conversation and literacy activities (Curtiss, 1977; B. Huang, 2014; D. H. Merritt & Klein, 2015; Newport, 1990). These children tend to catch up in basic language features.

The biological underpinnings of language are further validated with neurological research on regions of the brain. For most people, including the majority of right-handed children and deaf children who use a visual-manual sign system, the left side of the brain, known as the left *hemisphere*, dominates in language processing (Lazard, Innes-Brown, & Barone, 2014; A. J. Newman, Supalla, Hauser, Newport, & Bavelier, 2010). Within the left hemisphere, two regions specialize in language functions (see Figure 9.1). *Broca's area*, located near the forehead, plays a key role in producing speech, especially its literal meanings. *Wernicke's area*, behind the left ear, is involved in understanding speech. Areas in the right hemisphere offer complementary interpretations by sifting through implications of statements, perceiving humor and sarcasm, and keeping track of events described by the speaker (Neville & Bavelier, 2001; A. J. Newman et al., 2010; R. Ornstein, 1997; Sela, Panzer, & Lavidor, 2017).

Cognitive Process Theories

In contrast to Chomsky's position, cognitive process theorists assert that children are born not with one specialized language mechanism but rather with multiple perceptual abilities and intellectual processes, some specifically devoted to language and others being general-purpose thinking skills, the operations of both allowing for detection of patterns in the native language. Infants mentally churn through the speech they hear and infer statistical regularities in sequences of sounds, forms of speech, and uses of words. For instance, they learn that Mommy regularly says "Jess" when trying to get Daddy's attention and notice that the sound "D-a" occurs in speech but that "R-t" does not. Subsequently, children tailor their speech to conform to observed patterns, and their language skills improve accordingly.

The cognitive process model reveals that children become more proficient with language as they speak, listen, and ponder others' statements. Children attend to the separate elements in semantics, syntax, phonology, and pragmatics as they talk and listen to others (Gogate & Hollich, 2010; Laks, 2013; McMurray, Horst, & Samuelson, 2012). For example, children quickly learn that a request to a friend can be informal ("Hey, got a pencil I can use?"), whereas a request to an authority figure must be polite ("Mr. Evans, may I please borrow a pencil?").

Reasoning is another integral part of language learning (M. Atkinson, 1992; Frazier, Gelman, & Wellman, 2009; Landau, 2017). Young children form hypotheses about the meanings of new words by analyzing the circumstances of the conversation (Au & Glusman, 1990). In one investigation, researchers showed preschoolers an unfamiliar animal and consistently called it a *mido*. Later they presented a collection of odd-looking animals (including some midos) and asked the children to find a *theri* in the set (see Figure 9.2). Although the children had no information to guide their selection, they always chose an animal other than a mido. Apparently, they deduced that because the midos already had a name, a theri had to be a different kind of animal.

Certain discoveries with language are easier to make than others, contributing to the order in which children attain specific milestones. Children generally learn nouns before verbs, probably because they find it easier to map a word onto an object (e.g., *ball*) than onto a continuous stream of action (e.g., *throwing* the ball; Gentner, 2006; Golinkoff & Hirsh-Pasek, 2008; Waxman et al., 2013). After the first verbs enter children's speech, they find more and more words to label such conspicuous movements as an object *coming out* of a box and a classmate *walking to* school (Pulverman,

FIGURE 9.1 Primary language centers in the left side of the brain process literal meanings of words and phrases.

Wernicke's area translates sounds into interpretable speech; Broca's area permits production of speech. Areas in the right hemisphere (not shown here) take a more holistic approach with language and help make sense of non-literal information.

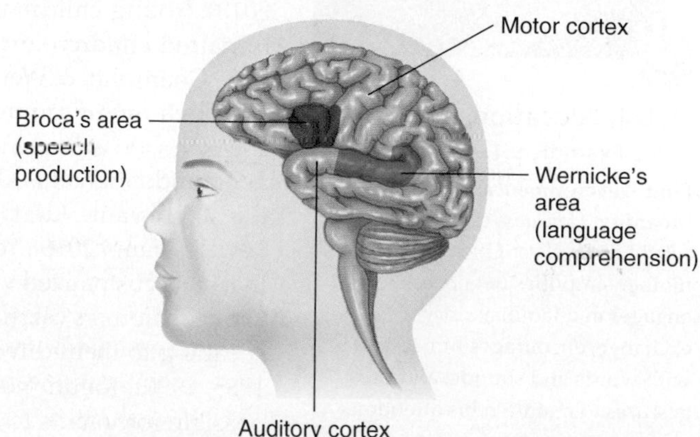

FIGURE 9.2 Which one of these is a *theri*?

Children are more likely to attach new words to objects for which they don't already have labels. In this situation, a child is likely to choose either the purple crocodile-like creature or the yellow dinosaur-like creature as being a *theri*.

After Au and Glusman (1990).

This is a *mido*.
Which one of these is a *theri*?

Song, Hirsh-Pasek, Pruden &, Golinkoff, 2014). As you might expect, children learn verbs for actions they can see (e.g., *running*) before actions they cannot see (e.g., *thinking*; Golinkoff & Hirsh-Pasek, 2008).

A strength of the cognitive process model is that it shows how children contribute to their own language learning. Children rely on what they already know when trying to decipher new language, as when they use existing vocabulary and familiar word order when guessing an unfamiliar term's meaning (Gleitman, Cassidy, Nappa, Papafragou, & Trueswell, 2005; Pinker, 1987). In the sentence, "Dog owners *adore* their pets," a child who has not previously encountered the word *adore* may surmise from word order and personal experience that the word probably refers to an affectionate response.

The cognitive process framework is a dominant force in contemporary explanations of language learning. Evidence that children use intelligent analytical strategies to determine language functions is compelling. Many fascinating questions guide research: How are neurological networks converted into attention to meaningful patterns in speech? How do children chunk information they hear? How do they blend their observations of the sounds a speaker makes with movements of his or her mouth? These and other unanswered questions motivate continued work by linguists, psychologists, anthropologists, and educators.

Sociocultural Theories

Whereas cognitive process theorists emphasize the intellectual operations involved in acquiring language, sociocultural theorists examine how social interactions foster language development. From this perspective children are *socialized* to use language (Cekaite, 2018; Ochs & Schieffelin, 1995; Salomo & Liszkowski, 2013; Serpell, 2017). **Language socialization** involves both explicit instruction about language (e.g., when parents insist that children say "please" and "thank you") and indirect means for fostering appropriate linguistic behaviors (e.g., when parents wait for children to take a turn in speaking, allow them to interject a few words, and expose them to the rhythms of interaction). Social interactions also provide a mechanism through which children *internalize* language. Consistent with Vygotsky's theory of cognitive development, children use words first in their interactions with others and then gradually incorporate words into thought processes (Hobson, 2004; K. Nelson, 1996a; Wernholm & Vigmo, 2015).

Language socialization begins in infancy. Adults have an intuitive sense of the challenges infants face and, depending on traditions in their society, may simplify their speech or explicitly teach verbal expressions. Many U.S. and European parents engage their infants in dyadic exchanges with short, simple, high-pitched language, with long pauses and gestures identifying the people or objects under discussion (Falk & Kello, 2017; M. Harris, 1992; B. McMurray, Kovack-Lesh, Goodwin, & McEchron, 2013). Young children find such **infant-directed speech** captivating; even hearing-impaired children are drawn to its animated features (S. Robertson, von Hapsburg, Hay, Champlin, & Werner, 2013).

MyLab Education
Video Example 9.1

Find Developmental Meaning *How does Corwin's mother adapt her speech for Corwin?* Corwin's mother simplifies her speech, engages in a familiar storybook exchange, encourages him to join in with words and sounds, and uses gestures to maintain his attention.

Such modifications can help with comprehension, for instance, by clarifying the speaker's focus of attention. When Grandma points to a piece of fruit and calls it an apple, her granddaughter is likely to remember it, particularly when Grandma repeats the word (G. A. Bryant, Liénard, & Barrett, 2012; B. McMurray et al., 2013; Schwab & Lew-Williams, 2016). Yet the neurological basis for language learning is sufficiently strong that such customized verbal interactions are not critical. Among the Kaluli in Papua New Guinea, mothers carry their infants around all day and hold infants facing outward, not speaking to them directly but allowing them to listen in on conversations (Schieffelin, 1985, 1990). Kaluli mothers do not intentionally ease the task of language yet make it possible for infants to eavesdrop and learn to speak a few words. When mothers hear infants' first words, they begin to ask infants to say certain phrases because they now see their children as having intentions to speak and learn language.

From a sociocultural perspective, *intersubjectivity*, the mutual awareness that two or more people are thinking about the same thing simultaneously, is foundational to language acquisition. For children to learn new words while interacting with others, they must be aware of their mutual focus (Mundy & Newell, 2007; Tomasello, 1999; Vuksanovic & Bjekic, 2013). As an illustration, imagine that a father and his 3-year-old daughter are shopping at the local supermarket. "Oh good," the father exclaims, "a carambola. I love carambolas!" If the daughter has never heard the word *carambola* before, she will likely look at her father's face and then follow his gaze to the object in question (in this case, a yellow-green star-shaped fruit). She is apt to do this only if she realizes that her father is looking at the object he is talking about.

Preparing for Your Licensure Examination

Your teaching test might ask you about cultural influences on language learning.

As early as the second year, and quite possibly before that, children use what they infer about other people's focus to assist in the interpretation of word meanings (Golinkoff & Hirsh-Pasek, 2006; Mundy & Newell, 2007; Tomasello, 1999). In one study, 18-month-olds were looking at one new toy while an adult looked at another (D. A. Baldwin, 1993). When the adult exclaimed, "A modi!" the children typically turned their attention to see what the adult was looking at. A short time later, when the children were asked to get the modi, they were most likely to choose the toy the adult had been looking at, even though they themselves had been looking at something different when they first heard the word.

A primary strength of the sociocultural framework is its clear commitment to the social origins of language acquisition. Language begins in every child's life as a tool for communication and evolves into a multifaceted capacity for information exchange, personal connection, self-control, and thought. A second strength of the sociocultural framework is its disclosure of many distinct styles in language learning. Children are flexible in their approaches to language learning, easily adapting to types of family interactions and cultural norms for communication.

Functionalism

Another important question about language involves its purpose: What does language help children accomplish in daily life? Some psychologists argue that over the course of evolution, human beings developed language skills because it served vital functions—hence the term **functionalism**. Language helps children to acquire knowledge, maintain productive relationships, control their behavior, and influence the actions of others (L. Bloom & Tinker, 2001; Karniol, 2010; Langacker, 2016; Tamis-LeMonda & Song, 2013). The British linguist **Michael Halliday** (1975) has offered several purposes of language for children:

- *Instrumental Functions.* Children use words to express needs and desires. One of the first functions children use language for is to ask for things—"juice," "blankie," or another wanted object.
- *Regulatory Functions.* Children soon try to make other people act in a certain way. When Mario attended preschool as a 3-year-old, he quickly learned such expressions as "No do dat no more!" and "Get outta here!" (Fantini, 1985, pp. 97–98).[2] We can reasonably infer that such phrases enabled Mario to assert his rights with classmates.
- *Interactional Functions.* Children use language to seek contact with others, as when a two-year-old boy who wants to be held by his grandfather says, "Up, Papa!"
- *Personal Functions.* Children express themselves individually with language—how they feel, what they believe, and how they see themselves. A seven-year-old girl may convey pride to her parents during a school event ("Look at my sculpture! I want to be an artist when I grow up.")
- *Heuristic Functions.* Children are active explorers of the world, and they quickly learn that asking questions is a good way to find out how things work.

[2] Excerpt from "Case Study: Mario" from *Language Acquisition of a Bilingual Child: A Sociological Perspective* by A. E. Fantini. Copyright © 1985 by Alvino E. Fantini. Reprinted by permission of the author.

- *Imaginative Functions.* Especially as they grow and are exposed to literature, poetry, and drama, children use language in creative ways—telling stories, making up jokes, and sharing fantasies with friends during pretend play.
- *Representational Functions.* Children use language to convey ideas—facts, impressions, and information acquired during academic lessons and everyday life.

Functionalist theorists also point out that language development is closely intertwined with—and, in fact, is critical for—development in other domains (L. Bloom & Tinker, 2001; Langacker, 1986). Thus, another outcome of language is the enhancement of cognitive development with symbols for representing events, exchanging information, and regulating personal behavior. Language is essential for moral development because conversations with others inform children about right and wrong and the underlying code of conduct they are expected to live by.

The principal merit of the functionalist framework is its identifications of the *purposes* of language. Language development is far more than acquiring knowledge about words and grammatical structures. Language transforms the child's mind and is a means for accomplishing personal goals. The initial function of sharing experiences with others is gradually supplemented with conveying respect, asserting individual rights, insulting others, expressing emotions, telling stories, and managing one's own behavior. Although the functionalist framework is not strong in identifying biological underpinnings or precise cognitive processes, its core ideas complement the nativist, cognitive process, and sociocultural frameworks.

Evaluating Theories of Language Development

The Basic Developmental Issues table "Contrasting Theories of Language Development" summarizes how nativism, cognitive process theories, sociocultural theories, and functionalism differ with respect to themes of nature and nurture, universality and diversity, and qualitative and quantitative change. An important difference among theoretical perspectives is their primary attention: Nativism focuses largely on syntactic development; cognitive processes document the detection of meaning in words and sounds of speech; sociocultural theories look closely at semantic development and pragmatic skills; and functionalism considers how motivation fits into the picture.

BASIC DEVELOPMENTAL ISSUES
Contrasting Contemporary Theories of Language Development

ISSUE	NATIVISM	COGNITIVE PROCESS THEORIES	SOCIOCULTURAL THEORIES	FUNCTIONALISM
Nature and Nurture	By and large, children develop language only when they are exposed to it; thus, environmental input is essential. But children also rely on one or more biological mechanisms that provide clues as to the underlying principles of language.	Language acquisition involves the activation of inherited brain circuits and the child's detection of regularities in language input (e.g., sounds that occur regularly in the native language, and clues in context that enable inferences about word meaning).	Sociocultural theorists don't discount the role of heredity, but they prioritize the social contexts and cultural legacy (e.g., culture-specific interpretations of phrases) that a society passes along from one generation to the next.	As children develop desires, ideas, and insights, they convey their thoughts with carefully chosen words. Growth is the result of heredity, environment, and children's reflection.
Universality and Diversity	Human languages have certain things in common (e.g., they contain words for actions [verbs] and people, places, and things [nouns]). Children speaking different languages reach milestones at similar ages. Diversity exists in the specific phonological, semantic, syntactic, and pragmatic patterns in particular languages.	Cognitive mechanisms that enable language acquisition (e.g., attention, analysis of speech sounds) are universally employed. Children's unique experiences, which vary across communities, lead to differences in the language(s) that children speak, their individual pathways toward proficiency, and concepts they communicate.	Some mechanisms that promote language development, for example, *intersubjectivity*, are universal across cultures. Different societies support these capacities in distinctive ways and cultivate their own linguistic practices. Cultures differ in the extent to which adults modify speech for young children.	The drive to understand and be understood is universal. Different cultural groups cultivate certain styles of communication more than others. Each culture uses unique traditions in communicating respect and telling stories.

BASIC DEVELOPMENTAL ISSUES
Contrasting Contemporary Theories of Language Development (Continued)

ISSUE	NATIVISM	COGNITIVE PROCESS THEORIES	SOCIOCULTURAL THEORIES	FUNCTIONALISM
Qualitative and Quantitative Change	Children acquire syntactic structures in a predictable order that has some stage-like properties. Young children proceed through one-word to two-word phases and later more complex constructions. If not exposed to conversation by the end of early childhood, a person's language growth requires laborious effort and yields only partial mastery.	Many changes in language development—for instance, growing vocabularies, refinement of word meanings, and increasingly correct pronunciation, come about in a quantitative fashion with certain advancements occurring before others based on simplicity of distinctions. Gradual maturation of the brain contributes to qualitative changes in language use.	As a qualitative change, *intersubjectivity* initially involves a sense of shared experience involving tangible objects and later incorporates a feeling of having common ground on how the social world works. Trend-like increases occur in the absorption of language conventions from the community.	Whereas a 2-year-old might simply ask for "More cookie?" A 15-year-old might ask, "When I'm old enough to drive, can I get a part-time job to buy a used car?" Qualitative changes occur in grammatical structures, and quantitative changes appear in sentence length.

Although theorists isolate single elements of children's language in order to make their analysis manageable, children embrace its full complexity, tackling the gamut of phonological, semantic, syntactic, and pragmatic rules as they speak and listen. Not only do children communicate according to basic principles governing their mother tongue; they also manage to improve their skills in the process. In the next section, we focus closely on the numerous developmental changes that occur in children's language.

Summary

Although modeling, reinforcement, and feedback play a modest role in language development, early theories based on such processes could not adequately account for the fact that most children acquire a native language in a very short period, with only limited guidance from adults. Several more recent theoretical perspectives have emerged, each focusing on a different aspect of language development. *Nativists* propose that young children have certain inherited abilities that facilitate language acquisition. *Cognitive process theorists* apply general principles of cognition (e.g., the importance of attention, the detection of patterns in language input) to explain how language develops. *Sociocultural theorists* emphasize the role that social interactions play in language learning. *Functionalists* propose that children are motivated to use language because it satisfies personal needs. To account for the range of advancements that occur in children's language development, scholars and practitioners are apt to draw from elements of two or more frameworks.

MyLab Education Self-Check 9.1

Developmental Trends in Language

9.2 Trace developmental changes in semantics, syntax, listening abilities, speaking skills, knowledge of pragmatics, and metalinguistic awareness.

Dramatic changes occur in language in the first few years of life. Children's first form of communication is crying. Soon after, they make eye contact, smile, coo, and babble. A bit later, they point and gesture, and, ultimately, speak and listen (Goldin-Meadow, 2006; Kraljević, Cepanec, & Šimleša, 2014; Tomasello, Carpenter, & Liszkowski, 2007). Let's look more carefully at the growth of language during infancy, childhood, and adolescence.

Preparing for Your Licensure Examination

Your teaching test might ask you to recognize key developmental milestones in learning language.

Semantic Development

Infants mentally categorize characteristics, objects, and creatures by 4 months of age (e.g., blue vs. green, dogs vs. cats); understand the meanings of a few words as early as 8 months of age; and say their first word at about 12 months (Fenson et al., 1994; M. Harris, 1992; Oller, Oller, & Oller, 2014; Poulin-Dubois & Pauen, 2017). By the time children are 16 to 18 months old, many have 50 words in their expressive vocabularies (Byrnes & Wasik, 2009; O'Grady, 1997). There is considerable variability from child to child, however. Mario did not say his first word until he was 16 months old, and by his second birthday he was using only 21 words (Fantini, 1985).

At some point during the end of the second year or beginning of the third year, there is a virtual explosion in vocabulary, with children using 30 to 50 new words a month and, later, as many as 20 new words *each day* (M. Harris, 1992; O'Grady, 1997). In the preschool years, children organize their knowledge of words into general categories (e.g., *juice*, *cereal*, and *morning* are all related to *breakfast*), hierarchies (e.g., *dogs* and *cats* are both *animals*), and other interword relationships (S. A. Gelman & Kalish, 2006; M. Harris, 1992). At 6 years of age, children's semantic knowledge typically includes 8,000 to 14,000 words, of which 2,600 are included in speech (Byrnes & Wasik, 2009; Carey, 1978). By sixth grade, they understand, on average, 50,000 words in what they hear and read, although they do not produce all of these words themselves. By the end of high school, vocabulary includes approximately 80,000 words (Owens, 2012).

This dramatic increase in vocabulary is the most obvious aspect of semantic development. Yet several other principles characterize vocabulary growth, as we now explain.

Children use a collection of strategies for learning the meanings of words. As children are identifying the specific words in speech, they must also zero in on their meanings. In some cases, adults provide instruction, perhaps by labeling objects or by asking questions ("Where is the _______________?") while looking at picture books with children (M. F. Collins, 2010; Dunham, Dunham, & Curwin, 1993; Manolitsis, Georgiou, & Parrila, 2011). More often, caregivers, teachers, and other individuals don't explicitly identify what they are referring to when they use new words. As a result, youngsters must infer the meaning from clues intrinsic to speech, from the contexts in which the words are used, and from their rudimentary reasoning abilities.

After children have acquired a basic vocabulary, they learn new words rapidly. By the time children are 2 or 3, they often infer a word's general meaning after only a few encounters or even one exposure—a process known as **fast mapping** (Carey & Bartlett, 1978; C. Kim, O'Grady, Deen, & Kim, 2017; Samuelson & McMurray, 2017). Young children seem to use a number of rules to fast-map word and syntactic meanings. Here are some key techniques:

- If I see several objects and know labels for all of them except one, the new word is probably the name of the unlabeled object. (Recall research involving the words *mido* and *theri*.)
- If someone uses a word while pointing to a particular object, the word probably refers to the *whole* object rather than to just a part of it.
- When a word is used to refer to a particular object or action, it refers to *similar* objects or actions as well.
- If a word is preceded by an article (e.g., "This is a *ball*"), it refers to a category of objects. If it has no article in front of it (e.g., "This is *Tobey*"), it is the name of a *particular* person, animal, or place (i.e., it is a proper noun) (Au & Glusman, 1990; K. W. Brady & Goodman, 2014; S. A. Gelman & Raman, 2003; S. A. Gelman & Taylor, 1984; Golinkoff, Hirsh-Pasek, Bailey, & Wenger, 1992; Markman, 1989; Samuelson & McMurray, 2017; Spiegel & Halberda, 2011; E. A. Walker, McGregor, Bacon, & Tobey, 2013).

Comprehension usually, but by no means always, precedes production. Psychologists studying language development frequently make a distinction between receptive and expressive language skills. **Receptive language** is the ability to understand what one hears and reads. In other words, it involves language *comprehension*. In contrast, **expressive language** is the ability to communicate effectively either orally or in writing. It involves language *production*. Essentially, receptive and expressive language skills develop hand in hand, with language comprehension facilitating language production, language production enhancing language comprehension, and both relying on cognitive abilities.

Yet there are occasions when comprehension or production can dominate in one situation or another. On other occasions, children use some words whose meanings they don't completely understand (Owens, 2012). Teresa recalls a 3-year-old preschooler in her class who talked about the "accoutrements" in her toy purse, presumably after hearing an adult use this word in a similar context (and yes, Teresa had to look up the word in the dictionary). Although the girl used the word appropriately, she presumably did not understand all its connotations. Her production exceeded her comprehension.

Children initially focus on lexical words; grammatical words come later. All languages have two main categories of words (Shi & Werker, 2001). **Lexical words** have some connection, either concrete or abstract, to objects, events, or circumstances in people's physical, social, and psychological worlds. They include nouns (e.g., *horse*, *freedom*), verbs (e.g., *swim*, *think*), adjectives (e.g., *handsome*, *ambiguous*), and adverbs (e.g., *quickly*, *intentionally*). **Grammatical words** (also known as *function words*) have little meaning by themselves but affect the meanings of other words or the interrelationships among words or phrases. They include articles (e.g., *a*, *the*), auxiliary verbs (e.g., *have* in *I have swum*), prepositions (e.g., *before*, *after*), and conjunctions (e.g., *however*, *unless*). By the time children are 6 months old, they can distinguish between lexical and grammatical words and show a distinct preference for lexical words (Bornstein et al., 2004; Shi & Werker, 2001).

MyLab Education
Video Example 9.2

Find Developmental Meaning *Is Corwin more advanced in receptive or expressive language?* Corwin can recognize words (e.g., cat, banana, dog) and point to relevant pictures that he is not yet able to label himself. In this respect, he has greater facility in understanding words (receptive language) than in saying them (expressive language).

Over time, children refine their understandings of lexical words. Children initially have a general idea of what certain words mean but define them imprecisely and use them incorrectly. One common error is **underextension**, in which children attach overly restricted meanings to words, leaving out some situations to which the words apply. For example, Jeanne once asked her son Jeff, then 6, to tell her what an *animal* is. He gave this definition:

> It has a head, tail, feet, paws, eyes, nose, ears, lots of hair.

Like Jeff, young elementary school children often restrict their meaning of *animal* primarily to nonhuman mammals, such as dogs and horses, and insist that fish, birds, insects, and people are *not* animals (Carey, 1985; Saltz, 1971). Another frequent error is **overextension**: Words are given meanings that are too broad and so are applied to inappropriate situations. For example, a child might say, "I'm *barefoot* all over!" or "I'll get up so early that it will still be *late*" (Chukovsky, 1968, p. 3; italics added).

In addition to underextending and overextending word meanings, children sometimes confuse the meanings of similar words. The following conversation illustrates 5-year-old Christine's confusion between *ask* and *tell*:

> Adult: Ask Eric his last name. [Eric Handel is a classmate of Christine's.]
> Christine: Handel.
> Adult: Ask Eric this doll's name.
> Christine: I don't know.
> Adult: Ask Eric what time it is.
> Christine: I don't know how to tell time.
> Adult: Tell Eric what class is in the library.
> Christine: Kindergarten.
> Adult: Ask Eric who his teacher is.
> Christine: Miss Turner. (dialogue from C. S. Chomsky, 1969, p. 55; format adapted)

Similarly, young children often confuse comparative words, sometimes interpreting *less* as "more" or thinking that *shorter* means "longer" (Owens, 2012; Palermo, 1974).

Children continue to have difficulty with grammatical words throughout the elementary and middle school years. Children's mastery of grammatical words typically evolves slowly over a period of several years. For instance, although 3-year-olds can distinguish between the articles *a* and *the*, children as old as 9 are occasionally confused about when to use each one (Reich, 1986). Children in the upper elementary and middle school grades, and occasionally at the high school level, have trouble with many conjunctions and adverbial phrases, such as *but*, *although*, *yet*, *however*, *honestly*, and *unless* (Ebbels, Marić, Murphy, & Turner, 2014; E. W. Katz & Brent, 1968). As an illustration, consider the following two pairs of sentences:

Jimmie went to school, but he felt sick.

Jimmie went to school, but he felt fine.

The meal was good, although the pie was bad.

The meal was good, although the pie was good.

Even 12-year-olds have trouble identifying the correct sentence in pairs like these, reflecting only a vague understanding of the connectives *but* and *although* (E. W. Katz & Brent, 1968). (The first sentence is correct in both cases.)

Refinements in verbal concepts occur throughout childhood, including during adolescence. As young people get older, they sharpen and expand their understandings of words through repeated encounters in conversation, books, and explicit instruction (Byrnes & Wasik, 2009; Carey & Bartlett, 1978; Samuelson & McMurray, 2017; Yildirim et al., 2014). They build on what they already know, adding nuances to existing concepts. As an example, consider how three children in the same family once defined the word *plant*:

Andrew (age 7): Something that people plant in a garden or somewhere.

Amaryth (age 10): A growing thing that's sometimes beautiful.

Anthony (age 13): A life-form that uses sunlight and carbon dioxide to live.

Notice how Andrew's definition is limited to contexts in which his parents and other people might have used the word. Amaryth's definition is more general, in that it includes a characteristic of all plants: growth. Only Anthony's definition includes characteristics that a biologist might identify. Presumably Anthony had acquired this understanding of the word *plant* in a science class.

Concrete words are understood before abstract words. Children's increasing ability to think abstractly is reflected in their semantic development (Anglin, 1977; Haskill & Corts, 2010; Quinn, 2007; Samuelson & McMurray, 2017). Young children in particular are apt to define words (even fairly abstract ones) in terms of the obvious, concrete aspects of their world. For example, when Jeanne's son Jeff was 4, he defined *summer* as the time of year when school is out and it is hot outside. By the time he was 12, he knew that scientists define summer in terms of the earth's tilt relative to the sun—a much more abstract notion.

Fostering Semantic Development

Language experts have identified several strategies that teachers, parents, and other caregivers can use to help children learn word meanings:

- **Talk regularly to, with, and around infants, toddlers, and preschool children.** Even when infants have not yet begun to talk, they learn a great deal from hearing their native language. Initially, they learn its basic characteristics, such as its typical rhythms and stress patterns and the range of sounds it includes. Later, as they begin to mentally "divide" speech into individual words, they draw inferences about what words mean. Although parents' simple sentences, talk about the here and now, and attention-grabbing tones attract infants into conversation, it's the richness of parents' language—the variety of words, complex syntactic structures, and so on—that facilitates vocabulary growth (B. Hart & Risley, 1995; Hoff & Naigles, 2002; McGillion, Pine, Herbert, & Matthews, 2017; Pan, Rowe, Singer, & Snow, 2005).

- **Invite children to listen to stories and later to read on their own.** Reading to young children expands their vocabularies, especially when periodically pausing to answer children's questions and explain unfamiliar words (Brabham & Lynch-Brown, 2002; Gómez, Vasilyeva, & Dulaney, 2017; Lugo-Neris, Jackson, & Goldstein, 2010). When children read themselves, they encounter a rich corpus of language. Avid readers learn many more new words and develop larger vocabularies than do peers who read infrequently (Fukkink & de Glopper, 1998; Swanborn & de Glopper, 1999; Zucker, Cabell, Justice, Pentimonti, & Kaderavek, 2013). As you can see in Artifact Example 9.1, 10-year-old Amaryth encountered several new words in her reading.

what dose worrisome meen?
what is and dose prevaricate mean?
Sobrquct?

MyLab Education
Artifact Example 9.1

Find Developmental Meaning *How does 10-year-old Amaryth respond to unfamiliar words?* Amaryth recognizes that a couple of words are new to her and realizes that she does not have enough information in the passage to decipher their meaning.

• **Define new words.** By the time children are school age, they often learn words more easily when told specifically what the words mean—in other words, when they are given definitions (Crevecoeur, Coyne, & McCoach, 2014; Tennyson & Cocchiarella, 1986). Most children can learn what a *circle* is and what *red* means even without definitions because roundness and redness are characteristics that are easily noticed. But the important characteristics of such conceptually based ideas as *polygon* and *fragile* are subtle, and for words like these, definitions can be useful.

• **Provide examples and nonexamples of new words.** Children often acquire a more accurate understanding of a word when they are shown several examples (Barringer & Gholson, 1979; Tennyson & Cocchiarella, 1986). Ideally, such exemplars should be as different from one another as possible so that they illustrate the word's entire range. If adults limit their examples of *animal* to dogs, cats, cows, and horses, children will understandably draw the conclusion that all animals have four legs and fur (a case of underextension). If instead adults also mention goldfish, robins, beetles, earthworms, and people as examples of *animals*, children are apt to realize that these creatures can differ considerably in physical appearance.

In addition to identifying examples, children benefit from learning nonexamples of a word, especially those that are "near misses" (Winston, 1973). For instance, to learn what a *salamander* is—an amphibian that looks like a cross between a frog and a lizard—a child might be shown several salamanders and be told what the characteristic features are. Next, the child could be shown such similar animals as a snake and a lizard and informed that these critters are "*not* salamanders." By presenting both examples and nonexamples, adults minimize the extent to which children are likely to overextend their use of words.

• **Give feedback to children when they use words incorrectly.** Misconceptions about word meanings reveal themselves in children's speech. Astute teachers listen closely not only to what children say but also to how they say and write about it. A preschooler might mistakenly refer to a rhinoceros as a "hippo," an elementary school student might deny that a square is a rectangle, and a high school student might use the term *atom* when she is really talking about molecules. In such situations adults should gently correct the misconceptions, perhaps by saying something along these lines: "A lot of people get hippos and rhinoceroses confused, because both of them are large gray mammals. This animal has a large horn on its nose, so it's a rhinoceros. Let's find a picture of a hippo and see how we can tell the difference."

Syntactic Development

Which one of the following sentences is grammatically correct?

- Growing children need nutritious food and lots of exercise.
- Experience students find to be many junior high school an unsettling.

You undoubtedly realized that the first sentence is grammatically correct and the second is not. But *how* were you able to tell the difference? Can you describe the specific grammatical rules you used to make your decisions?

Rules of syntax—the rules we use to combine words into meaningful sentences—are incredibly complex (e.g., N. Chomsky, 2006). Yet much of our knowledge about syntax is unconscious. Although we can produce acceptable sentences and understand others' syntactically correct sentences, we cannot always put our finger on exactly what it is we know about language that allows us to understand grammatical rules.

Despite the elusive nature of syntactic rules, children pick them up quickly. By the time they reach school age, children have mastered many of the basics of sentence construction (Christie, 2012; Haskill & Corts, 2010; McNeill, 1970). Grammar acquisition continues in school, with children filling in minor gaps in their syntactic knowledge throughout the elementary school years and, to a lesser extent, in the secondary school years as well. Following are noteworthy milestones in syntactic development over the course of childhood.

Early syntactic knowledge builds on an awareness of patterns in speech. In one study, 7-month-olds heard a series of "sentences," each composed of three nonsense syllables (e.g., *ga, na, ti, li*). Infants in Group 1 consistently heard them in a predictable "ABA" pattern (e.g., "Ga ti ga," "Li na li"), whereas infants in Group 2 heard them consistently in an "ABB" pattern (e.g., "Ga ti ti," "Li na na"; Marcus, Vijayan, Bandi Rao, & Vishton, 1999). After losing interest in whichever sentences they had heard, the babies were exposed to another series of "sentences" with new nonsense syllables. Some of these sentences followed the ABA pattern (e.g., "Wo fe wo"), whereas others followed the ABB pattern (e.g., "Wo fe fe"). The infants paid greater attention when listening to the new pattern, showing their distinction between familiar and unfamiliar structures.

First words emerge one by one. Initially, children use only single words to express their thoughts. At 18 months, Teresa's son Connor would simply say "mo" if he wanted *more* of whatever he was eating or playing with at the time. And like many toddlers, he would stretch out his arms and plead "Up!" when he wanted to be carried or cuddled. Developmental scientists sometimes use the word **holophrase** to refer to such one-word "sentences" (Byrnes & Wasik, 2009).

First grammars are simple and predictable. As toddlers begin to combine words into two-word "sentences" in the latter half of their second year, they use a limited number of grammatical forms (e.g., adjective adjective + noun noun), and their two-word combinations often reflect description ("Pillow dirty"), location ("Baby table"), and possession ("Adam hat"; R. Brown, 1973, p. 14). These early multiple-word sentences, known as **telegraphic speech**, include lexical words (rather than grammatical words) almost exclusively. By using such words, children maximize the meaning of their short sentences, just as many adolescents and adults do when they send text messages. As children's sentences lengthen, syntactic complexity progresses with the addition of a subject, a verb, and an object (e.g., "I ride horsie") or description of both an action and a location ("Put truck window," "Adam put it box"; R. Brown, 1973, p. 205). Sometime before age 3, children include grammatical words—*the, and, because*, and so on—in their sentences (O'Grady, 1997; Owens, 2012).

Young children increasingly attend to word order. By the time they are $1\frac{1}{2}$ children have a basic command of word order (Dove, 2012; Gertner, Fisher, & Eisengart, 2006; Hirsh-Pasek & Golinkoff, 1996). They know that "Big Bird is washing Cookie Monster" means something different from "Cookie Monster is washing Big Bird." Yet young children are sometimes misled by the order in which words appear (O'Grady, 1997). Many preschoolers apply a general rule that a pronoun refers to the noun that immediately precedes it. Consider the sentence "John said that Peter washed him." Many 4-year-olds think that *him* refers to *Peter* and hence conclude that Peter washed himself. Similarly, kindergartners are apt to have trouble with the sentence "Because she was tired, Mommy was sleeping" because no noun appears before *she*.

Children use prevalence and position of word combinations as clues to their functions. Some theorists suggest that acquiring syntax involves discovering the probabilities with which various word combinations appear in sentences (Dove, 2012; MacWhinney & Chang, 1995; Meylan, Frank, Roy, & Levy, 2017; Sirois, Buckingham, & Shultz, 2000). Children may notice that *the* is usually followed by names of things or by "describing" words (e.g., they might hear "the dog," "the picnic," or "the pretty hat"). In contrast, *the* is rarely followed by words that identify specific actions (e.g., they never hear "the do" or "the went").

Children attend to word meaning when figuring out syntactic rules. Children occasionally engage in **semantic bootstrapping**, the process of using word meanings as a basis for understanding syntactic categories (Abend, Kwiatkowski, Smith, Goldwater, & Steedman, 2017; Bates & MacWhinney, 1987; S. A. Gelman & Kalish, 2006; Pinker, 1984). They may notice that labels for people and concrete objects always serve particular functions in sentences, action words serve other functions, spatial-relationship and direction words serve still others, and so on. Through this process they gradually acquire an intuitive understanding of nouns, verbs, prepositions, and other parts of speech—an understanding that allows them to use words appropriately in sentences. When told that "The dog consumed his meal," children not familiar with the word *consumed* may correctly infer that the dog *did* something with his dinner, most likely eating it.

Children's questions increasingly honor syntactic rules. In some languages, it's easy to ask questions. In Chinese, for instance, a person can change a statement into a question simply by adding *ma* to the end of the sentence. In English, asking questions is more complicated, for one thing requiring a change to the order of the subject and verb (from "You are hungry" to "Are you hungry?"). When past tense is involved, asking a question requires putting the auxiliary verb but *not* the main verb first ("Have you eaten yet?"). And when something other than a yes or no answer is called for, a question word (e.g., *who, what, where, how*) must also appear at the beginning ("What did you eat?"). English-speaking children master these rules a step at a time. Initially, their questions may be nothing more than telegraphic sentences with a rise in pitch at the end (e.g., "Kitty go home?"; R. Brown, 1973, p. 141). At about age $2\frac{1}{2}$ they attach question words to the beginning, and sometime in their third year, they add an auxiliary verb such as *is* or *does*. By the time they are 5, most English-speaking children have mastered the correct syntax for questions (de Villiers, 1995).

Children learn general rules for word endings before they learn the many exceptions. Knowledge of syntax includes awareness of when to use word endings (suffixes) such as *s, er,* and *ed*. When children first learn the rules for using suffixes (e.g., *s* indicates plural, *er* indicates a comparison, and *ed* indicates past tense), they often apply these rules indiscriminately. Thus, a child might say "I have two *foots*," "Chocolate is *gooder* than vanilla," and "I *goed* to Grandma's house." This phenomenon, known as **overregularization**, is especially common during the preschool and early elementary years. It gradually diminishes as children master the irregular forms of words: The plural of *foot* is *feet*, the comparative form of *good* is *better*, the past tense of *go* is *went*, and so on (Blom, Paradis, Oetting, & Bedore, 2013; Cazden, 1968). Some mistakes continue to be made, however. Most high school students (and many adults as well) haven't completely mastered all irregularities in the English language (Marcus, 1996).

The ability to comprehend passive sentences evolves gradually during the preschool and elementary school years. In a passive sentence, the subject of the sentence is the recipient, rather than the agent, of the action conveyed by the verb. Passive sentences frequently confuse young children, who may incorrectly attribute the action to the subject. Consider these two sentences:

The boy is pushed by the girl.

The cup is washed by the girl.

Preschoolers are more likely to be confused by the first sentence—that is, to think that the boy is the one doing the pushing—than by the second sentence (Karmiloff-Smith, 1979). The first sentence has two possible "actors," but the second sentence has only one: Both boys and girls can push someone else, but cups can't wash girls. Complete mastery of passive sentences doesn't appear until the elementary school years (O'Grady, 1997; Perovic, Vuksanović, Petrović, & Avramović-Ilić, 2014; Sudhalter & Braine, 1985).

It takes time for children to comprehend sentences with multiple clauses. At about age 4, children begin to produce simple subordinate clauses, such as those that follow and modify nouns (e.g., "This is the toy *that I want*"; Owens, 2012, p. 298). Yet throughout the elementary school years children struggle to understand certain kinds of multiple-clause sentences. Sentences with one clause embedded in the middle of another are especially difficult, particularly if the noun tying the clauses together has a different function in each clause. Consider the sentence "The dog *that was chased by the boy* is angry" (Owens, 2012, p. 348). The dog is the subject of the main clause ("The dog . . . is angry") but is the recipient of the action in the embedded clause (". . . [dog] was chased by the boy"). Seventh-graders easily understand such sentences, but younger children over-rely on word order and conclude that the boy, rather than the dog, is angry.

Knowledge of syntactic rules continues to develop in the later elementary and secondary years. Beginning in the upper elementary and middle school grades, children may be taught to identify the various parts of a sentence (e.g., subject, direct object, prepositional phrase, and subordinate clause) about which they previously acquired intuitive knowledge. They study verb tenses (e.g., present, past, present progressive), which they have been using in everyday speech for some time. In middle school and high school, adolescents learn more subtle aspects of syntax, such as subject–verb and noun–pronoun agreement, correct uses of *that* versus *which* to introduce subordinate clauses, and functions of punctuation marks such as colons and semicolons (Alamargot et al., 2015). They rarely develop such knowledge on their own, however. Instead, most of their syntactic development during this period probably occurs as the result of formal instruction, especially through courses in language arts, English composition, and foreign languages (e.g., Pence & Justice, 2008; Riches, 2013).

Fostering Syntactic Knowledge

Especially as they are learning the more complex and subtle aspects of syntax, children and adolescents often benefit from ongoing instruction and practice with syntactic structures. The following are several examples of how caregivers and teachers can promote youngsters' syntactic development:

- **Expand on young children's telegraphic speech.** When young children speak in telegraphic sentences, caregivers can engage in **expansion** by repeating the sentences in a more mature form. When a toddler says, "Doggy eat," Mother might respond by saying, "Yes, the doggy is eating his dinner." Expansion gives children gentle feedback by fleshing out their own utterances and using more complex syntactic forms (C. Bouchard et al., 2010; Mermelshtine & Barnes, 2016; N. Scherer & Olswang, 1984).

- **With older children, teach irregular forms of verbs and comparative adjectives.** Children do not always hear the irregular forms of verbs and adjectives in everyday speech. Playmates may talk about what's *badder* or *worser*, and many adults confuse the past tenses of the verbs *lay* and *lie* (which are *laid* and *lay*, respectively). In elementary school, formal instruction in irregular forms is the only way that children discover the correct forms of certain words.

- **Classify sentence structures for children.** Having children examine and practice common syntactic structures (active and passive voice, independent and dependent clauses, etc.) has at least two benefits. First, children become better able to vary their sentence structure as they write—a strategy associated with more sophisticated writing (Beers & Nagy, 2009; Christie, 2012; Spivey, 1997). Second, learning the labels for such structures (e.g., *passive voice*) in English helps them acquire analogous structures in other languages.

- **Every now and then ask children to express their ideas with formal grammar.** In typical everyday conversation, adults and children alike use incomplete sentences and are lax in their adherence to grammatical rules (V. Cook & Newson, 1996; D. Lightfoot, 1999; K. Miller, 2013). But what's common in casual speech is often frowned on in writing and public speaking. In official communications (e.g., a letter to the editor of a local newspaper or a presentation to a large group), correct grammar is, in many people's minds, an indication that the writer or speaker is educated and credible (Purcell-Gates, 1995). Also important is that formal language allows the student to communicate ideas that are integral to advanced subject matter (Christie, 2012).

Development of Listening Skills

Children's ability to analyze speech is necessary for their oral comprehension. Other important parts include paying attention to the speaker, thinking about the implications of what has been said, *and* deciding how to respond. These and other skills appear in age-related trends.

Infants are drawn to human speech sounds. The basic elements of speech—all the consonants and vowels a language includes—are collectively known as **phonemes**. Phonemes are the smallest units of speech that indicate differences in meaning in a particular language. For instance, the word *bite* has three phonemes: a "buh" sound, an "eye" sound, and a "tuh" sound. If we change any one of these sounds—for instance, if we change *b* to *f (fight)*, long *i* to long *a (bait)*, or *t* to *k (bike)*—we get new words with different meanings.

At birth, infants can discriminate among a wide variety of phonemes, including many that they don't encounter in their native language (Jusczyk, 1995; Partanen, Pakarinen, Kujala, & Huotilainen, 2013; Werker & Lalonde, 1988). Newborn babies prefer to listen to their native language over other languages, suggesting that they have grown accustomed to the speech sounds they overheard as fetuses in their mother's womb (Huotilainen, 2013; Mehler et al., 1988; Moon, Lagercrantz, & Kuhl, 2013). Several months after birth, infants prefer words they have heard frequently, including their own names (Mandel, Jusczyk, & Pisoni, 1995).[3]

After months of listening to their native languages, infants can distinguish their sounds. By the time infants are a year old, they specialize in sounds that are prominent in their own languages (Gervain & Mehler, 2010; Jusczyk, 1997; Ortiz-Mantilla, Hämäläinen, Realpe-Bonilla, & Benasich, 2016). One-year-old infants in English-speaking countries continue to hear the difference between the "l" and "r" sounds, a distinction critical for making such discriminations as *lap* versus *rap* and *lice* versus *rice*. In contrast, Japanese children gradually lose the ability to make this distinction because the Japanese language treats the two sounds as a single phoneme. Comparably, babies in English-speaking societies lose the ability to pronounce "fu" as in Mount Fuji by using their lips alone, as if blowing out a candle.

Infants divide a continuous stream of speech into separate words. As infants listen to people speaking around them, they become familiar with the characteristic rhythm, stress patterns, and sound sequences in their native language (K. G. Estes, Evans, Alibali, & Saffran, 2007; R. H. Holt & Bent, 2017). Infants notice that some sound combinations regularly occur in sequence, whereas other combinations do not (Jusczyk, 1997). Consider the English statement, "Call Peter for dinner" ("C" [*Cuh*], "a" [*ahh*], and "l" [*ahl*]) flow easily together, but "l" (*luh*) and "p" (*puh*) do not, signaling to the listener that "call" is one word, and "cal<u>l</u>" and "<u>P</u>eter" are separate words. Similarly, "r" (*err*) and "f" (*fuh*) do not unfold fluently, providing a cue that "Pete<u>r</u>" and "<u>f</u>or" are separate words. By 6 to 8 months of age, infants are beginning to segment speech sounds into separate words (Aslin, Saffran, & Newport, 1998; Berdasco-Muñoz, Nishibayashi, Baud, Biran, & Nazzi, 2017).

A child's growing memory capacity allows for expansion in the amount of information that can be absorbed while listening. Working memory, that part of the memory system that holds and processes new information, is an important resource for language learning (Anthony, Lonigan, & Dyer, 1996; L. M. Archibald, 2017; Florit, Roch, Altoè, & Levorato, 2009). In the preschool years, children can pay attention for only brief periods, making it difficult for them to remember multi-step instructions (L. French & Brown, 1977). As working memory increases, children can attend to longer stretches of speech and as a result, they can understand and remember multistep directions better.

Children's prior knowledge affects how they make sense of oral language. Children can better understand a friend's story about a trip to a fast-food restaurant if they are familiar with what such visits entail. Knowledge of typical events enables children to draw inferences from the things they hear. Imagine that children are told that a father and a daughter have gone to the beach and, after placing their thermos and towels on the sand, they test the warmth of the water. Listeners who have previously gone to the beach will assume that father and daughter are sticking their toes in the seawater and not feeling the temperature of water in the thermos.

[3] If you are wondering how researchers know that infants are able to distinguish between particular sounds, their key method is to emit certain sounds and record the level of interest shown. When infants are interested in a particular sight or sound, they suck vigorously on a pacifier. As they grow accustomed to the stimulus, they look away and suck less, perking up again when a new or preferred stimulus is presented. Researchers measure infants' preferences by presenting a series of speech sounds or words, and when infants consistently suck harder to hear one type of sound (e.g., mother's voice, music, or a familiar story), the infant is said to be partial to it.

MyLab Education
Artifact Example 9.2

Find Developmental Meaning *How does 8-year-old Jeff portray a figure of speech that is common in English?* Jeff draws the literal meaning of the expression, "Your eyes are bigger than your stomach." Jeff reveals an emerging appreciation for how figurative speech illuminates a state of affairs, in this case, the desire for food exceeding a person's capacity to eat and digest it.

As children listen to a person talk, their interpretations depend, in part, on what else has been happening during the conversation. The spoken language itself offers some clues. Children do not necessarily focus on every little hum, hah, or syllable. Eighteen-month-old toddlers often guess the word a speaker is going to say after hearing only the first two phonemes (Fernald, Swingley, & Pinto, 2001). Children also assume that the speaker is talking about events in the environment they share. Information about shared roles in fantasy play helps with interpretation. Young children understand that playmates are pretending when they say that the doll baby is hungry. Older children realize that what a speaker says is different from what he or she actually means in cases of sarcasm (Airenti, 2016; M. Donaldson, 1978; Flavell, Miller, & Miller, 2002). When a classmate trips, spills his lunch, and says, "Oh, that's just *great*," an adolescent is likely to understand that the classmate is not really happy with the spill (Glenwright, Parackel, Cheung, & Nilsen, 2014),

Children gradually comprehend abstract and nonliteral concepts. As children move into the middle and secondary grades, they become better able to understand and explain **figurative speech**, phrases whose meaning transcends literal interpretation. Young adolescents understand that idioms, phrases with metaphorical meanings that have been historically established within a group of people, should not be taken at face value. A person who "hits the roof" doesn't really hit the roof, and someone who is "tied up" isn't necessarily bound with rope. In Artifact Example 9.2, you can see 8-year-old Jeff's whimsical drawing of the statement that someone's eyes are bigger than his or her stomach. Older children become progressively more adept at interpreting similes and metaphors (e.g., "Her hands are like ice," "Eugene is the Rock of Gibraltar"). In the late elementary years, they draw generalizations from such proverbs as "Look before you leap" and "Don't put the cart before the horse."

MyLab Education Application Exercise 9.1
Detect Developmental Levels
What developmental trend is suggested by a comparison between 10-year-old Kent's and 14-year-old Alicia's explanations of proverbs?

Children gradually learn to listen critically. Children fail to notice ambiguities and blatant inconsistencies in what they hear and read. **Comprehension monitoring**—the process of evaluating one's comprehension of oral and written material—develops slowly over childhood and well into the adolescent and adult years (Berkeley & Riccomini, 2013; Markman, 1979; Skarakis-Doyle & Dempsey, 2008). With cognitive development, scaffolding, and encouragement, children learn to compare and integrate separate assertions as they listen.

Children piece together how they are expected to listen at school. Children hear admonitions from teachers, parents, and other adults to stay quiet while they are talking. Children who ask questions, especially those who talk out of turn or seem disruptive, are reminded to remain silent until invited to speak (Bosacki, Rose-Krasnor, & Coplan, 2014). As a result, children in the early elementary grades believe they are good listeners when sitting quietly and not interrupting others. Older children (e.g., 10- and 11-year-olds) are more likely to recognize that good listening also requires mental engagement and comprehension skills (T. M. McDevitt, Spivey, Sheehan, Lennon,

& Story, 1990). In adolescence, youngsters realize that listening in an open-minded, nonjudgmental, and empathic manner is an important friendship skill (Imhof, 2001).

Children learn how to respond when a speaker doesn't make sense. Toddlers and young children may shrug their shoulders or say, "I don't know," when puzzled (P. L. Harris, Bartz, & Rowe, 2017). In school, many children believe that they should not ask for assistance when confused—it might seem disrespectful, make them look stupid, or violate a rule for working quietly. In a series of studies (T. M. McDevitt, 1990; T. M. McDevitt et al., 1990), children in Grades 1, 3, and 5 responded to the following dilemma:

> This is a story about a girl named Mary. Mary is at school listening to her teacher, Ms. Brown. Ms. Brown explains how to use a new computer that she just got for their classroom. She tells the children in the classroom how to use the computer. Mary doesn't understand the teacher's directions. She's confused. What should Mary do? (T. M. McDevitt, 1990, p. 570)

Some children responded that Mary should ask the teacher for further explanation. But others said that Mary should either listen more carefully or seek clarification from classmates. Many children, younger ones especially, believe it is not appropriate to ask a teacher for help, perhaps because they lack confidence or have previously been discouraged from asking questions at home or at school (Cluver, Heyman, & Carver, 2013; Marchand & Skinner, 2007; T. M. McDevitt, 1990; Puustinen, Lyyra, Metsäpelto, & Pulkkinen, 2008).

Promoting Listening Comprehension

During conversations and classroom lessons, adults can enhance children's capacity for effective listening. You can see examples of adults fostering relevant abilities in the Development-Enhancing Education feature, "Promoting Listening Skills in Children." In addition, consider these suggestions:

Development-Enhancing Education

Promoting Listening Skills in Children

Present only small amounts of information at one time.

- A preschool teacher helps the 3- and 4-year-olds in her class make "counting books." She has previously prepared nine sheets of paper (each with a different number from 1 to 9) for each count (two buttons for the "2" page, five pieces of macaroni for the "5" page, etc.). As she engages the children in the project, she describes only one or two steps at a time. (Early Childhood)
- As a kindergarten teacher reads aloud to children, she stops at the end of each page, allowing them time to absorb the segment. After brief comments from the children, the teacher resumes with the story. (Early Childhood)

Expect children to listen attentively for only short periods.

- A caregiver notices that babies in her care watch her face as she talks to them during diaper changes and bottle feedings. After a few moments of listening to her voice and looking at her expressions, babies are apt to look away. She continues to talk with them quietly but does not force interaction. (Infancy)
- A kindergarten teacher has learned that most of his students can listen quietly to books on tape for no more than 10 or 15 minutes at a stretch. He plans 10-minute sessions at the beginning of the school year and gradually lengthens the time over the next few months. (Early Childhood)

Discuss the components of good listening.

- A kindergarten teacher explains how children are to act during story time. After soliciting input from the children, the teacher posts several guidelines: (1) Pay attention to the story, (2) stay seated, (3) keep your hands to yourself, and (4) take your turn in discussions. (Early Childhood)
- A second-grade teacher explains to students that "good listening" involves more than just sitting quietly; it requires paying attention and trying to understand what the speaker is saying. After a police officer briefly describes bicycle safety, she asks the children to summarize what they heard and ask any questions they might have. (Middle Childhood)

Encourage particular courses of action when confused by a speaker.

- A preschool teacher tells children it is time for "free choice." The children move around the room and select one activity or another. When a boy who has recently

(continued)

moved to the school walks around aimlessly, the teacher talks with him privately, explaining what free choice means and encouraging him to ask questions when he doesn't understand something. (Early Childhood)

- At the beginning of the year, a middle school teacher explains to students that he will try to be clear in his explanations but there will be times when he forgets to mention key steps. Students have several tactics they can try when unclear about what to do—they can read the instructions he posts for every lesson, ask for help from another student, or ask him to clarify. He tells the students that he would rather they use these responses rather than remaining confused. (Early Adolescence)

- **Set up an environment that channels students' attention.** Schools are busy, noisy places. Throughout the day, chairs scrape, pencils drop, and classmates walk and talk. For young children in particular, focusing on speech amidst competing noises can be a challenge, and even some older students must try hard to ignore distractions (E. C. Thompson, Woodruff Carr, White-Schwoch, Otto-Meyer, & Kraus, 2017). Routines for how and when students use the restrooms, talk with classmates, and retrieve work materials keep distractions to a minimum. Natural light, ventilation, a blend of colors, and postings of children's artwork can create a comfortable environment for learning (P. Barrett, Zhang, Davies, & Barrett, 2015). Other aspects of the environment are ideally designed with children's age-related needs in mind, for example, with chairs and tables sized to children's bodies.

- **Give children practice in following instructions.** Initial expectations for children need to be simple, such as "Hang up your coat and then come sit down on the circle." Preschool teachers may introduce such games as "Simon Says" ("Simon Says, put your right hand over your eyes"), adding steps as children advance in relevant abilities. Other teachers ring bells or use hand signals to advise children of a change in activity (e.g., placing one hand on top of the other when it is time to sit quietly in their seats). After lunch or recess, teachers might turn down the lights, play music, encourage deep breathing, read a chapter from a book, or give them 10 minutes to read individually.

- **Align the length of presentations to students' attention span.** People of all ages can understand a message only when they are paying attention, and even with full concentration they can take in only so much information on a single occasion. Young children can handle only brief periods of oral instruction, and even older children benefit from reminders, handouts, and posters listing procedures for completing a project (e.g., Wasik, Karweit, Burns, & Brodsky, 1998).

- **Informally assess children's understanding.** Although children profit from being exposed to rich and varied language, adults must be careful to use familiar language when it is important for children to understand something, for example, directions for a high-stakes test or steps to take in an emergency. In such a situation, adults need to assess children's understandings, perhaps—depending on their age—by having them restate what they have heard in their own words, draw a picture, or demonstrate steps in a project (Jalongo, 2008).

- **Read to children.** Many parents tell young children stories, but some do not, perhaps because they have little free time, are not familiar with stories, or lack confidence in their reading abilities. Teachers can encourage parents to read to their children while also regularly reading to children in the classroom (M. Fox, 2013). Children learn to love literature, develop new vocabulary, and understand complex syntax from listening to stories.

- **Encourage critical listening.** Sometime around ages 3 to 6, children realize that what people say is not necessarily true (e.g., Koenig, Clément, & Harris, 2004; K. Lee, Cameron, Doucette, & Talwar, 2002). Yet throughout the elementary and secondary school years, youngsters sometimes have difficulty separating fact from fiction (Rozendaal, Buijzen, & Valkenburg, 2012). Even adolescents can be susceptible to verbal and visual persuasion, as for example, when seeing glamorous people drinking alcohol and smoking cigarettes in a movie (Grenard, Dent, & Stacy, 2013). Young people who are taught to be skeptical are more likely to find errors, falsehoods, ambiguities, and manipulation in what others say.

For example, when children are reminded that television commercials are designed to persuade them to buy something, they are less likely to be influenced by advertisers (Calvert, 2008; Halpern, 1998; D. F. Roberts, Christenson, Gibson, Mooser, & Goldberg, 1980).

• **Give children options for what to do when they are confused.** Depending on their experiences at home and in earlier grades, children might rather sit in silence than ask a question of a teacher or classmate. If questions are okay in your classroom, you can let children know. If you prefer that they wait until you are finished talking, advise them of this expectation. If you find that instructions must be repeated most of the time, consider supplementing oral instructions with steps summarized in handouts or on an electronic whiteboard.

Development of Speaking Skills

Children's growing proficiency in speech is the result of many things: better muscular control of the lips, tongue, and other parts of the vocal apparatus; more semantic and syntactic knowledge; increasing memory capacity; experience in formulating ideas; and an expanding awareness of what listeners are apt to know and believe. Following are key advancements in speech.

In the first year of life, children begin to make speech-like sounds. Between 1 and 2 months of age, they **coo**, making vowel sounds in a singsongy voice (e.g., "aaaaaaa," "ooooooo"). Sometime around 6 months, they **babble** by combining consonants and vowel sounds into repeated syllables (e.g., "mamamamama," "doodoodoo"). Babbling becomes increasingly speechlike, as infants fuse syllables into language-like utterances and drop sounds not present in their native language (J. L. Locke, 1993). Thus, infants first babble in a universal "language" that includes a range of phonemes and later shift to emitting sounds primarily in their native language. Children who are deaf and have signing parents go through a similar phase of spirited experimentation with manual signs, followed by a priority for gestures that resemble conventional signs (Oller et al., 2014).

MyLab Education
Video Example 9.3
Find Developmental Meaning *How might this little girl's gestures help her to communicate?* The girl uses hand movements to supplement her descriptions (e.g., in referring to carwash sponges and the surrounding area). Her gestures seem to serve a communicative function in supplementing words and a cognitive function in managing her answer.

Gestures precede and then supplement speech. During their first year of life, infants try to communicate through actions. An infant might put his fingers in his mouth to indicate that he wants something to eat. A toddler might wrinkle her nose and sniff as a way of "talking" about flowers. To some degree, the use of such gestures paves the way for later language development (Esteve-Gibert & Prieto, 2014; Goodwyn & Acredolo, 1998; V. Volterra, Caselli, Capirci, & Pizzuto, 2005). Youngsters don't entirely abandon gestures as they begin to speak, however. Gestures carry some of the meaning when a child cannot find the right words (Goldin-Meadow, 2017; Iverson & Goldin-Meadows, 2005).

Pronunciation improves in the early elementary years. As you have read, children say their first word sometime around their first birthday, and by age 2 or so most children talk a great deal. Yet children typically do not master all the phonemes of the English language until age 8 or so (Hulit & Howard, 2006; Owens, 2012). During the preschool years, children are likely to have difficulty pronouncing *r* and *th* (they might say "wabbit" instead of "rabbit" and "dat" instead of "that"). Most can make these sounds by the time they are 5 or 6, but may still have trouble with such complex consonant blends as *spl* and *thr* (Byrnes & Wasik, 2009; Eriks-Brophy, Gibson, & Tucker, 2013; Pence & Justice, 2008). Recall the kindergarten teacher's reference to Mario's "slight accent." Mario mastered Spanish pronunciation by age 3. A few months later, he could produce many of the additional phonemes required for English, while a few Spanish sounds occasionally crept into English words (Fantini, 1985).

Children's conversations advance in length, coherence, and conceptual depth. Early interchanges among children are brief. Most young children are quite willing to introduce new topics while talking with others and have difficulty sustaining a single topic (Brinton & Fujiki, 1984; K. Nelson, 1996a). As they grow older, they can carry on lengthier discussions about an issue or event. In adolescence, the content of their conversations becomes more personal and abstract (McAdams & McLean, 2013; Owens, 2012).

MyLab Education
Video Example 9.4
Find Developmental Meaning *How does this 7-year-old boy talk about his family?* The young man describes his family transitions with details that are meaningful to him.

Children learn to adapt their messages to the needs of listeners. Infants and young children use more words when others are present than when alone, giving their chatter a social quality. As they grow, they begin to change the way they speak based on salient characteristics of their listeners. Preschoolers use simpler language and more attention getters with infants than they do with adults and peers (Shatz & Gelman, 1973). Other aspects of adjusting to listeners' needs take longer to develop. Children in preschool and elementary school do not consistently take their listeners' visual perspectives into account and so provide inadequate information for helping listeners identify things they are talking about (Glucksberg & Krauss, 1967). A child might ask, "What's this?" without regard for whether the listener can see the object in question. As children grow older, they become better able to adjust messages to what particular listeners already know and are likely to understand (Aldrich, Tenenbaum, Brooks, Harrison, & Sines, 2011; T. M. McDevitt & Ford, 1987; Sonnenschein, 1988).

Over time, children gain competence in relaying events and imaginative stories. Beginning in the preschool years, children can tell a story, or **narrative**—an account of a sequence of events, either real or fictional, that are logically interconnected (McKeough, 1995; Sutton-Smith, 1986). Young children's narratives are quite brief and may simply link two events together, often about themselves, but by age 5 or 6, children recount many more details and often comment on the motivations of characters in their stories (K. Kelly & Bailey, 2013; Kemper, 1984; Nicolopoulou & Richner, 2007).

In addition to becoming more detailed, coherent, and sensitive to listeners' perspectives, children increasingly abide by cultural practices in speech. In her classic research, linguistic anthropologist **Shirley Brice Heath** (1983) identified two distinct styles of narrating events in working-class communities in the Piedmont Carolinas of the United States. In the predominantly European American community of Roadville, children relayed factual accounts of their personal experiences, whereas in the mostly African American community of Trackton, children told entertaining and far-fetched fictional stories. Children's narratives in many other cultures embody distinctive styles for communicating their imagination, experience, and values (M. Mills, Watkins, Washington, Nippold, & Schneider, 2013; Sterponi, 2010).

Creative and figurative expressions emerge in early childhood and develop further during adolescence. Many children enjoy "playing" with language (J. Thomas, 2012). Good friends might converse in "pig Latin" in which initial consonants are moved to the ends of words, and a long-*a* sound is added to each word. (As an illustration, the sentence *This sentence is written in pig Latin* would be "Is-thay entence-say is-ay itten-wray in-ay ig-pay atin-lay.") Many children delight in jokes and riddles that play on the multiple meanings of words or similar-sounding phrases ("How much do pirates pay for their earrings?" "A buccaneer"). Creative wordplay is especially common in many African American communities (e.g., Smitherman, 2007). It sometimes takes the form of **playing the dozens**, playful teasing of one another through creative insults—for example, "Your mama's so fat she's got to sleep in the Grand Canyon" (M. H. Goodwin, 2006, p. 232; J. Lee, 2009).

MyLab Education
Video Example 9.5
Find Developmental Meaning *Observe Corwin's turn-taking ability during interactions with his mother.* Corwin regularly makes cooing sounds after his mother says something to him.

Promoting Speaking Skills

To help children develop their speaking skills, teachers and other adults can give them opportunities to talk with and in front of others. The following strategies can be beneficial:

- **Invite infants to interact.** As early as 6 months, infants are able to take turns during verbal interactions, cooing or emitting a vocalization when caregivers pause in speech (de Barbaro, Johnson, & Deák, 2013; Masataka, 1992). Watch what happens when you gently pick up a well-rested baby, look him or her in the eyes, and speak softly and warmly. When a caregiver gently mimics the baby's vocalizations, the baby typically increases speechlike sounds (K. Bloom, Russell, & Wassenberg, 1987; J. L. Miller & Lossia, 2013).

- **Let children know when their statements are hard to understand.** People of all ages have trouble every now and then in communicating their thoughts clearly. Young children have particular difficulty because of their limited abilities to string complex ideas together and to addresses the knowledge base of their listeners. Asking questions or expressing confusion when children describe things ambiguously gradually helps them express their thoughts more more effectively (e.g., D. Matthews, Lieven, & Tomasello, 2007).

- **Ask children to recall events as well as make up stories.** A teacher might ask, "What did you do this weekend?" or say, "Make up a story about a child bringing a cow to show-and-tell." Giving children opportunities to relate events, either actual or imaginary, provides a context in which they can practice speaking (Hale-Benson, 1986; Hemphill & Snow, 1996; E. Levy & McNeill, 2013). Children's narrative skills can also be enhanced with practice and encouragement, especially when adults take time to listen, comment on characters, and ask for details (Mandel, Osana, & Venkatesh, 2013; McKeough, 1995; J. R. Price, Roberts, & Jackson, 2006). Consider how 6-year-old Leanne's ability to tell a story improved over a 2-month period as a result of specific instruction in telling stories:

> **Before instruction**:
> A girl—and a boy—and a kind old horse. They got mad at each other. That the end. (McKeough, 1995, p. 170)
> **After instruction**:
> Once upon a time there was a girl. She was playing with her toys and—um—she asked her mom if she could go outside—to play in the snow. But her mom said no. And then she was very sad. And—and she had to play. So she she [*sic*] asked her mom if she could go outside and she said yes. She jumped in the snow and she was having fun and she had an idea and she jumped in the snow and she feeled happy. (McKeough, 1995, p. 170)

- **Encourage creativity in oral language.** Linguistic creativity can be expressed in many ways, including through stories, poems, songs, rap, jokes, and puns. These forms of language not only encourage inventive language use but also help children identify parallels between different circumstances. Recognizing commonalities enables children to construct similes, metaphors, and other analogies. Some children have experience in exaggeration and hyperbole, features of speech that can be integrated into stories. Playful use of language can help children discover general characteristics of language, as an incident in Mario's childhood illustrates:

> Seven-year-old Mario tells his parents a joke that he has heard at school earlier in the day. He relates the joke in English: "What did the bird say when his cage got broken?" His parents have no idea what the bird said, so he tells them, "Cheap, cheap!"
>
> Mario's parents find the joke amusing, so he later translates it for the family's Spanish-speaking nanny: "*¿Qué dijo el pájaro cuando se le rompió la jaula?*" He follows up with the bird's answer: "*Barato, barato.*" Mario is surprised to discover that the nanny finds no humor in the joke. He knows that he has somehow failed to convey the point of the joke but cannot figure out where he went wrong. (Fantini, 1985, p. 72)[4]

The joke, of course, gets lost in translation. The Spanish word *barato* means "cheap" but has no resemblance to the sound that a bird makes. Only several years later did Mario understand that humor based in wordplay does not always translate from one language to another (Fantini, 1985). His eventual understanding of this principle was an aspect of his growing *metalinguistic awareness*, a topic we examine shortly.

Development of Pragmatics

The pragmatic features of language include verbal and nonverbal strategies for communicating effectively with others in settings where everyone has a unique perspective. Initiating conversations, changing the subject, asking for things politely, and arguing persuasively all require pragmatic knowledge. Also falling within the domain of pragmatics are **sociolinguistic behaviors**—the types of verbal interactions that are

[4] Excerpt from "Case Study: Mario" from *Language Acquisition of a Bilingual Child: A Sociological Perspective* by A. E. Fantini.

considered acceptable for a speaker in a particular setting depending on his or her age, gender, status, and familiarity with others.

Conversational Rules

Most children acquire conversational skills (e.g., asking how another is doing, prefacing a request with "please," and responding courteously to other people's questions) long before they reach school age. By and large, sociolinguistic conventions are learned in families and communities (Leech, Wei, Harring, & Rowe, 2017; Ochs, 2002; Rogoff, 2003). Children train one another informally, sometimes subtly and at other times bluntly, about what are and are not acceptable gestures for relating to one another. Adults occasionally teach sociolinguistic behaviors ("Say 'thank you' for the gift"). Modeling is also influential. Children mimic the way their parents answer the telephone, greet people on the street, and talk with relatives.

MyLab Education
Video Explanation 9.1
What kinds of pragmatic communication rules do children encounter at school?

Classroom Communication

Classrooms have their own patterns of communication. Mario, from our opening case study, once explained to his parents how his kindergarten teacher asked students to take turns when speaking in class (we present an English translation of Mario's Spanish):

> [A]t school, I have to raise my hand . . . and then wait a long, long time. And then the teacher says: "Now you can speak, Mario," and she makes the other children shut up, and she says, "Mario's speaking now." (Fantini, 1985, p. 83)[5]

Not all students notice these communication patterns, and some students will be newcomers in the school, making it important for teachers to model appropriate communication and to advise children of their expectations.

Speech Register

Another part of language development is becoming familiar with one or more **speech registers**, the styles of spoken language that are used by people who regularly interact in defined roles, take part in purposeful activities, and communicate with formality or informality. By communicating frequently, individuals in these situations come to share pronunciations, word choices, and other means for expressing their relationships (L. Wagner, Greene-Havas, & Gillespie, 2010). Teenagers talking on the basketball court and young people interviewing for a job use different registers. On the court, teenagers speak in a jocular fashion, interrupting one another, using their own lingo, and relying on shared understandings. The same youngsters at a job interview enact a polite and restrained tempo, are explicit in their descriptions, and pronounce words carefully. Young people use still other registers when talking with their parents, younger brothers and sisters, adults at school, and religious leaders.

Like so many achievements in language development, learning to use the right speech register takes time and practice. Conversation on the playground allows for spontaneity and laughter. In the classroom, children are to be attentive to rules as to how and when they ask a question and request help. The lunchroom is somewhere in between, allowing children to take initiative while keeping their voices down. Most children distinguish these different demands fairly quickly, but some, especially those with intellectual disabilities, have difficulties in adjusting speech to the demands of particular settings (Hatton, 1998; Mervis & Becerra, 2007).

Cultural Regularities in Conversation

Norms of communication—those unspoken rules about how conversations are supposed to take place—can seem obvious to teachers yet mysterious to students. As a result, teachers can easily misinterpret students' ways of talking. Misunderstandings are possible when a student violates typical speech acts, as when a child makes a request that seems presumptuous (e.g., saying "Gimme a pencil" rather than "May

[5] Excerpt from "Case Study: Mario" from *Language Acquisition of a Bilingual Child: A Sociological Perspective* by A. E. Fantini. Copyright © 1985 by Alvino E. Fantini. Reprinted by permission of the author.

I please have a pencil, Ms. Martinez?"). In reality, the child may not yet know polite forms for joining a conversation, expressing disagreement, or making a request of a teacher. It behooves teachers to learn about styles of communication that children bring from home and articulate their own expectations, such as occasions when children are to remain silent, speak out, answer in choral response, and wait to be called on before answering a question or making a comment. The following descriptions will sensitize you to distinctions in speech.

MyLab Education
Video Explanation 9.2
What norms of communication must second-language learners learn if they are to interact effectively with others at school?

Talking versus Being Silent. Relatively speaking, Western culture is a chatty one. People often say things to one another even when they have very little to communicate, making small talk as ways of making contact and filling awkward silences (Irujo, 1988; Trawick-Smith, 2014). In some African American communities, people speak frequently and often with a great deal of energy and enthusiasm (Gay, 2006; Lein, 1975). In certain other cultures, silence is golden. Many Brazilians and Peruvian individuals greet their guests silently. Some Arabic adults stop talking to indicate a desire for privacy, and people in several Native American communities value silence in certain circumstances (K. H. Basso, 1990; Menyuk & Menyuk, 1988; Trawick-Smith, 2014). These and other differences between ethnic groups are not absolute, of course. Thus, you can watch for variations in interactional styles among children and gently address individual characteristics. With one child, a teacher may slow down and speak softly, and with another, participate in a more animated discussion.

Relating to Adults. In many European American families, children feel they can speak freely when they have comments or questions. In many other communities, children learn early on that they should engage in conversation with adults only when their participation has been solicited. In such cultures, speaking directly to adults is seen as rude (Banks & Banks, 1995; Delgado-Gaitan, 1994; Paradise & Rogoff, 2009). Children also find out how adults expect them to learn new information and tasks. In some parts of Mexico and Alaska, children are expected to learn primarily by quietly observing adults and not asking questions or interrupting (García, 1994; Gutiérrez & Rogoff, 2003; Romero-Little, 2011).

Making Eye Contact. Among many people from European American backgrounds, looking someone in the eye is a way of indicating that they are trying to communicate or are listening intently. But for other people, especially some individuals with African American, Hispanic, and Native American backgrounds, a child who looks an adult in the eye is showing disrespect. Children in such cultures may be taught to look down in the presence of adults (Torres-Guzmán, 1998; Trawick-Smith, 2014). The following anecdote shows how an adult's recognition of culturally learned behavior can improve communication:

> A teacher [described a Native American] student who would never say a word, nor even answer when she greeted him. Then one day when he came in she looked in the other direction and said, "Hello, Jimmy." He answered enthusiastically, "Why hello Miss Jacobs." She found that he would always talk if she looked at a book or at the wall, but when she looked at him, he appeared frightened. (Gilliland, 1988, p. 26)

MyLab Education
Video Example 9.6
Find Developmental Meaning *What kind of support for learning occurs when children respond in unison to the teacher's prompts?* The children recite sentences containing new vocabulary and then answer questions about words.

Maintaining Personal Space. In numerous societies, such as in some African American and Turkish communities, people stand close together when they talk, and they touch one another frequently (Hale-Benson, 1986; Ozdemir, 2008). In contrast, numerous European Americans and Japanese Americans keep a fair distance from one another, maintaining **personal space**, especially when they don't know one another well (Trawick-Smith, 2014).

Responding Orally to Questions. A common interaction pattern in many Western classrooms is the **IRE cycle**: A teacher *initiates* an interaction by asking a question, a student *responds* to the question, and the teacher *evaluates* the response (Mehan, 1979). Similar interactions are frequently found in parent–child interactions in middle-income European American homes. These parents might ask their toddlers such questions as "Where's your nose?" and "What does a cow say?" and praise them for correct answers. But children from some other backgrounds are unfamiliar with such question-and-answer segments when they first come to school (Losey, 1995; Rogoff, 2003).

A number of classrooms use a different type of scripted response for students, in which students answer in unison. Many elementary-age schoolchildren are apt to be enthusiastic participants in such exchanges, especially after growing accustomed to the rhythms, and these interactions can be effective with rote learning (Hargreaves, 2012; McConney & Perry, 2011). They are less effective when the instructional methods require conceptual learning, in which the child must organize information mentally and relate it to what he or she already understands.

Answering Questions. Cultural groups also familiarize children with specific types of questions. European American parents frequently ask their children questions for which they already know the answers. Parents from a range of different cultures rarely ask such questions (Crago, Annahatak, & Ningiuruvik, 1993; Heath, 1989; Rogoff & Morelli, 1989). Parents in certain African American communities in the southeastern United States are more likely to ask questions involving comparisons and analogies. Rather than asking "What's that?" they may instead ask, "What's that *like*?" (Heath, 1980). Also, children in these communities are specifically taught *not* to answer questions from strangers about personal situations and home life (e.g., "What's your name?" "Where do you live?").

Participating in Classroom Discourse. Children are inclined to participate in classroom discussions when they have previously engaged in similar conversations. While interacting with parents, neighbors, and other children, children acquire familiarity with the tempo and rhythm of conversation. In some Australian Aboriginal, African American, Puerto Rican, and Jewish families, conversation consists of several people talking at once. People who wait for their turn might find themselves excluded from the discussion (Condon & Yousef, 1975; Farber, Mindel, & Lazerwitz, 1988; Rendle-Short & Moses, 2010). Children become accustomed to fast-paced conversation with overlapping speech and learn that it can be acceptable to interrupt others—an action that some teachers interpret as rudeness.

Within the classroom, children learn that teachers are authority figures who dictate who can speak when. Children infer that they are expected to act in a certain way during classroom lessons. Many conclude that it is safer to remain silent when teachers pose questions related to academic concepts, especially when queries are fired off rapidly. The typical **wait time** after teachers ask a question is a second or even less, at which point they either answer a question themselves or call on another student (Bilaloğlu, Aktaş Arnas, & Yaşar, 2017; M. B. Rowe, 1974, 1987). Children from many cultural backgrounds are more likely to answer questions when given several seconds to respond (C. A. Grant & Gomez, 2001; Tharp, 1989; Worley, 2012). The extended wait time communicates that teachers are serious about wanting their responses and gives the children needed time to formulate an answer. Of course, it is also important to respond to children's answers with kindness and diplomacy.

Teaching Sociolinguistic Rules in the Classroom

Teachers can try to identify and accept communication patterns children bring from home. With the Observation Guidelines table, "Identifying Cultural Differences in Sociolinguistic Conventions," you can practice identifying dimensions of communication that vary by culture.

It also makes sense to teach communication rules explicitly because children do not always notice certain ways of interacting; nor do they automatically adjust to them when first introduced. To help children abide by classroom communication rules, teachers can try several things:

- **Explain and demonstrate communication rules.** Children may find certain customs odd, such as raising their hands to speak. Explanations, reminders, and rewards for following these rules can convince students to practice the desired behaviors. Teachers might also model an action, for example, listening politely to a student during a

OBSERVATION GUIDELINES
Identifying Cultural Differences in Sociolinguistic Conventions

CHARACTERISTIC	LOOK FOR	EXAMPLE	IMPLICATION
Talkativeness	• *Frequent talking*, even about trivial matters, or • *Silence* unless something important needs to be said	When Muhammed unexpectedly stops talking to his peers and turns to read his book, the other children are puzzled.	Don't assume that a child's silence reflects apathy or rudeness. When children are talkative, explain customs for speaking and remaining silent in your classroom.
Style of Interacting with Adults	• *Willingness to initiate conversations* with adults, or • *Speaking to adults only when spoken to*	Elena is quiet in class and answers questions only when her teacher directs them specifically to her. At lunch and on the playground, she readily talks and laughs with friends.	If you think children may not understand a lesson, take them aside and ask a few questions to assess what they have learned. Provide additional instruction to address gaps in understanding.
Eye Contact	• *Looking others in the eye* when speaking or listening to them, or • *Looking down* or away in the presence of adults	Herman always looks at his feet when an adult speaks to him.	Do not assume that children aren't paying attention just because they fail to look at you.
Personal Space	• *Standing quite close* to a conversation partner, perhaps touching that person frequently, or • *Keeping distance* between oneself and others when talking with them	Michelle is noticeably uncomfortable when other people touch her.	Give children personal space during one-on-one interactions. To facilitate cross-cultural understanding, teach children that what constitutes personal space differs from culture to culture.
Responses to Questions	• *Answering questions readily*, or • *Failing to answer even very easy questions*	Leah never responds to "What is this?" questions, even when she knows the answers.	Be aware that some children are not accustomed to answering certain types of questions. Respect their privacy when they are reluctant to answer personal questions.
Wait Time	• *Waiting several seconds* before answering questions, or • *Not waiting at all*, and perhaps even interrupting others	Mario often interrupts his classmates during class discussions.	When addressing a question to a group of students, allow them time to think before calling on one to answer. Communicate a procedure for answering (e.g., hand raising and waiting to be called on).

presentation, pointing out the actions involved in respectful attention, and reminding students to practice these actions during show-and-tell activity. Teachers and other school professionals can help children to distinguish the requirements of various settings—it's okay to laugh and shout during recess but not during a reading lesson.

Preparing for Your Licensure Examination

Your teaching test might ask you about communication rules in the classroom.

• **Be flexible when children are adjusting to new communication rules.** Teachers can watch for children's use of communication conventions that are different from their own. Ms. Miller exhibits this perceptiveness when she realizes that one of her children, Ding Fang, seems to be following the Chinese custom of remaining silent during a threatening social situation:

Ms. Miller: What's going on over here? It seems like you two are having an argument.
Ding Fang: (Looks down, says nothing)
Maura: (In an angry tone) She took my car. (Now shouting at her peer) I was playing with that, you know!
Ding Fang: (Says nothing, does not establish eye contact)
Ms. Miller: Is that right, Ding Fang? Did you take Maura's car?
Ding Fang: (Remains silent)
Ms. Miller: Ding Fang? Can you tell me what happened?
Ding Fang: (Still silent)
Ms. Miller: Well, you don't seem to want to talk about it right now.
Ding Fang: (Remains silent; looks as if she might cry)
Ms. Miller: (Recognizes that Ding Fang is upset) You know, maybe this isn't such a good time to talk about it. Why don't we just go look at a book for a while. Would you like to do that? (Trawick-Smith, 2014, p. 297)[6]

[6] Excerpt from *Early Childhood Development: A Multicultural Perspective*, 6th Edition by Jeffrey Trawick-Smith. Copyright © 2014 by Jeffrey Trawick-Smith. Reprinted by permission of Pearson Education, Inc., Upper Saddle River, NJ.

Development of Metalinguistic Awareness

In the process of learning language, children acquire **metalinguistic awareness**, an understanding that language and its various components follow certain rules and achieve specific effects. Being able to reflect on language is important because an awareness of its constituent understandings (e.g., words are made up of syllables, speech is made up of segmented sounds, and sentences adhere to grammatical rules) contributes to the comprehension of complex verbal information and the acquisition of literacy skills.

Adults can foster metalinguistic awareness by drawing children's attention to language during age-appropriate activities. Playing with language through rhymes, chants, jokes, and puns seems to be especially instructive for preschool and elementary school children. Rhymes help children discover the relationships between sounds and letters. Jokes and puns help children discover that words and phrases can have more than one meaning (L. Bradley & Bryant, 1991; Cazden, 1976; Nwokah, Burnette, & Graves, 2013). Listening to stories also exposes children to the connection between print and spoken language (Ravid & Geiger, 2009; Yaden & Templeton, 1986).

MyLab Education
Video Example 9.7

Find Developmental Meaning *What literary techniques does this 13-year-old boy use in his story?* He uses a classic beginning ("There once was a small monkey") and dramatic phrases ("It's a crisis, a phenomenon, a catastrophe!").

With formal language instruction, adults can augment the metalinguistic awareness of older students and adolescents. By exploring parts of speech, sentence structures, and the like, young people gain a better grasp of the underlying structure of language. By reading and analyzing poetry and classic literature, they discover a variety of mechanisms (similes, metaphors, symbolism, and such transitional devices as "However, . . . ," "Equally important, . . . ," and "In short, . . . ") that a writer might use to convey connections between ideas.

In addition, second languages provide the impetus for children to identify commonalities and variations in different languages. Research consistently demonstrates that knowledge of two or more languages (bilingualism) promotes metalinguistic awareness (X. Chen et al., 2004; Reyes & Azuara, 2008; Zhang, Chin, & Li, 2017). As children learn two or more languages, they have occasions to compare the distinct methods of conveying meaning in different languages (e.g., how words are recorded in written script, how certain ideas are expressed, and how nouns are modified). Such reflections foster a conscious appreciation for the rules and conventions of languages. By the time Mario was 5, he showed considerable awareness of the nature of language:

> Mario was well aware that things were called in one of several possible ways, that the same story could be retold in another language (he was capable of doing this himself), and he knew that thoughts were convertible or translatable through other forms of expression. . . . He knew that a [language] could be varied so as to make it sound funny or to render its messages less transparent, such as in Pig Spanish. . . .
>
> [As Mario grew older,] he became increasingly analytical about the medium which so many take for granted as their sole form of expression. He demonstrated interest, for example, in the multiple meaning of some words ("'right' means three things"); and in peculiar usages ("Why do you call the car 'she'?"); as well as intuitions about the origins of words ("'soufflé' sounds French"). (Fantini, 1985, pp. 53–54)[7]

Promoting Metalinguistic Development

Factors that promote metalinguistic awareness—language play, reading experiences, formal instruction, and bilingualism—have several implications for teaching and working with children:

- **Arrange for children to identify and practice comprehension strategies.** Not every child spontaneously invents the processes needed for deciphering verbal information. Compared to typical learners, children who are autistic are less likely to grasp information that they listen to and read (Bodner, Engelhardt, Minshew, & Williams, 2015). Whereas these children may easily comprehend individual sentences,

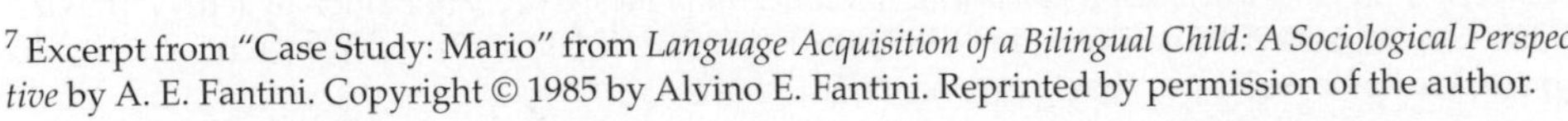

[7] Excerpt from "Case Study: Mario" from *Language Acquisition of a Bilingual Child: A Sociological Perspective* by A. E. Fantini. Copyright © 1985 by Alvino E. Fantini. Reprinted by permission of the author.

they do not necessarily see connections between separate assertions or come away with a coherent interpretation. As teachers read to children, they can periodically stop and discuss what is happening, for example, by asking children why characters might behave as they do (Roux, Dion, Barrette, Dupéré, & Fuchs, 2015). By providing such practice and labeling listening and reading techniques (e.g., inferring motivations, identifying the main point, looking for underlying themes in a passage), teachers can familiarize children with the strategies and their utility.

- **Explore multiple meanings in ambiguities, jokes, and riddles.** Having fun with language can be educational as well as entertaining. Teachers, parents, and other practitioners might ask children to identify the double meanings of such sentences as *He is drawing a gun* and *This restaurant even serves crabs* (Wiig, Gilbert, & Christian, 1978). Jokes and riddles provide another vehicle for exploring multiple meanings (Shultz, 1974; Shultz & Horibe, 1974; Yuill, 2009):

> Call me a cab.
> Okay, you're a cab.
> Tell me how long cows should be milked.
> They should be milked the same as short ones, of course.

- **Read literature whose authors play with language.** One of our favorite children's books is *The Phantom Tollbooth* (Juster, 1961), which has considerable fun with word meanings and common expressions. In one scene, the main character (Milo) asks for a square meal and is served (you guessed it) a plate "heaped high with steaming squares of all sizes and colors." Among the all-time classics in English wordplay are Lewis Carroll's *Alice's Adventures in Wonderland* and *Through the Looking Glass*. These books are packed with double word meanings, homonyms, and idioms, as the following excerpt from *Through the Looking Glass* illustrates:

> "But what could [a tree] do, if any danger came?" Alice asked.
> "It could bark," said the Rose.
> "It says, 'Boughwough!'" cried a Daisy. "That's why its branches are called boughs."

- **Encourage children to learn a second language.** Promoting metalinguistic awareness is just one of the benefits of learning a second language. In the next section, we look more closely at bilingualism.

Summary

Linguistic knowledge and skills improve throughout childhood. School-aged children add several thousand new words to their vocabulary each year. Over time, children rely less on word order and more on syntax to interpret other people's messages, and they comprehend and produce sentences with increasingly complex structures. Their conversations with others increase in length, they become better able to adapt the content of their speech to the characteristics of their listeners, and they become more aware of the unspoken social conventions that govern verbal interactions in their culture. They also acquire a growing understanding of the nature of language as an entity and a tool for communication.

MyLab Education Self-Check 9.2

Development of a Second Language

9.3 Summarize and apply research on second-language learning.

The majority of children around the world speaks two or more languages (McCabe et al., 2013). Educators have many occasions to support children's learning of multiple languages and understanding of academic content through one or more languages. Here we address children's general encounters with second-language learning and popular approaches in teaching second languages.

Experiences in Learning a Second Language

As you have learned, many children learn to speak two languages fluently. Like other **bilingual** individuals, Mario became accomplished in speaking both English and Spanish and learned to switch easily from one language to the other depending on the setting.

MyLab Education
Video Explanation 9.3
How do children who are second-language learners vary in their personal characteristics?

MyLab Education
Content Extension 9.1
Read about effective instruction for English language learners from diverse backgrounds.

In the United States, children who are proficient in their native language and not in English are referred to as **English language learners (ELLs)**. English language learners represent a rapidly expanding group of K–12 students. About 9.4% of children in U.S. public schools are English language learners, with California having the highest rate, at 22.4% (National Center for Education Statistics, 2017). U.S. children speak 350 different native languages, with Spanish being the most common language after English (C. B. Olson et al., 2012).

English language learners are a diverse lot. Some have recently arrived in the country and speak little English, whereas others show appropriate and even advanced proficiency in speaking English and display only minor delays, if any, in reading and writing (Bunch, 2013). A small proportion of English language learners grow up with well-to-do parents, attend nicely equipped schools, have tutors, and participate in enriching after-school activities. The majority of English language learners grow up in lower income families who must—because of their financial situations—rely on the schools for English instruction (C. B. Olson et al., 2012).

Advantages of Bilingualism

Being bilingual yields definite advantages. First and foremost, it allows children to maintain interpersonal relationships with family and other important people in their lives. Learning the ancestral language gives children access to cultural traditions and knowledge, perspectives that enrich their personal identity and flexibility in getting along with people who have grown up in a setting outside the mainstream society (Nieto, 1995; Torres-Guzmán, 1998).

Acquiring a second language also benefits children intellectually (Diaz, 1983; Stocco, Yamasaki, Natalenko, & Prat, 2014). Processes involved in learning two languages, using each in appropriate circumstances, and keeping two languages straight strengthen the brain's all-important *executive functions,* those deliberate thinking processes, such as planning and decision making, that allow a child to shift easily from one intellectual task to another (Arredondo, Hu, Satterfield, & Kovelman, 2017; Bialystok & Viswanathan, 2009; Marzecová et al., 2013). Bilingual children also tend to develop strong metalinguistic insights due to experiences in comparing expressions of a similar idea in two different languages (Bialystok, Peets, & Moreno, 2014; D. Rutgers & Evans, 2017).

Challenges Faced by Bilingual Children

Despite the advantages children enjoy while acquiring two languages, they also encounter clear-cut challenges. One is short-lived: Initial delays in language development, especially in vocabulary, sometimes occur, and words from one language can intrude as the child speaks in another language. By elementary school, bilingual children generally catch up with monolingual peers and easily keep the two languages separate (C. Baker, 1993; Bialystok, 2001; Fennell, Byers-Heinlein, & Werker, 2007).

MyLab Education
Video Example 9.8
Find Developmental Meaning *How does Mariana perceive other people's perceptions of her?* Mariana is aware of others' low expectations of her but does not let these views define her.

A more significant problem can occur if English language learners reach only partial mastery of each of their languages. If enrolled in schools that require English only, children may fail to make progress in their first language (J. Austin, Blume, & Sánchez, 2013). Arrested development in the native language can make it difficult for young people to converse easily with parents, unless the parents acquire English.

Finally, English language learners are often exposed to low expectations and even prejudice from others. A few teachers believe that these children do not belong in their classroom. Others assume that the children should be exposed to only limited academic content until fully proficient in English. If acted upon, these beliefs can seriously restrict children's opportunities for learning (Polat & Mahalingappa, 2013). English language learners themselves may at one time or another question their abilities.

Teaching a Second Language

Just as young children learn their native language through daily exposure and interaction, so, too, do they learn a second language, by being given frequent chances to speak it. When children begin to learn a second language in the elementary grades and later, they often learn it more quickly if their language-learning experiences are structured (Strozer, 1994). Of course, part of a high-quality language environment for bilingual children is acceptance of their need to communicate in their first language (Martínez-Álvarez & Ghiso, 2017). The methods by which children are taught a second language as well as engaged in their first language vary depending on school requirements, leadership within the school, prevailing ideas about bilingualism, and the language abilities of teachers. Cultural practices are also influential, as you can read more about in the Development in Culture feature, "Learning Second Languages in Cameroon."

Several approaches to second-language instruction have been used in schools, including bilingual education, submersion, structured English immersion programs, immersion, and foreign language instruction. The first three of these programs are typically used with English language learners, and the latter two programs are usually given to native English speakers learning a second language. Let's examine the characteristics of each.

In **bilingual education**, English language learners receive intensive instruction in English while studying other academic subject areas in their native language.

Development in Culture

Learning Second Languages in Cameroon

Educational anthropologist Leslie Moore spent several years in northern Cameroon, first as a Peace Corps volunteer and later as a researcher. During observations in Maroua, Cameroon, Moore observed children whose first language was Fulfulde and who were learning French at the local public school and Arabic during religious lessons (L. C. Moore, 2006, 2010, 2013).

Moore noticed similarities and differences in the ways that children were taught French and Arabic. In both cases, *guided repetition* was a primary way by which children learned the languages. Teachers would model a phrase and ask children to repeat it in unison. Children eagerly complied and gradually grew proficient in their pronunciation of both French and Arabic sounds, words, and phrases.

Yet the underlying purposes of learning French and Arabic were different and led to subtle distinctions in instruction. The purpose of learning French was to become educated within modern society. Children were taught French as a second language and were also taught their basic subjects in French. At school, instruction in French presumed that children had acquired sufficiently high levels of proficiency that they could understand the teacher's instructions and comprehend vocabulary in mathematics, civics, hygiene, and national culture.

The purpose of learning Arabic was more specific—it prepared children to recite the *Qur'an*, the Islamic book of sacred scriptures. Children did not learn to speak Arabic conversationally but rather memorized the particular phrases they needed to read along in the Qur'an. Children would recite verses from the Qur'an over and over, being careful to use appropriate intonations. Being able to recite the Qur'an prepared children to develop Muslim identities, including being reverent in matters of faith.

Heiner Heine/imageBROKER/Alamy Stock Photo

REPEAT AFTER ME. In Cameroon schools, imitation and rehearsal are primary means for learning second languages.

Moore identified advantages and disadvantages of guided repetition in the two contexts. Rote memorization appeared to work especially well in teaching children to recite the Qur'an because young children were expected to recite scripture as a matter of faith and not question its meaning. Guided repetition functioned reasonably well in the public school yet had definite limitations toward achieving advanced mastery of French. Many children did not develop the French expertise they needed to understand the challenging material in the upper school grades, and a high proportion of children repeated grades and dropped out of elementary school.

Children typically shift from taking only one or two courses in English to taking most of their courses in English. A common sequence in bilingual education is as follows:

Step One. Students join native English speakers for classes in subject areas that do not depend too heavily on language skills (e.g., art, music, physical education). They study other subject areas in their native language and also begin classes in *English as a Second Language* (ESL).

Step Two. Once students have acquired some English proficiency, instruction in English begins for one or two additional subject areas (perhaps for math and science).

Step Three. When it is clear that students can learn successfully in English in the subject areas identified in step 2, they join their English-speaking classmates in regular classes in these subjects.

Step Four. Eventually students are sufficiently proficient in English to join the mainstream in all subject areas and no longer require their ESL classes. (Krashen, 1996; A. M. Padilla, 2006; Valdés, Bunch, Snow, & Lee, 2005)

These four steps are generally carried out over 2 to 3 years. Yet children progress at different rates, and some students need more or less time. Pacing is important. Rushing students into English-only instruction when they have not yet achieved advanced levels in English is problematic when children do not have the comprehension skills to learn the course materials (Cummins, 1981; A. M. Padilla, 2006).

MyLab Education Application Exercise 9.2
Meet Individual Needs

How might the teacher, Angelica Reynosa, address individual differences in students' proficiency with English and Spanish?

In one variant of bilingual education, called *transitional bilingual education*, the teacher instructs children in regular subjects in their first language and teaches English as a separate subject. English is gradually incorporated into other subjects. In another type of program, *developmental bilingual education*, both the native language and English are maintained. Developmental bilingual teachers instruct the children in both languages for an indefinite period. In a related model, *dual-language instruction*, a mixed group of children who are native English speakers and others who are English language learners (and usually speak Spanish) receive instruction in both languages throughout their time in school. Dual-language programs have resulted in high levels of academic achievement, motivation, and student enthusiasm (Estrada, Gómez, & Ruiz-Escalante, 2009).

Despite the benefits that are found in bilingual education, many schools offer instruction in English only. Some schools have limited funds or an insufficient number of bilingual teachers given the number of children who speak one or more second languages. As a result, they may place English language learners in a regular classroom with native English speakers. In the **submersion approach**, children are essentially left to their own devices in acquiring English. In **structured English immersion** programs, children receive intensive instruction in English over a year or so. Teachers offer instruction in the English language as well as specially adapted instruction in English for the academic subjects (K. Clark, 2009). The main emphasis is on teaching in English, with educators hoping children will gain proficiency in English rapidly so that they can enter the regular classroom and catch up with classmates in academic subjects.

Two other programs are regularly used with native *English* speakers learning a second language. In **immersion** programs, children receive instruction in language arts in their first language and instruction in a second language in other subjects. Immersion programs begin as early as kindergarten and as late as sixth grade or after. For native English speakers, immersion in the second language for part or all of the school day helps students acquire basic proficiency in the language quickly, with any adverse effects on academic achievement being short-lived (Collier, 1992; T. H. Cunningham & Graham, 2000; Genesee, 1985; A. M. Padilla, 2006).

In traditional **foreign language instruction**, children are taught a second language as a subject, occasionally as early as elementary school and regularly in middle school and high school. Children receive instruction in the foreign language for approximately 20 to 50 minutes daily or a couple of times weekly. Instruction that is based on drills and grammatical lessons is generally less effective than lessons that emphasize cultural awareness, oral communication, and community involvement (Otto, 2010).

Which models are most effective, and why? Nonnative English speakers need to learn English so that they can master academic subjects and ultimately communicate with other English-speaking citizens, yet they also had best continue to communicate with family members, friends, and neighbors. If English language learners are taught exclusively in English, they are at risk for losing expertise in their native language before developing adequate proficiency in English—a phenomenon known as **subtractive bilingualism**—and their cognitive development will suffer in the process. In this regard, bilingual programs may be superior to submersion and structured English immersion models. Because bilingual education is designed to foster growth in *both* English and a child's native language, it is apt to promote academic as well as linguistic growth (Estrada et al., 2009; McBrien, 2005b; Pérez, 1998; Winsler, Díaz, Espinosa, & Rodriguez, 1999). Furthermore, bilingual programs, and especially dual-language instruction programs, tend not to isolate English language learners from their peers, a limitation that characterizes some English immersion models (Rios-Aguilar, González-Canche, & Moll, 2010).

For native English learners, immersion and foreign language instruction emphasizes conversation and ties to the culture of the new language community. Native English speakers who live in an English-speaking country and are immersed in a different language at school still have many opportunities—at home, with friends, and in the local community—to continue using and developing English.

Most English language learners are placed in regular classrooms without dedicated services, a condition that is due to budget restrictions and the prevailing belief that children should learn English as quickly as possible (Goldenberg, 2008; B. Peterson, 2017). Teachers in regular classrooms strive to support these children in learning English, studying academic subjects, and adjusting in school, as you can see in the Development-Enhancing Education feature "Working with English Language Learners."

Development-Enhancing Education

Working with English Language Learners

Ask parents about the languages children speak.

- A bilingual preschool teacher greets a new family in the Head Start center. As they get to know one another, she addresses the parents in their native Spanish language. She advises the parents about the activities and policies in the program and asks them about the child's interests, friendships, and family. She also asks about the child's routines in speaking English and Spanish—which languages are spoken at home, with friends, with neighbors, and so forth. (Early Childhood)
- At an initial meeting with a mother and father who recently moved into town with their two teenagers, the principal greets the parents with a few words in Spanish, warmly welcomes them to the school, and with assistance from the bilingual counselor, obtains information about the circumstances in which the students speak English and Spanish. (Late Adolescence)

Teach literacy skills in the student's native language.

- When working with students whose families have recently emigrated from Mexico, a first-grade teacher teaches basic letter–sound relationships and word decoding skills in Spanish

(continued)

(e.g., showing how the printed word *dos* can be broken up into the sounds "duh," "oh," and "sss"). (Middle Childhood)

- In a first-grade classroom, most of the children speak English but several speak Spanish or Vietnamese at home. The teacher makes read-along books available in English, Spanish, and Vietnamese and, with help of bilingual aides, posts the days of the week on the calendar and simple instructions on the board in the three languages. (Middle Childhood)

If you don't speak a student's native language, recruit parents, community volunteers, or other students to assist with communication.

- A high school has implemented a new Spanish Buddy program, in which bilingual high school students pair up with English language learners from Central America in a nearby elementary school. The high school students meet weekly with the children assigned to them. They talk informally with their elementary buddy at the beginning of each session and then read a story to him or her in Spanish. (Late Adolescence)
- A second-grade teacher invites the mother of a Salvadoran child to come to school and share traditions from her culture. The mother shares tamales with the class and talks about the different wrappers that people use to form the tamales, including corn husks, banana leaves, and paper. The children ask a lot of questions about the customs. (Middle Childhood)

When using English to communicate, speak more slowly than you might otherwise, and clearly enunciate each word.

- A third-grade teacher is careful that he says "going to" rather than "gonna" and "want to" rather than "wanna." At the same time, the teacher does not correct children speaking informally in dialects that use such pronunciation. She politely points out the differences when children are preparing essays in formal English. (Middle Childhood)
- A high school speech teacher provides a rubric for presentations. In addition to including criteria for organization, persuasive appeal, and an animated delivery, the teacher includes standards that benefit English language learners, especially requirements that key terms are defined in a handout and words are pronounced clearly. (Late Adolescence)

Use visual aids to supplement verbal explanations.

- Before introducing a lesson on the desert habitat, a fifth-grade teacher draws a picture of a desert on a poster, labels a few common plants and animals that live there, prepares a list of biological adaptations in harsh environments (e.g., conserving water, keeping predators away), and writes down vocabulary words (e.g., *desert*, *conserve*, *predator*). (Middle Childhood)
- A high school history teacher uses photographs she has downloaded from the Internet to illustrate a short lecture on ancient Egypt. She also includes key terms (e.g., *pyramid*, *sarcophagus*) on the electronic whiteboard. (Late Adolescence)

During small-group learning activities, periodically encourage same-language students to talk with one another in their native language.

- When a middle school science teacher assigns students into cooperative groups to study the effects of weight, length, and force onto a pendulum's oscillation rate, she puts three native Chinese speakers into a single group. She invites them to talk in either English or Chinese as they do their experiments. (Early Adolescence)
- A high school chemistry teacher asks a couple of Vietnamese students to brainstorm how chemistry is evident in contemporary Vietnamese society. The students share their ideas with other groups, who have been asked to identify how chemistry is influential in other societies. (Late Adolescence)

Have students work in pairs to make sense of textbook material.

- As two middle school students study a section of their geography textbook, one reads aloud while the other listens and takes notes. They frequently stop to talk about what's been read, and then they switch roles. (Early Adolescence)
- A high school literature teacher guides a small group of English language learners by asking them a series of questions about a novel. Students answer the questions and then give their own perspectives on dilemmas raised in the story. (Late Adolescence)

Invite students to read, write, and report about their native countries.

- A second-grade teacher asks children to write a report about people who have made a difference in the community in which their parents grew up. The teacher encourages the children to talk with their parents as well as to find books about their parents' culture from the library. (Middle Childhood).
- A middle school social studies teacher has students conduct research on a country from which they or their ancestors have immigrated. The students create posters to show what they have learned, and they proudly talk about their posters at "International Day." (Early Adolescence)

Sources: Agirdag (2009); Comeau, Cormier, Grandmaison, and Lacroix (1999); Ernst-Slavit and Mason (2012); Espinosa (2007); García (1995); B. Harris and Sullivan (2017); Herrell and Jordan (2004); Igoa (1995); Krashen (1996); McClelland (2001); McClelland, Fiez, and McCandliss (2002); National Center on Linguistic and Cultural Responsiveness (2014); A. M. Padilla (2006); Peregoy and Boyle (2008); Ramirez and Soto-Hinman (2009); Rothenberg and Fisher (2007); Slavin and Cheung (2005); Valdés et al. (2005).

Also, consider the following recommendations:

• **Honor children's right to speak in their first language.** Advocates for children have argued that speaking freely in one's home language is a fundamental right for children (Babaci-Wilhite, 2017; United Nations, 1990.). Speaking comfortably in their native tongue allows for allegiance to family and community, free expression of personal needs and perceptions, and access to the knowledge in the culture. Children should never be rebuked for using their mother tongue or for making mistakes when venturing to speak, write, and spell words in English.

MyLab Education
Video Example 9.9

Find Developmental Meaning *How might these activities help students learn English?* The children sing, march, and sign letters. They are exposed to certain words repeatedly and express themselves verbally.

• **Orient children to key information.** You can post a written schedule for the day on the board, let children know what your instructional objectives are, and provide written definitions for key vocabulary in English. For nonreaders, teachers can communicate the focus of lessons with verbal explanations, pantomime, videos, and, if possible, translations from other students in the class, classroom aides, or volunteers who speak the child's native language (Goldenberg, 2008; Haynes & Zacarian, 2010). Music and movement can also be incorporated into academic lessons, giving second-language learners entrée into the academic concepts.

• **Be explicit about concepts and skills.** In learning their first language, children use a process by which they easily recognize regularities in language. When learning a second language, the process is more deliberate, and teachers can assist by exposing children to English and clearly teaching them vocabulary, rules of grammar, and pragmatic conventions. This need is especially acute during academic learning—imagine the confusion an English language learner would have when introduced to *Pythagorean Theorem* without a definition. English language learners also appreciate explanations of idioms that pop up in literature or conversation ("That book is *over my head*," "Let me *sleep on it*," "I'm going to *call it a day*").

MyLab Education
Video Example 9.10

Find Developmental Meaning *How does the teacher affirm children's backgrounds?* Students are asked to tell about their lives, describe their family origins in English, and learn about the backgrounds of their classmates.

• **Scaffold children's attention to instructions.** Handouts with structured word frames can provide assistance in English while also prompting core ideas (e.g., "The three types of camouflage we examined were ______________, ______________, and ______________."). Written instructions that specify steps to completing a task are especially useful tools for English language learners who are not familiar with the progression of the lesson.

• **Get to know children and their families.** Teachers can learn a lot about children by asking them about where they and their parents were born. Parents can be invited to come to school and talk about their origins and the older generations. Given the distinct advantages to acquiring literacy skills in the native language, teachers might encourage parents to read to children in the family's first language.

• **Invite children to integrate phrases from their native language into their writing.** Teachers can honor children's language heritage by encouraging them to include conversational phrases from their native tongue into their writing.

MyLab Education
Application Exercise 9.3
Identify Development-Enhancing Education

Magali Williams, a bilingual resource teacher, explains to children how to incorporate a familiar style of speaking in a story.

• **Teach native English speakers a second language.** Given the benefits of bilingualism, the fact that we live in global society, and empirical verification that young children have an amazing capacity to learn language, it makes sense to introduce second languages in preschool or the elementary grades rather than waiting until middle or high school (Kalashnikova & Mattock, 2014; Roeper, 2012). Introducing a second language before high school has the advantages of enhancing fluency in pronunciation and fostering bilingualism (Berken, Gracco, & Klein, 2017).

Summary

Individuals easily learn two languages during infancy and early childhood. If they lack early exposure, they retain the ability to learn a second language later in childhood, and during adolescence and the adult years. Research consistently indicates that knowing two or more languages fosters important brain functions and promotes metalinguistic awareness. Several instructional models exist for teaching English to English language learners. Research is still ongoing, but serious concerns have been raised about the effectiveness of academic instruction for English language learners that is delivered solely in English. Nevertheless, it is common practice for English language learners to receive little assistance in their native language at school, and thus the classroom teacher is advised to consider the needs of these children in classroom lessons. It is important for second-language learners to develop advanced skills in their native language so that they may continue to communicate with family and community members.

MyLab Education Self-Check 9.3

Individuality in Language Development

9.4 Examine diversity and exceptionalities in language abilities.

Across a myriad of situations, children develop language skills that allow them to share their ideas and learn from what others say. Yet there are variations in children's language abilities that are important for educators to consider. In the remainder of this chapter, we examine characteristics that contribute to children's individuality as language learners.

Gender

As infants and toddlers, girls, on average, mature before boys in basic language milestones. Girls begin to speak about a month earlier, form sentences sooner, and have a larger vocabulary (M. Eriksson et al., 2012; Halpern & LaMay, 2000; Reznick & Goldfield, 1992). Once they enter school, girls outperform boys on tests of verbal ability, although boys eventually catch up. This early advantage is small, and plenty of boys have exemplary language skills that surpass those of most girls.

Boys and girls also differ in their instrumental goals for conversation. On average, boys see themselves as information providers and speak more directly and bluntly. Girls typically deepen relationships during intimate exchanges and are more likely to be indirect and tactful in their speech (Kyratzis & Tarım, 2010; Ladegaard & Bleses, 2003; Owens, 2012; Tannen, 1990). Girls can be at a disadvantage when they are in mixed-sex groups and feel intimidated about expressing themselves. Teachers can call on girls when boys are dominating the conversation, nurture assertiveness in girls, and encourage all children to learn patience when others are talking.

Family Income

As mentioned in the earlier discussion about nativism, children from diverse backgrounds reach language milestones at similar ages. However, children from higher-income homes tend to have larger vocabularies (B. Hart & Risley, 1995; M. C. Thomas, Forrester, & Ronald, 2013; Wasik & Bond, 2001). This difference is largely due to the quantity and complexity of language that parents use with children. Although most mothers in Western societies interact frequently with their children, on average mothers with high incomes talk with their young children for longer periods, ask more questions, elaborate to a greater extent on topics, and use a larger variety of words than do mothers with low incomes (B. Hart & Risley, 1999; Weisleder & Fernald, 2013; L. L. White, Alexander, & Greenfield, 2017).

Children from low-income families possess definite strengths in language that may not be as obvious as the large vocabulary of peers from well-educated families. They may possess imaginative storytelling abilities and talents with metaphors (Dudley-Marling & Lucas, 2009; Heath, 1983). Even when engaged in little conversation at home, young children growing up in economically disadvantaged families are generally quite able to develop strong verbal skills when immersed in language-rich schools (Obradović et al., 2009).

Ethnicity

As you have learned, sociolinguistic conventions, purposes of figurative language, and narrative styles differ from one group to another. Children from numerous ethnic groups use a form of English other than **Standard English** (sometimes known as Mainstream American English, United Kingdom Standard English, General Australian English, or another term, depending on country). Standard English is considered to be the type of English spoken by educated adults. In reality, few educated people speak this way at home but do use it in formal communications, in business settings, and in their writing. The style is perceived to be neutral to regional variations in the country. Standard English is valuable for children to learn, especially when their own ways of speaking are respected.

There are many other ways to speak English than the Standard variety. Many children living in the southern parts of the United States, numerous African American children, and children in various parts of England and other English-speaking countries use different **dialects**, forms of English (or another language) with unique pronunciations and syntactic structures. In Artifact Example 9.2, you can see evidence of the local dialect from the Northern Mariana Islands.

Yesterday I really have bad day. Because I break the window. When I knock at the door, knowbody was there. Then I knock at the window very hard it break. My mom got made at me. Because I break the window. I brack the window because my sister don't want to open the door. So I break the window.

MyLab Education
Artifact 9.3

Find Developmental Meaning *How might this written excerpt from a fifth-grade boy living in the Northern Mariana Islands in the Pacific Ocean reflect his local dialect?* The local dialect might explain why the boy blends present and past tenses in his description of an event. *Writing sample courtesy of the Commonwealth of the Northern Mariana Islands Public School System.*

Southern English is a dialect prevalent in southern regions of the United States. Although nonsoutherners may find this accent, with its infectious drawl, to be charming, they also see it as a reflection of lesser intelligence (Hudley & Mallinson, 2011). Examples of distinctive pronunciations include the following:

- The *z* sound is pronounced as *d* before nasal consonants (e.g., *wasn't* is pronounced "wadn't").
- The long *i* sound is typically pronounced as *ah* (e.g., *time* is pronounced "tom," *mile* is "mall").
- *Ing* is spoken as *in* (e.g., *walking* sounds like "walkin"). (Hudley & Mallinson, 2011)

African American English is another prevalent dialect. This dialect is often used in informal settings across the United States and especially in schools, churches, and other institutions that embrace African American cultures. Not all African Americans speak with an African American dialect, and those who do may confine its use to certain settings. Some White people living in communities with a high proportion of Black people also use the African American dialect (Hudley, 2009). Its unique language constructions include the following:

- The *th* sound at the beginning of a word is often pronounced as *d* (e.g., *that* is pronounced "dat").
- The *ng* sound at the end of a word is typically pronounced as *n* (e.g., *bringing* is pronounced "bringin").
- The *ed* ending on past-tense verbs is often dropped (e.g., "We walk to the park last night").
- The present- and past-tense forms of the verb *to be* are consistently *is* and *was*, even if the subject of the sentence is the pronoun *I* or a plural noun or pronoun (e.g., "I is runnin'," "They was runnin'").

- The verb is often dropped in simple descriptive sentences (e.g., "He a handsome man").
- The word *be* is used to indicate a constant or frequently occurring characteristic (e.g., "He be talking" describes someone who talks much of the time; Hudley & Mallinson, 2011; Hulit & Howard, 2006).

The African American and Southern English dialects are complex versions of English with their own grammatical rules (Fairchild & Edwards-Evans, 1990; D. Hill, 2013; B. Z. Pearson, Velleman, Bryant, & Charko, 2009). One dialect is not intrinsically better than another.

When children who use different dialects attend school together, teachers can put everyone at ease by explaining that all ways of speaking are valued and insisting that it is unacceptable to tease another student because of how he or she speaks (Bohney, 2016; B. Pearson, Conner, & Jackson, 2013). Teachers can explain what dialects are and suggest that it is fine to switch back and forth as appropriate (L. I. Johnson, Terry, Connor, & Thomas-Tate, 2017). They can also invite children to use local dialects in creative writing, informal classroom discussions, and other educational lessons (DeBose, 2007; Hudley & Mallinson, 2011; Ogbu, 1999, 2003; D. Paris, 2009). It is also in children's best interests to become familiar with Standard English. Standard English is generally preferred over other styles of language in written reports, business transactions, and conversations in higher education. Many of the textbooks, literature, and tests children read at school are written in Standard English, and as a result, those who have proficiency in Standard English have an easier time learning at school (Beneke & Cheatham, 2015).

Learning one or more dialects goes hand-in-hand with acquiring other aspects of language. In the Developmental Trends table "Language Skills at Different Age Levels," you can see the many milestones of language typically achieved during the childhood years.

DEVELOPMENTAL TRENDS

Language Skills at Different Age Levels

AGE	WHAT YOU MIGHT OBSERVE	DIVERSITY	IMPLICATIONS
Infancy (Birth–2 Years)	• Interest in listening to the human voice and exchanging vocalizations with adults • Repetition of vowel sounds (cooing) at age 1–2 months and consonant-vowel syllables (babbling) at about 6 months • Understanding of several common words at about 8 months • Speaking single words at about 12 months • Use of two-word combinations at about 18 months • Rapid increase in vocabulary in the second year	• In the latter half of the first year, babbling reflects phonemes of the native language. • More cautious children may wait a bit before beginning to speak. • Chronic ear infections can interfere with early language development. • Infants with severe hearing impairments may babble but not progress into words. • Cultural patterns affect how infants go about learning language (e.g., whether they primarily eavesdrop or interact with adults).	• Engage young infants in "conversations," using simplified and animated speech, and respond affectionately when they vocalize. • Label and describe the objects and events children observe. • Ask simple questions (e.g., "Is your diaper wet?" "What does a cow say?"). • Repeat and expand on children's early "sentences" (e.g., follow "Kitty eat" with "Yes, the kitty is eating his dinner"). • Teach simple hand signs that preverbal infants can use to communicate.
Early Childhood (2–6 Years)	• Rapid advances in vocabulary and syntax • Use of words through underextension (e.g., using "doggie" for the family pet and not for other dogs), overextension (e.g., *foots*, *gooder*, *goed*) • Confusion with comparatives such as *more* vs. *less* • Emphasis on word order and context over syntax in interpretation • Ability to talk about shared experiences • Understanding of "good listening" as being quiet • Initial awareness of words being made up of separate sounds • Difficulty pronouncing some phonemes and blends (e.g., *r*, *th*, *spl*)	• Children raised in bilingual environments may show slight delays in some aspects of language development, particularly vocabulary, but any delays are short-lived and rarely a cause for concern. • Major language impairments (e.g., abnormal syntactic constructions) reveal themselves in the preschool years and warrant referrals to a specialist. • The richness of parents' language affects their children's vocabulary growth. • On average, girls achieve language milestones before boys, but boys catch up within a couple of years.	• Read age-appropriate storybooks as a way of enhancing vocabulary. • Give tactful corrective feedback when children's use of words indicates inaccurate understandings. • Work on simple listening skills (e.g., sitting quietly, paying attention, asking questions when confused). • Ask follow-up questions to make sure that children accurately understand important messages. • Ask children to construct narratives about recent events (e.g., "Tell me about your camping trip last weekend"). • Teach children communication rules at school.

DEVELOPMENTAL TRENDS
Language Skills at Different Age Levels (Continued)

AGE	WHAT YOU MIGHT OBSERVE	DIVERSITY	IMPLICATIONS
Middle Childhood (6–10 Years)	• Increasing understanding of temporal words (e.g., *before*, *after*) and comparatives (e.g., *bigger*, *as big as*) • Incomplete knowledge of irregular word forms • Literal interpretation of messages (especially before age 9) • Pronunciation mastered by age 8 • Consideration of a listener's knowledge and perspective when speaking • Sustained conversations about concrete topics • Construction of narratives with plots and cause-and-effect relationships • Linguistic creativity and wordplay (e.g., rhymes, word games)	• Some minor language impairments (e.g., persistent articulation problems) are evident and can be addressed by specialists. • Children from certain groups (e.g., some children who are African American) show advanced ability to use figurative language (e.g., metaphor, hyperbole). • Bilingual children are apt to show advanced metalinguistic awareness. • Reading habits may affect children's metalinguistic awareness, vocabulary, and syntactic development. • Signing children exhibit metalinguistic awareness by identifying incorrectly formed signs.	• Use group discussions as a way to explore academic subject matter. • Have children create, illustrate, and present short stories. • Teach irregular word forms (e.g., the superlative form of *bad* is *worst*, the past tense of *bring* is *brought*). • Encourage jokes and rhymes that capitalize on double meanings and homonyms (sound-alike words). • When articulation problems are evident in the upper elementary grades, consult with a speech-language pathologist. • Teach children about dialects and ways they can enrich their stories with greetings and familiar sayings in local dialects.
Early Adolescence (10–14 Years)	• Increasing awareness of the terminology used in academic disciplines • Ability to understand complex, multiple-clause sentences • Emerging ability to look beyond literal interpretations; comprehension of simple proverbs • Growing capacity to carry on conversations about abstract topics • Significant growth in metalinguistic awareness	• Frequent readers tend to have large vocabularies. • Girls are more likely than boys to converse about intimate matters. • Certain adolescents (e.g., some African American teens) may bandy creative insults back and forth. • Adolescents may prefer to use their native *dialects* with peers and *Standard English in classroom lessons*.	• Use terminology from academic disciplines (e.g., *simile* in language arts, *theory* in science). • Arrange classroom debates that explore controversial issues. • Ask adolescents to consider underlying meanings of proverbs. • Teach students that dialects are rule-governed language systems that can be used in different contexts.
Late Adolescence (14–18 Years)	• Acquisition of terms related to specific academic disciplines • Subtle refinements in grammar, mostly as a result of formal instruction • Appropriate use of a variety of connectives (e.g., *although*, *however*, *nevertheless*) • General ability to understand figurative language (e.g., metaphors, proverbs, hyperbole)	• Boys are apt to communicate their thoughts in a direct and straightforward manner; girls are more likely to be indirect and tactful. • A preference for one's native dialect over Standard English continues into the high school years. • The kinds of slang vary depending on peer groups.	• Distinguish between similar abstract words (e.g., *weather* vs. *climate*, *velocity* vs. *acceleration*). • Explore complex syntactic structures (e.g., embedded clauses). • Talk about underlying meanings in poetry and fiction. • Encourage students to use local dialect in conversation and creative writing and Standard English in formal settings.

Sources: C. Baker (1993); Bruer (1999); Bruner (1983); Byrnes and Wasik (2009); N. Chomsky (1972); Flensborg-Madsen and Mortensen (2018); Hale-Benson (1986); Imhof (2001); Y.-S. Kim, Apel, and Al Otaiba (2013); J. L. Locke (1993); T. M. K. Nelson (1973); Nicolopoulou and Richner (2007); O'Grady (1997); Ortony, Turner, and Larson-Shapiro (1985); Owens (2015); Pence and Justice (2008); L. A. Petitto (1997); M. L. Rowe (2017); Short, Eadie, Descallar, Comino, and Kemp (2017); and A. Smith, Andrews, Ausbrooks, Gentry, and Jacobowitz (2013).

Exceptionalities in Language Development

As you have learned, individual children vary in in the pace, style, and dialects of language learning. A few children have language disorders and sensory shortcomings that limit their communication. Schoolwide and public health screenings, especially for infants and young children, are an important way to identify risk for basic hearing losses. These and additional kinds of speech and language problems can be assessed by audiologists and speech-language pathologists. Early assessment and intervention are important because children might otherwise be deprived of foundational academic learning and peer interaction.

Language Conditions

Some children develop normally in all respects except for language. Children with **specific language impairments** have delays or abnormalities in spoken language or in language comprehension that significantly interfere with competencies related to the following:

- Receptive language (e.g., inability to distinguish among different phonemes, difficulty understanding or remembering directions)
- Articulation (e.g., mispronunciations or omissions of certain speech sounds)
- Fluency (e.g., stuttering, an atypical rhythm in speech)
- Syntax (e.g., abnormal syntactic patterns, incorrect word order)
- Semantics (e.g., infrequent use of grammatical words, such as prepositions and conjunctions; frequent use of words with imprecise meanings, such as *thing* or *that*; difficulty interpreting words that have two or more meanings)
- Pragmatics (e.g., talking for long periods without letting others speak, failing to stick with the topic of conversation)

(American Speech-Language-Hearing Association, 1993; Claessen, Leitão, Kane, R., & Williams, 2013; Hulit & Howard, 2006; Jackson-Maldonado & Maldonado, 2017; Joanisse, 2007)

In comparison with typical peers, children with specific language impairments have greater difficulty in processing the quality, pitch, duration, intensity, and sequence of speech sounds (Corriveau, Pasquini, & Goswami, 2007; Thatcher, 2010). Some also have general learning problems with working memory or attentional self-control (Deacon et al., 2014; J. R. Johnston, 1997; Kapa, Plante, & Doubleday, 2017; Vugs, Hendriks, Cuperus, Knoors, & Verhoeven, 2017). In some cases, specific language impairments emerge because of a developmental disorder, such as autism, or an inherited condition, such as Down syndrome (D. Bishop, 2010; M. L. Rice, 2013). In other instances, struggles with language are due to a hearing loss or brain abnormality (Basu, Krishnan, & Weber-Fox, 2010; L. I. Halliday, Tuomainen, & Rosen, 2017; Korndewal et al., 2017). Often the exact cause of the impairment is unknown (M. M. Rice, 2016; P. P. Wang & Baron, 1997).

MyLab Education
Video Example 9.11
Find Developmental Meaning *How does his teacher facilitate La'Kori's language development?* La'Kori's teacher encourages him to repeat certain phrases and explains the meaning of words, enhancing his vocabulary, attention to grammar, and pronunciation.

Regardless of their origins, specific language impairments can be addressed effectively by teachers, trained speech and language specialists, and other school professionals. Some approaches apply broadly to a range of language impairments. For example, educators should try to remain patient when children struggle to communicate. Other tactics are tailored to the particular difficulties with language. With a child who stutters, a speech and language pathologist may encourage slow breathing, whereas a child who has difficulty with pronunciation may receive practice in making particular sounds. For another child whose language delay has contributed to weak social skills, a teacher may show him or her how to initiate a conversation or take turns during a conversation (Stanton-Chapman & Brown, 2015). You can find relevant strategies in the Development-Enhancing Education feature, "Working with Children Who Have Specific Language Impairments."

Development-Enhancing Education

Working with Children Who Have Specific Language Impairments

Be on the lookout for children who exhibit significant delays or other difficulties with language that are unusual for their age.

- A caregiver familiar with milestones in language development watches for unusual delays in children (e.g., absence of babbling, pointing, and gestures by the end of the first year; no words by 16 months; and no two-word phrases by the second year). Without overreacting, the caregiver advises parents of children who show major delays in language that a speech-language therapist could help determine whether treatment might be helpful. (Infancy)
- A preschool teacher consults a speech-language pathologist about a 4-year-old girl who communicates only by pointing and gesturing. "She's certainly not shy," the teacher explains. "She often tries to get other children's attention by poking them, and she loves to sit on my lap during story time." The consulting professional encourages the teacher to model social gestures and praise the little girl when she uses verbal gestures. (Early Childhood)

Encourage children to speak.

- A fourth-grade teacher has a student who repeats himself a lot, hesitates while speaking, changes the topic during the middle of a sentence, and says "um . . . " frequently.

The teacher offers discussion guidelines that are good practices for everyone and particularly helpful for students with a speech disorder, for example, by waiting patiently for the person with the floor to finish a sentence, looking at the speaker and keeping still, and valuing everyone's contribution to the conversation. (Middle Childhood)

- An 11-year-old boy has trouble pronouncing several blends of consonants (e.g., he says "thpethial" for *special*) and is meeting regularly with a speech therapist. His fifth-grade teacher encourages him to speak in class, especially in small-group settings. She models acceptance of his disability, and if a classmate makes fun of his speech, she takes the classmate aside and explains that all children have strengths and weaknesses, teasing about personal characteristics is not allowed, and everyone in her class deserves respect. (Early Adolescence)

Listen patiently.

- Before children read their stories aloud, an elementary teacher discusses expectations on how to listen. She tells the children that everyone is expected to listen quietly and to make comments, give compliments, and offer tactful suggestions that will help their classmates become better writers. (Middle Childhood)
- A high school student often struggles for several seconds midway through a sentence in articulating a particular word. Her teachers know that she is able to complete her thoughts if given the time. (Late Adolescence)

Politely ask for clarification when a message is unclear.

- A preschool teacher sits down with a child who has a language delay and helps him formulate his thoughts. The teacher comments on his actions and expands on his simple phrases. When she is confused by what he is trying to say, she asks for clarification, providing him with options if she can guess what he might be trying to say. When he says "whenchit," she asks, "Are you pretending that you are fixing the clock with a special wrench?" (Early Childhood)
- An 8-year-old boy often says "this" or "that thing there" when referring to objects in the classroom. Suspecting that he may have an undiagnosed language disability, his third-grade teacher talks with his parents and then refers him to a school psychologist for evaluation. In the meantime, the teacher expands on the boy's speech with the missing terms. (Middle Childhood)

Provide guidance on how to talk effectively with others.

- During storybook sharing, third-grade children form groups of two or three and talk about the books they had read. Before the groups meet, their teacher suggests that the way to be a good listener is to offer a compliment to the person who gives a report or to make a comment on a feature of the book that seems interesting. A girl with a language delay contributes to her group and receives constructive feedback from classmates. (Middle Childhood)
- A middle school girl dominates conversations in small-group discussions, rambling on at such length that her classmates have trouble getting a word in edgewise. Her teacher meets with her during lunch one day to remind her of the importance of letting everyone participate. Together they identify a strategy that will help her restrict her comments: Whenever she starts to speak, she will look at the second hand on her watch and yield the floor after no more than 30 seconds. (Early Adolescence)

Sources: L. Bloom and Lahey (1978); Otto (2010); J. R. Patton, Blackbourn, and Fad (1996); J. M. Rudolph (2017); Smith-Lock, Leitao, Lambert, and Nickels (2013); Turnbull, Turnbull, and Wehmeyer (2010).

Sensory Impairments and Other Language-Related Challenges

Children with visual impairments (e.g., blindness) typically have normal syntactic development but are apt to have more limited vocabularies than do sighted age-mates (M. Harris, 1992). Without seeing events around them, they do not have as many opportunities to make connections between words and the objects or concepts they represent (Hobson, 2004; M. B. Rowe, 1978).

Children with hearing impairments (e.g., deafness) are at risk for delays in syntactic and semantic development (M. Harris, 1992). Children who have been deaf from birth or soon thereafter typically need special training to develop proficiency in speaking. Yet these children are apt to show normal language development in *sign language* if family members and others use it as a primary means for communicating with them (Lederberg, Schick, & Spencer, 2013; E. L. Newport, 1990). Deaf infants who are regularly exposed to sign language often begin to "babble" with their hands at 7 to 10 months, are apt to sign their first word at around 18 to 22 months, and use multiword phrases soon thereafter. Like hearing children, signing children apply basic grammatical rules when signing and gradually add more sophisticated constructions (Goldin-Meadow, 2005; L. A. Petitto, 1997).

Many families with children who are deaf or hard of hearing turn to *hearing aids*, electronic devices that amplify sounds, or *cochlear implants*, tiny medical devices inserted into the inner ear that convert sounds to signals that the brain recognizes. When the hearing device is inserted within the first few years of life, and when parents often talk with children and expand on their speech (e.g., when the toddler says, "Me ookee," the father responds, "Do you want a cookie?"), language development is apt to proceed normally (I. Cruz, Quittner, Marker, & DesJardin, 2013). Another assistive device is the *frequency-modulated (FM) system*, in which the teacher wears a microphone and one or more children have receivers with sound levels that can be turned up or down.

Teachers, parents, and other adults can help children who are deaf or hard of hearing with measures customized to children's circumstances. Examples are presented in the Development-Enhancing Education feature "Working with Children with Hearing Impairments."

Two additional conditions affect language development and can be accommodated at school, inability to speak and nonverbal learning disorder. For students who are unable to speak, sometimes because of facial paralysis or an inability to control their mouth and vocal apparatus, the *sip-and-puff system* may be used for communication (Caltenco, Breidegard, Jönsson, & Struijk, 2012). Children learn to control a device, similar to a joystick, with their mouth, sipping (inhaling) and puffing (exhaling) to move the navigational system and on-screen keyboard. Children type messages, which are sometimes translated electronically into speech.

Students with a *nonverbal learning disorder* have trouble comprehending the meaning of nonverbal information—facial expressions, tone of voice, hand gestures, and body movements (Antshel & Khan, 2008; Cardillo, Mammarella, Garcia, & Cornoldi, 2017; Liddell & Rasmussen, 2005). The condition is thought to be neurologically based, possibly due to a genetic error in areas of the brain's right hemisphere, causing malfunctions in visual and spatial processing, drawing implications from related facts, reasoning about the meaning of events, and organizing information (Rissman, 2011). Although this condition is not recognized by all psychologists and psychiatrists, it is increasingly seen as a malady that affects learning and requires customized intervention

Development-Enhancing Education

Working with Children with Hearing Impairments

Intervene early to address correctable hearing impairments.

- Among the children in an infant room is a 2-year-old boy who is deaf. His mother expresses interest in a cochlear implant but cannot afford one. The boy's teacher and an audiologist locate a charitable organization that will pay for the cost of surgery. After the implant, the boy begins to hear the language around him, and his receptive and expressive language rapidly develop. (Infancy)
- A second-grade teacher wonders whether a boy in her class might have a hearing difficulty. She notices that he responds to her only when she is in face-to-face interaction with him. During large-group instruction, he does not follow directions without hearing them several times and seems to miss a lot of what she and classmates say. The teacher talks with the boy's parents, and together they decide to have him referred to a speech-language pathologist for testing. (Middle Childhood)

Communicate instruction through multiple modalities.

- During a large-group meeting of the class, a fifth-grade teacher places a girl with a hearing impairment nearby so that she has a good view of the teacher and can see the pictures clearly. (Middle Childhood)
- A 15-year-old who is deaf has a student aide who accompanies her to all of her classes and signs the teacher's lectures and explanations. Her teachers make sure that they communicate as much as possible through sight as well as sound. They write important points on the chalkboard and illustrate key ideas with pictures and graphics. (Late Adolescence)

Learn a few elements of American Sign Language and finger spelling, and teach them to classmates of signing children.

- A teacher in a combined first- and second-grade class has several students who are deaf, and she both speaks and signs to her class as she presents new information and describes assignments. All of her students know enough American Sign Language to use basic signs with one another. (Middle Childhood)
- An elementary school with a large population of children with hearing impairments offers a weekly workshop in American Sign Language. Several parents and other family members of children who sign attend, as do a few parents of hearing children who volunteer in the classroom and want to be able to communicate with all of the children. (Middle Childhood)

Sources: Bruer (1999); I. Cruz et al. (2013); Newport (1990); Otto (2010); and Svirsky Robbins, Kirk, Pisoni, and Miyamoto (2000).

Children with a nonverbal learning disorder challenge educators with their unique configurations of skills and weaknesses. They tend to have strong verbal skills and perform well academically in the elementary grades, during which time they rely on rote learning. They struggle in later grades, when it is necessary to integrate disparate sources of information and reflect on their meaning. Without a strong ability to put information into perspective, children with a nonverbal learning disorder may not understand jokes, metaphors, or sarcasm. They must exert exceptional effort to grasp cause and effect relationships, understand mathematics, and write legibly. Staying focused on complex tasks can also be difficult. Ways to help children with this condition include the following:

- Explanations of the underlying meaning of metaphors, themes in literature, and scientific discoveries
- Organizational tools, including calendars, clocks, and rubrics that spell out standards for an academic project
- Written deadlines that break up a complicated assignment into steps (e.g., for an essay, ask children to check off after they complete an outline of ideas, make a few notes on each topic, and prepare a first draft)
- Private discussions about peer relationships when children have not picked up cues from body language or grasped nonliteral statements (Cornoldi, Mammarella, & Fine, 2016; Eckerd, 2017; Vacca, 2001; R. V. Whitney & Whitney, 2008)

Summary

Children develop characteristic ways of speaking and listening. Subtle qualitative differences have been observed in the conversational styles of males and females. Children from higher socioeconomic-status backgrounds tend to have larger vocabularies, probably because they are exposed to a wider variety of words. Children from lower income backgrounds tend to have smaller vocabularies but show definite strengths in communication and are receptive to language-rich environments, especially during early childhood. Ethnic groups show differences in sociolinguistic behaviors, storytelling traditions, use of figurative language, and dialects.

Some children have disabilities that affect their language development that can be accommodated by educators. Specific language impairments include abnormalities in receptive or expressive language that significantly interfere with children's performance and accomplishments in and out of school. Children with hearing impairments and, to a lesser extent, those with visual impairments, may have more limited language proficiency because of reduced exposure to language or reduced awareness of its references in particular contexts. Children who cannot physically speak can use electronic devices for communication, and children with nonverbal learning disorders have good verbal skills but need help in perceiving facial expressions and the nonliteral meaning of a conversation.

MyLab Education Self-Check 9.4

Practicing For Your Licensure Examination

Many teaching tests require students to use what they have learned about child development in responses to brief vignettes and multiple-choice questions. You can practice for your licensure examination by reading the case study and answering the questions. After you submit responses to all the questions, you'll receive instant feedback.

Boarding School

Some parts of Alaska are so sparsely settled that building local high schools is not economically feasible. So in certain Native Alaskan communities, older students are sent to boarding school for their high school education. A high priority for teachers is to help students master Standard

English. With this information in mind, consider the following incident:

> Many of the students at the school spoke English with a native dialect and seemed unable to utter certain essential sounds in the English language. A new group of speech teachers was sent in to correct the problem. The teachers worked consistently with the students in an attempt to improve speech patterns and intonation, but found that their efforts were in vain.
>
> One night, the boys in the dormitory were seeming to have too much fun, and peals of laughter were rolling out from under the door. An investigating counselor approached cautiously and listened quietly outside the door to see if he could discover the source of the laughter. From behind the door he heard a voice, speaking in perfect English, giving instructions to the rest of the crowd. The others were finding the situation very amusing. When the counselor entered the room he found that one of the students was speaking. "Joseph," he said, "You've been cured! Your English is perfect." "No," said Joseph returning to his familiar dialect, "I was just doing an imitation of you." "But if you can speak in Standard English, why don't you do it all of the time?" the counselor queried. "I can," responded Joseph, "but it sounds funny, and I feel dumb doing it." (Garrison, 1989, p. 121)

Constructed-Response Question

1. Why might Joseph prefer his native dialect to Standard English?

Multiple-Choice Questions

2. The counselor told Joseph that he had "been cured." What belief about Joseph's native dialect does this statement reflect?

   a. The belief that Joseph's dialect was inferior to Standard English

   b. The belief that the dialect was a legitimate way of communicating if delivered with a Standard English accent

   c. The belief that the counselor could benefit from learning the Native American dialect

   d. The belief that acquiring a nonstandard dialect is the result of a physiological defect that can be treated medically

3. Considering the information in this chapter, how might teachers deal effectively with the language proficiencies of children in Joseph's school?

   a. Teachers can insist that children use only Standard English at school.

   b. Teachers can revert to teaching all subjects in the local dialect.

   c. Teachers can encourage Standard English in written work and in formal oral presentations but welcome the local dialect in creative writing and informal class discussions.

   d. Teachers can allow children to use the local dialect in formal communication and Standard English in letters home to families.

MyLab Education Licensure Practice 9.1

Key Concepts

phonology (p. 312)
semantics (p. 313)
syntax (p. 313)
pragmatics (p. 313)
native language (p. 313)
nativism (p. 314)
language acquisition device (p. 314)
language socialization (p. 316)
infant-directed speech (p. 316)
functionalism (p. 317)
fast mapping (p. 320)
receptive language (p. 320)
expressive language (p. 320)
lexical word (p. 321)
grammatical word (p. 321)
underextension (p. 321)
overextension (p. 321)
holophrase (p. 324)
telegraphic speech (p. 324)
semantic bootstrapping (p. 324)
overregularization (p. 325)
expansion (p. 326)
phonemes (p. 326)
figurative speech (p. 328)
comprehension monitoring (p. 328)
cooing (p. 331)
babbling (p. 331)
narrative (p. 332)
playing the dozens (p. 332)
sociolinguistic behaviors (p. 334)
speech register (p. 334)
norms of communication (p. 334)
personal space (p. 335)
IRE cycle (p. 335)
wait time (p. 336)
metalinguistic awareness (p. 338)
bilingualism (p. 340)
English language learner (ELL) (p. 340)
bilingual education (p. 341)
submersion approach (p. 342)
structured English immersion (p. 342)
immersion (p. 342)
foreign language instruction (p. 343)
subtractive bilingualism (p. 343)
Standard English (p. 347)
dialect (p. 347)
African American English (p. 347)
specific language impairment (p. 349)

Chapter Ten

Development in the Academic Domains

Bill Aron/PhotoEdit, Inc.

Objectives

10.1 Summarize and apply research on developmental trends in reading and writing.

10.2 Describe age-related advancements in children's mathematical and scientific competencies and instruction that inspires growth in these subjects.

10.3 Outline developmental changes in children's knowledge and skill in social studies and the arts, and summarize methods for fostering these capabilities.

Outline

CASE STUDY

Osvaldo's Story

Suzanne Peregoy, a specialist in language and literacy development, spent several days in a kindergarten classroom with English language learners. She observed the children's daily experiences in writing, listening to stories, and coordinating fantasy roles with peers in the dramatic play center (Peregoy & Boyle, 2008). During one language arts lesson, Suzanne asked the children if they might like to write a story in English that she could bring home to her husband. She handed out pieces of paper with blank spaces at the top for drawings and lines at the bottom for written text.

The children took pen to paper. Lisa wrote, "I love my mom," and illustrated her story with a picture of herself, her mother, and several hearts (Peregoy & Boyle, 2008, p. 153). Rosa drew her family of seven and filled in a few lines with evenly spaced block letters. Osvaldo was last to finish. He first wrote a series of letters, which were unintelligible to Suzanne, and then drew a boy with a soccer ball. Suzanne asked him several times what he was writing. He replied that he didn't know and eventually, after her persistent questioning, responded, "I won't know what my story is about until I finish my picture!" (Peregoy & Boyle, 2008, p. 153).

When Suzanne returned to the classroom at a later time, Osvaldo asked her, "How'd your daddy like the story?" (Peregoy & Boyle, 2008, p. 153). Osvaldo wanted to know how Suzanne's "daddy," meaning her husband, had interpreted his story.

- What did Osvaldo understand about writing?
- What kinds of writing skills will Osvaldo likely learn in the years ahead?

Osvaldo is learning to write. He realizes that stories are shared with an audience. He understands that readers have their own responses to stories. He appreciates that print and art can both be used to communicate. In the years ahead, Osvaldo will likely learn more about writing. He will continue to illustrate his stories while communicating more of his thoughts in words. With perceptive support from his teachers, he will learn to use conventional spelling, follow the rules of grammar and punctuation, and represent a topic cohesively.

In this chapter, we look at development in core academic disciplines. As children enter school, they, like Osvaldo, bring relevant knowledge to the tasks of learning to read, write, perform arithmetic, and understand geography, history, music, and art. Their initial ideas are simple and personal and gradually broaden into comprehensive concepts and skills. Notions such as *equivalence* in mathematics and *revolution* in social studies are first learned in concrete terms and later as abstract models. Likewise, rudimentary skills in recognizing letters and making letter–sound connections are acquired before such multistep proficiencies as decoding unfamiliar words in a text and synthesizing the main points of an essay (J. R. Kirby, Parrila, & Pfeiffer, 2003; McLachlan & Arrow, 2013; Pallante & Kim, 2013).

In an effective education, children encounter a reasonable sequence of academic lessons that allow them to extend what they know. Learning targets are sometimes framed as *standards*, the benchmarks within disciplines that school officials have selected for children to achieve over the school years (National Governors Association and Council of Chief State School Officers, 2014). Looking ahead to his first-grade year, Osvaldo will be expected to expand his narratives with details and prepare essays with a defined topic, supporting facts, and statement of closure (Common Core State Standards Initiative, 2018).

Yet standards are not necessarily congruent with children's abilities, interests, or age-related trajectories. Nor is the curriculum itself always well informed by how children learn to read, write, and understand academic concepts. Thus, teachers are apt to find that standards must be creatively transformed into child-friendly units and lessons. Fortunately, teachers generally have the flexibility to design lessons and adapt instruction to what they have learned about children's scholastic growth. To help you become acquainted with developmental journeys in key academic disciplines, we explain the milestones that children typically achieve in a few areas as well as the range of unique routes that occur.

Preparing for Your Licensure Examination

Your teaching test might ask you how to design instruction that promotes progress in academic standards.

Reading and Writing

10.1 Summarize and apply research on developmental trends in reading and writing.

Children's skills in reading and writing build on their knowledge of spoken language, especially, their awareness of the regularities of speech sounds, grammar, word meaning, and social rules. However, written language differs from spoken language in important ways. To learn to read and write, children must understand the relationships between how words sound and how they appear on paper. Children must also learn the nuances in their language's written symbol system, such as punctuation marks and upper- and lowercase letters, which have no direct counterparts in spoken language (Bolaños et al., 2013; Dávalos-Esparza, 2017; S. G. Paris & Cunningham, 1996).

Emergent Literacy

Through early exposure to reading and writing, young children learn many things about written language. For instance, they learn the following:

- Print conveys meaningful information.
- It is fun to read and listen to stories and books.
- Distinct kinds of printed matter (storybooks, newspapers, grocery lists, greeting cards, etc.) serve different purposes.
- Spoken language is transcribed according to certain rules (e.g., words are made up of discrete sounds that are represented with letters of the alphabet).
- Written language includes predictable elements and conventions (e.g., fairy tales often begin with "Once upon a time," and in English, writing proceeds from left to right and from the top to the bottom of the page) (W. Chong et al., 2014; Dougherty Stahl, 2014; S. G. Paris & Cunningham, 1996; Puranik, Phillips, Lonigan, & Gibson, 2018; Serpell, Baker, & Sonnenschein, 2005)

This knowledge about written language, known as **emergent literacy**, is the groundwork for reading and writing development.

Emergent literacy is often nurtured first at home. Young children whose parents read to them acquire prereading skills and learn to read and write more quickly than do peers without this exposure (Aram, Korat, & Hassunah-Arafat, 2013; Myrberg & Rosén, 2009; Sénéchal & LeFevre, 2002). The emotional connection to stories is another legacy of the good-night story. Children usually find it relaxing to listen to stories at their parents' knee and as a result often become enthusiastic readers themselves (L. Baker, Scher, & Mackler, 1997; Sukhram & Hsu, 2012; Vandermaas-Peeler, Nelson, Bumpass, & Sassine, 2009).

At school, teachers foster children's emergent literacy by making available age-appropriate reading and writing materials. They also demonstrate reading and writing activities, take children on trips to the library, talk about the things they themselves have read and written, and show that reading and writing are useful and enjoyable activities. But perhaps most important, they read regularly to children (L. Baker et al., 1997; Bingham, Venuto, Carey, & Moore, 2017; C. E. Huebner & Payne, 2010). Reading is especially valuable when adults exhibit sensitivity to children's interests, ask questions, invite comments, and connect the story to circumstances in children's lives (C. M. Edwards, 2014; C. E. Huebner & Payne, 2010).

Teachers and other caregivers can spot emergent literacy in children's actions with books and use of writing implements. The Observation Guidelines table "Assessing Emergent Literacy in Young Children" offers several ideas about what to watch for in the early childhood years.

OBSERVATION GUIDELINES
Assessing Emergent Literacy in Young Children

CHARACTERISTICS	LOOK FOR	EXAMPLE	IMPLICATION
Attitudes Toward Books	• *Looking through books* • *Interest and attentiveness* when adults read storybooks • *Eagerness to talk about stories* that are read to them	Martina often mentions the *Berenstain Bears* books that her father reads to her at home.	Devote a regular time to reading aloud, choose books with colorful pictures and imaginative story lines, and stop occasionally to discuss events in the story. Make regular trips to the library.
Behaviors with Books	• *Careful handling of books* (e.g., holding them right-side up, turning pages from left to right, not tearing pages) • *Pretend reading* by pointing at pages and talking about characters • *Referring to pictures* while mentally constructing events in a story • *Imitation of sounds* when coming across repeated phrases	Rusty has not heard many stories. He doesn't seem to know what to do with the books in his preschool classroom. He opens them haphazardly and sees nothing wrong with chewing on pages.	If children have had few experiences with books, occasionally read to them one-on-one or in small groups. Let them hold the books and turn the pages. Gently show them how to take care of books so that pages don't tear.
Letter and Word Recognition	• *Recognition of product names* in logos and other familiar contexts • *Correct identification* of a few alphabet letters • *Recognition of own name* in print	Katherine sees a take-out bag from a local fast-food restaurant and determines that it says "Burger King."	Prominently label coat hooks and other items that belong to children. Post the alphabet, and label major parts of the room (e.g., "sink," "art supplies," and "science area").
Writing Behaviors	• *Production of letter-like shapes* • *Writing in a left-to-right sequence* (in English and certain other languages) • *Ability to write some letters* correctly or almost correctly • *Ability to write own name*	Hank can write his name, but he frequently reverses the *N* and sometimes leaves it out the *A*.	Give children numerous opportunities to experiment with writing implements (paper, crayons, non-toxic markers, etc.). Invite children to trace and copy their names, and guide letter formation when children want help. Ask them to put their first names or initials on their artwork.
Knowledge About the Nature and Purposes of Written Language	• *Awareness that specific words are always spelled in the same way* • *Correct identification of reference materials*, perhaps calendars and computer manuals • *Pseudowriting* with intensity	When Shakira and Lucie pretend to shop, they create several squiggles on a piece of paper. They say that this is a list of items they need to get at the store.	Encourage play activities that involve pretend writing (e.g., preparing and delivering "letters" to friends or classmates). Let children see you engaging in a variety of reading and writing activities.

Sources: Cabell, Justice, Konold, and McGinty (2010); W. Chong et al. (2014); F. P. L. Hawkins (1997); McLane and McNamee (1990); M. M. Neumann (2018); S. G. Paris, Morrison, and Miller (2006); D. W. Rowe and Harste (1986; Serpell et al. (2005); Share and Gur (1999); and Sulzby (1985).

Letter Recognition and Phonological Awareness

Knowing letters and the sounds each one represents are obvious prerequisites for learning to read (M. Harris & Giannouli, 1999; Reutzel, Child, Jones, & Clark, 2014). Creative preschool teachers familiarize young children with lowercase and uppercase letters and encourage children to handle letters made out of felt, plastic, wood, and foam. The basic sounds of each letter are introduced after children recognize and name the letters. Another indispensable foundation is having strong **phonological awareness**, that is, the ability to hear the distinct sounds that make up words (Boscardin, Muthén, Francis, & Baker, 2008; D. V. Hayward et al., 2017; Reutzel et al., 2014). Phonological awareness includes specific skills such as these:

- Hearing distinct syllables within words (e.g., hearing "can" and "dee" as separate parts of *candy*)
- Dividing words into discrete word sounds, or *phonemes* (e.g., hearing the sounds "guh," "ay," and "tuh" in *gate*)[1]

[1]This aspect of phonological awareness is sometimes called *phonemic awareness*.

- Blending separate phonemes into meaningful words (e.g., recognizing that, when put together, the sounds "wuh," "eye," and "duh" make *wide*)
- Identifying words that rhyme (e.g., realizing that *cat* and *hat* end with the same sound).

Phonological awareness develops gradually during the preschool and early elementary years (Byrnes & Wasik, 2009; Lonigan, Burgess, Anthony, & Barker, 1998; Shing, 2013).

Most children can detect syllables within words by age 4, well before they begin school and start learning to read. Soon after, perhaps around age 5, they begin to realize that many syllables can be divided into two parts: an *onset* (one or more consonants that precede the vowel sound) and a *rime* (the vowel sound and any consonants that follow it). By the time they are 6 or 7, many children can identify the individual phonemes in spoken words. This last ability seems to emerge hand in hand with learning to read (Anthony & Francis, 2005; Goswami, 1999).

Children learn to distinguish speech sounds while listening to conversation. Attending to stories, listening to rhymes, and participating in various word games further promote a discerning ear for segmented speech sounds (Kuppen & Bourke, 2017; Muter, 1998; Shing, 2013). The Development-Enhancing Education feature "Promoting Phonological Awareness and Letter Recognition in Young Children" presents illustrations of useful strategies.

Preparing for Your Licensure Examination

Your teaching test might ask you about instructional strategies you could use to support children's phonological awareness and letter recognition.

Word Recognition

Many preschool children can correctly identify words in familiar contexts. For example, numerous young children correctly identify the word *stop* when it appears on a red,

Development-Enhancing Education

Promoting Phonological Awareness and Letter Recognition in Young Children

Read alphabet books with colorful pictures, amusing poems, or entertaining stories.

- A teacher reads *The Ocean Alphabet Book* (Pallotta & Mazzola, 1986) to an 18-month-old boy. It is the boy's favorite book, and he points at the pictures as his teacher reads the words. (Infancy)
- A preschool teacher shares *Alphabet Adventure* (A. Wood & Wood, 2001) with her group of 3-year-olds. The children eagerly follow along as the main character, "Little i," looks for her lost dot, and they delight in finding various letters on each page. (Early Childhood)

Have children find words that rhyme.

- A grandmother reads Dr. Seuss's (1968) *The Foot Book* to her 3-year-old granddaughter, stopping at the end of familiar phrases to allow the little girl to chime in with anticipated rhyming words. (Early Childhood)
- A kindergarten teacher challenges his students to think of at least five words that rhyme with *break*. (Early Childhood)

Ask children to identify words that begin (or end) with a particular sound.

- A preschool teacher invites children to join her in finding words that end with an "oo" sound. She says, "'Zoo' and the number 'two' end with an 'oo' sound. Can you think of other words that end with an 'oo' sound?" Children volunteer, "Achoo!," "Do," and "True." (Early Childhood)
- A first-grade teacher says, "Listen to the 'str' sound at the beginning of *string*. What are some other words that begin with 'str'?" (Middle Childhood)

Say a few words and ask children which one begins (or ends) in these sounds.

- After reading Robert McCloskey's (1948) book *Blueberries for Sal*, a preschool teacher asks his children, "Do you hear the difference between *kuplink*, *kuplank*, and *kuplunk*?" (Early Childhood)
- A second-grade teacher asks, "Listen carefully to these four words: *end*, *dent*, *bend*, and *mend*. Which one ends in a different sound than the others? Listen to them again before you decide: *end*, *dent*, *bend*, and *mend*." (Middle Childhood)

Have children practice forming alphabet letters.

- A preschool teacher gives children pieces of paper with large letters she has prepared with glue and colored sand. Children trace the letters with their fingers. (Early Childhood)
- A kindergarten teacher has children make letters with their bodies. One child stands with his arms outstretched like a *Y*, and two others bend over and clasp hands to form an *M*. (Early Childhood)

octagonal sign beside the road. They might also "read" the word *Cheerios* on a cereal box. And they know that a word at a fast-food restaurant is *McDonald's* when the *M* takes the form of the well-known golden arches (Ehri, 1994, 2014; Juel, 1991).

Sometime around age 5, children begin to look more closely at words. Initially, they are apt to focus on visually distinctive features, perhaps seeing the "tail" hanging down at the end of *dog* or the two "ears" sticking up in the middle of *rabbit*. Soon after, they begin to use some of letters' phonetic clues about what the word must be. For instance, they might read *box* by looking at the *b* and *x* and ignoring the *o* (Ehri, 1991, 2014).

Once children have mastered letter-sound relationships, they initially rely heavily on these relationships as they read (Byrnes & Wasik, 2009; Ehri, 1994; Farrington-Flint & Wood, 2007). Doing so allows them to identify such simple words as *cat*, *bed*, and *Jane*. With such a strategy, they have difficulty when they encounter words that violate pronunciation rules. For instance, using the rule that *ea* is pronounced "ee" (as in *meat* and *treat*), they might read *head* as "heed" or *sweater* as "sweeter." Some languages, including English, have so many irregularities that children must use additional cues besides the sounds of similar syllables. If they come to "stomach" and sound it out as "stow-match," they will be puzzled unless other cues suggest meaning (e.g., "My *stomach* reminded me that I was hungry").

By the middle elementary grades, most children have a basic **sight vocabulary**, which allows them to recognize a sizable number of words with little effort. That is, a good deal of word recognition has become *automatized*, in which children are able to respond efficiently to familiar tasks. When skills are well practiced, working memory is freed up for other challenging processes, including those required for comprehension (G. P. Moser, Morrison, & Wilcox, 2017). When they encounter words that are not yet in their sight vocabulary, they draw on letter-sound relationships, familiar prefixes and root words, common spelling patterns, and the meaning of other words in the passage (Ehri, 2014; Solity & Vousden, 2009).

Reading Comprehension

In its basic form, reading comprehension involves understanding the words and sentences on the page. For advanced readers, it also means going *beyond* the page to make inferences and predictions, identify main ideas, and detect the author's assumptions (Perfetti, 1985). Thus, reading comprehension is a very *constructive* process: Readers combine what they see on the printed page with their existing knowledge to derive meaning. Several advancements occur in reading comprehension.

Children's growing knowledge base facilitates reading comprehension. As children grow older, they become better able to understand what they read, in part, because they know more about the topics (Rayner, Foorman, Perfetti, Pesetsky, & Seidenberg, 2001). In fact, reading comprehension ability at *any* age is influenced by an understanding of relevant vocabulary and concepts (Lipson, 1983; Priebe, Keenan, & Miller, 2012; Swart et al., 2017). For example, when second-graders read about spiders, those who already know about their eight legs, fangs, and webs remember more and draw inferences more easily than peers who know less about these creatures (P. D. Pearson, Hansen, & Gordon, 1979). Therefore, it is often helpful to assess students' knowledge of basic terms—and fill in any substantive gaps—before assigning an essay or chapter.

MyLab Education Application Exercise 10.1
Meet Individual Needs

How does the teacher prepare students to read a book about natural resources?

Children become increasingly able to draw inferences from what they read. As they listen to stories, young children draw inferences about why people act as they do and why events unfold in certain ways (Lepola, Lynch, Laakkonen, Silvén, & Niemi, 2012; Tompkins, Guo, & Justice, 2013). Such inferences are not automatic. Some children need to be encouraged to think about connections between ideas and events. As they progress through the elementary grades, children find it easier to draw inferences and remember what they read (Bowyer-Crane & Snowling, 2010; S. G. Paris & Upton, 1976). Nevertheless, many older elementary school children continue to take things at face value, make little attempt to evaluate the quality of ideas, and fail to notice blatant contradictions (Markman, 1979; Vorstius, Radach, Mayer, & Lonigan, 2013; A. M.-Y Wong et al., 2017).

MyLab Education
Video Example 10.1

Find Developmental Meaning *How can teachers help elementary school children perceive the non-literal meaning of text?* In this video, bilingual third graders learn about making inferences while reading.

As youngsters reach adolescence and move into the secondary grades, most read written material with a critical eye (Chall, 1996). Nevertheless, encouragement to consider the meaning and implication of written passages is generally necessary. Young people who struggle may be receptive to talking about the meaning of passages with peers, especially when everyone is taught to ask one another questions about key points, the gist of what they read, and what might happen next in the material (Ciullo, Ortiz, Al Otaiba, & Lane, 2016).

Children become familiar with common structures in fictional and nonfictional texts. Most 5- and 6-year-olds distinguish between books that tell stories and those that provide information (S. L. Field, Labbo, & Ash, 1999). As children get older, they also learn how texts are organized, and this knowledge helps them make better sense of what they read. They acquire a **story schema** that represents components of fictional narratives (main characters, plot, problem resolution, etc.) and use this structure to understand a short story or novel (Graesser, Golding, & Long, 1991; Nwokah, Burnette, & Graves, 2013; N. L. Stein, 1982). With age, children also develop mental templates for nonfiction, such as an expository passage explaining a specific topic (G. G. Wallach & Ocampo, 2017). With a textbook, they might focus on headings and subheadings to help identify key ideas, look for a few details that support the main ideas, and quiz themselves as they read.

MyLab Education
Content Extension 10.1

Read more about developmental stages in reading skills.

Children develop metacognitive insights into reading. *Metacognition*, a person's understandings of his or her own cognitive processes and efforts to control these processes, is an important part of reading. One of the first aspects of metacognition to emerge is the recognition that reading involves more than identifying the words on a page—that it involves making *sense* of text. This awareness depends in part on how adults portray the process of reading to young children. When a researcher asked a first grader named Marissa if something she had just read made sense to her, the little girl responded, "What I read never makes sense. The teacher just gives us books so we can practice reading words—they don't have to make sense" (I. W. Gaskins, Satlow, & Pressley, 2007, pp. 196–197).

Effective readers obviously *do* realize that reading is a process of making sense (I. W. Gaskins et al., 2007; L. Snyder & Caccamise, 2010). As elementary school children gain experience in reading, and especially as they become familiar with expository text, they develop such basic comprehension strategies as skimming a chapter before reading it, asking themselves questions as they read, and identifying the main idea of a passage (J. B. Cobb, 2017; van den Broek, Lynch, Naslund, Ievers-Landis, & Verduin, 2003). Reading strategies, when supported, improve further in middle and high school. Trained high school students are able to monitor their comprehension and backtrack (i.e., reread) when they don't understand something (R. Garner, 1987; I. W. Gaskins et al., 2007). Not all adolescents use effective metacognitive reading strategies, of course, and those who do not tend to have difficulty in understanding and remembering what they read (Alvermann & Moore, 1991; Ortlieb, 2013).

Preparing for Your Licensure Examination

Your teaching test might ask you how to support children's metacognitive strategies in reading.

As young people move through the school years, they generally read with greater fluency and flexibility and comprehend increasingly challenging material. The Developmental Trends table "Reading at Different Age Levels" traces the development of reading over the course of childhood.

DEVELOPMENTAL TRENDS
Reading at Different Age Levels

AGE	WHAT YOU MIGHT OBSERVE	DIVERSITY	IMPLICATIONS
Infancy (Birth–2 Years)	• Manual exploration of cloth and cardboard books • Increasing enjoyment of stories • More concentration on pictures than story lines • Attention to and enjoyment of rhythm and rhymes in spoken language	• Individual infants vary in exposure to stories depending on habits of families. • Some toddlers who are read to regularly participate actively in reading (e.g., by pointing to and labeling objects in pictures), whereas others listen quietly.	• Read books with catchy rhythms and rhymes that attract attention and nurture phonological skills. • During story time, label and talk about pictures in books. Recognize that toddlers may not be able to sit still for an entire story.
Early Childhood (2–6 Years)	• Attention focused largely on pictures rather than print during adult reading (especially before age 6) • Incorporation of books and familiar story lines into play activities • Some knowledge of conventions of written language (e.g., left-to-right direction) by age 4 • Increasing familiarity with letters and letter–sound correspondences • Identification of a few words in well-known contexts (e.g., words on commercial products) • Use of a word's distinctive features (e.g., a single letter or overall shape) in attempts to identify it	• Children who have had little exposure to books are unfamiliar with sitting down for stories. • Some cultures emphasize oral language more than written language. • Parents who speak a language other than English may read to children in their native tongue, experiences that provide a foundation for literacy in English. • Some children begin school knowing the alphabet and have a small sight vocabulary. Others need to start from scratch in learning letter-sound connections.	• Read to young children using colorful books with high-interest content. • Teach letters of the alphabet through engaging activities. • Teach letter-sound relationships through storybooks, games, rhymes, and enjoyable writing activities. • Point out clues in a book (e.g., pictures, words they already know) when readers encounter unfamiliar words. • Encourage parents to read regularly to children and visit the local library. • Send home literacy bags containing a book and reading tips, asking parents to return the book the following week.
Middle Childhood (6–10 Years)	• Rapid growth in reading skills during this period • Ability to hear individual phonemes within words • Increasing proficiency in identifying unfamiliar words • Growing sight-word vocabulary, leading to greater reading fluency • Beginning of silent reading (at age 7 or 8) • Emerging ability to draw inferences • Tendency to take print at face value without critically evaluating the content or looking below the surface for underlying themes	• Children with deficits in phonological awareness have a difficult time learning to read fluently. • Children with hearing impairments may be delayed in mastering letter-sound relationships. • On average, girls develop reading skills earlier than boys. • Children vary in use of comprehension strategies. • Children with strong vocabularies may learn to read more easily than children with limited vocabularies.	• Explore "families" of words (e.g., "fight," "sight," and "light") that share similar sounds and spelling. • Assign well-written trade books (e.g., children's paperback novels) as soon as children are able to read them. • Engage children in discussions about books. Focus on interpretation, inferences, and speculation. • For delayed readers, teach phonological awareness, word identification skills, and basic comprehension strategies.
Early Adolescence (10–14 Years)	• Automatic recognition of common words • Ability to learn new information through reading • Expanding capacity for going beyond literal meaning • Developing metacognitive processes that aid comprehension (e.g., keeping track of emerging understandings, backtracking when confused, and becoming aware of gaps in comprehension)	• Adolescents with deficits in phonological awareness may lag behind in reading. • Individuals who were poor readers in elementary school often continue to be weak readers in adolescence. • Some individuals (e.g., students with intellectual disabilities) may read individual words yet not understand the passage. • Students with sensory challenges may lack understandings assumed by authors.	• Assign age-appropriate reading materials in academic areas while also providing scaffolding (e.g., questions to answer). • Explore classic works of poetry and fiction. • Seek advice and assistance from specialists to help promote the reading skills of youngsters who lag behind peers.
Late Adolescence (14–18 Years)	• Familiarity with abstract and discipline-specific words • Ability to consider multiple viewpoints about a topic • Ability to evaluate assertions in a text • Practice with new metacognitive reading strategies • Use of strategies for reading discipline-specific materials (e.g., looking for motivations in history and causal structures in science chapters)	• Poor readers draw few inferences from what they read and exert limited metacognitive control over reading. • Adolescents with reading disabilities may be frustrated when reading demanding text. • Girls are more likely than boys to enroll in advanced literature classes. • Many adolescents prefer to make their own choices rather than have books assigned to them.	• Encourage adolescents to draw inferences and make predictions from what they read. • Ask students to analyze classic works of poetry and fiction. • Supplement reading materials with prior discussions about themes and concepts students will encounter. • Scaffold reading assignments with learning objectives, comprehension questions, fill-in-the-blank outlines, and other guidelines.

Sources: K. Cain and Oakhill (1998); Chall (1996); Ehri (1994); Elleman (2017); Felton (1998); Hedges and Nowell (1995); Horowitz-Kraus, Schmitz, Hutton, & Schumacher (2017); P. Johnston and Afflerbach (1985); Y. Kim, Petscher, Schatschneider, and Foorman (2010); C. W. Little (2017); Logan et al. (2013); McBride-Chang and Treiman (2003); L. Reese, Garnier, Gallimore, and Goldenberg (2000); T. A. Roberts (2005); Treiman, Cohen, Mulqueeny, Kessler, and Schechtman (2007); Trelease (1982); and Wigfield, Eccles, and Pintrich (1996).

Reading in a Developmental System

From the perspective of the developmental system, children approach the task of reading as active agents embedded in, and interacting with, a dynamic learning environment. Thus, children draw from a wide range of factors—their intellectual talents, disabilities, interests, motivations, family practices with literacy, and cultural resources and traditions. The kind of reader a child becomes depends partly on support at home and school (e.g., the presence of age-appropriate books, expectations for independent reading), behaviors by classmates (e.g., whether friends talk about books they've read), and practices within the broader society (e.g., uses of literacy in an ethnic community; S. A. Hart, Soden, Johnson, Schatschneider, & Taylor, 2013; A. B. Jordan, 2005). With these and other factors impinging on reading development, the pace and trajectory of reading skills and habits can be quite varied. Let's look more closely at some of the factors that influence a child's reading.

Developmental Systems Prompt 10.1

Watch for individual children's selection of stories, historical accounts, autobiographies, and other types of nonfiction. What do these choices tell about children? What are the implications for the kinds of written materials that you can make available?

Biological Foundations of Reading Skill

Exceptional talents and serious delays in reading have moderate genetic underpinnings (J. M. Fletcher & Grigorenko, 2017; Logan et al., 2013). Children with certain genes develop robust networks of neurons in areas of the brain that interpret verbal information and in others that decode text. Children with different genes develop brain circuits that are less robust in support of reading skills. Strong and weak neurological conditions generate diiferent profiles in reading. Many (but not all) children who are later identified as gifted read early, and some read voraciously (Piirto, 1999; E. Rowe, Miller, Ebenstein, & Thompson, 2012). Children with intellectual disabilities learn to read more slowly and are apt to develop fewer effective reading strategies. In some instances, they develop excellent word identification skills yet understand little of what they read (Cossu, 1999).

Children with sensory disabilities face distinct challenges with reading. Youngsters who are visually impaired cannot see the printed page and may develop strong listening skills but limited knowledge about conventions of written language, such as the left-to-right progression of words, capitalization, and punctuation (M. Tobin & Hill, 2012; G. E. Tompkins & McGee, 1982). The world of literacy is available to these children when appropriate accommodations are made. Blind children who read in Braille, a form of written language encoded in raised dots and felt by the fingertips, have stronger comprehension skills when they gain high mastery of Braille than blind peers who remain novices at Braille (Ferrell, 2006). Children with hearing impairments who have learned a manual language (e.g., American Sign Language) cannot easily identify letter–sound relationships and may have limited knowledge of figurative language, such as metaphors, idioms, and symbolic themes in literature (J. F. Andrews & Mason, 1986; Guardino & Cannon, 2016). Nevertheless, young children with hearing loss are responsive to stories, especially when parents invite them to comment; those who use manual sign language gain strong literacy skills when educated in comprehensive and balanced reading programs taught through sign (DesJardin et al., 2014; van Staden, 2013).

Some children with learning disabilities have serious difficulties in learning to read. In its extreme form, this difficulty is known as **dyslexia**, a disability with a presumed biological basis that manifests itself in several ways (Galaburda & Rosen, 2001; Keenan & Meenan, 2014; Lohvansuu et al., 2018). Contrary to popular belief, dyslexia is typically *not* a problem of visual perception, such as reading words or letters backward. Instead, most children with dyslexia have deficits in phonological awareness (Keenan & Meenan, 2014; H. L. Swanson, Mink, & Bocian, 1999). A few have problems in identifying visual stimuli quickly, which results in difficulty automatizing connections between printed words and their meanings (Menghini et al., 2010; Wolf & Bowers, 1999). A number of children with reading disabilities have other information-processing difficulties, such as a small working memory capacity or tendency to process information slowly (Hulme & Snowling, 2013; Keenan & Meenan, 2014).

Gender

On average, girls read with greater skill than do boys (Chia & Kee, 2013; Cobb-Clark & Moschion, 2017; Weaver-Hightower, 2003). In the high school grades, girls are more likely than boys to enroll in advanced literature classes (Wigfield et al., 1996). Boys tend to have less interest in reading, in part because they find fewer books at school that pique their curiosity and also because they prefer to be physically active (Marinak & Gambrell, 2010; Senn, 2012). A 10th-grader named Devin expressed the latter reason this way: "Why should I want to read about doing things when I can actually *do* them?" (Newkirk, 2002, p. 54). Many boys prefer nonfiction to fiction and, when they do read novels, like to read books focused on action and adventure, science fiction, fantasy, comedy, and horror (Hébert & Pagnani, 2010; Senn, 2012). Some boys are interested in reading materials on the Internet, for example, the content of websites and gaming manuals.

Socioeconomic Background

On average, children from low-income families enter school with fewer literacy skills than is the case for children from middle- and upper-income families (Serpell et al., 2005). During the school years, less advantaged children have lower reading achievement than do their wealthier classmates, and as they progress through school, the disparity in reading ability increases (Jimerson, Egeland, & Teo, 1999; Portes, 1996).

Of course, delays in reading are not the inevitable outcome of growing up in a financially strapped family. Early reading intervention, in which a reading specialist provides literacy experiences and intensive instruction, can help young children catch up academically. Without such intensive literacy instruction, children's delays can escalate and become more difficult to treat (Y. Griffiths & Stuart, 2013). Another means of support involves educating parents about enriching activities they can do at home, for example, reading regularly to children and encouraging partnerships with teachers at school (Dumont, Trautwein, Nagy, & Nagengast, 2014; S. S. Park, Stone, & Holloway, 2017). In occasions of persistent delays, services need to be customized to build or compensate for underdeveloped skills (Y. Giffiths & Stuart, 2013).

Ethnicity and Culture

The interpretations that children make of what they read depend in large part on their cultural upbringing. As an example, Rosenna Bakari, a colleague of ours who specializes in African-centered education, describes an incident involving her 7-year-old daughter Nailah:

> [An event] that always stands out in my mind is a reading comprehension question that Nailah had in a workbook. The question asked why two brothers drew a line down the middle of a messy room to clean it. The answer was pretty obvious: The boys were dividing the room in half so that they could each clean their part. However, Nailah could not get to that answer no matter how I scaffolded her. When I told her the answer, she replied, "Why would they divide the room up? They should just both clean it together." I immediately realized that in her African-centered world, division rarely takes place. Most things in our house are communal. Each child is responsible for the other. So for her to get to that answer would have taken something beyond reasonable reading comprehension. She would have had to understand that there are people in the world who operate under different views about sharing and responsibility. That's a more difficult task for a seven-year-old. (R. Bakari, personal communication, 2002)

Literature that portrays cultures, ethnic groups, and individuals with specific characteristics (e.g., having a physical disability, being incarcerated as a youth, having two gay parents) can be of great interest to students. Access to books that represent characteristics similar to the children themselves can also motivate them and enhance their cultural knowledge (H. M. Kelley, Siwatu, Tost, & Martinez, 2015; Koss, Martinez, & Johnson, 2016). In a literature class with immigrant adolescents, a teacher might include books that feature the courage of refugees, for example, Dia Cha's *Dia's Story Cloth: The Hmong People's Journey of Freedom* (Cha, Cha, & Cha, 1999). In working with African American high school boys, one educator found that accounts of personal struggles by African American men were especially inspiring (A. W. Tatum, 2008). One boy, Quincy, previously a nonreader, spent all night reading after starting Anthony Davis and Jeffrey Jackson's (1998) book *"Yo, Little Brother . . . ": Basic Rules of Survival for Young African American Males*.

Promoting Reading Development

Traditionally, reading was taught during the elementary grades. Teachers hoped that middle school and high school students read well enough to learn successfully from textbooks and other printed materials. Research today indicates that this assumption is not warranted. Even many high school students have failed to master all of the skills involved in reading effectively (Robb, 2018). The Development-Enhancing Education feature "Promoting Effective Reading Comprehension Strategies" presents several suggestions for supporting literacy skills in elementary, middle, and high school.

Development-Enhancing Education

Promoting Effective Reading Comprehension Strategies

Teach reading comprehension skills in the subject areas.

- A middle school mathematics teacher demonstrates questions to ask oneself while reading narrative mathematical problems: Can I tell what this question is really asking? What other options are there to interpret the problem? What options do I have for solving it? How will I know if I have a good solution? (Early Adolescence)
- When a life skills instructor tells his students to read a section of the first aid manual, he suggests strategies to help them remember the material. For instance, as students begin each section, they should look at the heading and ask a question they think the section will answer. At the end of the section, they should stop and consider whether their question was answered. (Late Adolescence)

Model effective reading strategies.

- A girl in a seventh-grade history class reads aloud a passage describing how, during Columbus's first voyage across the Atlantic, many members of the crew wanted to turn around and return to Spain. Her teacher says, "Let's think of some reasons why the crew might have wanted to go home." One student responds, "Some of them might have been homesick." Another suggests, "Maybe they thought they'd never find their way back if they went too far." (Early Adolescence)
- A high school literacy teacher advises students that it may be difficult for them to keep track of all the characters in the novel they will be reading. She says, "When I was reading it, I had to jot down a few notes on who everyone was so I could follow the plot." (Late Adolescence)

Encourage children to relate what they are reading to things they already know.

- Children in a third-grade classroom are reading books on outer space. Before they begin reading a book, their teacher asks them to write answers to three questions: (a) What do you already know about outer space? (b) What do you hope to learn? and (c) Do you think what you learn in your books will change your perspective on space travel? (Middle Childhood)
- While reading autobiographies, students answer questions on a worksheet about basic aspects of the writers' lives (e.g., who was in their family, where they grew up, what kind of education they had). Students also write about how the authors' upbringing was similar to, and different from, their own. (Early Adolescence)

Arrange for children to discuss readings with classmates.

- A third-grade teacher invites children to learn about mollusks by reading a passage. Before beginning the passage, children ask one another about what they already know about mollusks and then stop at the end of each section to talk about what they have read and anticipate what they will learn about next. (Middle Childhood)
- A high school history teacher asks students to compare notes on what they have learned from reading letters from soldiers during the U.S. Civil War. The students form teams, with each group reading either letters from northern or southern soldiers, and then prepare skits with excerpts from the letters. (Late Adolescence)

Ask children to identify key elements in stories.

- A fourth-grade teacher instructs students to ask themselves a series of questions as they read stories: (a) Who is the main character? (b) Where and when did the story take place? (c) What did the main characters do? (d) How did the story end? and (e) How did the main character feel? (Middle Childhood)
- A high school literature teacher asks students to reflect on how the various genres they have examined during the year—short stories, poetry, dramatic texts, and novels—use particular strategies to convey mood and emotion. (Late Adolescence)

Suggest that children visualize what they are reading.

- A second-grade teacher asks children to come up with creative ways to represent characters in a story. Children

(continued)

draw characters with distressed facial expressions and also use various images, including a person falling off a cliff, a prison cell, and a fistfight, to show the turmoil in characters' lives. (Middle Childhood)

- When a high school English class reads Nathaniel Hawthorne's (1892) *The Scarlet Letter*, the teacher suggests that students envision what the two main characters, Arthur Dimmesdale and Hester Prynne, might look like. She then asks a few students to describe their mental images. (Late Adolescence)

Scaffold children's early efforts to use complex strategies.

- A middle school science teacher asks her students to write summaries of short textbook passages. She gives them four rules to follow: (a) Identify the most important ideas, (b) delete trivial details, (c) eliminate redundant information, and (d) identify relationships among the main ideas. (Early Adolescence)
- In a high school chemistry course, students use a computer program to structure their observations and notes. The program asks students to respond to questions such as these: What calculations are necessary? What data must be gathered? What steps are needed to gather the data? (Late Adolescence)

Sources: Dabarera, Renandya, and Zhang (2014); Gambrell and Bales (1986); I. W. Gaskins et al. (2007); Lupo, Strong, Lewis, Walpole, and McKenna (2018); Muijselaar et al. (2017); Pressley et al. (1994); Reutzel et al. (2014); Rinehart, Stahl, and Erickson (1986); Sejnost and Thiese (2010); Short and Ryan (1984); Senn (2012); and M. Stewart (2013).

Also consider the following strategies:

• **Foster emergent literacy in young children.** Reading aloud to young children is a crucial way to support their comprehension and motivation. Pausing to ask questions while reading to children fosters their active participation. Simple questions about what is happening in the story become stepping stones to inferences, such as thinking up a few reasons as to why a character might have acted as she did (Dougherty Stahl, 2014). Brief videos of familiar stories and wordless picture books can provide additional opportunities for building comprehension skills. Increasingly, parents engage young children with books and the alphabet on their mobile phones and tablets (M. M. Neumann & Neumann, 2017).

• **Advise parents how to read to young children.** Infants and children can acquire a love of reading, an enriched vocabulary, an ear for grammatically correct language, and other literacy skills from being read to on a regular basis (C. M. Edwards, 2014). Consider the following interaction between a mother and her toddler son:

Mother: Do you wanna see the cow? Would you like to read with Mama? You ready for the cow? Where is he? [turns the page] Huh! The cow says . . .
Child: Mooo!
Mother: What's that? [points to something in the book]
Child: Boon.
Mother: Balloon! We can count! One . . .
Child: Two.
Mother: Two! [reading book] This is my nose. Where's your nose?
Child: [touches his nose]
Mother: Nose! Where's your toes?
Child: [grabs his toes]
Mother: There's your toes!

Mother demonstrates enthusiasm for the book and uses its content to review object labels (*balloon*, *nose*, *toes*) and world knowledge (numbers, what a cow says) with her son. When parents use such strategies as they read, their children acquire larger vocabularies, increased knowledge of written language, and an appreciation for literature (Colmar, 2014; E. Reese, Sparks, & Leyva, 2010; Saracho, 2017; Whitehurst et al., 1994). Parents who are unaware of how children learn from storybook sessions can learn a lot about making bedtime stories educational by watching early childhood teachers reading to children.

• **Incorporate basic reading skills into engrossing activities.** Exercising the component skills of reading—relating letters to sounds, identifying simple words, finding main ideas, and so on—facilitates reading development (Ehri, 2014; Elbro & Petersen, 2004; Metsala & David, 2017). Preschool, kindergarten, and first-grade teachers conduct numerous activities that highlight letter–sound relationships and common words (McGeown & Medford, 2014; Stainthorp, Stuart, Powell, Quinlan, & Garwood, 2010).

One approach is to provide drill-and-practice activities—workbook exercises, flash cards, and so on—that help children automatize specific reading skills. Instruction in basic skills does not *have* to be dull, however. With a little thought, teachers, parents, and other adults can develop enjoyable, meaningful activities for nurturing reading skills. For instance, to promote phonological awareness in young children, adults might conduct a game of "20 Questions" (e.g., "I'm thinking of something in the room that begins with the letter *B*"). To foster word recognition, teachers might encourage children to create "sound boards" (e.g., identifying and listing words that end in "ack," perhaps *black*, *slack*, and *track*; Bear, Invernizzi, Templeton, & Johnston, 2008).

Some children cannot easily parse words into separate sounds or associate sounds with letter combinations (in the case of English and other alphabetic languages). For these children, extra practice in phonemic awareness (e.g., the sounds in *cat* are *c-a-t*) and phonics, in which sounds are mapped onto letters, may be worthwhile. In Artifact Example 10.1, you can see 7-year-old Meggie's exercise with words that have a long *o* and silent *e*.

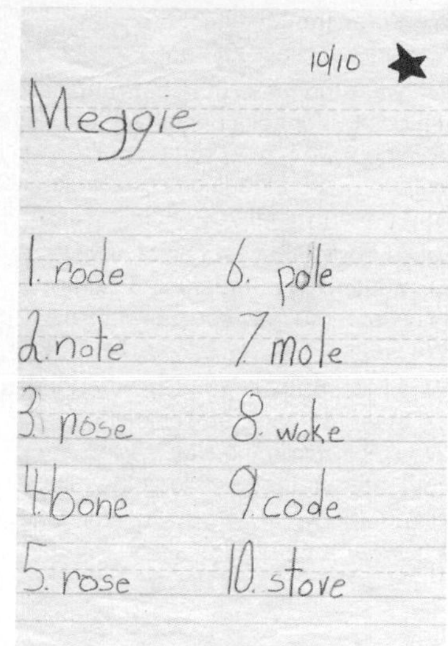

MyLab Education
Artifact Example 10.1

Find Developmental Meaning *What purpose does this assignment have for 7-year-old Meggie?* Meggie practices words with a long *o* sound and silent *e*, helping her to learn this spelling pattern in English.

- **Give children practice in reading aloud and silently.** When children learn to read orally with accuracy and expression, they are better able to comprehend text. Teachers can model how to read smoothly and give children plenty of guided practice in small groups (Driver, 2017; Ediger, 2011; Reutzel et al., 2014). In the elementary school years, teachers regularly arrange for children to select a book and sit down in a comfortable location in the classroom or library. Sometimes called independent reading, the endeavor is managed by teachers who make a range of books available and implement such accountability measures as having children write a summary or explain their story to peers in small groups (Sanden, 2012).

- **Address reading problems as early as possible.** If children struggle with reading, they are apt to avoid it when possible. As a result, the gap between them and their peers widens over time (Stanovich, 2000). To minimize delays, educators can help children make up reading deficits, ideally by first grade or before. Many children with early reading difficulties benefit from intensive training in letter recognition, phonological awareness, word identification, and comprehension strategies (Bursuck & Blanks, 2010; Hulme & Snowling, 2013; Lovett et al., 2017; D. C. Simmons et al., 2013).

- **Allow for choices in high-interest books.** Children read more energetically and persistently, use more advanced metacognitive strategies, and remember more content when they are interested in what they are reading than when they are not (R. C. Anderson, Shirey, Wilson, & Fielding, 1987; E. Fox, 2009; Repaskey, Schumm, & Johnson, 2017). As much as possible, then, teachers, parents, and other adults should make available reading lists, books, and resources that are likely to be relevant to young people's lives.

- **Conduct group discussions about novels.** Children often grasp written material more effectively when they discuss what they read with peers. Adults can form "book clubs" in which trained children lead small groups of classmates in discussions about specific books (Bean Thompson, 2013; Choi & Sachs, 2017; Kumasi, 2014; S. McMahon, 1992). Similarly, adults can hold "grand conversations" about a work of literature, asking youngsters to share their responses to open-ended questions, perhaps related to interpretations or critiques of parts of the novel (Dillon, O'Brien, Scharber, & Nichols-Besel, 2017; Eeds & Wells, 1989; E. H. Hiebert & Raphael, 1996). By tossing around interpretations of what they are reading, children model effective reading and listening strategies for one another (R. C. Anderson et al., 2001).

MyLab Education
Video Example 10.2

Find Developmental Meaning *How does the teacher foster children's familiarity with sounds in English?* The teacher emphasizes the beginning sounds of words.

- **Make available a range of media for self-expression.** Children might perform skits to illustrate stories, write personal letters to story characters, or create works of art that illustrate the setting of a novel. In Artifact Example 10.2, 16-year-old Jeff illustrates the meaning of a poem with two sides of a mask. Another avenue of self-expression is classroom blogs, in which the teacher and, in some cases, a student, pose thoughtful questions about a book they are all reading. They might speculate on what happens next in the story or why a character acted in a certain way (Stover, Yearta, & Harris, 2016).

We Wear the Mask
by Paul Laurence Dunbar

We wear the mask that grins and lies,
It hides our cheeks and shades our eyes,–
This debt we pay to human guile;
With torn and bleeding hearts we smile,
And mouth with myriad subtleties.

Why should the world be overwise,
In counting all our tears and sighs?
Nay, let them only see us, while
We wear the mask.

We smile, but, O great Christ, our cries
To thee from tortured souls arise.
We sing, but oh the clay is vile
Beneath our feet, and long the mile;
But let the world dream otherwise,
We wear the mask!

MyLab Education
Artifact Example 10.2

Find Developmental Meaning *What symbols does 16-year-old Jeff incorporate in his representation of Paul Laurence Dunbar's poem "We Wear the Mask"?* Jeff's brightly colored painting (at left) is the cheerful face ("mask") that its African American owner wore in public. The black face (at right) is the flip side of the mask, as viewed by the person wearing it. Depicted in the holes of the mask are a lynching (left eye), a whipping (right eye), a slave ship with someone being thrown overboard (mouth), and an African American woman and baby (nostrils), a regular outcome of White men's rape of women slaves.

- **Encourage reading outside of school.** Reading after school and during the summer months accounts for a significant portion of young people's growth in comprehension (D. P. Hayes & Grether, 1983; Springen, 2014; Tiruchittampalam, Nicholson, Levin, & Ferron, 2018). Providing books that children can take home encourages leisure reading and can significantly enhance comprehension skills (Koskinen et al., 2000). Visits to the local library can also encourage reading.

- **Invite bilingual children to read in two or more languages.** Even in an English-speaking country, reading instruction doesn't necessarily need to begin in English. By reading in their native language, they gain expertise and cultural knowledge. As bilingual children gain proficiency in English and tackle English reading materials, they apply relevant knowledge from their native language—in phonological awareness, vocabulary, and so on (Huennekens & Xu, 2010; C. P. Proctor, August, Carlo, & Snow, 2006; D. Zhang, Chin, & Li, 2017).

Writing Development

Children must synchronize numerous abilities as they write. Eye–hand coordination, a good hand grip on a writing implement, cognitive planning as to what to say, and knowledge of letters and words are all involved. Let's examine age-related trends that occur as children gain experience in writing.

Developmental Trends in Writing

Children write long before they reach school age, especially if they see people around them writing. By 18 months of age—sometimes even earlier—many toddlers scribble enthusiastically with crayons (McLane & McNamee, 1990; Winner, 2006). Children's early efforts with writing implements are largely exploratory, reflecting experimentation with different kinds of marks on paper. As they develop better eye–hand coordination, preschool children produce recognizable shapes. By age 3 or 4, their writing is clearly different from drawing (S. Graham & Weintraub, 1996; Otake, Treiman, & Yin, 2017; Sulzby, 1986). It may consist of wavy lines or connected loops that loosely resemble adults' cursive writing.

Children's early writing—or more accurately, *pseudowriting*—often reveals knowledge about written language, including the orientation and spacing of letters. Polishing one letter at a time, most children eventually achieve a standard of legibility with the entire alphabet (Puranik, Petscher, & Lonigan, 2013). Young children may include drawings and letters together, spontaneously shifting from one literate form to another, eagerly anticipating reactions from teachers and parents. As you may remember in our opening case study, Osvaldo combined print and art and was interested in how his audience responded to his story.

Progress in writing occurs on several fronts as youngsters gain experience in elementary, middle school, and high school. Children show improvements in spelling, grammar, and composition skills. By exposing children to good writing, pointing out ideal features, providing worksheets that specify steps in preparing various genres (e.g., in editing one's essay, reading it aloud and repairing parts that do not make sense), and giving feedback about their writing, teachers help children make progress (Jago, 2014; M. Shen & Troia, 2018).

MyLab Education Application Exercise 10.2
Identify Development-Enhancing Education

In this video, Alicia Sanchez, a fourth-grade teacher, encourages children to integrate emotionally rich descriptions into their writing.

Handwriting

During the elementary school years, children's handwriting gradually becomes smaller and more regular, and they shift from concentrating on forming each letter to writing entire words and sentences (S. Graham & Weintraub, 1996; Rumi, Toshihiro, & Kenryu, 2013). Little additional improvement in handwriting occurs after elementary school, although youngsters continue to simplify letters and write more efficiently (Olive, Favart, Beauvais, & Beauvais, 2009). Many educators now see keyboarding skills and proficient use of a word processor as invaluable tools for writing (ASCD, 2014). Skillful handwriting and keyboarding are important factors in writing because they allow students to focus attention on their thoughts instead of the transcription process (S. Graham, Harris, & Fink, 2000; Medwell & Wray, 2014).

Spelling

Phonological awareness is as important in spelling as it is in reading (Lennox & Siegel, 1998; Treiman & Kessler, 2013; C. C. Zhang, Bingham, & Quinn, 2017). Children learn proper spellings of a few words (such as their names) almost as soon as they learn how to write letters of the alphabet. But in their early writing they tend to engage in considerable guesswork about how words are spelled, creating **invented spellings** that capture certain sounds but not others (N. H. Clemens, Oslund, Simmons, & Simmons, 2014; Treiman, 1998). Consider the invented spellings in this kindergartner's creation entitled "My Garden" (note that "HWS" is *house*):

THIS IS A HWS
THE SUN
WL SHIN
ND MI
GRDN
WL GRO[2]
(Hemphill & Snow, 1996, p. 192)

As children develop greater phonological awareness, their spellings increasingly represent most or all of the phonemes they hear (Awramiuk, 2014; Hemphill &

[2]This is a house. The sun will shine, and my garden will grow.

Snow, 1996; C. C. Zhang, Bingham, et al., 2017). Sometime around first or second grade, they incorporate common letter patterns (e.g., *–ight*, *–ound*, and *–ing* in English) into unfamiliar words (Critten, Pine, & Steffler, 2007; Nation & Hulme, 1998). Children's ability to spell improves steadily, especially if they read and write regularly. Most children eventually memorize the spelling of words they use often (Rittle-Johnson & Siegler, 1999). To make more difficult words accessible, teachers expose children to selected word families (e.g., *fight* and *right*, *team* and *beam*) and rules (focusing on silent *e*, as in *came*, *hole*, and *smile*). Other teachers group children according to spelling proficiency and provide them with customized spelling lists and computer programs (B. McNeill & Kirk, 2014; Saine, Lerkkanen, Ahonen, Tolvanen, & Lyytinen, 2013).

Syntax and Grammar

As children grow older, they write in longer sentences and with more varied sentence structures. By the time they are 12 or 13 years old, the syntactic structures they use in written work are considerably more complex than those in speech. With age, too, comes an increasing ability to abide by punctuation and capitalization rules without reminders from adults (Feifer, 2013; R. B. Gillam & Johnston, 1992; Ravid & Zilberbuch, 2003). Regular reading and writing contribute to refinements in the mechanics of writing and in the effectiveness of expressing ideas. Teachers can guide students by drawing attention to the functions of parts of speech and the presence of grammatical expressions in books, articles, and students' own writing (J. Anderson, 2014; Furey, Marcotte, Wells, & Hintze, 2017).

Composition Skills

When preschool children engage in early writing activities at home, they often do so with a purpose in mind, such as labeling artwork or writing a letter to a grandparent. Only when children enter kindergarten or first grade do they write for writing's sake. Children's earliest compositions are usually narratives, such as recollections of personal experiences or short fictional stories (Hemphill & Snow, 1996).

In previous decades, expository writing (e.g., research reports, persuasive essays) was introduced late in schooling, in the upper elementary grades (Owens, 2008). Current views on writing instruction, including those guiding Common Core standards, give greater attention to writing across the curriculum, resulting in children in the early grades now being asked to write about their understandings in science, mathematics, and social studies. In the disciplines, students are taught how to write clearly and justify their conclusions (Alberti, 2012). The quality of students' compositions changes throughout the school years, and is reflected in the following progressions:

Children write about topics in greater depth as they grow older. When children of various ages are asked to write about a topic, the older ones include more ideas (de Milliano, van Gelderen, & Sleegers, 2012; Işıtan & Doğan, 2015; Zumbrunn & Bruning, 2013). Growth in the length and richness of writing continues throughout the school years. For instance, when writing persuasive essays, high school students include more arguments than do elementary and middle school students, and 12th-graders include more arguments than do 9th-graders (Knudson, 1992; McCann, 1989).

Children increasingly take their audience's perspective into account. As children become more capable of adapting speech to the characteristics of their listeners, they also attend to their readers' needs. Characters in a story must be introduced, for example, and the relationships between events must be explained. Young children realize that readers need to interpret their drawings and writing from their own perspectives, and as they grow, children envision their audience and tailor text accordingly (S. Graham, 2006; Perfetti & McCutchen, 1987; Peskin, Prusky, & Comay, 2014).

For some adolescents, a knowledge-telling approach gradually evolves into a knowledge-transforming approach. Young writers often compose a narrative or essay by writing down notes in the order in which they come to mind. Such an approach is known as **knowledge telling** (S. Graham, Harris, & Olinghouse, 2007; Scardamalia & Bereiter, 1986; Whitehead & Murphy, 2014). With age, experience, and practice with basic writing skills, young people become better able to communicate a meaningful perspective on a topic, one that helps potential readers *understand* the material, an approach known

FIGURE 10.1 Worksheet for Fourth Graders on Writing an Essay.

Teachers can scaffold students' academic writing with forms specifying steps and notes for completion.

Steps in Writing the Paper	Describe Your Steps
1. **Planning the Paper** Example: *I decided to write about wings of birds in a four-paragraph paper.*	Describe the focus and structure of your paper: ______________________ ______________________
2. **Generating Ideas** Example: *I used a concept map and then wrote an outline.*	Explain the strategy you used to develop your ideas: ______________________ ______________________
3. **Organizing Thoughts** Example: *I followed my outline.*	Identify your plan for organizing the sequence of ideas in your paper: ______________________ ______________________
4. **Writing the First Draft** Example: *I turned off my cell phone and took an hour to write down my thoughts.*	Summarize how you developed your first draft: __ ______________________
5. **Reviewing the Draft** Example: *I needed to fix the conclusion because it didn't make sense.*	Tell what you decided to change when you re-read your first draft: ______________________ ______________________
5. **Finalizing the Paper** Example: *I corrected a few spelling errors and changed the conclusion.*	Describe the changes you made when finalizing your essay: ______________________ ______________________

as **knowledge transforming**. It is challenging to write in such a manner that readers fully understand one's writing; plenty of feedback is needed for the novice writer (Olinghouse, Graham, & Gillespie, 2015).

With age and instruction comes a growing ability to write a clear and organized story, recollection, or composition. In the elementary grades, children use few if any devices to tie separate pieces of their creation together. They may write a story by beginning with "Once upon a time" and list a sequence of events that connect only loosely to one another, ending with "They lived happily ever after" (Boyle & Charles, 2011; McLane & McNamee, 1990). Their nonfiction, too, may be little more than a list of facts or events. Older students, especially adolescents, are more capable of analyzing and synthesizing their thoughts as they write. They compose more cohesive essays, in part because they now communicate coherently about causes for events and motivations of people (Byrnes & Wasik, 2009; McCutchen, 1987; Sun & Nippold, 2012).

With strategic guidance from adults, children gain metacognitive insights and control over their writing. Good writers think about a topic ahead of time and plan how they are going to render it. After preparing drafts, they critically evaluate their writing, looking not only for grammatical and spelling errors but also for omissions, ambiguities, logical flaws, and contradictions (Eunjyu, 2013; S. Graham, 2006; Tracy, Reid, & Graham, 2009). Such editing skills emerge slowly and are incomplete by the end of adolescence. In fact, young people typically find it difficult to identify problems in their writing, particularly those related to clarity (Berninger, Fuller, & Whitaker, 1996; Fitzgerald, 1987; Koutsoftas & Gray, 2013). In fact, students generally fail to revise their work unless urged to do so by an adult. When they *do* rewrite, they tend to make only small, superficial changes. With instruction in how to revise their written work, students are frequently able to improve their drafts (Tracy et al., 2009). Handouts specifying strategies for generating ideas and editing drafts can be useful (Babkie & Provost, 2002; L. Nguyen & Gu, 2013). An example for fourth-graders is included in Figure 10.1 (above).

With appropriate support from adults, children gradually learn to express themselves well. The Developmental Trends table "Writing at Different Age Levels" identifies accomplishments in writing seen during infancy and the preschool, elementary, middle, and secondary school years.

DEVELOPMENTAL TRENDS
Writing at Different Age Levels

AGE	WHAT YOU MIGHT OBSERVE	DIVERSITY	IMPLICATIONS
Infancy (Birth–2 Years)	• Development of eye–hand coordination, including the *pincer grasp*, in which infants use a thumb and forefinger to pick up and hold objects • Interest in mimicking "writing" by adults • Discovery of being able to make certain marks on paper with a crayon • Appearance of scribbling at 18 to 24 months	• Individual differences appear in advancement to fine motor skills. • Infants can imitate only what they see, so those who never watch anyone writing are unlikely to use crayons and other writing implements.	• Allow toddlers to manipulate small objects that do not present choking hazards. • Demonstrate how to make lines and shapes with writing implements. • Have a variety of tools available for scribbling (e.g., with fat crayons, washable markers, and butcher paper). • Tape writing paper to the table or floor to permit easy clean up.
Early Childhood (2–6 Years)	• Improving muscular control in writing and drawing • Pseudowriting (e.g., wavy lines, connected loops) during preschool activities • Awareness that writing proceeds from left to write in English • Ability to write own name (perhaps at age 3) • Ability to write most letters of the alphabet (at age 4 or later) • Invented spellings (at ages 5 to 6)	• Some cultures place greater emphasis on writing than others. • Some children have minimal exposure to written materials or letters. • Children with visual impairments are apt to have little awareness of print conventions (left-to-right progression, use of punctuation, etc.). • Children learning to write Chinese and Japanese characters find out about stroke order with forming characters.	• Make writing implements (pencils, markers, paper) easily accessible. • Give children opportunities to write their names and a few other words. • Have children act out stories they have orally composed. • Ask children to dictate stories, letters, poems, or reports for you to transcribe, and that they can later illustrate.
Middle Childhood (6–10 Years)	• Steady improvement in smoothness of handwriting; gradual decrease in handwriting size • Increasing application of letter-sound relationships and common letter patterns when spelling words • Predominance of narratives in writing • Increasing length in stories and reports as handwriting and spelling improve • Difficulty identifying problems (especially lack of clarity) in own writing • Emerging proficiency in keyboarding skill and use of word processing program	• Better readers tend to be better writers, presumably because language ability provides a foundation for both competencies. • Children with deficits in phonological awareness have a more difficult time learning to spell. • Girls show higher achievement in writing and spelling beginning in the elementary years. • Children with dyslexia and other learning disabilities often have poor handwriting skills. • Some children with learning disabilities have trouble with spelling and composing.	• Engage children in authentic writing activities (e.g., in writing letters to relatives or creating a newsletter). • Provide practice in spelling, grammar, and punctuation within authentic activities. • Explore how particular phonemes are spelled. • Introduce expository forms of writing (e.g., lab reports and social studies essays). • Include editing in the schedule; provide criteria for self-evaluation. • Use keyboards with large letters or tactile feedback for students with low vision, and use Braille typewriters with blind children.
Early Adolescence (10–14 Years)	• Automatized spelling of common words • Improvement in expository forms of writing • Planning ideas before beginning writing • Acting on knowledge of conventions about word endings and syllables • Use of longer and more complex syntactic structures • Tendency to not edit and revise unless required to do so	• Some students (e.g., those with learning disabilities) may continue to have difficulty with spelling and sentence structure. • A few adolescents write in their spare time (e.g., keeping diaries, writing notes to friends), whereas others write only when required at school. • Students may spend a lot of time composing instant text messages.	• Provide instruction in spelling, punctuation, and grammar, emphasizing functions in communicating meaning. • Teach persuasive and argumentative forms of writing. • Suggest a specific audience for whom to write. • Give feedback on first drafts, especially on clarity. • Encourage adolescents to use local dialects in creative writing projects.
Late Adolescence (14–18 Years)	• Ability to write about a particular topic in depth • More organized, unified, and interconnected essays than in previous years • Increasing tendency to knowledge-transform rather than knowledge-tell • More revisions than at younger ages, but with a focus on superficial rather than substantive problems	• Individuals with learning disabilities may focus largely on mechanics (e.g., correct spelling and grammar) while composing, perhaps because such skills are not yet automatized. • Individuals from some cultural backgrounds (e.g., a few from East Asian countries) may be reluctant to put thoughts on paper unless certain that their ideas are acceptable. • Students vary significantly in composition skills depending on their prior education.	• Assign and scaffold lengthy writing projects. • Teach specific strategies for organizing and synthesizing ideas. • Show examples of good writing (e.g., an essay that illustrates knowledge transforming). • For teens with language-based disabilities, provide resources such as spell checkers. • Encourage peers to evaluate one another's reports using prepared rubrics.

Sources: Beal (1996); Berninger et al. (1996); Broc et al. (2013); Byrnes (1996); Cameron, Hunt, and Linton (1996); Dien (1998); Donne (2012); Duarte Ribeiro and Loução Martins (2013); Erbeli, Hart, Kim, and Taylor (2017); J. M. Fletcher, Lyon, Fuchs, and Barnes (2007); Gentry (1982); Glaser and Brunstein (2007); S. Graham (2014); Halpern (2006); J. Hansen and Kissel (2009); Hedges and Nowell (1995); Hemphill and Snow (1996); Kellogg (1967); Lam and McBride (2018); MacArthur and Graham (1987); McLane and McNamee (1990); Rochat and Bullinger (1994); Shanahan and Tierney (1990); Smitherman (1994); Yaden and Templeton (1986); Young-Suk, Al Otaiba, Folsom, Greulich, and Puranik (2014).

Writing in a Developmental System

As you learned about reading, progress in writing is similarly influenced by the child's individual characteristics and experiences. Children observe their parents and other family members writing and later keep a journal at night, post personal updates on a social media account, or put writing to other purposes. At school, children are guided through formal writing assignments by teachers. Peers can also give one another tips and feedback (Alzahrani & Leko, 2018; Grünke, Wilbert, Tsiriotakis, & Agirregoikoa, 2017). In one study with fourth- and fifth-grade students, researchers focused on Juan, an English language learner who had previously failed to complete his written assignments. When an activity called for children to pair up for a writing assignment, Juan teamed up with his friend Ned and made much more progress than when on his own. In the following excerpt, the boys speculate about why turtles are disappearing, and Juan is motivated to take notes for the assignment:

> Ned: Another way he could get drown is a crab could get him.
>
> Juan: He puts his head in his shell?
>
> Ned: If he sticks his head in his shell, he can't get it out. Then it gets trapped. Then the crab will stick his claws inside it, and sometimes they eat turtles. They stick their claws inside and eat turtles. Sea turtles. He sticks his claws inside and gets the turtle's head and starts eating it. (Juan is writing.)
>
> Juan: Or . . . putting . . . his . . . head . . . in . . . his . . . shell . . . can drown him, too?
>
> Ned: What?
>
> Juan: Putting his head in his shell can drown him too?
>
> (Juan is writing. He continues his questioning to fill in the matrix where there are question marks.) (Bicais & Correia, 2008, p. 370)

The challenges inherent in writing a story, recording a personal memory, preparing a scientific report, or composing a persuasive essay are significant. Instruction is usually needed for proficient writing. Yet the kind of help that is needed varies among children. Some students exhibit extraordinary writing talent, even though they may choose to keep their writing private or anonymous on the Internet. For the majority of children, writing is a difficult endeavor, and for some, the tasks must be simplified, divided into separate steps, and sequenced carefully. Most children with intellectual disabilities and some with specific learning disabilities have problems in handwriting, spelling, and expressing themselves coherently (J. M. Fletcher et al., 2007). Children with writing delays typically focus their writing efforts on spelling, grammar, and punctuation (S. Graham, Schwartz, & MacArthur, 1993). The quality of their writing improves when demands on the mechanical aspects of writing are minimized (e.g., when they can dictate their stories and other compositions) and when they are given steps to follow as they write (Hallenbeck, 1996; R. J. Sawyer, Graham, & Harris, 1992).

Promoting Writing Development

Growth in writing requires a long-term effort. Psychologists and experienced educators have offered several suggestions for facilitating youngsters' writing development:

MyLab Education
Video Example 10.3

Find Developmental Meaning *How does Raike's teacher help her to reflect on her writing?* Raike's teacher asks about stories and essays she has written, what she thinks are the strengths of her writing, and what she hopes to improve on next year.

- **Provide tools for drawing and writing as soon as children are old enough to use them.** Quite early in life, children explore the outcomes of their hand movements in drawing, writing, and painting. For toddlers, the sensory experience of painting with wet fingertips is an obvious attraction, and gradually children attend to marks they make on the page. As fine motor skills, cognitive abilities, and knowledge of written symbols improve during the preschool years, children become increasingly able to produce recognizable shapes and letters.

As children grow older, additional tools can be made available. Crayons and paint brushes continue to have appeal, and pens and pencils are increasingly offered. Some children have the potential to be skilled writers but cannot form letters because of neuromuscular delays (McCarney, Peters, Jackson, Thomas, & Kirby, 2013). For these children, being able to type allows them to share creative works (Ashburner, Ziviani, & Pennington, 2012). Some educators now teach keyboarding with greater emphasis than on cursive, reasoning that there is not equal time for both and that facility on the computer is more important in our electronic age (Bauerlein, 2013).

• **Make assistive technologies, peer support, and digital resources available for children who are delayed in writing or find it motivating to use these tools.** Astute teachers may notice that one or more students are having trouble writing. Assessments from a psychologist, techniques from a special educator, and tools from an educational technologist can help classroom teachers exercise students' individual strengths in writing and work around their limitations (A. B. Coffin, Myles, Rogers, & Szakacs, 2016). Those students with learning disabilities who are not able to write or keyboard yet can dictate stories and essays might take advantage of voice-to-text conversion applications (I. Lee, 2013). Many students, including some with learning disabilities, benefit from computer applications that scaffold steps in outlining, taking notes, preparing a draft, and editing. Other students do not face a specific learning challenge and simply find it helpful and even inspiring to use technologies such as *iBooks Author*, an application by Apple, Inc. that allows students to create interactive books (Encheff, 2013). Other digital programs, such as a spell-checker, dictionary, thesaurus, grammar guide, and bibliography tool, can be made available when children need a little help with mechanics, word choice, and management of the document.

• **Implement authentic writing tasks.** Youngsters write more frequently and in a more organized and effective manner (e.g., knowledge-transforming) when they're interested in the topic and write for a "real" audience (not just for their teacher; S. L. Benton, 1997; Morales, 2017; S. Peterson, 2014). When one high school English teacher noticed that several capable students weren't completing assigned writing tasks, he asked them to write about their personal experiences and share their work on the Internet. The students began writing regularly, presumably because they could choose their topic and communicate with a real audience (R. Garner, 1998). Current events and personal circumstances likewise motivate communication about hopes, aspirations, and injustices (Chandler-Olcott, 2013). By the same token, students who are participating in service learning or internships have experiences that beg to be documented (Perren, Grove, & Thornton, 2013). In the Development in Culture feature "Summer Camp in Bosnia," a group of girls wrote stories for younger children.

Development in Culture

Summer Camp in Bosnia

Jacqueline Darvin, a college professor in literacy education, attended a conference one spring and became impressed with the work of the Global Children's Organization (GCO), a group of educators, professionals, and other volunteers offering summer camps for children growing up with unrest, violence, and intolerance (Darvin, 2009). Jacqueline learned that the GCO had implemented programs for children in Los Angeles and Northern Ireland and was planning a program in the former Yugoslavia. She joined the latter group and traveled to a summer camp in Bosnia.

Children at the Bosnian camp had grown up in communities afflicted with ethnic conflicts, high rates of unemployment, and political corruption. Children's families had strong allegiances as Bosnians, Bosnian Serbs, or Bosnian Croats, ethnic groups that had previously fought one another in a brutal war. Some of the children who attended camp had lost their parents in the war, and others had witnessed violence firsthand, sometimes at school.

At the camp, children were warmly welcomed in community-building exercises. Children also participated in numerous relaxing sports and leisure activities, including artwork, horseback riding, and hiking. Jacqueline's contribution to the activities was a literacy project. She invited the oldest girls at the camp (between 10 and 13 years old) to compose and illustrate books that they would share with younger children. Girls individually selected one of three themes to write about: peace and freedom, preservation of nature, or funny stories about horses. Children wrote their books in their native

Ladi Kirn/Alamy Stock Photo

SUMMER CAMP. These Bosnian children race on inflatable beach mattresses with new friends at summer camp.

Development in Culture

Summer Camp in Bosnia (continued)

Serbo-Croatian language, and English-speaking native speakers translated the books for Jacqueline.

A few girls wrote about horses, but the more popular themes were peace and friendship and the beauty of the natural world. An interest in developing new relationships with people from dissimilar backgrounds was evident in those who wrote about peace and friendship. Melita wrote about her desire to make friends with children from different backgrounds:

> When I was small, I always thought about meeting many friends and wanted to be surrounded by many people. Always, I was thinking and dreaming about this. I was in the dark, but one day, my eyes were opened. The people I met were different religions, from different countries, had different feelings, but the one thing we had in common was friendship and love. . . . It didn't matter that we had different colour skin, that we prayed to God in a different way and talked to Him about our eminent departure (from camp) and the pain we would feel. But sure enough, it was time to leave. We were all sad. But in a way, we were happy because we knew that we would see each other again and forever carry each other in our hearts.[a] (Darvin, 2009, p. 55)

Jacqueline had selected preservation of nature in Bosnia as a second option because of growing concerns there about pollution, water shortages, and illegal stripping of forests. Many children were aware of these concerns and appreciative of their time in the scenic rural setting. Children who selected this theme wrote about natural beauty. One student, Anela, communicated her sense of awe in a poem:

> One night,
> A little star was shining in the sky.
> In the morning,
> The birds woke up from their nests.
> The flowers bloomed from their green buds
> To please the missing stars.[a]
> (Darvin, 2009, p. 54)

As they prepared their books, the girls exchanged ideas and helped one another with illustrations. Local camp counselors assisted with spelling and grammar. As final touches, the girls wrote brief autobiographies, added photographs of themselves on the back covers, and laminated the books. Having completed the stories, the girls hosted a story hour for the 6- to 8-year-old children at camp. The girls were pleased with their accomplishments, and the younger children were impressed with the books.

[a]"Make Books, Not War: Workshops at a Summer Camp in Bosnia" by Jacqueline Darvin, from *Literacy*, March 17, 2009, Volume 43, Issue 1. Copyright © 2009 by Jacqueline Darvin. Reprinted with permission of LITERACY, a journal of the United Kingdom Literacy Association.

- **Scaffold children's writing efforts.** Given the many challenges of writing, especially for beginners, it can help to direct certain steps. Finding a structured writing task with tangible criteria can be helpful because clear goals make the writing task manageable. In addition, consider the following recommendations:

- Ask children to set specific goals for their writing.
- Help students organize their thoughts before beginning to write, perhaps asking them to talk about their ideas with a classmate or draw a picture of the characters or concepts they will be describing.
- Invite children to brainstorm ideas for communicating effectively (e.g., by using examples, analogies, and similes, as you can see in Artifact Example 10.3 on the next page).
- Post a *word wall*, a list of concepts being addressed in a particular unit (e.g., key terms in social studies), as a poster or list on the bulletin board.
- Ask children to keep a journal of their observations of a particular phenomenon (e.g., a record of plant growth for a science lesson).
- Guide children with questions they should address when writing a story (e.g., Who are the main characters? When and where does the story take place? What are the main characters trying to accomplish? What happens to them? How does the story end?).
- Identify elements for children to include in their assignment (e.g., in a persuasive essay, include a thesis statement, supporting arguments, and rebuttals to possible counterarguments).

MyLab Education
Video Example 10.4

Find Developmental Meaning *How does the high school teacher scaffold the writing of students who are learning English as a second language?* She makes the writing task manageable (by identifying the goal as writing an obituary), focused (with 5 Ws), and interactive (by having students work in pairs).

Like What...

hot like...
cold like...
sounds like...
tastes like...
feels like...
looks like...
smells like...
moves like...

Simile- comparison uses like or a:

SADNESS

Sadness is cold like an old empty house. It sounds like a cold winter wind. Sadness tastes like a glass of spoiled milk. It feels like an ice cub that been out of the refridgerator for two minutes. Sadness moves like a single leaf in the slow autumn wind. Sadness crawls across the floor hoping to go by unoticed.

MyLab Education
Artifact Example 10.3

Find Developmental Meaning *How has Charlotte's teacher guided students' writing?* Charlotte's teacher provided sentence stems that prompted children to generate similes. After 11-year-old Charlotte brainstormed similes for sadness, she wrote out her ideas.

- Suggest that children initially focus on communicating clearly; postpone attention to mechanics (e.g., spelling, punctuation) for later drafts.
- Provide questions that children should ask themselves as they review their writing (e.g., "Are my ideas logically organized?" "Do I have a topic sentence in each paragraph?").
- Ask children to collaborate on writing projects, including by reading and responding to one another's work.
- Encourage use of word processing programs while writing and editing.
- Allow children with limited writing skills to dictate rather than handwrite or keyboard stories. (ASCD, 2014; Benko, 2012; S. L. Benton, 1997; Boyle & Charles, 2011; Glaser & Brunstein, 2007; S. Graham & Perin, 2007; J. Hansen & Kissel, 2009; K. R. Harris & Graham, 1992; McLane & McNamee, 1990; Sitko, 1998; Sperling, 1996; Tracy et al., 2009; Zumbrunn & Bruning, 2013).

• **Include writing assignments in all areas of the curriculum.** Writing is an important form of communication for expressing insights about historical documents, scientific observations, artistic interpretations, and mathematical patterns. Writing takes different forms in separate disciplines, and students need to practice expressing their ideas in different fields. For example, a high school junior might during a three-week period prepare a critique of a novel, a science lab report, an analysis of historical documents, and a draft of a personal essay for college applications. Particularly at the secondary level, teachers need to teach writing skills that are conducive to expressing knowledge in the disciplines (De La Paz, 2005; D. Gillam, 2014; Sejnost & Thiese, 2010).

Summary

When young children have multiple experiences with reading materials, they learn a great deal about the nature of written language. They understand that spoken language is represented in consistent ways and that different kinds of printed materials serve distinct purposes. Such knowledge, known as *emergent literacy*, is an important foundation for the reading and writing skills children acquire in school. Skilled reading involves knowing letter–sound correspondences, recognizing words quickly, constructing meaning from paragraphs and longer passages, and regulating the reading process. Phonological awareness (hearing the distinct sounds within spoken words), word identification skills, and the automatic recognition of common words typically emerge by the early and middle elementary school years. Reading comprehension and metacognitive strategies develop throughout the school years.

Some children with sensory impairments or learning disabilities have more difficulty learning to read than do their nonlabeled peers. Researchers have also found gender, socioeconomic, and cultural factors in reading skill. Strategies for fostering reading include advising parents of strategies for effective storybook reading, reading to children at school, promoting their phonological awareness, providing access to authentic literature, making culturally relevant reading materials available, and engaging children in discussions about what they have read.

To become skillful writers, children must master not only handwriting and spelling but also methods for communicating thoughts clearly, including conventions for capitalization, punctuation, and syntax. Control of the entire writing effort is a challenge. Handwriting and keyboarding are usually mastered in the elementary grades, but other aspects of writing develop later. In the middle school and high school years, many youngsters gradually abandon a *knowledge-telling* approach to writing (in which they write ideas in whatever order the ideas come to mind) in favor of a *knowledge-transforming* approach (in which they conscientiously communicate with the reader's needs in mind). Self-evaluation and editing skills improve somewhat during adolescence.

To a considerable degree, writing development depends on children's general intellectual development, but some children have difficulty writing despite normal cognitive abilities. Teachers and other adults can promote writing development by introducing preschoolers to simple writing activities (e.g., making alphabet letters, encouraging pseudowriting in pretend play), assigning authentic writing tasks in the elementary and secondary grades, scaffolding everyone's writing efforts with age-appropriate structures, and assigning writing across the curriculum.

MyLab Education Self-Check 10.1

Mathematics and Science

10.2 Describe age-related advancements in children's mathematical and scientific competencies and instruction that inspires growth in these subjects.

Beginning in the first few years of life, children are intrinsically interested in the mathematical and scientific regularities in their world. At school, children extend their knowledge by counting, imagining quantities on a number line, employing the scientific method, and identifying properties in living and nonliving things. As students move through the grade levels, they find mathematics and science to be progressively challenging, yet having achieved a good foundation early on, and assuming that the subjects continue to be shown to be personally meaningful, they are likely to achieve the levels they need in our technologically advancing world.

Counting

Mathematics is a cluster of realms—arithmetic, algebra, geometry, statistics, and so on—each with its own methods for solving quantitative problems. Fundamental to mastering these distinct systems are abilities for perceiving magnitude, counting accurately, and gaining insight into the permutations of numbers and the integrity of mathematical principles.

From birth, children notice variations in quantity, size, volume, and magnitude. This sensitivity, which has a neurological basis, matures with development (Cantrell & Smith, 2013; Mou & vanMarle, 2014). By 5 or 6 months of age, infants spot the difference between two small collections that vary in amount (e.g., in sets of two and three objects), and they distinguish between large collections with visibly different amounts (e.g., a set of 16 dots and a set of 32 dots; Wynn, 1995; F. Xu & Spelke, 2000). It is an impressive feat and probably occurs because infants see differences in the spread or density of items before them. This ability to detect differences in magnitude through mental images that are not yet associated with numbers, words, or symbolic procedures for counting, has been labeled the **approximate number system** (Dehaene, 1997).

With experience, children's intuitions about magnitude strengthen and launch the next major development, counting. Counting makes it possible to distinguish between larger, nearly comparable quantities—say, between collections of eight versus nine objects (Lipton & Spelke, 2005). Children in Western cultures typically begin counting before their third birthday, and many 2- to 4-year-olds can count to 10 (S. Carey, Shusterman, Haward, & Distefano, 2017; Ginsburg, Cannon, Eisenband, & Pappas, 2006; Manfra, Dinehart, & Sembiante, 2014). Children first recall numbers by rote, without seeing connections to quantity (Geary, 2006; H. N. Nguyen, Laski, Thomson, Bronson, & Casey, 2017; Wynn, 1990). As a result, they may say two successive numbers (e.g., " . . . three, four . . . ") while pointing to a single object and so count it twice. By the time they are age 4 or 5, most children have mastered the essential principles of counting:

- *One-to-one principle.* Each object in the set being counted must be assigned one and only one number word. You would say "one" while pointing to one object, "two" while pointing to another object, and so on until every object has been counted exactly once.
- *Cardinal principle.* The last number word counted indicates the number of objects in the set. In other words, if you count from one to five when counting items, then there are five items in the set.

- *Order-irrelevance principle.* A set of objects has the same number regardless of the order in which individual objects are counted.

(Bryant & Nuñes, 2011; Gallistel & Gelman, 1992; S. Griffin, 2009; H. N. Nguyen et al., 2017; Sarnecka & Wright, 2013)

Initially children apply these principles primarily to small number sets (e.g., of 10 or fewer items), but within a few years they relate them to larger sets as well. As children work with two- and three-digit written numbers in the elementary grades, they increasingly master the correct sequence of numbers well into the hundreds (Case & Okamoto, 1996; W. Chan, Au, & Tang, 2014). Practice in counting with objects is an educationally worthwhile activity for children in preschool and kindergarten, with older students who have not yet had much practice in counting, and with children with disabilities that diminish their comprehension of numerical patterns (W. Chan et al., 2014; Jimenez & Kemmery, 2013; H. N. Nguyen et al., 2017). It takes time for them to gain an appreciation for the scale of large numbers, such as the populations of major cities, bacterial tallies in a petri dish, and distances between galaxies.

Mathematical Concepts

As children gain experience in counting objects, they develop a feeling for numbers. Early in the elementary years, they are receptive to learning the *part–whole principle*, the idea that any single number can be broken into two or more smaller numbers. For instance, 7 can be broken into 1, 2, and 4, or it can be seven 1s, a 3 and 4, and so on. The part–whole principle is central to children's understanding of addition and subtraction (Baroody, Tiilikainen, & Tai, 2006; Z. Cheng, 2012; Sophian & Vong, 1995). Children are receptive to this notion and fairly quickly act on it when dividing up sets.

Children gain other insights into numbers as they count, add, and subtract. For example, children initially come to believe the following:

- The smallest number is either 0 or 1.
- Numbers always become larger as they move away from zero.
- Addition to a number makes it larger.
- Subtraction from a number makes it smaller.

These principles apply to positive whole numbers but not to fractions, decimals, and negative numbers (Bofferding, 2014; Vosniadou & Brewer, 1992). Many children do not grasp this distinction; for them, every number is a whole number. Until well into their school years, children are confused by a fraction multiplying a whole number and yielding a smaller number (e.g., $\frac{1}{2} \times 50 = 25$). Reasoning about a *proportion*, the relative part of a whole, a notion reflected in fractions, ratios, and decimals, emerges gradually. As early as 6 months of age, infants show awareness of proportions—for instance, in distinguishing visual displays reflecting 2-to-1 and 4-to-1 ratios and in noticing a difference between containers that are $\frac{1}{4}$ and $\frac{3}{4}$ full of liquid (Denison & Xu, 2014; Jeong, Levine, & Huttenlocher, 2007; McCrink & Wynn, 2007). By about age 3 children can distinguish smaller and larger proportions in fractions of circles. In the early elementary grades children can understand simple, specific fractions (e.g., $\frac{1}{2}$ or $\frac{1}{3}$) if they can relate these portions to everyday objects (Empson, 1999; M. B. Wood, Olson, Freiberg, & Vega, 2013).

MyLab Education
Video Example 10.5
Find Developmental Meaning *How does the teacher facilitate students' understanding of proportions?* The teacher uses several strategies to make a lesson on proportions meaningful, including by reminding them of what they already know and walking through a series of fractions equivalent to $\frac{1}{4}$.

Even with a receptivity to the relative sizes of parts in a whole, students struggle with complex fractions and proportions until well into adolescence (Malone & Fuchs, 2017; Modestou & Gagatsis, 2010; Van Dooren, De Bock, Hessels, Janssens, & Verschaffel, 2005). Part of the problem is that they regularly misapply their knowledge of whole numbers (Ni & Zhou, 2005). For example, because 4 is greater than 3, students are apt to conclude that $\frac{1}{4}$ is greater than $\frac{1}{3}$. And because 256 is greater than 7, they are apt to think that 0.256 must be greater than 0.7. Instruction is instrumental to overcoming these conceptual barriers.

As children progress through school, they encounter additional challenging concepts. Middle school and high school math classes increasingly focus on abstract concepts, such as *pi* (π), *irrational numbers*, and *variable*. Mathematical principles, such as *the product of two negative numbers is a positive number* and *the angles of a triangle always have a total of 180°*, also are abstract. Given that such concepts are intangible, formal instruction with numerous examples is typically necessary (Chazan, Brantlinger, Clark, & Edwards, 2013; Geary, 1994; R. S. Nickerson, 2010).

Mathematical Operations

Mathematical procedures are learned hand in hand with relevant concepts. Two of the most basic operations are addition and subtraction. Infants have a preliminary understanding of these processes well before their first birthday (Christodoulou, Lac, & Moore, 2017; Slater, Bremner, Johnson, & Hayes, 2011; Wynn, 1992). Imagine that two Mickey Mouse dolls are placed on a table in front of you. An experimenter lowers a screen to block your view of the dolls, and then you watch the experimenter take one of the dolls from behind the screen and put it away. You assume that only one doll remains on the table, but as the screen is raised, you still see *two* dolls there. Even 5-month-olds show surprise at this outcome, indicating an awareness that something isn't as it should be.

By $2\frac{1}{2}$ or 3 years of age, children understand that adding objects to a set increases quantity and that subtracting objects decreases quantity (J. Huttenlocher, Jordan, & Levine, 1994). By age 3 or 4, many begin to apply their knowledge of counting to simple addition and subtraction problems, often using procedures that they develop on their own (Andres & Pesenti, 2015; Lafay, Thevenot, Castel, & Fayol, 2013; Siegler & Jenkins, 1989). Consider the problem *If I have 2 apples and you give me 3 more apples, how many apples do I have altogether?* A child might put up two fingers and then three more fingers and count all the fingers to reach the solution, "5 apples." Children also encounter simple division problems in the preschool years (e.g., when they must share food or toys with others), and even some 3-year-olds use counting to divide quantities equitably (K. Miller, 1989).

Somewhat later, children begin to use a *min* strategy in addition, in which they start with the larger of the two numbers (for the apple problem, they would start with 3) and then add on, one by one, the smaller number (e.g., counting "three apples . . . then four, five . . . five apples altogether"; Siegler & Jenkins, 1989). They might do something similar for subtraction, starting with the original number of objects and then counting down the number of objects removed: "Five . . . then four, three . . . three apples left." Children increasingly rely on memory of basic addition and subtraction facts (e.g., $2 + 3 = 5, 5 - 3 = 2$) and, with this advancement, depend less on fingers (Geary, Hoard, & Nugent, 2012; Siegler & Jenkins, 1989). Until children commit basic calculations to memory, higher mathematics is likely to elude them (S. Hopkins & Bayliss, 2017).

In North America, formal instruction in multiplication usually begins in first or second grade, when children try a mixture of strategies (J. B. Cooney & Ladd, 1992; Geary, 2006). When working with small numbers, they may simply use addition (e.g., solving '$3 \times 3 = ?$' by adding $3 + 3$ and then adding another 3 to the sum). Sometimes they count by twos, fives, or some other number (e.g., solving '$5 \times 4 = ?$' by counting "5, 10, 15, 20"). At other times they apply certain rules, such as *anything times zero is zero* or *anything times 1 is itself*. For most children, retrieval of basic multiplication facts slowly replaces strategies and rule-based derivations (D. H. Bailey, Littlefield, & Geary, 2012; J. B. Cooney, Swanson, & Ladd, 1988; De Brauwer & Fias, 2009).

Division is acquired slowly. As children tackle division problems, they often rely on their knowledge of other arithmetic facts, especially multiplication facts (e.g., if $5 \times 4 = 20$, then $20 \div 5 = 4$; Geary, 1994). With formal instruction and practice, processes become more accurate and efficient. Retrieval is not always possible with more complicated division problems (e.g., $1611 \div 3$), making it necessary for most children to divide numbers with pencil and paper in hand (Hickendorff, van Putten, Verhelst, & Heiser, 2010).

Integrated Competencies in Mathematics

Consider the question: Is 250 or 2,500 a better estimate of 51×49? If you apply your elementary school mathematics, you remember that in multiplying two 2-digit whole numbers you derive a number that has four digits. If you estimated the answer and did the actual calculations, you applied your understanding in, and skill with, multiplication. The answer is 2,499, making 2,500 the far better estimate. So far, we've described mathematical concepts and procedures separately, yet the two capacities are clearly intertwined (Rittle-Johnson, 2017).

26
+47
613

603
-305
208

MyLab Education
Artifact Example 10.4

Find Developmental Meaning *What kinds of procedures did the children seem to use in solving these two problems?* The child who solved the addition problem on the left simply put the sums of 6 + 7 (13) and 2 + 4 (6) side by side at the bottom. The child who solved the subtraction problem on the right apparently knew that borrowing was necessary to perform the subtraction in the ones column. Finding only a zero in the tens column, she instead borrowed "10" from the hundreds column. Thus, she subtracted 13 − 5 in the ones column and 5 − 3 in the hundreds column.

An underlying connection between concept and procedure exists with *place value*. When children encounter arithmetic problems involving two-digit or larger numbers, and especially when the problems involve "carrying" or "borrowing" across columns, they must apply knowledge of place value. The idea that digits reflect different quantities depending on column (whether they are in the ones column, tens column, and so on) is fairly abstract and one that many elementary school children struggle to understand (Byrge, Smith, & Mix, 2014; Fuson & Kwon, 1992). Certain activities contribute to children's understanding of place value, for example, counting the number of items in a collection, comparing amounts before and after something has been added or subtracted, and distinguishing place in two-digit numbers in worksheet problems; (Bofferding, 2014; Case & Okamoto, 1996; Case, Okamoto, Henderson, & McKeough, 1993; S. Griffin, 2009; S. Griffin, Case, & Siegler, 1994; Siegler & Lortie-Forgues, 2014). When children misunderstand this concept, they are apt to make errors in problems that require carrying or borrowing. In Artifact Example 10.4, you can see mistakes made by two children who retrieve basic math facts but make errors in carrying and borrowing procedures. Such mistakes are less frequent when children not only know *how* to carry and borrow but also know *why* carrying and borrowing are necessary.

Another important example of intertwining ideas and procedures is the *mental number line*. Children's image of numbers from low to high is a mental capacity that contributes to success in adding, subtracting, and comparing numbers (S. Griffin & Case, 1997). The multifaceted mental number line develops over a decade, with these interim milestones:

- As we explained previously, non-symbolic estimates of magnitude emerge in the first year of life. A toddler who likes fish-shaped crackers is likely to prefer the pile with 7 crackers over a nearby pile with only 3.
- Young children first say a few numbers they have heard (e.g., "Two!") and then recite numbers in ascendant order, as early efforts to count.
- Four-year-olds understand the difference between "a little" and "a lot" and recognize that adding objects to a collection leads to a higher number of total items and subtracting leads to fewer. They accurately count a small set of objects using the cardinal principle. Yet they cannot easily answer the question, "Which is more, five or six?" probably because getting to the answer exceeds their ability to juggle both counting and making a more-versus-less comparison.
- At age 6, children now have an elaborate mental number that facilitates their addition, subtraction, and comparisons of quantities. Children commonly can now do the following:
    - Understand and say the verbal numbers "one," "two," "three," and so on
    - Recognize the written numerals 1, 2, 3, etc.
    - Systematically count objects, saying each consecutive number as they touch or mentally tag the successive object in a group
    - Answer simple "Which is more?" questions
    - Use their fingers to represent small quantities (e.g., three fingers equal three objects)
    - Equate movement toward higher numbers with such concepts as "a lot," "more," and "bigger" and movement toward lower numbers with descriptions of "a little," "less," and "smaller"
    - Understand that movement from one number to the next is equivalent to either adding to the set or subtracting from it, depending on the direction of movement
- At age 8, children begin using two mental number lines simultaneously to solve mathematical problems. They can now answer such questions as "Which number is bigger, 32 or 28?" and "Which number is closer to 25, 21 or 18?" Such questions

require them to compare digits in the ones and tens columns in separate number lines. Many have an understanding of operations that require transformations across columns, such as "carrying 1" to the 10s column during addition or "borrowing 1" from the 10s column during subtraction.

- At age 10, children generalize relationships between two number lines to the entire number system. They now understand how the various columns (ones, tens, hundreds, etc.) relate to one another and can move back and forth among the columns. They can also answer such questions as "Which number is bigger, the difference between 29 and 13 or the difference between 25 and 8?" You can see how a child of this age might make this comparison in Figure 10.2.
- By the time students reach middle school, most are proficient in solving simple arithmetic problems with whole numbers. They now encounter a curriculum filled with proportions, negative numbers, square roots, exponents (e.g., -23, $\sqrt{18}$, 4^3), and unknown variables (e.g., x, y). Thus, students must shift their conception of a number line with whole numbers into a continuous and infinite line, inclusive of fractions, decimals, and negative numbers.

(Carr, 2012; Case & Okamoto, 1996; Case et al., 1993; Dehaene, 1997; S. Griffin, 2009; S. Griffin et al., 1994; Y. Liu, 2017)

FIGURE 10.2 Which number is bigger, **29 − 13 or 25 − 8?**

In this problem, children need to solve the two subtraction problems separately (top and middle number lines) and then compare the answers (bottom one). Facility with mental number lines is especially helpful as the numbers being compared become larger and the calculations more complex. (The two subtraction problems yield answers of 16 and 17, respectively, which means the second equation yields the larger number.)

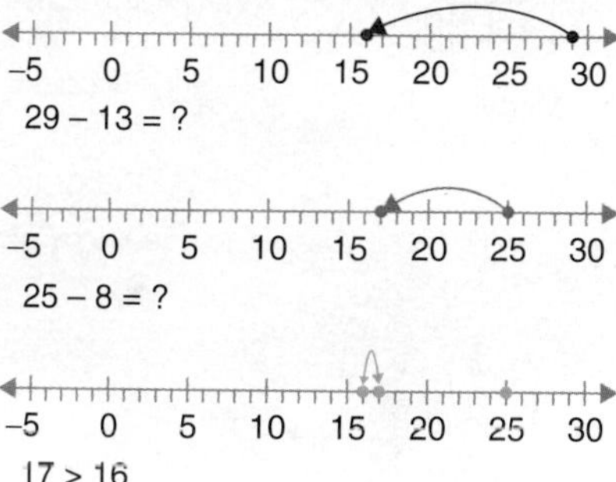

As young people move from arithmetic to advanced algebra, trigonometry, calculus, and statistics, they encounter concepts and procedures that transcend the mental number line. When they *cannot* make sense of mathematical procedures—perhaps because they haven't yet mastered the abstract concepts on which the procedures are based, or perhaps because no one has shown them why certain mathematical transformations are warranted and logical—they are apt to use the procedures incorrectly and fail to envision real-world applications. For example, some students who are not familiar with linear equations focus on finding a single value for x, even though the formula is intended to identify slope and intercept (Carr, 2012). Plugging in one value for x misrepresents the pattern in a scattering of values for paired variables, such as height and weight, in a data set.

One final type of integrated expertise is important to mention. Children's *metacognition* of mathematics refers to their awareness about how they think about mathematics and their proficiency in checking the accuracy and sensibility of mathematical calculations. Not only do youngsters need to understand the meaning of arithmetic calculations and advanced procedures, they need to plan, monitor, and assess their problem-solving efforts. Metacognitive oversight includes setting goals for a problem-solving task, monitoring the effectiveness of problem-solving strategies, and evaluating a final solution to determine whether it's a logical one (Cardelle-Elawar, 1992; Desoete, 2009; L. S. Fuchs et al., 2003). Only a child who reflects on his or her problem-solving efforts will recognize that a sum of 613 is *not* a reasonable answer to the problem $26 + 47 = ?$.

Mathematics in a Developmental System

Virtually all children are born with the capacity to detect variations in quantity. Yet youngsters differ considerably in the ways they go about learning mathematics, the specific purposes that they see mathematics being used around them, and the kind of instruction they receive at home and school.

Gender differences in mathematics exist but are small. Some researchers find a slight advantage for one gender or the other depending on the age-group, cultural setting, and task in question (Else-Quest, Hyde, & Linn, 2010; A. M. Gallagher & Kaufman, 2005). However, boys show greater *variability* in math. More boys than girls have exceptionally high mathematical ability, especially in high school, and more boys than girls have significant disabilities in this subject (Bergold, Wendt, Kasper, & Steinmayr, 2017; Forgasz & Hill, 2013; Halpern et al., 2007; Reigosa-Crespo et al., 2012). The prevalence of adolescent males at the upper end of the math-ability continuum may be partly due to biology and, in particular, to sex-related hormones (e.g., testosterone) that differentially affect brain development before and after puberty (Halpern, 1992; Hegarty & Kozhevnikov, 1999; Lippa, 2002). One specific area in which hormones come into

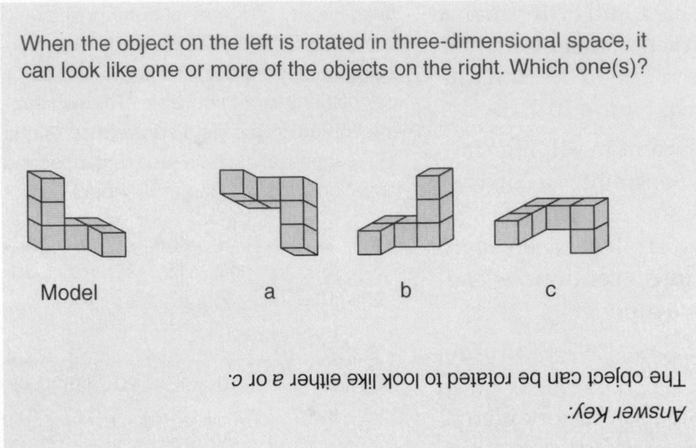

When the object on the left is rotated in three-dimensional space, it can look like one or more of the objects on the right. Which one(s)?
Model
a
b
c
Answer Key:
The object can be rotated to look like either a or c.

FIGURE 10.3 Example of a task requiring visual-spatial ability.

To perform well on this kind of task, children need to be able to rotate the figures mentally and identify the orientations among their parts.

Task modeled after Shepard and Metzler (1971).

play is in **visual-spatial ability**, the capacity to imagine and mentally manipulate two- and three-dimensional figures (see Figure 10.3). On average, boys and men perform better than girls and women on such measures, which gives them an advantage in certain mathematical tasks (Bakhiet & Lynn, 2015; Bull, Cleland, & Mitchell, 2013; Halpern et al., 2007; Hoppe et al., 2012).

Yet environmental factors also play a part in gender differences in mathematics. In many Western societies, mathematics has historically been viewed as a "male" domain. Some parents and teachers absorb this stereotype and expect boys to do better than girls in mathematics and offer them more encouragement (Bleeker & Jacobs, 2004; Espinoza, Arêas da Luz Fontes, & Arms-Chavez, 2014; Robinson-Cimpian, Lubienski, Ganley, & Copur-Gencturk, 2014; Tiedemann, 2000). Perhaps partly as a result of preferential treatment, boys tend to express greater confidence about their mathematical ability, even when actual achievement levels for the two genders are similar, with this difference emerging as early as first grade (Lindberg, Linkersdörfer, Ehm, Hasselhorn, & Lonnemann, 2013; Vermeer, Boekaerts, & Seegers, 2000).

Cultural practices and resources also affect learning in mathematics. For instance, 10- to 12-year-old candy sellers in Brazil are able to solve arithmetic and ratio problems with large numerical values, presumably due to their many experiences in calculating change and determining profits and losses in the marketplace (Saxe, 1988). Cultural practices in schools also affect mathematical competencies. Asian teachers are apt to provide thorough explanations of mathematical concepts, focus classroom discussions on making sense of problem-solving procedures, portray mathematics coherently, and assign a lot of math homework (Cai, Ding, & Wang, 2014; Schleppenbach, Perry, Miller, Sims, & Fang, 2007; J. Wang & Lin, 2005).

Curiously, even the terminology for numbers in a native language can influence mathematical development. Many theorists speculate that the structure of number words in Asian languages (Chinese, Japanese, Korean) facilitates children's mathematical development (Fuson & Kwon, 1992; K. F. Miller, Smith, Zhu, & Zhang, 1995; Miura & Okamoto, 2003). In these languages the base-10 number system is reflected in number words. The word for 11 is literally "ten-one," the word for 12 is "ten-two," and the word for 21 is "two-ten-one." Words for fractions reflect what a fraction *is*. For example, the word for $\frac{1}{4}$ is literally "of four parts, one." In contrast, English has many number words (e.g., *eleven, twelve, thirteen, twenty, thirty, one-half, one-fourth*) that don't reveal much about number structure.

Some children grasp challenging mathematics principles in a seemingly effortless fashion. A few children have learning disabilities that impede understanding of number concepts, automaticity of math facts, and quick arithmetic problem-solving. In an extreme form, these disabilities are known as **dyscalculia** (R. Cowan & Powell, 2014; N. C. Jordan, Hanich, & Kaplan, 2003; Monei & Pedro, 2017; Reigosa-Crespo et al., 2012). Dyscalculia is present in children who struggle to learn basic arithmetic and prefer to use finger counting of small numbers well into middle childhood. For most individuals with serious delays in mathematics, their condition is probably at least partly neurologically based. Interventions that incorporate extra practice with calculations and strategies in solving mathematical problems can provide children with dyscalculia valuable fortification to their fragile mathematical knowledge (Monei & Pedro, 2017).

With well-designed education, children around the world evolve from intuitive observers of simple mathematical patterns into disciplined thinkers who adeptly handle abstract mathematical relations. The Developmental Trends table "Mathematics at Different Age Levels" characterizes some of the benchmarks seen in infants, children, and adolescents.

DEVELOPMENTAL TRENDS
Mathematics at Different Age Levels

AGE	WHAT YOU MIGHT OBSERVE	DIVERSITY	IMPLICATIONS
Infancy (Birth–2 Years)	• An awareness that adding or subtracting something affects quantity (appearing at around 5 months) • Rudimentary ability to discriminate among different proportions (by 6 months) • Discrimination between changing states with increases versus decreases in total amount	• Some toddlers are familiar with small-number words (e.g., *two, three*) after parents use the words with them. • Children with visual impairments may have fewer chances to make more-versus-less comparisons. • Some families count objects in front of toddlers, talk about shapes, and point out different sizes and patterns in objects.	• Use small-number words (e.g., *two, three*) when talking with infants and doing so makes sense in the interaction. • Provide age-appropriate toys that encourage children to focus on size or quantity (e.g., nesting cups, stacking blocks). • Count objects in front of toddlers and use comparative words for size (e.g., *small* and *big*).
Early Childhood (2–6 Years)	• Conscious understandings that adding objects results in an increase and removing objects results in a decrease (by age $2\frac{1}{2}$ or 3) • Initial attempts at counting (at around age 3) • Increasing ability to count correctly (perhaps to 50 by age 5) • Emergence of self-constructed strategies for addition and subtraction (e.g., using fingers to count) • Some familiarity with division in everyday sharing tasks	• On average, children from middle-income families begin counting earlier than peers from low-income families. • Some children have daily experiences with blocks and other materials that exercise spatial skills. • On average, Chinese children count at a younger age than children whose native language is English. Transparent Chinese number words contribute to the advantage. • Young children receive varied encouragement to count, estimate, and do simple arithmetic.	• Occasionally ask mathematical questions (e.g., "How many are there?" "Where's the triangle?"). • In storybook reading sessions, occasionally read books with counting activities. • Use manipulatives (e.g., popsicle sticks) to facilitate counting and simple addition and subtraction. • Count steps, leaves, apple slices, and other common actions and objects. • Introduce a number line in your classroom, referring occasionally to its utility during arithmetic.
Middle Childhood (6–10 Years)	• Increasing ability to count correctly into the hundreds and beyond • Acquisition of more efficient addition and subtraction strategies, including retrieval of number facts • Increasing mastery of multiplication and division strategies • Growing understanding of place value and its relevance to carrying and borrowing • Some understanding of simple fractions • Basic ability to solve word problems	• Some 8-year-olds have simple additions and subtractions committed to memory whereas others count on fingers. • Children who speak certain Asian languages generally master multi-digit addition and subtraction earlier than English-speaking children. • Some children are confused when multiplying fractions and decimals, expecting that multiplication always generates larger numbers. • Some children dislike math after having been frustrated when trying to understand it.	• Help children understand the logic underlying basic mathematical procedures (e.g., show the relevance of the concept of *place value* in carrying and borrowing). • Provide frequent practice in basic arithmetic as a way of promoting automaticity. • Use number lines as a way of helping children understand how numbers of various kinds relate to one another. • Have low-achieving fourth and fifth graders tutor first and second graders in basic arithmetic skills.
Early Adolescence (10–14 Years)	• Increasing ability to understand abstract concepts (e.g., π, *variable*) • Growing understanding of and facility with proportions • Some naive beliefs about mathematics (e.g., that it involves memorizing procedures without necessarily understanding them)	• Young adolescents who have not yet automatized basic arithmetic facts struggle with challenging mathematical problems. • Some adolescents overgeneralize features of whole numbers to fractions and decimals. • Adolescents vary in their comprehension of abstract mathematical concepts.	• Conduct small-group activities in which students compare and explain personal approaches to solving a problem. • Teach metacognitive strategies for solving problems (e.g., identify the goal to be achieved, break a complex problem into smaller steps, consider whether the solution is reasonable).
Late Adolescence (14–18 Years)	• Increasing facility with abstract concepts and principles (e.g., unknowns such as x and y) • Difficulty translating word problems into algebraic expressions • Tendency for teens to memorize and carelessly apply mathematical procedures, rather than reflecting on what makes sense	• Individual differences in abilities increase during high school, due to "tracking" according to students' past achievement and the prevalence of elective mathematics courses. • Students who are struggling in mathematics may need tutoring to meet graduation requirements. • On average, girls are less confident than boys in mathematical ability even when achieving as well as or better than boys.	• Ask teenagers to apply their math skills to real-life contexts and problems. • Allow teens to use calculators with complex mathematical operations so as to allow for sufficient working memory capacity across the entire problem-solving effort. • Minimize competition for high grades (this strategy is especially important for girls). • Provide tutoring when necessary.

Sources: C. Björklund (2014); Brannon (2002); Bull and Lee (2014); Byrge et al. (2014); B. M. Byrne and Shavelson (1986); Cardelle-Elawar (1992); Carr and Biddlecomb (1998); Case and Okamoto (1996); J. B. Cooney and Ladd (1992); Davenport et al. (1998); De Corte, Greer, and Verschaffel (1996); Eccles, Freedman-Doan, Frome, Jacobs, and Yoon (2000); Empson (1999); Fuson and Kwon (1992); Gallistel and Gelman (1992); Geary (2006); Ginsburg et al. (2006); Greeno, Collins, and Resnick (1996); C. S. Ho and Fuson (1998); Klibanoff, Levine, Huttenlocher, Vasilyeva, and Hedges (2006); Krasa and Shunkwiler (2009); McCrink and Wynn (2004); K. Miller (1989); Schoenfeld (1988); Sedaghatjou and Campbell (2017); Siegler and Jenkins (1989); Trawick-Smith et al. (2017); Van Dooren et al. (2005); Wynn (1990); F. Xu and Spelke (2000); and Zamarian, Ischebeck, and Delazer (2009).

Promoting Advancements in Mathematics

Mathematical tools, many of which must be taught, help children make sense of numerical patterns. We offer the following suggestions for teachers to help children advance mathematically:

- **Teach preschool and kindergarten children to count and recognize numbers.** Adults can arrange activities involving counting, comparing quantities, adding, and subtracting, especially for children who face delays or have not had relevant experiences at home (Bird, 2009; Ginsburg, Lee, & Boyd, 2008). In preschool, children can count small blocks, steps on stairs, apple slices on the table, and the like. In kindergarten, children can count and compare numbers in board games and other structured tasks (Laski & Siegler, 2014).

- **Use objects and visual displays to illustrate mathematical concepts.** Beans, blocks, Cuisenaire rods, little plastic bears, and toothpicks bundled in groups of 10 can help children grasp the nature of addition, subtraction, place value, and fractions (C. Björklund, 2014; Fujimura, 2001; Fuson & Briars, 1990). Visual aids such as number lines, pictures of pizzas depicting fractions, and rudimentary line graphs can be instructive in the early elementary grades, and diagrams of geometric figures and more sophisticated graphs can facilitate understanding in secondary students (J. L. Schwartz, Yarushalmy, & Wilson, 1993; Steenpaß & Steinbring, 2014). In advanced mathematics, teachers can explain how concepts are relevant in physics, engineering, and computer science and show graphs with rates of change. A thorough explanation of the underlying relationships is usually necessary to make the concepts transparent.

- **Encourage visual-spatial thinking.** Although boys may have a slight advantage in visual-spatial thinking, structured experiences that *encourage* such representations can bring girls up to speed (Nuttall, Casey, & Pezaris, 2005; Sprafkin, Serbin, Denier, & Connor, 1983; Wilhelm, Jackson, Sullivan, & Wilhelm, 2013). In the preschool and early elementary grades, such experiences might involve blocks, Legos, puzzles, simple graphs, and basic measurement tools. As children move into the middle elementary grades and beyond, visual-spatial tasks might include analysis of complex graphs and three-dimensional geometry (Nuttall et al., 2005; Sandamas, Foreman, & Coulson, 2009; von Károlyi, 2013).

- **Guide children through steps to finding a solution.** Complex mathematical tasks put a strain on the child's working memory, concentration, and ability to shift strategies flexibly (Bull & Lee, 2014; H. L. Swanson, Jerman, & Zheng, 2008). A variety of tools are available to ease the burden. For children in the early elementary grades, tools include manipulatives and pencil and paper for keeping track of quantities, calculations, and other information. Once children have mastered basic mathematical facts and understand the logic behind arithmetic operations, they might use calculators or computers while working with large data sets (Horowitz, Darling-Hammond, & Bransford, 2005). Cognitive scaffolds are valuable as well. A teacher might encourage students to brainstorm possible approaches to problems, model problem-solving strategies, and teach techniques for checking progress (Calin-Jageman & Ratner, 2005; W. Chen, Rovegno, Cone, & Cone, 2012).

- **Supplement teacher-led lessons and hands-on activities with interactive technologies.** Several features of mathematics make it an appealing subject to reinforce with educational technology: Practice is essential at all levels of expertise, mathematical concepts can be portrayed with visual charts and demonstrations, concepts must be learned in a prescribed order, and individual differences of children's achievement are sizable. An increasing number of well-designed computer programs address these features with individualized instruction based on diagnostic assessments (A. Cheung & Slavin, 2013).

- **Foster metacognition in mathematics.** Adults can foster a strategic approach by verbalizing their own thoughts when solving a mathematical dilemma ("Hmm, one way I can solve this problem is to . . . "). They can also engage children in conversations about how they are approaching a mathematical problem, which features are relevant to calculations, and how they know the answer makes sense (Cornoldi, Carretti, Drusi, & Tencati, 2015). Errors can become a source of self-reflection so that children learn from their mistakes and from one another, especially when they get stuck (Bonnett, Yuill, & Carr, 2017).

- **Encourage children to invent, use, and defend their strategies.** As you have seen, young children often invent approaches (e.g., the *min* strategy) for adding and subtracting objects well before they have formal instruction in addition and subtraction. Rather than ignore methods children have developed on their own, teachers can encourage those that help them, even the primitive ones. As children acquire more efficient strategies over time, they gradually abandon the simpler ones (Geary, 1994; Siegler, 1989). Also beneficial is asking children to explain why they solved a problem as they did (Carr & Biddlecomb, 1998; Rittle-Johnson, 2006). You can see Noah's explanations as to how he solved a subtraction problem in Artifact Example 10.5.

- **Arrange for young people to use mathematical tools to the benefit of their community.** A few students enjoy the pure elegance of mathematical patterns, but many find mathematical endeavors to be motivating only when they see them in use. In fact, many students find mathematics appealing when they can integrate data into reports that serve the public good. Children can be asked to chart survey responses, measure water quality, and do other things that better conditions for people, animals, or the environment. These activities may be particularly motivating for students with backgrounds typically underrepresented in scientific, mathematical, and engineering fields (Bystydzienski & Brown, 2012; D. Cross et al., 2012).

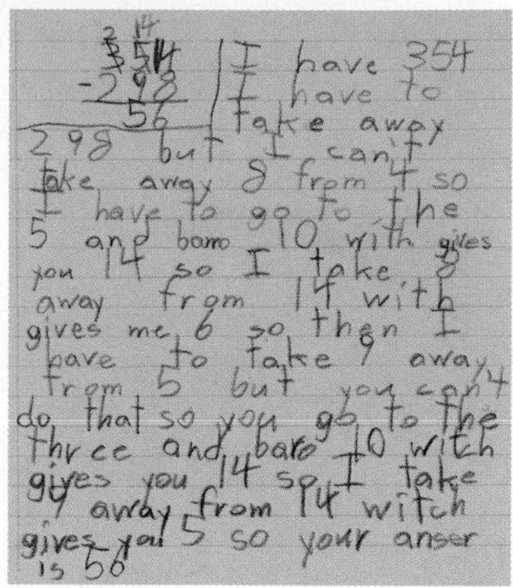

MyLab Education

Artifact Example 10.5

Find Developmental Meaning *How did Noah solve the subtraction problem, 354 – 298?* Noah applied a working knowledge of place value when solving the problem.

Children's Emerging Scientific Ideas

Scientists follow defined steps to discover the properties of nature. They formulate questions, separate and control variables, test hypotheses, make observations, and think through why certain results are obtained. With disciplined adherence to these procedures, scientists identify and explain what they observe. For children, learning about science involves being mentored into scientific reasoning and the laws it uncovers.

Of course, children approach the study of science with observations of their own. In examining children's scientific knowledge, many developmental scholars take a *theory theory* approach, in which children are presumed to construct (rather than absorb) ideas about physics, biology, and psychology (C. Cook, Goodman, & Schulz, 2011; Gopnik & Meltzoff, 1997). These intuitive understandings appear early in life and change systematically as children encounter new information. Expectations are shown by infants between 2 and 5 months when they show surprise by objects violating the laws of physics, rigged by the tricks of experimenters. These studies reveal infants' assumptions that an object maintains its shape as it moves, that two objects cannot occupy the same space at the same time, and that one object influences another only when the two come into contact (Baillargeon, 2004; T. L. Hubbard, 2013; Spelke, 1994).

As children get older, they construct increasingly elaborate theories of physics. Many school-aged children view all physical phenomena either as actual substances (i.e., touchable "things" in specific locations) or as properties of those substances (e.g., being hot or cold; Reiner, Slotta, Chi, & Resnick, 2000). This **substance schema** can be quite useful in explaining everyday events (e.g., holding a ball, touching a stove). Yet children overgeneralize it to such phenomena as light, which scientists explain as a different type of matter (Megalakaki, 2008; Reiner et al., 2000).

Another idea that children acquire quite early is the concept of *gravity*. At 3 or 4 months of age, children have some understanding that objects fall down (never up) when there is nothing to support them (Baillargeon, 1994). This "downward" view of gravity works quite well on a small scale. But imagine the situation depicted in Figure 10.4. A rock is dropped at the equator, at the entrances to two tunnels that go through the earth. Tunnel A comes out at the equator on the opposite side of the earth. Tunnel B comes out at the South Pole. Into which tunnel will the rock fall? Many middle school students say that the rock will fall into Tunnel B, apparently thinking that gravity always pulls something "down." They respond in this way even if they have explicitly learned that gravity pulls objects toward the center of the earth (Pulos, 1997).

FIGURE 10.4 Which way?

If a rock is dropped into a hole near the equator, into which of the two tunnels will it fall?

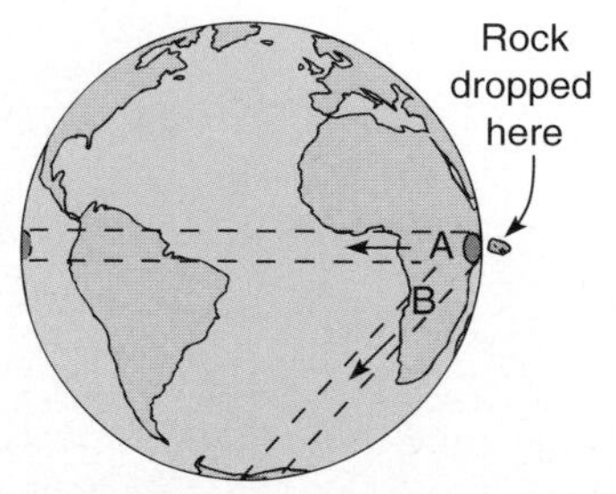

An important step in children's theory building is making a distinction between biological and nonbiological entities. By the time infants are 6 months old, most are aware that people and other animals move in ways that nonliving things do not. By age 3 or 4, children know that humans and other animals, but not nonliving objects, can move *themselves* and that living and nonliving entities change in different ways—living things grow, and nonliving things can increase in size, not by physiological processes (imagine a snowball or stream of water) (Jipson & Callanan, 2003; Massey & Gelman, 1988). At about age 4, children also realize that two living creatures in the same category, even if they look quite different, are apt to share characteristics—for instance, that a blackbird has more in common with a flamingo (because both are birds) than it does with a bat (S. A. Gelman & Markman, 1986). By the middle elementary school years, children understand that both plants and animals are defined largely by their genetic heritage and internal makeup—for instance, that round, reddish fruits that come from pear trees must be pears rather than apples.

Facilitating Conceptual Change in Science

Children undergo *conceptual change*, deliberate revision to their assumptions about a situation, when they encounter compelling evidence about the merits of a scientifically accurate explanation or another intellectually persuasive perspective. Conceptual change can be challenging because children invariably interpret new information from the perspective of what they already understand. Their receptivity to scientific descriptions depends in large part on their age, prior beliefs, and general experiences. Thus, methods in teaching science must be adapted to the needs of children at different grade levels.

In the preschool years, children need a wide berth in exploring the sensory world. They learn from watching water pouring through funnels, observing pets, looking at the moon and stars, and patting and mounding sand into hills and valleys. Teachers extend young children's scientific knowledge by providing age-appropriate materials, bringing nature into the classroom, inviting them to sort and classify objects, encouraging them to articulate their observations, and answering their innumerable questions (Moomaw, 2014).

As children encounter scientific concepts, they merge, and sometimes replace, their intuitive models with scientific concepts from school. What is needed in this transition is a lot of discussion, informal guidance, focused observations, and scientific themes integrated into lessons (National Science Teachers Association, 2014). Children might study light and shadows, plants, magnetism, animals, or the seasons over a several-week period, taking simple measurements and looking for patterns (Piasta, Pelatti, & Miller, 2014). Adults can guide the observations and interpretations that children make with systematic materials, forms for recording observations, discussions about evidence, and scientific explanations.

In the elementary school years, children continue to be curious about scientific matters, especially in the natural world. Living and nonliving things, first distinguished in infancy, are differentiated further. Living things are now seen to extend beyond animals to include plants; nonliving things refer to rocks, swing sets, imaginary friends, dead animals, and all sorts of other things (Carey, 1988; Opfer & Siegler, 2004). In the nonliving sphere, children enjoy learning about astronomy (e.g., phases of the moon, the structure of the earth, and energy in the sun), especially when teachers organize meaningful observations with flashlights, three-dimensional glasses, miniature solar systems, posters, and the like (Isik-Ercan, Zeynep Inan, Nowak, & Kim, 2014). Classification skills for both living and nonliving things are exercised regularly—from grouping similar birds by type of beak to distinguishing objects that are attracted to magnets from those that are not. Rudimentary reasoning about evidence is now possible (Elmesky, 2013).

In the secondary years, science becomes more detailed and technical. With the help of charts, pictures, microscopes, and other instruments, adolescents can learn about small structures, for example, cells, molecules, and atoms (Elmesky, 2013). With adequate explanations and supportive information, students can understand how complicated systems function (e.g., the circulatory system in the human body). A major challenge for secondary science teachers is protecting time to incorporate demonstrations, compare rival explanations, and generate reflection in students in the context of the enormous volume of facts that awaits them. In fact, students generally forget the scientific facts, laws, and summaries of theories they have studied unless given the chance to wrestle with relevant observations, data, and their implications for explanatory models (Akbas & Gençtürk, 2011; E. Kaya & Geban, 2012; Kuhn, 2011). Showing the relevance to current affairs can also be motivating. For example, climate change, reproductive technologies, and environmental toxins are regularly covered in the media and intrigue high school students, who may wish to study them in depth when given the chance (H. Morris, 2014).

Fostering Scientific Reasoning Skills

Even in the first year of life children are predisposed to identify cause-and-effect relationships in the world around them. But children's ability to think as scientists appears later, and then only gradually. **Scientific reasoning** encompasses a number of cognitive processes, including posing a question, planning an investigation, analyzing evidence, and drawing appropriate conclusions (Kuhn & Franklin, 2006; D. Mayer, Sodian, Koerber, & Schwippert, 2014). Common to the steps of the scientific method is a conscious intention to evaluate information critically.

Capacities to understand evidence, formulate hypotheses, and control variables emerge gradually over middle childhood and adolescence. Coming up with sound hypotheses depends on the ability to think abstractly because properties of nature are inferred from evidence rather than directly perceived. Critical thinking, when employed, enables students to entertain multiple explanations for what they see. Elementary school children often distinguish between experiments that do and do not control variables appropriately, yet they are apt to have trouble controlling variables in their *own* experiments—a task that requires them to keep track of several things simultaneously (Kuhn, Pease, & Wirkala, 2009; Metz, 2004). Thus, when learning about the germination of plant seeds, they might propose to compare two conditions, one on the windowsill with moderate light, daily water, and rich soil and the other in the closet, dark, dry, and placed in sand. The result may be predictable but constitutes a failure to anticipate rival explanations.

Although adolescents are more proficient than elementary school children in separating and controlling variables, they still have difficulty in identifying instrumental factors (Kuhn, Amsel, & O'Loughlin, 1988; Tsai, Chen, Chang, & Chang, 2013). They tend to test hypotheses they think are correct and ignore hypotheses that, in their minds, are *in*correct (Byrnes, 1996). Such *try-to-prove-what-I-already-believe* thinking reflects a *confirmation bias,* the tendency of people to favor information that is consistent with what they already believe. A confirmation bias appears not only when adolescents test hypotheses but also when they interpret data (Klaczynski, 2000; Kuhn et al., 1988; Kyza, 2009). In general, adolescents tend to overlook results that conflict with their favorite hypotheses and explain away unexpected results that they *cannot* ignore. For example, when students in a high school science laboratory observe results that contradict what they expected to happen, they might complain that "Our equipment isn't working right" or "I can never do science anyway" (Minstrell & Stimpson, 1996, p. 192).

Ultimately, students must discover that science is, like other disciplines, a dynamic body of ideas that evolve as new data come in. They must reflect on and critically evaluate their own beliefs. And, of course, they must be willing to change their views in the face of disconfirming evidence. Such understandings, abilities, and dispositions emerge gradually over childhood and adolescence (Gillies, Nichols, Burgh, & Haynes, 2014; Kuhn & Pearsall, 2000; Osterhaus, Koerber, & Sodian, 2017; C. Zimmerman, 2007). Giuliana, an eighth-grader, reveals beliefs about the evolving nature of scientific views:

> When the atom was discovered, it was considered the smallest particle, but now the quark's been discovered. What we believed before, now we don't believe anymore because the quark is smaller. Perhaps in fifty years' time an even smaller particle will turn up and then we'll be told that what we believed in before was false. It's really something to do with progress. (Mason, 2003, p. 223)

Youngsters' beliefs about science affect the approaches they take when they study. Students who believe that "knowing" science means understanding the relationships between concepts and evidence study more effectively than students who think that learning science means acquiring isolated facts (M. C. Linn, Songer, & Eylon, 1996; Yang & Tsai, 2010). Those who recognize that scientific theories inevitably change over time are more likely to evaluate theories (including their own) with a critical eye (Bereiter, 1994; M. C. Linn et al., 1996).

As you are learning, scientific development reflects transformations in reasoning skills, ideas about everyday phenomena, and reflections about scientific progress. The Developmental Trends table "Science at Different Age Levels" presents examples of the scientific skills that children of various ages are likely to exercise.

DEVELOPMENTAL TRENDS

Science at Different Age Levels

AGE	WHAT YOU MIGHT OBSERVE	DIVERSITY	IMPLICATIONS
Infancy (Birth–2 Years)	• Intuition of a few basic principles of physics (e.g., two objects cannot occupy the same space at the same time) • Emerging awareness that plants and animals are fundamentally different from nonliving things • Emerging ability to infer cause-and-effect relationships	• Infants differ in the number and diversity of opportunities to explore objects and surroundings. • Infants with sensory impairments (e.g., blindness, hearing loss) are limited in the scientific phenomena they can observe unless adults intervene with sensory-adapted materials.	• Put infants and toddlers in contexts in which they can safely explore and informally experiment with physical objects. • Let toddlers interact with small, gentle animals (e.g., rabbits, therapy dogs) under your close supervision.
Early Childhood (2–6 Years)	• Curiosity about the physical world, prompting them to make observations, tinker with objects, and ask questions of adults • Increasing differentiation between living and nonliving things (e.g., awareness that living things grow due to intrinsic physiological processes and nonliving things change with physical forces) • Increasing understanding that members of a biological category (e.g., *birds*) share characteristics despite differences in appearance	• Children in some cultures (e.g., Japanese children) are more likely to think of plants and nonliving objects as having "minds." • Children who grow up in inner-city environments may have little exposure to life cycles (e.g., calves being born, trees losing leaves in the fall and growing blossoms in the spring). • Some children develop intense interests in scientific and technological matters, such as dinosaurs or space travel.	• Read nonfiction picture books that depict wild and domesticated animals or other scientific topics of concern to children. • Take children to zoos, farms, arboretums, and other settings where they can see a variety of plants and animals. • Talk with children about natural phenomena, pointing out the physical properties of objects (e.g., some objects float and others sink). • Engage children in simple hands-on investigations of natural phenomena.
Middle Childhood (6–10 Years)	• Intuitive understanding that biological entities are defined by their genetic heritage and internal makeup • Tendency to think of all physical phenomena as having a physical and potentially touchable substance • Some ability to discriminate between valid and invalid tests of hypotheses but failure to control variables in own experiments	• Children differ in exposure to scientific concepts (e.g., through family visits to natural history museums and access to age-appropriate science books). • Some children view supernatural forces (e.g., God, the devil, witchcraft) as being responsible for natural disasters or illness. • Schools differ in how much and how well they teach elementary science.	• Have children conduct simple experiments with familiar materials; for example, have them raise sunflowers with varying amounts of light. • Obtain computer programs that let students "explore" human anatomy or "dissect" small animals in a virtual "laboratory." • Discuss scientific explanations for everyday observations. • Invite children to care for classroom pets.
Early Adolescence (10–14 Years)	• Occasional abstract thinking about scientific phenomena and separation and control of variables • Formulation and testing of hypotheses influenced by existing beliefs (confirmation bias) • Tendency to misapply scientific concepts (e.g., thinking that gravity pulls objects toward South Pole)	• Especially in adolescence, boys tend to have more positive attitudes toward science than do girls. Girls are more likely than boys to underestimate their scientific abilities. • Influences of religion on beliefs about natural phenomena (e.g., evolution) are noticeable in early adolescence.	• Have adolescents explore interests in science fair projects, scaffolding their efforts at forming hypotheses and controlling irrelevant variables. • Explain scientific data with charts and other concrete representations. • Ask students to collect and analyze data (e.g., water samples) from their community.

DEVELOPMENTAL TRENDS
Science at Different Age Levels (Continued)

AGE	WHAT YOU MIGHT OBSERVE	DIVERSITY	IMPLICATIONS
Late Adolescence (14–18 Years)	• Growing ability to understand abstract scientific concepts • Increasing skill in separating and controlling variables • Confirmation bias in experimentation and interpretation of results • Increasing awareness that science is a dynamic and changing discipline • Decline in interest in science unless students are allowed to pursue some of their own concerns	• On average, boys achieve at higher levels in the physical sciences, but the gender gap in science achievement has decreased in recent years. • Boys are more likely than girls to aspire to careers in science. • Cultures that place high value on honoring authority figures tend to promote belief that scientific findings should not be questioned unless disputed by religious doctrine.	• Accompany abstract explanations for scientific phenomena with diagrams, such as heat from molecules colliding being represented in a chart with balls and arrows. • Use scientific methods that permit students to make choices in topics • Emphasize utility of science for students' personal lives and the welfare of the community. • Arrange internships with scientists from diverse ethnic and cultural backgrounds.

Sources: Aldemir and Kermani (2017); Baillargeon (1994); Bandura, Barbaranelli, Caprara, and Pastorelli (2001); L. B. Cohen and Cashon (2006); E. M. Evans (2001); S. A. Gelman and Markman (1986); Halpern et al. (2007); Hatano and Inagaki (1996); Jipson and Callanan (2003); Klaczynski (2000); Kuhn et al. (2009); Larrain, Freire, and Howe (2014); Leaper and Friedman (2007); Lee-Pearce, Plowman, and Touchstone (1998); M. C. Linn and Muilenburg (1996); Massey and Gelman (1988); Metz (2004); Patall et al. (2017); Piasta, Pelatti, and Miller (2014); Pomerantz, Altermatt, and Saxon (2002); Pulos (1997); Qian and Pan (2002); Reiner et al. (2000); M. B. Rowe (1978); Schauble (1990); Spelke (1994); Stanovich, West, and Toplak (2012); Tamburrini (1982); Ullman (2010a); Vosniadou (1991); B. Y. White and Frederiksen (1998); and Wigfield et al. (1996).

Science Learning in a Developmental System

From a developmental systems perspective, children contribute to their own scientific knowledge by noticing patterns in the world and seeking out answers to things that perplex them. Some of the questions are affected by personal characteristics, including their interests, temperaments, abilities, and disabilities. Youngsters with sensory impairments have restricted firsthand experience with certain scientific phenomena unless adults supplement their exposure. For example, when a reference is made to the color of burning wood, a perceptive teacher might tell a child who is blind more about the appearance of wood on fire (M. B. Rowe, 1978).

As is true with mathematics, science-related fields, especially the physical sciences and engineering, have traditionally been regarded as "male" domains (Halpern et al., 2007; Marchand & Taasoobshirazi, 2013; Ullman, 2010a). Perhaps for this reason, boys tend to like science more than girls do, and they are more likely to aspire to careers in science (Bandura et al., 2001). On average, girls get higher grades in science than is the case for boys, but boys tend to come out slightly ahead on national science achievement tests, especially in the physical sciences (Halpern et al., 2007; Leaper & Friedman, 2007). Girls increase in their motivation in science under several conditions: being encouraged to invest their efforts, being exposed to women in scientific and technological fields, and taking classes that build on their concerns and interests (Pinkard, Erete, Martin, & de Royston, 2017; Ullman, 2010a).

Scientific topics learned in their families affect the child's interpretation of related views at school (Simpson & Parsons, 2008). Teachers can reach out to families to learn about their livelihoods, and when a community has shared knowledge about plants, animals, agriculture, a particular industry, mechanics, or construction, teachers can take the next step in adapting the curriculum to embrace and extend concepts with relevant scientific connections. In one school in Northern California, teachers invited children and parents who came from a predominantly Mien (Laotian) background to plant a garden and build a garden house at the school (Hammond, 2001). Families had extensive technological expertise from previous experiences in hunting, farming, preserving food, building houses, producing fabrics, forging metals, and creating elaborate jewelry. The Mien parents and children applied many of their indigenous abilities in planting the garden and building the house, creating a basis for discussion about scientific matters and motivating attendance at family science nights.

Cultural environments shape many beliefs about the biological and physical worlds. Japanese children are more likely than European American children to think of plants (e.g., a tree, a blade of grass) and certain nonliving objects as having a "mind" that thinks (M. Cole & Hatano, 2007; Hatano & Inagaki, 1996). Schools in China encourage respect for authority figures and downplay differences of opinion among experts. Possibly as a result, high school students in China are more likely than U.S. students to believe that science involves simple, undisputed facts rather than evolving perspectives and unresolved issues (Qian & Pan, 2002).

Religion comes into play for some youngsters as they develop ideas about the origins of life, the universe, and the ultimate causes of events. In the elementary grades, some children think that supernatural forces (e.g., God, the devil, witchcraft) are largely responsible for illness or natural disasters (O. Lee, 1999; Legare, Evans, Rosengren, & Harris, 2012). Young people's acceptance or rejection of Darwin's theory of evolution is closely connected to their religious positions about how human beings originated (E. M. Evans, 2001; Yasri & Mancy, 2014). Teachers should not challenge students' religious beliefs, but they can advise students about the compelling evidence related to scientific principles and theories (Hanley, Bennett, & Ratcliffe, 2014).

Educating Children in Science

In the first few years of life, children's science learning occurs through informal experiences. At this point, the best strategy is to provide objects and experiences—blocks, water tables, sand piles, field trips to farms and zoos, and so on—that help children acquire knowledge on which formal science instruction can later build. As we discussed previously, scaffolding with observations, classification of objects, and preliminary discussions about scientific concepts belong in early childhood.

Once children reach kindergarten or first grade, the curriculum addresses scientific topics overtly. At the elementary level, children learn that scientific knowledge is the outgrowth of disciplined inquiry. By having students engage in simple investigations from the very beginning of schooling, children gain experience with how scientists unravel mysteries in the world (Forsey, 2014; Khalid, 2010; Kuhn, 2007). As they proceed through elementary, middle, and high school, students ideally are given time to make observations, practice scientific skills, and update their understandings with new evidence, discussion, and exposure to formal scientific theories. Several instructional strategies facilitate scientific advancements:

- **Show children the relevance of science to what they already know.** Students are more likely to understand scientific concepts when teachers create a bridge between the formal curriculum and what they already understand. Depending on the age of students, teachers might ask children to draw pictures of concepts (e.g., on plant growth); talk about what they *know*, *want* to learn, and ultimately *learn (KWL)*; or write about the topic in a preassessment (Israel, Maynard, & Williamson, 2013).

- **Engage students in scientific investigations.** Preschool and kindergarten teachers can introduce children to the essence of scientific methods. Using reasonably familiar materials, such as rocks, rabbits, light, color, or objects that float, teachers can nurture young children's curiosity and help them make predictions about simple events, such as how long it will take for frog eggs to turn into adult frogs and what the different forms will look like during the lifecycle (Gerde, Schachter, & Wasik, 2013). As children advance through the grades, investigations become more structured. Unfortunately, many educational activities are little more than cookbook exercises. Ostensibly to simulate laboratory tests, teachers give students their objectives, materials, and instructions to follow step by step. Such lessons can help make scientific phenomena concrete yet can be weak in promoting conceptual change in students' ideas about scientific phenomena. Thus, laboratory activities by themselves are unlikely to foster scientific thinking processes (formulating and testing hypotheses, separating and controlling variables, and so on; Keil & Silberstein, 1996; M. J. Padilla, 1991; J. Singer, Marx, Krajcik, & Chambers, 2000). Discussions about gravity, photosynthesis, phases of the moon, or other concepts may be required such that students have a safe venue for articulating their ideas and having them challenged. Sometimes focused instruction with a series of explanations, hands-on lessons, diagrams, and readings must occur if students are to give up their ideas in favor of a scientific explanation.

To enhance the value of laboratory lessons, teachers should allow students to conduct experiments in which procedures and outcomes are not fully predetermined. For instance, teachers might ask students to address such questions as "Does one fast-food restaurant provide more meat in a hamburger than others?" or "Is the local drinking water really safe to drink?" (M. J. Padilla, 1991; J. Singer et al., 2000). Because youngsters typically need scaffolding for such activities, teachers may structure the various steps children should pursue during scientific inquiries. Examples include the following:

- Present situations in which only two or three variables need to be controlled.
- Provide guidance, hints, and feedback regarding the need to make observations objectively.
- Ask questions that encourage students to make predictions and critically analyze their observations (e.g., "What do you think will happen?" "What is your evidence?" "Do you see things that are inconsistent with what you predicted?"). (Byrnes, 1996; Carey, Evans, Honda, Jay, & Unger, 1989; Kuhn et al., 1988; Kuhn & Dean, 2005; Legaspi & Straits, 2011; Lorch et al., 2014; Minstrell & Stimpson, 1996; Thatch, 2008).

MyLab Education
Artifact Example 10.6

Find Developmental Meaning *How has 9-year-old Trisha's teacher guided her comprehension of cause-and-effect relationships?* By asking her to draw events in the water cycle, her teacher facilitates Trisha's understanding of its key processes.

• **Provide age-appropriate explanations for physical and biological phenomena.** Although youngsters can discover a great deal through experimentation, they also gain insights by studying the ideas, principles, and theories that scientists use to make sense of the world (Vygotsky, 1934/1986). Yet they need guidance in building mental frameworks of principles and causes in a scientific domain. Thus, teachers should not assume that their students are taking the bits and pieces they are learning and integrating them into conceptual models. To nudge children toward grasping scientific models, teachers often create visual models of relevant factors and their interrelationships. Scientifically accurate diagrams, flowcharts, and two- or three-dimensional models can help children make sense of trends (K. L. Cook, Bush, & Karp, 2016; Glynn, Yeany, & Britton, 1991a; Schwarz & White, 2005). Students themselves can draw pictures of causal forces, as you can see in 9-year-old Trisha's representation of the water cycle in Artifact Example 10.6.

• **Actively promote conceptual change.** Thanks to confirmation bias, youngsters are apt to seek out information that endorses, rather than contradicts, what they currently believe. Piquing students' interest about why the world works as it does sets the stage for conceptual change, as does inviting students to relax and speculate about alternative explanations (Hadjiachilleos, Valanides, & Angeli, 2013; Vosniadou & Mason, 2012). Perhaps one of the most effective approaches for facilitating conceptual change is to reason about competing perspectives within a classroom environment that communicates the message "It's okay to make errors and change our minds" (Minstrell & Stimpson, 1996; C. L. Smith, 2007; Vosniadou, 2009).

Several lessons may be needed when children resist compelling evidence suggesting that their beliefs are wrong. Take the example of young children's initial notion that the earth is a flat surface, not a solid sphere. Children live on an apparently level plane, so when first exposed to the notion that the earth is a round ball, they protect their prior belief by making subtle revisions of the earth being a hollow sphere with a flat surface inside or it being is a sphere with a flattened surface on its top (Vosniadou, 2009). It typically takes discussion and exposure to spherical models before children are able to accept the scientific view that the earth is a solid ball floating in space.

• **Ask students to write about scientific topics.** The journey from basic scientific knowledge to advanced expertise takes time. Assignments that require students to write up scientific reports with arguments for certain conclusions can help improve their scientific thinking. Sophisticated reasoning is challenging in any setting and all the more difficult while writing about ideas in science; therefore, it is necessary to give students many occasions to write, review exemplars of strong scientific reports, and get feedback on their drafts (Sampson, Enderle, Grooms, & Witte, 2013).

Summary

Children are attentive to quantity in the first year of life, and they learn to count when shown how to do so. Often, they create strategies for performing simple mathematical operations (e.g., adding and subtracting small numbers) on their own, but instruction is usually necessary for the construction of complex concepts and procedures. For optimal mathematical development, children should commit basic arithmetic to memory as well as truly understand (rather than simply memorize) mathematical procedures.

Some children have learning disabilities that impede their ability to automatize arithmetic facts or solve simple math problems, and others have little exposure to numbers and counting before beginning school. Gender and cultural differences in mathematics have been observed. Concrete manipulatives, encouragement to count and compare numbers of items, and visual aids facilitate children's mathematical development in the preschool and elementary years. Also, once children have mastered and automatized basic facts and skills, they are able to advance in their mathematical problem-solving abilities, especially when provided with effective instruction and tools that reduce demands on working memory.

Although children are born with the ability to apprehend basic principles of physics, by and large they acquire scientific knowledge through their informal experiences and formal instruction. As early as the preschool years, children form theories about categories of living creatures and cause-and-effect relationships in the physical world. The ability to reason as scientists do (e.g., formulating and testing hypotheses, drawing conclusions from data) develops gradually during childhood and improves in adolescence.

Children's individual abilities (e.g., visual-spatial skills) and disabilities (e.g., blindness) affect development in science, as do gender stereotypes and cultural beliefs. Authentic scientific investigations, age-appropriate explanations, and intentional efforts to bring about conceptual change enhance youngsters' scientific understandings and reasoning skills.

MyLab Education Self-Check 10.2

Social Studies and the Arts

10.3 Outline developmental changes in children's knowledge and skill in social studies and the arts, and summarize methods for fostering these capabilities.

In their studies of children's academic development, researchers have focused largely on reading, writing, mathematics, and science. Yet they have also learned a few things about children's development in social studies, art, and music. These latter subjects have the potential to broaden children's worlds and cultivate their citizenship, self-expression, and appreciation for beauty in human creations. We now look at trends in these areas.

Social Studies

Social studies, the interdisciplinary study of social science and humanities, is taught with the intention of preparing young people for responsible citizenship. In the United States, children are asked to embrace values for equality, justice, and freedom of thought and speech; other nations inculcate similar and sometimes distinct traditions, such as respect for a religious faith (International Bureau of Education, 2011; L. Martin & Smolen, 2010; National Council for the Social Studies, 2016; Puskás & Andersson, 2017). The social studies curriculum makes it possible for children to learn about their cultural heritage and the worldviews of people from different religions, ethnicities, and races.

Preparing for Your Licensure Examination

Your teaching test might ask you about instruction in an interdisciplinary unit.

Children's knowledge of social studies begins with an awareness of their own origins and those of family members. Sometime between ages 2 and 4, children construct an *autobiographical self:* They recall past events in their own lives and realize that they exist *in time*, with a past and a future as well as a present (Larkina, Merrill, & Bauer, 2017). In the elementary grades, awareness of ancestors tends to be concrete and simplistic. Children might conceptualize the birth of the United States as a single, specific event (e.g., the Boston Tea Party) or as involving the construction of new buildings (Ormrod, Jackson, Kirby, Davis, & Benson, 1999). In their middle school years, students are concerned with who they are and how they fit in society. Students of this age long to contribute to their community and may be motivated to learn about older people make a documentary about the needs of senior citizens, or serve in some other way (Swan, Karb, & Hofer, 2017). Many high school students take part in one or more extracurricular activities at school, have part-time jobs, and assume responsibility as a member of a faith community (Peck, Roeser, Zarrett, & Eccles, 2008). These involvements generate an insider's view of how institutions function and can pique students' interest in how governments at various levels operate.

In fact, students usually have little direct knowledge about the people they study in history. They haven't lived in the periods they examine, nor have they seen most of the locations they study. What they *can* build on is their knowledge of human beings. Thus, children can better understand historical events when they discover that figures from the past had beliefs and goals that were reasonable given the conditions of their lives (Bickford, 2013; Brophy, Alleman, & Knighton, 2009; Yeager et al., 1997). Children at various ages can benefit from a personalizing stance on social studies, with the specific methods adapted to their age. For young children, social studies is infused by fantasy play as a doctor, a firefighter, or a police officer and by visits from family members who talk about their countries of origin. In elementary school, children often enjoy acting out historical dramas and analyzing letters and documents from earlier times.

Many adolescents find history to be dull unless teachers show how the society they are studying is relevant to them—perhaps in stimulating their interest into the purpose of certain customs or the similarities between past and current struggles. Following are several additional strategies that encourage an up-and-close account of history:

- Assign works of fiction that realistically depict people in past times.
- Role-play family discussions of decisions during critical times in history (e.g., deciding whether to send a teenage son off to war).
- Ask children to analyze historical documents that represent conflicting perspectives on a historical event, encouraging them to speculate about how the experience of writers influenced their perspective.
- Have "journalists" (two or three students) interview people (other students) who imagine they have participated in a historical event.
- Assign readings from original documents, including diaries, letters, newspaper articles, and so on. (Bickford, 2013; Brophy & Alleman, 1996; Brophy et al., 2009; Brophy & VanSledright, 1997; Nokes, Dole, & Hacker, 2007; M. B. W. Wolfe & Goldman, 2005)

These instructional methods not only help students to see that the accomplishments and struggles of people from a certain era are relevant to them today, they also show them that there are a number of perspectives on this period.

MyLab Education Application Exercise 10.3
Detect Developmental Levels

How does this history teacher make the Jim Crow era personally meaningful to high school students?

Visual Arts

As budding artists, children exercise a variety of skills. They draw, paint, and sculpt, imagine new worlds, express their feelings, translate a mental image into a two- or three-dimensional likeness, practice fine motor skills, reason spatially, and explore the effects of texture, light, and color (Papandreou, 2014; Smutny & von Fremd, 2009).

MyLab Education
Video Example 10.6
Find Developmental Meaning *How does the teacher prepare students for drawing?* In this video, a teacher explains how to add definition and texture to artwork.

Artistic gestures begin as spontaneous scribbles by 1-year-olds and evolve quickly into deliberate marks on the page (Willcock, Imuta, & Hayne, 2011; Winner, 2006). At 2, children experiment with geometric figures, especially lines and circles. At 3, their repertoire of shapes includes squares, rectangles, triangles, crosses, and Xs, and they soon combine shapes into people, animals, and scenery (Golomb, 2004; Kellogg, 1967). Many early drawings are of a person, which might initially consist of a circle (depicting either a head or a head plus body) with a few facial features (e.g., eyes, mouth) and four lines (two arms, two legs) extending from the torso. With experience, preschoolers add features—hair, hands, fingers, and feet. Sometime around age 4, they combine drawings of objects to create pictures of groups or nature scenes. Initially, they may scatter things haphazardly around the page and eventually place objects in an orientation that is consistent with everyday reality. In the elementary grades, children become capable of producing a wide variety of shapes and contours, and their drawings become more detailed, realistic, and properly proportioned (N. R. Smith et al., 1998; Willcock et al., 2011; Winner, 2006). By the upper elementary grades, children portray depth in their drawings (Braine, Schauble, Kugelmass, & Winter, 1993).

Some youngsters draw and paint very little once they reach adolescence, especially if art is not a regular part of the school curriculum, and so their artistic skills may progress little further (Cohn, 2014; S. Moran & Gardner, 2006; Winner, 2006). Young adolescents frequently hold themselves to a high expectation for representing images and become disappointed when they cannot achieve realism (Luehrman & Unrath, 2006). Those who continue to create art refine their abilities and add texture, depth, perspective, and spatial relationships (N. R. Smith et al., 1998; Willats, 1995). They may also convey mood and emotion by selective use of shapes, notes, and color intensities (N. R. Smith et al., 1998).

Artistic techniques are highly valued and cultivated in some societies. If children receive extensive instruction in artistic techniques, as many children do in Japan and China, their drawings become elaborate, detailed, and true to life (Alland, 1983; Case & Okamoto, 1996; Cohn, 2014). By the middle elementary grades, some children mimic popular images in their local cultural environment, such as the drawings they see in comic books and magazines (B. Wilson, 1997; Winner, 2006). Images from history and social studies are also ripe for inspiration. In Artifact Example 10.7, you can see 15-year-old Berlinda's pencil-and-chalk drawing of pre-Columbian art.

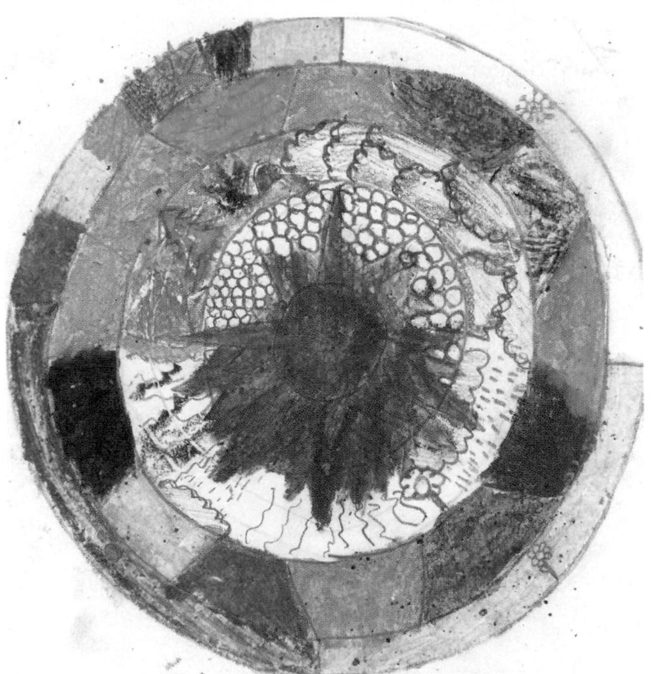

MyLab Education
Artifact Example 10.7
Find Developmental Meaning *What has 15-year-old Berlinda learned about people living in a pre-Columbian society?* Berlinda drew and colored this calendar, revealing an understanding of the significance of the sun and weather in the Mayan cosmic universe.

Music

Human beings of all ages enjoy music. Animated songs capture infants' attention and keep them on an even keel, perking them up a bit if they are low on energy and soothing them if they are overly aroused (Shenfield, Trehub, & Nakata, 2003). Five- to 24-month-old infants are more likely to sway, rock, and make other rhythmic movements to music rather than to speech (Zentner & Eerola, 2010). As youngsters grow older, and especially as they progress through the school years, they increasingly perceive patterns (melodies, keys, complex rhythms, etc.) instead of individual notes (Geist, Geist, & Kuznik, 2012; Gromko & Poorman, 1998).

At around age 2, children repeat some of the lyrics they hear. They soon add a rhythmic structure and an up-and-down "melody" of sorts. Preschool children love to learn new songs, and by the time they are 5 or 6, most can sing a recognizable tune and keep it largely within the right key and meter. With neuromuscular maturation and practice, young and elementary school children sing proficiently (Persellin & Bateman, 2009; Winner, 2006). For most youngsters, further development in singing and adoption of an instrument comes with training (D. J. Elliott, 1995; Miksza & Gault, 2014; Winner, 2006).

Individual children have varying abilities to hear and appreciate music. About 4% of children have **amusia** (or tone deafness), an inability to detect small changes in pitch that are common in melodies. These youngsters show little or no improvement in their perception of musical tones despite instruction and practice, suggesting that the ability to hear music *as* music may have a biological basis (Gardner, Torff, & Hatch, 1996; K. L. Hyde & Peretz, 2004; Lebrun, Moreau, McNally-Gagnon, Goulet, & Peretz, 2012). In contrast, some children not only hear but also *remember* subtle differences in pitch. Although most people can remember the relative pitches of notes in a melody, individuals with *absolute pitch* can also recall the *exact* pitch of a note they have heard in, say, a popular song (Shellenberg & Trehub, 2003). Absolute pitch is more common in infants and preschoolers than in older children or adults; thus, it seems that children lose this ability if it is not exercised (Miyazaki, Makomaska, & Rakowski, 2012; Saffran & Griepentrog, 2001).

MyLab Education
Video Example 10.7

Find Developmental Meaning *How does the teacher encourage preschool children's engagement with music?* The teacher invites singing and swaying to music.

Some children, including a few with autism and intellectual disabilities, have exceptional musical talents (Stanutz, Wapnick, & Burack, 2014). After watching a movie on television one evening, 14-year-old Leslie Lemke sat down at the family piano and played Tchaikovsky's Piano Concerto No. 1, which had been a soundtrack in the movie. He had never heard the concerto before that night, yet his rendition was flawless. Lemke became a world-renowned pianist, even though he has autism and an intellectual disability, is blind, and has never had a piano lesson (Treffert & Wallace, 2002).

Education in Social Studies and the Arts

The path to responsible citizenship is facilitated by knowledge of the diverse world in which we live and the struggles and accomplishments of our ancestors. Access to music, the arts, and other creative works enrich children's personal well-being. We close with these recommendations:

- **Implement rousing social studies lessons.** As children grow older, they become increasingly interested in how the social world works, including jobs adults take on, the processes by which governments balance rights and interests, and the customs practiced locally and around the world. Documents, experiences, data, and video clips on the Internet can provide intriguing material to read, analyze, and write about. A dynamic presentation in which children get firsthand experience with cultural materials can be instructional. Students might participate in skits, write and receive letters to pen pals in a foreign land, visit city council, compare conflicting perspectives in historical documents, and practice navigating the vicinity with compass and map. Cultural heritages and the unique experiences of diverse groups merit children's study, and if students find inspiring role models in the process, either in history or in their present community, they gain an important motivation for becoming responsible citizens.

- **Teach and advocate for the arts.** Music, drama, dance, sculpture, film production, and the visual arts transcend children's three primary domains of development—the physical, cognitive, and social-emotional areas. For example, children expressing themselves emotionally through artistic expression, sway to the beat of music in dance, and use abstract reasoning when comparing films for underlying themes and metaphors. The arts challenge children academically, help them refine motor skills, and allow self-expression. Curiously, the arts (and physical education) are among the first areas placed on the cutting board when budgets are slashed. Despite the excruciating trade-offs that must be weighed during tight times, a long-term perspective on children's well-being reveals significant value in these subjects.

Children undergo similar progressions in the arts as with other academic subjects, shifting from personal, concrete, and spontaneous approaches to abstract, comprehensive, and integrated frameworks and learning strategies. The Basic Developmental Issues table "Progressions in the Academic Domains" summarizes how three general themes—nature and nurture, universality and diversity, and qualitative and quantitative change—play out in academic subjects.

BASIC DEVELOPMENTAL ISSUES
Progressions in the Academic Domains

ISSUE	READING AND WRITING	MATH AND SCIENCE	SOCIAL STUDIES	ART AND MUSIC
Nature and Nurture	Although children are born ready to learn spoken language, facility in reading and writing is largely the result of exposure to printed materials and education. Nature can interfere with normal literacy development, however: Some children with biologically based disabilities have unusual difficulty in learning to read and write. Customized instruction, especially when initiated early in development, can help children overcome initial weaknesses.	Within the first few months of life, infants notice differences in quantity and, at some rudimentary level, understand basic principles of physics. Some theorists speculate that these early acquisitions reflect neurologically based knowledge. By and large, children's knowledge of numbers and scientific phenomena develops through experience and instruction, especially at the advanced levels. Mentoring of abstract knowledge can elicit sophisticated mathematical and scientific reasoning.	The bodies of knowledge and cognitive tools that children acquire in social studies are primarily the result of instruction and informal experiences in the family (e.g., with trips to historical sites, contact with other societies, use of maps on subway systems). Maturational processes partly determine the age at which children are able to think about historical time and understand the symbolism in maps and cultural traditions.	Hereditary and maturational factors play a role in artistic and musical development. Preschool children's ability to draw depends largely on maturation of fine motor skills. Most children have an appreciation for music, and some show exceptional talent even without a great deal of instruction. For the most part, advancements in art and music result from training, individual effort, and practice.
Universality and Diversity	Phonological awareness universally facilitates reading development even when written language is *not* based on how words are pronounced. Children learn to read and write more easily when words have highly regular and predictable spelling patterns. Children's literacy development depends on the extent to which adults model and encourage reading and writing.	Although children worldwide are aware of quantity, precision in counting and comparing quantities depends on transmission of number concepts and operations. Certain scientific knowledge (e.g., knowing that animals are different from inanimate objects) is similar worldwide. Several mental frameworks (e.g., beliefs about the origins of the human species) differ depending on religion and upbringing.	Children's construction of an autobiographical self is a universal foundation for historical knowledge. Given national differences in governments, variations in social studies knowledge can be significant. In industrialized societies, history is taught in school and can be meaningful to children when presented in a personally relevant way.	Virtually all cultures have traditions and creations in art and music. Artistic styles and musical patterns differ considerably from one society to the next, and development in these areas varies accordingly. Although preschoolers' drawings tend to be quite similar across cultures, by middle childhood their artwork begins to mimic images they see in their environment.
Qualitative and Quantitative Change	Literacy shows many qualitative changes. Children shift from a focus on word identification to concentration on comprehension (in reading), transition from knowledge telling to knowledge transforming (in writing), and increasingly incorporate metacognitive processes (in both reading and writing). Literacy development is quantitative in that children become able to recognize and spell more and more words, and basic reading and writing skills become increasingly automatized.	As children get older, they acquire more knowledge about mathematical and scientific concepts and principles—a progression reflecting quantitative change. They also acquire new and qualitatively different ways of thinking about math and science. Elementary school children begin to rely on retrieval rather than counting on fingers as they solve addition and subtraction problems. Scientific reasoning is gradually acquired (suggesting quantitative improvements), yet qualitative shifts to sophisticated thinking are possible.	A good deal of social studies knowledge develops quantitatively, in that children gradually acquire information about historical events. Qualitative changes are seen in how children *think* about history. With appropriate instruction children come to realize that knowledge of history is comprised of available accounts of what happened, many of which reflect a particular opinion on events. Their views on government sometimes shift from it being inaccessible to it being an entity that they can influence through voting, civic participation, and community service.	Many qualitative changes are seen in art and music development. With growth and experience, children's drawings embody a sense of composition (e.g., creating an organized scene rather than a random collection of objects), perspective, and texture. In the preschool years, songs start to reflect a consistent rhythm and key. Quantitative change is seen in children's increasing knowledge of musical notation and gradual improvement with a musical instrument.

Summary

Social studies, art, and music have received less attention in developmental research than have literacy, science, and mathematics, but researchers are finding age-related trends in these subject areas. Children in the early elementary grades are apt to struggle with historical time, and they may not appreciate that historical "knowledge" is a matter of perspective rather than fact. Educators can help children understand the traditions and motivations of other people by communicating the conditions of their lives.

Art and music are found in virtually all cultures, but the specific forms that they take differ considerably from one society to another. Infants around the world enjoy music, and children's early drawings of people are similar regardless of where they grow up. Advanced art and music abilities are largely dependent on instruction, available resources, and practice.

MyLab Education Self-Check 10.3

Practicing For Your Licensure Examination

Many teaching tests require students to apply their knowledge of child development in analyzing brief vignettes and answering multiple-choice questions. You can practice for your licensure examination by reading the following case study and answering a series of questions.

AP Calculus

Galen liked math but lacked confidence in his ability to handle difficult material. He eventually decided he would try the Advanced Placement (AP) Calculus class because he had heard good things about the teacher, Mr. Wagner.

As Galen settled into the class, he began to like the predictable format. For each lesson, Mr. Wagner began with a description of a specific concept in calculus and then asked students to complete a series of steps about it for homework. Homework took the form of an electronic journal entry, in which students prepared an overview of the concept (in an *Introduction*), explained its principles (in a *Research* section), clarified its meaning (in an *Interpretation*), and formulated relevant equations (in a final *Examples* section).

At the end of the year, students printed their homework assignments and bound them into a booklet with an essay they wrote about what they had learned from the class. Skim Galen's assignment (Figure A) and read an excerpt from his essay on the next page (Figure B). Unless you're a calculus buff, ignore the math equations, and focus instead on how the various sections were used to solidify students' understandings of the concepts and their applications.

FIGURE A Galen's homework.

For every concept in calculus, Galen and his classmates followed a template for analysis, in which they examined its meaning, principles, and implications.

Introduction

This journal discusses derivatives and their rules. Derivatives are key to measuring a *rate of change.* We also look at the tangent of a secant line, and how to determine a tangent to a function with a point.

Research

A Derivative is the rate of change of an output as a function of some input. $\frac{\Delta y}{\Delta x} = slope of chord$

The derivative equals the tangent of the secant line. It has the following forms:

$\frac{dy}{dx} = slope$ of tangent $\quad m_{tan} \lim_{h \to 0} \frac{f(x+h)-f(x)}{h} =$

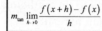

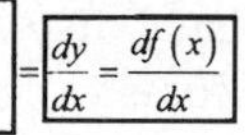
$\frac{dy}{dx} = \frac{df(x)}{dx}$

The derivative can be shown graphically as well. After all it is a *rate of change.*

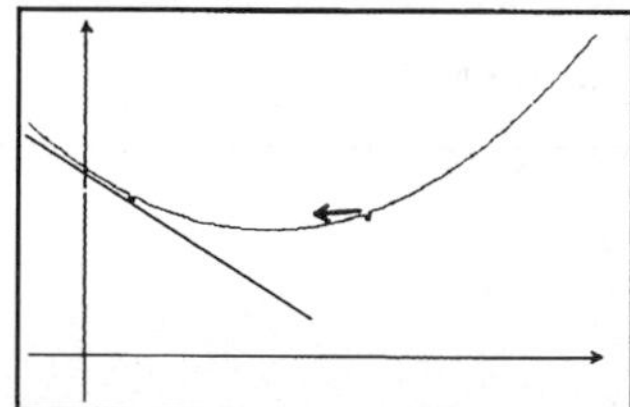

As these two point's distance gets closer to zero.

They start to form a tangent, and at zero there is a tangent to the secant line.

Research(cont.)

Determining the equation of a line tangent to a curve at a point:

1. Determine f(c) if needed.
2. Determine the derivative function.
3. Determine m=f'(c)
4. Determine b. (b = y - mx)

y = mx + b

m = f'(c) f(c)=y

b = y-mx

b = f(c) - f'(c)c

Interpretation

The derivative is a *rate of change.* It is the tangent to the secant line, that is created as two points on the secant line, get close together, *as their distance goes to zero.* The derivative takes the form of $\frac{dy}{dx}$ or $\frac{df(x)}{dx}$. They are really important in high end math, can be applied to anything that is changing at a constant rate.

??

Examples

a) $y = x^2 - 4x + 4$

$$\lim_{h \to 0} y' = \frac{((x+h)^2 - 4(x+h)+4)-(x^2-4x+4)}{h}$$

$$\lim_{h \to 0} y' = \frac{x^2 + 2xh + h^2 - 4x - 4h + 4 - x^2 + 4x - 4}{h}$$

$$\lim_{h \to 0} y' = \frac{2xh + h^2 - 4h}{h}$$

$$\lim_{h \to 0} y' = \frac{h(2x+h-4)}{h}$$

$$\lim_{h \to 0} y' = 2x + h - 4$$

$$\boxed{\lim_{h \to 0} y' = 2x - 4}$$

FIGURE B Galen's essay.

At the end of the school year, Galen wrote about how the structure of the assignments supported his understanding of the principles of calculus and their relevance for depicting physical forces such as acceleration.

What can I say about this year of AP Calculus? Let me start by saying how much I have learned and that I actually enjoyed learning the material. It's been an excellent year and we covered a lot of ground. I feel prepared for college calculus, and depending on my test score, may go to Calculus II at college. We learned about preliminary concepts (the pre-calc), limits, the derivative, the integral, and practical applications of each of those. For each unit we created journals to help us further understand the content. Overall I found the journals helpful but for most material it was overkill for me.

Mr. Wagner has been a great teacher. He makes the material understandable and interesting to learn. I like the routine he has for teaching to which we have grown accustomed. Each unit is separated into sections and each sub-section follows a similar pattern. We get a sheet to take notes over the smart notebook lesson we have in class, a homework assignment, and a quiz. This system worked really well for me and other students because we knew what to expect, and it was a good way to separate the learning into three parts—each part further bettering our understanding of the unit. . . .

The material we covered throughout the year is complex stuff and math that is used at a high level. The main applications that paralleled with real life patterns were derivation and integration. The derivative is a rate of change, the slope of the tangent line following the graph of a function. This is really important for instantaneous velocity, as the derivative of the position function is the velocity function, and the derivative of the velocity function is the acceleration function. . . . Also we learned how to determine the volume of a 3D shape using cross-sections and the integral. A real-life example could be finding the volume of a pond with the use of semi-circle cross-sections . . .

It's been a fun year, and it's made me appreciate how lucky I am to be learning such incredible things like calculus. The math we're doing is really complex and interesting and it's definitely not something everyone can do. We've been lucky to have a great teacher to teach us about the study of change. We've explored some real-life applications, while used as a high-level, it is math that is very important and helpful in our world.

Constructed-Response Question

1. What did Galen like about calculus and the way he was taught?

Multiple-Choice Questions

2. Would Mr. Wagner have been able to achieve similar results in calculus achievement with preschool children if he used the same instructional strategies with them?

a. No, because preschool children dislike mathematics.
b. Yes, because young children have the same ability as adolescents in acquiring challenging mathematical concepts.
c. No, because young children would rarely have the abstract reasoning abilities that are necessary for learning calculus.
d. Yes, because young children would easily translate abstract mathematics concepts into ideas that have a tangible basis in reality.

3. Which of the following instructional strategies was *not* one of the techniques summarized by Galen as being used by Mr. Wagner?

a. Encourage students to invent, use, and defend their own strategies.
b. As youngsters work on new and challenging mathematical problems, provide the scaffolding they need to find successful solutions.
c. Use visual displays to tie mathematical concepts and procedures to concrete reality.
d. Use concrete manipulatives when instructing children in mathematics.

MyLab Education Licensure Practice 10.1

Key Concepts

emergent literacy (p. 357)
phonological awareness (p. 358)
sight vocabulary (p. 360)
story schema (p. 361)
dyslexia (p. 363)
invented spelling (p. 369)
knowledge telling (p. 370)
knowledge transforming (p. 371)
approximate number system (p. 377)
visual-spatial ability (p. 382)
dyscalculia (p. 382)
substance schema (p. 385)
scientific reasoning (p. 387)
amusia (p. 395)

Chapter Eleven
Emotional Development

Comstock Images/Stockbyte/Getty Images

Objectives

11.1 Describe the central challenges in each of Erikson's eight stages of psychosocial development, and identify the strengths and limitations of the theory.

11.2 Summarize the developmental course of children's first attachments, distinguish four primary attachment styles, and explain the methods teachers and other practitioners can use to foster secure attachments in children.

11.3 Encapsulate developmental trends in children's emotional understanding and expression, and outline strategies for supporting children's emotional health.

11.4 Define key dimensions of temperament and personality, and generate techniques for embracing children's individuality.

11.5 Describe three frameworks for addressing emotional and behavioral problems and strategies for helping children with emotional conditions be successful at school.

CASE STUDY

Merv

Merv had had a difficult childhood growing up in an economically poor family in Hawaii. Her father was an alcoholic, and her mother had been anxious, depressed, and preoccupied with her own troubles. Neither parent took adequate care of Merv or her six brothers and sisters. Merv's parents regularly fought and occasionally struck Merv and the other children. Food, shoes, clothing, and basic school supplies were scarce. Other parents in their neighborhood considered Merv and her siblings to be unworthy playmates for their own children (Werner & Smith, 2001).

Remarkably, Merv beat the odds. By the time she reached her 40s, Merv was a productive, well-adjusted woman who worked as a parent educator and had been married since age 16 to "a pretty neat guy . . . a schoolteacher" (Werner & Smith, 2001, pp. 100–101). Merv and her husband raised their seven children in a manner that was gentle, patient, and loving. Merv remained close to her own brothers and sisters. She led a happy, fulfilled life.

Merv credited four childhood experiences with making her a strong and secure person. First of all, Merv had learned to work hard, as she described in this memory:

> As children, we took care of the yard, the house, the clothes, each other, and the cars. We did everything. My father cooked when there was something to cook, and my mother simply coped. . . . When things got rough, I learned to dig in my heels and say, "How am I going to make this happen?" versus "This is too hard, I quit." (Werner & Smith, 2001, pp. 95–96)[a]

Second, Merv had "caring and supportive people" to guide and nurture her (Werner & Smith, 2001, p. 96). Merv thrived on care she received from her grandmother Kahaunaele. During Merv's visits to Kahaunaele's house, Kahaunaele showered Merv with love, bathed the girl, and combed the tangles out of her long hair. Love from her grandmother came to be supplemented with kindness from several teachers and school staff. Merv's principal once said to her, "You are Hawaiian and you can be anything you choose to be" (Werner & Smith, 2001, p. 98). Merv was forever grateful for these words of encouragement.

Third, Merv received a good education. When she was 12 years old, she accepted an invitation to attend a prestigious school on another Hawaiian island. At the Kamehameha School, Merv was well cared for, academically and socially. Her life changed dramatically at age 16, however, when she became pregnant and was expelled from school for becoming an unwed mother. Merv married the father of her baby and was soon allowed to return when a school counselor went "out on a major limb" for her, having realized that she was "not a bad student. She just made a mistake" (Werner & Smith, 2001, p. 100).

Finally, Merv learned to trust that there is goodness in the world. Merv saw hope as a vital quality for all young people and noted that inspiration is found in a variety of places:

> Somewhere, someplace down the line, somebody had taught me, "There is somebody greater than us who loves you." And that is my hope and my belief. Whatever that translates for you—a belief in God, a belief in a religion, a goal, a dream, something that we can hang on to. As adults, we need to give our young people hope and something to hang on to. As young people, we need to find our own. (Werner & Smith, 2001, p. 101)

- What basic need did Merv have that was fulfilled by her grandmother, siblings, and people outside her family?
- What do Merv's childhood experiences suggest about how teachers and other practitioners can contribute to children's emotional development?

Every child needs to be loved. Merv's own parents neglected her, but her grandmother adored her, her brothers and sisters formed lasting bonds with her, and a few kindhearted educators provided her personal encouragement, advocacy, and a high-quality education. In this chapter you will find that affectionate care is the mainstay of children's first relationships. When children are treated with sensitivity, they learn to trust others, express their own needs, and empathize with others' feelings. You will learn that children do not always obtain adequate support to weather life's challenges. When adversities outweigh children's **coping skills**, their personal mechanisms for managing distress, the unfortunate outcome can be anxiety, depression, and health problems. Fortunately, teachers, counselors, and other practitioners can nurture children, ease their troubles, teach adaptive coping skills, and steer them toward a healthy future.

Outline

Erikson's Theory of Psychosocial Development

11.1 Describe the central challenges in each of Erikson's eight stages of psychosocial development, and identify the strengths and limitations of the theory.

Physical and cognitive abilities change dramatically during childhood. Learning to walk, run, talk, count, read, and write are important milestones. Yet equally momentous transformations occur in the social-emotional domain. To give you an overview of these significant social-emotional changes, we introduce Erikson's theory of psychosocial development.

Lessons Learned from Life's Challenges

Erik Erikson (1902–1994) was a *psychodynamic theorist* who believed that people grow from life's challenges. In his own youth, Erikson had struggled with who he was as a person. He often felt different from others, having been born to a single Danish mother in Germany during an era when two-parent families were the norm. Adding to his sense of uniqueness, he was Jewish but had blond hair and blue eyes, a rare combination of characteristics that puzzled other people and made him feel strange (Crain, 2011). Erikson had little interest in school and failed to earn a college degree. He grew by leaps and bounds and eventually became a well-known scholar of human development.

In his theory, Erikson suggested that people undergo eight "crises," dilemmas addressed in the form of **psychosocial stages**, between birth and old age (Erikson, 1963, 1966). Each crisis is a turning point, the resolution of which directs a person's future concerns. He called these eight predicaments *psychosocial* stages because the challenges represent qualitatively different concerns about oneself (*psycho*) and one's relationships with other people (*social*). Erikson observed that when individuals constructively address these challenges, they gain lasting personal assets. When their efforts fall short, people are apt to dwell on their problems. As they move from stage to stage, they build on accumulated assets and deficits, occasionally revisiting unresolved crises. Let's look at the potential outcomes of the eight stages.

Preparing for Your Licensure Examination

Your teaching test might ask you about the principles and implications of Erikson's theory.

Trust versus Mistrust (Infancy)

According to Erikson, infants' primary task is to learn whether they can trust other people. When caregivers can be depended on to feed a hungry stomach, change an uncomfortable diaper, and provide affection at regular intervals, an infant learns *trust*—that others are dependable. When caregivers ignore an infant's needs, are inconsistent in attention, or are abusive, the infant learns *mistrust*—that the world is an unpredictable and dangerous place.

Autonomy versus Shame and Doubt (Toddler Years)

As toddlers gain better control of their bodies, they become capable of satisfying their own needs. Toddlers learn to feed, wash, dress, and use the toilet. When parents and other caregivers encourage self-sufficient behavior, toddlers develop *autonomy*, a sense of being able to handle problems on their own. But when caregivers demand too much too soon, refuse to let children perform simple tasks, or ridicule early attempts at self-sufficiency, children instead develop *shame and doubt* about conducting themselves appropriately.

Initiative versus Guilt (Preschool Years)

If all goes well, children spend their infancy and toddler years learning that the world is a reasonably safe place where their daily needs can be met. Ideally, they also learn that certain people love them, and they can make things happen. With a growing drive toward independence, preschoolers develop their own ideas about activities they want to pursue. They undertake art projects, make houses and roadways in the sandbox, and share fantasies about being superheroes. When adults encourage such efforts, children develop *initiative*, the energy and motivation to undertake activities on their own. When adults discourage such activities, children may instead develop *guilt* about acting improperly.

Industry versus Inferiority (Elementary School Years)

When children reach elementary school, they are expected to master many new skills, and they soon learn that they can gain recognition from adults through academic, athletic, artistic, and civic-minded accomplishments. When children take pride in completed projects and are praised for achievements, they demonstrate *industry*, a pattern of working hard, gaining mastery of cultural tools, and persisting at complicated tasks. When children are ridiculed or punished for their efforts or when they find that they cannot meet adults' expectations, they may develop feelings of *inferiority* about their abilities.

Identity versus Role Confusion (Adolescence)

As they make the transition from childhood to adulthood, adolescents wrestle with questions about who they are and how they fit into the adult world. Values learned during childhood are now reassessed in light of an emerging motivation to take a stand on controversial issues, a sexual drive, and the desire to be true to oneself. Initially, youth experience *role confusion*—mixed feelings about the specific ways in which they fit into society—and may experiment with actions and attitudes (e.g., affiliating with various peer groups, trying sports and hobbies, and learning about the views of different political groups). In Erikson's view, most adolescents eventually achieve a sense of *identity* regarding who they are and where their lives are headed.

Intimacy versus Isolation (Young Adulthood)

Once people have established their identities, they are ready to make commitments to others. They become capable of *intimacy*—that is, they form close, reciprocal bonds (e.g., through friendships, marriage, or other intimate relationships) and willingly make the sacrifices and compromises that such relationships require. When people do not form these connections (perhaps because of their disregard for others' needs), a sense of *isolation* may result.

Generativity versus Stagnation (Middle Age)

During middle age, the primary developmental tasks are contributing to society and guiding future generations. When an individual gives something back, perhaps by raising a family, volunteering in the community, or serving others in a professional role, a sense of *generativity*, or productivity, results. In contrast, an individual who is self-centered and unable or unwilling to help others experiences *stagnation*—dissatisfaction with not having made a positive difference for others.

Integrity versus Despair (Retirement Years)

According to Erikson, the final developmental task is a retrospective one. As individuals look back on their past experiences, they develop feelings of contentment and *integrity* if they believe they have led a happy, productive life. Alternatively, they may develop a sense of *despair* if they look back on a life of disappointments and unachieved goals.

For Erikson, successful progress through each stage is not an absolute accomplishment but a matter of degree. In other words, people advance through each stage when they develop *more* of the positive tendency and *less* of the negative tendency. Erikson believed that having modest deficits that are balanced with adequate assets helps people respond sensibly to opportunities and threats in daily life. A young boy who has learned to trust his parents is hopeful when meeting a new teacher, yet having also known a few short-tempered grown-ups, he will be cautious until he gets to know the teacher better. Because his optimism is tempered with restraint, the boy is ready to form healthy relationships. In contrast, with too much of a deficit (e.g., when uneasiness outweighs peace of mind), a tipping point is reached, and the person becomes unhappy, isolated, and socially impaired.

Contemporary Perspectives on Erikson's Theory

Three strengths of Erikson's theory make it a compelling framework for human development. First, Erikson argued that important changes occur *throughout* the life span. Thanks, in part, to Erikson's theory, developmental scholars now accept that catalysts for growth surface at every age (e.g., with needs to be productive, define personal commitments, become intimate, and give something back to society). Second, Erikson focused on truly significant developments, including forming trusting relationships and establishing an identity (Marcia & Josselson, 2013; Vaughan & Rodriguez, 2013). Finally, Erikson's stages reflect the idea that development is a dynamic synthesis of nature, nurture, and the person's motivation to fulfill age-related needs (Dunkel & Sefcek, 2009; Knight, 2017). This portrayal of an individual actively pursuing personal goals, periodically reflecting on how things are going in life, and making adjustments with experience is consistent with contemporary developmental systems theory's focus on forces of change in the active person.

These strengths notwithstanding, Erikson's framework has limitations. For one thing, Erikson's observations of the human condition were largely anecdotal, and his conclusions, vague (Crain, 2011). The systematic results that have accumulated since Erikson formulated his theory indicate that his stages are probably not completely accurate descriptions of what happens at each age period. Erikson believed that most people achieve a sense of identity by the end of adolescence. In reality youth typically continue to wrestle with their personal commitments during the young adult years (Bartoszuk & Pittman, 2010; J. Kroger, 2004). Also problematic is that Erikson based his stages primarily on observations of men from a limited number of backgrounds. Women and individuals from non-Western cultures may face a different series of tasks than the ones Erikson identified. Although Erikson viewed culture as influential in age-related tasks, he probably underestimated just how differently various cultural groups think about their lives. For example, many cultures intentionally discourage self-assertiveness (autonomy) in young children, sometimes as a way of protecting them from dangers in the environment and at other times as a means for strengthening ties among family members (Kağitçibaşi 2007; Morelli & Rothbaum, 2007). You can see a summary of the research on Erikson's stages in Table 11.1.

Developmental Systems Prompt

Erikson's psychosocial theory, which reveals active changes across the life span, is compatible with the developmental system framework. In your work with students, consider age-related challenges that they feel compelled to resolve, such as how to be industrious or determine who they are as people.

Table 11.1 Developmental Research Related to Erikson's Stages

STAGE	AGE	RESEARCH
Trust vs. Mistrust	Birth to 1 year	Developmental investigations support Erikson's assertion that learning to trust is a fundamental acquisition for infants (Ainsworth, Blehar, Waters, & Wall, 1978; Bowlby, 1988; C. Green, Kalvaitis, & Worster, 2016; Klatzkin, Lieberman, & Van Horn, 2013). Although Erikson indicated that infancy was a critical time for developing a first trusting relationship, recent research indicates that children often get second chances. When infants receive unresponsive care, their first attachments are likely to be insecure, but if later care is warm, sensitive, and reliable, they are apt to develop secure relationships.
Autonomy vs. Shame and Doubt	1 to 3 years	Evidence supports Erikson's conclusion that toddlers have a strong will in acting without restriction. Toddlers are motivated to handle objects, walk on their own, and explore a home's forbidden areas. Yet not every culture agrees that autonomy is a virtue: Some groups see young children's drive for independence as an immature impulse (S. Griffith & Grolnick, 2014; Kağitçibaşi 2007).
Initiative vs. Guilt	3 to 5 years	Erikson aptly portrayed preschool-aged children as radiating a sense of purpose. Research confirms that young children show initiative in conversation, everyday tasks, and play. Erikson also paved the way for contemporary research on shame, doubt, and guilt. Developmental studies indicate that young children feel upset when they break a rule or fail to live up to a standard (Kagan, 1984; Kochanska, 1993; R. A. Thompson & Newton, 2010).
Industry vs. Inferiority	6 to 10 years	Erikson saw middle childhood as a period for completing demanding tasks proficiently. Cross-cultural research indicates that parents routinely assign chores to children in this age range, reflecting recognition of children's growing responsibility. Research also indicates that children compare their own abilities to those of peers and lose confidence when they come up short in domains that they value (J. S. Barnes & Spray, 2013; Harter, 2006; Roseth, Lee, & Saltarelli, 2018; W. Wu, West, & Hughes, 2010).
Identity vs. Role Confusion	10 to 20 years	Erikson's focus on identity has spawned a lot of research. Studies generally confirm Erikson's assertion that young people actively engage in soul-searching as to who they are, what they believe in, what it means to be a particular race and ethnicity, and where they are going in life (Marcia, 1980, 1988; M. B. Spencer, 2014). This preoccupation with identity extends for a longer period than Erikson proposed (Bartoszuk & Pittman, 2010).
Intimacy vs. Isolation	Young adulthood	Evidence confirms that taking part in intimate relationships is a common concern for young adults. However, some critics suggest that being closely connected with others is a human quality that transcends any single period (Gilligan, 1982). Furthermore, the early adult years are more complex than Erikson suggested. Young adults are concerned not only with finding a mate but also with getting a job and, in many cases, caring for their own children.
Generativity vs. Stagnation	Middle age	During middle age, most adults mobilize their lives to contribute to society, as Erikson proposed. One common critique of Erikson's theory is that he believed that men were primarily concerned with their careers and women with parenting their children. In Western cultures today, both career and family are serious concerns for men and women alike (Livingston, 2014; B. E. Peterson & Stewart, 1996).
Integrity vs. Despair	Retirement years	Looking back on one's life is an important task for many older adults, just as Erikson thought (R. N. Butler, 1963; Torges, Stewart, & Duncan, 2009). However, older adults tackle many other developmental tasks, including finding ways to cope with losses and make the best of their later years (Baltes, 1997; Ramírez, Ortega, Chamorro, & Colmenero, 2014). In other words, older adults live in the present as well as the past.

Despite holes in Erikson's theory, his framework offers a valuable perspective on human life. As we mentioned, Erikson's framework has several strengths, and it offers the additional advantage of inspiring optimism about the potential for growth in young people. Most educators agree with Erikson that youngsters can usually find the fortitude they need to transform life's challenges into such worthwhile assets as a healthy self-confidence, a commitment to productive social values, and a solid work ethic.

Although Erikson failed to provide detailed information about how to cultivate social-emotional skills in youngsters, other developmental scholars have taken up this cause. The focus of Erikson's first stage, a trusting relationship with caregivers, has been thoroughly examined by researchers, and we look at this topic shortly. Other key themes that Erikson examined—reflecting on one's personal characteristics, gaining satisfaction from completing difficult tasks, and forming close relationships with people outside the family—build on this security.

Summary

Erikson proposed that psychosocial characteristics emerge over the course of eight stages, with the first beginning in infancy and the last occurring in old age. Erikson blazed many trails for later developmental scholars; the volumes of research inspired by his work have shown that priorities change across major periods in life. Certain values embedded in Erikson's stages, such as personal identity and autonomy, vary in importance across cultures. Despite its flaws, Erikson's theory is well regarded due to its optimism that a person's initiative, warm relationships, and coping with adversity can yield good outcomes across the life span.

MyLab Education Self-Check 11.1

Attachment

11.2 Summarize the developmental course of children's first attachments, distinguish four primary attachment styles, and explain the methods teachers and other practitioners can use to foster secure attachments in children.

Erikson believed that the child's first task was to develop trust in a parent. Indeed, human beings of all ages have a fundamental need to feel socially connected to, and loved and respected by, other people. That is, they have a **need for relatedness** (Park, Crocker, & Vohs, 2006; S. Ward & Parker, 2013; Xiang, Ağbuğa, Liu, & McBride, 2017). This requirement is fulfilled with social bonds of various types, including family relationships, friendships, and romantic ties.

The Concept of Attachment

The child's first bond, called an **attachment**, is an enduring emotional tie that unites child to caregiver and has far-reaching effects on development (Ainsworth, 1973). In the past few decades, the dominant framework on infant–caregiver relationships has been **ethological attachment theory**, a perspective originally proposed by British psychiatrist **John Bowlby** (1907–1990) and later fleshed out by Canadian American psychologist **Mary Ainsworth** (1913–1999; Ainsworth, 1963, 1973; Ainsworth et al., 1978; Bowlby, 1951, 1958).

The attachment framework is couched in terms of *ethology*, a perspective in biology that examines the adaptive significance of behavior for the organism's survival in its natural environment. Ethological attachment theory suggests that the human capacity for close relationships evolved over millions of years. Severe environmental conditions in our ancestors' past made it necessary for small children to stay close to parents and for parents to watch over their children. These mutually close ties helped children survive their early years, develop into productive members of society, and nurture their own offspring. The biological capacity for attachment was presumably passed down from generation to generation.

What develops in infants is not simply a collection of discrete behaviors, such as crying when hungry, but also an underlying system for relating to parents. This system has four elements. First, infants learn to use their parents as a *safe haven*. Infants depend on parents for protection from harm and comfort when hunger, fatigue, and fear escalate to unmanageable levels. Second, infants use parents as a *secure base*. They relax in the presence of affectionate parents and venture here and there, crawling away and glancing back now and then for reassuring looks from Mom and Dad. Third, *proximity maintenance* means that infants are prone to explore surroundings and return to parents to share discoveries. Finally, *separation distress* refers to the fear, sadness, and anger that infants show when they cannot see or touch their parents. These four processes allow the infant to develop a relationship, gain a sense of security, get their needs met, stay safe, and engage with the world.

Formation of First Attachments

In the process of forming an attachment, infants learn a lot about themselves and other people. A baby slowly develops expectations about shared routines ("When Grandma says, 'Peekaboo,' I hide my eyes and laugh"), beliefs about other people ("Mommy takes care of me"), emotional connections ("I love my Daddy"), and sense of self ("I am lovable"). Emerging expectations are facilitated by maturation, cognitive development, and social experience. Bowlby believed that there are four phases in attachment development.

Pre-Attachment

From birth until about 6 to 12 weeks, infants use social signals (e.g., smiling, crying, and making eye contact) that elicit care from others. Babies initially treat adults in an equal opportunity fashion, allowing anyone with the right touch to comfort them (Schaffer, 1996). Yet rudimentary attachments are being formed in these early weeks as infants begin to recognize selected caregivers who respond affectionately to them.

Attachment-in-the-Making

From 6 to 12 weeks through 6 to 8 months after birth, infants learn that they cannot count on just anyone for attention, but instead turn to the few special people who regularly care for them. By the second or third month, infants smile selectively at people they know best, and a month or so later, laugh uproariously at good-humored antics (Bridgett, Laake, Gartstein, & Dorn, 2013; Camras, Malatesta, & Izard, 1991; Mireault et al., 2017). In the early months, adults carry the burden for maintaining a social exchange, but infants, when in the right mood, participate eagerly (Saarni, Campos, Camras, & Witherington, 2006). Sensitive caregivers notice when a baby is calm and alert, use the occasion to extend a greeting, and wait for a simple response. With experience, infants become familiar with the rhythms of these exchanges.

Clear-Cut Attachment

Between 6 to 8 months until a year and a half after birth, infants show a full-fledged attachment to one person or a small number of people, including, perhaps, a mother, a father, a grandparent, an employed caregiver, or some combination of these or other individuals. Attachments can be seen when infants reach out to be picked up by adored caregivers, protest when separated from them, and wriggle and coo when they walk into the room. When distressed, infants calm to comforting gestures from responsive parents. Just in time to accompany crawling, nature activates an adaptive emotional reaction, fear of the unknown. Rather than crawling off into the hinterlands, infants stick fairly close to familiar caregivers. When puzzling situations appear out of nowhere, such as a barking dog (woof!) or a jack-in-the-box's loud, unexpected effect (pop!), infants demand reassurance (now!).

Adults unknown to the baby now trigger fearful reactions. In the latter half of the first year of life and well into the second year, many infants exhibit **stranger anxiety**, fear of unfamiliar adults (Mangelsdorf, Shapiro, & Marzolf, 1995; Van Hulle, Moore, Lemery-Chalfant, Goldsmith, & Brooker, 2017). If the stranger has an unusual appearance and moves intrusively, fear can intensify into a red-faced, tearful, arm-flapping demand for safe haven from a familiar caregiver.

Reciprocal Relationship

From about 1½ to 2 years of age, infants employ budding cognitive abilities that allow them to infer parents' goals and plans. They now grasp some of the factors that determine the parent's coming and going, for example, mother's work schedule, and accordingly are less inclined to protest the separation. By the end of their first year, infants develop mental images of the care they have had from parents and other primary caregivers. Bowlby called these representations *working models* of attachments, which he considered to be rough templates for how activities with caregivers unfold (e.g., Grannie picks me up when I cry; Melinda plays peekaboo after my diaper change; Daddy rolls around the floor and laughs with me). These representations guide interactions with caregivers and give infants a sense of how they might best achieve an objective (e.g., being entertained or cuddled). Infants now actively participate in their relationships, taking turns in a conversation.

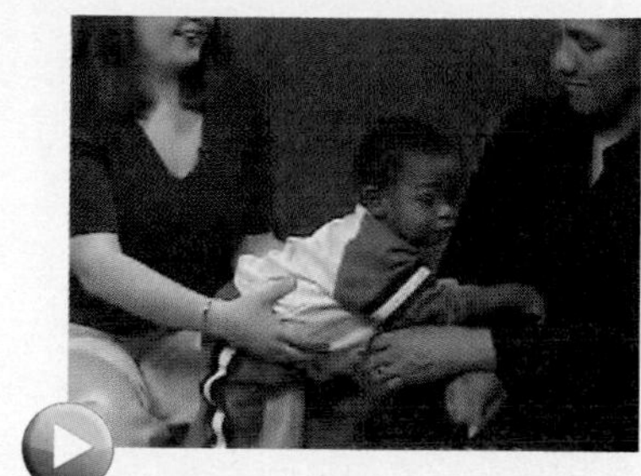

MyLab Education
Video Example 11.1

Find Developmental Meaning *How does the infant show wariness of an unfamiliar adult?* The little boy responds with fear and withdraws from the stranger's reach.

Attachments after Infancy

If parents have been sensitive and reliable, children will expect teachers and caregivers to be caring as well (L. J. Sherman, Rice, & Cassidy, 2015). As they interact with unfamiliar adults, children update their expectations for interactions. Gradually, children integrate separate bonds into a multifaceted understanding of different kinds of relationships (L. J. Sherman et al., 2015). They also draw conclusions about the degree to which others see them as acceptable partners, as worthy of love. The processes of reflecting on others and oneself are fundamental to other changes that take place during childhood and adolescence.

MyLab Education
Video Example 11.2

Find Developmental Meaning *How does Corwin contribute to the interaction with his mother?* Corwin vocalizes when his mother pauses, responding with words, sounds, and body movements.

Early Childhood

As they did in their infant days, young children rely on familiar caregivers for refuge when they are sick, scared, or distressed (S. F. Waters et al., 2010). Sensitive attention shifts from hands-on care (e.g., with feeding, diapering, and physically soothing the baby) to guidance with rules (e.g., "Please wash your hands before snack," and "Use your words"; Landry et al., 2014). Children take on a more mature role in relationships, talking with adults, hugging them back, and negotiating plans for the day. You can see "love notes" to mothers prepared by Ivy and Alex in Artifact Example 11.1.

Continuous contact with parents is no longer necessary. Protests over separations are fewer now, and stranger anxiety becomes less intense because children realize that they will be reunited with their parents shortly and that in the meantime relatives and caregivers will treat them well (Pinquart, Feußner, & Ahnert, 2013; Vu, 2015). Children begin to trust a number of teachers and classmates whom they find to be friendly and supportive (Ereky-Stevens, Funder, Katschnig, Malmberg, & Datler, 2018; Main & Cassidy, 1988; Schaffer, 1996). They are now able to balance personal desires with the perspectives of friends, endeavoring for solutions that meet everyone's needs (Groh et al., 2014; Howes, 1999; Kochanska & Kim, 2013).

MyLab Education
Artifact Example 11.1

Find Developmental Meaning *How did 3-year-old Ivy and 4-year-old Alex express their feelings for their mothers?* The two children chose the same graphic device, a stack of hearts, to represent the depth of their love for their mothers.

Middle Childhood and Adolescence

During the school years, youngsters typically remain close with parents, all the while growing attached to siblings, grandparents, extended family members, teachers, and classmates. Predictable separations (such as going to school each day or to summer camp for a week) worry a small number of elementary school children. The majority of school-aged children are secure enough that they feel safe with teachers and are able to concentrate on academic concepts (Geddes, 2017). Many adolescents become increasingly close to friends and romantic partners and prefer to receive attention from parents and teachers behind the scenes (Colley & Cooper, 2017; Elmore & Huebner, 2010; Mayseless, 2005; Venta, Shmueli-Goetz, & Sharp, 2014). In their desire for autonomy and close bonds with peers, teens prepare (consciously or not) for departure from the family nest.

Security in Attachment

The developmental course of attachments we have outlined is one that assumes dedication from parents, teachers, and other caregivers. Most adults responsible for children earn their trust, but in unfortunate exceptions, some do not.

If you look around at a group of toddlers or preschool children, you may notice variations in responses to being afraid, hurt, or upset. Some children find comfort in the reassuring arms of caregivers, a few are clingy and fretful, and one or two want to be left alone. To study such differences in the laboratory, Mary Ainsworth created a mildly stressful situation for 1-year-old infants. In a sequence of events, a mother and her infant were first brought to a playroom and left alone. A stranger (a research assistant) soon entered the room and attempted to play with the baby. After 3 minutes, the mother left, leaving the baby alone with the stranger. Subsequently, the mother returned and the stranger departed, leaving mother and baby together. Next, mother departed, with baby alone; the stranger returned at this point. Finally, the mother returned and the stranger departed (Ainsworth et al., 1978). This sequence, now known as the Strange Situation, has become a popular tool for assessing attachment in young children.

In the Strange Situation, attention is focused primarily on the child's behavior. Observers rate the child's attempts to seek contact with the caregiver, resistance to or avoidance of caregiver, exploration of toys in the room, and level of distress. From such ratings, the child is given one of several classifications:

MyLab Education
Video Example 11.3
Find Developmental Meaning *How does the infant respond to his father's departure and return?* The little boy becomes upset when his father leaves for a moment and is relieved when they are reunited.

- Infants who exhibit **secure attachment** use caregivers as a secure base. When caregivers are present, infants actively explore new toys and surroundings. When caregivers return after leaving the room, infants smile and talk to them, move over to greet them, or in other ways seek their proximity. About 60% to 70% of infants are classified as securely attached (Ainsworth et al., 1978; R. A. Thompson, 2006).
- Infants who exhibit **insecure-avoidant attachment** seem oblivious to a caregiver's presence. They fail to greet the caregiver and may even look away when reunited. Instead, they go about their business independently, and they are somewhat superficial in their interactions with toys. About 15% to 20% of children tested in Strange Situation studies appear insecure-avoidant (Ainsworth et al., 1978; R. A. Thompson, 2006).
- Infants who exhibit **insecure-resistant attachment** seem preoccupied with their caregivers yet are not easily comforted. When caregivers come back, the infants remain distressed and angry. They may rush to parents and other caregivers yet continue to cry and struggle to be released. Insecure-resistant infants comprise about 10 percent of participants in Strange Situation studies (Ainsworth et al., 1978; R. A. Thompson, 2006).
- More serious problems in attachment, which were not part of Ainsworth's original classification, have since been identified by other experts. A **disorganized and disoriented attachment** style has been documented, in which infants lack a coherent way of responding to worrisome events (Carlson, Hostinar, Mliner, & Gunnar, 2014; Granqvist et al., 2017; Main & Solomon, 1986, 1990; Zilberstein & Messer, 2010). Infants classified in this manner appear calm one moment, yet, without provocation, are scared or angry the next. Infants interrupt their own actions midstream, for example, by crawling toward caregivers and then suddenly freezing with apprehension. A very few children show *no* attachment behaviors or exhibit other extremely serious problems, such as displaying fear of familiar

caregivers rather than being comforted by them. Approximately 15% of children show a disorganized and disoriented attachment, no attachment, or another serious attachment problem (R. A. Thompson, 2006).

The Observation Guidelines table "Noticing Young Children's Attachment Behaviors" summarizes how children with particular kinds of attachments might act. In observing children, teachers and caregivers should guard against taking single responses from a child as an undisputable indicator of attachment security. They should instead look for patterns of behavior over time and consider their observations as tentative clues of the child's needs.

Attachment in a Developmental System

From a developmental systems perspective, the child contributes to his or her first relationships by relaxing when comforted, expressing positive regard, and taking an active role in interactions. These behaviors depend on the quality of the caregiver–child relationship, the child's individual characteristics, and the cultural setting.

OBSERVATION GUIDELINES
Noticing Young Children's Attachment Behaviors

CHARACTERISTIC	LOOK FOR	EXAMPLE	IMPLICATION
Secure Attachment	• *Active, intentional exploration* of the environment in the presence of a caregiver • *Protest at being separated from a caregiver*; ability to be soothed when the caregiver returns • *Initial wariness of strangers*, with eventual acceptance if reassured by a familiar caregiver	Luis cries when his father drops him off at the child care center in the morning. After a few minutes, he settles down and crawls to an affectionate teacher who is beginning to become an attachment figure for him.	It is natural for young children to resist separation from family members. Help little tykes establish a routine for saying good-bye in the morning, and give them extra attention during transitions. Reassure parents and describe the activities their children engage in after they relax.
Insecure-Avoidant Attachment	• *Superficial exploration* of the environment • *Indifference to a caregiver's departure*; failure to seek comfort upon the caregiver's return • *Apparent discomfort around strangers* but without an active resistance to their social overtures	Jennifer walks around her new child care center with a frown on her face. She parts easily with her mother and willingly explores her new environment, albeit without much enthusiasm. Jennifer glances up when her mother returns at the end of the day but doesn't seem overjoyed with mother's presence.	Children who seem aloof benefit from private and quiet signs of affection and eventually are likely to relax at school. For children who seem at ease with separation, support them throughout the day. Form your own affectionate relationships with them, knowing that such ties can evolve into secure bonds.
Insecure-Resistant Attachment	• *Clinginess* with caregiver • *Agitation and distress* at caregiver's departure; continued fussing after caregiver returns • *Apparent fear of strangers*; tendency to stay close to caregiver in new situation • Anxiety when left alone and sometimes in presence of caregiver	Irene tightly clutches her mother as the two enter the preschool room, and she stays close by as her mother signs her in for the morning. She is extremely upset when her mother leaves, seems to play with little enthusiasm, and remains agitated for a long time after their reunion later in the day.	If children appear anxious when they enter a new setting, give them extra time to separate from parents. Sometimes a "comfort" object from home (a teddy bear or blanket) can help. Be patient as you interact with children, knowing that they may eventually be able to form a secure bond with you.
Disorganized and Disoriented Attachment or Other Serious Attachment Problem	• *Unpredictable emotions* • *Cautious approaches* to caregivers, possibly indicative of fright • *Failure to contact caregiver* when distressed (after age 1) • *Reckless exploration* and failure to seek reassurance • *Reversed roles*, with excessive concern about caregiver • *No signs of attachment to* familiar caregivers and possible fear of them • *Indiscriminately friendly behavior* to new people and no preferences for familiar caregivers • *Signs of overwhelming grief* after the death of a primary caregiver	Myles seems lost at school. He arrives hungry, walks around aimlessly, and eventually sits and plays with blocks. He is aggressive with peers, and his teacher sees bruises on his arms.	Provide special attention to and closely monitor children who seem to have serious attachment problems. Be on the lookout for signs of abuse, and be ready to consult authorities. Work hard to establish positive, trusting relationships with children. Professional intervention may be necessary for the children and their families.

Sources: Ainsworth et al. (1978); J. Cassidy, Jones, and Shaver (2013); Gervai (2009); Granqvist et al. (2017); M. T. Greenberg (1999); Lundahl, Bettmann, Hurtado, and Goldsmith (2014); Main and Solomon (1986, 1990); Schuengel, de Schipper, Sterkenburg, and Kef (2013); Svanberg, Mennet, and Spieker (2010); R. A. Thompson (2006); and Zeanah (2000).

Developmental Systems Prompt

The formation of first attachments is a dynamic process for the child and his or her family. As you learn about factors that disrupt the process, such as turmoil in the family, consider the child's special needs for reassurance and, in serious cases, professional intervention for the family.

Quality of Caregiver–Child Relationship

The relationship between caregiver and child is the primary basis of attachment security. When caregivers are sensitive to young children, protect them from harm, respond sympathetically to their emotions, and provide for their needs, children are usually able to develop secure attachments (Farrow & Blissett, 2014; R. A. Thompson, 2006). Caregivers who are sensitively engaged show these qualities:

- *Contingent responses to infants' needs.* Caregivers establish routines for feeding, diapering, and holding infants. They do not run to every whimper, but they do notice and respond to infants' basic emotional reactions and are faithfully available when infants are in true anguish (M. Cassidy & Berlin, 1994; Farrow & Blissett, 2014; Morawska, Laws, Moretto, & Daniels, 2014; R. A. Thompson, Easterbrooks, & Padilla-Walker, 2003). For example, when introducing a new food, parents observe infants' facial expressions and their tasting and swallowing. Caregivers who are not responsive can be neglectful, intrusive, erratically available, and callous to infants' preferences and feelings.
- *Regular expressions of affection.* Caregivers dote on babies in a variety of ways that communicate love and pleasure in the interchange (Posada, 2013). Caregivers in some societies express affection through physical touch, for example, by gently carrying the baby most of the day and attending to discomfort by providing breast or bottle, shifting posture, and changing soiled diapers and clothing (H. Keller, 2017). In other societies, including in many Western families, parents carry the baby less often yet caress and rock him or her regularly, provide for physical needs, and smile, establish eye contact, and talk sweetly. Caregivers who fail to show affection may be withdrawn or even hostile and rejecting.
- *Openness to babies influencing the pace and direction of interaction.* Caregivers let infants take the lead on occasion. They note where infants are looking, watch their posture, look for emotional expressions, and recognize when infants want to interact (Farrow & Blissett, 2014; Isabella & Belsky, 1991; H. Keller, 2017; D. N. Stern, 1977). Adults act in synchrony, considering it a turn in the interaction when infants smile, move their hands, or babble. Caregivers who fail to show this quality intrusively redirect infants' attention, perhaps to the point that infants look away, cry, or go to sleep. They miss infants' subtle bids for attention, for example, by ignoring infants' attempts to make eye contact.

Children's Personal Characteristics

Children actively participate in their relationships with caregivers by making their needs known, relaxing when comforted, and reciprocating with affection. Infants' moods, gestures, and behaviors influence the manner in which caregivers interact with them. Whereas some infants fuss a lot when scared, others protest less adamantly. Infants who are exceptionally fearful and irritable can be difficult to care for, whereas those who are good natured and sociable invite positive, relaxed interactions (Brumariu & Kerns, 2013; R. A. Thompson, 2006).

For most children with disabilities, their special circumstances play only a minor role in the security of their attachments. Babies who are premature, delayed in developmental milestones, and unusually fussy are able to develop secure attachments as long as their needs are met with compassion (Spangler, 2013; van IJzendoorn, Goldberg, Kroonenberg, & Frenkel, 1992). Likewise, babies with chromosomal or genetic disorders or other disabilities typically form secure attachments when parents provide responsive care (E. A. Carlson, Sampson, & Sroufe, 2003). Children with Down syndrome are apt to form strong bonds with their parents even though their parents do not always recognize their subtle requests for comfort (Schuengel et al., 2013). The majority of children with autism become securely attached to their parents, even given the difficulty children have in understanding parents' eye contact and facial expressions (E. Perry & Flood, 2016). For a few children with disabilities, secure attachments are not easily formed because parents struggle to accept the diagnosis and find it taxing to meet their unique needs (Abubakar et al., 2013; E. Perry & Flood, 2016).

Culture and Community

Parents follow cultural practices in caring for infants, and the infants, in turn, grow accustomed to the style of interaction. Many Japanese, Indonesian, and Korean infants become upset when their mothers leave the room and take a while to calm down at their return (Jin, Jacobvitz, Hazen, & Jung, 2012; Miyake, Chen, & Campos, 1985; Takahashi, 1990). This reaction probably occurs because infants in these societies rarely separate from mothers, and when they do, it is in the care of close relatives (especially grandparents) rather than strangers (Saarni et al., 2006). In comparison, in Germany, many babies do not fret much when their mothers leave the room, nor do they move frantically toward mothers at their return (Grossmann, Grossmann, Huber, & Wartner, 1981; LeVine & Norman, 2008). German mothers regularly leave infants to do brief errands, and the infants grow used to being on their own for brief periods.

Cultures also prescribe appropriate methods for responding to infants' distress (Jin et al., 2012; Morelli & Rothbaum, 2007). Gusii mothers of Kenya continually hold, comfort, and watch their infants, who rarely cry (R. A. LeVine, 2004). These mothers are alarmed when they watch videos of Western mothers allowing infants to cry, even for a few moments. In comparison, some Western mothers believe that they are cultivating self-reliance when they allow infants to comfort themselves. Consider the experience of a German aunt who is caring for Karl, almost 2 years of age, while his parents are away on a 2-week vacation:

> "Oh, he's a good boy, but a bit fussy," his aunt says . . . . The aunt tells of how early he wakes up in the morning, at six o'clock, "but I'm not to take him out of bed, Sigrid (Karl's mother) said, he's to stay there until nine or he'll just get used to it and she won't have it; she's done that from when he was a baby." So Karl is kept in bed, he stays quiet, she doesn't know what he does, hears him move about in his bed, babbling to himself. (LeVine & Norman, 2008, p. 134)

Methods of communication with infants are culturally based. Earlier we suggested that societies differ in the degree to which they emphasize physical versus verbal contact. Let's illustrate what affectionate interactions look like in North America and Western Europe, where many parents respond tenderly to infants' cooing and babbling (P. M. Cole & Tan, 2007; H. Keller, 2017; R. A. Thompson & Virmani, 2010). Consider an affectionate interaction between a U.S. father and his 3-month-old daughter Toto after a family event. In the exchange, the father interacts good-naturedly with Toto, regularly waiting for, and then commenting on, her vocalizations:

Father: 5:30 p.m. Post-mortem on a party.
Toto: Eh.
Father: What was your reaction? What was your reaction? Did you like the food?
Toto: Ah! Ahaa ah.
Father: Yeah, that milk huh? It wasn't so bad, huh? And the guests—did you like the guests?
Toto: Eh.
Father: No, not so interesting.
Toto: Eh! Ah ah.
Father: What about the host and hostess?
Toto: Aha aaaaah!
Father: Yeah! Uncle Jim and Auntie Ann!
Toto: Aaah!
Father: Yeah, they're very nice.
Toto: Ha! Ha! Ha! Oh.
Father: Yeah; and did you enjoy yourself?
Toto: Aha! Aaah! Aaah!
Father: Yeah you had a good time. Well that's nice.
Toto: Ah haa!
Father: Well that's really nice.
Toto: Heheh! Ahh! Hehh!
Father: Did you think so as well? Yeah, I think so. Hmm? Yes?
Toto: Hah! Aaaah! Ah!

> Father: You didn't cry at all and you were very polite!
> (dialogue from Reissland, 2006, p. 44)

From this exchange and other similar interactions, Toto is learning that her father can be trusted to be warm, reliable, and respectful during her induction into communication.

The context in which the family lives is important in another respect. As you may know, it can be exhausting to care for a baby, and when parents in any society are isolated and under extreme stress, they easily become inconsiderate or even harsh in their caregiving. Although most parents are able to respond warmly to children's bids for affection, burdens can accumulate in parents' lives and spark anger, depression, insensitivity, and withdrawal (J. Patterson & Vakili, 2014). When community support is scarce and parents experience marital conflict, chronic illness, economic poverty, and substance abuse, they must make great effort to remain sensitive, especially with babies who are exceptionally needy, irritable, or muted in bids for affection.

Multiple Attachments

Early investigators focused on mothers as primary attachment figures, probably because women physically bear children and have historically done most of the feeding, bathing, and diapering (Ainsworth et al., 1978; Bowlby, 1969/1982). Increasingly, research has examined the significant roles that fathers, other caregivers, and siblings play as attachment figures.

When two parents are present in the home, infants frequently show an initial preference for one parent and soon welcome the second one as an attachment figure. Both parents are likely to instill secure attachments when they responsively attend to children's needs, express affection, and remain in children's lives for an extended time (Boldt, Kochanska, Yoon, & Koenig Nordling, 2014; Howes, 1999; R. A. Thompson et al., 2003). Nevertheless, mothers and fathers go about expressing their warmth in slightly different ways. Mothers tend to be more hands-on with infants, enthusiastic, verbal, and thoughtful about what infants might be experiencing, whereas fathers tend to engage infants in physical play, handling of toys, and exploration of the environment (M. E. Lamb & Lewis, 2004; Malmberg et al., 2007; Nordahl, Janson, Manger, & Zachrisson, 2014).

MyLab Education
Video Example 11.4
Find Developmental Meaning *How does the father in this video interact with his baby daughter?* The father dotes on 7-month-old Madison and anticipates her responses during a familiar exchange.

Contemporary researchers have found that infants also form attachments with siblings, grandparents, and other caregivers (E. Farmer, Selwyn, & Meakings, 2013; H. Keller, 2017; M. Lewis, 2005; Seibert & Kerns, 2009). Around the world, infants regularly form attachments with multiple figures. When infants are cared for by parents, siblings, extended family, and perhaps an employed caregiver, they may easily develop attachments to a handful of people. In one investigation with the Aka, a foraging people in a tropical region of Africa, infants exhibited attachments to 6 or more of the 20 people they interacted with on a daily basis (Meehan & Hawks, 2013).

Having a network of affectionate caregivers has benefits for children (Easterbrooks, Bartlett, Beeghly, & Thompson, 2013; C. B. Fisher, Jackson, & Villarruel, 1998; Howes, 1999; H. Keller, 2017). The various attachment figures in the child's network are apt to take on somewhat distinct roles. A 1-year-old crawls to Grandma when a stranger enters the family home; at 6, the same child seeks advice from his older sister about bullies on the playground; and at 14, the youngster talks with an uncle about career options. Relationships with all of these family members remain steady, but the particular kinds of support are differentially helpful over time. In addition to these focused roles, loving relatives and family friends can amplify support when parents are temporarily unable to meet the child's needs.

Attachments with Teachers

Attachments with teachers and employed caregivers serve a critical role for children. As is the case with parents, secure bonds with teachers and other professionals depend on responsive care and a sustained commitment (Ahnert, Pinquart, & Lamb, 2006; Howes, 1999). During the preschool and elementary years, children often develop close bonds with teachers, thriving on their warm care and feeling safe in their presence

(G. Cooper, Hoffman, & Powell, 2017; Cugmas, 2011; H. A. Davis, 2003). When parenting is abusive or otherwise problematic, a close bond with a teacher can alleviate the child's distress (Sabol & Pianta, 2012).

In the middle school years, adolescents spend a small portion of time with any single teacher, are in classes with large groups of students, and may feel anonymous at school. Therefore, close relationships with teachers are less common than before When adolescents have supportive relationships with their teachers, they tend to enjoy school, feel competent, and achieve at high levels academically (Al-Yagon, 2012; H. A. Davis, 2003; Roeser, Midgley, & Urdan, 1996). Unfortunately, obstacles to close relationships with teachers intensify in high school. High school students often find relationships with teachers to be adversarial—it's "us" against "them"—in part because they are perceived to be rebellious, independent, and resistant to close relationships (H. A. Davis, 2003). Yet good relationships with teachers clearly benefit youth. High school students who have supportive relationships with teachers and other mentors are more likely to be well adjusted and complete high school than students without such support (Cotterell, 1992; Georgiou, Demetriou, & Stavrinides, 2008).

MyLab Education
Video Example 11.5

Find Developmental Meaning *How does Auntie Spring console Matthew as he arrives at preschool?* Matthew protests separation from his mother and is soothed by Auntie Spring.

Attachment Security at School

A secure attachment during infancy has long-term benefits. In Western cultures, children who have been securely attached as infants tend to become relatively independent, empathic, and socially competent preschoolers (Sroufe, 1983; Sroufe, Egeland, Carlson, & Collins, 2005; Vaughn, Egeland, Sroufe, & Waters, 1979). In middle childhood and adolescence, they tend to be self-confident and cooperative with their parents, adjust easily to school environments, establish productive relationships with teachers and peers, do well on classroom tasks, and graduate from high school (Goffin, Boldt, & Kochanska, 2017; Groh et al., 2014; E. O'Connor & McCartney, 2006; Urban, Carlson, Egeland, & Sroufe, 1991). Security of attachment is also related to future relationships, with adults who had been securely attached as infants tending to look after their own children with sensitivity (Berlin, Cassidy, & Appleyard, 2008; Mikulincer & Shaver, 2013). The longterm advantages differ slightly in other cultures. For Japanese children, close and affectionate relationships with caregivers foster an appreciation for caregivers' benevolence and a desire to act harmoniously with others (Morelli & Rothbaum, 2007).

An important mechanism by which first attachments affect later social behavior is through the working models of relationships we introduced earlier. As children have contact with primary caregivers, they form mental representations of the degree to which their needs are met (Bowlby, 1969/1982, 1973; R. M. Ryan, Stiller, & Lynch, 1994). Especially when they are young, children's understanding of relationships is largely unconscious yet influential to their style of interacting (S. C. Johnson et al., 2010; Maier, Bernier, Pekrun, Zimmermann, & Grossmann, 2004). For example, children with secure attachments are inclined to forgive friends and teachers for misunderstandings; those with insecure or disorganized attachments may remain suspicious or on guard.

Even as children are strongly influenced by their first relationships, they remain amenable to new kinds of bonds. In one investigation, when parents were initially harsh and insensitive but later became affectionate and responsive, their children were likely to develop increasingly productive social skills (NICHD Early Child Care Research Network, 2006b). In another study, many children who had been raised in orphanages with perfunctory care were able to form secure bonds with responsive adoptive parents (Carlson et al., 2014). The reverse trend also occurs, although perhaps less often. Some young people who had been securely attached and later lived through one or more traumatic events (perhaps a parent's death, their abuse, or violence between the parents) became overwhelmed with stress and did not establish healthy relationships later in life (M. Lewis, Feiring, & Rosenthal, 2000; Mikulincer & Shaver, 2007; E. Waters, Merrick, Treboux, Crowell, & Albersheim, 2000).

Thus, as youngsters grow older, relationships with teachers and friends and, eventually, romantic partners, provide opportunities for new types of attachments (Arriaga, Kumashiro, Simpson, & Overall, 2018; M. W. Baldwin, Keelan, Fehr, Enns, & Koh-Rangarajoo, 1996; C. Chow & Ruhl, 2014). Children supplement their initial mental representation of what interpersonal relationships are like with new understandings of being in a relationship. Eventually, these various mental representations become integrated into the child's personality (R. A. Thompson, 2006). In other words, children may initially develop trust in a parent and later become trusting people.

At the beginning of the school year, teachers and counselors may notice variations in students' interactions. Imagine you are getting to know students in your third-grade classroom. You might encounter profiles such as the following:

- Oscar seems happy about being in third grade. School is a safe place. He trusts you. You find Oscar to be likable, and he takes your suggestions about his schoolwork seriously. You notice that he has a few good friends with whom he affiliates at recess and lunch. After his Nana died, he sits with you during lunchtime, shows you her memorial photographs, and tells you about her. Oscar appears to use behaviors that anticipate a secure attachment.
- Elia quietly settles into third grade. She appears businesslike and needs no one's help—or so she says. She is uncomfortable when you stand near her desk. Elia has a few classmates whom she seems to like, but she spends most of her time by herself. She gets annoyed when you hand back her work with comments and recommendations for improvement. Elia's behaviors are consistent with an insecure-avoidant style.
- Marissa is the first child you notice in the morning because she is waiting at the classroom door. She is worried about one thing or another—where she can store her lunchbox, whether she will be able to check out books from the library, and where she will sit. During lessons, Marissa seems preoccupied and, on the playground, clingy with her friend Biba. Marissa exhibits behaviors exemplifying an insecure-resistant style.
- Every morning, Jeremy smiles at you and his classmates. Yet his approachability appears to be a self-serving mechanism for getting what he wants—part of his classmates' lunch, approval from adults, etc. After a few months, Jeremy has not made any friends and appears tense, lonely, and erratic. When frustrated, he lashes out at classmates, hides in the bathroom, and calls you names. Jeremy shows behaviors consistent with a disorganized attachment.

Each of these students, and the others in your classroom, require your sensitivity if they are to feel safe with you and one another. Oscar is hitting the ground running, but for Elia, Marissa, and Jeremy, it may take months of reassurance from teachers and participation in age-appropriate routines (Geddes, 2017; P. Nash, 2017). The teacher's persistence in being warm and available allows a troubled child to construct a new model for relationships, one in which it is possible to relax in the teacher's care.

Implications of Attachment Research

As you have learned, infants' attachments at home provide the foundation for future relationships. This foundation can be rebuilt if it's shaky, and it must occasionally be bolstered if, despite a solid beginning, it weakens in adverse circumstances. The Development-Enhancing Education feature "Offering Warm and Sensitive Care to Infants and Toddlers" illustrates high-quality care at this age. Teachers and other school professionals can also support the attachments of older children, as you can see in the following recommendations:

- **Be patient as students get to know you.** Students who feel insecure at school may appear anxious, aloof, tentative, unruly, or superficially friendly (García Sierra, 2012). Given their fear in entering your classroom, insecure children are likely to appreciate it when you put them at ease. Your warm greetings, expressions of care, provisions for an engaging curriculum, protection from harm, and calm discipline are fodder for secure relationships. Yet it takes time for children to construct a new working model for relationships. Try not to take it personally when students are wary of you for the initial weeks or months of school.

- **Nurture bonds in children of all ages.** The need for close attachments does not end with infancy. Children stand to gain immensely by having high-quality

DEVELOPMENT-ENHANCING EDUCATION

Offering Warm and Sensitive Care to Infants and Toddlers

Meet infants' needs in a timely fashion.

- An infant program has one caregiver for every three infants, a ratio that helps ensure no one is left unattended for long. When it is impossible to tend immediately to the needs of individual children, a caregiver reassures them that their needs are important and that she will be there as soon as possible. (Infancy)
- A mother is talking on her cell phone when her baby begins to cry. The mother tells her friend that she will call her back after she gives her baby a bottle and rocks him to sleep. (Infancy)

Respond positively to new abilities.

- Caregivers in one center cheer on milestones, including advances in crawling, first steps, and first words. They share their delight with family members and are sensitive to the desire of parents to be among the first to witness the advancement: "Raj is getting ready to walk, isn't he!" (Infancy)
- A father notices that his 6-month-old son has begun to flip over from back to front. The father gets on the floor beside his son and imitates his roll over. Together they laugh as they move back and forth. (Infancy)

Be polite but matter-of-fact when referring to infants' bodies.

- The director of an infant program trains staff members to use neutral terms for body functions. She asks a new teacher to not use the term "stinky baby," but instead to make a simple statement that an infant's diaper needs to be changed. (Infancy)
- A grandfather notices that his grandson has diarrhea and is developing diaper rash. As he changes the baby's diaper, he tells him, "Your bottom is getting very sore. I'm going to put some ointment on you after I wipe your bottom." (Infancy)

Set limits and redirect unacceptable behavior in a firm, but gentle way.

- The director of an infant-toddler program reminds teachers that their role is one of a *nurturer* who helps children learn self-control rather than an *authority figure* who doles out punishments. He suggests, "Tell children what they *can* do instead of telling them what they *cannot* do. You might say, 'Walk inside, please. Run outside.'" (Infancy)
- A quick-moving toddler has managed to unplug a humidifier and spill water from the tank. Her caregiver removes her from the scene and inserts safety plugs into the socket. She tells the little girl, "I made a mistake by placing the humidifier where you could reach it. Let me put it somewhere else so you don't get hurt." (Infancy)

Structure the environment so that infants can maintain stable relationships with caregivers.

- An infant-toddler program is arranged into separate rooms so that each caregiver has a small number of children with whom to interact. Toddler teachers make a point to visit the infant room occasionally to get to know children who will soon move to their room. (Infancy)
- In one child-care center, caregivers arrange children into groups that stay together; as the infants outgrow the "Infant Room," for example, they "graduate" together to the "Toddler Room," and their caregiver goes with them. (Infancy)

relationships with their teachers during the elementary, middle, and high school years. In general, teachers and caregivers find it easiest to become acquainted with children in elementary school. However, teachers at the older levels can express their concern for individual students and get to know those they advise or see often (H. A. Davis, 2003). Many secondary schools make it a policy that every student has at least one advocate who checks in with him or her periodically. Adults can further promote ties among classmates, for example, by structuring group work and giving them a chance to become involved in clubs and sports teams.

- **When children undergo a family disruption, provide extra attention.** Children invariably want to stay connected with parents who move away for one reason or another. When parents are divorcing and agree to share custody of their children, teachers can send home copies of newsletters to both and invite each to meetings. Counselors can talk with parents about practical ways to facilitate rotations between households (J. B. Kelly & Lamb, 2000). When a parent is deployed in the military, hospitalized after surgery, incarcerated, employed out of state, or recently deceased, teachers can reassure children, watch for distress (e.g., regressing in basic skills, such as losing bladder control or struggling to sleep at nap time), and, when suffering persists, look into counseling at the school (Lieberman & Van Horn, 2013; Shear & Shair, 2005).

• **Encourage multiple attachments.** In the child care center and at school, children may talk about a variety of people in their lives (e.g., brothers and sisters, aunts and uncles, grandparents, and neighbors). Teachers and other practitioners can encourage children to invite these important individuals to school events and orientation meetings. Educators can further help children by establishing a productive classroom environment that fosters relationships among students. Children with insecure attachments to parents may not find it easy to brush off teasing from classmates, and thus, a classroom goal of treating one another with respect is valuable (Scharf, 2014).

• **Advocate for stability in caregivers.** Children find it disruptive when a devoted teacher is present one day only to vanish the next. Rates of turnover in preschools are high because the position of early childhood teacher is misconceived to be an easy job, is not paid well compared to other professions, and does not universally require advanced education. School and center leaders can promote a stable early childhood staff by paying a competitive wage, enforcing minimal education requirements (e.g., in some U.S. states, bachelor's degree or course work in early childhood education), and investing in professional development (Blank, 2010; J. Cassidy et al., 2013; Dennis & Horn, 2014; S. Wagner et al., 2013).

• **As you notice signs of insecurity, step up the give-and-take.** Warm and consistent routines, especially during arrivals and departures, help insecure children to adjust well to the demands of school (C. S. Cain, 2006; Mercer, 2006). Depending on the age of the child, you might sit together during a relaxing activity, perhaps building blocks, tossing a ball back and forth, and walking and talking on school grounds. Because children who are anxious sometimes demand a lot of attention, you can intersperse reassurance with invitations to take on independent challenges, such as persisting with a difficult assignment, sitting beside a classmate at lunch, or speaking in front of the class.

• **Encourage parents to respect children's self-initiated actions.** One of the most effective tactics family educators can use with insensitive parents is to *show* them (in person or through videotapes) how children enjoy caring gestures during such routine games as playing peekaboo or tossing the ball back and forth (Bakermans-Kranenburg, van IJzendoorn, & Juffer, 2003; A. Carr, 2014; Svanberg et al., 2010). Mental health programs that have generated improvements in parents' responsivity, consistency, and warmth with children have focused on following the child's lead during an interaction, avoiding interactions that could be frightening (e.g., speaking harshly), remaining focused on the child rather than drifting off into daydreams, and comforting the child during upsetting experiences (Granqvist et al., 2017).

• **Coach parents in thinking about infants' understanding of events.** Parents do not always understand what makes their babies "tick" ("Why does Mike keep jumping out of his crib? Every time he does this, he gets hurt. What is he *thinking*?"). Professionals can share ideas about infants' motives, feelings, and understandings to help parents appreciate how babies might view the world ("Mike is one determined little guy, isn't he? He really wants to explore his environment!"). When parents learn to reflect on how infants feel and construe events, attachments tend to become more secure (Koren-Karie, Oppenheim, Dolev, Sher, & Etzion-Carasso, 2002).

• **Advise parents about the special needs of children with disabilities.** Some parents feel overwhelmed by the challenge of raising a child with a disability. Teachers and caregivers can help parents recognize their child's distinctive ways of expressing emotions. You might ask parents of a blind girl if she enjoys exploring their faces with her hands. Similarly, you could point out to parents of a child with Down syndrome that children with this condition may show discomfort in subtle, rather than insistent, ways, and they appreciate the chance every now and then to control the pace of the exchange (D. Howe, 2006; Schuengel et al., 2013).

• **Reach out to recently appointed parent figures.** When children are removed from families by social service authorities because of maltreatment, neglect, drug abuse, or criminal activity, they can find the transition to be traumatic (Chisholm, Carter,

Ames, & Morison, 1995; Marcovitch et al., 1997; Zilberstein & Messer, 2010). Professionals can let new families know what to expect. Foster parents of an 8-year-old boy might be advised to expect temper tantrums and to respond firmly and affectionately. Foster parents can be trained to communicate their expectations for controlled behavior, follow through with agreed-on consequences to misbehavior, and persist with showing affection, even before the child feels safe enough to reciprocate with caring concern. New parents who are under excessive **stress**, the physiological response of feeling worried, tense, and pressured, may benefit from counseling or other therapy (J. Patterson & Vakili, 2014).

• **Address the needs of the family when parents struggle with their own unmet emotional needs.** Mental health problems, including substance abuse, are a major factor in harsh, intrusive, and abusive parenting. When parents are anxious or depressed, they are at risk for becoming unresponsive, inconsistent, and hostile toward their children, which, in turn, can trigger sadness and withdrawal in children (Burrous, Crockenberg, & Leerkes, 2009; Teti, Gelfand, Messinger, & Isabella, 1995). Professional intervention that helps parents cope can be a necessary first step in them shifting to an involved, affectionate parenting style (Benoit & Parker, 1994; Main, Kaplan, & Cassidy, 1985). During the period in which a parent receives mental health treatment, the other parent or another family member can be advised to use tender and responsive care.

• **Collaborate with colleagues when attachment problems are serious.** It takes a team of school professionals to guide, love, and discipline a child whose social-emotional development has been seriously undermined at home. For one child, the team might be composed of the following:

- The child him or herself, who is being asked to grow and change
- Trained foster parents, who take the child into their home and enlist cooperation in household activities, chores, and family meals
- The parents, who try to rebuild their lives and prepare for the child's return
- A counselor, who allows the child to talk about rejection, betrayal, or other hurtful experience, and also nurtures his or her coping skills
- A school nurse, who monitors the child's health and medication
- A special educator, who scaffolds progress in areas of academic weakness
- A school psychologist, who consults on matters of independence and discipline
- A classroom teacher, who befriends the child, integrates him or her into a productive learning situation, and enforces rules in a uniform way (C. S. Cain, 2006; Zilberstein & Messer, 2010).

Everyone has a job in steering the child onto a healthy trajectory, using methods that support a positive adjustment.

Summary

Ideally, children's first attachments are close and enduring bonds between themselves and their parents and other caregivers. Sensitive and responsive attention is the crucial ingredient for secure attachments and is reciprocated with children's affection. Secure attachments in the early years lead to positive social-emotional outcomes in later life. Attachments manifest themselves somewhat differently in different cultures, and the security of children's attachments can change over time.

Teachers and other professionals can develop their own positive relationships with children. Sensitive and ongoing care of individual children is the backbone of high-quality relationships with them. Educators can watch for significant social-emotional challenges faced by children, address these appropriately, and seek professional guidance when necessary.

MyLab Education Self-Check 11.2

Emotion

11.3 Encapsulate developmental trends in children's emotional understanding and expression, and outline strategies for supporting children's emotional health.

Emotions (sometimes referred to as *affective states*) are the feelings, both physiological and psychological, that people have in response to events that are personally relevant to their needs and goals (Campos, Frankel, & Camras, 2004). Emotions energize thoughts and behavior according to present circumstances (Goleman, 1995; Muris & Meesters, 2014). *Sadness* leads a child to find comfort from others and reassess whether a goal is possible, *anger* spurs a child to try a new tactic or abandon an unrealistic goal, and *happiness* prompts a child to share positive feelings with others and repeat a pleasurable experience in the future (Saarni et al., 2006). These and other emotions are described in the Observation Guidelines table "Assessing Emotion in Children."

Emotions Go to School

Classroom teachers and other school personnel have many occasions to observe children's emotions. A student arriving in the morning might be happy or anxious or feel a combination of affective states. When the student falls short on a test, he or she might become sad or disappointed, and after an argument with a friend, angry. Such emotions are a routine part of the student's day and generate opportunities for self-expression, problem solving, and learning. They can also be a distraction, as when a girl is enraged and shouts at her teacher and classmates. Likewise, emotions can influence learning, as when a depressed boy slumps in his chair and wanders off mentally. In fact, there is a strong association between the emotional health of children and their level of academic achievement. Those with advanced coping skills are likely to perform well on academic tasks (Edossa, Schroeders, Weinert, & Artelt, 2018; Paunesku et al., 2015; Pekrun, Lichtenfeld, Marsh, Murayama, & Goetz, 2017; Voltmer & von Salisch, 2017).

Teachers and other school professionals regularly notice children's emotions (Bridgeland, Bruce, & Hariharan, 2013). Many educators realize that social-emotional skills can be taught, and numerous schools have begun to invest in structured programs shown to be effective in fostering children's social-emotional skills (Krachman, LaRocca, & Gabrieli, 2018). An important foundation for professionals is an understanding of age-related advancements in children's emotional capacities.

Developmental Changes in Emotions

How youngsters express, understand, and cope with emotions changes with age and experience. Emotional development is characterized by the following trends.

Infants begin life with a few basic emotions and gradually experience additional feelings. *Distress*, *contentment*, and *interest* are felt within the first 6 months of life (Braungart-Rieker, Hill-Soderlund, & Karrass, 2010; Easterbrooks et al., 2013; Emde, Gaensbauer, & Harmon, 1976). Distress takes a few different forms. Newborns cry in alarm after a sudden noise, with urgency to mounting hunger, and in pain while suffering abdominal gas. Hungry babies most certainly feel pleasure when they feed. A small smile may occur when infants are relaxed, happy, or enchanted with animated people. Infants show interest by watching objects carefully, inspecting their arms and legs, mouthing fingers and toes, and tilting their head to listen to the fine points of speech and music. As they mature, infants add to their store of emotions. Simple distress can become true *anger* when desires are obstructed: Daddy does not come immediately to pick up baby, and Mommy does not indulge baby's desire to press buttons on her mobile phone. Infants show their anger by crying, thrashing, and looking directly, with accusation, at caregivers. Infants tend to show *fear* during the second half of the first year, as occurs in stranger anxiety (see the earlier discussion). Animals and objects that move in unexpected ways also scare infants.

OBSERVATION GUIDELINES
Assessing Emotion in Children

CHARACTERISTIC	LOOK FOR	EXAMPLE	IMPLICATION
Happiness	• *Smiles* • *Laughter* • *Spontaneity*	Paul, age 17, relaxes with his friends during the school's end-of-year athletic field day. He is happy about having schoolwork over and looks forward to his summer job, paychecks, and freedom.	Happiness helps people enjoy life and seek pleasurable experiences. Help children find appropriate outlets to express joy, and celebrate with them. Encourage them to talk about things they are happy about.
Anger	• *Frowns and angry expressions* • *Increased heartrate, respiration, and muscle tension* • *Possible retaliation* toward the source of anger	Aranya, age 14, is furious that she wasn't admitted into a fun and challenging elective course when her two closest friends were. Aranya is angry with the principal, whom she thinks dislikes her.	Anger helps people deal with obstacles to their goals, often spurring them to try new tactics. Help youngsters express their anger appropriately and redirect their energy toward reasonable solutions.
Fear	• *Frightened expression* • *Withdrawal* from circumstances • *Physiological responses*, such as sweating, twitches, and nervous behavior	Tony, age 2½, sits on his mat, eyes wide, body tense. He stares at a new poster of a clown in his preschool classroom. He is scared, runs to his teacher, and buries his head in her lap.	Fear occurs when people feel threatened and believe that their safety and well-being are at stake. Fear motivates people to flee, seek support, and fight back. Offer children ideas about how to cope with their worries.
Sadness	• *Sad expression* • *Crying* • *Pouting* • *Being quiet* • *Possible withdrawal* from a situation	Greta, age 15, sits quietly on a bench near her locker. With her head hung low, she rereads the letter from a cheerleading organization. She has not been admitted to a prestigious cheerleading summer camp.	People are sad when they cannot attain a desired goal or when they experience a loss, such as a friend moving to a distant city. Sadness causes people to reassess their goals. Ask children how they are doing, let them regroup, and encourage them to join activities.
Disgust	• *Wrinkled nose* • *Remarks such as "Phew!"* • *Withdrawal* from the source of displeasure	Norton, age 8, looks skeptically at the meal he has just received in the school cafeteria. He wrinkles his nose and averts his gaze from the "tuna melt" on his plate.	Disgust occurs when people encounter food, smells, and sights they find repulsive. Respect children's feelings of disgust, but also encourage them to reflect on why they might find substances offensive.
Anxiety	• *Frequent worrying* • *Excessive fidgeting*, hand wringing, or nail biting • *Avoidance* of source of anxiety	Tanesha, age 16, has to give an oral presentation to her class. She has spent hours preparing but is worried that, when standing by herself in front of the group, she might get so nervous that she forgets what she needs to say.	As long as it is not excessive, anxiety can spur people to avoid problems and achieve valued goals. Teach youngsters strategies that keep anxiety at a manageable level, as well as tactics that help them achieve their goals.
Shame	• *Signs of embarrassment* • *Attempts to withdraw* from a situation • *Looking down and away* from other people	Luke, age 9, is stunned. He's just had an accident, urinating on the floor. He had felt a bit antsy beforehand but wasn't aware that he needed to use the toilet. Now 20 pairs of eyes are glued on him.	When children feel ashamed, they know they are not meeting a community's ideals. Shame is more motivating when it comes from within rather than another's ridicule. Help children redirect their behavior to meet desired standards.
Guilt	• *Sad expression* • *Self-conscious demeanor* • *Possible concern* for a person who has been harmed	A. J., age 12, regrets bad-mouthing his friend Pete. A. J. sinks down low in his chair, feeling remorse for what he said behind Pete's back that caused his friend's sadness.	Guilt occurs when people do something that violates personal standards. It leads people to right a wrong and protect others. Suggest to children that they can behave differently next time.
Pride	• *Happy expression* • *Desire to show off* work and accomplishments to other people	Jacinda, age 5, is beaming. For the last 20 minutes, she's painstakingly pasted sequins, stars, and feathers onto a mask. Her final product is a colorful, delicately adorned creation. She displays her happiness with an ear-to-ear grin.	People are proud when they earn others' respect and meet personal goals. Pride fosters the commitment to achieving high standards and sharing accomplishments with others. Validate children's joy when they accomplish something meaningful for them.

Note: Adaptive functions of emotions are based on concepts in Saarni et al. (2006).

Infants watch others' emotions. The capacity to detect basic emotions in others is present in infancy (Bischof-Köhler, 2012; Haviland & Lelwica, 1987; Heck, Hock, White, Jubran, & Bhatt, 2016; Hutman & Dapretto, 2009). This ability is illustrated by the **emotional contagion** of babies: When one starts crying, others join in (Eisenberg, 1992; Hatfield, Cacioppo, & Rapson, 1994). Reflexive crying is not the same as a true empathic response, however, in which a person is aware of, and concerned with, another's distress. Rather, it is the primitive emotional response of sharing another's distress, much like your own experience in yawning after having witnessed another in the same act. Within the first few months of life, infants react to the emotional expressions of caregivers in meaningful ways. If they see their father looking in their direction with a smile on his face, they may jiggle arms and legs in excitement of playtime. While interacting with a parent, older sibling, or teacher, infants gradually synchronize eye contact and facial expressions with those of their social partner (Easterbrooks et al., 2013).

Toddlers guide their actions in part on other people's facial expressions, mannerisms, and tone of voice. Toward the end of the first year, infants monitor others' emotions, particularly those of parents and trusted caregivers, when they are not sure of how to respond. Infants show *social referencing* early in their second year: They watch their parents' faces and body language and listen to emotional tones in their voices in a novel situation (Boccia & Campos, 1989; Easterbrooks et al., 2013). A 16-month-old girl may glance at Mommy's face when a new babysitter enters the house. By determining whether Mommy is smiling or frowning, the little girl knows how to respond.

Young children gradually expand their emotions to include self-conscious feelings. Simple affective states such as fear, anger, and pleasure in infancy are supplemented with **self-conscious emotions** in early childhood. These affective states reflect awareness of social standards (M. Lewis, 1993, 2014; Parisette-Sparks, Bufferd, & Klein, 2017; R. A. Thompson & Newton, 2010). Self-conscious emotions include guilt, embarrassment, and pride. Teresa recalls early displays of guilt in both of her sons. As preschoolers, the boys would often respond angrily when misbehavior resulted in their being sent to their room or having a privilege taken away. Occasionally they'd swat at her or stomp out of the room and return a while later, looking at her face and affectionately rubbing her arm as they apologized.

Beginning in early childhood, children contemplate the nature and causes of emotions. As early as age 2 or 3, children talk about emotions that they and others experience ("Daniel got mad and pushed me"), and they realize that emotions are connected to people's desires ("Kurt loves to go down the slide and was mad he didn't get a turn"; Bretherton, Fritz, Zahn-Waxler, & Ridgeway, 1986; Easterbrooks et al., 2013). By middle childhood, they realize that their own interpretations of a situation determine how they feel about it and that other people may have different views and, as a result, different feelings ("Arlene feels bad because she thinks I don't like her"; P. L. Harris, 1989). Children also learn to connect words for emotions (*happy, sad, angry,* etc.) with particular facial expressions and the conditions under which these emotions are elicited.

Children realize that they and others sometimes project misleading emotional expressions. By middle childhood, children appreciate that emotional expressions do not always reflect people's true feelings (Saarni et al., 2006; Selman, 1980). A 9-year-old may observe his neighbor's cheerful demeanor and realize that because her brother passed away yesterday, she is probably sad inside. During middle childhood, children also understand that they and other people can have ambivalent feelings (S. K. Donaldson & Westerman, 1986; Zajdel, Bloom, Fireman, & Larsen, 2013). A 10-year-old girl may love her father but be angry with him for moving out of the house; she may like going to see him during custodial visits but not like the turmoil the visits evoke in her.

Concern for others' feelings develops with age. **Empathy**, the ability to recognize and share the feelings of another person, helps a child get along with other people (Eisenberg, Eggum, & Edwards, 2010; Hoffman, 1991). In their first months, infants cry reflexively at hearing others in distress, at 6 months, they gesture to someone in distress, and between 8 and 12 months, they appear uncomfortable when another child is hurt (Davidov, Zahn-Waxler, Roth-Hanania, & Knafo, 2013). In the second year, toddlers show empathic concern by patting a distressed friend on the face or back (Zahn-Waxler, 1991). By the third year, children console injured age-mates by expressing sympathy through facial expressions and comforting words. Empathy advances during the elementary school years, with children gaining cognitive skills for identifying others' perspectives and inferring the kinds of support that might alleviate the distress. Adolescents improve in their ability to understand other people's innermost feelings, even those whom they have never met. This capacity can extend to animals, as well.

This developmental course for empathy does not occur universally. Children whose parents have been insensitive, neglectful, or abusive are at risk for insecure attachments and a blunted capacity for compassion. They have missed out on loving interactions that reflect mutual concern: "Mommy and Daddy love me, and I love them" (Farrant, Devine, Maybery, & Fletcher, 2012; Feldman, 2007; Kochanska, 2002). Without a capacity for emotional engagement, children are not likely to feel concerned about others. A few children are born with fragile neurological connections for sensing others' feelings, thereby dampening their sympathy for others in distress (P. D. Hastings, Miller, Kahle, & Zahn-Waxler, 2014). Failure to develop empathy is associated with conduct problems in children: being aggressive at school, bullying others, destroying property, lying and stealing, breaking classroom rules, and being truant from school (Malti, Chaparro, Zuffianò, & Colasante, 2016).

MyLab Education
Video Example 11.6

Find Developmental Meaning *How does empathy play a role in Brendan's vision of neighborhood improvements?* Brendan expresses empathic concern for injured birds.

A physiological system for responding to stress is formed. Emotions are processed in part by the *hypothalamic–pituitary–adrenocortical (HPA) axis*, the body's method for registering stress and mobilizing the body for action. This system is activated during the prenatal period and matures in early childhood (R. Thompson, 2014). When a child encounters a threat in the environment (perhaps an unfamiliar adult entering the room), the *hypothalamus*—an almond-sized structure in the brain involved with eating, sleeping, and maintaining body temperature—is put on alert to galvanize the *pituitary*, a pea-sized gland that sends instructions to other glands producing hormones. Once stimulated, the pituitary releases a substance that triggers the *adrenocortical glands*, small organs near each kidney, to produce cortisol. The release of cortisol mobilizes the child's energy, suppresses the immune response, and arouses the cardiovascular system, effects that together prompt a focus on the threat and a quick reaction if necessary.

This system works well in mobilizing escape from danger, yet when overloaded, health is compromised. Those who are exposed to excessive levels of stress have trouble relaxing, live with a constant sense of dread, and remain ever alert to potential danger (J. E. Carroll et al., 2013; S. B. Johnson, Riley, Granger, & Riis, 2013). Chronic stress undermines immune functions, elevates blood pressure, and increases inflammatory tendencies in the body, which, in childhood, can cause joint pain, stomach aches, and other health problems and, in adulthood, arthritis and heart disease. Stress reactions can be repaired to a large extent when children participate in effective interventions focusing on caring relationships and relaxation (Slopen, McLaughlin, & Shonkoff, 2014).

Children gradually learn to regulate their emotions. Initially spontaneous, emotions become targets of personal control. A major accomplishment in childhood is **emotional regulation**, the ability to moderate affective states and change how they are experienced (Eisenberg, Hofer, & Vaughn, 2007). Emotional regulation has its origins in caregiving, wherein parents and other caregivers relieve infants of unpleasant sensations, such as hunger, pain, or fear. Infants themselves ease up on their crying, allow themselves to relax, close their eyes, sigh, and nestle into the arms of the adult. Infants gradually become more intentional in self-soothing, for example, by tugging at an ear, sucking on a thumb or fingers, and snuggling up with a favorite blanket.

Assuming that young children continue to receive gentle and loving care, they slowly add to their regulatory processes (A. S. Morris, Criss, Silk, & Houltberg, 2017). Children identify their feelings using particular words (e.g., being "annoyed") and talk themselves through challenging situations (e.g., while trying not to shed tears at a movie, telling oneself that the story is not true; P. M. Cole, Armstrong, & Pemberton, 2010). They learn to modulate their emotional expressions based on their understanding of how others interpret a situation. They may smile at a friend who has been quiet lately, hide their jealousy over a former boyfriend's current love interest, and feign happiness when receiving a disagreeable gift from a well-meaning relative (Webb, Gallo, Miles, Gollwitzer, & Sheeran, 2012).

Coping skills develop from infancy through adolescence. Coping skills are vital forms of emotional regulation, which, when effective, lead to progressive relaxation (Cummings, Braungart-Rieker, & Schudlich, 2013; Laurent, 2014; Muris & Meesters, 2014). The self-soothing actions of infants are a primitive but effective coping skill (P. M. Cole et al., 2010). They may suck on a thumb, avert their gaze from a stranger, or crawl away from a scary toy (Cummings et al., 2013; Macklem, 2008; Mangelsdorf et al., 1995).

Preparing for Your Licensure Examination

Your teaching test might ask you about self-regulation.

During early childhood, distraught children seek support from adults who have proven trustworthy. Guidance from parents helps young children expand on their coping strategies (Cummings et al., 2013; S. Meyer, Raikes, Virmani, Waters, & Thompson, 2014). Parents may reappraise the situation, reason through why events unfolded as they did, suggest that an alleged combatant is really a just an unhappy friend, and recommend a few possible tactics. Here a mother suggests a few actions for her young child:

Child: [crying] Mommy!
Mother: Are you okay?
Mother: You want a tissue?
Mother: Can I kiss it and make it better?
Mother: You want to get your baby and make it better?
Mother: Hug your baby.
Mother: Wanna hug your baby? (P. M. Cole et al., 2010, pp. 67–68)

During middle childhood, parents serve an important role by expressing negative emotions verbally: "I'm angry that you promised to make dinner but didn't do it." Children may subsequently use a similar strategy with peers: "I'm angry that you said I could have a turn, and you didn't keep your promise." Some youngsters talk themselves through challenging situations as an adult might have done for them in the past, nudging them to persist on a difficult assignment (K. L. Day & Smith, 2013). Seven-year-old Miguel reflects on how he controls his temper in Artifact Example 11.2.

MyLab Education
Artifact Example 11.2

Find Developmental Meaning *How does 7-year-old Miguel try to regulate his emotions?* Miguel comments on his efforts to express anger appropriately by avoiding hitting and shouting.

Adolescents realize that when they are upset they have a range of choices. They might substitute one activity for another (e.g., watching baseball on television after an injury rather than trying to play the game themselves), ask for support from peers or adults, wait it out, or change the way they think about a troubling situation (e.g., by trying to forget about it, go to sleep, or reappraise the situation by focusing on its positive features; E. L. Davis, Levine, Lench, & Quas, 2010; P. M. Cole et al., 2011). They also try such strategies as distracting themselves with a movie or electronic game, planning how to avoid the problem in the future, or watching how peers solve similar dilemmas. A few strategies will prove counterproductive. Some students wait for problems to go away, whether or not this is a realistic possibility (Zimmer-Gembeck & Skinner, 2008). Other young people ruminate over difficulties to such an extent that they become anxious or depressed. Sometimes young people complain, feel sorry for themselves, blame others, withdraw socially, deny that anything is wrong, or alter unpleasant moods with drugs and alcohol.

MyLab Education Application Exercise 11.1
Detect Developmental Levels
Listen to a young girl and an older adolescent boy talk about emotions and coping strategies.

The adolescent years unleash intense pressures that test coping skills. Concerns about fitting in at school, making mistakes in front of others, being ridiculed by peers, completing difficult homework, deciding on a career, and having an ideal body type intensify during adolescence (Bokhorst, Westenberg, Oosterlaan, & Heyne,

2008; Giletta et al., 2018; Moksnes, Espnes, & Haugan, 2014). Other pressures arise at home. As youngsters become more independent, they sometimes find themselves in disputes with parents (Arnett, 1999; Moksnes et al., 2010). Some young people find community life stressful because of the violence, unrest, and discrimination that they see around them (Conner-Warren, 2014). These and other pressures can provoke a great deal of worry. In Artifact Example 11.3, you can see 17-year-old Jeff's portrayal of the pressures he felt during his senior year of high school. Fortunately, Jeff and many young people are able to draw from their store of coping skills and reduce their apprehension (Orkibi, Hamama, Gavriel-Fried, & Ronen, 2018).

MyLab Education
Artifact Example 11.3

Find Developmental Meaning *How does Jeff feel about the multitude of challenges he faces?* Late one night, 17-year-old Jeff put his schoolwork aside to create this metaphorical self-portrait. At the time, he was dealing with a challenging course load, due dates for college applications, and being a confidante for several troubled friends. Because he had difficulty drawing human figures, he combined two favorite things—a soft drink can and black-and-white cowhide—to represent himself. Jeff appears to feel pressured with a range of demands. A cage and gigantic boulder pin Jeff in, and he cannot join his peers (represented by other soft drink cans) who frolic in the distance.

Emotions in the Developmental System

Children actively feel, reflect on, and regulate their emotions, drawing from personal characteristics and experiences in the settings in which they spend time. As you have learned, experiences in families and at school influence children's emotional skills. You have also found that children's personal characteristics (some inherited) contribute to emotional expression. Other factors that strongly influence children's emotions include gender, culture, and socioeconomic status.

Gender

At birth, male and female babies are similar in emotional states; any gender differences are subtle and situation dependent (J. E. O. Blakemore, Berenbaum, & Liben, 2009; Eisenberg, Martin, & Fabes, 1996). After the age of 2, small average differences emerge. Boys show more anger than girls beginning in early childhood, and girls show more positive emotions overall but also more sadness, fear, and guilt from the elementary grades onward (Blakemore et al., 2009; Chaplin & Aldao, 2013; Eisenberg et al., 1996). Some girls are inclined to dwell on their problems rather than take action or distract themselves. Such a ruminating style is a risk factor for depression (Nolen-Hoeksema, Morrow, & Fredrickson, 1993; K. D. Rudolph, Davis, & Monti, 2017). Boys are more apt to put on a self-confident front when they feel vulnerable (Blakemore et al., 2009; Chaplin & Aldao, 2013; Ruble, Martin, & Berenbaum, 2006). This style, too, has its disadvantages, especially when boys feel pressured to live up to unrealistic standards of strength.

Biology contributes to these gender differences in emotions. Rising hormone levels at puberty are associated with intensified activity in emotional areas of the brain, increased moodiness and depression in girls, and aggressiveness and rebelliousness in boys (Buchanan, Eccles, & Becker, 1992; Goddings, Burnett Heyes, Bird, Viner, & Blakemore, 2012; Klapwijk et al., 2013). Socialization also is a factor in gender differences in emotional responding. Parents are more likely to talk about fear and sadness with daughters and anger with sons (Bardack & Obradović, 2017; Kennedy Root & Denham, 2010; Malatesta & Haviland, 1982). Adolescent girls tend to respond to other girls' concerns with sympathy, whereas boys are more apt to respond to one another with disregard or teasing (Klimes-Dougan et al., 2014).

Developmental Systems Prompt

While interacting individually with children, be fully present with them, in the moment, focused on their well-being, and attentive to their unique ways of expressing themselves.

Culture

The language children speak defines aspects of emotion that are important in their culture. In English, words for emotions—for example, being anxious, happy, or excited—focus on internal, private states (Boiger, De Deyne, & Mesquita, 2013; Kagan, 2010). Some other languages emphasize the bodily sensations of emotions, such as being dizzy, having a headache, or feeling a racing heartbeat. A language also encodes nuances of emotion that are relevant in a culture. A child speaking English may hear about someone being "ashamed," whereas a child speaking Chinese encounters five distinct terms for shame, words that each communicate different causes of and responses to personal transgressions (H. Frank, Harvey, & Verdun, 2000).

Children also learn about emotions from how they see other people expressing themselves. Children in *individualistic* cultures are encouraged to express the full gamut of their emotions, including happiness, pride, frustration, and anger, as it is considered healthy to reveal one's innermost feelings (Boiger et al., 2013; Morelli & Rothbaum, 2007). In contrast, *collectivistic* cultures disapprove of displays of anger, frustration, and pride because they reflect self-absorption and disrupt a group's harmony.

Socioeconomic Status

Family income has a complicated relationship to emotional development. Children living in families facing economic hardships are at heightened risk for emotional and behavioral problems. Children whose families have low incomes are more prone to anxiety, depression, and behavior problems (e.g., physical aggression) than are children from advantaged backgrounds (Devenish, Hooley, & Mellor, 2017; Kagan, 2010; Schibli, Wong, Hedayati, & D'Angiulli, 2017; Tolani & Brooks-Gunn, 2006). They have more than their share of reasons to feel sad, fearful, and angry, including when watching their parents struggle to meet ends and encountering violence and drug addiction in their neighborhoods. As you have learned, excessive stress can become problematic for children. Educators, physicians, and mental health specialists are beginning to understand that reducing high levels of stress is of great consequence for children's health and learning ability.

Of course, not every child who grows up in a low-income environment is emotionally burdened. Many, perhaps most, children who face financial hardships receive stable, loving care from families and in the process acquire good coping skills. In our opening case study, Merv was able to leverage loving care from her grandmother, siblings, and a few teachers as she built a happy and responsible life. In fact, children from certain low-income backgrounds receive such loving, stable, and attentive care that they develop excellent coping skills (E. Chen & Miller, 2012). A group of children whose parents emigrated from Mexico to the United States with limited financial resources were shown to have fewer emotional and behavioral problems than is the case with American-born children (Espinosa, 2008).

Nor are children from middle- and high-income backgrounds immune to stress. Some middle-income parents project their own perfectionistic aspirations onto children, expecting children to follow unrealistic developmental timetables, such as reading at 3 years. When children fail to meet these timetables, overzealous parents may become overly critical, take control over children's free time, and insist on skill-based activities, including sports, tutoring, and music (Hyson, Hirsh-Pasek, Rescorla, Cone, & Martell-Boinske, 1991; S. Wheeler, 2014). Children may worry about parents' expectations, particularly when they think they are not measuring up (Hilt, Cha, & Nolen-Hoeksema, 2008; M. Levine, 2006).

Promoting Children's Emotional Development

An understanding of emotions helps educators to support children. The Basic Developmental Issues table "Attachment and Emotional Development" shows how attachments and emotions draw from nature and nurture, show universality and diversity, and exhibit qualitative and quantitative change. Nature furnishes children with inclinations to form attachments and express emotions. Nurture translates these abstract capacities into real-life relationships and coping skills. We offer the following suggestions for promoting children's emotional well-being:

- **Help crying infants find comfort.** Caregivers can do several things to help infants in distress. First, they can strive to give timely reassurance—not always immediately, because they may have other demands, but not so delayed that infants' crying escalates into real suffering. Second, caregivers can nurture actions that infants themselves use to reduce stress. Searching for a favorite blanket, putting a finger in the mouth, and tugging at an ear are positive signs that infants are learning to soothe themselves. Third, caregivers can consciously invite a baby to join them in a calm state—by showing the baby a smiling face, holding him or her close to the chest, and breathing in a shared rhythm (Gonzalez-Mena, 2002). Fourth, caregivers can investigate why an infant might be crying and try to meet the unfilled need or remove the source of pain. Finally, caregivers should try to stay calm and not take it personally—infants sometimes cry despite the most sensitive care.

BASIC DEVELOPMENTAL ISSUES
Attachment and Emotional Development

ISSUE	ATTACHMENT	EMOTIONAL DEVELOPMENT
Nature and Nurture	Children are biologically predisposed to form close bonds with their parents and other primary caregivers (reflecting nature), but they are more likely to form secure bonds with adults who have showered them with love (nurture). Parents, in turn, are by nature predisposed to care for their offspring, but they learn specific ways of raising children from other family members and from the community and culture in which they live.	The full range of emotions is made possible by human genetic instructions; the brain is wired to experience anger, pleasure, fear, and so on. Genetic factors also affect individual differences in temperament (e.g., activity level and ways of responding to new stimuli). Nurture affects how emotions are expressed. Children learn to control the expression of negative emotions by observing other people and practicing coping skills.
Universality and Diversity	The predisposition to form close social-emotional bonds is universal. Sensitive care is the common route to healthy attachments. However, not every child receives this responsive attention and thus not everyone forms secure attachments. Being clingy and demanding may help infants who live in an environment with scarce resources. Similarly, being able to form multiple relationships enhances adjustment when numerous caregivers are present during the early years.	All children experience such basic emotions as happiness, sadness, anger, and fear. The tendency for emotional states to energize particular responses (e.g., fleeing in response to fear) is also universal. Substantial diversity is present in how children regulate their emotions (e.g., when trying to relax or conceal their true feelings). Some children are more likely than others to respond to social situations in a positive, upbeat fashion.
Qualitative and Quantitative Change	The development of attachments largely reflects quantitative change: Children gradually become more active as social partners, initiating conversations and other exchanges, taking turns to keep interactions going, and so on. Qualitative change occurs when young children, who have previously leaped into the arms of strangers, suddenly display stranger anxiety.	Children gradually gain the knowledge and skills needed to assess others' emotions. By watching facial expressions, listening to tones of voice, and drawing inferences from behaviors, children learn how others express and control emotions. The emergence of self-conscious emotions (pride, guilt, etc.) represents a qualitative change that reflects a new awareness of social standards.

- **Notice children's facial expressions and invite them to say how they feel.** Adults who respond sympathetically to upset children essentially tell them that feelings matter and can be dealt with constructively. Beginning in early childhood, children can learn the labels and implications of particular feelings: "I know you were angry with Davis for pulling your hair. You did a good job with using your words to tell him how you felt." As children grow, adults can coach them in fine-tuning emotional displays to the particular social situation. Blowing up about a low test score will not be well received by anyone, but expressing disappointment privately can lead to productive problem solving as to how to prepare for the next examination. Writing about one's feelings can at times be therapeutic as well.

- **Create a warm and inclusive atmosphere at school.** Children learn most effectively when they are calm, happy, or excited about an activity (Bauminger & Kimhi-Kind, 2008; Linnenbrink & Pintrich, 2004; M. Rasmussen & Laumann, 2013). Traditions that begin and end the day, including greeting students by their preferred names, enhance a sense of belonging. Establishing pleasant routines, such as a late-afternoon meeting in which children take turns telling about their day, encourages self-reflection, self-expression, and respect for one another (Walkley & Cox, 2013). Clear expectations that no one should be teased or mocked help children settle down and concentrate on school work. The classroom itself, with attractive plants and decorations, a child-friendly organization (e.g., with labeled buckets for supplies), age-appropriate furniture, and a secluded area with pillows and rugs, invites children to relax and focus on learning.

- **Cultivate empathy.** With a child who seems uncaring of others, you can model appropriate reactions when someone is hurt, talk about the injured person's feelings, and encourage the child to offer help and show sympathy. Children may lack relevant socialization at home and yet remain amenable to learning about others' perspectives from teachers, foster parents, extended family members, and counselors. For example, in the classroom and on the playground, teachers can gently remind a self-centered child to consider the feelings of an upset classmate (Luke & Banerjee, 2012). With children who are outright callous of others' feelings, professional treatment is likely to be necessary (A. Carr, 2014; Happé & Frith, 2013).

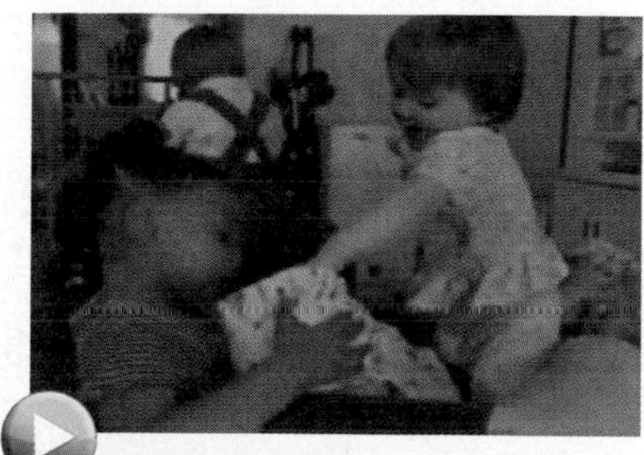

MyLab Education
Video Explanation 11.1
What kinds of emotionally significant events do children experience in a preschool classroom?

• **Take note of your own emotions.** What makes you happy, disappointed, tired, and angry in working with children? Practitioners often find themselves frustrated by the people they serve (Button, 2007; B. Davis, 2001). Teachers sometimes become angry with rude children, harried parents, unrealistic external mandates, and inadequate resources for schools. Frustration is a natural emotion but must be handled with care. Exploding at the nearest bystander or retreating into personal despair are *not* good ideas; counting to 10 and finding a colleague to talk with *can* be helpful in preserving one's mental health.

• **Model and encourage appropriate ways for dealing with negative emotions.** Youngsters often struggle with how to deal with anger, fear, and sadness; they can benefit from seeing adults express these emotions appropriately (Delaney, 2006; W. S. Pollack, 2010). Teresa remembers how her fifth-grade teacher expressed anger: Rather than raising her voice, she lowered it to a whisper. The teacher's approach worked well: Students sensed her disappointment, responded with concern, and tried to make amends. Educators can boost the gains of modeling controlled, honest emotions by offering an explanation: "I'm really angry now. Let's talk this out when we've all calmed down."

MyLab Education Application Exercise 11.2
Meet Individual Needs
How does (counselor) Rocky coach 8-year-old Noah in expressing his feelings?

LaST NiT I Krid MY SeLF To SLeP.

MyLab Education
Artifact Example 11.4

Find Developmental Meaning *How did 8-year-old Noah feel about his parents' recent divorce?* In this journal entry, 8-year-old Noah reveals his sadness about the change in his family.

What Hits Me

Feeling excitment bubble inside know something great is waiting to happen to you. Feeling scared or nervous, want to dive under the covers and go back to sleep even though it is 8:30 and it is almost time to go to school. Feeling sad because your parents got divorced and you dad just moved out of the house. Feeling scared and excited at same time because you have discovered something that's mysterious and you are ditermind to figur it out.

MyLab Education
Artifact Example 11.5

Find Developmental Meaning *What emotions does 10-year-old Shea feel?* Shea talks about excitement, fright, and nervousness.

• **Offer age-appropriate outlets for emotional expression.** When children are young, they usually find safe outlets in play to communicate their feelings. Through fantasies with peers, they work through fear and conflict, perhaps as monsters, superheroes, or bad guys (Kohlberg & Fein, 1987; Mathieson & Banerjee, 2010; Mooney, 2014). For older children, writing about feelings, perhaps in essays or journals, or expressing emotions in artwork, dance, or music, can be therapeutic. In Artifact Examples 11.4 and 11.5, Noah uses his journal as a time to reflect on his feelings and Shea writes about her recent feelings.

• **Discuss emotions of characters in literature and ancestors in history.** Stories provide occasions to live vicariously through a character's emotions (Fleer & Hammer, 2013; Mar & Oatley, 2008). As young children become familiar with fairy tales, fables, and short stories, for example, in *The Empty Pot* (Demi, 1990), they share fear, anger, love, and other strong feelings with classmates and with the adult telling the story; in the process they grow accustomed to embracing emotions in social situations (Fleer & Hammer, 2013). In *Frog and Toad Are Friends* (Lobel, 1979), a book suitable for 4- to 8-year-olds, Frog waits impatiently to play with his hibernating friend, Toad, and plays a trick on him to get him up early. The story provides a forum for discussions about feelings that may arise between friends, such as resentment at being teased or misled (Solomon, Watson, Battistich, Schaps, & Delucchi, 1992). Meanwhile, older children and adolescents might read firsthand accounts of historical events and talk through how people in various contexts have responded emotionally to hostilities and inequities (Maguth, Boit, Muenz, & Smith, 2015). Students can also focus on story characters and historical figures who act out of compassion for others.

• **Ask children to consider how people might feel in particular situations.** Children can practice analyzing particular situations and considering how those involved might feel. In Figure 11.1, you can see one situation that an elementary school counselor asks children to pretend they face. Adults can assure children that anger, fear, guilt, and other feelings are reasonable reactions in certain situations. In addition, they can ask children to think about how they should act when they have uncomfortable feelings of their own.

MyLab Education Application Exercise 11.3
Identify Development-Enhancing Education

Watch English/Language Arts teacher Myrlene Schenck ask her fifth-grade students to identify characters who were benevolent.

- **Expect to see cultural variations in emotions.** Some cultures encourage open communication about feelings, whereas others actively discourage emotional expressiveness. Adults working with children from diverse cultures must be mindful of such differences when interpreting children's feelings (Trommsdorff & Heikamp, 2013). A girl who is poker-faced when eliminated from a school spelling bee may choose not to show her deep disappointment, reflecting the emotional restraint she has learned at home. A sympathetic teacher who notices her stiff reaction will find a moment later in the day to speak privately with her, congratulate her on her effort, and advise her about other competitions in the future.

- **Encourage boys and girls to look beyond stereotyped ways for responding to distress.** Concerned educators can look for occasions when children use gender-traditional methods of coping that actually worsen matters for them. Adults might watch for occasions when girls are ruminating over problems and help them work through their feelings, tackle the problems, and get on with life. Similarly, when boys seem to be trying hard to brush off a significant loss, adults can acknowledge that the event is likely to be upsetting but can be addressed with such coping skills as confiding in friends or writing about the situation.

- **Help children relax.** When stress is long-lasting, anxiety easily results. **Anxiety** is an emotional condition characterized by worry and apprehension, often about future events with unknown outcomes. Children who are anxious may experience such physiological symptoms as muscle tension and headaches and have trouble concentrating. Educators can do a variety of things to help keep anxiety at a manageable level. Deep breathing, stretching, yoga, outdoor recess, and mentally retreating with a good book are all good routines. When teachers assign oral reports, they can encourage students to create index cards or other memory "crutches." Before giving an important test (such as end-of-year state examinations), teachers can administer practice tests that show what to expect. In general, teachers should communicate realistic expectations for classroom performance and provide the support students need to *meet* those expectations.

- **Address the special needs of children experiencing excessive stress.** Children who live in constant anguish cannot easily focus on school subjects, get the rest they need, or remain patient when provoked (Ursache & Raver, 2014). Fortunately, children retain the ability to acquire new coping strategies even after having grown accustomed to less healthy ones. New relationships that are warm, responsive, and stable help children who overreact to challenging situations to calm down with new coping skills (P. A. Fisher Gunnar, Dozier, Bruce, & Pears, 2006; Samuels & Blitz, 2014). Teachers can encourage concentration, acknowledge improvements in attention, and give students plenty of brief breaks. Should the opportunity arise, teachers can also advise parents of educationally worthwhile activities that reduce stress. Sharing a good-night story has payoffs in young children's literacy development and also reduces stress in children and parents (Zajicek-Farber, Mayer, & Daughtery, 2012). Adolescents who have experienced long-term stress have the same needs as younger children in that they require ongoing considerate care. Specially trained counselors, foster parents, and teachers can help anxious, irritable, and distrustful adolescents distinguish situations that are truly threatening from those that are not and guide them in expressing emotions in accordance with the situation (Catania, Hetrick, Newman, & Purcell, 2011; Dozier & Fisher, 2014).

FIGURE 11.1 Respecting others' privacy.

Counselors can ask children to pretend they are characters in particular situations and help them talk about how they might feel and respond.

Marissa and Wendy Sue have been good friends for a long time. Marissa told Lucy about Wendy Sue's family. Wendy Sue had asked her not to tell anyone.

• **Look into research-based programs for fostering emotional development.** To have a significant impact on children's emotional expression, school personnel can implement a systematic program for educating children in an environment that is warm, open, and instructive on handling feelings (Case-Smith, 2013; Fishbein et al., 2016; S. H. Landry et al., 2014). One illustration of a comprehensive emotional education program is the *Promoting Alternative Thinking Strategies (PATHS)* curriculum (Domitrovich, Cortes, & Greenberg, 2007). Second- and third-grade children are taught that all feelings are okay, that some feelings are comfortable and others uncomfortable, that feelings can help children learn what to do in certain situations, and that some ways of dealing with emotions are better than others. Children keep a record of their feelings and use a poster showing a traffic signal as a guide to regulating their responses. Teachers encourage children to refer to the steps on a poster: to stop and calm down (red), consider their options (yellow), and try a plan (green). This program has been shown to increase emotional understanding and decrease problem behaviors in children with diverse ability levels.

• **When children appear indifferent to classmates, cultivate empathy and reinforce good behavior.** Impairment in empathy is worrisome because it is a major risk factor for conduct problems in childhood and violent and criminal acts in adulthood (Reidy et al., 2017). Interventions in early childhood have good prospects for enhancing empathy when they focus on forming secure attachments, learning about emotions, and using helpful rather than hurtful behaviors. Facilitating compassion is more difficult in elementary school and later grades (Elizur, Somech, & Vinokur, 2017). School-aged children who have been systematically deprived of affection do not know how to care for others; they may hit a peer who has been hurt rather than offer sympathy (Volling, 2001). At school, educators can try to get to know the children, model sympathetic reactions to someone who has been hurt, talk about the injured person's feelings, ask them how they might feel in similar situations, and reward cooperation. Intensive counseling can work with older children when it addresses missing skills.

For young people who are callous to other people's pain, professional intervention may include making eye contact, inferring what others are experiencing, reinforcing good behavior, and anticipating positive consequences for moral actions (Moul, Hawes, & Dadds, 2015). In the classroom, no student can be allowed to hurt another, making it important to monitor aggressive actions, impose restrictions on hurtful behavior, and reward cooperation. Punishment does not seem to be effective with children who are callous, yet they are motivated to earn rewards, and self-interest can be the lynchpin for change (D. J. Hawes, Price, & Dadds, 2014). In other words, these young people can earn privileges for treating others kindly, and in the process, experience the satisfaction of behaving morally, even when other people's feelings do not yet resonate with them.

Summary

Emotions have adaptive functions for young people, helping them decide how to direct their attention and which goals to pursue. Children become increasingly able to regulate their emotions in ways that are both socially acceptable and personally satisfying. Individual differences in emotional functioning are the result of both biology (e.g., genetic instructions for neurotransmitters and gender-specific hormones) and environment (e.g., socialization by parents, peers, and culture).

Classrooms are fertile environments for emotions. Children arrive at school with certain coping skills and stress responses that affect their ability to concentrate, remember information, and make friends. Teachers, counselors, and other school leaders can teach children how to express themselves according to cultural practices and personal needs. School personnel can emphasize that all emotions are okay and that what needs to be learned is how to manage them. For children who do not readily show concern for the plights of others, professional interventions can be effective, especially when conducted when children are young.

MyLab Education Self-Check 11.3

Temperament and Personality

11.4 Define key dimensions of temperament and personality, and generate techniques for embracing children's individuality.

Visit any group of children—perhaps at a local child care center, a school, or an after-school program—and you are bound to notice dramatic differences in children's energy, mood, spontaneity, and attention to academic tasks. Such differences reflect children's *temperaments* and *personalities*. *Temperament* refers to a child's typical and somewhat stable ways of responding to events, novel stimulation, and personal impulses (Cummings et al., 2013; Kagan & Fox, 2006; M. R. Klein et al., 2018; Rothbart, Sheese, & Conradt, 2009). Individual differences in temperament are present even in infancy. Some infants are fussy and demanding; others are cheerful and easily pacified. Temperament has a genetic basis, as we shall see, but it also is very much affected by children's relationships and experiences.

As children grow older, they develop distinctive ways of behaving, thinking, and feeling. That is, they develop unique **personalities**. Temperament affects personality: A child who is timid relates to people and events differently than one who is socially confident (Cummings et al., 2013). But personality includes more than temperament. Personality is affected by children's intellectual interests and the many habits they acquire while growing up, for example, in fulfilling family obligations, dealing with stressful situations, interacting with others, managing personal belongings, and spending leisure time.

Both temperament and personality reflect how individual children respond to emotions, form relationships, and act within schools and other group settings. Temperament may be especially helpful to consider when children are infants and toddlers; personality can be more relevant as youngsters move into their later childhood and adolescent years. Let's look more closely at both concepts and consider their implications for educators.

Dimensions to Children's Personal Characteristics

Temperament and personality are each made up of constellations of independent dimensions. Individual children may have a lot, a little, or an in-between amount of each characteristic.

Temperament

Much of the initial work on temperament was done using parents' reports and researchers' observations of infants' typical behaviors. Parents and researchers judged the extent to which the infants were active and adaptable to change. In considering the dramatic individual differences that emerged from this analysis, experts realized that infants' temperaments partly determine the care that works best for them (A. Thomas & Chess, 1977).

Infants who exhibit a high activity level (squirming a lot, wiggling while having a diaper change) may benefit from many opportunities for safe exploration. For children with low activity levels, adults might need to slow down their pace, enjoy quiet interaction with them, and only then invite more active play. Thus, children's well-being depends to some extent on the *goodness of fit* between their temperament and the particular environment in which they are raised (Chess & Thomas, 1992). Having a good fit does not mean that the adult shares the same temperament with the child but rather that the adult warmly accepts and accommodates the child's personal rhythms and dispositions.

Recent research has focused on the neurological basis of temperament. American psychologist **Mary Rothbart** and her colleagues suggest that temperaments emerge as children's brains develop distinctive capacities for responding to impulses and regulating attention, emotion, and activity (Rothbart, 2007, 2012; Rothbart & Bates, 2006; Rothbart et al., 2009). At birth, children react rather automatically to changes in stimuli by crying, thrashing their limbs, and looking away. As they grow, they develop new ways to deal with sensations and environmental demands. Fear prompts children to be wary of potentially dangerous things, whereas a sense of initiative incites children to explore the world. Restraint emerges gradually, as children learn to direct their attention and actions flexibly, according to social rules and anticipated consequences. These distinctive capacities (i.e., reacting automatically, withdrawing out of fear, exploring with enthusiasm, and directing activity intentionally) are housed in different parts of the brain.

According to Rothbart and her colleagues, children may be low or high, or somewhere in between, on three dimensions of temperament:

- Children who score high on *extraversion/surgency* show high levels of optimistic anticipation, impulsivity, activity, and sensation seeking, and they smile and laugh often.
- Children who score high on *negative affectivity* are shy and often fearful, frustrated, sad, uncomfortable, and not easily soothed.
- Children who show high levels of *effortful control* are proficient in strategically focusing and shifting their attention. They effectively plan for the future, suppress inappropriate responses, and take pleasure in complex and novel stimuli.

These three temperamental dimensions are fairly stable, partly due to genetic factors, as shown by identical twins reared in different homes developing similar temperaments (N. D. Henderson, 1982; J. J. Li & Lee, 2014). Children's genetic makeup affects their temperaments through effects on brain chemistry, such as the potency of certain neurotransmitters, the levels of cortisol released during stressful situations, and the comparative level of activity between the two sides of the brain (Cummings et al., 2013; Kagan, Snidman, Vahn, & Towsley, 2007; Rothbart et al., 2009).

Children's environments also remain fairly similar over time and are a second route to stability in temperament. The typical ways in which parents express or withhold affection and respond to children's emotional expressions show some consistency over time. Parents who are unsupportive are apt to have children who become increasingly irritable and aggressive (Briley & Tucker-Drob, 2014; Fanti & Henrich, 2010). Continuity in neighborhoods and communities, for example, with long-lasting poverty, unemployment, and drug addiction, contribute to children being nervous a good portion of the time (N. A. Marshall et al., 2018).

Children's environments also cause changes in children's temperaments. Separate societies encourage distinct types of initiative. In Western cultures, children are expected to be reasonably outgoing with peers. When parents encourage quiet and reserved children to interact with peers and develop independence, the children are apt to become socially confident (Arcus, 2001; Feng, Shaw, & Moilanen, 2011; N. A. Fox, Henderson, Rubin, Calkins, & Schmidt, 2001; J. S. Grady, Karraker, & Metzger, 2012). In China, acting in a socially restrained manner is valued (Coplan, Liu, Cao, Chen, & Li, 2017). You can learn more about the manifestations of shyness in the Development in Culture feature "Temperament in China."

Personality

Over time, a child integrates biologically based emotional tendencies with experience, relationships, and intellectual interests. The result is a distinctive and somewhat stable personality. A child who is passionate about finding order in the material world may, as a 4-year-old, have an insatiable curiosity for dinosaurs; as an 8-year-old, be fascinated with space and aeronautics; as a 12-year-old, learn all he can about bridges and buildings; as a 16-year-old, become an expert in computers; and as a young man, prepare for a career in environmental engineering.

Despite their relative stability, children's personalities change slightly (and sometimes dramatically) in response to the demands of particular situations. A 12-year-old girl may be typically sociable (e.g., talking frequently, smiling at others, and befriending peers) yet find it difficult to make new friends when her family moves across the country and encounters unfamiliar customs and values. Children reveal certain parts of their personality in some settings more than others. An 8-year-old boy may be spontaneous and cheerful on the playground but distracted and agitated in the classroom.

Development In Culture

Temperament in China

China has a population of over 1.3 billion people, 265 million of whom are children ranging in age from infancy through 14 years (X. Chen & Wang, 2010). Fifty-six separate ethnic groups exist in China, and the country is rapidly shifting from reliance on a centrally planned financial system to a market economy with international ties.

Obviously, children throughout China are exposed to distinct customs. Yet several cultural beliefs and practices pervade family and community life across China. Confucianism offers prominent guidelines (X. Chen & Wang, 2010). Confucius (551–479 BC) was an influential philosopher who lived during a time of significant social upheaval as China was making the transition from slavery to a feudal society, and he espoused practices for maintaining a harmonious social order. Moral standards in Confucianism include benevolence, righteousness, politeness, and wisdom. Children are expected to pledge obedience and respect to their parents. Parents, in turn, must guide and discipline their children. Children are similarly expected to respect their teachers and other authority figures and be considerate of peers.

Taoism is another prevalent belief system in China. Taoism advocates personal harmony in being soft and tender (X. Chen & Wang, 2010). People are advised to be flexible, adjust to life circumstances, and refrain from struggles over material wealth. In the ideologies of both Confucianism and Taoism, children are directed to be calm, honorable, and attentive to the needs of the group. Children require a lot of guidance from adults before they reliably overcome their own impulses and defer to the needs of others. This socialization begins early. Chinese parents regularly encourage young children to tone down emotional expressions into muted, socially acceptable levels. In one experimental study, Chinese infants produced less facial movement, fewer smiles, and less crying than did European American infants (Camras et al., 1998).

Chinese parents also encourage children to temper their independent exploratory behaviors. In an observational study, 2-year-old Chinese children were more likely than Canadian children of the same age to stay close to mothers in the presence of a stranger or unfamiliar toys (X. Chen et al., 1998). Chinese children are expected to abide by basic rules even when parents are not present to oversee their conduct. In an experimental study, Chinese toddlers more willingly put away toys without their mother's intervention than did Canadian toddlers (X. Chen et al., 2003).

As they grow older, Chinese children prefer controlled behavior in peers. Shy Chinese preschool children are more likely to be accepted by peers than are shy Canadian children (X. Chen, DeSouza, Chen, & Wang, 2006). However, it appears that shyness is manifested in multiple ways in China (Y. Xu, Farver, Chang, Zhang, & Yu, 2007). Children who exhibit *regulated shyness* show social restraint that is consistent with Chinese customs. They do not draw attention to themselves, are modest and unassuming, and are considerate of peers. In comparison, children who exhibit *anxious shyness* are overwhelmed with negative emotions and find it difficult to behave appropriately in social settings. These children find it too stressful to enter peer groups and instead stay on the periphery. Regulated-shy children have an advantage over anxious-shy children in China, probably because children with the former characteristics are able to insinuate themselves into groups whereas the latter are not (Y. Xu et al., 2007).

Curiously, biological factors may play a small role in Chinese children being emotionally controlled. Genetic factors appear partly responsible for Chinese infants displaying fewer smiles and withdrawing more vigorously from stressful circumstances than is the case with Caucasian infants (Kagan, 2010). Thus, it seems that Chinese society extends a biologically based temperament for emotional restraint with cultural values for social harmony and personal serenity.

Madeleine Jettre/dbimages/Alamy Stock Photo

SERENITY. This young boy walks quietly with his grandmother in Shaxi Village in the Yunnan Province of China.

Recognizing that a child's personality changes somewhat over time and across situations, psychologists have found five relatively constant dimensions of personality:

- *Extraversion*—extent of being socially outgoing
- *Agreeableness*—extent of being warm and sympathetic

- *Conscientiousness*—extent of being persistent and organized
- *Neuroticism*—extent of being anxious and fearful
- *Openness*—extent of being curious and imaginative

These five dimensions were originally identified in adults, but they characterize children as well (A. D. Haan, Deković, den Akker, Stoltz, & Prinzie, 2013; John, Caspi, Robins, Moffitt, & Stouthamer-Loeber, 1994; G. Stoll et al., 2017). Just as there is a certain constancy in temperament, personality is persistent over the years, stability that is partly because of genetics and partly because of consistency in children's environments.

MyLab Education
Content Extension 11.1
Read about another theoretical model of children's personality.

Helping Children Be Themselves

Teachers can plan lessons and activities that address the varied temperaments and personalities of youngsters in their care. Here are some suggestions:

• **Identify the kinds of temperaments that you naturally prefer, as well as those that push your buttons.** Many teachers prefer to work with children who are curious, happy, obedient, industrious, cooperative, intelligent, cautious, and efficient (Keogh, 2003; S. McClowry et al., 2013; Meisgeier & Kellow, 2015; Wentzel, 2000). Teachers generally find it less rewarding to work with children who are distracted, angry or irritable, disruptive, and exceptionally assertive. Teachers also are less proficient in managing the misbehavior of children they perceive to be difficult. When teachers come to realize that they automatically (and often unconsciously) respond in certain ways to particular temperaments, they can take the first steps toward holding their biases in check. This insight can motivate professional development in managing irritable and noncompliant children and fostering their emotional regulation.

• **Adjust to young children's stylistic behavior.** Warmly accepting children's personal ways of regulating their attention is an important service adults can offer children (Rudasill, Gallagher, & White, 2010). To meet the needs of active infants, caregivers might permit them to explore. With older children, teachers can observe children's focus of attention, remind those who are distractible to stay engaged in lessons, and offer opportunities for free choice. Infants who show a lower activity level let the world come to them (A. Thomas & Chess, 1977; Zero to Three: National Center for Infants, Toddlers, and Families, 2002). Caregivers might sit quietly with infants, talk softly about pictures in a book, and acknowledge their interests in toys.

• **Consider children's temperaments when forming groups.** Teachers can help children who are shy or impulsive by pairing them with peers who compensate with an outgoing personality and ability to take projects step by step. A first-grade teacher might plan a Halloween activity of making "dirt" cake, knowing she can count on one boy to be methodical in measuring ingredients and pair him with another boy who will attack the project enthusiastically but without restraint. Together, they might make a good team. Because there is never any guarantee that temperamentally dissimilar children will work effectively together, experienced teachers must monitor the evolving dynamics of groups and make changes as needed.

• **Allow children to play to their natural strengths, but also encourage them to try new strategies every now and then.** Permitting children to choose from among a few specified options is an important way to respect children's individuality. When children are asked to report on a book they have read, they might have an array of formats, such as a written analysis, poster, or oral presentation. However, children are naturally inclined to remain in their comfort zone and can benefit from practice with less developed talents. Hence, a child who has trouble concentrating may be taught to use attention-focusing strategies, and a child who chooses books impulsively might be asked to prepare a checklist of desirable topics for selecting a new book at the library.

• **Communicate your expectations about acceptable behaviors.** When adults make expectations explicit and consistently enforce compliance, children with many kinds of temperaments and personalities thrive (Denno, Carr, & Bell, 2010;

Keogh, 2003). Those who are apprehensive about doing the right thing can be assured that they are acting in an acceptable manner. Others who are inclined to act impulsively can be reminded of rules, consequences for misbehavior, and strategies for keeping track of their behavior.

• **Set up reasonable routines.** Most children prefer a schedule that is somewhat predictable (H. A. Davis, 2003). Children adjust to activities more easily when they know what to expect, for example, when they know that after they arrive at school in the morning, they are to place their backpacks and jackets in designated places, go straight to their desks, and begin writing an entry in their class journals. Children also need to be advised of procedures in the classroom, such as how to line up or disperse for lunch, and the circumstances under which they can sharpen pencils, use the restroom, and ask for assistance.

• **Help children cope with changes in routines.** Children with certain temperaments and personalities (for instance, those who are timid or irritable) may find alterations to routines to be difficult (Keogh, 2003). To help these children, educators can tell them ahead of time about anticipated modifications in staff, schedules, or rules. Elementary school children can be introduced to a substitute teacher the week before their regular teacher departs on family leave. Middle school adolescents can be shown the blueprints for a new auditorium before the existing structure is leveled, and high school students should receive a copy of a new code of conduct before it is instituted. When changes *cannot* be anticipated ahead of time, children appreciate hearing as soon as possible about alterations, especially those changes that affect them personally.

• **Arrange the classroom to minimize disruptions.** Cleared pathways between desks, protected spaces in high-traffic areas, and separate areas for relaxation can minimize tussles among children who are easily frustrated, lacking in social skills, or simply tired (Emmer, Evertson, & Worsham, 2000; Tassoni, 2013). Children who are easily distracted by noise might occasionally be allowed to complete assignments in the school library.

• **Make appropriate adjustments for children who show unusually high or low levels on personality dimensions.** Children with exceptionally low or high in personality characteristics stand out from other children. These children need to be accepted for who they are but also guided in study skills, peer relationships, emotional expression, and motivation to follow rules. Let's consider how educators might adjust to unusual levels of the personality dimensions we introduced earlier:

- *Extraversion.* Extraverted children are active, assertive, emotionally expressive, talkative, enthusiastic, and socially outgoing. They often appreciate opportunities to work on projects with peers. Teachers might occasionally offer a public forum (such as a dramatic performance) for self-expression. Teachers can intersperse opportunities for physical movement around quiet activities to give these children needed exercise. Some exuberant children need gentle reminders from teachers to stay focused and listen to others (Rimm-Kaufman et al., 2002). Children who are shy may benefit from private conversations with teachers and friendly invitations from peers and adults to join an activity.
- *Agreeableness.* Agreeable children are warm, responsive, generous, kind, sympathetic, and trusting. They may be pleased when adults and other children notice and comment on their cooperative spirit. Children who are not prone to be agreeable or socially sensitive may benefit if teachers encourage them to compliment peers, share toys, offer comfort to others in distress, and voice opinions without insulting people. Extremely irritable children are at risk for developing behavior problems but have the ability to adjust well when assisted by knowledgeable teachers, counselors, psychologists, and doctors (Aman et al., 2009; Ehrler, Evans, & McGhee, 1999; A. E. West & Weinstein, 2012).
- *Conscientiousness.* Conscientious children are attentive, persistent in activities, organized, and responsible. Teachers can admire their determination and organization and point out how their style pays off in well-designed work products. Children who follow lower standards can be taught to set ambitious goals, resist counterproductive urges, and monitor their progress (Muris, Meesters, & Rompelberg, 2006).

- *Neuroticism.* Neurotic children are anxious, fearful, lacking in confidence, and self-pitying. These children need support in dealing with negative feelings (Kwok, Hughes, & Luo, 2007). They also need encouragement to try challenging tasks they might otherwise avoid. Children who are relaxed and confident thrive when given continuous support from adults. No one is self-assured all the time, however, and adults can express extra support when normally confident children face momentous losses, personal failures, or traumatic events.
- *Openness.* Children who are open are curious, eager to explore their world, and imaginative. They can be encouraged to exercise their skills in many contexts. However, curious children are not always motivated to achieve in school and may need encouragement to tackle conventional academic assignments (Abe, 2005). Those who are less driven to explore art, literature, history, and the scientific world may need to be persuaded of the intrigue, beauty, and relevance of academic fields.

• **Recognize the complexity of children's personalities.** The various dimensions of temperament and personality combine in a myriad of creative ways that can both delight and tax adults. A teacher may have one child who is socially outgoing but a bit anxious and not terribly agreeable; another child who is self-confident and conscientious but somewhat conforming and slow to exercise her imagination; another who is curious and thoughtful, worries constantly, and craves approval from adults; and many other children, each with an individual profile. Every child has special needs when it comes to temperament and personality.

The Developmental Trends table "Emotional and Personal Characteristics at Different Age Levels" captures what you have learned about children's attachment, emotional qualities, and temperaments and personalities. By now it should be abundantly clear that children are well served when adults appreciate their individual qualities, a mindset that is all the more crucial when children have serious emotional problems, a theme we explore in the final section.

DEVELOPMENTAL TRENDS

Emotional and Personal Characteristics at Different Age Levels

AGE	WHAT YOU MIGHT OBSERVE	DIVERSITY	IMPLICATIONS
Infancy (Birth–2 Years)	• Seeking contact with a caregiver when afraid, hurt, or hungry; being sufficiently relaxed in the presence of caregiver to explore the environment • Distress at separation from caregiver • Crying and smiling gradually supplemented with laughter, hand gestures, and words • Beginning ability to soothe self by sucking thumb, hugging favorite blankets, pulling on ear, and so on • Emergence of personal rhythms in eating, sleeping, and exploring	• Some babies have multiple attachments and move easily from one caregiver to another, whereas others have a single close attachment and strongly protest separation from this person. • Some cultures encourage small children to express all of their feelings, including anger and sadness. Other cultures place group harmony above self-expression and discourage expression of anger, teach restraint, and identify the behaviors needed in a healthy group.	• Try to remain calm when infants and toddlers cry and shout. • Be responsive and sensitive to the needs of infants—they are learning to trust you as you satisfy their needs. • Ask for guidance when you encounter infants who appear to have serious attachment problems. • Provide infants with lots of reassurance during separation distress. • Tell parents what you do to comfort their child and how long it takes for him or her to settle down after the morning drop-off.
Early Childhood (2–6 Years)	• Desire to be close to parents when afraid, hurt, or uncertain • Ability to talk about and accept where parents go during a temporary separation • Attachments to multiple people, including mother, father, siblings, extended family members, and teachers • Wide variety of emotions (e.g., happiness, sadness, fear, anger, disgust) • Familiarity with and use of labels for basic emotions • Self-conscious emotions (e.g., pride, embarrassment, guilt)	• Children vary in the number of close attachments they form, the extent to which they are calm with familiar caregivers, and their responses to strangers. Some cling tightly to caregivers; others venture confidently to explore new environments and greet strangers. • Children vary in how they express their emotions. Some are controlled, especially in masking anger and sadness. Others are more expressive. • Children with chronically stressed families may find it challenging to concentrate.	• Be patient in interacting with young children; some form attachments quickly, while others take weeks or months before bonding with teachers. • Teach appropriate ways of handling negative emotions. Encourage children to "use their words" rather than push, hit, or shout when angry. • Foster empathy by being kind, modeling sympathetic responses, and discussing the needs of people facing hardship. Seek intervention for children who are indifferent to others' feelings.

DEVELOPMENTAL TRENDS
Emotional and Personal Characteristics at Different Age Levels (Continued)

AGE	WHAT YOU MIGHT OBSERVE	DIVERSITY	IMPLICATIONS
Middle Childhood (6–10 Years)	• Continued close relationships with family members • Increasing number of bonds with people outside the family, including peers, teachers, and other adults • Increasing ability to regulate emotions • Broadening of coping skills to include asking for help from peers and teachers • Blossoming into a one-of-a-kind personality, especially when supported by parents and teachers	• Some children are traumatized with major family disruptions (e.g., divorce of parents, death or illness of a family member). • Changes in family membership may undermine children's security, usually temporarily, but sometimes for a longer period. • Some children have strong role models for emotional regulation. Others see parents and other adults exploding and getting violent.	• Incorporate emotions into the curriculum; examine the feelings of characters in literature and history. • Model appropriate ways of expressing feelings. • Respect cultural differences in regulating emotions. • Try to form good relationships with all children in your care. • Ask for guidance from other professionals when children appear callous to the feelings of classmates.
Early Adolescence (10–14 Years)	• Frequent fluctuations in mood, partly as a result of hormonal changes and an increasing number of stressful experiences at home and in school • Careful regulation of emotions in public (e.g., hiding excitement about a good grade in order to be acceptable to peers) • Shift in confiding in parents to using a wider support system that includes parents, friends, and teachers	• Individual adolescents differ in the extent to which they conform to typical gender roles in expressing emotions. • Most adolescents expand coping skills in middle school, but some internalize stress (e.g., with depression or anxiety). Others respond with negative behaviors (e.g., hurting others or breaking the law). • The onset of puberty can be a troubling time for some young people.	• Be a supportive listener when young people want to share their anxieties. • Keep in mind that some moodiness is normal in the middle school grades. Talk with parents or the school counselor about the emotional well-being of youngsters who seem especially troubled. • Give young people a chance to express their empathy through service learning in their community.
Late Adolescence (14–18 Years)	• Seeking emotional intimacy with same-sex and opposite-sex peers • Continued attachments to parents, but with strong preferences for affection to be demonstrated in private • Increasing ability to be comforted by peers when distressed • Development of new strategies for coping with stress and negative emotions • Occasionally intense stress as adolescents endeavor to meet graduation requirements, maintain good relationships with peers, and stay in good standing with parents.	• For some adolescents, relationships with parents are tense and offer little reassurance. • Some adolescents use drugs and alcohol to deal with negative emotions. • Some adolescents (girls especially) ruminate over small setbacks and disappointments. • Some adolescents (boys especially) project the impression that they are not bothered by losses, disappointments, and embarrassments. • Volunteering youth may discover that they can effectively help others in need.	• When adolescents are in minor conflicts with parents, help them see that parents want the best despite their different perspective. • Refer youngsters to a school counselor when family relationships deteriorate significantly or youngsters show signs of depression. • Ask adolescents to reflect on the emotional experiences of fictional characters and historical figures. • Teach new coping skills to troubled teens. • Try out yoga and reflective breathing to help students relax.

Summary

Children are born with individual dispositions to respond to the world and express their emotions in certain ways. These constitutional inclinations, called temperaments, are affected by experience and social relationships. Children exercise their temperamental dimensions, integrating their stylistic behaviors, intellectual interests, and social habits, while emerging as distinctive personalities. Teachers and other practitioners help children when they effectively accommodate unique temperaments and personalities.

MyLab Education Self-Check 11.4

Caring for Children with Emotional Problems

11.5 Describe three frameworks for addressing emotional and behavioral problems and strategies for helping children with emotional conditions be successful at school.

Some children have more than their share of negative experiences, to the point where their ability to tackle everyday problems is weakened. As you saw with Merv's experience in the opening case study, many children overcome significant obstacles, especially those with steady support—at home, in school, in the community—ideally, in multiple places. In the remainder of this chapter, we examine serious emotional conditions and explain three frameworks for supporting children.

Support for Children through Special Education

The first framework for supporting children with emotional needs is the field of special education. When difficulties in adjustment are a long-term situation and hinder learning at school, children may be considered to have an **emotional or behavioral disorder** (EBD). The U.S. Department of Education (USDOE) defines emotional disturbance as a condition that has been present over a long period of time, has adversely affected academic performance, and is considered a disability (USDOE, 2004). Special educational services are mandated when the student has an emotional or behavioral disorder and one or more of the following characteristics:

- An inability to learn that cannot be explained by intellectual, sensory, or health factors
- An inability to build or maintain satisfactory interpersonal relationships with peers and teachers
- Inappropriate types of behavior or feelings under normal circumstances
- A pervasive mood of unhappiness or depression
- A tendency to develop physical symptoms or fears associated with personal or school problems (USDOE, 2004)

Children with schizophrenia, who have aberrations in thought and perception and see or hear things that are not present in reality, are likewise considered to have an emotional disorder. Children who are undergoing temporary adjustment difficulties, such as becoming withdrawn for several months after the family's relocation, are not classified as having an emotional disorder unless they meet one or more of the USDOE criteria.

Children who have EBD generally use either an externalizing or internalizing orientation for dealing with personal problems. Children who externalize are aggressive, defiant, disorderly, and prone to difficulties in academic achievement and peer relationships (Trach, Lee, & Hymel, 2018). Children who internalize are frequently sad, anxious, depressed, and fearful, and they lack age-typical social skills and are at risk for becoming victimized by peers (Trach et al., 2018). Externalizing problems are more obvious than internalizing disorders due to their disruptive qualities. Nevertheless, internalizing problems are serious for the students who have them.

Students who are documented as having an EBD in the United States are to receive special education services at school. Personalized goals for the student are developed after discussion with him or her and the family, a school counselor, an advisor and classroom teacher, and other school personnel with relevant expertise. Students might pursue such goals as expressing feelings appropriately, following the teacher's directions, being honest when in trouble, not hitting classmates or calling them names, coping with unsettling events, or respecting others' property and space. Depending on the severity of symptoms, students will stay in the regular classroom, be placed in a small group of students with a special education teacher, or be individually pulled out of the classroom for counseling. The school's services are usually offered on a long-term basis.

The Three-Tiered Model of Social-Emotional Learning

In addition to providing special education services to individual children who are classified as emotionally disturbed, educators can make social-emotional learning a priority for everyone at school. Cultivation of a caring and compassionate environment helps all children, including those with emotional problems. Not everyone needs the same intensity of support, therefore, educators target varied needs in an efficient manner.

Preparing for Your Licensure Examination

Your teaching test might ask you about how you can help children with emotional and behavioral disorders.

The three-tiered hierarchy has become a well-regarded model for providing comprehensive support to students. Numerous three-tiered programs have proved effective; here we illustrate the School-Wide Positive Behavior Support (SWPBS; National Technical Assistance Center on Positive Behavioral Interventions and Supports, 2018). Fundamental to the SWPBS and other three-tiered frameworks are policies, curricula, and classroom routines that foster emotional health, kindness, and good behavior (Macklem, 2011). In Figure 11.2, this foundation is shown in Tier 1 at the bottom of the pyramid of social-emotional interventions, signifying the universal cultivation of cooperation, compassion, and responsibility. In SWPBS programs, behaviors that exemplify these dispositions are illustrated at school. For example, in the Woodlawn Middle School, students are expected to be respectful (e.g., by listening politely and speaking respectfully in the classroom and speaking in conversational tones in the cafeteria), responsible (e.g., by reporting vandalism in the lavatory and using hallway lockers at their designated time), and safe (e.g., by keeping hands, feet, and objects to oneself in the classroom and refraining from running in the hallway; Woodlawn Middle School, n.d.).

In the SWPBS curriculum, educators accommodate three levels of readiness in becoming cooperative, compassionate, and responsible. Tier 1 sets the expectations for a safe, nurturing, and productive learning environment. Most students learn and abide by these rules, yet a few do not (Fossum, Handegård, & Drugli, 2017). Approximately 10% to 15% of students regularly commit minor offenses, some of which merit a visit to the principal's office; these students are referred for Tier 2 support (M. K. Burns, Deno, & Jimerson, 2007). Students in Tier 2 are given an opportunity to learn missing social-emotional skills, typically in small groups and with guidance from adults. One measure in Tier 2 is the Check In/Check Out program, in which students begin the morning with a school professional, briefly chat with him or her, and pick up a point sheet, which they bring to other staff who make notes on difficulties and accomplishments.

FIGURE 11.2 Hierarchy of educational interventions for emotional well-being.

In the three-tiered model of social-emotional learning, students universally receive lessons in emotional literacy and standards for behavior (Tier 1). A small number of students commit transgressions that put them at risk for more serious problems. The school arranges for small-group exercises addressing the difficulties students are experiencing and often provides counseling (Tier 2). A few students exhibit more serious behaviors consistent with having a mental health disorder. The school provides an intensive intervention, inclusive of individual counseling and a personalized treatment plan for their work at school (Tier 3; National Technical Assistance Center on Positive Behavioral Interventions and Supports, 2018).

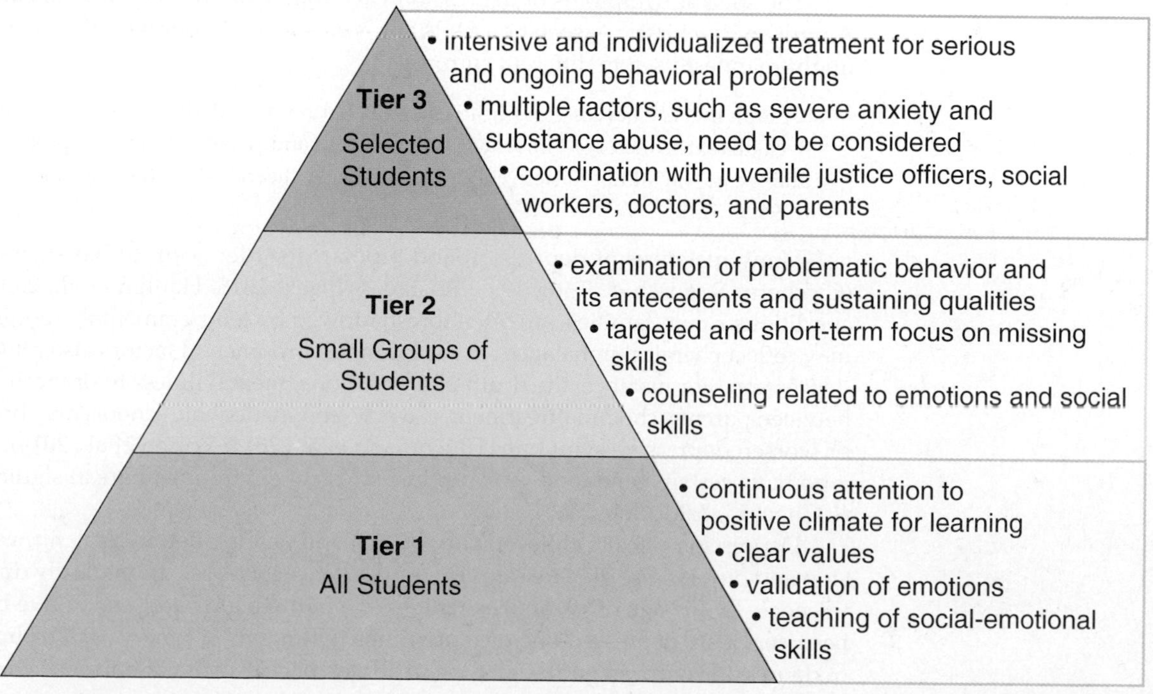

At the end of the day, students return to the adult seen in the morning and together they examine progress.

A smaller number of students exhibit even more worrying behaviors and are eligible for Tier 3 services. Approximately 5% to 10% of students perform actions that interfere with their learning and the welfare of others (M. K. Burns et al., 2007). For example, one student disliked mathematics, which he found incomprehensible, and started to shout at the teacher and throw objects at classmates. Everyday discipline had no effect. Students in Tier 3 may receive counseling, develop a plan for reaching personal goals (e.g., tell an adult when bothered by a classmate or walk away rather than explode in anger), participate in training activities, and log behaviors relevant to desired targets. Educators also consult with probation officers, psychiatrists, and social workers on matters of mutual concern, such as when a new medication to quell anxiety diminishes a student's concentration at school. Students in Tier 3 may or may not be obtaining services within the special education system.

Medical Model of Emotional Conditions

Our final framework for understanding emotional conditions is the medical model. Medical researchers have long sought to understand the physiological basis of emotional difficulties and the treatments that alleviate them. They have conceptualized the tendency to feel negative emotions (e.g., sadness, anger, or fear) to an extreme degree as a sickness that can be treated with medication, counseling, behavioral change, and other clinical methods. Approximately 25% of children in the United States are affected by a mental health problem, in which their thinking, feeling, mood, and ability to relate to others are disrupted for one or more periods (Braaten, 2011; Tolani & Brooks-Gunn, 2006). Here we look at three conditions—depression, anxiety, and conduct disorder.

Depression

People with **depression** feel exceptionally sad, discouraged, and hopeless; they may also feel restless, sluggish, helpless, worthless, or unusually guilty. Children with depression may be unresponsive to caregivers, withdraw from social interactions with peers, report such physical complaints as headaches and stomach pain, and be perpetually sad or irritable (Alba, Calvete, Wante, Van Beveren, & Braet, 2018; Braaten, 2011; A. Carr, 2014). Depressed youngsters may have trouble concentrating, keeping up with usual activities, eating, and sleeping (American Psychiatric Association, 1994). A variation of depression, *bipolar disorder*, occurs when individuals experience periods of extreme elation and hyperactivity as well as phases of deep depression.

The specific symptoms of depression vary somewhat from culture to culture. The American Psychiatric Association (APA) provides several examples of how depression might manifest itself in different cultures:

> Complaints of "nerves" and headaches (in Latino and Mediterranean cultures), of weakness, tiredness, or "imbalance" (in Chinese and Asian cultures), of problems of the "heart" (in Middle Eastern cultures), or of being "heartbroken" (among Hopi). (APA, 1994, p. 324)

Many instances of depression and bipolar disorder seem to have genetic roots (Cicchetti, Rogosch, & Toth, 1997; Fristad & Black, 2018; Hankin et al., 2009). These conditions run in families, are often foreshadowed by temperamental moodiness, and may reflect chemical imbalances in the brain. Environmental factors also play a role in depression. For instance, the death of a loved one, mental illness in or marital conflict between parents, child maltreatment, poverty, and inadequate schools may bring about or worsen depressive symptoms (Buchmann et al., 2014; Vrijsen et al., 2014). Children who have certain genes and grow up in a stressful environment are at significant risk (J. Chen, Li, & McGue, 2013).

Depression rates in children vary by age and gender. Before adolescence, depression and bipolar disorder are rare. Their prevalence increases dramatically during adolescence. By the age of 19, approximately one in three girls and one in five boys have been seriously depressed one or more times (Oltmanns & Emery, 2007). Higher rates of depression occur in girls beginning in adolescence because of hormone changes and the tendency of girls to dwell on their problems (Hilt & Nolen-Hoeksema, 2009). When children succumb to extreme stress with a depressive episode, the event alters their neurological chemistry, making it more likely that they will suffer another depressive episode in the future (Akiskal & McKinney, 1973; Luby, 2010).

Youth with serious depression or bipolar disorder are at risk for considering or committing suicide (Ordaz, Goyer, Ho, Singh, & Gotlib, 2018; M. G. Sawyer et al., 2010; Shilubane et al., 2014). The overwhelming despair and high frequency of suicide that accompany depression make it a condition that educators must take seriously. Through their daily contact with youngsters, teachers have numerous opportunities to observe children's moods and so may become aware of a possible depression. (Friends and family, though they have closer ties to youngsters, may not comprehend or accept how serious the problem is.) Educators will want to offer emotional comfort to young people who appear troubled, and they should consult with principals and counselors if they suspect severe depression or another serious emotional disturbance.

Anxiety Disorder

In its milder forms, anxiety is a common and very "normal" emotion. But some people, including some children and adolescents, fuss and fret excessively and find it difficult to control their worrisome thoughts and feelings; in other words, they have an **anxiety disorder** (APA, 2000; A. Carr, 2014). Children with a *generalized anxiety* disorder worry unreasonably about a wide variety of things, including their academic achievement and potentially catastrophic events such as wars or hurricanes. Other individuals have specific anxiety disorders, perhaps worrying constantly about such things as gaining weight, having a serious illness, being away from family and home, feeling embarrassed in public, flying on an airplane, or being scared to go to school (A. Carr, 2014; Heeren & McNally, 2018; Ollendick, Costa, & Benoit, 2010).

As you might expect, nature and nurture both contribute to anxiety disorders. These disorders have a genetic basis and run in families (Hudson et al., 2013; Last, Hersen, Kazdin, Francis, & Grubb, 1987; Ogliari et al., 2010; Shackman et al., 2017). Family environment also plays a role. Some evidence suggests that a number of anxious children have had insecure attachments to their parents and have been exposed to aloof and critical parenting or to exceedingly controlling and intrusive parenting (Cooper-Vince, Pincus, & Comer, 2014; Havinga, Boschloo, Hartman, & Schoevers, 2018; Luijk et al., 2010; P. S. Moore, Whaley, & Sigman, 2004). With these types of care, children worry about their ability to make independent decisions and handle threatening situations.

Conduct Disorder

When children display a chronic pattern of misbehavior and show little shame or guilt about their wrongdoings, they may be identified as having a **conduct disorder**. Youngsters who display a conduct disorder ignore the rights of others in ways that are unusual for their age. Common symptoms include aggression toward people and animals (e.g., initiating physical fights, forcing someone into sexual activity, torturing animals), destruction of property (e.g., setting fires, painting graffiti), theft and deceitfulness (e.g., breaking into cars, lying about shoplifting so as not to be caught), and serious violations of rules (e.g., ignoring reasonable curfews, being truant from school; APA, 2000; A. Carr, 2014; Gelhorn et al., 2009). Approximately 2% to 6% of school-aged youth could be classified as having a conduct disorder, with rates being three or four times higher for boys than for girls (Kazdin, 1997).

One or two antisocial acts do not make a conduct problem. Conduct disorders are more than a matter of "kids being kids" or "sowing wild oats." Instead, they represent a deep-seated and persistent disregard for the rights and feelings of others. Youth with conduct disorders tend to see the world through conflict-colored glasses, for example, by assuming that others have hostile intentions toward them (Dodge et al., 2003). Given the serious problems that children and adolescents with a conduct disorder exhibit at school, they are likely to be referred for special education, the Tier 3 counseling and individualized services we explained earlier, or other intensive interventions available at school.

Conduct disorder is especially worrisome (and likely to foreshadow adjustment problems in the adult years) when it begins prior to adolescence (J. G. Barrett, 2005; D. Shaw, 2013). Youngsters who exhibit conduct disorders beginning in childhood are likely to have many problems in adulthood, including antisocial and criminal behavior, frequent changes in employment, high divorce rates, little participation in families and community groups, and early death. In contrast, conduct disorders that don't emerge until adolescence are often the result of affiliation with peers who engage in delinquent behavior. Late-onset offenders usually mature and find new social contacts, shedding their antisocial ways.

As is true for other emotional disorders, biology may be *partly* to blame for conduct disorders. Children with conduct disorders have difficulty inhibiting aggressive impulses, perhaps as a result of brain damage or other neurological conditions (Fishbein et al., 2006; S. White et al., 2013). Families are influential as well: Conduct disorders are relatively common when parents provide little affection, abuse children, and are highly critical and harsh in their physical punishment (G. R. Patterson, DeBaryshe, & Ramsey, 1989; Rolon-Arroyo, Arnold, Breaux, & Harvey, 2018; Tuvblad, Bezdjian, Raine, & Baker, 2013). Neighborhoods can also be a factor in conduct disorders, as when children witness violence in their communities and later become physically aggressive themselves (Ridenour, Clark, & Cottler, 2009; Shahinfar, Kupersmidt, & Matza, 2001).

Supporting Youngsters with Emotional and Behavioral Problems

Young people who are struggling with anxiety and depression are often helped in counseling and other mental health treatments. Sensitive and consistent attention from teachers and other school staff can be part of the solution. Consider these strategies:

- **Communicate that you care for children.** Having a supportive relationship with a teacher protects a child from everyday stresses and increases the chances that the child adjusts well at school (Rueger, Chen, Jenkins, & Choe, 2014; Valiente, Lemery-Chalfant, Swanson, & Reiser, 2008; M. Zee & Koomen, 2017). Many youngsters with emotional disorders have few positive ties with individuals outside of school, and so their relationships with caring teachers, school counselors, and other skilled professionals are critical. The many "little things" educators and other practitioners do each day, including greeting youngsters warmly, expressing concern when they seem worried, and lending an ear when they want to share hopes or frustrations, can make the world of difference for children (S. C. Diamond, 1991).

- **Convey positive expectations for healthy emotional expression, moral behavior, and good relationships.** When reading about Tier 1 interventions, you learned about the advantages of universal expectations for constructive emotional expression and mutually respectful behavior. There are a numerous social-emotional programs that serve this function, and educators are advised to select ones with documented success. Yet even if a systematic social-emotional program is not implemented at your school, you can nevertheless do a lot to promote growth. Because children with emotional problems have difficulty in finding and keeping friends, teachers can coach them in basic social skills, such as resolving conflicts by talking through the issues, avoiding accusations, and focusing on solutions (Asher & Coie, 1990; Gillham, Reivich, Jaycox, & Seligman, 1995; Kingery, Erdley, Marshall, Whitaker, & Reuter, 2010; Marquez et al., 2014).

- **Provide extra structure for youngsters who are highly anxious.** Apprehensive children perform better in well-structured environments, such as classrooms in which expectations for academic achievement and social behavior are communicated directly (Sieber, O'Neil, & Tobias, 1977; Stipek, 1993). When they know what to expect and how they will be evaluated, young people are more inclined to relax, enjoy themselves, and learn. In a preschool program designed to help children manage their anxiety, called FRIENDS, children learn to attend to their *Feelings, Relax,* think about their *Inner* feelings, *Explore* plans, motivate themselves with comments about having done *Nice* work, remind themselves *"Don't* forget to practice," and *Stay* calm (Anticich, Barrett, Silverman, Lacherez, & Gillies, 2013).

• **Respect children's autonomy.** Every child needs to be able to make choices. Some students, especially those who consistently defy authority figures, often behave less appropriately when adults try to control them. With these youngsters, it is important that practitioners not get into power struggles, situations where only one person wins and the other loses (S. C. Diamond, 1991). Instead, adults can try to create situations in which children conform to expectations yet also know they have some control over what happens to them.

• **Share your ideas on how a child can be supported.** Parents whose children have emotional and behavioral problems may appreciate advice. Depending on the particular challenges children face, parents may benefit from guidance in establishing clear rules, recognizing children's good behaviors, disciplining them, and helping them manage feelings (Garland, Augustyn, & Stein, 2007; Rosenblum & Muzik, 2014). Family educators play a special role in coaching parents to try new childrearing methods, ones that guide parents in understanding how children's emotions affect their behavior and can be expressed productively.

• **Be alert for signs that a student is contemplating suicide.** Seriously depressed youngsters may fail to reach out for help when they believe that no one cares about them or that they should be able to solve problems on their own. A few are worried that people would think less of them if they were to disclose their personal anguish (Freedenthal & Stiffman, 2007). Informed professionals keep alert to the signs that troubled students give off (consciously or not) that they may be thinking about taking their own lives. Warning signs include the following:

- Signs of depression, hopelessness, and helplessness
- Abrupt withdrawal from social relationships (possibly after being rejected by peers or breaking up with a boyfriend or girlfriend)
- Disregard for personal appearance
- Serious health problems (e.g., a debilitating injury from an accident or a chronic condition resulting from an eating disorder)
- A dramatic personality change
- A sudden elevation in mood
- A preoccupation with death and morbid themes
- Serious problems at school, home, or in the community (e.g., expulsion from school, death of a friend, pregnancy, or arrest for illegal behavior)
- Overt or veiled threats (e.g., "I won't be around much longer")
- Actions that indicate "putting one's affairs in order" (e.g., giving away prized possessions)
- Substance abuse
- Repeated self-injury
- Preference for certain kinds of music (e.g., heavy metal rock music with morbid themes)
- Efforts to obtain suicidal means (e.g., medications, ropes, or guns)
- In some cases, impulsive personality (M. M. Jensen, 2005; L. L. Kerns & Lieberman, 1993; Ordaz et al., 2018; Taliaferro & Muehlenkamp, 2014)

Adults must take these behaviors seriously, particularly if they see more than one of the signs on the list. Educators should show genuine concern for potentially suicidal youngsters and seek help from a school psychologist or counselor *immediately* (McCoy, 1994; Spirito, Valeri, Boergers, & Donaldson, 2003).

Summary

Children with emotional disorders may obtain services through one or more professional frameworks. Children who are classified within the special education system receive accommodations for an emotional disturbance. Three-tier interventions provide basic education about emotions and establish high standards of conduct for everyone and, for those who need it, specialized support. The medical model offers information about the symptoms and treatment of depression, anxiety, and conduct disorders. Teachers are likely to have children coping with emotional problems in their classroom and can offer reassurance, communicate expectations for appropriate behavior, and address personal concerns, such as getting along with peers and having some control over everyday decisions.

MyLab Education Self-Check 11.5

Practicing For Your Licensure Examination

Many teaching tests require students to apply what they have learned about child development to brief vignettes and multiple-choice questions. You can practice for your licensure examination by reading the following case study and answering a series of questions.

The Girly Shirt

Eight-year-old Tim caused quite a disruption in class this morning. His teacher, Amy Fox, isn't quite sure why things got out of hand, and so she is meeting with Tim while the rest of the class is at lunch to learn what happened.

Ms. Fox: Things got out of control in class this morning, didn't they, Tim?

Tim: I guess they did.

Ms. Fox: Tell me what happened.

Tim: John and Steven were teasing me about my shirt. They really made me mad.

Ms. Fox: They were teasing you about your shirt? What did they say?

Tim: That it's too pink. That it's a "girly" color.

Ms. Fox: Really? I don't think it's too "girly" at all. In fact, I rather like that color on you. But anyway, you say the boys teased you about it. What did you do then?

Tim: I yelled at them. Then when you gave me that dirty look, they kept on laughing, and so I kept on yelling.

Ms. Fox: I see. John and Steven were certainly wrong to tease you about your clothes. I'll speak to them later. But right now I'm concerned about how you reacted to the situation. You were so loud that the class couldn't possibly continue with the lesson.

Tim: I know. I'm sorry.

Ms. Fox: I appreciate your apology, Tim. And I'd like to make sure that the next time someone hurts your feelings—maybe intentionally, maybe not—you don't blow up the way you did today. Let's come up with a plan for how you might keep your temper under better control.

Constructed-Response Question

1. What type of plan might be effective in helping Tim control his anger?

Multiple-Choice Questions

2. What aspect of emotional development is Tim struggling with in this incident?
   a. Emotional regulation, because he is having trouble controlling his temper
   b. Emotional contagion, because he is absorbing the feelings of the other boys
   c. Empathy, because he, like the other boys, disliked his shirt
   d. Insecure attachment, because he is not able to use his peers as a safe haven

3. Let's assume that Tim has been somewhat irritable since infancy. What factors might account for this temperament?
   a. Tim's temperament is the outgrowth of his unique genetic profile.
   b. Tim's temperament is the result of harsh and punitive parenting.
   c. Tim's temperament is the complex result of his genetic disposition, his relationships, and his own choices and experiences.
   d. Temperament changes dramatically from day to day and week to week; therefore, it is not possible to identify any factors that account for consistency in his irritability.

MyLab Education Licensure Practice 11.1

Key Concepts

coping skills (p. 401)
psychosocial stages (p. 401)
need for relatedness (p. 405)
attachment (p. 405)
ethological attachment theory (p. 405)
stranger anxiety (p. 406)
secure attachment (p. 408)
insecure-avoidant attachment (p. 408)
insecure-resistant attachment (p. 408)
disorganized and disoriented attachment (p. 408)
emotion (p. 418)
emotional contagion (p. 419)
self-conscious emotion (p. 420)
empathy (p. 420)
emotional regulation (p. 421)
anxiety (p. 427)
personality (p. 429)
emotional or behavioral disorder (p. 436)
depression (p. 438)
anxiety disorder (p. 439)
conduct disorder (p. 439)

Chapter Twelve
Self and Social Understanding

Jamie Gril/JGI/Blend Images/Getty Images

Objectives

12.1 Trace key developments in children's ideas about themselves, and explain strategies teachers use to foster healthy self-perceptions.

12.2 Discuss changes in social cognition during childhood, and identify ways in which teachers nurture social understandings.

CASE STUDY

Theodore

At age 16, Theodore had an assignment to write about who he was as a person. Following is his response:

Hello. I'm Theodore. I am 16 years old and come from America. I'm a very happy person and have an optimistic view on life. Although life can be very challenging and confusing at times, I always think to myself it will be all right later on. I think everybody is equal and everybody should be treated the same, even though this is close to impossible.

I love to hang out with my friends and family. I think family is one of the most important things in life. I love my family and feel very lucky, and I am very appreciative for all they have done for me. Not everybody can have such a loving family though, and that makes me very sad. Occasionally I get great urges to go out and try to help people all around the world who are in need of support. But also at times I feel very helpless, and I feel like I can't do much to help, which makes me upset. Living in a small city in America is very great, but I know there is more out there in the world, and I wish I could experience living in a developing country. I have been able to travel to several countries and have friends around the world that I keep in contact with on Facebook.

I am just a sort-of average kid who is medium in height and underweight. I have longish brown hair and big feet. I like girls and some like me back. I love to play video games and watch movies. I also like to play any kind of sports with my friends, especially Ultimate Frisbee.

I have no idea what I will be when I grow up. I am interested in SO many things, and it seems I will never be able to narrow it down. I am interested in computers/engineering, being a medical doctor of sorts, being an airplane pilot, and more. My biggest dream in life is to travel around the world as much as I can and learn about people, culture, food, history, language, religions, everything else I can learn about, everywhere in the world.

Throughout my life I have changed a lot physically and mentally. I look at the world very differently than I did even a few months ago, and I will probably think differently a couple months down the road. I grow more and more patient and less egocentric every day. I think I am going in the right direction except for a few things. Although I am smart and get good grades, I could work a lot harder in school and on other academic things. I could do extra homework. I find it hard to muster the gumption to work harder and do more academic things such as enter a spelling bee or science contest or something.

Well that's who I am today. Ask me again in a couple of years and see what I say!

- What does Theodore say about himself?
- How does Theodore think about his social world?

Outline

Each child is born with a starter kit for social life—preferences for looking at faces (especially the eyes and mouth), listening to voices, and joining in a conversation (Govrin, 2018; Happé & Frith, 2014). In the process of communicating with other people, children become aware of themselves and the behavior of others. Early perceptions are simple and concrete, such as recognizing one's name and the physical features of others, and they evolve into abstract reflections, as in Theodore's gratitude for the blessings he has with his family and community.

In addition to thinking about themselves, children become perceptive of what makes others act as they do. Theodore mentions that he is becoming less egocentric. He uses his perspective-taking skills with family and friends and also with people in other societies. He feels a commitment to helping others in need. Having a sense of self and an inclination to consider the needs of others helps Theodore, and other young people, get along in society.

In this chapter, you will learn that a few children face challenges in developing a positive self-concept. In absorbing others' messages about their value as human beings, some children conclude that they are incapable, unattractive, and unwanted. A few others have difficulty grasping the viewpoints of other people. Without the ability to recognize others' beliefs, ideas, and wishes, children find the social world strange and themselves excluded. Fortunately, it is possible for adults to help children in recognizing their worth and in considering other people's perspectives. We examine practical applications of social perceptions in the context of developmental trends and exceptionalities.

Sense of Self

12.1 Trace key developments in children's ideas about themselves, and explain strategies teachers use to foster healthy self-perceptions.

Children develop knowledge, beliefs, judgments, and feelings about themselves, sentiments collectively known as a **sense of self**. Particular elements of self-perceptions go by a variety of names, including self-concept, self-esteem, and self-worth. In general, one's *self-concept* addresses the question, "Who am I?" Self-concept includes understandings of one's own characteristics, strengths, and weaknesses ("I am a Puerto Rican American"; "My nose is crooked"). The terms *self-esteem* and *self-worth* are synonyms that address the question, "How good am I as a person?" They include judgments and feelings about one's value and worth (e.g., "I am proud to be Puerto Rican and American"; "I hate my crooked nose!").

Children's self-concept and self-worth are closely related (Byrne, 2002; Harter, 2012). Children who focus largely on their negative features tend to believe they are undeserving human beings. Those who hold favorable impressions of their characteristics tend to have high self-esteem. In this chapter, we examine self-concept and self-esteem together, often calling them self-perceptions but occasionally using one or another when distinctions in the research merit their separation.

Purpose of the Self

Children's sense of self serves several functions. It helps children understand things that happen to them ("Other kids ask me to join their teams, so I must be good at sports"). It motivates them to engage in behaviors that others approve ("If I'm nice to Russ, maybe he'll ask me to play with him"). It influences their reactions to events ("I'm upset that I'm not reading as well as my classmates"). And once they begin to look seriously at their *future self*, they can make choices appropriate to their goals ("To become a veterinarian, I need to take a biology class").

Perhaps most important, a sense of self helps a person find a comfortable niche in a complex world, a place in which the individual feels capable, cared for, and respected. Many psychologists believe that human beings have a basic need to think of themselves as competent, likable, and well-intentioned individuals (Covington, 1992; Marshall, Parker, Ciarrochi, & Heaven, 2014; Tatlow-Golden & Guerin, 2017). Although children cannot always feel good about themselves, they usually try to protect their self-image.

Preparing for Your Licensure Examination

Your teaching test might ask you why children's self-perceptions are integral to their adjustment at school.

To maintain strong self-worth, children use a variety of tactics, including affiliating with other individuals who treat them kindly and putting themselves in situations where they can be successful.

Factors Influencing Self-Perceptions

Self-concept emerges in the arms of parents. When caregivers regularly nurture infants with affection and responsive care, infants learn not only that their caregivers love them but that they themselves are worthy of being loved (Bretherton, 1991). As children grow, parents enhance children's sense of self, specifically their self-esteem, by treating them warmly and communicating expectations for mature behavior. Parents who accept children as they are—applauding their abilities and taking *in*abilities in stride—are likely to have offspring with high self-esteem. Parents who punish children for things they do not or cannot do, without also praising them for hard work and things they've done well, are apt to have offspring with low self-esteem (Ahmann, 2014; Baek & Yoo, 2017; Harter, 1999).

Generally speaking, children's self-esteem reflects the extent to which children feel accepted by important people in their lives (Gruenenfelder-Steiger, Harris, & Fend, 2016). Adults outside the family become increasingly influential as children spend more time away from home. Teachers, school nurses, and other practitioners foster a positive sense of self when they have high yet realistic expectations for performance; empathize with children who are lonely, anxious, and depressed; and offer needed support to children to withstand hardships and succeed on difficult tasks (Baek & Yoo, 2017; M. J. Harris & Rosenthal, 1985; Olowokere & Okanlawon, 2014).

Having friends is a critical component in how most children feel about themselves. Friends essentially communicate that children are worthy partners for free time and, as they grow, for honest and open discussions (Corsano, Musetti, Caricati, & Magnani, 2017). Participation in one or more large social groups—gatherings of youngsters who affiliate in clubs, in homes, or on the streets—also influences sense of self, especially in adolescence (Birkeland, Breivik, & Wold, 2014; Lave & Wenger, 1991). Many young people additionally associate with others on social networking sites and online communities on the World Wide Web; in the process, they gain a sense of being part of a circle of friends (R. K. Baker & White, 2010; Best, Manktelow, & Taylor, 2014; Ranzini & Hoek, 2017). In high school, students absorb some of the benefits from being part of their school's athletic team, musical club, other extracurricular activity, or a community service project. When young people feel excluded from traditional means of achievement, they may seek social acceptance elsewhere, in such groups as gangs (Barbieri, Clipper & Vasquez, 2016).

Age-mates contribute to a child's sense of self in another way: They provide information about what he or she "should" be able to do. As you will learn, by the elementary school years, how children see themselves is affected by how peers see them (Ehm, Lindberg, & Hasselhorn, 2014; Guay, Boivin, & Hodges, 1999). Children who achieve at higher levels than age-mates develop a more positive sense of self than do those who fall short. Peers may seek out a child's help on an assignment or ridicule him or her in front of others (Bogart et al., 2014; Dweck, 2000).

The school itself provides a context in which children make sense of their accomplishments. Academically, children base their self-perceptions on a growing record of performance (Damon, 1991; M. Seaton, Parker, Marsh, Craven, & Yeung, 2014). Children are more likely to believe they will succeed in school and later in college if they have been mostly successful in previous work. Those children who struggle recurrently may view their abilities as limited and their academic future as bleak. In the minds of children, their ability to meet standards and their impressions of how classmates judge their abilities become intertwined. Tom, a second-grader who had dyslexia, once described how he felt when struggling with reading in first grade:

> I falt like a losr. Like nobad likde me. I was afrad then kais wod tec me. Becacz I wased larning wale . . . I dan not whet to raed. I whoe whte to troe a book it my mom.
>
> *(I felt like a loser. Like nobody liked me. I was afraid that kids would tease me. Because I wasn't learning well . . . I did not want to read. I would want to throw a book at my mom.)*
> (N. F. Knapp, 2002, p. 74)

Obviously, no child wants to feel like a loser. Children work hard to protect themselves from negative information about their abilities and worth. Thus, they may explain their shortcomings in ways that allow them to maintain a positive self-image (Crocker & Major, 1989). A middle school boy who has prepared intensively for an oral presentation is surprised with a low score and wonders whether the teacher was really paying attention. Or he may realize that he forgot to include a vital element, such as an ending conclusion, which he will try to remember next time. Although these two interpretations have different implications, neither undermines his self-worth. In the following example, you can see 10-year-old David give an upbeat spin on why he doesn't recall as many words as he expects to. He predicts that he might recall 12 out of 12 words but actually recalls only 3. Here is David's positive interpretation:

David: Okay, shirt, carrot, bed. I'm sorry, I can't remember the rest of it. It's just, I don't know. My brain was turned off right now. I use it a lot during school hours so then I just like to relax. . . .

Interviewer: What did you do to remember the ones that you remembered?

David: Even though I said 12, I was just trying to challenge myself a little.

MyLab Education
Video Example 12.1

Find Developmental Meaning
How does David interpret his failure to remember as many words as he had anticipated? David puts a positive spin on not remembering many words. Realizing that he was not paying attention, he knows he should exert more effort in a future memory task to better his chances of success.

The need to protect oneself is so strong that it sometimes leads children to create obstacles that give them an excuse for failing. In other words, youngsters occasionally do things that actually *undermine* their chances of success—a phenomenon known as **self-handicapping**. Self-handicapping takes a variety of forms, including the following:

- *Reducing effort.* Putting forth an obviously insufficient amount of effort to succeed
- *Setting unattainably high goals.* Working toward goals that even the most capable individuals couldn't achieve
- *Taking on too much.* Assuming so many responsibilities that no one could possibly accomplish them all
- *Procrastinating.* Putting off a task until success is virtually impossible
- *Cheating.* Presenting others' work as one's own
- *Using alcohol or drugs.* Taking substances that will inevitably reduce performance (Covington, 1992; Shih, 2009; K. Snyder, Malin, Dent, & Linnenbrink-Garcia, 2014; Urdan, Ryan, Anderman, & Gheen, 2002)

It might seem paradoxical that youngsters who want to be successful would actually undermine their own accomplishments. But if they believe they are unlikely to succeed no matter what they do—and especially if failure will reflect poorly on their intelligence—these tactics increase their chances of *justifying* failure. Self-handicapping is seen as early as elementary school and becomes increasingly common in the high school and college years (Alesi, Rappo, & Pepi, 2012; Urdan, 2004). In extreme cases, students become anxious or depressed and decide that further effort is futile and that they should look in other arenas for chances to be successful (E. E. Rosenberg, Burt, Forehand, & Paysnick, 2016). Depending on the opportunities available, they might invest their efforts in other subjects, such as physical education or music, or alternatively drop out of school.

So far our discussion has focused primarily on the effects of experience on self-perception—that is, on children's processing of encounters in social and school environments. Biology has an impact as well. Self-esteem has a hereditary basis in that people who share many genes tend to view themselves in a similarly positive or negative way (H. Chen et al., 2013; Raevuori et al., 2007). Genes probably affect self-esteem indirectly through their effects on complex characteristics (e.g., temperaments, motor skills, and cognitive abilities and disabilities) that contribute to performance in social, athletic, and academic pursuits. Physical appearance also makes a difference: Adults and peers alike respond more favorably and expect higher levels of intelligence from children who are physically attractive (R. A. Gordon, Crosnoe, & Wang, 2013; S. H. W. Mares, de Leeuw, Scholte, & Engels, 2010; Talamas, Mavor, Axelsson, Sundelin, & Perrett, 2016).

Developmental Trends in the Self

Children's physical, cognitive, and social abilities change with age, and their perceptions of themselves shift accordingly. Researchers have observed the following developmental trends in sense of self.

Children construct increasingly abstract, integrated, and multifaceted understandings of who they are. Young children define themselves with a few specific, concrete, easily observable characteristics. In the preschool and early elementary grades, students can distinguish between a few general aspects of themselves, for example, how competent they are in daily activities and how much family and friends like them (Davis-Kean & Sandler, 2001; E. Reese, Yan, Jack, & Hayne, 2010). As they grow older, they make finer discriminations (Harter, 2012; Kuzucu, Bontempo, Hofer, Stallings, & Piccinin, 2014). By the upper elementary grades, they realize that they may be more or less advanced in their academic work, athletic activities, classroom behavior, likability among peers, and physical attractiveness. By adolescence, they develop self-perceptions about competence at adultlike tasks and romantic appeal. Adolescents also begin to describe themselves as reflecting intangible qualities, for example, as being "tech savvy" or "moody" (D. Hart, 1988; Meadows, 2010).

Most youngsters adopt standards for evaluating their appearance and accomplishments that they have learned from others. Psychologists specializing in the self suggest that children internalize some of other people's ideas about desirable characteristics and behaviors (Burton & Mitchell, 2003; J. L. Williams & Smalls-Glover, 2014). As youngsters acquire such criteria, their self-esteem is increasingly based on *self*-judgments rather than others' judgments. A boy whose parents regularly praise him for his high grades is likely to begin judging *himself* by the grades he earns. You can see such internalization in the following example with 15-year-old Greg:

Interviewer:	What are the things that make you want to do well in school?
Greg:	My parents. [*Both laugh.*]
Interviewer:	Okay.
Greg:	My parents mostly. . . . And myself . . . sometimes.
Interviewer:	Okay. How do your parents influence you wanting to do well in school?
Greg:	I don't know. They did well so they want me to . . . .
Interviewer:	You said that sometimes you also want to do well for you. Can you tell me more about that?
Greg:	'Cause, I mean, you feel better if you get all As than Cs or Fs.

Yet the standards that youngsters internalize are not always realistic or productive. A girl whose friends place a premium on fashion-magazine standards for beauty may think she is "fat" even when she is dangerously underweight—a misperception commonly seen in youngsters who have eating disorders (Attie, Brooks-Gunn, & Petersen, 1990; Nanu, Tăut, & Băban, 2013). Likewise, a student who expects to earn perfect marks in school is bound to run into disappointment at one time or another.

MyLab Education
Video Example 12.2

Find Developmental Meaning
How is Greg navigating a transition in values for academic achievement? Originally perceiving high grades to be his parents' goals, Greg realizes that he now likes to get good grades.

Children become increasingly committed to chosen standards. Youngsters generally have high self-esteem when they evaluate themselves as being strong in domains that are important to them. For some, academic achievement may be the overriding factor, whereas for others, popularity with peers may be more influential. Some children invest in athletic accomplishments, and others may value their contributions to family or community. And for many youngsters around the world, physical attractiveness contributes heavily to self-esteem (D. Hart, 1988; Harter, 2012).

Despite experiencing a general trend toward becoming progressively more certain of their own personal standards, some youngsters remain heavily dependent on others' opinions well into adolescence. They may be so preoccupied with approval from others that they base their own self-worth largely on what others think of them—or at least on what *they think* others think (Dweck, 2000; Ghoul, Niwa, & Boxer, 2013; Harter, Stocker, & Robinson, 1996; Ishizu, 2017). Teenagers who have such **contingent self-worth** are often on an emotional roller coaster, feeling elated one day and devastated the next, depending on how classmates, parents, and teachers have recently treated them.

As children grow older, their feelings of self-worth depend more on peers' behaviors and opinions. In the early years, parents and other family members are key players in shaping children's sense of self. As children spend more time away from home, however, they become more aware of and concerned about what nonfamily members—and especially peers—think of them (Birkeland et al., 2014; Richman, Hope, & Mihalas, 2010). Whereas parents often express approval for good behavior and high academic achievement, peers tend to prefer physical attractiveness, athleticism, and being a reliable confidant and fun playmate. Peers by no means replace the influence of parents, however. Well into the adolescent years, youngsters' self-perceptions continue to be strongly affected by parents (B. B. Chen, 2017; S. M. Cooper & Smalls, 2010; Harter, 2012).

Children increasingly behave in ways that mirror their self-perceptions. Those who see themselves as "good students" are more apt to pay attention in class, use effective learning strategies, and tackle challenging tasks, whereas those who believe they are "poor students" are apt to misbehave in class, study infrequently, and avoid difficult subject matter. Children who see themselves as friendly and likable are apt to reach out to classmates, ask for help when needed, or run for student council, whereas those who believe they are disliked may keep to themselves or behave aggressively toward age-mates. As you might guess, children who routinely *under*estimate their ability avoid the many challenges necessary for cognitive, social, and physical growth (Assor & Connell, 1992; D. Phillips & Zimmerman, 1990). These children are at risk for developing depression and other mental health problems (Nuijens, Teglasi, & Hancock, 2009; van Tuijl, de Jong, Sportel, de Hullu, & Nauta, 2014).

Children's sense of worth becomes more stable over time. Beginning in middle childhood, self-esteem becomes fairly stable, such that those with positive self-perceptions tend to continue to see themselves in favorable terms (J. Kim & Cicchetti, 2009; R. W. Robins & Trzesniewski, 2005). Likewise, children who think poorly of themselves in elementary school generally have relatively low self-esteem in high school and adulthood. Several factors contribute to the stability of self-perceptions:

- Children usually behave in ways consistent with what they believe about themselves, and their behaviors are apt to produce reactions from others that confirm these self-concepts.
- Children tend to seek out information that confirms what they already believe. Those with positive self-perceptions are more likely to attend to feedback about their strengths, whereas others with negative self-perceptions focus on their weaknesses (S. Epstein & Morling, 1995; R. T. Liu, Kraines, Massing-Schaffer, & Alloy, 2014).
- The elementary school environment tends to be relatively consistent from year to year. During this period, children compare their levels of performance to those of classmates and find that their standing remains fairly steady (J. M. Chung, Hutteman, van Aken, & Denissen, 2017).
- Children seldom put themselves in situations where they believe they won't succeed, thus minimizing the chances of discovering that they *can* perform well in a previously difficult domain. If a middle school student believes he is a poor athlete and so refuses to go out for the baseball team, he may never learn that, in fact, he has the potential to become a good player.
- Many factors affecting self-esteem—inherited abilities and disabilities, parents' encouragement, physical attractiveness, and so on—remain relatively stable throughout childhood (Goleniowska, 2014; O'Malley & Bachman, 1983; Raevuori et al., 2007).

This is *not* to say that once children acquire an unfavorable sense of self, they will always think poorly of themselves. Quite the contrary can be true, especially with new circumstances—including being put in situations where they are shown how to succeed and coaxed into taking risks (Marsh & Craven, 1997; Rönnau-Böse & Fröhlich-Gildhoff, 2009). In fact, with multiple challenges in the adolescent years, including puberty, disagreements with parents, prospects for sexual intimacy, enticements to partake in risky behaviors, and growing demands in schoolwork, self-esteem can fluctuate from day to day, week to week, and month to month (J. M. Chung et al., 2017). As young people weather these developmental challenges and enter young adulthood, they become reasonably consistent in their views about themselves.

Characteristics of the Self During the Developmental Periods

The developmental trends just listed reflect gradual changes in sense of self over time. We now look at unique aspects of self-perceptions during the five age periods.

Preparing for Your Licensure Examination

Your teaching test might ask you about how children's self-perceptions change with age.

Infancy (Birth–Age 2)

The first elements of a sense of self emerge during infancy. Through repeated physical experiences, babies discover that they have bodies that bring them discomfort (through hunger, fatigue, and injury) and pleasure (through feeding, sucking thumbs, and snuggling in the arms of caregivers; R. A. Thompson, 2006). Infants form impressions of themselves as being lovable (or not) based on their relationships with parents and other primary caregivers. Infants who form secure bonds are apt to develop positive self-perceptions, whereas others who form insecure attachments are less likely to view themselves as favorably.

In the first year, a range of experiences feed self-awareness. As they drop a ball, kick a mobile, and engage a parent with a cry or smile, infants realize that their behavior elicits particular effects (Ciaunica & Fotopoulou, 2017; R. A. Thompson & Virmani, 2010). Imitations of other people's facial expressions nourish their early sense of self; likewise, they notice and appreciate when adults imitate their behavior (Kristen-Antonow, Sodian, Perst, & Licata, 2015; Langfur, 2013; Meltzoff, 2007). As they mimic others' expressions (e.g., opening and closing their mouth, sticking out their tongue, laughing in unison with others), it dawns on them that they and other people are separate entities. Late in the first year, activities involving joint attention come into play. When Mommy and baby examine a toy together, baby shifts her gaze between the toy and Mommy's face. Baby begins to learn that she has a sense of "we-ness" with her mother (Emde & Buchsbaum, 1990). Thus, infants integrate rudimentary perceptions of separateness *and* interpersonal connection into their sense of who they are.

In the second year, infants begin to recognize themselves in the mirror. In a clever study of self-recognition, babies 9 to 24 months were placed in front of a mirror (M. Lewis & Brooks-Gunn, 1979; R. A. Thompson & Virmani, 2010). Their mothers wiped their faces and left a red mark on their noses. Older infants, especially those 15 months or older, touched their noses when noticing their reflections, as if they understood that the reflected images belonged to them. Of course, this sense of self is spontaneous and fleeting—reflecting a dawning awareness of the self in action, not an introspective this-is-me-and-I-have-these-qualities self-image. Relevant to their emerging sense of self, infants gain a feeling of mastery—confidence in action—as they exert desired effects on objects, for instance, by releasing levers, bouncing balls, activating music, and pulling Auntie's hair.

Early Childhood (Ages 2–6)

In early childhood, language acquisition and other cognitive developments permit advancements in the self. Once children talk, their self-awareness becomes more obvious. Children begin to refer to themselves by the pronouns *I* and *me*, and at ages 2 and 3 commonly exclaim "Mine!" during tussles with siblings and peers (Brownell, Iesue, Nichols, & Svetlova, 2013; L. Levine, 1983). Learning about what is *mine* is a natural part of development and probably a precursor to sharing. Young children also increasingly assert their competence and independence (e.g., by refusing assistance with putting on their jackets) and articulate their self-awareness by labeling emotions (e.g., "Happy me").

Another acquisition that depends on cognitive development is the *autobiographical self*, the child's memory of important events in his or her life. Children's early recollections take the form of sparse and fragmented snippets that don't hang together in a meaningful way. On average, children remember few if any events that occurred before age $3\frac{1}{2}$. Their recall of events before age 2 is virtually nonexistent. Memories of events become increasingly detailed and integrated during the preschool years as children talk about their experiences with other people (Fivush & Nelson, 2004; Schröder, Kärtner, & Keller, 2015; Q. Wang, 2013).

MyLab Education
Content Extension 12.1

Learn how a sense of self in early childhood contributes to productive peer relations.

Young children's conceptions of themselves draw on another cognitive advancement, the adoption of standards for behavior, appearance, personality, and intelligence. Initially, they see themselves largely in terms of obvious physical characteristics and simple psychological traits (Damon & Hart, 1988; Harter, 2012). As they learn from caregivers what things are "good" and "bad," they apply these standards in evaluating themselves (Eisenberg, Spinrad, Valiente, & Duckworth, 2014; Kagan, 1981). Often they feel sad or angry when they don't measure up. A 4-year-old boy may become quite frustrated when he has set the goal of being a tall-tower-builder and inadvertently knocks over his blocks half-way through the construction.

Young children are apt to focus more on what they do well than on what they do poorly, and so they are inclined to think rather highly of themselves (Jacobs, Lanza, Osgood, Eccles, & Wigfield, 2002; Salley, Vannatta, Gerhardt, & Noll, 2010). By and large, most young children have upbeat self-concepts and high self-esteem. Often they believe that they are more capable than they really are (Harter, 2012; Lockhart, Chang, & Story, 2002). Such optimism is perhaps due to their tendency to base self-assessments on continuing improvements in "big boy" and "big girl" activities. Their overconfidence is mostly beneficial in that it motivates them to persist at challenging tasks (Bjorklund & Green, 1992; Pintrich & Schunk, 2002). They downplay areas that give them trouble (e.g., "Math is dumb"). However, looking at the world through rose-colored glasses is not universal: Children who have had negative early social experiences with parents, as when neglected, are not prone to this optimistic bias (Tomlinson, Keyfitz, Rawana, & Lumley, 2017).

Middle Childhood (Ages 6–10)

During middle childhood, children see themselves in complex physical and psychological terms. Elementary school children remain fairly optimistic but become more conscious that they do some things well and other things poorly (Bong, Cho, Ahn, & Kim, 2012; H. W. Marsh et al., 2018; H. W. Marsh & Craven, 1997; Wigfield, 1994). In Artifact Example 12.1, Shea's poem reveals her multifaceted view of herself.

As children progress through the elementary grades, they have many opportunities to compare themselves with others, and they become cognitively adept at *making* such comparisons. Most youngsters now receive doses of critical feedback from teachers and observe peers outshining them some of the time. Their self-assessments reflect a decline from the overconfidence of the preschool years to the upbeat but realistic levels of middle childhood (Bong et al., 2012; H. W. Marsh & Hau, 2003). Becoming more sensible about talents and limitations probably helps children choose age-appropriate activities and work toward achievable goals (Baumeister, Campbell, Krueger, & Vohs, 2003; Harter, 2012).

Song of Myself

I am Shea
Above me are the bright colored leaves on the trees
Below me are seeds waiting to become flowers next spring
Before me are years to come full of new things to be learned
Behind me are memories I've forgotten
All around me are my friends lending me a helping hand
I see children having fun
I smell the sweet scent of flowers
I hear the birds talking to each other
I feel the fur of a helpless baby bunny
I move like wind as I run through the grass
I am old like the planets who have been here from the beginning
I am young like a seed waiting to sprout
I am the black of a panda's patches
I am the gold of the sun
I am thegreen of a cat's eye
I am the many colors of the sunset
I am a parrot, kangaroo, tiger, turtle
I am kind, responsible, pretty, smart
I think, plan, help, research
I give ideas to people that need them
I fear lightning
I believe that we all are equal
I remember my dreams
I dream of bad things as well as the good
I do not understand why some people pollute the Earth
I am Shea, a child of honesty
May I walk in peace

MyLab Education
Artifact Example 12.1

Find Developmental Meaning Shea wrote this poem about herself using "stems" provided by her teacher (e.g., "Above me . . . ," "I feel . . . ," "I am . . . ," and "I dream . . . "). The assignment allows children in this period to reflect on numerous facets of themselves.

Early Adolescence (Ages 10–14)

By the time they enter middle school, at around age 10, young students have had many chances to reflect on who they are as individuals. They have learned to apply standards of importance to them—perhaps being academically strong, attractive in physical appearance, popular with peers, and honorable in serving the community. Yet life does not stand still. The many transformations they now face as young adolescents challenge their self-image, and they must form new ideals. Puberty heightens introspection in young people, who respond to the momentous changes with assessments of how they look and feel as emerging adults. To achieve a mature self, they must think more deeply about where they are going in life. The shift from child to adult requires imagination as to what the future holds, as you can see in 10-year-old Alex's drawings in Artifact Example 12.2. Given the inherent difficulty in deciding on a career, adolescents can learn from assignments that invite exploration of a range of fields, jobs, and practical duties. Students might visit work sites, take on job shadowing, in which they observe the everyday duties of a seasoned professional, and internships, in which they are given duties to perform in a work setting, possibly over a summer or academic term (J. M. Holland, 2011; J. Newman & Hubner, 2012).

A drop in self-esteem often occurs at about the time that youngsters move from elementary school to middle or junior high school; this drop is sometimes more pronounced for girls (Cai, Wu, Luo, & Yang, 2014; Coelho, Marchante, & Jimerson, 2017; Marsh, 1990b; Santo et al., 2013). The average achievement levels in the school become salient to adolescents, who figure out where they stand in the hierarchy of academic accomplishments, with those spotting below-par performance tending to adjust expectations downward (H. W. Marsh et al., 2018). The physiological changes of puberty are another factor in the decline. Self-evaluations depend increasingly on perceptions of appearance and popularity, and boys and girls alike tend to think of themselves as becoming less attractive once they reach adolescence (Gatti, Ionio, Traficante, & Confalonieri, 2014; Harter, Whitesell, & Junkin, 1998). Changes in the school environment, such as disrupted friendships, superficial teacher–student relationships, and rigorous academic standards, also have a negative impact (Eccles & Midgley, 1989; Morin, Maïano, Marsh, Nagengast, & Janosz, 2013).

MyLab Education
Artifact Example 12.2

Find Developmental Meaning Ten-year-old Alex envisions who he might become in the future. The wide-ranging roles Alex envisions for himself (some fanciful) suggest that he has broad interests and will likely need to explore multiple fields and careers.

Self-examination in early adolescence changes in two additional ways. First, youngsters become more concerned with how others see them (Harter, 2012). They may initially go to extremes, thinking that everyone else's attention is focused squarely on them (Alberts, Elkind, & Ginsberg, 2007; J. Martin & Sokol, 2011). This self-centered quality of adolescence is sometimes called the **imaginary audience**. Because they believe they are the center of attention, teenagers (girls especially) are often preoccupied with their physical appearance and can be quite self-critical. Many adolescents change the way they speak and act according to who they are with at the time. The dynamic of an imaginary audience also operates on social networking sites (Ranzini & Hoek, 2017). Anticipating that they are being judged by friends and unknown followers, young people present themselves in a style that they believe will generate positive reactions.

The young adolescent's preoccupation with self also leads to an exaggeration of individuality. In the **personal fable**, teenagers can feel as if they are completely unlike anyone else (Bester, 2013; Elkind, 1981a; P. L. Hill & Lapsley, 2011). They are apt to think their own feelings are unique—that the people around them have never had such experiences. Hence, they may insist that no one else, least of all parents and teachers, can possibly know how they feel. They may also believe that they have special powers and are invulnerable to harm. This feeling of invulnerability affects adolescents' behavior on the Internet (Cingel, Krcmar, & Olsen, 2015). Not realizing the dangers that exist with disclosures of one's name, residence, and image, some young people reveal personal information, as with their names, addresses, and nude photographs. Use of social networking also put students at risk for **cyberbullying**, in which they are harassed, threatened, or embarrassed by another person via online technologies. Ironically, the misconception that the Internet is anonymous can trigger bullying behavior, as when students make rude remarks about others.

Adults should keep in mind that modest levels of personal fable and the imaginary audience serve valuable functions for adolescents. Being somewhat—but not excessively—self-centered may help adolescents navigate physical, social, and academic expectations (C. T. Barry & Kauten, 2014). The personal fable—in particular, the sense of invulnerability—may encourage young people to venture out and try new things (Bjorklund & Green, 1992; Lapsley, 1993). The imaginary audience keeps youngsters "connected" to their larger social context. Because they attend to how others judge their actions, they are apt to behave in ways that their society views favorably (Lapsley, 1993; R. M. Ryan & Kuczkowski, 1994). At some point, both the imaginary audience and personal fable outlive their purposes for most teens because these tendencies diminish in late adolescence and early adulthood (Krauss Whitbourne, 2016; Lapsley, 1993; P. D. Schwartz, Maynard, & Uzelac, 2008).

Late Adolescence (Ages 14–18)

As their worlds expand, teenagers have a greater variety of social experiences with people from diverse backgrounds. With their growing ability to reflect on their own behaviors, they become consciously aware that they are taking on different personalities when interacting with parents, teachers, friends, and romantic partners. Teens may also discover parts of themselves that they do not like. Furthermore, their sense of self may include qualities that they perceive to be somewhat contradictory (Garn, McCaughtry, Martin, Shen, & Fahlman, 2012; D. Hart, 1988; Villalobos Solís, Smetana, & Tasopoulos-Chan, 2017). The inconsistencies can be a source of confusion, as a ninth-grader revealed:

> I really don't understand how I can switch so fast from being cheerful with my friends, then coming home and feeling anxious, and then getting frustrated and sarcastic with my parents. Which one is the *real* me? (Harter, 1999, p. 67)

As high school students wrestle with the question, *Who is the real me?* they gradually broaden their self to accommodate a range of personas (Harter, 2012). For instance, they may amend self-perceptions of being both "cheerful" and "depressed" by concluding that they are "moody" or explain inconsistent behaviors by deciding they are "flexible" or "open-minded."

In the process of reconciling their "multiple selves," older adolescents make progress toward establishing an **identity**, a self-constructed definition of who they are, what they find important, what they believe, and what they plan to become. In Erik Erikson's historically significant theory of human development, adolescents' search for identity is a pivotal challenge. Contemporary research indicates that before youngsters achieve a true sense of their adult identity, most need considerable time to explore career options, political views, religious convictions, and so on. Canadian psychologist **James Marcia** (1980, 1991; Marcia & Josselson, 2013) identified four distinct patterns of behavior that characterize the search for identity:

- *Identity diffusion.* The adolescent has made no commitment to a particular career path or ideological belief system. Possibly there has been some haphazard experimentation with roles or beliefs, but the adolescent has not yet embarked on a serious exploration of issues related to self-definition.
- *Foreclosure.* The adolescent has made a commitment to an occupation and a particular set of beliefs. The choices have been made without much deliberation or exploration of other possibilities; rather, they have been based largely on what others (especially parents) have prescribed.
- *Moratorium.* The adolescent has no strong commitment to a career or set of beliefs but is actively exploring a variety of values and career tracks.
- *Identity achievement.* The adolescent has previously gone through a period of moratorium and emerged with a clear choice regarding a small range of occupations as well as a commitment to particular political and religious beliefs.

Marcia's framework presumes that some exploration is necessary. Foreclosure—identity without prior exploration—rules out potentially more productive alternatives, and identity diffusion leaves young people without a clear sense of direction. Being in moratorium can be an uncomfortable experience for adolescents (consider the uneasiness that Theodore, in the introductory case study, expressed with not yet having decided on a career path), but it is often an important step in achieving a healthy identity (Marcia, 1988; Marcia & Josselson, 2013).

In fact, for most older high school students, the search for identity is hardly complete. Even so, their self-esteem has largely recuperated from the unsettling experiences of the middle school and early high school years (Harter, 2012). Several developmental advancements contribute to this rebound. Most older adolescents have acquired the social skills they need to get along well with others. They have accepted the apparent inconsistencies in their self-perceptions and have considerable autonomy in choosing activities at which they are likely to succeed. And they increasingly judge themselves based on their *own* (rather than other people's) standards. When adolescents find others who share their passion for a particular direction, pastime, or field of study, they gain a feeling of camaraderie, as you can see in 17-year-old Kiley's reflections on her affiliations at school in Artifact Example 12.3.

Even as older adolescents move toward independence, their attachments to family members, especially parents, continue to play a significant role for them. Adolescents who have strong emotional bonds with sensitive parents tend to have high self-esteem (Duineveld, Parker, Ciarrochi, Ryan, & Salmela-Aro, 2017; R. M. Ryan & Lynch, 1989; Wouters, Doumen, Germeijs, Colpin, & Verschueren, 2013). The emotional support gives adolescents license to explore various aspects of their developing identities (Mullis, Graf, & Mullis, 2009). Other parenting styles (e.g., uninvolved, controlling, or rejecting parenting) can cause adolescents to feel alienated from parents and susceptible to the opinions of others; these adolescents are more likely to have the *contingent self-worth* you read about earlier (Josselson, 1988; Wouters et al., 2013).

It was during high school that I discovered who I was. Freshman and sophomore year I was a hermit crab, slowly trying to change to a new shell. I was eager to make the process yet I was yearning for something to hold on to help ease the way. For me my path of stepping stones was the — High School music department.

When I walked into chorus my freshman year, I was petrified. I felt like I was involved in a cult of some sort. Everyone either seemed extremely friendly or in love with the music department. I have to admit that at first I thought that the music department was pretty lame. Everyday I would walk in and see everyone hugging their friends or people crying on each other's shoulders, what was this? Everyone seemed so dependent on each other. I had my thoughts of quitting; I didn't know a lot of people and wasn't excited at the thought of making friends with them either, but I stuck it out, singing has always been my passion and I wasn't about to never perform again. This is who I was, I wasn't about to let some crazy group of people intimidate me.

By the middle of my sophomore year I was a full time band geek; besides the fact that I wasn't even in the band. I finally let my walls cave in and let the music department be my second home. I loved it. I could come in during the middle of a bad school day and always find a friend, always have someone their for me. The seniors in the rest of the school always seemed so big, so intimidating, but when I walked through the doors of the music department everyone was equal; there were no judgments and everyone felt welcome.

The music department changed me. I am no longer shy or timid but I am me to the fullest extent of the word. I now have the ability to walk into a group of people and make friends instantly. The music department helped me realize that performing is my passion, it's what I love; it's who I am. I am now ready to go audition, to go out and show the world what I am made of. Throughout high school nothing else has made such a lasting impression on me, I am not going to sit back one day as a mother and tell my children about my freshman PE class; my only eventful memories are contained within the walls of the music department. . . .

The music department has given me the strength to move on. When I am nervous I know I can always think back to my — years, and the confidence that slowly grew with the help of loving arms. I may be unsure about the future but I am excited. I will always remember the friends I made, the confidence I earned, and the love I shared within the four years; or better yet the four solid walls of the — High School music department.

MyLab Education

Artifact Example 12.3

Find Developmental Meaning In one of her 11th-grade classes, 17-year-old "Kiley" (a pseudonym) wrote the essay shown here. (We have blanked out the name of Kiley's school and left spelling and grammar errors intact.) Kiley overcame her reservations about the music community and embraced support from fellow musicians.

As you have learned, self-perceptions change dramatically by age. The Developmental Trends table "The Self at Different Age Levels" encapsulates the self-perceptions you might see, and the responses you might make, with children in each developmental period.

DEVELOPMENTAL TRENDS
The Self at Different Age Levels

AGE	WHAT YOU MIGHT OBSERVE	DIVERSITY	IMPLICATIONS
Infancy (Birth–2 Years)	• Increasing awareness of being separate from caregivers (in the first year) • Emerging awareness of having an impact on other people and environment (especially at the end of the first year) • Increasing recognition of self in mirror (in the second year) • A few first-person pronouns, such as *I, me, mine* (late in the second year)	• The quality of caregiving influences infants' belief that they are worthy of love. • The regularity with which adults comment on infants' images in mirrors and refer to their facial features (e.g., "We'd better wipe your runny nose") may affect self-recognition.	• Communicate affection by cuddling and talking to infants and attending to their physical needs in a timely and consistent manner. • Talk with infants and toddlers about their bodily features and possessions ("Where's your nose?"). • Celebrate baby's physical milestones (e.g., "Well look at you turning over! I see you wriggling away.")
Early Childhood (2–6 Years)	• Frequent use of *I*, *me*, and *mine*, especially at ages 2 and 3 • Emergence of an autobiographical self (beginning at age 3 or 4) • Concrete self-descriptions (e.g., "I'm a boy," "I'm pretty") • Overconfidence about what tasks can be accomplished ("Watch me jump to the moon!")	• Children whom others treat affectionately tend to develop a positive sense of self. Those who are rejected, ridiculed, or ignored have a harder time seeing themselves in favorable terms. • Some children gain an emerging awareness that they belong to a particular racial or ethnic group (by about age 5).	• Acknowledge children's possessions, yet encourage turn taking and sharing of classroom toys. • Engage children in retellings of recent events. • Don't disparage children's lofty ambitions ("I'm going to be president!"), but focus their efforts on accomplishing short-term goals.
Middle Childhood (6–10 Years)	• Increasing distinction among various aspects of oneself (e.g., among academic performance, athletic ability, and personal likability) • Increasing tendency to base self on how one's own performance compares with that of peers • Internalization of others' standards for performance (continues into adolescence) • Generally good self-esteem unless confronted with harsh environments	• Different children place greater or lesser importance on specific domains (e.g., on academic performance vs. athletic prowess) in deriving an overall sense of self-worth. • In middle childhood, girls evaluate their physical appearance less favorably than boys do. • Boys and girls who feel rejected at home or with peers are apt to develop low self-esteem.	• Support accomplishments across areas (e.g., in physical activities, social relationships, and specific academic subjects). • Help children find arenas in which they can be especially successful. • When appropriate, allow choice (e.g., after reading a novel, allowing students to prepare either a cartoon strip of key scenes, a narrated soundtrack with dialogue, or an essay on the meaning of the resolution).
Early Adolescence (10–14 Years)	• Increasing tendency to define oneself in the abstract rather than with concrete characteristics • Possible drop in self-esteem after the transition to middle or junior high • Heightened sensitivity to what others think of them *(imaginary audience)*, leading to a preoccupation with appearance • Belief in oneself as overly unique *(personal fable)*, occasionally leading to feelings of invulnerability	• Drops in self-esteem, when large and not followed by a rebound, can signal a problem. • Many youngsters prioritize desired standards based on gender stereotypes (e.g., boys see themselves as good in mathematics and science, girls see themselves as good in reading) even when actual achievement levels are similar. • Members of ethnic groups vary in how their ethnicity plays a role in core identity.	• When students are making the transition to middle school or junior high, be supportive and optimistic about their potential for success. • Ease the transitions to middle school by making sure that every student has an advocate. • Be patient when adolescents show self-consciousness; give them strategies for presenting themselves well to others (e.g., how they might introduce themselves to unfamiliar peers).
Late Adolescence (14–18 Years)	• Decrease in the self-consciousness that was obvious in early adolescence • Reconciliation of many apparent contradictions in oneself • Concern with identity issues: Who am I? What do I believe? What course should my life take?	• Adolescents whose self-worth depends heavily on others' behaviors and opinions (those who have *contingent self-worth*) are more susceptible to mood swings and peer pressure. • Some adolescents accept the professional goals that parents offer. Others engage in more soul-searching as they piece together their own identity. • Gender non-conforming youth defy traditional gender roles through clothing, hairstyle, and actions.	• Provide opportunities for adolescents to explore diverse belief systems and try on a variety of occupational "hats." • Be on the lookout for teens whose self-worth seems especially dependent on peers' opinions; help them discover areas of talent that can generate a stable sense of self-worth. • Encourage students to keep a journal and prepare an autobiography.

Self in a Developmental System

Self-perceptions become progressively multifaceted, abstract, and integrated. Against this backdrop of developmental advancement are significant individual differences, which emerge in response to personal characteristics, affiliations with groups, and other factors. American psychologist **Margaret Beale Spencer** has developed an informative framework, the *Phenomenological Variant of Ecological Systems Theory* (PVEST), which examines processes in defining a sense of self. According to Spencer's theory, children develop self-perceptions as they interact with social partners, use available resources, build on their assets, confront their risks, develop coping skills, and achieve personal outcomes (see Figure 12.1). Spencer's framework emphasizes the individuality that emerges in identity development.

Spencer views her theory as a *bioecological* framework because it extends Urie Bronfenbrenner's (1979; Bronfenbrenner & Morris, 2006) concept that children are influenced by biological dispositions, affecting their interests, learning, and personality, and their relationships with families, friends, and others in the community.

Developmental Systems Prompt

Students develop a sense of self while reflecting on their experiences in complex social environments. You can help them interpret hardships constructively, in light of their strengths, supportive relationships, and ability to bounce back from adversity.

FIGURE 12.1 Emerging identities in contexts of protection and risk.

In the example, 8-year-old Jerry has a close relationship with his grandfather, his primary guardian. When he and his grandfather move to a new city, Jerry feels unsettled and anxious for the first few months. He gradually adjusts to the new school and learns to cope with support from a new friend and teacher. Jerry begins to identify as a good student and becomes an active participant at school.

Based on information in M. B. Spencer (2006) and Spencer and Swanson (2013).

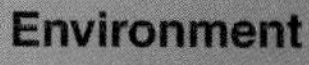

Environment

Protective factors
(e.g., family support and economic stability, children's intelligence and physical attractiveness)

Risk factors
(e.g., unstable family conditions; parents with limited education; discrimination in society; stereotypes about ethnicity, gender, culture, religion, and immigration)

Outcome

School achievement
School completion
Dropping out of school
Employment
Incarceration
Friendships
Stable family relationships
Estrangement from family
Poor health
Teenage pregnancy

Identity

Self as learner
Self as member of one or more ethnic groups
Self as male or female
Self as critic of society
Self as contributor to the community

Stress

Change in family income
Ongoing economic poverty
Change in family membership
Change in school
Move to a new neighborhood

Coping

Engagement in, or avoidance of, school
Risk-taking behavior
Interactions with family and friends
Help-seeking with extended family
Solicitation of support from teachers

According to Spencer, children encounter both *risk factors* (e.g., growing up in poverty and dealing with discrimination) and *protective factors* (e.g., being intelligent and having involved parents and dedicated teachers). In Spencer's model, society treats children differently according to salient characteristics such as race and ethnicity. Many African American children regularly confront prejudice and discrimination. Yet as a group, African American children are apt to enjoy numerous advantages, for example, strong extended family support, an active spiritual life, good coping skills, and supportive neighbors (E. McGee & Spencer, 2014; M. B. Spencer, 2006). In comparison, many European American children benefit from access to a high-quality education and ample family income yet struggle with life's challenges, stresses that are evident in the comparatively high suicide rates in White youth (National Institute of Mental Health, 2008b; M. B. Spencer, 2006).

In the PVEST model, children do not passively succumb to the pressures of external circumstances. Instead, they actively interpret the implications of events. One boy welcomes the addition of a new father figure into the family, as he perceives his mother's new husband as an affectionate provider who is concerned with his welfare. Another boy feels threatened by the presence of his new stepfather, whom he sees as an interloper trying to displace his birth father. Spencer's point is that individual children facing the same objective circumstances show distinctly different responses.

While children are dealing with daily challenges, they try out an array of *coping skills*, behavioral strategies for overcoming stressful circumstances. Children often develop adaptive coping skills that allow them to make the best of a difficult situation. Occasionally they develop maladaptive habits that hinder their adjustment. One adolescent girl responds to decreased attention from her parents (due to a new job or a family crisis) by spending more time with grandparents and asking for help from a teacher. A second girl reacts to the same situation by staying away from home, associating with deviant peers, and getting into trouble.

As children exercise coping skills, they build and rebuild their personal *identity*. Children may see themselves as strong or weak learners, as vital members of families or as rejected children, and as productive members of society or as rebels who engage in illegal activities. These and other identities solidify and affect children's adjustment. An adolescent boy who sees himself as an academically talented student will likely try to get good grades and earn a high school diploma. A boy who sees himself as a renegade may drop out of school. The developmental outcomes that youngsters attain, in turn, determine their new environments. An adolescent girl who is on track to earn her high school diploma now thinks about working in her aunt's hair salon as she attends college. Her cousin has been charged with vandalism, burglary, and assault, and now spends most of her time with peers who commit delinquent acts.

Identity, then, is the outcome of many experiences and also serves as a catalyst for future endeavors. Let's look more closely at three characteristics that Spencer and colleagues suggest are integral to personal identity: gender, ethnicity, and culture.

Gender

From an early age, children show an interest in gender. As they grow, they figure out what gender means for them.

Preparing for Your Licensure Examination

Your teaching test might ask you about gender differences in psychological characteristics.

Developmental Understanding of Gender. By the end of the first year, infants can distinguish male and female faces, and by age $2\frac{1}{2}$, most children know that they are a "boy" or a "girl" (J. E. O. Blakemore, Berenbaum, & Liben, 2009; Kohlberg, 1966). After children understand that there is a distinction between males and females, they become alert to the properties of gender and the implications for themselves. By age 4 or 5, children understand that gender is permanent—that boys do not become girls if they grow their hair long and wear ribbons and that girls do not become boys if they cut their hair short and wear boys' clothes (Bem, 1989; Ruble et al., 2007).

As children become increasingly aware of the typical characteristics of males and females, they begin to pull their knowledge together into self-constructed understandings, or **gender schemas**, of "what boys and men are like" and "what girls and women are like." These gender schemas become part of their self-concept and standards for behavior—how they should dress, what toys they should play with, and what interests and academic subject areas they should pursue (Bem, 1981; Halim et al., 2014; Ruble, Martin, & Berenbaum, 2006). Thus, although they know biology plays a decisive role in gender, they accentuate their masculinity or femininity with clothing, pastimes, and mannerisms (Halim et al., 2014).

With the onset of puberty, being "male" or "female" takes on new meaning. Many youngsters show a surge in gender-specific interests at this time (Ruble et al., 2006; Steensma, Kreukels, de Vries, & Cohen-Kettenis, 2013). Girls may have heightened concerns for their appearance, and boys may develop an unprecedented fascination with sports. To affirm their masculinity or femininity, many adolescents shy away from behaviors more closely associated with the opposite sex. Particularly in the older school years, girls show less interest and confidence in subject areas that have been historically preferred by boys—for instance, in mathematics, science, and sports (Barkatsas, Kasimatis, & Gialamas, 2009; E. M. Evans, Schweingruber, & Stevenson, 2002; Kessels, Heyder, Latsch, & Hannover, 2014; Leaper & Friedman, 2007). As a result of aligning their behavior and interests with others of the same gender, adolescents firm up their **gender identity** and embrace themselves as male, female, or an alternate gender (Steensma et al., 2013).

Origins of Gender Differences in Interests, Abilities, and Behavior. The consistency of psychological differences between the sexes raises questions about how these patterns originate. Biology clearly has a strong influence. The brain is first marked "male" or "female" by subtle differences in anatomy during prenatal development (J. E. O. Blakemore et al., 2009; Steensma et al., 2013). At puberty, gender differences in the brain are amplified as hormones augment physical characteristics. In a few cases these hormones increase the likelihood of problems. In boys, these rising hormones are associated with increased aggression—a stereotypically male characteristic—and in girls, with depression—a condition that is more prevalent in females. Despite these biological differences, boys and girls are remarkably similar in their intellectual profiles (J. S. Hyde, 2005).

Other people play a role by encouraging children to think about males and females in traditional ways. Family and peers model gender-typical behavior, reinforce children for "staying within bounds," and punish them (e.g., by ridicule or exclusion) when they violate accepted gender roles (Cassano & Zeman, 2010; Pipher, 1994). A boy who cries after breaking his arm may be called a "sissy," and a girl who excels in mathematics might be teased for being a "math geek." Society influences children's roles through gender-typical jobs (backhoe operators are almost always men) and priorities of the sexes ("Why don't you gals go shopping and let us guys watch the game?"; Halim, Ruble, & Tamis-Lemonda, 2013; Tennenbaum & Leaper, 2002).

Much of the pressure to act "appropriately" for one's gender comes from within rather than from others (Bem, 1981). The tendency for children and adolescents to conform to their own ideas about appropriate behaviors is known as **self-socialization**. Even when teachers actively encourage children to engage in non-gender-stereotypical activities (boys playing with dolls, girls playing with toy cars.), children experiment and soon revert to their earlier, more gender-stereotypical ways (Lippa, 2002). It is important to avoid criticizing children for cross-gender behaviors, an overture that happens surprisingly often. In fact, children acquire valuable skills when they cross traditional boundaries, for example, when girls learn about propulsion from toy rockets and boys acquire social abilities when pretending to care for dolls (Dinella, Weisgram, & Fulcher, 2017; Freeman, 2007).

Children Who Do Not Follow Typical Gender Roles. Thus far, we have spoken of gender identity as an either–or proposition, but, of course, not every child develops the gender identity that conforms to biological sex. A few boys settle into a pattern of consistently presenting themselves as girls, and likewise, a small number of girls portray themselves as boys. *Gender-nonconforming children* express their gender in ways that do not correspond with society's expectations for individuals with a given chromosomal sex (D. Chen, Edwards-Leeper, Stancin, & Tishelman, 2018). Some youngsters exhibit characteristics of both sexes, as when a middle school boy shows the traditionally masculine qualities of being assertive and strong and also the conventionally feminine characteristics of being an emotionally expressive and compassionate caregiver of younger siblings. Other gender-nonconforming children prefer to present themselves in neutral or mixed terms, as does a high school girl who cuts her hair short, wears lipstick, and chooses as her daily attire a baseball cap, T-shirt, jeans, and athletic shoes. Some children are puzzled by gender stereotypes and do not feel that they are boys *or* girls.

Children who are *transgender* strongly affirm that their gender identity differs from their sex assigned at birth, and many of these children ask for medical treatment during or after puberty to bring their bodies into closer alignment with this identity (D. Chen et al., 2018). A four-year-old boy may tell his parents "I am a girl," and likewise, a girl may advise her parents that she really is a boy. Before puberty, transgender children may transition socially to the gender with which they identify, wearing hairstyles and clothing typical of their felt gender. Some parents arrange for their children to make the transition over the summer and return to school with the new identity in the Fall.

The long-term trajectory of these children cannot be certain. Some children engage in gender-atypical behavior and later identify with their sex assigned at birth. According to the American Academy of Pediatrics (2018), this reversal most often happens around age 9 or 10, although it is not clear whether these children are spontaneously changing their identity or are hiding their true self due to social pressure. When a young adolescent has been steadfast in a nonconforming identity since early childhood, he or she is unlikely to change (American Academy of Pediatrics, 2018). Many gender-nonconforming children grow up and remain transgender or emerge as gay, lesbian, or bisexual teens, adolescents who are attracted to members of the same sex or both sexes.

Increasingly, parents, physicians, psychologists, and educators endorse the rights of children to live according to the gender identity that they endorse (D. Chen et al., 2018; L. Simons, Schrager, Clark, Belzer, & Olson, 2013). Such support can be crucial, as gender-nonconforming children are at serious risk for depression, anxiety, and other mental health problems, especially when shamed by parents, teachers, and peers for what is perceived to be an odd or immoral appearance. Adding to the complications of sorting out who they are meant to be, gender nonconforming youth may encounter peers who are rude, abusive, and even violent with them. Obviously, threatening behaviors must be squashed at school. Teachers and other practitioners can accept gender nonconforming children for who they are: young people driven to explore their sense of self (Singh, Meng, & Hansen, 2014).

For most children who are gender nonconforming, the origins of their characteristics are uncertain. However, it has been shown that hormones, genetic factors, and other circumstances influence gender identity (Steensma et al., 2013). During prenatal development, uncommon genes can lead to deficiencies in male and female hormones in the baby's brain. In one case, a girl fetus is exposed to an unusual dosage of male hormones in utero; during childhood, the girl progressively feels more male than female. In another pregnancy, a boy fetus is exposed to a preponderance of female hormones; although he has male genitalia, he later develops definite feminine characteristics in clothing preferences, mannerisms, and interests. A small number of children are born with ambiguous genitalia; for example, a girl who has female chromosomes and internal female organs is born with what appears to be a male penis. Historically, doctors believed it was in children's interests to declare one sex and not tell the children about their situation. Such a decision is made more thoughtfully today, as children may feel that something is wrong with them and not have the basis to make sense of these feelings.

Although factors causing a young person's nonconforming gender identity are not fully certain, when it persists into adolescence, this condition almost certainly has biological origins and cannot be changed with training, persuasion, religious conversion, or medical treatment (American Academy of Pediatrics, 2018). Schools can be helpful by training teachers and staff about the condition, making literature available in the nurse's office, discouraging harassment, and creating an open and accepting climate for young people to talk through the issues they are facing.

Ethnicity

Another aspect of the self *is ethnic identity*, the awareness of, and pride in, one's ethnic heritage, coupled with a willingness to adopt values and behaviors that are characteristic of individuals with this ethnicity (Adams-Bass, Stevenson, & Kotzin, 2014; C. S. Brown, 2017; Phinney, 1989). It has been suggested that the development of ethnic identity resembles James Marcia's stages of general identity formation. Children begin by absorbing the messages that parents and other trusted caregivers offer about their ethnicity, in much the same way that they might accept their parents' religious faith or job advice (leading to foreclosure in ethnic identity; S. J. Schwartz et al., 2014). During middle childhood and adolescence, young people become keenly attentive to its implications for themselves (reflecting a moratorium in ethnic identity). Ultimately, adolescents resolve what their ethnicity means for their personal identity (reflecting ethnic identity achievement; Phinney, 1989).

Research with children backs up this basic sequence from awareness to exploration to a commitment to belonging to one or more ethnic groups. By the time children reach kindergarten or first grade, they are aware that they belong to a different "group" than some of their age-mates. Several characteristics make them ethnically identifiable in a crowd, including their skin color, facial features, and language. In elementary school, many children accurately classify themselves as African, Mexican, Laotian, and so on and know some of the traditions of their group (Adams-Bass et al., 2014; C. S. Brown, 2017; R. D. Parke & Clarke-Stewart, 2011; Sheets, 1999). Parents and other family members give them labels (*Black, Chinese, Mexican American*, etc.) that communicate that they are special in an important way. By early adolescence, youngsters actively consider how their lives are affected by being a member of one or more ethnic groups. By late adolescence, large numbers of youngsters have achieved a consistent ethnic identity.

Of course, the ethnic identity that young people develop depends on the messages they encounter. Youngsters who develop a clear ethnic identity are likely to have experienced gestures by parents that encourage allegiance to the group. Many African American parents speak with pride about their heritage, inform children about the valiant struggles of their ancestors, and teach them how to cope with racial prejudice (Adams-Bass et al., 2014; D. Hughes, 2003). Many Puerto Rican and Dominican families transmit cultural pride by posting flags, inviting extended family over for traditional meals, speaking Spanish, and celebrating the religious and political holidays of their native lands (Csizmadia, Kaneakua, Miller, & Halgunseth, 2013; Pahl & Way, 2006).

Not all the messages that children receive are positive ones, however. Unfortunately, numerous children from ethnic minority and immigrant families are victims of prejudicial remarks. Sozan, an adolescent girl whose family members were Kurdish refugees to the United States, regularly heard classmates criticize her thick eyebrows and the scarf she wore out of respect for her religion, suggesting that she was bald and had a "unibrow" (i.e., one long eyebrow extending across her forehead; McBrien, 2005a, p. 66). These were deeply hurtful comments, yet Sozan held onto her faith and customs, as you can see in her self-portrait in Artifact Example 12.4.

Children from ethnic minority backgrounds typically consider their cultural background to be a more central feature of their self-concept than do children from majority backgrounds (Aboud, 1988; Kiang & Fuligni, 2010; K. L. Turner & Brown, 2007). European American children tend to see their ethnicity as the norm and are not strongly motivated to learn more about it. Children from other ethnicities realize that they are different and are interested in learning about family origins. In the process of exploring their ancestry, children of color regularly develop more positive self-perceptions than do children from majority groups, possibly because they benefit from overtures from families that portray their heritage in a positive light (Adams-Bass et al., 2014; H. Cooper & Dorr, 1995). When they struggle and achieve despite discrimination, children of color are proud of themselves. Nevertheless, those who are victimized repeatedly can become stressed and discouraged. In fact, exposure to discrimination creates risks for low academic achievement, anxiety, and depression (Perreira, Kiang, & Potochnick, 2013; Scrimin, Moscardino, & Natour, 2014; T.-C. Yang & Chen, 2018).

Children who have more than one ancestry, perhaps because of growing up in an immigrant or *multiethnic* family, are especially keen to explore their various

MyLab Education
Artifact Example 12.4

Find Developmental Meaning How does Sozan see herself? Sozan views herself as a young Muslim woman who is committed to her cultural heritage and also wants to take advantage of customs in the United States.

"Sozan Self-Portrait from Dissertation" from DISCRIMINATION AND ACADEMIC MOTIVATION IN ADOLESCENT REFUGEE GIRLS by J. L. McBrien (Unpublished doctoral dissertation, Emory University, Atlanta, GA) DISSERTATION ABSTRACTS INTERNATIONAL SECTION A: HUMANITIES AND SOCIAL SCIENCES, 66 (95–4). Copyright © 2005 by J. Lynn McBrien. Reprinted with permission.

heritages. Children with multiethnic backgrounds slowly learn about their two or more ethnic or racial heritages, determine how they are different and alike from others, synthesize their separate heritages into a self-concept, and call on distinct parts of their backgrounds depending on the occasion (A. M. Lopez, 2003; Manzi, Ferrari, Rosnati, & Benet-Martinez, 2014; B. D. Tatum, 1997). Consider Alice, who migrated from China to the United States at age 8. Although she gained fluency in English fairly quickly, for several years she had trouble reconciling the Chinese and American aspects of herself:

> [A]t home my parents expect me to be not a traditional Chinese daughter . . . but they expect things because I was born in China and I am Chinese. And at school, that's a totally different story because you're expected to behave as an American. You know, you speak English in your school; all your friends speak English. You try to be as much of an American as you can. So I feel I'm caught somewhere in between. . . . I feel I can no longer be fully Chinese or fully American anymore. (Igoa, 1995, p. 85)

After exploring numerous options for self-expression, many teens with multiethnic backgrounds ultimately construct a strong, multifaceted ethnic identity.

For the most part, students with a positive ethnic identity (including those with a strong multiethnic identity) perform well academically (Chavous et al., 2003; Costigan, Hua, & Su, 2010). Having a clear ethnic identity is linked to high self-esteem and a willingness to help other people (Corenblum, 2014; Phinney, Cantu, & Kurtz, 1997). Other findings indicate that young people with a strong ethnic identity are less likely to partake in illicit drugs and other perilous behaviors (Brook, Chenshu, Finch, & Brook, 2010; Umaña-Taylor & Alfaro, 2006). Apparently, pride in one's ethnic heritage serves as an emotional "buffer" against insults and discrimination (Romero & Roberts, 2003).

Occasionally, people outside the family (and, rarely, other family members) communicate that aspects of a child's ethnic heritage are undesirable, a destructive message that obviously upsets the child (C. Brown & Brown, 2014; C. R. Cooper, Jackson, Azmitia, Lopez, & Dunbar, 1995). For example, a light-skinned girl with an African American mother and European American father might be told that she can "pass" as white, denigrating her mother's origins. Teachers, of course, must insist that children not ridicule classmates about their ethnic heritage. By establishing an inclusive environment, teachers lessen negative pressures on children with diverse and multidimensional ethnicities (C. S. Brown, 2017; Perreira et al., 2013).

Culture

Cultures tell children what they should think about, how they should relate to other people, and what it means to be a good person. These core lessons are integrated into children's sense of self (Morelli & Rothbaum, 2007; R. A. Thompson & Virmani, 2010).

Separate cultures differ in the extent to which they encourage children to attend to personal needs (those of the individual self) or other people's needs (those of the collective group). Some societies (e.g., many groups in North America) place a lot of emphasis on personal needs. In *individualistic societies*, parents, teachers, and other adults encourage children to focus on their own wishes, motivations, and emotions (Markus & Hamedani, 2007; Rudy, Carlo, Lambert, & Awong, 2014). Children are encouraged to become personally confident. In comparison, children in *collectivistic societies* place more emphasis on fitting into an esteemed group. Adults in these latter cultures encourage children to take pride in the accomplishments of their families and communities (Banks & Banks, 1995; A. O. Harrison, Wilson, Pine, Chan, & Buriel, 1990). Children are more willing to acknowledge their weaknesses than is true for individualistic groups, perhaps because admitting personal limitations is a sign of humility (a desirable quality) rather than an indication of poor self-esteem (Brophy, 2004).

As a result of being socialized in any society, children learn to think of themselves as having personal qualities and as being an integral part of a community. A 6-year-old European American girl describes herself primarily in individual terms, being smart and a member of a sports team, whereas a Chinese boy of the same age mentions some of his own talents but emphasizes his ties to family (Q. Wang, 2006). Thus, children from both individualistic and collectivistic societies are likely to embrace both personal qualities and interpersonal connections, even though the emphasis varies. In our opening case study, Theodore described himself as having individual qualities (e.g., being smart, not as academically motivated as he might be) and as being closely connected with family and friends.

The earlier anecdote about Sozan reveals that the process of incorporating cultural beliefs into a sense of self is enriched by, and occasionally complicated by, exposure to two or more cultures. Around the world, many children of immigrant families are exposed to their family's native customs as well as to the new community's way of life (Hernandez, 2010). When children are exposed to two or more backgrounds at home, they generally take an approach that is adaptive and resourceful, drawing here and there from the various traditions they have encountered, depending on the demands of the situation. You can read about how children actively acquire the customs of a new society in the Development and Culture feature "At Home in Ireland."

Enhancing Children's Sense of Self

As with all areas of development, adults are more effective in nurturing children's sense of self when they understand how children think, feel, and express themselves. In the Observations Guidelines table "Observing Indicators of Children's Self-Perceptions," you can see some of the ways that children reveal how they see themselves. As you develop this awareness, you will also find occasions to affirm their sense of self-worth. Consider trying one or more of the following strategies:

Development in Culture

At Home in Ireland

In the 19th and 20th centuries, millions of Irish citizens, including Teresa's four grandparents, emigrated from Ireland to other countries in search of employment. Decades later, and with a strong educational system, the economic environment had changed dramatically. By the middle 1990s, Ireland boasted low unemployment, modest corporate tax rates, and a well-educated workforce. Not only did many Irish emigrants return home, but the "Celtic Tiger," as Ireland came to be called, also took in a record-breaking number of immigrants, with a large proportion coming from Eastern Europe, especially Poland.

A previously homogenous country composed primarily of fair-skinned individuals of Roman Catholic faith, Ireland welcomed the newcomers with interest, sympathy, and trepidation. To learn about people's adjustment to the changes, two researchers conducted interviews with native Irish, immigrants, and asylum seekers living in refugee hostels in Cork, a large city in the southwest of the country (O'Sullivan-Lago & de Abreu, 2010).

Many of those interviewed expressed uncertainty about rapid changes in Ireland. One native Irishman, Dermot, lamented the break from the past, worrying that long-standing Irish customs would be replaced by practices from other countries. Alejandro, an immigrant from Galicia, an autonomous community in northern Spain, was torn between his allegiance to Galicia and his recognition that he now felt at home in his adopted city of Cork. Alike, an asylum seeker, was apprehensive about her personal future, worried as to whether she would be able to make Ireland her permanent home.

Schools were commonly seen as a place of integration for children. Irishman Dermot observed that children from different backgrounds were easily integrated into the classroom. Asylum seeking parents were eager to see their children attend school and acquire Irish accents and customs. Jumoke was enthusiastic that her daughter, who could already speak Arabic and English, would acquire an Irish accent.

Some of the immigrants and asylum seekers believed that in order for their children to fit in, their families would need to give up some of their own traditions. Children in immigrant families eagerly practiced new customs, such as Irish sports, as they interacted with peers. Their parents were more hesitant in acquiring new customs. Thus, children essentially led the way in the family's assimilation, with parents marveling at the speed with which children acquired an Irish accent, made friends, and became proficient in local sports. Despite a dramatic downturn in the Irish economy in the late 2000s, many immigrants and refugees decided to remain in Ireland, in large part due to their children having made good adjustments there.

Barry Mason/Alamy Stock Photo

IRRESISTIBLE FUN. These Irish children are members of a neighborhood hockey club and participants in St. Patrick's Day festivities. Their enjoyable antics would likely entice local immigrant children to join in.

- **Communicate a genuine interest in children's well-being.** As children hear what adults say about them, they wonder, "What do these things mean about me?" We urge all adults, but especially teachers, school nurses, and counselors, to think carefully about what they say and do to children. Messages of affection and high regard come in a variety of forms, including the following:
  - Giving children a smile and warm greeting at the beginning of the day
  - Complimenting children on a special talent, a new skill, or exceptional effort
  - Asking children to talk about important events in their lives
  - Being a good listener when children appear angry or upset
  - Being well prepared for lessons and other activities with children
  - Including children in decision making and in evaluations of their performance
  - Expressing sensitivity to the stressful circumstances children encounter
  - Acknowledging that children occasionally have an "off" day and not holding it against them (L. H. Anderman, Patrick, Hruda, & Linnenbrink, 2002; Cushman & Cowan, 2010; H. A. Davis, 2003; Olowokere & Okanlawon, 2014)

OBSERVATION GUIDELINES

Watching for Indicators of Children's Self-Perceptions

CHARACTERISTIC	LOOK FOR	EXAMPLE	IMPLICATION
Self-Concept	• *Increased time spent looking in mirror* and inspecting one's image (in infancy) • *Verbal references to self* (e.g., "I," "mine") (in infancy and early childhood) • *Self-assessments in areas of proficiency and weakness* (e.g., "I'm good at math but bad at reading") (in middle childhood and adolescence)	Eighteen-month-old Sierra stands at the full-length mirror. She looks up and down at her reflection, smiles, and, after noticing a scrape on her knee in the mirror, bends down to touch her leg and says, "Ouch."	Express a genuine interest in every individual child. Encourage young children's emerging insights into their sense of self (e.g., "Look who's in the mirror!" and "I see you copying me! Can you make your hands do this?"). As children grow, compliment them on accomplishments, extra effort on tasks, and effective learning strategies.
Self-Worth	• *Comments on the self's inherent goodness or capability* (e.g., "I'm a good boy") • *Attempts to protect the self from threatening information* (e.g., anger at hearing critical comments after a flawed high-jump attempt, or such self-handicapping gestures as not studying for a challenging test) • *Changes in mood* depending on recent treatment by peers (reflecting *contingent self-worth*)	After receiving his mathematics score, 13-year-old Emmett crumples up the paper and throws it in the trash. The next time he has a mathematics test, he does not study at all, even though he knows he's confused about the math concepts.	Encourage children to take disappointments in stride. Suggest that although they may not have done as well on a particular task, with renewed effort, a change in tactics, and perhaps a little assistance, they have the ability to progress. Provide a range of activities so that everyone has a chance to excel in one or more areas of learning.
Autobiographical Self	• *Conversations with parents about past family events* in which the child participated • *Recollections about personally significant events* or family celebrations	Five-year-old Jeremiah draws a picture of himself with his parents, two sisters, and the family dog in front of a farm. He explains that his family used to live in rural Idaho and then moved to the Oregon coast when his parents changed jobs.	Create assignments that allow children to reflect on their family origins and early experiences. Have kindergarten children bring in photographs of themselves as babies and preschoolers. Ask older children to write essays about their early years.
Gender Schema	• *Insistence that boys must act one way and girls another* (especially in early childhood) • *Selection of toys that are stereotypical for one's gender*, for example, toy cars, blocks, and action figures by boys and dolls and board games by girls • *Heightened interest in same-sex role models* in magazines and other media during adolescence	In her spare time, 13-year-old Janice likes to browse through her mother's fashion magazines. She looks for tips on how to apply cosmetics, meet boys, and interact with others. Her older brother Reggie reads their father's automotive mechanics magazines.	Recognize that during various points in development, children may go through phases of rigidly endorsing traditional gender roles. When you can, communicate that both men and women have a range of opportunities in life and that few individuals can live up to the media's standards of attractiveness. Be aware of the special needs of gender-nonconforming children.
Identity	• *Early in identity formation, varied levels of concern about the future*: —Questions about jobs —Noncritical acceptance of career goals suggested by parents —Expression of a desire to define lifelong goals • *During late adolescence, serious attempts to form an identity*: —Active search of careers, political viewpoints, and religious faiths —Occasional well-justified political beliefs and plans for future occupations	Mr. Decker asks the ninth-graders in his advisee group to write a brief essay about the kinds of jobs they find appealing. Some of the students write about jobs their parents currently have; others write little, having apparently not given the matter much thought. He brings in the school counselor to talk about processes in finding a career, administers a few career inventories, and helps students arrange visits and internships in local industries, clinics, agencies, and companies.	Give children opportunities to examine and try out a variety of adult roles. With young children, rotate props through a housekeeping area (e.g., dress-up clothes and equipment that might be found in a police station, gas station, or doctor's office). With older children, ask parents to come to school to talk about their jobs. With adolescents, arrange internships in local businesses, community agencies, and other institutions.
Ethnic Identity	• *Comments about being a member of an ethnic group* • *Growing preference for customs in one's own group* (e.g., with meal practices, holiday celebrations, tastes in music and art) • *Practice* with ethnic cooking and other traditions • *Frustration* with discrimination toward one's ethnic group	Fourteen-year-old Diego is proud of his Latino heritage. He follows many of his parents' Mexican traditions, loves Mexican food, and regularly watches Spanish-speaking programs on television. Diego is incensed by the derogatory names for Latinos used by a few students at his high school.	Foster pride by welcoming ethnic traditions at school. Encourage youngsters to write about ethnic customs in assignments, and infuse multicultural material into instruction. Establish cooperative groups that cross ethnic lines and ensure that children from different backgrounds take on responsible positions. Adamantly discourage ethnic slurs.

• **Hone in on age-related developments.** Adults are most likely to help children when they cherish the qualities children are in the midst of acquiring—perhaps a sense of mastery in inserting blocks into slots during infancy ("Look what you can do!"), cooperation during early childhood ("You are so nice to share your car!"), a multifaceted self-concept during middle childhood ("Keyboarding seems to be easier for you than writing your story in cursive."), adjustment to a new school in early adolescence ("You seem to be settling in well to the new school. Is there anything I can help with?"), and exploration of career goals in late adolescence ("One of your options for the senior project is to do an internship.").

• **Promote success on academic, social, and physical tasks.** Experiences with success are powerful catalysts for positive self-perceptions in academic domains, such as mathematics or music (Bong, Cho, Ahn, & Kim, 2012; Damon, 1991; Marsh & Craven, 1997). Thus, teachers should gear assignments to youngsters' capabilities, for instance, by making sure that they have already mastered prerequisite concepts and skills. However, success at very easy activities is unlikely to have much of an impact. Mastering the significant challenges in life—earning the hard-won successes that come only with effort and persistence—cultivates resilient self-perceptions (Dweck, 2000; Winne, 1995a). Teachers are most likely to bolster youngsters' sense of self when they assign challenging tasks and provide the structure youngsters need to accomplish them successfully. They should also help young people keep little "failures" in stride: Mistakes are an inevitable part of learning something new. Overall, youngsters are likely to be optimistic about their chance for success if they see they are making regular progress—if they continually make gains through effort and practice. They are *un*likely to be optimistic if they focus their attention on how their age-mates are surpassing them (Deci & Ryan, 1992; Duijnhouwer, Prins, & Stokking, 2012; Stipek, 1996).

• **Be honest about children's shortcomings, and provide ample guidance for overcoming them.** Youngsters are likely to be successful over the long run if they come to grips with weaknesses. If adults give only positive feedback—and especially if they provide inflated evaluations of performance—children may be unaware of areas that need improvement (Dweck, 2000; Paris & Cunningham, 1996). And when adults praise children for successes on easy tasks, children may conclude that they are not capable of handling anything more difficult, or, alternatively, may come to believe that they must always achieve at high levels (Brummelman, Thomaes, Orobio de Castro, Overbeek, & Bushman, 2014; Pintrich & Schunk, 2002). Realistically, adults need to give children negative as well as positive feedback. When feedback must include information about shortcomings, the best approach is to give it within the context of high (yet achievable) expectations for future performance (Deci & Ryan, 1985; Pintrich & Schunk, 2002). Following are examples of how a teacher might put a positive spin on negative feedback:

- "You're usually a very kind person, but you hurt Jenny's feelings by making fun of her new outfit. Perhaps you can think of a good way to make her feel better."
- "In the first draft of your research paper, many of your paragraphs don't lead logically to the ones that follow. A few headings and transitional sentences would make the world of difference. Let's find a time to discuss how you might use these techniques to improve your paper."

When children have long-standing difficulties in certain domains, discovering that their failures are due to a disability, such as dyslexia or attention-deficit hyperactivity disorder (ADHD), sometimes helps repair damage to self-esteem. Such a realization helps children make sense of *why* they can't perform certain tasks as well as peers. It can also spur on children to identify coping strategies. In the following reflection, one young adolescent boy reveals how, in coming to terms with his dyslexia, he's acquired a healthy sense of self despite the disability:

> Dyslexia is your brain's wired differently and there's brick walls for some things and you just have to work either around it or break it. I'm dyslexic at reading that means I need a little bit more help. If you have dyslexia the thing you have to find is how to get over the hump, the wall. Basically you either go around it and just don't read and get along in life without it or you break down the wall. (Zambo, 2003, p. 10)

Keep in mind that it can be detrimental if children are given labels for their conditions without simultaneously being taught strategies for overcoming their difficulties.

• **Provide opportunities to explore a wide variety of activities.** Not all students can achieve at superior levels in the classroom, nor can they all be superstars on the playing field. Youngsters are more likely to have a positive sense of self if they find an activity—perhaps singing, gardening, student government, or competitive jump-roping—in which they shine (Harter, 1999; Ruiz-Gallardo, Verde, & Valdés, 2013). Exposures to the world of work can also be informative. By exploring different fields and zeroing in on a few possible career paths, young people take another important step toward forming an adult identity. Although students may not uncover the perfect job during community visits, job shadows, and internships, they are apt to imagine themselves in certain situations, reflect on job requirements, and analyze the fit between their personality and duties of various jobs.

• **Consider the unique needs of girls and boys.** Many youngsters place little value on characteristics that they think are "appropriate" for members of the opposite sex. In addition, they may place high value on qualities they think they need to be "feminine" or "manly." Some teenage girls strive for impossible standards of physical beauty, and some teenage boys worry that they are maturing too slowly and lack the height and build of age-mates. With these points in mind, adults might occasionally use different tactics in nurturing the self-esteem of girls and boys. They might help girls identify realistic standards by which to judge their physical appearance. Given girls' tendency to react negatively to failures, adults might encourage them to pat themselves on the back for their many successes, even those (and perhaps *especially* those) in traditionally male domains such as science and mathematics. Boys, too, have special needs. Many boys are often brought up to believe they should be "tough" and hide feelings of self-doubt or inadequacy. Adults may want to acknowledge a boy's "softer" sides—for instance, his compassion and skill in interacting with small children.

• **Communicate respect for diverse ethnic and cultural backgrounds.** Although most educators are aware of the need to respect diversity in children's backgrounds, they do not always know how best to show this regard. An important first step, of course, is understanding the traditions, values, and priorities of ethnic and cultural groups. In addition to showing appreciation for children's native languages and dialects, educators can communicate respect for diverse groups through strategies such as these:

- Treat all children as full-fledged members of the classroom and community rather than as exotic "curiosities" who come from a strange and separate world.
- Call children by given names unless they specifically request otherwise (see Artifact Example 12.5).
- Look at historical and current events from diverse perspectives—for instance, by considering American, European, African, and Arabic perspectives on recent events in the Middle East.
- In prominent places in school hallways, classrooms, and the library, post pictures related to children's cultures.
- Make assignments in which children can explore their family heritage.
- Expose children to the accomplishments of numerous ancestral cultures in readings and activities.
- Visit the communities in which children live, and invite their families to school to share their talents, origins, and traditions.
- Create situations in which youngsters from diverse backgrounds must collaborate to achieve success—for example,

I had lots of friends back home, and I remember all of them, we used to play soccer together. I have also friends here now, well... mostly classmates.

School is OK but there is one thing that bothers me. My name is Mohammed, no other. Here, my teacher calls me Mo, because there are five other kids with the same name. My friends sometimes call me M J, which is not too bad, but I wish they will call me by my real name. I like what my grandma called me: "Mamet." I like how she used to say it. One thing makes me really mad. I have a pen pal called Rudy. He lives in Toronto. Once I showed his letter to my teacher and she said: "That is nice name." Now, all my friends call me Rudy. I hate it, because that's not me, that's not my name. My name is "MO-HA-MMED." Do you understand me?

MyLab Education
Artifact Example 12.5

Find Developmental Meaning Mohammed and his family immigrated to Canada as refugees. How does he feel about his teacher and classmates using nicknames in reference to him? Mohammed has a strong preference that others use his proper name, which seems to be an important part of his identity.

Source: Reprinted with permission of "Refugee Children in Canada: Searching for Identity," by A. M. Fantino and A. Colak, 2001, Child Welfare, 80, pp. 591–592, a publication of the Child Welfare League of America.

through cooperative group activities or community service projects. (Banks & Banks, 1995; Branch, 1999; C. S. Brown, 2017; Fantino & Colak, 2001; García, Arias, Murri, & Serna, 2010; Howard, 2007; Ladson-Billings, 1994; A. Romero, Edwards, Fryberg, & Orduña, 2014; Villegas & Lucas, 2007; S. C. Wong, 1993)

In their efforts to be sensitive to children's cultural backgrounds, some well-meaning practitioners make the mistake of thinking of children as belonging exclusively to a single ethnic or cultural group. In this age of increasing multiracial ethnicities and multicultural families, youngsters do not want to be pigeonholed. Teachers need to keep in mind that many of their students have a multifaceted ethnic, racial, cultural, and religious heritage, and students want to be integral parts of the multiple groups in which they spend time, including the dominant society (Borrero & Yeh, 2011; Csizmadia et al., 2013; A. M. Lopez, 2003). It also is worth bearing in mind that children of any ethnic heritage, however simple or complex, may or may not exhibit typical characteristics of people with shared ancestry. When they are raised in multiple traditions, students may draw selectively on customs depending on the situation.

- **Cultivate gratitude and hope.** Students can become more optimistic when they take a moment to count their blessings (Shoshani & Steinmetz, 2014). They can be encouraged to keep journals in which they regularly describe good things in their lives. They might also be encouraged to write about their strengths and how they have applied them recently to overcome a problem. Or they could reflect on tactics to try with a challenge they are currently facing.

- **Give youngsters second chances to develop healthy self-perceptions.** Adolescents who struggle academically or have friendships with antisocial peers are apt to see themselves as disconnected from school. These self-perceptions are not easily changed, but concerted efforts from a teacher sometimes have desirable effects. In one instance a group of adolescents with learning disabilities were moved from one school (Piney Ridge), where they were failing, to another school in which teachers got to know them individually (Youngblood & Spencer, 2002). With time the adolescents came to see themselves as capable academically and socially, as one boy explains:

Interviewer:	What makes you. . . . Why do you think there's a difference between the student helping each other in this program and not helping each other at Piney?
Rashae:	Because they're. . . . Well half of them over there criminal. They're like they just got out of jail or whatever. I mean, they just. . . . I think Piney Ridge like a school for bad kids.
Interviewer:	So why do you think they're more likely to help you over here?
Rashae:	Because everybody over here nice. They don't think about just they self. Think about other people in the class. . . . Well we help one another in the class work or out of class. (dialogue from Youngblood & Spencer, 2002, p. 103)

- **Enforce no-teasing zones for physical conditions.** Criticism about children's appearance and disabilities can have a devastating effect on self-perceptions. Some children look different from peers as a result of disabilities, being exceptionally thin or heavy, or having an unusual physical feature—perhaps a large nose, skinny legs, facial birthmark, chubby abdomen, *cleft lip* (an opening in the child's upper lip that extends upward to the nose), or fitful limbs because of *cerebral palsy* (a condition characterized by impaired muscle control as a result of oxygen deprivation to the brain during or around the time of birth). Teresa remembers walking in a local park with a few elementary school children with intellectual disabilities and physical deformities. They encountered a group of preschool children also on a walk. The younger children became visibly frightened when one student made grunting noises and walked on his toes. One little girl cried as Teresa's students walked by. Their preschool teacher managed to comfort them, and off they went.

As children grow older, they begin to verbalize observations of physical differences. Private conversations can address children's natural curiosity yet also inform them that another child might feel uncomfortable with their comments. In middle childhood, a matter-of-fact explanation is sometimes helpful ("No, Janie does not have makeup on her face. It's a beauty mark she was born with"). Students in this age range are usually mature enough to recognize that other people can be hurt by comments about their imperfections. They can also learn to stand up as bystanders when they hear rude remarks about others' appearance.

Unfortunately, some children knowingly criticize peers based on what they look like. Rather than simply responding to ridicule, teasing, or bullying as it occurs, proactive teachers begin the school year with firm prohibitions (K. Shore, 1998). In addition, with approval from parents of a child with a physical disability, teachers can explain the condition to students (e.g., "Brendan will be joining our class next week. He cannot walk because his spine did not fuse properly before birth. He is in a wheelchair. We're going to move one of the computer stations to allow him to move around. He's a great kid. I can't wait for you to meet him!"). Of course, it is also important to communicate that students with disabilities are similar in most other ways and have numerous strengths (e.g., "Brendan and his family recently moved here from Chicago. Get this: He was a semifinalist in a youth competition for *League of Legends*. He's also athletic and loves to play basketball. Who would like to sit near him at lunch?").

- **Put self-esteem in proper perspective.** Popular educational literature overrates self-esteem, sometimes to the point where it becomes the primary target of intervention (Dweck, 2000). Certainly we want children to feel good about themselves, but increasing evidence suggests that efforts to enhance self-esteem as *the* goal can be ineffective for several reasons (Baumeister et al., 2003; Meadows, 2010). First, children appreciate optimistic evaluations from adults but are more likely to be convinced of their own capability when watching themselves reach high standards. Thus, rather than telling children that they are smart and good, it makes more sense to create conditions in which children are able to achieve success. Second, high self-esteem seems to be closely linked to personal happiness, yet, counter to society's expectations, it does *not* protect young people from risks in life. Self-esteem is more accurately conceived as a resource for weathering adversity. It is not tool for resisting temptation, therefore, students with high self-esteem do not avoid drugs any more than youngsters with low self-esteem (Baumeister et al., 2003; R. Lewandowski et al., 2014). Hence, other developmental outcomes must receive equal billing. Third, a few children with an inflated sense of self are aggressive and callous to the feelings of others (Baumeister et al., 2003). Thus, rather than simply being told how good they are, these children need to encounter expectations for respecting the needs of other people. Finally, not every culture aspires to high self-esteem, at least as self-esteem is typically conceptualized in Western cultures. Other communities socialize children to focus on being humble and courteous to friends, family members, and adults in authority.

Summary

Children's *sense of self* includes beliefs about who they are as people (self-concept) and judgments about their value (self-esteem or self-worth). Most children interpret events in ways that allow them to maintain a positive self-image. Realistic self-perceptions, or perhaps self-perceptions that are just slightly inflated, are optimal in that they encourage children to set their sights on achievable challenges.

To a considerable degree, children's sense of self is based on their own prior successes and failures. Other people also play a role, either by treating children in ways that communicate high or low regard or (in the case of peers) by demonstrating the kinds of things children "should" be able to do at a certain age. Membership in various groups (e.g., athletic teams, ethnic groups, friends through social media) also has an impact, as do gender, culture, physical appearance, disabilities, and inherited characteristics. With age, children construct increasingly complex and multifaceted understandings of who they are as people. In the early years, their self-perceptions are fairly simplistic, concrete, and categorical (e.g., "I have brown eyes"; "I'm a boy"). But as they acquire the capacity for abstract thought, their self-descriptions include inferred psychological qualities (e.g., "thoughtful," "dependable"). Adolescents also begin to wrestle with who they ultimately want to become as human beings. Individual differences in self-perceptions become sizable and are linked to coping skills and direction in life.

Teachers and other professionals can support children's self-perceptions by treating students with compassion and arranging for instruction and experiences that are

MyLab Education
Video Example 12.3

Find Developmental Meaning *How does Wanda Owens-Morabito invite her seventh- and eighth-grade students to talk about their cultural origins?* Learn about the Road of Life, a community-building activity in which young adolescents portray their geographical and cultural origins and share this information with other students.

growth-promoting. When students have not achieved well at school, teachers can adjust assignments and monitor performance so that students will begin to succeed and see themselves as competent learners. Students must not be able to tease or harass one another based on gender, ethnicity, appearance, religion, or other factors.

MyLab Education Self-Check 12.1

Social Cognition

12.2 Discuss changes in social cognition during childhood, and identify ways in which teachers nurture social understandings.

As children reflect on their own thoughts, feelings, and personal characteristics, it dawns on them that other people have qualities that differ from their own. Most children devote a lot of mental energy to **social cognition**, their speculations about what other people are thinking, feeling, and wanting to do. As you might expect, social cognition has many facets. We begin our discussion with an analysis of children's understanding of what other people think. We next examine biases in children's thinking that can lead to prejudice. Finally, we consider variations that exist in children's social-cognitive abilities and outline the many things adults can do to foster these social understandings.

Understanding What Others Think

Just as children construct theories about their physical and biological surroundings, so, too, do they construct explanations about the psychological world. Gradually, they develop a **theory of mind** that explains people's mental and emotional states—their thoughts, beliefs, feelings, motives, intentions, and so on. Children apply intuitive principles of psychology to themselves, as we examined in the previous section, and to others as well, as we explain here. While interacting with others, children step into their shoes and look at events from their vantage points. Such **social perspective taking** helps children make sense of actions that might otherwise be puzzling. As children gain practice in inferring others' people points of view, they are able to relate to others more sympathetically and in a balanced way that fulfills their motivations as well helps others achieve their desires (Caputi, Lecce, Pagnin, & Banerjee, 2012; R. D. Parke & Clarke-Stewart, 2011). A series of developments make it possible for students to assert themselves and respect others.

Infancy (Birth–Age 2)

Infants quickly discover that, unlike inanimate objects, people are active, expressive, and responsive (Bardi, 2017; Mandler, 2007a; Poulin-Dubois, Frenkiel-Fishman, Nayer, & Johnson, 2006). In the latter part of their first year, they begin to realize that people have an "inner life" that objects do not have. By about 9 or 10 months, infants achieve *intersubjectivity*, an awareness that they share a focus of attention with social partners. At about the same time or shortly thereafter, they acquire an awareness of **intentionality**. That is, they know that other people behave in order to accomplish certain goals, and they draw inferences about people's intentions from their actions in reaching for, pointing at, and gazing at objects (Beier & Carey, 2014; Carruthers, 2013).

In the second year, infants become increasingly mindful of other people's mental states. Infants as young as 12 months engage in *social referencing*, the tendency to watch an adult react to an unfamiliar person, object, or event in a manner that shows comfort, fear, or agitation and then show the same kind of response. By 18 months, children know that their own actions influence other people's emotions and behaviors. Infants are likely to offer an adult a food item to which the adult has previously reacted favorably, even though they themselves dislike that kind of food (Repacholi & Gopnik, 1997). Early comforting gestures may reflect an attempt to consider another person's perspective. In other situations, toddlers may use information about someone's perspective for personal gain or to annoy him or her (J. Dunn & Munn, 1985; Flavell,

Miller, & Miller, 2002; P. L. Harris, 2006; Paulus, 2014). As a toddler, Jeanne's daughter Tina occasionally ran into the street and then looked tauntingly back at Mom as if to say, "Look at what I'm doing! I know this upsets you! Catch me if you can!"

Early Childhood (Ages 2–6)

In the preschool years, children become increasingly aware of other people's mental states. Beginning at age 2 (sometimes even earlier), children spontaneously use words that refer to desires and emotions (e.g., *want, feel, sad*), and by age 3, mental state words such as *think, know*, and *remember* (Bartsch & Wellman, 1995; Lagattuta, 2014). By the time children are 3, they also realize that the mind is distinct from the physical world—that *thoughts, memories*, and *dreams* are not tangible entities (J. A. Baird & Astington, 2005; Wellman & Estes, 1986; Woolley, 1995).

In trying to understand why other people act as they do, young children are initially attentive to what others want—a desire to eat another cookie, finish up the ironing, or watch a video on a mobile device. In the third and fourth year, children develop an appreciation that others have *desires* that differ from their own (P. L. Harris, 2006). Preschoolers are often eager to learn why people do the things they do, as this conversation between $2\frac{1}{2}$-year-old Adam and his mother illustrates:

> Adam: Why she write dat name?
> Mother: Because she wanted to.
> Adam: Why she wanted to?
> Mother: Because she thought you'd like it.
> Adam: I don't want to like it. (Wellman, Phillips, & Rodriguez, 2000, p. 908)

Inherent in Adam's question, *Why she write dat name?* is an advancement in theory of mind: Preschoolers become increasingly aware of connections between other people's desires and their understanding of the situation. After gaining an appreciation that they and other people have *desires*, young children gradually gain an understanding of other people's *knowledge* (P. L. Harris, 2006; Saracho, 2014). Initially, preschoolers have trouble looking inward and describing their own thoughts, and they may mistakenly assume that what *they* know is what other people know as well. Consider the following situation:

> Max puts a piece of chocolate in the kitchen cupboard and then goes out to play. While he is gone, his mother discovers the chocolate and moves it to a drawer. When Max returns later, where will he look for his chocolate? (based on Wimmer & Perner, 1983)

Max will look in the cupboard, of course, because that's where he thinks the chocolate is. However, 3-year-olds are quite certain he will look in the drawer, where the chocolate is actually located. Not until age 4 or 5 do children appreciate a *false belief*: They realize that circumstances may reasonably lead people to believe something different from what they know to be true (Laranjo, Bernier, Meins, & Carlson, 2014; Oktay-Gür Schulz, & Rakoczy, 2018; M. Rhodes & Wellman, 2013; Wimmer & Perner, 1983).

Children gain proficiency in inferring people's intentions and other mental states in part from cues in their behavior (Astington & Pelletier, 1996; Fireman & Kose, 2010; Saracho, 2014). Look at the two scenarios in Figure 12.2. *Which boy would like to swing?* The boy in the lower picture is the one who has an *intention* of using the swing. Most 5-year-olds correctly answer the question we've just asked you, but few 3-year-olds do (Astington, 1991).

FIGURE 12.2 Which boy would like to swing?

Children who can correctly answer this question can distinguish between intention and behavior.

"Which Boy Wants to Swing" by J. W. Astington, from "Intention in the Child's Theory of Mind" from Children's Theories of Mind: Mental States and Social Understanding by D. Frye. Illustration copyright © 2009 by J. W. Astington. Reprinted with permission via Copyright Clearance Center.

Middle Childhood (Ages 6–10)

As children reach the elementary grades, they become capable of sophisticated inferences about people's mental states. They realize that people's facial expressions, statements, and actions do not always reflect their true thoughts and feelings (Flavell et al., 2002; Gnepp, 1989). A person may intentionally lie about a situation to mislead someone else, and another person who appears happy may actually be sad.

Middle childhood heralds deeper understanding of the nature of thinking. Children now understand that people *interpret* an event rather than simply "record" it, a phenomenon that allows for differences in perspectives among people (Chandler & Boyes, 1982; P. L. Harris, 2006). Children also recognize that people's thoughts and feelings are often closely intertwined. Thus different thoughts about a situation lead to different feelings about it (P. L. Harris, 1989; Y. Wu & Schulz, 2017). A 9-year-old might say, "Arlene feels bad because she thinks I don't like her. I *do* like her, though."

Middle childhood brings another change in theory of mind. Children at this age sometimes use information they have gleaned about peers', siblings', and adults' knowledge and vulnerabilities to outwit, tease, and manipulate them (Lonigro, Laghi, Baiocco, & Baumgartner, 2014). Thus, theory of mind is a tool that allows children to comprehend and accommodate the needs of their social partners, yet it can be—and is—occasionally applied to outwit, tease, or manipulate someone else. In a situation of conflicting perspective, in which a child has the ability to help a peer but also has a self-serving motivation, theory of mind is not sufficient to prompt cooperative behavior (Doenyas, 2017). Children must also focus on the motivation to do the right thing.

Early Adolescence (Ages 10–14)

Fueled by maturation of the brain, perspective taking continues to develop during the adolescent years (Blakemore & Mills, 2014; Smetana & Villalobos, 2009; Will, Crone, Lier, & Güroğlu, 2018). Several social networks in the brain are put into overdrive, empowering a heightened sensitivity to social interaction. Young people find intensified pleasure in contact with peers and become more interested in figuring out what makes other people think and feel as they do.

Adolescents appreciate that people can have mixed feelings about events and other individuals (Harter & Whitesell, 1989; Rostad & Pexman, 2014). They realize that a person may simultaneously have multiple, and possibly incompatible, intentions (Chandler, 1987). They become increasingly thoughtful about the divergent perspectives that people may have about a single event, as you can see in Artifact Example 12.6. In general, young adolescents find it easier to think about the perspectives of people they know and like, presumably because these individuals have shared their views in the past (T. G. O'Connor & Hirsch, 1999; Smetana & Villalobos, 2009).

Courtesy of their expanding reasoning abilities, working memory capacity, social awareness, and neurological maturation, young adolescents engage in **recursive thinking** (Müeller & Overton, 2010; Perner & Wimmer, 1985; van den Bos, van Duijvenvoorde, & Westenberg, 2016). That is, they now contemplate what other people might be thinking about them and eventually reflect on their own and other people's thoughts through multiple iterations (e.g., "You think that I think that you think . . ."). This is not to say that adolescents always use this capacity. In fact, thinking only about one's own perspective, without regard for the perspectives of others, is a common phenomenon in the early adolescent years (recall our earlier discussion of the *imaginary audience*).

Late Adolescence (Ages 14–18)

Older adolescents can draw on a rich knowledge base derived from numerous social experiences, and so they become ever more skillful at identifying people's psychological characteristics, intentions, and needs (Eisenberg, Carlo, Murphy, & Van Court, 1995; Paget, Kritt, & Bergemann, 1984). More challenging social situations involving disagreements among friends, alliances and betrayals, and assurances and broken promises demand high-level perspective-taking skills. High school students become increasingly attuned to complex

We were playing freeze tag one day at recess. Leslie got tagged and asked me to step on her shadow before anyone else. I stepped on Becca's shadow before I stepped on Leslie's and she got mad. I told Leslie to stop being so selfish and bratty. She took it extremely personally and stormed off, told a teacher, and called her mom.

I later appologized and we became friends again. I invited her to my birthday and she came but I could tell she felt uncomfortable. So, I decided to do makeovers. I was playing around with lipsticks and accidentally messed up on Leslie's makeover, but laughed because I knew it could be fixed. She ran to see the "damage" in the mirror, started to cry, and called her mom and left.

From then on, I've never really understood her and we've never been close. We see eachother and say "hi" in the halls, but that's it.

MyLab Education
Artifact Example 12.6

Find Developmental Meaning Why are some people difficult to understand? In this reflective essay, 13-year-old Georgia expresses dismay over an acquaintance's interpretation of events.

dynamics—the combination of thoughts, feelings, present circumstances, and past experiences—in behavior (Fett et al., 2014; Selman, 1980; Tynes, 2007). What we see emerging in the high school years, then, is a budding psychologist: an individual who can be quite astute in deciphering and explaining the motives and actions of others.

MyLab Education
Application Exercise 12.1
Identify Development-Enhancing Education
Watch as a high school English teacher, Sue Southam, asks her students to imagine the perspectives of characters in Nathaniel Hawthorne's The Scarlet Letter.

Social Perspective Taking in Action

Taking the perspective of another person is not simply an intellectual exercise. Drawing inferences about other people's thoughts, desires, and intentions allows children to predict their behavior and determine how to adjust to these needs. When children lack the capacity to infer other people's intentions, they would not know whether a nurse is trying to help or hurt them while rubbing ointment on their scraped knee. Similarly, they may wrongly assume that a classmate who bumped into them on the lunch line purposefully spilled their juice. As young people grow, adeptness in understanding other people enhances their proficiencies in finding fair and mutually acceptable solutions during conflicts and in getting along with people from diverse cultures (Galinsky et al., 2015; Kam, Guntzviller, & Pines, 2017; Van Lissa, Hawk, & Meeus, 2017).

Let's look more closely at this critical human capacity through the lens of American psychologist **Robert Selman's** theory of social perspective. After asking children to anticipate the perspectives of different people in a particular situation, Selman found developmental trends in children's thinking. Consider the following situation:

> Holly is an 8-year-old girl who likes to climb trees. She is the best tree climber in the neighborhood. One day while climbing down from a tall tree she falls off the bottom branch but does not hurt herself. Her father sees her fall. He is upset and asks her to promise not to climb the trees any more. Holly promises.
>
> Later that day, Holly and her friends meet Sean. Sean's kitten is caught up in a tree and cannot get down. Something has to be done right away or the kitten may fall. Holly is the only one who climbs trees well enough to reach the kitten and get it down, but she remembers her promise to her father. (Selman & Byrne, 1974, p. 805)

Children are asked if Holly understands Sean's feelings about the kitten, if Sean realizes why it will be difficult for Holly to decide whether or not to climb up the tree, and what Holly believes her father will think if he learns she does climb the tree. To answer these questions, you must look at the situation from the perspectives of three different people: Sean, Holly, and Holly's father. By presenting situations like this one and asking children to view them from various perspectives, Selman (1980; Selman & Schultz, 1990) found that with age, children show an increasing ability to take and act on the perspective of others. He described a series of five levels in perspective taking:

- *Level 0: Egocentric perspective taking.* Children are aware of physical differences among people but have little awareness of psychological differences. They are incapable of looking at a situation from anyone's perspective but their own (hence the reference to Level 0). As an example, 3-year-old Andrea assumes that her preschool friends know how scared she is about climbing on the jungle gym. Hence, she expresses indignation when Rose and Sue Ann ask her to climb with them.
- *Level 1: Subjective perspective taking.* Children realize that people have different thoughts and feelings as well as different physical features. However, they view

someone else's perspective in a relatively simplistic, one-dimensional fashion (e.g., a person is simply happy, sad, or angry) and equate behavior with underlying feelings (e.g., a happy person will smile, and a sad person will pout or cry). For instance, 8-year-old Li-Wen realizes that her friend Tony is sad about his grandfather's recent death but does not understand that he also feels relief that his grandfather's suffering is over.

- *Level 2: Second-person, reciprocal perspective taking.* Children realize that people occasionally have mixed feelings about an event—for instance, that Holly might feel both compassion for the kitten and uneasiness about breaking her promise to her father. At this level, children also understand that people may feel differently than their behaviors indicate and that others sometimes do things they didn't really want or intend to do. Eleven-year-old Peter understands that his friend Mark has misgivings about his decision to experiment with inhalants. Peter perceives reservation in Mark's voice and body language as he tells about recent escapades.
- *Level 3: Third-person, mutual perspective taking.* Youngsters can take an outsider's perspective of interpersonal relationships: They can look at their own interactions with another person as a third individual might. They appreciate the need to satisfy both their own and another's needs simultaneously and therefore readily grasp the advantages of cooperation, compromise, and trust. To illustrate, two high school freshmen, Jasmine and Alethea, discover that they've each arranged a homecoming party for the same night. They learn that they've each sent invitations to friends that they share. Because they were both looking forward to hosting a party, they discuss options for rescheduling one of the parties or co-hosting the event.
- *Level 4: Societal, symbolic perspective taking.* Adolescents begin to realize that people are affected by many factors in their environments and, furthermore, that they are not always aware of why they act as they do. In their psychology course, high school seniors Kent and Joaquin are preparing a joint oral report on social persuasion. They find magazine advertisements that are geared toward teens and discuss images and feelings that advertisers are trying to arouse in their age group.

Selman has nicely captured the essence of developmental trends in perspective taking, but he underestimated young children's capabilities. Even young preschoolers realize that another person can see an object only if he or she is looking in its direction and has a clear, unobstructed view. Older preschoolers also grasp that the same object may look different to people viewing it from separate angles—for example, that a book that is right-side up to one person will be upside down to someone sitting across the table (Flavell, 2000). Furthermore, in their daily communication, children appear to listen to what other people say, respond appropriately, and take into account how their listeners might be thinking and feeling (Garvey & Hogan, 1973; Rozendaal & Baker, 2010).

Selman's theory is limited in another way. The early versions of his theory imply that progress through the levels is almost inevitable. In more recent work, Selman has conceded that children's social awareness is not guaranteed by basic maturational processes and instead is highly dependent on experience (Selman, 2003). For example, Selman and his colleagues have found that children use their past encounters with teasing when thinking about others' motives (Dray, Selman, & Schultz, 2009; S. L. Katz, Selman, & Mason, 2008).

Practically speaking, Selman's work suggests that adults can nudge young people toward slightly more advanced thinking—perhaps one level up in perspective taking. To illustrate, preschool teachers might point out how classmates' perspectives differ from children's own feelings (Level 1). Adults who work with students in the elementary grades can discuss situations in which people may have mixed feelings—situations such as going to a new school, trying a difficult but enjoyable sport, or celebrating a holiday without a favorite family member present (Level 2). Adults who work with adolescents might, either informally (e.g., in free-flowing conversations) or formally

MyLab Education
Application Exercise 12.2
Detect Developmental Levels

In this video, a preschool teacher encourages three young girls to consider one another's point of view after a conflict on the playground.

DEVELOPMENTAL TRENDS
Social Cognition at Different Age Levels

AGE	WHAT YOU MIGHT OBSERVE	DIVERSITY	IMPLICATIONS
Infancy (Birth–2 Years)	• Awareness of one's ability to share a focus of attention with a caregiver *(intersubjectivity)* • Observation of other people's emotional reactions, followed by the child having a similar response *(social referencing)* • Emerging realization that other people have desires different from one's own	• Infants who receive inadequate care at home may be delayed in intersubjectivity and social referencing. • Infants who are autistic may avoid eye contact with caregivers and fail to see the connection between where others are pointing and what they are thinking about.	• Get to know infants as individuals and the kinds of social interactions that each of them enjoys. • Use words such as *like, want*, and *think* in descriptions of yourself and children. • Patiently explain why you prohibit dangerous activities in order for children to understand your reasoning.
Early Childhood (2–6 Years)	• Increasing use of "feeling" and "thinking" words (e.g., *want, sad, know*) • Growing realization that the mind does not always represent events accurately (e.g., a person may have a false belief) • Growing ability to take others' perspectives	• Children whose parents talk frequently about thoughts and feelings tend to have a more advanced theory of mind. • Children with certain cognitive impairments (e.g., autism) and those with reduced exposure to language (e.g., as a result of hearing impairments) tend to have a delayed theory of mind.	• Talk about people's thoughts, feelings, perspectives, and needs. • Establish fun routines (e.g., tossing a ball back and forth, jointly turning the pages of a book) with children who find it difficult to synchronize their behavior with others. • Recognize that territorial behaviors are common in early childhood, yet look for opportunities to share.
Middle Childhood (6–10 Years)	• Recognition that people's actions do not always reflect their true thoughts and feelings • Growing realization that other people interpret (rather than simply remember) their experiences • Softening of rigid stereotypes of particular groups of people (for most children)	• Compared to peers, children with certain disabilities (e.g., attention-deficit hyperactivity disorder [ADHD], autism, and general intellectual disability) have difficulty in making accurate inferences about other people's motives and intentions. • Children whose families or communities consistently promote unflattering images of other ethnic groups may have strong prejudices.	• Assist children in their attempts to discern the viewpoints of characters in stories and public figures during tragedies and political events. • When addressing the experiences of a particular ethnic group (perhaps their literary accomplishments or struggles in past events), expose children to individuals within the group who hold distinctly different perspectives.
Early Adolescence (10–14 Years)	• Recognition that people have multiple and occasionally conflicting feelings and motives • Emerging ability to think recursively about one's own and others' thoughts	• Some adolescents become so concerned about how other people see them that they succumb to peer pressure and take extreme measures to please them. • Intellectual disabilities may hinder adolescents' capacity to consider multiple points of view.	• Conduct discussions that require adolescents to look at controversial issues from multiple perspectives. • Do not tolerate ethnic jokes or other remarks that show prejudice toward one or more ethnic groups.
Late Adolescence (14–18 Years)	• Recognition that people are products of their environment and that past events, and that present circumstances influence personality and behavior • Use of a peer group as a forum for self-exploration and self-understanding • Increasing awareness that members of any single category of people (e.g., women, individuals with disabilities) can be very different from one another	• Most high school students use their social perspective-taking abilities constructively, but a few students use their inferences about other people's vulnerabilities to inflict harm on them. • Adolescents who are familiar with people from diverse cultures may find it relatively easy to infer the perspectives of others from different backgrounds.	• Talk about other people's complex and sometimes incompatible motives, perhaps while examining contemporary issues, historical events, or works of fiction. • Assign autobiographies and other readings that depict individuals who have actively worked for the greater good of society, asking students to write about the motivations, beliefs, and ideas of these individuals.

(e.g., in a high school psychology class), explore the many ways in which people are affected by experience (Level 4).

The various progressions in social cognition reveal that it's a long road from infants' initial flickers of social awareness to adolescents' far-reaching insights into how minds coordinate mental states. In the Developmental Trends table "Social Cognition at Different Age Levels," you can see some of the primary accomplishments and manifestations of diversity across the childhood years.

Social-Cognitive Bias and Prejudice

By now you have insights into just how much mental work is involved in thinking about social situations. Yet, people often take shortcuts to ease the load on their memory and make their dealings with others more efficient (K. L. Mosier, 2013; Tversky & Kahneman, 1990). Many of these shortcuts reflect **social-cognitive biases**, predispositions to interpret or respond to social situations in particular ways. For example, a child might assume that another person's action reflects his or her typical behavior (Seiver, Gopnik, & Goodman, 2013). Eight-year-old Dwight observes a new boy arguing with his friend on the playground and jumps to the conclusion that the boy is a bully.

Most social-cognitive biases are a minor nuisance; they lead to small distortions in thinking but don't cause grave harm. A few, however, have serious consequences. Children occasionally jump to hasty conclusions about others based on group membership (e.g., gender, ethnicity, sexual orientation, religious affiliation). In other words, they respond on the basis of a **stereotype**, a rigid, simplistic, and erroneous characterization of a particular group. Often a stereotype encompasses a host of negative attributes (e.g., "stingy," "lazy," "promiscuous") and leads children to exhibit negative attitudes, feelings, and behaviors—that is, **prejudice**—toward the group.

The roots of stereotypes and prejudice lie in the natural tendency of human beings to categorize experience. In their first few years, children learn that people belong to different groups, such as boys and girls, and "Blacks" and "Whites." Many preschoolers can distinguish members of various ethnic groups (Aboud, 1988). As children form these social categories, they are apt to favor their own group and expect less desirable characteristics from individuals in other groups, especially if the groups clash over resources or territories (Aboud, 2005; Aboud & Spears Brown, 2013; R. D. Parke & Clarke-Stewart, 2011). By age 4, children show definite biases about social groups, expecting that members of their own community are better in some way than individuals from other groups (Aboud & Spears Brown, 2013).

On average, stereotypes and prejudice decrease as children move through the elementary grades (D. E. Carter, Detine-Carter, & Benson, 1995; F. H. Davidson, 1976). This decline is probably due to children's increasing realization that social categories have their limits. Many children slowly realize that individuals who share membership in a category (e.g., "girls") are similar in some ways but very different in others. Other individual factors strengthen stereotypes, and so some children show an increase in prejudice as they reach early adolescence (Aboud, 2005; J. H. Pfeifer, Brown, & Juvonen, 2007). Parents may incite prejudice through words and deeds—for instance, by telling ethnic jokes, restricting playmates to same-race peers, expressing negative attitudes about other races, affiliating with individuals only from their own in-group, and enrolling their children in schools with as little diversity as possible (Allport, 1954; Ashmore & DelBoca, 1976; Degner & Dalege, 2013; Meeusen, 2014). Popular images in television and other media—where males are depicted as strong and aggressive, females weak and passive, and members of certain ethnic groups are unimportant characters or "bad guys"—also have an impact (Durkin, Nesdale, Dempsey, & McLean, 2012; Huston et al., 1992).

By adolescence and probably before, children who are victims of prejudice are well aware when others' treatment of them is unfair (Phinney & Tarver, 1988; E. Seaton, Yip, Morgan-Lopez, & Sellers, 2012). Over time they acquire a variety of strategies—seeking the support and companionship from other group members, forming a positive ethnic identity, and so on—for coping with prejudice and discrimination (Forsyth & Carter, 2012; Swim & Stangor, 1998). Even so, young people who are victims of prejudice are more likely than peers to become ill or depressed and are at risk for achieving at lower levels in school (English, Lambert, & Ialongo, 2014; B. D. Tatum, 1997).

Developmental Systems Prompt

Children's personal characteristics and experiences in social groups affect how they understand other people. With children who regularly misunderstand other people, teach missing skills to the extent possible.

Social Cognition in a Developmental System

From the beginning of life, children are actors and observers during interactions with other people. They are naturally driven to figure out what makes other people act as they do, and a maturing brain and exposure to mental terms facilitate their ability to construe others' inner states. The specific psychological processes that children learn depend on their personal characteristics and experiences in complex environments. Let's look at two qualities affecting social cognition: having certain exceptionalities and growing up in particular social settings.

Exceptionalities Affecting Social Cognition

Some children with disabilities are disadvantaged in their understanding of other people, in large part because their brains do not allow them to easily recognize faces, engage in eye contact, imagine other people's perspectives, and detect emotions. Children with *Fragile X syndrome*, who typically have intellectual disabilities and social anxiety, perform at relatively low levels on theory-of-mind tasks (P. Lewis et al., 2006; Losh, Martin, Klusek, Hogan-Brown, & Sideris, 2012). When children do not have a way to communicate early in life (e.g., when born deaf to hearing parents who do not sign), they miss out on discussions about "thinking," "feeling," "wanting," and the like, and their theory of mind is delayed (C. C. Peterson, 2002; Rieffe & Wiefferink, 2017; Sundqvist, Lyxell, Jönsson, & Heimann, 2014). Some children with ADHD find it difficult to take the perspective of other people, possibly because of having impaired brain circuits for social reasoning. This difficulty, coupled with a weakness in inhibiting disruptive behaviors, gives children with ADHD the reputation of being undesirable social partners (Maoz et al., 2014; Stormont, 2001).

Children with **autism spectrum disorders** have an especially difficult time with social cognition. Children with these conditions have a serious impairment in social communication and exhibit restricted, repetitive behaviors (e.g., repeatedly flipping through the pages of a book or running water over one's hands; American Psychiatric Association, 2013; Waterhouse & Gillberg, 2014). The variation in social-cognitive, language, and intelligence in children with autism is large; each child with the condition is said to be somewhere on the *spectrum*. Most children with autism are diagnosed by age 3, by which time they have noticeable delays in reciprocal interaction, communication, language, imitation, and imaginative play. Children in this heterogeneous group commonly have an intellectual disability, yet a few have average or superior intelligence. Children with *Asperger's syndrome* are similar to peers with autism in that they have limitations with social abilities and display repetitive behaviors, but unlike many others with autism, their intelligence and language abilities are normal.

Preparing for Your Licensure Examination

Your teaching test might ask you about the characteristics of children with autism and Asperger's syndrome.

Educators who work effectively with autistic children attend to the full range of their individual abilities and limitations. Fundamental to successful instruction, interaction, and guidance is a sensitivity to children's struggles in grasping the motivations, feelings, and perspectives of other people. Imagine that you are a student with this difficulty and do not understand why a teacher is reading a story to you, why a classmate always says, "good morning" as you arrive at school, or why a classmate shows a furled eyebrow when you sit next to him. Without social cognition, these interactions would be puzzling. Common to autism spectrum disorders are significant deficits in social cognition (e.g., in self-awareness, theory of mind, and perspective taking) and social skills (e.g., in gaining entry into a peer group, interacting appropriately, and negotiating during disagreements; Baron-Cohen, Tager-Flusberg, & Cohen, 1993; A. Samson et al., 2014). Although children with autism typically form close attachments to parents, they often prefer to be alone and have difficulty in making friends (Bauminger-Zviely & Agam-Ben-Artzi, 2014; Hobson, 2004). Temple Grandin, a brilliant woman who has gained international prominence as a designer of livestock facilities, recalls what it was like to be a child with autism:

> From as far back as I can remember, I always hated to be hugged. I wanted to experience the good feeling of being hugged, but it was just too overwhelming. It was like a great, all-engulfing tidal wave of stimulation, and I reacted like a wild animal. . . .
>
> When I was little, loud noises were also a problem, often feeling like a dentist's drill hitting a nerve. They actually caused pain. I was scared to death of balloons popping, because the sound was like an explosion in my ear. Minor noises that most people can tune out drove me to distraction. (Grandin, 1995, pp. 63, 67)

There has been a great deal of research and speculation about the origins of autism. A couple of factors, including errors in particular genes and exposure to viruses during the prenatal period, are implicated in the emergence of an unusual brain development. It appears that multiple parts of the brain are affected. Neurons in social areas of the brain have been found to be weakly connected and show comparatively little activity in autistic children (Hudac et al., 2017; Strzelecka, 2014; Vanderwert & Nelson, 2014). At least some children with autism have larger-than-usual brains by the first year of life (suggesting excessive propagation of neurons and failure of synaptic pruning mechanisms). Autistic children also develop abnormal structures in the cerebellum (which modulates controlled movements), brainstem (which controls automatic functions necessary for survival, including breathing, digestion, and circulation of blood), and the front part of the cortex (which controls planning, inhibiting of automatic responses, and coordinating of complex, multistep actions; Fan, Decety, Yang, Liu, & Cheng, 2010; Minshew & Williams, 2007; Ozonoff, 2010). A particular type of brain cell, the *mirror neuron*, may also contribute to autistic disorders (Rizzolatti & Fabbri-Destro, 2010). **Mirror neurons** are specialized brain cells that grow in the premotor area of the brain, where planning, selecting, and implementing actions are supported. The same sets of mirror neurons are activated when a person performs a certain act, such as reaching for a cup or clapping one's hands, as when the person observes someone else carrying out the same behaviors (J. T. Kaplan & Iacoboni, 2006; McGregor & Gribble, 2015). Mirror neurons play a role in imitation and also allow for reasonable inferences about how another person feels when carrying out familiar movements. Similarly, the same parts of the brain involved in making facial expressions are also used while observing others' facial expressions. The role of mirror neurons in autistic children's ability to grasp other people's perspectives is not definite, yet preliminary evidence suggests that mirror neurons in autistic children fire only when they perform an activity, not when they see another person do it (Oberman & Ramachandran, 2015). Other data indicate that individuals with severe autistic symptoms have few mirror neurons and show additional underpinnings in the brain that cause social-cognitive deficits (Fründt et al., 2018). 1234

Despite their unusual brain systems, and perhaps in part because of them, children with autism have notable strengths. Some autistic children form deep connections with animals, such as horses or dogs, learn new skills quickly, solve mathematical problems insightfully, and benefit from the advocacy of devoted families (B. L. Hawkins, Ryan, Cory, & Donaldson, 2014; Iuculano et al., 2014; Sarahan & Copas, 2014; J. J. Xue, Ooh, & Magiati, 2014). Having weak connections across separate areas of the brain enables individuals with autism to concentrate on specific domains that do not require much cross-talk (Casanova, 2008). Occasionally, children with autism exhibit *savant syndrome*, in that they possess an extraordinary talent that stands in sharp contrast to their other limited abilities (Treffert, 2014; Winner, 2000).

Many children with one of the autism spectrum disorders are in the regular classroom for all or part of the school day. Teachers can help them feel secure by keeping the classroom layout and schedule consistent. Especially with young autistic children, teachers can establish one-on-one relationships with them, perhaps initially sitting beside them, expressing an interest in their handling of objects, and encouraging (but not demanding) give-and-take in interactions (American Speech-Language-Hearing Association, 2018; Schreibman, 2008; Wieder, Greenspan, & Kalmanson, 2008). To help facilitate children's limited theory of mind, teachers can teach vocabulary for such internal mental processes as "thinking," "wishing," and "remembering." Finally, many autistic children benefit from training in planning, learning strategies, and self-evaluation of performance (Cote et al., 2014; El Zein, Solis, Vaughn, & McCulley, 2014). Such strategies can help children achieve at higher levels and gain a sense of self-determination (Seo, 2014).

Explicit training in social abilities is usually necessary. Educators can advise youngsters about what to expect during upcoming social events, for example, that they will sit with peers during a school play or hold hands with another child during a field trip. They can discourage actions that other youngsters find disturbing, such as repetitive behaviors, so as to increase their peer acceptance (Turnbull, Turnbull, & Wehmeyer, 2010). They can also teach appropriate ways to secure peers' attention, take turns in conversation, refrain from dominating the discussion, ask for something politely, and participate in pretend play with friends (Y. Chang, et al., 2014; K. Chung et al., 2007; Meadan, Angell, Stoner, & Daczewitz, 2014). Some teachers set up buddy arrangements, in which a child without a serious disability is trained to interact during a lesson with a child with autism, and they maintain mutual attention and comment on ongoing activities (Kohler, Greteman, Raschke, & Highnam, 2007). School counselors can prompt targeted behaviors with handheld tablets and video recordings of children using social skills (Auger, 2013).

Social Setting

The people with whom children spend time, and the practices they follow, nurture social cognitive development. Discussions with adults about what people think, feel, want, and so on enhance children's awareness of thoughts and emotions (J. M. Jenkins, Turrell, Kogushi, Lollis, & Ross, 2003; Ziv, Smadja, & Aram, 2013). Parents who comment on differing points of view during family discussions help children realize that multiple perspectives legitimately exist (Astington & Pelletier, 1996; Taumoepeau & Ruffman, 2008). In the early years, sociodramatic play activities, in which children take on a defined role and coordinate it with others' positions ("mommy," "doctor," etc.), help children imagine others' thoughts and feelings (Lillard, 1998; Saracho, 2014). Arguments with siblings provide an especially motivating context in which to use perspective-taking skills (McAlister & Peterson, 2013; Randell & Peterson, 2009).

Culture makes certain aspects of another person's thinking salient. Universally, another person's perspective is important, and children exposed to a wide range of cultural customs acquire a theory of mind at similar ages (D. Liu, Wellman, Tardif, & Sabbagh, 2008; Shahaeian, Nielsen, Peterson, & Slaughter, 2014). Children first learn about other people's desires and then develop additional social cognitive abilities that are a priority in their culture. After grasping that other people are motivated to fulfill their desires, Chinese children next develop an appreciation that people can be either knowledgeable or ignorant, whereas children in the United States and Australia next come to realize that different people have varying beliefs about matters (Wellman, Fang, Liu, Zhu, & Zhu, 2006).

Cultures also influence *how much* children think about other people's thoughts and feelings (Lillard, 1999). Some cultures frequently explain people's behaviors in terms of mental events, whereas others focus on external circumstances. In the United States, children who live in urban areas regularly refer to people's psychological states when explaining good and bad behaviors (e.g., "He helped me catch bugs, because he and I like to catch bugs"). In contrast, children in rural areas are more likely to attribute people's behaviors to situational factors (e.g., "She helped me pick up my books, because if she didn't I would have missed the bus"). The latter approach is also common in many Southeast Asian cultures (J. G. Miller, 1987).

As you have learned in this chapter, a sense of self and basic social understandings about other people derive from both nature *and* nurture. In the Basic Developmental Issues table "Comparing Sense of Self and Social Cognition," you can see other ways that the two characteristics reflect developmental dimensions.

BASIC DEVELOPMENTAL ISSUES
Comparing Sense of Self and Social Cognition

ISSUE	SENSE OF SELF	SOCIAL COGNITION
Nature and Nurture	Human beings appear to have an inborn need to think of themselves as competent, likable, and worthy individuals. A positive sense of self is fostered in environments wherein adults encourage children's attainment of mature standards for behavior and arrange for them to make steady progress.	The ability to consider other people's perspectives (their intentions, desires, and thoughts) depends on having a normally maturing human brain. The capacities of theory of mind and social perspective taking are nurtured by social experiences with other people and, in particular, with exposure to different viewpoints.
Universality and Diversity	General developmental trends in self-perceptions are fairly universal. Most children first develop simple views of the self and then see the self in more complex terms. For example, children progressively integrate their many discrete self-perceptions into general abstractions of their qualities. Diversity emerges due to unique experiences in families and peer groups. Variations are also reflected in the self-perceptions of boys and girls from different cultures and distinct ethnic groups.	Theory of mind appears to be a universal capacity. A few children (e.g., some with autism or serious intellectual disabilities) exhibit delays in understanding other people's desires, intentions, thoughts, and feelings. Diversity is present in the age at which children acquire specific elements of theory of mind and is tied to opportunities to hear about other people's ideas, desires, and feelings and cultural practices that foster conjectures into other people's perspectives.
Qualitative and Quantitative Change	Infants' awareness of themselves, arising from experiences with bodily sensations and shared focus of attention with caregivers, is transformed qualitatively when they begin to speak about thoughts and feelings with others. Qualitative changes also occur when adolescents fold separate selves into unified abstract models of their characteristics. Quantitative changes occur as children increase their knowledge about things that they are good at and activities for which they lack proficiency.	A series of qualitative changes, for example, in the acquisition of *intersubjectivity* and *social referencing*, sets the stage for an awareness that other people have their own perspectives. Qualitative changes also occur in abilities to coordinate multiple perspectives and meet personal needs in a complex social environment. Quantitative changes are evident in increasingly sophisticated understandings of other people's thoughts, intentions, and feelings.

Fostering the Development of Social Cognition

The research findings just reviewed have implications for teachers and other adults who work with children. We recommend the following strategies for facilitating children's social cognitive understandings.

- **Talk about mental concepts in age-appropriate ways.** Adults can talk with children about others' perspectives. For example, together they might speculate about what other people (e.g., peers, figures in historical events, fictional characters) think about past events. Adults should try to gear such discussions to children's capabilities. Preschoolers understand such straightforward feelings as being *sad, disappointed*, and *angry* (Saarni, Campos, Camras, & Witherington, 2006). Adolescents have sufficiently advanced cognitive and social reasoning capabilities that they can consider abstract and complex psychological qualities (e.g., being *passive aggressive* or having an inner *moral compass*).

- **Encourage children to look at situations from other people's perspectives.** Classrooms and other group settings provide many opportunities for children to look at the world as others do, and over time such opportunities enhance children's theory of mind and perspective-taking capabilities. The Development-Enhancing Education feature "Encouraging Social Perspective Taking" illustrates effective strategies.

- **Help children tune in to the nonverbal cues that can help them "read people's minds."** Some children readily pick up on body language. Other children are less perceptive. The latter group can benefit from explicit instruction in signals they might look for—the furrowed brow that indicates confusion, the restless agitation that indicates frustration or impatience, the "silent treatment" that suggests anger, and so on (e.g., Franco, Davis, & Davis, 2013; Minskoff, 1980).

- **Coach children who face substantial delays with psychological concepts.** Children who are obstructed in theory of mind may need systematic exposure to psychological words and explanations (e.g., *wanting, thinking*, and *believing*). Paula,

Development-Enhancing Education

Encouraging Social Perspective Taking

Ask children to share their interpretations with one another.

- A first-grade teacher finds several children arguing over why Serena fell during a game of tag. The teacher comforts Serena and then asks the children about what happened. Some believe she stumbled over loose shoelaces, others argue that one of the other girls got in her way, and one boy thinks Serena wasn't looking where she was going. The teacher suggests that each of them may be partly right. He also urges them to be more careful when they play running games, because it is easy to bump into one another by accident. (Middle Childhood)
- After a field trip to a local museum, a high school art teacher asks her students to share their interpretations of how the artists have combined colors in their paintings. The students learn that some of them thought the color combinations were aesthetically vibrant and appealing, whereas others thought the palettes were garish. (Late Adolescence)

Encourage children to speculate about characters' thoughts, emotions, and motives in literature.

- As a teacher in a child-care center reads a story to a group of young children, she occasionally stops to ask questions about what the different characters might be thinking and feeling. While reading *The Berenstain Bears' Trouble with Pets* (Berenstain & Berenstain, 1990), she asks, "Why does the Bear family let Little Bird fly away?" and "How do you think Mama and Papa Bear feel when Lady makes a mess in the living room?" (Early Childhood)
- In *The Corn Grows Ripe* by Dorothy Rhoads (1956), Tigre, a 12-year-old Mayan boy living in the Yucatán, must take on new responsibilities when his father is injured. Mr. Torres assigns the book to his middle school students and leads a discussion about Tigre's new responsibilities. The students express a variety of opinions about how they would feel about taking on these new duties. (Early Adolescence)

Ask children to consider the perspectives of people they don't know very well.

- A preschool teacher makes a batch of cookies for senior citizens who regularly come to their class to read to children. The children prepare baskets for their senior friends, place a few cookies in each, and insert thank-you notes. She says to the children, "Imagine how surprised our senior friends are going to be! How do you think they might feel when they see the baskets?" (Early Childhood)
- During a discussion of a recent earthquake in South America, an eighth-grade social studies teacher asks students to imagine how people must feel when they lose their home and possessions and don't know whether their loved ones are dead or alive. (Early Adolescence)

a 9-year-old girl with fetal alcohol syndrome, was delayed in her cognitive and language development, had trouble interacting with other children, and rarely used terms for her own or others' mental states (Timler, Olswang, & Coggins, 2005). An intervention was designed to foster Paula's awareness of these characteristics. Paula and two other children met with a speech-language specialist over several weeks and considered how characters in hypothetical scenarios might have thought about the events. After a few weeks, Paula regularly used mental state terms in her speech:

> "I *know* Marco didn't let me play soccer unless I gave him one dollar bill."
>
> "The teacher *thought* I was making this story up and I'm trying to get him in trouble because he told her a lie."
>
> "I *know* because I saw the toilet paper in the boy's hand."
>
> "She *knows* that we got the wrong pizza because we were arguing about where we wanted to go and we went to Dominoes."
>
> (Timler et al., 2005, p. 81)

- **Promote an inclusive setting.** Creating a warm and respectful climate for children from diverse backgrounds takes ongoing work (Andreouli, Howarth, & Sonn, 2014). Certain procedures are essential, especially having a code of conduct that prohibits name-calling on the basis of ethnicity, race, gender, religion, socioeconomic status, abilities and disabilities, and other social categories. Also worthwhile is establishing affirmative values, such as respecting people regardless of their backgrounds, a quality that can be infused into resources and curricula (e.g., by screening books for ethnic stereotypes), outreach to families (e.g., by inviting parents and guardians to share their upbringings, jobs, and special talents in the classroom), and classroom traditions (e.g., by morning greetings, afternoon farewells, and regular class meetings).

Preparing for Your Licensure Examination

Your teaching test might ask you about steps in fostering an inclusive climate at school.

• **Break down stereotypes and reduce prejudice.** One effective strategy is to encourage children to see people as *individuals*—as human beings with their own unique strengths and weaknesses—rather than as members of particular groups (C. D. Lee & Slaughter-Defoe, 1995; Spencer & Markstrom-Adams, 1990). Another strategy is to increase interpersonal contacts among people from diverse groups (and ideally to create a sense that "we are all in this together") through cooperative activities, community service projects, or pen pal relationships (Koeppel & Mulrooney, 1992; Rutland, Killen, & Abrams, 2010). As children gain contact with people from unfamiliar groups, they tend to see one another as more similar than they previously thought, and prejudices often dissipate (Stathi, Cameron, Hartley, & Bradford, 2014). Cross-racial friendships are fostered when children notice one another's talents, hear about individual characteristics, and find that they can depend on one another during collaborative projects.

MyLab Education
Application Exercise 12.3
Meet Individual Needs
How does this adolescent girl describe her ethnic culture?

Adults should challenge any stereotypes and prejudicial attitudes they encounter in children's speech or actions. If a teenager talks about "lazy migrant workers," a teacher might respond by saying, "I wonder where that idea came from. Migrant workers are often up before dawn and pick fruits and vegetables until dusk. Many take other demanding jobs when the growing season is over." Notice how the teacher confronts the "lazy migrant worker" misconception matter-of-factly and does not assume that the teen's remark has malicious intent. Playing on their desire to appear tolerant and open-minded may be more effective than chastising them for attitudes they have not carefully thought through (Dovidio & Gaertner, 1999). Some educators have found it effective to train children to intervene when they hear prejudicial remarks (Aboud & Fenwick, 1999; Dessel, 2010).

Summary

As children grow older, they become more attuned to and interested in the mental lives of those around them. In the process of developing a *theory of mind*, they gradually learn that people have thoughts, feelings, and motives different from their own and that these internal states can be complex and at times contradictory. Children also become increasingly skilled in taking the perspectives of others. Yet youngsters' growing beliefs about other people may also include rigid stereotypes about certain groups, leading them to act in prejudicial ways.

Classrooms and other group settings are important contexts in which children develop awareness of other people's needs and perspectives. Teachers and other adults can foster greater knowledge in numerous ways—for instance, by talking frequently about people's thoughts and feelings, exposing students to multiple perspectives about particular topics and events, and confronting their inaccurate and counterproductive stereotypes.

MyLab Education Self-Check 12.2

Practicing for your Licensure Examination

Many teaching tests require students to apply what they have learned about child development to brief vignettes and multiple-choice questions. You can practice for your licensure examination by reading the following case study and answering a series of questions.

Two Histories

Rachel Stephanie Bolden-Kramer is an adolescent from San Francisco, California. In her poem, *Two Histories*, Rachel tells her experience of having a dual ethnic heritage:

> Daddy wanted to name me Wilhemina after his mother.
> You know you're supposed to name your baby after someone who's gone.
> Not alive.
> But then my mother protested.
> I should carry her mother's name, Anne.
> "Rachel" kept me from the arguments and sour family disputes.
> But did it compromise or anger both sides?
> And that's what I'm stuck with,
> Every day
> Every move
> I'm a compromise
> Light skin
> But thick bone structure
> Half 'n half Jewish girl who fights for BSU[a]
> Latke and greens
> The horah and the butterfly
> Act White
> Won't date Black men
> Think she's better
> Has good hair
> Looks more Latina than half-breed
> But that boy always called me mixed in such an ugly way
> Some say, "Nigga get off the swing"
> Others say, "You're really not like those other Black people"
> And I get told it's better to pretend I'm White
> But I got two histories in me
> Both enslaved
> And both warriors.
> Rachel Stephanie Bolden-Kramer[a]
> (WritersCorps, 2003, pp. 39–40)

Constructed-Response Question

1. What challenges and assets did Rachel have in forming an ethnic identity?

Multiple-Choice Questions

2. How might the developmental theorist James Marcia describe Rachel's ethnic identity formation?

a. Rachel is in a state of *diffusion*, in which she has failed to embark on a serious exploration of her ethnic identity.

b. Rachel is in *foreclosure*, a state of committing to a vision of her ethnicity established for her by her parents.

c. Rachel spent several years in *identity achievement*, embracing clear commitments to her ethnic identity, before entering *foreclosure*, the condition of committing to particular ideals and ways of life established for her by her parents.

d. Rachel went through a period of *moratorium*, in which she actively searched for the meaning of her ethnic identity and now seems to be in *identity achievement*.

3. How would you describe Rachel's development from the perspective of Margaret Beale Spencer's framework of identity development?

a. Rachel had *protective factors*, supportive parents who shared their cultural values and traditions with her and her own personal insight and resolve. Rachel also faced the *risk factor* of having bigoted and insensitive peers.

b. As Rachel reflected on her ethnic identity and relationships with peers and family members, she developed *coping skills*.

c. In the process of developing coping skills, Rachel gained a sense of her own *ethnic identity*.

d. All of the above.

[a]"Two Histories" by Rachel Stephanie Bolden-Kramer from *Paint Me Like I Am: Teen Poems from Writerscorps*.

MyLab Education Licensure Practice 12.1

Key Concepts

sense of self (p. 446)
self-handicapping (p. 448)
contingent self-worth (p. 449)
imaginary audience (p. 453)
personal fable (p. 453)
cyberbullying (p. 453)
identity (p. 454)
gender schema (p. 458)
gender identity (p. 459)
self-socialization (p. 459)
social cognition (p. 470)
theory of mind (p. 470)
social perspective taking (p. 470)
intentionality (p. 470)
recursive thinking (p. 472)
social-cognitive bias (p. 476)
stereotype (p. 476)
prejudice (p. 476)
autism spectrum disorders (p. 477)
mirror neuron (p. 478)

Chapter Thirteen

Self-Regulation and Motivation

Hero Images/Getty Images

Learning Objectives

13.1 Identify developmental trends in self-regulation, and implement practical applications for cultivating this important capacity.

13.2 Differentiate between extrinsic and intrinsic motivation, and identify factors influencing the manifestations of each.

13.3 Describe the kinds of goals children set and the explanations they make for how well they achieve their goals.

13.4 Summarize strategies for motivating children at school.

CASE STUDY

Making Kites

Janet Keany teaches a mathematics class for fifth- and sixth-graders who have a history of poor performance.[a] She has recently shown her students how concepts in geometry relate to aerodynamics, emphasizing that the size and shape of an object affect its flight. As a follow-up to the lesson, she asks her students to experiment with sizes and shapes as they each design a kite.

The kite project lasts several days. A researcher observes the class throughout the project and interviews the students afterward. She finds that different students take different approaches to the task and have widely varying perspectives about it. A girl named Sara approaches the task as a scientist might: She is keenly interested in creating an aerodynamic design and realizes that doing so will take time and patience. She redesigns her kite three times to make it as aerodynamic as possible. After the project, she summarizes her results:

> I wasn't completely successful, because I had a few problems. But I realized that most scientists, when they try experiments, well, they're not always right. . . . [I]f I can correct myself on [errors] then I don't really mind them that much. I mean, everybody learns from their mistakes. I know I do. . . . I think mistakes are actually good, to tell you the truth. . . . When I had my test flights, the shape flew really, really well, and I was going to stick with that shape. . . . I had no doubts because I knew that I could really do it; I knew I could put this together really well, 'cause I had a lot of confidence in myself. . . . (D. K. Meyer, Turner, & Spencer, 1997, pp. 511–512)

Unlike Sara, Amy sticks with a single design throughout the project even though she has trouble getting her kite to fly. Later, Amy tells the researcher:

> I knew from the start what shape I wanted. Once I had the materials it was very easy to make the kite . . . . [T]here wasn't enough wind for the kites to fly. (D. K. Meyer et al., 1997, pp. 510, 513)

The researcher asks Amy how important the project was to her and whether she ever takes risks at school. She responds:

> I feel lazy because I don't like to make challenges for myself, to make goals. I just like to do it as I go along, not make goals or challenges. . . . I like to do well for [the teacher] and my parents, and myself, I guess. . . . [I]f it doesn't affect my grade, whether I do this or not, if I totally fail and do everything wrong, if it doesn't affect my grade, then I'll [take risks]. (D. K. Meyer et al., 1997, pp. 510, 512)

Had her kite flown, how might Amy have explained it? Amy tells the researcher that it would probably have been "beginner's luck" (D. K. Meyer, Turner, & Spencer, 1994, D. K. Meyer et al., 1997).

- What differences do you notice in how the two girls approach the kite-making activity?
- What goals do Sara and Amy pursue as they create their kites? What challenges do they each overcome?
- How does Sara explain her success? How does Amy explain her failure?

As Sara and Amy developed plans for their kites, carried them out, and reflected on their kites' fitness to fly, they exhibited varying levels of deliberation. Their intentional actions were acts of *self-regulation*, the multifaceted capacity for thoughtful self-control over behavior, feelings, and learning. Both girls exhibited this capacity to some degree. The project took several days, and the girls had to concentrate on the design, creation, testing, and revision of their kites. In distinctive ways, the girls showed **motivation**, the driving force that energizes, directs, and sustains behavior toward chosen ends. Sara wanted an operational kite; Amy, a passing grade.

Children's academic performance is an outgrowth of their goals, enjoyment in learning, value in achievement, and confidence in an ability to grow intellectually. Sara

[a]Although the case is real, "Janet Keany" is a pseudonym.

Outline

is willing to experiment and make mistakes, processes that allow her to learn and construct the best kite possible, whereas Amy prefers an easier course of action that meets minimum expectations. Sara interprets her mistakes as clues to aerodynamics. Amy completes the first design she considered; she has no real commitment to producing an operational kite. Sara attributes her successful kite to her own effort and ability whereas Amy concludes that her failure is because of poor weather conditions.

In this chapter, we examine the development of self-regulation and motivation, two related capacities that contribute to educational success. Children are confronted daily with competing demands for their attention, and they regularly encounter obstacles to learning. As a result, they must have a reasonably strong motivation to persevere. To keep going, students need optimistic views about what they can accomplish in reading, mathematics, other subjects, and future careers. When strongly motivated, young people are generally willing to perform the conscious, calculated actions of self-regulation—in setting goals, developing plans, resisting distractions, overcoming obstacles, and keeping track of progress.

Self-Regulation

13.1 Identify developmental trends in self-regulation, and implement practical applications for cultivating this important capacity.

Children use self-regulation skills every day. A 3-year-old boy arrives at his new preschool, holding back tears as he waves good-bye to his mother. Kindergarten children stand in line for outdoor play, folding their arms to prevent accidental bumping. Fourth-grade students concentrate on a teacher's explanations rather than look out the window. Adolescents in a composition class plan their report and add interim deadlines into their calendars.

To stay focused and resist counterproductive impulses, children draw on neurological networks that govern the direction and flow of their voluntary activity (Heatherton, 2011; Mittal, Russell, Britner, & Peake, 2013). These brain circuits are known as *executive functions* because the child manages his or her mental processes in a top-down manner, with a particular goal in mind, much as a business executives traditionally controlled operations in a company. The self-regulatory capabilities that rely on executive functions include the following:

- *Setting goals:* identifying and striving for self-chosen goals and standards
- *Planning ahead:* thinking through various means for tackling a project and making a commitment to getting started in a certain way
- *Controlling impulses:* resisting sudden urges to engage in forbidden or counterproductive behaviors
- *Managing emotions:* modulating the expression of affective states so that conveyed feelings are true to self and expressed appropriately
- *Motivating oneself:* creating conditions that make a task more engaging or rewarding
- *Deploying mental processes:* directing and monitoring attention and learning strategies in ways that achieve personal goals
- *Tracking progress:* keeping tabs on the results of one's efforts and making adjustments as necessary

These skills do not appear overnight. The immature brain does not easily inhibit behaviors that are dominant or bring instant reward. It takes time for children to think through options and prioritize those that generate better future outcomes. In fact, executive functions strengthen over a whopping two and a half decades of life (S. J. Taylor, Barker, Heavey, & McHale, 2013). Let's look at age-related advancements in self-control and how other aspects of self-regulation unfold.

Growth in Self-Regulation

Infants try to moderate their environment when it is loud, aversive, repetitive, or unpleasant. In the first year, infants look away from things they don't want to see

(Eisenberg, Spinrad, Valiente, & Duckworth, 2014). Also, in the first year, infants exhibit self-soothing actions, such as pulling at an ear, sucking a thumb, or snuggling into a favorite blanket when distressed. In the second year, they speed up or go slow in their locomotion depending on interests and circumstances. Toddlers develop an intensified motivation to make their *own* choices. Some parents in Western cultures complain about the "terrible twos," a period between the second and third birthdays when toddlers become angry when restricted from their wishes, often staging a tantrum.

Children learn to control when and where they pursue their desires. During early childhood, most children develop a rudimentary ability to **delay gratification**, the forgoing of small, immediate rewards in favor of more substantial consequences down the road (L. Green, Fry, & Myerson, 1994; Suor, Sturge-Apple, & Jones-Gordils, 2018; B. E. Vaughn, Kopp, & Krakow, 1984). Delay of gratification was operationalized in a classic experiment by **Walter Mischel,** an Austrian-born American psychologist, and his colleagues. Four-year-old children were individually asked by a researcher to choose between having one marshmallow now or several marshmallows in 15 minutes. Most children chose to wait for the larger reward, but several asked for the one marshmallow *now* (Mischel & Ebbesen, 1970; Mischel, Shoda, & Rodriguez, 1989). Of course, choosing deferment is one thing; sticking with that plan is another.

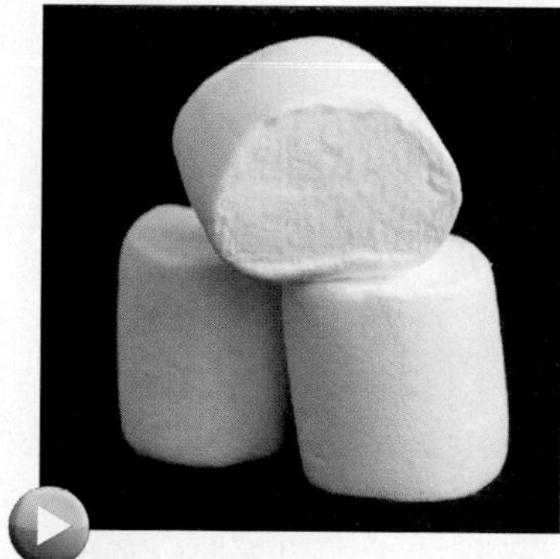

MyLab Education
Video Explanation 13.1
How do young children behave when they are tempted to eat marshmallows yet trying to resist immediate gratification? Children participate in the classic marshmallow task, and psychologist Walter Mischel explains its significance.[1]

While waiting for the marshmallows, many children used creative techniques to distract themselves, for example, by talking, singing, or playing games with their hands and feet. About 30 percent of children were able to resist the temptation for an immediate award for a full 15 minutes. It is a simple task, for sure, yet behavior during it is associated with later literacy and mathematics skills and productive peer relationships (Jaramillo, Rendón, Muñoz, Weis, & Trommsdorff, 2017). Delay of gratification is also predictive of adjustment in adolescence, including coping with frustration, getting along with others, and achieving academically; in adulthood, self-restraint on the childhood measure is associated with having high educational achievement, good health, adaptive stress-reduction skills, and an optimal weight (Eigsti et al., 2006; Mischel et al., 1989; Lamm et al., 2017; Montroy, Bowles, Skibbe, & Foster, 2014; Schlam, Wilson, Shoda, Mischel, & Ayduk, 2013; Shoda, Mischel, & Peake, 1990).

Self-regulation advances simultaneously on three fronts. Behaviorally, children must learn to sit when required to do so and inhibit such actions as shouting out an answer when the classroom rule is to wait to be called on. Children must also take turns, share toys, and abstain from hitting irksome classmates. *Emotionally*, children learn to express their feelings in a balanced and culturally acceptable manner, neither keeping them bottled up nor exploding disruptively. *Cognitively*, children must attend to academic lessons, including ones that they do not enjoy, and set specific learning goals, develop plans, monitor progress, and make adjustments as warranted. Self-regulation in each of these domains is essential for adjustment at school (Dent & Koenka, 2016; Williford, Whittaker, Vitiello, & Downer, 2013; L. J. Woodward, Lu, Morris, & Healey, 2017).

Children improve in their ability to guide actions in light of future consequences. As you have learned, the young child is incited to earn an immediate reward. Part of the reason is that the present looms large; the future is ephemeral (Schuitema, Peetsma, & van der Veen, 2014). Children slowly conceive of themselves in both the present and future and consider the two time frames when choosing a response. They learn to avoid inappropriate acts, such as grabbing a toy out of the hands of a classmate, in part due to their awareness of consequences to self and to the other child. They also become better able to think through several steps and use this planning ability while making decisions (P. Anderson, Anderson, & Lajoie, 1996; Krikorian & Bartok, 1998). By early elementary school, children can imagine more than one way to handle situations and compare the merits and disadvantages of each (C. Moore, 2010). As you might expect, it is not always easy to think realistically about the future. Young people cannot always mentally project themselves in time, and numerous high school students do not find it easy to imagine what they will do and become later in life (Schuitema et al., 2014).

[1]Should this YouTube video not work for you, which might be the case in certain countries, try searching for one of the many other videos that are available on Mischel's marshmallow task.

Children increasingly talk their way, and eventually think their way, through situations. The *inner speech* that the famous Russian psychologist and educator **Lev Vygotsky** (1896–1934) described is a key mechanism by which children regulate their behavior (Vygotsky, 1934/1986). As children acquire language skills, they talk themselves through new challenges (in tying shoes: "Put one lace over and then under the other; then make a loop . . . "). They internalize their self-talk, first whispering to themselves and eventually *mentally* telling themselves what they should do. Children also repeat the advice they have heard from others, either verbally or mentally (in putting on a cardigan: "Put one arm in first, then the next, now button it up from the bottom upward"). Self-talk helps children complete simple physical tasks; later, it helps them achieve difficult interpersonal and academic goals, for instance, resolving conflicts and studying for a classroom test (Alarcón-Rubio, Sánchez-Medina, & Prieto-García, 2014; Aziz, Fletcher, & Bayliss, 2016; Berk, 1994).

External standards are slowly internalized. Developing a **conscience**—an internalized sense of right and wrong—is crucial to good behavior. A conscience first emerges out of the child's close relationship with parents, in which the child slowly accepts family rules as his or her own (Goffin, Boldt, & Kochanska, 2017; Hoffman, 1979; R. A. Thompson, 2014). Yet even when children have developed a disposition to obey, they are driven to express their own strong wills. Thus, the internalization of family rules occurs slowly, one responsibility at a time.

Children comply with simple requests and restrictions by 12 to 18 months old (Kopp, 1982). As they become increasingly verbal, they use self-talk to prevent themselves from engaging in prohibited behaviors when caregivers are absent—for instance, saying "no" or "can't" to themselves as they reach for an electric outlet (Kochanska, 1993). By age 3 or 4, many children invent strategies for following rules. If they are asked to wait for a short time, they might invent games or sing to themselves to pass the time more quickly (Mischel & Ebbesen, 1970). If a playmate has an enticing toy, they may turn away and engage in an alternative activity so as to lessen the impulse to grab it (Kopp, 1982). Continued neurological maturation and experience enable persistence toward goals in new contexts. For example, a 10-year-old boy may turn down an invitation to hang out with a good friend after school because he had previously agreed to look after his younger brother.

Children increasingly make judgments about how well they are performing a task. Infants do not evaluate their own behavior, nor do they show much concern about how others assess it. In contrast, 2-year-olds often seek adults' approval for their actions (Stipek, Recchia, & McClintic, 1992). Sometime around age 3, children show signs of judging their own performance. They look happy when they're successful and sad when they fail (Heckenhausen, 1984; J. Ross, 2017). As children move through the preschool, elementary, and middle school years, they show a marked increase in self-assessment (A. D. Elder, 2010; van Kraayenoord & Paris, 1997). Parents have praised certain behaviors and criticized others, teachers have evaluated their academic performance, and peers have let them know which of their social gestures are polished or awkward. Children reflect on these comments; internalize commitments to being a good friend, student, and son or daughter; and evaluate how they measure up to—or fall short of—basic standards for conduct and performance.

Willpower builds in early and middle childhood and then takes a temporary dip during adolescence. Although neurological circuits for self-regulation have been taking shape throughout childhood, the teenage brain undergoes a dramatic rewiring that initially weakens self-control in select domains (M. A. Kuhn, Ahles, Aldrich, Wielgus, & Mezulis, 2017; R. C. Lorenz et al., 2014). Maturation in the brain intensifies the pleasure a young person experiences when taking risks, especially in the presence of peers. In these conditions, youngsters are at risk for acting rashly. Many adolescents succumb to temptations; some do so frequently. Yet with further maturation, coaching from adults, support from peers, personal resolve, and practice, adolescents strengthen their willpower and stay focused on long-term goals.

Self-Regulation in a Developmental System

The many facets of self-regulation draw on nature and nurture. Although virtually all children develop executive functions, significant individual differences arise in how robust these brain circuits become (Eisenberg, Duckworth, Spinrad, & Valiente, 2014; Hrabok & Kerns, 2010). Partly as a result of genetic factors, young children with impulsive temperaments have trouble inhibiting inappropriate behaviors as they move into elementary school (Eigsti et al., 2006; Leve et al., 2013). As part of their unique heredity, these children are inclined to be inattentive, irritable, and easily distracted from goals and mental challenges (M. A. Bell & Deater-Deckard, 2007). Children with disabilities—for instance, some with brain injuries, learning delays, or mental illness—may struggle with foresight and self-discipline and require support in planning ahead, considering what might happen in a situation, and putting the brakes on impulsive behavior (Gligorović & Đurović, 2014; Meltzer, 2007).

Environmental factors—especially socialization practices—play a strong role in children's self-regulatory profile. Infants are characteristically present in the moment, spontaneous, and largely unable to manage their moods. Parents take on the role of baby-regulator, keeping him or her safe, teaching self-care, and lessening fear, distress, and pain. Contrary to occasional concerns in Western society that cuddling a baby generates self-centeredness, research indicates that sensitive comforting does *not* cause dependence, selfishness, or immaturity. Instead, responsive care facilitates well-being and secure attachments to parents (Eisenberg et al., 2014; Pallini, Chirumbolo, Morelli, Baiocco, Laghi, & Eisenberg, 2018). In loving relationships, children learn to tone down their distress (with comforting care from parents), focus on valued activities, and take on increasing responsibility across a multitude of endeavors.

Developmental Systems Prompt

Self-regulation is made possible by brain circuits that support goal-directed behavior. You can scaffold students' self-regulation by providing assistance with goal-setting, planning, focusing, shifting attention, and recovering from setbacks.

In early childhood, caregiver sensitivity is a major catalyst for self-regulation. Attention to the child's needs is especially valuable when accompanied by expectations for mature behavior—for example, to wear a helmet while riding a bicycle, make the bed in the morning, and kneel in church at the right times. During the preschool years, most parents socialize children to live up to standards for social behavior—being polite, responsible, and the like (Gralinski & Kopp, 1993; Hrabok & Kerns, 2010). When parents, teachers, and other adults have warm and stable relationships with children, set reasonable expectations for behavior, and take everyone's needs into consideration, they create ideal conditions for making good choices (Eisenberg et al., 2014; Luthar & Eisenberg, 2017; B. J. Zimmerman, 2004).

The cultural values and traditions that children acquire also affect how children regulate their thinking, feeling, and behavior. Children want to fit in to their community and are motivated to emulate how familiar people go about routine tasks, talk about their goals, exert effort, and address obstacles along the way (Jaramillo et al., 2017; M. M. McClelland, Geldhof, Cameron, & Wanless, 2015). Some cultural groups in Asia and Africa place a high priority on self-discipline (P. M. Cole & Tamang, 2001; Trommsdorff, 2012). Even as toddlers, children are strongly encouraged to control their feelings, minimizing the "terrible twos" phenomenon we mentioned earlier (D. Y. F. Ho, 1994). From the beginning of life, children in these cultures are expected to preserve harmony in the family, respect their elders, and abide by the wishes of authority figures. Thus, young children learn to temper self-interest, curb emotions that might upset others, act responsibly, and fulfill the desires of authority figures (Jaramillo et al., 2017). Children raised in rural Cameroonian Nso farming families are expected to be self-controlled early in life. Consequently, young children in the Nso exhibit strong abilities to delay gratification (abilities that are verified in an experiment similar to the marshmallow task, with treats changed to small donuts in accord with local preferences; Lamm et al., 2017).

In comparison, children in many Western societies are socialized to express personal feelings and to develop a strong sense of autonomy and accomplishment. For these children, putting up a stink when their intentions are thwarted is a natural extension of their drive for independence (Jaramillo et al., 2017). In an urban area of Germany, children who were raised to be autonomous by middle-class families were more likely than children from the Nso society to give in to cravings for treats (for the German children, a lollipop or a chocolate bar) after only a few minutes (Lamm et al., 2017). In addition, there were differences in coping strategies in the two groups. The Nso children relaxed easily as they waited, whereas the German children battled a gnawing urge for candy as they fidgeted, walked around, and distracted themselves.

Finally, children living in economically disadvantaged families sometimes strain with self-regulation skills (A. L. Roy & Raver, 2014). Pressures on parents—long work hours, difficulty in affording necessities, and countless daily hassles—can be overwhelming and diminish their sensitivity, patience, and conversation with children. In response, children may not get the chance to calm down, plan ahead, or think through challenges. Those who experience multiple traumatic events, such as abuse, neglect, and family violence, are at risk for developing problems with anxiety and chronic illness. Children who experience high levels of stress over a lengthy period of time, unaccompanied by ample comfort, are apt to develop a physiological stress system that remains in overdrive, which puts them at risk for chronic illness and mental health problems (J. L. Cameron, Eagleson, Fox, Hensch, & Levitt, 2017; Condon, Sadler, & Mayes, 2018). Under *toxic stress*, children lose mental energy for executive functions and struggle to exercise self-control.

Fortunately, many children from low-income families develop heavy-duty self-regulatory skills, in large part because of personal resilience and strong support from parents, teachers, counselors, and other concerned adults (G. W. Evans & Fuller-Rowell, 2013; Raver, 2012; Sciaraffa, Zeanah, & Zeanah, 2017). This support can be enough to tame children's out-of-control stress reactions and fortify them for new challenges. Interventions that convince parents to avoid harsh parenting, express affection, communicate realistic standards, and use firm discipline, can culminate in more opportunities for children to exercise self-regulation skills. (Luthar & Eisenberg, 2017).

Preparing for Your Licensure Examination

Your teaching test might ask you about educational practices supporting self-regulation.

Promoting Self-Regulation

As you have learned, self-control, the ability to plan for the future, and other aspects of self-regulation are responsive to intervention. We offer the following recommendations:

- **Invite young children to plan activities.** As you have learned, delay of gratification and related executive functions are present but fragile in the preschool years. Teachers can ask young children to articulate their choices when entering play or free time or when starting a school project. When children stray from their professed goals, teachers can ask them how they might address distractions and return to their goals. Teachers can also encourage children to persist on artwork, puzzles, and other learning tasks and to squelch impulses to thump annoying classmates (Ursache, Blair, & Raver, 2012).

- **Immerse children in an environment that scaffolds the full range of self-regulation abilities.** Several programs illustrate support for children in setting goals, persisting on tasks, and inhibiting automatic responses (Ursache et al., 2012). In the *Research-Based Developmentally Informed (REDI) Head Start* project, children encounter a comprehensive preschool curriculum that focuses on fostering self-control in behavior and emotions (Bierman et al., 2014). Children are taught how they can express feelings, resolve disagreements with peers, and stop and think before acting. Compared to peers enrolled in another preschool program, REDI children were more engaged with the curriculum and less aggressive with peers.

Participants in other high-quality preschools in the United States have gained advantages intellectually, socially, emotionally, and behaviorally. Part of the reason seems to be that the preschools foster children's self-regulation, which, in turn, precipitate all sorts of benefits (Goodwin & Miller, 2013). In the *High/Scope* program in Ypsilanti, Michigan, preschool children from low-income families acquired language, cognitive abilities, and reasoning skills, and they planned and exercised self-control (Belfield, Nores, Barnett, & Schweinhart, 2008; Schweinhart, 2006). More of the High/Scope students went on to graduate from high school than did peers without this intervention. As adults, High/Scope graduates were more likely to be employed, and they earned more, were arrested less, and used less government assistance.

• **Teach self-regulatory skills to children who had a rough start in first relationships.** In the *Kids in Transition to School* (KITS) program, children in foster care who are getting ready for kindergarten are trained in self-regulation, early literacy, and prosocial skills (Pears et al., 2013). Children in the KITS program are taught how to concentrate, sit still, and wait their turn. In literacy, they are taught letter naming, phonological skills, print conventions, and comprehension abilities. In the prosocial domain, children are educated about sharing and getting along with others. Children who participated in the KITS program have acquired stronger self-regulatory and literacy skills (but did not differ in prosocial skills) compared to other children in foster care who received regular services from the child welfare system.

• **With older students, explain your expectations for desired behaviors.** Students are in a better position to make wise choices when they know what is expected and can be certain that particular actions will yield desired outcomes (Bronson, 2000; Holler & Greene, 2010; Meltzer, Pollica, & Barzillai, 2007). Communicating guidelines for behavior, routines, techniques for approaching assignments, and locations of needed items (pencils, hole punchers, dictionaries, etc.) improve conduct and reduce needs for adult supervision.

• **Provide children of all ages with choices.** Although young children inevitably require guidance to stay safe, they also benefit from making choices (Holler & Greene, 2010; Perry, VandeKamp, Mercer, & Nordby, 2002). A teacher might invite young children to select an activity for structured free time, perhaps in the puzzle area, dramatic play center, sensory table, or block zone. Children of older ages might choose either individual reading, journaling, or working on homework during flexible times. Such choices are vetted by teachers ahead of time. Educators create rules for taking turns and sharing materials, put dangerous objects out of reach, designate areas for messy undertakings (e.g., painting, working with clay), and ask students to sign in and out when using laboratory equipment (Bronson, 2000). Independent assignments, computer-based academic programs, group projects, and homework sometimes help students know how to proceed (H. Cooper, Robinson, & Patall, 2006; Corno & Mandinach, 2004; Landry & Smith, 2010). When children make shortsighted choices, adults can offer constructive feedback that will scaffold, rather than dampen, children's independent action.

• **Create checklists for guiding completion of a task.** Some middle and high school students lose track of materials and assignments, not because they are unmotivated but because they have poor organizational skills. For these students, mechanisms for keeping track of homework and due dates can be helpful (Belfiore & Hornyak, 1998). In one intervention, students asked the teacher for assistance when they needed it and learned to reward themselves (e.g., playing a board game or spending time on a computer) when they finished a task. Initially, the teacher needed to monitor whether checklists accurately reflected what children had accomplished, but eventually oversight was not necessary. In Figure 13.1, you can see a checklist for elementary children focused on being prepared for the first lesson of the day. Teachers can also use checklists as steps for completing lengthy projects, for example, in dividing up a writing assignment into brainstorming ideas, identifying key concepts, writing topic sentences, adding evidence, filling in the gaps, and editing (Meltzer, 2010).

• **Provide guidance when, and only when, children need it.** Being self-regulating doesn't necessarily always mean doing something independently. It also involves knowing when assistance is needed and seeking it out (Karabenick & Sharma, 1994; Kaya & Kablan, 2013). Accordingly, teachers might welcome any reasonable requests for help and not convey the message that children are "dumb" or bothersome for asking (R. S. Newman & Schwager, 1992). Sometimes, however, children ask for help when they really just want attention or companionship. If a 4-year-old asks for help on a puzzle, an astute preschool teacher might, after watching the child at work, say, "I don't think you need help with this. But I can keep you company for a few minutes if you'd like" (Bronson, 2000).

• **Use suggestions rather than direct commands as much as possible.** Children are more likely to internalize guidelines for behavior when adults elicit children's perspectives, make recommendations on how to accomplish goals, and provide a rationale

FIGURE 13.1 Daily Checklist.

Elementary school students can practice their self-regulatory processes by reporting on relevant actions.

Student's Name ______________________ **Date** ____________

Step	Yes	No	Teacher's Comment
1. I took my homework out of my backpack and put it in the basket.			
2. I took out my journal and pen and placed them on the table.			
3. I hung up my sweater or jacket on the coat rack.			
4. I took a deep breath and sat down.			
5. I said good morning to classmates at my table.			
6. I looked at the bulletin board to find out which topic I should write about in my journal.			

for why certain behaviors are unacceptable (Baraldi & Iervese, 2010; Hoffman, 1975). Younger children respond more favorably to suggestions that are concrete rather than abstract. To avoid incidents of bumping and pushing in the cafeteria, for example, teachers at one school asked students to imagine they had "magic bubbles" around them. The students could keep their bubbles from "popping" if they kept a safe distance between themselves and others. This simple strategy resulted in fewer behavior problems at lunchtime (Sullivan-DeCarlo, DeFalco, & Roberts, 1998).

- **Teach specific self-regulation skills.** Children become more self-regulating when they learn methods for directing their behavior. Particular strategies can be taught as follows:

  - **Self-monitoring**. Children aren't always aware of how frequently they do something wrong or how infrequently they do something right. To help them become aware of their actions, adults can ask them to observe and record their own behavior. Such self-focused observation and record keeping often bring about significant improvements in children's academic and social behaviors (Roebers, Krebs, & Roderer, 2014; J. R. Sullivan & Conoley, 2004; Webber, Scheuermann, McCall, & Coleman, 1993). Initially some children may need assistance in monitoring their behavior, for example, whether they have stayed on task during a lesson (DuPaul & Hoff, 1998).
  - **Self-instructions**. Sometimes children need a reminder about how to respond in particular situations. By teaching specific ways of talking themselves through an endeavor, adults give them a means through which they remind *themselves* about appropriate actions. Such a strategy is often effective with young children and especially those with poor impulse control (Ennis & Jolivette, 2014; Meichenbaum, 1985). For example, a teacher might give a child a line drawing of an ear as a reminder to listen quietly during storybook reading (A. Diamond et al., 2007). Checklists, assessment rubrics (with defined standards), and lists of steps are worthwhile for older students.
  - **Self-motivation**. Children may appreciate strategies to keep themselves motivated during dull but important tasks. For example, they might identify several reasons why completing an activity will help them over the long run. They might embellish a task to make it more interesting. Or they might learn how to divide a lengthy assignment into a number of small pieces and then reward themselves after completing each part (Wery & Thomson, 2013; B. J. Zimmerman & Cleary, 2009).
  - **Self-evaluation**. To become truly self-regulating, children must acquire reasonable criteria by which to guide and judge their accomplishments. For instance, teachers might ask students to reflect on improvement ("What can we do that we didn't do before?") or complete self-assessment instruments that show what to look for in performance (Panadero, Tapia, & Huertas, 2012; S. G. Paris & Ayres, 1994). At the secondary school level (and perhaps even sooner), students might play a role in identifying the criteria by which their performance is reasonably evaluated.

MyLab Education
Video Example 13.1

Find Developmental Meaning
How does Brandon use a gadget to help maintain his attention? Brandon explain how he checks his attention and registers his progress each time the gadget buzzes, and in the process makes progress toward an award.

MyLab Education Application Exercise 13.1
Identify Development-Enhancing Education
Second-grade student Keenan and her teacher discuss her goals and progress in reading and writing.

• **Tailor support to the needs of children with disabilities.** Independence is a major concern for children with disabilities, especially because adults are apt to monitor their behavior closely (Sands & Wehmeyer, 1996; H. Wu & Chu, 2012). Adults can help by taking a long-term perspective and arranging for independent activities in which they are available to remind students of procedures. For instance, one teacher asks a student with an intellectual disability to take the daily attendance sheet to the office and reminds her that as soon as she has done so, she should return immediately to class (Patton, Blackbourn, & Fad, 1996). Another teacher gives a student who is blind a chance to explore the classroom before the others students have arrived, locating objects in the classroom (wastebasket, pencil sharpener, etc.) and identifying distinctive sounds (e.g., the buzz of a wall clock) that help the student get his bearings (J. W. Wood, 1998).

• **Demonstrate your own willpower.** Adults promote self-regulation by modeling controlled behaviors (A. M. Jones, 2017; M. R. Sanders & Mazzucchelli, 2013; B. J. Zimmerman & Cleary, 2009). In a variant on the classic marshmallow task introduced previously, fourth- and fifth-graders watched adult models make a series of choices between small, immediate rewards and more valuable, postponed ones (e.g., plastic chess pieces available on that day versus wooden ones that they could have in 2 weeks). Some children observed a model choosing the immediate rewards (e.g., saying, "Chess figures are chess figures. I can get much use out of the plastic ones right away" (Bandura & Mischel, 1965, p. 701). Others observed a model choosing the deferred rewards (e.g., saying, "The wooden chess figures are of much better quality, more attractive, and will last longer. I'll wait 2 weeks for the better ones" (Bandura & Mischel, 1965, p. 701). Immediately after they observed the models, and on a second occasion several weeks later, the children were asked to choose between small, immediate rewards and larger, deferred ones (e.g., a small plastic ball now or a much larger one in 2 weeks). The children were more likely to delay gratification if they had seen the model do likewise. In other contexts, an adult might make remarks such as the following:

- "That was a delicious cookie! I'd like another but I won't take it because I want to be healthy."
- "Let's talk about it later. I'm angry now and need to cool down first."
- "I know those word problems take a while to finish. One thing I do with a big project is break it up and take a quick break when I'm halfway through; I will reward myself when I'm all finished."
- "I'd love to go to the concert this weekend, but I'm almost done with the last section of my master's thesis."
- "I'll be more proficient on this new computer program if I browse through the instructions before trying to use it."

• **Shield adolescents from their unique vulnerabilities.** Adolescents have more advanced cognitive skills than do younger children but face definite challenges in resisting temptations. Particular areas in the brain mature unevenly during adolescence, causing some vexing problems with self-regulation (A. A. Baird, 2010; Ernst & Hardin, 2010; Van Leijenhorst & Crone, 2010). During adolescence, neurological circuits for emotions, sensitivity to rewards, and social interests outpace networks for judgment and restraint. As a result, adolescents find it difficult to stay focused on academic tasks when peers entice them with high-spirited adventures. On school grounds, risky activities must be discouraged and group activities supervised. Many secondary teachers provide outlets for social needs by arranging for students to work together in teams (Dyson & Plunkett, 2012; Slavin, Lake, & Groff, 2009).

As you have learned, adults play a crucial role in fostering children's initiative. The Development-Enhancing Education feature "Teaching Self-Regulation Skills" includes several illustrations of effective strategies.

Development-Enhancing Education

Teaching Self-Regulation Skills

Have children observe and record their own activities.

- When a third-grade student has trouble staying on task, her teacher asks her to stop every 10 minutes (with aid of an egg timer) and determine whether she has been on task. The student uses the checklist to record her observations. Within a couple of weeks, the student's on-task behavior has noticeably improved. (Middle Childhood)

Every ten minutes, put a mark to show how well you have been staying on task.

+ means you were almost always on task
1/2 means you were on task about half the time
– means you were hardly ever on task

9:00-9:10	9:10-9:20	9:20-9:30	9:30-9:40	9:40-9:50	9:50-10:00
+	+	–	+	1/2	–
10:00-10:10	10:10-10:20	10:20-10:30	10:30-10:40	10:40-10:50	10:50-11:00
1/2	–	recess		+	1/2
11:00-11:10	11:10-11:20	11:20-11:30	11:30-11:40	11:40-11:50	11:50-12:00

- A high school adviser notices that one of his students is getting low grades. After a discussion with him, the adviser finds he often forgets to do his homework or turn it in. The teacher develops a weekly calendar with the boy and checks with him to see that he has written due dates on the calendar and crosses off assignments as he gives them to teachers. (Late Adolescence)

Teach instructions children can apply themselves.

- A counselor helps a fifth-grader control his impulsive behavior on multiple-choice tests by having him mentally say to himself as he reads each question: "Read the entire question. Then look at each answer carefully and decide whether it is correct or incorrect. Then choose the answer that seems most correct." (Middle Childhood)
- A high school history teacher advises his students of what they can do to begin their homework. She tells them, "Remind yourself to use the **POM** strategy: **P**repare your learning space, **O**rganize your materials, and **M**inimize distractions by turning the television off, silencing your cell phone, and getting to work." (Late Adolescence)

Help children identify ways to make tedious tasks more rewarding.

- A third-grade teacher suggests that students practice the week's spelling words at home every night. "That might not sound like much fun," she says, "but it's an important thing to do. Who can think of a way to make spelling practice more fun?" One student suggests writing out words in rainbow colors or spelling them in crossword puzzles. Another suggests trying to think of sentences that spell words with first letters—for example, *"Eighty-nine overweight unicorns get hiccups"* spells *enough*. (Middle Childhood)
- A high school chemistry teacher explains the order of elements in the periodic table and encourages students to attend to atomic number (across) and chemical characteristics (down). He demonstrates how sodium and lithium react when dropped in water to help students visualize the properties of these elements. When students study the table, they remember properties of elements that they have observed. (Late Adolescence)

Teach children to reward themselves for appropriate behavior.

- A middle school teacher suggests that her students are more likely to develop regular study habits if they make a favorite activity—for example, shooting baskets or watching television—contingent on completing homework. (Early Adolescence)
- A high school geography class has been fascinated with lessons on immigration. After moving to a unit on maps, the teacher finds that students have lost their enthusiasm. The teacher acknowledges that certain geography topics are more interesting than others. To help them stay engaged, he offers a reward (a pizza party, free period, or choice for an upcoming topic) that they can earn when everyone has completed the mapping project. (Late Adolescence)

Encourage children to evaluate their own performance.

- A middle school mathematics teacher has students grade their own mathematics homework. After totaling up their points, students enter their scores in an electronic log. Students also write a few comments on how they are doing and whether they need help with any concepts. Those who need assistance see the teacher during the last 10 minutes of class. (Early Adolescence)
- Early in the season, the coach of a boys' baseball team videotapes each athlete as he practices batting, pitching, and fielding ground balls. The coach models good form for each of the activities and lists several things the boys should look for as they watch themselves on tape. (Late Adolescence)

Summary

With age and experience, most children become increasingly able to direct and control their own behavior. They learn to restrain their impulses, internalize adults' rules and restrictions, and evaluate their performance using appropriate criteria. Yet progress with self-regulation is gradual, and setbacks are common. Even at the high school level, youngsters can be inattentive and hasty with peers. Adults promote self-regulation by establishing guidelines for behavior, listening to children's perspectives, and providing a reasonable rationale for required behavior. Adults can model self-regulating behaviors, give children age-appropriate opportunities for independence, and teach such specific skills as self-monitoring, self-instructions, self-motivation, and self-evaluation.

MyLab Education Self-Check 13.1

Extrinsic and Intrinsic Motivation

13.2 Differentiate between extrinsic and intrinsic motivation, and identify factors influencing the manifestations of each.

Virtually all children are motivated in one way or another. Mia excels in athletics and works out daily in hopes of winning a prize at an upcoming race. Achilles is enchanted with science and seeks out challenging course work in physics and engineering.

Sometimes youngsters have strong **extrinsic motivation**. Like Mia, they are motivated to attain or avoid certain consequences in the outside world. Children may complete a classroom assignment in order to get adult approval (as Amy did in the opening case), or they may try to earn passing grades to avoid punishment from family. At other times youngsters have deep **intrinsic motivation**. Like Achilles, they are motivated by factors within themselves or inherent in a task they are performing. They might read a book simply for the pleasure it brings, experiment with kite shapes to find out which one flies best (as Sara did), or return a wallet to its owner consistent with a moral code.

Preparing for Your Licensure Examination

Your teaching test might ask you to distinguish between extrinsic and intrinsic motivation.

Both extrinsic and intrinsic motivation can spur children to acquire new knowledge and engage in productive behaviors. But intrinsic motivation has numerous advantages over extrinsic motivation. Intrinsically motivated children are eager to learn classroom material, tackle assigned tasks, use effective learning strategies, and achieve at high levels. In contrast, extrinsically motivated children may have to be enticed or prodded, are apt to study classroom topics only superficially, and are often inclined to perform only easy tasks and meet minimal classroom requirements (Froiland & Oros, 2014; A. E. Gottfried, Fleming, & Gottfried, 2001; R. M. Ryan & Deci, 2009). Extrinsic motivation has its own advantages, however. Knowing that children will work hard to achieve certain rewards, teachers and other practitioners can promote mature behavior with incentives. We examine that issue now.

Factors Affecting Extrinsic Motivation

Human beings of all ages usually behave in ways that bring desired results. In an early theory of learning known as *operant conditioning*, American behaviorist **B. F. Skinner**

(1904–1990) proposed that children engage in behaviors that lead to pleasant consequences, which he called **reinforcers** (e.g., Skinner, 1953, 1968). From Skinner's perspective, people actively choose behaviors that are currently being reinforced or have been reinforced in the past. Miguel might practice the piano regularly if his parents compliment his efforts. Brigita might throw frequent temper tantrums if her fits are the only way she can get special toys or privileges. Peter might misbehave in class if doing so gains him attention from his teacher or classmates. The last of these examples illustrates an important point: Reinforcers are not always what we would typically think of as "rewards." The attention Peter gets for misbehavior may seem unpleasant to others: Peter's teacher scolds him for acting out, and classmates gasp and shake their heads. But if Peter's misbehaviors increase as a result, then the attention is indeed the reinforcer.

Concepts in behavioral learning. In early infancy, children are largely concerned with **primary reinforcers**, those rewards that satisfy built-in needs or desires. Some primary reinforcers, such as food and drinks, are essential for health. Others, such as physical affection, cuddling, and smiles, are more social in nature and are said to become quickly associated with primary reinforcers (Eby & Greer, 2017; Harlow & Zimmerman, 1959; Vollmer & Hackenberg, 2001). A child might discover that approval from Mother often comes with a candy treat or that a good grade frequently leads to hugs from Father. Through such associations, consequences such as praise, money, good grades, and attention (sometimes even attention in the form of a scolding) become reinforcing in their own right. That is, they become **secondary reinforcers**. Because secondary reinforcers are consequences that children *learn* to appreciate, and because children have widely different upbringings, the effectiveness of any one of them will differ considerably from one child to the next.

Although Skinner argued that direct reinforcement was necessary for changing children's behavior, social learning theorists have found that children's motivation is affected not only by personal experience but also by the consequences *other people* receive in a relevant situation (Bandura, 1965, 1977). In other words, observed consequences may affect children vicariously. In **vicarious reinforcement**, a child who observes a peer being reinforced for doing something is likely to behave similarly.

Reinforcement in the classroom. Principles of reinforcement are an invaluable part of any teacher's toolkit, especially when children's need to become self-regulating is valued (Austin & Bevan, 2011; DeLeon, Bullock, & Catania, 2013; Kamps, 2002). In order to use reinforcement effectively, teachers and other practitioners must identify the type of behavior they would like children to achieve—perhaps remaining in their seat during a lesson (rather than getting up and wandering around the room). Then, to give children a realistic chance of achieving the standard, teachers may establish interim targets whose mastery gets them closer to mature behavior. Thus, although Ms. Owens might prefer for her first-grade students to be on task for the entire school day, she would begin with a briefer time frame, say, a 20-minute interval, and advise students of the need to work quietly. She then might walk around the room and put a gold star on the papers of children who have stayed on task, praising them, and saying, "Tom, I like the way you are working so carefully on your assignment. Good job!"

These techniques have become an especially valuable resource for children with special needs. Educator Ann Turnbull and her colleagues illustrate the process with Jane, an adolescent girl with autism, for whom learning how to care for herself and manage a household are priorities. Jane wants approval from her teacher, and thus praise is the reinforcer (A. P. Turnbull, Turnbull, & Wehmeyer, 2010). In the process of learning to sort silverware, Jane is first shown a *discriminative stimulus*, a reminder that a particular response is necessary. Next, she emits the desired *response* of placing the utensils in their proper places and finally receives *reinforcement*, verbal praise. Here's how Jane is coached in sorting silverware:

Preparing for Your Licensure Examination

Your teaching test might ask you how reinforcement can be implemented in the classroom.

> You lay a spoon, a fork, and a knife in front of her and provide a discriminative stimulus by saying, "Jane, show me the spoon." Most likely, Jane will point to or touch one of the utensils, or, if she is not certain, not respond at all. If she points to the spoon, you immediately praise her, saying, "Great job, Jane! That's right, that's the spoon." Your

praise constitutes the reinforcing stimulus. If she points to a different utensil or to none of them, she does not get your reinforcer (verbal praise); instead, you prompt her again to identify the spoon. Eventually, if you reinforce ("Great job!"), her correct response (pointing to the spoon) to your discriminative stimulus ("Show me the spoon"), while ignoring or not reinforcing Jane's other responses, she will respond more consistently to the stimulus with the appropriate response. (A. P. Turnbull et al., 2010, p. 322)

The characteristics of children shape how reinforcement is implemented. For young children, immediate reinforcement is effective in managing behavior, given their limited ability to delay gratification (J. C. Coleman et al., 2013). Desires for types of rewards vary by age and individual preference, making it worthwhile to ask students about their preferences. Some teachers administer surveys to students to get feedback on options—would they like puzzles, 15 minutes of free time, popcorn, or something else? (Panahon & Martens, 2013). With students who are seriously disruptive, the teacher usually consults a psychologist or special educator, sometimes with help from parents, and designs a customized plan for reinforcing appropriate actions.

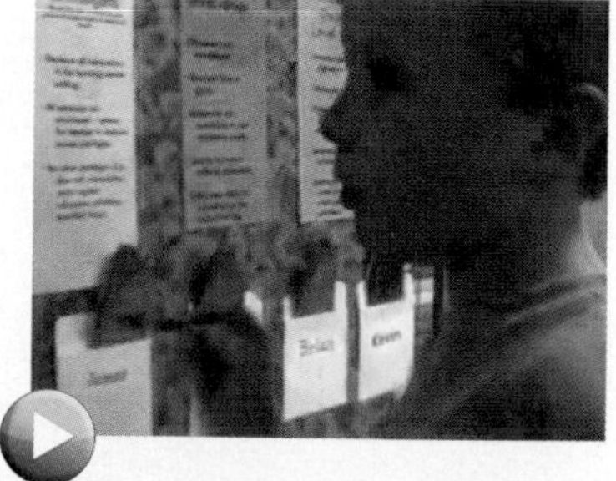

MyLab Education
Video Example 13.2

Find Developmental Meaning *How does teacher Kimberly Rich motivate her students to use good behaviors?* Hunter, Clay, and Dylan explain the tokens that they earn for good behaviors, such as raising a hand to speak, working quietly, staying in seat, and avoiding unwanted behaviors, including physical aggression, not submitting homework, and failing to comply with the teacher's instructions.

Punishment at school. Once in a while children are neither intrinsically motivated to acquire important skills nor responsive to simple reinforcement. In rare cases when children persist with a particular misbehavior despite adults' best efforts, punishment is used. Psychologists define **punishment** as a consequence that *decreases* the frequency of the response it follows.[2] Whereas children are likely to behave in ways that lead to reinforcement, they are *un*likely to behave in ways that lead to punishment. Punishment of undesirable responses (e.g., engaging in off-task behaviors during a lesson), especially when combined with reinforcement of more productive responses (e.g., sitting attentively during the lesson), can bring about improvements in children's behavior (Minshawi et al., 2014; Walters & Grusec, 1977). In working with children with serious behavioral problems, teachers may award points (reinforcement) for appropriate behaviors and take away points (punishment) for misbehaviors. After a certain time interval (perhaps at the end of the day or week), children can exchange the points they've accumulated for small toys or privileges. Taking away previously earned points for unacceptable behavior (a strategy called *response cost*) can be effective in bringing about behavior change (Eluri, Andrade, Trevino, & Mahmoud, 2016; Landrum & Kauffman, 2006; K. D. O'Leary & O'Leary, 1972).

However, punishment is a tool of last resort. Punishment does not, by itself, teach a more productive behavior and can have unwanted effects. Punishment that is aggressive, inflicts physical or psychological harm, or involves suspension or expulsion from school has been shown to be ineffective (S. A. Hemphill & Schneider, 2013; Kennedy-Lewis & Murphy, 2016; Luiselli, 2009). After extreme punishment, students may reduce the targeted behavior temporarily yet also feel angry and humiliated and eventually exhibit increases in antagonistic behavior. Thus, compliance is short-lived and accompanied by negative feelings. Suspensions and expulsions are also problematic because students are deprived of valuable educational experiences.

Children sometimes reduce a certain behavior after observing others being punished for it. In **vicarious punishment**, a child who sees a peer being punished for a particular behavior is unlikely to behave in that way. For example, children might learn

MyLab Education
Content Extension 13.1

Learn more about types, effects, and uses of punishment.

MyLab Education Application Exercise 13.2
Meet Individual Needs

Mr. Wimberley uses proactive discipline with two disputing boys while simultaneously conducting a lesson in his sixth-grade classroom.

[2]Be aware that the term *negative reinforcement* is *not* a synonym for punishment. Negative reinforcement increases rather than decreases a behavior it follows by removing an unpleasant stimulus and causing a sense of relief in the person. Punishment decreases the behavior it follows.

that a teammate who pushed another player on the playing field was benched the next game. With this knowledge, they make an effort to control their temper on the field. When possible, teachers should avoid punishment in favor of techniques that foster students' problem-solving, self-control, and reinforcement.

Factors Affecting Intrinsic Motivation

Although children actively select behaviors that maximize rewards and minimize punishments, they also consider internal factors—especially, their personal interests. As the following principles reveal, some of the factors underlying intrinsic motivation are at work early in life, whereas others emerge as children learn more about themselves and the world.

Children have a natural predisposition to explore their environment. Following in Jean Piaget's (1896–1980) footsteps, many developmental theorists believe that children are naturally curious about their world and actively seek out information to make sense of it (Alvarez & Booth, 2014; Oudeyer & Smith, 2016; R. M. Ryan & Deci, 2009; Taffoni et al., 2014). Infants constantly experiment with objects to discover their properties and effects. Later, as children gain proficiency in their native language, they also ask questions (e.g., "How do they make statues?" "Why does it rain sometimes?") to satisfy their curiosity (Callanan & Oakes, 1992, p. 218; Kemler Nelson, Egan, & Holt, 2004).

Children strive for consistency when trying to understand the world. Jean Piaget suggested that another factor driving a child's learning is *disequilibrium*, an inconsistency between new information and what the child believes to be true. According to Piaget, disequilibrium causes mental discomfort and spurs the child to integrate, reorganize, and, in some cases, replace existing schemes with new ideas and procedures that better explain the puzzling information. Like Piaget, many contemporary developmental theorists believe that beginning early in life, human beings have an innate need to see the world as being governed by consistent, coherent, and reasonable principles (Bronson, 2000; B. Hayes & Rehder, 2012; Keil, 2010; K. L. Steiner & Pillemer, 2018). Thus, the need to construct clear and lucid mental frameworks is a major impetus in children's learning.

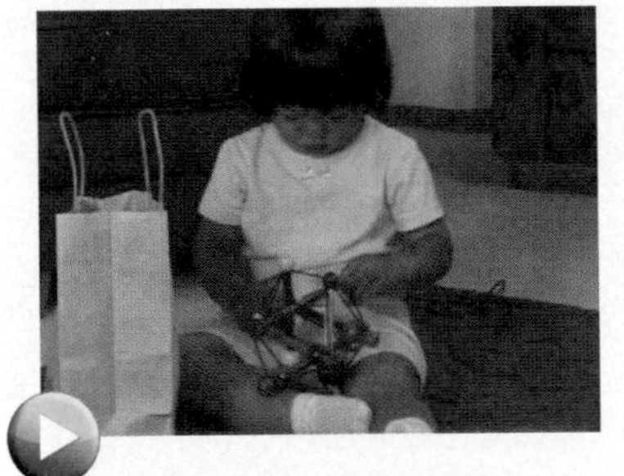

MyLab Education
Video Example 13.3

Find Developmental Meaning
A young child explores a toy with intrinsic motivation. Maddie inspects the pieces, compressibility, sounds, and shapes of a toy.

Children choose activities at which they think they can be successful. Some psychologists propose that an important source of intrinsic motivation is an innate need to feel *competent*—to believe that one can deal effectively with the environment (Malboeuf-Hurtubise, Joussemet, Taylor, & Lacourse, 2018; K. Richards & Levesque-Bristol, 2014; R. M. Ryan & Deci, 2009). A need for competence pushes children to acquire increasingly effective ways for dealing with their surroundings. It may be one important reason why we human beings have, over the course of time, been able to adapt successfully to many different habitats (R. White, 1959). As you can see in the following example, 9-year-old Elena expresses interest and confidence in mathematics, her favorite subject:

> Interviewer: What do you like best about school?
> Elena: I like PEAK [a program for students identified as gifted]. It's this thing where you go to this program. It's for smart kids who have, like, good ideas for stuff you could do. And so they make it more challenging for you in school. So instead of third-grade math, you get fourth-grade math.

To maintain their sense of competence, children are apt to choose and persist at activities for which they have high **self-efficacy**—that is, on activities at which they believe they can be successful (Bandura, 1997, 2012; Schunk & Pajares, 2009). In the opening case study, Sara reveals a high sense of self-efficacy about building a kite: "I had no doubts because I knew that I could really do it; I knew I could put this together really well" (D. K. Meyer et al., 1997, p. 512). Once youngsters have high self-efficacy for a task or activity, they eagerly seek out challenges that will enhance their skills and knowledge.

MyLab Education
Video Example 13.4

Find Developmental Meaning
What motivates 9-year-old Elena in mathematics? Elena reveals a desire to be challenged.

When children have *low* self-efficacy in an area, they may try to avoid it as much as possible. A student with a reading disability reveals one strategy:

> When it comes time for reading I do everything under the sun I can to get out of it because it's my worst nightmare to read. I'll say I have to go to the bathroom or that

> I'm sick and I have to go to the nurse right now. My teacher doesn't know that I'll be walking around campus. She thinks I am going to the bathroom or whatever my lame excuse is. All I really want to do is get out of having to read. (Zambo & Brem, 2004, p. 5)

Children prefer activities for which they have autonomy. As early as 6 months of age, infants become frustrated when a parent stops them from moving their arms freely or when a device they've learned to operate successfully stops playing music (Braungart-Rieker, Hill-Soderlund, & Karrass, 2010; M. W. Sullivan & Lewis, 2003). By 14 months, infants actively resist parents' requests that would prevent them from reaching their immediate goal (e.g., "Put the cookie down"; Dix, Stewart, Gershoff, & Day, 2007). In general, children are more intrinsically motivated when they have a **sense of self-determination** (R. M. Ryan & Deci, 2009; Sebire, Jago, Fox, Edwards, & Thompson, 2013). A child who thinks, "I *want* to do this," or "I'd *like* to learn more about that," has a feeling of self-determination. A child who thinks, "I *must* do this," or "*My teacher wants* me to learn that," thinks that someone else is directing the course of events.

Developmental Trends in Intrinsic Motivation

A child's intrinsic motivation is a vital capacity that evolves with age and experience. Let's consider major changes.

As children grow older, their interests become increasingly stable. When we say that children have an *interest* in a topic or activity, we mean that they find it intriguing or rewarding in and of itself. Interest, then, is an important form of intrinsic motivation. Psychologists distinguish between two general types of *interest* (Hidi, Renninger, & Krapp, 2004; Middleton, 2013; Schiefele, 2009). **Situational interest** is evoked by something in the environment—something that is perhaps new, unusual, or surprising. In contrast, **personal interest** comes from within the child and is largely unrelated to immediate circumstances.

MyLab Education
Video Example 13.5

Find Developmental Meaning
How does Alicia exhibit a need for self-determination? Alicia has a strong preference for choosing her own books.

In infancy and early childhood, interests are mostly situational and short-lived. Young children are readily attracted to novel, attention-getting stimuli and events for, say, a few seconds or minutes (Courage, Reynolds, & Richards, 2006; Elkins, 2013). Sometimes these encounters plant the seeds from which longer term personal interests grow (Hidi & Renninger, 2006). By middle and upper elementary grades, children express personal interests, for instance, in animal life, mechanical movements, music, or dinosaurs, that persist over a period of time and ultimately become parts of children's identities (J. M. Alexander, Johnson, Leibham, & Kelley, 2008; Hidi et al., 2004; Middleton, 2013). Joey displayed an exceptional interest in art beginning at age 3. As you can see in Artifact Example 13.1, he had a long-term interest in drawing the human form and, later, in fashion design.

Age 8

Age 11

Age 17

MyLab Education
Artifact Example 13.1

Find Developmental Meaning *What kind of interest does Joey seem to have in drawing the human form?* Joey has a long-term personal interest, accompanied by a growing artistic talent.

Children increasingly pursue activities that have instrumental value. A task or activity has **value** when children like the benefits of performing it (Dweck & Elliott, 1983; Fan & Wolters, 2014; M. Wang & Eccles, 2013; Wigfield & Eccles, 2000). A boy who wants to be smart and thinks that he can achieve this goal will place a premium on academic success. Other activities have high value because they are means to an end. As much as she disliked mathematics, Jeanne's daughter Tina struggled through math classes throughout high school because many colleges require four years of math. Still other activities are valued because they bring enjoyment (Eccles & Wigfield, 1985; Zhu, Sun, Chen, & Ennis, 2012). An adolescent may value watching movies or reading novels for the sheer pleasure of these activities.

The value that children place in schoolwork changes developmentally. In the elementary grades, children primarily choose activities that are interesting and enjoyable. As they reach adolescence and proceed through the secondary grades, they increasingly choose activities that, in their minds at least, will be instrumental for achieving personal goals (Eccles, Wigfield, & Schiefele, 1998; Wigfield, Tonks, & Eccles, 2004). The value that students place in school is critical during the older adolescent years when students have the option to leave school. When high school students fail to see academic achievement as helping them in the future, they are at risk for dropping out of school (Legault, Green-Demers, & Pelletier, 2006).

Over time, children internalize the desire to engage in activities promoted by adults. As children grow older, most adopt at least some of the values and priorities of the people around them. Such **internalized motivation** typically develops gradually, perhaps in the sequence depicted in Figure 13.2 (R. M. Ryan & Deci, 2009). Initially, children engage in some activities primarily because of the external consequences that result. Students may do schoolwork to earn praise or avoid being punished for poor grades. With time other people's approval becomes increasingly important to children. Eventually children internalize the "pressure" to perform certain activities and see these activities as important in their own right. Such internalization of values is most likely to occur if adults do the following:

- Engage in valued activities themselves.
- Provide a warm, supportive, and structured environment for children.
- Offer enough autonomy that children feel self-determining.

(Eisenberg, Duckworth, Spinrad, & Valiente, 2014; J. E. Jacobs, Davis-Kean, Bleeker, Eccles, & Malanchuk, 2005; R. M. Ryan, Connell, & Grolnick, 1992; R. M. Ryan & Deci, 2000; K. M. Sheldon, 2013)

FIGURE 13.2 Emergence of internalized motivation.

Children shift from external pressure to internal motivation in certain endeavors.

Source: Based on Ryan, R. M., & Deci, E. L. (2009). Promoting self-determined school engagement. In K. R. Wentzel & A. Wigfield (Eds.), *Handbook of motivation at school* (pp. 171–195). New York, NY: Routledge.

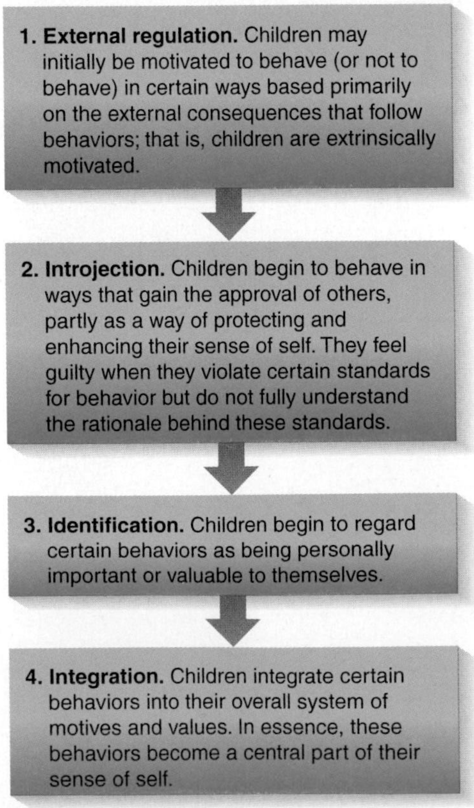

1. **External regulation.** Children may initially be motivated to behave (or not to behave) in certain ways based primarily on the external consequences that follow behaviors; that is, children are extrinsically motivated.
2. **Introjection.** Children begin to behave in ways that gain the approval of others, partly as a way of protecting and enhancing their sense of self. They feel guilty when they violate certain standards for behavior but do not fully understand the rationale behind these standards.
3. **Identification.** Children begin to regard certain behaviors as being personally important or valuable to themselves.
4. **Integration.** Children integrate certain behaviors into their overall system of motives and values. In essence, these behaviors become a central part of their sense of self.

Some of our readers may realize that internalized motivation sounds similar to intrinsic motivation. Certainly internalized motivation is a *form* of intrinsic motivation in that it comes from inside the child rather than from things in the here-and-now environment. But in one important way it is different from other forms of intrinsic motivation. Intrinsic motivation arises spontaneously within the child (e.g., curiosity about an intriguing object) and can increase or decrease unpredictably. In contrast, because internalized motivation eventually becomes an integral part of a child's sense of self, it remains fairly stable and dependable over time (Otis, Grouzet, & Pelletier, 2005; Reeve, Deci, & Ryan, 2004; R. M. Ryan & Deci, 2009).

Intrinsic motivation for learning school subject matter declines during the school years. Young children are often eager to learn new things at school. Sometime in elementary school, children become less intrinsically motivated to learn classroom topics (Corpus, McClintic-Gilbert, & Hayenga, 2009; Gillet, Vallerand, & Lafrenière, 2012; Spinath & Steinmayr, 2012). Intrinsic motivation may become especially low when youngsters are anxious, such as when they make the transitions to middle and high school (Eccles & Roeser, 2009; Wigfield, Byrnes, & Eccles, 2006). Intrinsic interest in academic subjects declines further in high school (Gnambs & Hanfstingl, 2016).

The decline in intrinsic motivation for academic subjects appears to be due to several factors. As children move through the grade levels, evidence mounts that they are not necessarily as competent as some of their peers, and with this awareness they may shy away from activities for which they have little sense of competence (Gnambs, & Hanfstingl, 2016; Harter, 1992, 1996; Wigfield et al., 2006). Frequent reminders of the importance of good grades for promotion, graduation, and college admission can actually undermine students' intrinsic motivation and sense of self-determination (Deci & Ryan, 1992; Eccles & Roeser, 2009). In addition, as young people grow older, they may become increasingly impatient with highly structured, repetitive activities, especially those delivered in a take-it-or-leave-it fashion (Battistich, Solomon, Kim, Watson, & Schaps, 1995; Headden, 2013). The following interview with a high school student named Alfredo illustrates this last point:

Adult: Do you think your classes are interesting?

Alfredo: Some of them are. But some of them are boring. You go to the same class every day and you just do the same type of work every day. Like biology, I like [the teacher of this] class. She's about the only one I like. And last year I had the same problem. The only class I liked last year was science. . . . We used to do different things every day . . . but like classes like Reading, you go inside, read a story with the same person every day. That's boring.

Adult: That's boring? So will you just not show up?

Alfredo: No, I'll go but I won't do nothing sometimes. (dialogue from Way, 1998, p. 198)

OBSERVATION GUIDELINES

Recognizing Intrinsic Motivation in Children's Behaviors

CHARACTERISTIC	LOOK FOR	EXAMPLE	IMPLICATION
Inquisitiveness	• *Eagerness to explore* and learn • *Fascination* with objects, other people, or both • *Frequent thoughtful questions* • *Lack of concern* about external rewards for learning	Jamie often takes great interest in the new toys he finds at preschool. He is especially drawn to objects that come apart and can be reassembled.	Pique children's curiosity with puzzling situations, unusual phenomena, and opportunities to explore in a safe environment.
High Self-Efficacy	• *Confidence* in executing a series of actions and obtaining desired results • *Obvious pleasure during learning* • *Eagerness to tackle challenging topics* and activities • *Willingness* to make mistakes	Luana delights in tackling the brainteasers that her math teacher occasionally assigns for extra credit.	Give children the support they need to succeed at challenging tasks. Use evaluation procedures that do not penalize mistakes.
Autonomy	• *Pursuit of self-chosen activities* • *Willingness to engage in minimally structured tasks* • *Sensitivity to issues with control*	Mark, Reggie, and Cynthia form a rock band and practice together every chance they get. They actively seek out "gigs" at school and in the community.	Provide opportunities for children to pursue self chosen activities. Give them only as much structure as they need to achieve learning outcomes.
Effective Learning Strategies	• *Focus on making sense of subject matter*, rather than on rote memorization of facts • *Persistence* in trying to solve difficult problems and understand complex ideas • *Practice of learning strategies*, such as elaboration and visualization of new material and giving extra attention to difficult ideas	Lenesia reads an assigned chapter in her geography textbook. Despite reading the section on mountain formation several times, she remains uncertain about how folded mountains form. The following day she asks her teacher to explain the process.	In instruction and assessment activities, emphasize genuine understanding and integration of the subject matter, rather than rote memorization of isolated facts. Explicitly teach learning strategies and methods for monitoring their effectiveness.
Long-Term Interests	• *Consistent selection of a particular topic* when choices are given • *Frequent initiation of activities* in a particular domain	Whenever his after-school group goes to the local library, Connor looks for books about military battleships and aircraft.	Relate subject matter to children's interests. Give them occasional choices regarding topics they study and methods for demonstrating their knowledge.
Priorities	• *Consistent pursuit of certain activities* and disregard of alternatives • *Apparent adoption of other people's values* (e.g., a strong work ethic) as one's own, reflecting internalized motivation	Audrey is clearly frustrated when unexpected events at home prevent her from doing an assignment as thoroughly as she'd like. "Even though I got an A," she says later, "I didn't do as well as I *could* have with more time."	Encourage activities that will be in youngsters' best interest over the long run. Do so in a warm, supportive environment in which youngsters have input into decision making.

Despite the typical downward trend in intrinsic motivation, some students remain interested in academic subjects throughout the school years, especially if they have internalized the importance of school learning, encounter optimal levels of challenge, are reasonably successful, and recognize the relevance of academic concepts for their interests (Eccles & Roeser, 2009; Froiland & Oros, 2014; Garon-Carrier et al., 2016; Otis et al., 2005). Virtually all children have intrinsic motivation for *some* activities—perhaps for skateboarding, dancing, or playing electronic games. The Observation Guidelines table "Recognizing Intrinsic Motivation in Children's Behaviors" on page 501 lists characteristics and behaviors to look for.

The interplay between extrinsic and intrinsic motivation affects academic learning. Intrinsic and extrinsic motivations develop hand in hand and occasionally interact such that one or the other takes precedence. A girl who originally likes to dance for the challenge and pleasure of movement may become increasingly motivated by accolades from her parents, instructor, and the audience. A boy who is at first dependent on reinforcement for good behavior may ultimately decide that he likes to cooperate on his own accord. The Basic Developmental Issues table "Contrasting Extrinsic and Intrinsic Motivation" explains how these two types of motivation relate to children's growth.

The combinations of intrinsic and extrinsic motivators that impel children's performance set the stage for their future efforts. It is an experienced teacher, for sure, who can adeptly capitalize on children's intrinsic interests, nurture their internalized motivations, and manage the classroom without appearing too controlling. Later in this chapter, we give you recommendations for using effective motivational strategies. For now, keep in mind that there are connections among intrinsic motivation, extrinsic motivation, and self-regulation. Children who have been encouraged to explore their personal interests as well as exhibit good conduct at school are generally ready to try self-regulatory skills—to set learning goals, plan, carry out steps toward task completion, solve problems as they arise, and evaluate progress. The techniques we summarized previously, such as giving children independence and teaching them skills in self-monitoring, self-instructions, self-motivation, and self-evaluation, promote strategic learning.

BASIC DEVELOPMENTAL ISSUES

Contrasting Extrinsic and Intrinsic Motivation

ISSUE	EXTRINSIC MOTIVATION	INTRINSIC MOTIVATION
Nature and Nurture	Reinforcement is a strong influence on children's behavior. Primary reinforcers satisfy inborn and presumably inherited needs (e.g., hunger, thirst). Secondary reinforcers acquire reinforcing effects through association with primary reinforcers.	Children have a natural curiosity about the world. Desires to feel competent and resolve inconsistencies are inborn. Other factors that contribute to intrinsic motivation, such as confidence in a particular ability, depend on experience.
Universality and Diversity	By and large, primary reinforcers are universal. Secondary reinforcers (e.g., praise) are *learned*; thus, their effectiveness differs from child to child. Individual differences also exist in the types of rewards children find desirable.	Innate sources of motivation, such as curiosity and the need to feel competent, are universal, as is the goal-directed nature of human behavior. Yet individuals have diverse interests, values, and goals.
Qualitative and Quantitative Change	Children typically improve in delay of gratification, a trend that reflects quantitative change. Rewiring of the brain during adolescence temporarily reduces self-control in situations of heightened emotion. Children change qualitatively in responses to potential awards. A child who appreciates a teacher's praise in elementary school may later, as an adolescent, *avoid* compliments due to fear of peer ridicule.	As a qualitative change, children shift from pursuing their own interests to internalizing some of the priorities and values of people around them. As a quantitative trend, intrinsic motivation for learning subject matter declines over the school years.

Summary

Motivation energizes, directs, and sustains behavior. It can be either extrinsic (evoked largely by the external consequences that behaviors bring) or intrinsic in focus (emanating from characteristics within a person or inherent in a task being performed). On average, children who are intrinsically motivated use more effective learning strategies and achieve at higher levels than those who are extrinsically motivated.

One key factor in extrinsic motivation is the extent to which either primary reinforcers (things that satisfy built-in biological needs) or secondary reinforcers (things that have become reinforcing through frequent association with other reinforcing consequences) are offered contingently to the appearance of various behaviors. With age, children become increasingly able to forgo small, immediate rewards in favor of larger, delayed ones. An additional source of extrinsic motivation is punishment: Children tend to avoid behaviors that have previously led to unpleasant consequences either for themselves or for others.

Research on intrinsic motivation has implications for fostering children's perceptions of competence and control. The principles of reinforcement are invaluable to professionals, especially in managing groups of children. Throughout their work, educators strive to maintain an orderly environment that is conducive to learning yet also makes self-regulation a priority.

MyLab Education Self-Check 13.2

Goals and Explanations

13.3 Describe the kinds of goals children set and the explanations they make for how well they achieve their goals.

Psychologists believe that human beings are purposeful in nature. Children set goals and choose behaviors they hope will achieve their desired ends (Boekaerts, 2009; Dweck & Elliott, 1983; E. Higgins & Scholer, 2015). Some goals ("I want to finish reading my dinosaur book") are transitory desires. Others ("I want to be a paleontologist") are enduring. Seeing purpose in activity also extends to interpretations of performance and achievement. Children are prompted to explain to themselves why they accomplished a goal and why, in other circumstances, they struggled without meeting it.

Development of Goals

Short-term goals emerge in the first year of life. When one end of a string is attached to a 2-month-old baby's foot and the other to a mobile, the baby soon realizes that foot motion makes the mobile move (Mash, Bornstein, & Banerjee, 2014; Rovee-Collier, 1999; Rovee-Collier & Cuevas, 2009). The infant begins to shake his or her foot vigorously, apparently as a way to attain interesting visual displays. As infants develop their motor skills (reaching, grabbing, crawling, etc.), they become capable of getting things they want. The "terrible twos" that we touched on earlier is a manifestation of a surging drive to achieve personal objectives. Babies also learn to coordinate their intentions with those of others (e.g., wishing to share a book with Mommy or explore a new toy together with Daddy; Tomasello & Gonzalez-Cabrera, 2017).

As children mature neurologically, they pursue longer-term goals. Being happy and healthy, doing well in school, learning about the world, getting along with peers, bringing honor to the family, and having a romantic partner are just a few of the possibilities (M. E. Ford, 1996; Schutz, 1994; Taffoni et al., 2014). Children also progressively discriminate among objectives and pursue multiple ends simultaneously. For example, whereas a third-grade boy simply wants to join a summer baseball team, a year later he wants to stay on the team, improve his batting average, and play shortstop (Bürger & Schmitt, 2017). Let's examine two categories of goals that are important at school, achievement goals and social goals, after which we delve deeper into developmental changes in goal-directed activities and children's perceptions of their accomplishments and struggles.

Achievement Goals

Students have a range of reasons for wanting to achieve at school. **Achievement goal theory** is a conceptual framework for distinguishing adaptive and maladaptive motivations for academic success (Dweck, 1986; Hornstra, Majoor, & Peetsma, 2017; Nicholls, 1984; Pintrich, 2003).

In the opening case study, Sara is primarily concerned with constructing a kite that flies well, and she redesigns it three times to make it more aerodynamic. She doesn't mind occasional stumbling blocks: "I mean everybody learns from their mistakes. I know I do" (D. K. Meyer et al., 1997, p. 511). Amy sticks with her initial design, one that is easy to make but never gets off the ground. She says that she is primarily concerned with pleasing her teacher and parents, acknowledges that she rarely takes risks if a good grade is at stake, and then adds, "I feel lazy because I don't like to make challenges for myself, to make goals. I just like to . . . do it as I go along, not make goals or challenges" (D. K. Meyer et al., 1997, p. 510).

Both girls want to do well in school; that is, they both have *achievement goals*. However, their reasons for wanting to do well are quite different. Sara has a **mastery goal**: She wants to acquire new knowledge related to kite construction, and to do so she must inevitably make a few mistakes. Amy has a **performance goal**: She wants to present herself as competent in the eyes of others and so tries to avoid making mistakes (Dweck & Master, 2009; Mega, Ronconi, & De Beni, 2014; Nicholls, 1984).[3]

Considerable research indicates that with most academic challenges, mastery goals are optimal. To the extent that students have mastery goals, they engage in the very activities that will help them learn: They pay attention at school, study hard, and learn from their mistakes. Furthermore, they have a healthy perspective on learning, effort, and failure: They realize that learning is a process of trying hard, gaining knowledge from mistakes, and persevering despite temporary setbacks (E. M. Anderman & Maehr, 1994; Lüftenegger, van de Schoot, Schober, Finsterwald, & Spiel, 2014).

Especially as they grow older, children often focus on one of two performance goals. In a **performance-approach goal**, the focus is on achieving positive outcomes, such as good grades, adult approval, or respect from classmates. In a **performance-avoidance goal**, the focus is more on *avoiding undesirable* outcomes, such as exhibiting poor performance in public or being the subject of peer ridicule. Performance goals sometimes have an element of social comparison, in that children are concerned with how their accomplishments match up to those of their peers (A. J. Elliot & McGregor, 2000; Maehr & Zusho, 2009).

When children in Western societies pursue performance goals—especially those with performance-*avoidance* themes—they may be so concerned about how others evaluate them that they shy away from challenging tasks that could help them master new skills (Dweck, 1986; Schweinle, Berg, & Sorenson, 2013; Urdan, 1997). Performance-*approach* goals are a mixed bag: They sometimes have positive effects, spurring children on to achieve at high levels, possibly because they embody a desire to improve a skill and an interest in how classmates are accomplishing this goal (Harackiewicz, Barron, Pintrich, Elliot, & Thrash, 2002; Linnenbrink, 2005; Maehr & Zusho, 2009). The disadvantage of performance-approach goals is that a concentration on the consequences of achievement distracts them from using effective learning strategies.

When children in non-Western societies pursue achievement, other considerations come into play. Mastery goals appear to have the same meaning across cultures but performance goals can vary in repercussions (R. B. King, 2016; Y. Qu & Pomerantz, 2015). Performance-avoidance goals, which have negative effects in many children, reflect a concern for not bringing dishonor to the family in collectivist societies. You may recall from other readings that collectivist societies hold high priority for respect within the family, whereas individualist societies emphasize autonomy and individual accomplishment. Failing publicly brings dishonor to loved ones in the former culture and shame to self in the latter.

[3]You may sometimes see the term *learning goal* or *task involvement* instead of *mastery goal* and the term *ego involvement* instead of *performance goal* (e.g., Dweck & Elliott, 1983).

Mastery goals, performance-approach goals, and performance-avoidance goals are not necessarily mutually exclusive, probably in any society. On many occasions children have two or even all three of these aspirations (Covington & Müeller, 2001; Hornstra et al., 2017; Meece & Holt, 1993). Most young children seem to be primarily concerned with mastery goals. But by the time they reach second grade, American students begin to show signs of having performance goals as well, and such goals become increasingly prevalent as they move into middle and high school (Eccles & Midgley, 1989; Nicholls, Cobb, Yackel, Wood, & Wheatley, 1990). The greater emphasis on performance goals at older ages is due partly to growing awareness of how one's performance compares with that of peers and to an increasing focus on grades and test scores at upper grade levels (Bounoua et al., 2012; Duchesne & Ratelle, 2010; Nicholls et al., 1990).

MyLab Education
Video Explanation 13.2
Are mastery goals possible in a calculus class? Jennifer McDaniel, an AP calculus teacher, motivates her students with primarily mastery goals and secondarily performance goals.

Social Goals

Human beings have a basic *need for relatedness*—they want to feel socially connected with, and get the love and respect of, other people. For infants and toddlers, this need is reflected in attempts to engage other people by crying, smiling, eye contact, imitation, and social exchanges. For school-aged children and adolescents, it may be reflected in the high priority they put on interacting with friends, sometimes at the expense of finishing chores, schoolwork, or other assigned tasks (Rodkin, Ryan, Jamison, & Wilson, 2013; Wigfield, Eccles, Mac Iver, Reuman, & Midgley, 1991). In the following example, 15-year-old Greg reveals the importance of social relationships in his life at school:

> Interviewer: What do you like best about school?
> Greg: Lunch.
> Interviewer: Lunch?
> Greg: All the social aspects. . . . Just friends and cliques. . . .

Like Greg, many high school students find the nonacademic aspects of school to be the most enjoyable parts of the day (Otis et al., 2005).

Consistent with their need for relatedness, children are apt to have a variety of **social goals**, perhaps including the following:

- Forming and maintaining friendly or intimate relationships with other people
- Gaining other people's approval
- Helping one another achieve their goals
- Becoming part of a mutually supportive peer group
- Achieving status and prestige within the group
- Meeting social obligations and keeping interpersonal commitments
- Assisting and supporting others, and ensuring their welfare (Beier, Over, & Carpenter, 2014; Berndt & Keefe, 1996; Dowson & McInerney, 2001; M. E. Ford & Smith, 2009)

MyLab Education
Video Example 13.6
Find Developmental Meaning
What does 15-year-old Greg like most about school? Greg talks about social contacts.

Young people's social goals affect their behavior in the classroom and in other group settings. Those who are seeking friendly relationships with peers or are concerned about others' welfare may enjoy such activities as cooperative learning and peer tutoring (Allodi, 2010; Dowson & McInerney, 2001; R. King, McInerney, & Watkins, 2012). If they want to gain adults' attention and approval, they are apt to strive for good grades and shoot for performance goals (Hinkley, McInerney, & Marsh, 2001). Those concerned with looking good in front of peers might study hard or not, depending on academic accomplishments of the peers they wish to impress.

Development of Aspirations

Children's goals advance along three dimensions. The first shift is the transition from simple to complex. The single desires of infancy are gradually transformed into multiple goals across different areas. In the school years, children are likely to juggle several distinct aims. Sometimes they find activities that allow them to achieve several goals simultaneously. They might satisfy both achievement goals and social goals by forming a study group to prepare for an exam. At other times they may believe they have to abandon one goal to satisfy the other (Boekaerts, 2009; Phelan, Yu, & Davidson, 1994).

Teachers regularly encounter students' complex goal orientations and realize they need to help students amend or make the best of goal combinations. A few youngsters who want to do well in school may choose not to perform at their best when friends don't value academic achievement. Teachers may encourage them to affiliate with different peers in an extracurricular setting, put them in a leadership position with younger children, enlist their service in a community project, or otherwise enlist their collaboration with nondeviant peers. The instructional and management demands are also worth the teacher's review. Students are more likely to try hard when assignments entice them to learn new skills (thus encouraging mastery), when they have occasional group projects (thus helping them meet social goals), and when the evaluation system allows for mistakes (thus helping them meet performance goals) (Midgley, 2002).

The second dimension of developmental change embodies an increase in reflection about goals. Children are at first spontaneous in their intentional behavior and gradually become more deliberate. For example, as students pursue multiple goals, they think about the demands for, and tradeoffs with, certain goal combinations. Students with mastery goals may find that the demands of school lead them to focus on performance goals (e.g., getting good grades) rather than studying the subject matter as thoroughly as they'd like. Brian, a junior high school student, expresses his ambivalence about striving for performance goals over mastery goals:

> I sit here and I say, "Hey, I did this assignment in five minutes and I still got an A on it." I still have a feeling that I could do better, and it was kind of cheap that I didn't do my best and I still got this A. . . . I think probably it might lower my standards eventually, which I'm not looking forward to at all. . . . I'll always know, though, that I have it in me. It's just that I won't express it that much. (S. Thomas & Oldfather, 1997, p. 119)

Finally, students shift from focusing on desires in the here and now to mobilizing multi-step plans for achieving future goals. Young children imagine what they might do in the months, years, and decades ahead, but they frequently change their mind about plans. For example, a 4-year-old may want to be a firefighter one week and professional basketball player the next. Older children are more capable of looking realistically at the future. In the later elementary school years, children begin to formulate and perseverate with long-term goals, perhaps going to college, becoming a musician, or having children (Harter, 1999; Oyserman & Markus, 1993; Usinger & Smith, 2010). These intentions are important because they affect motivations at school and upcoming career decisions.

The process of career development can be quite lengthy and requires support along the way. Children initially absorb information about typical occupations held by men and women in their society (R. B. Miller & Brickman, 2004). A little later, perhaps in middle childhood and early adolescence, children speculate about careers that seem feasible for them (Bandura, 1986). These initial interests are by no means firm commitments but, rather, are general judgments of potentially desirable jobs. Young people's selections are based in part on their perceptions of what they like and are capable of doing (e.g., whether they enjoy working with people or have the mental discipline for software development). Young people consider prevalent jobs in their community, costs of training or college, approval from peers, and proficiency in mathematics or other crucial subjects (Beal & Crockett, 2013). By mid- to late adolescence, many (although by no means all) young people settle in on a narrower range of careers (Marcia, 1980). Such preferences allow for serious steps in career exploration, such as selecting engineering classes necessary for admission into flight school.

Children's Explanations for Performance

In the opening case study, Amy had not gotten her kite to fly. Even though she has put little effort into conceiving and constructing the kite, she chalks up her failure to insufficient wind and speculates that a successful kite would have been a matter of luck. In contrast, Sara, who has created a more aerodynamic kite, takes ownership of both her success ("I knew that I could really do it") and her little failures along the way ("I mean, everybody learns from their mistakes"; Meyer et al., 1997, p. 511).

Like Amy and Sara, other children are driven to make sense of their accomplishments and setbacks. In part because of their past experiences in an area—for example, in mathematics, literacy, a second language, soccer, or basketball—children develop beliefs, ideas, and implicit theories about personal abilities, success in overcoming difficulties, and prospects for achievement next time. Scholars concerned with motivation have examined how children conceptualize their achievement and the implications of these beliefs for their performance, persistence, and learning strategies. Let's examine the types of explanations children make, the implications of these interpretations, and their developmental progressions:

Children form a variety of **attributions** *about the causes of events in their lives.* They develop beliefs about why they do well or poorly on classroom assignments, why they are popular or have trouble making friends, why they are skilled athletes or total klutzes, and so on. They may attribute their successes and failures to such factors as aptitude (how smart or proficient they are), effort (how hard they're trying), other people (how well an instructor teaches or likes them), task difficulty (how easy or hard something is), luck, mood, illness, fatigue, or physical appearance. Such attributions differ from one another in three general ways (Frijters et al., 2018; Pasta, Mendola, Longobardi, Prino, & Gastaldi, 2013; Roque, Lemos, & Gonçalves, 2014; Weiner, 1986, 2000, 2004):

- *Internal versus external.* Children may attribute the causes of events to factors within themselves (*internal* things) or to factors outside themselves (*external* things). In the opening case study, Sara's attributions are internal, whereas Amy's are mostly external.
- *Stable versus unstable.* Children may believe either that events are due to *stable* factors, which probably won't change much in the near future, or to *unstable* factors, which do vary from one occasion to the next. Sara attributes her success to her own relatively stable ability ("I knew that I could really do it"). In contrast, Amy's explanations of "not enough wind" and "beginner's luck" are based on unstable factors that change unpredictably.
- *Controllable versus uncontrollable.* Children may attribute events to *controllable* factors, which they can influence and change, or to *uncontrollable* factors, which they cannot influence. Sara clearly sees herself in charge of her success ("I knew I could put this together really well, 'cause I had a lot of confidence in myself"), whereas Amy has no control over weather conditions or a lucky break.

Children's attributions are self-constructed *interpretations* that don't always match reality. In general, children attribute their successes to internal causes (e.g., high ability, hard work) and their failures to external causes (e.g., bad luck, other people's behaviors; Marsh, 1990a; Whitley & Frieze, 1985). By patting themselves on the back for the things they do well and putting the blame elsewhere for poor performance, they maintain a sense of competence (Clifford, 1990; Frijters et al., 2018; S. G. Paris & Byrnes, 1989). Yet youngsters are most likely to be successful over the long run when they attribute successes and failures alike to *internal and controllable factors*—that is, to things they are doing or might do differently.

Children increasingly distinguish among different causes. Up until age 5 or 6, children don't discriminate among the possible causes of their successes and failures—effort, ability, luck, task difficulty, and so on (S. Graham & Williams, 2009; Nicholls, 1990). Especially troublesome for young children is the distinction between effort and ability. At about age 6, children begin to recognize that effort and ability are separate qualities. At this point they believe that people who try hardest are those who have the greatest ability and that effort is the primary determiner of successful outcomes. At about age 9, they begin to understand that effort and ability can compensate for each other: Students with less ability may have to exert greater effort to achieve the same outcomes as their more able peers. By about age 13, children clearly differentiate between effort and ability. They realize that people differ both in their capacity to perform a task and in the effort they exert. They also realize that a lack of ability sometimes precludes success no matter how much exertion—that some people simply don't have what it takes to accomplish certain things.

Preparing for Your Licensure Examination

Your teaching test might ask you about the role that attributions play in achievement.

Children settle into patterns of making certain kinds of attributions. When young people have frequent success in new endeavors, they gain confidence that they can master a variety of tasks. They attribute their accomplishments to their own ability and effort and have an *I can do it* attitude known as a **mastery orientation**. Yet other youngsters, especially those who encounter a consistent string of failures, become increasingly pessimistic about their chances for future success. They develop an *I can't do it* attitude known as **learned helplessness**.

Even when children with a mastery orientation and those with learned helplessness initially have equal ability, those with a mastery orientation behave in ways that cause higher achievement over the long run. In particular, they set ambitious goals, seek out new challenges, and persist in the face of obstacles. Children with learned helplessness behave quite differently. Because they underestimate their ability, they set goals they can easily accomplish, avoid challenges that might enhance their learning, and respond to failure in counterproductive ways (e.g., giving up quickly; Altermatt & Broady, 2009; Seligman, 1991; Ulusoy & Duy, 2013).

Occasionally preschoolers develop learned helplessness about a particular activity if they consistently fail at it, and they may conclude that they are basically "bad" or "dumb" children (Altermatt & Broady, 2009; Burhans & Dweck, 1995). By age 5 or 6, a few children begin to show an inclination toward learned helplessness. They express little confidence about tackling challenging tasks and quickly abandon activities at which they initially struggle (McMillan & Jarvis, 2013; D. I. Ziegert, Kistner, Castro, & Robertson, 2001). By and large, however, children seldom exhibit extreme forms of learned helplessness before age 8, perhaps because they still believe that success is due largely to their own efforts (Eccles et al., 1998; Lockhart, Chang, & Story, 2002; S. G. Paris & Cunningham, 1996). Feelings of helplessness are more common in adolescence. Some adolescents believe they have no control over things that happen to them and are at a loss on how to achieve (Ciarrochi & Heaven, 2008; C. Peterson, Maier, & Seligman, 1993).

Children develop outlooks on their capacity for getting better at skills. Some children develop a **growth mind-set** (previously known as an *incremental view* of ability), thinking that they will almost certainly become proficient in an activity if they try hard, use good strategies, and persevere. Others have a **fixed mind-set** (previously known as an *entity view*), believing that their capacity to perform various tasks is an inherited trait or is in some other way beyond their control (Dweck, 2000, 2017; Dweck & Master, 2009).

The distinction between growth and fixed explanations, spearheaded by American psychologist **Carol Dweck** and her colleagues, has garnered much attention in recent years. According to Dweck, mind-sets function as personal theories that emerge as children take on learning challenges (Dweck, 2017). Children who find the process, including challenges and inevitable mistakes, intrinsically enjoyable develop a growth mind-set. They come to see their intelligence as something that they can improve, and they relish the process of doing so. Other children who dislike making errors and find learning to be a means to an end develop a fixed mind-set. For these children, it is risky and unpleasant to be faced with an intellectual challenge. They might find—and others could notice—that they simply do not have what it takes to succeed. Children with these two different mind-sets are not necessarily different in their actual intelligence, yet those with a growth mind-set use more active self-regulatory learning processes (e.g., setting goals and using mastery-oriented learning strategies) and achieve at higher levels academically (Burnette, O'Boyle, VanEpps, Pollack, & Finkel, 2013; Dweck, 2017)

The developmental story by which children embrace one mind-set or another is still being revealed, but some trends have been identified. In the elementary grades, children attribute their successes to effort and hard work, and so they are usually optimistic about their chances for success and may work harder when they fail. By adolescence, students attribute success and failure more to ability and other factors they see as beyond their control. To some degree, then, children move from growth mind-sets in the elementary years to a fixed mind-set in adolescence (Dweck, 2000; Nicholls, 1990; Throndsen, 2011). Probably for this reason, adolescents are more discouraged by stumbling blocks than happens with elementary school children (Eccles & Wigfield, 1985; Pressley, Borkowski, & Schneider, 1987).

Yet there are also individual differences and domain effects in mind-sets. Some young people continue to hold a growth mind-set throughout high school. Others gradually discover the impact of hard work and effective learning strategies as they move through high school. Adolescents who have a growth mind-set are more likely to have mastery goals, seek out challenges that will enhance their competence, take reasonable risks with new strategies, try new approaches, persist in the face of difficulty, and achieve at high levels (Blackwell, Trzesniewski, & Dweck, 2007; Dweck, 2017; Dweck, Mangels, & Good, 2004; Revelle, 2013). You may also notice that children can hold different mind-sets in different areas (Dweck, 2017). Hence, a girl might have a growth mind-set in mathematics and a fixed mind-set about her athletic ability.

*Experience, reflection, and socialization play a part in attributions, mind-sets, and other mental frameworks***.** To a significant degree, children's attributions are the result of their previous successes and failures (Covington, 1987; Hornstra, van der Veen, Peetsma, & Volman, 2013; Pasta et al., 2013). Those who usually succeed when they give a task their best shot are likely to believe that success is due to internal factors such as effort and smart strategies. Those who frequently fail despite considerable effort are likely to believe that success is due to something beyond their control—perhaps an innate weakness or to such external factors as bad luck or a teacher's arbitrary judgments.

Children also pick up on other people's beliefs about why they have done well or poorly (Cimpian, Arce, Markman, & Dweck, 2007; S. Graham & Williams, 2009; Hareli & Weiner, 2002). Sometimes others' attributions are quite explicit, as the following statements illustrate:

- "That's wonderful. Your hard work has really paid off, hasn't it?" *(effort)*
- "You did it! You're so smart!" *(fairly stable ability)*
- "Hmmm, maybe this just isn't something you're good at." *(ability once again)*
- "Maybe you're just having a bad day." *(luck)*

A combination of observing chronic failure in oneself and hearing unflattering attributions from others can be devastating, as a journal entry by a high school student with an undiagnosed learning disability reveals:

> When I told one teacher in jr. high that I thought I had dyslexia, he told me that I was just lazy. Yeah, right! Me, lazy? I would end up with the same routine before every vocabulary test or important assignment. I would spend a week trying to memorize words that, no matter what I did, I couldn't spell right. On test days, I would turn in the test, and get an F. All I could do was hope that I'd do better on the next one.
>
> It only got worse in high school, where there were more spelling and essay tests, with more complicated words that seemed too impossible to memorize. Finally, I just started to think, "Why should I even try? I am just going to end up with an 'F' anyway." It seems that an "F" was going to symbolize what I would end up in the future. (The Freedom Writers, 1999, p. 147)

In some instances, adults communicate attributions indirectly. When adults criticize and express anger about children's poor performance, they imply that children have the ability to master the task and simply aren't trying hard enough. When they instead express pity, they imply that low ability is the reason for the failure (Vlachou, Eleftheriadou, & Metallidou, 2014; Weiner, 1984). Adults communicate low ability, too, when they praise easy successes, provide unneeded assistance on easy tasks, or allow children to abandon challenging ones (Droe, 2013; Hokoda & Fincham, 1995; Schunk & Pajares, 2004).

Interventions targeting children's mind-sets have proved to be influential. In one investigation, Dweck and her colleagues conducted a training program with seventh-graders in mathematics. A group of students who were taught to use study skills and informed about how the brain changes with practice, just as muscles strengthen with exercise, were compared with a similar group of students who received study skill practice alone (Blackwell et al., 2007). The first group of students increased in their growth mind-sets and outperformed the control group in mathematics achievement.

Motivation in a Developmental System

Children's personal characteristics and experiences affect their goals, attributions, implicit theories, and other aspects of motivation. Maturational states and personal preferences affect the tangible rewards and activities that individuals find reinforcing. Temperament partly determines inclinations to act on curiosity or, alternatively, to stay on the sidelines of activities (Keogh, 2003). Children with attention-deficit hyperactivity disorder (many of whom have poor impulse control) are apt to have difficulty delaying gratification (Chelonis et al., 2011; Curchack-Lichtin, Chacko, & Halperin, 2014). Some children with significant physical disabilities have a reduced sense of self-determination because other people play a prominent role in meeting their needs (Luckner & Sebald, 2013; Sands & Wehmeyer, 1996). Children with intellectual disabilities or learning disabilities may show signs of learned helplessness if their past efforts at school have met with failure (E. Carter, Weir, Cooney, Walter, & Moss, 2012; Hersh, Stone, & Ford, 1996).

Developmental Systems Prompt

Children's individual characteristics and experiences at home affect their motivational states, goals, attributions, and mind-sets. As you interact with children, consider the interests, values, and beliefs about achievement that they developed during their upbringing.

Children also have unique motivations associated with being boys or girls and as participants in cultural and ethnic groups. Let's examine these patterns.

Gender

Boys and girls have somewhat different motivational patterns. On average, young boys are more likely to develop interests that involve a specific topic (e.g., about frogs, dinosaurs, space travel, or a particular sport). In contrast, young girls show more interest in literacy and creative activities such as drawing and painting (J. M. Alexander et al., 2008; Baroody & Diamond, 2013; K. E. Johnson, Alexander, Spencer, Leibham, & Neitzel, 2004). In the elementary grades, boys and girls find greater or lesser value in academic domains depending, in part, on whether they view particular subjects as appropriate for their gender. Many children (but certainly not all) perceive some subjects (e.g., writing, music) to be for girls and others (e.g., math, science) to be for boys (Eccles et al., 1998; C. L. Martin & Ruble, 2010).

Generally girls are more concerned with doing well in school. They are more engaged in classroom activities, work more diligently on school assignments, and are more likely to graduate from high school (A. L. Duckworth & Seligman, 2006; Halpern, 2006). An advantage in attentional self-control seems to be part of the reason that girls earn higher grades than boys (A. L. Duckworth et al., 2015). Despite girls' higher achievement, they tend to have less confidence about their abilities. When researchers compare girls and boys who have equal achievement, they find that girls typically have higher self-efficacy in stereotypically feminine domains (e.g., reading, writing, the arts) and that boys have higher self-efficacy, especially in stereotypically masculine domains (e.g., science and mathematics; Andrade, Wang, Du, & Akawi, 2009; Diseth, Meland, & Breidablik, 2014; Wigfield et al., 2006). In addition, girls (especially high-achieving girls) are more easily discouraged by failure than are boys (Dweck, 2000). Researchers have observed a tendency for boys to attribute their successes to ability and their failures to lack of effort, thus displaying the attitude that *I know I can do this if I work at it*. Girls tend to show the reverse pattern: They attribute their successes to effort and their failures to lack of ability, believing that *I don't know whether I can keep on doing it, because I'm not very good at this type of thing*. When encountering failure, boys are apt to have a growth mind-set, and girls a fixed mind-set (they are stuck with what they have; Chedzoy & Burden, 2009; Dweck, 2000).

Preparing for Your Licensure Examination

Your teaching test might ask about gender differences in motivation.

Historically, boys had more ambitious career aspirations than did girls (Deaux, 1984; Lueptow, 1984). In recent years, many girls—especially those in Western countries—have set their sights on challenging professions (Bandura, Barbaranelli, Caprara, & Pastorelli, 2001; Lapan, Tucker, Kim, & Kosciulek, 2003). But even as traditional boundaries delineating "appropriate" professions for men and for women have begun to dissolve, many adolescents continue to limit themselves to gender-stereotypical careers (Lippa, 2002; Weisgram, Bigler, & Liben, 2010). Gender patterns in career choices are also partly due to differences in confidence in achieving in relevant domains (Bandura et al., 2001; Heilbronner, 2013; Jacobs, Lanza, Osgood, Eccles, & Wigfield, 2002). In addition, girls are more likely than boys to be attracted to helping professions (e.g., teaching, counseling) and to be concerned about balancing career with family life (Cinamon & Rich, 2014; Mahaffy & Ward, 2002).

Culture and Ethnicity

Children everywhere are naturally curious about the physical world and the society in which they live. Similarly, all children want to make at least some of their own decisions. And, of course, every child is motivated to accomplish something—whether succeeding in school, learning a second or third language, helping their family, or preparing for a future career path.

Each culture fosters motivational qualities in ways that fit with its prevailing worldviews, loyalties, and traditions. Earlier we mentioned that performance-avoidance goals have different implications in children with individualist and collectivist orientations. Another important manifestation of culture is the difference between groups in the form of their self-determination (d'Ailly, 2003; J. Kim, Schallert, & Kim, 2010). Adults in some Native American communities express confidence in young children by giving them a lot of freedom to make choices (Deyhle & LeCompte, 1999). Some African American parents believe that young children should be closely supervised because of concerns for their safety (Hale-Benson, 1986; S. B. Richman & Mandara, 2013). In some Asian cultures, young people prefer that trusted adults make important choices for them (Iyengar & Lepper, 1999; N. Zhou, Lam, & Chan, 2012).

Children from many—probably most—cultural groups place high value on getting a good education (Gallimore & Goldenberg, 2001; K. Griffin, del Pilar, McIntosh, & Griffin, 2012; Okagaki, 2001). But to some degree, different groups encourage distinct educational values. Many people in China, Japan, and Russia emphasize learning for learning's sake: With knowledge comes personal growth, better understanding of the world, and greater potential to contribute to society. Important for these cultures, too, are hard work and persistence in academic studies (Hess & Azuma, 1991; Hufton, Elliott, & Illushin, 2002; J. Li, 2006). Many students from American backgrounds are less likely to be diligent when classroom topics have little intrinsic appeal, but they often find worth in academic assignments that pique their curiosity, independent thinking, and critical analysis (Hess & Azuma, 1991; Kuhn & Park, 2005).

Preparing for Your Licensure Examination

Your teaching test might ask you how children acquire motivation in a cultural context.

Attributions for academic tasks are also socialized during everyday tasks, for example, when adults offer explanations about why children might not have succeeded at a task. Students from Asian cultures are more likely to attribute classroom success and failure to controllable factors (e.g., effort) than are students brought up in Western cultures (Muramoto, Yamaguchi, & Kim, 2009; Weiner, 2004). Thus, many Asian children are urged to try harder and be more careful.

Finally, children's cultural experiences inform them of the kinds of goals that are feasible to pursue. A girl in one community may envision herself as an astronaut, a computer programmer, or a civil engineer, whereas a girl in another community looks forward to becoming a weaver or a midwife. In the Development in Culture feature "Achievement Orientation in Tanzania," you can read about aspects of achievement perceived by a group of rural Tanzanian children.

As you have learned, motivation changes with age and also responds systematically to experience. The Developmental Trends table "Motivation at Different Age Levels" identifies motivational characteristics and the types of diversity you are likely to see in children of different age groups.

Summary

Children direct their behavior toward personal objectives and increasingly pursue long-term goals. When they enter school, most children want to do well but significant individual differences exist in how they go about achieving academic goals. Some children want to acquire new knowledge and skills (i.e., they have *mastery goals*) whereas others want to look good or avoid looking bad in front of classmates, teachers, and family (i.e., they have *performance goals*). Children's social goals are also important and can be accommodated by thoughtful teachers.

Among factors influencing children's motivation are the attributions children make regarding their successes and failures in particular activities. Children are most optimistic when they attribute both successes and failures to internal factors that they

Development in Culture

Achievement Orientation in Tanzania

How can an adult determine what a child wants to accomplish in life? Simply asking children to describe their goals is an option, but this method has disadvantages. Many children feel uncomfortable sharing private dreams and fears with a stranger. Others cannot easily respond to abstract questions about events that have not yet taken place.

Priya Nalkur, an expert in human development, was aware of difficulties in assessing children's ideas about achievement yet committed to examining these ideas in children from the Kilimanjaro region of Tanzania, Africa (Nalkur, 2009). She needed a strategy that would put children at ease, give them something concrete to respond to, and allow them to use a familiar means of expression. She decided to interact individually with children, show them pictures of people engaged in a task, and ask them to make up stories about what was going on in the pictures.

In her research, Nalkur invited children to examine three cards drawn of human figures with east African features and clothing. Picture 1 had a boy sitting at his desk and staring at a violin, Picture 2 showed a young woman carrying books and looking off into a field, and Picture 3 had a man hanging onto a suspended rope with his hand. Nalkur selected these pictures because they typically elicit motivational themes. Young people are apt to project their own desires into their interpretations of the drawings.

Nalkur encouraged children to develop stories that explained what the person in the card was doing before, during, and after the scene in the picture. She believed that the method would provide a comfortable context for children, who could focus on meaningful stimuli and create stories, a tradition that is celebrated in their culture. To further create a relaxing atmosphere, Nalkur enlisted the help of a small group of cooperating children who led warm-up games before child participants looked at the pictures and told their stories.

Anup Shah/Photodisc/Getty Images

LIVING IN THE PRESENT, PREPARING FOR THE FUTURE. This Maasai boy proudly wears the traditional clothing of his tribe. He is developing an outlook on the future that is infused with cultural values and practices.

Nalkur drew from three groups of research participants. "Street children" lived primarily on the streets, in some cases having lost parents to acquired immunodeficiency syndrome (AIDS) or leaving home themselves because of abuse. "Former street children" were those who had previously slept on the streets and had been in a shelter for at least 1 year at the time of the interview. "Schoolchildren" lived with families and attended school. Nalkur decided to include only boys in her sample because street children in Tanzania are mainly boys. One hundred eighty-three boys from ages 11 to 18 participated, with roughly a third in each of the groups.

Children's stories regularly included the theme of *maisha magumu*, a feeling of having a "difficult life"[a] (Nalkur, 2009, p. 1013). Children were affected by widespread frustration among adults regarding the local economy and its inadequate employment, health care, and education. Yet children also conveyed resilience. They demonstrated a faith in their own self-reliance and communicated a belief that they could overcome difficult challenges in life.

As you might expect, the particular achievement orientations that children expressed varied by group. Street children expressed hope in the future and in other people's obligation for making life better for them. Although their aspirations were for a bright future, the street children did not seem to know how to achieve their goals. They often talked about troubled characters who were unaware of how to get ahead. Former street children told stories about taking charge of their lives. Friends and adults outside the family played an important role. Schoolchildren told stories that linked hard work to academic achievement. They talked about jobs, performance in school, and effort in studying. The schoolchildren were aware of temptations around them and strategies for taking control of their lives, as seen in one student's story:

> There was once a young man who was a thief. Together with his friends, he made others join their behavior. He lived a very difficult life, and eventually decided to join adult education to avoid getting a bad name in the community. He became very keen in studying to have a better future. He in turn motivated his friends who were thieves to not continue with that lifestyle. He told them to continue with education so as not to have a bad reputation. Eventually, they too got educated and worked to improve the community as a whole. (12 years, Picture 3)[a] (Nalkur, 2009, p. 1023).

In her interpretations of responses, Nalkur realized that children's achievement orientations arose from experience. Street children expressed hope for protection from harm yet did not know how to achieve their goals. Former street children's emphasis on friendship may have derived from their recognition that it was primarily other children who could be counted on for affection. Finally, the schoolchildren saw a clear connection between being well educated and having a good life.

[a]Excerpt from "Achievement Orientations and Strategies: A Cultural Comparison of Tanzanian Street Children, Former Street Children, and School-Going Children" by Priya G. Nalkur, from *Journal of Cross-Cultural Psychology*, November 2009, Volume 40(6), 324–332.

DEVELOPMENTAL TRENDS

Motivation at Different Age Levels

AGE	WHAT YOU MIGHT OBSERVE	DIVERSITY	IMPLICATIONS
Infancy (Birth–2 Years)	• Curiosity about objects and people • Enthusiasm for moving body parts, handling objects, and exploring the environment through locomotion • Some goal-directed behavior as early as 3 months • Little interest in praise, especially in the first year; greater appreciation of praise after age 1	• Temperament and culture influence infants' willingness to experiment with toys. • Attachment security influences infants' exploration. • Infants with significant disabilities may show less interest in exploration than do peers without disabilities.	• Create a predictable, affectionate environment in which children feel comfortable exploring. • Provide new and unusual objects that pique children's curiosity. • Identify objects and events that can capture the interest of infants with disabilities.
Early Childhood (2–6 Years)	• Preference for small and immediate rewards over larger and delayed ones • Overconfidence about one's ability to perform new tasks • Strong motivation to learn the causal properties of objects and events • Rapidly changing, situation-dependent interests • Focus on obtaining the approval of adults more than that from peers • Focus on mastery (rather than performance) goals • Little understanding of reasons for successes and failures	• Individual differences in desires for social interaction are evident as early as 3 or 4. • Children who begin school without knowledge of colors, shapes, letters, and numbers may notice differences between their abilities and those of peers, setting the stage for weak self-efficacy. • Learned helplessness occasionally appears as early as age 4 or 5 after a history of failure. • Some children develop what becomes a stable interest.	• Provide a wide variety of interesting toys, storybooks, props for dramatic play, and other equipment. • Praise (or in some other way reinforce) desired behaviors as they occur. • Provide the guidance children need in order to experience success more often than failure. • Address delays in literacy, numeracy, self-regulation, and other school-readiness skills.
Middle Childhood (6–10 Years)	• Increasing ability to delay gratification • Emerging awareness of how one's own performance compares with that of peers; more realistic assessment of abilities • Increasing prevalence of performance goals • Increasing distinction between effort and ability as causes of success and failure; tendency to attribute successes to hard work	• As a result of low self-efficacy, children with learning delays have less intrinsic motivation to learn academic subject matter. • Some bright, talented girls are reluctant to do their best because of concerns about appearing unfeminine. • Children with certain disabilities are likely to develop learned helplessness for academic achievement.	• Communicate that with appropriate effort, strategy, and support, virtually *all* children can master academic knowledge and skills. • Focus children's attention on the progress they are making, rather than on how their performance compares to that of peers. • Stress the value of learning for the intrinsic pleasure it brings.
Early Adolescence (10–14 Years)	• Increasing interest in social activities; intensified concern with approval from peers • Declining sense of competence, often accompanying the transition to middle school or junior high • Decline in intrinsic motivation to learn school subject matter; stronger performance goals • Increasing belief that skill is the result of stable factors (e.g., inherited ability) rather than effort and practice • Growing motivation to achieve in stereotypically gender-appropriate domains	• Students who are gifted may show passions for learning in areas of interest, for example, making films or doing mathematical puzzles. • Some adolescents believe that high achievement can interfere with popularity. • Adolescents from a few ethnic groups (e.g., some from a few Asian societies) place high value on adult approval. • Some individuals develop learned helplessness in academic matters and consider dropping out of school.	• Evaluate adolescents on the basis of how well they are achieving instructional objectives, not on how well their performance compares with that of classmates. • Assign cooperative group projects that allow adolescents to interact with one another, display unique talents, and contribute to the group. • When youngsters exhibit a pattern of failure, provide needed support to become successful in endeavors.
Late Adolescence (14–18 Years)	• Ability to postpone immediate pleasures in order to gain long-term rewards • Increasing stability of interests and priorities • Increasing focus on the utilitarian value of activities • Tendency to attribute performance levels more to ability than to effort • Tentative decisions about career areas	• Girls work harder on school assignments and are more likely to graduate from high school than are boys. • Adolescents from some Asian cultures often attribute successes and failures to effort rather than to natural talent. • Many teens have career aspirations that are stereotypically gender appropriate.	• Point out the relevance of academic domains for long-term goals. • Create assignments in which adolescents can apply academic content to real-world adult tasks. • Allow teens to pursue personal interests within the context of academic domains. • Set up internships to explore career interests.

Sources: Alvarez and Booth (2014); Atun-Einy, Berger, and Scher (2013); Bandura et al. (2001); L. A. Bell (1989); Burhans and Dweck (1995); L. Coleman and Guo (2013); H. Cooper and Dorr (1995); Corpus et al. (2009); Deshler and Schumaker (1988); Dweck and Master (2009); Eccles and Midgley (1989); Eccles and Roeser (2009); Fewell and Sandall (1983); S. Graham (1989); L. Green, Fry, and Myerson (1994); Halpern (2006); Harter (1996); J. E. Jacobs et al. (2002); Jacobsen, Lowery, and DuCette (1986); K. E. Johnson et al. (2004); Juvonen (2000); Leaper and Friedman (2007); Legare (2014); Lillard (1997); Lockhart et al. (2002); Nicholls (1990); Otis et al. (2005); S. G. Paris and Cunningham (1996); Portes (1996); Rovee-Collier (1999); R. M. Ryan and Deci (2009); Schultz and Switzky (1990); Schunk and Pajares (2009); Seligman (1991); Vaughn et al. (1984); Wigfield et al. (2006); and D. I. Ziegert, Kistner, Castro, and Robertson (2001).

can control (e.g., amount of effort and use of good strategies). Ultimately, some children acquire a general *I can do it* attitude (a *mastery orientation*), whereas others acquire an *I can't do it even if I try* attitude (*learned helplessness*). Children's mind-sets about intellectual growth or fixed status are connected with their goals and learning strategies; the growth mind-set is more favorable in an achievement setting.

Children's motivational goals and beliefs are affected by personal characteristics and experiences. Children's temperaments and any disabilities they might have affect how they display their curiosity as well as their ability to delay gratification and exercise self-determination. Boys and girls exhibit a few differences in motivation, particularly in their interests, academic aspirations, and confidence. Cultural values partly determine how children express their autonomy, persist with tasks, make attributions, and form aspirations for the future. During childhood, students' goals become multifaceted, future-oriented, and intertwined with reflection.

MyLab Education Self-Check 13.3

Motivating Children at School

13.4 Summarize strategies for motivating children at school.

A common misconception about motivation is that it is something children "carry around" inside them, such that some students are consistently motivated to learn at school and others are not. As you learned with intrinsic motivation, it is true that some sources of motivation come from within. However, it's equally true that youngsters' immediate environments have dramatic effects on their motivation to learn. Such environment-dependent motivation is known as **situated motivation** (D. T. Hickey & Granade, 2004; Järvelä, Järvenoja, & Malmberg, 2012; S. G. Paris & Turner, 1994). When children are enticed to collaborate on challenging activities they have a choice in, they are likely to find pleasure and a sense of competence in task completion (Eccles, 2007; Hidi & Renninger, 2006). The following strategies are recommended for fostering situated motivation at school:

- **Focus on promoting intrinsic (rather than extrinsic) motivation.** Externally imposed consequences—praise, money, good grades, and so on—often bring about desired changes in children's behavior. Such reinforcers have disadvantages, however. Although they provide a source of extrinsic motivation, they can undermine children's *intrinsic* motivation if children perceive them to be controlling, manipulative, or in some other way limiting of their self-determination (R. M. Ryan & Deci, 2009; Vansteenkiste, Lens, & Deci, 2006). Furthermore, externally imposed reinforcers may communicate the message that assigned tasks are unpleasant chores (why else would a reinforcer be necessary?) rather than activities to be carried out for their own sake (B. A. Hennessey, 1995; Stipek, 1993).

Ideally, teachers, parents, and other adults focus children's attention *not* on the external consequences of their efforts but on the internal pleasures (enjoyment, satisfaction, pride, etc.) that accompany participation in the learning activities. Adults can also increase children's intrinsic motivation for learning important topics and skills using strategies such as these:

- Communicating enthusiasm for a topic
- Piquing curiosity with new and intriguing objects and phenomena
- Incorporating fantasy, adventure, and suspense into activities
- Creating disequilibrium by presenting puzzling phenomena
- Getting children physically involved with a topic (e.g., through role-playing or hands-on experimentation)
- Relating important skills and subject matter to children's interests and goals

- Offering choices when several alternatives will be equally effective in helping children acquire desired skills
- Accentuating children's choice in studying material (e.g., "You've selected some interesting books to read")
- Identifying areas in which each child can be especially successful.
- Encouraging children to set personal goals for learning more about subjects in which they are interested (Brophy, 2004; Froiland, Oros, Smith, & Hirchert, 2012; Martens, de Brabander, Rozendaal, Boekaerts, & van der Leeden, 2010; Patall, Cooper, & Wynn, 2008; R. M. Ryan & Deci, 2009; Schraw, Flowerday, & Lehman, 2001)

• **Enhance children's self-efficacy for mastering important knowledge and skills.** One critical way to enhance children's self-efficacy in reading, mathematics, or another academic domain is, of course, to help them achieve success in that realm—for instance, by tailoring instruction to their ability levels, scaffolding their efforts, and so on (Lodewyk & Winne, 2005; Schunk & Pajares, 2009). Another effective approach is to show them *other people's* successes. When children see peers of similar age and ability accomplish a task, they are more likely to believe that they, too, can accomplish it (Schunk & Hanson, 1985).

• **Maintain children's sense of self-determination when giving instructions.** Every group needs a few rules and procedures to ensure smooth-running activities. Similarly, teachers and other professionals must often impose restrictions on how children carry out assigned tasks. The trick is to present rules, procedures, guidelines, and structure without communicating an intention to *control* children's behavior. Instead, adults should present these things as *information*—for instance, as conditions that help children accomplish important goals (Froiland et al., 2012; Hagger, Chatzisarantis, Barkoukis, Wang, & Baranowski, 2005; R. M. Ryan & Deci, 2009). Following are examples:

- "We can make sure everyone has an equal chance to speak if we listen without interrupting."
- "I'm giving you a particular format to follow when you do your math homework. If you use this format, it will be easier for me to figure out which concepts you understand and which ones you need more help with—and I'll be able to give you better guidance."
- "Let's remember that other children will be using the same paints and brushes later today, so we need to make sure everything we use is in tip-top shape when we're done. It's important, then, that we clean the brushes thoroughly when we're done painting."
- "I'm available to give you a few hints if you need it, but see if you can work through the problems on your own before coming to me."

• **Encourage children to shoot for objectives that they can reasonably attain.** Children often respond favorably to goals they set for themselves (Boekaerts, 2009; Lens, 2001; Wentzel, 1999). Yet many children have trouble conceptualizing future accomplishments (e.g., getting a good education, going to medical school; Bandura, 1997; Husman & Freeman, 1999; Usinger & Smith, 2010). They may initially respond more favorably to short-term, concrete goals—perhaps learning a certain number of math facts in a given week, getting the next belt in karate, or earning a merit badge in a scout troop (R. B. Miller & Brickman, 2004; Schunk & Rice, 1989). By working toward a series of short-term goals, youngsters get regular feedback about progress, acquire a greater sense of self-efficacy for mastering new skills, and achieve at higher levels (Iselin, Mulvey, Loughran, Chung, & Schubert, 2012; Schunk, 1996). Children's attainment of short-term goals thus puts them closer to realizing the long-term goals they have set for their future selves. In Artifact Example 13.2, 10-year-old Amaryth outlines her goals in sports and science.

As students reach adolescence, their expanding capacity for abstract thought allows them to envision long-term goals (e.g., winning a spot on a varsity sports team or having a career in journalism). Yet perhaps as a result of low self-efficacy or limited financial resources, some set their sights quite low. Teachers and other practitioners should not only encourage these young people to think ambitiously but also convince them that high goals are achievable. When encouraging girls to consider stereotypically masculine career paths, adults might provide examples of women who have led successful lives in those careers. When encouraging teens from low-income families to think about college, adults might assist them with scholarship applications and scheduling appointments with financial aid officers.

• **Encourage mastery goals as well as (ideally even more than) performance goals.** To some degree, performance goals are inevitable. Students invariably look to their peers' performance when evaluating their own accomplishments, and many gateways into the adult world (e.g., gaining admission to college or getting a job) are competitive. In some cultures, performance goals are intertwined with respect for family. Yet teachers probably do youngsters a disservice when they focus too much on "looking good," surpassing peers, or having proud parents. When adults instead explain how certain knowledge is useful, highlight progress, and acknowledge that learning entails effort and mistakes, they are emphasizing mastery goals that will enhance achievement (Bong, 2001; Brophy, 2004; Tas & Cakir, 2014).

• **Downplay the seriousness of failures.** Students are more apt to accept responsibility for their failures—and therefore to learn from them—if adults don't make a big deal of mistakes and give them numerous opportunities to improve assignments (Ames, 1992; Dweck & Master, 2009; Katkovsky, Crandall, & Good, 1967). In some instances, adults may also find it appropriate to focus children's attention on the *processes* they use to tackle problems rather than on the final outcome of their efforts. A teacher may occasionally give instructions like these:

> It doesn't matter at all how many you get right. In fact, these problems are kind of hard. I'm just interested in learning more about what [you] think about while [you're] working on problems like these. I want you to focus on the problem and just say out loud whatever you're thinking while you're working—whatever comes into your head. (Stipek & Kowalski, 1989, p. 387)

MyLab Education

Artifact Example 13.2

Find Developmental Meaning *How does ten-year-old Amaryth describe how she worked toward goals at school?* Amaryth reports that she set the target of making at least three soccer goals in the following four weeks and went on to make five. Her second goal was to earn two As across four subject areas, and she indicated that she achieved this goal as well. She concluded that next time she could be more ambitious in setting goals and might use a calendar for keeping track of progress.

Preparing for Your Licensure Examination

Your teaching test might ask you about educational strategies for supporting children's self-determination.

• **Help youngsters meet their social goals.** One of the reasons adolescents concentrate on performance goals is that making a good impression helps them gain acceptance from peers. Adolescents encounter most of their friends at school and naturally make social goals a high priority there (B. B. Brown, Eicher, & Petrie, 1986; Rodkin, Ryan, Jamison, & Wilson, 2013; Wentzel & Wigfield, 1998). The Development-Enhancing Education feature "Helping Children Meet Their Social Goals" suggests several ways in which educators can address social needs within academic instruction.

• **Focus children's attention on trying hard, using an effective strategy, and making personal progress.** When commenting on children's successes, probably the best approach is to mention such controllable factors as effort and learning strategies (Dweck & Master, 2009; Gunderson et al., 2013; Weiner, 1984). In this way, adults provide assurance that children are certainly capable of succeeding with hard work and perseverance. A teacher might say

- "You've done very well. I can see that you've been trying very hard to get better."
- "Your project shows good strategies and a lot of hard work."

Development-Enhancing Education

Helping Children Meet Their Social Goals

Continually communicate the message that you like and respect the young people with whom you are working.

- A second-grade teacher tells a student that she saw his karate exhibition at the local mall over the weekend. "Wow! How did you learn to punch and kick like that? she asks. "How many years have you been studying karate?" (Middle Childhood)
- A high school teacher reads about a group of students at school who produce informal movies in their free time and post them on YouTube. "I watched some of your movies," he says to one of the students. "Very clever. Let me know when you post new videos." (Late Adolescence)

Plan learning tasks that involve social interaction.

- A sixth-grade social studies teacher incorporates classroom debates, small-group discussions, and cooperative learning tasks into each month's lesson plans. (Early Adolescence)
- A high school chemistry teacher forms cooperative groups for conducting experiments. Every student is assigned a role essential to the lesson—manager of equipment, recorder of notes, checker of observations, or spokesperson to the class. Students rotate through each of the roles. (Late Adolescence)

Get youngsters involved in large projects in which they must work together.

- The eighth-graders at a middle school are sharply divided socially, and some students are excluded. The school music teacher suggests that a production of the musical *You're a Good Man, Charlie Brown* become a project for the entire class. All eighth-graders are either in the cast or working on costumes, scenery, or lighting. The ambitious scope of the project and the fact that the class's efforts will be on public display instill a cohesive class spirit, with formerly popular and unpopular students working respectfully with one another. (Early Adolescence)
- An environmental studies club organizes a Green Day for the school. Students post flyers and Facebook requests for everyone to bring in objects that can be recycled, repurposed, or safely disposed. Students, teachers, and staff bring in used batteries, printer cartridges, eyeglasses, and cell phones. (Late Adolescence)

Teach youngsters approaches for presenting themselves well to others.

- A preschool teacher welcomes a new boy, Fernando, to the classroom and introduces him to the other children. After noticing that he seems to be shy, the teacher observes his exceptional skill in building intricate block structures. She encourages a few other builders to admire his work, "Look at the amazing space station Fernando is making. I bet he could use help from other engineers." (Early Childhood)
- As fourth-graders prepare for upcoming oral reports on their small-group science projects, the teacher offers suggestions for capturing the audience's interest. "You might present a puzzling question," she says. "Or you might show them something that will surprise them." (Middle Childhood)

Give praise in private when a student is sensitive to peers' reactions.

- Laura, a girl in middle school, has worked hard as student body president. Her adviser, Mr. Gomez, has observed the results of her efforts in inspiring officers to work together. Realizing that Laura would want to give credit to others in her group, Mr. Gomez takes her aside to compliment her on her initiative. (Early Adolescence)
- A high school English teacher reads a particularly creative story written by a young man who, she knows, is concerned about maintaining his "cool" image. On the second page of his story (which the student's classmates are unlikely to see), she writes, "Tony, I think your essay's good enough to enter in the state writing contest. Can we meet before or after school to talk about the contest?" (Late Adolescence)

Respect individual differences.

- A preschool teacher notices that some of his students have a greater need for social contact than others. Some enjoy cooperative play activities, whereas others are more interested in experimenting with physical objects. He is careful not to interrupt those happily engrossed in play or experimentation. (Early Childhood)
- An elementary student whose parents recently divorced is getting accustomed to the new routines. His father picks him up on Mondays through Wednesdays and his mother on Thursdays and Fridays. The boy places great importance on his social life and wants to continue to see friends after school. When he is going home with a friend for afternoon play, his teacher watches to make sure he takes his overnight bag if it's a day when he is shifting between his mother's and father's homes. (Middle Childhood)

Sources: M. E. Ford and Smith (2007), Hamre and Pianta (2005); Harter (1999); Juvonen (2000, 2006); Ladd, Herald-Brown, and Kochel (2009); Ormrod (2008); R. J. Stevens and Slavin (1995); M. Thompson and Grace (2001; school play example); Rodkin et al. (2013); Wentzel and Wigfield (1998); and Wigfield, Eccles, & Pintrich, 1996).

When identifying possible causes for failures, adults can focus primarily on increasing effort and improving strategies (Brophy, 2004; Cimpian et al., 2007; Dweck, 2000). Following are examples:

- "The more you practice, the better you will get."
- "Perhaps you need to study a little each night rather than waiting until the night before. And let's talk about how you might also study *differently* than you did last time."

When children's failures are consistently attributed to controllable factors such as lack of effort or ineffective strategies, and when amplified energy and new techniques do, in fact, produce success, children often work harder, persist longer in the face of failure, and seek help when they need it (Dweck & Master, 2009; Eccles & Wigfield, 1985).

The most effective feedback—no matter whether it commends successes or identifies weaknesses—also maintains children's sense of self-determination. More specifically, it provides information about children's performance and does *not* convey a desire to control the behavior (Deci, 1992; Standage, Cumming, & Gillison, 2013). In complimenting a student who has written a good persuasive essay, a teacher might say, "Your arguments are well organized and quite convincing" (emphasis on what the student has done well), rather than saying, "Good job in following my guidelines" (emphasis on following the teacher's instructions). In admonishing students for off-task behavior during a cooperative learning activity, a teacher might ask, "Are you guys going to have time to work on your project tonight if you don't finish it during class?" (emphasis on students' own time management concerns) rather than saying, "How many times do I have to remind this group to *get to work*?" (emphasis on keeping the students under control).

- **Teach children to give themselves encouraging attribution messages.** Numerous investigations have shown that children can be taught more productive attributions, often generating higher achievement and more persistence in the face of failure (e.g., Chodkiewicz & Boyle, 2014; Dweck, 1975). In these *attribution retraining* studies, children are asked to engage in a particular task (e.g., reading challenging texts, solving arithmetic problems, constructing geometric puzzles), with occasional failures interspersed among frequent successes. Within this context, one viable approach for changing attributions is for an adult to interpret each success in terms of high effort or good strategy and each failure due to insufficient effort or ineffective strategies. Even more effective is teaching children to attribute their *own* successes and failures to high effort and specific strategies (Dweck & Master, 2009; Fowler & Peterson, 1981).

- **Use praise that validates hard work and successful strategies.** Some students with weak academic skills have special educational needs. Extensive research on praise has found that children with delays learn to be sensitive to adults' compliments. Adults should generally avoid praise for intelligence, as in "You're such a smart kid!" This flattering remark, however well intentioned, is interpreted as intelligence being fixed, which decreases children's confidence in expansion of abilities in the future. In comparison, telling children that they must have tried hard or used a particularly effective problem-solving strategy helps them focus in on factors that they can control (Esparza, Shumow, & Schmidt, 2014; E. A. Gunderson et al., 2013). Adults should also try to be specific in describing the child's accomplishment. Telling a sixth-grader that his essay is convincing with its vivid details is more informative than telling him, "Good job!"

- **Use extrinsic reinforcers when necessary.** Despite adults' best efforts, children sometimes have little interest in acquiring knowledge or skills critical for later success. To encourage learning or desired behaviors in such situations, adults may have to provide extrinsic reinforcers—not only praise but also free time, grades, special privileges, or points toward a small prize. How can adults use such reinforcers without undermining intrinsic motivation? One effective strategy is to reinforce children not simply for doing something but for doing it *well*. Another is to communicate that an extrinsic reinforcer is merely a concrete acknowledgment of a significant progress or achievement—an accomplishment about which children should feel proud (Brophy, 2004; J. Cameron, 2001). Especially when working with youngsters from cultures that place a high priority on family or community ties, adults might point out the positive impact that children's actions have on other people (Abi-Nader, 1993; Dien, 1998; Suina & Smolkin, 1994). A teacher might say, "Everyone in school will appreciate the beautiful murals you have painted in the hallway."

MyLab Education Application Exercise 13.3
Detect Developmental Levels
Watch a first-grade teacher, Michelle Kern, motivate children as members of four-person groups preparing books on the desert.

A more controversial use of extrinsic reinforcers is to pay students for earning advanced test scores or high grades or attending tutoring sessions (R. Wright, 2009). Cash incentives have been tried in school districts in schools serving predominantly low-income students in several large U.S. cities, including New York City, Chicago, and Washington, D.C. Proponents of cash incentives have argued that low-income students need financial support so that they can afford to study after school rather than work long hours in part-time jobs. Others suggest that students from low-income families do not receive the same financial advantages as students from wealthier backgrounds and therefore appreciate financial incentives. So far the evidence on the impact has been mixed, with some studies indicating higher performance among those receiving incentives and others not finding an advantage (Bettinger, 2012; J. Henderson, 2009). We have reservations about their effectiveness given that incentives work best when children have control over the target behavior and are rewarded in the near future, not years later. Educators are also concerned that if funding for these programs dries up, students will probably decrease their efforts.

- **Be attentive to the needs of students who are behind in academic skills.** Some students with delayed academic skills have learning disabilities or other special educational needs. Others have limited proficiency in English or a background that is not understood or embraced at school. Still others encounter serious personal problems (e.g., a pregnancy, an arrest, a parent's incarceration), do not have friends at school, or come from home environments in which academic success is not encouraged (Behnke, Gonzalez, & Cox, 2010; Hirschfield, 2009; Makarova & Herzog, 2013; Steinberg, Blinde, & Chan, 1984). Regardless of the reasons for delayed progress, students who fail to acquire minimum academic skills are at risk for dropping out of school (Boling & Evans, 2008; Fortin, Marcotte, Diallo, Potvin, & Royer, 2013).

Low-achieving students come from all socioeconomic levels, but youngsters from low-income families, in particular, are likely to leave school before high school graduation (Rumberger, 1995; Suh, Suh, & Houston, 2007). Boys are more likely to drop out than girls, and African Americans, Hispanic Americans, and Native Americans have higher dropout rates than other groups (A. Edwards, 2014; Oguntoyinbo, 2009; Roderick & Camburn, 1999). Of course, low-achieving students almost always have the ability to succeed when supported by concerned professionals. The motivational strategies we've listed in the preceding pages are especially important for students who are low achieving. The Development-Enhancing Education feature "Encouraging Students Who Are Achieving at Low Levels" offers additional suggestions.

Summary

To some degree, children's intrinsic motivation to tackle an activity depends on factors that develop gradually over time (e.g., self-efficacy, sense of self-determination, a

Development-Enhancing Education

Encouraging Students Who Are Achieving at Low Levels

Make the curriculum relevant to students' lives.

- In a unit on the physics of sound, a junior high school science teacher shows students how basic principles reveal themselves in rock music. On one occasion the teacher brings in a guitar and explains why holding a string at different points along its neck creates different frequencies and therefore higher and lower notes. (Early Adolescence)
- A middle school social studies teacher invites students to select an autobiography from an assortment of books written from a range of backgrounds. Students regularly choose books written by individuals who share their cultural experiences. (Early Adolescence)

Use students' strengths to promote high self-efficacy.

- An elementary school serving predominantly families from low-income backgrounds forms a singing group (the "Jazz Cats") for which students must try out. The group performs at a variety of community events, and the students are recognized for their talent. Group members exhibit confidence in their musical abilities, improvement in other school subjects, greater teamwork, and leadership skills. (Middle Childhood)
- A middle school science teacher encourages her students to enter a local science fair. Several students participate, and they design innovative projects such as ones focused on chemical analyses of water from local estuaries or migration patterns of bees during periods of restricted access to pollen. After participating in the fair, students become more motivated in science. (Early Adolescence)

Provide extra support for academic success.

- At the beginning of class each day, a middle school teacher distributes a general outline that guides students' note taking. She also writes two or three questions on the board that students should be able to answer at the end of the lesson. (Early Adolescence)
- A high school algebra teacher arranges with his principal to hire a tutor for students who are struggling in mathematics. The tutor works after school to offer help with homework. A local electronics company sponsors snacks for the students to munch on during the drop-in tutoring sessions. (Late Adolescence)

Communicate optimism about students' chances for career success.

- A kindergarten teacher equips the dramatic play area in her classroom with supplies and clothing from a wide array of professions—an airplane pilot's cap, a doctor's stethoscope, a beautician's hairbrush and rollers, a cash register with play money, and so forth. "What will you pretend to be today?" she asks the children. After they make their selections, she comments, "Isn't it wonderful to think about jobs you could have when you grow up?" (Early Childhood)
- A mathematics teacher in a low-income, inner-city high school recruits students to participate in an intensive math program. The teacher and students work evenings, Saturdays, and vacations, and all of them later pass the Advanced Placement calculus exam. (Late Adolescence)

Show students that they are personally responsible for their successes.

- A high school teacher says to a student, "Your essay about recent hate crimes is powerful. You've given the topic a lot of thought, and you've mastered several of techniques of persuasive writing. I'd like you to think seriously about submitting your essay to the local paper for its editorial page. Can we spend some time during lunch tomorrow fine-tuning the grammar and spelling?" (Late Adolescence)
- "Every single student in my advisee group is capable of going to college or a vocational program," an adviser tells his high school students at the beginning of the year. "But getting into college and choosing a major will be easier for you if you start planning now." During the year, students take a career inventory of interests; arrange for an internship with a professional in a field of personal interest; and search through catalogs from local colleges, universities, and vocational programs. (Late Adolescence)

Get students involved in extracurricular activities.

- A middle school encourages its students to get involved in at least one extracurricular activity. Students can choose from athletic teams, an astronomy club, band, color guard, a hip-hop dance group, honor societies, science club, student council, yearbook, Peers for Peace, school newspaper, gay–straight alliance, and Ultimate Frisbee team. Each of the groups recruits members at the beginning of the year and conducts a membership drive halfway through the year. (Early Adolescence)
- A high school adviser encourages a student with a strong throwing arm to go out for the school baseball team and introduces the student to the baseball coach. The coach, in turn, expresses his enthusiasm for having the student join the team and asks several current team members to welcome him. (Late Adolescence)

Involve students in school policy and management decisions.

- A teacher in a third-grade classroom encourages children to organize a Valentine's Day party. With a little guidance from their teacher, children form several small groups, each tasked with a job—bringing in decorations, asking parents to send in a drink or snack, creating bags for each child to store goodies, and typing up a list of children's names for those preparing Valentine's Day cards. (Middle Childhood)

- Students and teachers at one high school hold regular "town meetings" to discuss how groups are operating and how disputes can be resolved. Meetings are democratic, with students and teachers alike having one vote apiece, and the will of the majority being binding. (Late Adolescence)

Sources: Alderman (1990); L. W. Anderson and Pellicer (1998); Behnke et al. (2010); Christenson and Thurlow (2004); Cosden, Morrison, Albanese, and Macias (2001); Fredricks, Blumenfeld, and Paris (2004); S. Goldstein and Brooks (2006); Hamre and Pianta (2005); A. Higgins (1995; town meetings example); Jenlink (1994; Jazz Cats example); M. S. Knapp, Turnbull, and Shields (1990); Lee-Pearce, Plowman, and Touchstone (1998); Milner (2006); A. Smith and Thomson (2014); and Towne (2009).

mastery orientation) and is affected by experience. Piquing youngsters' curiosity and interest, helping them be successful in their efforts to master new skills, enhancing their sense of autonomy, and encouraging the formation of specific goals are a few of the things adults can do to enhance youngsters' motivation to engage in productive activities. Teachers can exercise diplomacy in remarks about students' performance. They can emphasize factors that students can control and that will promote effective learning.

MyLab Education Self-Check 13.4

Practicing For Your Licensure Examination

Many teaching tests require students to apply their knowledge of child development in analyzing brief vignettes and answering multiple-choice questions. You can practice for your licensure examination by reading the following case study and answering a series of questions.

Tears of Pearls

When students in a sixth-grade class don't turn in homework assignments, a teacher intern insists that they write a 200-word essay explaining the missing homework and describing how they plan to be more diligent next time. In an essay shown on the next, 11-year-old Andrea explains why she didn't turn in her analysis of the lyrics to the song "Tears of Pearls," by the Australian singing duo Savage Garden. Read Andrea's essay and then answer the questions that follow it.

Constructed-Response Question

1. What kinds of benefits might Andrea gain from preparing this essay?

Multiple-Choice Questions

2. What does Andrea say that indicates she is developing self-regulatory skills in completing her school assignments?

200 word essay

I am very sorry this happened. I feel guilty that I forgot to pass the assignment Tears of Pearls in. Every time in social studies I will make sure I passed in all my assignments so that this will not happen again. I understand how hard it is for you to keep track of two classes work and I think it is a good idea you are doing this. I wish I wasn't so forgetful. Hopefully this will not happen to me again. Every night I will check my social studies folder to make sure the homework is complete. Now all I have to do is get it to school and put it in the pass in box. It was complete but I just forgot to pass it in. Every night I do my homework and my mom checks it and it goes in my back pack but sometimes I just forget to give it to you. I'm sorry. I really am. It is sometimes hard for us kids sometimes too. It is sometimes hard for us kids to be prepared but I guess that's just something we'll have to learn before middle school! Oh and sometimes we're packed with homework and the next day its hard to get it back together and into your and Mrs. Copeland's hands as soon as possible (A.S.A.P.). Like I said it's hard for you too and I can understand, but sometimes things (other) things are hard for us too. For the third time im really am sorry

sincerly,
Andrea

a. Andrea reported that she completed the assignment (reflecting her desire to be conscientious) but forgot to turn it in.

b. Andrea felt guilty about not getting her homework in on time.

c. Andrea reports that her mother checks her homework and that they put it in her backpack.

d. All of the above.

3. What evidence is there that Andrea still needs help in regulating her learning at school?

a. Andrea forgets to turn in her homework.

b. Andrea relies on her mother to check her homework.

c. Andrea expresses uncertainty as to how to proceed.

d. All of the above.

MyLab Education Licensure Practice 13.1

Key Concepts

motivation (p. 485)
delay of gratification (p. 487)
conscience (p. 488)
self-monitoring (p. 492)
self-instructions (p. 492)
self-motivation (p. 492)
self-evaluation (p. 492)
extrinsic motivation (p. 495)
intrinsic motivation (p. 495)
reinforcer (p. 495)
primary reinforcer (p. 496)
secondary reinforcer (p. 496)
vicarious reinforcement (p. 496)
punishment (p. 497)
vicarious punishment (p. 497)
self-efficacy (p. 498)
sense of self-determination (p. 499)
situational interest (p. 499)
personal interest (p. 499)
value (p. 500)
internalized motivation (p. 500)
achievement goal theory (p. 504)
mastery goal (p. 504)
performance goal (p. 504)
performance-approach goal (p. 504)
performance-avoidance goal (p. 504)
social goal (p. 505)
attribution (p. 507)
mastery orientation (p. 508)
learned helplessness (p. 508)
growth mind-set (of ability) (p. 508)
fixed mind-set (of ability) (p. 508)
situated motivation (p. 514)

Chapter Fourteen
Moral Development

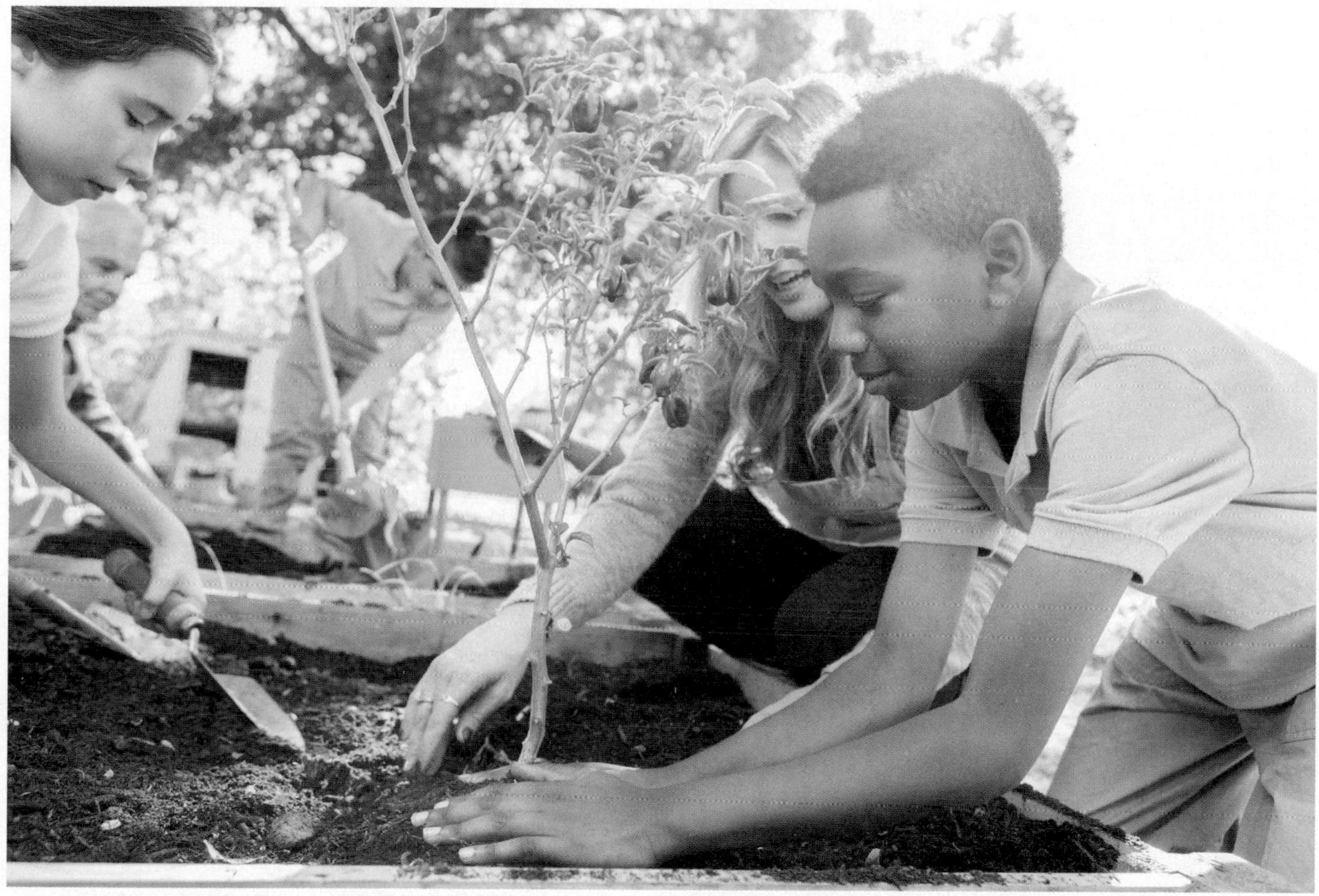

Steve Debenport/E+/Getty Images

Learning Objectives

14.1 Describe developmental trends in children's moral reasoning and factors that facilitate these progressions.

14.2 Identify key influences on the development of prosocial and aggressive behaviors, including methods at school that promote good behavior and safe school environments.

CASE STUDY

Changing the World, One City at a Time

Alice Terry had worked as a middle school teacher with gifted and talented students in a rural area of Georgia. Over the years, Alice gave her students a chance to work on projects addressing pressing needs in their community by restoring buildings, preparing a waste management plan, and designing a walking tour past historic buildings and monuments (A. W. Terry, 2000, 2001, 2003, 2008; A. W. Terry & Panter, 2010).

After her middle students completed the projects, they talked with Alice about what they had learned. Students reported that they acquired numerous benefits from participating in the projects, often gaining a sense of purpose in their work. Now in high school, several adolescents who had renovated a theater described their accomplishments:

> "Makes you feel like you have a—" Trina interrupted.
>
> "A place in life," Kevin continued. "We, like, have our—we have, like, a place. No, not a place, but we have a a—a mark."
>
> Anna blurted out, "We left our mark, yeah!"
>
> "Our mark. When we were eighth graders," Kevin added, "we really made a difference."
>
> "We'll go back," Ann responded, "and probably find some of our signatures somewhere."
>
> "Our footprints are in there," Kevin mused. "Our breath will still be there"[a] (A. W. Terry, 2000, p. 126).

Along with gaining a sense of purpose, the adolescents acquired valuable social insights about relationships with peers. Students realized that they had to consider how their moods affected others:

> "You can't be in a grouchy mood and do stuff like this," Anna began, "'cause folks are just gonna get mad at you—you can't do that . . . . You got to have a good attitude about it."
>
> Kevin interjected, "Everybody has to have a good attitude."
>
> Anna added, "Or nothing will get done." (A. W. Terry, 2000, p. 124)

A related social lesson was that cooperation was imperative to the group's progress. When asked to advise other adolescents who would be working on community service projects, the students emphasized teamwork:

> "Learn to . . . work together," Kevin advised.
>
> Anna added, "Work hard."
>
> "Get along. To just, um, use their time wisely so they can get the most out of the project," Trina remarked. (A. W. Terry, 2000, p. 126)

In addition, students learned about themselves. Kat, now a young woman, used to be impatient with her teammates and recalled lessons in self-control and tolerance:

> "I used to just blow up at people . . . . I guess we were working in such close quarters that, you know, if somebody that you didn't like was there, they were going to breathe on you at some point. You were going to have to put up with it." (A. Terry, 2000, pp. 126–127)

- What did Alice Terry understand about the moral needs of young people?
- What skills did the adolescents learn as they participated in community service projects?

Children easily learn moral values, yet now and again, they need guidance in treating one another humanely. In the introductory case study, Alice Terry understood that adolescents could benefit from an opportunity to work together and serve their community. As a result of their experiences, these young people learned important lessons—that

[a]Excerpts from "An Early Glimpse: Service Learning from an Adolescent Perspective" by A. W. Terry, from *Journal of Secondary Gifted Education*, Vol. 11, Issue 3, pp. 124, 126–128, 303–304. Copyright © 2000 by Prufrock Press, Inc. Reprinted with permission of Prufrock Press, Inc. http://www.prufrock.com, Editor: Alice W. Terry.

their community needed them, that they had to compromise to achieve common goals, and that they could derive satisfaction from their collective accomplishments.

In this chapter, we examine children's moral development. We look specifically at children's reasoning about right and wrong and their tendencies to help and occasionally hurt others. As you have discovered with other aspects of development, teachers and other professionals play a vital role in morality. They help children to act decently, responsibly, and honorably.

Outline

Moral Reasoning

14.1 Describe developmental trends in children's moral reasoning and factors that facilitate these progressions.

Moral development involves acquiring standards about right and wrong and acting in accordance with these standards. Three influential theories, by Piaget, Kohlberg, and Elliot Turiel, explain regularities in children's moral reasoning.

Piaget's Theory of Moral Development

After observing children's social games (e.g., playing with marbles) and interviewing children about people's wrongdoings, the pioneering theorist **Jean Piaget** (1896–1980) proposed that children construct increasingly mature understandings of "good" and "bad" behavior (Piaget, 1960b). In the early elementary years, children believe that behaviors that are "bad" or "naughty" are those that cause serious damage or harm. Thus, a young child might say that a person who accidentally broke 15 dishes was more badly behaved than a person who intentionally broke one dish. By the upper elementary grades, children consider people's motives when evaluating behaviors. At this age, they would see the person who intentionally broke one dish as the guiltier party.

Piaget noticed additional changes in the ideas that children formed about moral issues. For preschoolers, "good" behavior consists of obeying authority figures. Around age 5, children begin to judge what is good and appropriate based on established *rules* for behavior. At this point, they see regulations as firm dictates to be obeyed without question. Piaget called rule-based morality *moral realism*. Sometime around age 8 or 9, children begin to recognize that rules are created primarily to help people get along and can be changed if everyone agrees to the change.

Many developmental scholars accept Piaget's premise that children construct their own ideas about moral behavior—often as a result of having discussions with others—rather than automatically internalize moral guidelines from adults (Hoffman, 2000; Kohlberg, 1984; Vozzola, 2014). Theorists agree that development of children's moral understandings depends on cognitive advancements, such as the awakening of social perspective taking and abstract thought (Eisenberg, 1995; Kohlberg, 1969).

Nevertheless, modern researchers have found that Piaget was not fully accurate about how and when moral reasoning emerges. Children rarely see an adult's rules as the be-all and end-all of morality. Even preschoolers recognize that certain behaviors (e.g., pushing others or damaging their property) are wrong even if an adult tells them otherwise (Nucci, 2009; Tisak, 1993; Turiel, 1983). In part, children learn about right and wrong from their own feelings. In fact, new evidence indicates that infants react emotionally to simple acts of aggression and unequal distribution of goods (Sommerville & Ziv, 2018; Van de Vondervoort & Hamlin, 2018). Thus, children's moral intuitions appear in the first years of life and provide a foundation for the rules they will later follow.

Preparing for Your Licensure Examination

Your teaching test might ask you to describe how moral development is a constructive process that depends on experience and reflection.

Despite limitations in Piaget's framework, there is much to be learned from asking children how they think about moral issues. In the next section we discuss a prominent theorist, Lawrence Kohlberg, who worked in Piaget's footsteps and identified significant changes in moral thinking during childhood, adolescence, and adulthood.

Kohlberg's Theory of Moral Development

When the cognitive-developmental psychologist **Lawrence Kohlberg** (1927–1987) first began to examine early theorists' descriptions of children's moral development, he was disappointed with what he read (Kohlberg, 1963, 1964). At the time, several outspoken theorists (e.g., Sigmund Freud and B. F. Skinner) argued that people behave morally because of pressure from others. Kohlberg rejected this idea, siding instead with Piaget's view that individuals develop their own ideas about proper courses of action. Yet, whereas Piaget studied moral development as one of several topics he examined, Kohlberg made moral thinking his life's work and created a detailed account of his research.

Kohlberg was the first researcher to look in depth at the age-related ways in which people analyze hypothetical conflicts. Consider the following situation:

> In Europe, a woman was near death from a rare form of cancer. There was one drug that the doctors thought might save her, a form of radium that a druggist in the same town had recently discovered. The druggist was charging $2,000, ten times what the drug cost him to make. The sick woman's husband, Heinz, went to everyone he knew to borrow the money, but he could only get together about half of what the drug cost. He told the druggist that his wife was dying and asked him to sell it cheaper or let him pay later. But the druggist said no. So Heinz got desperate and broke into the man's store to steal the drug for his wife. (Kohlberg, 1984, p. 186)

Should Heinz have stolen the drug? What would you have done if you were Heinz? Which is worse, stealing something that belongs to someone else or letting another person die a preventable death, and why? The story of Heinz and his dying wife is an example of a **moral dilemma**, a situation in which two or more people's rights or needs are at odds and for which there is no clear-cut right or wrong solution. Following are three boys' responses to Heinz's dilemma. We have given the boys fictitious names so that we can talk about their individual responses.

> *Andrew (a fifth grader):* Maybe his wife is an important person and runs a store, and the man buys stuff from her and can't get it any other place. The police would blame the owner that he didn't save the wife. He didn't save an important person, and that's just like killing with a gun or a knife. You can get the electric chair for that. (Kohlberg, 1981, pp. 265–266)
>
> *Vlad (a high school student):* If he cares enough for her to steal for her, he should steal it. If not he should let her die. It's up to him. (Kohlberg, 1981, p. 132)
>
> *Hector (a high school student):* In that particular situation Heinz was right to do it. In the eyes of the law he would not be doing the right thing, but in the eyes of the moral law he would. If he had exhausted every other alternative I think it would be worth it to save a life. (Kohlberg, 1984, pp. 446–447)

Each boy offers a different reason why or why not Heinz should steal the lifesaving drug. Andrew suggests that the druggist (whom he calls the owner) needs to be punished for not saving a life. Vlad takes a self-serving view, proposing that the decision to either steal or not steal the drug depends on how much Heinz loves his wife. Only Hector considers the value of human life in justifying why Heinz should break the law.

After obtaining hundreds of responses to moral dilemmas from children and adults, Kohlberg proposed that the development of moral reasoning is characterized by a sequence of six stages grouped into three levels: preconventional, conventional, and postconventional morality (Colby, Kohlberg, Gibbs, & Lieberman, 1983; Kohlberg, 1963, 1976, 1984; see Table 14.1). **Preconventional morality** is the earliest and least mature form of moral reasoning in that a child has not yet adopted or internalized society's conventions for what is right or wrong—hence the label *preconventional*. Andrew's response is a good example of preconventional, Stage 1 thinking, in that he focuses on the consequences (death in the electric chair) of not providing the medicine. Kohlberg classified Vlad's response as a preconventional Stage 2 response. Vlad is beginning to recognize the importance of saving someone else's life, but the decision to do so ultimately depends on whether Heinz loves his wife. In other words, his decision depends on *his* feelings alone.

Conventional morality is characterized by acceptance of society's conventions regarding right and wrong. At this level, an individual obeys rules even when there are no consequences for obedience or disobedience. Adherence to rules is rigid, however, and its fairness is seldom questioned. In contrast, people who exhibit **postconventional morality** view rules as useful mechanisms that are created to maintain the social order and protect human rights rather than as absolute dictates that must be obeyed without

Table 14.1 Kohlberg's Levels and Stages of Moral Reasoning

LEVEL	AGE RANGE	STAGE	NATURE OF MORAL REASONING
Level I: Preconventional Morality	Seen in preschool children, most elementary school students, some junior high school students, and a few high school students	Stage 1: Punishment-avoidance and obedience	People make decisions based on what is best for themselves, without regard for others' needs or feelings. They obey rules only if enforced by more powerful individuals; they may disobey if they aren't likely to get caught. "Wrong" behaviors are those that will be punished.
		Stage 2: Exchange of favors	People recognize that others have needs. They may try to satisfy others' needs if their own requirements are met ("You scratch my back, I'll scratch yours"). They continue to define right and wrong primarily in terms of consequences to themselves.
Level II: Conventional Morality	Seen in a few older elementary school students, some junior high school students, and many high school students (Stage 4 typically does not appear until the high school years.)	Stage 3: Good boy/good girl	People make decisions based on what actions will please others, especially authority figures and others with high status (e.g., teachers, popular peers). They are concerned about maintaining relationships through sharing, trusting, and being loyal, and they take other people's perspectives into account when making decisions.
		Stage 4: Law and order	People look to society for guidelines about right or wrong. They know rules are necessary for keeping things running smoothly and believe it is their "duty" to obey them. However, they perceive rules to be inflexible; they don't necessarily recognize that as society's needs change, rules should change as well.
Level III: Postconventional Morality	Rarely seen before college (Stage 6 is extremely rare even in adults.)	Stage 5: Social contract	People recognize that rules represent agreements among many individuals about appropriate behavior. Rules are seen as potentially useful mechanisms that can maintain the general social order and protect individual rights, rather than as absolute dictates that must be obeyed because they are "the law." People also recognize the flexibility of rules, with those that no longer serve society's best interests needing to be changed.
		Stage 6: Universal ethical principles	Stage 6 is a hypothetical, "ideal" stage that few people reach. Those who reason at this stage believe in a few abstract, universal principles (e.g., equality of all people, respect for human dignity, commitment to justice) that transcend existing norms and rules. They answer to a strong inner conscience and disobey laws that violate their ethical principles.

Sources: Colby and Kohlberg (1984); Colby et al. (1983); and Kohlberg (1976, 1984, 1986).

question. Postconventional individuals live by their own abstract principles about right and wrong—ethics that include such basic human rights as life, liberty, and justice. They may disobey rules inconsistent with their principles, as we see in Hector's Stage 5 response to the Heinz dilemma: "In the eyes of the law he would not be doing the right thing, but in the eyes of the moral law he would." Rules can and should be changed if they fail to protect people's rights with justice and equity.

A great deal of research on moral development has followed on the heels of Kohlberg's work. Kohlberg's basic idea that moral development is a constructive process has stood the test of time—theorists remain intrigued with children's intrinsic desire to analyze behavior as right or wrong (Nucci, 2006; Thornberg, 2010; Turiel, 2008a). And generally speaking, children and adolescents make advancements in the order that Kohlberg proposed (Colby & Kohlberg, 1984; Nucci, 2009; Stewart & Pascual-Leone, 1992). Kohlberg recognized that ranges in moral reasoning at a given age can be significant, especially among older students. In the high school classroom, each of the three levels of reasoning may be evident.

Nevertheless, psychologists have identified several weaknesses in Kohlberg's theory. One set of problems is related to how Kohlberg defined morality. For one thing, Kohlberg included both *moral issues* (e.g., causing harm) and *social conventions* (e.g., having rules to help society run smoothly) in his framework of morality, yet as you will find out, children view these two domains differently. In addition, he largely overlooked one very important aspect of morality: that of showing others compassion (Gilligan, 1982, 1987). Although Kohlberg acknowledged that moral thinking is saturated with emotions, he gave priority to cognitive processes. Today's scholars find that emotions (e.g., empathy and guilt) are strong influences on moral thought and behavior (Arsenio & Lemerise, 2010; Laible, Murphy, & Augustine, 2014; Turiel & Killen, 2010). In fact, it now appears that emotions, not cognitive insights, jump-start moral reflections in children.

Another limitation of Kohlberg's theory is his proposal that environmental factors have only a modest impact on moral development. Kohlberg assumed that children's moral thinking advances through personal introspection, sometimes including ruminations of what peers have said, but largely without assistance. Yet recent research indicates that children are very much influenced by peers, adults, and their many cultural experiences (Grusec, 2006; Malti, Eisenberg, Kim, & Buchmann, 2013; Recchia, Wainryb, Bourne, & Pasupathi, 2014; R. A. Thompson, 2012). The social context is important in another way that was also largely ignored by Kohlberg. As they come to understand right and wrong, children are strongly affected by interpersonal dynamics (Minnameier & Schmidt, 2013; Rest, Narváez, Bebeau, & Thoma, 1999). For example, children are more inclined to judge lying as immoral if it causes someone harm than if it has no adverse effect—that is, if it is just a "white lie" (Turiel, Smetana, & Killen, 1991). A theoretical implication of contextual effects is that children draw from networks of moral ideas and values, not from a single stage-related position (U. Kaplan & Tivnan, 2014; Turiel, 2018). Children weigh what they know about participants in the situation given their existing moral understandings; in the process they form complicated moral judgments.

Social Domain Theory of Moral Development

Preparing for Your Licensure Examination

Your teaching test might ask you about the basic tenets and educational implications of Kohlberg's theory of moral development.

American psychologist **Elliott Turiel** and his colleagues have followed the leads of Jean Piaget and Lawrence Kohlberg in examining children's beliefs about the appropriateness of people's actions (Jambon & Smetana, 2014; Turiel, 2008b, 2018; Turiel & Killen, 2010). The unique contribution that Turiel and his collaborators have made has been to demonstrate that young children easily discriminate morality from concerns about society's conventions—an ability that was largely overlooked by Kohlberg. By comparing children's responses to carefully defined moral and social-conventional violations, Turiel and his colleagues have been able to demonstrate capabilities in reasoning that were not evident in Kohlberg's data and, in the process, have expanded our understanding of children's context-sensitive reasoning about right and wrong.

Let's examine some of the distinctions that children learn to make, which we find in three domains. Young children understand that **moral transgressions** (e.g., hitting others, stealing their belongings, and calling them nasty names) are wrong because they cause harm, violate human rights, and run counter to basic principles of equality, freedom, or justice (J. G. Miller, 2007; Nucci, 2009; Recchia et al., 2014; Turiel, 2018). Preschool and kindergarten children also realize that **conventional transgressions** (e.g., talking back to adults or burping at meals) violate widely held understandings about how one should act. These transgressions are wrong but not intrinsically harmful to other people. Conventional transgressions are usually specific to a particular culture. Although burping is frowned on in mainstream Western culture, people in some cultures burp as a compliment to the chef. Moreover, young children see some choices, such as selecting a friend, as a **personal matter**; therefore, determining what is a good choice is up to the individual. The ability to distinguish moral violations, conventional transgressions, and personal choices appears to be universal, as you can learn more about in the Development in Culture feature "Moral Development in Colombia."

Development in Culture

Moral Development in Colombia

Children around the world develop common ideas as well as some divergent views about social responsibility. Evidence of universality is present in the widespread ability of children to distinguish between moral, social, and personal actions (Jambon & Smetana, 2014; Turiel, 2006b; Wainryb, 2006). By the preschool years, children realize that moral violations (e.g., hitting and pushing or taking another's belongings) are hurtful acts that are rarely justified. Young children consider violations of social conventions (e.g., failing to say "please" or "thank you" or ignoring table etiquette) to be disrespectful but not as reprehensible as moral violations. With reference to the personal domain (e.g., selecting a friend or choosing a hairstyle), children typically say that individuals themselves should make their own decisions.

Roberto Orrú/Alamy Stock Photo

LEARNING RIGHT FROM WRONG. These Colombian children have daily experiences that help them acquire important moral and social understandings.

Alicia Ardila-Rey and her colleagues in Colombia, South America, have delved into these understandings. As with children in many other cultures, Colombian children differentiate domains of social action. In one study, interviewers read stories to 3- to 7-year-old Colombian children from middle-class families (Ardila-Rey & Killen, 2001). Stories portrayed hypothetical children who were at odds with teachers over moral issues (e.g., hitting another child), social-conventional conflicts (e.g., drinking milk standing up rather than following the classroom's custom of consuming beverages sitting down), and personal disagreements (e.g., choosing to sit next to another classmate rather than the one chosen for the child by the teacher during story time). Interviewers asked children about the proper course of action for teachers to take when the hypothetical children failed to live up to teachers' wishes.

The Colombian children stated that teachers should offer explanations when children violated moral rules. They believed that the children had misbehaved because they were young and uninformed, not because they were intentionally disobedient. Therefore, the imaginary children were thought to need guidance, not punishment. In comparison, the interviewed children believed teachers should negotiate with children who violated social-conventional rules or insisted on pursuing personal actions disapproved of by teachers. From the children's perspective, teachers should advise students about social-conventional and personal domains and allow students to make their own decisions. In the following responses, children defended the rights of peers to exercise their independence in personal matters:

> "Children have their own rights, they have the right to choose what to play with" *("Los niños tienen sus propios derechos; ellos tienen derecho de jugar a lo que quieran jugar")*. "It is the child's play, not the teacher's play. The child can do whatever she wants to do" *("Es el juego de la niña, no es el juego de la profesora. La niña puede jugar a lo que ella quiera")*. "They can't force you to sit with a friend who is not your friend" *("A uno no lo pueden obligar a*

(continued)

sentarse con un amigo que no es su amigo"). (Ardila-Rey & Killen, 2001, p. 253)

Other research shows diversity in Colombian children's views about conduct. In one investigation about moral transgressions, 6- to 12-year-old Colombian children were recruited from two towns: Chía, a small and peaceful rural community with an educated population, and Soacha, a densely populated and economically impoverished community with high rates of crime and violence (Ardila-Rey, Killen, & Brenick, 2009). The vast majority of children from both groups saw hitting and refusing to share toys as wrong. The two groups differed in views about hitting or not sharing when another person had been aggressive ("Would it be okay to do it if they had teased or hurt her first? Why?" "Would it be okay to hit her back? Why?"; Ardila-Rey et al., 2009, p. 189). Compared to children in Chía, who had grown up in a relatively peaceful setting, children from Soacha, who had been exposed to a lot of violence, more often responded that hitting and not sharing would be acceptable if the other person had acted aggressively or selfishly.

These and other studies indicate that Colombian children from very different backgrounds believe that they should be given latitude in making their own social decisions and should abide by moral rules that protect the welfare of other people. Subtle variations exist in children's beliefs about the circumstances in which moral rules can be ignored. Children who have been exposed to excessive levels of violence are more inclined than peers in peace abiding communities to excuse aggressive and selfish acts when that individual's own rights have been violated.

Research in support of social domain theory reveals that children construct understandings of rules from everyday experiences. When a person hurts someone else, the victim tends to express anger, pain, or sadness, and adults may point out negative outcomes of the inappropriate acts (J. Dunn, 2006; Parke & Clarke-Stewart, 2011; Recchia et al., 2014; Turiel, 2018). Conversely, children notice that when someone violates a social convention, people's responses tend to be less strident and focus instead on the rules that have been broken.

These understandings are initially simple and concrete. During early childhood, children describe violations in the moral domain as tangible harm to others (e.g., hurting their feelings or causing an injury). Older children express additional concerns with inequality, social exclusion, and other abstract concepts (Smetana, 2006). Similarly, children's awareness of social conventions is rudimentary in early childhood and increases during the elementary and secondary school years (Helwig & Jasiobedzka, 2001; Mullins & Tisak, 2006; Turiel, 2006b). A young child may suggest that it is wrong to call a teacher by his or her first name because of the school's custom of using titles "Mr.," "Miss," "Mrs.," and "Ms.," whereas an older child may explain that failing to use the proper title is disrespectful (Turiel, 1983). Concerns about the personal domain, initially focusing on choosing one's own friends and clothing, later expand with matters related to safety, comfort, and health (Thornberg, 2010; Tisak & Turiel, 1984).

Children's judgments expand with their growing awareness that there are varying perspectives on rights and responsibilities. Thus, children come to realize that there can be multiple views on right and wrong. Adolescents may realize that a teacher's decision to place boys and girls into separate groups can be evaluated from different perspectives (Killen, Margie, & Sinno, 2006). Morally, it might be considered unfair when one gender or the other is denied an equal opportunity for learning. In conventional terms, the decision might be considered acceptable because separating boys and girls is a common practice that sometimes generates advanced learning. In the personal domain, the decision might be considered an imposition that violates individuals' rights to select their own groups.

Children also learn that culture contributes to diversity in moral perspectives. In addition to distinguishing moral, conventional, and personal violations, children around the world learn culture-*specific* ways of classifying rules and violations. Social conventions in some areas of India include women wearing a *sari* (traditional apparel draped around the body) and a *bindi* (a forehead decoration), whereas some Mennonite and Amish women in the United States and Canada wear long dresses and bonnets (Parke & Clarke-Stewart, 2011). Such variations in dress are not simply fashion statements; they uphold the social order. Moral rules also vary somewhat across culture. In Hindu society, fish is considered a "hot" food that would stimulate sexual desire and is not to be consumed by widows who should be seeking salvation for their deceased husbands (Shweder, Mahapatra, & Miller, 1987). Widows in Western cultures historically did not refrain from eating fish but instead wore black for a time and followed other customs for showing grief.

Social domain theory has inspired an impressive volume of studies portraying children as perceptive evaluators of social action. As a limitation, this perspective has not yet yielded much research about links among moral thinking, emotions, and behavior. Fortunately, scholars in the field have begun to make strides in illuminating these important connections (Arsenio & Lemerise, 2010; Dahl, Sherlock, Campos, & Theunissen, 2014; Smetana & Killen, 2008; Turiel & Killen, 2010).

Each of the theories we examined offers important lessons about children's moral reasoning. Piaget uncovered constructive processes in moral imperatives, Kohlberg identified developmental shifts in thinking about rights and rules, and Turiel discovered specialized domains that children distinguish. Despite progress in the field, we do not yet have a comprehensive theory that incorporates the various insights and merges them with recent evidence on emotions, behavior, and upbringing related to morality. We hope that a future framework of moral development that is more encompassing will be available to guide educational applications. In the meantime, teachers and other school professionals can learn about children's moral progressions and the conditions that foster growth. Let's look at some of the primary age-related trends in personal integrity.

Developmental Trends in Morality

Many contemporary developmental psychologists believe that moral development involves gradual expansions in understanding rather than hard-and-fast stages. The following developmental trends appear in children's moral reasoning and behavior.

Children begin using internal standards at an early age. Indeed, children distinguish right and wrong before age 2 (Kochanska, Casey, & Fukumoto, 1995; Kochanska & Kim, 2014; R. A. Thompson & Newton, 2010; Van de Vondervoort & Hamlin, 2018). Toddlers may wince, cover their eyes or ears, or cry when they witness an aggressive interaction. They also differentiate what's "good" and "bad," for example, looking at a broken object and saying, "Uh-oh!" (Kagan, 1984; S. Lamb & Feeny, 1995). By age 3 or 4, children understand that causing physical harm to another person is wrong regardless of what authority figures might tell them (Helwig, Zelazo, & Wilson, 2001; Smetana, 1981; Turiel, 2006b). A little later they recognize that causing another person psychological harm through teasing or name-calling is also wrong (Jambon & Smetana, 2014).

MyLab Education
Video Example 14.1

Find Developmental Meaning
How does Corwin show an emerging standard as to how blocks should look? Corwin reacts to the fallen tower.

Children's emotions affect their moral responses. Certain emotions accompany and incite moral action. Children show signs of **guilt**—a feeling of discomfort when they know that they have inflicted damage or caused someone else suffering—as early as 22 months (Kochanska, Gross, Lin, & Nichols, 2002). This capacity increases over the childhood years and seems to be an essential part of having a conscience. Feeling remorse deters future wrongdoing; children who are especially prone to feeling culpable tend to refrain from serious misbehaviors (Colasante & Malti, 2017; Kochanska et al., 2002; W. Roberts, Strayer, & Denham, 2014; Tangney & Dearing, 2002). Excessive levels of guilt can be detrimental, however, leading children to become self-berating and depressed (Luby et al., 2009; Tully & Donohue, 2017; Zahn-Waxler & Kochanska, 1990).

Children also develop a capacity for **shame**, the feeling of being embarrassed or humiliated when failing to meet basic standards of behavior. Precursors to shame emerge during early childhood and evolve into conscious emotions in middle childhood. Toddlers sometimes avoid adults or appear anxious when they have done something wrong, and children reliably exhibit shame by the middle elementary grades (Barrett, 2005; Damon, 1988; Hoffman, 1991). Feeling shame does not inhibit wrongdoing as effectively as does guilt, however. In fact, some young people who are ashamed act out disruptively, aggressively, or even criminally (MacDermott, Gullone, Allen, King, & Tonge, 2010; Mazzone, Camodeca, & Salmivalli, 2018; Muris & Meesters, 2014).

Guilt and shame occur when children believe they have done something wrong. In contrast, *empathy*, the capacity to experience the same feelings as another person, and **sympathy**, a genuine feeling of compassion for another person's distress, motivate moral behavior intended to diminish the person's suffering. Precursors to empathy operate when infants cry spontaneously and show worried expressions in the presence of a person in distress. In later infancy and early childhood, cooperative gestures (e.g., patting, verbalizing concern, and bringing objects of comfort to a person) appear. Kindheartedness deepens and motivates helpful behaviors during middle childhood and adolescence (Ongley & Malti, 2014; J. Xu, Saether, & Sommerville, 2016; Zahn-Waxler, Radke-Yarrow, Wagner, & Chapman, 1992).

Of course, children do not always feel benevolent, even when they have learned to be sympathetic. In the primary grades, children show empathy mostly for people they know, including friends and classmates. But by the upper elementary and secondary school grades, youngsters also feel empathy for people they *don't* know—perhaps for the economically poor, homeless, or individuals in catastrophic circumstances (Eisenberg, 1982; Hoffman, 1991; Markstrom, Huey, Stiles, & Krause, 2010). In the opening case study, adolescents felt empathic for unfamiliar people in their community, wishing to preserve historical landmarks and natural resources for everyone's benefit.

Children's understanding of fairness evolves throughout early and middle childhood. The ability to share with others depends on a sense of **distributive justice**, the commitment to principles for sharing a valued commodity (food, toys, playground equipment, etc.). Notions of distributive justice emerge early and evolve over time (Damon, 1977; Gummerum, Keller, Takezawa, & Mata, 2008; Gunzburger, 1977; Kienbaum & Wilkening, 2009; C. E. Smith & Warneken, 2016; Sommerville, 2018). Infants have a basic expectation of fairness when they see goods being handed out. For example, they might look longer when an adult gives seven blocks to one child and three to another than when he or she gives each five blocks. In the preschool years, children continue to value equal distribution, even though it can be difficult for them to live up to this principle when they themselves stand to receive a larger share of a desired commodity. By the early elementary grades, children believe in *parity*: They base their judgments about fairness on strict equality (a desired commodity is divided into equal portions). Sometime around age 8, children begin to take merit and special needs into account consistently. They show glimmers of *equity*, thinking that people who contribute more to the group should reap a greater portion of the group's rewards and that people who are economically poor might be given more resources than others.

Children supplement reasoning with other considerations when deciding how to behave. Children who reason at higher Kohlbergian stages are less likely to cheat, insult others, or engage in delinquent activities and more likely to protect people in need (Kohlberg, 1975; Kohlberg & Candee, 1984). Yet as boys and girls think about responding to others, additional factors besides fairness, justice, and welfare come into play. Their perspective-taking and emotions (in particular, their guilt, empathy, and sympathy) influence decisions to behave morally (Batson, 1991; Damon, 1988; Lonigro, Laghi, Baiocco, & Baumgartner, 2014). Personal goals affect moral behavior as well. Although children may want to do the right thing, they also care about others approving of their actions and other consequences to their behavior. Children are apt to behave in accordance with moral standards if the benefits are high ("Will other people like me better?") and the personal costs are low ("How much will I be inconvenienced?"; Batson & Thompson, 2001; Narváez & Rest, 1995; Nunner-Winkler, 2007). In the opening case study, group solidarity and shared pride partly compensated for hard work in resolving interpersonal differences.

As you have learned, a constellation of moral understandings, emotions, and behaviors emerges gradually in children. The Developmental Trends table "Moral Reasoning and Behavior at Different Age Levels" describes advancements you are likely to see in infancy, childhood, and adolescence.

Morality in a Developmental System

Children contribute to their own moral development with a number of processes—by complying with adults' rules, misbehaving, feeling guilty about misdeeds, and thinking about violations as moral, conventional, or personal matters. Children's neurological growth and their personal characteristics and experiences also influence their moral reasoning and behavior.

DEVELOPMENTAL TRENDS

Moral Reasoning and Behavior at Different Age Levels

AGE	WHAT YOU MIGHT OBSERVE	DIVERSITY	IMPLICATION
Infancy (Birth–2 Years)	• Acquisition of basic standards for behavior (e.g., saying "uh-oh!" after breaking an object) • Attention to adults' responses to broken objects, spilled drinks, and injured people • Distress when witnessing someone getting hurt	• In the second year, children label objects and events in ways that reflect cultural standards (e.g., *good, bad, dirty, boo-boo*). • Toddlers who are fearful and inhibited get upset when parents respond harshly to their wrongdoings. • Toddlers whose parents have been sensitive with them begin to share objects.	• Consistently discourage behaviors that cause harm or distress to others (e.g., hitting or biting peers). • Acknowledge undesirable events (e.g., spilled milk or a broken object), but don't overreact or communicate that children are inadequate for having caused them.
Early Childhood (2–6 Years)	• Some awareness that behaviors causing physical or psychological harm are morally wrong • Guilt for misbehaviors (e.g., damaging a valuable object, hitting a younger brother) • Greater concern for one's own needs than those of others; complaining "It's not fair" when resources are not distributed equally • Realization that some misbehaviors are moral transgressions, whereas others are conventional violations or personal decisions	• Some cultures emphasize training in moral values; for example, in many Hispanic communities, a child who is *bien educado* (literally, "well educated") knows right from wrong and behaves accordingly. • Children who show greater evidence of guilt about transgressions are more likely to adhere to rules for behavior. • At ages 2 and 3, girls are more likely to show guilt than are boys; boys catch up around age 4.	• Make standards for behavior clear. • Have a discussion with children about how they interpret and follow general rules. • Invite children to give input into classroom rules. • When children misbehave, give reasons why such behaviors are unacceptable, focusing on the harm they have caused others (see discussion on parents' use of *induction*) on pages 534–535).
Middle Childhood (6–10 Years)	• Distributive justice increasingly taking into account differing contributions and circumstances (e.g., a child who has been recently hospitalized might get an early turn at a favorite chore) • Increasing empathy for unknown individuals who are suffering or needy • Feelings of shame, as well as guilt, for moral wrongdoings	• Some cultures place greater emphasis on ensuring people's individual rights, whereas others place greater value on the welfare of the community as a whole. • Children whose parents explain *why* certain behaviors are unacceptable show more advanced moral development.	• Talk about how rules enable classrooms to run more smoothly. • Present simple moral dilemmas similar to circumstances children might encounter themselves (e.g., "What should a girl do when she has forgotten her lunch money and finds a dollar bill on the floor under a classmate's desk?").
Early Adolescence (10–14 Years)	• Tendency to think of moral rules as standards that should be followed • New inclinations to disobey classroom rules but ability to appreciate how disruptions affect other people when these are pointed out • Belief that troubled individuals (e.g., the homeless) are entirely responsible for their own fate	• Sometime around puberty, some youngsters begin to incorporate moral traits into their sense of self. • Youngsters' religious faith (e.g., their beliefs in an afterlife) influences their judgments about what behaviors are morally right and wrong. • Many middle school students are idealistic and expect fairness at school and in their community.	• Involve adolescents in group projects that benefit their school or community. • Encourage adolescents to think about how society's laws and practices affect people in need (e.g., individuals who are economically disadvantaged). • When imposing discipline for moral transgressions, point out harm caused to others. • Talk about moral issues, for example, a recent increase in acts of disrespect at school.
Late Adolescence (14–18 Years)	• Understanding that rules and conventions help society run smoothly • Increasing concern about doing one's duty rather than pleasing authority figures • Genuine empathy for people in distress • Belief that society has an obligation to help those in need	• For some older adolescents, high moral values are a central part of their overall identity; these individuals show a strong commitment to helping those less fortunate than themselves. • Adolescents who focus on their own needs are likely to engage in antisocial activities. • Some high school students can be rude and disruptive to teachers and classmates.	• Explore moral issues in social studies, science, and literature. • Give teenagers a political voice in decision making at school and elsewhere. • Explain why it is necessary to maintain academic integrity, monitor test-taking, and offer to help struggling students. • Get help yourself from colleagues or counselors when you find students to be rude and unresponsive.

Sources: Chandler and Moran (1990); Damon (1988); DeVries and Zan (2003); Eisenberg and Fabes (1998); Farver and Branstetter (1994); Flanagan and Faison (2001); D. Hart and Fegley (1995); Helwig and Jasiobedzka (2001); Hoffman (1975, 1991); Kochanska et al. (1995, 2002); Kohlberg (1984); D. L. Krebs and Van Hesteren (1994); Kurtines, Berman, Ittel, and Williamson (1995); S. Lamb and Feeny (1995); Lapsley and Carlo (2014); Laupa and Turiel (1995); Nucci (2009); Rizzo and Bosacki (2013); Schonert-Reichl (1993); Smetana and Braeges (1990); Sommerville (2018); R. A. Thompson and Newton (2010); Triandis (1995); Turiel (2006a, 2018); Vozzola (2014); Yates and Youniss (1996); Yau and Smetana (2003); and Zahn-Waxler et al. (1992).

Brain Maturation

The human brain encodes moral sensitivities from birth. Empathy has roots in networks of neurons that form impressions of another person's emotions (de Souza, 2014; Missana, Grigutsch, & Grossmann, 2014). The ability to distinguish moral and social-conventional events also has a neurological basis. Moral transgressions are naturally offensive and easy to detect, whereas violations of social conventions require a mental search through learned social rules (Lahat, Helwig, & Zelazo, 2013). Maturation of the cerebral cortex also provides the basis for inhibiting shortsighted, self-centered impulses, such as lashing out at an annoying classmate (Chiasson, Vera-Estay, Lalonde, Dooley, & Beauchamp, 2017). Growth in the brain likewise improves the ability to read others' mental states and think through consequences before acting, capacities that contribute to doing the right thing.

Of course, having a healthy brain with robust networks of neurons registering moral issues does not guarantee that children will do the right thing when given a choice. When empathy fails to develop normally or when parents are callous, indifferent, or harsh, moral capacities may be delayed (de Souza, 2014; Frick, Ray, Thornton, & Kahn, 2014). For some children, exceptional levels of guidance must be given if they are to acquire normal moral abilities. Specific areas (e.g., those that support thoughts about other people's perspectives) are weak in children with certain disabilities (Happé & Frith, 2014).

Developmental Systems Prompt 14.1

Personal characteristics, culture, and experience influence children's moral thought and action. You can scaffold moral development when you ask children how they see right and wrong. You can also introduce slightly more advanced moral reasoning to them, communicate the expectation that everyone treats one another with respect, and encourage actions that would be helpful to others.

Intellectual Abilities

Let's return once again to Hector's response to the Heinz dilemma: "In the eyes of the law he would not be doing the right thing, but in the eyes of the moral law he would." Advanced moral reasoning, involving thoughtful consideration of moral standards and such ideals as equality, justice, and basic human rights, requires reflection about multidimensional ideas (Kohlberg, 1976; Turiel, 2002). Children who are intellectually gifted are, on average, more likely than peers to analyze moral issues and address injustices (Schwenck et al., 2014; L. K. Silverman, 1994). In comparison, those with an intellectual disability tend to reason at lower levels regarding moral issues (Langdon, Clare, & Murphy, 2010).

Yet cognitive skills do not *guarantee* moral development. It is quite possible to think abstractly and yet reason in a self-centered, "preconventional" manner (Kohlberg, 1976). In other words, having a basic intellectual capacity is a necessary but insufficient condition for the development of moral reasoning.

Identity

Gaining a sense of oneself as a person who is caring, honest, and respectful of others' rights is an important achievement in moral development. Children are more likely to engage in compassionate action when they see themselves as capable of helping other people—in other words, when they are confident about their ability to make a positive difference (Narváez & Rest, 1995). This capacity begins in early childhood when children see themselves doing the right thing—even when no one is looking. In adolescence, youngsters typically integrate a commitment to moral values into their personal goals (Arnold, 2000; S. A. Hardy, Walker, Olsen, Woodbury, & Hickman, 2014; Heiphetz, Strohminger, Gelman, & Young, 2018). Those who think of themselves as moral, caring individuals place a high priority on acting the part. In middle and high school, acts of compassion are not limited to friends and acquaintances but frequently extend to the community at large, as was the case with young people in the opening case study.

Parenting

The nature of the parent–child relationship and the type of discipline a parent uses affect moral development. Having a warm relationship with parents motivates the child to notice and follow family rules (Kochanska & Kim, 2014; R. A. Thompson & Newton, 2010). Of course, no child adheres to a stringent moral code all of the time, and the way a parent responds to misbehavior influences children's future decisions. Parents who are consistent, warm, and levelheaded in their discipline promote children's attention to moral standards and inclinations to follow them. In comparison, severe punishment, especially physical punishment, focuses children on their own distress and not on why they should improve their behavior (Hoffman, 1975; Nucci, 2001).

Children are more likely to act with kindness when parents invite them to think about the harm that certain behaviors have caused for *others*. Giving children reasons why certain behaviors are unacceptable, with a focus on other people's perspectives, is known as **induction** (Hoffman, 1975). Consider these examples:

- "Having your hair pulled the way you just pulled Mai's can be really painful."
- "You probably hurt John's feelings when you call him names like that."
- "This science project you've just ridiculed may not be as fancy as yours, but I know that Michael spent many hours working on it and was quite proud of what he'd done."

Consistent use of induction in disciplining children, especially when accompanied by *mild* punishment for misbehavior—for instance, insisting that children make amends for their wrongdoings—promotes compliance with rules and empathy, compassion, and altruism (Hoffman, 1975; Patrick & Gibbs, 2012; R. A. Thompson & Newton, 2010). In contrast, power-assertive techniques, in which parents impose their will through spanking, making threats, expressing anger, and issuing commands (e.g., "Do this because I say so!"), are relatively *in*effective in promoting moral development (Damon, 1988; Kochanska et al., 2002; Labella & Masten, 2018; Zhou et al., 2002).

Parents also help their children live up to moral responsibility by talking about recent events in which children acted in consideration of, or with disregard for, the needs of others. These conversations are not strictly disciplinary but rather occasions for making sense of a morally charged event. When parents draw attention to how other people were helped or hurt by something the child did, he or she is apt to form a strong conscience (Laible & Thompson, 2000; Recchia et al., 2014; R. A. Thompson & Newton, 2010).

Interactions with Peers

Children receive numerous moral lessons while interacting with age-mates. As infants play with other children, they may notice others' reactions when they grab a toy or push them away. Beginning in the preschool years and continuing through middle childhood and adolescence, issues related to sharing, cooperation, and negotiation occur during group activities (Damon, 1981; Galliger, Tisak, & Tisak, 2009; K. McDonald, Malti, Killen, & Rubin, 2014). Conflicts frequently arise as a result of disagreements, disregard for one another's feelings, concerns about betrayal, and exclusion from social groups (Feigenberg, King, Barr, & Selman, 2008; Killen & Nucci, 1995; K. McDonald et al., 2014). To learn to resolve interpersonal conflicts successfully, children must engage in social perspective taking, show consideration for others' feelings, refrain from jumping to conclusions, and respect everyone's rights (Killen & Nucci, 1995; Komolova, Wainryb, & Recchia, 2017; Raikes, Virmani, Thompson, & Hatton, 2013; E. Singer & Doornenbal, 2006).

Gender

On average, girls are more likely than boys to express guilt, shame, empathy, and sympathy—emotions associated with moral behavior (Alessandri & Lewis, 1993; Apavaloaie, Page, & Marks, 2014; Mestre, Samper, Frías, & Tur, 2009; Roos, Hodges, & Salmivalli, 2014; Zahn-Waxler & Robinson, 1995). Girls' greater tendency to communicate guilt and shame may be related to their general inclination to attribute personal failures to internal qualities.

Do girls and boys also *reason* differently? In presenting a variety of moral dilemmas to young adults of both genders, Kohlberg found that females reasoned, on average, at Stage 3, whereas males were more likely to reason at Stage 4 (Kohlberg & Kramer, 1969). Yet psychologist **Carol Gilligan** has argued that Kohlberg's stages do not adequately describe female moral development (Gilligan, 1982, 1987; Gilligan & Attanucci, 1988). In particular, Gilligan has suggested that Kohlberg's stages reflect a **justice orientation**—an emphasis on fairness and equal rights—that better characterizes males' moral reasoning. In contrast, girls are socialized to take a **care orientation** toward moral issues—that is, to focus on interpersonal relationships and responsibility for others' well-being. The following dilemma can elicit either a justice orientation or a care orientation:

The Porcupine Dilemma

A group of industrious, prudent moles have spent the summer digging a burrow where they will spend the winter. A lazy, improvident porcupine who has not prepared a winter shelter approaches the moles and pleads to share their burrow. The moles take pity on the porcupine and agree to let him in. Unfortunately, the moles did not anticipate the problem the porcupine's sharp quills would pose in close quarters. Once the porcupine has moved in, the moles are constantly being stabbed. The question is, what should the moles do? (Meyers, 1987, p. 141, adapted from Gilligan, 1985).

People with a justice orientation are apt to look at this situation in terms of someone's rights being violated. They might point out that the burrow belongs to the moles, and so the moles can legitimately throw the porcupine out. If the porcupine refuses to leave, the moles might harm or perhaps even kill him. In contrast, people with a care orientation are likely to show compassion when dealing with the porcupine. They might suggest that the moles cover the porcupine with a blanket so his quills won't annoy anyone (D. T. Meyers, 1987).

Gilligan has raised a good point: There is more to moral thinking than justice. By including compassion as well as respect for others' rights, she has broadened our conception of what morality encompasses (Milanowicz & Bokus, 2013; L. J. Walker, 1995). However, most investigations do not find major gender differences in moral reasoning (Leman & Björnberg, 2010; L. J. Walker, 1991, 2006). Minor differences (usually favoring females) sometimes emerge in early adolescence but disappear by late adolescence (Basinger, Gibbs, & Fuller, 1995). Furthermore, males and females typically incorporate both justice and care into their moral reasoning, applying different orientations (sometimes one, sometimes the other, sometimes both) to different moral problems (Rothbart, Hanley, & Albert, 1986; Smetana, Killen, & Turiel, 1991; L. J. Walker, 2006). Such findings are sufficiently compelling that Gilligan herself has acknowledged that both justice and care orientations are frequently seen in males and females alike (L. M. Brown, Tappan, & Gilligan, 1995; Gilligan & Attanucci, 1988).

MyLab Education
Content Extension 14.1
Learn more about Gilligan's justice and care orientations.

Deliberations over Moral Issues

Kohlberg proposed that children grow morally when confronting moral dilemmas that are not easily reconciled with their current stage of moral reasoning—in other words, when they encounter situations that create disequilibrium. Discussions of moral issues appear to promote moral reasoning, especially when children are exposed to a position that's slightly more advanced than their present viewpoint (DeVries & Zan, 1996; Nucci, Creane, & Powers, 2015; Power, Higgins, & Kohlberg, 1989; Schlaefli, Rest, & Thoma, 1985). Teachers can integrate dilemmas into the curriculum, for example, by asking children whether it is right to steal food from a store to feed a hungry person (a moral issue), wear casual clothing to a formal event (a conventional issue), or wear a shirt with a rock band logo (a personal issue; Nucci, 2009).

Religious Doctrine

Having a religious faith or ethical position plays an integral role in the moral development of many children. Even though religious beliefs do not typically enhance moral reasoning as Kohlberg defined it, perhaps most of the time these beliefs do contribute to moral development by providing a compelling rationale for acting humanely (Fasoli, 2017; Needham-Penrose & Friedman, 2012; L. J. Walker & Reimer, 2006). Kohlberg's decision that justice, equality, and freedom must be espoused independently of a religious position in order to be considered advanced moral reasoning has been interpreted as a bias by scholars (Cullen, 1998; Moroney, 2006).

Despite the prevalent role of religion in justifying moral positions, having a religious faith has not been found to be crucial to moral advancement. Many children raised without a religious faith develop age-typical moral standards (McGowan, 2007; Norenzayan, 2014). Nor does religion ensure a moral orientation in a serious matter. In a few unfortunate cases, children are taught to use their faith as a justification for mistreating others, as has occurred in some White supremacy groups and terrorist organizations (P. E. King & Benson, 2006; J. Miller, 2013).

Culture

Each cultural group has unique standards for distinguishing between behaviors that are right or wrong. Consequently, there are differences by culture in moral behavior and reasoning. In many cultures, lying to avoid punishment for inappropriate behavior is considered wrong, but in some societies it is a legitimate way of saving face (Triandis, 1995).

Likewise, many cultures emphasize the importance of being considerate of other people (e.g., "Please be quiet so that your sister can study"), whereas others emphasize the importance of tolerating annoying behavior (e.g., "Please try not to let your brother's radio bother you when you study"; M. L. Fuller, 2001; H. L. Grossman, 1994). Likewise, some societies teach children to emphasize the rights of individuals and others a sense of duty to family and society or adherence to a sacred order (Haidt, 2008; J. G. Miller, 2007; Turiel, 2006a). Although many people in mainstream Western societies believe that males and females should have equal rights and opportunities, many Hindu people in India believe that a woman's obedience to her husband is vital to the moral order (Nucci, 2001; Shweder et al., 1987).

Despite these variations, separate cultures usually encourage a few common principles. Protecting others from harm is a universal value. Most cultures value both individual rights and concern for others (Turiel, 2006a; Turiel, Killen, & Helwig, 1987). And as you learned previously, children around the world distinguish moral, conventional, and personal issues. Children also commonly attend to the demands of situations, focusing on justice in some circumstances, compassion in others, and a balance between the two when possible (Lapsley & Carlo, 2014; J. G. Miller, 2007; Turiel, 1998; Turiel et al., 1987).

Promoting Moral Development

Preparing for Your Licensure Examination

Your teaching test might ask you about the breadth of variables that influence children's moral development.

Several educational strategies have been shown to promote moral reasoning and behavior. Consider the following recommendations:

- **Ask children for input on rules.** Children can gain insight into how communities function when they reflect on classroom rules (DeVries & Zan, 2003; F. C. Power & Scott, 2014). From such discussions they might learn that some children feel bullied and want to be protected with rules against harassment and the communication of expectations that classmates act respectfully. At the beginning of the school year, teachers frequently invite children to suggest classroom rules for helping everyone feel safe and be able to learn effectively. As the year progresses, children might give input into how to resolve sticky situations that arise during accidents, disputes, and distractions. Even preschool and kindergarten children can offer pragmatic solutions to realistic problems. When one educator asked preschoolers what it meant to abide by their classroom rule of not hurting their newly hatched chicks, the children came up with a combination of reasonable procedures, including picking up chicks carefully, not squeezing them, and not dropping them (DeVries & Zan, 2003). In the process of talking about rules, children are apt to feel included in the governance of the classroom.
- **Explain why certain behaviors are acceptable and others are not.** Adults must make it clear that some behaviors (e.g., shoving, making racist remarks, bringing weapons to school) are not acceptable under any circumstance. A preschool teacher might say, "If we throw the blocks, someone may get hurt" (Bronson, 2000, p. 206). An elementary school teacher might remind students, "We walk when we are in line so nobody gets bumped or tripped" (Bronson, 2000, p. 205). Children are also able to learn from classmates' descriptions of how they feel when they're teased (Doescher & Sugawara, 1989; Hoffman, 1991). With a bit of empathy, perpetrators of teasing may think twice next time, and bystanders may realize they need to intervene. In addition, adults can encourage children to make amends for misdeeds (Nucci, 2001). A middle school teacher might say, "I'm sure you didn't mean to hurt Jamal's feelings, but he's pretty upset about what you said. What might you do or say to make him feel better?" Adults also need to explain that some behaviors are appropriate in certain situations and restricted in others. Copying a classmate's work may be permissible when a student is in the process of learning but is unacceptable (constituting fraud) during tests of what a student has learned (Thorkildsen, 1995).
- **Discuss moral dilemmas with children.** Moral dilemmas often arise in conjunction with inappropriate behaviors at school (e.g., hitting, ridicule, and theft). One effective approach is to form a *just community*, in which students and their teachers hold regular "town meetings" to discuss recent interpersonal conflicts and establish rules that help students become more responsible (e.g., A. Higgins, 1995; Oser, Althof, & Higgins-D'Alessandro, 2008; Power et al., 1989).

Teachers and other professionals do several things to ensure that these discussions are productive (Nucci, 2001; Reimer, Paolitto, & Hersh, 1983; Thornberg, 2010). First, they create a trusting and nonthreatening atmosphere in which children feel free to express their ideas without censure or embarrassment. Second, they help children identify key aspects of a dilemma, including the perspectives of the individuals involved. Third, they encourage children to explore the underlying basis of their thinking. For example, adults might encourage children to look at a behavior from the extent to which moral concerns, conventions, and personal choice are all involved (Nucci & Weber, 1991). Although classmates who deface their school building with graffiti might believe they are engaging in creative self-expression (personal choice), they are also breaking a rule (convention), disregarding other students' rights to study in a clean setting (justice), and thumbing their noses at those around them (care).

• **Identify moral issues in the curriculum.** An English class studying works of Shakespeare might debate whether Hamlet was justified in killing Claudius as revenge for the murder of his father (Nucci, 2009). A science class might discuss the ethical issues involved in using laboratory rats to study the effects of cancer-producing agents. Classroom discussions can also help young people distinguish among moral, conventional, and personal matters in historical events. In American history a teacher might ask students to reflect on why George Washington refused to accept a letter from King George II of England. In Washington's mind, the letter violated an important social convention because it was addressed to "Mr. George Washington" rather than "President George Washington," thereby failing to recognize his status as leader of a legitimate nation (Nucci, 2001, 2006). Likewise, students might discuss moral dimensions in John Brown's 19th-century violent campaigns against slavery in the United States by considering the suffering inflicted on freedom fighters and oppressors (Nucci, 2001, 2006).

Preparing for Your Licensure Examination

Your teaching test might ask how you would facilitate discussions with children about social, moral, and personal issues.

• **Challenge children's moral reasoning with slightly more advanced positions.** Kohlberg's stages (see Table 14.1 on page 527) provide a useful framework for identifying moral arguments that provoke disequilibrium in youngsters. In particular, Kohlberg suggested that teachers offer reasoning that is one stage above a child's current thinking. Imagine that a teenage boy who is concerned primarily with gaining peer approval (Stage 3) often lets a popular cheerleader copy his homework. His teacher might present law-and-order logic (Stage 4), suggesting that a homework assignment has been designed to help students learn more effectively, especially when completed with minimal assistance. If adults present arguments at a level that is too high, then children will have trouble understanding the logic and therefore disregard the argument (Boom, Brugman, & van der Heijden, 2001; Narváez, 1998).

• **Encourage children to invite excluded classmates to participate in activities.** In almost every school, some children are excluded from social groups. Such rejection can occur as a result of prejudice, with students occasionally perceiving peers with disabilities, those from low-income backgrounds, and individuals from different ethnic groups as undesirable playmates (Killen, Mulvey, & Hitti, 2013; Killen & Smetana, 2010). Complicating matters, many children view the issue of selecting peers to eat lunch with or sit next to on the bus as their personal choice. Thus, they may feel justified when banning certain peers from their play. Teachers can appeal to children's sense of fairness by pointing out that their classroom is a place where *all* children belong; they can help by inviting children who are left out to sit with them at lunch, join them on the playground, and come to their birthday party. Teachers can also appeal to children's empathy by explaining that excluded classmates are likely to feel hurt by the slight.

• **Establish cooperative learning groups.** For certain lessons, teachers can arrange cooperative learning groups. Oftentimes, a teacher puts children together in four-person groups and assigns a role to each, perhaps timekeeper, recorder, materials manager, and spokesperson (Brame & Biel, 2015). The roles rotate regularly such that every child spends time in each position. The teacher gives students feedback periodically as to how well they had been working together, and students are evaluated on group projects and individual reports. Cooperative learning groups can be an effective way to promote academic learning and the inclusion of children who are different in some way from others, perhaps because they are learning English, are an ethnic minority, or have a disability

(Garrote, Dessemontet, & Opitz, 2016). When cooperative groups work as intended, children see one another contributing to everyone's accomplishments.

• **Involve children in community service.** As you've learned, youngsters are more likely to act morally when they see themselves as honest, fair, just, and compassionate. Young people are more likely to be confident in helping others when they have guidance. Through ongoing **service learning**—food and clothing drives, visits to homes for the elderly, community cleanup efforts, and so on—students can learn that they have the skills to help those less fortunate than themselves. In the process, many think of themselves as concerned citizens (Nucci, 2001; O'Flaherty, Liddy, Tansey, & Roche, 2011; Youniss & Yates, 1999). Even elementary school children can become more empathic by holding a clothing drive for a homeless shelter, hosting a toy drive for hospitalized children, planting flowers at their school, and so on (K. E. Scott & Graham, 2015). To gain full advantage of service learning, students need to have choice in the projects they take on, reflect on what they accomplished at the completion of the project, and either write about or discuss their experiences with others (T. Gross, 2010; D. Hart, Atkins, & Donnelly, 2006; Morimoto & Friedland, 2013; Nucci, 2006; Preus, Payne, Wick, & Glomski, 2016; J. Terry, Smith, & McQuillin, 2014).

• **Foster religious tolerance.** In the United States, the First Amendment to the Constitution requires that matters of church and state be kept separate. Many other nations offer similar protections. Under such a mandate, public school teachers can discuss religion within the context of social studies or other appropriate academic topics. What is not allowed is incorporating religious practices into school activities in a way that shows preference for one religion over another; also discouraged is expressing a preference for religion over atheism (or vice versa). Many school districts have policies that prohibit name-calling related to religious beliefs, practices, and affiliations. Teaching respect for diverse religious perspectives is not the same as accepting the legitimacy of all customs justified by religious beliefs. Adults will certainly want to question practices that blatantly violate people's basic human rights. It *does* mean, however, that everyone must work hard to understand others' behaviors within the context of their religious beliefs.

• **Appeal to children's emotional sensitivities.** Kohlberg's theory of moral development has been enormously influential, as you have learned, but its historical focus on cognition has eclipsed the role of emotions in moral reasoning and behavior (Lapsley & Carlo, 2014). Virtually all children are born with neurologically based emotional capacities that, with affectionate care, connect up with brain circuits for cognitive abilities (for moral reasoning) and procedural skills (for helping and hurting behaviors). Teachers can strengthen these neurological connections by asking children how they felt during difficult circumstances, inquiring into other people's experiences, and encouraging children to join them in small acts of kindness.

• **Discourage cheating.** *Cheating* refers to the deliberate act of breaking a rule and misrepresenting oneself as playing fair in order to gain an advantage. Academic cheating, in which children falsely pass off someone else's schoolwork as their own, is common in schools, especially in the middle and high school grades (X. Ding et al., 2014; Muñoz-García & Aviles-Herrera, 2014). Students cheat by sharing answers and accessing information from prohibited sources (e.g., by getting answers on the Internet, paying others to write essays for them, and hiding such contraband resources as definitions, equations, or formulas).

From a moral perspective, cheating is wrong because students deceive the teacher as to who completed the schoolwork. The result is that the teacher obtains inaccurate indicators of students' abilities and makes decisions (e.g., who receives a high school diploma) that are unfair (Muñoz-García & Aviles-Herrera, 2014). Students are harmed by cheating when dishonesty becomes a habit because they reduce their effort at school and come to see themselves as lacking in integrity. Children do not automatically understand the moral implications of cheating, however. For many young people, cheating does not hurt anyone, certainly not in the same way as pushing classmates off the swing or stealing their lunch. Some see cheating as a reasonable way to complete difficult assignments, cope with anxiety, exercise weak skills, and finish requirements early (Hensley, 2013; F. Power & Power, 2006).

Children need to be taught why cheating is wrong. Consider the following tactics for fostering academic honesty:

- *Develop an honor code.* Honor codes assert a school body's commitment to live by virtues of academic honesty. Teachers can talk about the honor code with children, describing its intentions and helping them connect abstract values with relevant behaviors, for example, respecting other people's creativity by not copying their statements word for word.
- *Establish a climate of learning that is conducive to academic integrity.* Academic integrity means being honest and responsible in school assignments. These virtues are more likely to develop when teachers explain them and motivate students with interesting and relevant material (Sorenson & Goldsmith, 2012). In other words, children are less likely to cheat when they are motivated to learn the material.
- *Explain the different forms of cheating, tactics that school personnel take to identify them, and penalties that students suffer when caught.* Students need to learn what plagiarism is, why it is wrong, and how they can avoid it. In many situations it is fine for children to share ideas with one another, and therefore they need to know why and when they must work on their own.
- *Empathize with students about the pressures they experience in schoolwork.* A primary reason children cheat is that they want to do well on their assignments, do not know how to study, and are worried about their performance. Answering their questions about schoolwork and reassuring them that they can talk with you is an important step in taking the desperation out of assignments.
- *Supervise tests, watch for plagiarism, and be vigilant for other types of cheating.* Students are less likely to cheat when they think they might be caught, and therefore teachers are advised to monitor tests, walk around the room, and look for banned resources, such as cell phones, that are common devices for accessing prohibited information.
- *Follow through with penalties.* Given how prevalent cheating is, penalties should be serious but not severe. For instance, students might be asked to redo assignments they have plagiarized in a first offense and receive a zero on a second offense. Students who persist with dishonest behaviors after being chastised may require counseling and other interventions, as this type of behavior is associated with later problems in the adult years (G. E. Miller, 1987).

Children's understanding of cheating develops as they grow, especially when adults nurture their honesty, draw attention to the negative side-effects of cheating, and take reasonable precautions to reduce access to prohibited resources.

MyLab Education Application Exercise 14.1
Detect Developmental Levels

How do children reason about why it would be okay or not okay for Steve to cheat? Children of various ages reason about why it would be wrong to cheat on a test.

Summary

An ability to distinguish between right and wrong emerges early in life and continues to develop over time. Infants are uncomfortable when they witness others being hurt. Most preschoolers are aware that actions that cause significant physical or psychological harm are wrong even if an authority figure tells them otherwise. Young children distinguish transgressions that violate moral rules from actions that are inconsistent with conventional social practices and from decisions that are generally considered a matter of personal choice. As children get older, they better understand fairness and feel guilt, shame, and empathy about moral wrongdoings. As they advance in cognitive skills, and especially as they become capable of abstract thought, young people reason about moral issues in more sophisticated ways, and they are more likely to behave in accordance with moral principles. Nevertheless, even at the high school level, youngsters do not always take the moral high road because personal needs and self-interests enter into their decisions.

To some degree, different cultures foster distinct moral values, yet virtually all societies recognize fairness, justice, and concern for others. Adults can promote young people's moral development by explaining why certain behaviors are unacceptable (in that they cause harm to another person or jeopardize his or her rights), engaging youngsters in discussions about moral dilemmas, exposing them to slightly more advanced moral perspectives, getting them actively involved in service to others, and teaching them not to teach.

MyLab Education Self-Check 14.1

Prosocial Behavior and Aggression

14.2 Identify key influences on the development of prosocial and aggressive behaviors, including methods at school that promote good behavior and safe school environments.

Children's helping and hurting behaviors have an impact on other people's well-being and therefore have moral implications. **Prosocial behavior** is an action intended to promote the welfare of another person, perhaps by sharing, teaching, or comforting. **Aggression** is an action intentionally taken to hurt another person either physically (e.g., hitting, shoving, or fighting) or psychologically (e.g., embarrassing, insulting, or ostracizing). Let's consider the typical developmental course of these behaviors, their origins, and their educational implications.

Development of Prosocial Behavior

Even young infants are attuned to others' distress, for example, they may cry when they hear other babies crying (Eisenberg, 1992; Hatfield, Cacioppo, & Rapson, 1994). True prosocial behaviors appear in the first year (M. Carpenter, Uebel, & Tomasello, 2013; Farver & Branstetter, 1994; Hammond, Al-Jbouri, Edwards, & Feltham, 2017; Jing, Saether, & Sommerville, 2016; Kärtner, Keller, & Chaudhary, 2010; Zahn-Waxler et al., 1992). Before their first birthday, infants extend their limbs to make it easier for parents to put on their clothes, and they occasionally put away their toys and wipe down a high chair surface (Hammond et al., 2017). Toddlers spontaneously give adults or peers assistance with everyday tasks, and they might offer their favorite blanket or teddy bear to someone who appears unhappy or in pain.

As a general rule, children become more attentive to others' welfare—for instance, they become increasingly generous—as they grow older, especially when parents are affectionate and encourage their helpfulness (C. A. Brownell, Svetlova, Anderson, Nichols, & Drummond, 2013; Eisenberg, 1982; K. K. Williams & Berthelsen, 2017). The endearing gestures of infancy and early childhood give way to more thoughtful assistance in the elementary school years and afterwards.

Children become more prosocial, in part, because they recognize an increasing number of reasons for helping others. Some motivations are self-serving. Helpful gestures are more common when benefits outweigh the costs—for instance, when children think the beneficiary might eventually do them a favor in return (Eisenberg, Fabes, Schaller, Carlo, & Miller, 1991; L. Peterson, 1980). A 3-year-old boy brings a toy to a distressed peer, hoping the other child will stop his annoying crying. A 7-year-old girl tutors a classmate with schoolwork in order to gain her teacher's approval.

Genuine concern about others deepens during childhood and becomes a serious motive for prosocial behavior. In the process of putting themselves in someone else's shoes, children experience that person's feelings—that is, they have *empathy*. Many children who behave prosocially feel *sympathy*, a concern for another that does not necessarily involve sharing the same feeling as that person (Batson, 1991; A. Edwards et al., 2014; Eisenberg, Eggum, & Edwards, 2010). Empathy and sympathy are powerful motivators for prosocial behavior, and the relationships among empathy, sympathy, and prosocial behavior are complex. Empathy is not present with every good turn, and when it is, it by itself is insufficient to generate truly helpful actions. Children need to be capable of determining what support is needed and finding a way to provide it. Some students are sympathetic toward the plight of others but do not step forward because of their uncertainty over *how* to lend a hand. Sometimes children are empathic toward another's distress yet consumed by their own distress and consequently unable to act responsibly (Eisenberg et al., 2010).

An additional factor in prosocial development is growth in knowledge about what can be accomplished for persons in need. Children are more likely to help another individual if they themselves have been the cause of the person's pain or distress (Eisenberg, 1995). Thus, feeling guilty is one precipitator of prosocial behavior (Eisenberg et al., 2010). Another is seeing the person as being worthy of their help. Children are more likely to behave prosocially if others' misfortunes are the result of an accident, disability, or other uncontrollable circumstance, rather than the result of something the distressed people might be construed as having brought upon themselves (Eisenberg & Fabes, 1998; S. Graham, 1997).

Finally, children increasingly formalize their sense of responsibility to help others. As they grow older, children increasingly help others as a result of a

OBSERVATION GUIDELINES

Assessing Children's Prosocial Development

CHARACTERISTIC	LOOK FOR	EXAMPLE	IMPLICATION
Hedonistic Orientation *(common in preschool and the early elementary grades)*	• Tendency to help others only when one can simultaneously address one's own needs • Prosocial behaviors directed primarily toward familiar adults and peers	Several preschoolers are at a table drawing pictures. Peter is using the only black crayon at the table. Alaina asks him for the crayon so she can color her dog black, telling him, "I just need it for a second." Ignoring her, Peter continues to use the black crayon for several minutes.	Point out that other people have legitimate needs, and emphasize the importance of fairness and the value in helping others. For example, ask children to be "reading buddies" for younger children, explaining that doing so will help them become better readers themselves.
Superficial Needs-of-Others Orientation *(common in the elementary grades)*	• Some willingness to help others even at personal sacrifice • Only superficial understanding of others' perspectives	During an annual holiday toy drive, many children in a third-grade class contribute toys they have outgrown. They seem happy to do so, commenting that "Poor kids need toys too" and "This doll will be fun for somebody else to play with."	Commend youngsters for altruistic behaviors, and ask them to speculate on how their actions help recipients (e.g., "Can you imagine how the children will feel when they get your toys? Most of them escaped the flood with only the clothes on their backs.").
Stereotyped, Approval-Focused Orientation *(seen in some elementary and secondary students)*	• Tendency to behave prosocially as a means to gain others' approval • Simplistic, stereotypical views of what "good" and "bad" people do	When walking to school, Cari sees Stanley stumble and accidentally drop his backpack in a puddle. She stops, asks if he's okay, and helps him wipe off his backpack. As she describes the incident to her teacher, she says, "Maybe he'll be my friend now. Anyway, it's nice to help someone."	Provide opportunities for youngsters to engage in prosocial activities. Choose activities that are apt to be enjoyable and in other ways rewarding in and of themselves.
Empathic Orientation *(common in the secondary grades)*	• Genuine empathy for other people's distress, even when one does not know the people personally • Willingness to help without regard for consequences to oneself	Members of a high school club coordinate a schoolwide garage sale, with proceeds going to help pay the medical expenses of a classmate with a rare form of cancer. Students collect contributions and use their own money for supplies to make the fund-raiser a success.	Alert youngsters to circumstances in which people's basic needs are not being met or in which human rights are being violated. Ask youngsters to brainstorm ways in which they might, in some small way, make a difference for people living in these circumstances.
Internalized-Values Orientation *(seen in a small minority of high school students)*	• Generalized concern for equality, dignity, human rights, and the welfare of society as a whole • Commitment to helping others integrated into one's sense of self	Franklin spends much of his free time working with Habitat for Humanity, an organization of volunteers who build houses for low-income families. "It's everyone's responsibility to help one another," he says.	Create assignments—public service projects, fund-raisers, and so on—in which youngsters with an internalized-values orientation can invest in prosocial activities with peers.

Sources: First two columns based on Eisenberg (1982), Eisenberg et al. (1995), and Eisenberg, Lennon, and Pasternack (1986).

commitment to being compassionate. American psychologist **Nancy Eisenberg** and her colleagues have identified five different levels, or *orientations*, to prosocial behavior. Eisenberg asked children about whether peers in a scenario should choose between fulfilling their own desires or helping others in need. For example, when Mary is on her way to a birthday party, she comes across a child who has been injured in a fall. Should she stop to help or keep going to the party? Eisenberg found age-related changes in reasoning about their responses, producing a continuum from self-interest to caring for others. Children do not go through the orientations in a lockstep manner, however. Their behavior is apt to reflect two or more orientations in any particular time period, even as they increasingly exhibit more advanced orientations (Eisenberg, Carlo, Murphy, & Van Court, 1995; Eisenberg, Fabes, & Spinrad, 2006; Eisenberg, Miller, Shell, McNalley, & Shea, 1991). These orientations are described in the Observation Guidelines table "Assessing Children's Prosocial Development" on the previous page.

Piecing together the different data on children's prosocial behavior, we see that children try to help others from the first year of life. Children are motivated in their prosocial behavior by feelings of empathy or sympathy, and occasionally by a self-serving desire. Not every attempt by children to help others results in a beneficial effect, yet as their prosocial reasoning advances, children become better able to comfort and care for others.

Development of Aggression

Unfortunately, some children find that aggression is more satisfying than prosocial behavior. **Physical aggression** is an action that can cause bodily injury. Examples are hitting, pushing, fighting, and using weapons. **Relational aggression** is an action that can adversely affect friendships. Examples are name-calling, spreading unflattering rumors, and ostracizing a peer from a desirable social group.

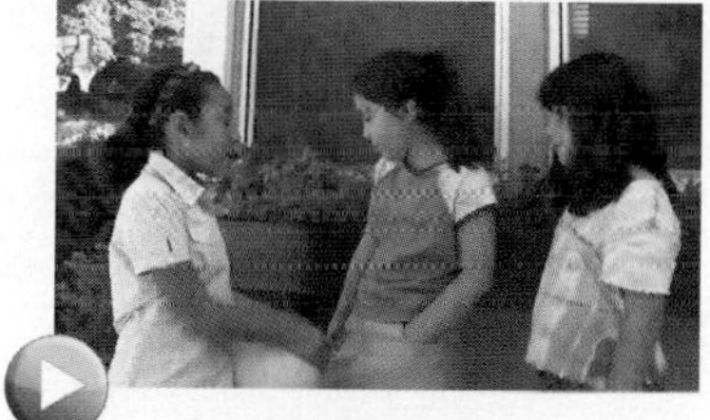

MyLab Education
Video Example 14.2
Find Developmental Meaning
How do children exhibit relational aggression during unstructured peer interaction? A girl slights her friend by running off with another girl.

The capacity for aggression emerges early. By the latter half of the first year, infants show anger toward caregivers who prevent them from reaching the objects they desire (Hay, 2017; Lorber, Del Vecchio, & Smith Slep, 2014; C. R. Stenberg & Campos, 1990). As they approach their first birthday, infants may swat at others, bite, or pull the hair of someone who obstructs their actions (e.g., grabbing and shaking a rattle; Caplan, Vespo, Pedersen, & Hay, 1991; Dodge, Coie, & Lynam, 2006; Hay, 2017). In their second year, children forcefully remove a toy that an age-mate took from them. By 18 months, children occasionally hit, kick, push, and bite others (Nærde, Ogden, Janson, & Daae Zachrisson, 2014; Tremblay et al., 2004).

Conflicts over possessions are common during the preschool years, and children struggle not to hit or grab (S. Jenkins, Bax, & Hart, 1980). For most children, physical aggression declines after early childhood, probably for several reasons: Children learn to control their impulses, acquire better strategies for resolving conflicts, and become increasingly proficient at relational aggression (Dodge et al., 2006; Flanders et al., 2010; Mischel, 1974). A decline in physical aggression is not universal, however. When children remain physically aggressive after the transition into kindergarten, they are at risk for problems in social adjustment, peer acceptance, and relationships with teachers (Gower, Lingras, Mathieson, Kawabata, & Crick, 2014).

MyLab Education
Video Example 14.3
Find Developmental Meaning
How might a teacher of young children nurture self-control during scuffles with age-mates? A young boy starts to push and grab before being reminded to use his words.

Children who fail to show the expected decline in fighting usually exhibit one of two profiles. Children who exhibit **reactive aggression** hit, push, and shove primarily in response to frustration, anger, or provocation (Crick & Dodge, 1996; Hubbard, Morrow, Romano, & McAuliffe, 2010; Poulin & Boivin, 1999). When an age-mate teases a child for losing a game, the child may impulsively punch the teaser. Children who engage primarily in **proactive aggression** deliberately initiate aggressive behaviors—physical aggression, relational aggression, or both—as a means of obtaining desired goals. For example, a child may callously push an age-mate out of the way at a vending machine when he hears that there is only one remaining can of soda.

Proactively aggressive children sometimes funnel hurtful actions toward one or a few specific peers, and those who do are known as **bullies**. Bullies, like other aggressive children, have problems handling emotions, especially anger. They have weak social skills and are less empathic than age-mates. Yet bullies have unique characteristics not shared with other aggressive children. Bullies are selective. They develop a peculiar relationship with their victims, whom they repeatedly humiliate, threaten, and intimidate. Many bullies who pick on certain children were previously victimized themselves (and are sometimes called bully-victims). Bullies can also become victims later on, as a result of weak social skills.

Bullies and other aggressive children may have one or more of the following limitations:

- *They misinterpret social cues.* Children who are either physically or relationally aggressive tend to interpret others as having hostile intentions, especially when such behaviors are ambiguous in intent. This **hostile attributional bias** is especially prevalent in children who are prone to *reactive* aggression (Cicchetti, Murray-Close, Cillessen, Lansu, & Van Den Berg, 2014; Crick & Dodge, 1996; Dodge et al., 2003; A. L. C. Fung, 2017; A. Law & Fung, 2013). Thus, if a clumsy peer bumps gently into a reactively aggressive child, the aggressive child may assume that the act was deliberately hurtful, retaliating with a push.
- *They prioritize self-serving goals.* For most young people, establishing and maintaining interpersonal relationships are high priorities. For aggressive children, self-serving goals—perhaps maintaining an inflated self-image, seeking revenge, or gaining power and prestige—may take precedence (Crick & Dodge, 1996; K. L. McDonald, Baden, & Lochman, 2013).
- *They have rudimentary social problem-solving skills.* Aggressive children often have little knowledge of how to persuade, negotiate, or compromise, and they resort to hitting, shoving, and barging into play (Priddis, Landy, Moroney, & Kane, 2014).
- *They believe that their hurtful actions are justified.* Many aggressive children believe that violence and other forms of aggression are acceptable ways of resolving conflicts and retaliating for others' misdeeds. They may believe they need to teach someone a "lesson." Those who display high rates of *proactive* aggression are apt to believe that aggressive action will yield positive results—for instance, that it will enhance their social status (Hubbard et al., 2010).
- *They are morally disengaged.* By early adolescence, aggressive young people rationalize their aggressive behaviors by reframing them (perhaps the person deserved it, or maybe the victim was not really hurt all that much), blaming the victim, and minimizing their own role in the transgression (Bandura, 2016; Paciello, Masi, Clemente, Milone, & Muratori, 2017; Ribeaud & Eisner, 2015).
- *They use multiple outlets.* Aggressive children pester peers in multiple ways. They ridicule age-mates in the classroom, spread rumors on the lunch line, and send embarrassing images of classmates over social media (Bauman, 2011; Compton, Campbell, & Mergler, 2014; Solomontos-Kountouri, Tsagkaridis, Gradinger, & Strohmeier, 2017). *Cyberbullies* provoke anguish in their victims with accusations and threats.

We'd be remiss if we did not consider the special needs of children who are routinely victimized by bullies. Any child can become the butt of jokes at one time or another, but there are some common characteristics of children who are regular targets of bullies. Compared to peers, they are shy, immature, anxious, friendless, lacking in self-confidence, and unaccustomed to defending themselves (Bierman, 2004; Marsh, Parada, Yeung, & Healey, 2001; Pellegrini, Bartini, & Brooks, 1999). Some have disabilities, are overweight, or are gay, lesbian, bisexual, or transgender (Juvonen & Graham, 2014).

Children who are mistreated benefit from guidance, sympathy, and reassurance that the bully will not be allowed to intimidate them anymore. Teachers and counselors can comfort victims and, when necessary, teach them skills in self-defense, negotiation, and self-assertion. Intervention is important because children who have been bullied are at risk for anxiety, depression, other mental health problems, chronic health conditions, and conflicts in intimate relationships (W. E. Copeland et al., 2014; Sigurdson, Wallander, & Sund, 2014; Wolke, Lereya, Fisher, Lewis, & Zammit, 2014).

MyLab Education Application Exercise 14.2
Meet Individual Needs

How does a girl who has been bullied describe the motivations of bullies and the experience of victims? A girl interprets the bullying dynamic.

Bystanders to bullying have their own needs. They may be distressed about seeing another child harmed and then afterward feel guilty that they did not intervene and worry they might be next (Pozzoli, Gini, & Thornberg, 2017). Some bystanders encourage the bully by laughing at his or her acts of ridicule. School professionals must vehemently discourage bullying, monitor aggression over time, and educate everyone about how to respond to intimidation.

As you have learned, helping and hurting behaviors change steadily over the childhood years. In the Developmental Trends table "Prosocial and Aggressive Behavior at Different Age Levels," we present characteristics that teachers and other practitioners are likely to see, as well as common forms of diversity in the age-groups.

Prosocial Behavior and Aggression in a Developmental System

Children's helping and hurting behaviors emerge out of multiple factors—heredity, biological factors, childrearing practices, modeling, peer relationships, emotional

DEVELOPMENTAL TRENDS
Prosocial and Aggressive Behavior at Different Age Levels

AGE	WHAT YOU MIGHT OBSERVE	DIVERSITY	IMPLICATION
Infancy (Birth–2 Years)	• Cooperation in first year as parents diaper, feed, and clothe infants • Appearance of simple prosocial behaviors (e.g., offering a teddy bear to a crying child) in second year • Anger at caregivers who prevent reaching desired objects • Conflicts with peers about toys and other objects • Occasional biting, hitting, or scratching of peers	• Infants are more inclined to show prosocial actions when caregivers model these behaviors. • Some children have "difficult" temperaments; they may be especially contrary in the second year, biting others or exhibiting frequent temper tantrums.	• Allow infants to interact with one another under your supervision. • Verbalize sympathy toward an injured child within earshot of the other children. • Warmly acknowledge infants' helping. • Provide duplicates of favorite toys and create separate areas for quiet play and active movement. • Tell toddlers that hitting is hurtful and provokes consequences (e.g., brief time-out). Demonstrate gentle touch instead.
Early Childhood (2–6 Years)	• Basic signs of empathy for people in distress • Rudimentary sharing and coordination of play activities • Attempts to comfort people in distress, especially those whom children know well; comforting strategies not always effective • Occasional aggressive struggles over possessions • Emerging ability to inhibit aggressive impulses	• Children who are impulsive may use more physical aggression than those who are patient and self-controlled. • Children are more apt to behave prosocially if they are reinforced for such behavior. • On average, boys are more physically aggressive than are girls.	• Recognize that selfish and territorial behaviors are common in early childhood. • Model sympathetic responses; explain how you are helping out. • Encourage children to comfort a distressed peer. • Praise controlled and constructive responses to frustration. • Comfort victims of aggression, and administer punishment to perpetrators.

(continued)

DEVELOPMENTAL TRENDS

Prosocial and Aggressive Behavior at Different Age Levels (Continued)

AGE	WHAT YOU MIGHT OBSERVE	DIVERSITY	IMPLICATION
Middle Childhood (6–10 Years)	• Growing repertoire of conflict resolution skills • Increasing empathy for unknown individuals who are suffering or needy • Growing desire to help others as a goal in and of itself • Decrease in overt physical aggression, accompanied by a rise in relational aggression (e.g., ostracizing and ridiculing others) and covert antisocial behaviors (e.g., lying, stealing)	• Children whose parents value prosocial behavior are more likely to express concern for others. • Some children consistently misinterpret peers' thoughts and motives (e.g., by interpreting accidents as deliberate attempts to cause harm). • A few children become increasingly aggressive in the elementary grades. • Some children are regularly victimized (e.g., those without friends or with disabilities).	• Ask disagreeing children to consider a rival's perspective, and together generate solutions that address everyone's needs. • Draw attention to a consoled child's relief ("Look how much better Sally feels now that you've apologized for hurting her feelings"). • Make sure children understand rules for behavior, and respond to aggression with consequences. • Coach victimized children with self-assertion and social skills. • With help from a psychologist, plan interventions for exceptionally aggressive children.
Early Adolescence (10–14 Years)	• Idealism about a community being respectful and caring • Kindness to others, especially friends and loved ones in trouble • Decline in physical aggression • Frequent teasing and taunting of peers; occasional sexual harassment • Bullying using social network sites and cell phones • Occasional name-calling of teachers and other adults	• Some adolescents develop a concern for younger children, animals, old people, or others. • A large number of young people make fun of peers, sometimes persistently. • Adolescents with conduct disorders may show deficits in empathy. • Bullying behavior in some youngsters temporarily increases after the transition to middle school or junior high.	• Communicate that giving, sharing, and caring for others are high priorities. • Keep a watchful eye on students' activities between classes and during afternoon dismissal; make it clear that aggression is *not* acceptable on school grounds. • Talk with adolescents about their peer relationships and pressures on them to conform.
Late Adolescence (14–18 Years)	• For many, decreasing aggressive behavior, often after forming intimate relationships with others • Relational aggression in the form of teasing, excluding others, or cyberbullying • Ability to offer constructive help to others as individuals or members of volunteer groups	• Some high school students are committed to making the world a better place. • On average, youngsters who live in violent neighborhoods are more apt to be aggressive than are peers in safer neighborhoods. • Violence-prone adolescents may believe that hitting another person is reasonable retribution for unjust actions. • Substance abuse and sexual activity can be factors in aggression.	• Encourage community service and other work. in helping others. Ask adolescents to discuss their experiences with others or in written essays. • Enforce prohibitions against bringing weapons to school. • Provide intensive treatment to young people who exhibit heightened aggression.

experiences, and cognitive reflections. In this section we look at key influences on children's prosocial and aggressive behavior.

Developmental Systems Prompt 14.2

Prosocial behavior and aggression are affected by nature, nurture, and experience. When children require assistance in becoming more helpful and less hurtful, intervene in a manner that is developmentally appropriate, addresses their individual characteristics, sets realistic standards for growth, and is sensitive to their upbringing.

Biological Factors

From an evolutionary perspective, both prosocial and aggressive inclinations contributed to survival in the human species (Hoffman, 1981; McCullough, Kurzban, & Tabak, 2011; Meloni, 2013). Prosocial behavior provides the basis for close relationships, promotes group cohesion, and helps people pull together in harsh conditions. Squabbling and warfare cause people to spread apart (thereby improving their chances of finding food and other essential resources) and, in times of battle, to compete such that only the strongest members survive and, later pass on their genes in sturdy offspring.

An evolutionary perspective of such behaviors is, of course, speculative. Twin studies provide more convincing evidence that both prosocial and aggressive behaviors have biological origins. Monozygotic (identical) twins tend to be more similar than dizygotic (fraternal) twins with respect to altruistic behavior, empathy for others, and aggression (Brendgen, 2014; Eisenberg et al., 2006; Lacourse et al., 2014; Knafo-Noam, Uzefovsky, Israel, Davidov, & Zahn-Waxler 2015; Rushton, Fulkner, Neal, Nias, & Eysenck, 1986). The full range of genes that affect children's tendencies to be helpful or hurtful has not been documented, yet it is known that genes direct hormones and areas in the brain that handle emotions and interpretation of social cues.

A few factors in heightened aggression have been identified. Chemical substances in the brain, partly guided by genes, affect children's dispositions for seeking out novel stimulation, inhibiting impulses, coping with frustration, and lashing out at others (E. Baker, Shelton, Baibazarova, Hay, & van Goozen, 2013; Gorodetsky et al., 2014). On average, males are more aggressive than females, and after puberty, males with high testosterone levels tend to be more aggressive than those with lower levels (Carney & Mason, 2010; Susman et al., 1987). Young people with damage to the front of the brain's cortex, which is involved in planning, behavior control, and toning down the emotional amygdala center, display heightened aggression (Bertsch et al., 2013; Pennington & Bennetto, 1993; Raine & Scerbo, 1991; S. F. White et al., 2016).

Parenting

Close relationships are powerful catalysts for helping and hurting behaviors. Children whose parents are sensitive, compassionate, and responsive tend to become empathic, cooperative, and helpful themselves (Hammond et al., 2017; Healy, Sanders, & Iyer, 2014; R. A. Thompson & Newton, 2010). Children are more likely to be cooperative with others when parents exhibit an *authoritative* parenting style—that is, when parents are warm and loving, hold high standards for behavior, and tell them why certain behaviors are unacceptable (Baumrind, Larzelere, & Owens, 2010; Hoffman, 1988; Padilla-Walker, Carlo, Christensen, & Yorgason, 2012). Children likewise become more prosocial when parents enlist their help in looking after younger siblings and doing household chores (Carlo, Koller, Raffaelli, & de Guzman, 2007; Whiting & Whiting, 1975).

Children whose parents are harsh or neglectful are at definite risk for becoming aggressive and developing mental health problems. Hostile parents embolden children to hurt others, particularly with using reactive aggression, in that children grow accustomed to letting their frustrations escalate into attacks on others (Fite et al., 2010). Frequent physical punishment breeds aggression, and so occasionally does very *permissive* parenting, presumably because children are left to their own devices in dealing with negative urges (Ehrenreich, Beron, Brinkley, & Underwood, 2014; Straus, 2000).

In addition to socializing children's prosocial and aggressive behavior through discipline and hands-on care, parents engage children in social learning. Children who observe sympathetic and generous models tend to be more helpful than those without such exposure (R. Elliott & Vasta, 1970; M. Mares, Palmer, & Sullivan, 2008). Children notice and later emulate a parent's charitable acts. Through similar processes, children who observe aggressive models show a greater-than-average number of antagonistic acts (C. A. Anderson et al., 2003; Febres et al., 2014; Huesmann, Dubow, & Boxer, 2011).

Over the short run, children engage in more prosocial behavior if they are rewarded (e.g., with candy or praise) for such behavior (Eisenberg, Fabes, Carlo, & Karbon, 1992; Ramaswamy & Bergin, 2009). However, rewards are counterproductive later on, possibly because children begin to perform prosocial actions primarily to benefit themselves ("I gave her my candy because I knew Dad would give me an even bigger treat for sharing"; Eisenberg & Fabes, 1998; Szynal-Brown & Morgan, 1983). Aggressive behavior can be reinforced by its outcomes: It may enable children to gain desired objects or get revenge (Crick & Dodge, 1996; Lochman, Wayland, & White, 1993).

School, Culture, and Society

Schools are busy environments with frequent acts of kindness and rudeness. Children are more likely to engage in prosocial behaviors, as well as integrate compassion into their identity, when teachers and other adults encourage empathy for others (Krishnakumar, Narine, Roopnarine, & Logie, 2014; Youniss & Yates, 1999). Conversely, young people who regularly encounter mild aggression at school, typically in the form of racial and sexual harassment, bullying, and vandalism, are likely to conclude that hostility is a natural part of life (J. K. Bayer et al., 2018; Bibou-Nakou, Asimopoulos, Hatzipemou, Soumaki, & Tsiantis, 2014; Frey, Newman, & Onyewuenyi, 2014; Garbarino, Bradshaw, & Vorrasi, 2002).

Neighborhoods can also influence helping and hurting behaviors (Su, Mrug, & Windle, 2010). Community violence is associated with proactive aggression, presumably because some young people who witness violent events eventually commit aggressive

MyLab Education
Artifact 14.1
Find Developmental Meaning
How does 6-year-old Myron imagine a superhero on television? In his drawing, Myron has given the superhero a large weapon.

acts of their own (Fite et al., 2010). Exposure to high rates of violence on television and in electronic games also increases children's aggression. Decades of evidence from all sorts of methodologies indicate that witnessing a lot of violence in electronic media can make young people more aggressive, especially when they start out more antagonistic than age-mates (Hartmann, Krakowiak, & Tsay-Vogel, 2014). Children's own temperament, motivation, history of acting forcefully, and child-rearing experiences affect how much they are affected by violent content. In his artwork in an Artifact Example 14.1, 6-year-old Myron shows his receptivity to an image of a powerful, gun-toting superhero.

The child's culture likewise determines targets of, and circumstances for, compassion and aggression. In some societies mealtime is an occasion to lavish loving attention on guests (Barlow, 2010). Many children see their families caring for infants, grandparents, and neighbors in need. A culture also defines justifiable occasions for hurting others. In a study comparing peer relationships in American and Japanese fourth-graders, both groups used relational aggression, for example, in excluding other children from their play groups. Despite the similarities of the behavior, exclusion was considered serious in the Japanese population and normal in the American people (Kawabata, Crick, & Hamaguchi, 2010). Japanese children high in relational aggression felt depressed, whereas comparable American children did not, presumably because of the stronger emphasis on intimacy and harmony in Japanese relationships.

Gender

Beginning in the preschool years, boys hit, push, and punch more than girls (Dodge et al., 2006; Eagly, 1987; Hay et al., 2011). Boys' greater inclination toward physical aggression is the result of both biological factors (recall the link between testosterone and aggression) and socialization (parents are more likely to allow aggression in sons than in daughters; J. E. O. Blakemore, Berenbaum, & Liben, 2009; Condry & Ross, 1985). Some evidence indicates that boys also engage in more name-calling and exclusionary behavior than do girls (Artz, Kassis, & Moldenhauer, 2013). Furthermore, boys tend to be more assertive than girls. In mixed-sex groups, boys sometimes dominate activities, take charge of needed equipment, and get their way when group members disagree (Jovanovic & King, 1998). Such assertiveness is nurtured in same-sex groups because boys' friendships typically involve more conflict and competition than is the case with girls' friendships (Eisenberg, Martin, & Fabes, 1996; Leaper & Smith, 2004). In comparison, girls make frequent small concessions to keep the peace (P. M. Miller, Danaher, & Forbes, 1986; Rudolph, Caldwell, & Conley, 2005).

Individual Profiles

The many separate effects on children's social behaviors mount over time, crystallizing into relatively stable patterns of helping and hurting behaviors (Knafo, Zahn-Waxler, Van Hulle, Robinson, & Rhee, 2008; Lacourse et al., 2014; Laninga-Wijnen, Harakeh, Dijkstra, Veenstra, & Vollebergh, 2018). Thus, expressions of kindness or antagonism can become habitual for children as they settle into peer groups, take on particular roles, and practice social gestures.

MyLab Education
Video Example 14.4
Find Developmental Meaning
What goals does this mother have for her family? The mother and counselor discuss the son's aggression toward animals and possible goals for him and his sister. (The counselor also works directly with the son.)

For children who are seriously deficient in compassion, stability is not an ideal condition. Impairments in empathy and aggression are associated with problems in adjustment, peer relationships, and academic achievement (Eisenberg et al., 2010; S. Kim, Kim, & Kamphaus, 2010; Priddis et al., 2014). Children who are hostile when they are young (e.g., regularly hitting others) are at risk for becoming violent in adolescence and adulthood (e.g., participating in gang fights and physical assaults; C. A. Anderson et al., 2003; Di Giunta et al., 2010; Ladd & Burgess, 1999). Counseling with children can be effective in enhancing empathy, regulating anger, and reducing aggressive behaviors, although its efficacy in addressing animal cruelty is less certain (T. R. Howe, 2014; T. L. Hughes, Tansy, & Fallon, 2017; S. E. McDonald et al., 2017).

Both prosocial behavior and aggression can be seen at one time or another in youngsters of various ages and backgrounds. You can read about other similarities between these two types of behavior in the Basic Developmental Issues table "Comparing Prosocial Behavior and Aggression."

BASIC DEVELOPMENTAL ISSUES
Comparing Prosocial Behavior and Aggression

ISSUE	PROSOCIAL BEHAVIOR	AGGRESSION
Nature and Nurture	The capacity for prosocial behavior is a natural, inborn human characteristic, but individual children have unique genetically based qualities that predispose them to varying degrees of altruism. Affectionate caregiving, prosocial role modeling, and explicit requests to consider the needs of others are effective ways to encourage prosocial behavior.	The capacity for aggression has a biological basis. Temperamental dispositions, hormone levels, and neurological structures in the brain influence aggressiveness in individual children. Families, peers, neighbors, the media, and social institutions (e.g., schools) foster aggression (or restraint) through modeling, reinforcement, discussion, and discipline.
Universality and Diversity	The capacity for prosocial behavior is universal in the human species. Furthermore, people in most cultures become increasingly prosocial as they mature. Significant diversity exists in the extent to which cultural groups encourage prosocial activities (e.g., sharing, nurturing) and expose children to prosocial behavior and advice about how to care for people in need.	Aggressive behavior is universal in human beings. Some developmental sequences in aggressive expression, such as a gradual shift from physical aggression to verbal aggression, are ubiquitous. Diversity is present in the ways that children express aggression, in the amount of aggression they encounter in the environment, and in the extent to which aggression is condoned.
Qualitative and Quantitative Change	Qualitative changes occur in children's understanding of why helping others is valuable. Young children often help to gain rewards or approval, whereas older children and adolescents are more likely to assist out of a genuine concern for others in need. Quantitative increases occur in children's knowledge of, and ability to carry out, effective prosocial strategies.	A gradual shift from physical aggression in early childhood to more verbal and relational forms of aggression in later years reflects a qualitative change. The shift from being a victim of bullying to also becoming a perpetrator occurs every now and then and reflects a qualitative change. The gradual decline in physical aggression in most children later in childhood reveals a quantitative reduction.

Sources: Dodge et al. (2006); Eisenberg et al. (2010); and Eisenberg and Fabes (1998).

Encouraging Children to Act with Compassion and Curb Aggressive Impulses

Teachers and other practitioners who work with young people have many opportunities to foster prosocial skills and discourage aggressive behaviors. You can see illustrations of educators fostering productive social capacities in the Development and Practice feature "Promoting Prosocial Skills and Discouraging Aggression." In addition, consider the following strategies:

Development-Enhancing Education
Promoting Prosocial Skills and Discouraging Aggression

Talk about other people's feelings in a sympathetic manner.

- A kindergarten teacher notices that Farai is standing next to Ivan in the block area. The teacher says to Ivan, "It looks like Farai would like to help you build your tower. What do you think?" (Early Childhood)
- When reading a story about a homeless child, Lia, a second-grade teacher, pauses and asks children to reflect on the girl's needs: "Lia is trying to figure out how her new classroom operates. How do you think she feels on her first day of school? " (Middle Childhood)

Communicate your concern for others who are hurt, and enlist children's support in caring for these individuals.

- A preschool teacher sympathizes with a boy who has skinned his knee. She brings out the first-aid kit and asks another child to get a bandage as she applies the antiseptic. (Early Childhood)
- A high school English teacher walks over to Abril and Maddie, who has recently broken her leg. "Good morning, young ladies. Today we're going to be doing a few activities that involve moving around the room. Abril, would you mind helping Maddie carry her belongings when we shift seats?" (Late Adolescence)

Acknowledge children's good deeds.

- When a third-grade teacher notices a child helping a classmate confused by an assignment, she comments, "Thank you for helping Amanda, Jack. You're always ready to lend a hand." (Middle Childhood)
- In an advising session with Jerald, a middle school teacher asks him about his goals for the year. The teacher is delighted to hear about Jerald's volunteer work as a swim instructor for children with disabilities. The teacher encourages him, "Jerald, that's good work. Can you write a story for the school newspaper?" (Early Adolescence)

(continued)

Ask children to brainstorm approaches to solving moral dilemmas.

- A middle school teacher presents a situation to his class: "Imagine that one of your classmates comes up to you and asks if she can copy your homework. You don't want to let her copy it. How might you refuse her request?" (Early Adolescence)
- A boy in a middle school literature class is doing a class project on a book he recently read. He downloads a pirated copy of the movie that was based on the book. His teacher comments that showing a scene from the movie could inspire a lot of interesting discussions, but the clip cannot be shown because doing so would violate the rights of people who made the movie. The boy says he will find a nonpirated source for the clip. (Early Adolescence)

Give concrete feedback about appropriate and inappropriate social behaviors.

- A fifth-grade teacher takes Marshall aside after he exercises self-restraint during a difficult social interaction. Previously aggressive, Marshall counted to 10 and walked away after Tanner called him a "douchebag." The teacher acknowledged his self-control: "Way to go, Marshall. What Tanner did was wrong, and you handled the situation very well." (Middle Childhood)
- During a cooperative learning activity, a high school teacher notices that the members of one group are getting angry. After briefly listening to their discussion, the teacher reminds them, "As we agreed yesterday, it's okay to criticize ideas, but it's *not* okay to criticize people." (Late Adolescence)

Encourage children to think carefully before acting in difficult social situations.

- A soccer coach finds that several of her 9-year-old players respond rashly to any physical contact. They hit or yell at another player who unintentionally bumps into them on the playing field. The coach teaches the athletes four steps to follow in such situations: (a) think about what happened, (b) list three different ways to respond, (c) predict what might happen with each response, and (d) choose the best tactic. (Middle Childhood)
- With a rise in bullying in their school, teachers talk with children about what bullying is and how to handle being a victim of, or bystander to, harassment. One teacher tells her class, "No one needs to put up with bullying. If someone is picking on you, you can tell that person to stop it, but it's also important to step in when you see *someone else* being bullied. Say something. Tell the bully to stop it." (Middle Childhood)

- **Treat children compassionately.** The root of empathy is love, and children are especially inclined to be kind to others when they themselves have been treated warmly, gently, and with sensitivity. Infant caregivers set the stage for productive social behaviors by interacting responsively with babies in their care, tending patiently to their needs, and comforting them when in distress (Gonzalez-Mena, 2010). As children grow older, adults can show compassion by asking them about their activities, acknowledging their progress, and forgiving rather than shaming those who make mistakes (Sanders, 2010).
- **Expose children to prosocial behavior.** When adults model gestures of kindness, children are likely to respond similarly. Teachers occasionally invite public servants and members of charitable organizations to talk about rewards in community service (Honig, 2009). Teachers can also share histories of altruistic movements, such as rescuers of Jewish people during the Holocaust and the generosity of the Choctaw Nation, a Native American tribe that sent aid to Ireland during the Great Famine of the 1840s, having recently struggled through their own famine (Nucci, 2009).
- **Give concrete guidelines for behavior.** Children should consistently hear the message that they must handle conflicts nonviolently. An important first step is to establish rules that prohibit physical aggression and possession of weapons. Behaviors that cause psychological harm—malicious gossip, prejudicial remarks, sexual harassment, intimidation, ostracism, and so on—must also be off-limits. Teachers and other professionals must consistently enforce these rules in the classroom, on the playground, in the lunchroom, and during extracurricular activities (Grumm & Hein, 2013; Juvonen, Nishina, & Graham, 2000; Learning First Alliance, 2001).
- **Label appropriate behaviors as they occur.** Teachers can heighten children's awareness of effective social skills by validating good behaviors (Sanders, 2010; Vorrath, 1985; Wittmer & Honig, 1994). A teacher might say, "Thank you for *sharing* your art materials," or "I think that you two were able to write a more imaginative short story by *cooperating* on the project." Experts have found, too, that acknowledging children's

decency (their generosity, empathy, etc.) has beneficial effects (Dunsmore, 2015; Grusec & Redler, 1980; R. S. L. Mills & Grusec, 1989). Eight-year-olds who are told "You're the kind of person who likes to help others whenever you can" or "You are a very helpful person" are more likely to share their belongings.

- **Create occasions for caring for others.** A preschool teacher might set up the pretend play area as an animal shelter, a doctor's office, a baby's room, a grocery store, or another setting that elicits compassionate behavior. A teacher might offer subtle suggestions with prosocial themes: "My Grandma is preparing food baskets to take to people in need. I think I'll help her by buying some canned goods at your grocery store" (Sanders, 2010, p. 51). A school might sponsor an annual clothing drive for individuals in the community who are homeless or abused, and a teacher might take his class to bring cookies to senior citizens at a local retirement home (N. E. Wallace, 2006).

MyLab Education
Video Example 14.5

Find developmental meaning
How does kindergarten teacher Cecilia Fowler encourage children to be helpful to one another? She and a few students explain the Kindness Quilt Project.

- **Implement cooperative learning group activities.** Earlier, in the context of fostering the inclusion of children who might otherwise be left on the periphery of social interaction, we recommended cooperative learning groups. This instructional method has also been shown to be effective in enhancing prosocial behavior and curbing aggression. In cooperative learning activities, youngsters can practice help-giving, help-seeking, and conflict resolution skills (Choi, Johnson, & Johnson, 2011; Webb & Farivar, 1994). Working on tasks that require a number of different skills can foster an appreciation for the strengths that children with diverse backgrounds contribute (E. G. Cohen, 1994; Lotan, 2006). Cooperative activities are most successful when children have a structure to follow (e.g., when each group member is given a specific role to perform) and are given guidelines about desirable behavior (E. G. Cohen, 1994; Pescarmona, 2014). For example, children could be told that everyone is expected to participate and that disagreement is permissible but hitting, shoving, and calling one another derogatory names are not. Because children can easily lapse into negative behaviors, it is essential for teachers to listen in regularly to the conversations of children and intervene when interactions deteriorate.

- **Document a child's improper behavior.** If a child regularly exhibits hurtful behaviors, an adult should record their form (e.g., Is the child biting, pushing, or name-calling?) and the kinds of situations in which they occur (e.g., Did the child act to gain resources or prestige, or alternatively is he or she reacting out of frustration? Does he or she choose the same or different victim each time? Is there a particular time of day or setting in which the child is prone to act out?). This information can be used to formulate a plan that discourages the aggression and teaches the child missing skills. For example, a teacher might make extra efforts to calm an unsettled child during transitions. Another teacher might coach a boy in the skill of compromise when he grabs toys rather than taking turns or sharing.

Preparing for Your Licensure Examination

Your teaching test might ask you about fostering prosocial behavior and discouraging aggressive behavior in the learning environment.

- **Implement an antibullying program proven to reduce the intimidation of vulnerable students.** Several school programs have been designed to reduce the frequency of bullying (Menard & Grotpeter, 2014; Morgan, 2012). Yet some of these programs have not yielded intended effects and, in a few cases, have actually led to increases in aggressive incidents. In programs that have been successful, clear expectations are established for bullying, consequences are given as soon as possible, and victims are reassured (Morgan, 2012). Antibullying programs also educate children on the need to step forward as a bystander and tell the perpetrator to stop.

MyLab Education Application Exercise 14.3
Identify Development-Enhancing Education

Listen to Ms. Salazar talk with her middle school students about their experiences in being bullied and what they can do next time.

- **Develop a peer mediation program.** Children often benefit from training in **peer mediation**, a protocol for intervening in peers' disputes (Daunic & Smith, 2010;

M. Deutsch, 1993; Linnemeier, 2012). During their preparation, youngsters learn how to help peers resolve conflicts by asking opposing sides to express their points of view and talk through a reasonable resolution. In one study (D. W. Johnson, Johnson, Dudley, Ward, & Magnuson, 1995), students in Grades 2 through 5 were trained to help peers resolve interpersonal conflicts by asking opposing sides to do the following:

1. Define the conflict (the problem).
2. Explain their own perspectives and needs.
3. Explain the *other* side's perspectives and needs.
4. Identify at least three possible solutions to the conflict.
5. Reach an agreement that addresses the needs of both parties.

Students took turns serving as mediator for their classmates, such that everyone had experience resolving the conflicts of others. As a result, students more frequently resolved their *own* interpersonal conflicts in ways that addressed the needs of both parties, and they were less likely to ask for adult intervention than were students who had not had mediation training.

Peer mediation is most effective when youngsters of diverse ethnic backgrounds, socioeconomic groups, and achievement levels serve as mediators. It seems to work best for relatively small, short-term interpersonal problems (hurt feelings, conflicts over use of limited academic resources, etc.). A peer mediation program requires a lengthy training and entails a commitment from students and financial investment from the schools. Schools need to be prepared with additional violence prevention tactics if a safe school environment is to be established. As another limitation, even the most proficient of peer mediators are ill prepared to handle emotionally charged conflicts, such as interactions that involve sexual harassment, violence, or homophobia (Casella, 2001; K. M. Williams, 2001).

- **Intervene at all ages and especially when children are young.** Even when infants and young children have gotten off to a shaky start, perhaps having been neglected, abused, or submitted to family violence, they remain capable of learning new ways of relating to others. Yet those who are born with an irritable, impulsive temperament are at heightened risk when their parents have been impatient, coercive, or aloof with them. In that situation, children have intense needs to be cared for lovingly, calmly, and with lessons in self-control. Children who display reactive aggression need practice in coping effectively with anger, in identifying others' perspective and motivations, and in dealing with conflicts before they escalate (Hubbard et al., 2010). Children who exhibit reactive aggression also need practice in negotiation, turn-taking, sharing, and other productive social skills. Because proactively aggressive children can be callous and unemotional with others, adults need to guide their attention to the feelings of others (Maldonado-Molina, Reingle, Tobler, Jennings, & Komro, 2010). Some chronically aggressive individuals do not reduce their hostile behaviors until the early adult years, after they have found a reason—perhaps a job or intimate partner—to shape up their behavior. Those with severe problems, including the potential to become violent, require immediate and intensive support, a topic we get to shortly.

Creating a Safe and Nurturing School Environment

Students can achieve at optimal levels at school only if they feel safe. Security is achieved, in part, by schoolwide programs that promote a peaceful, mutually respectful climate and offer extra guidance to those students who struggle with impulsivity, hostility, aggression, and weak social skills. Educators, mental health experts, and developmental scholars have found that intervening with students at three levels of social-emotional abilities can improve conduct, enhance emotional regulation, and boost academic learning (August, Piehler, & Miller, 2018). The three-tiered model sets the groundwork for mental health with a whole-school commitment to being a caring community. It is supplemented in evidence-based programs that address needs of young people who break rules and discipline and violate others' rights. The framework, depicted in Figure 14.1, has been successful in meeting a wide range of needs related to academic learning, mental health, and reduction of aggression (Dwyer & Osher, 2000; B. B. Nelson et al., 2013; Stanton-Chapman, Walker, Voorhees, & Snell, 2016; H. M. Walker

FIGURE 14.1 Hierarchy of school interventions for mental health and positive behavior.

In the three-tiered model of support for social-emotional development, students universally receive lessons in emotional literacy and standards for behavior (Tier 1). A small number of students commit conduct transgressions that put them at risk for more serious problems. The school arranges for small-group exercises addressing the difficulties students are experiencing and often provides counseling (Tier 2). A few students exhibit dangerous behaviors, including using a weapon at school, consistent with having a mental health disorder. The school provides an intensive intervention, inclusive of individual counseling and a personalized treatment plan for their work at school (Tier 3).

Source: Based on National Technical Assistance Center on Positive Behavioral Interventions and Supports (2018). About us. Retrieved March 2, 2018 from https://www.pbis.org/about-us)

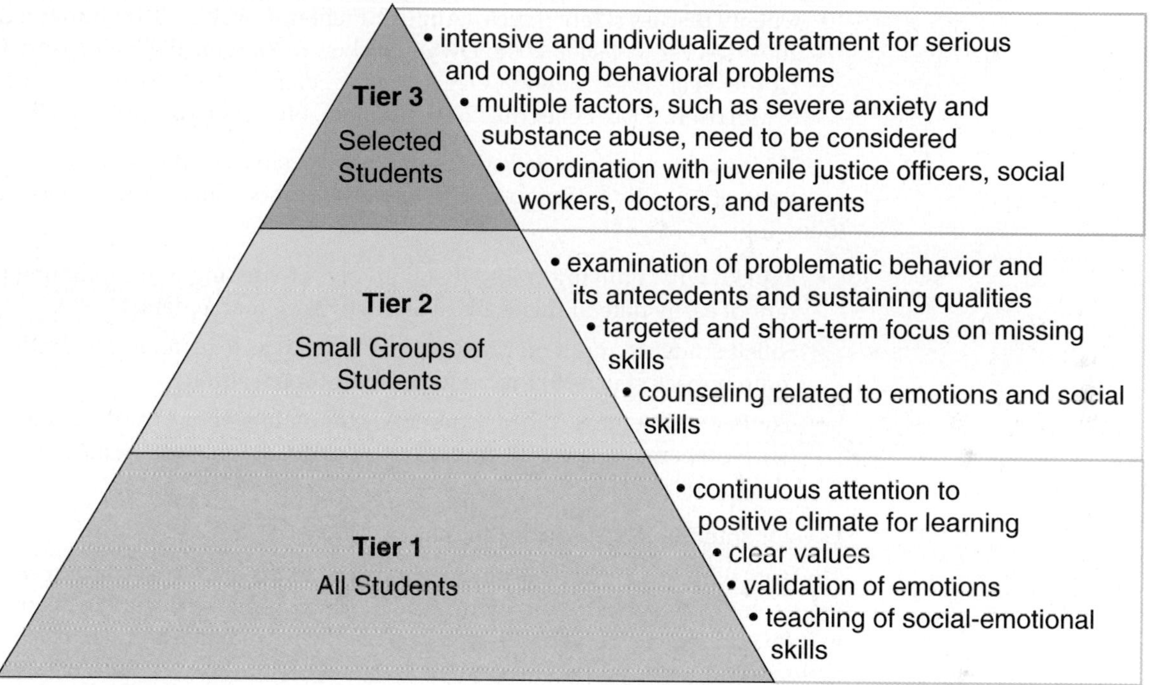

et al., 1996).[1] (represented at the bottom of the pyramid) follow expectations for appropriate behavior, whereas a few must be coached in social skills, either in small groups (middle level) or through individualized, intensive counseling (top level).

Level I: Creating a Healthy School Environment

All children need to be able to interact in a school in which they feel safe, find that good behaviors are rewarded, and see hurtful behaviors discouraged. Creating a peaceful, nonviolent school environment is a long-term effort with the following strategies:

- Make a joint, schoolwide commitment to supporting *all* students' academic learning, personal growth, and social success.
- Explicitly teach school values (e.g., for kindness and inclusion) and the code of conduct (e.g., for not harassing anyone at school).
- Provide a challenging and engaging curriculum.
- Form caring, trusting faculty–student relationships.
- Insist on genuine respect—among students as well as faculty—for people of diverse backgrounds, races, and ethnicities.
- Teach children to understand their emotions and express them productively.
- Encourage children to take the perspective of age-mates and adults, especially in circumstances of a conflict.
- Establish schoolwide practices that foster appropriate behavior (e.g., give clear guidelines for behavior, consistently enforce penalties for infractions, and deliver instruction in productive social and problem-solving skills).

[1] If you read Chapter 11, you will recognize this model as a method for nurturing healthy emotional development and addressing disorders.

- Involve students in decision making about school policies and procedures.
- Provide mechanisms through which students can communicate their concerns openly and without fear of reprisal.
- Model, recognize, and teach prosocial behaviors (e.g., sharing, helping, cooperation).
- Establish close working relationships with community agencies and families.
- Reach out to families, advise them of services in their community, and offer workshops in identifying anxiety in children and setting age-appropriate limits on disruptive behavior.
- Openly discuss safety issues. (August, Piehler, & Miller, 2018; Burstyn & Stevens, 2001; Dwyer & Osher, 2000; Dwyer, Osher, & Warger, 1998; Gregory et al., 2010; Horner et al., 2004; Mendez, Ogg, Loker, & Fefer, 2013; Morrison, Furlong, D'Incau, & Morrison, 2004; Pellegrini, 2002; Sprague, Nishioka, & Smith, 2007)

The final strategy on the list—an open discussion of safety issues—encompasses a variety of specific techniques. For example, school faculty members can do the following:

- Explain what bullying is (i.e., that it involves harassing or intimidating peers who cannot easily defend themselves) and why it is unacceptable.
- Solicit students' input on potentially unsafe areas (e.g., an infrequently used restroom or back stairwell) that require faculty supervision.
- Convey willingness to hear students' complaints about troublesome classmates (such concerns can provide important clues about which students are most in need of assistance).

Level II: Intervening Early for Students at Risk

Students who fail to develop productive social skills are at risk for developing more worrisome problems. These students may be identified as having adjustment difficulties in managing anger, coping with a traumatic event, making friends, or feeling scared and sad at school. Students are assigned to a small group and an instructor or therapist who provides social skills training, counseling, or coaching in emotional regulation. Training is scripted in a manual, and the program unfolds over a multiweek period. School staff can also get to know students' interests and encourage their participation in extracurricular activities. These interventions are most effective when they occur early—before students go too far down the path of antisocial behavior or a serious psychiatric condition—and when delivered by a multidisciplinary team of qualified professionals (Dryfoos, 1997; Dwyer & Osher, 2000; Priddis et al., 2014).

Level III: Providing Intensive Intervention for Students in Trouble

For a few students, intensive professional intervention is necessary. Children who are exceptionally aggressive may have a weak empathic capacity, limited desire to follow school rules, delayed interpersonal skills, and limited restraint in social situations. They may have been abused themselves and later act out the destructive overtures used on them. Forceful behaviors may initially occur due to lapses of self-control and later solidify into habits of hurting others. A few students develop an explosive temper or deep-seated disregard for others' welfare, possibly triggered by serious problems at home. Other young people may be identified for a Tier 3 intervention because of a significant mental health problem, such as depression, anxiety, or bipolar disorder. These youth may or may not have acted out aggressively but are similar to aggressive youth in their need for comprehensive services. A few additional students are referred because of chronic misbehavior in the classroom that does not improve with a Tier 2 intervention.

Preparing for Your Licensure Examination

Your teaching test might ask you about enlisting counselors, school psychologists, other school personnel, law enforcement officials, and other professionals in support of, and guidance for, potentially violent youth.

Tier 3 interventions are individualized programs. A common Tier 3 objective is to reduce the anxiety of students. Students learn to recognize physiological sensations that accompany emotions, identify situations that are likely to cause fear and panic, and practice talking themselves through difficult situations. With students who have been consistently or callously aggressive, schools may work closely with mental health clinics, police and probation officers, and social services to teach new skills to students at high risk for violence and protect others from harm (M. T. Greenberg et al., 2003; Hyman et al., 2006; Rollison et al., 2013; Sprague & Horner, 2012). Parents may be taught how to coach their children in conflict resolution and productive emotional expression.

Through their daily interactions with students, teachers may notice certain characteristics that suggest a need for an intensive intervention. Teachers should consult with principals if they notice several of these warning signs:

- *Social withdrawal.* Over time, a student interacts less frequently with teachers and peers. A student may express the belief that he or she is friendless, disliked, or unfairly picked on.
- *Rapid decline in academic performance.* A student shows a dramatic change in academic performance and seems unconcerned about doing well. Cognitive and physical factors (e.g., learning disabilities, ineffective study strategies, brain injury) have been ruled out as causes of the decline.
- *Poor coping skills.* A student has little ability to deal with frustration, takes the smallest affront personally, and has trouble bouncing back after disappointment. He or she frequently responds with uncontrolled anger to minor injustices and innocent bystanders.
- *Sense of superiority, self-centeredness, and lack of empathy.* A student depicts himself or herself as smarter or otherwise better than peers, is preoccupied with personal needs, and has little regard for others' perspectives.
- *Lengthy grudges.* A student is unforgiving of others' transgressions, even after considerable time has elapsed.
- *Violent themes in drawings and written work.* Violence predominates in a student's artwork, stories, and journal entries, with certain individuals (e.g., a parent or classmate) being regularly targeted in these fantasies. (Keep in mind that *occasional* violence in writing and art is not unusual, especially for boys.)
- *Intolerance for differences.* A student shows intense disdain for and prejudice toward people of a certain race, ethnicity, gender, sexual orientation, religion, or disability.
- *History of violence, aggression, and other discipline problems.* A student has a long record of destructive or cruel behaviors extending over several years.
- *Association with violent peers.* A student associates regularly with a gang or other antisocial peer group.
- *Violent role models.* A student may speak with admiration about Satan or Hitler or another malevolent figure.
- *Preoccupation with violent media.* A student who enjoys the blood and gore of a video game may become physically aggressive, although there are plenty of young people who consume violent media and do not become violent.
- *Repeated victimization of other students.* A student who has bullied one or more other children is at risk for committing additional violence in the future.
- *Frequent alcohol or drug use.* A student who abuses alcohol or drugs may have reduced self-control; in some cases, substance abuse signals a mental illness.
- *Access to firearms.* A student has easy access to guns and ammunition and may regularly practice using them.
- *Threats of violence.* A student has openly expressed the intent to harm someone else. ***This warning sign alone requires immediate action.***
- *Threats of suicide.* A student has talked or written about his own suicide. ***This warning sign alone also requires immediate action.***

(Bondü & Scheithauer, 2014; Dwyer et al., 1998; M. L. Mitchell & Brendtro, 2013; Ormrod, 2011; O'Toole, 2000; Vossekuil, Fein, Reddy, Borum, & Modzeleski, 2004)

By themselves, most of the signs are unlikely to foreshadow a violent attack, but several of them in combination necessitate consultation with a specially trained professional. As noted, a student's stated intention to harm self or another should *always* be considered seriously.

Gang-Related Problems

One manifestation of aggression at schools is gang-related hostilities. A gang is a group of young people and sometimes family members; it has a unique identity, claims jurisdiction over a region, and commits criminal activities, including thefts, harassment, drug dealings, sexual assault, and shootings. Children who join gangs generally want protection yet end up experiencing sexual assault, other kinds of violence, and access to illegal drugs (Petering, Rhoades, Winetrobe, Dent, & Rice, 2017; S. E. Reid & Listwan, 2018). Although gangs are more prevalent in low-income, inner-city schools, they are increasingly found in suburban and rural schools as well (M. E. Buckle & Walsh 2013; Estrada, Gilreath, Astor, & Benbenishty, 2016; Howell & Lynch, 2000; Sharkey, Shekhtmeyster, Chavez-Lopez, Norris, & Sass, 2011).

The three-level approach to combating school violence just described goes a long way toward preventing and suppressing gang activities. Level I activities that ensure children have good relationships at school and access to an engaging curriculum discourage children from joining gangs in the first place (Sharkey et al., 2011). The Level II strategy of teaching students how to regulate emotions and encouraging their involvement in extracurricular activities may also preempt gang initiation (Sharkey et al., 2011). As suggested in our discussion of Level III, students who are already exhibiting violent behavior need intensive intervention to reduce aggressive acts and avoid the gang.

It is important to limit the influence of gangs already present within the school setting. Gang involvement puts young people in harm's way and exposes classmates to negative behaviors. Young people who enter gangs are exposed to harassment, violence, criminal activity, and disengagement from school by other members (Forber-Pratt & Espelage, 2018). When gangs are in the community, educators usually take measures to communicate that schools are neutral territories that do not favor one gang or another and, in fact, prohibit all signs of gang affiliation. Specific strategies include the following:

- Develop, communicate, and enforce clear-cut policies regarding potential threats to school safety.
- Identify the specific nature and scope of gang activity in the student population.
- Forbid clothing, jewelry, and behaviors that signify membership in a particular gang (e.g., bandanas, shoelaces in gang colors, certain hand signs).[2]
- Actively mediate between-gang and within-gang disputes. (Kodluboy, 2004; Sharkey et al., 2011)

In the last of these strategies—mediation—either adults or peers might serve as mediators, provided that they are familiar with relevant cultures and issues of gangs (Kodluboy, 2004; Tron, 2013). Another promising strategy has been to develop a *youth court* at school or in the community, in which students serve as jurors and sometimes as judges, attorneys, and clerks in hearing the case of disputing age-mates (H. A. Cole & Heilig, 2011). Students who participate in a youth court hearing become less likely to repeat aggressive behavior. Young people in gangs need to see that they belong at school, have decent relationships with classmates and teachers, and find academic learning relevant to their interests and aspirations (Kronholz, 2011).

Summary

Most children become increasingly prosocial and less aggressive over the years, with such changes being partly the result of perspective taking, empathy, and sympathy. However, some children display troublesome levels of physical or relational aggression, perhaps partly as a result of temperamental characteristics, aggressive role models, and counterproductive social cognitive processes. These youngsters often need guidance from caring adults who scaffold their means for feeling empathy, resolving conflicts, and curbing aggressive tendencies.

[2]A potential problem with this strategy is that it may violate students' civil liberties. For guidance on how to walk the line between ensuring students' safety and giving them reasonable freedom of expression, see Kodluboy (2004) and Rozalski and Yell (2004).

The three-tier intervention model has been implemented in schools as a systematic method for setting foundations for good behavior and allowing for more intensive measures when empathy is impaired, helpful behaviors are below expected levels, and aggression is potentially dangerous. The three-tier intervention can prevent and diminish gang activity, which if not mitigated can cause anxiety at school and an increase in gang membership. Programs in the three tiers must each be evaluated because their impact can be either effective or ineffective depending on services and matches with students' assets and limitations.

MyLab Education Self-Check 14.2

Practicing For Your Licensure Examination

Many teaching tests require students to apply their knowledge of child development in analyzing brief vignettes and answering multiple-choice questions. You can practice for your licensure examination by reading the following case study and answering a series of questions.

Gang Mediation

At Washington Middle School, many students belonged to one of several gangs that seemed to "rule the school." Fights among rival gangs were common, and non-gang members were frequent victims of harassment (Sanchez & Anderson, 1990). School officials tried a variety of strategies to keep the gang-related behavior in check—mandating dress codes, conducting weapon searches, counseling or suspending chronic troublemakers, and so on—but without success.

In desperation, two school counselors suggested that the school implement a peer mediation program. The program began by focusing on the three largest gangs, which were responsible for most of the trouble on school grounds. Interpersonal problems involving two or more gangs would be brought to a mediation team, comprised of five school faculty members and three representatives from each of the three gangs.

The mediation team committed to addressing the problems that were brought to them. They were to conduct their business out of mutual respect. Everyone was to avoid calling anyone names and criticizing one another. During conversations, one person was to speak at a time. There were to be no weapons brought to the hearings. Honesty was expected, and the sessions were to be kept confidential until an agreement was reached or mediation was called off. All team members would have to agree to and sign off on any decisions that the team reached. However, participation in the process was voluntary, and students could withdraw at any time.

To lay the groundwork for productive discussions, faculty members of the mediation team met separately with each of the three gangs to establish feelings of rapport and trust and to explain how the mediation process would work. After considerable discussion and venting of hostile intergroup feelings, many gang members agreed to try the new approach. Meanwhile, the buzz throughout the student body was that something extraordinary was occurring at Washington.

Mediation sessions were held in a conference room, with team members sitting around a large table so that they could maintain eye contact with one another. In the first session, common grievances were aired. Students agreed that they didn't like being put down or intimidated, that they worried about their physical safety, and that they all wanted one another's respect. Curiously, each gang also complained that the school administration showed preferential treatment for the *other* gangs. Through all of this, the students got one message loud and clear: They could speak freely and honestly at the meeting, without fear of reprisal from faculty members or other students.

In several additional meetings during the next 2 weeks, the team reached an agreement that a number of behaviors would be unacceptable at school: There would be no put-downs, name-calling, hostile looks, threats, shoving, or gang graffiti. After the final meeting, each gang was separately called into the conference room. Its representatives on the mediation team explained the agreement, and other members of the gang were asked to sign it. Despite some skepticism, most members of all three gangs signed the agreement.

A month later, it was clear that the process had been successful, at least in improving the school's social climate over the short term. Members of rival gangs nodded pleasantly to one another or gave one another friendly greetings as they passed in the hall. Gang members no longer felt compelled to hang out in groups for safety's sake. Members of two of the gangs were seen playing soccer together one afternoon. And there had been no gang-related arguments all month. (Sanchez & Anderson, 1990)

Constructed-Response Question

1. Why do you think the mediation approach was successful when other approaches had failed? Draw on what you've learned about moral development, and identify at least three possible reasons.

Multiple-Choice Questions

2. Considering the recommendations in this chapter on creating a safe school environment, which of the following strategies might reasonably supplement the mediation program used in this school?

   a. Look carefully at the curriculum to make sure it is engaging for students.
   b. Advise students about extracurricular activities that might be of personal interest to them.
   c. Provide individual counseling for students who have previously exhibited violent behavior.
   d. All of the above

3. Given what you learned about aggression, which of the following explanations most accurately accounts for the reasons that children in the gangs at Washington Middle School might have become aggressive?

   a. As is the case with all children, gang members can be persuaded to do anything that adults want them to do.
   b. The children were probably affected by a combination of factors, perhaps including exposure to parents and peers who handled their conflicts aggressively, dispositions that put them at risk for responding impulsively, and their own habits and interpretations of social events.
   c. The children's genes, which made them irritable and impulsive, can be considered fully responsible for their aggressive style of interacting.
   d. None of the above

MyLab Education Licensure Practice 14.1

Key Concepts

moral development (p. 525)
moral dilemma (p. 526)
preconventional morality (p. 526)
conventional morality (p. 526)
postconventional morality (p. 526)
moral transgression (p. 528)
conventional transgression (p. 529)
personal matter (p. 529)
guilt (p. 531)
shame (p. 531)
sympathy (p. 532)
distributive justice (p. 532)
induction (p. 534)
justice orientation (p. 535)
care orientation (p. 535)
service learning (p. 539)
prosocial behavior (p. 541)
aggression (p. 541)
physical aggression (p. 543)
relational aggression (p. 543)
reactive aggression (p. 543)
proactive aggression (p. 543)
bully (p. 543)
hostile attributional bias (p. 544)
peer mediation (p. 551)

Chapter Fifteen

Peers, Schools, and Society

Ariel Skelley/Digital Vision/Getty Image

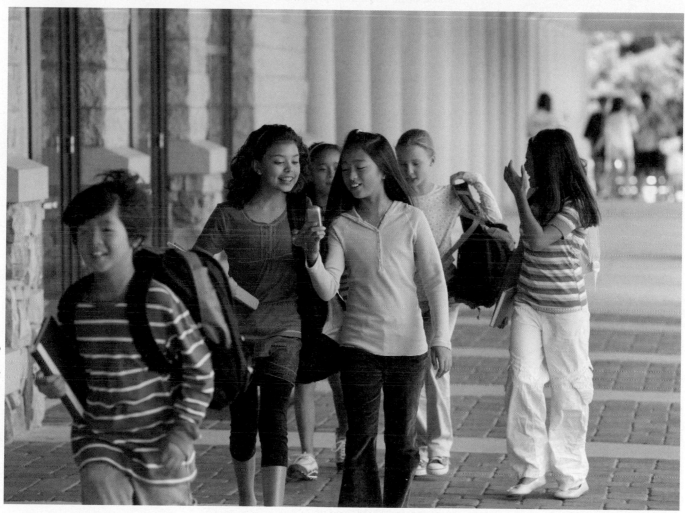

Learning Objectives

15.1 Characterize friendships and other peer affiliations in childhood, including the manner in which relationships change developmentally and can be fostered by teachers and other professionals.

15.2 Discuss three characteristics of school environments that affect children positively.

15.3 Describe how a society's services, the media, and interactive technologies influence children's learning and behavior.

CASE STUDY

One Girl, Three High Schools

When I [Teresa] sat down with 17-year-old Catherine[1] and asked her to describe high school, Catherine smiled and asked, "Which one?"

I smiled back. "How many were there?"

She laughed: "I'm on my third. Third one's the charm, right?"

"Definitely," I answered. "You've made it this far. Can you start with school number one?"

"My first high school was okay," Catherine explained. "I liked algebra . . . quadratic equations, all that. My teacher sent me to represent the school at a state contest. I liked art as well. I got to design a book and illustrate a poem. Shakespeare was dull. The teacher focused on symbols and ignored the stories—the characters and their relationships. But I basically liked the school. I had good friends. Teachers cared about us. Unfortunately, the school closed at the end of my freshman year." Her tone lowered, and she looked down, "Enter school number two . . . ."

"A tough time?" I asked.

"Yeah," Catherine answered. "The second school was a hard place. Not socially, because many of my friends went with me. But the atmosphere was bad. Classes were boring. Students goofed off. I read novels in class. Teachers did nothing. In Geometry [class] I drew pictures. Our history teacher shouldn't have been teaching. He'd been a missionary in Chile for 30 years and became a teacher because he knew the principal. He was . . . weird . . . disturbed. And the principal was a real . . . "

I waited. She gathered her thoughts and continued: "The principal used some of the kids to tell on the others. Yeah . . . and one teacher was really depraved. He pretended to be Hitler, and got students to salute him . . . The principal did . . . . nothing . . . " Her voice trailed off.

I absorbed what she was saying.

Catherine sighed. "I told my parents I wanted to leave. They weren't happy. But they figured out it was better for me to finish school *somewhere* than to drop out. They eventually let me leave."

"And school number three? What's it like?" I asked.

"It's really big. No one knows me here . . . . My real friends are in other schools. Some have already graduated. The teachers give us a lot of choices, but I can't tell if that's because they like us [the students] or just can't be bothered. In my P.E. class, I'm allowed to run instead of join in dorky games. I run around the track, the fields, local neighborhoods. I like the freedom. The only personal contact I've had is in my writing class. We keep a journal, and our teacher reads it. My teacher wrote to me that she saves my journal for last because I write about real things. She and I have never talked, though."

"Do you have an advisor?" I asked.

"I don't think so," she answered quietly.

"A counselor?" I followed up.

"Well, yeah, I saw him once. I took a career inventory and found out that my interest in mechanical things is at the one percentile," Catherine laughed. "So I guess I won't be an engineer."

"And now what?" I wondered.

"I've been accepted into college," Catherine answered. "It must have been my SATs[2]—not my grades." She laughed. "After my freshman year, I stopped studying. I read a lot, though, things that are not required. That helps me with tests. College will be different, I hope. At least I can learn about things I care about." She looked up and smiled.

- How did Catherine perceive her three schools?
- What challenges did she face?

In the opening case study, 17-year-old Catherine was at risk for dropping out of high school. In her travails through secondary school, she experienced three settings, which she found to offer varying levels of support. The first and third schools offered

[1]Catherine is a pseudonym.

[2]The SAT is a college admission test published by the College Board.

her acceptable levels of encouragement from friends and teachers. The second's moral limitations undermined her engagement in school. Fortunately, her algebra teacher recognized her talent, as did her writing teacher, both validating her abilities. Friends were a critical part of her life and a source of stability as she moved between schools.

Other students, like Catherine, are deeply affected by their school's atmosphere, relationships, and opportunities for a relevant and challenging education. In this chapter you will find that educational settings can be positive catalysts for growth, and other elements of society, including peers, the media, interactive technologies, and after-school programs, have the potential to promote healthy development.

Outline

Peers

15.1 Characterize friendships and other peer affiliations in childhood, including the manner in which relationships change developmentally and can be fostered by teachers and other professionals.

Peers, people of approximately the same age and position within a social group, make unique contributions to development—effects that supplement rather than duplicate those from relationships with family and adults. In the next few pages, we examine peer relationships, including their functions, constituent social skills, and forms.

Functions of Peer Relationships

Companionship with peers is one of children's top priorities. When peer relationships are warm and cordial, they serve several beneficial functions.

Peers offer emotional support. The presence of familiar peers helps children relax in new environments and cope with mild aggression and other stresses (Asher & Parker, 1989; Buhs, Koziol, Rudasill, & Crockett, 2018; K. Snow & Mann-Feder, 2013; Wentzel, 1999). In our opening case study, Catherine felt supported through school transitions by having close friends. As a general rule, children who have peers to turn to have higher self-esteem, fewer emotional problems (such as depression), and higher engagement with, and achievement in, school (Buhrmester, 1992; Cappella, Kim, Neal, & Jackson, 2013; Erath, Flanagan, Bierman, & Tu, 2010; Graber, Turner, & Madill, 2016). In Artifact Example 15.1, 7-year-old Madison shows her close friendship with Katherine.

MyLab Education
Artifact Example 15.1

Find Developmental Meaning *How does 7-year-old Madison feel about Katherine?* Madison drew a picture of herself holding hands with friend Katherine and wrote that she cried when they were separated, a sign of their emotional bond.

Peers serve as partners for practicing social skills. When children interact with peers, they enter social exchanges on more or less equal footing. Friendships are by choice, and no individual has absolute power over another. Equality does not mean that friends have the same abilities or roles within the relationship, but true friends care for one another and accept each other's inherent goodness, motives, and talents. By satisfying their own needs while also maintaining productive relationships with others, children acquire such fundamental skills as taking the perspective of others and talking through hurt feelings (K. L. McDonald, Malti, Killen, & Rubin, 2014; Selman, 2003; Sutton-Smith, 1979).

Peers train one another for social life. Children socialize one another in several ways (Guyer & Jarcho, 2018; Hartup, 2009; Rubin, Bukowski, & Parker, 2006; Shi & Xie, 2014). Peers stipulate options for leisure time, perhaps jumping rope in a vacant lot, getting together in a study group, or smoking cigarettes on the street corner. They offer new ideas, presenting arguments for becoming a vegetarian or helping out in an animal rescue center. They serve as role models, showing what is possible and what is admirable. Peers reinforce one another for acting in ways deemed appropriate for their age, gender, ethnic group, and cultural background. And they sanction one another, through ridicule, gossip, or ostracism, for stepping outside acceptable bounds.

Peers contribute to a sense of identity. Associations with peers help children decide who they are and what they want to become (Bukowski & Raufelder, 2018; Clemens, Shipp, & Pisarik, 2008; Zosuls, Field, Martin, Andrews, & England, 2014). Young people learn a lot about themselves and their identity in peer groups, and, especially in adolescence, they gain a sense of affinity with like-minded individuals. For instance, when Jeanne's son Alex was in middle school, he and his friends were avid skateboarders and spent long hours at a local ramp practicing and refining their technique. Alex proudly labeled himself a "skater" and wore the extra-large T-shirts and wide-legged pants that conveyed this identity.

Children help one another make sense of their lives. During conversations with peers, children share ideas that help one another interpret confusing and troubling events. Children may talk about similar experiences in confronting a grouchy classmate, dealing with a difficult teacher, or being punished by parents. Informative conversations occur throughout childhood and take on special significance during adolescence, when teenagers are changing rapidly and long for reassurance from others facing similar challenges (Richard & Schneider, 2005; H. S. Sullivan, 1953).

Peers achieve common ways of looking at the world. Getting together regularly, children come to share views on the world. A long-standing group works out rules, often unspoken expectations and interpretations—a **peer culture**—that influence how everyone behaves (P. Davidson & Youniss, 1995; A. Lynch, Lerner, & Leventhal, 2013; Nijnatten, Matarese, & Noordegraaf, 2017; C. Simmons, 2014). You can read more about this aspect of children's lives in the Development and Culture feature "Peer Culture in the United States and Italy."

Development in Culture

Peer Culture in the United States and Italy

William Corsaro is an American sociologist, a scientist who studies people's interactions in groups. Corsaro's interest is in how children relate to one another at school. In a series of *ethnographies* in the United States and Italy, he spent months becoming familiar with preschool children's routines, the subtleties in their exchanges, and the purpose of their customs.[a] He gained children's confidence by sitting down beside them, quietly watching and listening, and letting them react to him. Occasionally, he joined in their play, always following their leads.

Children in both societies gradually accepted Corsaro. In preschools in the United States, children came to think of Corsaro as "Big Bill," whom they readily welcomed into their playgroups (Corsaro, 2003, p. 7).[b] The children eventually insisted that he sit with them during birthday parties and that their parents include him in plans for cookies, cupcakes, and Valentine cards. In Italian preschools, children initially treated Corsaro as "an incompetent adult" because of his lack of fluency with the Italian language (Corsaro, 2003, p. 15).[a] Children teased Corsaro when he made mistakes in speaking Italian and regularly taught him new phrases. Corsaro recalled strides in winning over the children:

ArenaCreative/Fotolia

PEER CULTURE IN ITALY. These Italian children are exchanging secrets built on their shared understandings and customs.

> I was sitting on the floor with two boys (Felice and Roberto) and we were racing some toy cars around in circles. Felice was talking about an Italian race car driver as we played, but because he was talking so fast I could understand only part of what he was saying. At one point, however, he raced his car into a wall and it flipped over. Then I clearly heard him say "*Luis è morto*," and I knew this meant, "He's

dead." I guessed that Felix must be recounting a tragic accident in some past Grand Prix event. At that moment I remembered and used a phrase that I had learned in my first Italian course: "*Che peccato!*" ("What a pity!"). Looking up in amazement Felice said, "Bill! Bill! *Ha ragione! Bravo Bill!*" ("Bill! Bill! He's right! Way to go, Bill!"). "*Bravo, Bill!*" Roberto chimed in. (Corsaro, 2003, pp. 17–18)[b]

As a result of his extended time with children in both settings, Corsaro gained an insider's perspective on their *peer cultures* (Corsaro, 2003; Corsaro & Eder, 1990). During their time together, children in the two societies developed their own informal routines. In one American preschool, children became excited when they heard the noises of trash collectors attaching the dumpster to a lift. The truck was visible from the top of the jungle gym, and whichever child noticed it coming shouted to the others that the "garbage man" had arrived (Corsaro, 2003, p. 49).[b] Others quickly climbed the bars to get a good look, and they cheered in unison and made sound effects as the driver grabbed the container and emptied its contents. Every day the routine was the same, as it was a year later when Corsaro observed a second group of children at the school.

Other themes that regularly guided children's play were those of being scared and finding protection. Children would take turns pretending to be monsters; others would chase or flee from monsters and find safe haven in a home base. Another dynamic that pervaded children's play was making friends and protecting existing friendships. Concerns with loyalty and rivalry were regularly borne out in interactions in young children.

Finally, children conspired in acts of mischief. For example, children tried to convince teachers that it was acceptable to run inside because they were pretending to be police chasing robbers. Toy weapons were not allowed in school, yet children pretended to shoot one another by pointing and cocking their fingers. A couple of children brought in contraband toys and candy and shared items with one another, out of sight of teachers. Other children shirked their responsibilities at cleanup time by surreptitiously moving from an area that they had messed up to another tidier location, where they would be absolved from housework.

Many aspects of children's peer culture were unknown to teachers. Although some of children's routines, such as sharing contraband toys, might have been considered objectionable had they been identified, peer culture overall was a constructive way for children to learn how to act in a group.

[a] In an ethnography, a researcher spends an extended time observing a group of people behaving in their natural environment. The researcher documents the activities and interprets them from the perspective of the participants.

[b] Excerpts from *We're Friends, Right?: Inside Kids' Culture* by William A. Corsaro. Copyright © 2003 by William A. Corsaro. Reprinted with permission by the National Academy of Sciences, Courtesy of the National Academies Press, Washington, D.C.

Social Skills

Children are most likely to develop productive relationships when they have acquired age-typical **social skills**, procedures that facilitate smooth and friendly interactions with others. Children who are adept in social skills are generally perceptive of other people's needs, able to establish and maintain high-quality relationships, and motivated to curb aggression. In other words, they are *socially competent* (B. E. Vaughn et al., 2009). Compared to children who are deficient in social skills, socially competent children achieve at higher levels academically, enjoy high self-esteem, have friends, are happier at school, are better able to deal with anger and frustration, exhibit fewer problem behaviors, and have better school attendance (Berkovits & Baker, 2014; Bornstein, Hahn, & Haynes, 2010; R. Carter, Halawah, & Trinh, 2018).

Preparing for Your Licensure Examination

Your teaching test might ask about developmental trends in social skills and peer relationships.

Developmental Trends in Social Skills

Socially competent children acquire skills as they interact with peers during each of the developmental periods:

Infancy (birth–2 years). Infants acquire basic social skills while interacting with parents. They are gradually able to coordinate eye contact, smiles, and utterances. In the latter half of the first year, infants who spend time with other small children may babble, smile at one another, and look where others point (Eckerman, 1979; D. Wittmer, 2012). As toddlers, children imitate one another, offer each other toys, and cooperate in simple tasks and play activities (P. L. Harris, 2006; Howes & Matheson, 1992; Meadows, 2010). These are not simply responsive behaviors—instead, infants and toddlers are actually forming

MyLab Education
Video Example 15.1

Find Developmental Meaning
What indicators of parallel play do you see? Children play side by side but do not converse or coordinate their activities.

MyLab Education
Video Example 15.2

Find Developmental Meaning
What aspects of cooperative play occur? Two young boys join forces in building a house, deciding where to place the parts, working through differences, and interacting occasionally with two nearby boys who provide props.

relationships with peers—seeking out one another and even finding comfort from a familiar tyke when adjusting to a new room at the child-care center (D. F. Hay, Caplan, & Nash, 2018; S. L. Recchia & Dvorakova, 2012).

Early Childhood (2–6 years). Having capacities for rudimentary conversation and shared attention, young children are prepared to interact more effectively with age-mates, especially within the context of play. One early researcher identified six different kinds of behaviors in children age 2 to 5 (Parten, 1932). These categories, which reflect increasing social interaction, are described in the Observation Guidelines table "Watching the Social Aspects of Young Children's Play."

Across the early childhood years, children typically become more interactive in their play (Gottman, 1983; Howes & Matheson, 1992; Meadows, 2010). The imagination and social coordination that characterize cooperative play make it an important activity of early childhood. In one form of cooperative play, *sociodramatic play*, children assume complementary pretend roles and carry out a logical sequence of actions. In the following scenario, we see Eric and Naomi, longtime friends, assuming the roles of husband and wife. Naomi is making plans to go shopping:

N: I'm buying it at a toy store, to buy Eric Fisher a record 'cause he doesn't have a . . .
E: What happened to his old one?
N: It's all broken.
E: How did it get all broken?
N: Ah, a robber stealed it, I think. That's what he said, a robber stealed it.
E: Did he see what the action was? You know my gun is in here, so could you go get my gun? It's right over there, back there, back there, not paper . . . did you get it?

OBSERVATION GUIDELINES
Watching the Social Aspects of Young Children's Play

CHARACTERISTIC	LOOK FOR	EXAMPLE	IMPLICATION
Unoccupied Behavior	• *Failure to engage in any activity*, either with or without another individual • *Aimless wandering* • *Quiet sitting and staring*	During free-play time, Donald often retreats to a corner of the play yard, where he sits quietly either running his fingers through the dirt or staring off into space.	Allow private time for relaxation. If the child is receptive, engage him or her with intriguing toys or include in a small-group activity. Consult with a specialist if unoccupied behavior is persistent.
Solitary Play	• *Absorption* in one's own playthings • *Apparent lack of awareness* of other children's presence	Although Laura and Erika are sitting next to each other in the sandbox, they are facing in opposite directions. Laura is digging a large hole for her pond, and Erika is making roads with a toy bulldozer.	Keep in mind that children's independent play has value for them. Occasionally present new toys or games that encourage participation by several children.
Onlooker Behavior	• *Unobtrusive observation* of other children's play activities • *Quiet looking* at nearby children	As three of his classmates play "store," Jason quietly watches them from the side of the room.	Ask the child if he or she would like to play with the other children. If so, ask the others quietly if the onlooker might join in.
Parallel Play	• *Playing next to another child*, but with little or no interaction • *Similarities in the behaviors of two or more children* who are playing near one another	Naticia and Leo are both making "skyscrapers" with wooden blocks. Sometimes one child looks at what the other is doing, and occasionally one child makes a tower similar to the other's construction.	Comment that both children are doing something similar. Gently suggest an enjoyable activity that incorporates what both children are doing, but don't force interaction.
Associative Play	• *Some talking and sharing* of objects with another child • *Occasional comments* about what other child is doing	Several children are working at the same table creating animals from Play-Doh. They occasionally ask for a particular color ("Gimme the red") or make remarks about others' creations ("You made a kitty just like I did").	Keep in mind that associative play is often a productive way for children to get to know one another. Once children feel comfortable together, you can suggest an activity that would encourage cooperative behavior.
Cooperative Play	• *Active sharing* of toys and coordination of activities • *Taking on specific roles* related to a common theme	Sheldon sets up a "doctor's office" and Jan comes to visit him with her teddy bear, who has a "sore throat." Sheldon puts a tongue depressor to the bear's mouth and instructs it to "Say 'aahh.'"	Provide a variety of toys and other objects that are best used in group play—balls, props for playing "house" and "store," and so on.

Source: First two columns based on Parten (1932).

N: Yes, I found the robbers right in the closet.
E: Good, kill 'em.
N: I killed 'em.
E: Already?
N: Yes, so quick they can't believe it. (Gottman, 1986, p. 191)

Sociodramatic play activities contribute to children's growing social competence. In this kind of play children coordinate their perspectives, share fantasies, and take turns (Karabon, 2017; Meadows, 2010; Rubin et al., 2006; C. Simmons, 2014). They agree on individual roles ("I'll be the warrior"; "Okay, I'll be the chief"), props ("The log can be our base"), and rules that govern actions ("We'll let Frances play, but she has to be the horse").

During sociodramatic play, children exercise skills in assertiveness, negotiation, conflict resolution, and self-regulation (G. Anderson, Spainhower, & Sharp, 2014; Banerjee, Alsalman, & Alqafari, 2016; Cordoni, Demuru, Ceccarelli, & Palagi, 2016; Göncü, 1993). Many learn to become progressively more polite in making requests. A 3-year-old is apt to be a bit bossy ("Give me the red one"; "You hafta . . . "), whereas 5- and 6-year-olds are more likely to use hints and suggestions ("Would you like . . . ?" "Let's . . . "; Parkhurst & Gottman, 1986, p. 329). Through negotiating roles and story lines, they discover the advantages of compromise ("I want to be the Mommy, you're the baby"; "No, you were the mommy last time, so it's *my* turn"; "Okay, but next time I get to be the mommy"). Children learn how to give one another emotional support by recognizing one another's actions and creations ("That's pretty") and expressing sympathy for a playmate's distress ("Don't worry about that, it'll come off"; Gottman, 1983, p. 58; Rubin et al., 2006). An outcome of close coordination in activities is found in Artifact Example 15.2, a drawing created by two friends during afternoon play.

MyLab Education
Video Example 15.3

Find Developmental Meaning
What gestures do 4-year-old Acadia and Cody use to nurture their friendship? They make explicit reference to their friendship ("Let's go, Cody, my best friend"), encourage one another to climb ("This is gonna be cool!"), admit when they're wrong ("Silly me, I forget everything"), and come to agreement about which slide to go down ("Yeah. Let's do it").

Despite its exercise of social, cognitive, and physical skills, sociodramatic play is probably not crucial for every child's development (Lillard et al., 2013). Other kinds of play have important benefits, especially at younger ages. Parallel play, although seemingly nonsocial, has definite value: Children use it to learn more about peers' interests (Bakeman & Brownlee, 1980; Rubin et al., 2006). Solitary play is not only used by very young children but is sometimes preferred by older children who are less social than peers (Coplan, Ooi, Rose-Krasnor, & Nocita, 2014). Some children regularly play with peers but also prefer time alone for exploring the properties of objects and improving their proficiency in handling tools, natural specimens, and toys (A. D. Pellegrini, 2013).

MyLab Education
Artifact Example 15.2

Find Developmental Meaning
Alex (age 5) and Davis (age 6) drew this picture, which they called "Our Robot." Might the boys be friends? The fact that the boys drew the picture together, with its common theme, used a title that reflects shared possession, and jointly signed it are clues to their friendship.

Middle Childhood (6–10 years). Once children begin elementary school, about 30 percent of their interactions are with peers (Rubin et al., 2006). Many interactions at school are in activities in which they are learning academic skills together. As a result of these social experiences, children become aware that some behaviors with peers are acceptable whereas others are not. With a growing awareness of others' opinions, most children become eager to behave in socially acceptable ways. Children also become concerned with rights within the group. Conflicts inevitably arise, and it is easier said than done to resolve disagreements equitably (Frederickson & Simmonds, 2008; Newcomb & Bagwell, 1995; Salvas et al., 2014). Children discover that such negative strategies as sulking ("I'm going home!"), threatening ("I'm never gonna play with you again!"), and hitting ("Take that!") rarely work. By experimenting with other strategies and improving their capacity for social perspective taking, most children become proficient at maintaining amicable relationships with age-mates. You can see a 10-year-old boy's representation of the emotional difficulties and relief related to settling an argument with a good friend in Artifact Example 15.3.

Whereas preschool children are apt to get together in groups of two or three and engage in free-flowing fantasy, elementary school children convene in larger groups. Children affiliate in these networks at recess, in the neighborhood, and in after-school teams and activities. Various roles emerge as children interact, with one or more individuals dominating and a few unhealthy associations emerging, notably social exclusions and bully–victim relationships, in which one child has more power and repeatedly picks on the other.

MyLab Education
Artifact Example 15.3

Find Developmental Meaning *Ten-year-old Jacob drew a child getting into an argument with a friend and coming to a mutually acceptable solution. What does Jacob understand about conflict resolution?* In his, artwork Jacob reveals an awareness that arguing with friends is unpleasant but that disputes can be resolved to everyone's satisfaction.

In informal settings, such as on the playground or at one another's homes, children of this age frequently play games with established rules. Verbal contests (e.g., "Twenty Questions," "I Spy"), board games, computer games, and team sports are common (Hartup, 1984; N. Howe & Leach, 2018; Knowles, Parnell, Stratton, & Ridgers, 2013). By participating in such activities, children discover how to use rules to their own advantage ("If I put another house on Boardwalk, you have to pay me double the next time you land on it"). They learn how to form alliances ("I'll run behind him, and then you pass me the ball over his head"). And they develop strategies for dealing with ambiguous situations ("It was *in*!" "Are you kidding? It was *out*!" "Okay, we'll say it's out, but next time *I* get to decide!").

Early Adolescence (10–14 years). A major task during young adolescence is identifying peers at school with whom to affiliate. Young people tend to attract social partners who are similar to them in key ways—in their academic achievement, ethnicity, appearance (e.g., how much they weigh), and behavior (e.g., how altruistic and aggressive they are; B. W. Domingue et al., 2018; Echols & Graham, 2013; Traylor, Williams, Kenney, & Hopson, 2016). As students get to know one another and gel as a group, they view outsiders as different from themselves. Young adolescents have a tendency to pigeonhole classmates with such labels as "brains," "jocks," "skaters," and "geeks" (B. B. Brown & Dietz, 2009; Wölfer & Scheithauer, 2014).

Once students reach puberty, they increasingly rely on peers for emotional support (G. H. Brody et al., 2014; Golden, Griffin, Metzger, & Cooper, 2018; Levitt, Guacci-Franco, & Levitt, 1993). Many reveal their innermost thoughts to familiar peers during face-to-face conversations and with contacts over the Internet (Dolev-Cohen & Barak, 2013; Levitt et al., 1993). As their tendency for self-disclosure expands, young adolescents become self-conscious about what others think of them. Age-mates frequently exert **peer pressure** by encouraging adolescents to behave in certain ways and not others. Youngsters who have poor relationships with their families, live in economically disadvantaged neighborhoods, and base their self-esteem on other people's opinions are especially vulnerable to peer pressure (Erwin, 1993; Matjasko, Needham, Grunden, & Farb, 2010). Yet young people obviously make their own choices and imitate peers' behavior selectively, as this reflection by a youngster reveals:

> There's all this crap about being accepted into a group and struggling and making an effort to make friends and not being comfortable about your own self-worth as a human being. You're trying very hard to show everyone what a great person you are, and the best way to do that is if everyone else is drinking therefore they think that's the thing to do, then you might do the same thing to prove to them that you have the same values that they do and therefore you're okay. At the same time, the idea of peer pressure is a lot of bunk. What I heard about peer pressure all the way through school is that someone is going to walk up to me and say, "Here, drink this and you'll be cool." It wasn't like that at all. You go somewhere and everyone else would be doing it and you'd think, "Hey, everyone else is doing it and they seem to be having a good time—now why wouldn't I do this?" In that sense, the preparation of the powers that be, the lessons that they tried to drill into me, they were completely off. They had no idea what we are up against. (C. Lightfoot, 1992, p. 240)

Because much of the motivation to conform to peers' standards comes from within rather than from others, young people who have a firm sense of their own identity are better able than insecure peers to resist the urge to imitate others' characteristics (K. A. Buck, Kretsch, & Harden, 2013; Hartup, 1983).

Late Adolescence (14–18 years). Older adolescents spend almost a third of their waking hours interacting with peers (Rubin et al., 2006). Teenagers spend little time with adults and very little time *exclusively* with an adult, such as a parent or teacher (Csikszentmihalyi, 1995; Csikszentmihalyi & Larson, 1984). In their many interactions, adolescents help one another define who they are as individuals. They talk through their values and aspirations and use peers as a forum for self-exploration (Gottman & Mettetal, 1986; Meadows, 2010). Because adolescents choose their confidantes, intimate conversations tend to be supportive. Adolescents provide one another with temptations to engage in risky behaviors, but they also encourage sharing, cooperation, ethical decisions, and community involvement (Capone, Donizzetti, & Petrillo, 2018; Wentzel, 2014).

Emerging abstract reasoning allows older adolescents to think of other people as unique individuals rather than as members of a group. Older teens become increasingly aware of the characteristics they share with people from diverse backgrounds. Perhaps as a result, ties to sharply divided groups dissipate, hostilities soften, and youngsters become more flexible about the people with whom they associate (B. B. Brown & Dietz, 2009; Shrum & Cheek, 1987). One graduate of a racially mixed high school put it this way:

> Senior year was wonderful, when the black kids and the white kids got to be friends again, and the graduation parties where everyone mixed . . . . It was so much better. (T. Lewin, 2000, p. 20)

A Developmental System for Acquiring Social Skills

The particular social skills that children develop depend not only on their age but also on their individual features and shared experiences. Social skills are strongly influenced by personal characteristics, gender, family interactions, and culture.

Developmental Systems Prompt

Social skills emerge in unique cultural settings. As you teach children to be friendly to others, join a conversation, work out disagreements, or express their feelings constructively, give them occasions to practice the new skills in familar settings.

Personal characteristics. Children's biological predispositions play a definite role in their peer relationships. Children who are born with a tendency to be impulsive and irritable are at risk for becoming disruptive, insensitive, and aggressive in their peer relationships (Berdan, Keane, & Calkins, 2008; Boivin et al., 2013; Latham, Mark, & Oliver, 2018). Those who are especially shy and withdrawn may also have trouble because they fail to initiate contact with peers. Of course, with support, virtually all children are capable of forming close peer relationships.

On average, children with high intelligence (e.g., youngsters whom school personnel have identified as gifted) have good social skills. Yet some youngsters with highly advanced intellectual abilities have trouble maintaining effective interpersonal relationships because they feel *very* different from their peers, have parents who rebuff them, or are in an educational setting where they are outcasts (Olszewski-Kubilius, Lee, & Thomson, 2014; Winner, 1997). Children with lower intelligence find it more difficult than peers to understand how other people think, interpret their emotional expressions, and carry on conversations (Stichter, Herzog, Kilgus, & Schoemann, 2018). Many children with disabilities have good interpersonal skills, but some do not. Children with significant sensory or physical disabilities may have few opportunities to interact with peers. Children who have impaired social cognition—for instance, those with a significant intellectual disability or one of the *autism spectrum disorders*, in which they exhibit off-putting repetitive behaviors and have difficulty understanding other people, often have deficiencies in social skills (E. W. Carter et al., 2014; S. Greenspan & Granfield, 1992; Stichter et al., 2018). A child who is autistic may fail to express empathy to distressed peers, carry on a one-sided conversation, and exhibit tantrums when frustrated. Youngsters with chronic emotional and behavioral problems (e.g., conduct disorders) are apt to have difficulty making and keeping friends, usually because of having poor social problem-solving skills (Asher & Coie, 1990; Renk, White, Scott, & Middleton, 2009).

Gender. Beginning in preschool, boys and girls tend to segregate into same-gender groups (Paley, 1984; Parke & Clarke-Stewart, 2011; Sallquist, DiDonato, Hanish, Martin, & Fabes, 2012; Xiao, Cook, Martin, Nielson, & Field, 2018). In sociodramatic play, girls enact scenarios that are relatively calm and sedate (e.g., playing house or school). In contrast, boys introduce elements of adventure and danger (e.g., playing cops and robbers or fighting intergalactic battles). As boys grow older they continue to place a high priority on physical action. Girls spend much more time simply talking, sharing personal concerns, telling secrets, offering emotional support, and so on (Berndt, 1992; Rose & Smith, 2009). Girls feel more attached to peers than do boys and are also more sensitive to subtle, nonverbal messages (body language; J. H. Block, 1983; Gorrese & Ruggieri, 2012). On average, girls are slightly more kind and considerate, yet boys regularly show their "softer" sides, displaying affection and sympathy appropriate for the occasion (Baillargeon et al., 2011; Eisenberg & Fabes, 1998).

Family and community experiences. Children learn a great deal about how to get along with others at home and generalize these interactions to classmates (D. J. Dickson, Huey, Laursen, Kiuru, & Nurmi, 2018; Hosokawa & Katsura, 2017). When parents are responsive and sensitive, children are likely to be considerate with peers. In addition, many families promote their children's peer relationships directly by setting up get-togethers with peers. Parents also coach children in social skills, for example, encouraging them to take turns instead of fighting over toys (Healy, Sanders, & Iyer, 2014; Russell & Finnie, 1990). Contact with peers is also influenced by local circumstances. Generally, children in working-class and middle-class neighborhoods have numerous peers who live nearby (G. W. Ladd, 2005). Some parents living in economically disadvantaged communities restrict children's free time with peers because of dangers in the neighborhood. In affluent communities, few families with children are apt to live nearby, and parents may not have time to chauffeur children around to social events (Medrich, 1981). Numerous parents from all backgrounds overcome barriers to social contact for their children, especially when children request get-togethers.

Culture. To some degree, cultural groups model particular styles of relating to other people. For example, children in China, especially in the rural areas, are encouraged to be shy, whereas those in Israel are encouraged to be assertive (X. Chen, Wang, & Wang, 2009; Krispin, Sternberg, & Lamb, 1992). Parents also arrange or prohibit contact with peers depending on customs. In North America, parents value the ability of their children to get along with peers, and they encourage children's friendships with "playdates," appointments for their children to get together at one house or the other. Japanese children have less free time than do U.S. children and fewer chances to interact with peers in informal settings; they acquire valuable interaction skills at school, where teachers cultivate a commitment to kind and sensitive treatment of classmates, including those with disabilities (Kayama & Haight, 2013; Rothbaum, Pott, Azuma, Miyake, & Weisz, 2000).

Types of Affiliations with Peers

Children affiliate with one another in four distinct ways. First, they select social partners with whom to affiliate informally, often on a short-term basis, for example, by choosing whom to sit next to at lunchtime, with the result that some children are regularly accepted as buddies and others are not. Second, young people form friends with whom they share secrets and pastimes. Third, young people form larger social groups, especially during the older childhood and adolescent years. Finally, they become partners in romance. Let's examine the qualities of these kinds of social contact.

Social Partners in Informal Interactions

Children make many choices for age-mates they would like to affiliate with when walking home after school, doing homework, going to birthday parties, and the like. Socially skilled children—those who are trusting, cooperative, and responsive with others—are frequently approached by peers and invited into social interaction (Blandon, Calkins, Grimm, Keane, & O'Brien, 2010; J. Chin, 2014; Santos, Vaughn, Peceguina, & Daniel, 2014). Developmental researchers examine *peer acceptance* by asking children in a classroom to confidentially nominate individual classmates with whom they would like to interact and others whom they would prefer to avoid. Researchers collect nominations and classify each child into one of five groups: *popular*, *rejected*, *neglected*, *controversial*, and *average* (Coie, Dodge, & Coppotelli, 1982; Dishion, Kim, Stormshak, & O'Neill, 2014; Rubin et al., 2006). Researchers then compare the features of children in each classification.

Children who are well liked by peers are considered **popular**. When researchers ask children to identify classmates they would most like to do something with, children don't necessarily choose those whom they and their teachers perceive to be the most admired members of the student body (Lafontana & Cillessen, 1998; Parkhurst & Hopmeyer, 1998). When we talk about *popular children* in terms of peer acceptance, we are usually describing young people who are well liked, kind, and trustworthy rather than those who hold obvious high-status positions, such as head cheerleader or football quarterback. Children who are well accepted by peers typically have good social skills. They know how to initiate and sustain conversations, refrain from talking only about their own needs, detect the subtle social cues that others give off, adjust their behaviors to changing circumstances, and share, cooperate, and empathize with others (Oortwijn, Boekaerts, Vedder, & Fortuin, 2008; Santos et al., 2014).

Children who are frequently excluded by peers are known as **rejected children**. Rejected children generally have poor social skills—for example, they may persistently draw attention to themselves and act impulsively and disruptively in the classroom (Asher & Renshaw, 1981; G. Ladd, Ettekal, Kochenderfer-Ladd, Rudolph, & Andrews, 2014; Putallaz & Heflin, 1986). Some rejected children are aggressive, placing a higher priority on acquiring objects and gaining power over others than on maintaining congenial interpersonal relationships (Dodge, Bates, & Pettit, 1990; Parke & Clarke-Stewart, 2011). Other rejected children appear immature, insensitive, inattentive, strange, or exceptionally timid (Bierman, 2004). Some have an obvious disability (Voyer, Tessier, & Nadeau, 2017). Rejected children's tendency to alienate others leaves them few opportunities to develop the social skills they desperately need, and many feel lonely and become targets of bullying behaviors (Beeri & Lev-Wiesel, 2012; Coie & Cillessen, 1993).

A third group of children consists of **neglected children**, those whom age-mates rarely select as peers they would either most like or least like to do something with (Asher & Renshaw, 1981). Many neglected children are quiet and keep to themselves. Some prefer to be alone, others do not know how to go about making friends, and still others may be quite content with one or two close friends (Parke & Clarke-Stewart, 2011). Neglected status is often only a temporary situation; children categorized as neglected at one time are not always so categorized in follow-up assessments (Rubin et al., 2006; S. Walker, 2009).

A fourth category, **controversial children**, includes youngsters who are very well liked by some peers and intensely disliked by others. Controversial children are apt to have characteristics of both popular and rejected children. For example, they may be aggressive on some occasions and helpful at other times (Coie & Dodge, 1988). The fifth group consists of children who, for lack of a better term, are known simply as *average*: Some peers like them and others don't but without the intensity of feelings shown for popular, rejected, or controversial children and without the invisibility of neglected children.

Because of its apparent effects on children, peer acceptance is an important quality for adults to monitor. In the Observation Guidelines table "Noticing Children's Level of Peer Acceptance," we present common characteristics of popular, rejected, neglected, controversial, and average children and suggest basic strategies for supporting students with these varying levels of peer acceptance.

OBSERVATION GUIDELINES

Noticing Children's Level of Peer Acceptance

CHARACTERISTIC	LOOK FOR	EXAMPLE	IMPLICATION
Popular Children	• *Good communication skills* • *Sensitivity and responsiveness* to others' needs • *Willingness to assimilate* into ongoing activities • *Signs of leadership potential*	On the playground, 8-year-old Daequan moves easily from one group to another. Before joining a conversation, he listens and adds a relevant comment. He doesn't draw much attention to himself but is well liked by most classmates.	Use popular children as leaders when trying to change others' behavior. For example, when starting a recycling program, ask a well-regarded student to help get the program off the ground.
Rejected Children	• *For some, high rates of aggression* • *For others, immature, anxious, or impulsive behavior, including disruptions in class*	Most children dislike 10-year-old Terra. She frequently calls classmates insulting nicknames, threatens to beat them up, and noisily intrudes into their private conversations.	Help rejected children learn basic social skills, such as how to initiate a conversation. Place them in cooperative groups with classmates who are likely to be accepting.

(continued)

OBSERVATION GUIDELINES
Noticing Children's Level of Peer Acceptance (continued)

CHARACTERISTIC	LOOK FOR	EXAMPLE	IMPLICATION
Rejected Children (continued)	• *For still others, unusually shy and withdrawn behavior or presence of a serious disability* • *Unwillingness of other children* to play or work with them • *In some cases, appearance of being strange and annoying*		With aggressive children, give appropriate consequences and teach strategies for controlling impulses. Publicly compliment rejected children on things they do well. Consult counselors when rejected children fail to respond to your gestures.
Neglected Children	• *Tendency to be relatively quiet*; little or no disruptive behavior • *Fewer-than-average interactions* with age-mates but possible friendships with one or two peers • *For some, anxiety* about interacting with others • *Possible temporary* neglected status	Fourteen-year-old Sedna is initially reserved at her new school. She eats her lunch and walks home alone. Later in the year, she seems happier and more involved in school activities.	Identify group activities in which neglected children might feel comfortable. Arrange situations in which shy children with similar interests can get to know one another.
Controversial Children	• *Acceptance by some peers, rejection by others* • *Aggression and disruptive behavior in some situations, yet helpfulness, cooperation and sensitivity in others*	Thirteen-year-old Marcus is usually charming and cheerful, but occasionally he makes jokes at someone else's expense. His sunny personality impresses many classmates, yet his biting humor offends others.	Let controversial children know in no uncertain terms when their behaviors are inappropriate, but acknowledge their effective social skills as well.
Average Children	• *Tendency to be liked by some peers but disliked by others* • *Average interpersonal skills* (e.g., typical levels of prosocial behavior and aggression) • *Ability to find a comfortable social niche*	Five-year-old Joachim doesn't attract much attention to himself. He's made a few friends in kindergarten and seems to get along fairly well with them, but he sometimes has trouble handling disagreements.	Help average children refine emerging social skills. Encourage them to be tactful, honest, and kind. Acknowledge sensitivity, cooperation, and leadership, and teach alternatives to hurting and selfish behavior.

Sources: Bierman (2004); Coie and Dodge (1988); Coie and Kupersmidt (1983); Dodge (1983); G. Ladd et al. (2014); Parke and Clarke-Stewart (2011); Putallaz and Gottman (1981); Rubin et al. (2006); Santos et al. (2014); Voyer, Tessier, and Nadeau (2017); and S. Walker (2009).

Friendships

In addition to wanting to be included by peers in everyday activities, children invariably hope to have one or more friends. Some of these friendships are brief liaisons; others last a lifetime. Many are casual; a few are deep and intimate. Some children have a large number of friends; others invest steadfastly in one or two close ones. Despite coming in varied types, friendships have four common qualities that distinguish them from other peer relationships.

My best friend is brian and we have had many fun times together with my other friends (anthony and arthur) too. We have been friends since 1st grade, He has always been in my class those years, so has arthur and anthony, We have had sad and happy times/adventures, We sometimes argued. We would play hide and seek and get soda and other things at the moble home park. We both enjoyed hamster as pets. Sometimes he came to my house to play

MyLab Education
Artifact Example 15.4

Find Developmental Meaning *How did 10-year-old Joseph spend time with his friend Brian?* Joseph describes a wide range of activities that they participated in together.

Friendships are voluntary relationships. Children often spend time with peers through happenstance: Perhaps they ride the same school bus, are members of a class, or join a given sports team. In contrast, children *choose* their friends. Children make active efforts to affiliate with friends, and two or more youngsters typically remain pals as long as they continue to enjoy one another's company, manage to get together, and resolve their differences amicably.

Friendships are powered by shared routines. Friends establish traditions that are meaningful and mutually enjoyable. Over time, friends talk through their likes and dislikes, establishing common ground about many topics (Sorşana, Guizard, & Trognon, 2013; Suttles, 1970). Children talk, smile, and laugh more often with friends than with nonfriends, and they engage in more complex fantasy play with them (J. G. Parker, 1986). In Artifact Example 15.4, 10-year-old Joseph writes about the fun activities he and his friend Brian have enjoyed together.

Friendships are reciprocal relationships. In the time they spend together, friends address one another's needs (J. L. Epstein, 1986; J. Neal, Neal, & Cappella, 2014). Although friends take on slightly different roles in their relationship, generally they are equal partners. One friend may instigate fun activities, and the other may be an especially sympathetic listener, with both styles reflecting personal characteristics, perceptions of the partner's needs, and mutual regard.

Friendships offer ongoing, dependable support. Friends help each other cope with stressful events by providing reassurance (Berndt & Keefe, 1995; Cranley Gallagher, 2013). Because friends have an emotional investment in their relationship, they work hard to look at situations from each other's point of view and resolve disputes that threaten to be divisive. As a result, they practice perspective taking and conflict resolution (Basinger, Gibbs, & Fuller, 1995; Calder, Hill, & Pellicano, 2013; DeVries, 1997).

The distinct qualities of friendship we have examined evolve with maturation and experience. Friendships begin with mutual enjoyment and slowly incorporate loyalty, trust, intimacy, compromise, and repairs after misunderstandings. Let's look more carefully at their manifestation during the developmental periods.

Infancy (birth–2 years). Primitive relationships among peers emerge during infancy. In the beginning, social interests are fleeting, and infants are as likely to crawl over one another as to pass a toy back and forth. Yet as infants grow, develop basic cognitive and language skills, and become familiar with one another, they smile, watch one another's faces, study others' actions, and try to coordinate play (Gonzalez-Mena, 2012; D. F. Hay et al., 2018; Rubin et al., 2006). When Teresa's son Connor was 9 months old, he became friendly with Patrick, another boy of the same age at his child-care center. The two boys established familiar play routines, often laughing and chasing one another while crawling around the room. Although they weren't yet speaking, and they certainly didn't swap secrets, they were attuned to one another's behaviors. Such social interests solidify, and in their second year, toddlers make social overtures often, carry on complex interactions, and display positive emotions with peers whom they know and like (Howes, 1988).

Early Childhood (2–6 years). In the preschool years children infuse language, fantasy, and play into social interactions with familiar peers. When 3- and 4-year-olds are interacting with friends rather than with other age-mates, they are more likely to offer social greetings, share materials, carry on conversation, engage in complex play, and exhibit good social skills (C. Carter & Nutbrown, 2016; Charlesworth & LaFreniere, 1983; Hoyte, Torr, & Degotardi, 2014). Friends are usually motivated to work through disagreements, and in the process, children assert themselves while also showing regard for friends (Hartup & Laursen, 1991). This capacity to balance fulfillment of personal needs with concern for the rights of others is generalizable to all sorts of future relationships. Children like to spend time with their friends, as you can see in Artifact Example 15.5.

MyLab Education
Artifact Example 15.5

Find Developmental Meaning
Four-year-old Dana drew a picture of herself and her friend Dina. The two girls met in child care and became close companions until their families moved to separate towns. How might the girls respond to one another when they later attended summer camp? Not shown in the picture, the girls happily renewed their friendship when reunited at summer camp.

Middle Childhood (6–10 years). During the elementary school years, children continue to act differently with friends than with nonfriends. With friends they are more likely to express their feelings and ask about one another's emotional states (Newcomb & Bagwell, 1995; Newcomb & Brady, 1982). In elementary school, friends develop trust and loyalty, and many, girls especially, use self-disclosure as a strategy with friends (Diaz & Berndt, 1982; Rotenberg & Boulton, 2013; Swenson & Rose, 2009). Friendships are more stable in middle childhood than they were in the preschool years, and children are more deliberate in selecting playmates with qualities similar to their own (Berndt & Hoyle, 1985; Rubin, Lynch, Coplan, Rose-Krasnor, & Booth, 1994). Children typically choose friends of their own gender, in part, because same-gender peers are more likely to share interests and pastimes (Gottman, 1986; Zosuls et al., 2014). Ten-year-old Andres shows his affection for buddies in his drawing in Artifact Example 15.6. A few children at this age make friends with children of the opposite gender, and such relationships are valuable in promoting social perspective taking and flexible communication skills (McDougall & Hymel, 2007). Children who fail to make any friends at school are at risk for loneliness and adjustment problems (D. Wang & Fletcher, 2017).

MyLab Education
Artifact Example 15.6

Find Developmental Meaning *Ten-year-old Andres drew a picture of himself with two of his buddies. How is the friendship among the three boys typical of elementary and middle school?* Many close friendships in these age ranges occur among children of the same gender.

Early Adolescence (10–14 years). Differences in relationships between friends and nonfriends intensify during early adolescence (Basinger et al., 1995; J. G. Parker & Gottman, 1989). Many young adolescents let down their guard and reveal their vulnerabilities to close friends, even as they try to maintain self-confidence in front of other age-mates. Adolescents also confront feelings of possessiveness over friends (J. G. Parker, Kruse, & Aikins, 2010). As friendship pairs and triads of buddies fuse into broader collections of age-mates, adolescents have a chance to learn that friendships don't have to be exclusive. In middle schools with a diverse ethnic population, students often develop friendships with individuals who are from a different background, a situation that can benefit everyone's mental health and feeling of being welcome in a strong, inclusive community (S. Graham, 2018).

Late Adolescence (14–18 years). Older adolescents are selective in their choice of friends (J. L. Epstein, 1986). Gone are the days when they run out of fingers as they count off their "close" friends, except, of course, on social media, where friends multiply. In face-to-face relationships, older teenagers tend to nurture connections with a few friends that they keep over time, in some cases throughout their lifetimes. They frequently turn to friends for emotional support in times of trouble and engage in lengthy discussions about personal problems and possible solutions (Asher & Parker, 1989; Weeks & Pasupathi, 2010). When young people cannot easily turn to parents to reason through personal problems, friends often provide an open-minded ear and words of comfort (Espinoza, Gillen-O'Neel, Gonzales, & Fuligni, 2013).

As you have learned, friendship is a wonderful human capacity whose initial flickers can be seen in babies who come to enjoy one another's antics. The capacity expands throughout childhood and adolescence with the accompaniment of social skills, companionship, and commitments to abstract ideas about intimacy and trust.

MyLab Education Application Exercise 15.1
Detect Developmental Levels

How do 6-year-old Ying-Yu and 17-year-old Paul conceptualize friendship? Listen to a young child and older adolescent explain friendship and conflict resolution.

Social Groups

Another kind of peer affiliation occurs in middle childhood and adolescence. As a result of their expanding social contacts, youngsters form large social groups that regularly fraternize (Knifsend & Juvonen, 2014; Rubin et al., 2006). Initially, these groups are collections of single-gender friendships. In adolescence they often include both boys and girls. Youngsters' social groups vary considerably in size, function, and character. Many have the following attributes.

Group members develop a common culture. As you have learned, children who choose to affiliate with one another develop common routines and ways of thinking about their lives. This shared culture gives group members a sense of community, belonging, and identity. Identification with a group also prompts young people to notice that they and other members of their same group have certain characteristics in common that differ from other groups.

Group members socialize one another to follow group norms. Group members encourage conformity by reinforcing certain behaviors and discouraging others (Clasen & Brown, 1985; Deutsch, Steinley, & Slutske, 2014). Fortunately, many groups embrace productive characteristics, such as honesty, fairness, cooperation, academic achievement, and a sense of humor (Damon, 1988; Padilla-Walker & Carlo, 2014). Others, however, encourage unproductive behaviors, such as threatening classmates, making fun of those with disabilities, and using drugs (B. B. Brown, 1993; Deutsch et al., 2014). Of course, young people do not passively become what fellow group members want them to be. In fact, youngsters generally affiliate with peers who have similar characteristics and pressure themselves to adopt norms (Gottman & Mettetal, 1986; Gremmen, Dijkstra, Steglich, & Veenstra, 2017; Kwon & Lease, 2009).

Group members influence youngsters more strongly in some areas of life than others. Young people rarely accept a peer's suggestions without question (B. B. Brown, 1990; Padilla-Walker & Carlo, 2007). Instead, they typically evaluate what peers ask them to do, often with memories of advice they previously received from family members, teachers, and others. Peer groups are particularly influential in matters of style—for example, in dress, music, and social activities. In contrast, parents, teachers, and other adults continue to be influential in views about education, morality, religion, and careers (E. C. Cook, Buehler, & Henson, 2009; Hartup, 1983).

Group members develop a sense of unity. Once youngsters gel as a group, they prefer members to nonmembers, and they develop feelings of loyalty to individuals within the group. In some cases they also feel hostility toward members of other groups and view them as competitors or unworthy human beings (Sherif, Harvey, White, Hood, & Sherif, 1961; L. K. Taylor et al., 2014). Such feelings toward *out-groups* are particularly intense when two or more groups battle over reputation or resources, as rival athletic teams and adolescent gangs often do.

Dominance hierarchies emerge in the group. When children's groups continue for any length of time, a pecking order, or **dominance hierarchy**, gradually evolves (J. L. Martin, 2009; Strayer, 1991). Some group members rise to the top, leading the way and making decisions for everyone. Other group members are followers: They look to those around them for guidance on how to behave and assume lesser roles in the group's activities. Sometimes less dominant individuals find unique positions within the group, perhaps the proverbial clown, daredevil, nursemaid, or brainiac. When interactions become tightly controlled by position, those lower in the pecking order are at risk for being ignored, ostracized, and bullied (Garandeau, Lee, & Salmivalli, 2014).

Once youngsters reach puberty, social groups become a salient feature of their worlds. Developmental researchers have described several kinds of groups that are significant during middle school, junior high, and high school: cliques and crowds, and subcultures.

Cliques and Crowds. **Cliques** are moderately stable friendship groups of three to nine individuals, often of the same gender. Cliques provide the basis for many voluntary social interactions during childhood and adolescence (X. Chen, Chang, & He, 2003; Kwon, Lease, & Hoffman, 2012). Clique boundaries tend to be fairly rigid and exclusive (some people are in; others are out), and membership affects social status and level of influence.

Children begin to form cliques as early as first grade, as dyads of friends affiliate with other dyads (Witvliet, van Lier, Cuijpers, & Koot, 2010). Cliques are moderately stable, with many children often affiliating with the same group for a year or more. A certain number enter and exit groups during the year. As children grow, they become increasingly concerned with being accepted into a clique. Young adolescents wonder about their social standing: "Who likes me?" "Will I be popular at my new school?" "Why didn't Sal invite me to his party?" (Gavin & Furman, 1989). When they leave one clique to join another, they and their previous friends may feel betrayal, hurt, and jealousy (Kanner, Feldman, Weinberger, & Ford, 1987). Occasionally, friends within a clique tease and pester one another, and this experience can be hurtful for those being victimized (Closson & Watanabe, 2018).

Cliques decline in prevalence during the adolescent years and are replaced by **crowds**, larger collections of individuals who are defined by others according to the

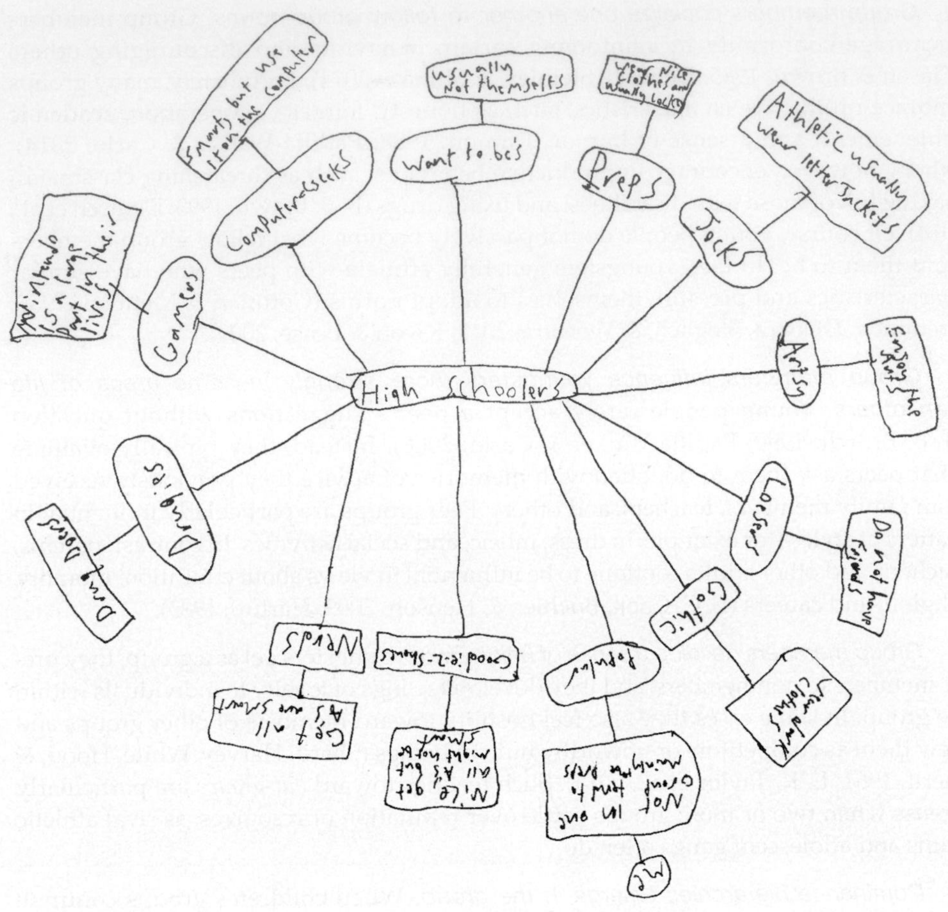

MyLab Education
Artifact Example 15.7

Find Developmental Meaning *Fourteen-year-old Connor diagrammed the student groupings he observed during his freshman year in high school. In his inner circle he labeled the different groups (e.g., preps, jocks, gamers), and in the outer circle he described each one (e.g., "wear nice clothes and usually cocky," "athletic, usually wear letter jackets," "Nintendo is a large part in their lives"). What does the network suggest about Connor's interest in social groups at school?* Connor is struck by clusters of students distinguished by their interests and appearance.

group's reputation (B. B. Brown & Dietz, 2009). Like cliques, crowds provide support to young people and opportunities to practice social skills. Crowds tend to disband during the final 2 years of high school when young people feel freer to act as individuals and intermingle with people from different backgrounds. In Artifact Example 15.7 (above), Connor diagrams the types of crowds he noticed his first year of high school.

Subcultures. A large number of adolescents affiliate with a well-defined **subculture**, a group that resists the dominant culture by adopting a significantly different way of life (Czymoniewicz-Klippel, 2013; J. S. Epstein, 1998). Some subcultures are tightly knit groups, and others are loosely configured, with members coming and going. Some subcultures are relatively benign; for instance, a middle school skateboarders' subculture may simply espouse a mode of dress and recreational pastime. Other subcultures, such as those that promote drug use, engage in criminal activity, hurt themselves, or endorse racist and anti-Semitic behaviors (e.g., skinheads), are worrisome (C. C. Clark, 1992; Intravia, Wolff, Stewart, & Simons, 2014). Following are a few of the many sub-cultural groups with which young people affiliate:

- **Hip-Hop.** Students who endorse the Hip-Hop culture are drawn to music with a percussive rhythm, also known as rap, a style that is thought to reflect authentic experiences of people living in urban communities. Themes of the music include social issues, especially regarding frustrations with discrimination, drugs, and violence. Educators have objected to some themes, such as contempt for women, even while other empowering themes have become a bridge for connecting to certain youth.

- **Goths.** Students who identify as Goth may dress in black clothing, wear dark eye and pale face makeup, and adorn themselves with silver piercings and tattoos. They share preferences for Gothic music, resonate to dark and pessimistic themes, and dwell on romantic and horror stories from the 19th century. Students who identify as Goths may be drawn to use drugs and hurt themselves (e.g., by cutting their skin when anxious and depressed because paradoxically this action makes them feel better).

- **Pro-Ana.** Students who follow the Pro-Ana movement typically have an eating disorder, such as *anorexia nervosa*, in which they eat little or nothing for weeks or months and seriously jeopardize their own health. Followers, who are primarily girls, seek the advice and support of likeminded individuals who wish to be extremely thin and are accessible in digital chatrooms.

- **Gangs.** A **gang** is a cohesive group characterized by initiation rites, distinctive colors and symbols, alleged ownership of a territory, feuds with rival groups, and criminal activity, including selling drugs, brandishing weapons, and intimidating peers. Gangs have well-defined dominance hierarchies, strict rules, and stiff penalties for breaking them. Once confined to a few neighborhoods in inner cities, gangs have now become widespread, especially in lower-income inner-city areas but also increasingly in suburbs and rural areas. (Bobakova, Geckova, Klein, van Dijk, & Reijneveld, 2015; G. H. Brown, Brunelle, & Malhotra, 2017; A. Campbell, 1984; Gilman, Hill, Hawkins, Howell, & Kosterman, 2014; Gover, Jennings, & Tewksbury, 2009; Kodluboy, 2004; Melde, Taylor, & Esbensen, 2009; National Drug Intelligence Center, 2008; Parks, 1995; Rojek, Petrocelli, & Oberweis, 2010; Rutledge, Rimer, & Scott, 2008; R. Young, Sproeber, Groschwitz, Preiss, & Plener, 2014).

Romantic Liaisons and Relationships

Starry-eyed desires create an entirely different kind of peer connection. Awareness of romantic intimacy emerges in early childhood. Many children, especially those living in traditional two-parent families, believe that getting married and having children is a normal and inevitable part of growing up. In Artifact Example 15.8, 5-year-old Alex draws his image of his parents on their wedding day. Children sometimes act out their fantasies in play, as this episode involving Eric and Naomi illustrates:

E: Hey, Naomi, I know what we can play today.
N: What?
E: How about, um, the marry game. You like that.
N: Marry?
E: How about baker or something? How about this. Marry you? OK, Naomi, you want to pretend that?
N: Yes.
E: OK, Naomi, do you want to marry me?
N: Yeah.
E: Good, just a minute, Naomi, we don't have any marry place.
N: We could pretend this is the marry place.
E: Oh, well, pretend this, ah, there'll have to be a cake.
N: The wedding is here first.
E: OK, but listen to this, we have to have a baby, oh, and a pet.
N: This is our baby. (Gottman, 1986, p. 157)

Consistent with what we have learned about cognitive abilities at this age, young children's understandings of courtship and marriage are simple and concrete. In the preceding scenario, Naomi and Eric focus on having a "marry place" and wedding cake. Such fantasies help young children anticipate their eventual entry into romantic relationships.

MyLab Education
Artifact Example 15.8

Find Developmental Meaning
What does Alex (age 5) show in his picture of his parents getting married? Like many preschoolers, Alex sees a wedding as a happy and significant event for the couple.

Dating. As children grow, they gradually expand on their ideas about what it means to participate in romantic relationship. Many begin to date. Prior to puberty, some children practice courtship behaviors, with girls vying for the attention of boys by using cosmetics and choosing clothing that make them look older and (they think) prettier, and with boys flaunting whatever manly airs they can muster (Elkind, 1981b; Giordano, 2003). The early romances of late middle childhood and early adolescence often exist more in youngsters' minds than in reality, as the following conversation between two young teenage girls illustrates:

A: How's Lance [*giggle*]? Has he taken you to a movie yet?
B: No. Saw him today but I don't care.
A: Didn't he say anything to you?
B: Oh . . .
A: Lovers!
B: Shut up!
A: Lovers at first sight! [*Giggle.*]
B: [*Giggle.*] Quit it! (Gottman & Mettetal, 1986, p. 210; reprinted with the permission of Cambridge University Press)

Building on its initial manifestations in fantasy, romantic conduct follows a developmental course. In the upper elementary grades and middle school, students develop crushes and get together in mixed-sex groups, if their culture approves of such affiliations) (Beckmeyer & Malacane, 2018). In high school, dating becomes common, sometimes as dyads and at other times in groups. Some romantic relationships become serious, especially later in high school (Connolly & McIsaac, 2009; Rubin et al., 2006). The transition between infatuation to amorous relationships usually takes several years. Not rushing through these steps is associated with being positively adjusted, probably because youngsters need more time to build the skills required for intimate relationships, such as sharing expectations, asserting personal needs, and coping with hurt or angry feelings (Beckmeyer & Malacane, 2018).

In determining how to act in romantic relationships, young people begin with the social skills that they have gained in close relationships. Adolescents with secure attachments to family members are likely to have successful dating experiences, probably because they have greater self-confidence, better social skills, and more experience in trusting relationships (W. A. Collins & Sroufe, 1999; Rauer, Pettit, Lansford, Bates, & Dodge, 2013). Adolescents who are accustomed to a balanced give-and-take at home use this same method with romantic partners, negotiating what movie to see, which party to attend, and so on. In contrast, teenagers who have seen family violence may hit and push partners or, conversely, tolerate partners' aggressive behavior ("He didn't mean it"; "She was drunk"; "He'll outgrow it"; D. A. Wolfe & Wekerle, 1997). Young people also select from among patterns they have absorbed about intimacy, perhaps being loyal to a partner, "hooking up" (being intimate on a onetime basis with someone who is not a dating partner) or having a "friendship with benefits" (a casual relationship in which partners are sexually active but not committed to one another; Connolly & McIsaac, 2009).

Adolescents' romantic relationships offer advantages. Being in a twosome fulfills needs for companionship, affection, security, and social status (W. A. Collins & Sroufe, 1999; Connolly & McIsaac, 2009). Such relationships also provide opportunities for young people to experiment with new interactional styles and to examine previously unexplored aspects of their identity. At the same time, romantic relationships can wreak havoc with adolescents' emotions (W. A. Collins & van Dulmen, 2006; Ha, Dishion, Overbeek, Burk, & Engels, 2014). Young people may find it exciting and frustrating to enter (and exit) romantic liaisons. In some cases the emotional highs and lows that come with romance—the roller-coaster rides between exhilaration and disappointment—cloud judgment, trigger depression, and distract young people from schoolwork (Beckmeyer & Malacane, 2018; Ha et al., 2014; Larson, Clore, & Wood, 1999).

Sexual Intimacy. Both genders have a capacity for sexual arousal before puberty (Conn & Kanner, 1940; de Graaf & Rademakers, 2006). Children occasionally look at or touch one another in private places and play games with sexual overtones (e.g., strip poker, playing doctor; Dornbusch et al., 1981; Leander, Larsen, & Munk, 2018). However, sexual contact before adolescence typically lacks the erotic features present in later development, by which time young people have developed the physical structures and physiological impetus to become sexually active.

As they mature, adolescents try to come to terms with their emerging sexuality. They must accept their changing bodies, cope with unanticipated feelings of desire, and reconcile the conflicting messages they get from home, peers, religious groups, and the media as to the circumstances in which varying degrees of sexual intimacy are appropriate (Brooks-Gunn & Paikoff, 1993). For many adolescents, sexual intimacy goes hand in hand with, and is a natural outgrowth of, long-term romantic relationships (Graber, Britto, & Brooks-Gunn, 1999). For others, it is something that should be saved for the "right moment" and marriage. And for a few, sexual intimacy is completely separate from romantic involvement. For these individuals, it may be a means of enhancing social standings with peers, experimenting with a risky activity, exploring sexual orientations, gaining others' affection, or simply feeling physical pleasure (W. A. Collins & Sroufe, 1999; Peltzer, 2010; Woody, D'Souza, & Russel, 2003).

In a few cases, young people progress to sexual intercourse during their first intimate encounter. More commonly, they follow a developmental sequence. Young people typically begin with hand-holding and a simple kiss and then add more personal contacts. Despite increases in casual sex, adolescents usually initiate sexual intercourse only after several years of intimate exploration (Connolly & McIsaac, 2009; DeLamater & MacCorquodale, 1979; Victor, 2012).

Sexual maturation is a natural process, yet it is not a simple matter for adults to address. With young children, parents mention sexuality, especially, where babies come from—in general terms—in the context of love and marriage, names of body parts, and restrictions to which private parts can be touched by others (K. A. Martin & Torres, 2014). No one knows how best to handle adolescent sexuality—not parents or teachers and certainly not adolescents themselves. Many adults ignore the topic, assuming (or perhaps hoping) it's not yet relevant for adolescents in their care. Even teenagers who have open relationships with their parents have few chances to talk about sex (Brooks-Gunn & Furstenberg, 1990; Farringdon, Holgate, McIntyre, & Bulsara, 2014). Usually, young people learn about sex from the media and one another.

Sexual Orientation and Gender Identity. By **sexual orientation**, we mean the particular sex(es) to whom an individual is romantically attracted. A small but significant percentage of adolescents find themselves sexually attracted to their own gender either instead of or in addition to the opposite gender. Although it has been difficult to establish precise figures, researchers have estimated that 2% to 4% of young people report being gay, lesbian, or bisexual, with an additional few percentages either having some degree of same-sex attractions while continuing to identify primarily as heterosexual or realizing as adults that they are homosexual or bisexual (J. M. Bailey, Dunne, & Martin, 2000; L. M. Diamond, 2013; Savin-Williams, 2005).

It has become increasingly clear that sexual orientation is, at least, partly determined by biological factors (Savin-Williams & Diamond, 1997; VanderLaan, Blanchard, Wood, & Zucker, 2014). Some evidence for a genetic component comes from twin studies: Monozygotic (identical) twins are more similar in their sexual orientation and gender identity than are dizygotic (fraternal) twins (Dawood, Bailey, & Martin, 2009; Gabard, 1999). Genes affect levels of steroids and hormones in the prenatal environment, which bathe the brain circuits that will later define sexual orientation and gender identity (LeVay, 2011; Q. Rahman & Wilson, 2003). Certain aspects of the mother's physiology may also play a role. For example, boys who have numerous older brothers are more likely to become homosexual, presumably because their mothers' bodies became reactive to male hormones in later pregnancies and produced substances diminishing the masculinity of the fetus's developing brain (VanderLaan et al., 2014).

Regardless of the exact factors determining sexual orientation and gender identity, it seems clear that these important aspects of human development are not the outcomes of conscious deliberation. Many homosexual and bisexual young people recall feeling different from peers since childhood (D. A. Anderson, 1994; Carver, Egan, & Perry, 2004; Kenneady & Oswalt, 2014). Adolescence can be a particularly confusing time for them, as they struggle to form an identity while feeling isolated from peers (Needham & Austin, 2010; C. J. Patterson, 1995). When their attractions to same-gender peers become stronger, they may initially work hard to discount such sentiments. At an older age, they are apt to accept some aspects of their homosexuality and later "come out" and identify fully and openly with other gay, lesbian, bisexual, or transgender individuals.

Schools are not necessarily friendly environments for gay youth. When the topic of homosexuality comes up in the school curriculum, it is usually within the context of acquired immunodeficiency syndrome (AIDS) and other risks (Gowen & Winges-Yanez, 2014; Malinsky, 1997). Unfortunately, adolescents with a homosexual, bisexual, or transgender orientation are often harassed by peers and occasionally victimized in hate crimes (Elze, 2003; McGuire, Anderson, Toomey, & Russell, 2010). Under such circumstances some gay, lesbian, bisexual, and transgender youth become "silent, invisible, and fearful" (M. B. Harris, 1997, p. xxi). Feeling that school is not a safe place for them to be, numerous youth stay home or drop out of school (C. Burton, Marshal, & Chisolm, 2014; Elia, 1994).

Despite these social hardships, most gay, lesbian, and transgender youths have good mental health and find the support they need, especially when they tell others about their orientation (Kosciw, Palmer, & Kull, 2015; Savin-Williams, 1989). Rates of depression and anxiety are higher than usual in gay, lesbian, bisexual, and transgender youth than in other young people, and much of this adjustment problem is due to the heartache of ostracism from peers and family (K. Richmond, Carroll, & Denboske, 2010). In Artifact Example 15.9, 19-year-old Michael describes his journey to self-acceptance.

As long as I can remember, I always felt a little different when it came to having crushes on other people. When I was in elementary school I never had crushes on girls, and when I look back on that time now, I was probably most attracted to my male friends. I participated in some of the typical "boy" activities, like trading baseball cards and playing video games, but I was never very interested in rough sports. I often preferred to play with the girls in more role-playing and cooperative games. Of course, I didn't understand much about sex or gender roles at the time. I just figured I would become more masculine and develop feelings for the opposite sex after going through puberty.

To my dismay, middle school and the onset of puberty only brought more attention to my lack of interest in girls. The first time I thought about being gay was when I was in 6th grade, so I was probably 11 or 12 years old at the time. But in my mind, being gay was not an option and I began to expend an incredible amount of energy repressing my developing homosexual urges. In 7th grade, I had my first experience with major depression. Looking back on it, I am almost positive that being gay was the immediate cause of the depression. . . . When I finally recovered from the episode a few months later, I did my best to move on with my life and forget about my problems with sexuality. I continued to repress my feelings through high school, a task that became more and more difficult as the years went by. I never really dated any girls and my group of friends in high school was highly female. When I was 16, a junior in high school, I had another more severe bout of depression. . . . I continued to be ashamed of my feelings and refused to even tell my psychologist about concerns over my sexuality. After finally emerging from my depression, I came to somewhat of an agreement with myself. I decided that I would simply put my conflict on hold, hoping it would resolve itself. Unfortunately, I still held on to the hope that it would resolve itself in heterosexuality and I remained distraught by my feelings. I finally came out during my freshman year at [college] with the support of my friends and an extremely accepting social environment.

Having exposure to the homosexual lifestyle in college is what finally made me realize that I could have a normal life and that I would not have to compromise my dreams because of it. Even though my high school was relatively liberal and very supportive of different backgrounds, there was very little discussion about homosexuality, even in health class. We had visibly gay teachers, but it was rarely openly talked about. I think the reason it took me so long to accept my sexuality was simply because I had no exposure to it while growing up. It angers me that people refer to homosexuality as a lifestyle choice because I had no choice over my sexuality. I spent seven years of my life denying my homosexuality, and believe me, if there had ever been a choice between gay or straight during that time, I would have chosen straight in a second. Today I can't imagine my life without being gay and I would never choose to be straight.

Essay used with permission.

MyLab Education

Artifact Example 15.9

Find Developmental Meaning *After a year of college, 19-year-old Michael wrote this essay about coming of age as a young man. What kind of journey to self-acceptance did Michael have?* Read Michael's poignant memories of challenges he overcame to develop a healthy identity.

Fostering Productive Peer Relationships

Group environments for children—classrooms, schools, after-school programs, and so forth—are valuable settings for fostering children's social skills, peer acceptance, and friendships. Thoughtful guidance is particularly important for youngsters who are socially isolated or rejected by peers. We offer the following suggestions:

- **Set up situations in which youngsters can enjoy interactions with one another.** Teachers can arrange structured cooperative learning activities with shared responsibilities. Likewise, teachers can provide play equipment such as balls and climbing structures that lend themselves to coordinated interaction (Slavin, 1990; Stanton-Chapman, 2014). Adults might also ask youngsters to read to a peer with a visual impairment, sign to a child with hearing loss, provide tutoring to a classmate with a learning disability, or take notes for a child with a physical impairment. To encourage cooperation, teachers can acknowledge mutual benefits ("Thanks, Jamie, for helping Branson—he really appreciates your assistance, and you seemed to have learned a lot by explaining concepts to him").

- **Encourage respect for one another.** Adults who successfully promote friendships across diverse backgrounds consistently communicate that all members of their community are welcome (Allodi, 2010; Battistich, Solomon, Kim, Watson, & Schaps, 1995). Fernando Arias, a high school vocational education teacher, put it this way:

> In our school, our philosophy is that we treat everybody the way we'd like to be treated . . . . Our school is a unique situation where we have pregnant young ladies who go to our school. We have special education children. We have the regular kids, and we have the drop-out recovery program . . . we're all equal. We all have an equal chance. And we have members of every gang at our school, and we hardly have any fights, and there are close to about 300 gangs in our city. We all get along. It's one big family unit it seems like. (Turnbull, Pereira, & Blue-Banning, 2000, p. 67)

Preparing for Your Licensure Examination

Your teaching test might ask about what teachers and other practitioners can do to facilitate productive peer interactions.

- **Teach children how to interact productively.** School is a unique context for peer interaction. Schools attract significant diversity in experience, skill sets, and personal characteristics, yet individual students are generally unprepared for the variations they will encounter. Many need to be coached, especially in showing acceptance and kindness to one another. Another aspect of the school's peer context is the public arena in which students perform academically. Even though scores and grades are handed out privately, children notice how well they and peers are doing in mathematics, reading, and other subjects. In setting up group work, teachers can communicate expectations for behavior when working together.

MyLab Education
Video Example 15.4

Find Developmental Meaning
How does this elementary school teacher foster children's social skills? Watch how the teacher explains the purpose and methods of constructive criticism during a literacy lesson.

- **Help children ease into social groups.** Young children who are shy or new to a community can benefit from intercession by educators. In the following anecdote, Mrs. Kusumoto, a Japanese preschool teacher, skillfully models desired behaviors and helps one child, Fumiko, enter a group of peers:

> Mrs. Kusumoto helps Fumiko put a cha-cha-cha tape in the portable cassette player, and calls a second girl to come over and join them on a small stage made of blocks. The two girls and Mrs. Kusumoto stand on the stage, singing and shaking their maracas. Then Mrs. Kusumoto steps down and faces them, singing along and encouraging them to continue. After a few minutes she attempts to melt away. The girls continue singing briefly, but when the song ends the second girl runs off, leaving Fumiko alone and unoccupied. She looks for Mrs. Kusumoto and begins following her around again. Mrs. Kusumoto approaches a small group of girls who are playing house, asking them: "Would you like to invite this girl over for dinner? After giving the concert, she is very hungry." One of the girls nods silently. Fumiko smiles and enters the "house." She stands there uncertainly, saying nothing. Mrs. Kusumoto inquires, "Fumiko-chan. Have you had your dinner? Why don't you join us? Don't you want something to eat? It looks good." Fumiko nods and the girls bring her a couple [of] dishes of clay "food." Mrs. Kusumoto looks on briefly, then moves quietly out of the scene. (Holloway, 2000, pp. 100–101)

MyLab Education
Video Example 15.5
Find Developmental Meaning
How does elementary school teacher Kimberly Rich encourage children's social skills? She describes social behaviors in tangible terms and has the children practice them.

As Mrs. Kusumoto's gestures demonstrate, teachers can sometimes gently coax children into cooperative play. Children naturally insist on choosing their own friends outside of school (Hollingsworth & Buysse, 2009; Stanton-Chapman, 2014).

- **Teach social skills and problem-solving strategies.** By participating in and reflecting on interactions, many youngsters develop proficient social behaviors. But other youngsters—perhaps because of limited opportunities to interact with age-mates, poor role models at home, or a cognitive disability—know little about initiating conversations, exchanging compliments, or offering emotional support. Some also lack productive strategies for solving social problems. They may barge into a game without asking or respond to teasing with aggression. Teachers and counselors can coach social skills, perhaps advising a child, "To join a conversation, stand for a moment next to the other students, listen, and watch for a time when you might say something relevant." When students fail to respond to informal coaching, individual counseling can be helpful (Goertz-Dorten et al., 2018).

- **Minimize barriers to social interaction.** Children are less likely to interact with peers when physical, linguistic, or social barriers stand in the way (Anaby et al., 2013; Bobzien et al., 2013; Matheson, Olsen, & Weisner, 2007). A middle school student who cannot not negotiate the cafeteria steps with her wheelchair might easily eat lunch alone. Educators can be on the lookout for such impediments and campaign for an appropriate accommodation. They can also teach youngsters some basic vocabulary and simple phrases in one another's native tongues.

MyLab Education
Content Extension 15.1
Learn more about how to help children with disabilities be included in social interaction with peers.

- **Cultivate empathy for peers with special needs.** Some children feel resentment or anger because of their belief that peers with special needs should be able to control inappropriate behaviors (Juvonen, 1991). In fact, classmates are less tolerant of peers with cognitive difficulties or emotional and behavioral disorders than they are of peers with obvious physical disabilities (Madden & Slavin, 1983; Ysseldyke & Algozzine, 1984). Through paired or small-group activities, adults can show nondisabled students that peers with disabilities have many of the same talents, thoughts, feelings, and desires that they themselves have (E. W. Carter, Asmus, & Moss, 2013; Staub, 1998).

- **Recruit students to serve as buddies to a child with special needs.** A teacher might train students to tutor a peer with a disability, showing them how to explain concepts, review the classmate's comprehension of a concept, and encourage his or her participation (E. W. Carter et al., 2013; S. Clarke & Duda, 2018; Płatos & Wojaczek, 2018). Other strategies are to ask students to invite a peer with a disability to have lunch with them or check on a classmate's activities during particular times of the day. Students with disabilities can benefit from this assistance educationally as well as socially, and buddies can acquire a deeper commitment to inclusion (E. W. Carter et al., 2013).

- **Be a backup system when peer relationships aren't going well.** Disruptions in peer relationships—perhaps because of interpersonal conflicts or a friend's relocation to a distant city—can trigger emotional distress (Wentzel, 2009). Warm, supportive adults can lessen the pain when a child has no close friends nearby (Guay, Boivin, & Hodges, 1999; Wentzel, 1999). Such sympathetic overtures are especially important for children who have little support at home and might otherwise turn to deviant peers for attention (Parks, 1995). Good relationships with teachers often have the effect of putting children at ease; as a result, children who previously had difficulties in making friends now may reach out to teachers (De Laet et al., 2014). It's important for an educator to balance gestures of kindness for a neglected child with subtle efforts at his or her inclusion with classmates. In other words, positive peer relationships should remain a long-term goal even as a teacher reaches out to the excluded student.

- **Be aware of family influences on children's peer relationships.** Family practices strongly influence children's interactions with peers. Some parents are protective and rarely allow children to play with peers outside the family, whereas others actively arrange time with friends (A. C. Fletcher, Bridges, & Hunter, 2007). Children who have not had much experience with peers can nevertheless gain valuable experience in groups at school, particularly when teachers quietly insinuate them into existing groups. For example, a teacher might sit with a few children at lunch and, when noticing a socially inexperienced child eating alone, ask him or her to join them (e.g., "Sasha, we're talking about our pets. Would you like to tell us about your new puppy").

- **Provide the specific kinds of support that rejected children need most.** A first step in helping rejected children is to determine the reasons why other children find them unpleasant to be around (Bierman, & Powers, 2009). As you have learned, rejected children might be aggressive, have limited social skills, or use coercive behaviors to get their way. Other rejected children have trouble asserting their desires and opinions. Having a reputation as being odd or weird is another risk factor for becoming excluded or victimized (Hoglund & Chisholm, 2014). Even after children show improvements in social behavior, peers may continue to dislike them (Bierman, Miller, & Staub, 1987; Prinstein, Rancourt, Guerry, & Browne, 2009). Once educators understand exactly what is missing from a rejected child's skill set, they can take steps to help him or her acquire the missing competencies. To improve children's reputations, adults can create structured cooperative learning groups in which formerly ostracized children can use their newly developed social skills and show peers that they are now good companions.

- **Accept the legitimacy of romantic preoccupations.** When young people reach puberty, they become engrossed in who harbors secret yearnings for whom, whether the targets of desire reciprocate with affection, and which friends are sexually active. Some young people attract a series of steady admirers, whereas others are inexperienced in, possibly even indifferent to, the world of romance. And, as mentioned earlier, a small percentage of adolescents will have yearnings for members of their own gender. As a practitioner working with young people, you may find the undercurrent of romantic desire to be a distraction. While focusing young people on academic learning, you can nevertheless accept that infatuations are a healthy part of coming-of-age.

- **Be supportive when young people are dissolving romantic relationships.** To some adults the romantic bonds and breakups of adolescents seem trivial, but they can cause considerable stress. Adolescents may feel deep humiliation after rejection by a romantic partner or a profound sense of loss at the end of long-term relationship. In such situations teachers and counselors can help adolescents sort through their feelings and look forward with optimism to new relationships (Bannister, Jakubec, & Stein, 2003; Larson et al., 1999). In such situations, students might benefit from therapy from a counselor, nonjudgmental conversations with a teacher, healthy relationships with other classmates, and informal occasions to express their feelings in diaries, journals, music, or other avenues (Boniel-Nissim & Barak, 2013; A. Sparks, Lee, & Spjeldnes, 2012).

- **Explain what sexual harassment is and why it must be prohibited.** **Sexual harassment** is any action that a targeted person can reasonably construe as hostile, humiliating, or sexually offensive (Sjostrom & Stein, 1996). It is a form of discrimination and therefore is prohibited by the laws of many nations, including the United States. Sexual harassment can be a problem at the late elementary, middle school, and high school levels, when youngsters are developing an interest in sexual matters. Youngsters must be advised that sexual harassment will not be tolerated. They should be informed that under no circumstances may they degrade one another—by words, gestures, or actions—with regard to physical traits or sexual orientation. An example of a description of sexual harassment for young people appears in Figure 15.1.

- **Advise young people about human sexuality.** A conventional belief has held that education about human sexuality is the prerogative of parents and has no place in schools. Typically, if sex education is a part of the school curriculum at all, it focuses on the biological aspects of sexual intercourse and offers little information to help teens make sense of physical intimacy. Adolescents' participation in a sex education curriculum usually requires parents' approval, and many parents are loath to give it. Less controversial alternatives include making developmentally appropriate literature accessible in school libraries and letting adolescents know that school counselors and nurses are available to talk about sexual health. Educators need to be prepared to answer a range of questions, including how young people can protect their health during intimate

FIGURE 15.1 It's no joke.

Example of how teachers and school counselors might describe sexual harassment in language that children and adolescents understand.

Source: *Excerpt from "Stop Sexual Harassment in Schools" by Nan Stein, from* USA Today, *May 18, 1993. Copyright © 1993 by Nan Stein, Ed.D. Used with permission of the author.*

SEXUAL HARASSMENT: IT'S NO JOKE!

- **Sexual harassment is unwanted and unwelcomed sexual behavior** which interferes with your right to get an education or to participate in school activities. In school, sexual harassment may result from someone's words, gestures or actions (of a sexual nature) that make you feel uncomfortable, embarrassed, offended, demeaned, frightened, helpless or threatened. If you are the target of sexual harassment, it may be very scary to go to school or hard to concentrate on your school work.
- **Sexual harassment can happen once, several times, or on a daily basis.**
- **Sexual harassment can happen any time and anywhere** in school—in hallways or in the lunchroom, on the playground or the bus, at dances or on field trips.
- **Sexual harassment can happen to anyone!** Girls and boys both get sexually harassed by other students in school.
- **Agreement isn't needed.** The target of sexual harassment and the harasser do not have to agree about what is happening; sexual harassment is defined by the girl or boy who is targeted. The harasser may tell you that he or she is only joking, but if their words, gestures or actions (of a sexual nature) are making you uncomfortable or afraid, then you're being sexually harassed. You do not have to get others, either your friends, teachers or school officials, to agree with you.
- **No one has the right to sexually harass another person!** School officials are legally responsible to guarantee that all students, you included, can learn in a safe environment which is free from sexual harassment and sex discrimination. If you are being sexually harassed, your student rights are being violated. Find an adult you trust and tell them what's happening, so that something can be done to stop the harassment.
- **Examples of sexual harassment in school:**
  - touching, pinching, and grabbing body parts
  - being cornered
  - sending sexual notes or pictures
  - writing sexual graffiti on desks, bathroom walls or buildings
  - making suggestive or sexual gestures, looks, jokes, or verbal comments (including "mooing," "barking" and other noises)
  - spreading sexual rumors or making sexual propositions
  - pulling off someone's clothes
  - pulling off your own clothes
  - being forced to kiss someone or do something sexual
  - attempted rape and rape

REMEMBER: SEXUAL HARASSMENT IS SERIOUS AND AGAINST THE LAW!

contact, extricate themselves from destructive relationships, rebound from a breakup, and tell parents about being gay.

• **Protect the rights of gay, lesbian, bisexual, and transgender youth.** Teachers and other adults sometimes overhear students teasing a classmate who violates traditional gender roles or speaks openly about attraction to same-sex individuals. Unfortunately, some educators tolerate these remarks and contribute to an environment that is hostile to gay, lesbian, bisexual, and transgender students. One transgender adolescent observed, "[Teachers] should actually speak up, because I've been in a lot of classrooms where stuff is said, and the teachers don't do [anything]. And if they did, it would stop right there" (McGuire et al., 2010, p. 1183). Young adolescence is a peak period for harassment of sexual minority youth, although derisive remarks about non-traditional gender appearances and mannerisms are occasionally made from preschool through high school (Merrin et al., 2018). Students who are homosexual or different in some other ways from peers adjust more easily when teachers create an explicitly welcome environment for all youth, in which teachers accept individuals for who they are and intervene when they hear a young person being teased or harassed.

• **Make appropriate referrals when necessary.** Teachers occasionally learn unexpectedly about youngsters' personal lives. Students may tell teachers they are pregnant, have a pregnant girlfriend, have been raped or sexually abused, or have a sexually transmitted infection. Educators must fulfill legal obligations to contact law enforcement or community agencies about possible rape, abuse, or hate crimes. Some situations, such as a sexually transmitted infection, do not require contact with parents and, instead, merit referrals for the young person. Although students may feel embarrassed about their health circumstances, it sometimes makes sense to advise them to talk with family members.

As you have learned, adults can do many things to foster productive peer relationships. In the Developmental Trends table "Peer Relationships at Different Age

Levels," you can review typical features and variations in affiliations among children of different ages.

Summary

Peers serve important functions in social-emotional development. Not only do they offer companionship, but they also create contexts for practicing social skills, making sense of social experiences, and acquiring certain values. Peer relationships change systematically throughout childhood; activities tend to shift from simple gestures and imitation (infancy), to pretend play (early childhood), to structured group games (middle childhood), to social activities within cliques and crowds (early adolescence), and finally to larger, mixed-gender groups (late adolescence). Friendships are especially important peer relationships for emotional support and motivations to resolve conflicts in mutually satisfying ways.

Although preschoolers and elementary school children have an interest in romantic relationships, young people do not understand intimacy until they reach adolescence. As they go through puberty, they must come to terms with their changing bodies, sexual drives, and sexual attraction to peers. Romances, either actual or imagined, can delight youngsters but also put emotions in turmoil. Some adolescents experiment with sexual contact with little information about potential risks. Others wrestle with sexual feelings for same-gender peers. As adolescents experience a range of new feelings, they are apt to appreciate adults' sensitivity.

DEVELOPMENTAL TRENDS
Peer Relationships at Different Age Levels

AGE	WHAT YOU MIGHT OBSERVE	DIVERSITY	IMPLICATION
Infancy (Birth–2 Years)	• Growing interest in other infants in the child care setting • Beginning attempts to make contact with familiar infants by looking at their faces and smiling at them • Occasional laughing, chasing, and passing of toys back and forth • In second year, side-by-side play and awareness of one another's actions	• Some infants have not had social experiences with siblings or other children; they may need time to adjust to the presence of peers at the child care center. • Security of attachment to caregivers may affect infants' interaction with peers. • Infants who are temperamentally shy, fearful, or inhibited may be wary of other children.	• Place small babies side by side when they are calm and alert. • Talk about what other children are doing (e.g., "Look at how Willonda spins the beads on her toy"). • Supervise infants to prevent them from hurting one another. Redirect them when they accidentally bump into others.
Early Childhood (2–6 Years)	• Increasing frequency and complexity of interactions with familiar peers • Developing preferences for being with certain peers during play activities • Rudimentary friendships based on proximity (e.g., formation of friendships with neighbors and classmates) • Involved conversations and imaginative fantasies with friends	• Children who have had enjoyable experiences with peers find it easier to make new friends at school. • Children who have sociable and easygoing temperaments tend to form and keep friends more easily than those who are shy, aggressive, anxious, or high-strung.	• Help shy children gain entry into groups, especially if they have had limited social experience. • When necessary, help children resolve conflicts with friends, but encourage them to identify solutions that benefit everyone. Let them do as much of the negotiation as possible.
Middle Childhood (6–10 Years)	• Concern about being accepted by peers • Tendency to assemble in larger groups as dyads of friends intermingle • Less need for adult supervision than previously • Outdoor peer groups structured with games and sports • Increase in gossip about unliked peers • Some exclusion, with friends reluctant to let outsiders to join their activities • Predominance of same-gender friendships	• Boys tend to play in larger groups than girls do. • Some children are temperamentally cautious and timid; they may stand at the periphery of a group. • Some children are actively rejected by peers, perhaps because they are perceived as odd, immature, or socially unskilled.	• Supervise peer relationships from a distance; intervene when a conflict escalates. • Tactfully facilitate the entry of isolated children into ongoing games, cooperative learning groups, and informal lunch gatherings. • Teach rejected children how to interact appropriately with peers.

(continued)

DEVELOPMENTAL TRENDS
Peer Relationships at Different Age Levels (continued)

AGE	WHAT YOU MIGHT OBSERVE	DIVERSITY	IMPLICATION
Early Adolescence (10–14 Years)	• Presence of peer interactions in a variety of contexts (e.g., competitive sports, extracurricular activities, parties) • Heightened concern about acceptance and popularity among peers • Fads and conformity in dress and communication styles • Same-gender cliques, often restricted to members of a single ethnic group • Increasing intimacy, self-disclosure, and loyalty among friends • New interest in members of opposite gender; for gay and lesbian youths, in same gender • For some, initiation of dating, often within the context of larger group activities	• Many young adolescents are socially minded; others are quieter and more reserved. • Gossiping and social exclusion continue in some groups. • A few young adolescents become involved in gangs or other subcultural groups. • A small number of young adolescents are sexually active. • A minority of adolescents begin to construct an identity as gay, lesbian, bisexual, or transgender.	• Make classrooms affirming places for all adolescents. Create an atmosphere of respect for students from all sorts of backgrounds. • Do not tolerate name calling, insensitive remarks, or sexual harassment. • Provide appropriate places for adolescents to hang out before and after school. • Identify mechanisms (e.g., cooperative learning groups, public service projects) through which teenagers can work together. • On some occasions, decide which students will fraternize; on others, let them choose work partners. • Sponsor after-school activities (e.g., in sports, music, or interest areas).
Late Adolescence (14–18 Years)	• Emerging understanding that relationships with new friends do not threaten long-standing friendships • Increasing dependence on friends for advice and support • Less cliquishness and greater tendency to affiliate in large and less exclusive crowds • Increasing amount of time in mixed-gender groups • Many social activities unsupervised by adults	• Some teenagers have parents who monitor their whereabouts; others have little adult supervision. • Adolescents' choices of friends affect their leisure activities, risk-taking behaviors, and attitudes toward schoolwork. • Teens attracted to same-gender peers face unique challenges in constructing adult identities, especially if others are not accepting of the orientation.	• In literature and history, assign readings with themes of interest to adolescents (e.g., loyalty and self-disclosure). • Encourage adolescents to join extracurricular activities that make them feel an integral part of their school. • Sponsor dances and other supervised social events that give adolescents opportunities to get together.

MyLab Education Self-Check 15.1

Schools

15.2 Discuss three characteristics of school environments that affect children positively.

Schools are entrusted with educating children and nurturing their welfare. To the extent that educators align environments with students' age-related needs, they are likely to be successful in fostering growth. The concept of **stage–school fit** was identified by American educational psychologist **Jacquelynne Eccles** and her colleagues and encapsulates the match between students' age-related needs and their experiences in learning academically, relating to others, feeling connected, developing a sense of self, and acting with self-control (Eccles et al., 1993, 1996). Children who attend schools that match their age-related needs achieve at higher levels than peers who do not (Bahena, Schueler, McIntyre, & Gehlbach, 2016; Eccles et al., 1993, 1996).

To accomplish stage–school fit, educators must think holistically about students' cognitive, social-emotional, and physical qualities. What this means is that the overall structure of the school and its curriculum design, management structure, services for young people, and transitions between grades must periodically be reviewed and adjusted according to the needs of students. Let's look at four characteristics of schools that have potential to fit with children's developmental needs: (1) fostering a sense of community; (2) implementing effective processes in guiding learning and behavior; (3) issuing clear, age-appropriate, and affirming socialization messages; and (4) being proactive during developmental transitions.

The School as a Community

Educators foster a **sense of community** in schools when students, teachers, and other staff share goals, validate one another's efforts, and articulate that everyone makes an important contribution (Capone et al., 2018; Garcia-Reid, Peterson, Reid, & Peterson, 2013; D. Kim, Solomon, & Roberts, 1995; Sayer, Beaven, Stringer, & Hermena, 2013). When schools cultivate a sense of community, students exhibit prosocial behavior, positive attitudes about school, intrinsic motivation, and high achievement. A sense of community is associated with lower rates of disruptive classroom behavior, emotional distress, truancy, violence, drug use, and dropping out of school (D. Kim et al., 1995; O'Brennan & Furlong, 2010; Sayer et al., 2013). Educators set the tone for a positive school community with a good climate and healthy traditions.

Classroom Climate

Teachers foster a productive climate when they establish a warm, affectionate atmosphere in the classroom, show that they care for children individually, and express their interest in children's learning. Students thrive when their classrooms exhibit the following features:

- Teachers let students know that they care about them individually and collectively. They keep the door open, metaphorically, for students to express their worries, struggles, and hopes for the future.
- Students feel safe; they know that they can make mistakes without being ridiculed and that they can seek help from others when they need it. Nor will they be physically hurt by classmates.
- Teachers adopt an *authoritative* approach to classroom management, set clear guidelines for behavior and, in the process, consider students' needs and involve them in decision making.
- Teachers provide sufficient order and structure to guide classroom assignments while also giving students opportunities to engage in self-chosen and self-directed activities.
- Teachers encourage children to work toward shared goals, giving them the sense that they are a bonded group.
- Teachers implement fun routines, perhaps arranging for enjoyable games during recess or classroom activities.

MyLab Education
Video Example 15.6
Find Developmental Meaning *How does this middle school convey a commitment to safety?* Note the clean and orderly classrooms, the presence of students' work, and a poster espousing a commitment to mutual respect.

Classrooms that reflect these principles promote well-being and strong educational outcomes. Under these conditions, students are able to concentrate and draw from sufficient energy. They practice new skills, feel needed, perceive themselves as capable, achieve at high academic levels, and act in a socially competent manner (G. A. Davis & Thomas, 1989; Scott-Little & Holloway, 1992; H. K. Wilson, Pianta, & Stuhlman, 2007). When other aspects of children's lives are troubled—for instance, when children are depressed, have strained family relationships, live in violent neighborhoods, or are confronted with a natural disaster—perceived support from teachers helps youngsters feel safe, competent, and understood (Loukas, Roalson, & Herrera, 2010; E. P. Smith, Boutte, Zigler, & Finn-Stevenson, 2004; Spilt, Leflot, & Colpin, 2018). Positive relationships with teachers are also associated with high levels of achievement (Cadima et al., 2018; Maulana, Opdenakker, & Bosker, 2014).

Preparing for Your Licensure Examination

Your teaching test might ask about strategies for establishing a productive classroom environment.

School Traditions

Teachers can foster a sense of community by encouraging children to participate actively in school activities and day-to-day operations. Schools that operate as true communities encourage everyone to work together (Battistich et al., 1995; Battistich, Solomon, Watson, & Schaps, 1997; Cemalcilar, 2010; Rothstein-Fisch & Trumbull, 2008). Several strategies are helpful in creating this school spirit:

- Soliciting students' ideas about school activities, such as how Valentine's Day might be observed
- Creating mechanisms through which students can help make the school run smoothly and efficiently (e.g., assigning various helper roles to students on a rotating basis)

- Emphasizing prosocial values in school codes of conduct, in newsletters, and on bulletin boards
- Providing public recognition of students' contributions to the overall success of the classroom and school
- Creating schoolwide traditions that are fun for youngsters and their families, such as carnivals and field days (D. Kim et al., 1995; Lickona, 1991; Osterman, 2000)

Classroom Processes that Guide Learning and Behavior

Teachers and other school staff influence children based on how well prepared they are to work with them. Educator **Robert Pianta** and his colleagues have found three dimensions to be important: instructional methods that help students make adequate academic progress, sensitive interactions that address children's emotional needs, and an organized classroom that supports children's good behavior, attention, and engagement (Downer, Booren, Lima, Luckner, & Pianta, 2010; Hamre, Hatfield, Pianta, & Jamil, 2014; Jerome, Hamre, & Pianta, 2009). These three dimensions are interrelated, and we focus here on their impact on children.

Instructional Methods

When instruction is effective, it allows children not only to be mentored in intellectual skills but also to feel supported. Teachers foster a sense of community in students when they use methods that are active, engaging, challenging, and cooperative. In one instructional model, children form a **community of learners**, a classroom arrangement in which students help one another achieve learning goals. A community of learners has these characteristics:

- All students are active participants in activities.
- Collaboration among two or more students is a common occurrence and plays a key role in learning.
- Diversity in students' interests and progress is expected and respected.
- Everyone is a potential resource for the others; different individuals are likely to serve as resident experts on different occasions, depending on the topics and tasks at hand.
- The teacher guides the overall design of classroom activities, and students contribute to their implementation.
- Students regularly critique one another's work, giving feedback in such a way that recipients feel affirmed and ready to improve their performance.
- The process of learning is emphasized as much as, and sometimes more than, the finished product. (Boersma, ten Dam, Wardekker, & Volman, 2016; A. L. Brown & Campione, 1994; Campione, Shapiro, & Brown, 1995; Rogoff, 1994; Sewell, 2011)

Preparing for Your Licensure Examination

Your teaching test might ask about instructional methods that engage children in learning.

The outcomes of community-of-learner groups are often quite positive. Communities of learners promote complex thinking processes and are highly motivating for students (A. L. Brown & Campione, 1994; Jaber & Hammer, 2016; Sewell, St George, & Cullen, 2013; Turkanis, 2001). Students in these groups occasionally insist on going to school even when they are ill, and they become disappointed when the school year ends (Rogoff, 1994).

MyLab Education Application Exercise 15.2

Identify Development-Enhancing Education

Students in Mr. Chris Gammon's seventh-grade social studies class are actively engaged in interactive projects.

Skilled and Sensitive Interactions

Throughout their development, students benefit from kindness at school. The value of a close relationship with a teacher is especially pronounced. Positive connections with teachers are associated with academic learning, prosocial behavior, and involvement in after-school activities (McNally & Slutsky, 2018). Children feel bolstered by this support and acquire expectations for treating others warmly (Luckner & Pianta, 2011).

Teachers and other school staff invariably want to support all of their students, yet they do not always realize that certain students are difficult for them to understand. For example, educators may find it challenging to relate to children from ethnic and cultural backgrounds different from their own. Likewise, students who have certain disabilities or are prone to misbehave can be tricky for teachers to like. This situation is problematic because being deprived of a good relationship with a teacher is an obstacle to school success. Children who do not feel supported by their teachers are at risk for academic failure. It is incumbent on teachers to seek guidance when they find themselves disliking certain children (Early, Maxwell, Ponder, & Yi, 2017).

A Well-Run Classroom

An organized school gives students many chances to concentrate. Disruptions are minimized, and students know what to do at any given time. They have chances to exercise age-related abilities for mature behavior. They get plenty of practice in regulating their own behavior and are allowed to make choices within reasonable boundaries (Luckner & Pianta, 2011). Teachers redirect students when they stray from expectations, including standards of conduct for interacting with classmates.

Socialization in Schools

Classrooms are busy places that require courtesy if smooth operations are to occur. Thus, teachers encourage children to follow certain behaviors (e.g., showing politeness by saying "please" and "thank you") and avoid others (e.g., hitting other children). Educational professionals also transmit information about expectations for behavior and achievement at school.

School Values

Teachers begin to socialize children at the moment of school entry, typically expecting and rewarding behaviors such as these:

- Showing respect for authority figures
- Controlling impulses
- Following instructions
- Completing assigned tasks in a timely manner
- Working independently
- Cooperating with classmates
- Striving for academic excellence

Children cope most effectively when teachers openly communicate such expectations. However, much of the time teachers do not remember to articulate their standards. Teachers' unstated desires for behavior are sometimes known as the *hidden curriculum* (Anyon, 1988; Moyse & Porter, 2015; K. Rahman, 2013).

A teacher's hidden curriculum may or may not be consistent with sound developmental principles. A teacher may emphasize the importance of always getting the right answer, of doing tasks in only one way, or of getting things done as quickly as possible, as the following dialogue between a teacher and several students illustrates:

Teacher: I will put some problems on the board. You are to divide.
Child: We got to divide?
Teacher: Yes.
Several children: [*Groan*] Not again, Mr. B., we done this yesterday.

Child: Do we put the date?

Teacher: Yes. I hope we remember we work in silence. You're supposed to do it on white paper. I'll explain it later.

Child: Somebody broke my pencil. [*Crash*—a child falls out of his chair.]

Child: [*repeats*] Mr. B., somebody broke my *pencil!*

Child: Are we going to be here all morning? (Anyon, 1988, p. 367)

In this situation the teacher presents math problems as things that need to be done—not as tasks that might actually have some benefit—and children clearly have little interest in completing them. Children may or may not find it easy to live up to teachers' expectations, but they are more likely to be successful in the classroom if they are at least *aware* of the standards. Teachers can socialize children in three ways:

- **Tell children about desired behavior.** Children come to school with their own habits and do not easily decipher how students are supposed to communicate in groups, ask for help, express their confusion, and so forth. In general, children find it easier to act in acceptable ways when teachers explain their expectations, post important rules for behavior on a bulletin board, and disseminate rules in simple handouts (Gettinger & Kohler, 2006).

- **Ask children about their perceptions of classroom rules.** Children actively interpret classroom events and, when asked, offer informed points of view about classroom operations. In one study in Sweden, children viewed teachers as being hypocritical by asking them not to chew gum but then surreptitiously chewing gum themselves (Thornberg, 2008). In one conversation with a researcher, three 11-year-old boys complained about having to go outside during breaks, saying that they did not get headaches when they stayed inside even though this was the reason given by teachers for the outside activities. A more thorough discussion between the teachers and children might have led to a mutually respectful understanding and perhaps even plans that everyone found reasonable.

- **Offer extra help to students who find it difficult to recognize expectations at school.** Some youngsters, perhaps because of a cognitive or social-emotional disability, find it challenging to determine which behaviors are appropriate in certain situations and which are unacceptable. A child with Asperger syndrome, a type of autism spectrum disorder, might need to be told that although squealing on the playground is considered fun, shouting inside the classroom will annoy others (Myles & Simpson, 2001). Strategies that appear effective in making the hidden curriculum transparent include role-playing, asking children to speculate about proper courses of action in particular settings, and conducting "social autopsies"—conversations with the child about social mistakes and better courses of action for the future (Myles & Simpson, 2001).

Teachers' Expectations about Abilities of Students

As we have seen, teachers have expectations for how students should behave in the classroom. But teachers also form expectations about how individual students are *likely* to perform. In many instances teachers size up their students fairly accurately: They know which ones need help with reading skills, which other ones have trouble working together in a cooperative group, and so on, and they adapt their instruction accordingly (Alber-Morgan, 2010; Goldenberg, 1992; Zhu, Urhahne, & Rubie-Davies, 2018).

But teachers occasionally make inaccurate assessments. They are apt to underestimate the abilities of students who have the following characteristics:

- Are overweight or physically unattractive
- Misbehave frequently in class
- Speak in dialects other than Standard English
- Are members of ethnic minority groups
- Are recent immigrants
- Come from low-income backgrounds
- Have a disability

(R. E. Bennett, Gottesman, Rock, & Cerullo, 1993; Licona, 2013; McGillicuddy & Devine, 2018; J. Oakes & Guiton, 1995; J. Peterson, Puhl, & Luedicke, 2012; Ritts, Patterson, & Tubbs, 1992; Speybroeck et al., 2012)

Teachers with low expectations for students are apt to offer them few opportunities for speaking in class and may ask them easy questions, give little feedback, and present them with few, if any, challenging assignments (Rosenthal, 1994; Straehler-Pohl, Fernández, Gellert, & Figueiras, 2014). In contrast, teachers with high expectations for students generally create a warmer classroom climate, interact with students frequently, provide more opportunities for students to respond, and give positive feedback (Rubie-Davies, 2007).

Most children are well aware of teachers' differential treatment within the classroom and use these observations to draw inferences about their own and classmates' abilities (R. Butler, 1994; Good & Nichols, 2001; Thys & Van Houtte, 2016; Weinstein, 1993). Children also make inferences about their own abilities from the kind of remarks teachers make to them. Those who routinely receive low-ability messages from teachers begin to see themselves as incapable. Underestimated students may exert little effort on academic tasks and frequently misbehave (Murdock, 1999; Rattan, Good, & Dweck, 2012). In some cases, teachers' expectations lead to a **self-fulfilling prophecy**: What teachers expect students to achieve becomes what students actually achieve.

Communicating High Expectations

A characteristic found in effective schools is high expectations for student performance (Roderick & Camburn, 1999; Sheras & Bradshaw, 2016). Even when students' initial academic performance is low, educators must remember that cognitive abilities can and do change, especially when the environment is conducive to growth. We suggest two strategies to help teachers maintain a realistic yet optimistic outlook on what young people can accomplish.

• **Learn more about students' backgrounds.** Adults are most likely to develop low expectations for students' performance when they have biases about ethnic and socioeconomic groups (J. Leonard & Martin, 2013; Reyna, 2000). Preconceptions are often the result of ignorance about students' home environments (K. Alexander, Entwisle, & Thompson, 1987; J. Leonard & Martin, 2013). Self-education is key: Teachers and other school personnel might take part in workshops about the cultures and communities they serve, and they could attend community events such as festivals and musical performances. With such exposure, it becomes easier to grasp the origins of children's behavior at school. With a clear picture of students' families, activities, and values, educators are far more likely to think of students as *individuals*—each with a unique set of talents and skills—rather than as members of a stereotyped group.

• **Collaborate with colleagues to maximize children's success.** Educators are more likely to have high expectations when they are confident in their ability to foster students' academic and social success (Ashton, 1985; L. Wilson, 2007). Consider the case of one inner-city high school. For many years, teachers at the school believed that their low-achieving students were unmotivated to learn. Teachers also saw themselves, their colleagues, and school administrators as ineffective in facilitating students' success. To counteract such tendencies, the school faculty began holding regular 2-hour meetings in which they did the following:

- Read research related to low-achieving and at-risk students
- Explored hypotheses about why their students were having difficulty
- Developed, refined, and evaluated innovative strategies for helping students succeed
- Established a collaborative atmosphere in which, working together, they could take positive action

Such meetings led to the teachers forming higher expectations for students' achievement and better understanding what they themselves could do to help students achieve (Weinstein, Madison, & Kuklinski, 1995).

Transitions in Schools

Entering a new school requires youngsters to adjust to peers and teachers, academic expectations, and activities in the building. After their initial adjustment, students continue to confront changes in the school environment, including establishing relationships with peers and teachers. Let's look at the age-related qualities of different school levels.

Elementary Schools

In most Western societies, children begin elementary school at age 5 or 6, when society declares them "ready" for learning. Children generally find it easier to adjust to school when they enter with expected academic skills. Those who have been encouraged to listen to stories and use complex language at home usually adapt easily to a school's literacy curriculum. Likewise, children who have had many experiences with peers and an academically informed curriculum tend to adjust quickly to the social environment. In part because of having had scaffolded experiences with peers, children who have been in preschool make better social adjustments and achieve at higher levels in first grade than do children from similar backgrounds who did not attend preschool (J. Chen, Claessens, & Msall, 2014; Consortium of Longitudinal Studies, 1983; Temple, Reynolds, & Arteaga, 2010).

In the process of attending school, children adjust to its regulatory atmosphere. Elementary classrooms tend to be more regimented than the cozy settings of family, child care, and preschool. As a result, when children first enter elementary school, one of their challenges is learning the procedures of the "big kids" school (Corsaro & Molinari, 2005). Here's how first-grader Sofia described school rules to her mother and an interviewer:

Mother: Do you know the rules? What are the rules in first grade?
Sofia: You cannot run in the corridors, you cannot hurt anyone, you have to raise your hand before talking, you cannot lose toys.
Interviewer: You know all the rules!
Sofia: Then you cannot walk around, you cannot shout in the bathroom.
Interviewer: You know everything.
Mother: And then? Perhaps you must wait your turn.
Sofia: And then, you have to be silent, write the date. That's all. (Corsaro & Molinari, 2005, pp. 74–75)

Certainly school is more than jumping through hoops, yet the regulatory aspect of schools is necessary. Therefore, every child is expected to follow rules, and it can be a major challenge for children to do the expected thing at the right time. To help children adjust to new classrooms, teachers generally offer lots of reassurance, especially during those initial weeks and months when children feel uneasy. Many schools offer orientations and encourage children and families to visit the classrooms before school begins. We authors recall that our children had elementary teachers who invited them to visit school in the spring or summer when student placements were announced and sent friendly letters before the school year began.

During the period of settling in, children get to know their teacher. Interactions are frequent enough that relationships begin to form, and these bonds are an important factor in children's adjustment. In the elementary grades, each child is one of 15 to 30 students whom a teacher usually gets to know fairly well. Teachers can make these relationships positive by reaching out to children individually, getting to know their names, noticing what they do well, and encouraging them to persist during setbacks. Also easing children's adjustment is the teacher's attention to individual academic needs. Especially important are efforts to appropriately assist children without grade-level academic knowledge, social skills, and self-control.

Secondary Schools

Young people make two major transitions at the secondary level. First, beginning at Grade 5, 6, or 7, many students move from elementary to either middle school or junior high school. Second, at Grade 9 or 10, students move from middle or junior high school to high school. As they progress through these upper grade levels, students attend separate classes, each with its own teacher. The three secondary configurations—middle, junior high, and high school—have distinctive features but share qualities that distinguish them from elementary schools. A typical secondary school is unlike an elementary school in these ways:

- The school is larger and has more students.
- Teacher–student relationships are more superficial than they were in elementary school.
- There is more whole-class work and less individualized instruction that takes into account a student's needs.
- Classes are less socially cohesive; students may not know their classmates well and be reluctant to call on them for assistance.
- Competition among students (e.g., for popular classes or spots on an athletic team) is more common, especially in high school.
- Students have more responsibility for their own learning; for instance, they sometimes have relatively unstructured assignments to be accomplished over a 2- or 3-week period and must take the initiative to seek help if they are struggling.
- Standards for assigning grades are more rigorous, so students may earn lower grades than they did in elementary school. Grades are often assigned on a comparative basis, with only the highest-achieving students getting As and Bs. (Brewin & Statham, 2011; A. J. Davidson, Gest, & Welsh, 2010; Eccles & Midgley, 1989; Eccles & Roeser, 2011; Raccanello, Brondino, & Bernardi, 2013; Roderick & Camburn, 1999; Véronneau & Dishion, 2011; Wigfield, Eccles, & Pintrich, 1996)

Many educators lament the mismatch between the secondary environment and the needs of adolescents. At a time when adolescents are self-conscious, uncertain, driven to make their own decisions, and confronted with tumultuous changes in their bodies and social relationships, their contact with teachers is superficial and sometimes adversarial. To combat potential feelings of anonymity and disengagement, some high schools arrange for every teacher to take responsibility for a small group of students whom he or she gets to know individually. Advisors can orient students to the layout and customs of the school and talk regularly with them about how they are doing in classes, what study skills they are using, how well they are progressing toward graduation requirements, and how they are getting on with classmates (Patel, 2014; Uvaas, 2010).

Fortunately, many schools are finding ways to welcome entering students and personalize learning environments. The Development-Enhancing Education feature "Easing School Transitions" illustrates several strategies for helping youngsters adjust to new schools.

Development-Enhancing Education

Easing School Transitions

Make contact with children before the beginning of school.

- In April a kindergarten teacher invites prospective students and their parents to come to an orientation in her classroom. The teacher arranges for snacks to be served and reserves time for a brief presentation and exploration of the room. (Early Childhood)
- Late in the summer, a high school teacher sends his homeroom students a letter introducing himself and welcoming them to his room. He talks about the fun things he has done over the summer, including traveling, camping, reading, and volunteering in a community garden. He mentions his academic interests and tells students he looks forward to hearing about their summer. (Late Adolescence)

Provide a means through which every student can feel a part of a small, close-knit group.

- A physical education teacher arranges for students to work on motor skills in small groups. Students stay in the groups for several weeks and learn how to coach one another. During each lesson, students praise each another on a particular aspect of the skill (e.g., dribbling or throwing a ball) that they are doing well and offer a suggestion on one feature that could be improved. (Middle Childhood)
- In September a middle school math teacher establishes *base groups* of three or four students who provide assistance to one another. At the beginning or end of every class period, the teacher gives students in the base groups 5 minutes to help one another with homework assignments. (Early Adolescence)

(Continued)

Development-Enhancing Education *(Continued)*

Find time to meet one on one with every student.

- An elementary teacher holds individual conferences with children twice a year. The teacher looks through representative works that they have created but also makes a point to ask them how they feel about school and relationships with peers. (Middle Childhood)
- Early in the school year, a middle school social studies teacher holds individual meetings with his students. In these meetings he searches for common interests that he and his students share and encourages students to talk with him whenever they need help at school. Throughout the semester he continues to touch base with students individually (often during lunch or before or after school) to see how they are doing. (Early Adolescence)

Give young people the extra support they may need to master academic concepts and study skills.

- An after-school program offers a comprehensive array of services to middle school students. Students receive tutoring in core subjects as well as opportunities to participate in leisure activities. Professionals in the community serve as mentors, and students discuss goals for the future and strategies for resisting negative temptations (T. E. Hanlon, Simon, O'Grady, Carswell, & Callaman, 2009). (Early Adolescence)
- A high school implements a homework hotline staffed by a teacher and a group of honor students. Teachers in the school make a point of encouraging students to evaluate how well they are keeping up with their work and to ask for help when necessary (McCarthy & Kuh, 2005). (Late Adolescence)

Summary

Schools are influential contexts for children and adolescents. Schools not only prepare youngsters with essential academic skills but also serve as complex social environments that communicate how welcome youngsters are and how likely they are to succeed. Ideally, schools offer children a sense of community, deliver affirming messages about learning, and support them as they transition into new academic environments.

MyLab Education Self-Check 15.2

Society

15.3 Describe how a society's services, the media, and interactive technologies influence children's learning and behavior.

As you have learned, youngsters acquire many skills, beliefs, and attitudes during ongoing interactions in the family, at school, and with peers. Children also learn from others in **society**—an enduring group of people who are socially and economically organized into institutions. We now examine effects of society's services and digital media.

Services for Children and Adolescents

The time that children spend outside of school is crucial to their development. Child care and after-school activities are especially influential outlets for time.

Child Care

Many young children are in the care of adults other than their parents for a significant portion of time. Children are attended to in a range of settings, from family homes to commercial buildings, and with caregivers who differ in experience, education, and level of dedication. Such variations raise concerns about the degree to which children are cared for in a manner that is affectionate, safe, and age-appropriate (Brauner, Gordic, & Zigler, 2004; H. F. Ladd, Muschkin, & Dodge, 2014; Õun, Tuul, Tera, Sagen, & Mägi, 2018).

Advocates for high standards in child care have two primary ways of defining quality. *Structural measures* include such objective indicators as caregivers' training and experience, child-to-caregiver ratios, staff turnover, and number and complexity of toys and equipment (Ghazvini & Mullis, 2002; Jeon, Buettner, & Hur, 2014). Early childhood specialists recommend that the child-to-caregiver ratio be no more than three infants or six toddlers to each adult (Bredekamp & Copple, 1997). *Process measures* of quality include sensitive care of children, affectionate child–caregiver relationships, productive child–peer interactions, and developmentally appropriate activities (Jeon et al., 2014; NICHD Early Child Care Research Network, 2006a; Õun et al., 2018). As an indication of high-quality processes, the schedules of activities in a toddler room might be fairly predictable from day to day but also flexible enough to be guided by individual needs (Bredekamp & Copple, 1997). Thus, toddlers might be offered two snacks over the span of the morning, even though only a few choose to eat twice.

In reality, indicators of structure and process are related. Low child-to-staff ratios, small group sizes, and advanced levels of caregiver education are associated with responsive interactions with children (Bigras et al., 2010; Howes, Smith, & Galinsky, 1995). When caregivers have too many children to care for, their style of interacting with individuals becomes rushed and mechanical (Pessanha et al., 2017).

Research confirms that high-quality child care affords advantages. Infants and small children typically develop secure attachments to employed caregivers who are warm, sensitive, and consistently involved in their care (Altenhofen, Clyman, Little, Baker, & Biringen, 2013; Barnas & Cummings, 1994). Children advance developmentally in cognitive, linguistic, literacy, and social skills while in good care, with the greatest benefits occurring in children whose families have been inattentive (Jeon et al., 2014; Sylva, Melhuish, Sammons, Siraj-Blatchford, & Taggart, 2004).

In unfortunate circumstances, child care creates risks if not actual harm. Exposure to child care at a young age and for long hours on average increases children's aggression and noncompliance slightly (Belsky & Eggebeen, 1991; M. E. Lamb & Ahnert, 2006; NICHD Early Child Care Research Network, 2002). These effects are not always seen and, when they are, are smaller for high-quality than for low-quality care (Rusby, Jones, Crowley, & Smolkowski, 2013). Enrollment in low-quality care, in which adults are brusque, nonresponsive, or overly critical and in which the environment is dangerous, can lead to the child's distress, boredom, physical injuries, and negative social behaviors.

After-School Programs and Extracurricular Activities

Depending on an assortment of factors, including students' age and interests, parents' income and work schedules, the selection of school programs, and community resources, children have out-of-school activities that may or may not be safe, educational, and health-promoting. Not every parent has access to affordable care, and as youngsters grow, they naturally want to care for themselves (Ceglowski, Shears, & Furman, 2010). Frequent *self-care* is a concern during the preschool and early elementary years because children do not reliably anticipate or avoid hazardous situations. Children may open the door when a stranger rings the doorbell and forget what they have left on the stove. They can be worried and lonely, and without adult monitoring, they are apt to skip homework and chores (Venter & Rambau, 2011). Beginning in the early adolescent years, lack of supervision in the after-school hours is associated with risky behaviors (J. Greenberg, 2014).

Self-care arrangements are generally more effective when parents explain safety procedures, convey clear and firm expectations for behavior, and monitor children's activities by calling them on the telephone or by having another family member, such as a grandparent, check on them (Atherton, Schofield, Sitka, Conger, & Robins, 2016; Mahoney & Parente, 2009; Steinberg, 1986). Communities can help by providing safe, fun, and supervised activities. Young people who have productive outlets for their free time—perhaps in clubs, sports leagues, dance and martial arts lessons, scout troops, and so on—are apt to acquire valuable skills and avoid serious trouble.

The effects of after-school and extracurricular programs are difficult to determine because comparison groups are not available. Despite a lack of certainty about causal effects, a growing body of research suggests that participation in well-designed after-school and summer activities foster children's cognitive and social-emotional development. Academically oriented programs appear to cultivate positive feelings about school, better school attendance, higher grades and achievement, superior classroom behavior, greater conflict resolution skills, and decreased tension with family members (Dryfoos, 1999; Granger, 2008; Téllez & Waxman, 2010). High school students who participate in their school's extracurricular activities are more likely than nonparticipants to achieve at high levels and graduate from high school. They are also less likely to smoke cigarettes, use alcohol or drugs, exhibit anxiety, join gangs, engage in criminal activities, and become teenage parents (Biddle, 1993; Dimech & Seiler, 2010; L. L. Myers, 2013). After-school programs focusing on the full spectrum of children' needs (e.g., in developing close relationships with adults, social skills with peers, sustained attention for homework, and judgment in decision making) have been shown to be especially beneficial for the academic, social, and personal adjustment of young people living in economic poverty (S. L. Frazier, Mehta, Atkins, Hur, & Rusch, 2013).

After-school and summer programs vary in their focus, yet most espouse a commitment to assigning an adult advocate who gets to know each student. In addition, effective programs include these features:

- Breadth of activities, including recreation, academic and cultural enrichment, and opportunities for the pursuit of individual interests
- Chances for meaningful participation in authentic activities, such as building a fort, planting a garden, reading to younger children, or registering voters
- Opportunities for success, perhaps in domains in which youngsters have previously unrecognized talents
- Access to areas of enrichment, such as advanced technologies, that help build valuable skills
- Positive interactions and relationships with both adults and peers
- Emotionally supportive interactions with familiar adults
- Clear limits, with youngsters actively participating in the establishment of rules
- High regard for young people's diverse cultural beliefs and practices
- Options for physical activity (C. R. Cooper, Denner, & Lopez, 1999; Durlak, Mahoney, Bohnert, & Parente, 2010; Gesell et al., 2013; Kerewsky & Lefstein, 1982; Lefstein & Lipsitz, 1995; Noam & Bernstein-Yamashiro, 2013; E. P. Smith & Bradshaw, 2017; Vickery, 2014)

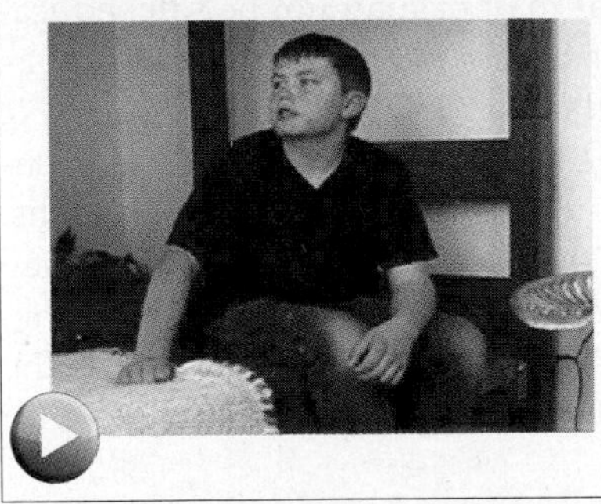

MyLab Education Application Exercise 15.3

Meet Individual Needs

Listen to 12-year-old Colin describe what he does outside school. How might his activities affect his learning at school?

Another influential experience in after-school hours, especially for high school students, is the part-time job. Being employed allows for practice in getting to work on time, adhering to the requirements of a position, being polite in a business setting, and managing money. With limited work hours (e.g., 10 to 15 hours per week), adolescents usually have adequate time to study and remain involved in school activities (Mortimer, Shanahan, & Ryu, 1994; Staff, Messersmith, & Schulenberg, 2009; Steinberg, Brown, Cider, Kaczmarek, & Lazzaro, 1988). Comparatively, spending time in employment seems to be more advantageous to adolescents than long periods of unsupervised contact with peers (K. K. Lee, Lewis, Kataoka, Schenke, & Vandell, 2018). However, many adolescents work long hours in tedious jobs that fail to inculcate a motivation to work hard. Excessively long work hours put young people at risk for poor school achievement, reduced times for extracurricular activities, and drug and alcohol use (Staff et al., 2009).

Even though the effects of after-school activities, extracurricular activities, and employment are hard to pin down, their potential benefits *seem* strong and merit investment from schools and communities. The Development-Enhancing Education feature "Arranging Before- and After-School Experiences" suggests strategies for educators and other practitioners to help young people make good use of their nonschool time.

Development-Enhancing Education

Arranging Before- and After-School Experiences

Help children navigate transitions between school and out-of-school care.

- After school a kindergarten teacher walks outside to make sure that each child connects with family members or carpool drivers, gets on the appropriate bus or van, or begins walking home. (Early Childhood)
- A teacher in an after-school elementary program asks arriving children to unpack their homework and put it in a special folder. After children have eaten, rested, and gotten a chance to play for a half hour or so, the teacher pulls out assignments and helps the children get started with their homework. (Middle Childhood)

Sponsor after-school clubs at your school.

- A middle school offers several clubs for students to participate in after school. Popular options include a Hispanic cultures club, athletic teams, an honor society, a band, a community service group, and the yearbook staff. (Early Adolescence)
- Most of the teachers in a high school serve as sponsors for one or more after-school activities. The school offers traditional high school clubs, such as band, a theater group, competitive sports, and a debate society, and also invites students to help initiate new activities, for example, Ultimate Frisbee and a community service organization. (Late Adolescence)

Inform parents and guardians about youth initiatives in their area.

- At a parent–teacher–student conference, a middle school teacher describes clubs and sports programs available at the school, as well as recreational and service opportunities in the local community. (Early Adolescence)
- A high school includes a page on its website with links to various clubs, leisure activities, and extracurricular options at school and in the community. During an advising session early in the year, teachers invite students to check out the options. (Late Adolescence)

Establish a team of school personnel and after-school providers to ensure that programs meet children's physical, social-emotional, and academic needs.

- Two teachers, the principal, and the director of an after-school program meet regularly to discuss space, resources, and ways that the after-school program can give children needed rest, relaxation, snacks, and tutoring. (Middle Childhood)
- A middle school principal invites community leaders to offer a brief presentation to students and parents. The community leaders inform everyone about the various youth centers and leisure activities that are available in the area. (Early Adolescence)

Interactive Technologies

Around the world, children use a growing collection of **interactive technologies**—computers, video games, mobile devices, tablets, and cell phones (also known as cellular phones or mobile phones), and other digital tools. Children use electronic technologies for several purposes, especially communication, information seeking, and entertainment.

Personal and Social Uses of Digital Media

Young people today have access to a wide range of digital technologies. In the classroom, teachers may notice children sending *texts*, brief written messages that appear alone or are accompanied by photos or videos. Other regular pastimes are watching video clips, playing electronic games, and accessing *social networking sites* (websites that permit students to communicate with selected individuals, share photographs and update information about their activities, and participate in focused interest groups; examples include Facebook, MySpace, Big Tent, Tumblr, and WeChat).

Preparing for Your Licensure Examination

Your teaching test might ask about using the Internet and other digital tools to enrich the learning environment for students.

In their use of digital technologies, students learn to express themselves to a wide, diverse, and largely anonymous audience. Many students contribute to *blogs* (personalized websites that allow documentation of a person's ideas, images, and events and that permit comments from visitors), Twitter (blogs with characters up to 140 characters in length), and *wikis* (interlinked websites that are created and edited with simple programming languages; F. W. Baker, 2010). By describing their experiences, adolescents learn about themselves—who they are and what they stand for (K. Davis, 2010). Frequently they project one or more *personas* (perhaps representing themselves with a different age, gender, or background), thereby gaining insights into other people, discovering new parts of themselves, and figuring out who they are becoming.

Young people actively engage with others in a range of social purposes. To a large degree, computers and their progeny have changed the way youngsters relate to one another. For example, young people gain a sense of friendship with other youth they have never met and team up with others in online games (Leung & McBride-Chang, 2013). An 18-year-old senior, Natalie, expressed the value of communicating with her friends on LiveJournal:

> I mean it's great because I love being able to, I guess, empathize with stuff that [my friends are] going through, and then they get to read stuff that I'm going through and give—like commenting—"hey, do you want to talk through this?" or something, and that's really helpful. (K. Davis, 2010, p. 157).

Being able to post messages on a website adds a measure of distance, such that young people write things that they would rarely say in face-to-face communication or over the phone. Middle school and high schools students may number their social media "friends" in the hundreds, even though they have only four or five close friends in their daily, nonelectronic lives (S. Quinn & Oldmeadow, 2013). To some degree, the purposes to which children put social media depend on their personality (Hollenbaugh & Ferris, 2014). Young people who are socially outgoing create an active community on social media, whereas those who are introverted or insecure are more selective and post less flamboyant information about themselves.

A few negative things happen in the virtual world. Some young people spend so much time interacting online that they have little time remaining for play or other interactions with peers. The desire to stay connected in a virtual world can lead to excessively long hours on a smartphone and little time interacting directly with family and peers (Coyne, Padilla-Walker, & Holmgren, 2018; Pontes, 2017). A few youngsters develop bad habits in communication, such as *flaming* (i.e., verbally ridiculing someone in a public electronic site), *trolling* (i.e., making an inflammatory remark to provoke an argument), *hacking* into secured sites to disrupt services or spread computer viruses, and *plagiarizing* the work of others (Hellenga, 2002). Other risks include facing public rebuke and ostracism online and being manipulated by adult predators (Sittichai & Smith, 2018; Wolak, Finkelhor, Mitchell, & Ybarra, 2010).

Watching Television, Movies, and Video Clips

Many developmental experts conclude that television is detrimental for infants, whose foremost needs are for close bonds with caregivers and active exploration of the environment (Courage & Setliff, 2010). Heavy viewing by older children is also a concern, especially when it interferes with physical activity and peer interaction (Caroli, Argentieri, Cardone, & Masi, 2004). A little TV viewing after infancy seems okay, especially when the content is supervised.

Fortunately, many programs aired on television have educationally worthwhile content. *The Magic School Bus*, *Sesame Street*, *Reading Rainbow*, *Between the Lions*, and *Bill Nye the Science Guy* teach children vocabulary, word recognition, reading concepts, problem-solving skills, and scientific principles (D. R. Anderson, 2003; Kirkorian, Wartella, & Anderson, 2008; J. Sherry, 2013). Programs that model prosocial behaviors, for example, *Mister Rogers' Neighborhood*, *Sesame Street*, *Saved by the Bell*, and *Smurfs*, teach children valuable social skills (D. R. Anderson, 2003; C. G. Christensen & Myford, 2014; C. F. Cole, Labin, & del Rocio Galarza, 2008).

Unfortunately, counterproductive content coexists with, and potentially overshadows, socially responsible material. Television programs, movies, and video games show ethnic minorities infrequently and, when they do, with grossly stereotypical characters—for instance, women as airheads, men as brutes, and people with dark skin as thugs (Eisenberg, Martin, & Fabes, 1996; Kahlenberg & Hein, 2010). Such offensive portrayals can easily instill impressionable children with misconceptions. Furthermore, when youngsters repeatedly view slender and athletically toned actors, actresses, and rock stars, they may develop a standard of physical attractiveness that is not realistic for their own body frame (Anschutz, Engels, Van Leeuwe, & Van Strien, 2009). Advertisements on television and Internet websites cultivate desires for sugary cereals, fast food, clothing, and toys—items not necessarily in children's long-term interests (Buijzen & Valkenburg, 2003; Gbadamosi, 2018; S. Reese, 1996; D. M. Thomson, 2010).

Excessively violent and gruesomely graphic scenes are a serious concern. In fact, violence can be found in a large percentage of television programs and video games (C. A. Anderson et al., 2003; Comstock & Scharrer, 2006; Holtz & Appel, 2011). In one investigation, 8- to 12-year-old children were randomly assigned to play either violent or nonviolent video games (Gentile, Bender, & Anderson, 2017). Those who played violent games were found to emit higher levels of the stress hormone cortisol than those who played nonviolent games. Repeated exposure to violent acts on television seems to make children more aggressive and may be particularly harmful to those already predisposed to be combative (Comstock & Scharrer, 2006; Eron, 1980; Holtz & Appel, 2011). Children inclined to solve conflicts in physically aggressive ways are prone to choose programs with violent content *and* become *more aggressive* after viewing them. In addition, heavy viewing of televised violence and excessive use of violent video games may desensitize children to acts of violence; recurring viewing of violence seems to erode children's empathy for victims of real aggressive acts (Lemmens, Valkenburg, & Peter, 2011; B. J. Wilson, 2008).

MyLab Education
Artifact Example 15.10
Find Developmental Meaning
Gene drew this picture of his video game equipment from memory. What does his drawing show? Gene is familiar with the apparatus and a game's combat theme.

Playing Interactive Games

Interactive games played on consoles, computers, and handheld devices are an especially popular source of entertainment among Western youth, especially among boys in middle childhood and adolescence (Hamlen, 2011; D. F. Roberts & Foehr, 2008). Youngsters with access to video games spend numerous hours clutching controllers as they engage in virtual punching matches, motorcycle races, and explorations of mythical environments. In Artifact Example 15.10, Gene drew a picture of his video game controller with a character reaching out to punch someone. And six-year-old Brent shows his enthusiasm for video games when he says,

> I usually play video games. There's this army game and snowboard game and . . . and a game called "Smash Brothers." . . . They're cool.

The appeal of video games derives largely from their strikingly effective instructional qualities. Video games allow children to pursue a tangible goal, implement continually evolving strategies, make steady progress, experience success, use increasingly advanced tools, and obtain personalized feedback at every step (Gentile & Gentile, 2008; Hamlen, 2011). Numerous nonviolent and creative video games are available, and youngsters practice focusing and shifting attention, solving problems, and exercising spatial and visual-attention skills (Greenfield, DeWinstanley, Kilpatrick, & Kaye, 1996; Griffiths, 2010; Rothbart & Posner, 2015; Sherry, 2016). Children themselves report benefits from playing video games, including having fun, enjoying the challenge, cooperating with peers, making friends, expressing creativity, and trying out new identities (Granic, Lobel, & Engels, 2014; C. K. Olson, 2010). They feel united with characters in the game and experience emotional rhythms as they win and lose. They get frustrated while dealing with difficult challenges and feel happiness when overcoming barriers, performing increasingly well, and achieving their goals (A. Sanders, 2016). Particular games, such as those with health-promotion themes, can teach children valuable skills in caring for themselves, eating healthfully, and managing health conditions (Baranowski et al., 2011; Henkemans et al., 2017; D. A. Lieberman, 1997).

Nevertheless, playing video games can become a time-consuming habit, and overuse is a concern when it leads children to curtail social interaction, healthful physical activity, and completion of homework and family chores. Playing video games can give young people relief from stress and a rewarding sense of accomplishment; for most children, it is probably part of a healthy diet of leisure activities. In a few cases, children come to

MyLab Education
Video Example 15.7

Find Developmental Meaning
Brent talks about activities he enjoys after school, on the weekend, and over the summer. What is it about video games that he likes? Brent names the digital games he played and finds them "cool."

prioritize video games over other pursuits, and the desire to improve a score and conquer virtual worlds intensifies, becomes compulsive, and reduces opportunities to practice versatile coping skills, such as blowing off steam on the athletic field or talking over anxieties with friends (Plante, Gentile, Groves, Modlin, & Blanco-Herrera, 2018; Pontes, 2017).

Using Digital Technologies at School

Personal computers and other electronic devices have numerous applications in the classroom. Through e-mail, web-based chat rooms, and electronic bulletin boards, students communicate with peers, teachers, and other adults to analyze data, exchange perspectives, build on others' ideas, and solve problems (McCombs & Vakili, 2005; M. Scherer, 2011; Subrahmanyam & Greenfield, 2012). A class itself can have a website, allowing students to monitor announcements, turn in assignments, and make comments on a shared bulletin board (L. S. Dunn, 2011).

Well-constructed software and interactive systems give students a curriculum with personalized lessons and steady feedback. Serious educational games, for example, *The Great Entomologist Escape*, expose users to worthwhile scientific information. In *The Great Entomologist Escape*, created by a high school science teacher, students pretend to be the lead scientist who must learn about ants and solve various practical problems (Annetta, 2010). Examples of dynamic, interactive websites include those of the National Library of Virtual Manipulatives,[3] Cells Alive,[4] National Geographic Creature Feature,[5] and Math in Daily Life[6] (Coiro & Fogleman, 2011). *Epistemic games*, electronic games that allow users to practice the thinking skills of experts in one or more fields, are becoming increasingly popular. In Sim City 4, students function as urban planners in designing simulated residential areas, commercial areas of cities, railways, airports, power plants, and other infrastructures for the locality. As they gain experience with the game, students solve complex real-world problems and learn about science, technology, and society (Salmani Nodoushan, 2009). Examples of other epistemic games are Age of Empires (focusing on history), Microsoft Flight Simulator (drawing from knowledge of aircraft flight, airports, and climatic conditions), and Digital Zoo (using principles of biomechanical engineering and animal physiology).

Implications of Digital Media for School

If utilized properly, electronic media and technologies contribute immensely to the education of children. We offer the following suggestions:

MyLab Education
Video Example 15.8

Find Developmental Meaning
How do children use digital technologies in their lesson? Watch children searching for videos about worms on the Internet.

- **Encourage children to express themselves creatively.** Many young people like to reveal their thoughts, feelings, and imagination to one another through social media. Teachers can enlist this motivation for educational purposes. For example, students might interpret a poem in the context of their own lives, articulate opinions about a community issue, or become pen pals with students in another country. In the classroom, students can be quite inventive while using flexible applications, for example, representing themselves and their ideas in creative blends of photographs, videos, icons, text, and art. In the process of projecting themselves, students gain personal satisfaction, communicate who they are to others, and acquire sophisticated technology skills.

- **Select technologies that meet instructional objectives.** Countless educational resources are available on the Internet and in commercial software to address a range of instructional objectives. Many educational packages, especially in reading and mathematics, allow children to practice skills that they are ready to learn and for which they need more practice. Yet teachers can also use the Internet innovatively by having children conduct research, collaborate with others, and analyze information on a particular topic.

- **Use video segments that illustrate elusive concepts.** Some television programs and videos can make abstract concepts more understandable. For instance, when Teresa

[3]See http://nlvm.usu.edu/en/nav/vlibrary.html.

[4]See http://www.cellsalive.com.

[5]See http://kids.nationalgeographic.com/kids/animals/creaturefeature.

[6]See http://www.learner.org/interactives/dailymath.

and a coleader guided a group of sixth and seventh graders in a discussion of George Bernard Shaw's (1916) play *Pygmalion*, everyone struggled to make sense of characters' dialects. The group watched segments of *My Fair Lady*, a movie based on the play, and found the dialects much easier to understand.

• **Select technologies based on students' age-typical abilities and interests.** Young children are curious about what they can do on cell phones, tablets, laptops, and desktops—on virtually any interactive devices for which they are given access. During preschool and kindergarten, children are able to practice basic skills in recognizing the alphabet, counting, and even simple programming. Yet children in this age range learn by exploring the environment, interacting with adults and peers, asking questions, and listening to stories. With their keen interest in digital technologies, young children can easily spend more time with digital technologies than is healthy. As children grow older, and certainly into adolescence, they have more capacity to benefit from interactive technologies yet even then need guidance to avoid overuse.

• **Teach critical analysis of information on the Internet, television, and film.** Basic media literacy requires students to learn of inaccuracies on the World Wide Web and to rely on certain sites more than others. Data provided on websites of government agencies and well-respected nonprofit organizations might be fairly reliable, but opinion pieces on someone's personal web page may not be (Ostenson, 2014). With information on the Internet exploding, youngsters must be taught how to find, retrieve, organize, synthesize, and evaluate the information they find (M. M. Neumann, Finger, & Neumann, 2017). Educators can teach youngsters how to watch television with a critical eye (Calvert, 2008). They might help young children understand that television commercials aim to persuade them to buy something, perhaps toys, cereal, or hamburgers. They can point out subtle advertising ploys for older children, such as the use of color, physically attractive models, and endorsements by famous actors and athletes. And they can advise young people of stereotypes and negative portrayals of men and women, certain ethnic groups, and various professions.

• **Teach children etiquette, civic-mindedness, and safety on the Internet.** Educators can help students learn to be polite and restrained with postings. Teachers can likewise talk with students about the kinds of information that is appropriate and risky to share. Many, probably most, students need to be advised about the possible long-term harm that can befall them if they portray themselves too candidly. To make these issues concrete, teachers might show how other people can track their images and explain how employers perform electronic searches on job applicants (Richardson, 2011; Van Ouytsel, Walrave, & Ponnet, 2014).

• **Teach children to manage their use of digital media such that they remain safe, healthy, and in good standing for future careers.** Educators can help students learn about appropriate and inappropriate uses of digital technologies. *Take the Challenge* is a 6-week curriculum that was developed for middle school students to build their capacity to monitor their use of digital media such that their actions, Internet presence, and time investment are in their personal best interests. As part of the program, students learn about the negative effects of excessive screen time and gain practice in restricting their time with digital technologies (Bickham, Hswen, Slaby, & Rich, 2018). Participants in the program are found to decrease their time watching television and to increase their hours of sleep. A similar curriculum, the *Student Media Awareness to Reduce Television* (SMART) program has been developed for elementary students and has likewise had good effects on students' sleep, diet, and social skills (T. N. Robinson & Borzekowski, 2006).

Educators can design their own methods for guiding digital media use. In Figure 15.2, you can see a form that allows high school students to set goals with digital media and keep track of their progress. In this example, a student sets three goals—for reducing gaming time, reviewing the content of personal accounts, and managing emotional responses to annoying texts, emails, and social network remarks. Other goals might be established, such as trying out advanced search tips, evaluating the credibility of claims on websites, developing video-editing and production skills, and examining digital material for bias.

FIGURE 15.2 Self-Regulation of Media Use.

Students set one to four goals with digital media and then track their progress toward these ends over a 2-week period.

Form for Self-Regulation of Digital Media

Goal	Week 1	Week 2	Student's Evaluation	Teacher's Comment
Goal 1: Reduce screen time between Weeks 1 and 2 on school days by 20% (for health class.)	Monday: 8 hours Tuesday: 7 hours Wednesday: 9 hours Thursday: 6 hours Friday: 13 hours Total: 44 hours	Monday: 9 hours Tuesday: 7 hours Wednesday: 5 hours Thursday: 5 hours Friday: 8 hours Total: 34 hours	I decreased my screen time by 22.7%. Monday and Tuesday were regular days when I didn't reduce the time. On Wednesday and Thursday, I set an alarm, and that worked. Friday was hard because I felt like staying up late gaming.	*Did you want to set an alarm to stop gaming Monday through Thursday? Maybe a later alarm on Friday?*
Goal 2: Do an audit of my social media accounts (for career development course).	Review social media accounts, including those on old platforms, from the perspective of potential employers.	Deleted a few embarrassing posts and added community service to my Facebook account. Examined Snapchat, Instagram, Tumblr, and Reddit and thought they were okay.	My image is fine but kind of goofy.	*How might you use your accounts while applying to colleges?*
Goal 3: Tone down my embarrassment, sadness, anxiety, and anger when reading rude remarks in texts, email, and posts on social networking sites (homeroom class).	I noticed that someone said I looked fat in a birthday photo of me in my Facebook account.	When I found the comment, I replied "Get lost." Then I deleted the comment.	It was annoying to see the comment, but it didn't make me really sad, just a little annoyed and then proud for sticking up for myself and using self-control.	*Well done. Come talk with me if you want.*

• **Make advanced technology available to children with limited access.** Although children from middle- and upper-income families are apt to have access to personal computers at home, similar access is less common for children from low-income families. Yet computer expertise, including being able to find, comprehend, and evaluate information on the Internet, is increasingly critical for everyone's success. Fortunately, digital technologies are becoming more and more affordable, and school districts can sometimes make available laptops and handheld devices and offer instruction in technology applications (Scherer, 2011). A preschool teacher might teach children how to play computer games that give practice in emergent literacy skills, and an after-school tutor might show young people how to use the Internet while completing homework.

• **Discourage youngsters from using technologies for aggressive purposes.** Many educators have had some success in persuading children that the glamorous, humorous, and pervasive manner in which violence is shown on television is misleading (Rosenkoetter, Rosenkoetter, Ozretich, & Acock, 2004). You might point out that, contrary to typical television scenes, violence is usually *not* an effective way to handle disagreements and often creates additional problems. You could also explain to children that violence is an eye-catching and unrealistic element that television producers use to attract audiences and make money.

Teachers and other adults must advise young people to refrain from *cyberbullying*, the sending or posting of harmful messages in public places on the Internet (Hinduja & Patchin, 2011; Willard, 2007). Adults must also discourage young people from posting racist messages or profanity in their blogs and from sending unflattering photographs of others or demeaning messages over cell phones. Finally, some young people also need to be reminded to refrain from sending mocking or threatening statements as text messages or instant messages (Willard, 2007).

• **Encourage parents to monitor children's interpretation of the Internet and television.** At meetings and school events and in newsletters, educators can encourage parents to set specific television-viewing limits for their children. For instance, if parents find their children watch television 4 or 5 hours a day, they might want to set a 2-hour limit. Parents may also find it informative to watch a few television programs with their children. In the process, parents can discover how their children interpret what they watch and provide a reality check when characters consistently violate norms for appropriate behavior ("Do you think people should really insult one another like that?"). Parents can also familiarize themselves with websites their children visit and consider using Internet filters or blocks. They can be advised to talk with their children about who is on their buddy list and discourage any meetings with online acquaintances. In addition, parents can learn common acronyms in contemporary use, for example, LOL (laugh out loud), TTYL (talk to you later), PAW (parents are watching), A/S/L (age, sex, and location), and WTGP (want to go private?); National Center for Missing and Exploited Children, 2004.

As you have learned, children grow up in a complex social world. The Basic Developmental issues table "Social Contexts of Child Development" synthesizes the effects of peers, schools, and society on children from the perspective of nature and nurture, universality and diversity, and qualitative and quantitative change.

BASIC DEVELOPMENTAL ISSUES

Social Contexts of Child Development

ISSUE	INFLUENCES OF PEERS, SCHOOL, AND SOCIETY
Nature and Nurture	In ideal circumstances, peers offer children emotional support, a safe forum for polishing social skills, and reassurance during shared transitions. Teachers communicate expectations about children's abilities, implement classroom traditions, organize learning groups, and cultivate a sense of belonging at school. Society has institutions that care for children, technological systems that permit widespread communication, and media that transmit content about expected behaviors for people with various characteristics. *Nature* provides a necessary foundation for children's social development with a biologically based desire to interact with other people. Maturational changes are evident in evolving peer relationships. Advancements in language and the ability to take others' perspectives improve conflict resolution with peers. Individual differences that derive partly from genes (e.g., temperaments, appearance, and some disabilities) affect children's peer relationships and social acceptance.
Universality and Diversity	*Universality* is present in benefits children gain from being liked by peers, having relationships with caring adults outside the family (e.g., teachers and child care providers), participating in a school setting where they achieve and feel that they belong, and having safe and interesting options for free time. *Diversity* occurs in the particular social skills children develop, the extent to which peers find them likable partners, the suitability of children's environments (e.g., the quality of child care centers), and the degree to which young people engage in risky behaviors (e.g., committing crimes with fellow gang members, engaging in unprotected sexual contact, or hurting themselves).
Qualitative and Quantitative Change	Children undergo several *qualitative* transformations in their social relationships. Infants form associations with peers during fleeting exchanges. These ties become rich language-based and stable relationships during early and middle childhood, and close friendships, cliques, and romantic relationships during late childhood and adolescence. Other qualitative overhauls occur in the onset of sexual feelings for peers of opposite gender (or in some instances, same gender) and in youngsters' uses of media (e.g., initially preferring television and video games and later choosing e-mail and chat rooms). Children also exhibit gradual, *quantitative* changes in peer relationships, styles of behaving in schools, and uses of society's institutions. Children gradually refine their skills for interacting with peers, and once they adjust to a new school, slowly learn to follow its rules and expectations.

Summary

Society plays an important role through its provision of services to children. Groups of children spend time in child care settings that vary in quality—from those that are well staffed and properly trained in responsive and developmentally appropriate care to those that are overcrowded, neglectful, and harsh in caregiving. Child care, after-school programs and extracurricular activities can bolster the development of youngsters when they include stable, affectionate relationships with adults and peers and options for productive pastimes.

Children spend many hours watching television and using computers of various kinds. Televisions, computers, tablets, cell phones, and other media have considerable potential to foster children's cognitive development, but their benefits have not yet been fully realized, and they are accompanied by risks. Violent and stereotypical content in the media can be a minor or serious problem for young people, depending on their preexisting characteristics. Young people enjoy self-expression on social media sites but sometimes acquire bad habits on the Internet, saying things that are rude to others, leaving themselves open to others' cruel remarks or exploitation, and spending so much time on the Internet that they neglect their sleep, homework, physical activity, and face-to-face friendships.

MyLab Education Self-Check 15.3

Practicing For Your Licensure Examination

Many teaching tests require students to apply their knowledge of child development in analyzing brief vignettes and answering multiple-choice questions. You can practice for your licensure examination by reading the following case study and answering a series of questions.

Aaron and Cole

Aaron and Cole became friends when they were both students in Mr. Howard's fifth-grade class. Although Aaron was in most respects a typical fifth grader, Cole had significant developmental delays. Special educator Debbie Staub (1998) described Cole's special educational needs and his strengths as follows:

> Cole has limited expressive vocabulary and uses one- or two-word sentences. He does not participate in traditional academic tasks, although he is included with his typically developing schoolmates for the entire school day. Cole has a history of behavioral problems that have ranged from mild noncompliance to adult requests to serious aggressive and destructive behavior such as throwing furniture at others. In spite of his occasional outbursts, however, it is hard not to like him. Cole is like an eager toddler who finds wonder in the world around him. The boys he has befriended in Mr. Howard's class bring him great joy. He appreciates their jokes and harmless teasing. Cole would like nothing better than to hang out with his friends all day, but if he had to choose just one friend, it would be Aaron. (D. Staub, 1998, p. 76)[a]

Throughout their fifth- and sixth-grade years, Aaron was both a good friend and a caring mentor to Cole. Without prompting from adults, Aaron helped Cole with his work, included him in games at recess, and generally watched out for him. Aaron also assumed responsibility for Cole's behavior by explaining to Cole how his actions affected others. The following excerpt from a classroom observation illustrates Aaron's gentle way with Cole:

> Cole was taking Nelle's [a classmate's] things out of her bag and throwing them on the floor. As soon as Aaron saw, he walked right over to Cole and started talking to him. He said, "We're making a new rule—no being mean." Then he walked with Cole to the front of the room and told him to tell another boy what the new rule was. Cole tapped the boy's shoulder to tell him but the boy walked away. Cole looked confused. Aaron smiled and put his hand on Cole's shoulder and told him, "It's okay. Just remember the rule." Then he walked Cole back to Nelle's stuff and quietly asked Cole to put everything back. (D. Staub, 1998, pp. 77–78)

Aaron, too, benefited from the friendship, as his mother explained: "Our family has recently gone through a tough divorce and there are a lot of hurt feelings out there for everyone. But at least when Aaron is at school he feels good about being there and I think a big reason is because he has Cole and he knows that he is an important person in Cole's life" (D. Staub, 1998, pp. 90–91).

Dr. Staub observed that, despite their developmental differences, the boys' relationship was in many respects a normal one:

> I asked Mr. Howard once, "Do you think Cole's and Aaron's friendship looks different from others' in your class?" Mr. Howard thought for a moment before responding: "No, I don't think it looks that different. Well, I was going to say one of the differences is that Aaron sometimes tells Cole to be quiet, or 'Hey Cole, I gotta do my work!' But I don't know if that is any different than what he might say to Ben leaning over and interrupting him. I think I would say that Aaron honestly likes Cole and it's not because he's a special-needs kid." (D. Staub, 1998, p. 78)

Aaron and Cole remained close until Cole moved 30 miles away at the beginning of seventh grade.

Constructed-Response Question

1. In what ways did Aaron and Cole's friendship promote each boy's social-emotional development?

Multiple-Choice Questions

2. What did Aaron do that helped Cole become more socially competent with other peers?

   a. Aaron helped Cole to be accepted by peers by convincing Cole to join him in some risky behaviors.

   b. Aaron did Cole's homework so that Cole looked more capable in front of peers.

   c. Aaron encouraged Cole to avoid other children and remain his friend exclusively.

   d. Aaron coached Cole in such social skills as controlling his temper and remaining friendly with peers.

3. Aaron's and Cole's teacher, Mr. Howard, seemed to be supportive of the boys' friendship. Considering the perspectives in this chapter, what might Mr. Howard have done if he were committed to establishing an effective classroom climate?

   a. Communicate genuine caring and respect for all students.

   b. Encourage students to pursue common goals.

   c. Implement some fun routines on a regular basis.

   d. All of the above.

MyLab Education Licensure Practice 15.1

Key Concepts

peer culture (p. 562)
social skills (p. 563)
peer pressure (p. 566)
popular children (p. 569)
rejected children (p. 569)
neglected children (p. 569)
controversial children (p. 569)
dominance hierarchy (p. 573)
clique (p. 573)
crowd (p. 573)
subculture (p. 574)
gang (p. 575)
sexual orientation (p. 577)
sexual harassment (p. 581)
sense of community (p. 585)
community of learners (p. 586)
self-fulfilling prophecy (p. 589)
stage–school fit (p. 584)
society (p. 592)
interactive technology (p. 595)

Glossary

accommodation Process of responding to a new event by either modifying an existing scheme or forming a new one.

acculturation Process of taking on the customs and values of a new culture.

achievement goal theory A conceptual framework for distinguishing adaptive and maladaptive motivations for accomplishing academic standards and battling obstacles to success.

action research Systematic study of an issue or problem by a teacher or other practitioner, with the goal of bringing about more productive outcomes for children.

adaptive behavior Behavior related to self-care, daily living skills, getting along in society, and exhibiting appropriate conduct in social situations.

addiction Physical and psychological dependence on a substance, such that increasing quantities must be taken to produce the desired effect and withdrawal produces adverse physiological and psychological effects.

African American English Dialect of some African American communities that includes pronunciations, idioms, and grammatical constructions different from those of Standard English.

aggression Action intentionally taken to hurt another either physically or psychologically.

alleles Genes located at the same point on corresponding (paired) chromosomes and related to the same physical characteristic.

amusia Inability to detect the small changes in pitch that are common in melodies; an extreme form of tone deafness.

anorexia nervosa Eating disorder in which a person eats little or nothing for weeks or months and seriously jeopardizes his or her health.

antisocial behavior actions children intentionally perform to hurt other people, disrupt others' activities, and show disobedience to parents and other caregivers.

anxiety An emotional state characterized by ongoing worry and apprehension.

anxiety disorder Chronic emotional condition characterized by excessive, debilitating worry.

apprenticeship Mentorship in which a novice works intensively with an expert to learn how to accomplish complex tasks in a particular domain.

appropriation Gradual adoption of (and perhaps also adaptation of) other people's ways of thinking and behaving for one's own purposes.

approximate number system The early ability to detect differences in magnitude through mental images not yet associated with numbers, words, or symbolic procedures for counting.

assessment Task that children complete and adults use to make judgments of children's knowledge, abilities, and other characteristics.

assimilation Form of acculturation in which a person totally embraces a culture, abandoning a previous culture in the process.

assimilation In Piaget's theory, process of responding (either physically or mentally) to a new event in a way that is consistent with an existing scheme.

astrocyte Glial cell that regulates blood flow in the brain, brings nutrients to and metabolizes chemicals for neurons, and communicates with other similar cells and with neurons.

attachment An enduring emotional tie uniting one person to another.

attention-deficit hyperactivity disorder (ADHD) Disability characterized by inattention, hyperactivity, or impulsive behavior, or by all of these characteristics.

attribution Belief about the cause of one's own or another person's success or failure.

authentic activity Instructional activity similar to one that a child might eventually encounter in the outside world.

authoritarian parenting style Parenting style characterized by strict expectations for behavior and rigid rules that children are required to obey without question.

authoritative parenting style Parenting style characterized by emotional warmth, high expectations, consistent enforcement of rules, explanations regarding the reasons behind these rules, and the inclusion of children in decision making.

autism spectrum disorders Disorders marked by impaired social cognition, social skills, and social interaction, as well as by repetitive behaviors; extreme forms are often associated with significant cognitive and linguistic delays and highly unusual behaviors.

autobiographical self Mental "history" of important events in one's life.

automatization Process of becoming able to respond quickly and efficiently while mentally processing or physically performing certain tasks.

axon Armlike part of a neuron that sends information to other neurons.

babbling Repeating certain consonant-vowel syllables over and over (e.g., "mamamama"); common in the latter half of the first year.

behaviorism Theoretical perspective in which children's behavioral and emotional responses change as a direct result of particular environmental stimuli.

bicultural orientation Form of acculturation in which a person is familiar with two cultures and selectively draws from the values and traditions of one or both cultures depending on the context.

bilingual education Approach to second-language instruction in which students are instructed in academic subject areas in their native language while simultaneously being taught to speak, read, and write in a second language.

bilingualism Knowing and speaking two languages fluently.

biological theory Theoretical perspective that focuses on inherited physiological structures of the body and brain that support survival, growth, and learning.

bulimia Eating disorder in which a person, in an attempt to be thin, eats a large amount of food, and then purposefully purges it from the body by vomiting or taking laxatives.

bully Child or adolescent who frequently threatens, harasses, or causes physical or psychological injury to particular peers.

care orientation Focus on nurturance and concern for others in moral decision making.

case study Naturalistic research study in which investigators document a single person's or a small group's experiences in depth over a period.

central conceptual structure Integrated network of concepts and cognitive processes that forms the basis for much of one's thinking, reasoning, and learning in a specific content domain.

central executive Component of the human information processing system that oversees the flow of information throughout the system and enacts cognitive strategies.

cephalocaudal trend Vertical ordering of motor skills and physical development; order is head first to feet last.

child development Study of the persistent, cumulative, and progressive changes in the physical, cognitive, and social-emotional development of children and adolescents.

child maltreatment Adverse treatment of a child in the form of neglect, physical abuse, sexual abuse, or emotional abuse.

chromosome Rodlike structure that resides in the nucleus of every cell of the body and contains genes that guide growth and development; each chromosome is made up of DNA and other biological instructions.

class inclusion Recognition that an object simultaneously belongs to a particular category and to one of its subcategories.

clinical method Procedure in which an adult probes a child's reasoning about a task or problem, tailoring questions to what the child has previously said or done in the interview.

clique Moderately stable friendship group of perhaps three to nine members.

co-action Complex process by which genes and environmental experiences merge in the child's brain and body as influences on the child's characteristics.

codominance Situation in which the two genes of an allele pair, although not identical, both have some influence on a characteristic.

cognitive apprenticeship Mentorship in which an expert and a novice work together on a challenging task and the expert suggests ways to think about the task.

cognitive development Systematic changes in reasoning, concepts, memory, language, and intellectual skills.

cognitive process theory Theoretical perspective that focuses on the precise nature of human mental representations and operations.

cognitive science An interdisciplinary field drawing from research in psychology, neuroscience, linguistics, anthropology, artificial intelligence, and philosophy and examining the representations and operations of the human mind.

cognitive strategy Specific mental process that people intentionally use to acquire or manipulate information.

cognitive tool Concept, symbol, strategy, or other culturally constructed mechanism that helps people think more effectively.

cognitive-developmental theory Theoretical perspective that focuses on major transformations to the underlying structures of thinking over the course of development.

collectivistic culture Culture that encourages obedience to and dependence on authority figures and being honorable, cooperative, and invested in group accomplishments.

community The local neighborhood and surrounding areas in which a child grows up and in which the family interacts on a daily basis.

community of learners A classroom in which teacher(s) and students actively and collaboratively work to help one another learn.

comprehension monitoring The process of evaluating one's comprehension of oral messages or written material.

conceptual change Revision of one's knowledge and understanding of a topic in response to new information about the topic.

conduct disorder Chronic emotional condition characterized by lack of concern for the rights of others.

conscience An internalized sense of right and wrong for guiding and evaluating one's behavior.

conservation Realization that if nothing is added or taken away, an amount stays the same regardless of any alterations in shape or arrangement.

constructivism Theoretical perspective proposing that learners construct a body of knowledge and beliefs, rather than absorbing information exactly as it is received.

contexts The broad social environments, including family, schools, neighborhoods, community organizations, culture, ethnicity, and society at large, that influence children's development.

contingent self-worth Overall sense of self that is highly dependent on others' opinions.

control group Group of participants in a research study who do not receive the treatment under investigation; often used in an experimental study.

controversial children Children whom some peers really like and other peers strongly dislike.

conventional morality In Kohlberg's theory, acceptance of society's conventions regarding right and wrong; behaving to please others or to live up to society's expectations for appropriate behavior.

conventional transgression In social domain theory, action that violates society's general guidelines (often unspoken) for socially acceptable behavior.

cooing Making and repeating vowel sounds (e.g., "oooooo"); common in early infancy.

coparents The two (or more) parents who share responsibility for rearing their children.

coping skills Personal mechanisms for managing distress.

correlational study Research study that explores relationships among variables.

cortex Part of the forebrain that enables conscious thinking processes, including executive functions.

creativity The valuable process of generating novel and worthwhile solutions to a person's goals, needs, and problems.

cross-sectional study Research study in which the performance of individuals at different ages is compared at a single point in time.

crowd Large collection of adolescents who share certain characteristics, tend to affiliate together, and are defined by others according to their reputations.

crystallized intelligence Knowledge and skills accumulated from one's prior experience, schooling, and culture.

cultural bias Extent to which an assessment offends or unfairly penalizes some individuals because of their ethnicity or cultural background, gender, or socioeconomic status.

culture The values, traditions, and symbol systems of a long-standing social group that give purpose and meaning to children's daily activities and interpersonal relationships.

cyberbullying Use of digital technologies to harass, threaten, or embarrass another person.

delay of gratification Forgoing small immediate rewards for larger ones at a future time.

dendrite Branchlike part of a neuron that receives information from other neurons.

depression An emotional condition characterized by lasting sadness, discouragement, hopelessness, and, in children, irritability.

development-enhancing education Schooling whose qualities of being warm, individualized, age appropriate, culturally inclusive, and academically challenging foster both scholastic achievement in children and their growing capacities in the cognitive, physical, and social-emotional domains.

developmental milestone A major physical, cognitive, or social-emotional skill that is age-related and appears as part of a predictable sequence of skills.

developmental systems theory Theoretical perspective that focuses on the multiple factors, including the child's activity and systems inside and outside the child, that combine to influence development.

dialect Form of a language characteristic of a particular geographic region or ethnic group.

differentiation A gradual transition from general possibility to specialized functioning over the course of development.

digital literacy The ability to retrieve, interpret, evaluate, create, and communicate information from interactive computer resources and technologies.

discrimination The unfair treatment to people sharing a certain characteristic, such as race or ethnicity.

disequilibrium State of being unable to address new events with existing schemes.

disorganized and disoriented attachment Attachment classification in which children lack a single coherent way of responding to attachment figures.

distributed intelligence Thinking facilitated by physical objects and technology, social support, and concepts and symbols of one's culture.

distributive justice Beliefs about what constitutes people's fair share of a valued commodity.

diversity In a particular aspect of human development, the varied ways in which individuals progress.

dizygotic twins Twins that began as two separate zygotes and so are as genetically similar as two siblings conceived and born at different times.

DNA A spiral-staircase–shaped molecule that guides the production of proteins needed by the body for growth and development; short for deoxyribonucleic acid.

dominance hierarchy Relative standing of group members in terms of such qualities as leadership and social influence.

dominant gene Gene that overrides any competing instructions in an allele pair.

dynamic assessment Systematic examination of how a child's knowledge or reasoning may change as a result of learning a specific task or performing it with adult guidance.

dyscalculia Inability to master basic numerical concepts and operations in a developmentally typical time frame despite normal instruction.

dyslexia Inability to master basic reading skills in a developmentally typical time frame despite normal reading instruction.

educational equality Aspiration for all children to receive the same high standard of schooling effectiveness.

educational equity Aspiration for all children to receive a high-quality education that is tailored to their individual needs.

egocentrism Inability of a child in Piaget's preoperational stage to view situations from another person's perspective.

elaboration Process of using prior knowledge to embellish new information and learn it more effectively.

embryo During prenatal weeks 2 through 8, the developing offspring that is in the process of forming major body structures and organs.

emergent literacy Knowledge and skills that lay a foundation for reading and writing; typically develops in the preschool years from early experiences with written language.

emotion Affective response to an event that is personally relevant to one's needs and goals.

emotional contagion Tendency for infants to cry spontaneously when they hear other infants crying.

emotional intelligence The ability to perceive, understand, and regulate affective feelings.

emotional or behavioral disorder Disability classification reflecting a disturbance of mood, inappropriate behavior, and/or difficulty in maintaining relationships, problems that are manifested over a long time and warrant thoughtful planning and accommodation at school.

emotional regulation Strategies to manage affective states.

empathy Capacity to experience the same feelings as another person, especially when the feeling is pain or distress.

English language learner (ELL) School-aged child who is not fully fluent in English because his or her family speaks a language other than English at home.

epigenetic changes Long-lasting modifications to switches on chromosomes that turn genes on and off as a result of the child's unique experiences with nutrition, exercise, sleep, stress, caregiving, and exposure to toxins.

equilibration Movement from equilibrium to disequilibrium and back to equilibrium; a process that promotes the development of increasingly complex forms of thought and knowledge.

equilibrium State of being able to address new events using existing schemes.

ethnicity Affiliation with other people with whom the child identifies as having a common heritage, geographical origin, language, religious faith, and other characteristics.

ethnography Naturalistic research study in which investigators spend an extensive period documenting the cultural patterns of a group of people in everyday settings.

ethological attachment theory Theoretical perspective that emphasizes the benefits to children derived from close bonds with caregivers, particularly protection from harm and a secure base from which to explore the environment.

executive functions Purposeful and goal-directed intellectual processes (e.g., planning, decision making) made possible by higher brain structures.

expansion Repetition of a child's short utterances in more complete and grammatically correct forms.

experimental study Research study in which a researcher manipulates one aspect of the environment (a treatment), controls other aspects of the environment, and assesses the treatment's effects on participants' behavior.

expressive language Ability to communicate effectively through speaking and writing.

extrinsic motivation Motivation provoked by the external consequences that certain behaviors bring.

family Two or more people who live together and are related by such enduring factors as birth, marriage, adoption, or long-term mutual commitment.

family structure The residents in a family home, including heads of household, other close family members, and children.

fast mapping Inferring a word's general meaning after a single exposure.

fetus During prenatal week 9 until birth, the developing offspring that grows in size and weight and in sensory abilities, brain structures, and organs needed for survival.

figurative speech Speech that communicates meaning beyond a literal interpretation of its words.

fine motor skills Small, precise movements of particular parts of the body, especially the hands.

fixed mind-set (of ability) Belief that ability is a "thing" that is relatively permanent and unchangeable.

fluid intelligence Ability to acquire knowledge quickly and thereby adapt effectively to new situations.

Flynn effect Gradual increase in intelligence test performance observed in many countries during the past several decades.

forebrain Part of the brain responsible for complex thinking, emotions, and motivation.

foreign language instruction Approach to second-language instruction in which native English speakers receive lessons in a new language for less than an hour once or twice a week or occasionally more often.

functionalism Theoretical perspective of language development that emphasizes the purposes language serves for human beings.

g General factor in intelligence that influences performance in a wide variety of tasks and content domains.

gamete Reproductive cell that, in humans, contains 23 chromosomes rather than the 46 chromosomes present in other cells in the body; a male gamete (sperm) and a female gamete (ovum) join at conception.

gang Cohesive social group characterized by initiation rites, distinctive colors and symbols, territorial orientation, feuds with rival groups, and criminal activity.

gender identity Personal embracement of the self as male, female, or an alternate gender.

gender schema Self-constructed body of beliefs about the traits and behaviors of males or females.

gene Basic unit of heredity in a living cell; genes are made up of DNA and contained on chromosomes.

giftedness Unusually high ability in one or more areas, to the point where children require special educational services to help them meet their full potential.

glial cell Cell in the brain that provides structural or functional support for, and in some cases the direction to, one or more neurons.

goal-directed behavior Intentional behavior aimed at bringing about an anticipated outcome.

grammatical word Nonlexical word that affects the meanings of other words or the interrelationships among words in a sentence.

gross motor skills Large movements of the body that permit locomotion through and within the environment.

grounded theory study Naturalistic research study in which investigators develop and elaborate new theories while comparing data (such as interview statements from participants) to the researchers' emerging interpretations.

growth mind-set (of ability) Belief that one's ability can and does improve with effort and practice.

growth spurt Rapid increase in height and weight during puberty.

guided participation The child's active immersion in cultural activities, typically with considerable direction from an adult or other individual with relevant expertise; children are given increasing responsibility and independence as they gain experience and proficiency.

guilt Feeling of discomfort when one inflicts damage or causes someone else pain or distress.

habituation Changes in children's physiological responses to repeated displays of the same stimulus, reflecting loss of interest.

hindbrain Part of the brain controlling the basic physiological processes that sustain survival.

holistic perspective of child development Framework for thinking about the child from a comprehensive vantage point, such that his or her full range of cognitive, physical, and social-emotional functions are considered simultaneously.

holophrase A single word used to express a complete thought; commonly observed in children's earliest speech.

hostile attributional bias Tendency to interpret others' behaviors as reflecting hostile or aggressive intentions.

identity Self-constructed definition of who one is, what things one finds important, what one believes, and what goals one wants to accomplish in life.

imaginary audience Belief that one is the center of attention in any social situation.

immersion Approach to second-language instruction in which native English speakers hear and speak the second language almost exclusively in the classroom.

implicit bias The relatively unconscious judgments people make about individuals with a particular characteristic such as race, gender, or religious faith.

individual constructivism Theoretical perspective that focuses on how people independently construct meaning from their experiences.

individualistic culture Culture that encourages independence, self-assertion, competition, and expression of personal needs.

Individualized Education Plan In the United States, a plan for a child with an eligible disability, developed by the child's classroom teacher, other professionals, and parents that defines the child's current intellectual and social abilities, academic goals for the year, desirable activities and accommodations for helping him or her succeed, and methods for assessing the child's progress.

induction Act of explaining why a certain behavior is unacceptable, usually with a focus on the pain or distress that someone has caused another.

infant-directed speech Short, simple, high-pitched speech often used when talking to young children.

infantile amnesia General inability to recall events that have occurred in the early years of life.

information processing theory A family of related theoretical perspectives that focus on the specific ways in which people mentally acquire, interpret, and remember information.

inner speech "Talking" to oneself mentally rather than aloud as a way of guiding oneself through a task.

insecure-avoidant attachment Attachment classification in which children appear somewhat indifferent to attachment figures.

insecure-resistant attachment Attachment classification in which children are preoccupied with their attachment figures but gain little comfort from them when distressed.

integration An increasing coordination of body parts over the course of development.

intellectual disability Disability marked by significantly below-average general intelligence and deficits in adaptive behavior.

intelligence Ability to apply past knowledge and experiences flexibly to accomplish challenging new tasks.

intelligence test General measure of current cognitive functioning, used primarily to predict academic achievement over the short run.

intentionality Engagement in an action congruent with one's purpose or goal.

interactive technology Array of electronic, digitally based machines that are operated dynamically by a person whose commands determine emerging program sequences.

internalization In Vygotsky's theory, the gradual evolution of external, social activities into internal, mental activities.

internalized motivation Adoption of behaviors that others value, whether or not one's immediate environment reinforces those behaviors.

intersubjectivity Awareness of shared perceptions and understandings that provide the foundation for social interaction.

interview Data-collection technique that obtains self-report data through face-to-face conversation.

intrinsic motivation Motivation resulting from personal characteristics or from factors inherent in the task being performed.

invented spelling A child's early, self-constructed word spelling, which may reflect only some of the word's phonemes.

IQ score Score on an intelligence test, determined by comparing one's performance with the performance of same-age peers

IRE cycle Adult–child interaction pattern marked by adult initiation, child response, and adult evaluation; in Western cultures, such a pattern is often seen in instructional settings.

joint attention Phenomenon in which two people (e.g., a child and a caregiver) simultaneously focus on the same object or event, monitor each other's attention, and coordinate their responses.

justice orientation Focus on individual rights in moral decision making.

knowledge base One's knowledge about specific topics and the world in general.

knowledge telling Writing down ideas in whatever order they come to mind, with little regard for communicating the ideas effectively.

knowledge transforming Writing about ideas in such a way as to intentionally help the reader understand them.

language acquisition device Biologically built-in mechanism hypothesized to facilitate language learning.

language socialization Direct and indirect means through which other people teach children the language and verbal behaviors deemed to be appropriate in their culture.

learned helplessness General belief that one is incapable of accomplishing tasks and has little or no control of the environment.

learning disability Significant deficit in one or more cognitive processes to the point where special educational services are required.

left hemisphere Left side of the cortex; largely responsible for sequential reasoning and analysis, especially in right-handed people.

lexical word Word that in some way represents an aspect of one's physical, social, or psychological world.

long-term memory Component of memory that holds knowledge and skills for a relatively long period.

longitudinal study Research study in which the performance of a single group of people is tracked over a period.

mastery goal Desire to acquire additional knowledge or master new skills (also known as a learning goal).

mastery orientation General belief that one is capable of accomplishing challenging tasks, accompanied by an intent to master such tasks.

maturation Genetically guided changes that occur over the course of development.

mediated learning experience Discussion between an adult and a child in which the adult helps the child make sense of an event they have mutually experienced.

mediation In Vygotsky's theory, a process through which adults help children make culturally appropriate sense of experiences, perhaps by attaching labels to objects or explaining the nature of certain phenomena.

meiosis The process of cell division and reproduction by which gametes are formed.

menarche First menstrual period in an adolescent female.

metacognition Knowledge and beliefs about one's own cognitive processes, as well as efforts to regulate those cognitive processes to maximize learning and memory.

metacognitive awareness Extent to which one is able to reflect on the nature of one's own thinking processes.

metalinguistic awareness Extent to which one consciously understands and thinks about the nature and functions of language.

midbrain Part of the brain that coordinates communication between the hindbrain and forebrain.

mindfulness A state of quiet calm in which a person focuses on the present moment and, while experiencing it, his or her cognitive, emotional, and physiological conditions.

mirror neuron Specialized cell in the brain that fires either when the person performs a particular act or observes another individual performing the same act.

mitosis The process of cell duplication by which chromosomes are preserved and a human being or other biological organism can grow.

monozygotic twins Twins that began as a single zygote and so share the same genetic makeup.

moral development Advancements in reasoning and behaving in accordance with culturally prescribed or self-constructed standards of right and wrong.

moral dilemma Situation in which there is no clear-cut answer regarding the morally right thing to do.

moral transgression In social domain theory, action that causes damage or harm or in some other way infringes on the needs and rights of others.

motivation State that energizes, directs, and sustains behavior.

multifactorial trait Particular characteristic determined by many separate genes combining in influence with environmental factors.

myelination The growth of a fatty sheath around neurons that allows them to transmit messages quickly.

narrative Verbal account of a temporal sequence of logically interconnected events; a story.

native language The first language a child learns.

nativism Theoretical perspective proposing that some knowledge is biologically built in and available at birth or soon thereafter.

nature Inherited characteristics that affect development.

need for relatedness Fundamental need to feel socially connected to, and loved and respected by, other people.

neglected children Children whom peers rarely select as someone they would either most like or least like to do something with.

neo-Piagetian theory Theoretical perspective that combines elements of Piaget's theory with more contemporary research findings and suggests that development in specific content domains is often stagelike in nature.

neuron Cell that transmits information to other cells; also called a nerve cell.

niche construction A child's active shaping of the environment through behaviors, activities, and choices in accordance with personal, genetically based tendencies.

niche-picking Tendency to actively seek out environments that match one's inherited abilities.

norms of communication Unspoken cultural rules about how conversations are supposed to take place in certain settings and among people of various positions and roles.

nurture Environmental conditions that affect development.

obesity Condition in which a person's body mass index, a measure of weight in relation to height, is at or above the 95th percentile for someone of the same age and gender.

object permanence Realization that objects continue to exist even when they are out of sight.

observation Data-collection technique whereby a researcher carefully watches and documents the behaviors of participants in a research study.

operation In Piaget's theory, an organized and integrated system of logical thought processes.

organization Process of identifying interrelationships among pieces of information as a way of learning them more effectively.

overextension Overly broad meaning for a word, such that it is used in situations to which it does not apply.

overregularization Use of a syntactic rule in situations where an exception to the rule applies.

parenting style Predominant pattern of behaviors that a parent uses to nurture and discipline his or her children.

peer culture General set of rules, expectations, and interpretations that influence how members of a particular peer group behave.

peer mediation Approach to conflict resolution in which one child or adolescent (the mediator) asks peers in conflict to express their differing viewpoints and then work together to identify an appropriate compromise.

peer pressure Tactics used to encourage some behaviors and discourage others in age-mates.

perception Interpretation of stimuli that the body has sensed.

performance goal Desire to demonstrate high ability and make a good impression.

performance-approach goal Desire to look good and receive favorable judgments from others.

performance-avoidance goal Desire not to look bad or receive unfavorable judgments from others.

permissive parenting style Parenting style characterized by emotional warmth but few expectations or standards for children's behavior.

personal fable Belief held by many adolescents that they are unique beings invulnerable to normal risks and dangers.

personal interest Long-term, relatively stable interest in a particular topic or activity.

personal matter In social domain theory, action that is considered a choice that an individual can make without consulting others.

personal space A child's personally and culturally preferred distance from other people during social interaction.

personality Characteristic way a person behaves, thinks, and feels.

phonemes Smallest units of a spoken language that signify differences in meaning.

phonological awareness Ability to hear the distinct sounds of which spoken words are composed.

phonology The sound system of a language; how words sound and are produced.

physical aggression Action that can potentially cause bodily injury (for example, hitting or scratching another person).

physical development Systematic changes of the body and brain and age-related changes in motor skills and health behaviors.

physiological measure Direct assessment of physical development or specific aspect of physiological functioning.

playing the dozens Friendly, playful exchange of insults, common in some African American communities; also called joaning or sounding.

polygenic inheritance Genetic influence in which a wide range of genes contributes to the manifestation of a characteristic.

popular children Children whom many peers like and perceive to be kind and trustworthy.

postconventional morality In Kohlberg's theory, behaving in accordance with self-developed abstract principles regarding right and wrong.

pragmatics Conventions and strategies used in effective and socially acceptable verbal interactions.

preconventional morality In Kohlberg's theory, a lack of internalized standards about right and wrong; making decisions based on what is best for oneself, without regard for others' needs and feelings.

prejudice Display of negative attitudes, feelings, and behaviors toward individuals because of their affiliation with a group that is presumed to be inferior to others.

premature infant Infant born early (before 37 weeks of prenatal growth) and sometimes with serious medical problems.

prenatal development Systematic growth of a human offspring that takes place between fertilization and birth.

primary reinforcer Stimulus or event that satisfies a built-in biological need.

proactive aggression Deliberate aggression against another as a means of obtaining a desired goal.

prosocial behavior Action intended to benefit another person (for example, sharing with or helping another person).

proximodistal trend Inside-outside ordering of motor skills and physical development; order is inside first and outside last.

psychodynamic theory Theoretical perspective that focuses on how early experiences and internal conflicts affect social and personality development.

psychosocial stages In Erikson's theory, eight periods of life that involve age-related challenges.

puberty Physiological changes that occur during adolescence and lead to reproductive maturation.

punishment Consequence of a response that leads to a decrease in the frequency of that response.

qualitative change Relatively dramatic developmental change that reflects considerable reorganization in functioning.

quantitative change Developmental change that involves a series of minor, trendlike modifications.

quasi-experimental study Research study in which one or more experimental treatments are administered but in which random assignment to groups is not possible.

questionnaire Data-collection technique that obtains self-report data through a paper-and-pencil inventory.

race Affiliation with other people with whom the child has shared physical features such as skin color, eye color, hair texture, and facial bone structure.

reactive aggression Aggressive response to frustration or provocation.

reasoning The ability to think logically and weigh evidence reasonably when drawing conclusions.

receptive language Ability to understand the language one hears or reads.

recessive gene Gene that influences growth and development primarily when the other gene in the allele pair is identical to it.

reciprocal teaching Approach to teaching reading comprehension in which students take turns asking teacher-like questions of their classmates.

recursive thinking Thinking about what other people may be thinking about oneself, possibly through multiple iterations.

reflex Automatic motor response to a particular kind of stimulus.

rehearsal Attempt to learn and remember information by repeating it over and over.

reinforcer Consequence of a response that leads to an increase in the frequency of that response.

rejected children Children whom many peers identify as being unfavorable social partners.

relational aggression Action that can adversely affect interpersonal relationships (for example, calling another person names or socially excluding the person).

reliability Extent to which a data-collection technique yields consistent, dependable results that are only minimally affected by temporary and irrelevant influences.

resilience Ability of some youngsters (often enhanced with environmental support) to thrive despite adverse environmental conditions.

right hemisphere Right side of the cortex; largely responsible for simultaneous processing and synthesis, especially in right-handed people.

rough-and-tumble play Playful physical "fighting" common in early and middle childhood.

rubric A list of the ideal features of an assessment, often used by students in completing a task and by teachers in evaluating students' performance.

sample Participants in a research study whose characteristics are often assumed to indicate how a larger population of individuals would be.

scaffolding Support mechanism, provided by a more competent individual, that helps a child successfully perform a task within his or her zone of proximal development.

schema Tightly integrated set of ideas about a specific object or situation.

scheme In Piaget's theory, an organized group of similar actions or thoughts that are used repeatedly in response to the environment.

schizophrenia A psychiatric condition characterized by irrational ideas and disorganized thinking.

scientific method Multistep process of using critical thinking in defining a research question, collecting evidence, and determining implications of the results for theory and new questions.

scientific reasoning Cognitive processes central to conducting scientific research and interpreting findings appropriately.

script Schema that involves a predictable sequence of events related to a common activity.

secondary reinforcer Stimulus or event that becomes reinforcing over time through its association with one or more other reinforcers.

secure attachment Attachment classification in which children use attachment figures as a source of comfort in times of distress and as a secure base from which to explore.

selective adoption Form of acculturation in which a person assumes some customs of a new culture while also retaining some customs of a previous culture.

self-conscious emotion Affective state that reflects awareness of a community's social standards (e.g., pride, guilt, shame).

self-efficacy Belief that one is capable of executing certain behaviors or reaching certain goals.

self-evaluation Judging one's own performance in accordance with predetermined criteria.

self-fulfilling prophecy Phenomenon in which an adult's expectations for a child's performance bring about that level of performance.

self-handicapping Action that undermines one's own success as a way of protecting self-worth during difficult tasks.

self-instruction Specific directions that one gives oneself while performing a complex behavior; a form of self-talk.

self-monitoring Process of observing and recording one's own behavior.

self-motivation Intentionally using certain strategies to keep oneself on task during a dull but important activity.

self-regulated learning Directing and controlling one's own cognitive processes in order to learn successfully.

self-regulation The processes by which children direct their actions, learning, and emotions in accordance with personal goals and standards.

self-report Data-collection technique whereby participants are asked to describe their own characteristics and performance.

self-socialization Tendency to integrate personal observations and others' input into self-constructed standards for behavior and to choose actions consistent with those standards.

self-talk Talking to oneself as a way of guiding oneself through a task.

semantic bootstrapping Using knowledge of word meanings to derive knowledge about syntactic categories and structures.

semantics The meanings of words and word combinations.

sensation Physiological detection of stimuli in the environment.

sense of community In a classroom or school, a collection of widely shared beliefs that students, teachers, and other staff have common goals, support one another's efforts, and make important contributions to everyone's success.

sense of self Knowledge, beliefs, judgments, and feelings about oneself as a person.

sense of self-determination Belief that one has some choice and control regarding the future course of one's life.

sensitive period A period in development when certain environmental experiences have a more pronounced influence than is true at other times.

sensory register Component of memory that holds incoming information in an unanalyzed form for a very brief time (2 to 3 seconds or less).

separation Form of acculturation in which a person fails to learn or accept any customs and values from a new cultural environment.

service learning Activity that promotes learning and skill development through volunteerism or community service.

sexual harassment Form of discrimination in which a target individual perceives another's actions or statements to be hostile, humiliating, or offensive, especially pertaining to physical appearance or sexual matters.

sexual orientation Particular genders to which an individual is romantically and sexually attracted.

shame Feeling of embarrassment or humiliation after failing to meet certain standards for moral behavior.

sight vocabulary Words that a child can immediately recognize while reading.

situated motivation Phenomenon in which aspects of the immediate environment enhance motivation to learn particular things or behave in particular ways.

situational interest Interest evoked temporarily by something in the environment.

social cognition Process of thinking about how other people are likely to think, act, and react and choosing one's own interpersonal behaviors accordingly.

social constructivism Theoretical perspective that focuses on people's collective efforts to impose meaning on the world.

social desirability Tendency of children to give answers that will be perceived favorably by others.

social goal Goal related to establishing or maintaining relationships with other people.

social learning theory Theoretical perspective that focuses on how children's beliefs and goals influence their actions and how they often learn by observing others.

social perspective taking Imagining what someone else might be thinking or feeling.

social referencing Looking at someone else (e.g., a caregiver) for clues about how to respond to a particular object or event.

social skills Strategies used to interact effectively with others.

social-cognitive bias Mental shortcut used when thinking about other people or social events.

social-emotional development Systematic changes in emotions, self-concept, motivation, social relationships, and moral reasoning and behavior.

socialization Systematic efforts by other people and institutions to prepare youngsters to act in ways deemed by society to be appropriate and responsible.

society The relatively large and enduring collection of people who live in the same region and share government services, economic markets, legal systems, and medical care.

sociocognitive conflict Situation in which one encounters and has to wrestle with ideas and viewpoints of others different from one's own.

sociocultural theory Theoretical perspective that focuses on children's learning of tools, thinking processes, and communication systems through practice in meaningful tasks with other people.

sociodramatic play Play in which children take on specific roles and act out a scenario of imaginary events.

socioeconomic status (SES) One's general standing in an economically stratified society, encompassing family income, type of job, and education level.

sociolinguistic behaviors Types of verbal interactions that are considered socially acceptable in society for a speaker in a particular setting depending on his or her age, gender, status, and familiarity with others.

specific language impairment Disability characterized by abnormalities in producing or understanding spoken language to the point where special educational services are required.

speech register The style of spoken language used by people who interact regularly in a particular setting, follow certain roles, and embody a defined level of formality.

spermarche First ejaculation in an adolescent male.

stage A period of development characterized by a qualitatively distinct way of behaving or thinking.

stage theory Theory that describes development as involving a series of qualitatively distinct changes.

stage–school fit Match between students' age-related needs and the offerings at school nurturing academic learning, relationships with others, a sense of connection with the school, positive self-perceptions, and self-control.

Standard English Form of English generally considered acceptable in school (as reflected in textbooks, grammar instruction, etc.) and in other formal institutions by teachers and others.

standardized achievement test Formal assessment of knowledge and skills in carefully defined academic areas that is administered under controlled conditions.

state of arousal Physiological condition of sleepiness or wakefulness.

stepfamily Family created when one parent–child(ren) group combines with another parent figure and any children in his or her custody.

stereotype Rigid, simplistic, and erroneous characterization of a particular group.

stereotype threat Reduction in performance (often unintentional) as a result of a belief that one's group typically performs poorly.

story schema Knowledge of the typical elements and sequence of a narrative.

stranger anxiety Fear of unfamiliar adults in the latter half of the first year and into the second year of life.

stress The physiological responses to being worried, tense, and pressured.

structured English immersion Approach to second-language instruction for English language learners in which the children receive intensive lessons in English for a year or so and are then placed in the regular classroom.

subculture Group that resists the ways of the dominant culture and adopts its own norms for behavior.

submersion approach Approach to second-language instruction in which English language learners are placed in the regular classroom and expected to acquire the new language simply through exposure.

substance schema General view of all physical phenomena as being either touchable substances or properties of those substances.

subtractive bilingualism Phenomenon in which immersion in a new-language environment leads to deficits in one's native language.

sudden infant death syndrome (SIDS) Death of an infant in the first year of life, typically during sleep, that cannot be explained by a thorough medical examination; the risk of SIDS is highest between 2 and 4 months of age.

symbol Mental entity that represents an external object or event, typically without reflecting its perceptual and behavioral qualities.

symbolic thought Ability to mentally represent and think about external objects and events.

sympathy Feeling of sorrow and concern about another's problems or distress.

synapse Junction between two neurons.

synaptic pruning A process in brain development whereby many previously formed synapses wither away, especially if they have not been used frequently.

synaptogenesis A process in brain development whereby many new synapses appear during the first few years of life.

syntax Rules consistently used to put words together into sentences.

telegraphic speech Short, grammatically incomplete sentences that include lexical (rather than grammatical) words almost exclusively; common in toddlers.

temperament A child's characteristic ways of responding to emotional events, novel stimuli, and personal impulses.

teratogen Potentially harmful substance that can cause damaging effects during prenatal development.

test Instrument designed to assess knowledge, abilities, or skills in a consistent fashion across individuals.

theory Integrated collection of principles and explanations regarding a particular phenomenon.

theory of mind Awareness that people have an inner, psychological life (thoughts, beliefs, feelings, etc.).

theory theory Theoretical perspective proposing that children construct increasingly integrated and complex understandings of physical and mental phenomena.

toxic stress After a lengthy period of distress in childhood, unaccompanied by adequate reassurance, the emerging disorder of becoming hypervigilant, having difficulty in learning and coping, and developing risks for heart disease, depression, and substance abuse.

transgender identity Deeply felt sense of having a gender that is different than the one assigned at birth (i.e., a child born as a boy with a self-identity as a girl, and a child born as a girl with a self-identity as a boy).

traumatic brain injury (TBI) Hits or jolts to the head that alter brain functioning and result in an injury that ranges from a mild concussion to a severe head wound.

underextension Overly restricted meaning for a word that excludes some situations to which the word applies.

uninvolved parenting style Parenting style characterized by a lack of emotional support and a lack of standards regarding appropriate behavior.

universal design Type of instructional modifications in which teachers compare the needs of individual learners to the demands of the curriculum and make adjustments to the way knowledge is represented, the knowledge structures that are used, and the choices that are possible for the learners to display their skills and understandings.

universality In a particular aspect of human development, the commonalities seen in the way virtually all individuals progress.

validity Extent to which a data-collection technique actually assesses what the researcher intends for it to assess.

value Belief that a particular activity has direct or indirect benefits.

vicarious punishment Phenomenon in which a child decreases a certain response after seeing someone else punished for that response.

vicarious reinforcement Phenomenon in which a child increases a certain response after seeing someone else reinforced for that response.

visual-spatial ability Ability to imagine and mentally manipulate two- and three-dimensional figures.

wait time The length of time a teacher pauses, after either asking a question or hearing a student's comment, before saying something.

working memory Component of memory that enables people to actively think about and process a small amount of information.

zone of proximal development (ZPD) Range of tasks that one cannot yet perform independently but can perform with the help and guidance of others.

zygote Cell formed when a male sperm fertilizes a female ovum; with reasonably healthy genes and nurturing conditions in the uterus, it may develop into a fetus and be born as a live infant.

References

Abbate-Daga, G., Marzola, E., Amianto, F., & Fassino, S. (2016). A comprehensive review of psychodynamic treatments for eating disorders. *Eating and Weight Disorders, 21*, 553–580. doi:10.1007/s40519-016-0265-9

Abdul Aziz, S., Fletcher, J., & Bayliss, D. M. (2017). Self-regulatory speech during planning and problem-solving in children with SLI and their typically developing peers. *International Journal of Language & Communication Disorders, 52*, 311–322. doi:10.1111/1460-6984.12273

Abe, J. A. A. (2005). The predictive validity of the five-factor model of personality with preschool age children: A nine year follow-up study. *Journal of Research in Personality, 39*, 423–442.

Abel, E. M., Chung-Canine, U., & Broussard, K. (2013). A quasi-experimental evaluation of a school-based intervention for children experiencing family disruption. *Journal of Evidence-Based Social Work, 10*, 136–144. doi:10.1080/15433714.2012.663666\

Abelev, M. S. (2009). Advancing out of poverty: Social class worldview and its relation to resilience. *Journal of Adolescent Research, 24*(1), 114–141.

Abend, O., Kwiatkowski, T., Smith, N. J., Goldwater, S., & Steedman, M. (2017). Bootstrapping language acquisition. *Cognition, 164*, 116–143. http://dx.doi.org/10.1016/j.cognition.2017.02.009

Abi-Nader, J. (1993). Meeting the needs of multicultural classrooms: Family values and the motivation of minority students. In M. J. O'Hair & S. J. Odell (Eds.), *Diversity and teaching: Teacher education yearbook I (pp. 212–236)*. Fort Worth, TX: Harcourt Brace Jovanovich.

Abikoff, H., Gallagher, R., Wells, K. C., Murray, D. W., Huang, L., Lu, F., & Petkova, E. (2013). Remediating organizational functioning in children with ADHD: Immediate and long-term effects from a randomized controlled trial. *Journal of Consulting and Clinical Psychology, 81*, 113–128. doi:10.1037/a0029648

Abitbol Avtzon, S. (2013). Effect of neuroscience-based cognitive skill training on growth of cognitive deficits associated with learning disabilities in children grades 2–4. *Dissertation Abstracts International Section A, 73*.

Aboud, F. E. (1988). *Children and prejudice*. New York, NY: Basil Blackwell.

Aboud, F. E. (2005). The development of prejudice in childhood and adolescence. In J. F. Dovidio, P. Glick, & L. A. Rudman (Eds.), *On the nature of prejudice: Fifty years after Allport* (pp. 310–326). Malden, MA: Blackwell.

Aboud, F. E., & Fenwick, V. (1999). Exploring and evaluating school-based interventions to reduce prejudice. *Journal of Social Issues, 55*, 767–785. doi:10.1111/0022-4537.00146

Aboud, F. E., & Spears Brown, C. (2013). Positive and negative intergroup contact among children and its effect on attitudes. In G. Hodson & M. Hewstone (Eds.), *Advances in intergroup contact* (pp. 176–199). New York, NY: Psychology Press.

Aboud, F. E., & Yousafzai, A. K. (2015). Global health and development in early childhood. *Annual Review of Psychology, 66*, 433–457. doi:10.1146/annurev-psych-010814-015128

Abubakar, A., Alonso-Arbiol, I., Van de Vijver, F., Murugami, M., Mazrui, L., & Arasa, J. (2013). Attachment and psychological well-being among adolescents with and without disabilities in Kenya: The mediating role of identity formation. *Journal of Adolescence, 36*, 849–857.

Abushaikha, L., & Massah, R. (2013). Perceptions of barriers to paternal presence and contribution during childbirth: An exploratory study from Syria. *Birth: Issues in Perinatal Care, 40*(1), 61–66. doi:10.1111/birt.12030

Acevedo-Polakovich, I., Cousineau, J., Quirk, K., Gerhart, J., Bell, K., & Adomako, M. (2014). Toward an asset orientation in the study of U.S. Latina/o youth: Biculturalism, ethnic identity, and positive youth development. *Counseling Psychologist, 42*, 201–229.

Ackerman, C. M., & Fifield, A. (2005). *Education policy brief: Gifted and talented education*. Retrieved from http://www.rdc.udel.edu/policy_briefs/v19_May.pdf

Ackerman, P. L., & Lohman, D. F. (2006). Individual differences in cognitive functions. In P. A. Alexander & P. H. Winne (Eds.), *Handbook of educational psychology* (2nd ed., pp. 139–161). Mahwah, NJ: Erlbaum.

Adam, E. K. (2004). Beyond quality: Parental and residential stability and children's adjustment. *Current Directions in Psychological Science, 13*, 210–213.

Adam, E. K., Snell, E. K., & Pendry, P. (2007). Sleep timing and quantity in ecological and family context: A nationally representative time-diary study. *Journal of Family Psychology, 21*, 4–19.

Adamović, T. T., Sovilj, M. M., Ribarić-Jankes, K. K., Ljubić, A. A., & Antonović, O. O. (2013). 30. Comparative analysis of reflexes tested in babies immediately after birth. *Clinical Neurophysiology, 124*(7), e16. doi:10.1016/j.clinph.2012.12.039

Adams, B. (2008). Here comes the sun. *Science and Children, 46*(1), 56–58.

Adams-Bass, V., Stevenson, H., & Kotzin, D. (2014). Measuring the meaning of black media stereotypes and their relationship to the racial identity, black history knowledge, and racial socialization of African American youth. *Journal of Black Studies, 45*, 367–395.

Adamson, L. B., & McArthur, D. (1995). Joint attention, affect, and culture. In C. Moore & P. J. Dunham (Eds.), *Joint attention: Its origins and role in development* (pp. 205–221). Hillsdale, NJ: Erlbaum.

Adhikari, D. D. (2016). Reinforcement of correct answers raised stage of performance in traditional nonliterate Nepalese adults. *Behavioral Development Bulletin, 21*(1), 44–49. doi:10.1037/bdb0000018

Adolph, K. E., & Berger, S. E. (2011). Physical and motor development. In M. H. Bornstein & M. E. Lamb (Eds.), *Cognitive development: An advanced textbook* (pp. 257–318). New York, NY: Psychology Press.

Affenito, S., Thompson, D., Dorazio, A., Albertson, A., Loew, A., & Holschuh, N. (2013). Ready-to-eat cereal consumption and the school breakfast program: Relationship to nutrient intake and weight. *Journal of School Health, 83*(1), 28–35.

Afflerbach, P., Cho, B., Kim, J., Crassas, M., & Doyle, B. (2013). Reading: What else matters besides strategies and skills? *Reading Teacher, 66*, 440–448. doi:10.1002/TRTR.1146

Agarwal, P. K., Finley, J. R., Rose, N. S., & Roediger, H. L. (2017). Benefits from retrieval practice are greater for students with lower working memory capacity. *Memory, 25*, 764–771. doi:10.1080/09658211.2016.1220579

Agirdag, O. (2009). All languages welcomed here. *Educational Leadership, 66*(7), 20–25.

Agnich, L. E., Schueths, A. M., James, T. D., & Klibert, J. (2016). The effects of adoption openness and type on the mental health, delinquency, and family relationships of adopted youth. *Sociological Spectrum, 36*, 321–336. doi:10.1080/02732173.2016.1198950

Agostino, A., Johnson, J., & Pascual-Leone, J. (2010). Executive functions underlying multiplicative reasoning: Problem type matters. *Journal of Experimental Child Psychology, 105*, 286–305.

Ahern, A. L., & Hetherington, M. M. (2006). The thin ideal and body image: An experimental study of implicit attitudes. *Psychology of Addictive Behaviors, 20*, 338–342.

Ahmann, E. (2014). Encouraging positive behavior in "challenging" children: The Nurtured Heart Approach™. *Pediatric Nursing, 40*(1), 38–42.

Ahnert, L., Pinquart, M., & Lamb, M. E. (2006). Security of children's relationships with nonparental care providers: A meta-analysis. *Child Development, 74*, 664–679.

Ainsworth, M. D. S. (1963). The development of infant–mother interaction among the Ganda. In B. M. Foss (Ed.), *Determinants of infant behavior* (Vol. 2, pp. 67–104). New York, NY: Wiley.

Ainsworth, M. D. S. (1973). The development of infant–mother attachment. In B. Caldwell & H. Ricciuti (Eds.), *Review of child development research* (Vol. 3, pp. 1–94). Chicago, IL: University of Chicago Press.

Ainsworth, M. D. S., Blehar, M. C., Waters, E., & Wall, S. (1978). *Patterns of attachment*. Hillsdale, NJ: Erlbaum.

Airenti, G. (2016). Playing with expectations: A contextual view of humor development. *Frontiers in Psychology, 7*, Article ID 1392.

Akbas, Y., & Gençtürk, E. (2011). The effect of conceptual change approach to eliminate 9th grade high school students' misconceptions about air pressure. *Educational Sciences: Theory & Practice, 11*(4), 2217–2222.

Akiba, D., & García Coll, C. (2003). Effective interventions with children of color and their families: A contextual developmental approach. In T. B. Smith (Ed.), *Practicing multiculturalism: Internalizing and affirming diversity in counseling and psychology* (pp. 148–177). Boston, MA: Allyn & Bacon.

Akiskal, H. S., & McKinney, W. T. (1973). Depressive disorders: Toward a unified hypothesis. *Science, 162*, 20–29.

Al-Yagon, M. (2012). Adolescents with learning disabilities: Socioemotional and behavioral functioning and attachment relationships with fathers, mothers, and teachers. *Journal of Youth and Adolescence, 41*, 1294–1311. doi:10.1007/s10964-012-9767-6

Alamargot, D., Flouret, L., Larocque, D., Caporossi, G., Pontart, V., Paduraru, C., . . . Fayol, M. (2015). Successful written subject–verb agreement: An online analysis of the procedure used by students in Grades 3, 5 and 12. *Reading and Writing, 28*, 291–312. http://dx.doi.org.unco.idm.oclc.org/10.1007/s11145-014-9525-0

Alan Guttmacher Institute. (2001). *Can more progress be made? Teenage sexual and reproductive behavior in developed countries*. Retrieved from http://www.guttmacher.org/pubs/summaries/euroteens_summ.pdf

Alanís, I. (2013). Where's your partner? Pairing bilingual learners in preschool and primary grade dual language classrooms. *Young Children, 68*(1), 42–46.

Alarcón, G., Cservenka, A., & Nagel, B. J. (2017). Adolescent neural response to reward is related to participant sex and task motivation. *Brain and Cognition, 111*, 51–62. doi:10.1016/j.bandc.2016.10.003

Alarcón-Rubio, D., Sánchez-Medina, J. A., & Prieto-García, J. R. (2014). Executive function and verbal self-regulation in childhood: Developmental linkages between partially internalized private speech and cognitive flexibility. *Early Childhood Research Quarterly, 29*, 95–105. doi:10.1016/j.ecresq.2013.11.002

Alba, J., Calvete, E., Wante, L., Van Beveren, M.-L., & Braet, C. (2018). Early maladaptive schemas as moderators of the association between bullying victimization and depressive symptoms in adolescents. *Cognitive Therapy and Research, 42*(1), 24–35. http://dx.doi.org.unco.idm.oclc.org/10.1007/s10608-017-9874-5

Alber-Morgan, S. (2010). *Using RTI to teach literacy to diverse learners, K–8: Strategies for the inclusive classroom*. Thousand Oaks, CA: Corwin.

Alberti, S. (2012). Making the shifts. *Educational Leadership, 70*(4), 24–27.

Alberts, A., Elkind, D., & Ginsberg, S. (2007). The personal fable and risk-taking in early adolescence. *Journal of Youth and Adolescence, 36*, 71–76.

Aldemir, J., & Kermani, H. (2017). Integrated STEM curriculum: Improving educational outcomes for Head Start children. *Early Child Development & Care, 187*, 1694–1706. doi:10.1080/03004430.2016.1185102

Alderman, M. K. (1990). Motivation for at-risk students. *Educational Leadership, 48*(1), 27–30.

Aldrich, N. J., Tenenbaum, H. R., Brooks, P. J., Harrison, K., & Sines, J. (2011). Perspective taking in children's narratives about jealousy. *British Journal of Developmental Psychology, 29*, 86–109. doi:10.1348/026151010X533238

Alesi, M., Rappo, G., & Pepi, A. (2012). Self-esteem at school and self-handicapping in childhood: Comparison of groups with learning disabilities. *Psychological Reports, 111*, 952–962. doi:10.2466/15.10.PR0.111.6.952-962

Alessandri, S. M., & Lewis, M. (1993). Parental evaluation and its relation to shame and pride in young children. *Sex Roles, 29*, 335–343.

Alexander, J. M., Johnson, K. E., Leibham, M. E., & Kelley, K. (2008). The development of conceptual interests in young children. *Cognitive Development, 23*, 324–334.

Alexander, K., Entwisle, D., & Thompson, M. (1987). School performance, status relations, and the structure of sentiment: Bringing the teacher back in. *American Sociological Review, 52*, 665–682.

Alexander, P. A., Graham, S., & Harris, K. R. (1998). A perspective on strategy research: Progress and prospects. *Educational Psychology Review, 10*, 129–154.

Algood, C. L., Harris, C., & Hong, J. (2013). Parenting success and challenges for families of children with disabilities: An ecological systems analysis. *Journal of Human Behavior in the Social Environment, 23*, 126–136.

Algozzine, B., Babb, J., Algozzine, K., Mraz, M., Kissel, B., Spano, S., & Foxworth, K. (2011). Classroom effects of an Early Childhood Educator Professional Development Partnership. *NHSA Dialog, 14*, 246–262.

Alhaqbani, A., & Riazi, M. (2012). Metacognitive awareness of reading strategy use in Arabic as a second language. *Reading in a Foreign Language, 24*, 231–255.

Alison, J., Negley, S., & Sibthorp, J. (2013). Assessing the social effect of therapeutic recreation summer camp for adolescents with chronic illness. *Therapeutic Recreation Journal, 47*(1), 35–46.

Alland, A. (1983). *Playing with form*. New York, NY: Columbia University Press.

Allara, E., Angelini, P., Gorini, G., Bosi, S., Carreras, G., Gozzi, C. . . . Faggiano, F. (2015). A prevention program for multiple health-compromising behaviors in adolescence: Baseline results from a cluster randomized controlled trial. *Preventive Medicine: An International Journal Devoted to Practice and Theory, 71*, 20–26. doi:10.1016/j.ypmed.2014.12.002

Alleyne, V. (2006). Locked up means locked out: Women, addiction and incarceration. *Women & Therapy, 29*(3/4), 181–194. doi:101300/J015v29n0310

Allodi, M. W. (2010). Goals and values in school: A model developed for describing, evaluating and changing the social climate of learning environments. *Social Psychology of Education, 13*, 207–235. doi:10.1007/s11218-009-9110-6

Allport, G. W. (1954). *The nature of prejudice*. Reading, MA: Addison-Wesley.

Altenhofen, S., Clyman, R., Little, C., Baker, M., & Biringen, Z. (2013). Attachment security in three-year-olds who entered substitute care in infancy. *Infant Mental Health Journal, 34*, 435–445. doi:10.1002/imhj.21401

Alter, A. L., Aronson, J., Darley, J. M., Rodriguez, C., & Ruble, D. N. (2010). Rising to the threat: Reducing stereotype threat by reframing the threat as a challenge. *Journal of Experimental Social Psychology, 46*, 166–171. doi:10.1016/j.jesp.2009.09.014

Altermatt, E. R., & Broady, E. F. (2009). Coping with achievement-related failure: An examination of conversations between friends. *Merrill-Palmer Quarterly, 55*, 454–487.

Altvater-Mackensen, N., Jessen, S., & Grossmann, T. (2017). Brain responses reveal that infants' face discrimination is guided by statistical learning from distributional information. *Developmental Science, 20*(2), 1–8. doi:10.1111/desc.12393

Alvarez, A. L., & Booth, A. E. (2014). Motivated by meaning: Testing the effect of knowledge-infused rewards on preschoolers' persistence. *Child Development, 85*, 783–791. doi:10.1111/cdev.12151

Alvarez, C., Salavati, S., Nussbaum, M., & Milrad, M. (2013). Collboard: Fostering new media literacies in the classroom through collaborative problem solving supported by digital pens and interactive whiteboards. *Computers & Education, 63*, 368–379. doi:10.1016/j.compedu.2012.12.019

Alvermann, D. E., & Moore, D. W. (1991). Secondary school reading. In R. Barr, M. L. Kamil, P. B. Mosenthal, & P. D. Pearson (Eds.), *Handbook of reading research* (Vol. II, pp. 951–983). New York, NY: Longman.

Alwadei, A. H., Benini, R., Mahmoud, A., Alasmari, A., Kamsteeg, E.-J., & Alfadhel, M. (2016). Loss-of-function mutation in RUSC2 causes intellectual disability and secondary microcephaly. *Developmental Medicine & Child Neurology, 58*, 1317–1322. doi:10.1111/dmcn.13250

Alzahrani, T., & Leko, M. (2018). The effects of peer tutoring on the reading comprehension performance of secondary students with disabilities: A systematic review. *Reading &*

Writing Quarterly, 34(1), 1–17. doi:10.1080/10573569.2017.1302372

Aman, M. G., McDougle, C. J., Scahill, L., Handen, B., Arnold, L. E. A., Johnson, C., . . . Wagner, A. (2009). Medication and parent training in children with pervasive developmental disorders and serious behavior problems: Results from a randomized clinical trial. *Journal of the American Academy of Child & Adolescent Psychiatry, 48*, 1143–1154.

Ambrose, D., Allen, J., & Huntley, S. B. (1994). Mentorship of the highly creative. *Roeper Review, 17*, 131–133.

American Academy of Pediatrics Committee on Pediatric AIDS and Committee on Infectious Diseases. (1999). Issues related to human immunodeficiency virus transmission in schools, child care, medical settings, home, and community. *Pediatrics, 104*, 318–324.

American Academy of Pediatrics Committee on Sports Medicine and Fitness. (2000). Intensive training and sports specialization in young athletes. *Pediatrics, 106*, 154–157.

American Academy of Pediatrics Task Force on Infant Sleep Position and Sudden Infant Death Syndrome. (2000). Changing concepts of sudden infant death syndrome: Implications for infant sleeping environment and sleep position. *Pediatrics, 105*, 650–656.

American Academy of Pediatrics. (2016). *American Academy of Pediatrics supports childhood sleep guidelines*. Retrieved January 28, 2017 from https://www.aap.org/en-us/about-the-aap/aap-press-room/pages/American-Academy-of-Pediatrics-Supports-Childhood-Sleep-Guidelines.aspx

American Academy of Pediatrics. (2018). *Gender non-conforming and transgender children*. Retrieved March 24, 2018, from https://www.healthychildren.org/English/ages-stages/gradeschool/Pages/Gender-Non-Conforming-Transgender-Children.aspx

American Association on Intellectual and Developmental Disabilities. (2013). *Definition of intellectual disability*. Retrieved from http://aaidd.org/intellectual-disability/definition#.UsEC9mRDtsg

American Educational Research Association. (2000). *Position on high-stakes testing*. Retrieved from http://www.aera.net/AboutAERA/AERARulesPolicies/AERAPolicyStatements/PositionStatementonHighStakesTesting/tabid/11083/Default.aspx

American Library Association (2011). *Digital literacy definition*. Retrieved from http://connect.ala.org/node/181197.

American Pregnancy Association. (2013a). *Ultrasound: Sonogram*. Retrieved from http://americanpregnancy.org/prenataltesting/ultrasound.html

American Pregnancy Association. (2013b). *Childbirth education classes*. Retrieved from http://americanpregnancy.org/labornbirth/childbirtheducation.html

American Psychiatric Association. (1994). *Diagnostic and statistical manual of mental disorders* (4th ed.). Washington, DC: Author.

American Psychiatric Association. (2000). *Diagnostic and statistical manual of mental disorders* (4th ed., text rev.). Washington, DC: Author.

American Psychiatric Association, DSM-5 Task Force. (2013). *Diagnostic and statistical manual of mental disorders* (5th ed.). Arlington, VA: American Psychiatric Publishing, Inc.

American Psychological Association. (2002). Ethical principles of psychologists and code of conduct. *American Psychologist, 57*, 1060–1073.

American Psychological Association. (2016). *Marriage and divorce*. Retrieved from http://www.apa.org/topics/divorce/

American Speech-Language-Hearing Association, 2018. *Austin spectrum disorder: Treatment*. Retrieved March 27, 2018, from https://www.asha.org/PRPSpecificTopic.aspx?folderid=8589935303§ion=Treatment

American Speech-Language-Hearing Association. (1993). Definitions of communication disorders and variations. *ASHA, 35*(Suppl. 10), 40–41.

Ames, C. (1984). Competitive, cooperative, and individualistic goal structures: A cognitive-motivational analysis. In R. Ames & C. Ames (Eds.), *Research on Motivation in Education: Vol. 1. Student motivation* (pp. 177–207). San Diego, CA: Academic Press.

Ames, C. (1992). Classrooms: Goals, structures, and student motivation. *Journal of Educational Psychology, 84*, 261–271.

Anaby, D., Hand, C., Bradley, L., DiRezze, B., Forhan, M., DiGiacomo, A., & Law, M. (2013). The effect of the environment on participation of children and youth with disabilities: A scoping review. *Disability and Rehabilitation: An International, Multidisciplinary Journal, 35*, 1589–1598. doi: 10.3109/09638288.2012.748840

Anastasi, A., & Urbina, S. (1997). *Psychological testing* (7th ed.). Upper Saddle River, NJ: Prentice Hall.

Anderman, E. M. (2012). Adolescence. In K. R. Harris, S. Graham,T. Urdan, A. G. Bus, S. Major, & H. L. Swanson (Eds.), *APA Educational Psychology Handbook, Vol. 3. Application to teaching and learning* (pp. 43–61). Washington, DC: American Psychological Association. doi:10.1037/13275-003

Anderman, E. M., & Maehr, M. L. (1994). Motivation and schooling in the middle grades. *Review of Educational Research, 64*, 287–309.

Anderman, L. H., Patrick, H., Hruda, L. Z., & Linnenbrink, E. A. (2002). Observing classroom goal structures to clarify and expand goal theory. In C. Midgley (Ed.), *Goals, goal structures, and patterns of adaptive learning* (pp. 243–278). Mahwah, NJ: Erlbaum.

Anderson, C. A., Berkowitz, L., Donnerstein, E., Huesmann, L. R., Johnson, J. D., Linz, D., . . . Wartella, E. (2003). The influence of media violence on youth. *Psychological Science in the Public Interest, 4*, 81–110.

Anderson, D. A. (1994). Lesbian and gay adolescents: Social and developmental considerations. *The High School Journal, 77* (1, 2), 13–19.

Anderson, D. R. (2003). The Children's Television Act: A public policy that benefits children. *Applied Developmental Psychology, 24*, 337–340.

Anderson, E. K. Jr. (2013). The experiences of teachers serving learning disabled students in special education: A phenomenological study. *Dissertation Abstracts International, 73*.

Anderson, E. R., & Greene, S. M. (2013). Beyond divorce: Research on children in repartnered and remarried families. *Family Court Review, 51*, 119–130. doi:10.1111/fcre.12013'

Anderson, G., Spainhower, A., & Sharp, A. (2014). "Where do the bears go?" The value of child-directed play. *Young Children, 69*(2), 8–14.

Anderson, J. (2014). What writing is & isn't. *Educational Leadership, 71*(7), 10–14.

Anderson, J., Ellefson, J., Lashley, J., Miller, A., Olinger, S., Russell, A., . . . Weigman, J. (2010). The Cornerhouse forensic interview protocol: RATAC. *Thomas M. Cooley Journal of Practical & Clinical Law, 12*, 193–331.

Anderson, J. C. (1983). *The architecture of cognition*. Cambridge, MA: Harvard University Press.

Anderson, K. E., Lytton, H., & Romney, D. M. (1986). Mothers' interactions with normal and conduct-disordered boys: Who affects whom? *Developmental Psychology, 22*, 604–609.

Anderson, L. W., & Pellicer, L. O. (1998). Toward an understanding of unusually successful programs for economically disadvantaged students. *Journal of Education for Students Placed at Risk, 3*, 237–263.

Anderson, P., Anderson, V., & Lajoie, G. (1996). The Tower of London Test: Validation and standardization for pediatric populations. *Clinical Neuropsychologist, 10*(1), 54–65.

Anderson, R. C., Nguyen-Jahiel, K., McNurlen, B., Archodidou, A., Kim, S.-Y., Reznitskaya, A., . . . Gilbert, L. (2001). The snowball phenomenon: Spread of ways of talking and ways of thinking across groups of children. *Cognition and Instruction, 19*, 1–46.

Anderson, R. C., Shirey, L., Wilson, P., & Fielding, L. (1987). Interestingness of children's reading materials. In R. Snow & M. Farr (Eds.), *Aptitude, Learning, and Instruction: III. Cognitive and affective process analyses* (pp. 287–299). Hillsdale, NJ: Erlbaum.

Andrade, H. L., Wang, X., Du, Y., & Akawi, R. L. (2009). Rubric-referenced self-assessment and self-efficacy for writing. *Journal of Educational Research, 102*, 287–301. doi:10.3200/JOER.102.4.287-302

Andre, L., Durksen, T., & Volman, M. L. (2017). Museums as avenues of learning for children: A decade of research. *Learning Environments Research, 20*(1), 47–76. doi:10.1007/s10984-016-9222-9

Andreouli, E., Howarth, C., & Sonn, C. (2014). The role of schools in promoting inclusive communities in contexts of diversity. *Journal of Health Psychology, 19*(1), 16–21.

Andres, M., & Pesenti, M. (2015). Finger-based representation of mental arithmetic. In R. C. Kadosh & A. Dowker (Eds.), *Oxford library of psychology. The Oxford handbook of numerical cognition* (pp. 67–88). New York, NY: Oxford University Press.

Andrews, J. F., & Mason, J. M. (1986). Childhood deafness and the acquisition of print concepts. In D. B. Yaden, Jr., & S. Templeton (Eds.), *Metalinguistic awareness and beginning literacy: Conceptualizing what it means to read and write* (pp. 277–290). Portsmouth, NH: Heinemann.

Andriessen, J. (2006). Arguing to learn. In R. K. Sawyer (Ed.), *The Cambridge handbook of the learning sciences* (pp. 443–459). Cambridge, England: Cambridge University Press.

Aneni, E. C., Hamer, D. H., & Gill, C. J. (2013). Systematic review of current and emerging strategies for reducing morbidity from malaria in sickle cell disease. *Tropical Medicine & International Health, 18*(3), 313–327. doi:10.1111/tmi.12056

Ang, S., Rodgers, J., & Wänström, L. (2010). The Flynn effect within subgroups in the U.S.: Gender, race, income, education, and urbanization differences in the NLSY-Children data. *Intelligence, 38*, 367–384.

Angacian, S., Bray, M. A., Kehle, T. J., Byer-Alcorace, G., Theodore, L. A., Cross, K., & DeBiase, E. (2015). School-based intervention for social skills in children from divorced families. *Journal of Applied School Psychology, 31*(4), 315–346.

Anglin, J. M. (1977). *Word, object, and conceptual development.* New York, NY: Norton.

Anjum, A., Gait, P., Cullen, K. R., & White, T. (2010). Schizophrenia in adolescents and young adults. In J. E. Grant & M. N. Potenza (Eds.), *Young adult mental health* (pp. 362–378). New York, NY: Oxford University Press.

Annetta, L. A. (2010). The "I's" have it: A framework for serious educational game design. *Review of General Psychology, 14*, 105–112. doi:10.1037/a0018985

Ansalone, G. (2006). Perceptions of ability and equity in the U.S. and Japan: Understanding the pervasiveness of tracking. *Radical Pedagogy, 8*(1), 1–1.

Anschutz, D., Engels, R., Van Leeuwe, J., & Van Strien, T. (2009). Watching your weight? The relations between watching soaps and music television and body dissatisfaction and restrained eating in young girls. *Psychology & Health, 24*, 1035–1050. doi:10.1080/08870440802192268

Anthony, J. L., & Francis, D. J. (2005). Development of phonological awareness. *Current Directions in Psychological Science, 14*, 255–259.

Anthony, J. L., Lonigan, C. J., & Dyer, S. M. (1996, April). *The development of reading comprehension: Listening comprehension or basic language processes?* Paper presented at the annual meeting of the American Educational Research Association, New York, NY.

Anticich, S. J., Barrett, P. M., Silverman, W., Lacherez, P., & Gillies, R. (2013). The prevention of childhood anxiety and promotion of resilience among preschool-aged children: A universal school based trial. *Advances in School Mental Health Promotion, 6*, 93–121. doi:10.1080/1754730X.2013.784616

Antony, M. M. (2014). "It's not religious, but it's spiritual": Appropriation and the universal spirituality of yoga. *Journal of Communication & Religion, 37*(4), 63–81.

Antshel, K. M., & Khan, F. M. (2008). Is there an increased familial prevalence of psychopathology in children with nonverbal learning disorders? *Journal of Learning Disabilities, 41*(3), 208–217. http://dx.doi.org.unco.idm.oclc.org/10.1177/0022219408317546

Anyon, J. (1988). Social class and the hidden curriculum of work. In G. Handel (Ed.), *Childhood socialization* (pp. 357–382). New York, NY: Aldine de Gruyter.

Aoki, C., Romeo, R. D., & Smith, S. S. (2017). Adolescence as a critical period for developmental plasticity. *Brain Research, 1654*(Part B), 85–86. doi:10.1016/j.brainres.2016.11.026

Apavaloaie, L., Page, T., & Marks, L. D. (2014). Romanian children's representations of negative and self-conscious emotions in a narrative story. *Europe's Journal of Psychology, 10*, 318–335. doi:10.5964/ejop.v10i2.704

Aram, D., Korat, O., & Hassunah-Arafat, S. (2013). The contribution of early home literacy activities to first grade reading and writing achievements in Arabic. *Reading & Writing, 26*, 1517–1536. doi:10.1007/s11145-013-9430-y

Arbib, M. (Ed.). (2005). *Action to language via the mirror neuron system.* New York, NY: Cambridge University Press.

Archer, S. L., & Curtin, S. (2011). Perceiving onset clusters in infancy. *Infant Behavior & Development, 34*, 534–540. doi:10.1016/j.infbeh.2011.07.001

Archibald, L. M. D. (2017). Working memory and language learning: A review. *Child Language Teaching and Therapy, 33*(1), 5–17. http://dx.doi.org/10.1177/0265659016654206

Arcus, D. M. (1991). *Experiential modification of temperamental bias in inhibited and uninhibited children* (Unpublished doctoral dissertation). Harvard University, Cambridge, MA.

Arcus, D. M. (2001). Inhibited and uninhibited children: Biology in the social context. In T. D. Wachs & G. A. Kohnstamm (Eds.), *Temperament in context* (pp. 43–60). Mahwah, NJ: Erlbaum.

Ardila-Rey, A., & Killen, M. (2001). Middle class Colombian children's evaluations of personal, moral, and social-conventional interactions in the classroom. *International Journal of Behavioral Development, 25*, 246–255. doi:10.1080/01650250042000221

Ardila-Rey, A., Killen, M., & Brenick, A. (2009). Moral reasoning in violent contexts: Displaced and non-displaced Colombian children's evaluations of moral transgressions, retaliation, and reconciliation. *Social Development, 18*, 181–209. doi:10.1111/j.1467-9507.2008.00483.x

Arias Pablopulos, C. C. (2016). Investigating the use of the clinical interview method in an elementary mathematics methods course. *Dissertation Abstracts International Section A: Humanities and Social Sciences, 76*(7-A(E)).

Ark, T. J. (2017). Promoting digital access and equity. *School Administrator, 74*(3), 22–26.

Armstrong, T. (2009). *Multiple intelligences in the classroom.* Alexandria, VA: Association for Supervision and Curriculum Development.

Arnett, J. J. (1999). Adolescent storm and stress, reconsidered. *American Psychologist, 54*, 317–326.

Arnold, C. (2015). A way into a child's world. *Nursery World (MA Education Limited), 115* (4371), 23–25.

Arnold, M. L. (2000). Stage, sequence, and sequels: Changing conceptions of morality, post-Kohlberg. *Educational Psychology Review, 12*, 365–383.

Aronson, S. R., & Huston, A. C. (2004). The mother–infant relationship in single, cohabiting, and married families: A case for marriage? *Journal of Family Psychology, 18*, 5–18.

Arredondo, M. M., Hu, X., Satterfield, T., & Kovelman, I. (2017). Bilingualism alters children's frontal lobe functioning for attentional control. *Developmental Science, 20*(3), 1–15. doi:10.1111/desc.12377

Arriaga, X. B., Kumashiro, M., Simpson, J. A., & Overall, N. C. (2018). Revising working models across time: Relationship situations that enhance attachment security. *Personality and Social Psychology Review, 22*(1), 71–96.

Arsenio, W. F., & Lemerise, E. A. (2010). Introduction. In W. F. Arsenio & E. A. Lemerise (Eds.), *Emotions, aggression, and morality in children: Bridging development and psychopathology* (pp. 3–9). Washington, DC: American Psychological Association.

Artman, L., & Cahan, S. (1993). Schooling and the development of transitive inference. *Developmental Psychology, 29*, 753–759.

Artz, S., Kassis, W., & Moldenhauer, S. (2013). Rethinking indirect aggression: The end of the mean girl myth. *Victims & Offenders, 8*, 308–328. doi:10.1080/15564886.2012.756842

Asakura, N., & Inui, T. (2016). A Bayesian framework for false belief reasoning in children: A rational integration of theory-theory and simulation theory. *Frontiers in Psychology, 7*, Article ID 2019.

Asatryan, S. A. (2016). Activities contributing a great deal to the students' interactive skills in foreign language classes. *BCES Conference Proceedings, 14*(2), 16–22.

ASCD. (2014). Double take: The writing standards—and evidence-based practices. *Educational Leadership, 71*(7), 8.

Ashburner, J., Bennett, L., Rodger, S., & Ziviani, J. (2013). Understanding the sensory experiences of young people with autism spectrum disorder: A preliminary investigation. *Australian Occupational Therapy Journal, 60*, 171–180. doi:10.1111/1440-1630.12025

Ashburner, J., Ziviani, J., & Pennington, A. (2012). The Introduction of keyboarding to children with autism spectrum disorders with handwriting difficulties: A help or a hindrance? *Australasian Journal of Special Education, 36*(1), 32–61. doi:10.1017/jse.2012.6

Asher, S. R., & Coie, J. D. (Eds.). (1990). *Peer rejection in childhood*.Cambridge, England: Cambridge University Press.

Asher, S. R., & Parker, J. G. (1989). Significance of peer relationship problems in childhood. In B. H. Schneider, G. Attili, J. Nadel, & R. P. Weissberg (Eds.), *Social competence in developmental perspective* (pp. 5–23). Dordrecht, the Netherlands: Kluwer.

Asher, S. R., & Renshaw, P. D. (1981). Children without friends: Social knowledge and social skill training. In S. R. Asher & J. M. Gottman (Eds.), *The development of children's friendships* (pp. 273–296). Cambridge, England: Cambridge University Press.

Ashkenazi, S., Black, J. M., Abrams, D. A., Hoeft, F., & Menon, V. (2013). Neurobiological underpinnings of math and reading learning disabilities. *Journal of Learning Disabilities, 46*, 549–569.

Ashmore, R., & DelBoca, F. (1976). Psychological approaches. In P. A. Katz (Ed.), *Elimination of racism* (pp. 73–123). New York, NY: Pergamon.

Ashton, P. (1985). Motivation and the teacher's sense of efficacy. In C. Ames & R. Ames (Eds.), *Research on Motivation in Education: Vol. 2. The classroom milieu (pp. 141–174)*. Orlando, FL: Academic Press.

Aslin, R. N. (2014). Infant learning: Historical, conceptual, and methodological challenges. *Infancy, 19*(1), 2–27. doi:10.1111/infa.12036

Aslin, R. N., Saffran, J. R., & Newport, E. L. (1998). Computation of conditional probability statistics by 8-month-old infants. *Psychological Science, 9*, 321–324.

Assis Gomes, C. M., de Araújo, J., Gomes Ferreira, M., & Golino, H. (2014). The validity of the Cattell-Horn-Carroll model on the intra-individual approach. *Behavioral Development Bulletin, 19*(4), 22–30.

Association for Childhood Education International. (2009). *Preparation of elementary teachers* (ACEI position paper). Retrieved from http://www.acei.org/prepel.htm

Association for Middle Level Education. (2011). *Study guide for This We Believe: Keys to educating young adolescents*. Retrieved from http://www.amle.org/AboutAMLE/ThisWeBelieve/tabid/1273/Default.aspx

Assor, A., & Connell, J. P. (1992). The validity of students' self-reports as measures of performance affecting self-appraisals. In D. H. Schunk & J. L. Meece (Eds.), *Student perceptions in the classroom* (pp. 25–47). Hillsdale, NJ: Erlbaum.

Astington, J. W. (1991). Intention in the child's theory of mind. In C. Moore & D. Frye (Eds.), *Children's theories of mind* (pp. 157–172). Hillsdale, NJ: Erlbaum.

Astington, J. W., & Pelletier, J. (1996). The language of mind: Its role in teaching and learning. In D. R. Olson & N. Torrance (Eds.), *The handbook of education and human development: New models of learning, teaching and schooling* (pp. 593–619). Cambridge, MA: Blackwell.

Atherton, O. O., Schofield, T. J., Sitka, A., Conger, R. D., & Robins, R. W. (2016). Unsupervised self-care predicts conduct problems: The moderating roles of hostile aggression and gender. *Journal of Adolescence, 48*, 1–10. doi:10.1016/j.adolescence.2016.01.001

Atkinson, J., & Braddick, O. (2012). Visual attention in the first years: Typical development and developmental disorders. *Developmental Medicine & Child Neurology, 54*, 589–595. doi:10.1111/j.1469-8749.2012.04294.x

Atkinson, M. (1992). *Children's syntax: An introduction to principles and parameters theory*. Oxford, England: Blackwell.

Atkinson, R. C., & Shiffrin, R. M. (1968). Human memory: A proposed system and its control processes. In K. Spence & J. Spence (Eds.), *The psychology of learning and motivation* (Vol. 2, pp. 89–195). New York, NY: Academic Press.

Attie, I., Brooks-Gunn, J., & Petersen, A. (1990). A developmental perspective on eating disorders and eating problems. In M. Lewis & S. M. Miller (Eds.), *Handbook of developmental psychopathology* (pp. 409–420). New York, NY: Plenum Press.

Atun-Einy, O., Berger, S., & Scher, A. (2013). Assessing motivation to move and its relationship to motor development in infancy. *Infant Behavior & Development, 36*, 457–469. doi:10.1016/j.infbeh.2013.03.006

Au, T. K., & Glusman, M. (1990). The principle of mutual exclusivity in word learning: To honor or not to honor? *Child Development, 61*, 1474–1490.

Auger, R. W. (2013). Autism spectrum disorders: A research review for school counselors. *Professional School Counseling, 16*, 256–268.

August, G. J., Piehler, T. F., & Miller, F. G. (2018). Getting "smart" about implementing multi-tiered systems of support to promote school mental health. *Journal of School Psychology, 66*, 85–96. http://dx.doi.org.unco.idm.oclc.org/10.1016/j.jsp.2017.10.001

Augustine, E., Smith, L. B., & Jones, S. S. (2011). Parts and relations in young children's shape-based object recognition. *Journal of Cognition & Development, 12*, 556–572. doi:10.1080/15248372.2011.560586

Austeng, M., Akre, H., Falkenberg, E., Øverland, B., Abdelnoor, M., & Kværner, K. (2013). Hearing level in children with Down syndrome at the age of eight. *Research in Developmental Disabilities, 34*, 2251–2256. doi:10.1016/j.ridd.2013.04.006

Auster, C. J., & Mansbach, C. S. (2012). The gender marketing of toys: An analysis of color and type of toy on the Disney store website. *Sex Roles, 67*(7–8), 375–388. doi:10.1007/s11199-012-0177-8.

Austin, J., Blume, M., & Sánchez, L. (2013). Syntactic development in the L1 of Spanish-English bilingual children. *Hispania, 96*, 542–561. doi:10.1353/hpn.2013.0091

Austin, J. L., & Bevan, D. (2011). Using differential reinforcement of low rates to reduce children's requests for teacher attention. *Journal of Applied Behavior Analysis, 44*, 451–461.

Austin, S. B., Ziyadeh, N. J., Forman, S., Prokop, L. A., Keliher, A., & Jacobs, D. (2008). Screening high school students for eating disorders: Results of a national initiative. *Preventing Chronic Disease, 5*(4). Retrieved from http://www.cdc.gov/pcd/issues/2008/oct/07_0164htm

Austin, W. G. (2012). Relocation, research, and child custody disputes. In K. Kuehnle & L. Drozd (Eds.), *Parenting plan evaluations: Applied research for the family court* (pp. 540–559). New York, NY: Oxford University Press.

Averill, R., Anderson, D., Easton, H., Te Maro, P., Smith, D., & Hynds, A. (2009). Culturally responsive teaching of mathematics: Three models from linked studies. *Journal for Research in Mathematics Education, 40*, 157–186.

Aviezer, O., Sher-Censor, E., & Stein-Lahad, T. (2017). Earliest memories in Israeli kibbutz upbringing: It is parental engagement that makes a difference. *Memory*, 25(10), 1375–1389.http://dx.doi.org.unco.idm.oclc.org/10.1080/09658211.2017.1307991

Awramiuk, E. (2014). Invented spelling—a window on early literacy. *EDUKACJA Quarterly, 130*(5), 112–123.

Ayoub, C. C. (2006). Adaptive and maladaptive parenting: Influence on child development. In H. E. Fitzgerald, R. Zucker, & K. Freeark (Eds. in Chief), & N. F. Watt, C. Ayoub, R. H. Bradley, J. E. Puma, & W. A. LeBouef (Vol. Eds.), *The Crisis in Youth Mental Health: Critical Issues and Effective Programs: Vol. 1. Early intervention programs and policies* (pp. 121–413). Westport, CT: Praeger.

Aziz, S. A., Fletcher, J., & Bayliss, D. M. (2016). The effectiveness of self-regulatory speech training for planning and problem solving in children with specific language impairment. *Journal of Abnormal Child Psychology, 44*, 1045–1059.

Azzam, A. M. (2009/2010). Finding our way back to healthy eating: A conversation with David A. Kessler. *Educational Leadership, 67*(4), 6–10.

Baams, L., Dubas, J. S., Overbeek, G., & Van Aken, M. A. G. (2015). Transitions in body and behavior: A meta-analytic study on the relationship between pubertal development and adolescent sexual behavior. *Journal of Adolescent Health, 56*, 586–598. doi:10.1016/j.jadohealth.2014.11.019

Babaci-Wilhite, Z. Z. (2017). A rights-based approach to science literacy using local languages: Contextualising inquiry-based learning in Africa. *International Review of Education/Internationale Zeitschrift Für Erziehungswissenschaft, 63*, 381–401. doi:10.1007/s11159-017-9644-3

Babkie, A. M., & Provost, M. C. (2002). 20 ways to—select, write, and use metacognitive strategies in the classroom.

Intervention in School & Clinic, 37, 173–177. doi:10.1177/105345120203700307

Baddeley, A. (1981). The concept of working memory: A view of its current state and probable future development. *Cognition, 10*(1–3), 17–23.

Baek, S., & Yoo, H. (2017). Ecological factors influencing emotional/behavioral problems and self-concept in adolescents from low-income families in South Korea. *Issues in Mental Health Nursing, 38*, 733–741.

Bahena, S., Schueler, B. E., McIntyre, J., & Gehlbach, H. (2016). Assessing parent perceptions of school fit: The development and measurement qualities of a survey scale. *Applied Developmental Science, 20*, 121–134. doi:10.1080/10888691.2015.1085308

Bailey, D. H., Littlefield, A., & Geary, D. C. (2012). The codevelopment of skill at and preference for use of retrieval-based processes for solving addition problems: Individual and sex differences from first to sixth grades. *Journal of Experimental Child Psychology, 113*(1), 78–92. doi:10.1016/j.jecp.2012.04.014

Bailey, J. A., Hill, K. G., Guttmannova, K., Oesterle, S., Hawkins, J., Catalano, R. F., & McMahon, R. J. (2013). The association between parent early adult drug use disorder and later observed parenting practices and child behavior problems: Testing alternate models. *Developmental Psychology, 49*, 887–899. doi:10.1037/a0029235

Bailey, J. M., Dunne, M. P., & Martin, N. G. (2000). Genetic and environmental influences on sexual orientation and its correlates in an Australian twin sample. *Journal of Personality and Social Psychology, 78*, 524–536.

Baillargeon, R. (1994). How do infants learn about the physical world? *Current Directions in Psychological Science, 3*, 133–140.

Baillargeon, R. (2004). Infants' physical worlds. *Current Directions in Psychological Science, 13*, 89–94.

Baillargeon, R. H., Morisset, A., Keenan, K., Normand, C. L., Jeyaganth, S., Boivin, M., & Tremblay, R. E. (2011). The development of prosocial behaviors in young children: A prospective population-based cohort study. *The Journal of Genetic Psychology: Research and Theory on Human Development, 172*, 221–251. doi:10.1080/00221325.2010.533719

Baines, E., & Blatchford, P. (2011). Children's games and playground activities in school and their role in development. In A. D. Pellegrini (Ed.), *Oxford library of psychology. The Oxford handbook of the development of play* (pp. 260–283). New York, NY: Oxford University Press.

Baird, A. A. (2010). The terrible twelves. In P. D. Zelazo, M. Chandler, & E. Crone (Eds.), *Developmental social cognitive neuroscience (The Jean Piaget Symposium Series*, pp. 191–207). New York, NY: Psychology Press.

Baird, J. A., & Astington, J. W. (2005). The development of the intention concept: From the observable world to the unobservable mind. In R. R. Hassin, J. S. Uleman, & J. A. Bargh (Eds.), *The new unconscious* (pp. 256–276). New York, NY: Oxford University Press.

Bakari, R. (2000). *The development and validation of an instrument to measure preservice teachers' attitudes toward teaching African American students* (Unpublished doctoral dissertation). University of Northern Colorado, Greeley.

Bakeman, R., & Brownlee, J. R. (1980). The strategic use of parallel play: A sequential analysis. *Child Development, 51*, 873–878.

Baker, C. (1993). *Foundations of bilingual education and bilingualism.* Clevedon, England: Multilingual Matters.

Baker, D. D., Eslinger, P. J., Benavides, M., Peters, E., Dieckmann, N. F., & Leon, J. (2015). The cognitive impact of the education revolution: A possible cause of the Flynn Effect on population IQ. *Intelligence, 49*, 144–158. doi:10.1016/j.intell.2015.01.003

Baker, E., Shelton, K. H., Baibazarova, E., Hay, D. F., & van Goozen, S. M. (2013). Low skin conductance activity in infancy predicts aggression in toddlers 2 years later. *Psychological Science, 24*, 1051–1056. doi:10.1177/0956797612465198

Baker, F. S. (2013). Making the quiet population of internationally adopted children heard through well-informed teacher preparation. *Early Child Development and Care, 183*, 223–246. doi:10.1080/03004430.2012.669757

Baker, F. W. (2010). Media literacy: 21st century literacy skills. In H. H. Jacobs (Ed.), *Curriculum 21: Essential education for a changing world* (pp. 133–152). Alexandria, VA: Association for Supervision and Curriculum Development.

Baker, L., Scher, D., & Mackler, K. (1997). Home and family influences on motivations for reading. *Educational Psychologist, 32*, 69–82.

Baker, R. K., & White, K. M. (2010). Predicting adolescents' use of social networking sites from an extended theory of planned behaviour perspective. *Computers in Human Behavior, 26*, 1591–1597.

Bakermans-Kranenburg, M. J., van IJzendoorn, M. H., & Juffer, F. (2003). Less is more: Meta-analyses of sensitivity and attachment interventions in early childhood. *Psychological Bulletin, 129*, 195–215.

Bakhiet, S. A., & Lynn, R. (2015). Sex differences on the Wechsler Intelligence Scale for Children–III in Bahrain and the United States. *Psychological Reports, 117*, 794–798. doi:10.2466/03.17.PR0.117c26z9

Bal, M. I., Sattoe, J. N. T., Roelofs, P. D. D. M., Bal, R., van Staa, A., &Miedema, H. S. (2016). Exploring effectiveness and effective components of self-management interventions for young people with chronic physical conditions: A systematic review. *Patient Education and Counseling, 99*, 1293–1309. doi:10.1016/j.pec.2016.02.012

Baldwin, D. A. (1993). Early referential understanding: Infants' ability to recognize referential acts for what they are. *Developmental Psychology, 29*, 832–843.

Baldwin, M. W., Keelan, J. P. R., Fehr, B., Enns, V., & Koh-Rangarajoo, E. (1996). Social-cognitive conceptualization of attachment working models: Availability and accessibility effects. *Journal of Personality and Social Psychology, 71*, 94–109.

Ball, J. W., Bindler, R. C., & Cowen, K. J. (2010). *Child health nursing: Partnering with children and families* (2nd ed.). Upper Saddle River, NJ: Pearson Education.

Ball, L. C., Cribbie, R. A., & Steele, J. R. (2013). Beyond gender differences: Using tests of equivalence to evaluate gender similarities. *Psychology of Women Quarterly, 37*(2), 147–154. doi:10.1177/0361684313480483

Balliet, D., Wu, J., & De Dreu, C. K. W. (2014). Ingroup favoritism in cooperation: A meta-analysis. *Psychological Bulletin, 140*(6), 1556-1581. doi:10.1037/a0037737

Balog, H. (2010). A comparison of maternal and child intonation: Does adult input support child production? *Infant Behavior & Development, 33*, 337–345.

Baltes, P. B. (1997). On the incomplete architecture of human ontogeny: Selection, optimization, and compensation as a foundation of developmental theory. *American Psychologist, 52*, 366–380.

Baltes, P. B., Lindenberger, U., & Staudinger, U. M. (2006). Life span theory in developmental psychology. In W. Damon & R. M. Lerner (Eds. in Chief) & R. M. Lerner (Vol. Ed.), *Handbook of Child Psychology: Vol. 1. Theoretical models of human development* (6th ed., pp. 569–664). Hoboken, NJ: Wiley.

Bandura, A. (1965). Influence of models' reinforcement contingencies on the acquisition of imitative responses. *Journal of Personality and Social Psychology, 1*, 589–595.

Bandura, A. (1977). *Social learning theory.* Englewood Cliffs, NJ: Prentice Hall.

Bandura, A. (1986). *Social foundations of thought and action: A social cognitive theory.* Englewood Cliffs, NJ: Prentice Hall, Inc.

Bandura, A. (1997). *Self-efficacy: The exercise of control.* New York, NY: Freeman.

Bandura, A. (2006). Toward a psychology of human agency. *Perspectives on Psychological Science, 1*, 164–180.

Bandura, A. (2012). Social cognitive theory. In P. M. Van Lange, A. W. Kruglanski, & E. Higgins (Eds.), *Handbook of theories of social psychology* (Vol. 1, pp. 349–373). Thousand Oaks, CA: Sage.

Bandura, A. (2016). *Moral disengagement: How people do harm and live with themselves.* New York, NY: Worth Publishers.

Bandura, A., Barbaranelli, C., Caprara, G. V., & Pastorelli, C. (2001). Self-efficacy beliefs as shapers of children's aspirations and career trajectories. *Child Development, 72*, 187–206.

Bandura, A., & Mischel, W. (1965). Modification of self-imposed delay of reward through exposure to live and symbolic models. *Journal of Personality and Social Psychology, 2,* 698–705.

Banerjee, R., Alsalman, A., & Alqafari, S. (2016). Supporting sociodramatic play in preschools to promote language and literacy skills of English language learners. *Early Childhood Education Journal, 44,* 299–305.

Banks, J. A. (1994). *An introduction to multicultural education.* Needham Heights, MA: Allyn & Bacon.

Banks, J. A., & Banks, C. A. M. (Eds.). (1995). *Handbook of research on multicultural education.* New York, NY: Macmillan.

Bannister, E. M., Jakubec, S. L., & Stein, J. A. (2003). "Like, what am I supposed to do?": Adolescents' health concerns in their dating relationships. *Canadian Journal of Nursing Research, 35*(2), 16–33.

Barab, S. A., & Plucker, J. A. (2002). Smart people or smart contexts? Cognition, ability, and talent development in an age of situated approaches to knowing and learning. *Educational Psychologist, 37,* 165–182.

Baraldi, C., & Iervese, V. (2010). Dialogic mediation in conflict resolution education. *Conflict Resolution Quarterly, 27,* 423–445. doi:10.1002/crq.20005

Baranowski, T., Baranowski, J., Thompson, D., Buday, R., Jago, R., Griffith, M. J., . . . Watson, K. B. (2011). Video game play, child diet, and physical activity behavior change: A randomized clinical trial. *American Journal of Preventive Medicine, 40*(1), 33–38. doi:10.1016/j.amepre.2010.09.029

Barber, J. G., & Delfabbro, P. H. (2004). *Children in foster care.* New York, NY: Routledge.

Barbieri, N., Clipper, S. J., & Vasquez, A. G. (2016). Adolescent gang membership and differences in ethnic identity, esteem, and efficacy. *Deviant Behavior, 37,* 1429–1442. http://dx.doi.org.unco.idm.oclc.org/10.1080/01639625.2016.1185870

Bardack, S., & Obradović, J. (2017). Emotional behavior problems, parent emotion socialization, and gender as determinants of teacher–child closeness. *Early Education and Development, 28,* 507–524.

Bardi, L. (2017). Biological motion perception. In B. Hopkins, E. Geangu, & S. Linkenauger (Eds.), *The Cambridge encyclopedia of child development* (pp. 271–276). New York, NY: Cambridge University Press. http://dx.doi.org.unco.idm.oclc.org/10.1017/9781316216491.047

Barga, N. K. (1996). Students with learning disabilities in education: Managing a disability. *Journal of Learning Disabilities, 29,* 413–421.

Barkatsas, A., Kasimatis, K., & Gialamas, V. (2009). Learning secondary mathematics with technology: Exploring the complex interrelationship between students' attitudes, engagement, gender and achievement. *Computers & Education, 52*(3), 562–570.

Barker, C. E., Bird, C. E., Pradhan, A., & Shakya, G. (2007). Support to the Safe Motherhood Programme in Nepal: An integrated approach. *Reproductive Health Matters, 15*(30), 1–10.

Barker, L. A. (2016). Working memory in the classroom: An inside look at the central executive. *Applied Neuropsychology: Child, 5,* 180–193. doi:10.1080/21622965.2016.1167493

Barkley, R. A. (1998). *Attention-deficit hyperactivity disorder: A handbook for diagnosis and treatment* (2nd ed.). New York, NY: Guilford Press.

Barlow, K. (2010). Sharing food, sharing values: Mothering and empathy in Murik society. *Ethos, 38,* 339–353. doi:10.1111/j.1548-1352.2010.01154.x

Barnas, M. V., & Cummings, E. M. (1994). Caregiver stability and toddlers' attachment-related behaviors towards caregivers in day care. *Infant Behavior and Development, 17,* 141–147.

Barnes, J. S., & Spray, C. M. (2013). Social comparison in physical education: An examination of the relationship between two frames of reference and engagement, disaffection, and physical self-concept. *Psychology in the Schools, 50,* 1060–1072. doi:10.1002/pits.21726'

Barnes, M., Davis, K., Mancini, M., Ruffin, J., Simpson, T., & Casazza, K. (2016). Setting adolescents up for success: Promoting a policy to delay high school start times. *Journal of School Health, 86,* 552–557. doi:10.1111/josh.1240

Barnett, J. E. (2001, April). *Study strategies and preparing for exams: A survey of middle and high school students.* Paper presented at the annual meeting of the American Educational Research Association, Seattle, WA.

Barnett, W. S. (1992). Benefits of compensatory preschool education. *Journal of Human Resources, 27,* 279–312.

Barnyak, N., & McNelly, T. (2016). The Literacy skills and motivation to read of children enrolled in Title I: A comparison of electronic and print nonfiction books. *Early Childhood Education Journal, 44,* 527–536. doi:10.1007/s10643-015-0735-0

Baron-Cohen, S., Tager-Flusberg, H., & Cohen, D. J. (1993). *Understanding other minds: Perspectives from autism.* Oxford, England: Oxford University Press.

Baroody, A. E., & Diamond, K. E. (2013). Measures of preschool children's interest and engagement in literacy activities: Examining gender differences and construct dimensions. *Early Childhood Research Quarterly, 28,* 291–301. doi:10.1016/j.ecresq.2012.07.002

Baroody, A. J., Tiilikainen, S. H., & Tai, Y.-C. (2006). The application and development of an addition goal sketch. *Cognition and Instruction, 24,* 123–170.

Barrett, J. G. (2005). Conduct disorders. In C. B. Fisher & R. M. Lerner(Eds.), *Encyclopedia of applied developmental science* (Vol. 1, pp. 294–295). Thousand Oaks, CA: Sage.

Barrett, J. G. (2005). Conduct disorders. In C. B. Fisher & R. M. Lerner (Eds.), *Encyclopedia of applied developmental science* (Vol. 1, pp. 294–295). Thousand Oaks, CA: Sage.

Barrett, P., Zhang, Y., Davies, F., & Barrett, L. (2015). *Clever classrooms.* Manchester, England: University of Salford. Retrieved from http://www.salford.ac.uk/cleverclassrooms/1503-Salford-Uni-Report-DIGITAL.pdf

Barringer, C., & Gholson, B. (1979). Effects of type and combination of feedback upon conceptual learning by children: Implications for research in academic learning. *Review of Educational Research, 49,* 459–478.

Barry, C. T., & Kauten, R. L. (2014). Nonpathological and pathological narcissism: Which self-reported characteristics are most problematic in adolescents? *Journal of Personality Assessment, 96,* 212–219. doi:10.1080/00223891.2013.830264

Barth, A. E., & Elleman, A. (2017). Evaluating the impact of a multistrategy inference intervention for middle-grade struggling readers. *Language, Speech, and Hearing Services in Schools, 48*(1), 31–41.

Barth, R. P. (2009). Preventing child abuse and neglect with parent training: Evidence and opportunities. *Future of Children, 19*(2), 95–118.

Barton, K. C., & Levstik, L. S. (1996). "Back when God was around and everything": Elementary children's understanding of historical time. *American Educational Research Journal, 33,* 419–454.

Bartoszuk, K., & Pittman, J. F. (2010). Profiles of identity exploration and commitment across domains. *Journal of Child and Family Studies, 19,* 444–450.

Bartsch, K., & Wellman, H. M. (1995). *Children talk about the mind.* New York, NY: Oxford University Press.

Bascandziev, I., & Harris, P. L. (2016). The beautiful and the accurate: Are children's selective trust decisions biased? *Journal of Experimental Child Psychology, 152,* 92–105. doi:10.1016/j.jecp.2016.06.017

Basinger, K. S., Gibbs, J. C., & Fuller, D. (1995). Context and the measurement of moral judgment. *International Journal of Behavioral Development, 18,* 537–556.

Basso, K. H. (1984). Stalking with stories: Names, places, and moral narratives among the Western Apache. In E. M. Bruner & S. Plattner (Eds.), *Text, play and story: The construction and reconstruction of self and society* (pp. 19–55). Washington, DC: American Ethnological Society.

Basso, K. H. (1990). "To give up on words": Silence in Western Apache culture. In D. Carbaugh (Ed.), *Communication textbook series: Intercultural communication. Cultural communication and intercultural contact* (pp. 303-320). Hillsdale, NJ, US: Lawrence Erlbaum Associates, Inc. (Reprinted from Southwest Journal of Anthropology, 1970, 26, 213-230)

Basu, M., Krishnan, A., & Weber-Fox, C. (2010). Brainstem correlates of temporal auditory processing in children with specific language impairment. *Developmental Science, 13,* 77–91.

Bates, E., & MacWhinney, B. (1987). Competition, variation, and language learning. In B. MacWhinney (Ed.), *Mechanisms of language acquisition* (pp. 157–193). Hillsdale, NJ: Erlbaum.

Bates, T. C., Lewis, G. J., & Weiss, A. (2013). Childhood socioeconomic status amplifies genetic effects on adult intelligence. *Psychological Science, 24,* 2111–2116.

Batson, C. D. (1991). *The altruism question: Toward a social-psychological answer.* Hillsdale, NJ: Erlbaum.

Batson, C. D., & Thompson, E. R. (2001). Why don't moral people act morally? Motivational considerations. *Current Directions in Psychological Science, 10,* 54–57.

Battistich, V. (2003). Effects of a school-based program to enhance prosocial development on children's peer relations and social adjustment. *Journal of Research in Character Education, 1*(1), 1–17.

Battistich, V., Solomon, D., Kim, D., Watson, M., & Schaps, E. (1995). Schools as communities, poverty levels of student populations, and students' attitudes, motives, and performance: A multilevel analysis. *American Educational Research Journal, 32,* 627–658.

Battistich, V., Solomon, D., Watson, M., & Schaps, E. (1997). Caring school communities. *Educational Psychologist, 32,* 137 151.

Bauer, K. W., Hearst, M. O., Escoto, K., Berge, J. M., & Neumark-Sztainer, D. (2012). Parental employment and work-family stress: Associations with family food environments. *Social Science & Medicine, 75,* 496–504. doi:10.1016/j.socscimed.2012.03.026

Bauer, P. J., DeBoer, T., & Lukowski, A. F. (2007). In the language of multiple memory systems: Defining and describing developments in long-term declarative memory. In L. M. Oakes & P. J. Bauer (Eds.), *Short- and long-term memory in infancy and early childhood: Taking the first steps toward remembering* (pp. 240–270). New York, NY: Oxford University Press.

Bauer, P. J., & Dow, G. A. (1994). Episodic memory in 16- and 20-month-old children: Specifics not generalized, but not forgotten. *Developmental Psychology, 30,* 403–417.

Bauerlein, V. (2013, January 31). The new scripts for teaching handwriting is no script at all. *Wall Street Journal—Eastern Edition,* A1–A12.

Baum, J., & Bird, B. (2010). The successful intelligence of high-growth entrepreneurs: Links to new venture growth. *Organization Science, 21*(2), 397–412. doi:10.1287/orsc.1090.0445

Bauman, S. (2011). *Cyberbullying: What counselors need to know.* Alexandria, VA: American Counseling Association.

Baumeister, R. F., Campbell, J. D., Krueger, J. I., & Vohs, K. D. (2003). Does high self-esteem cause better performance, interpersonal success, happiness, or healthier lifestyles? *Psychological Science in the Public Interest, 4*(1), 1–44.

Bauminger-Zviely, N., & Agam-Ben-Artzi, G. (2014). Young friendship in HFASD and typical development: Friend versus non-friend comparisons. *Journal of Autism & Developmental Disorders, 44,* 1733–1748. doi:10.1007/s10803-014-2052-7

Bauminger, N., & Kimhi-Kind, I. (2008). Social information processing, security of attachment, and emotion regulation in children with learning disabilities. *Journal of Learning Disabilities, 41,* 315–332.

Baumrind, D. (1967). Child care practices anteceding three patterns of preschool behavior. *Genetic Psychology Monographs, 75,* 43–88.

Baumrind, D. (1971). Current patterns of parental authority. *Developmental Psychology Monographs, 4*(1), 103.

Baumrind, D. (1980). New directions in socialization research. *American Psychologist, 35,* 639–652.

Baumrind, D. (1989). Rearing competent children. In W. Damon (Ed.), *Child development today and tomorrow* (pp. 349–378). San Francisco, CA: Jossey-Bass.

Baumrind, D. (1991). Parenting styles and adolescent development. In R. Lerner, A. C. Petersen, & J. Brooks-Gunn (Eds.), *The encyclopedia of adolescence (pp. 746–758).* New York, NY: Garland Press.

Baumrind, D. (2013). Authoritative parenting revisited: History and current status. In R. E. Larzelere, A. Morris, & A. W. Harrist (Eds.), *Authoritative parenting: Synthesizing nurturance and discipline for optimal child development* (pp. 11–34). Washington, DC: American Psychological Association. doi:10.1037/13948-002

Baumrind, D., Larzelere, R. E., & Owens, E. B. (2010). Effects of preschool parents' power assertive patterns and practices on adolescent development. *Parenting: Science and Practice, 10,* 157–201. doi:10.1080/15295190903290790

Baurain, C., & Nader-Grosbois, N. (2013). Theory of mind, socio-emotional problem-solving, socio-emotional regulation in children with intellectual disability and in typically developing children. *Journal of Autism and Developmental Disorders, 43,* 1080–1097. doi:10.1007/s10803-012-1651-4

Bayazit, I. (2013). An investigation of problem solving approaches, strategies, and models used by the 7th and 8th grade students when solving real-world problems. *Educational Sciences: Theory & Practice, 13,* 1920–1927. doi:10.12738/estp.2013.3.1419

Bayer, J. K., Mundy, L., Stokes, I., Hearps, S., Allen, N., & Patton, G. (2018). Bullying, mental health and friendship in Australian primary school children. *Child and Adolescent Mental Health.* Advance online publication. http://dx.doi.org.unco.idm.oclc.org/10.1111/camh.12261

Bayley, N. (2005). *Bayley Scales of Infant Development* (3rd ed.). San Antonio, TX: Psychological Corporation.

Bayley, N. (2006). *Bayley Scales of Infant and Toddler Development—Third edition: Administration manual.* San Antonio, TX: Harcourt Assessment.

Beach, S. R. H., Barton, A. W., Lei, M. K., Mandara, J., Wells, A. C., Kogan, S. M., & Brody, G. H. (2016). Decreasing substance use risk among African American youth: Parent-based mechanisms of change. Prevention Science, 17, 572–583. doi:10.1007/s11121-016-0651-6

Beal, C. R. (1996). The role of comprehension monitoring in children's revision. *Educational Psychology Review, 8,* 219–238.

Beal, S., & Crockett, L. (2013). Adolescents' occupational and educational goals: A test of reciprocal relations. *Journal of Applied Developmental Psychology, 34,* 219–229. doi:10.1016/j.appdev.2013.04.005

Bean Thompson, S. (2013). Don't forget the tweens. *Public Libraries, 52*(6), 29–30.

Bear, D. R., Invernizzi, M., Templeton, S., & Johnston, F. (2008). *Words their way: Word study for phonics, vocabulary, and spelling instruction* (4th ed.). Upper Saddle River, NJ: Pearson Prentice Hall.

Bearison, D. J. (1998). Pediatric psychology and children's medical problems. In W. Damon (Series Ed.), & I. E. Sigel, & K. A. Renninger (Vol. Eds.), *Handbook of Child Psychology: Vol. 4. Child psychology in practice* (5th ed., pp. 635–711). New York, NY: Wiley.

Beauchaine, T. P., Gatzke-Kopp, L., Neuhaus, E., Chipman, J., Reid, M., & Webster-Stratton, C. (2013). Sympathetic- and parasympathetic-linked cardiac function and prediction of externalizing behavior, emotion regulation, and prosocial behavior among preschoolers treated for ADHD. *Journal of Consulting and Clinical Psychology, 81*(3), 481–493. doi:10.1037/a0032302

Bebko, J. M., McMorris, C. A., Metcalfe, A., Ricciuti, C., & Goldstein, G. (2014). Language proficiency and metacognition as predictors of spontaneous rehearsal in children. *Canadian Journal of Experimental Psychology/Revue canadienne de psychologie expérimentale, 68*(1), 46–58. doi:10.1037/cep0000013

Beckert, T. E., Strom, P. S., Strom, R. D., Darre, K., & Weed, A. (2008). Single mothers of early adolescents: Perceptions of competence. *Adolescence, 43*(170), 275–290.

Beckmeyer, J., & Malacane, M. (2018). Patterns of adolescents' romantic activities: Associations with psychosocial adjustment. *Journal of Child and Family Studies.* Advance online publication. http://dx.doi.org.unco.idm.oclc.org/10.1007/s10826-018-1108-2

Beeri, A., & Lev-Wiesel, R. (2012). Social rejection by peers: A risk factor for psychological distress. *Child and Adolescent Mental Health, 17,* 216–221. doi:10.1111/j.1475-3588.2011.00637.x

Beers, S. F., & Nagy, W. E. (2009). Syntactic complexity as a predictor of adolescent writing quality: Which measures? Which genre? *Reading and Writing*, *22*, 185–200.

Behnke, A. O., Gonzalez, L. M., & Cox, R. B. (2010). Latino students in new arrival states: Factors and services to prevent youth from dropping out. *Hispanic Journal of Behavioral Sciences*, *32*, 385–409. doi:10.1177/0739986310374025

Behrens, K. Y., Haltigan, J. D., & Bahm, N. I. G. (2016). Infant attachment, adult attachment, and maternal sensitivity: Revisiting the intergenerational transmission gap. *Attachment & Human Development*, *18*, 337–353. doi:10.1080/14616734.2016.1167095

Bei, B., Byrne, M. L., Ivens, C., Waloszek, J., Woods, M. J., Dudgeon, P., . . . Allen, N. B. (2013). Pilot study of a mindfulness-based, multi-component, in-school group sleep intervention in adolescent girls. *Early Intervention in Psychiatry*, *7*, 213–220.

Beier, J. S., & Carey, S. (2014). Contingency is not enough: Social context guides third-party attributions of intentional agency. *Developmental Psychology*, *50*, 889–902. doi:10.1037/a0034171

Beier, J. S., Over, H., & Carpenter, M. (2014). Young children help others to achieve their social goals. *Developmental Psychology*, *50*, 934–940. doi:10.1037/a0033886

Beijers, R., Cillessen, L., & Zijlmans, M. A. C. (2016). An experimental study on mother-infant skin-to-skin contact in full-terms. *Infant Behavior & Development*, *43*, 58–65. doi:10.1016/j.infbeh.2016.01.001

Bekkhus, M., Rutter, M., Barker, E. D., & Borge, A. I. H. (2011). The role of pre- and postnatal-timing of family risk factors on child behavior at 36 months. *Journal of Abnormal Child Psychology*, *39*, 611–621. doi:10.1007/s10802-010-9477-z

Belenky, M. F., Bond, L. A., & Weinstock, J. S. (1997). *A tradition that has no name: Nurturing the development of people, families, and communities.* New York, NY: Basic Books.

Belfield, C. R., Nores, M., Barnett, S., & Schweinhart, L. (2008). The High/Scope Perry Preschool Program: Cost-benefit analysis using data from the age-40 follow-up. In A. Schmitz & R. R. Zerbe (Eds.), *Applied benefit-cost analysis* (Elgar Reference Collection, International Library of Critical Writings in Economics, Vol. 231, pp. 103–131). Cheltenham, England, and Northampton, MA: Elgar.

Belfiore, P. J., & Hornyak, R. S. (1998). Operant theory and application to self-monitoring in adolescents. In D. H. Schunk & B. J. Zimmerman (Eds.), *Self-regulated learning: From teaching to self-reflective practice (pp. 184–202).* New York, NY: Guilford Press.

Bell, L. A. (1989). Something's wrong here and it's not me: Challenging the dilemmas that block girls' success. *Journal for the Education of the Gifted*, *12*, 118–130.

Bell, M. A., & Deater-Deckard, K. (2007). Biological systems and the development of self-regulation: Integrating behavior, genetics, and psychophysiology. *Journal of Developmental and Behavioral Pediatrics*, *28*, 409–420.

Bell, N. L., McConnell, J. E., Lassiter, K. S., & Matthews, T. (2013). The validity of the Universal Nonverbal Intelligence Test with the Woodcock-Johnson III Tests of Achievement. *North American Journal of Psychology*, *15*, 243–256.

Bell, R. Q. (1988). Contributions of human infants to caregiving and social interaction. In G. Handel (Ed.), *Childhood socialization* (pp. 103–122). New York, NY: Aldine de Gruyter.

Bell, S. M. (2017). Two nonverbal screeners: The Universal Multidimensional Abilities Scales and the Universal Nonverbal Intelligence Test-Group Abilities Test. In R. S. McCallum (Ed.), *Handbook of nonverbal assessment* (pp. 217–227). Cham, Switzerland: Springer International Publishing. http://dx.doi.org/10.1007/978-3-319-50604-3_13

Belsky, J., & Eggebeen, D. (1991). Early and extensive maternal employment and young children's socio-emotional development: Children of the National Longitudinal Survey of Youth. *Journal of Marriage and Family*, *53*, 1083–1098.

Belsky, J., Gilstrap, B., & Rovine, M. (1984). The Pennsylvania Infant and Family Development Project, I: Stability and change in mother–infant and father–infant interaction in a family setting at one, three, and nine months. *Child Development*, *55*, 692–705.

Bem, S. L. (1981). Gender schema theory: A cognitive account of sex typing. *Psychological Review*, *88*, 354–364.

Bem, S. L. (1989). Genital knowledge and gender constancy in preschool children. *Child Development*, *60*, 649–662.

Benbenishty, R., & Schmid, H. (2013). Public attitudes toward the identification and reporting of alleged maltreatment cases among social groups in Israel. *Children and Youth Services Review*, *35*, 332–339. doi:10.1016/j.childyouth.2012.11.013

Benbow, C. P., & Lubinski, D. (2009). Extending Sandra Scarr's ideas about development to the longitudinal study of intellectually precocious youth. In K. McCartney, & R. A. Weinberg (Eds.), *Annual meeting of the Association for Psychological Science (APS), 19th, May 2007, Washington, DC, US; This festschrift for Sandra Scarr was organized and presented at the aforementioned conference* (pp. 231–252). New York, NY: Psychology Press.

Beneke, M. M., & Cheatham, G. G. (2015). Speaking up for African American English: Equity and inclusion in early childhood settings. *Early Childhood Education Journal*, *43*, 127–134. doi:10.1007/s10643-014-0641-x

Benko, S. L. (2012). Scaffolding: An ongoing process to support adolescent writing development. *Journal of Adolescent & Adult Literacy*, *56*, 291–300. doi:10.1002/JAAL.00142

Benn, P. (2016). Expanding non-invasive prenatal testing beyond chromosomes 21, 18, 13, X and Y. *Clinical Genetics*, *90*, 477-485. doi:10.1111/cge.12818

Benner, A. D., Boyle, A. E., & Sadler, S. (2016). Parental involvement and adolescents' educational success: The roles of prior achievement and socioeconomic status. *Journal of Youth and Adolescence*, *45*, 1053–1064. doi:10.1007/s10964-016-0431-4

Bennett, A., Bridglall, B. L., Cauce, A. M., Everson, H. T., Gordon, E. W., Lee, C. D., . . . Stewart, J. K. (2007). Task force report on the affirmative development of academic ability: All students reaching the top: Strategies for closing academic achievement gaps. In E. W. Gordon & B. L. Bridglall (Eds.), *Affirmative development: Cultivating academic ability* (pp. 239–275). Lanham, MD: Rowman.

Bennett, R. E., Gottesman, R. L., Rock, D. A., & Cerullo, F. (1993). Influence of behavior perceptions and gender on teachers' judgments of students' academic skill. *Journal of Educational Psychology*, *85*, 347–356.

Benoit, D., & Parker, K. C. (1994). Stability and transmission of attachment across three generations. *Child Development*, *65*, 1444–1456.

Benson, N. N., Kranzler, J. H., & Floyd, R. G. (2016). Examining the integrity of measurement of cognitive abilities in the prediction of achievement: Comparisons and contrasts across variables from higher-order and bifactor models. *Journal of School Psychology*, *58*, 1–19. doi:10.1016/j.jsp.2016.06.001

Benton, S. L. (1997). Psychological foundations of elementary writing instruction. In G. D. Phye (Ed.), *Handbook of academic learning: Construction of knowledge* (pp. 235–264). San Diego, CA: Academic Press.

Berdan, L. E., Keane, S. P., & Calkins, S. D. (2008). Temperament and externalizing behavior: Social preference and perceived acceptance as protective factors. *Developmental Psychology*, *44*, 957–968. doi:10.1037/0012-1649.44.4.957

Berdasco-Muñoz, E., Nishibayashi, L.-L., Baud, O., Biran, V., & Nazzi, T. (2017). Early segmentation abilities in preterm infants. *Infancy*, *23*(2), 268–287.

Bereiter, C. (1994). Implications of postmodernism for science, or, science as progressive discourse. *Educational Psychologist*, *29*, 3–12.

Berencsi, A., Gombos, F., & Kovács, I. (2016). Capacity to improve fine motor skills in Williams syndrome. *Journal of Intellectual Disability Research*, *60*, 956–968. doi:10.1111/jir.12317

Berenstain, S., & Berenstain, J. (1990). *The Berenstain bears' trouble with pets.* New York, NY: Random House.

Berge, J. M., MacLehose, R. F., Larson, N., Laska, M., & Neumark-Sztainer, D. (2016). Family food preparation and its effects on adolescent dietary quality and eating patterns. *Journal of Adolescent Health*, *59*, 530–536. doi:10.1016/j.jadohealth.2016.06.007

Bergen, D., & Fromberg, D. P. (2009). Play and social interaction in middle childhood. *Phi Delta Kappan*, *90*, 426–430.

Berger-Jenkins, E. E., Jarpe-Ratner, E., Giorgio, M., Squillaro, A., McCord, M., & Meyer, D. (2017). Engaging caregivers in school-based obesity prevention initiatives in a predominantly Latino immigrant community: A qualitative analysis. *Journal of Nutrition Education & Behavior*, *49*(1), 53–59.e1. doi:10.1016/j.jneb.2016.08.004

Berger, L. M., Paxson, C., & Waldfogel, J. (2009). Income and child development. *Children and Youth Services Review*, *31*, 978–989.

Berger, R. (2000). Remarried families of 2000: Definitions, descriptions, and interventions. In W. C. Nichols, M. A. Pace-Nichols, D. S. Becvar, & A. Y. Napier (Eds.), *Handbook of family development* (pp. 371–390). New York, NY: Wiley.

Bergeron, R., & Floyd, R. G. (2006). Broad cognitive abilities of children with mental retardation: An analysis of group and individual profiles. *American Journal on Mental Retardation*, *111*, 417–432.

Bergin, C. A., & Bergin, D. A. (2009/2010). Sleep: The E-zzz intervention. *Educational Leadership*, *67*(4), 44–47.

Bergold, S., Wendt, H., Kasper, D., & Steinmayr, R. (2017). Academic competencies: Their interrelatedness and gender differences at their high end. *Journal of Educational Psychology*, *109*, 439–449.http://dx.doi.org.unco.idm.oclc.org/10.1037/edu0000140

Berk, L. E. (1994). Why children talk to themselves. *Scientific American*, *271*, 78–83.

Berkeley, S., & Riccomini, P. J. (2013). QRAC-the-code: A comprehension monitoring strategy for middle school social studies textbooks. *Journal of Learning Disabilities*, *46*, 154–165. doi:10.1177/0022219411409412

Berken, J. A., Gracco, V. L., & Klein, D. (2017). Early bilingualism, language attainment, and brain development. *Neuropsychologia*, *98*, 220–227.

Berkovits, L., & Baker, B. (2014). Emotion dysregulation and social competence: Stability, change and predictive power. *Journal of Intellectual Disability Research*, *58*, 765–776. doi:10.1111/jir.12088

Berlin, L. J., Cassidy, J., & Appleyard, K. (2008). The influence of early attachments on other relationships. In J. Cassidy & P. R. Shaver (Eds.), *Handbook of attachment: Theory, research, and clinical applications* (2nd ed., pp. 333–347). New York, NY: Guilford Press.

Berliner, D. (2009). *Poverty and potential: Out-of-school factors and school success*. Boulder, CO, and Tempe, AZ: Education and the Public Interest Center & Education Policy Research. Retrieved from http://epicpolicy.org/publication/poverty-and-potential

Bernard, M., & Popard Newell, E. (2013). Students affected by neglect. In E. Rossen & R. Hull (Eds.), *Supporting and educating traumatized students: A guide for school-based professionals* (pp. 203–217). New York, NY: Oxford University Press.

Bernard, R. S., Cohen, L. L., & Moffet, K. (2009). A token economy for exercise adherence in pediatric cystic fibrosis: A single-subject analysis. *Journal of Pediatric Psychology*, *34*, 354–365.

Berndt, T. J. (1992). Friendship and friends' influence in adolescence. *Current Directions in Psychological Science*, *1*, 156–159.

Berndt, T. J., & Hoyle, S. G. (1985). Stability and change in childhood and adolescent friendships. *Developmental Psychology*, *21*, 1007–1015.

Berndt, T. J., & Keefe, K. (1995). Friends' influence on adolescents' adjustment to school. *Child Development*, *66*, 1312–1329.

Berndt, T. J., & Keefe, K. (1996). Friends' influence on school adjustment: A motivational analysis. In J. Juvonen & K. R. Wentzel (Eds.), *Social motivation: Understanding children's school adjustment* (pp. 248–278). Cambridge, England: Cambridge University Press.

Berninger, V. W., Fuller, F., & Whitaker, D. (1996). A process model of writing development across the life span. *Educational Psychology Review*, *8*, 193–218.

Berrick, J. D., & Hernandez, J. (2016). Developing consistent and transparent kinship care policy and practice: State mandated, mediated, and independent care. *Children & Youth Services Review*, *68*, 24–33. doi:10.1016/j.childyouth.2016.06.025

Bertenthal, B. I., Campos, J. J., & Kermoian, R. (1994). An epigenetic perspective on the development of self-produced locomotion and its consequences. *Current Directions in Psychological Science*, *3*, 140–145.

Bertera, E. M., & Crewe, S. (2013). Parenthood in the twenty-first century: African American grandparents as surrogate parents. *Journal of Human Behavior in the Social Environment*, *23*, 178–192. doi:10.1080/10911359.2013.747348

Berthold, K., & Renkl, A. (2009). Instructional aids to support a conceptual understanding of multiple representations. *Journalof Educational Psychology*, *101*(1), 70–87.

Bertsch, K., Grothe, M., Prehn, K., Vohs, K., Berger, C., Hauenstein, K., . . . Herpertz, S. C. (2013). Brain volumes differ between diagnostic groups of violent criminal offenders. *European Archives of Psychiatry and Clinical Neuroscience*, *263*, 593–606. doi:10.1007/s00406-013-0391-6

Best, P., Manktelow, R., & Taylor, B. (2014). Online communication, social media and adolescent wellbeing: A systematic narrative review. *Children & Youth Services Review*, *41*, 27–36.

Bester, G. (2013). Adolescent egocentrism in a learning context. *Africa Education Review*, *10*, 393–409.

Bettinger, E. (2012). Paying to learn: The effect of financial incentives on elementary school test scores. *Review of Economics & Statistics*, *94*, 686–698.

Betts, K. S. (2013). Lasting Impacts: Pre- and Postnatal PBDE Exposures Linked to IQ Deficits. *Environmental Health Perspectives*, *121*(2), A58.

Bhatia, V. K., & Ebooks, C. (2014). *The Routledge handbook of language and professional communication*. New York, NY: Routledge.

Bialystok, E. (2001). *Bilingualism in development: Language, literacy, and cognition*. Cambridge, England: Cambridge University Press.

Bialystok, E., Peets, K., & Moreno, S. (2014). Producing bilinguals through immersion education: Development of metalinguistic awareness. *Applied Psycholinguistics*, *35*, 177–191. doi:10.1017/S0142716412000288

Bibace, R., & Walsh, M. E. (1981). Children's conceptions of illness. In R. Bibace & M. E. Walsh (Eds.), *New directions for child development: Children's conceptions of health, illness, and bodily functions* (pp. 31–48). San Francisco, CA: Jossey-Bass.

Bialystok, E., & Viswanathan, M. (2009). Components of executive control with advantages for bilingual children in two cultures. *Cognition*, 112(3), 494–500.

Bibou-Nakou, I. I., Asimopoulos, C. H., Hatzipemou, T. H., Soumaki, E. E., & Tsiantis, J. J. (2014). Bullying in Greek secondary schools: Prevalence and profile of bullying practices. *International Journal of Mental Health Promotion*, *16*(1), 3–18. doi:10.1080/14623730.2013.857824

Bicais, J., & Correia, M. G. (2008). Peer-learning spaces: A staple in English language learners' tool kit for developing language and literacy. *Journal of Research in Childhood Education*, *22*, 363–375.

Bickford III, J. (2013). Initiating historical thinking in elementary schools. *Social Studies Research & Practice*, *8*(3), 60–77.

Bickham, D. D., Hswen, Y., Slaby, R. G., & Rich, M. (2018). A preliminary evaluation of a school-based media education and reduction intervention. *Journal of Primary Prevention*, *39*, 229–245. doi:10.1007/s10935-018-0510-2

Biddle, S. J. (1993). Children, exercise and mental health. *International Journal of Sport Psychology*, *24*, 200–216.

Biduła, S. P., & Króliczak, G. (2015). Structural asymmetry of the insula is linked to the lateralization of gesture and language. *European Journal of Neuroscience*, *41*, 1438–1447. doi:10.1111/ejn.12888

Bierman, K. L. (2004). *Peer rejection: Developmental processes and intervention strategies*. New York, NY: Guilford Press.

Bierman, K. L., & Powers, C. J. (2009). Social skills training to improve peer relations. In K. H. Rubin, W. M. Bukowski, & B. Laursen (Eds.), *Handbook of peer interactions, relationships, and groups* (pp. 603–621). New York, NY: Guilford Press.

Bierman, K. L., & Torres, M. (2016). Promoting the development of executive functions through early education and prevention programs. In J. A. Griffin, P. McCardle, & L. S. Freund (Eds.), *Executive function in preschool-age children: Integrating measurement, neurodevelopment, and translational research* (pp. 299–326). Washington, DC, US: American Psychological

Association. http://dx.doi.org.unco.idm.oclc.org/10.1037/14797-014

Bierman, K. L., Miller, C. L., & Staub, S. D. (1987). Improving the social behavior and peer acceptance of rejected boys: Effect of social skill training with instructions and prohibitions. *Journal of Consulting and Clinical Psychology, 55*, 194–200.

Bierman, K. L., Nix, R. L., Heinrichs, B. S., Domitrovich, C. E., Gest, S. D., Welsh, J. A., & Gill, S. (2014). Effects of Head Start REDI on children's outcomes 1 year later in different kindergarten contexts. *Child Development, 85*, 140–159. doi:10.1111/cdev.12117

Bigelow, A. E., & Best, C. (2013). Peek-a-what? Infants' response to the still-face task after normal and interrupted peek-a-boo. *Infancy, 18*, 400–413. doi:10.1111/j.1532-7078.2012.00124.x

Bigner, B. J. (2006). *Parent–child relations: An introduction to parenting* (7th ed.). Upper Saddle River, NJ: Pearson Merrill Prentice Hall.

Bigras, N., Bouchard, C., Cantin, G., Brunson, L., Coutu, S., Lemay, L., . . . Charron, A. (2010). A comparative study of structural and process quality in center-based and family-based child care services. *Child & Youth Care Forum, 39*, 129–150. doi:10.1007/s10566-009-9088-4

Bikic, A., Reichow, B., McCauley, S. A., Ibrahim, K., & Sukhodolsky, D. G. (2017). Meta-analysis of organizational skills interventions for children and adolescents with Attention-Deficit/Hyperactivity Disorder. *Clinical Psychology Review, 52*, 108–123. doi:10.1016/j.cpr.2016.12.004

Bilaloğlu, R. G., Aktaş Arnas, Y., & Yaşar, M. (2017). Question types and wait-time during science related activities in Turkish preschools. *Teachers and Teaching: Theory and Practice, 23*, 211–226. http://dx.doi.org/10.1080/13540602.2016.1203773

Binet, A., & Simon, T. (1948). The development of the Binet-Simon Scale, 1905–1908. In W. Dennis (Ed.), *Readings in the history of psychology* (pp. 412–424). East Norwalk, CT US: Appleton-Century-Crofts. doi:10.1037/11304-047

Bingham, G. E., Jeon, H., Kwon, K., & Lim, C. (2017). Parenting styles and home literacy opportunities: Associations with children's oral language skills. Infant & Child Development, 26(5), n/a-N.PAG. doi:10.1002/icd.2020

Bingham, G. E., Venuto, N., Carey, M., & Moore, C. (2017). Making it REAL: Using informational picture books in preschool classrooms. *Early Childhood Education Journal*, 46(5), 467–475.

Bird, R. (2009). *Overcoming difficulties with number: Supporting dyscalculia and students who struggle with math.* Los Angeles, CA: Sage.

Birkeland, M., Breivik, K., & Wold, B. (2014). Peer acceptance protects global self-esteem from negative effects of low closeness to parents during adolescence and early adulthood. *Journal of Youth & Adolescence, 43*, 70–80.

Bischof-Köhler, D. (2012). Empathy and self-recognition in phylogenetic and ontogenetic perspective. *Emotion Review, 4*(1), 40–48. doi:10.1177/1754073911421377

Bishop, D. (2010). Specific language impairment. In C. L. Cooper, J. Field, U. Goswami, R. Jenkins, & B. Sahakian (Eds.), *Mental capital and well-being* (pp. 767–773). Ames, IA: Wiley-Blackwell.

Bishop, E. G., Cherny, S. S., Corley, R., Plomin, R., DeFries, J. C., & Hewitt, J. K. (2003). Development genetic analysis of general cognitive ability from 1 to 12 years in a sample of adoptees, biological siblings, and twins. *Intelligence, 31*, 31–49.

Bivens, J. A., & Berk, L. E. (1990). A longitudinal study of the development of elementary school children's private speech. *Merrill-Palmer Quarterly, 36*, 443–463.

Björklund, C. (2014). Less is more—mathematical manipulatives in early childhood education. *Early Child Development & Care, 184*, 469–485. doi:10.1080/03004430.2013.799154

Bjorklund, D. F. (1987). How age changes in knowledge base contribute to the development of children's memory: An interpretive review. *Developmental Review, 7*, 93–130.

Bjorklund, D. F. (1997). The role immaturity in human development. *Psychological Bulletin, 122*, 153–169. doi:10.1037/0033-2909.122.2.153

Bjorklund, D. F., & Causey, K. B. (2018). *Children's thinking: Cognitive development and individual differences.* Thousand Oaks, CA: Sage.

Bjorklund, D. F., & Green, B. L. (1992). The adaptive nature of cognitive immaturity. *American Psychologist, 47*, 46–54.

Bjorklund, D. F., Dukes, C., & Brown, R. D. (2009). The development of memory strategies. In M. L. Courage & N. Cowan (Eds.), *The development of memory in infancy and childhood* (pp. 145–175). New York, NY: Psychology Press.

Bjorklund, D. F., Periss, V., & Causey, K. (2009). The benefits of youth. *European Journal of Developmental Psychology, 6*, 120–137.

Blachford, S. L. (2002). *The Gale encyclopedia of genetic disorders.* Detroit, MI: Gale Group.

Blackwell, L. S., Trzesniewski, K. H., & Dweck, C. S. (2007). Implicit theories of intelligence predict achievement across an adolescent transition: A longitudinal study and an intervention. *Child Development, 78*, 246–263. http://dx.doi.org.unco.idm.oclc.org/10.1111/j.1467-8624.2007.00995.x

Blad, E. (2015). Withholding recess as discipline in decline. *Education Week, 34*(27), 1–14.

Blain-Brière, B., Bouchard, C., Bigras, N., & Cadoret, G. (2014). Development of active control within working memory: Active retrieval versus monitoring in children. *International Journal of Behavioral Development, 38*, 239–246. doi:10.1177/0165025413513202

Blair, C. (2002). School readiness: Integrating cognition and emotion in a neurobiological conceptualization of children's functioning at school entry. *American Psychologist, 57*, 111–127.

Blair, C., Ursache, A., Greenberg, M., Vernon-Feagans, L., & Family Life Project Investigators. (2015). Multiple aspects of self-regulation uniquely predict mathematics but not letter–word knowledge in the early elementary grades. *Developmental Psychology, 51*, 459–472. doi:10.1037/a0038813

Blake, M., Waloszek, J. M., Schwartz, O., Raniti, M., Simmons, J. G.,Blake, L., . . . Allen, N. B. (2016). The SENSE study: Post intervention effects of a randomized controlled trial of a cognitive–behavioral and mindfulness-based group sleep improvement intervention among at-risk adolescents. *Journal of Consulting and Clinical Psychology, 84*, 1039–1051. doi:10.1037/ccp0000142

Blake, S., & Giannangelo, D. M. (2012). Creativity and young children: Review of literature and connections to thinking processes. In O. N. Saracho (Ed.), *Contemporary perspectives on research in creativity in early childhood education* (pp. 293–315). Charlotte, NC: Information Age Publishing.

Blakemore, C. (1976). The conditions required for the maintenance of binocularity in the kitten's visual cortex. *Journal of Physiology, 261*, 423–444.

Blakemore, J. E. O., Berenbaum, S. A., & Liben, L. S. (2009). *Gender development.* New York, NY: Psychology Press.

Blakemore, S., & Mills, K. L. (2014). Is adolescence a sensitive period for sociocultural processing? *Annual Review of Psychology, 65*, 187–207. doi:10.1146/annurev-psych-010213-115202

Blandon, A. Y., Calkins, S. D., Grimm, K. J., Keane, S. P., & O'Brien, M. (2010). Testing a developmental cascade model of emotional and social competence and early peer acceptance. *Development and Psychopathology, 22*, 737–748. doi:10.1017/S0954579410000428

Blank, J. (2010). Early childhood teacher education: Historical themes and contemporary issues. *Journal of Early Childhood Teacher Education, 31*, 391–405. doi:10.1080/10901027.2010.523772

Blatchford, P., Baines, E., & Pellegrini, A. (2003). The social context of school playground games: Sex and ethnic differences, and changes over time after entry to junior school. *British Journal of Developmental Psychology, 21*, 481–505.

Blaustein, M. E., & Kinniburgh, K. M. (2017). Attachment, self-regulation, and competency (ARC). In M. A. Landolt, M. Cloitre, & U. Schnyder (Eds.), *Evidence-based treatments for trauma related disorders in children and adolescents* (pp. 299–319). Cham, Switzerland: Springer International Publishing. http://dx.doi.org.unco.idm.oclc.org/10.1007/978-3-319-46138-0_14

Bleeker, M. M., & Jacobs, J. E. (2004). Achievement in math and science: Do mothers' beliefs matter 12 years later? *Journal of Educational Psychology, 96*, 97–109.

Blevins, C. (2010). *Math lesson plan.* Retrieved from http://www.athens.edu/vinsobm/lesson_5.html

Blissett, J., & Fogel, A. (2013). Intrinsic and extrinsic influences on children's acceptance of new foods. *Physiology & Behavior, 121,* 89–95. http://dx.doi.org.unco.idm.oclc.org/10.1016/j.physbeh.2013.02.013

Blitz, L. V., Anderson, E. M., & Saastamoinen, M. (2016). Assessing perceptions of culture and trauma in an elementary school: Informing a model for culturally responsive trauma-informed schools. *Urban Review, 48,* 520–542. doi:10.1007/s11256-016-0366-9b

Block, J. H. (1983). Differential premises arising from differential socialization of the sexes: Some conjectures. *Child Development, 54,* 1335–1354.

Blom, E., Paradis, J., Oetting, J., & Bedore, L. (2013). Past tense production by English second language learners with and without language impairment. *Journal of Speech, Language & Hearing Research, 56,* 281–294. doi:10.1044/1092-4388(2012/11-0112)

Bloom, B. S. (1964). *Stability and change in human characteristics.* New York, NY: Wiley.

Bloom, K., Russell, A., & Wassenberg, K. (1987). Turn taking affects the quality of infant vocalizations. *Journal of Child Language, 14,* 211–227.

Bloom, L., & Lahey, M. (1978). *Language development and language disorders.* New York, NY: Wiley.

Bloom, L., & Tinker, E. (2001). The intentionality model and language acquisition. *Monographs of the Society for Research in Child Development, 66*(4, Serial No. 267).

Blumberg, S. J., Zablotsky, B., Avila, R. M., Colpe, L. J., Pringle, B. A., & Kogan, M. D. (2016). Diagnosis lost: Differences between children who had and who currently have an autism spectrum disorder diagnosis. *Autism, 20,* 783–795. doi:10.1177/1362361315607724

Blustein, C. C., Carter, E. W., & McMillan, E. D. (2016). The voices of parents. *Journal of Special Education, 50,* 164–177. doi:10.1177/0022466916641381

Bobakova, D. D., Geckova, A. M., Klein, D., van Dijk, J. P., & Reijneveld, S. A. (2015). Fighting, truancy and low academic achievement in youth subcultures. *Young, 23,* 357–372. doi:10.1177/1103308815596905

Bobzien, J., Richels, C., Raver, S. A., Hester, P., Browning, E., & Morin, L. (2013). An observational study of social communication skills in eight preschoolers with and without hearing loss during cooperative play. *Early Childhood Education Journal, 41,* 339–346. doi:10.1007/s10643-012-0561-6

Boccia, M., & Campos, J. J. (1989). Maternal emotional signals, social referencing, and infants' reactions to strangers. In N. Eisenberg (Ed.), *New directions for child development* (Vol. 44, pp. 25–49). San Francisco, CA: Jossey-Bass.

Bock, J., & Johnson, S. E. (2004). Subsistence ecology and play among the Okavango Delta peoples of Botswana. *Human Nature, 15,* 63–81.

Bodner, K., Engelhardt, C., Minshew, N., & Williams, D. (2015). Making inferences: Comprehension of physical causality, intentionality, and emotions in discourse by high-functioning older children, adolescents, and adults with autism. *Journal of Autism & Developmental Disorders, 45,* 2721–2733. doi:10.1007/s10803-015-2436-3

Bodrova, E., & Leong, D. J. (1996). *Tools of the mind: The Vygotskian approach to early childhood education.* Upper Saddle River, NJ: Merrill/Prentice Hall.

Bodrova, E., & Leong, D. J. (2009). Tools of the mind: A Vygotskian-based early childhood curriculum. *Early Childhood Services: An Interdisciplinary Journal of Effectiveness, 3,* 245–262.

Bodrova, E., Leong, D., & Akhutina, T. (2011). When everything new is well-forgotten old: Vygotsky/Luria insights in the development of executive functions. *New Directions for Child & Adolescent Development, 2011*(133), 11–28. doi:10.1002/cd.301

Bodrow, W., & Magalashvili, V. (2009). Knowledge visualization in IT-based discovery learning. *Communication and Cognition, 42*(1&2), 101–112.

Boekaerts, M. (2006). Self-regulation and effort investment. In W. Damon & R. M. Lerner (Eds. in Chief), & K. A. Renninger & I. E. Sigel (Vol. Eds.), *Handbook of Child Psychology, Vol. 4. Child psychology in practice* (pp. 345–377). New York, NY: Wiley.

Boekaerts, M. (2009). Goal-directed behavior in the classroom. In K. R. Wenzel & A. Wigfield (Eds.), *Handbook of motivation at school (Educational Psychology Handbook Series,* pp. 105–122). New York, NY: Routledge/Taylor & Francis Group.

Boersma, A., ten Dam, G., Wardekker, W., & Volman, M. (2016). Designing innovative learning environments to foster communities of learners for students in initial vocational education. *Learning Environments Research, 19*(1), 107–131. http://dx.doi.org.unco.idm.oclc.org/10.1007/s10984-015-9203-4

Bofferding, L. (2014). Negative integer understanding: Characterizing first graders' mental models. *Journal for Research in Mathematics Education, 45,* 194–245.

Bogart, L. M., Elliott, M. N., Klein, D. J., Tortolero, S. R., Mrug, S., Peskin, M. F., . . . Schuster, M. A. (2014). Peer victimization in fifth grade and health in tenth grade. *Pediatrics, 133,* 440–447. doi:10.1542/peds.2013-3510

Bohney, B. B. (2016). Moving students toward acceptance of "other" Englishes. *English Journal, 105*(6), 66–71.

Boiger, M., De Deyne, S., & Mesquita, B. (2013). Emotions in "the world": Cultural practices, products, and meanings of anger and shame in two individualist cultures. *Frontiers in Psychology, 4,* 1–14.

Boivin, M., Brendgen, M., Vitaro, F., Dionne, G., Girard, A., Pérusse, D., & Tremblay, R. (2013). Strong genetic contribution to peer relationship difficulties at school entry: Findings from a longitudinal twin study. *Child Development, 84,* 1098–1114. doi:10.1111/cdev.12019

Bokhorst, C. L., Westenberg, P. M., Oosterlaan, J., & Heyne, D. A. (2008). Changes in social fears across childhood and adolescence: Age-related differences in the factor structure of the Fear Survey Schedule for Children—Revised. *Journal of Anxiety Disorders, 22,* 135–142.

Bolaños, D., Cole, R. A., Ward, W. H., Tindal, G. A., Schwanenflugel, P. J., & Kuhn, M. R. (2013). Automatic assessment of expressive oral reading. *Speech Communication, 55,* 221–236. doi:10.1016/j.specom.2012.08.002

Boldt, L. J., Kochanska, G., Yoon, J., & Koenig Nordling, J. (2014). Children's attachment to both parents from toddler age to middle childhood: Links to adaptive and maladaptive outcomes. *Attachment & Human Development, 16,* 211–229. doi:10.1080/14616734.2014.889181

Boling, C. J., & Evans, W. H. (2008). Reading success in the secondary classroom. *Preventing School Failure, 52*(2), 59–66. doi:10.3200/PSFL.52.2.59-66

Boncoddo, R., Dixon, J. A., & Kelley, E. (2010). The emergence of a novel representation from action: Evidence from preschoolers. *Developmental Science, 13,* 370–377. doi:10.1111/j.1467-7687.2009.00905.x

Bond, C., Symes, W., Hebron, J., Humphrey, N., Morewood, G., & Woods, K. (2016). Educational interventions for children with ASD: A systematic literature review 2008–2013. *School Psychology International, 37,* 303–320. doi:10.1177/0143034316639638

Bondü, R., & Scheithauer, H. (2014). Leaking and death-threats by students: A study in German schools. *School Psychology International, 35,* 592–608. doi:10.1177/0143034314552346

Bong, M. (2001). Between- and within-domain relations of academic motivation among middle and high school students: Self-efficacy, task-value, and achievement goals. *Journal of Educational Psychology, 93,* 23–34.

Bong, M., Cho, C., Ahn, H., & Kim, H. (2012). Comparison of self-beliefs for predicting student motivation and achievement. *Journal of Educational Research, 105,* 336–352. doi:10.1080/00220671.2011.627401

Boniel-Nissim, M., & Barak, A. (2013). The therapeutic value of adolescents' blogging about social–emotional difficulties. *Psychological Services, 10,* 333–341. doi:10.1037/a0026664

Bonnett, V. V., Yuill, N., & Carr, A. (2017). Mathematics, mastery and metacognition: How adding a creative approach can support children in maths. *Educational & Child Psychology, 34*(1), 83–93.

Bonta, B. D. (1997). Cooperation and competition in peaceful societies. *Psychological Bulletin, 121,* 299–320.

Boom, J., Brugman, D., & van der Heijden, P. G. M. (2001). Hierarchical structure of moral stages assessed by a sorting task. *Child Development, 72,* 535–548.

Borgen, W., & Hiebert, B. (2014). Orienting educators to contemporary ideas for career counseling: An illustrative example. In G. Arulmani, A. J. Bakshi, F. L. Leong, & A. G. Watts (Eds.), *Handbook of career development: International perspectives* (pp. 709–726). New York, NY: Springer Science Business Media. doi:10.1007/978-1-4614-9460-7_40

Borkowski, J. G., Bisconti, T., Willard, C. C., Keogh, D. A., Whitman, T. L., & Weed, K. (2002). The adolescent as parent: Influences on children's intellectual, academic, and socioemotional development. In J. G. Borkowski, S. L. Ramey, & M. Bristol-Power (Eds.), *Parenting and the child's world: Influences on academic, intellectual, and social-emotional development* (pp. 161–184). Mahwah, NJ: Erlbaum.

Bornovalova, M. A., Cummings, J. R., Hunt, E. E., Blazei, R. R., Malone, S. S., & Iacono, W. G. (2014). Understanding the relative contributions of direct environmental effects and passive genotype–environment correlations in the association between familial risk factors and child disruptive behavior disorders. *Psychological Medicine, 44*, 831–844.

Bornstein, M. H., Cote, L. R., Maital, S., Painter, K., Sung-Yun, P., Pascual, L., . . . Vyt, A. (2004). Cross-linguistic analysis of vocabulary in young children: Spanish, Dutch, French, Hebrew, Italian, Korean, and American English. *Child Development, 75*, 1115–1139. doi:10.1111/j.1467-8624.2004.00729.x

Bornstein, M. H., Hahn, C., & Haynes, O. M. (2010). Social competence, externalizing, and internalizing behavioral adjustment from early childhood through early adolescence: Developmental cascades. *Development and Psychopathology, 22*, 717–735. doi:10.1017/S0954579410000416

Bornstein, M. H., Jager, J., & Putnick, D. L. (2013). Sampling in developmental science: Situations, shortcomings, solutions, and standards. *Developmental Review, 33*(4), 357–370. doi:10.1016/j.dr.2013.08.003

Bornstein, M., Hahn, C., & Wolke, D. (2013). Systems and cascades in cognitive development and academic achievement. *Child Development, 84*, 154–162. doi:10.1111/j.1467-8624.2012.01849.x

Borrero, N. E., & Yeh, C. J. (2011). The multidimensionality of ethnic identity among urban high school youth. *Identity, 11*, 114–135. doi:10.1080/15283488.2011.555978

Borst, G., Poirel, N., Pineau, A., Cassotti, M., & Houdé, O. (2013). Inhibitory control efficiency in a Piaget-like class-inclusion task in school-age children and adults: A developmental negative priming study. *Developmental Psychology, 49*, 1366–1374. doi:10.1037/a0029622

Bos, H. (2013). Lesbian-mother families formed through donor insemination. In A. E. Goldberg & K. R. Allen (Eds.), *LGBT-parent families: Innovations in research and implications for practice* (pp. 21–37). New York, NY: Springer Science Business Media. doi:10.1007/978-1-4614-4556-2_2

Bosacki, S., Rose-Krasnor, L., & Coplan, R. (2014). Children's talking and listening within the classroom: teachers' insights. *Early Child Development & Care, 184*, 247–265. doi:10.1080/03004430.2013.781165

Boscardin, C. K., Muthén, B., Francis, D. J., & Baker, E. L. (2008). Early identification of reading difficulties using heterogeneous developmental trajectories. *Journal of Educational Psychology, 100*, 192–208.

Botellero, V. L., Skranes, J., Bjuland, K. J., Løhaugen, G. C., Håberg, A. K., Lydersen, S., . . . Martinussen, M. (2016). Mental health and cerebellar Vol. during adolescence in very-low-birth-weight infants: A longitudinal study. *Child and Adolescent Psychiatry and Mental Health, 10*, Article ID 6. doi:10.1186/s13034-016-0093-8

Bøttcher, L., & Dammeyer, J. (2012). Disability as a dialectical concept: Building on Vygotsky defectology. *European Journal of Special Needs Education, 27*, 433–446. doi:10.1080/08856257.2012.711958

Bouchard, C., Bigras, N., Cantin, G., Coutu, S., Blain-Brière, B., Eryasa, J., . . . Brunson, L. (2010). Early childhood educators' use of language-support practices with 4-year-old children in child care centers. *Early Childhood Education Journal, 37*, 371–379.

Bouchard, T. J. (2014). Genes, evolution and intelligence. *Behavior Genetics, 4*, 549–577. doi:10.1007/s10519-014-9646-x

Bouchard, T. J., & McGue, M. (1981). Familial studies of intelligence: A review. *Science, 212*, 1056.

Bouchard, T. J., Jr. (1997). IQ similarity in twins reared apart: Findings and responses to critics. In R. J. Sternberg & E. L. Grigorenko (Eds.), *Intelligence, heredity, and environment* (pp. 126–160). Cambridge, England: Cambridge University Press.

Boucher, O., Muckle, G., Jacobson, J. L., Carter, R., Kaplan-Estrin, M., Ayotte, P., Dewailly, Ã., & Jacobson, S. W. (2014). Domain-specific effects of prenatal exposure to PCBs, mercury, and lead on infant cognition: Results from the environmental contaminants and child development study in Nunavik. *Environmental Health Perspectives, 122*(3), 310-316. doi:10.1289/ehp.1206323

Bounoua, L., Cury, F., Regner, I., Huguet, P., Barron, K. E., & Elliot, A. J. (2012). Motivated use of information about others: Linking the 2 × 2 achievement goal model to social comparison propensities and processes. *British Journal of Social Psychology, 51*, 626–641.

Bouta, H., & Retalis, S. (2013). Enhancing primary school children collaborative learning experiences in maths via a 3D virtual environment. *Education & Information Technologies, 18*, 571–596. doi:10.1007/s10639-012-9198-8

Boutte, G. S., & McCormick, C. B. (1992). Authentic multicultural activities: Avoiding pseudomulticulturalism. *Childhood Education, 68*(3), 140–144.

Bowlby, J. (1951). *Maternal care and mental health*. Geneva, Switzerland: World Health Organization.

Bowlby, J. (1958). The nature of the child's tie to his mother. *International Journal of Psycho-Analysis, 39*, 350–373.

Bowlby, J. (1973). *Attachment and Loss: Vol. 2. Separation: Anxiety and anger*. New York, NY: Basic Books.

Bowlby, J. (1982). *Attachment and Loss: Vol. 1. Attachment* (2nd ed.). New York, NY: Basic Books. (Original work published 1969)

Bowlby, J. (1988). *A secure base: Parent–child attachment and healthy human development*. New York, NY: Basic Books.

Bowman-Perrott, L., Davis, H., Vannest, K., Williams, L., Greenwood, C., & Parker, R. (2013). Academic benefits of peer tutoring: A meta-analytic review of single-case research. *School Psychology Review, 42*(1), 39–55.

Bowman, D., & Popp, P. A. (2013). Students experiencing homelessness. In E. Rossen & R. Hull (Eds.), *Supporting and educating traumatized students: A guide for school-based professionals* (pp. 73–92). New York, NY: Oxford University Press.

Bowyer-Crane, C., & Snowling, M. J. (2010). Turning frogs into princes: Can children make inferences from fairy tales? *Reading and Writing, 23*(1), 19–29.

Boyette, A. H. (2016). Children's play and culture learning in an egalitarian foraging society. *Child Development, 87*, 759–769. doi:10.1111/cdev.12496

Boykin, A. W. (1994). Harvesting talent and culture: African-American children and educational reform. In R. J. Rossi (Ed.), *Schools and students at risk: Context and framework for positive change (pp. 116–138)*. New York, NY: Teachers College Press.

Boyle, B., & Charles, M. (2011). "The three hags and Pocohontas": How collaboration develops early years writing skills. *Literacy, 45*(1), 10–18. doi:10.1111/j.1741-4369.2011.00576.x

Braaten, E. B. (2011). *How to find mental health care for your child*. Washington, DC: American Psychological Association.

Brabham, E. G., & Lynch-Brown, C. (2002). Effects of teachers' reading-aloud styles on vocabulary acquisition and comprehension of students in the early elementary grades. *Journal of Educational Psychology, 94*, 465–473.

Bracken, B. A., & McCallum, R. S. (1998). *Universal Nonverbal Intelligence Test*. Itasca, IL: Riverside.

Bracken, B. A., & McCallum, R. S. (2009). Universal Nonverbal Intelligence Test (UNIT). In J. A. Naglieri & S. Goldstein (Eds.), *Practitioner's guide to assessing intelligence and achievement* (pp. 291–313). Hoboken, NJ: Wiley.

Bracken, B. A., McCallum, R. S., & Shaughnessy, M. F. (1999). An interview with Bruce A. Bracken and R. Steve McCallum, authors of the Universal Nonverbal Intelligence Test (UNIT). *North American Journal of Psychology, 1*, 277–288.

Bradley, L., & Bryant, P. (1991). Phonological skills before and after learning to read. In S. A. Brady & D. P. Shankweiler (Eds.), *Phonological processes in literacy* (pp. 47–45). Hillsdale, NJ: Erlbaum.

Bradley, R. H., & Caldwell, B. M. (1984). The relation of infants' home environments to achievement test performance in first grade: A follow-up study. *Child Development, 55*, 803–809.

Bradley, R. H., Corwyn, R. F., McAdoo, H., & Coll, C. (2001). The home environments of children in the United States: Part I. Variations by age, ethnicity, and poverty status. *Child Development, 72*, 1844–1867.

Brady, K. W., & Goodman, J. C. (2014). The type, but not the amount, of information available influences toddlers' fast mapping and retention of new words. *American Journal of Speech-Language Pathology, 23*, 120–133. doi:10.1044/2013

Braine, L. G., Schauble, L., Kugelmass, S., & Winter, A. (1993). Representation of depth by children: Spatial strategies and lateral biases. *Developmental Psychology, 29*, 466–479.

Brainerd, C. J. (2003). Jean Piaget, learning research, and American education. In B. J. Zimmerman & D. H. Schunk (Eds.), *Educational psychology: A century of contributions* (pp. 251–287). Mahwah, NJ: Erlbaum.

Braithwaite, D. W., Tian, J., & Siegler, R. S. (2018). Do children understand fraction addition? *Developmental Science, 21*(4), 1-9. doi:10.1111/desc.12601

Brame, C.J. and Biel, R. (2015). *Setting up and facilitating group work: Using cooperative learning groups effectively*. Retrieved from http://cft.vanderbilt.edu/guides-sub-pages/setting-up-and-facilitating-group-work-using-cooperative-learning-groups-effectively/

Branch, C. (1999). Race and human development. In R. H. Sheets & E. R. Hollins (Eds.), *Racial and ethnic identity in school practices: Aspects of human development* (pp. 7–28). Mahwah, NJ: Erlbaum.

Brannon, M. E. (2002). The development of ordinal numerical knowledge in infancy. *Cognition, 83*, 223–240.

Branstetter, S. A., & Furman, W. (2013). Buffering effect of parental monitoring knowledge and parent-adolescent relationships on consequences of adolescent substance use. *Journal of Child and Family Studies, 22*, 192–198. doi:10.1007/s10826-012-9568-2

Brant, A. M., Haberstick, B. C., Corley, R. P., Wadsworth, S. J., DeFries, J. C., & Hewitt, J. K. (2009). The developmental etiology of high IQ. *Behavior Genetics, 39*, 393–405.

Braswell, G. S., & Callanan, M. A. (2003). Learning to draw recognizable graphic representations during mother–child interactions. *Merrill-Palmer Quarterly, 49*, 471–494.

Brauner, J., Gordic, B., & Zigler, E. (2004). Putting the child back into child care: Combining care and education for children ages 3–5. *Social Policy Report, 18, 1, 3-15.* Ann Arbor, MI: Society for Research in Child Development.

Braungart-Rieker, J. M., Hill-Soderlund, A. L., & Karrass, J. (2010). Fear and anger reactivity trajectories from 4 to 16 months: The roles of temperament, regulation, and maternal sensitivity. *Developmental Psychology, 46*, 791–804. doi:10.1037/a0019673

Braza, P., Carreras, R., Muñoz, J. M., Braza, F., Azurmendi, A., Pascual-Sagastizábal, E., . . . Sánchez-Martín, J. R. (2015). Negative maternal and paternal parenting styles as predictors of children's behavioral problems: Moderating effects of the child's sex. *Journal of Child and Family Studies, 24*, 847–856. doi:10.1007/s10826-013-9893-0

Brazelton, T. B. (2009). The role of the Neonatal Behavioral Assessment Scale: Personal reflections. In J. K. Nugent, B. J. Petrauskas, & T. B. Brazelton (Eds.), *The newborn as a person* (pp. 278–286). Hoboken, NJ: Wiley.

Breckenridge, K., Braddick, O., & Atkinson, J. (2013). The organization of attention in typical development: A new preschool attention test battery. *British Journal of Developmental Psychology, 31*(3), 271–288. doi:10.1111/bjdp.12004

Bredekamp, S. (2011). *Effective practices in early childhood education: Building a foundation*. Upper Saddle River, NJ: Pearson Education.

Bredekamp, S., & Copple, C. (Eds.). (1997). *Developmentally appropriate practice in early childhood programs* (3rd ed.). Washington, DC: National Association for the Education of Young Children.

Bremner, J. G., Slater, A. M., & Johnson, S. P. (2015). Perception of object persistence: The origins of object permanence in infancy. *Child Development Perspectives, 9*(1), 7-13. doi:10.1111/cdep.12098

Bremner, J. G., Slater, A. M., Mason, U. C., Spring, J., & Johnson, S. P. (2016). Limits of object persistence: Young infants perceive continuity of vertical and horizontal trajectories, but not 45-degree oblique trajectories. *Infancy*. Advance online publication. doi:10.1111/infa.12170

Brendgen, M. (2014). The interplay between genetic factors and the peer environment in explaining children's social adjustment. *Merrill-Palmer Quarterly, 60*, 101–109.

Brener, N. D., Eaton, D. K., Kann, L. K., McManus, T. S., Lee, S. M., Scanlon, K. S., . . . O'Toole, T. P. (2013). Behaviors related to physical activity and nutrition among U.S. high school students. *Journal of Adolescent Health, 53*(4), 539–546. http://dx.doi.org.unco.idm.oclc.org/10.1016/j.jadohealth.2013.05.006

Brenick, A. A., Shattuck, J. J., Donlan, A. A., Duh, S. S., & Zurbriggen, E. Z. (2014). Empowering children with safety-skills: An evaluation of the Kidpower Everyday Safety-Skills Program. *Children & Youth Services Review, 44*, 152–162. doi:10.1016/j.childyouth.2014.06.007

Bretherton, I. (1991). Pouring new wine into old bottles: The social self as internal working model. In M. R. Gunnar & L. A. Sroufe (Eds.), *Self processes and development: The Minnesota Symposia on Child Development* (Vol. 23, pp. 1–42). Hillsdale, NJ: Erlbaum.

Bretherton, I., Fritz, J., Zahn-Waxler, C., & Ridgeway, D. (1986). Learning to talk about emotions: A functionalist perspective. *Child Development, 57*, 529–548.

Brewin, M., & Statham, J. (2011). Supporting the transition from primary school to secondary school for children who are looked after. *Educational Psychology in Practice, 27*, 365–381. doi:10.1080/02667363.2011.624301

Bridgeland, J., Bruce, M., & Hariharan, A. (2013). *The missing piece: A national teacher survey on how social and emotional learning can empower children and transform schools.* Chicago, IL: Collaborative for Academic, Social, and Emotional Learning and Civic Enterprises. Retrieved from https://www.casel.org/wp-content/uploads/2016/01/the-missing-piece.pdf

Bridgett, D. J., Laake, L. M., Gartstein, M. A., & Dorn, D. (2013). Development of infant positive emotionality: The contribution of maternal characteristics and effects on subsequent parenting. *Infant & Child Development, 22*, 362–382. doi:10.1002/icd.1795

Brietzke, E., Moreira, C. L. R., Toniolo, R. A., & Lafer, B. (2011). Clinical correlates of eating disorder comorbidity in women with bipolar disorder type I. *Journal of Affective Disorders, 130*(1–2), 162–165. doi:10.1016/j.jad.2010.10.020

Brighton, C. B., Moon, T. R., & Huang, F. L. (2015). Advanced readers in Reading First classrooms. *Journal for the Education of the Gifted, 38*, 257–293. doi:10.1177/0162353215592501

Briley, D. A., & Tucker-Drob, E. M. (2013). Explaining the increasing heritability of cognitive ability across development: A meta-analysis of longitudinal twin and adoption studies. *Psychological Science, 24*, 1704–1713. doi:10.1177/0956797613478618

Briley, D. A., & Tucker-Drob, E. M. (2014). Genetic and environmental continuity in personality development: A meta-analysis. *Psychological Bulletin, 140*, 1303–1331.

Brinch, C. N., & Galloway, T. A. (2012). Schooling in adolescence raises IQ scores. *Proceedings of the National Academy of Sciences of the United States of America, 109*, 425–430. doi:10.1073/pnas.1106077109

Brinton, B., & Fujiki, M. (1984). Development of topic manipulation skills in discourse. *Journal of Speech and Hearing Research, 27*, 350–358.

Brintworth, K., & Sandall, J. (2013). What makes a successful home birth service: An examination of the influential elements by review of one service. *Midwifery, 29*, 713–721. doi:10.1016/j.midw.2012.06.016

Broc, L., Bernicot, J., Olive, T., Favart, M., Reilly, J., Quémart, P., & Uzé, J. (2013). Lexical spelling in children and adolescents with specific language impairment: Variations with the writing situation. *Research in Developmental Disabilities, 34*, 3253–3266. doi:10.1016/j.ridd.2013.06.025

Brock, R. L., & Kochanska, G. (2016). Interparental conflict, children's security with parents, and long-term risk of internalizing problems: A longitudinal study from ages 2 to 10. *Development and Psychopathology, 28*(1), 45–54. doi:10.1017/S0954579415000279

Brody, G. G., Tianyi, Y., Beach, S. H., Kogan, S. M., Philibert, R. A., & Windle, M. (2014). Harsh parenting and adolescent health: A longitudinal analysis with genetic moderation. *Health Psychology, 33*(5), 401-409.

Brody, G. H., Lei, M., Chae, D. H., Yu, T., Kogan, S. M., & Beach, S. H. (2014). Perceived discrimination among African American adolescents and allostatic load: A longitudinal analysis with buffering effects. *Child Development, 85*, 989–1002. doi:10.1111/cdev.12213

Brody, G. H., Stoneman, Z., & McCoy, J. K. (1994). Forecasting sibling relationships in early adolescence from child temperament and family processes in middle childhood. *Child Development, 65*, 771–784.

Brody, G. H., Yu, T., & Beach, S. R. H. (2016). Resilience to adversity and the early origins of disease. *Development and Psychopathology, 28*(4, Pt. 2), 1347–1365. doi:10.1017/S0954579416000894

Brody, N. (1992). *Intelligence.* New York, NY: Academic Press.

Brody, N. (1997). Intelligence, schooling, and society. *American Psychologist, 52*, 1046–1050.

Brody, N. (2004). Review of "Emotional Intelligence: Science and Myth." *Intelligence, 32*(1), 109–111. doi:10.1016/S0160-2896(03)00059-X

Brody, N. (2006). Geocentric theory: A valid interpretation of Gardner's theory of intelligence. In J. A. Schaler (Ed.), *Howard Gardner under fire: The rebel psychologist faces his critics* (pp. 73–94). Chicago, IL: Open Court.

Brodzinsky, D. M. (2006). Family structural openness and communication openness as predictors in the adjustment of adopted children. *Adoption Quarterly, 9*(4), 1–19.

Bronfenbrenner, U. (1979). *The ecology of human development: Experiments by nature and design.* Cambridge, MA: Harvard University Press.

Bronfenbrenner, U. (1999). Is early intervention effective? Some studies of early education in familial and extra-familial settings. In A. Montagu (Ed.), *Race and IQ* (expanded ed., pp. 343–378). New York, NY: Oxford University Press.

Bronfenbrenner, U. (2001). The bioecological theory of human development. In N. J. Smelser & P. B. Baltes (Eds.), *International encyclopedia of the social and behavioral sciences* (Vol. 10, pp. 6963–6970). New York, NY: Elsevier.

Bronfenbrenner, U. (2005). *Making human beings human: Bioecological perspectives on human development.* Thousand Oaks, CA: Sage.

Bronfenbrenner, U., & Morris, P. A. (2006). The bio-ecological model of human development. In W. Damon & R. M. Lerner (Eds. in Chief) & R. M. Lerner (Vol. Ed.), *Handbook of Child Psychology: Vol. 1. Theoretical models of human development* (6th ed., pp. 793–828). Hoboken, NJ: Wiley.

Bronfenbrenner, U., Alvarez, W. F., & Henderson, C. R., Jr. (1984). Working and watching: Maternal employment status and parents' perceptions of their three-year-old children. *Child Development, 55*, 1362–1379.

Bronson, M. B. (2000). *Self-regulation in early childhood: Nature and nurture.* New York, NY: Guilford Press.

Brook, J., Chenshu, Z., Finch, S., & Brook, D. (2010). Adolescent pathways to adult smoking: Ethnic identity, peer substance use, and antisocial behavior. *American Journal on Addictions, 19*, 178–186.

Brookhart, S. (2013). Assessing Creativity. *Educational Leadership, 70*(5), 28–34.

Brooks-Gunn, J. (2003). Do you believe in magic? What we can expect from early childhood intervention programs. *Social Policy Report, 17*(1).

Brooks-Gunn, J., & Furstenberg, F. F. (1990). Coming of age in the era of AIDS: Puberty, sexuality, and contraception. *Milbrank Quarterly, 68*(Suppl. 1), 59–84.

Brooks-Gunn, J., & Paikoff, R. L. (1992). Changes in self-feelings during the transition toward adolescence. In H. R. McGurk (Ed.), *Childhood social development: Contemporary perspectives* (pp. 63–97). Hillsdale, NJ: Erlbaum.

Brooks-Gunn, J., Klebanov, P. K., & Duncan, G. J. (1996). Ethnic differences in children's intelligence test scores: Role of economic deprivation, home environment, and maternal characteristics. *Child Development, 67*, 396–408.

Brooks, R., & Meltzoff, A. N. (2014). Gaze following: A mechanism for building social connections between infants and adults. In M. Mikulincer & P. R. Shaver (Eds.), *Mechanisms of social connection: From brain to group* (pp. 167–183). Washington, DC: American Psychological Association. doi:10.1037/14250-010

Brophy, J. E. (2004). *Motivating students to learn* (2nd ed.). Mahwah, NJ: Erlbaum.

Brophy, J. E., & Alleman, J. (1996). *Powerful social studies for elementary students.* Fort Worth, TX: Harcourt Brace.

Brophy, J. E., Alleman, J., & Knighton, B. (2009). *Inside the social studies classroom.* New York, NY: Routledge.

Brophy, J. E., & VanSledright, B. (1997). *Teaching and learning history in elementary schools.* New York, NY: Teachers College Press.

Brouzos, A., Misailidi, P., & Hadjimattheou, A. (2014). Associations between emotional intelligence, socio-emotional adjustment, and academic achievement in childhood: The influence of age. *Canadian Journal of School Psychology, 29*(2), 83–99. doi:10.1177/0829573514521976

Brown, A. L., & Campione, J. C. (1994). Guided discovery in a community of learners. In K. McGilly (Ed.), *Classroom lessons: Integrating cognitive theory and classroom practice* (pp. 229–270). Cambridge, MA: MIT Press.

Brown, A. L., & Palincsar, A. S. (1987). Reciprocal teaching of comprehension strategies: A natural history of one program for enhancing learning. In J. Borkowski & J. D. Day (Eds.), *Cognition in special education: Comparative approaches to retardation, learning disabilities, and giftedness* (pp. 81–132). Norwood, NJ: Ablex.

Brown, B. B. (1990). Peer groups and peer culture. In S. S. Feldman & G. R. Elliott (Eds.), *At the threshold: The developing adolescent* (pp. 171–196). Cambridge, MA: Harvard University Press.

Brown, B. B. (1993). School culture, social politics, and the academic motivation of U.S. citizens. In T. M. Tomlinson (Ed.), *Motivating students to learn: Overcoming barriers to high achievement (pp. 63–98).* Berkeley, CA: McCutchan.

Brown, B. B., & Dietz, E. L. (2009). Informal peer groups in middle childhood and adolescence. In K. H. Rubin, W. M. Bukowski, & B. Laursen (Eds.), *Handbook of peer interactions, relationships, and groups* (pp. 361–376). New York, NY: Guilford Press.

Brown, B. B., Eicher, S. A., & Petrie, S. (1986). The importance of peer group ("crowd") affiliation in adolescence. *Journal of Adolescence, 9*, 73–96.

Brown, C. S. (2017). School context influences the ethnic identity development of immigrant children in middle childhood. *Social Development, 26*, 797–812. http://dx.doi.org.unco.idm.oclc.org/10.1111/sode.12240

Brown, C., & Brown, B. (2014). On passing (or not): Developing under multicultural heritages. *Journal of the American Academy of Child & Adolescent Psychiatry, 53*, 603–605. doi:10.1016/j.jaac.2014.02.011

Brown, C., & Chu, H. (2012). Discrimination, ethnic identity, and academic outcomes of Mexican immigrant children: The importance of school context. *Child Development, 83*, 1477–1485. doi:10.1111/j.1467-8624.2012.01786.x

Brown, G. H., Brunelle, L. M., & Malhotra, V. (2017). Tagging: Deviant behavior or adolescent rites of passage? *Culture & Psychology, 23*, 487–501. http://dx.doi.org.unco.idm.oclc.org/10.1177/1354067X16660852

Brown, J. V., Bakeman, R., Coles, C. D., Platzman, K. A., & Lynch, M. E. (2004). Prenatal cocaine exposure: A comparison of 2-year-old children in parental and nonparental care. *Child Development, 75*, 1282–1295.

Brown, L. F., Pridham, K. A., & Brown, R. (2014). Sequential observation of infant regulated and dysregulated behavior following soothing and stimulating maternal behavior during feeding. *Journal for Specialists in Pediatric Nursing, 19*, 139–148. doi:10.1111/jspn.12062

Brown, L. M., Tappan, M. B., & Gilligan, C. (1995). Listening to different voices. In W. M. Kurtines & J. L. Gewirtz (Eds.), *Moral development: An introduction* (pp. 311–335). Boston, MA: Allyn & Bacon.

Brown, R. (1973). *A first language: The early stages.* Cambridge, MA: Harvard University Press.

Brown, R., & Hanlon, C. (1970). Derivational complexity and order of acquisition in child speech. In J. R. Hayes (Ed.), *Cognition and the development of language* (pp. 11–54). New York, NY: Wiley.

Brown, S., Gutiérrez, J., & Alibali, M. (2016, November 3). "Relational" equity: Elementary students co-construct a social-mathematical power dynamic during collaborative engagement on equivalence tasks. In M. B. Wood, E. E. Turner, M. Civil, & J. A. Eli (Eds.). (2016). *Proceedings of the 38th annual meeting of the North American Chapter of the International Group for the Psychology of Mathematics Education.* Tucson, AZ: The University of Arizona.

Browne, J., O'Brien, M., Taylor, J., Bowman, R., & Davis, D. (2014). 'You've got it within you': The political act of keeping a wellness focus in the antenatal time. *Midwifery, 30*, 420–426. doi:10.1016/j.midw.2013.04.003

Brownell, C. A., Iesue, S. S., Nichols, S. R., & Svetlova, M. (2013). Mine or yours? Development of sharing in toddlers in relation to ownership understanding. *Child Development, 84*, 906–920. doi:10.1111/cdev.12009

Brownell, C. A., Svetlova, M., Anderson, R., Nichols, S. R., & Drummond, J. (2013). Socialization of early prosocial behavior: Parents' talk about emotions is associated with sharing and helping in toddlers. *Infancy, 18*(1), 91–119. doi:10.1111/j.1532-7078.2012.00125.x

Brownell, M. T., Mellard, D. F., & Deshler, D. D. (1993). Differences in the learning and transfer performance between students with learning disabilities and other low-achieving students on problem-solving tasks. *Learning Disabilities Quarterly, 16*, 138–156.

Bruer, J. T. (1999). *The myth of the first three years: A new understanding of early brain development and lifelong learning.* New York, NY: Free Press.

Brumariu, L., & Kerns, K. (2013). Pathways to anxiety: Contributions of attachment history, temperament, peer competence, and ability to manage intense emotions. *Child Psychiatry & Human Development, 44*, 504–515.

Brummelman, E., Thomaes, S., Orobio de Castro, B., Overbeek, G., & Bushman, B. (2014). "That's not just beautiful—That's incredibly beautiful!" The adverse impact of inflated praise on children with low self-esteem. *Psychological Science, 25*, 728–735.

Brunelle, S., Herrington, S., Coghlan, R., & Brussoni, M. (2016). Play worth remembering: Are playgrounds too safe? *Children, Youth & Environments, 26*(1), 17–36.

Bruner, J. S. (1983). The acquisition of pragmatic commitments. In R. M. Golinkoff (Ed.), *The transition from prelinguistic to linguistic communication* (pp. 27–42). Hillsdale, NJ: Erlbaum.

Bruner, J. S., & Sherwood, V. (1976). Early rule structure: The case of "peekaboo." In R. Harre (Ed.), *Life sentences* (pp. 55–62). London, England: Wiley.

Bruni, O., & Angriman, M. (2017). Pediatric insomnia. In S. Nevšímalová & O. Bruni (Eds.), *Sleep disorders in children* (pp. 155–184). Cham, Switzerland: Springer International Publishing. http://dx.doi.org.unco.idm.oclc.org/10.1007/978-3-319-28640-2_9

Bryan, J., & Henry, L. (2008). Strengths-based partnerships: A school-family-community partnership approach to empowering students. *Professional School Counseling, 12*, 149–156.

Bryan, T., Burstein, K., & Bryan, J. (2001). Students with learning disabilities: Homework problems and promising practices. *Educational Psychologist, 36*, 167–180.

Bryant, G. A., Liénard, P., & Barrett, H. (2012). Recognizing infant-directed speech across distant cultures: Evidence from Africa. *Journal of Evolutionary Psychology, 10*, 47–59. doi:10.1556/JEP.10.2012.2.1

Bryant, P., & Nuñes, T. (2011). Children's understanding of mathematics. In U. Goswami (Ed.), *The Wiley-Blackwell handbook of childhood cognitive development* (2nd ed., pp. 549–573). Malden, MA: Wiley-Blackwell.

Buchanan, C. M., Eccles, J. S., & Becker, J. B. (1992). Are adolescents the victims of raging hormones: Evidence for activational effects of hormones on moods and behaviors at adolescence. *Psychological Bulletin, 111*, 62–107.

Buchmann, A. F., Holz, N., Boecker, R., Blomeyer, D., Rietschel, M., Witt, S. H., . . . Laucht, M. (2014). Moderating role of FKBP5 genotype in the impact of childhood adversity on cortisol stress response during adulthood. *European Neuropsychopharmacology, 24*, 837–845. doi:10.1016/j.euroneuro.2013.12.001

Buck, G. A., Cook, K. L., Quigley, C. F., Prince, P., & Lucas, Y. (2014). Seeking to improve African American girls' attitudes toward science. *Elementary School Journal, 114*(3), 431–453.

Buck, K. A., Kretsch, N., & Harden, K. (2013). Positive attentional bias, attachment style, and susceptibility to peer influence. *Journal of Research on Adolescence, 23*, 605–613. doi:10.1111/jora.12026

Buckle, M. E., & Walsh, D. S. (2013). Teaching responsibility to gang-affiliated Youths. *JOPERD: The Journal of Physical Education, Recreation & Dance, 84*(2), 53–58.

Budd, G. M., & Volpe, S. L. (2006). School-based obesity prevention: Research, challenges, and recommendations. *Journal of School Health, 76*, 485–495.

Buettner, C., Hur, E., Jeon, L., & Andrews, D. (2016). What are we teaching the teachers? Child development curricula in US higher education. *Child & Youth Care Forum, 45*(1), 155–175. doi:10.1007/s10566-015-9323-0

Bugental, D. (2009). Predicting and preventing child maltreatment: A biocognitive transactional approach. In A. Sameroff (Ed.), *The transactional model of development: How children and contexts shape each other* (pp. 97–115). Washington, DC: American Psychological Association.

Buhrmester, D. (1992). The developmental courses of sibling and peer relationships. In F. Boer & J. Dunn (Eds.), *Children's sibling relationships: Developmental and clinical issues* (pp. 19–40) Hillsdale, NJ: Erlbaum.

Buhs, E. S., Koziol, N. A., Rudasill, K. M., & Crockett, L. J. (2018). Early temperament and middle school engagement: School social relationships as mediating processes. *Journal of Educational Psychology, 110*, 338–354. http://dx.doi.org.unco.idm.oclc.org/10.1037/edu0000224

Buijzen, M., & Valkenburg, P. M. (2003). The effects of television advertising on materialism, parent–child conflict, and unhappiness: A review of research. *Applied Developmental Psychology, 24*, 437–456.

Buka, S. L., Cannon, T. D., Torrey, E. F., Yolken, R. H., and the Collaborative Study Group on the Perinatal Origins of Severe Psychiatric Disorders (2008). Maternal exposure to herpes simplex virus and risk of psychosis among adult offspring. *Biological Psychiatry, 63*, 809–815.

Bukowski, W. M., & Raufelder, D. (2018). Peers and the self. In W. M. Bukowski, B. Laursen, & K. H. Rubin (Eds.), *Handbook of peer interactions, relationships, and groups* (pp. 141–156). New York, NY: Guilford Press.

Bukstein, O. C., & Deas, D. (2010). Substance abuse and addictions. In M. K. Dulcan (Ed.), *Dulcan's textbook of child and adolescent psychiatry* (pp. 241–258). Arlington, VA: American Psychiatric Publishing.

Bull, R., & Lee, K. (2014). Executive functioning and mathematics achievement. *Child Development Perspectives, 8*(1), 36–41. doi:10.1111/cdep.12059

Bull, R., Cleland, A. A., & Mitchell, T. (2013). Sex differences in the spatial representation of number. *Journal of Experimental Psychology, 142*, 181–192. doi:10.1037/a0028387

Bunch, G. (2013). Pedagogical language knowledge: Preparing mainstream teachers for English learners in the new standards era. *Review of Research in Education, 37*, 298–341. doi:10.3102/0091732X12461772

Bürger, K., & Schmitt, M. (2017). Students' multiple state goals as a function of appraisals, trait goals, and their interactions. *Contemporary Educational Psychology, 51*, 464–481. http://dx.doi.org.unco.idm.oclc.org/10.1016/j.cedpsych.2017.09.006

Burhans, K. K., & Dweck, C. S. (1995). Helplessness in early childhood: The role of contingent worth. *Child Development, 66*, 1719–1738.

Burnette, J. L., O'Boyle, E. H., VanEpps, E. M., Pollack, J. M., & Finkel, E. J. (2013). Mind-sets matter: A meta-analytic review of implicit theories and self-regulation. *Psychological Bulletin, 139*, 655–701. http://dx.doi.org.unco.idm.oclc.org/10.1037/a0029531

Burns, C. E., Brady, M. A., Dunn, A. M., & Starr, N. B. (2000). *Pediatric primary care: A handbook for nurse practitioners* (2nd ed.). Philadelphia, PA: Saunders.

Burns, M. K, Deno, S., & Jimerson, S. R. (2007). Toward a unified model of Response to Intervention. In S. R. Jimerson, M. K. Burns, & A. M. VanDerHeyden (Eds.), *Handbook of response to intervention: The science and practice of assessment and intervention* (pp. 428–440). New York, NY: Springer.

Burrous, C. E., Crockenberg, S. C., & Leerkes, E. M. (2009). Developmental history of care and control, depression and anger: Correlates of maternal sensitivity in toddlerhood. *Infant Mental Health Journal, 30*, 103–123.

Burstyn, J. N., & Stevens, R. (2001). Involving the whole school in violence prevention. In J. N. Burstyn, G. Bender, R. Casella, H. W. Gordon, D. P. Guerra, K. V. Luschen, et al. (Eds.), *Preventing violence in schools: A challenge to American democracy* (pp. 139–158). Mahwah, NJ: Erlbaum.

Bursuck, B., & Blanks, B. (2010). Evidence-based early reading practices within a response to intervention system. *Psychology in the Schools. Special Issue: Literacy and Disabilities, 47*(5), 421–431.

Burton, C., Marshal, M., & Chisolm, D. (2014). School absenteeism and mental health among sexual minority youth and heterosexual youth. *Journal of School Psychology, 52*(1), 37–47. doi:10.1016/j.jsp.2013.12.001

Burton, S., & Mitchell, P. (2003). Judging who knows best about yourself: Developmental change in citing the self across middle childhood. *Child Development, 74*, 426–443.

Butler, D. L., Schnellert, L., & Cleary, T. (Ed). (2015). Success for students with learning disabilities: What does self-regulation have to do with it? In T. J. Cleary (Ed.), *Self-regulated learning interventions with at-risk youth: Enhancing adaptability, performance, and well-being* (Applying Psychology in the Schools, pp. 89–111). Washington, DC, US: American Psychological Association. http://dx.doi.org/10.1037/14641-005

Butler, R. (1994). Teacher communication and student interpretations: Effects of teacher responses to failing students on attributional inferences in two age groups. *British Journal of Educational Psychology, 64*, 277–294.

Butler, R. N. (1963). The life review: An interpretation of reminiscence in the aged. *Psychiatry, 26*, 65–76.

Button, R. E. (2007). Teachers' anger, frustration, and self-regulation. In P. A. Schutz & R. Pekrun (Eds.), *Emotion in education* (Educational Psychology Series, pp. 259–274). San Diego, CA: Elsevier Academic Press.

Butzer, B., LoRusso, A. M., Windsor, R., Riley, F., Frame, K., Khalsa, S. B. S., & Conboy, L. (2017). A qualitative examination of yoga for middle school adolescents. *Advances in School Mental Health Promotion, 10*, 195–219. doi:10.1080/1754730X.2017.1325328

Byard, E., Kosciw, J., & Bartkiewicz, M. (2013). Schools and LGBT-parent families: Creating change through programming and advocacy. In A. E. Goldberg & K. R. Allen (Eds.), *LGBT-parent families: Innovations in research and implications for practice* (pp. 275–290). New York, NY: Springer Science Business Media. doi:10.1007/978-1-4614-4556-2_18

Byrge, L., Smith, L. B., & Mix, K. S. (2014). Beginnings of place value: How preschoolers write three-digit numbers. *Child Development, 85*, 437–443. doi:10.1111/cdev.12162

Byrne, B. M. (2002). Validating the measurement and structure of self-concept: Snapshots of past, present, and future research. *American Psychologist, 57*, 897–909.

Byrne, B. M., & Shavelson, R. J. (1986, April). *On gender differences in the structure of adolescent self-concept.* Paper presented at the annual meeting of the American Educational Research Association, San Francisco, CA.

Byrne, J., Hauck, Y., Fisher, C., Bayes, S., & Schutze, R. (2014). Effectiveness of a mindfulness-based childbirth education pilot study on maternal self-efficacy and fear of childbirth. *Journal of Midwifery & Women's Health, 59*, 192–197.

Byrnes, J. P. (1996). *Cognitive development and learning in instructional contexts.* Boston, MA: Allyn & Bacon.

Byrnes, J. P., & Wasik, B. A. (2009). *Language and literacy development: What educators need to know.* New York, NY: Guilford Press.

Bystydzienski, J., & Brown, A. (2012). "I just want to help people": Young women's gendered engagement with engineering. *Feminist Formations, 24*(3), 1–21. doi:10.1353/ff.2012.0027

Cabell, S. Q., Justice, L. M., Konold, T. R., & McGinty, A. S. (2010). Profiles of emergent literacy skills among preschool children who are at risk for academic difficulties. *Early Childhood Research Quarterly, 26*(1), 1–14.

Cacchione, T. (2013). The foundations of object permanence: Does perceived cohesion determine infants' appreciation of the continuous existence of material objects? *Cognition, 128*, 397–406. doi:10.1016/j.cognition.2013.05.006

Cacchione, T., Schaub, S., & Rakoczy, H. (2013). Fourteen-month-old infants infer the continuous identity of objects on the basis of nonvisible causal properties. *Developmental Psychology, 49*, 1325–1329. doi:10.1037/a0029746

Cadima, J., Barros, S., Ferreira, T., Serra-Lemos, M., Leal, T., & Verschueren, K. (2018). Bidirectional associations between vocabulary and self-regulation in preschool and their interplay with teacher–child closeness and autonomy support. *Early Childhood Research Quarterly.* Advance online publication. http://dx.doi.org.unco.idm.oclc.org/10.1016/j.ecresq.2018.04.004

Cai, H., Wu, M., Luo, Y. L., & Yang, J. (2014). Implicit self-esteem decreases in adolescence: A cross-sectional study. *PLoS ONE, 9*(2), 1–5. doi:10.1371/journal.pone.0089988

Cai, J., Ding, M., & Wang, T. (2014). How do exemplary Chinese and U.S. mathematics teachers view instructional coherence? *Educational Studies in Mathematics, 85*, 265–280. doi:10.1007/s10649-013-9513-3

Cain, C. S. (2006). *Attachment disorders: Treatment strategies for traumatized children.* Lantham, MD: Jason Aronson Publishing.

Cain, K., & Oakhill, J. (1998). Comprehension skill and inference-making ability: Issues of causality. In C. Hulme & R. M. Joshi (Eds.), *Reading and spelling: Development and disorders* (pp. 329–342). Mahwah, NJ: Erlbaum.

Calder, L., Hill, V., & Pellicano, E. (2013). "Sometimes I want to play by myself": Understanding what friendship means to children with autism in mainstream primary schools. *Autism: The International Journal of Research & Practice, 17*, 296–316. doi:10.1177/1362361312467866

Calin-Jageman, R. J., & Ratner, H. H. (2005). The role of encoding in the self-explanation effect. *Cognition and Instruction, 23*, 523–543.

Callanan, M. A., & Oakes, L. M. (1992). Preschoolers' questions and parents' explanations: Causal thinking in everyday activity. *Cognitive Development, 7*, 213–233.

Callister, L., Corbett, C., Reed, S., Tomao, C., & Thornton, K. G. (2010). Giving birth: The voices of Ecuadorian women. *Journal of Perinatal & Neonatal Nursing, 24*, 146–154.

Callister, L., Eads, M., & See Yeung, P. (2011). Perceptions of giving birth and adherence to cultural practices in Chinese women. MCN: *American Journal of Maternal Child Nursing, 36*, 387–394.

Caltenco, H. A., Breidegard, B., Jönsson, B., & Struijk, L. N. S. A. (2012). Understanding computer users with tetraplegia: Survey of assistive technology users. *International Journal of Human-Computer Interaction, 28*, 258–268. http://dx.doi.org .unco.idm.oclc.org/10.1080/10447318.2011.586305

Calvert, S. L. (2008). Children as consumers: Advertising and marketing. *Future of Children, 18*(1), 205–234.

Calvin, C. M., Fernandes, C., Smith, P., Visscher, P. M., & Deary, I. J. (2010). Sex, intelligence and educational achievement in a national cohort of over 175,000 11-year-old schoolchildren in England. *Intelligence, 38*, 424–432.

Cameron, C. A., Hunt, A. K., & Linton, M. J. (1996). Written expression as recontextualization: Children write in social time. *Educational Psychology Review, 8*, 125–150.

Cameron, C. E., Cottone, E. A., Murrah, W. M., & Grissmer, D. W. (2016). How are motor skills linked to children's school performance and academic achievement? *Child Development Perspectives, 10*(2), 93–98. doi:10.1111/cdep.12168

Cameron, J. (2001). Negative effects of reward on intrinsic motivation—a limited phenomenon: Comment on Deci, Koestner, and Ryan (2001). *Review of Educational Research, 71*, 29–42.

Cameron, J. L., Eagleson, K. L., Fox, N. A., Hensch, T. K., & Levitt, P. (2017). Social origins of developmental risk for mental and physical illness. *The Journal of Neuroscience, 37*, 10783–10791.

Camilleri, B., & Botting, N. (2013). Beyond static assessment of children's receptive vocabulary: The dynamic assessment of word learning (DAWL). *International Journal of Language & Communication Disorders, 48*, 565–581. doi:10.1111/1460-6984.12033

Campbell, A. (1984). *The girls in the gang: A report from New York City*. New York, NY: Basil Blackwell.

Campbell, D. T., & Stanley, J. C. (1963). Experimental and quasi-experimental designs for research on teaching. In N. L. Gage (Ed.), *Handbook of research on teaching* (pp. 171–246). Chicago, IL: Rand McNally.

Campbell, F. A., Ramey, C. T., Pungello, E., Sparling, J., & Miller-Johnson, S. (2002). Early childhood education: Young adult outcomes from the Abecedarian Project. *Applied Developmental Science, 6*, 42–57.

Campbell, F., Conti, G., Heckman, J. J., Moon, S. H., Hyeok, S., Pungello, E., & Pan, Y. (2014). Early childhood investments substantially boost adult health. *Science, 343*(6178), 1478–1484. doi:10.1126/science.1248429

Campbell, L., Campbell, B., & Dickinson, D. (1998). *Teaching and learning through multiple intelligences* (2nd ed.). Boston, MA: Allyn & Bacon.

Campione, J. C., Shapiro, A. M., & Brown, A. L. (1995). Forms of transfer in a community of learners: Flexible learning and understanding. In A. McKeough, J. Lupart, & A. Marini (Eds.), *Teaching for transfer: Fostering generalization in learning (pp. 35–68)*. Mahwah, NJ: Erlbaum.

Campos, J. J., Frankel, C. B., & Camras, L. (2004). On the nature of emotion regulation. *Child Development, 75*, 377–394.

Camras, L. A., Malatesta, C., & Izard, C. (1991). The development of facial expressions in infancy. In R. S. Feldman & B. Rime (Eds.), *Fundamentals of nonverbal behavior: Studies in emotion and social interaction* (pp. 73–105). New York, NY: Cambridge University Press.

Camras, L. A., Oster, H., Campos, J., Campos, R., Ujiie, T., Miyake, K., . . . Meng, Z. (1998). Production of emotional facial expressions in European American, Japanese, and Chinese infants. *Developmental Psychology, 34*, 616–628.

Cañada, F. F, González-Gómez, D., Airado-Rodríguez, D., Niño, L. M., & Acedo, M. D. (2017). Change in elementary school students' misconceptions on material systems after a theoretical-practical instruction. *International Electronic Journal of Elementary Education, 9*, 499–510.

Cano, F., García, Á., Berbén, A. G., & Justicia, F. (2014). Science Learning: A path analysis of its links with reading comprehension, question-asking in class and science achievement. *International Journal of Science Education, 36*, 1710–1732. doi:10.1080/09500693.2013.876678

Cantrell, L., & Smith, L. B. (2013). Open questions and a proposal: A critical review of the evidence on infant numerical abilities. *Cognition, 128*, 331–352. doi:10.1016/j.cognition.2013.04.008

Cantrell, L., Boyer, T. W., Cordes, S., & Smith, L. B. (2015). Signal clarity: An account of the variability in infant quantity discrimination tasks. *Developmental Science, 18*, 877–893. doi:10.1111/desc.12283

Cao, T. H., Jung, J., & Lee, J. (2017). Assessment in gifted education: A review of the literature from 2005 to 2016. *Journal of Advanced Academics, 28*, 163–203. doi:10.1177/1932202X17714572

Capatosto, K. (2015, July). *Implicit bias strategies: Addressing implicit bias in early childhood education*. Retrieved from http://kirwaninstitute.osu.edu/wp-content/uploads/2016/04/Implicit-Bias-Strategies-Early-Childhood.pdf

Caplan, M., Vespo, J. E., Pedersen, J., & Hay, D. F. (1991). Conflict over resources in small groups of 1- and 2-year-olds. *Child Development, 62*, 1513–1524.

Capone, V., Donizzetti, A. R., & Petrillo, G. (2018). Classroom relationships, sense of community, perceptions of justice, and collective efficacy for students' social well-being. *Journal of Community Psychology, 46*, 374–382. http://dx.doi.org.unco.idm.oclc.org/10.1002/jcop.21943

Cappella, E., Kim, H., Neal, J. W., & Jackson, D. R. (2013). Classroom peer relationships and behavioral engagement in elementary school: The role of social network equity. *American Journal of Community Psychology, 52*, 367–379. doi:10.1007/s10464-013-9603-5

Capron, C., & Duyme, M. (1989). Assessment of effects of socio-economic status on IQ in a full cross-fostering study. *Nature, 340*(6234), 552–554.

Caputi, M., Lecce, S., Pagnin, A., & Banerjee, R. (2012). Longitudinal effects of theory of mind on later peer relations: The role of prosocial behavior. *Developmental Psychology, 48*(1), 257–270. doi:10.1037/a0025402

Cardelle-Elawar, M. (1992). Effects of teaching metacognitive skills to students with low mathematics ability. *Teaching and Teacher Education, 8*, 109–121.

Cardillo, R. R., Mammarella, I. C., Garcia, R. B., & Cornoldi, C. (2017). Local and global processing in block design tasks in children with dyslexia or nonverbal learning disability. *Research in Developmental Disabilities, 64*, 96–107. doi:10.1016/j.ridd.2017.03.011

Carey, S. (1978). The child as word learner. In M. Halle, J. Bresnan, & G. Miller (Eds.), *Linguistic theory and psychological reality* (pp. 264–293). Cambridge, MA: MIT Press.

Carey, S. (1985). *Conceptual change in childhood*. Cambridge, MA: MIT Press.

Carey, S. (1988). Are children fundamentally different kinds of thinkers and learners than adults? In K. Richardson & S. Sheldon (Eds.), *Cognitive development to adolescence: A reader* (pp. 105–138). Hillsdale, NJ: Erlbaum.

Carey, S., & Bartlett, E. (1978). Acquiring a single new word. *Papers and Reports on Child Language Development, 15*, 17–29.

Carey, S., Evans, R., Honda, M., Jay, E., & Unger, C. (1989). "An experiment is when you try it and see if it works": A study of Grade 7 students' understanding of the construction of scientific knowledge. *International Journal of Science Education, 11*, 514–529.

Carey, S., Shusterman, A., Haward, P., & Distefano, R. (2017). Do analog number representations underlie the meanings of young children's verbal numerals? *Cognition, 168*, 243–255.

Carla, B. (2003). Natural birthing lessons from Nepal. *British Journal of Midwifery, 11*(8), 492–495.

Carlisi, C. O., Pavletic, N. N., & Ernst, M. M. (2013). New perspectives on neural systems models of adolescent behavior: Functional brain connectivity. *Neuropsychiatrie De L'enfance Et De L'adolescence, 61*(4), 209–218. doi:10.1016/j.neurenf.2013.02.003

Carlo, G., Koller, S., Raffaelli, M., & de Guzman, M. R. T. (2007). Culture-related strengths among Latin American families: A case study of Brazil. *Marriage and Family Review, 41*, 335–360.

Carlson, E. A., Hostinar, C. E., Mliner, S. B., & Gunnar, M. R. (2014). The emergence of attachment following early social deprivation. *Development & Psychopathology, 26*, 479–489. doi:10.1017/S0954579414000078

Carlson, E. A., Sampson, M. C., & Sroufe, L. A. (2003). Implications of attachment theory and research for developmental-behavioral pediatrics. *Journal of Developmental and Behavioral Pediatrics, 24*, 364–379.

Carlson, N. R. (2014). *Foundations of behavioral neuroscience* (9th ed.). Boston, MA: Pearson.

Carlson, S. M., White, R. E., & Davis-Unger, A. C. (2014). Evidence for a relation between executive function and pretense representation in preschool children. *Cognitive Development, 29*, 1–16. doi:10.1016/j.cogdev.2013.09.001

Carmona, S., Proal, E., Hoekzema, E. A., Gispert, J., Picado, M., Moreno, I., . . . Vilarroya, C. (2009). Ventro-striatal reductions underpin symptoms of hyperactivity and impulsivity in attention-deficit/hyperactivity disorder. *Biological Psychiatry, 66*, 972–977.

Carnell, S., Kim, Y., & Pryor, K. (2012). Fat brains, greedy genes, and parent power: A biobehavioural risk model of child and adult obesity. *International Review of Psychiatry, 24*(3), 189–199. doi:10.3109/09540261.2012.676988

Carney, D. R., & Mason, M. F. (2010). Decision making and testosterone: When the ends justify the means. *Journal of Experimental Social Psychology, 46*, 668–671. doi:10.1016/j.jesp.2010.02.003

Carolan, B. V. (2016). Unequal academic achievement in high school: The mediating roles of concerted cultivation and close friends. *British Journal of Sociology of Education, 37*, 1034–1055. doi:10.1080/01425692.2015.1013085

Caroli, M., Argentieri, L., Cardone, M., & Masi, A. (2004). Role of television in childhood obesity prevention. *International Journal of Obesity, 28*, S105–S108.

Carpenter, M., Uebel, J., & Tomasello, M. (2013). Being mimicked increases prosocial behavior in 18-month-old infants. *Child Development, 84*, 1511–1518. doi:10.1111/cdev.12083

Carpenter, S., Cepeda, N., Rohrer, D., Kang, S., & Pashler, H. (2012). Using spacing to enhance diverse forms of learning: Review of recent research and implications for instruction. *Educational Psychology Review, 24*, 369–378. doi:10.1007/s10648-012-9205-z

Carr, A. (2014). The evidence base for family therapy and systemic interventions for child-focused problems. *Journal of Family Therapy, 36*, 107–157. doi:10.1111/1467-6427.12032

Carr, J. (2012). Six weeks to 45 years: A longitudinal study of a population with Down syndrome. *Journal of Applied Research in Intellectual Disabilities, 25*, 414–422. doi:10.1111/j.1468-3148.2011.00676.x

Carr, M. (2010). The importance of metacognition for conceptual change and strategy use in mathematics. In H. S. Waters & W. Schneider (Eds.), *Metacognition, strategy use, and instruction* (pp. 176–197). New York, NY: Guilford Press.

Carr, M. (2012). Critical transitions: Arithmetic to algebra. In K. R. Harris, S. Graham, T. Urdan, A. G. Bus, S. Major, & H. L. Swanson (Eds.), *APA Educational Psychology Handbook, Vol. 3. Application to teaching and learning* (pp. 229–255). Washington, DC: American Psychological Association. doi:10.1037/13275-010

Carr, M., & Biddlecomb, B. (1998). Metacognition in mathematics from a constructivist perspective. In D. J. Hacker, J. Dunlosky, & A. C. Graesser (Eds.), *Metacognition in educational theory and practice* (pp. 69–91). Mahwah, NJ: Erlbaum.

Carr, M., & Schneider, W. (1991). Long-term maintenance of organizational strategies in kindergarten children. *Contemporary Educational Psychology, 16*, 61–72.

Carroll, J. E., Gruenewald, T. L., Taylor, S. E., Janicki-Deverts, D., Matthews, K. A., & Seeman, T. E. (2013). Childhood abuse, parental warmth, and adult multisystem biological risk in the Coronary Artery Risk Development in Young Adults study. *PNAS—Proceedings of the National Academy of Sciences of the United States of America, 110*, 17149–17153. doi:10.1073/pnas.1315458110

Carruthers, P. (2013). Mindreading in infancy. *Mind & Language, 28*, 141–172. doi:10.1111/mila.12014

Carter, C., & Nutbrown, C. (2016). A pedagogy of friendship: Young children's friendships and how schools can support them. *International Journal of Early Years Education, 24*, 395–413. http://dx.doi.org.unco.idm.oclc.org/10.1080/09669760.2016.1189813

Carter, D. E., Detine-Carter, S. L., & Benson, F. W. (1995). Interracial acceptance in the classroom. In H. C. Foot, A. J. Chapman, & J. R. Smith (Eds.), *Friendship and social relations in children* (pp. 117–143). New Brunswick, NJ: Transaction.

Carter, E. W., Asmus, J., & Moss, C. (2013). Fostering friendships: Supporting relationships among youth with and without developmental disabilities. *Prevention Researcher, 20*(2), 14–17.

Carter, E. W., Common, E. A., Sreckovic, M. A., Huber, H. B., Bottema-Beutel, K., Gustafson, J., . . . Hume, K. (2014). Promoting social competence and peer relationships for adolescents with autism spectrum disorders. *Remedial & Special Education, 35*, 91–101. doi:10.1177/0741932513514618

Carter, E. W., Weir, K., Cooney, M., Walter, M. J., & Moss, C. (2012). Fostering self-determination among children and youth with disabilities: Learning from parents. *Exceptional Parent, 42*(3), 13–17.

Carter, K. R. (1991). Evaluation of gifted programs. In N. Buchanan & J. Feldhusen (Eds.), *Conducting research and evaluation in gifted education: A handbook of methods and applications.* New York, NY: Teachers College Press.

Carter, K. R., & Ormrod, J. E. (1982). Acquisition of formal operations by intellectually gifted children. *Gifted Child Quarterly, 26*, 110–115.

Carter, R., Halawah, A., & Trinh, S. L. (2018). Peer exclusion during the pubertal transition: The role of social competence. *Journal of Youth and Adolescence, 47*(1), 121–134. http://dx.doi.org.unco.idm.oclc.org/10.1007/s10964-017-0682-8

Carter, R., Jaccard, J., Silverman, W. K., & Pina, A. A. (2009). Pubertal timing and its link to behavioral and emotional problems among 'at risk' African American adolescent girls. *Journal of Adolescence, 32*, 467–481.

Carver, P. R., Egan, S. K., & Perry, D. G. (2004). Children who question their heterosexuality. *Developmental Psychology, 40*(1), 43–53.

Casagrande, M., Martella, D., Ruggiero, M. C., Maccari, L., Paloscia, C., Rosa, C., & Pasini, A. (2012). Assessing attentional systems in children with attention deficit hyperactivity disorder. *Archives of Clinical Neuropsychology, 27*(1), 30–44. doi:10.1093/arclin/acr085

Casanova, M. F. (2008). The significance of minicolumnar size variability in autism: A perspective from comparative anatomy. In A. W. Zimmerman (Ed.), *Autism: Current theories and evidence* (pp. 349–360). Totowa, NJ: Humana Press. doi:10.1007/978-1-60327-489-0_16

Case-Smith, J. (1996). Fine motor outcomes in preschool children who receive occupational therapy services. *American Journal of Occupational Therapy, 50*, 52–61.

Case-Smith, J. (2013). Systematic review of interventions to promote social-emotional development in young children with or at risk for disability. *American Journal of Occupational Therapy, 67*, 395–404. doi:10.5014/ajot.2013.004713

Case, R. (1980). Implications of a neo-Piagetian theory for improving the design of instruction. In J. R. Kirby & J. B. Biggs (Eds.), *Cognition, development, and instruction* (pp. 161–186). New York, NY: Academic Press.

Case, R. (1985). *Intellectual development: Birth to adulthood.* Orlando, FL: Academic Press.

Case, R. (1991). *The mind's staircase: Exploring the conceptual underpinnings of children's thought ad knowledge.* Hillsdale, NJ: Erlbaum.

Case, R., & Okamoto, Y., in collaboration with Griffin, S., McKeough, A., Bleiker, C., Henderson, B., & Stephenson, K. M. (1996). The role of central conceptual structures in the development of children's thought. *Monographs of the Society for Research in Child Development, 61*(1–2, Serial No. 246).

Case, R., Okamoto, Y., Henderson, B., & McKeough, A. (1993). Individual variability and consistency in cognitive development: New evidence for the existence of central conceptual structures. In R. Case & W. Edelstein (Eds.), *The new structuralism in cognitive development: Theory and research on individual pathways* (pp. 71–100). Basel, Switzerland: Karger.

Casella, R. (2001). The cultural foundations of peer mediation: Beyond a behaviorist model of urban school conflict. In J. N. Burstyn, G. Bender, R. Casella, H. W. Gordon, D. P. Guerra, K. V. Luschen, et al. (Eds.), *Preventing violence in schools: A challenge to American democracy* (pp. 159–179). Mahwah, NJ: Erlbaum.

Casey, B. J., Giedd, J. N., & Thomas, K. M. (2000). Structural and functional brain development and its relation to cognitive development. *Biological Psychology, 54*, 241–257.

Caspi, A., McClay, J., Moffitt, T., Mill, J., Martin, J., Craig, I. W., . . . Poulton, R. (2002). Role of genotype in the cycle of violence in maltreated children. *Science, 297*(5582), 851–854. doi:10.1126/science.1072290

Caspi, A., Sugden, K., Moffitt, T. E., Taylor, A., Craig, I. W., Harrington, J., . . . Poulton, R. (2003). Influence of life stress on depression: Moderation by the polymorphism in the 5-HTT gene. *Science, 30*, 1386–1389.

Cassano, M. C., & Zeman, J. L. (2010). Parental socialization of sadness regulation in middle childhood: The role of expectations and gender. *Developmental Psychology, 46*, 1214–1226.

Cassidy, A. R. (2016). Executive function and psychosocial adjustment in healthy children and adolescents: A latent variable modelling investigation. *Child Neuropsychology, 22*, 292–317. doi:10.1080/09297049.2014.994484

Cassidy, J., Jones, J. D., & Shaver, P. R. (2013). Contributions of attachment theory and research: A framework for future research, translation, and policy. *Development & Psychopathology, 25*(4 Pt. 2), 1415–1434. doi:10.1017/S0954579413000692

Cassidy, M., & Berlin, L. J. (1994). The insecure-ambivalent pattern of attachment: Theory and research. *Child Development, 65*, 971–991.

Catania, L. S., Hetrick, S. E., Newman, L. K., & Purcell, R. (2011). Prevention and early intervention for mental health problems in 0–25 year olds: Are there evidence-based models of care? *Advances in Mental Health, 10*(1), 6–19. doi:10.5172/jamh.2011.10.1.6

Cates, J. A., & Weber, C. (2012). A substance use survey with old order Amish early adolescents: Perceptions of peer alcohol and drug use. *Journal of Child & Adolescent Substance Abuse, 21*, 193–203. doi:10.1080/10678 28X.2012.689935

Cattell, R. B. (1963). Theory of fluid and crystallized intelligence: A critical experiment. *Journal of Educational Psychology, 54*, 1–22.

Cattell, R. B. (1980). The heritability of fluid, *gf*, and crystallised, *gc*, intelligence, estimated by a least squares use of the MAVA method. *British Journal of Educational Psychology, 50*, 253–265.

Cattell, R. B. (1987). *Intelligence: Its structure, growth, and action.* Amsterdam, the Netherlands: North-Holland.

Cazden, C. B. (1968). The acquisition of noun and verb inflections. *Child Development, 39*, 433–448.

Cazden, C. B. (1976). Play with language and meta-linguistic awareness: One dimension of language experience.In J. Bruner, A. Jolly, & K. Sylva (Eds.), *Play: Its role in development and evolution* (pp. 603–608). New York, NY: Basic Books.

Ceci, S. J. (2003). Cast in six ponds and you'll reel in something: Looking back on 25 years of research. *American Psychologist, 58*, 855–864.

Ceci, S. J., & Roazzi, A. (1994). The effects of context on cognition: Postcards from Brazil. In R. J. Sternberg & R. K. Wagner (Eds.), *Mind in context: Interactionist perspectives on human intelligence* (pp. 74–101). Cambridge, England: Cambridge University Press.

Ceci, S. J., & Williams, W. M. (1997). Schooling, intelligence, and income. *American Psychologist*, 52, 1051–1058. doi:10.1037/0003-066X.52.10.1051

Ceci, S. J., Rosenblum, T. B., & Kumpf, M. (1998). The shrinking gap between high- and low-scoring groups: Current trends and possible causes. In U. Neisser (Ed.), *The rising curve: Long-term gains in IQ and related measures* (pp. 287–302). Washington, DC: American Psychological Association.

Ceglowski, D., Shears, J., & Furman, R. (2010). "I want child care he's gonna be happy in": A case study of a father's child care experiences. *Early Education and Development, 21*(1), 1–20. doi:10.1080/10409280902783467

Cekaite, A. (2018). Microgenesis of language creativity: Innovation, conformity and incongruence in children's language play. *Language Sciences, 65*, 26–36. http://dx.doi.org.unco.idm.oclc.org/10.1016/j.langsci.2017.01.007

Cemalcilar, Z. (2010). Schools as socialisation contexts: Understanding the impact of school climate factors on students' sense of school belonging. *Applied Psychology, 59*, 243–272. doi:10.1111/j.1464-0597.2009.00389.x

Center for Children and Families. (2013). *How to establish a daily report card.* Retrieved from http://ccf.buffalo.edu/pdf/school_daily_report_card.pdf

Center for History and New Media. (2006). *Teaching American history: Conflict and consensus. Key moments in U.S. history.* Retrieved from http://chnm.gmu.edu/mcpstah/lessonplans/1950-to-present/?planid26

Centers for Disease Control and Prevention. (2005). *Nutrition and the health of young people.* Atlanta, GA: Author.

Centers for Disease Control & Prevention (2009a). *Birth to 24 months: Boys.* Retrieved from https://www.cdc.gov/growthcharts/data/who/grchrt_boys_24lw_100611.pdf

Centers for Disease Control & Prevention (2009b). *Birth to 24 months: Girls.* Retrieved from https://www.cdc.gov/growthcharts/data/who/grchrt_girls_24lw_9210.pdf

Centers for Disease Control and Prevention. (2009c). *Understanding child maltreatment.* Retrieved fromhttp://www.cdc.gov/violenceprevention/pdf/CM-FactSheet-a.pdf

Centers for Disease Control and Prevention. (2010). *The association between school based physical activity, including physical education, and academic performance.* Atlanta, GA: U.S. Department of Health and Human Services; 2010. Retrieved from https://www.cdc.gov/healthyschools/pecat/pa-pe_paper.pdf

Centers for Disease Control and Prevention. (2011). School health guidelines to promote healthy eating and physical activity. *Morbidity and Mortality Weekly Report, 60*(5). Retrieved from http://www.cdc.gov/mmwr/pdf/rr/rr6005.pdf

Centers for Disease Control and Prevention. (2013). *Child maltreatment: Consequences.* Retrieved from http://www.cdc.gov/violenceprevention/childmaltreatment/consequences.html

Centers for Disease Control and Prevention. (2013a). Adolescent and school health standard 6. Retrieved from http://www.cdc.gov/healthyyouth/sher/standards/6.htm

Centers for Disease Control and Prevention. (2013b). *About BMI for children and teens.* Retrieved from http://www.cdc.gov/healthyweight/assessing/bmi/childrens_bmi/about_childrens_bmi.html

Centers for Disease Control and Prevention. (2013c). *Overweight and obesity. Childhood obesity facts.* Retrieved from http://www.cdc.gov/obesity/data/childhood.html

Centers for Disease Control and Prevention. (2013d). *Progress on childhood obesity: Many states show declines.* Retrieved from http://www.cdc.gov/VitalSigns/ChildhoodObesity/

Centers for Disease Control and Prevention. (2013e). *Injury prevention and control: Data and statistics.* Retrieved from http://www.cdc.gov/injury/wisqars/LeadingCauses.html

Centers for Disease Control and Prevention. (2013f). *Injury prevention and control: Traumatic brain injury.* Retrieved from http://www.cdc.gov/traumaticBrainInjury/causes.html

Centers for Disease Control and Prevention. (2013g). *Injury prevention and control.* Retrieved from http://www.cdc.gov/traumaticbraininjury/prevention.html

Centers for Disease Control and Prevention (2015a). *Body Mass Index (BMI) Measurement in Schools.* Retrieved from https://www.cdc.gov/healthyschools/obesity/BMI/BMI_measurement_schools.htm

Centers for Disease Control and Prevention (2015b). *Health schools: Physical activity facts.* Retrieved from https://www.cdc.gov/healthyschools/physicalactivity/facts.htm

Centers for Disease Control and Prevention. (2016, June 10). *Youth risk behavior surveillance—United States, 2015. Morbidity and Mortality Weekly Report, 65*(6). Retrieved from https://www.cdc.gov/mmwr/volumes/65/ss/pdfs/ss6506.pdf

Central Intelligence Agency. (2010, January 15). *The world factbook. South Asia: Nepal.* Retrieved from https://www.cia.gov/library/publications/the-world-factbook/geos/np.html

Cermak, L. S., & Craik, F. I. M. (Eds.). (1979). *Levels of processing in human memory.* Hillsdale, NJ: Erlbaum.

Cha, D., Cha, C., & Cha, N. T. (1999). *Dia's story cloth: The Hmong People's Journey of Freedom.* New York, New York: Lee & Low Books.

Chall, J. S. (1996). *Stages of reading development* (2nd ed.) Fort Worth, TX: Harcourt, Brace.

Champagne, F. A. (2009). Beyond nature vs. nurture: Philosophical insights from molecular biology. *Observer, 22*(4), 4, 27–28.

Champion, J. (2013). Stories from a Mexican American Partera: Life on the Texas–Mexico border. *Journal of Transcultural Nursing, 24*, 94–102. doi:10.1177/1043659612452003

Chan, W., Au, T. K., & Tang, J. (2014). Strategic counting: A novel assessment of place-value understanding. *Learning & Instruction, 29*, 78–94. doi:10.1016/j.learninstruc.2013.09.001

Chandler-Olcott, K. (2013). Expanding what it means to make evidence-based claims. *Journal of Adolescent & Adult Literacy, 57*, 280–288. doi:10.1002/jaal.252

Chandler, M. J. (1987). The Othello effect: Essay on the emergence and eclipse of skeptical doubt. *Human Development, 30*, 137–159.

Chandler, M., & Boyes, M. (1982). Social-cognitive development. In B. Wolman (Ed.), *Handbook of developmental psychology* (pp. 387-402). Upper Saddle River, NJ: Prentice Hall.

Chandler, M., & Moran, T. (1990). Psychopathy and moral development: A comparative study of delinquent and nondelinquent youth. *Development and Psychopathology, 2*, 227–246.

Chang, M., Paulson, S. E., Finch, W., Mcintosh, D. E., &Rothlisberg, B. A. (2014). Joint confirmatory factor analysis of the Woodcock-Johnson Tests of Cognitive Abilities, Third Edition, and the Stanford-Binet Intelligence Scales, Fifth Edition, with a preschool population. *Psychology in the Schools, 51*(1), 32–57. doi:10.1002/pits.21734

Chang, N. (2012). What are the roles that children's drawings play in inquiry of science concepts? *Early Child Development and Care, 182*(5), 621–637. doi:10.1080/03004430.2011.569542

Chang, Y., Laugeson, E., Gantman, A., Ellingsen, R., Frankel, F., & Dillon, A. (2014). Predicting treatment success in social skills training for adolescents with autism spectrum disorders: The UCLA Program for the Education and Enrichment of Relational Skills. *Autism: The International Journal of Research & Practice, 18*, 467–470.

Chant, R. H. (2009). Developing involved and active citizens: The role of personal practical theories and action research in a standards-based social studies classroom. *Teacher Education Quarterly, 36*(1), 181–190.

Chao, R. K. (1994). Beyond parental control and authoritarian parenting style: Understanding Chinese parenting through the cultural notion of training. *Child Development, 65*, 1111–1119.

Chao, R. K. (2000). Cultural explanations for the role of parenting in the school success of Asian-American children. In R. D. Taylor & M. C. Wang (Eds.), *Resilience across contexts: Family, work, culture, and community* (pp. 333–363). Mahwah, NJ: Erlbaum.

Chaplin, T. M., & Aldao, A. (2013). Gender differences in emotion expression in children: A meta-analytic review. *Psychological Bulletin, 139*, 735–765. doi:10.1037/a0030737

Chapman, M. (1988). *Constructive evolution: Origins and development of Piaget's thought.* Cambridge, England: Cambridge University Press.

Charkaluk, M., Marchand-Martin, L., Ego, A., Zeitlin, J., Arnaud, C., Burguet, A., . . . Pierrat, V. (2012). The influence of fetal growth reference standards on assessment of cognitive and academic outcomes of very preterm children. *Journal of Pediatrics, 161*, 1053–1058. doi:10.1016/j.jpeds.2012.05.037

Charlesworth, W. R. (1994). Charles Darwin and developmental psychology: Past and present. In R. D. Parke, P. A. Ornstein, J. R. Rieser, & C. Zahn-Waxler, *A century of developmental psychology* (pp. 77–102). Washington, DC: American Psychological Association.

Charlesworth, W. R., & LaFreniere, P. (1983). Dominance, friendship, and resource utilization in preschool children's groups. *Ethology and Sociobiology, 4*, 175–186.

Chaudhary, M., & Gupta, A. (2012). Children's influence in family buying process in India. *Young Consumers, 13*, 161–175. doi:10.1108/17473611211233512

Chavous, T. M., Bernat, D. H., Schmeelk-Cone, K., Caldwell, C. H., Kohn-Wood, L., & Zimmerman, M. A. (2003). Racial identity and academic attainment among African American adolescents. *Child Development, 74*, 1076–1090.

Chazan-Cohen, R., Jerald, J., & Stark, D. R. (2001). A commitment to supporting the mental health of our youngest children. *Zero to Three, 22*(1), 4–12.

Chazan, D., Brantlinger, A., Clark, L. M., & Edwards, A. R. (2013). What mathematics education might learn from the work of well-respected African American mathematics teachers in urban schools. *Teachers College Record, 115*(2), 1–40.

Chedzoy, S., & Burden, R. (2009). Primary school children's reflections on physical education lessons: An attributional analysis and possible implications for teacher action. *Thinking Skills and Creativity, 4*, 185–193. doi:10.1016/j.tsc.2009.09.008

Cheek, J., Abrams, E. M., Lipschitz, D. L., Vago, D. R., & Nakamura, Y. (2017). Creating novel school-based education programs to cultivate mindfulness in youth: What the letters told us. *Journal of Child and Family Studies.* Advance online publication. doi:10.1007/s10826-017-0761-1

Chelonis, J. J., Johnson, T. A., Ferguson, S. A., Berry, K. J., Kubacak, B., Edwards, M. C., & Paule, M. G. (2011). Effect of methylphenidate on motivation in children with attention-deficit/hyperactivity disorder. *Experimental and Clinical Psychopharmacology, 19*, 145–153. doi:10.1037/a0022794

Chen, B.-B. (2017). Parent–adolescent attachment and academic adjustment: The mediating role of self-worth. *Journal of Child and Family Studies, 26*, 2070–2076. http://dx.doi.org.unco.idm.oclc.org/10.1007/s10826-017-0728-2

Chen, D., Edwards-Leeper, L., Stancin, T., & Tishelman, A. (2018). Advancing the practice of pediatric psychology with transgender youth: State of the science, ongoing controversies, and future directions. *Clinical Practice in Pediatric Psychology, 6*, 73–83. http://dx.doi.org.unco.idm.oclc.org/10.1037/cpp0000229

Chen, E., & Miller, G. E. (2012). "Shift-and-persist" strategies: Why low socioeconomic status isn't always bad for health. *Perspectives on Psychological Science, 7*, 135–158. doi:10.1177/1745691612436694

Chen, H., Pine, D. S., Ernst, M., Gorodetsky, E., Kasen, S., Gordon, . . . Cohen, P. (2013). The MAOA gene predicts happiness in women. *Progress in Neuro-Psychopharmacology & Biological Psychiatry, 40*, 122–125. doi:10.1016/j.pnpbp.2012.07.018

Chen, J.-Q. (2009). China's assimilation of MI theory in education: Accent on the family and harmony. In J.-Q. Chen, S. Moran, & H. Gardner (Eds.), *Multiple intelligences around the world* (pp. 29–42). San Francisco, CA: Jossey-Bass.

Chen, J., & Gardner, H. (2012). Assessment of intellectual profile: A perspective from multiple-intelligences theory. In D. P. Flanagan & P. L. Harrison (Eds.), *Contemporary intellectual assessment: Theories, tests, and issues* (3rd ed., pp. 145–155). New York, NY: Guilford Press.

Chen, J., Claessens, A., & Msall, M. E. (2014). Prematurity and school readiness in a nationally representative sample of Australian children: Does typically occurring preschool moderate the relationship? *Early Human Development, 90*(2), 73–79. doi:10.1016/j.earlhumdev.2013.09.015

Chen, J., Li, X., & McGue, M. (2013). The interacting effect of the BDNF Val66Met polymorphism and stressful life events on adolescent depression is not an artifact of gene-environment correlation: evidence from a longitudinal twin study. *Journal of Child Psychology & Psychiatry, 54*, 1066–1073.

Chen, L.-L., Su, Y.-C., Su, C.-H., Lin, H.-C., & Kuo, H.-W. (2008). Acupressure and meridian massage: Combined effects on increasing body weight in premature infants. *Journal of Clinical Nursing, 17*, 1174–1181.

Chen, M. J., Gruenewald, P. J., & Remer, L. G. (2009). Does alcohol outlet density affect youth access to alcohol? *Journal of Adolescent Health, 44*, 582–589.

Chen, W.-C. (2016). The role of grandparents in single-parent families in Taiwan. *Marriage & Family Review, 52*(1–2), 41–63. doi:10.1080/01494929.2015.1073654

Chen, W., Rovegno, I., Cone, S., & Cone, T. (2012). An accomplished teacher's use of scaffolding during a second-grade unit on designing games. *Research Quarterly for Exercise & Sport, 83*, 221–234.

Chen, X., & Wang, L. (2010). China. In M. H. Bornstein (Ed.), *Handbook of cultural developmental science* (pp. 429–444). New York, NY: Psychology Press.

Chen, X., Anderson, R. C., Li, W., Hao, M., Wu, X., & Shu, H. (2004). Phonological awareness of bilingual and monolingual Chinese children. *Journal of Educational Psychology, 96*, 142–151.

Chen, X., Chang, L., & He, Y. (2003). The peer group as a context: Mediating and moderating effects on the relations between academic achievement and social functioning in Chinese children. *Child Development, 74*, 710–727.

Chen, X., DeSouza, A. T., Chen, H., & Wang, L. (2006). Reticent behavior and experiences in peer interactions in Chinese and Canadian children. *Developmental Psychology, 42*, 656–665.

Chen, X., Hastings, P. D., Rubin, K. H., Chen, H., Cen, G., & Stewart, S. L. (1998). Child-rearing attitudes and behavioral inhibition in Chinese and Canadian toddlers: A cross-cultural study. *Developmental Psychology, 34*, 677–686.

Chen, X., Rubin, K. H., Liu, M., Chen, H., Wang, L., Li, D., . . . Boshu, L. (2003). Compliance in Chinese and Canadian toddlers: A cross-cultural study. *International Journal of Behavioral Development, 27*, 428–436.

Chen, X., Wang, L., & Wang, Z. (2009). Shyness-sensitivity and social, school, and psychological adjustment in rural migrant and urban children in china. *Child Development, 80*, 1499–1513. doi:10.1111/j.1467-8624.2009.01347.x

Chen, Y., McAnally, H., & Reese, E. (2013). Development in the organization of episodic memories in middle childhood and adolescence. *Frontiers in Behavioral Neuroscience, 7*, 1-9, Article ID 84.

Chen, Z., Sanchez, R. P., & Campbell, T. (1997). From beyond to within their grasp: The rudiments of analogical problem solving in 10- and 13-month-olds. *Developmental Psychology, 33*, 790–801.

Cheng, Z. (2012). Teaching young children decomposition strategies to solve addition problems: An experimental study. *Journal of Mathematical Behavior, 31*(1), 29–47. doi:10.1016/j.jmathb.2011.09.002

Chess, S., & Thomas, A. (1992). Interactions between offspring and parents in development. In B. Tizard & V. P. Varma (Eds.), *Vulnerability and resilience in human development: A festschrift for Ann and Alan Clarke* (pp. 72–87). London, England: Jessica Kingsley Publishers.

Chesworth, L. (2016). A funds of knowledge approach to examining play interests: Listening to children's and parents' perspectives. *International Journal of Early Years Education, 24*, 294–308. doi:10.1080/09669760.2016.1188370

Chetland, E., & Fluck, M. (2007). Children's performance on the "give x" task: A microgenetic analysis of 'counting' and 'grabbing' behavior. *Infant and Child Development. Special Issue: Using the Microgenetic Method to Investigate Cognitive Development, 16*(1), 35–51.

Cheung, A., & Slavin, R. (2013). The effectiveness of educational technology applications for enhancing mathematics achievement in K–12 classrooms: A meta-analysis. *Educational Research Review, 9*, 88–113. doi:10.1016/j.edurev.2013.01.001

Cheung, H. H.-P. (2009). Multiple intelligences in China: Challenges and hopes. In J.-Q. Chen, S. Moran & H. Gardner (Eds.), *Multiple intelligences around the world* (pp. 43–54). San Francisco, CA: Jossey-Bass.

Cheyney, M., Burcher, P., & Vedam, S. (2014). A crusade against home birth. *Birth: Issues In Perinatal Care, 41*(1), 1–4. doi:10.1111/birt.12099

Chi, M. T. H. (1978). Knowledge structures and memory development. In R. S. Siegler (Ed.), *Children's thinking: What develops?* (pp. 73-96). Hillsdale, NJ: Erlbaum.

Chia, N., & Kee, N. (2013). Gender differences in the reading process of six-year-olds in Singapore. *Early Child Development & Care, 183*, 1432–1448. doi:10.1080/03004430.2013.788812

Chiasson, V., Vera-Estay, E., Lalonde, G., Dooley, J. J., & Beauchamp, M. H. (2017). Assessing social cognition: Age-related changes in moral reasoning in childhood and adolescence. *Clinical Neuropsychologist, 31*, 515–530. http://dx.doi.org.unco.idm.oclc.org/10.1080/13854046.2016.1268650

ChildTrends. (2014). *World family map*. Retrieved from http://worldfamilymap.ifstudies.org/2014/wp-content/uploads/2014/06/WFM-2014-Final_ForWeb.

Chin, J. (2014). Young children's trust beliefs in peers: Relations to social competence and interactive behaviors in a peer group. *Early Education And Development, 25*, 601–618. doi:10.1080/10409289.2013.836698

Chisholm, K., Carter, M. C., Ames, E. W., & Morison, S. J. (1995). Attachment security and indiscriminately friendly behavior in children adopted from Romanian orphanages. *Development and Psychopathology, 7*, 283–297.

Chiu, M. M. (2007). Families, economies, cultures, and science achievement in 41 countries: Country-, school-, and student-level analyses. *Journal of Family Psychology, 21*, 510–519.

Chodkiewicz, A., & Boyle, C. (2014). Exploring the contribution of attribution retraining to student perceptions and the learning process. *Educational Psychology in Practice, 30*(1), 78–87. doi:10.1080/02667363.2014.880048

Choi, J., & Sachs, G. T. (2017). Adolescent multilinguals' engagement with religion in a book club. *Journal of Adolescent & Adult Literacy, 60*, 415–423. doi:10.1002/jaal.591

Choi, J., Johnson, D. W., & Johnson, R. (2011). Relationships among cooperative learning experiences, social interdependence, children's aggression, victimization, and prosocial behaviors. *Journal of Applied Social Psychology, 41*, 976–1003. doi:10.1111/j.1559-1816.2011.00744.x

Chomsky, C. S. (1969). *The acquisition of syntax in children from 5 to 10*. Cambridge, MA: MIT Press.

Chomsky, N. (1959). Review of B. F. Skinner's *Verbal Behavior*. *Language, 35*, 26–58.

Chomsky, N. (1965). *Aspects of the theory of syntax*. Cambridge, MA: MIT Press.

Chomsky, N. (1972). *Language and mind* (enlarged ed.). San Diego, CA: Harcourt Brace Jovanovich.

Chomsky, N. (1976). *Reflections on language*. London, England: Temple Smith.

Chomsky, N. (2006). *Language and mind* (3rd ed.). Cambridge, England: Cambridge University Press.

Chomsky, N. (2017). The language capacity: architecture and evolution. *Psychonomic Bulletin & Review, 24*, 200–203.

Chong, W., Moore, D. W., Nonis, K. P., Tang, H., Koh, P., & Wee, S. (2014). Mission I'm possible: Effects of a community-based project on the basic literacy skills of at-risk kindergarteners. *Infants & Young Children, 27*(1), 60–73. doi:10.1097/IYC.0b013e3182a60281

Chow, C., & Ruhl, H. (2014). Friendship and romantic stressors and depression in emerging adulthood: Mediating and moderating roles of attachment representations. *Journal of Adult Development, 21*, 106–115. doi:10.1007/s10804-014-9184-z

Christensen, C. G., & Myford, C. M. (2014). Measuring social and emotional content in children's television: An instrument development study. *Journal of Broadcasting & Electronic Media, 58*(1), 21–41. doi:10.1080/08838151.2013.875024

Christenson, S. L., & Thurlow, M. L. (2004). School dropouts: Prevention, considerations, interventions, and challenges. *Current Directions in Psychological Science, 13*, 36–39.

Christenson, S., Palan, R., & Scullin, S. (2009). Family–school partnerships: An essential component of student achievement. *Principal Leadership, 9*(9), 10–16.

Christie, F. (2012) The overall trajectory in language learning in school. *Language Learning, 62*, 187–224. doi:10.1111/j.1467-9922.2011.00683.x

Christie, J. F., & Johnsen, E. P. (1983). The role of play in social-intellectual development. *Review of Educational Research, 53*, 93–115.

Christodoulou, J. J., Lac, A., & Moore, D. S. (2017). Babies and math: A meta-analysis of infants; simple arithmetic competence. *Developmental Psychology, 53*, 1405–1417. doi:10.1037/dev0000330

Christoffersen, M. (2012). A study of adopted children, their environment, and development: A systematic review. *Adoption Quarterly, 15*(3), 220–237. doi:10.1080/10926755.2012.700002

Christopher, C., Saunders, R., Jacobvitz, D., Burton, R., & Hazen, N. (2013). Maternal empathy and changes in mothers' permissiveness as predictors of toddlers' early social competence with peers: A parenting intervention study. *Journal of Child & Family Studies, 22*(6), 769–778. doi:10.1007/s10826-012-9631-z

Chukovsky, K. (1968). *From two to five* (M. Morton, Trans.). Berkeley: University of California Press.

Chung, J. M., Hutteman, R., van Aken, M. A. G., & Denissen, J. J. A. (2017). High, low, and in between: Self-esteem development from middle childhood to young adulthood. *Journal of Research in Personality, 70*, 122–133. http://dx.doi.org.unco.idm.oclc.org/10.1016/j.jrp.2017.07.001

Chung, K., Reavis, S., Mosconi, M., Drewry, J., Matthews, T., & Tassé, M. J. (2007). Peer-mediated social skills training program for young children with high-functioning autism. *Research in Developmental Disabilities, 28*, 423–436. doi:10.1016/j.ridd.2006.05.002

Ciarrochi, J., & Heaven, P. C. L. (2008). Learned social hopelessness: The role of explanatory style in predicting social support during adolescence. *Journal of Child Psychology and Psychiatry, 49*, 1279–1286. doi:10.1111/j.1469-7610.2008.01950.x

Ciaunica, A., & Fotopoulou, A. (2017). The touched self: Psychological and philosophical perspectives on proximal intersubjectivity and the self. In C. Durt, T. Fuchs, & C. Tewes (Eds.), *Embodiment, enaction, and culture: Investigating the constitution of the shared world* (pp. 173–192). Cambridge, MA, US: MIT Press.

Cicchetti, D., Hetzel, S., Rogosch, F. A., Handley, E. D., & Toth, S. L. (2016a). An investigation of child maltreatment and epigenetic mechanisms of mental and physical health risk. *Development and Psychopathology, 28*(4, Pt. 2), 1305–1317. doi:10.1017/S0954579416000869

Cicchetti, D., McGowan, P. O., & Roth, T. L. (2015). Epigenetic pathways through which experiences become linked with biology. *Development & Psychopathology, 27*, 637–648. doi:10.1017/S0954579415000206

Cicchetti, D., Murray-Close, D., Cillessen, A. N., Lansu, T. M., & Van Den Berg, Y. M. (2014). Aggression, hostile attributions, status, and gender: A continued quest. *Development & Psychopathology, 26*, 635–644. doi:10.1017/S0954579414000285

Cicchetti, D., Rogosch, F. A., & Toth, S. L. (1997). Ontogenesis, depressotypic organization, and the depressive spectrum. In S. S. Luthar, J. A. Burack, D. Cicchetti, & J. R. Weisz (Eds.), *Developmental psychopathology: Perspectives on adjustment, risk, and disorder* (pp. 273–313). Cambridge, England: Cambridge University Press.

Cicchetti, D., Spencer, M., & Swanson, D. (2013). Opportunities and challenges to the development of healthy children and youth living in diverse communities. *Development & Psychopathology, 25*(4, Pt. 2), 1551–1566. doi:10.1017/S095457941300076X

Cimpian, A., Arce, H.-M. C., Markman, E. M., & Dweck, C. S. (2007). Subtle linguistic cues affect children's motivation. *Psychological Science, 18*, 314–316.

Cinamon, R., & Rich, Y. (2014). Work and family plans among at-risk Israeli adolescents: A mixed-methods study. *Journal of Career Development, 41*, 163–184. doi:10.1177/0894845313507748

Cingel, D. P., Krcmar, M., & Olsen, M. K. (2015). Exploring predictors and consequences of Personal Fable ideation on Facebook. *Computers in Human Behavior, 48*, 28–35. http://dx.doi.org.unco.idm.oclc.org/10.1016/j.chb.2015.01.017

Ciullo, S., Ortiz, M. B., Al Otaiba, S., & Lane, K. L. (2016). Advanced reading comprehension expectations in secondary school: Considerations for students with emotional or behavior disorders. *Journal of Disability Policy Studies, 27*(1), 54–64. http://dx.doi.org.unco.idm.oclc.org/10.1177/1044207315604365

Claessen, M., Leitão, S., Kane, R., & Williams, C. (2013). Phonological processing skills in specific language impairment. *International Journal of Speech-Language Pathology, 15*, 471–483. doi:10.3109/17549507.2012.753110

Claeys, J. (2013). Theory and research: The nexus of clinical inference. *Journal of Psychoeducational Assessment, 31*, 170–174. doi:10.1177/0734282913478037

Clair, L., Jackson, B., & Zweiback, R. (2012). Six years later: Effect of family involvement training on the language skills of children from migrant families. *School Community Journal, 22*(1), 9–19.

Clark, B. (1997). *Growing up gifted* (5th ed.). Upper Saddle River, NJ: Merrill/Prentice Hall.

Clark, C. C. (1992). Deviant adolescent subcultures: Assessment strategies and clinical interventions. *Adolescence, 27*(106), 283–293.

Clark, D. B. (2006). Longitudinal conceptual change in students' understanding of thermal equilibrium: An examination of the process of conceptual restructuring. *Cognition and Instruction, 24*, 467–563.

Clark, K. (2009). The case for structured English immersion. *Educational Leadership, 66*(7), 42–46.

Clark, N. M., Gong, M., & Kaciroti, N. (2014). A model of self-regulation for control of chronic disease. *Health Education & Behavior, 41*, 499–508. doi:10.1177/1090198114547701

Clark, P., & Zygmunt, E. (2014). A close encounter with personal bias: Pedagogical implications for teacher education. *Journal of Negro Education, 83*, 147–161. doi:10.7709/jnegroeducation.83.2.0147

Clarke, S., & Duda, M. A. (2018). PBS goes to middle school: Building capacity of peer buddies to implement a PBS intervention with fidelity. *Behavior Analysis in Practice.* Advance online publication. http://dx.doi.org.unco.idm.oclc.org/10.1007/s40617-018-0253-9

Clasen, D. R., & Brown, B. B. (1985). The multidimensionality of peer pressure in adolescence. *Journal of Youth and Adolescence, 14*, 451–468.

Clemens, E. V., Shipp, A. E., & Pisarik, C. T. (2008). MySpace as a tool for mental health professionals. *Child and Adolescent Mental Health, 13*(2), 97–98.

Clemens, N. H., Oslund, E. L., Simmons, L. E., & Simmons, D. (2014). Assessing spelling in kindergarten: Further comparison of scoring metrics and their relation to reading skills. *Journal of School Psychology, 52*(1), 49–61. doi:10.1016/j.jsp.2013.12.005

Clifford, M. M. (1990). Students need challenge, not easy success. *Educational Leadership, 48*(1), 22–26.

Closson, L. M., & Watanabe, L. (2018). Popularity in the peer group and victimization within friendship cliques during early adolescence. *The Journal of Early Adolescence, 38*, 327–351. http://dx.doi.org.unco.idm.oclc.org/10.1177/0272431616670753

Cluss, P. A., Fee, L., Culyba, R. J., Bhat, K. B., & Owen, K. (2014). Effect of food service nutrition improvements on elementary school cafeteria lunch purchase patterns. *Journal of School Health, 84*, 355–362. doi:10.1111/josh.12157

Cluver, A., Heyman, G., & Carver, L. J. (2013). Young children selectively seek help when solving problems. *Journal of Experimental Child Psychology, 115*, 570–578. doi:10.1016/j.jecp.2012.12.011

Cobb-Clark, D., & Moschion, J. (2017). Gender gaps in early educational achievement. *Journal of Population Economics, 30*, 1093–1134. doi:10.1007/s00148-017-0638-z

Cobb, J. B. (2017). Investigating reading metacognitive strategy awareness of elementary children: A developmental continuum emerges. *Journal of Research in Childhood Education, 31*, 401–418. http://dx.doi.org.unco.idm.oclc.org/10.1080/02568543.2017.1309481

Cochran-Smith, M., & Lytle, S. (1993). *Inside out: Teacher research and knowledge.* New York, NY: Teachers College Press.

Cody, H., & Kamphaus, R. W. (1999). Down syndrome. In S. Goldstein & C. R. Reynolds (Eds.), *Handbook of neurodevelopmental and genetic disorders* (pp. 385–405). New York, NY: Guilford Press.

Coelho, V. A., Marchante, M., & Jimerson, S. R. (2017). Promoting a positive middle school transition: A randomized-controlled treatment study examining self-concept and self-esteem. *Journal of Youth and Adolescence, 46*, 558–569.

Coffin, A. B., Myles, B. S., Rogers, J., & Szakacs, W. (2016). Supporting the writing skills of individuals with autism spectrum disorder through assistive technologies. In T. A. Cardon (Ed.), *Technology and the treatment of children with autism spectrum disorder* (Autism and Child Psychopathology Series, pp. 59–73). Cham, Switzerland: Springer International Publishing. http://dx.doi.org.unco.idm.oclc.org/10.1007/978-3-319-20872-5_6

Cohen, E. G. (1994). Restructuring the classroom: Conditions for productive small groups. *Review of Educational Research, 64*, 1–35.

Cohen, L. B., & Cashon, C. H. (2006). Infant cognition. In W. Damon & R. M. Lerner (Eds. in Chief) & D. Kuhn & R. S. Siegler (Vol. Eds.), *Handbook of Child Psychology: Vol. 2. Cognition, perception, and language* (6th ed., pp. 214–251). Hoboken, NJ: Wiley.

Cohn, N. (2014). Framing "I can't draw": The influence of cultural frames on the development of drawing. *Culture & Psychology, 20*(1), 102–117. doi:10.1177/1354067X13515936

Coie, J. D., & Cillessen, A. H. N. (1993). Peer rejection: Origins and effects on children's development. *Current Directions in Psychological Science, 2*, 89–92.

Coie, J. D., & Dodge, K. A. (1988). Multiple sources of data on social behavior and social status. *Child Development, 59*, 815–829.

Coie, J. D., & Kupersmidt, J. (1983). A behavioral analysis of emerging social status in boys' groups. *Child Development, 54*, 1400–1416.

Coie, J. D., Dodge, K. A., & Coppotelli, H. (1982). Dimensions and types of social status: A cross-age perspective. *Developmental Psychology, 18*, 557–570.

Coie, J. D., Dodge, K. A., Terry, R., & Wright, V. (1991). The role of aggression in peer relations: An analysis of aggression episodes in boys' play groups. *Child Development, 62*, 812–826.

Coiro, J., & Fogleman, J. (2011, February). Using websites wisely. *Educational Leadership, 68*(5), 34–38.

Colasante, T., & Malti, T. (2017). Resting heart rate, guilt, and sympathy: A developmental psychophysiological study of physical aggression. *Psychophysiology, 54*, 1770–1781. http://dx.doi.org.unco.idm.oclc.org/10.1111/psyp.12915

Colby, A., & Kohlberg, L. (1984). Invariant sequence and internal consistency in moral judgment stages. In W. M. Kurtines & J. L. Gewirtz (Eds.), *Morality, moral behavior, and moral development (pp. 41–51).* New York, NY: Wiley.

Colby, A., Kohlberg, L., Gibbs, J., & Lieberman, M. (1983). A longitudinal study of moral judgment. *Monographs of the Society for Research in Child Development, 48*(1–2, Serial No. 200).

Cole, C. F., Labin, D. B., & del Rocio Galarza, M. (2008). Begin with the children: What research on *Sesame Street's* international coproductions reveals about using media to promote a new more peaceful world. *International Journal of Behavioral Development, 32*, 359–365. doi:10.1177/0165025408090977

Cole, H. A., & Heilig, J. V. (2011). Developing a school-based youth court: A potential alternative to the school to prison pipeline. *Journal of Law & Education, 40*, 305–321.

Cole, M. (2006). Culture and cognitive development in phylogenetic, historical and ontogenetic perspective. In W. Damon & R. M. Lerner (Series Eds.) & D. Kuhn & R. Siegler (Vol. Eds.), *Handbook of Child Psychology: Vol. 2. Cognition, perception, and language* (6th ed., pp. 636–683). New York, NY: Wiley.

Cole, M., & Hatano, G. (2007). Cultural-historical activity theory: Integrating phylogeny, cultural history, and ontogenesis in cultural psychology. In S. Kitayama & D. Cohen (Eds.), *Handbook of cultural psychology* (pp. 109–135). New York, NY: Guilford Press.

Cole, P. M., & Tamang, B. L. (2001). Nepali children's ideas about emotional displays in hypo-thetical challenges. *Developmental Psychology, 34*, 640–646.

Cole, P. M., & Tan, P. Z. (2007). Emotion socialization from a cultural perspective. In J. E. Grusec & P. D. Hastings (Eds.), *Handbook of socialization: Theory and research* (pp. 516–542). New York, NY: Guilford Press.

Cole, P. M., Armstrong, L. M., & Pemberton, C. K. (2010). The role of language in the development of emotion regulation. In S. D. Calkins & M. A. Bell (Eds.), *Child development at the intersection of emotion and cognition* (pp. 59–77). Washington, DC: American Psychological Association.

Cole, P. M., Tan, P. Z., Hall, S. E., Zhang, Y., Crnic, K. A., Blair, C. B., & Li, R. (2011). Developmental changes in anger expression and attention focus: Learning to wait. *Developmental Psychology, 47*, 1078–1089. doi:10.1037/a0023813

Coleman, J. C., Crosby, M. G., Irwin, H. K., Dennis, L. R., Simpson, C. G., & Rose, C. A. (2013). Preventing challenging behaviors in preschool: Effective strategies for classroom teachers. *Young Exceptional Children, 16*(3), 3–10. doi:10.1177/1096250612464641

Coleman, L., & Guo, A. (2013). Exploring children's passion for learning in six domains. *Journal for the Education of The Gifted, 36*, 155–175. doi:10.1177/0162353213480432

Coley, R. L., & Chase-Lansdale, P. L. (1998). Adolescent pregnancy and parenthood. *American Psychologist, 53*, 152–166.

Colley, D., & Cooper, P. (2017). Models of emotional development. In D. Colley & P. Cooper (Eds.), *Attachment and emotional development in the classroom: Theory and practice* (pp. 11–36). London, England: Jessica Kinglsey.

Collier, V. P. (1992). The Canadian bilingual immersion debate: A synthesis of research findings. *Studies in Second Language Acquisition, 14*, 87–97.

Collin-Vézina, D. (2013). Students affected by sexual abuse. In E. Rossen & R. Hull (Eds.), *Supporting and educating traumatized students: A guide for school-based professionals* (pp. 187–202). New York, NY: Oxford University Press.

Collins, A. (2006). Cognitive apprenticeship. In R. K. Sawyer (Ed.), *The Cambridge handbook of the learning sciences* (pp. 47–60). Cambridge, England: Cambridge University Press.

Collins, A., Brown, J. S., & Newman, S. E. (1989). Cognitive apprenticeship: Teaching the crafts of reading, writing, and mathematics. In L. B. Resnick (Ed.), *Knowing, learning, and instruction: Essays in honor of Robert Glaser* (pp. 453-494). Hillsdale, NJ: Erlbaum.

Collins, M. F. (2010). ELL preschoolers' English vocabulary acquisition from storybook reading. *Early Childhood Research Quarterly, 25*(1), 84–97.

Collins, W. A., & Sroufe, L. A. (1999). Capacity for intimate relationships: A developmental construction. In W. Furman, B. B. Brown, & C. Feiring (Eds.), *The development of romantic relationships in adolescence* (pp. 125–147). Cambridge, England: Cambridge University Press.

Collins, W. A., & van Dulmen, M. (2006). "The course of true love(s)?": Origins and pathways in the development of romantic relationships. In A. C. Crouter & A. Booth (Eds.), *Romance and sex in adolescence and emerging adulthood: Risks and opportunities* (pp. 53–86). Mahwah, NJ: Erlbaum.

Colmar, S. (2014). A parent-based book-reading intervention for disadvantaged children with language difficulties. *Child Language Teaching & Therapy, 30*(1), 79–90. doi:10.1177/0265659013507296

Colombo, J. (1993). *Infant cognition: Predicting later intellectual functioning.* Newbury Park, CA: Sage.

Colombo, J., Brez, C. C., & Curtindale, L. M. (2013). Infant perception and cognition. In R. M. Lerner, M. Easterbrooks, J. Mistry, & I. B. Weiner (Eds.), *Handbook of Psychology, Vol. 6: Developmental psychology* (2nd ed., pp. 61–89). Hoboken, NJ: Wiley.

Comalli, D. M., Keen, R., Abraham, E. S., Foo, V. J., Mei-Hua, L., & Adolph, K. K. (2016). The development of tool use: Planning for end-state comfort. *Developmental Psychology, 52*, 1878–1892. doi:10.1037/dev0000207

Comeau, L., Cormier, P., Grandmaison, É., & Lacroix, D. (1999). A longitudinal study of phonological processing skills in children learning to read in a second language. *Journal of Educational Psychology, 91*, 29–43.

Common Core State Standards Initiative (2018). English language arts standards in writing: Grade 1. Retrieved January 2, 2018 from http://www.corestandards.org/ELA-Literacy/W/1/#CCSS.ELA-Literacy.W.1.1

Compton, L., Campbell, M. A., & Mergler, A. (2014). Teacher, parent and student perceptions of the motives of cyberbullies. *Social Psychology of Education. 17*(3), 383-400. http://dx.doi.org.unco.idm.oclc.org/10.1007/s11218-014-9254-x

Comstock, G., & Scharrer, E. (2006). Media and popular culture. In W. Damon & R. M. Lerner (Series Eds.) & K. A. Renninger & I. E. Sigel (Vol. Eds.), *Handbook of Child Psychology: Vol. 3. Social, emotional, and personality development* (6th ed., pp. 817–863). New York, NY: Wiley.

Condon, E. M., Sadler, L. S., & Mayes, L. C. (2018). Toxic stress and protective factors in multi-ethnic school age children: A research protocol. *Research in Nursing & Health, 41*, 97-106.

Condon, J. C., & Yousef, F. S. (1975). *An introduction to intercultural communication.* Indianapolis, IN: Bobbs-Merrill.

Condry, J. C., & Ross, D. F. (1985). Sex and aggression: The influence of gender label on the perception of aggression in chilren. *Child Development, 56*, 225–233.

Conn, J., & Kanner, L. (1940). Spontaneous erections in childhood. *Journal of Pediatrics, 16*, 237–240.

Conner-Warren, R. (2014). Effects of cumulative trauma load on perceptions of health, blood pressure, and resting heart rate in urban African American youth. *Journal for Specialists in Pediatric Nursing, 19*, 127–138. doi:10.1111/jspn.12063

Conner, B. T., Hellemann, G. S., Ritchie, T. L., & Noble, E. P. (2010). Genetic, personality, and environmental predictors of drug use in adolescents. *Journal of Substance Abuse Treatment, 38*, 178–190.

Conners, G. P., Veenema, T. G., Kavanagh, C. A., Ricci, J., & Callahan, C. M. (2002). Still falling: A community-wide infant walker injury prevention initiative. *Patient Education and Counseling, 46*, 169–173. doi:10.1016/S0738-3991(01)00210-5

Connolly, J. A., & McIsaac, C. (2009). Romantic relationships in adolescence. In R. M. Lerner, & L. Steinberg (Eds.), *Handbook of Adolescent Psychology, Vol. 2. Contextual influences on adolescent development* (3rd ed., pp. 104–151). Hoboken, NJ: Wiley.

Consortium of Longitudinal Studies. (Ed.). (1983). *As the twig is bent: Lasting effects of preschool programs.* Mahwah, NJ: Erlbaum.

Contento, I. R., Koch, P. A., Lee, H., Sauberli, W., & Calabrese-Barton, A. (2007). Enhancing personal agency and competence in eating and moving: Formative evaluation of a middle school curriculum—Choice, control, and change. *Journal of Nutrition Education & Behavior, 39*, S179–S186.

Cook-Cottone, C. P. (2017). *Mindfulness and yoga in schools: A guide for teachers and practitioners.* New York, NY: Springer.

Cook-Cottone, C. P., Tribole, E., & Tylka, T. L. (2013). Pillar II: Healthy physical activity. In *Healthy eating in schools: Evidence-based interventions to help kids thrive* (pp. 107–122). Washington, DC US: American Psychological Association. doi:10.1037/14180-006

Cook, C., Goodman, N. D., & Schulz, L. E. (2011). Where science starts: Spontaneous experiments in preschoolers' exploratory play. *Cognition, 120*, 341–349. doi:10.1016/j.cognition.2011.03.003

Cook, E. C., Buehler, C., & Henson, R. (2009). Parents and peers as social influences to deter antisocial behavior. *Journal of Youth and Adolescence, 38*, 1240–1252.

Cook, K., Bush, S., & Karp, K. (2016). Clarifying confusing science rules, vocabulary & diagrams. *American Biology Teacher* (University of California Press), *78*, 676–678. doi:10.1525/abt.2016.78.8.676

Cook, V., & Newson, M. (1996). *Chomsky's universal grammar: An introduction* (2nd ed.). Oxford, England: Blackwell.

Cooklin, A. R., Westrupp, E. M., Strazdins, L., Giallo, R., Martin, A., & Nicholson, J. M. (2016). Fathers at work: Work–family conflict, work–family enrichment and parenting in an Australian cohort. *Journal of Family Issues, 37*, 1611–1635. doi:10.1177/0192513X14553054

Cooney, J. B., & Ladd, S. F. (1992). The influence of verbal protocol methods on children's mental computation. *Learning and Individual Differences, 4*, 237–257.

Cooney, J. B., Swanson, H. L., & Ladd, S. F. (1988). Acquisition of mental multiplication skill: Evidence for the transition between counting and retrieval strategies. *Cognition and Instruction, 5*, 323–345.

Cooper-Vince, C., Pincus, D., & Comer, J. (2014). Maternal intrusiveness, family financial means, and anxiety across childhood in a large multiphase sample of community youth. *Journal of Abnormal Child Psychology, 42*, 429–438.

Cooper, C. R., Denner, J., & Lopez, E. M. (1999, Fall). Cultural brokers: Helping Latino children on pathways toward success. *The Future of Children: When School Is Out, 9*, 51–57.

Cooper, C. R., Jackson, J. F., Azmitia, M., Lopez, E., & Dunbar, N. (1995). Bridging students' multiple worlds: African American and Latino youth in academic outreach programs. In R. F. Macias & R. G. Garcia-Ramos (Eds.), *Changing schools for changing students: An anthology of research on language minorities* (pp. 211–234). Santa Barbara: University of California Linguistic Minority Research Institute.

Cooper, G., Hoffman, K., & Powell, B. (2017). Circle of security in child care. *Zero to Three, 37*(3), 27–34.

Cooper, H., & Dorr, N. (1995). Race comparisons on need for achievement: A meta-analytic alternative to Graham's narrative review. *Review of Educational Research, 65*, 483–508.

Cooper, H., Robinson, J. C., & Patall, E. A. (2006). Does homework improve academic achievement? A synthesis of research, 1987–2003. *Review of Educational Research, 76*, 1–62.

Cooper, S. M., & Smalls, C. (2010). Culturally distinctive and academic socialization: Direct and interactive relationships with African American adolescents' academic adjustment. *Journal of Youth and Adolescence, 39*, 199–212.

Cooperrider, K., & Goldin-Meadow, S. (2017). When gesture becomes analogy. *Topics in Cognitive Science, 9*(3), 719-737. http://dx.doi.org.unco.idm.oclc.org/10.1111/tops.12276

Coopersmith, S. (1967). *The antecedents of self-esteem.* San Francisco, CA: Freeman.

Copeland, W. E., Wolke, D., Lereya, S., Shanahan, L., Worthman, C., & Costello, E. (2014). Childhood bullying involvement predicts low-grade systemic inflammation into adulthood. *PNAS: Proceedings Of The National Academy of Sciences of the United States of America, 111*, 7570–7575. doi:10.1073/pnas.1323641111

Coplan, R. J., Liu, J., Cao, J., Chen, X., & Li, D. (2017). Shyness and school adjustment in Chinese children: The roles of teachers and peers. *School Psychology Quarterly, 32*, 131–142. http://dx.doi.org.unco.idm.oclc.org/10.1037/spq0000179

Coplan, R. J., Ooi, L. L., Rose-Krasnor, L., & Nocita, G. (2014). "I want to play alone": Assessment and correlates of self-reported preference for solitary play in young children. *Infant & Child Development, 23*, 229–238. doi:10.1002/icd.1854

Corbin, J. M., & Strauss, A. (2008). *Basics of qualitative research: Techniques and procedures for developing grounded theory* (3rd ed.). Los Angeles, CA: Sage.

Cordoni, G., Demuru, E., Ceccarelli, E., & Palagi, E. (2016). Play, aggressive conflict and reconciliation in pre-school children: What matters? *Behaviour, 153*(9–11), 1075–1102. http://dx.doi.org.unco.idm.oclc.org/10.1163/1568539X-00003397

Corenblum, B. (2014). Relationships between racial-ethnic identity, self-esteem and in-group attitudes among First Nation children. *Journal of Youth & Adolescence, 43*, 387–404. doi:10.1007/s10964-013-0081-8

Corno, L., & Mandinach, E. B. (2004). What we have learned about student engagement in the past twenty years. In D. M. McNerney & S. Van Etten (Eds.), *Big theories revisited* (pp. 299–328). Greenwich, CT: Information Age.

Cornoldi, C. (2010). Metacognition, intelligence, and academic performance. In H. S. Waters & W. Schneider (Eds.), *Metacognition, strategy use, and instruction* (pp. 257–277). New York, NY: Guilford Press.

Cornoldi, C., Carretti, B., Drusi, S., & Tencati, C. (2015). Improving problem solving in primary school students: The effect of a training programme focusing on metacognition and working memory. *British Journal of Educational Psychology, 85*, 424–439. doi:10.1111/bjep.12083

Cornoldi, C., Mammarella, I. C., & Fine, J. G. (2016). *Nonverbal learning disabilities.* New York, NY: Guilford Press.

Corpus, J., McClintic-Gilbert, M., & Hayenga, A. (2009). Within-year changes in children's intrinsic and extrinsic motivational orientations: Contextual predictors and academic outcomes. *Contemporary Educational Psychology, 34*, 154–166. doi:10.1016/j.cedpsych.2009.01.001

Corrigall, K. A., & Schellenberg, G. (2015). Predicting who takes music lessons: Parent and child characteristics. *Frontiers in Psychology, 6*, Article ID 282.

Corriveau, K., Pasquini, E., & Goswami, U. (2007). Basic auditory processing skills and specific language impairment: A new look at an old hypothesis. *Journal of Speech, Language, and Hearing Research, 50*, 647–666.

Corsano, P., Musetti, A., Caricati, L., & Magnani, B. (2017). Keeping secrets from friends: Exploring the effects of friendship quality, loneliness and self-esteem on secrecy. *Journal of Adolescence, 58*, 24–32. http://dx.doi.org.unco.idm.oclc.org/10.1016/j.adolescence.2017.04.010

Corsaro, W. A. (2003). *We're friends, right? Inside kids' culture.* Washington, DC: Joseph Henry Press.

Corsaro, W. A., & Eder, D. (1990). Children's peer cultures. *Annual Review of Sociology, 16*, 197–220.

Corsaro, W. A., & Molinari, L. (2005). *I compagni: Understanding children's transition from preschool to elementary school.* New York, NY: Teachers College Press.

Cortese, S. (2013). Gym for the attention-deficit/hyperactivity disorder brain? Still a long run ahead. . . . *Journal of the American Academy of Child & Adolescent Psychiatry, 52*, 894–896. doi:10.1016/j.jaac.2013.06.011

Cosden, M., Morrison, G., Albanese, A. L., & Macias, S. (2001). When homework is not home work: After-school programs for homework assistance. *Educational Psychologist, 36*, 211–221.

Cossu, G. (1999). The acquisition of Italian orthography. In M. Harris & G. Hatano (Eds.), *Learning to read and write: A cross-linguistic perspective* (pp. 10–33). Cambridge, England: Cambridge University Press.

Costigan, C. L., Hua, J. M., & Su, T. F. (2010). Living up to expectations: The strengths and challenges experienced by Chinese Canadian students. *Canadian Journal of School Psychology, 25*, 223–245.

Cote, D., Jones, V., Barnett, C., Pavelek, K., Nguyen, H., & Sparks, S. (2014). Teaching problem solving skills to elementary age students with autism. *Education & Training in Autism & Developmental Disabilities, 49*, 189–199.

Cotterell, J. L. (1992). The relation of attachments and supports to adolescent well-being and school adjustment. *Journal of Adolescent Research, 7*, 28–42.

Council for Exceptional Children. (1995). *Toward a common agenda: Linking gifted education and school reform.* Reston, VA: Author.

Council on Early Childhood, & Council on School Health. (2016). The pediatrician's role in optimizing school readiness. *Pediatrics, 138*, e1-e7. doi:10.1542/peds.2016-2293

Courage, M. L., & Adams, R. J. (1990). Visual acuity assessment from birth to three years using the acuity card procedures: Cross-sectional and longitudinal samples. *Optometry and Vision Science, 67*, 713–718.

Courage, M. L., & Setliff, A. E. (2010). When babies watch television: Attention-getting, attention-holding, and the implications for learning from video material. *Developmental Review, 30*, 220–238. doi:10.1016/j.dr.2010.03.003

Courage, M. L., Reynolds, G. D., & Richards, J. E. (2006). Infants' attention to patterned stimuli: Developmental change from 3 to 12 months of age. *Child Development, 77*, 680–695.

Covington, M. V. (1987). Achievement motivation, self-attributions, and the exceptional learner. In J. D. Day & J. G. Borkowski (Eds.), *Intelligence and exceptionality (pp. 355–389).* Norwood, NJ: Ablex.

Covington, M. V. (1992). *Making the grade: A self-worth perspective on motivation and school reform.* Cambridge, England: Cambridge University Press.

Covington, M. V., & Müeller, K. J. (2001). Intrinsic versus extrinsic motivation: An approach/avoidance reformulation. *Educational Psychology Review, 13*, 157–176.

Cowan, N. (2014). Working memory underpins cognitive development, learning, and education. *Educational Psychology Review, 26*, 197–223. doi:10.1007/s10648-013-9246-y

Cowan, R., & Powell, D. (2014). The contributions of domain-general and numerical factors to third-grade arithmetic skills and mathematical learning disability. *Journal of Educational Psychology, 106*, 214–229. doi:10.1037/a0034097

Cox, C. B. (2000). *Empowering grandparents raising grandchildren.* New York, NY: Springer.

Cox, M. E., Orme, J. G., & Rhoades, K. W. (2003). Willingness to foster children with emotional or behavioral problems. *Journal of Social Service Research, 29*, 23–51.

Coyne, S. M., Padilla-Walker, L. M., & Holmgren, H. G. (2018). A six-year longitudinal study of texting trajectories during adolescence. *Child Development, 89*(1), 58–65. http://dx.doi.org.unco.idm.oclc.org/10.1111/cdev.12823

Crago, M. B. (1988). *Cultural context in communicative interaction of Inuit children* (Order No. NL48660). Available from ProQuest Dissertations & Theses Global. (275849665). Retrieved from https://unco.idm.oclc.org/login?url=https://search-proquest-com.unco.idm.oclc.org/docview/275849665?accountid=12832

Crago, M. B., Allen, S. E. M., & Hough-Eyamie, W. P. (1997). Exploring innateness through cultural and linguistic variation. In M. Gopnik (Ed.), *The inheritance and innateness of grammars* (pp. 70–90). New York, NY: Oxford University Press.

Crago, M. B., Annahatak, B., & Ningiuruvik, L. (1993). Changing patterns of language socialization in Inuit homes. *Anthropology and Education Quarterly, 24*, 205–223.

Craig, L., & Powell, A. (2013). Non-parental childcare, time pressure and the gendered division of paid work, domestic work and parental childcare. *Community, Work & Family, 16*(1), 100–119. doi:10.1080/13668803.2012.722013

Crain, W. (2011). *Theories of development: Concepts and applications* (6th ed.). Upper Saddle River, NJ: Pearson Prentice Hall.

Cranley Gallagher, K. (2013). Guiding children's friendship development. *Young Children, 68*(5), 26–32.

Crevecoeur, Y. C., Coyne, M. D., & McCoach, D. (2014). English language learners and English-Only learners' response to direct vocabulary instruction. *Reading & Writing Quarterly, 30*(1), 51–78. doi:10.1080/10573569.2013.758943

Crick, N. R., & Dodge, K. A. (1996). Social information-processing mechanisms in reactive and proactive aggression. *Child Development, 67*, 993–1002.

Criss, M. M., Pettit, G. S., Bates, J. E., Dodge, K. A., & Lapp, A. L. (1992). Family adversity, positive peer relationships, and children's externalizing behavior: A longitudinal perspective on risk and resilience. *Child Development, 73*, 1220–1237.

Critten, S., Pine, K., & Steffler, D. (2007). Spelling development in young children: A case of representational redescription? *Journal of Educational Psychology, 99*, 207–220.

Crocker, J., & Major, B. (1989). Social stigma and self-esteem: The self-protective properties of stigma. *Psychological Review, 96*, 608–630. http://dx.doi.org.unco.idm.oclc.org/10.1037/0033-295X.96.4.608

Croker, S., & Buchanan, H. (2011). Scientific reasoning in a real-world context: The effect of prior belief and outcome on children's hypothesis-testing strategies. *British Journal of Developmental Psychology, 29*, 409–424. doi:10.1348/026151010X496906

Cronin, D. (2003). *Diary of a worm.* New York, NY: Harper Collins.

Crosnoe, R. (2009). Family–school connections and the transitions of low-income youths and English language learners from middle school to high school. *Developmental Psychology, 45*(4), 1061–1076.

Crosnoe, R., & Elder, G. H., Jr. (2004). Family dynamics, supportive relationships, and educational resilience during adolescence. *Journal of Family Issues, 25*, 571–602.

Crosnoe, R., & Huston, A. C. (2007). Socioeconomic status, schooling, and the developmental trajectories of adolescents. *Developmental Psychology, 43*, 1097–1110.

Cross, D., Adefope, O., Rapacki, L., Hudson, R., Lee, M. Y., & Perez, A. (2012). Success made probable: Creating equitable mathematical experiences through project-based learning. *Journal of Urban Mathematics Education, 5*(2), 55–86.

Cross, J., Bugaj, S. J., & Mammadov, S. (2016). Accepting a scholarly identity. *Journal for the Education of the Gifted, 39*(1), 23–48. doi:10.1177/0162353215624162

Crowl, A., Ahn, S., & Baker, J. (2008). A meta-analysis of developmental outcomes for children of same-sex and heterosexual parents. *Journal of GLBT Family Studies, 4*(3), 385–407. doi:10.1080/15504280802177615

Crowley, K., & Jacobs, M. (2002). Building islands of expertise in everyday family activity. In G. Leinhardt, K. Crowley, & K. Knutson (Eds.), *Learning conversations in museums* (pp. 333–356). Mahwah, NJ: Erlbaum.

Crum, W. (2010). Foster parent parenting characteristics that lead to increased placement stability or disruption. *Children and Youth Services Review, 32*, 185–190. doi:10.1016/j.childyouth.2009.08.022

Cruz, I., Quittner, A. L., Marker, C., & DesJardin, J. L. (2013). Identification of effective strategies to promote language in deaf children with cochlear implants. *Child Development, 84*, 543–559. doi:10.1111/j.1467-8624.2012.01863.x

Csikszentmihalyi, M. (1995). Education for the twenty-first century. *Daedalus, 124*(4), 107–114.

Csikszentmihalyi, M., & Larson, R. (1984). *Being adolescent: Conflict and growth in the teenage years.* New York, NY: Basic Books.

Csizmadia, A., Kaneakua, J. P., Miller, M., & Halgunseth, L. C. (2013). Ethnic-racial socialization and its implications for ethnic minority children's adjustment in middle childhood. *Journal of Communications Research, 5*, 227–242.

Cugmas, Z. (2011). Relation between children's attachment to kindergarten teachers, personality characteristics and play activities. *Early Child Development & Care, 181*, 1271–1289. doi:10.1080/03004430.2010.523993

Cullen, B. (1998). Teaching the faith with humility: Indoctrination versus education. *Lutheran Education, 134*(2), 77–89.

Cummings, E. M., & Merrilees, C. E. (2010). Identifying the dynamic processes underlying links between marital conflict and child adjustment. In M. S. Schulz, M. K. Pruett, P. K. Kerig, & R. D. Parke (Eds.), *Strengthening couple relationships for optimal child development: Lessons from research and intervention* (pp. 27–40). Washington, DC: American Psychological Association.

Cummings, E., Braungart-Rieker, J. M., & Schudlich, T. (2013). Emotion and personality development. In R. M. Lerner, M. Easterbrooks, J. Mistry, & I. B. Weiner (Eds.), *Handbook of Psychology, Vol. 6. Developmental psychology* (2nd ed., pp. 215–241). Hoboken, NJ: Wiley.

Cummins, J. (1981). Age on arrival and immigrant second language learning in Canada: A reassessment. *Applied Linguistics, 2*, 132–149.

Cunningham, T. H., & Graham, C. R. (2000). Increasing native English vocabulary recognition through Spanish immersion: Cognate transfer from foreign to first language. *Journal of Educational Psychology, 92*, 37–49.

Cunningham, W. A., & Zelazo, P. D. (2010). The development of iterative reprocessing: Implications for affect and its regulation. In P. D. Zelazo, M. Chandler, & E. Crone (Eds.), *Developmental social cognitive neuroscience* (pp. 81–98). New York, NY: Psychology Press.

Curchack-Lichtin, J., Chacko, A., & Halperin, J. (2014). Changes in ADHD symptom endorsement: Preschool to school age. *Journal of Abnormal Child Psychology, 42*, 993–eg1004. doi:10.1007/s10802-013-9834-9s

Curci, A., Lanciano, T., Soleti, E., Zammuner, V., & Salovey, P. (2013). Construct validity of the Italian version of the Mayer–Salovey–Caruso Emotional Intelligence Test (MSCEIT) v2.0. *Journal of Personality Assessment, 95*, 486–494. doi:10.1080/00223891.2013.778272

Curcio, A. L., Knott, V. E, & Mak, A. S. (2015). Why do young people engage in delinquency and problem drinking? Views from adolescents and stakeholders. *Australian Psychologist, 50*, 350–361. doi:10.1111/ap.12118

Curley, J. P., & Champagne, F. A. (2016). Influence of maternal care on the developing brain: Mechanisms, temporal dynamics and sensitive periods. *Frontiers in Neuroendocrinology, 40*, 52–66. doi:10.1016/j.yfrne.2015.11.001

Curtin, K. C., Schweitzer, A., Tuxbury, K., & D'Aoust, J. A. (2016). Investigating the factors of resiliency among exceptional youth living in rural underserved communities. *Rural Special Education Quarterly, 35*(2), 3–9.

Curtiss, S. (1977). *Genie: A psycholinguistic study of a modern-day "wild child."* New York, NY: Academic Press.

Curwood, J., Magnified, A., & Lammers, J. C. (2013). Writing in the wild: Writers' motivation in fan-based affinity spaces. *Journal of Adolescent & Adult Literacy, 56*, 677–685. doi:10.1002/JAAL.192

Cushman, P., & Cowan, J. (2010). Enhancing student self-worth in the primary school learning environment: Teachers' views and students' views. *Pastoral Care in Education, 28*, 81–95.

Czymoniewicz-Klippel, M. T. (2013). Bad boys, big trouble: Subcultural formation and resistance in a Cambodian village. *Youth & Society, 45*, 480–499.

d'Ailly, H. (2003). Children's autonomy and perceived control in learning: A model of motivation and achievement in Taiwan. *Journal of Educational Psychology, 95*, 84–96.

D'Souza, H., & Karmiloff-Smith, A. (2017). Neurodevelopmental disorders. *WIREs Cognitive Science, 8*(1–2), 1–10. doi:10.1002/wcs.1398

Dabarera, C., Renandya, W. A., & Zhang, L. (2014). The impact of metacognitive scaffolding and monitoring on reading comprehension. *System, 42*, 462–473. doi:10.1016/j.system.2013.12.020

Dahl, A., Campos, J. J., Anderson, D. I., Uchiyama, I., Witherington, D. C., Ueno, M., . . . Barbu-Roth, M. (2013). The epigenesis of wariness of heights. *Psychological Science, 24*, 1361–1367. doi:10.1177/0956797613476047

Dahl, A., Sherlock, B. R., Campos, J. J., & Theunissen, F. E. (2014). Mothers' tone of voice depends on the nature of infants' transgressions. *Emotion, 14*, 651–665. doi:10.1037/a0036608

Dahl, R. (1964). *Charlie and the chocolate factory* (J. Schindelman, Ill.). New York, NY: Knopf.

Dahl, R. E., & Lewin, D. S. (2002). Pathways to adolescent health: Sleep regulation and behavior. *Journal of Adolescent Health, 31* (6 Suppl.), 175–184.

Dahlin, B., & Watkins, D. (2000). The role of repetition in the processes of memorizing and understanding: A comparison of the views of Western and Chinese secondary students in Hong Kong. *British Journal of Educational Psychology, 70*, 65–84.

Daley, T. C., Whaley, S. E., Sigman, M. D., Espinosa, M. P., & Neumann, C. (2003). IQ on the rise: The Flynn effect in rural Kenyan children. *Psychological Science, 14*, 215–219.

Dallaire, D. H., & Wilson, L. C. (2010). The relation of exposure to parental criminal activity, arrest, and sentencing to children's maladjustment. *Journal of Child and Family Studies, 19*, 404–418. doi:10.1007/s10826-009-9311-9

Dalton, T. C. (2005). Arnold Gesell and the maturation controversy. *Integrative Physiological & Behavioral Science, 40*(4), 182–204.

Damon, W. (1977). *The social world of the child.* San Francisco, CA: Jossey-Bass.

Damon, W. (1984). Peer education: The untapped potential. *Journal of Applied Developmental Psychology, 5*, 331–343.

Damon, W. (1988). *The moral child: Nurturing children's natural moral growth.* New York, NY: Free Press.

Damon, W. (1991). Putting substance into self-esteem: A focus on academic and moral values. *Educational Horizons, 70*(1), 12–18.

Damon, W., & Hart, D. (1988). *Self-understanding in childhood and adolescence.* New York, NY: Cambridge University Press.

DanceSafe. (2000a). *What is LSD?* Retrieved from http://www.dancesafe.org/documents/druginfo/lsd.php

DanceSafe. (2000b). *What is speed?* Retrieved from http://www.dancesafe.org/documents/druginfo/speed.php

Daniel, J. (2009). Intentionally thoughtful family engagement in early childhood education. *Young Children, 64*(5), 10–14.

Danish, J. J., Saleh, A., Andrade, A., & Bryan, B. (2017). Observing complex systems thinking in the zone of proximal development. *Instructional Science, 45*(1), 5–24. doi:10.1007/s11251-016-9391-z

Danner, F. W., & Day, M. C. (1977). Eliciting formal operations. *Child Development, 48*, 1600–1606.

Darling-Hammond, L., & Bransford, J. (Eds.). (2005). *Preparing teachers for a changing world: What teachers should learn and be able to do.* San Francisco, CA: Jossey-Bass/Wiley.

Darling, S., Parker, M., Goodall, K. E., Havelka, J., & Allen, R. J. (2014). Visuospatial bootstrapping: Implicit binding of verbal working memory to visuospatial representations in children and adults. *Journal of Experimental Child Psychology, 119*, 112–119. doi:10.1016/j.jecp.2013.10.004

Darvin, J. (2009). Make books, not war: workshops at a summer camp in Bosnia. *Literacy, 43*(1), 50–59. doi:10.1111/j.1741-4369.2009.00483.x

Daryanani, I., Hamilton, J. L., Abramson, L. Y., & Alloy, L. B. (2016). Single mother parenting and adolescent psychopathology. *Journal of Abnormal Child Psychology, 44*, 1411–1423. doi:10.1007/s10802-016-0128-x

Daunic, A. P., & Smith, S. W. (2010). Conflict resolution, peer mediation, and bullying prevention. In B. Algozzine, A. P. Daunic, & S. W. Smith (Eds.), *Preventing problem behaviors: Schoolwide programs and classroom practices* (2nd ed., pp. 113–132). Thousand Oaks, CA: Corwin.

Dauvier, B., Bailleux, C., & Perret, P. (2014). The development of relational integration during childhood. *Developmental Psychology, 50*, 1687–1697. doi:10.1037/a0036655

Dávalos-Esparza, D.-A. (2017). Children's reflections on the uses and functions of punctuation: The role of modality markers. *Infancia y Aprendizaje/Journal for the Study of Education and Development, 40*(3), 429–466.

Davenport, E. C., Jr., Davison, M. L., Kuang, H., Ding, S., Kim, S., & Kwak, N. (1998). High school mathematics course-taking by gender and ethnicity. *American Educational Research Journal, 35*, 497–514.

Davidov, M., Zahn-Waxler, C., Roth-Hanania, R., & Knafo, A. (2013). Concern for others in the first year of life: Theory, evidence, and avenues for research. *Child Development Perspectives, 7*, 126–131. doi:10.1111/cdep.12028

Davidse, N., de Jong, M., Bus, A., Huijbregts, S., & Swaab, H. (2011). Cognitive and environmental predictors of early literacy skills. *Reading and Writing, 24*, 395–412. doi:10.1007/s11145-010-9233-3

Davidson, A. J., Gest, S. D., & Welsh, J. A. (2010). Relatedness with teachers and peers during early adolescence: An integrated variable-oriented and person-oriented approach. *Journal of School Psychology, 48*, 483–510. doi:10.1016/j.jsp.2010.08.002

Davidson, F. H. (1976). Ability to respect persons compared to ethnic prejudice in childhood. *Journal of Personality and Social Psychology, 34,* 1256–1267.

Davidson, M. R., London, M. L., & Ladewig, P. A. W. (2008). *Olds' maternal-newborn nursing and women's health across the lifespan.* Upper Saddle River, NJ: Pearson Prentice Hall.

Davidson, P., & Youniss, J. (1995). Moral development and social construction. In W. M. Kurtines & J. L. Gewirtz (Eds.), *Moral development: An ntroduction (pp. 289–310).* Boston, MA: Allyn & Bacon.

Davies, D., Jindal-Snape, D., Collier, C., Digby, R., Hay, P., & Howe, A. (2013). Creative learning environments in education—A systematic literature review. *Thinking Skills & Creativity, 8,* 80–91. doi:10.1016/j.tsc.2012.07.004

Davies, P. T., Cicchetti, D., Hentges, R. F., & Sturge-Apple, M. L. (2013). The genetic precursors and the advantageous and disadvantageous sequelae of inhibited temperament: An evolutionary perspective. *Developmental Psychology, 49,* 2285–2300. doi:10.1037/a0032312

Davis-Kean, P. E., & Sandler, H. M. (2001). A meta-analysis of measures of self-esteem for young children: A framework for future measures. *Child Development, 72,* 887–906.

Davis, A. C., & Jackson, J.W. (1998). *"Yo, little brother": Basic rules of survival for young African American males.* Chicago, IL: African American Images.

Davis, B. (2001). The restorative power of emotions in Child Protective Services. *Child and Adolescent Social Work Journal, 18,* 437–454.

Davis, D. A., & Davis, S. (2012). Morocco. In J. Arnett (Ed.), *Adolescent psychology around the world* (pp. 47–59). New York, NY: Psychology Press.

Davis, E. L., Levine, L. J., Lench, H. C., & Quas, J. A. (2010). Metacognitive emotion regulation: Children's awareness that changing thoughts and goals can alleviate negative emotions. *Emotion, 10,* 498–510.

Davis, G. A., & Rimm, S. B. (1998). *Education of the gifted and talented* (4th ed.). Boston, MA: Allyn & Bacon.

Davis, G. A., & Thomas, M. A. (1989). *Effective schools and effective teachers.* Needham Heights, MA: Allyn & Bacon.

Davis, H. A. (2003). Conceptualizing the role and influence of student–teacher relationships on children's social and cognitive development. *Educational Psychologist, 38,* 207–234.

Davis, K. (2010). Coming of age online: The developmental underpinnings of girls' blogs. *Journal of Adolescent Research, 25*(1), 145–171. doi:10.1177/0743558409350503

Davis, M., Figueroa Velez, D., Guevarra, R., Yang, M., Habeeb, M., Carathedathu, M., & Gandhi, S. (2015). Inhibitory neuron transplantation into adult visual cortex creates a new critical period that rescues impaired vision. *Neuron, 86,* 1055–1066. doi:http://dx.doi.org/10.1016/j.neuron.2015.03.062

Davis, V. (2012). Interconnected but underprotected? Parents' methods and motivations for information seeking on digital safety issues. *Cyberpsychology, Behavior, and Social Networking, 15*(12), 669–674. doi:10.1089/cyber.2012.0179

Dawood, K., Bailey, J. M., & Martin, N. G. (2009). Genetic and environmental influences on sexual orientation. In Y. Kim (Ed.), *Handbook of behavior genetics* (pp. 269–279). New York, NY: Springer Science + Business Media. doi:10.1007/978-0-387-76727-7_19

Dawson-McClure, S., Calzada, E., Huang, K., Kamboukos, D., Rhule, D., Kolawole, B., . . . Brotman, L. (2014). A population-level approach to promoting healthy child development and school success in low-income, urban neighborhoods: Impact on parenting and child conduct problems. *Prevention Science,* doi:10.1007/s11121-014-0473-3

Day, K. L., & Smith, C. L. (2013). Understanding the role of private speech in children's emotion regulation. *Early Childhood Research Quarterly, 28,* 405–414. doi:10.1016/j.ecresq.2012.10.003

de Barbaro, K., Johnson, C. M., & Deák, G. O. (2013). Twelve-month 'social revolution' emerges from mother-infant sensorimotor coordination: A longitudinal investigation. *Human Development, 56,* 223–248. doi:10.1159/000351313

De Brauwer, J., & Fias, W. (2009). A longitudinal study of children's performance on simple multiplication and division problems. *Developmental Psychology, 45,* 1480–1496.

de Carvalho, J. S., Pinto, A. M., & Marôco, J. (2017). Results of a mindfulness-based social-emotional learning program on Portuguese elementary students and teachers: A quasi-experimental study. *Mindfulness, 8,* 337–350. doi:10.1007/s12671-016-0603-z

de Clerck, I., Pettinato, M., Verhoeven, J., & Gillis, S. (2017). Is prosodic production driven by lexical development? Longitudinal evidence from babble and words. *Journal of Child Language, 44,* 1248–1273. http://dx.doi.org/10.1017/S0305000916000532

De Corte, E., Greer, B., & Verschaffel, L. (1996). Mathematics teaching and learning. In D. C. Berliner & R. C. Calfee (Eds.), *Handbook of educational psychology* (pp. 491–549). New York, NY: Macmillan.

de Graaf, H., & Rademakers, J. (2006). Sexual behavior of prepubertal children. *Journal of Psychology and Human Sexuality, 18*(1), 1–21.

de Heering, A., Turati, C., Rossion, B., Bulf, H., Goffaux, V., & Simion, F. (2008). Newborns' face recognition is based on spatial frequencies below 0.5 cycles per degree. *Cognition, 106,* 444–454.

de Jong, T., & van Joolingen, W. R. (1998). Scientific discovery learning with computer simulations of conceptual domains. *Review of Educational Research, 68,* 179–201.

De La Paz, S. (2005). Effects of historical reasoning instruction and writing strategy mastery in culturally and academically diverse middle school classrooms. *Journal of Educational Psychology, 97,* 139–156.

De Laet, S., Doumen, S., Vervoort, E., Colpin, H., Van Leeuwen, K., Goossens, L., & Verschueren, K. (2014). Transactional links between teacher–child relationship quality and perceived versus sociometric popularity: A three-wave longitudinal study. *Child Development, 85,* 1647–1662.

De Lisi, R., & Golbeck, S. L. (1999). Implications of Piagetian theory for peer learning. In A. M. O'Donnell & A. King (Eds.), *Cognitive perspectives on peer learning* (pp. 3–37). Mahwah, NJ: Erlbaum.

de Milliano, I., van Gelderen, A., & Sleegers, P. (2012). Patterns of cognitive self-regulation of adolescent struggling writers. *Written Communication, 29,* 303–325. doi:10.1177/0741088312450275

De Neve, D., & Devos, G. (2017). How do professional learning communities aid and hamper professional learning of beginning teachers related to differentiated instruction? *Teachers & Teaching, 23,* 262–283. doi:10.1080/13540602.2016.1206524

De Pedro, K., Astor, R., Benbenishty, R., Estrada, J. r., Smith, G., & Esqueda, M. (2011). The children of military service members: Challenges, supports, and future educational research. *Review of Educational Research, 81,* 566–618.

de Souza, M. (2014). The empathetic mind: The essence of human spirituality. *International Journal of Children's Spirituality, 19*(1), 45–54. doi:10.1080/1364436X.2014.897221

de Villiers, J. (1995). Empty categories and complex sentences: The case of wh- questions. In P. Fletcher & B. MacWhinney (Eds.), *The handbook of child language* (pp. 508–540). Oxford, England: Blackwell.

de Weerdt, F., Desoete, A., & Roeyers, H. (2013). Behavioral inhibition in children with learning disabilities. *Research in Developmental Disabilities, 34,* 1998–2007. doi:10.1016/j.ridd.2013.02.020

de Wit, C. C., Sas, T. J., Wit, J. M., & Cutfield, W. S. (2013). Patterns of catch-up growth. *Journal of Pediatrics, 162,* 415–420. doi:10.1016/j.jpeds.2012.10.014

Deacon, S., Cleave, P. L., Baylis, J., Fraser, J., Ingram, E., & Perlmutter, S. (2014). The representation of roots in the spelling of children with specific language impairment. *Journal of Learning Disabilities, 47,* 13–21.

Deák, G. O., Triesch, J., Krasno, A., de Barbaro, K., & Robledo, M. (2013). Learning to share: The emergence of joint attention in human infancy. In B. Kar (Ed.), *Cognition and brain development: Converging evidence from various methodologies* (pp. 173–210). Washington, DC: American Psychological Association. doi:10.1037/14043-010

Deater-Deckard, K. (2009). Parenting the genotype. In K. McCartney & R. A. Weinberg (Eds.),

Experience and development: A festschrift in honor of Sandra Wood Scarr (pp. 141–161). New York, NY: Psychology Press.

Deater-Deckard, K., Dodge, K., Bates, J., & Pettit, G. (1996). Physical discipline among African American and European American mothers: Links to children's externalizing behaviors. *Developmental Psychology, 32*, 1065–1072.

Deaux, K. (1984). From individual differences to social categories: Analysis of a decade's research on gender. *American Psychologist, 39*, 105–116.

DeBose, C. E. (2007). The Ebonics phenomenon, language planning, and the hegemony of Standard English. In H. S. Alim & J. Baugh (Eds.), *Talkin Black talk: Language, education, and social change* (pp. 30–42). New York, NY: Teachers College Press.

DeCasper, A. J., & Fifer, W. P. (1980). Of human bonding: Newborns prefer their mothers' voices. *Science, 208*, 1174–1176.

Deci, E. L. (1992). The relation of interest to the motivation of behavior: A self-determination theory perspective. In K. A. Renninger, S. Hidi, & A. Krapp (Eds.), *The role of interest in learning and development (pp. 43–70).* Hillsdale, NJ: Erlbaum.

Deci, E. L., & Ryan, R. M. (1985). *Intrinsic motivation and self-determination in human behavior.* New York, NY: Plenum Press.

Deci, E. L., & Ryan, R. M. (1992). The initiation and regulation of intrinsically motivated learning and achievement. In A. K. Boggiano & T. S. Pittman (Eds.), *Achievement and motivation: A social-developmental perspective* (pp. 3–36). Cambridge, England: Cambridge University Press.

Degner, J., & Dalege, J. (2013). The apple does not fall far from the tree, or does it? A meta-analysis of parent–child similarity in intergroup attitudes. *Psychological Bulletin, 139*, 1270–1304. doi:10.1037/a0031436

Dehaene, S. (1997). *The number sense: How the mind creates mathematics.* London: Penguin

Deitrick, L. M., & Draves, P. R. (2008). Attitudes toward doula support during pregnancy by clients, doulas, and labor-and-delivery nurses: A case study from Tampa, Florida. *Human Organization, 67*, 397–406.

DeLamater, J., & MacCorquodale, P. (1979). *Premarital sexuality: Attitudes, relationships, behavior.* Madison: University of Wisconsin Press.

Delaney, K. R. (2006). Following the affect: Learning to observe emotional regulation. *Journal of Child and Adolescent Psychiatric Nursing, 19*(4), 175–181.

DeLeon, I. G., Bullock, C. E., & Catania, A. (2013). Arranging reinforcement contingencies in applied settings: Fundamentals and implications of recent basic and applied research. In G. J. Madden, W. V. Dube, T. D. Hackenberg, G. P. Hanley, & K. A. Lattal (Eds.), *APA Handbook of Behavior Analysis, Vol. 2. Translating principles into practice* (pp. 47–75). Washington, DC: American Psychological Association. doi:10.1037/13938-003

Delgado-Gaitan, C. (1994). Socializing young children in Mexican-American families: An intergenerational perspective. In P. M. Greenfield & R. R. Cocking (Eds.), *Cross-cultural roots of minority child development* (pp. 55–86). Hillsdale, NJ: Erlbaum.

DeLisle, J. R. (1984). *Gifted children speak out.* New York, NY: Walker.

DeLoache, J. S. (2011). Early development of the understanding and use of symbolic artifacts. In U. Goswami (Ed.), *The Wiley-Blackwell handbook of childhood cognitive development* (2nd ed., pp. 312–336). Malden, MA: Wiley-Blackwell.

DeLoache, J. S., & Todd, C. M. (1988). Young children's use of spatial categorization as a mnemonic strategy. *Journal of Experimental Child Psychology, 46*, 1–20.

DeLoache, J. S., Cassidy, D. J., & Brown, A. L. (1985). Precursors of mnemonic strategies in very young children's memory. *Child Development, 56*, 125–137.

DeLoache, J. S., Miller, K. F., & Rosengren, K. S. (1997). The credible shrinking room: Very young children's performance with symbolic and nonsymbolic relations. *Psychological Science, 8*, 308–313.

Demarest, R. J., & Charon, R. (1996). *An illustrated guide to human reproduction and fertility control.* New York, NY: Parthenon.

Demetriou, A. (2000). Organization and development of self-understanding and self-regulation. In M. Boekaerts, P. Pintrich, & M. Zeidner (Eds.), *Handbook of self-regulation* (pp. 209–251). San Diego, CA: Academic Press.

Demetriou, A., Mouyi, A., & Spanoudis, G. (2008). Modelling the structure and development of g. *Intelligence, 36*, 437–454.

Demi (1990). *The empty pot.* New York, NY: H. Holt.

Dempster, F. N., & Corkill, A. J. (1999). Interference and inhibition in cognition and behavior: Unifying themes for educational psychology. *Educational Psychology Review, 11*, 1–88.

Denckla, M. B. (2007). Executive function: Binding together the definitions of attention-deficit/-hyperactivity disorder and learning disabilities. In L. Meltzer (Ed.), *Executive function in education: From theory to practice* (pp. 5–18). New York, NY: Guilford Press.

Denison, S., & Xu, F. (2014). The origins of probabilistic inference in human infants. *Cognition, 130*, 335–347. doi:10.1016/j.cognition.2013.12.001

Denmark, N., & Harden, B. (2012). Un día en la vida: The everyday activities of young children from Central American immigrant families. *Early Child Development and Care, 182*, 1523–1543. doi:10.1080/03004430.2011.630073

Dennis, L., & Horn, E. (2014). The effects of professional development on preschool teachers' instructional behaviours during storybook reading. *Early Child Development & Care, 184*, 1160–1177. doi:10.1080/03004430.2013.853055

Denno, D. M., Carr, V., & Bell, S. H. (2010). *Addressing challenging behaviors in early childhood settings: A teacher's guide.* Baltimore, MD: Paul H. Brookes.

Dent, A. L., & Koenka, A. C. (2016). The relation between self-regulated learning and academic achievement across childhood and adolescence: A meta-analysis. *Educational Psychology Review, 28*, 425–474.

Désert, M. M., Préaux, M. M., & Jund, R. R. (2009). So young and already victims of stereotype threat: Socio-economic status and performance of 6 to 9 years old children on Raven's progressive matrices. *European Journal of Psychology of Education - EJPE (Instituto Superior De Psicologia Aplicada), 24*, 207–218.

Deshler, D. D., & Schumaker, J. B. (1988). An instructional model for teaching students how to learn. In J. L. Graden, J. E. Zins, & M. J. Curtis (Eds.), *Alternative educational delivery systems: Enhancing instructional options for all students (pp. 391–411).* Washington, DC: National Association of School Psychologists.

DesJardin, J. L., Doll, E. R., Stika, C. J., Eisenberg, L. S., Johnson, K. J., Ganguly, D., . . . Henning, S. C. (2014). Parental support for language development during joint book reading for young children with hearing loss. *Communication Disorders Quarterly, 35*, 167–181. doi:10.1177/1525740113518062

DeSocio, J. (2015). A call to action: Reducing toxic stress during pregnancy and early childhood. *Journal of Child & Adolescent Psychiatric Nursing, 28*(2), 70–71. doi:10.1111/jcap.12106

Desoete, A. (2009). Metacognitive prediction and evaluation skills and mathematical learning in third-grade students. *Educational Research and Evaluation, 15*(5), 435–446.

Desrosiers, T., Herring, A., Shapira, S., Hooiveld, M., Luben, T., Herdt-Losavio, M., . . . Olshan, A. (2012). Paternal occupation and birth defects: Findings from the National Birth Defects Prevention Study. *Occupational & Environmental Medicine, 69*, 534–542.

Dessel, A. (2010). Prejudice in schools: Promotion of an inclusive culture and climate. *Education and Urban Society, 42*, 407–429. doi:10.1177/0013124510361852

Destan, N. & Roebers, C. (2015). What are the metacognitive costs of young children's overconfidence?. *Metacognition & Learning, 10*, 347–374. doi:10.1007/s11409-014-9133-z

Deutsch, A. R., Steinley, D., & Slutske, W. S. (2014). The role of gender and friends' gender on peer socialization of adolescent drinking: A prospective multilevel social network analysis. *Journal of Youth and Adolescence, 43*, 1421–1435. doi:10.1007/s10964-013-0048-9

Deutsch, M. (1993). Educating for a peaceful world. *American Psychologist, 48*, 510–517.

Devenish, B., Hooley, M., & Mellor, D. (2017). The pathways between socioeconomic status and adolescent outcomes: A systematic review. *American Journal of Community Psychology, 59*(1/2), 219–238. doi:10.1002/ajcp.12115

Devereaux, Y., & Sullivan, H. (2013). Doula support while laboring: Does it help achieve a more natural birth? *International Journal of Childbirth Education, 28*(2), 54–61.

Devlin, B., Daniels, M., & Roeder, K. (1997). The heritability of IQ. *Nature, 388*(6641), 468–471.

DeVries, R. (1997). Piaget's social theory. *Educational Researcher, 26*(2), 4–17.

DeVries, R., & Zan, B. (1996). A constructivist perspective on the role of the sociomoral atmosphere in promoting children's development. In C. T. Fosnot (Ed.), *Constructivism: Theory, perspectives, and practice* (pp. 103–119). New York, NY: Teachers College Press.

DeVries, R., & Zan, B. (2003). When children make rules. *Educational Leadership, 61*(1), 64–67.

Deyhle, D., & LeCompte, M. (1999). Cultural differences in child development: Navajo adolescents in middle schools. In R. H. Sheets & E. R. Hollins (Eds.), *Racial and ethnic identity in school practices: Aspects of human development* (pp. 123–139). Mahwah, NJ: Erlbaum.

Di Giunta, L., Pastorelli, C., Eisenberg, N., Gerbino, M., Castellani, V., & Bombi, A. S. (2010). Developmental trajectories of physical aggression: Prediction of overt and covert antisocial behaviors from self and mothers' reports. *European Child & Adolescent Psychiatry, 19*, 873–882. doi:10.1007/s00787-010-0134-4

Di Santo, A. d., Timmons, K., & Pelletier, J. (2016). 'Mommy that's the exit.': Empowering homeless mothers to support their children's daily literacy experiences. *Journal of Early Childhood Literacy, 16*(2), 145–170. doi:10.1177/1468798415577872

Dia Cha. (1996). *Dia's story cloth: The Hmong people's journey of freedom.* New York, NY: Lee & Low Books.

Diamond, A., Barnett, W. S., Thomas, J., & Munro, S. (2007). Preschool program improves cognitive control. *Science, 318*(5855), 1387–1388. doi:10.1126/science.1151148

Diamond, L. M. (2013). Sexual-minority, gender-nonconforming, and transgender youths. In D. S. Bromberg & W. T. O'Donohue (Eds.), *Handbook of child and adolescent sexuality: Developmental and forensic psychology* (pp. 275–300). San Diego, CA: Elsevier Academic Press. http://dx.doi.org.unco.idm.oclc.org/10.1016/B978-0-12-387759-8.00011-8

Diamond, M., & Hopson, J. (1998). *Magic trees of the mind.* New York, NY: Dutton.

Diamond, S. C. (1991). What to do when you can't do anything: Working with disturbed adolescents. *Clearing House, 64*, 232–234.

Diamond, U., Bartolo, C. A., Badin, E., & Shatkin, J. P. (2017). Almost psychiatry: The impact of teaching child and adolescent mental health studies to undergraduate college students. *Academic Psychiatry, 41*(5), 574–581. http://dx.doi.org.unco.idm.oclc.org/10.1007/s40596-017-0680-x

Dias, N. M., & Seabra, A. G. (2017). Intervention for executive functions development in early elementary school children: effects on learning and behaviour, and follow-up maintenance. *Educational Psychology, 37*, 468–486. doi:10.1080/01443410.2016.1214686

Diaz, R. M. (1983). Thought and two languages: The impact of bilingualism on cognitive development. In E. W. Gordon (Ed.), *Review of research in education* (Vol. 10, pp. 23–54). Washington, DC: American Educational Research Association.

Diaz, R. M., & Berndt, T. J. (1982). Children's knowledge of best friend: Fact or fancy? *Developmental Psychology, 18*, 787–794.

Dibbens, L. M., Heron, S. E., & Mulley, J. C. (2007). A polygenic heterogeneity model for common epilepsies with complex genetics. *Genes, Brain & Behavior, 6*, 593–597.

Dick-Read, G. (1944). *Childbirth without fear.* New York, NY: Harper & Brothers.

Dickens, W. T., & Flynn, J. R. (2001). Heritability estimates versus large environmental effects: The IQ paradox resolved. *Psychological Review, 108*, 346–369.

Dickson, D. J., Huey, M., Laursen, B., Kiuru, N., & Nurmi, J. E. (2018). Parent contributions to friendship stability during the primary school years. *Journal of Family Psychology, 32*, 217–228. http://dx.doi.org.unco.idm.oclc.org/10.1037/fam0000388

Dien, T. (1998). Language and literacy in Vietnamese American communities. In B. Pérez (Ed.), *Sociocultural contexts of language and literacy* (pp. 123–162). Mahwah, NJ: Erlbaum.

Dierssen, M. (2012). Down syndrome: The brain in trisomic mode. *Nature Reviews Neuroscience, 13*, 844–858. doi:10.1038/nrn3314

Dillon, D. R., O'Brien, D. G., Scharber, C., & Nichols-Besel, K. (2017). Motivating boys to read: Guys Read, a summer library reading program for boys. *Children & Libraries: The Journal of the Association for Library Service to Children, 15*(2), 3–8.

Dimech, A. S., & Seiler, R. (2010). The association between extra-curricular sport participation and social anxiety symptoms in children. *Journal of Clinical Sport Psychology, 4*, 191–203.

Dinella, L. M., Weisgram, E. S., & Fulcher, M. (2017). Children's gender-typed toy interests: Does propulsion matter? *Archives of Sexual Behavior, 46*, 1295–1305. http://dx.doi.org.unco.idm.oclc.org/10.1007/s10508-016-0901-5

Dineva, E., & Schöner, G. (2018). How infants' reaches reveal principles of sensorimotor decision making. *Connection Science, 30*(1), 53–80. http://dx.doi.org.unco.idm.oclc.org/10.1080/09540091.2017.1405382

Ding, X., Omrin, D., Evans, A., Fu, G., Chen, G., & Lee, K. (2014). Elementary school children's cheating behavior and its cognitive correlates. *Journal of Experimental Child Psychology, 121*, 85–95.

DiPietro, J. A. (2004). The role of prenatal maternal stress in child development. *Current Directions in Psychological Science, 13*, 71–74.

diSessa, A. A. (1996). What do 'just plain folk' know about physics?. In D. R. Olson & N. Torrance (Eds.) *The handbook of education and human development: New models of learning, teaching and schooling* (pp. 709–730). Malden, MA: Blackwell.

diSessa, A. A. (2007). An interactional analysis of clinical interviewing. *Cognition and Instruction, 25*, 523–565.

diSessa, A. A., Gillespie, N. M., & Esterly, J. B. (2004). Coherence versus fragmentation in the development in the concept of force. *Cognitive Science, 28*, 843–900.

Diseth, Å., Meland, E., & Breidablik, H. J. (2014). Self-beliefs among students: Grade level and gender differences in self-esteem, self-efficacy and implicit theories of intelligence. *Learning and Individual Differences, 35*, 1–8.

Dishion, T. J., Kim, H., Stormshak, E. A., & O'Neill, M. (2014). A brief measure of peer affiliation and social acceptance (PASA): Validity in an ethnically diverse sample of early adolescents. *Journal of Clinical Child and Adolescent Psychology, 43*, 601–612. doi:10.1080/15374416.2013.876641

Distelmaier, F., Haack, T. B., Catarino, C. B., Gallenmüller, C., Rodenburg, R. J., Strom, T. M., . . . Klopstock, T. (2015). MRPL44 mutations cause a slowly progressive multisystem disease with childhood-onset hypertrophic cardiomyopathy. *Neurogenetics, 16*, 319–323. doi:10.1007/s10048-015-0444-2

Dix, T., Stewart, A. D., Gershoff, E. T., & Day, W. H. (2007). Autonomy and children's reactions to being controlled: Evidence that both compliance and defiance may be positive markers in early development. *Child Development, 78*, 1204–1221.

Dixon, L., Skinner, J., & Foureur, M. (2013a). The emotional and hormonal pathways of labour and birth: Integrating mind, body and behaviour. *New Zealand College of Midwives Journal, 48*, 15–23.

Dixon, L., Skinner, J., & Foureur, M. (2013b). Women's perspectives of the stages and phases of labour. *Midwifery, 29*(1), 10–17. doi:10.1016/j.midw.2012.07.001

Dixon, P., Humble, S., & Chan, D. W. (2016). How children living in poor areas of Dar Es Salaam, Tanzania perceive their own multiple intelligences. *Oxford Review of Education, 42*, 230–248. doi:10.1080/03054985.2016.1159955

Do, K. T., & Galván, A. (2016). Neural sensitivity to smoking stimuli is associated with cigarette craving in adolescent smokers. *Journal of Adolescent Health, 58*, 186–194. doi:10.1016/j.jadohealth.2015.10.004

Dodge, K. A. (1983). Behavioral antecedents of peer social status. *Child Development, 54,* 1386–1399.

Dodge, K. A., Bates, J. E., & Pettit, G. S. (1990). Mechanisms in the cycle of violence. *Science, 250,* 1678–1683.

Dodge, K. A., Coie, J., & Lynam, D. (2006). Aggression and antisocial behavior in youth. In W. Damon & R. M. Lerner (Series Eds.) & N. Eisenberg (Vol. Ed.), *Handbook of Child Psychology: Vol. 3. Social, emotional, and personality development* (6th ed., pp. 719–788). New York, NY: Wiley.

Dodge, K. A., Lansford, J. E., Burks, V. S., Bates, J. E., Pettit, G. S., Fontaine, R., & Price, J. (2003). Peer rejection and social information-processing factors in the development of aggressive behavior problems in children. *Child Development, 74,* 374–393.

Doenyas, C. (2017). Self versus other oriented social motivation, not lack of empathic or moral ability, explains behavioral outcomes in children with high theory of mind abilities. *Motivation and Emotion, 41,* 683–697. http://dx.doi.org.unco.idm.oclc.org/10.1007/s11031-017-9636-4

Doescher, S. M., & Sugawara, A. I. (1989). Encouraging prosocial behavior in young children. *Childhood Education, 65,* 213–216.

Dolan, M. M., Casanueva, C., Smith, K. R., & Bradley, R. H. (2009). Parenting and the home environment provided by grandmothers of children in the child welfare system. *Children and Youth Services Review, 31,* 784–796.

Dolev-Cohen, M., & Barak, A. (2013). Adolescents' use of instant messaging as a means of emotional relief. *Computers in Human Behavior, 29*(1), 58–63.

Domellöf, M., & Szymlek-Gay, E. A. (2012). Iron nutrition and neurodevelopment in young children. In L. Riby, M. Smith & J. Foster (Eds.), *Nutrition and mental performance: A lifespan perspective* (pp. 13–28). New York, NY: Palgrave Macmillan.

Dominé, F., Berchtold, A., Akré, C., Michaud, P.-A., & Suris, J.-C. (2009). Disordered eating behaviors: What about boys? *Journal of Adolescent Health, 44,* 111–117.

Domingue, B. W., Belsky, D. W., Fletcher, J. M., Conley, D., Boardman, J. D., & Harris, K. M. (2018). *The social genome of friends and schoolmates in the National Longitudinal Study of Adolescent to Adult Health.* PNAS: Proceedings of the National Academy of Sciences of the United States of America, 115, 702–707. http://dx.doi.org.unco.idm.oclc.org/10.1073/pnas.1711803115

Domitrovich, C. E., Cortes, R. C., & Greenberg, M. T. (2007). Improving young children's social and emotional competence: A randomized trial of the preschool "PATHS" curriculum. *Journal of Primary Prevention, 28,* 67–91.

Donaldson, M. (1978). *Children's minds.* New York, NY: Norton.

Donaldson, S. K., & Westerman, M. A. (1986). Development of children's understanding of ambivalence and causal theories of emotion. *Developmental Psychology, 22,* 655–662.

Donne, V. (2012). Keyboard instruction for students with a disability. *Clearing House, 85,* 201–206. doi:10.1080/00098655.2012.689784

Dornbusch, S. M., Carlsmith, J. M., Gross, R. T., Martin, J. A., Jennings, D., Rosenberg, A., & Duke, P. (1981). Sexual development, age, and dating: A comparison of biological and social influences upon one set of behaviors. *Child Development, 52,* 179–185.

Dornbusch, S. M., Ritter, P. L., Leiderman, P. H., Roberts, D. F., & Fraleigh, M. J. (1987). The relation of parenting style to adolescent school performance. *Child Development, 58,* 1244–1257.

dos Santos, E., de Kieviet, J. F., Königs, M., van Elburg, R. M., & Oosterlaan, J. (2013). Predictive value of the Bayley Scales of Infant Development on development of very preterm/very low birth weight children: A meta-analysis. *Early Human Development, 89,* 487–496. doi:10.1016/j.earlhumdev.2013.03.008

Dougherty Stahl, K. A. (2014). Fostering inference generation with emergent and novice readers. *Reading Teacher, 67,* 384–388. doi:10.1002/trtr.1230

Douglas, E. M. (2017). *Child maltreatment fatalities in the United States: Four decades of policy, program, and professional responses.* New York, NY: Springer Science + Business Media. doi:10.1007/978-94-017-7583-0

Dove, G. (2012). Grammar as a developmental phenomenon. *Biology & Philosophy, 27,* 615–637. doi:10.1007/s10539-012-9324-4

Dovidio, J. F., & Gaertner, S. L. (1999). Reducing prejudice: Combating intergroup biases. *Current Directions in Psychological Science, 8,* 101–105.

Downer, J. T., Booren, L. M., Lima, O. K., Luckner, A. E., & Pianta, R. C. (2010). The individualized classroom assessment scoring system (inCLASS): Preliminary reliability and validity of a system for observing preschoolers' competence in classroom interactions. *Early Childhood Research Quarterly, 25*(1), 1–16. doi:10.1016/j.ecresq.2009.08.004

Downes, M., Bathelt, J., & De Haan, M. (2017). Event-related potential measures of executive functioning from preschool to adolescence. *Developmental Medicine & Child Neurology, 59,* 581–590. doi:10.1111/dmcn.13395

Downey, D. B., Condron, D. J., & Yucel, D. (2015). Number of siblings and social skills revisited among American fifth graders. *Journal of Family Issues, 36*(2), 273–296. doi:10.1177/0192513X13507569

Downey, J. (2000, March). *The role of schools in adolescent resilience: Recommendations from the literature.* Paper presented at the International Association of Adolescent Health, Washington, DC.

Dowson, M., & McInerney, D. M. (2001). Psychological parameters of students' social and work avoidance goals: A qualitative investigation. *Journal of Educational Psychology, 93,* 35–42.

Doyle, P. A., Bird, B. C., Appel, S., Parisi, D., Rogers, P., Glarso, R., . . . Birkhead, G. (2006). Developing an effective communications campaign to reach pregnant women at high risk of late or no prenatal care. *Social Marketing Quarterly, 12*(4), 35–50.

Dozier, M., & Fisher, P. (2014). Neuroscience enhanced child maltreatment interventions to improve outcomes. *Social Policy Report, 28*(1), 25–27.

Dray, A. J., & Selman, R. L., & Schultz, L. H. (2009). Communicating with intent: A study of social awareness and children's writing. *Journal of Applied Developmental Psychology, 30,* 116–128.

Driessnack, M. and Gallo, A. M. (2013). Children 'draw-and-tell' their knowledge of genetics. *Pediatric Nursing, 39*(4), 173–180.

Driver, T. (2017). Every voice heard. *Reading Teacher, 70,* 747–748. doi:10.1002/trtr.1571

Droe, K. (2013). Effect of verbal praise on achievement goal orientation, motivation, and performance attribution. *Journal of Music Teacher Education, 23*(1), 63–78. doi:10.1177/1057083712458592

Dryfoos, J. G. (1997). The prevalence of problem behaviors: Implications for programs. In R. P. Weissberg, T. P. Gullotta, R. L. Hamptom, B. A. Ryan, & G. R. Adams (Eds.), *Enhancing children's wellness* (Vol. 8, pp. 17–46). Thousand Oaks, CA: Sage.

Dryfoos, J. G. (1999, Fall). The role of the school in children's out-of-school time. *The Future of Children: When School Is Out, 9,* 117–134.

Duarte Ribeiro, L., & Loução Martins, A. (2013). Specific learning disabilities: Evidence from third grade students' handwriting performance. *Special Education, 2,* 158–163.

Duchesne, S., & Ratelle, C. (2010). Parental behaviors and adolescents' achievement goals at the beginning of middle school: Emotional problems as potential mediators. *Journal of Educational Psychology, 102,* 497–507. doi:10.1037/a0019320

Duckworth, A. L., & Seligman, M. E. P. (2005). Self-discipline outdoes IQ in predicting academic performance of adolescents. *Psychological Science, 16,* 939–944.

Duckworth, A. L., & Seligman, M. E. P. (2006). Self-discipline gives girls the edge: Gender in self-discipline, grades, and achievement test scores. *Journal of Educational Psychology, 98,* 198–208.

Duckworth, A. L., Shulman, E. P., Mastronarde, A. J., Patrick, S. D., Zhang, J., & Druckman, J. (2015). Will not want: Self-control rather than motivation explains the female advantage in report card grades. *Learning and Individual Differences, 39,* 13–23.

Dudley-Marling, C., & Lucas, K. (2009). Pathologizing the language and culture of poor children. *Language Arts, 86*, 362–370.

Duijnhouwer, H., Prins, F., & Stokking, K. (2012). Feedback providing improvement strategies and reflection on feedback use: Effects on students' writing motivation, process, and performance. *Learning & Instruction, 22*, 171–184. doi:10.1016/j.learninstruc.2011.10.003

Duineveld, J. J., Parker, P. D., Ciarrochi, J., Ryan, R. M., & Salmela-Aro, K. (2017). The link between perceived maternal and paternal autonomy support and adolescent well-being across three major educational transitions. *Developmental Psychology, 53*, 1978–1994. doi:10.1037/dev0000364

Dumont, H., Trautwein, U., Nagy, G., & Nagengast, B. (2014). Quality of parental homework involvement: Predictors and reciprocal relations with academic functioning in the reading domain. *Journal of Educational Psychology, 106*, 144–161. doi:10.1037/a0034100

Duncan, G. (2013, April). *Enhancing well-being of children and youth living in poverty*. Paper presented at the annual meeting of the American Educational Research Association, San Francisco, CA.

Duncheon, J. C., & Tierney, W. G. (2013). Changing conceptions of time: Implications for educational research and practice. *Review of Educational Research, 83*, 236–272. doi:10.3102/0034654313478492

Dunham, P. J., Dunham, F., & Curwin, A. (1993). Joint-attentional states and lexical acquisition at 18 months. *Developmental Psychology, 29*, 827–831.

Dunham, Y., & Olson, K. R. (2016). Beyond discrete categories: Studying multiracial, intersex, and transgender children will strengthen basic developmental science. *Journal of Cognition & Development, 17*, 642–665. doi:10.1080/15248372.2016.1195388

Dunkel, C. S., & Sefcek, J. A. (2009). Eriksonian lifespan theory and life history theory: An integration using the example of identity formation. *Review of General Psychology, 13*(1), 13–23.

Dunn, J. (1984). *Sisters and brothers*. Cambridge, MA: Harvard University Press.

Dunn, J. (2006). Moral development in early childhood and social interaction in the family. In M. Killen & J. G. Smetana (Eds.), *Handbook of moral development* (pp. 331–350). Mahwah, NJ: Erlbaum.

Dunn, J. (2007). Siblings and socialization. In J. E. Grusec & P. D. Hastings (Eds.), *Handbook of socialization: Theory and research* (pp. 309–327). New York, NY: Guilford Press.

Dunn, J., & Munn, P. (1985). Becoming a family member: Family conflict and the development of social understanding in the second year. *Child Development, 56*, 480–492.

Dunn, L. S. (2011, February). Making the most of your class website. *Educational Leadership, 68*(5), 60–62

Dunsmore, J. C. (2015). Effects of person- and process-focused feedback on prosocial behavior in middle childhood. *Social Development, 24*(1), 57–75.

DuPaul, G., & Hoff, K. (1998). Reducing disruptive behavior in general education classrooms: The use of self-management strategies. *School Psychology Review, 27*, 290–304.

Duquette, C. (2016). A study of inclusive practices. *Journal of Research in Special Educational Needs, 16*, 111–115. doi:10.1111/1471-3802.12132

Durand, V. M. (1998). *Sleep better: A guide to improving sleep for children with special needs*. Baltimore, MD: Paul H. Brookes.

Durkin, K., Nesdale, D., Dempsey, G., & McLean, A. (2012). Young children's responses to media representations of intergroup threat and ethnicity. *British Journal of Developmental Psychology, 30*, 459–476. doi:10.1111/j.2044-835X.2011.02056.x

Durlak, J. A., Mahoney, J. L., Bohnert, A. M., & Parente, M. E. (2010). Developing and improving after-school programs to enhance youth's personal growth and adjustment: A special issue of AJCP. *American Journal of Community Psychology, 45*, 285–293. doi:10.1007/s10464-010-9298-9

Dush, C. (2013). Marital and cohabitation dissolution and parental depressive symptoms in fragile families. *Journal of Marriage and Family, 75*(1), 91–109.

Dweck, C. S. (1975). The role of expectations and attributions in the alleviation of learned helplessness. *Journal of Personality and Social Psychology, 31*, 674–685.

Dweck, C. S. (1986). Motivational processes affecting learning. *American Psychologist, 41*, 1040–1048.

Dweck, C. S. (2000). *Self-theories: Their role in motivation, personality, and development*. Philadelphia, PA: Psychology Press.

Dweck, C. S. (2008). Brainology: Transforming students' motivation to learn. *Independent School, 67*, 110–119.

Dweck, C. S. (2009). Foreword. In F. D. Horowitz, R. F. Subotnik & D. J. Matthews (Eds.), *The development of giftedness and talent across the life span* (pp. xi–xiv). Washington, DC: American Psychological Association.

Dweck, C. S. (2010). Even geniuses work hard. *Educational Leadership, 68*(2), 16–20.

Dweck, C. S. (2012). Mindsets and human nature: Promoting change in the Middle East, the schoolyard, the racial divide, and willpower. *American Psychologist, 67*, 614–622. doi:10.1037/a0029783

Dweck, C. S. (2017). The journey to children's mindsets—and beyond. *Child Development Perspectives, 11*, 139–144. http://dx.doi.org.unco.idm.oclc.org/10.1111/cdep.12225

Dweck, C. S., & Elliott, E. S. (1983). Achievement motivation. In E. M. Hetherington (Ed.), *Handbook of Child Psychology: Vol. 4. Socialization, personality, and social development* (4th ed., pp. 643–691). New York, NY: Wiley.

Dweck, C. S., & Master, A. (2009). Self-theories and motivation: Students' beliefs about intelligence. K. R. Wentzel & A. Wigfield (Eds.), *Handbook of motivation at school* (pp. 123–140). New York, NY: Routledge/Taylor & Francis Group.

Dweck, C. S., Mangels, J. A., & Good, C. (2004). Motivational effects on attention, cognition, and performance. In D. Y. Dai & R. J. Sternberg (Eds.), *Motivation, emotion, and cognition: Integrative perspectives on intellectual functioning and development* (pp. 41–55). Mahwah, NJ: Erlbaum.

Dwyer, K., & Osher, D. (2000). *Safeguarding our children: An action guide*. Washington, DC: U.S. Departments of Education and Jstice, American Institutes for Research. Retrieved from http://www.ed.gov/pubs/edpubs.html

Dwyer, K., Osher, D., & Warger, C. (1998). *Early warning, timely response: A guide to safe schools*. Washington, DC: U.S. Department of Education. Retrieved from http://www.ed.gov/offices/OSERS/OSEP/earlywrn.html

Dykens, E. M., & Cassidy, S. B. (1999). Prader-Willi syndrome. In S. Goldstein & C. R. Reynolds (Eds.), *Handbook of neurodevelopmental and genetic disorders* (pp. 525–554). New York, NY: Guilford Press.

Dyson, M., & Plunkett, M. (2012). Making a difference by embracing cooperative learning practices in an alternate setting: An exciting combination to incite the educational imagination. *Journal of Classroom Interaction, 47*(2), 13–24.

Eagly, A. H. (1987). *Sex differences in social behavior: A social-role interpretation*. Hillsdale, NJ: Erlbaum.

Eamon, M. K., & Mulder, C. (2005). Predicting anti-social behavior among Latino young adolescents: An ecological systems analysis. *American Journal of Orthopsychiatry, 75*, 117–127.

Early, D. M., Maxwell, K. L., Burchinal M., Alva, S., Bender, R. H., Bryant, D., . . . Zill, N. (2007). Teachers' education, classroom quality, and young children's academic skills: Results from seven studies of preschool programs. *Child Development, 78*, 558–580.

Early, D. M., Maxwell, K. L., Ponder, B. D., & Pan, Y. (2017). Improving teacher-child interactions: A randomized controlled trial of Making the Most of Classroom Interactions and my teaching partner professional development models. *Early Childhood Research Quarterly, 38*, 57–70. http://dx.doi.org.unco.idm.oclc.org/10.1016/j.ecresq.2016.08.005

Easterbrooks, M., Bartlett, J., Beeghly, M., & Thompson, R. A. (2013). Social and emotional development in infancy. In R. M. Lerner, M. Easterbrooks, J. Mistry, & I. B. Weiner (Eds.), *Handbook of Psychology, Vol. 6. Developmental psychology* (2nd ed., pp. 91–120). Hoboken, NJ: Wiley.

Ebbels, S. H., Marić, N., Murphy, A., & Turner, G. (2014). Improving comprehension in adolescents with severe receptive language impairments: a randomized control trial of intervention for coordinating conjunctions. *International Journal of Language & Communication Disorders, 49*(1), 30–48. doi:10.1111/1460-6984.12047

Ebersbach, M. (2016). Development of children's estimation skills: The ambiguous role of their familiarity with numerals. *Child Development Perspectives, 10*, 116–121. doi:10.1111/cdep.12172

Eby, C. M., & Greer, R. D. (2017). Effects of social reinforcement on the emission of tacts by preschoolers. *Behavioral Development Bulletin, 22*(1), 23–43.

Eccles, J. J., & Roeser, R. W. (2011). Schools as developmental contexts during adolescence. *Journal of Research on Adolescence, 21*(1), 225–241. doi:10.1111/j.1532-7795.2010.00725.x

Eccles, J. S. (2007). Families, schools, and developing achievement-related motivations and engagement. In J. E. Grusec & P. D. Hastings (Eds.), *Handbook of socialization: Theory and research* (pp. 665–691). New York, NY: Guilford Press.

Eccles, J. S., & Midgley, C. (1989). Stage-environment fit: Developmentally appropriate classrooms for young adolescents. In C. Ames & R. Ames (Eds.), *Research on Motivation in Education: Vol. 3. Goals and cognition* (pp. 13–44). San Diego, CA: Academic Press.

Eccles, J. S., & Roeser, R. W. (2009). Schools, academic motivation, and stage-environment fit. In R. M. Lerner & L. Steinberg (Eds.), *Handbook of adolescent psychology: Individual bases of adolescent development* (pp. 404–434). Hoboken, NJ, US: John Wiley & Sons Inc. http://dx.doi.org.unco.idm.oclc.org/10.1002/9780470479193.adlpsy001013

Eccles, J. S., & Wigfield, A. (1985). Teacher expectations and student motivation. In J. B. Dusek (Ed.), *Teacher expectancies (pp. 185–226).* Hillsdale, NJ: Erlbaum.

Eccles, J. S., Flanagan, C., Lord, S., Midgley, C., Roeser, R., & Yee, D. (1996). Schools, families, and early adolescents: What are we? *Journal of Developmental and Behavioral Pediatrics, 17*, 267–276. http://dx.doi.org.unco.idm.oclc.org/10.1097/00004703-199608000-00011

Eccles, J. S., Freedman-Doan, C., Frome, P., Jacobs, J., & Yoon, K. S. (2000). Gender-role socialization in the family: A longitudinal approach. In T. Eckes & H. M. Trautner (Eds.), *The developmental social psychology of gender* (pp. 333–360). Mahwah, NH: Erlbaum.

Eccles, J. S., Midgley, C., Wigfield, A., Buchanan, C. M., Reuman, D., Flanagan, C., & Mac Iver, D. (1993). Development during adolescence: The impact of stage-environment fit on young adolescents' experiences in schools and in families. *American Psychologist, 48*, 90–101. http://dx.doi.org.unco.idm.oclc.org/10.1037/0003-066X.48.2.90

Eccles, J. S., Wigfield, A., & Schiefele, U. (1998). Motivation to succeed. In W. Damon (Series Ed.) & N. Eisenberg (Vol. Ed.), *Handbook of Child Psychology: Vol 3. Social, emotional, and personality development* (5th ed., pp. 1017–1095). New York, NY: Wiley.

Echols, L., & Graham, S. (2013). Birds of a different feather: How do cross-ethnic friends flock together? *Merrill-Palmer Quarterly, 59*, 461–488.

Eckerd, M. (2017). *Help the school help your child with NLD*. Retrieved on from http://www.smartkidswithld.org/getting-help/nld/help-school-help-child-nld/

Eckerman, C. O. (1979). The human infant in social interaction. In R. Cairns (Ed.), *The analysis of social interactions: Methods, issues, and illustrations* (pp. 163–178). Hillsdale, NJ: Erlbaum.

Edelstein, W. (2015). Education for democracy: Cooperation, participation and civic engagement in the classroom. In C. Psaltis, A. Gillespie, & A.-N. Perret-Clermont (Eds.), *Social relations in human and societal development* (pp. 19–31). London, England: Palgrave Macmillan.

Ediger, M. (2011). Shared reading, the pupil, and the teacher. *Reading Improvement, 48*(2), 55–58.

Edmunds, A. L., & Edmunds, G. A. (2005). Sensitivity: A double-edged sword for the pre-adolescent and adolescent gifted child. *Roeper Review, 27*(2), 69–77.

Edossa, A. K., Schroeders, U., Weinert, S., & Artelt, C. (2018). The development of emotional and behavioral self-regulation and their effects on academic achievement in childhood. *International Journal of Behavioral Development, 42*, 192–202. doi:10.1177/0165025416687412

Edwards, A. (2014). African-American male student perceptions about factors related to why black boys drop out of secondary school. *Dissertation Abstracts International Section A, 74*.

Edwards, A., Eisenberg, N., Spinrad, T. L., Reiser, M., Eggum-Wilkens, N. D., & Liew, J. (2015). Predicting sympathy and prosocial behavior from young children's dispositional sadness. *Social Development, 24*(1), 76–94. http://dx.doi.org.unco.idm.oclc.org/10.1111/sode.12084

Edwards, C. (2014). Maternal literacy practices and toddlers' emergent literacy skills. *Journal of Early Childhood Literacy, 14*(1), 53–79. doi:10.1177/1468798412451590

Edwards, O. W., & Taub, G. E. (2009). A conceptual pathways model to promote positive youth development in children raised by their grandparents. *School Psychology Quarterly, 24*, 160–172.

Eeds, M., & Wells, D. (1989). Grand conversations: An explanation of meaning construction in literature study groups. *Research in the Teaching of English, 23*, 4–29.

Ehm, J., Lindberg, S., & Hasselhorn, M. (2014). Reading, writing, and math self-concept in elementary school children: Influence of dimensional comparison processes. *European Journal of Psychology of Education, 29*, 277–294. doi:10.1007/s10212-013-0198-x

Ehrenberg, M., Regev, R., Lazinski, M., Behrman, L. J., & Zimmerman, J. (2014). Adjustment to divorce for children. In L. Grossman & S. Walfish (Eds.), *Translating psychological research into practice* (pp. 1–7). New York, NY: Springer Publishing Co.

Ehrenreich, S. E., Beron, K. J., Brinkley, D. Y., & Underwood, M. K. (2014). Family predictors of continuity and change in social and physical aggression from ages 9 to 18. *Aggressive Behavior, 40*(5), 421–439. http://dx.doi.org.unco.idm.oclc.org/10.1002/ab.21535

Ehri, L. (2014). Orthographic mapping in the acquisition of sight word reading, spelling memory, and vocabulary learning. *Scientific Studies of Reading, 18*(1), 5–21. doi:10.1080/10888438.2013.819356

Ehri, L. C. (1994). Development of the ability to read words: Update. In R. B. Ruddell, M. R. Ruddell, & H. Singer (Eds.), *Theoretical models and processes of reading* (4th ed., pp. 323–358). Newark, DE: International Reading Association.

Ehrler, D. J., Evans, J. G., & McGhee, R. L. (1999). Extending big-five theory into childhood: A preliminary investigation into the relationship between big-five personality traits and behavior problems in children. *Psychology in the Schools, 36*, 451–458.

Eigsti, I., Zayas, V., Mischel, W., Shoda, Y., Ayduk, O., Dadlani, M. B., . . . Casey, B. J. (2006). Predicting cognitive control from preschool to late adolescence and young adulthood. *Psychological Science, 17*, 478–484. doi:10.1111/j.1467-9280.2006.01732.x

Einarsson, I. i., Jóhannsson, E., Daly, D., & Arngrímsson, S. Á. (2016). Physical activity during school and after school among youth with and without intellectual disability. *Research in Developmental Disabilities, 56*, 60–70. doi:10.1016/j.ridd.2016.05.016

Eisenberg, N. (1982). The development of reasoning regarding prosocial behavior. In N. Eisenberg (Ed.), *The development of proocial behavior (pp. 219–249).* New York, NY: Academic Press.

Eisenberg, N. (1992). *The caring child.* Cambridge, MA: Harvard University Press.

Eisenberg, N. (1995). Prosocial development: A multifaceted model. In W. M. Kurtines & J. L. Gewirtz (Eds.), *Moral development: An introduction* (pp. 401–429). Boston, MA: Allyn & Bacon.

Eisenberg, N. (2006). Emotion-related regulation. In H. E. Fitzgerald, B. M. Lester, & B. Zuckerman (Vol. Eds.), & H. E. Fitzgerald, R. Zucker, & K. Freeark (Eds. in Chief), *The Crisis in Youth Mental Health: Critical Issues and Effective Programs. Vol. 1. Childhood disorders* (pp. 133–155). Westport, CT: Praeger.

Eisenberg, N., & Fabes, R. A. (1998). Prosocial development. In W. Damon (Series Ed.) & N. Eisenberg (Vol. Ed.), *Handbook of Child Psychology: Vol. 3. Social, emotional, and personality development* (pp. 701–778). New York, NY: Wiley.

Eisenberg, N., Carlo, G., Murphy, B., & Van Court, N. (1995). Prosocial development in late adolescence: A longitudinal study. *Child Development, 66*, 1179–1197.

Eisenberg, N., Duckworth, A. L., Spinrad, T. L., & Valiente, C. (2014). Conscientiousness: Origins in childhood? *Developmental Psychology, 50,* 1331–1349. http://dx.doi.org.unco.idm.oclc.org/10.1037/a0030977

Eisenberg, N., Eggum, N. D., & Edwards, A. (2010). Empathy-related responding and moral development. In W. F. Arsenio & E. A. Lemerise (Eds.), *Emotions, aggression, and morality in children: Bridging development and psychopathology* (pp. 115–135). Washington, DC: American Psychological Association.

Eisenberg, N., Fabes, R. A., & Spinrad, T. L. (2006). Prosocial development. In N. Eisenberg, W. Damon, R. M. Lerner (Eds.), *Handbook of Child Psychology: Vol. 3, Social, emotional, and personality development* (6th ed., pp. 646–718). Hoboken, NJ: Wiley.

Eisenberg, N., Fabes, R. A., Carlo, G., & Karbon, M. (1992). Emotional responsivity to others: Behavioral correlates and socialization antecedents. In N. Eisenberg & R. A. Fabes (Eds.), *New directions in child development* (No. 55, pp. 57–73). San Francisco, CA: Jossey-Bass.

Eisenberg, N., Fabes, R. A., Schaller, M., Carlo, G., & Miller, P. A. (1991). The relations of parental characteristics and practices to children's vicarious emotional responding. *Child Development, 62,* 1393–1408.

Eisenberg, N., Hofer, C., & Vaughan, J. (2007). Effortful control and its socioemotional consequences. In J. J. Gross (Ed.), *Handbook of emotion regulation* (pp. 287–306). New York, NY: Guilford Press.

Eisenberg, N., Lennon, R., & Pasternack, J. F. (1986). Altruistic values and moral judgment. In N. Eisenberg (Ed.), *Altruistic emotion, cognition, and behavior* (pp. 115–159). Hillsdale, NJ: Erlbaum.

Eisenberg, N., Martin, C. L., & Fabes, R. A. (1996). Gender development and gender effects. In D. C. Berliner & R. C. Calfee (Eds.), *Handbook of educational psychology (pp. 358–396).*

Eisenberg, N., Miller, P. A., Shell, R., McNalley, S., & Shea, C. (1991). Prosocial development in adolescence: A longitudinal study. *Developmental Psychology, 27,* 849–857.

Eisenberg, N., Spinrad, T. L., Valiente, C., & Duckworth, A. L. (2014). Conscientiousness: Origins in childhood? *Developmental Psychology, 50,* 1331–1349. doi:10.1037/a0030977

Ekelin, M., Crang-Svalenius, E., & Dykes, A. K. (2004). A qualitative study of mothers' and fathers' experiences of routine ultrasound examination in Sweden. *Midwifery, 20,* 335–344.

Ekinci, B. (2014). The relationships among Sternberg's triarchic abilities, Gardner's multiple intelligences, and academic achievement. *Social Behavior & Personality: An International Journal, 42,* 625–633. doi:10.2224/sbp.2014.42.4.625

El Zein, F., Solis, M., Vaughn, S., & McCulley, L. (2014). Reading comprehension interventions for students with autism spectrum disorders: A synthesis of research. *Journal of Autism & Developmental Disorders, 44,* 1303–1322. doi:10.1007/s10803-013-1989-2

Elbro, C., & Petersen, D. K. (2004). Long-term effects of phoneme awareness and letter sound training: An intervention study with children at risk for dyslexia. *Journal of Educational Psychology, 96,* 660–670.

Elder, A. D. (2010). Children's self-assessment of their school work in elementary school. *Education 3–13, 38*(1), 5–11. doi:10.1080/03004270802602044

Elia, J. P. (1994). Homophobia in the high school: A problem in need of a resolution. *Journal of Homosexuality, 77*(1), 177–185.

Elish-Piper, L., Matthews, M., & Risko, V. (2013). Invisibility: An unintended consequence of standards, tests, and mandates. *Journal of Language & Literacy Education / Ankara Universitesi SBF Dergisi, 9*(2), 4–23.

Elizur, Y., Somech, L. Y., & Vinokur, A. D. (2017). Effects of parent training on callous-unemotional traits, effortful control, and conduct problems: Mediation by parenting. *Journal of Abnormal Child Psychology, 45*(1), 15–26. http://dx.doi.org.unco.idm.oclc.org/10.1007/s10802-016-0163-7

Elkind, D. (1981a). *Children and adolescents: Interpretive essays on Jean Piaget* (3rd ed.). New York, NY: Oxford University Press.

Elkind, D. (1981b). *The hurried child: Growing up too fast too soon.* Reading, MA: Addison-Wesley.

Elkind, D. (2012, January–February). The many modes of experience and learning: The grandmasters of ECE. *Exchange,* no. 203, 8–10.

Elkins, A. (2013). Environments that inspire. *Teaching Young Children, 6*(5), 14–17.

Elledge, L. l., Elledge, A., Newgent, R., Cavell, T., Elledge, L. C., Elledge, A. R., . . . Cavell, T. A. (2016). Social risk and peer victimization in elementary school children: The protective role of teacher-student relationships. *Journal of Abnormal Child Psychology, 44,* 691–703. doi:10.1007/s10802-015-0074-z

Elleman, A. M. (2017). Examining the impact of inference instruction on the literal and inferential comprehension of skilled and less skilled readers: A meta-analytic review. *Journal of Educational Psychology, 109,* 761–781. http://dx.doi.org.unco.idm.oclc.org/10.1037/edu0000180

Elliot, A. J., & McGregor, H. A. (2000, April). Approach and avoidance goals and autonomous-controlled regulation: Empirical and conceptual relations. In A. Assor (Chair), *Self-determination theory and achievement goal theory: Convergences, divergences, and educational implications.* Symposium conducted at the annual meeting of the American Educational Research Association, New Orleans, LA.

Elliott, D. J. (1995). *Music matters: A new philosophy of music education.* New York, NY: Oxford University Press.

Elliott, R., & Vasta, R. (1970). The modeling of sharing: Effects associated with vicarious reinforcement, symbolization, age, and generalization. *Journal of Experimental Child Psychology, 10,* 8–15.

Elliott, S. N., Kurz, A., & Neergaard, L. (2012). Large-scale assessment for educational accountability. In K. R. Harris, S. Graham, T. Urdan, A. G. Bus, S. Major, & H. Swanson (Eds.), *APA Educational Psychology Handbook, Vol. 3. Application to teaching and learning* (pp. 111–138). Washington, DC: American Psychological Association. doi:10.1037/13275-006

Elliott, S., & Elliott, G. (2014). Chess, contest, and English. *English Journal, 103*(3), 87–93.

Elmesky, R. (2013). Building capacity in understanding foundational biology concepts: A K-12 learning progression in genetics informed by research on children's thinking and learning. *Research in Science Education, 43,* 1155–1175. doi:10.1007/s11165-012-9286-1

Elmore, C. A., & Gaylord-Harden, N. K. (2013). The influence of supportive parenting and racial socialization messages on African American youth behavioral outcomes. *Journal of Child and Family Studies, 22,* 63–75. doi:10.1007/s10826-012-9653-6

Elmore, G. M., & Huebner, E. S. (2010). Adolescents' satisfaction with school experiences: Relationships with demographics, attachment relationships, and school engagement behavior. *Psychology in the Schools, 47,* 525–537.

Else-Quest, N. M., Hyde, J. S., & Linn, M. C. (2010). Cross-national patterns of gender differences in mathematics: A meta-analysis. *Psychological Bulletin, 136,* 103–127.

Eluri, Z., Andrade, I., Trevino, N., & Mahmoud, E. (2016). Assessment and treatment of problem behavior maintained by mand compliance. *Journal of Applied Behavior Analysis, 49,* 383–387.

Elze, D. E. (2003). Gay, lesbian, and bisexual youths' perceptions of their high school environments and comfort in school. *Children and Schools, 25,* 225–239.

Emde, R. N., & Buchsbaum, H. (1990). "Didn't you hear my mommy?" Autonomy with connectedness in moral self-emergence. In D. Cicchetti & M. Beeghly (Eds.), *The self in transition: Infancy to adulthood* (pp. 35–60). Chicago, IL: University of Chicago Press.

Emde, R., Gaensbauer, T., & Harmon, R. (1976). *Emotional expression in infancy: A biobehavioral study* (Psychological Issues, Vol. 10, No. 37). New York, NY: International Universities Press.

Emmer, E. T., Evertson, C. M., & Worsham, M. E. (2000). *Classroom management for secondary teachers* (5th ed.). Boston, MA: Allyn & Bacon.

Empson, S. B. (1999). Equal sharing and shared meaning: The development of fraction concepts in a first-grade classroom. *Cognition and Instruction, 17,* 283–342.

Encheff, D. (2013). Creating a science e-book with fifth grade students. *Techtrends: Linking Research & Practice to Improve Learning, 57*(6), 61–72. doi:10.1007/s11528-013-0703-8

Engel, S. (2011). Children's need to know: Curiosity in schools. *Harvard Educational Review, 81,* 625–645.

Engel, S. (2015). *The hungry mind: The origins of curiosity in childhood*. Cambridge, MA: Harvard University Press.

Engeland, A., Bjørge, T., Daltveit, A., Skurtveit, S., Vangen, S., Vollset, S., & Furu, K. (2013). Effects of preconceptional paternal drug exposure on birth outcomes: Cohort study of 340 000 pregnancies using Norwegian population-based databases. *British Journal of Clinical Pharmacology, 75*, 1134–1141. doi:10.1111/j.1365-2125.2012.04426.x

Engelhardt, L. E., Mann, F. D., Briley, D. A., Church, J. A., Harden, K. P., & Tucker-Drob, E. M. (2016). Strong genetic overlap between executive functions and intelligence. *Journal of Experimental Psychology: General, 145*, 1141–1159.

English, D. J. (1998). The extent and consequences of child maltreatment. *The Future of Children: Protecting Children from Abuse and Neglect, 8*(1), 39–53.

English, D., Lambert, S., & Ialongo, N. (2014). Longitudinal associations between experienced racial discrimination and depressive symptoms in African American adolescents. *Developmental Psychology, 50*, 1190–1196.

Ennis, R., & Jolivette, K. (2014). Existing research and future directions for self-regulated strategy development with students with and at risk for emotional and behavioral disorders. *Journal of Special Education, 48*(1), 32–45. doi:10.1177/0022466912454682

Eppig, C., Fincher, C. L., & Thornhill, R. (2010). Parasite prevalence and the worldwide distribution of cognitive ability. *Proceedings of the Royal Society, B, 277, 3801–3808.*

Epstein, J. L. (1986). Friendship selection: Developmental and environmental influences. In E. Mueller & C. Cooper (Eds.), *Process and outcome in peer relationships* (pp. 129–160). New York, NY: Academic Press.

Epstein, J. L. (1996). Perspectives and previews on research and policy for school, family, and community partnerships. In A. Booth & J. F. Dunn (Eds.), *Family–school links: How do they affect educational outcomes? (pp. 209–246).* Mahwah, NJ: Erlbaum.

Epstein, J. L. (2001). Building bridges of home, school, and community: The importance of design. *Journal of Education for Students Placed at Risk, 6*(1/2), 161–168.

Epstein, J. L., Galindo, C. L., & Sheldon, S. B. (2011). Levels of leadership: Effects of district and school leaders on the quality of school programs of family and community involvement. *Educational Administration Quarterly, 47*, 462–495. doi:10.1177/0013161X10396929

Epstein, J. S. (1998). Introduction: Generation X, youth culture, and identity. In J. S. Epstein (Ed.), *Youth culture: Identity in a postmodern world* (pp. 1–23). Malden, MA: Blackwell.

Epstein, S., & Morling, B. (1995). Is the self motivated to do more than enhance and/or verify itself? In M. H. Kernis (Ed.), *Efficacy, agency, and self-esteem* (pp. 9–30). New York, NY: Plenum Press.

Erath, S. A., Flanagan, K. S., Bierman, K. L., & Tu, K. M. (2010). Friendships moderate psychosocial maladjustment in socially anxious early adolescents. *Journal of Applied Developmental Psychology, 31*(1), 15–26. doi:10.1016/j.appdev.2009.05.005

Erbeli, F., Hart, S. A., Kim, Y. G., & Taylor, J. (2017). The effects of genetic and environmental factors on writing development. *Learning & Individual Differences, 59*, 11–21. doi:10.1016/j.lindif.2017.08.005

Ereky-Stevens, K., Funder, A., Katschnig, T., Malmberg, L.-E., & Datler, W. (2018). Relationship building between toddlers and new caregivers in out-of-home childcare: Attachment security and caregiver sensitivity. *Early Childhood Research Quarterly, 42*, 270–279. http://dx.doi.org.unco.idm.oclc.org/10.1016/j.ecresq.2017.10.007

Eriks-Brophy, A., Gibson, S., & Tucker, S. (2013). Articulatory error patterns and phonological process use of preschool children with and without hearing loss. *Volta Review, 113*, 87–125.

Eriksen, H., Kesmodel, U., Wimberley, T., Underbjerg, M., Kilburn, T., & Mortensen, E. (2012). Effects of tobacco smoking in pregnancy on offspring intelligence at the age of 5. *Journal of Pregnancy, 2012*, 1–9. doi:10.1155/2012/945196

Erikson, E. H. (1963). *Childhood and society* (2nd ed.). New York, NY: Norton.

Erikson, E. H. (1966). *Eight ages of man. International Journal of Psychiatry*, 2(3), 281–300.

Eriksson, M., Marschik, P. B., Tulviste, T., Almgren, M., Pérez Pereira, M., Wehberg, S.,... Gallego, C. (2012). Differences between girls and boys in emerging language skills: Evidence from 10 language communities. *British Journal of Developmental Psychology, 30*, 326–343. doi:10.1111/j.2044-835X.2011.02042.x

Ernst-Slavit, G. & Mason, M. (2012). *Making your first ELL home visit: A guide for classroom teachers.* Retrieved from http://www.colorincolorado.org/article/59138/

Ernst, M., & Hardin, M. (2010). Neurodevelopment underlying adolescent behavior. In P. D. Zelazo, M. Chandler, & E. Crone (Eds.), *Developmental social cognitive neuroscience. The Jean Piaget symposium series* (pp. 165–189). New York, NY: Psychology Press.

Eron, L. D. (1980). Prescription for reduction of aggression. *American Psychologist, 35*, 244–252.

Eron, L. D. (1987). The development of aggressive behavior from the perspective of a developing behaviorism. *American Psychologist, 42*, 435–442.

Erwin, P. (1993). *Friendship and peer relations in children.* Chichester, England: Wiley.

Esnaola, I., Revuelta, L., Ros, I., & Sarasa, M. (2017). The development of emotional intelligence in adolescence. *Anales de Psicología, 33*, 327–333.

Esparza, J., Shumow, L., & Schmidt, J. (2014). Growth mindset of gifted seventh grade students in science. *NCSSSMST Journal, 19*(1), 6–13.

Espinosa, L. (2007). English-language learners as they enter school. In R. Pianta, M. Cox, & K. Snow (Eds.), *School readiness and the transition to kindergarten in the era of accountability* (pp. 175–196). Baltimore, MD: Paul H. Brookes.

Espinosa, L. (2008). *Challenging common myths about young English language learners* (FCD Policy Brief: Advancing PK–3; No. 8). New York, NY: Foundation for Child Development.

Espinoza, G., Gillen-O'Neel, C., Gonzales, N. A., & Fuligni, A. J. (2013). Friend affiliations and school adjustment among Mexican-American adolescents: The moderating role of peer and parent support. *Journal of Youth and Adolescence. 43*(12), 1969-1981. http://dx.doi.org.unco.idm.oclc.org/10.1007/s10964-013-0023-5

Espinoza, P., Arêas da Luz Fontes, A., & Arms-Chavez, C. (2014). Attributional gender bias: Teachers' ability and effort explanations for students' math performance. *Social Psychology of Education, 17*, 105–126. doi:10.1007/s11218-013-9226-6

Esser, M. B., Rao, G. N., Gururaj, G., Murthy, P., Jayarajan, D., Sethu, L., . . . Collaborators Group on Epidemiological Study of Patterns and Consequences of Alcohol Misuse in India. (2016). Physical abuse, psychological abuse and neglect: Evidence of alcohol-related harm to children in five states of India. *Drug and Alcohol Review, 35*, 530–538. doi:10.1111/dar.12377

Estes, K. G., Evans, J. L., Alibali, M. W., & Saffran, J. R. (2007). Can infants map meaning to newly segmented words? Statistical segmentation and word learning. *Psychological Science, 18*, 254–260.

Esteve-Gibert, N., & Prieto, P. (2014). Infants temporally coordinate gesture-speech combinations before they produce their first words. *Speech Communication, 57*, 301–316. doi:10.1016/j.specom.2013.06.006

Estrada, J. J., Gilreath, T. D., Astor, R. A., & Benbenishty, R. (2016). A statewide study of gang membership in California secondary schools. *Youth & Society, 48*, 720–736. doi:10.1177/0044118X14528957

Estrada, V. L., Gómez, L., & Ruiz-Escalante, J. A. (2009). Let's make dual language the norm. *Educational Leadership, 66*(7), 54–58.

Eunjyu, Y. (2013). Empowering at-risk students as autonomous learners: Toward a metacognitive approach. *Research & Teaching in Developmental Education, 30*(1), 35–45.

Evans, D. W., & Marsh, H. L. (2017). A brief introduction to early forms of non-verbal social cognition. *Infant Behavior & Development, 48*(Part A), 2–4. http://dx.doi.org/10.1016/j.infbeh.2016.11.012

Evans, E. M. (2001). Cognitive and contextual factors in the emergence of diverse belief systems: Creation versus evolution. *Cognitive Psychology, 42*, 217–266.

Evans, E. M., Schweingruber, H., & Stevenson, H. W. (2002). Gender differences in interest and knowledge acquisition: The United States, Taiwan, and Japan. *Sex Roles, 47*, 153–167.

Evans, G. W., & Fuller-Rowell, T. E. (2013). Childhood poverty, chronic stress, and young adult working memory: The protective role of self-regulatory capacity. *Developmental Science, 16*(5), 688–696. doi:10.1111/desc.12082

Evans, G. W., & Kim, P. (2007). Childhood poverty and health: Cumulative risk exposure and stress dysregulation. *Psychological Science, 18*, 953–957.

Evans, G. W., & Schamberg, M. A. (2009). Childhood poverty, chronic stress, and adult working memory. *PNAS Proceedings of the National Academy of the United States, 106*, 6545–6549.

Evans, J. L., Hahn, J. A., Lum, P. J., Stein, E. S., & Page, K. (2009). Predictors of injection drug use cessation and relapse in a prospective cohort of young injection drug users in San Francisco, CA (UFO Study). *Drug and Alcohol Dependence, 101*, 152–157.

Fadiman, A. (1997). *The spirit catches you and you fall down: The Hmong child, her American doctors, and the collision of two cultures.* New York, NY: Noonday Press/Farrar.

Fagan, J. F. (2011). Intelligence in infancy. In R. J. Sternberg & S. B. Kaufman (Eds.), Cambridge handbooks in psychology. *The Cambridge handbook of intelligence* (pp. 130–143). Cambridge, England: Cambridge University Press. http://dx.doi.org/10.1017/CBO9780511977244.008

Fahrmeier, E. D. (1978). The development of concrete operations among the Hausa. *Journal of Cross-Cultural Psychology, 9*, 23–44.

Fairchild, H. H., & Edwards-Evans, S. (1990). African American dialects and schooling: A review. In A. M. Padilla, H. H. Fairchild, & C. M. Valadez (Eds.), *Bilingual education: Issues and strategies* (pp. 75–86). Newbury Park, CA: Sage.

Fais, L., Kajikawa, S., Shigeaki, A., & Werker, J. F. (2009). Infant discrimination of a morphologically relevant word-final contrast. *Infancy, 14*, 488–499.

Falbo, T., & Polit, D. (1986). A quantitative review of the only child literature: Research evidence and theory development. *Psychological Bulletin, 100*, 176–189.

Falch, T., & Sandgren Massih, S. (2011). The effect of education on cognitive ability. *Economic Inquiry, 49*(3), 838–856. doi:10.1111/j.1465-7295.2010.00312.x

Falk, S., & Kello, C. T. (2017). Hierarchical organization in the temporal structure of infant-direct speech and song. *Cognition, 163*, 80–86. http://dx.doi.org.unco.idm.oclc.org/10.1515/cog-2016-0004

Fan, W., & Wolters, C. A. (2014). School motivation and high school dropout: The mediating role of educational expectation. *British Journal of Educational Psychology, 84*(1), 22–39. doi:10.1111/bjep.12002

Fan, Y., Decety, J., Yang, C., Liu, J., & Cheng, Y. (2010). Unbroken mirror neurons in autism spectrum disorders. *Journal of Child Psychology and Psychiatry, 51*, 981–988.

Fanti, K. A., & Henrich, C. C. (2010). Trajectories of pure and co-occurring internalizing and externalizing problems from age 2 to age 12: Findings from the National Institute of Child Health and Human Development Study of Early Child Care. *Developmental Psychology, 46*, 1159–1175.

Fantini, A. E. (1985). *Language acquisition of a bilingual child: A sociolinguistic perspective.* Clevedon, England: Multilingual Matters.

Fantino, A. M., & Colak, A. (2001). Refugee children in Canada: Searching for identity. *Child Welfare, 80*, 587–596.

Farber, B., Mindel, C. H., & Lazerwitz, B. (1988). The Jewish American family. In C. H. Mindel, R. W. Habenstein, & R. Wright (Eds.), *Ethnic families in America: Patterns and variations* (pp. 400–437). New York, NY: Elsevier.

Farmer, E., Selwyn, J., & Meakings, S. (2013). "Other children say you're not normal because you don't live with your parents." Children's views of living with informal kinship carers: Social networks, stigma and attachment to carers. *Child & Family Social Work, 18*(1), 25–34. doi:10.1111/cfs.12030

Farr, R. H. (2016). Does parental sexual orientation matter? A longitudinal follow-up of adoptive families with school-age children. *Developmental Psychology*. Advance online publication. doi:10.1037/dev0000228

Farr, R. H., & Patterson, C. J. (2013). Lesbian and gay adoptive parents and their children. In A. E. Goldberg & K. R. Allen (Eds.), *LGBT-parent families: Innovations in research and implications for practice* (pp. 39–55). New York, NY: Springer Science + Business Media. doi:10.1007/978-1-4614-4556-2_3

Farrant, B. M., Devine, T. J., Maybery, M. T., & Fletcher, J. (2012). Empathy, perspective taking and prosocial behaviour: The importance of parenting practices. *Infant & Child Development, 21*, 175–188. doi:10.1002/icd.740

Farrell, A. D., Erwin, E. H., Bettencourt, A., Mays, S., Vulin-Reynolds, M., Sullivan, T., . . . Meyer, A. (2008). Individual factors influencing effective nonviolent behavior and fighting in peer situations: A qualitative study with urban African American adolescents. *Journal of Clinical Child and Adolescent Psychology, 37*(2), 397–411.

Farringdon, F., Holgate, C., McIntyre, F., & Bulsara, M. (2014). A level of discomfort! Exploring the relationship between maternal sexual health knowledge, religiosity and comfort discussing sexual health issues with adolescents. *Sexuality Research & Social Policy: A Journal of the NSRC, 11*(2), 95–103. doi:10.1007/s13178-013-0122-9

Farrington-Flint, L., & Wood, C. (2007). The role of lexical analogies in beginning reading: Insights from children's self-reports. *Journal of Educational Psychology, 99*, 326–338.

Farrow, C., & Blissett, J. (2014). Maternal mind-mindedness during infancy, general parenting sensitivity and observed child feeding behavior: A longitudinal study. *Attachment & Human Development, 16*, 230–241. doi:10.1080/14616734.2014.898158

Farver, J. A. M., & Branstetter, W. H. (1994). Preschoolers' prosocial responses to their peers' distress. *Developmental Psychology, 30*, 334–341.

Farver, J. M., & Shin, Y. L. (1997). Social pretend play in Korean- and Anglo-American preschoolers. *Child Development, 68*(3), 544–556.

Farver, J. M., Xu, Y., Lonigan, C. J., & Eppe, S. (2013). The home literacy environment and Latino head start children's emergent literacy skills. *Developmental Psychology, 49*(4), 775–791. doi:10.1037/a0028766

Fasoli, A. D. (2017). Moral responsibility, personal regulation, and helping others: A cultural approach to moral reasoning in U.S. Evangelical Christian cultures. *Culture & Psychology, 23*, 461–486. http://dx.doi.org.unco.idm.oclc.org/10.1177/1354067X17692117

Fausel, D. F. (1986). Loss after divorce: Helping children grieve. *Journal of Independent Social Work, 1*(1), 39–47.

Fearrington, J. Y., Parker, P. D., Kidder-Ashley, P., Gagnon, S. G., McCane-Bowling, S., & Sorrell, C. A. (2014). Gender differences in written expression curriculum-based measurement in third- through eighth-grade students. *Psychology in The Schools, 51*(1), 85–96. doi:10.1002/pits.21733

Febres, J., Shorey, R., Zucosky, H., Brasfield, H., Vitulano, M., Elmquist, J., . . . Stuart, G. L. (2014). The relationship between male-perpetrated interparental aggression, paternal characteristics, and child psychosocial functioning. *Journal of Child & Family Studies, 23*, 907–916. doi:10.1007/s10826-013-9748-8

Federal Interagency Forum on Child and Family Statistics. (2013b). *Table FAM1.B Family structure and children's living arrangements: Detailed living arrangements of children by gender, race and Hispanic origin, age, parent's education, and poverty status, 2011.* Retrieved from http://www.childstats.gov/americaschildren/tables/fam1b.asp

Federal Interagency Forum on Child and Family Statistics. (2013c). *Special 1.A/C Adoption: Number and percentage of children ages 0–17 who are adopted and percentage of adopted children ages 0–17 who are of a different race than their adoptive parent by region and state, 2008.* Retrieved from http://www.childstats.gov/americaschildren11/tables/special1ac.asp.

Feifer, S. G. (2013). Psychopathology of disorders of written expression and dysgraphia. In A. S. Davis (Ed.), *Psychopathology of childhood and adolescence: A neuropsychological approach* (pp. 145–157). New York, NY: Springer Publishing Co.

Feigenberg, L., King, M., Barr, D., & Selman, R. (2008). Belonging to and exclusion from the peer group in schools: influences on adolescents' moral choices. *Journal of Moral Education, 37*, 165–184. doi:10.1080/03057240802009306

Feinberg, M. E., Kan, M. L., & Goslin, M. C. (2009). Enhancing coparenting, parenting, and child self-regulation: Effects of family foundations 1 year after birth. *Prevention Science, 10*(3), 276–285.

Feinberg, M. E., Kan, M. L., & Hetherington, E. M. (2007). The longitudinal influence of coparenting conflict on parental negativity and adolescent adjustment. *Journal of Marriage and Family, 69*, 687–702.

Feinman, S. (1992). *Social referencing and the social construction of reality in infancy.* New York, NY: Plenum Press.

Feldhusen, J. F. (1989). Synthesis of research on gifted youth. *Educational Leadership, 26*(1), 6–11.

Feldhusen, J. F., Van Winkle, L., & Ehle, D. A. (1996). Is it acceleration or simply appropriate instruction for precocious youth? *Teaching Exceptional Children, 28*(3), 48–51.

Feldman, R. (2007). Mother-infant synchrony and the development of moral orientation in childhood and adolescence: Direct and indirect mechanisms of developmental continuity. *American Journal of Orthopsychiatry, 77*, 582–597. doi:10.1037/0002-9432.77.4.582

Felner, R. D., & DeVries, M. (2013). Poverty in childhood and adolescence: A transactional-ecological approach to understanding and enhancing resilience in contexts of disadvantage and developmental risk. In S. Goldstein & R. B. Brooks (Eds.), *Handbook of resilience in children* (2nd ed., pp. 105–126). New York, NY: Springer Science + Business Media. doi:10.1007/978-1-4614-3661-4_7

Felton, R. H. (1998). The development of reading skills in poor readers: Educational implications. In C. Hulme & R. M. Joshi (Eds.), *Reading and spelling: Development and disorders* (pp. 329–342). Mahwah, NJ: Erlbaum.

Felver, J. C., Celis-de Hoyos, C. E., Tezanos, K., & Singh, N. N. (2016). A systematic review of mindfulness-based interventions for youth in school settings. *Mindfulness, 7*(1), 34–45. doi:10.1007/s12671-015-0389-4

Feng, X., Shaw, D., & Moilanen, K. (2011). Parental negative control moderates the shyness-emotion regulation pathway to school-age internalizing symptoms. *Journal of Abnormal Child Psychology, 39*, 425–436.

Fennell, C. T., Byers-Heinlein, K., & Werker, J. F. (2007). Using speech sounds to guide word learning: The case of bilingual infants. *Child Development, 78*, 1510–1525.

Fennimore, B. S. (2013). Honoring women who must raise their children alone. In J. Pattnaik (Ed.), *Father involvement in young children's lives: A global analysis* (pp. 169–179). New York, NY: Springer Science + Business Media. doi:10.1007/978-94-007-5155-2_10

Fenson, L., Dale, P., Reznick, J., Bates, E., Thal, D., & Pethick, S. (1994). Variability in early communicative development. *Monographs of the Society for Research in Child Development, 59*(5, Serial No. 242).

Fenton, A. A., & McFarland-Piazza, L. (2014). Supporting early childhood preservice teachers in their work with children and families with complex needs: A strengths approach. *Journal of Early Childhood Teacher Education, 35*(1), 22–38. doi:10.1080/10901027.2013.874384

Fernald, A., Swingley, D., & Pinto, J. P. (2001). When half a word is enough: Infants can recognize spoken words using partial phonetic information. *Child Development, 72*, 1003–1015.

Ferrell, K. (2006). Evidence-based practices for students with visual disabilities. *Communication Disorders Quarterly, 28*(1), 42–48.

Fetro, J. V., Givens, C., & Carroll, K. (2009). Coordinated school health: Getting it all together. *Educational Leadership, 67*(4), 32–37.

Fett, A. J., Shergill, S. S., Gromann, P. M., Dumontheil, I., Blakemore, S., Yakub, F., & Krabbendam, L. (2014). Trust and social reciprocity in adolescence—A matter of perspective-taking. *Journal of Adolescence, 37*, 175–184. doi:10.1016/j.adolescence.2013.11.011

Feuerstein, R. (1979). *The dynamic assessment of retarded performers: The Learning Potential Assessment Device, theory, instruments, and techniques.* Baltimore, MD: University Park Press.

Feuerstein, R., & Falik, L. D. (2010). Learning to think, Thinking to learn: A comparative analysis of three approaches to instruction. *Journal of Cognitive Education & Psychology, 9*(1), 4–20. doi:10.1891/1945-8959.9.1.4

Feuerstein, R., Feuerstein, R., & Gross, S. (1997). The Learning Potential Assessment Device. In D. P. Flanagan, J. L. Genshaft, & P. L. Harrison (Eds.), *Contemporary intellectual assessment: Theories, tests, and issues* (pp. 297–313). New York, NY: Guilford Press.

Fewell, R. R., & Sandall, S. R. (1983). Curricula adaptations for young children: Visually impaired, hearing impaired, and physically impaired. *Curricula in Early Childhood Special Education, 2*(4), 51–66.

Fiedler, E. D., Lange, R. E., & Winebrenner, S. (1993). In search of reality: Unraveling the myths about tracking, ability grouping and the gifted. *Roeper Review, 16*(1), 4–7.

Field, S. L., Labbo, L. D., & Ash, G. E. (1999, April). *Investigating young children's construction of social studies concepts and the intersection of literacy learning.* Paper presented at the annual meeting of the American Educational Research Association, Montreal, Quebec, Canada.

Field, T. (2001). Massage therapy facilitates weight gain in preterm infants. *Current Directions in Psychological Science, 10*, 51–54.

Field, T., Woodson, R., Greenberg, R., & Cohen, D. (1982). Discrimination and imitation of facial expressions by neonates. *Science, 218*, 179–181.

Fields, R. D. (2009). *The other brain: From dementia to schizophrenia, how new discoveries are revolutionizing medicine and science.* New York, NY: Simon & Schuster.

Finders, M., & Lewis, C. (1994). Why some parents don't come to school. *Educational Leadership, 51*(8), 50–54.

Finkelhor, D., Ormrod, R., Turner, H., & Hamby, S. L. (2005). The victimization of children and youth: A comprehensive, national study. *Child Maltreatment, 10*(1), 5–25.

Fiorello, C. A., & Primerano, D. (2005). Research into practice: Cattell-Horn-Carroll cognitive assessment in practice: Eligibility and program development issues. *Psychology in the Schools, 42*, 525–536.

Fireman, G. D., & Kose, G. (2010). Perspective taking. In E. H. Sandberg & B. L. Spritz (Eds.), *A clinician's guide to normal cognitive development in childhood* (pp. 85–100). New York, NY: Routledge/Taylor & Francis Group.

Firkowska-Mankiewicz, A. (2011). Adult careers: Does childhood IQ predict later life outcome? *Journal of Policy & Practice in Intellectual Disabilities, 8*(1), 1–9. doi:10.1111/j.1741-1130.2011.00281.x

Fischer, K. W. (2008). Dynamic cycles of cognitive and brain development: Measuring growth in mind, brain, and education. In A. M. Battro, K. W. Fischer, & P. J. Lena (Eds.), *The educated brain* (pp. 127–150). New York, NY: Cambridge University Press.

Fischer, K. W., & Immordino-Yang, M. H. (2002). Cognitive development and education: From dynamic general structure to specific learning and teaching. In E. Lagemann (Ed.), *Traditions of scholarship in education* (pp. 1–55). Chicago, IL: Spencer Foundation.

Fischer, K. W., Stein, Z., & Heikkinen, K. (2009). Narrow assessments misrepresent development and misguide policy: Comment on Steinberg, Cauffman, Woolard, Graham, and Banich (2009). *American Psychologist, 64*, 595–600.

Fishbein, D. H., Domitrovich, C., Williams, J., Gitukui, S., Guthrie, C., Shapiro, D., & Greenberg, M. (2016). Short-Term intervention effects of the PATHS Curriculum in young low-income children: Capitalizing on plasticity. *Journal of Primary Prevention, 37*, 493–511. doi:10.1007/s10935-016-0452-5

Fishbein, D. H., Hyde, C., Eldreth, D., Paschall, M. J., Hubal, R., Das, A., . . . Yung, B. (2006). Neurocognitive skills moderate urban male adolescents' responses to preventive intervention materials. *Drug and Alcohol Dependence, 82*(1), 47–60.

Fisher, C. B., Jackson, J. F., & Villarruel, F. A. (1998). The study of African American and Latin American children and youth. In W. Damon (Series Ed.) & R. M. Lerner (Vol. Ed.), *Handbook of Child Psychology: Vol. 1. Theoretical models of human development* (5th ed., pp. 1145–1207). New York, NY: Wiley.

Fisher, C. B., Jackson, J. F., & Villarruel, F. A. (1998). The study of African American and Latin American children and youth. In W. Damon (Series Ed.) & R. M. Lerner

(Vol. Ed.), *Handbook of Child Psychology: Vol. 1. Theoretical models of human development* (5th ed., pp. 1145–1207). New York, NY: Wiley.

Fisher, D., & Frey, N. (2007). *Checking for understanding: Formative assessment techniques for your classroom.* Alexandria, VA: Association for Supervision and Curriculum Development.

Fisher, P. A., Gunnar, M. R., Dozier, M., Bruce, J., & Pears, K. C. (2006). Effects of therapeutic interventions for foster children on behavioral problems, caregiver attachment, and stress regulatory neural systems. *Annals of the New York Academy of Sciences, 1094,* 215–225. doi:10.1196/annals.1376.023

Fisher, P. A., Kim, H. K., & Pears, K. C. (2009). Effects of Multidimensional Treatment Foster Care for Preschoolers (MTFC-P) on reducing permanent placement failures among children with placement instability. *Children and Youth Services Review, 31,* 541–546.

Fite, P. J., Vitulano, M., Wynn, P., Wimsatt, A., Gaertner, A., & Rathert, J. (2010). Influence of perceived neighborhood safety on proactive and reactive aggression. *Journal of Community Psychology, 38,* 757–768. doi:10.1002/jcop.20393

Fitzgerald, J. (1987). Research on revision in writing. *Review of Educational Research, 57,* 481–506.

Fitzpatrick, C., McKinnon, R. D., Blair, C. B., & Willoughby, M. T. (2014). Do preschool executive function skills explain the school readiness gap between advantaged and disadvantaged children? *Learning & Instruction, 30,* 25–31. doi:10.1016/j.learninstruc.2013.11.003

Fitzsimmons, P., Leddy, D., Johnson, L., Biggam, S., & Locke, S. (2013). The moon challenge. *Science & Children, 51*(1), 36–41.

Fivush, R. (2009). Sociocultural perspectives on autobiographical memory. In M. L. Courage & N. Cowan (Eds.), *The development of memory in infancy and childhood* (pp. 283–301). New York, NY: Psychology Press.

Fivush, R., & Nelson, K. (2004). Culture and language in the emergence of autobiographical memory. *Psychological Science, 15,* 573–577.

Fivush, R., Haden, C., & Adam, S. (1995). Structure and coherence of preschoolers' personal narratives over time: Implications for childhood amnesia. *Journal of Experimental Child Psychology, 60,* 32–56.

Flanagan, C. A., & Faison, N. (2001). Youth civic development: Implications of research for social policy and programs. *Social Policy Report, 15*(1), 1–14.

Flanagan, D., Alfonso, V., & Reynolds, M. (2013). Broad and narrow CHC Abilities measured and not measured by the Wechsler Scales: Moving beyond within-battery factor analysis. *Journal of Psychoeducational Assessment, 31*(2), 202–223. doi:10.1177/0734282913478047

Flanagan, S. M., Greenfield, S., Coad, J., & Neilson, S. (2015). An exploration of the data collection methods utilised with children, teenagers and young people (CTYPs). *BMC Research Notes, 8*(1), 1–14. doi:10.1186/s13104-015-1018-

Flanders, J. L., Simard, M., Paquette, D., Parent, S., Vitaro, F., Pihl, R. O., et al. (2010). Rough-and-tumble play and the development of physical aggression and emotion regulation: A five-year follow-up study. *Journal of Family Violence, 25*(4), 357–367. doi:10.1007/s10896-009-9297-5

Flannery, L. P., & Bers, M. (2013). Let's Dance the "Robot Hokey-Pokey"!: Children's programming approaches and achievement throughout early cognitive development. *Journal of Research on Technology in Education, 46*(1), 81–101.

Flavell, J. H. (2000). Development of children's knowledge about the mental world. *International Journal of Behavioral Development, 24*(1), 15–23.

Flavell, J. H., Friedrichs, A. G., & Hoyt, J. D. (1970). Developmental changes in memorization processes. *Cognitive Psychology, 1,* 324–340. doi:10.1016/0010-0285(70)90019-8

Flavell, J. H., Green, F. L., & Flavell, E. R. (1995). Young children's knowledge about thinking. *Monographs of the Society for Research in Child Development, 60*(1, Serial No. 243).

Flavell, J. H., Miller, P. H., & Miller, S. A. (2002). *Cognitive development* (4th ed.). Upper Saddle River, NJ: Prentice Hall.

Flay, B. R., & Allred, C. G. (2003). Long-term effects of the Positive Action program. *American Journal of Health Behavior, 27*(1), 6–21.

Fleer, M., & Hammer, M. (2013). Emotions in imaginative situations: The valued place of fairytales for supporting emotion regulation. *Mind, Culture & Activity, 20,* 240–259. doi:10.1080/10749039.2013.781652

Fleischer, C. (2016). Everyday advocacy: The new professionalism for teachers. *Voices from the Middle, 24*(1), 19–23, 28. Retrieved from http://0-search.proquest.com.source.unco.edu/docview/1815704128?accountid=12832

Fleming, D. (2002). *Alphabet under construction.* New York, NY: Henry Holt.

Flensborg-Madsen, T., & Mortensen, E. L. (2017). Predictors of motor developmental milestones during the first year of life. *European Journal of Pediatrics, 176,* 109–119. doi:http://dx.doi.org/10.1007/s00431-016-2817-4

Flensborg-Madsen, T. T., & Mortensen, E. L (2018). Associations of early developmental milestones with adult intelligence. *Child Development, 89*(2), 638–648.

Fletcher, A. C., Bridges, T. H., & Hunter, A. G. (2007). Managing children's friendships through interparental relationships: Roles of ethnicity and friendship context. *Journal of Marriage and Family, 69,* 1135–1149.

Fletcher, J. M., & Grigorenko, E. L. (2017). Neuropsychology of learning disabilities: The past and the future. *Journal of the International Neuropsychological Society, 23,* 930–940.

Fletcher, J. M., Lyon, G. R., Fuchs, L. S., & Barnes, M. A. (2007). *Learning disabilities: From identification to intervention.* New York, NY: Guilford Press.

Fletcher, K. L., & Bray, N. W. (1996). External memory strategy use in preschool children. *Merrill-Palmer Quarterly, 42,* 379–396.

Florit, E., Roch, M., Altoè, G., & Levorato, M. C. (2009). Listening comprehension in preschoolers: The role of memory. *British Journal of Developmental Psychology, 27,* 935–951.

Flouri, E. E., & Sarmadi, Z. (2016). Prosocial behavior and childhood trajectories of internalizing and externalizing problems: The role of neighborhood and school contexts. *Developmental Psychology, 52*(2), 253–258. doi:10.1037/dev0000076

Floyd, R. G., Bergeron, R., & Alfonso, V. C. (2006). Cattell-Horn-Carroll cognitive ability profiles of poor comprehenders. *Reading and Writing, 19,* 427–456.

Fluke, J. D., Corwin, T. W., Hollinshead, D. M., & Maher, E. J. (2016). Family preservation or child safety? Associations between child welfare workers' experience, position, and perspectives. *Children and Youth Services Review, 69,* 210–218. doi:10.1016/j.childyouth.2016.08.012

Flynn, E. G., Laland, K. N., Kendal, R. L., & Kendal, J. R. (2013). Developmental niche construction. *Developmental Science, 16,* 296–313. doi:10.1111/desc.12030

Flynn, J. R. (1987). Massive IQ gains in 14 nations: What IQ tests really measure. *Psychological Bulletin, 101,* 171–191.

Flynn, J. R. (2007). *What is intelligence? Beyond the Flynn effect.* New York, NY: Cambridge University Press.

Fodor, J. A. (2000). *The mind doesn't work that way: The scope and limits of computational psychology.* Cambridge, MA: The MIT Press.

Follan, M., & McNamara, M. (2014). A fragile bond: adoptive parents' experiences of caring for children with a diagnosis of reactive attachment disorder. *Journal of Clinical Nursing, 23,* 1076–1085. doi:10.1111/jocn.12341

Fong, K. (2016). Child welfare involvement and contexts of poverty: The role of parental adversities, social networks, and social services. *Children and Youth Services Review.* Advance online publication. doi:10.1016/j.childyouth.2016.10.011

Fonner, V. A., Armstrong, K. S., Kennedy, C. E., O'Reilly, K. R., & Sweat, M. D. (2014). School based sex education and HIV prevention in low- and middle-income countries: A systematic review and meta-analysis. *PLoS ONE, 9*(3), 1–18. doi:10.1371/journal.pone.0089692

Fontaine, K. L. (2011). *Complementary and alternative therapies for nursing practice* (3rd ed.). Upper Saddle River, NJ: Pearson Education.

Food Allergy Research & Education (2017). *Resources for schools.* Retrieved from http://www.foodallergy.org/resources/schools?

Forber-Pratt, A. A., & Espelage, D. L. (2018). A qualitative investigation of gang presence and sexual harassment in a middle school. *Journal of Child & Family Studies, 27*, 1929–1939. doi:10.1007/s10826-017-1012-1

Forbes, M. L., Ormrod, J. E., Bernardi, J. D., Taylor, S. L., & Jackson, D. L. (1999, April). *Children's conceptions of space, as reflected in maps of their hometown.* Paper presented at the annual meeting of the American Educational Research Association, Montreal, Canada.

Ford, L., & Dahinten, V. S. (2005). Use of intelligence tests in the assessment of preschoolers. In D. P. Flanagan & P. L. Harrison (Eds.), *Contemporary intellectual assessment: Theories, tests,*

Ford, M. E. (1996). Motivational opportunities and obstacles associated with social responsibility and caring behavior in school contexts. In J. Juvonen & K. R. Wentzel (Eds.), *Social motivation: Understanding children's school adjustment* (pp. 126–153). Cambridge, England: Cambridge University Press.

Ford, M. E., & Smith, P. R. (2007). Thriving with social purpose: An integrative approach to the development of optimal human functioning. *Educational Psychologist, 42*, 153–171.

Ford, M. E., & Smith, P. R. (2009). Commentary: Building on a strong foundation: Five pathways to the next level of motivational theorizing. K. R. Wentzel & A. Wigfield (Eds.), *Handbook of motivation at school* (pp. 265–275). New York, NY: Routledge/Taylor & Francis Group.

Forgasz, H., & Hill, J. (2013). Factors implicated in high mathematics achievement. *International Journal of Science & Mathematics Education, 11*, 481–499. doi:10.1007/s10763-012-9348-x

Forman, H. (2015). Events and children's sense of time: A perspective on the origins of everyday time-keeping. *Frontiers in Psychology, 6*, Article ID 259.

Forsey, K. (2014). Taking the new curriculum outdoors. *Primary Science, 132*, 9–11.

Forsyth, J., & Carter, R. (2012). The relationship between racial identity status attitudes, racism-related coping, and mental health among black Americans. *Cultural Diversity & Ethnic Minority Psychology, 18*, 128–140.

Fortin, L., Marcotte, D., Diallo, T., Potvin, P., & Royer, É. (2013). A multidimensional model of school dropout from an 8-year longitudinal study in a general high school population. *European Journal of Psychology of Education—EJPE, 28*, 563–583. doi:10.1007/s10212-012-0129-2

Forum on Child and Family Statistics. (2016). *America's children in brief: Key national indicators of well-being, 2016.* Retrieved from https://www.childstats.gov/americaschildren/press_release.asp

Forum on Child and Family Statistics. (2016a). *Pop3 race and Hispanic origin composition: Percentage of U.S. children ages 0–17 by race and Hispanic origin, 1980–2015 and projected 2016–2050.* Retrieved from http://www.childstats.gov/americaschildren/tables/pop3.asp

Forum on Child and Family Statistics. (2016b). *Table FAM1.A Family structure and children's living arrangements: Percentage of children ages 0–17 by presence of parents in household and race and Hispanic origin, 1980–2015.* Retrieved from http://www.childstats.gov/americaschildren/tables/fam1a.asp

Forum on Child and Family Statistics. (2016c). *Table FAM1.B Family structure and children's living arrangements: Detailed living arrangements of children by gender, race and Hispanic origin, age, parent's education, and poverty status, 2015.* Retrieved from http://www.childstats.gov/americaschildren/tables/fam1b.asp

Forum on Child and Family Statistics. (2016d). *Child poverty.* Retrieved from http://www.childstats.gov/americaschildren/eco1.asp

Forum on Child and Family Statistics. (2016e). *CON1.A Child poverty: Percentage of children ages 0–17 living below selected poverty levels by selected characteristics, 1980–2014.* Retrieved from http://www.childstats.gov/americaschildren/tables/econ1a.asp

Fossum, S., Handegård, B. H., & Drugli, M. B. (2017). The incredible years teacher classroom management programme in kindergartens: Effects of a universal preventive effort. *Journal of Child and Family Studies, 26*, 2215–2223. http://dx.doi.org.unco.idm.oclc.org/10.1007/s10826-017-0727-3

Fowler, J. W., & Peterson, P. L. (1981). Increasing reading persistence and altering attributional style of learned helpless children. *Journal of Educational Psychology, 73*, 251–260.

Fowler, R. C. (2017). Reframing the debate about the relationship between learning and development: An effort to resolve dilemmas and reestablish dialogue in a fractured field. *Early Childhood Education Journal, 45*, 155–162. doi:10.1007/s10643-015-0770-x

Fox, E. (2009). The role of reader characteristics in processing and learning from informational text. *Review of Educational Research, 79*, 197–261.

Fox, M. (2013). What next in the read-aloud battle? Win or lose? *Reading Teacher, 67*(1), 4–8. doi:10.1002/TRTR.1185

Fox, N. A., Henderson, H. A., Rubin, K. H., Calkins, S. D., & Schmidt, L. A. (2001). Continuity and discontinuity of behavioral inhibition and exuberance: Psychophysiological and behavioral influences across the first 4 years of life. *Child Development, 72*, 1–21.

Franco, J. H., Davis, B. L., & Davis, J. L. (2013). Increasing social interaction using prelinguistic milieu teaching with nonverbal school-age children with autism. *American Journal of Speech-Language Pathology, 22*, 489–502. doi:10.1044/1058-0360(2012/10-0103)

Frank, C. (1999). *Ethnographic eyes: A teacher's guide to classroom observation.* Portsmouth, NH: Heinemann.

Frank, H., Harvey, O. J., & Verdun, K. (2000). American responses to five categories of shame in Chinese culture: A preliminary cross-cultural construct validation. *Personality and Individual Differences, 28*, 887–896.

Frank, J. L., Kohler, K., Peal, A., & Bose, B. (2017). Effectiveness of a school-based yoga program on adolescent mental health and school performance: Findings from a randomized controlled trial. *Mindfulness, 8*, 544–553. doi:10.1007/s12671-016-0628-3

Frazier, B. N., Gelman, S. A., & Wellman, H. M. (2009). Preschoolers' search for explanatory information within adult-child conversation. *Child Development, 80*, 1592–1611.

Frazier, S. L., Mehta, T. G., Atkins, M. S., Hur, K., & Rusch, D. (2013). Not just a walk in the park: Efficacy to effectiveness for after school programs in communities of concentrated urban poverty. *Administration and Policy in Mental Health and Mental Health Services Research, 40*, 406–418. doi:10.1007/s10488-012-0432-x

Frederickson, N. L., & Simmonds, E. A. (2008). Special needs, relationship type and distributive justice norms in early and later years of middle childhood. *Social Development, 17*, 1056–1073. doi:10.1111/j.1467-9507.2008.00477.x

Frederiksen, N. (1984). Implications of cognitive theory for instruction in problem-solving. *Review of Educational Research, 54*, 363–407.

Fredricks, J. A., Blumenfeld, P. C., & Paris, A. H. (2004). School engagement: Potential of the concept, state of the evidence. *Review of Educational Research, 74*, 59–109.

Freeark, K. (2006). Adoption and youth: Critical issues and strengths-based programming to address them. In K. Freeark & W. S. Davidson (Eds.), *The Crisis in Youth Mental Health: Critical Issues and Effective Programs: Vol. 3. Issues for families, schools, and communities* (pp. 121–146). Westport, CT: Praeger/Greenwood.

Freedenthal, S., & Stiffman, A. R. (2007). "They might think I was crazy": Young American Indians' reasons for not seeking help when suicidal. *Journal of Adolescent Research, 22*, 58–77.

Freeman, N. K. (2007). Preschoolers' perceptions of gender appropriate toys and their parents' beliefs about genderized behaviors: Miscommunication, mixed messages, or hidden truths? *Early Childhood Education Journal, 34*, 357–366. http://dx.doi.org.unco.idm.oclc.org/10.1007/s10643-006-0123-x

French, L., & Brown, A. (1977). Comprehension of "before" and "after" in logical and arbitrary sequences. *Journal of Child Language, 4*, 247–256.

Freud, S. (1905). *Three contributions to the theory of sex. The basic writings of Sigmund Freud* (A. A. Brill, Trans.). New York, NY: The Modern Library.

Freud, S. (1960). *The ego and the id* (J. Riviere, Trans.). New York, NY: Norton. (Original work published 1923)

Freud, S. (1965). *The origin and development of psychoanalysis*. New York, NY: Henry Regnery (Gateway Editions). (Original work published 1910)

Frey, K. S., Newman, J., & Onyewuenyi, A. C. (2014). Aggressive forms and functions on school playgrounds: Profile variations in interaction styles, bystander actions, and victimization. *The Journal of Early Adolescence, 34*, 285–310. doi:10.1177/0272431613496638

Frick, P. J., Ray, J. V., Thornton, L. C., & Kahn, R. E. (2014). Annual research review: A developmental psychopathology approach to understanding callous-unemotional traits in children and adolescents with serious conduct problems. *Journal of Child Psychology and Psychiatry, 55*, 532–548. doi:10.1111/jcpp.12152

Friedrich, M., & Friederici, A. D. (2017). The origins of word learning: Brain responses of 3-month-olds indicate their rapid association of objects and words. *Developmental Science, 20*(2), 1–13. doi:10.1111/desc.12357

Frijters, J. J., Tsujimoto, K. K., Boada, R. R., Gottwald, S. S., Hill, D. D., Jacobson, L. J., . . . Gruen, J. J. (2018). Reading related causal attributions for success and failure: Dynamic links with reading skill. *Reading Research Quarterly, 53*(1), 127–148. doi:10.1002/rrq.189

Fristad, M. A., & Black, S. R. (2018). Mood disorders in childhood and adolescence. In J. N. Butcher & P. C. Kendall (Eds.), *APA handbook of psychopathology: Child and adolescent psychopathology* (APA Handbooks in Psychology Series, pp. 253–277). Washington, DC: American Psychological Association. http://dx.doi.org.unco.idm.oclc.org/10.1037/0000065-013

Froiland, J., & Oros, E. (2014). Intrinsic motivation, perceived competence and classroom engagement as longitudinal predictors of adolescent reading achievement. *Educational Psychology, 34*, 119–132. doi:10.1080/01443410.2013.822964

Froiland, J., Oros, E., Smith, L., & Hirchert, T. (2012). Intrinsic motivation to learn: The nexus between psychological health and academic success. *Contemporary School Psychology, 16*, 91–100.

Frost, J. L., Shin, D., & Jacobs, P. J. (1998). Physical environments and children's play. In O. N. Saracho & B. Spodek (Eds.), *Multiple perspectives on play in early childhood education* (pp. 255–294). Albany: State University of New York Press.

Fruchter, N. (2007). *Urban schools, public will: Making education work for all our children*. New York, NY: Teachers College Press.

Fründt, O., Schulz, R., Schöttle, D., Cheng, B., Thomalla, G., Braaß, H., . . . Münchau, A. (2018). White matter microstructure of the human mirror neuron system is related to symptom severity in adults with autism. *Journal of Autism and Developmental Disorders, 48*, 417–429. http://dx.doi.org.unco.idm.oclc.org/10.1007/s10803-017-3332-9

Fry, A. F., & Hale, S. (1996). Processing speed, working memory, and fluid intelligence. *Psychological Science, 7*, 237–241.

Fuchs, L. S., Fuchs, D., Prentice, K., Burch, M., Hamlett, C. L., Owen, R., & Schroeter, K. (2003). Enhancing third-grade students' mathematical problem solving with self-regulated learning strategies. *Journal of Educational Psychology, 95*, 306–315.

Fuhs, M., & Day, J. D. (2011). Verbal ability and executive functioning development in preschoolers at Head Start. *Developmental Psychology, 47*, 404–416. doi:10.1037/a0021065

Fujimura, N. (2001). Facilitating children's proportional reasoning: A model of reasoning processes and effects of intervention on strategy change. *Journal of Educational Psychology, 93*, 589–603.

Fujioka, T., Mourad, N., & Trainor, L. J. (2011). Development of auditory-specific brain rhythm in infants. *European Journal of Neuroscience, 33*, 521–529. doi:10.1111/j.1460-9568.2010.07544.x

Fukkink, R. G., & de Glopper, K. (1998). Effects of instruction in deriving word meanings from context: A meta-analysis. *Review of Educational Research, 68*, 450–469.

Fuller, M. L. (2001). Multicultural concerns and classroom management. In C. A. Grant & M. L. Gomez (Eds.), *Campus and classroom: Making schooling multicultural* (pp. 109–134). Upper Saddle River, NJ: Merrill/Prentice Hall.

Fuller, R. G., Campbell, T. C., Dykstra, D. I. Jr., & Stevens, S. M. (2009). The learning cycle: College teaching and the development of reasoning. In R. G. Fuller, T. C. Campbell, D. I. Dykstra Jr., & S. M. Stevens (Eds.), *College teaching and the development of reasoning: Science and engineering education sources* (pp. 115–133). Charlotte, NC: Information Age Publishing.

Fung, A. L. C. (2017). Reducing schoolchildren with reactive aggression through child, parent, and conjoint parent–child group interventions: A longitudinal outcome effectiveness study. *Family Process*. Advance online publication. http://dx.doi.org.unco.idm.oclc.org/10.1111/famp.12323

Furey, W. M., Marcotte, A. M., Wells, C. S., & Hintze, J. M. (2017). The effects of supplemental sentence-level instruction for fourth-grade students identified as struggling writers. *Reading & Writing Quarterly, 33*, 563–578. doi:10.1080/10573569.2017.1288591

Furnham, A., & Cheng, H. (2013). Factors influencing adult earnings: Findings from a nationally representative sample. *The Journal of Socio-Economics, 44*, 120–125. doi:10.1016/j.socec.2013.02.008

Fusarelli, L. D. (2015). Child welfare, education, inequality, and social policy in comparative perspective. *Peabody Journal of Education, 90*(5), 677–690. doi:10.1080/0161956X.2015.1087779

Fusaro, M., & Nelson, C. A. III. (2009). Developmental cognitive neuroscience and education practice. In O. A. Barbarin & B. H. Wasik (Eds.), *Handbook of child development and early education: Research to practice* (pp. 57–77). New York, NY: Guilford Press.

Fuson, K. C., & Briars, D. J. (1990). Using a base-ten blocks learning/teaching approach for first- and second-grade place-value and multidigit addition and subtraction. *Journal for Research in Mathematics Education, 21*, 180–206.

Fuson, K. C., & Kwon, Y. (1992). Korean children's understanding of multidigit addition and subtraction. *Child Development, 63*, 491–506.

Gabard, D. L. (1999). Homosexuality and the Human Genome Project: Private and public choices. *Journal of Homosexuality, 37*, 25–51.

Gagne, J. R., & Saudino, K. J. (2016). The development of inhibitory control in early childhood: A twin study from 2-3 years. *Developmental Psychology, 52*, 391–399. doi:10.1037/dev0000090

Gagnon, S. G., Huelsman, T. J., Kidder-Ashley, P., & Ballard, M. (2009). Student–teacher relationships matter: Moderating influences between temperament and preschool social competence. *Psychology in the Schools, 46*, 553–567.

Gainotti, G. (2007). Face familiarity feelings, the right temporal lobe and the possible underlying neural mechanisms. *Brain Research Reviews, 56*, 214–235.

Galaburda, A. M., & Rosen, G. D. (2001). Neural plasticity in dyslexia: A window to mechanisms of learning disabilities. In J. L. McClelland & R. S. Siegler (Eds.), *Mechanisms of cognitive development: Behavioral and neural perspectives* (pp. 307–323). Mahwah, NJ: Erlbaum.

Galinsky, A. D., Todd, A. R., Homan, A. C., Phillips, K. W., Apfelbaum, E. P., Sasaki, S. J., . . . Maddux, W. W. (2015). Maximizing the gains and minimizing the pains of diversity: A policy perspective. *Perspectives on Psychological Science, 10*, 742–748. http://dx.doi.org.unco.idm.oclc.org/10.1177/1745691615598513

Gallagher, A. M., & Kaufman, J. C. (Eds.) (2005). *Gender differences in mathematics: An integrative psychological approach*. Cambridge, England: Cambridge University Press.

Gallahue, D. L., & Ozmun, J. C. (1998). *Understanding motor development: Infants, children, adolescents, adults*. Boston, MA: McGraw-Hill.

Galliger, C., Tisak, M., & Tisak, J. (2009). When the wheels on the bus go round: Social interactions on the school bus. *Social Psychology of Education, 12*(1), 43–62. doi:10.1007/s11218-008-9072-0

Gallimore, R., & Goldenberg, C. (2001). Analyzing cultural models and settings to connect minority achievement and school improvement research. *Educational Psychologist, 36*, 45–56.

Gallimore, R., & Tharp, R. (1992). Teaching mind in society: Teaching, schooling, and literate discourse. In L. C. Moll (Ed.),*Vygotsky and education: Instructional implications and applications of sociohistorical psychology* (pp. 175–205). New York, NY: Cambridge University Press.

Gallistel, C. R., & Gelman, R. (1992). Preverbal and verbal counting and computation. *Cognition, 44*, 43–74.

Gallistel, C. R., Brown, A. L., Carey, S., Gelman, R., & Keil, F. C. (1991). Lessons from animal learning for the study of cognitive development. In S. Carey & R. Gelman (Eds.), *Epigenesis of mind: Essays on biology and cognition (pp. 3–36).* Hillsdale, NJ: Erlbaum.

Gallo, A. M., Hadley, E. K., Angst, D. B., Knafl, K. A., & Smith, C. A. M. (2008). Parents' concerns about issues related to their children's genetic conditions. *Journal for Specialists in Pediatric Nursing, 13*(1), 4–14.

Galotti, K. M., Komatsu, L. K., & Voelz, S. (1997). Children's differential performance on deductive and inductive syllogisms. *Developmental Psychology, 33,* 70–78.

Galupo, M. P., Cartwright, K. B., & Savage, L. S. (2010). Cross-category friendships and postformal thought among college students. *Journal of Adult Development* 17(4), 208–214. doi:10.1007/s10804-009-9089-4

Gambrell, L. B., & Bales, R. J. (1986). Mental imagery and the comprehension-monitoring performance of fourth- and fifth-grade poor readers. *Reading Research Quarterly, 21,* 454–464.

Ganiban, J. M., Ulbricht, J., Saudino, K. J., Reiss, D., & Neiderhiser, J. M. (2011). Understanding child-based effects on parenting: Temperament as a moderator of genetic and environmental contributions to parenting. *Developmental Psychology, 47,* 676–692.

Gao, M., Maynard, K. R., Chokshi, V., Song, L., Jacobs, C., Wang, H., . . . Lee, H.-K. (2014). Rebound potentiation of inhibition in juvenile visual cortex requires vision-induced BDNF expression. *The Journal of Neuroscience, 34*(32), 10770-10779. http://dx.doi.org.unco.idm.oclc.org/10.1523/JNEUROSCI.5454-13.2014

Garandeau, C. F., Lee, I. A., & Salmivalli, C. (2014). Inequality matters: Classroom status hierarchy and adolescents' bullying. *Journal of Youth and Adolescence, 43,* 1123–1133. doi:10.1007/s10964-013-0040-4

Garbarino, J., & Abramowitz, R. H. (1992). Sociocultural risk and opportunity. In J. Garbarino (Ed.), *Children and families in the social environment* (pp. 35–70). New York, NY: Aldine de Gruyter.

Garbarino, J., Bradshaw, C. P., & Vorrasi, J. A. (2002). Mitigating the effects of gun violence on children and youth. *The Future of Children, 12*(2), 73–85.

Garces-Bacsal, R. (2011). Socioaffective issues and concerns among gifted Filipino children. *Roeper Review: A Journal on Gifted Education, 33,* 239–251. doi:10.1080/02783193.2011.603112

Garces, E., Thomas, D., & Currie, J. (2002). Longer-term effects of Head Start. *American Economic Review, 92,* 999–1012.

García Coll, C. G., & Marks, A. K. (2009). *Immigrant stories: Ethnicity and academics in middle childhood.* New York, NY: Oxford University Press.

García Coll, C., Lamberty, G., Jenkins, R., McAdoo, H. P., Crnic, K., Wasik, B. H., & Vásquez García, H. (1996). An integrative model for the study of developmental competencies in minority children. *Child Development, 67,* 1891–1914.

García Sierra, P. (2012). Attachment and preschool teacher: An opportunity to develop a secure base. *International Journal of Early Childhood Special Education, 4*(1), 1–16.

Garcia-Reid, P., Peterson, C., Reid, R. J., & Peterson, N. (2013). The protective effects of sense of community, multigroup ethnic identity, and self-esteem against internalizing problems among Dominican youth: Implications for social workers. *Social Work in Mental Health, 11,* 199–222. doi:10.1080/15332985.2013.774923

García, E. E. (1994). *Understanding and meeting the challenge of student cultural diversity.* Boston, MA: Houghton Mifflin.

García, E. E. (1995). Educating Mexican American students: Past treatment and recent developments in theory, research, policy, and practice. In J. A. Banks & C. A. M. Banks (Eds.), *Handbook of research on multicultural education* (pp. 372–387). New York, NY: Macmillan.

García, E. E., & Jensen, B. (2007). Helping young Hispanic learners. *Educational Leadership, 64*(6), 34–39.

García, E., Arias, M., Murri, N., & Serna, C. (2010). Developing responsive teachers: A challenge for a demographic reality. *Journal of Teacher Education, 61*(1/2), 132–142.

Gardner, H. (1983). *Frames of mind: The theory of multiple intelligences.* New York, NY: Basic Books.

Gardner, H. (1993). *Multiple intelligences: The theory in practice.* New York, NY: Basic Books.

Gardner, H. (1995). Reflections on multiple intelligences: Myths and messages. *Phi Delta Kappan, 77,* 200–209.

Gardner, H. (1999). *Intelligence reframed: Multiple intelligences for the 21st century.* New York, NY: Basic Books.

Gardner, H. (2003). *Multiple intelligences after twenty years.* Paper presented at the annual meeting of the American Educational Research Association, Chicago, IL. Retrieved February 25, 2008, from http://www.pz.harvard.edu/PIs/HG_MI_after_20_years.pdf

Gardner, H. (2006). Replies to my critics. In J. A. Schaler (Ed.), *Howard Gardner under fire: The rebel psychologist faces his critics* (pp. 277–344). Chicago, IL: Open Court.

Gardner, H. (2008). *The 25th anniversary of the publication of Howard Gardner's* Frames of mind: The theory of multiple intelligences. Retrieved from http://www.howardgardner.com

Gardner, H. (2009). Birth and the spreading of a "meme." In J.-Q. Chen, S. Moran, & H. Gardner (Eds.), *Multiple intelligences around the world* (pp. 3–16). San Francisco, CA: Jossey-Bass.

Gardner, H. (2011). The theory of multiple intelligences. In M. Gernsbacher, R. W. Pew, L. M. Hough, & J. R. Pomerantz (Eds.), *Psychology and the real world: Essays illustrating fundamental contributions to society* (pp. 122–130). New York, NY: Worth Publishers.

Gardner, H. (2016). Multiple intelligences: Prelude, theory, and aftermath. In R. J. Sternberg, S. T. Fiske, & D. J. Foss (Eds.), *Scientists making a difference: One hundred eminent behavioral and brain scientists talk about their most important contributions* (pp. 167–170). New York, NY: Cambridge University Press.

Gardner, H., & Hatch, T. (1990). Multiple intelligences go to school: Educational implications of the theory of multiple intelligences. *Educational Researcher, 18*(8), 4–10.

Gardner, H., & Moran, S. (2006). The science of multiple intelligences theory: A response to Lynn Waterhouse. *Educational Psychologist, 41*(4), 227–232.

Gardner, H., Torff, B., & Hatch, T. (1996). The age of innocence reconsidered: Preserving the best of the progressive traditions in psychology and education. In D. R. Olson & N. Torrance (Eds.), *The handbook of education and human development: New models of learning, teaching and schooling* (pp. 28–55). Cambridge, MA: Blackwell.

Garland, A., Augustyn, M., & Stein, M. T. (2007). Disruptive and oppositional behavior in an 11-year-old boy. *Journal of Developmental and Behavioral Pediatrics, 28,* 406–408.

Garn, A., McCaughtry, N., Martin, J., Shen, B., & Fahlman, M. (2012). A Basic Needs Theory investigation of adolescents' physical self-concept and global self-esteem. *International Journal of Sport & Exercise Psychology, 10,* 314–328.

Garner, A. S., Shonkoff, J. P., Siegel, B. S., Dobbins, M. I., Earls, M. F., McGuinn, L., . . . Wood, D. L. (2012). Early childhood adversity, toxic stress, and the role of the pediatrician: Translating developmental science into lifelong health. *Pediatrics, 129*(1), e224–e231. doi:10.1542/peds.2011-2662

Garner, R. (1987). Strategies for reading and studying expository texts. *Educational Psychologist, 22,* 299–312.

Garner, R. (1998). Epilogue: Choosing to learn or not-learn in school. *Educational Psychology Review, 10,* 227–237.

Garon-Carrier, G., Boivin, M., Guay, F., Kovas, Y., Dionne, G., Lemelin, J.-P., . . . Tremblay, R. E. (2016). Intrinsic motivation and achievement in mathematics in elementary school: A longitudinal investigation of their association. *Child Development, 87,* 165–175.

Garrison, L. (1989). Programming for the gifted American Indian student. In C. J. Maker & S. W. Schiever (Eds.), *Critical Issues in Gifted Education: Vol. 2. Defensible programs for cultural and ethnic minorities* (pp. 79–90). Austin, TX: Pro-Ed.

Garrison, L. (1989). Programming for the gifted American Indian student. In C. J. Maker & S. W. Schiever (Eds.), Critical *Issues in Gifted Education: Vol. 2. Defensible programs for cultural and ethnic minorities* (pp. 79–90). Austin, TX: Pro-Ed.

Garrote, A., Dessemontet, R. S., Opitz, E. M. (2016). Facilitating the social participation of pupils with special educational needs in mainstream schools: A review of school-based interventions, *Educational Research Review, 20*, 12–23. doi:10.1016/j.edurev.2016.11.001.

Garvey, C., & Hogan, R. (1973). Social speech and social interaction: Egocentrism revisited. *Child Development, 44*, 562–568. doi:10.2307/1128013

Gaskins, I. W., Satlow, E., & Pressley, M. (2007). Executive control of reading comprehension in the elementary school. In L. Meltzer (Ed.), *Executive function in education: From theory to practice* (pp. 194–215). New York, NY: Guilford Press.

Gassman-Pines, A. (2015). Effects of Mexican immigrant parents' daily workplace discrimination on child behavior and family functioning. *Child Development, 86*(4), 1175–1190. doi:10.1111/cdev.12378

Gatti, E., Ionio, C., Traficante, D., & Confalonieri, E. (2014). "I like my body; therefore, I like myself": How body image influences self-esteem-A cross-sectional study on Italian adolescents. *Europe's Journal of Psychology, 10*, 301–317. doi:10.5964/ejop.v10i2.703

Gaumon, S., Paquette, D., Cyr, C., Émond-Nakamura, M., & St-André, M. (2016). Anxiety and attachment to the mother in preschoolers receiving psychiatric care: The father–child activation relationship as a protective factor. *Infant Mental Health Journal, 37*, 372–387. doi:10.1002/imhj.21571

Gaunt, K. D. (2006). *The games Black girls play: Learning the ropes from double-dutch to hip-hop.* New York, NY: New York University Press.

Gauvain, M. (2001). *The social context of cognitive development.* New York, NY: Guilford Press.

Gauvain, M. (2009). Social and cultural transactions in cognitive development: A cross-generational view. In A. Sameroff (Ed.), *The transactional model of development: How children and contexts shape each other* (pp. 163–182). Washington, DC: American Psychological Association.

Gauvain, M., & Parke, R. D. (2010). Socialization. In M. H. Bornstein (Ed.), *Handbook of cultural developmental science* (pp. 239–258). New York, NY: Psychology Press.

Gauvain, M., & Perez, S. M. (2015). The socialization of cognition. In J. E. Grusec & P. D. Hastings (Eds.), *Handbook of socialization: Theory and research* (pp. 566–589). New York, NY, US: Guilford Press.

Gauvain, M., Perez, S. M., & Beebe, H. (2013). Authoritative parenting and parental support for children's cognitive development. In R. E. Larzelere, A. Morris, & A. W. Harrist (Eds.), *Authoritative parenting: Synthesizing nurturance and discipline for optimal child development* (pp. 211–233). Washington, DC: American Psychological Association. doi:10.1037/13948-010

Gavin, L. A., & Fuhrman, W. (1989). Age differences in adolescents' perceptions of their peer groups. *Developmental Psychology, 25*, 827–834.

Gay, G. (2006). Connections between classroom management and culturally responsive teaching. In C. M. Evertson & C. S. Weinstein (Eds.), *Handbook of classroom management: Research, practice, and contemporary issues* (pp. 343–370). Mahwah, NJ: Erlbaum.

Gbadamosi, A. (2018). The changing landscape of young consumer behaviour. In A. Gbadamosi (Ed.), *Young consumer behaviour: A research companion* (pp. 3–22). New York, NY: Routledge/Taylor & Francis Group.

Geary, D. C. (1994). *Children's mathematical development: Research and practical applications.* Washington, DC: American Psychological Association.

Geary, D. C. (2006). Development of mathematical understanding. In W. Damon & R. M. Lerner (Series Eds.), & D. Kuhn & R. Siegler (Vol. Eds.), *Handbook of Child Psychology: Vol. 1. Cognition, perception, and language* (6th ed., 777–810). New York, NY: Wiley.

Geary, D. C., Hoard, M. K., & Nugent, L. (2012). Independent contributions of the central executive, intelligence, and in-class attentive behavior to developmental change in the strategies used to solve addition problems. *Journal of Experimental Child Psychology, 113*(1), 49–65. doi:10.1016/j.jecp.2012.03.003

Geddes, H. (2017). Attachment behavior and learning. In D. Colley & P. Cooper (Eds.), *Attachment and emotional development in the classroom: Theory and practice* (pp. 37–48). London, UK: Jessica Kinglsey.

Geist, K., Geist, E., & Kuznik, K. (2012). The patterns of music. *Young Children, 67*(1), 74–79.

Gelhorn, H., Hartman, C., Sakai, J., Mikulich-Gilbertson, S., Stallings, M., Young, S., . . . Crowley, T. (2009). An item response theory analysis of conduct disorder. *Journal of the American Academy of Child & Adolescent Psychiatry, 48*, 42–50.

Gelman, R., & Baillargeon, R. (1983). A review of some Piagetian concepts. In J. H. Flavell & E. M. Markman (Eds.), *Handbook of Child Psychology: Vol. 3. Cognitive development* (pp. 167–230). New York, NY: Wiley.

Gelman, S. A., & Kalish, C. W. (2006). Conceptual development. In W. Damon & R. M. Lerner (Series Eds.), & D. Kuhn & R. Siegler (Vol. Eds.), *Handbook of Child Psychology: Vol. 1. Cognition, perception, and language* (6th ed., pp. 687–733). New York, NY: Wiley.

Gelman, S. A., & Markman, E. M. (1986). Categories and induction in young children. *Cognition, 23*, 183–209.

Gelman, S. A., & Raman, L. (2003). Preschool children use linguistic form class and pragmatic cues to interpret generics. *Child Development, 74*, 308–325.

Gelman, S. A., & Taylor, M. (1984). How two-year-old children interpret proper and common names for unfamiliar objects. *Child Development, 55*, 1535–1540.

Gelman, S. A., Ware, E. A., Manczak, E. M., & Graham, S. A. (2013). Children's sensitivity to the knowledge expressed in pedagogical and nonpedagogical contexts. *Developmental Psychology, 49*, 491–504. doi:10.1037/a0027901

Genesee, F. (1985). Second language learning through immersion: A review of U.S. programs. *Review of Educational Research, 55*, 541–561.

Genesoni, L., & Tallandini, M. A. (2009). Men's psychological transition to fatherhood: An analysis of the literature, 1989–2008. *Birth, 36*, 305–317.

Gentile, D. A., & Gentile, J. R. (2008). Violent video games as exemplary teachers: A conceptual analysis. *Journal of Youth and Adolescence, 37*, 127–141.

Gentile, D. A., Bender, P. K., & Anderson, C. A. (2017). Violent video game effects on salivary cortisol, arousal, and aggressive thoughts in children. *Computers in Human Behavior, 70*, 39–43. http://dx.doi.org.unco.idm.oclc.org/10.1016/j.chb.2016.12.045

Gentner, D. (2006). Why verbs are hard to learn. In K. Hirsh-Pasek & R. M. Golinkoff (Eds.), *Action meets word: How children learn verbs* (pp. 544–564). New York, NY: Oxford University Press.

Gentry, R. (1982). An analysis of the developmental spellings in *Gnys at Wrk. The Reading Teacher, 36*, 192–200.

Genzuk, M. (1999). Tapping into community funds of knowledge. In *Effective strategies for English language acquisition: Curriculum guide for the professional development of teachers grades kindergarten through eight* (pp. 9–21). Los Angeles, CA: Los Angeles Annenberg Metropolitan Project, ARCO Foundation. Retrieved from http://www-bcf.usc.edu/~genzuk/Genzuk_ARCO_Funds_of_Knowledge.pdf

George, L. (2005). Lack of preparedness: Experiences of first-time mothers. *American Journal of Maternal/Child Nursing, 30*, 251–255.

Georgiou, S., Demetriou, A., & Stavrinides, P. (2008). Attachment style and mentoring relationships in adolescence. *Educational Psychology, 28*, 603–614.

Geraci, A. (2009/2010). Good food in the city. *Educational Leadership, 67*(4), 12–16.

Gerde, H., Schachter, R., & Wasik, B. (2013). Using the scientific method to guide learning: An integrated approach to early childhood curriculum. *Early Childhood Education Journal, 41*(5), 315–323. doi:10.1007/s10643-013-0579-4

Gershoff, E. T., Aber, J. L., & Raver, C. C. (2005). Child poverty in the United States: An evidence-based conceptual framework for programs and policies. In R. M. Lerner, F. Jacobs, & D. Wertlieb (Eds.), *Applied developmental science: An advanced textbook* (pp. 269–324). Thousand Oaks, CA: Sage.

Gershoff, E. T., & Grogan-Kaylor, A. (2016). Spanking and child outcomes: Old controversies and new meta-analyses. *Journal of Family Psychology, 30*(4), 453–469.

Gerson, S. A., & Woodward, A. L. (2013). The goal trumps the means: Highlighting goals is more beneficial than highlighting means in means-end training. *Infancy, 18*, 289–302. doi:10.1111/j.1532-7078.2012.00112.x

Gertner, Y., Fisher, C., & Eisengart, J. (2006). Learning words and rules: Abstract knowledge of word order in early sentence comprehension. *Psychological Science, 17*, 684–691.

Gervai, J. (2009, September 4). Environmental and genetic influences on early attachment. *Child and Adolescent Psychiatry and Mental Health*, 3: 25. doi:10.1186/1753-2000-3-25

Gervain, J., & Mehler, J. (2010). Speech perception and language acquisition in the first year of life. *Annual Review of Psychology, 61*, 191–218.

Gesell, A. (1928). *Infancy and human growth.* New York, NY: Macmillan.

Gesell, S. B., Sommer, E. C., Lambert, E., de Andrade, A., Whitaker, L., Davis, L., . . . Barkin, S. L. (2013). Comparative effectiveness of after-school programs to increase physical activity. *Journal of Obesity*, 1–8. doi:10.1155/2013/576821

Gettinger, M., & Kohler, K. M. (2006). Process-outcome approaches to classroom management and effective teaching. In C. M. Evertson & C. S. Weinstein (Eds.), *Handbook of classroom management: Research, practice, and contemporary issues* (pp. 73–95). Mahwah, NJ: Erlbaum.

Ghazvini, A., & Mullis, R. L. (2002). Center-based care for young children: Examining predictors of quality. *Journal of Genetic Psychology, 163*, 112–125.

Ghoul, A., Niwa, E. Y., & Boxer, P. (2013). The role of contingent self-worth in the relation between victimization and internalizing problems in adolescents. *Journal of Adolescence, 36*, 457–464. doi:10.1016/j.adolescence.2013.01.007

Giammarco, E. A. (2016). The measurement of individual differences in morality. *Personality & Individual Differences, 88*, 26–34. doi:10.1016/j.paid.2015.08.039

Gibson, E. J., & Walk, R. D. (1960). The "visual cliff." *Scientific American, 202*(4), 64–71.

Giletta, M., Slavich, G. M., Rudolph, K. D., Hastings, P. D., Nock, M. K., & Prinstein, M. J. (2018). Peer victimization predicts heightened inflammatory reactivity to social stress in cognitively vulnerable adolescents. *Journal of Child Psychology and Psychiatry, 59*, 129–139.

Gillam, D. (2014). Strategies for writing in the science classroom. *Science & Children, 51*(7), 95–96.

Gillam, R. B., & Johnston, J. R. (1992). Spoken and written language relationships in language/learning-impaired and normal achieving school-age children. *Journal of Speech and Hearing Research, 35*, 1303–1315.

Gillet, N., Vallerand, R., & Lafrenière, M. (2012). Intrinsic and extrinsic school motivation as a function of age: the mediating role of autonomy support. *Social Psychology of Education, 15*, 77–95. doi:10.1007/s11218-011-9170-2

Gillham, J. E., Reivich, K. J., Jaycox, L. H., & Seligman, M. E. P. (1995). Prevention of depressive symptoms in schoolchildren: Two-year follow-up. *Psychological Science, 6*, 343–351.

Gillies, R. M., Nichols, K., Burgh, G., & Haynes, M. (2014). Primary students' scientific reasoning and discourse during cooperative inquiry-based science activities. *International Journal of Educational Research, 63*, 127–140. doi:10.1016/j.ijer.2013.01.001

Gilligan, C. (1982). *In a different voice: Psychological theory and women's development.* Cambridge, MA: Harvard University Press.

Gilligan, C. F. (1985, March). *Keynote address at the Conference on Women and Moral Theory*, Stony Brook, NY.

Gilligan, C. F. (1987). Moral orientation and moral development. In E. F. Kittay & D. T. Meyers (Eds.), *Women and moral theory* (pp. 19–33). Totowa, NJ: Rowman & Littlefield.

Gilligan, C. F., & Attanucci, J. (1988). Two moral orientations. In C. F. Gilligan, J. V. Ward, & J. M. Taylor (Eds.), *Mapping the moral domain: A contribution of women's thinking to psychological theory and education.* Cambridge, MA: Center for the Study of Gender, Education, and Human Development (distributed by Harvard University Press).

Gilliland, H. (1988). Discovering and emphasizing the positive aspects of the culture. In H. Gilliland & J. Reyhner (Eds.), *Teaching the Native American (pp. 21–36).* Dubuque, IA: Kendall/Hunt.

Gilman, A. B., Hill, K. G., Hawkins, J., Howell, J. C., & Kosterman, R. (2014). The developmental dynamics of joining a gang in adolescence: Patterns and predictors of gang membership. *Journal of Research on Adolescence, 24*, 204–219. doi:10.1111/jora.12121

Ginsburg, H. P. (2009). The challenge of formative assessment in mathematics education: Children's minds, teachers' minds. *Human Development, 52*, 109–128.

Ginsburg, H. P., Cannon, J., Eisenband, J., & Pappas, S. (2006). Mathematical thinking and learning. In K. McCartney & D. Phillips (Eds.), *Blackwell handbook of early childhood development* (pp. 208–229). Malden, MA: Blackwell.

Ginsburg, H. P., Lee, J. S., & Boyd, J. S. (2008). Mathematics education for young children: What it is and how to promote it. *Social Policy Report, 22*(1).

Gioia, G. A. (2016). Medical-school partnership in guiding return to school following mild traumatic brain injury in youth. *Journal of Child Neurology, 31*, 93–108. doi:10.1177/0883073814555604

Giordano, P. C. (2003). Relationships in adolescence. *Annual Review of Sociology, 29*, 257–281.

Glahn, D. C., & Burdick, K. E. (2011). Clinical endophenotypes for bipolar disorder. In H. K. Manji & C. A. Zarate Jr. (Eds.), *Behavioral neurobiology of bipolar disorder and its treatment* (pp. 51–67). New York, NY: Springer Science.

Gläscher, J., Rudrauf, D., Colom, R., Paul, L. K., Tranel, D., Damasio, H., & Adolphs, R. (2010). Distributed neural system for general intelligence revealed by lesion mapping. *Proceedings of the National Academy of Sciences of the United States of America, 107*, 4705–4709.

Glaser, C., & Brunstein, J. C. (2007). Improving fourth-grade students' composition skills: Effects of strategy instruction and self-regulation procedures. *Journal of Educational Psychology, 99*, 297–310.

Glasgow, J. N. (1994). Action research changes cultural attitudes. *Teaching Education, 6*, 41–48.

Gleitman, L. R., Cassidy, K., Nappa, R., Papafragou, A., & Trueswell, J. C. (2005). Hard words. *Language Learning and Development, 1*(1), 23–64.

Glenwright, M., Parackel, J. M., Cheung, K. R. J., & Nilsen, E. S. (2014). Intonation influences how children and adults interpret sarcasm. *Journal of Child Language, 41*, 472–484. http://dx.doi.org/10.1017/S0305000912000773

Glick, J. E., & Bates, L. (2010). Diversity in academic achievement: Children of immigrants in U.S. schools. In E. L. Grigorenko & R. Takanishi (Eds.), *Immigration, diversity, and education* (pp. 112–129). New York, NY: Routledge.

Gligorović, M. M., & Ðurović, N. (2014). Inhibitory control and adaptive behaviour in children with mild intellectual disability. *Journal of Intellectual Disability Research, 58*, 233–242. doi:10.1111/jir.12000

Glucksberg, S., & Krauss, R. M. (1967). What do people say after they have learned to talk? Studies of the development of referential communication. *Merrill-Palmer Quarterly, 13*, 309–316.

Glynn, S. M., Yeany, R. H., & Britton, B. K. (1991a). A constructive view of learning science. In S. M. Glynn, R. H. Yeany, & B. K. Britton (Eds.), *The psychology of learning science* (pp. 3–19). Mahwah, NJ: Erlbaum.

Glynn, S. M., Yeany, R. H., & Britton, B. K. (Eds.) (1991b). *The psychology of learning science.* Hillsdale, NJ: Erlbaum.

Gnambs, T., & Hanfstingl, B. (2016). The decline of academic motivation during adolescence: An accelerated longitudinal cohort analysis on the effect of psychological need satisfaction. *Educational Psychology, 36*, 1691–1705.

Gnanasekaran, S., Choueiri, R., Neumeyer, A., Ajari, O., Shui, A., & Kuhlthau, K. (2016). Impact of employee benefits on families with children with autism spectrum disorders. *Autism, 20*(5), 616-622. doi:10.1177/1362361315598891

Gnepp, J. (1989). Children's use of personal information to understand other people's feelings. In C. Saarni & P. L. Harris (Eds.), *Children's understanding of emotion* (pp. 151-180). Cambridge, England: Cambridge University Press.

Goddings, A.-L., & Giedd, J. N. (2014). Structural brain development during childhood and adolescence. In M. S. Gazzaniga & G. R. Mangun (Eds.), *The cognitive neurosciences* (pp. 15–22). Cambridge, MA: MIT Press.

Goddings, A., Burnett Heyes, S., Bird, G., Viner, R. M., & Blakemore, S. (2012). The relationship between puberty and social emotion processing. *Developmental Science, 15*, 801–811. doi:10.1111/j.1467-7687.2012.01174.x

Goeke-Morey, M. C., Papp, L. M., & Cummings, E. (2013). Changes in marital conflict and youths' responses across childhood and adolescence: A test of sensitization. *Development and Psychopathology, 25*, 241–251. doi:10.1017/S0954579412000995

Goertz-Dorten, A., Benesch, C., Berk-Pawlitzek, E., Faber, M., Hautmann, C., Hellmich, M., . . . Doepfner, M. (2018). Efficacy of individualized social competence training for children with oppositional defiant disorders/conduct disorders: A randomized controlled trial with an active control group. *European Child & Adolescent Psychiatry*. Advance online publication. http://dx.doi.org.unco.idm.oclc.org/10.1007/s00787-018-1144-x

Goff, K., & Torrance, E. (2002). *Abbreviated Torrance Test for Adults Manual*. Bensenville, IL: Scholastic Testing Service.

Goffin, K. C., Boldt, L. J., & Kochanska, G. (2017). A secure base from which to cooperate: Security, child and parent willing stance, and adaptive and maladaptive outcomes in two longitudinal studies. *Journal of Abnormal Child Psychology*. Advance online publication.

Gogate, L. J., & Hollich, G. (2010). Invariance detection within an interactive system: A perceptual gateway to language development. *Psychological Review, 117*(2), 496–516. doi:10.1037/a0019049

Goh, S., Dong, Z., Zhang, Y., DiMauro, S., & Peterson, B. S. (2014). Mitochondrial dysfunction as a neurobiological subtype of autism spectrum disorder: Evidence from brain imaging. *JAMA Psychiatry, 71*, 665–671. doi:10.1001/jamapsychiatry.2014.179

Goharpey, N., Crewther, D. P., & Crewther, S. G. (2013). Problem solving ability in children with intellectual disability as measured by the Raven's Colored Progressive Matrices. *Research in Developmental Disabilities, 34*, 4366–4374. doi:10.1016/j.ridd.2013.09.013

Golay, P., & Lecerf, T. (2011). Orthogonal higher order structure and confirmatory factor analysis of the French Wechsler Adult Intelligence Scale (WAIS-III). *Psychological Assessment, 23*(1), 143–152. doi:10.1037/a0021230

Goldberg, A. E. (2007). (How) does it make a difference? Perspectives of adults with lesbian, gay, and bisexual parents. *American Journal of Orthopsychiatry, 77*(4), 550–562. doi:10.1037/0002-9432.77.4.550

Golden, A. R., Griffin, C. B., Metzger, I. W., & Cooper, S. M. (2018). School racial climate and academic outcomes in African American adolescents: The protective role of peers. *Journal of Black Psychology, 44*(1), 47–73. http://dx.doi.org.unco.idm.oclc.org/10.1177/0095798417736685

Goldenberg, C. (1992). The limits of expectations: A case for case knowledge about teacher expectancy effects. *American Educational Research Journal, 29*, 517–544.

Goldenberg, C. (2008). Teaching English language learners: What the research does—and does not—say. *American Educator*, 2(2), 8–23, 42–44.

Goldin-Meadow, S, (2005). What language creation in the manual modality tells us about the foundations of language. *Linguistic Review, 22*, 199–225.

Goldin-Meadow, S. (1997). When gestures and words speak differently. *Current Directions in Psychological Science, 6*, 138–143.

Goldin-Meadow, S. (2006). Talking and thinking with our hands. *Current Directions in Psychological Science, 15*, 34–39.

Goldin-Meadow, S. (2017). What the hands can tell us about language emergence. *Psychonomic Bulletin & Review, 24*(1), 213–218. http://dx.doi.org.unco.idm.oclc.org/10.3758/s13423-016-1074-x

Goldin-Meadow, S., Shield, A., Lenzen, D., Herzig, M., & Padden, C. (2012). The gestures ASL signers use tell us when they are ready to learn math. *Cognition, 123*, 448–453. doi:10.1016/j.cognition.2012.02.006

Goldstein, S., & Brooks, R. B. (Eds.) (2006). *Handbook of resilience in children*. New York, NY: Springer.

Goleman, D. (1995). *Emotional intelligence*. New York, NY: Bantam Books.

Goleniowska, H. (2014). The importance of developing confidence and self-esteem in children with a learning disability. *Advances in Mental Health & Intellectual Disabilities, 8*, 188–191. doi:10.1108/AMHID-09-2013-0059

Golinkoff, R. M., & Hirsh-Pasek, K. (2006). Baby wordsmith: From associationistic to social sophisticate. *Current Directions in Psychological Science, 15*, 30–33.

Golinkoff, R. M., & Hirsh-Pasek, K. (2008). How toddlers begin to learn verbs. *Trends in Cognitive Sciences, 12*, 397–403.

Golinkoff, R. M., Hirsh-Pasek, K., Bailey, L., & Wenger, N. (1992). Young children and adults use lexical principles to learn new nouns. *Developmental Psychology, 28*, 99–108.

Golomb, C. (2004). *The child's creation of a pictorial world* (2nd ed.). Mahwah, NJ: Erlbaum.

Golombok, S., Mellish, L., Jennings, S., Casey, P., Tasker, F., & Lamb, M. E. (2014). Adoptive gay father families: Parent–child relationships and children's psychological adjustment. *Child Development, 85*, 456–468. doi:10.1111/cdev.12155

Gomby, D. S., Culross, P. L., & Behrman, R. E. (1999). Home visiting: Recent program evaluations—Analysis and recommendations. *The Future of Children. Home Visiting: Recent Program Evaluations, 9*(1), 4–26.

Gómez, L. E., Vasilyeva, M., & Dulaney, A. (2017). Preschool teachers' read-aloud practices in Chile as predictors of children's vocabulary. *Journal of Applied Developmental Psychology, 52*, 149–158.

Göncü, A. (1993). Development of intersubjectivity in the dyadic play of preschoolers. *Early Childhood Research Quarterly, 8*, 99–116.

Göncü, A., & Gauvain, M. (2012). Sociocultural approaches to educational psychology: Theory, research, and application. In K. R. Harris, S. Graham, T. Urdan, C. B. McCormick, G. M. Sinatra, & J. Sweller (Eds.), *APA Educational Psychology Handbook, Vol. 1. Theories, constructs, and critical issues* (pp. 125–154). Washington, DC: American Psychological Association. doi:10.1037/13273-006

Gonzales-Backen, M. A. (2013). An application of ecological theory to ethnic identity formation among biethnic adolescents. *Family Relations, 62*(1), 92–108. doi:10.1111/j.1741-3729.2012.00749.x

Gonzalez-Mena, J. (2002). *The child in the family and the community* (3rd ed.). Upper Saddle River, NJ: Merrill/Prentice Hall.

Gonzalez-Mena, J. (2010). Compassionate roots begin with babies. *Exchange, 32*(3), 46–49.

Gonzalez-Mena, J. (2012). On the way to friendship: Growing peer relationships among infants and toddlers. *Exchange, 205*, 48–50.

Gonzalez, L. (2011). Class placement and academic and behavioral variables as predictors of graduation for students with disabilities. *Dissertation Abstracts International Section A, 71*.

González, N., Moll, L. C., & Amanti, C. (2005). Introduction: Theorizing practices. In N. González, L. C. Moll, & C. Amanti (Eds.), *Funds of knowledge: Theorizing practices in households, communities, and classrooms* (pp. 1–24). Mahwah, NJ: Erlbaum.

Good, T. L., & Nichols, S. L. (2001). Expectancy effects in the classroom: A special focus on improving the reading performance of minority students in first-grade classrooms. *Educational Psychologist, 36*, 113–126.

Good, T. L., McCaslin, M. M., & Reys, B. J. (1992). Investigating work groups to promote problem solving in mathematics. In J. Brophy (Ed.), *Advances in Research on Teaching: Vol. 3. Planning and managing learning tasks and activities (pp. 115-160)*. Greenwich, CT: JAI Press.

Gooding, J., & Metz, B. (2011). From misconceptions to conceptual change. *Science Teacher, 78*(4), 34–37.

Goodwin, B., & Miller, K. (2013). Creativity requires a mix of skills. *Educational Leadership, 70*(5), 80–83.

Goodwin, M. H. (2006). *The hidden life of girls: Games of stance, status, and exclusion*. Malden, MA: Blackwell.

Goodwyn, S. W., & Acredolo, L. P. (1998). Encouraging symbolic gestures: A new perspective on the relationship between gesture and speech. In J. M. Iverson & S. Goldin-Meadow (Eds.), *Nature and functions of gesture in children's communication* (pp. 61–73). San Francisco, CA: Jossey-Bass.

Gopnik, A. (2009a, August 1). Babies rule! *New Scientist, 203*(2719), 44–45.

Gopnik, A. (2009b). Rational constructivism: A new way to bridge rationalism and empiricism. *Behavioral and Brain Sciences, 32*, 208–209.

Gopnik, A. (2009c, August 16). Your baby is smarter than you think. *New York Times*.

Gopnik, A., & Meltzoff, A. N. (1997). *Words, thoughts, and theories*. Cambridge, MA: MIT Press.

Gopnik, A., & Wellman, H. M. (2012). Reconstructing constructivism: Causal models, Bayesian learning mechanisms, and the theory theory. *Psychological Bulletin, 138*, 1085–1108. doi:10.1037/a0028044

Gordon, R. A., Crosnoe, R., & Wang, X. (2013). Physical attractiveness and the accumulation of social and human capital in adolescence and young adulthood: Assets and distractions. *Monographs of the Society for Research in Child Development, 78*(6), 1–137.

Gorodetsky, E., Bevilacqua, L., Carli, V., Sarchiapone, M., Roy, A., Goldman, D., & Enoch, M. A. (2014). The interactive effect of MAOA-LPR genotype and childhood physical neglect on aggressive behaviors in Italian male prisoners. *Genes, Brain & Behavior, 13*, 543–549. doi:10.1111/gbb.12140

Gorrese, A., & Ruggieri, R. (2012). Peer attachment: A meta-analytic review of gender and age differences and associations with parent attachment. *Journal of Youth and Adolescence, 41*, 650–672. doi:10.1007/s10964-012-9759-6

Goswami, U. (1999). The relationship between phonological awareness and orthographic representation in different orthographies. In M. Harris & G. Hatano (Eds.), *Learning to read and write: A cross-linguistic perspective* (pp. 134–156). Cambridge, England: Cambridge University Press.

Goswami, U. (2011). *Inductive and deductive reasoning*. In U. Goswami (Ed.), *The Wiley-Blackwell handbook of childhood cognitive development* (2nd ed., pp. 399–419). Malden, MA: Wiley-Blackwell.

Gottfredson, L. (2003). Dissecting practical intelligence theory: Its claims and evidence. *Intelligence, 31*, 343–397.

Gottfried, A. E., Fleming, J. S., & Gottfried, A. W. (1994). Role of parental motivational practices in children's academic intrinsic motivation and achievement. *Journal of Educational Psychology, 86*, 104–113.

Gottfried, A. E., Fleming, J. S., & Gottfried, A. W. (2001). Continuity of academic intrinsic motivation from childhood through late adolescence: A longitudinal study. *Journal of Educational Psychology, 93*(1), 3–13.

Gottfried, A. W., Gottfried, A. E., & Guerin, D. W. (2009). Issues in early prediction and identification of intellectual giftedness. In F. D. Horowitz, R. F. Subotnik, & D. J. Matthews (Eds.), *The development of giftedness and talent across the life span* (pp. 43–56). Washington, DC: American Psychological Association.

Gottfried, A. W., Gottfried, A. E., Bathurst, K., & Guerin, D. W. (1994). *Gifted IQ: Early developmental aspects*. New York, NY: Plenum Press.

Gottlieb, G., Wahlsten, D., & Lickliter, R. (2006). The significance of biology for human development: A developmental psychobiological systems view. In W. Damon & R. M. Lerner (Eds. in Chief) & R. M. Lerner (Vol. Ed.), *Handbook of Child Psychology: Vol. 1. Theoretical models of human development* (6th ed., pp. 210–257). Hoboken, NJ: Wiley.

Gottman, J. M. (1983). How children become friends. *Monographs of the Society for Research in Child Development, 48*(3, Serial No. 201).

Gottman, J. M. (1986). The world of coordinated play: Same- and cross-sex friendship in young children. In J. M. Gottman & J. G. Parker (Eds.), *Conversations of friends: Speculations on affective development* (pp. 139–191). Cambridge, England: Cambridge University Press.

Gottman, J. M., & Mettetal, G. (1986). Speculations about social and affective development: Friendship and acquaintanceship through adolescence. In J. M. Gottman & J. G. Parker (Eds.), *Conversations of friends: Speculations on affective development* (pp. 192–237). Cambridge, England: Cambridge University Press.

Gottwald, J. M., De Bortoli Vizioli, A., Lindskog, M., Nyström, P., L. Ekberg, T., von Hofsten, C., & Gredebäck, G. (2017). Infants prospectively control reaching based on the difficulty of future actions: To what extent can infants' multiple-step actions be explained by Fitts' law? *Developmental Psychology, 53*(1), 4–12. doi:10.1037/dev0000212

Gover, A. R., Jennings, W. G., & Tewksbury, R. (2009). Adolescent male and female gang members' experiences with violent victimization, dating violence, and sexual assault. *American Journal of Criminal Justice, 34*, 103–115. doi:10.1007/s12103-008-9053-z

Govrin, A. (2018). The attachment approach to moral judgment. In K. Gray & J. Graham (Eds.), *Atlas of moral psychology* (pp. 440–450). New York, NY: Guilford Press.

Gowen, L., & Winges-Yanez, N. (2014). Lesbian, gay, bisexual, transgender, queer, and questioning youths' perspectives of inclusive school-based sexuality education. *Journal of Sex Research, 51*, 788–800. doi:10.1080/00224499.2013.806648

Gower, A. L., Lingras, K. A., Mathieson, L. C., Kawabata, Y., & Crick, N. R. (2014). The role of preschool relational and physical aggression in the transition to kindergarten: Links with social-psychological adjustment. *Early Education and Development, 25*, 619–640. doi:10.1080/10409289.2014.844058

Graber, J. A., Britto, P. R., & Brooks-Gunn, J. (1999). What's love got to do with it? Adolescents' and young adults' beliefs about sexual and romantic relationships. In W. Furman, B. B. Brown, & C. Feiring (Eds.), *The development of romantic relationships in adolescence* (pp. 364–395). Cambridge, England: Cambridge University Press.

Graber, R., Turner, R., & Madill, A. (2016). Best friends and better coping: Facilitating psychological resilience through boys' and girls' closest friendships. *British Journal of Psychology, 107*, 338–358. http://dx.doi.org.unco.idm.oclc.org/10.1111/bjop.12135

Grady, J. S., Karraker, K., & Metzger, A. (2012). Shyness trajectories in slow-to-warm-up infants: Relations with child sex and maternal parenting. *Journal of Applied Developmental Psychology, 33*, 91–101. http://dx.doi.org.unco.idm.oclc.org/10.1016/j.appdev.2011.11.002

Graesch, A. P. (2009). Material indicators of family busyness. *Social Indicators Research, 93*, 85–94.

Graesser, A., Golding, J. M., & Long, D. L. (1991). Narrative representation and comprehension. In R. Barr, M. L. Kamil, P. B. Mosenthal, P. Pearson(Eds.), *Handbook of reading research* (Vol. 2, pp. 171–205). Hillsdale, NJ: Lawrence Erlbaum.

Graff, G. (2014). The intergenerational trauma of slavery and its aftermath. *The Journal of Psychohistory, 41*(3), 181–197.

Graham, S. (1989). Motivation in Afro-Americans. In G. L. Berry & J. K. Asamen (Eds.), *Black students: Psychosocial issues and academic achievement (pp. 10–16)*. Newbury Park, CA: Sage.

Graham, S. (1997). Using attribution theory to understand social and academic motivation in African American youth. *Educational Psychologist, 32*, 21–34.

Graham, S. (2006). Writing. In P. A. Alexander & P. H. Winne (Eds.), *Handbook of educational psychology* (2nd ed., pp. 457–478). Mahwah, NJ: Erlbaum.

Graham, S. (2009). Giftedness in adolescence: African American gifted youth and their challenges from a motivational perspective. In F. D. Horowitz, R. F. Subotnik, & D. J. Matthews (Eds.), *The development of giftedness and talent across the life span* (pp. 109–129). Washington, DC: American Psychological Association.

Graham, S. (2014). The use of multiple forms of assessment in the service of writing. *Literacy Research & Instruction, 53*, 96–100. doi:10.1080/19388071.2014.868249

Graham, S. (2016). Commentary: The role of race/ethnicity in a developmental science of equity and justice. *Child Development, 87*, 1493–1504. doi:10.1111/cdev.12602

Graham, S. (2018). Race/ethnicity and social adjustment of adolescents: How (not if) school diversity matters. *Educational Psychologist, 53*(2), 64–77. http://dx.doi.org.unco.idm.oclc.org/10.1080/00461520.2018.1428805

Graham, S. A., San Juan, V., & Khu, M. (2017). Words are not enough: How preschoolers' integration of perspective and emotion informs their referential understanding. *Journal of Child Language, 44*, 500–526. doi:10.1017/S0305000916000519

Graham, S., & Perin, D. (2007). A meta-analysis of writing instruction for adolescent students. *Journal of Educational Psychology, 99*, 445–476.

Graham, S., & Weintraub, N. (1996). A review of handwriting research: Progress and prospects from 1980 to 1994. *Educational Psychology Review, 8*, 7–87.

Graham, S., & Williams, C. (2009). An attributional approach to motivation in school. In K. R. Wentzel & A. Wigfield (Eds.), *Handbook of motivation at school* (pp. 11–33). New York, NY: Routledge.

Graham, S., Harris, K. R., & Fink, B. (2000). Is handwriting causally related to learning to write? Treatment of handwriting problems in beginning writers. *Journal of Educational Psychology, 92*, 620–633.

Graham, S., Harris, K. R., & Olinghouse, N. (2007). Addressing executive function problems in writing: An example from the self-regulated strategy development model. In L. Meltzer (Ed.), *Executive function in education: From theory to practice* (pp. 216–236). New York, NY: Guilford Press.

Graham, S., Schwartz, S. S., & MacArthur, C. A. (1993). Knowledge of writing and the composing process, attitude toward writing, and self-efficacy for students with and without learning disabilities. *Journal of Learning Disabilities, 26*, 237–249.

Gralinski, J. H., & Kopp, C. B. (1993). Everyday rules for behavior: Mothers' requests to young children. *Developmental Psychology, 29*, 573–584. doi:10.1037/0012-1649.29.3.573

Grammer, J. K., Purtell, K. M., Coffman, J. L., & Ornstein, P. A. (2011). Relations between children's metamemory and strategic performance: Time-varying covariates in early elementary school. *Journal of Experimental Child Psychology, 108*(1), 139–155. doi:10.1016/j.jecp.2010.08.001

Grammer, J., Coffman, J., & Ornstein, P. (2013). The effect of teachers' memory-relevant language on children's strategy use and knowledge. *Child Development, 84*, 1989–2002. doi:10.1111/cdev.12100

Grand, R. (2016). A collective case study of expectant father fears. *Dissertation Abstracts International Section A: Humanities and Social Sciences*, 77(3-A(E)).

Grandin, T. (1995). *Thinking in pictures and other reports of my life with autism.* New York, NY: Random House.

Granger, R. C. (2008). After-school programs and academics: Implications for policy, practice, and research. *Social Policy Report, 22*(2).

Granic, I., Lobel, A., & Engels, R. E. (2014). The benefits of playing video games. *American Psychologist, 69*(1), 66–78. doi:10.1037/a0034857

Granqvist, P., Sroufe, L. A., Dozier, M., Hesse, E., Steele, M., van IJzendoorn, M., . . . Duschinsky, R. (2017). Disorganized attachment in infancy: A review of the phenomenon and its implications for clinicians and policy-makers. *Attachment & Human Development, 19*, 534–558. http://dx.doi.org.unco.idm.oclc.org/10.1080/14616734.2017.1354040

Grant, C. A., & Gomez, M. L. (2001). *Campus and classroom: Making schooling multicultural* (2nd ed.). Upper Saddle River, NJ: Merrill/Prentice Hall.

Grant, H., & Dweck, C. (2001). Cross-cultural response to failure: Considering outcome attributions with different goals. In F. Salili & C. Chiu (Eds.), *Student motivation: The culture and context of learning* (pp. 203–219). Dordrecht, the Netherlands: Kluwer Academic.

Grant, R., Gracy, D., Goldsmith, G., Shapiro, A., & Redlener, I. E. (2013). Twenty-five years of child and family homelessness: Where are we now? *American Journal of Public Health, 103*(S2), e1–e10. doi:10.2105/AJPH.2013.301618

Graue, M. E., & Walsh, D. J. (1998). *Studying children in context.* Thousand Oaks, CA: Sage.

Graves, S. L., Jr., & Nichols, K. (2016). Intellectual assessment of ethnic minority children. In S. L. Graves & J. J. Blake (Eds.), *Applying psychology in the schools book series. Psychoeducational assessment and intervention for ethnic minority children: Evidence-based approaches* (pp. 61–76). Washington, DC: American Psychological Association. http://dx.doi.org/10.1037/14855-005

Graziano, P. A., Garb, L. R., Ros, R., Hart, K., & Garcia, A. (2016). Executive functioning and school readiness among preschoolers with externalizing problems: The moderating role of the student–teacher relationship. *Early Education & Development, 27*, 573–589. doi:10.1080/10409289.2016.1102019

Gredler, M. E., & Shields, C. C. (2008). *Vygotsky's legacy: A foundation for research and practice.* New York, NY: Guilford Press.

Green, C. (2012). Listening to children: Exploring intuitive strategies and interactive methods in a study of children's special places. *International Journal of Early Childhood, 44*, 269–285. doi:10.1007/s13158-012-0075-9

Green, C., Kalvaitis, D., & Worster, A. (2016). Recontextualizing psychosocial development in young children: A model of environmental identity development. *Environmental Education Research, 22*, 1025–1048. http://dx.doi.org.unco.idm.oclc.org/10.1080/13504622.2015.1072136

Green, L., Fry, A. F., & Myerson, J. (1994). Discounting of delayed rewards: A life-span comparison. *Psychological Science, 5*, 33–36.

Green, Y. R., & Gray, M. (2013). Lessons learned from the Kinship Education and Support Program (KEPS): Developing effective support groups for formal kinship caregivers. *Social Work with Groups: A Journal of Community and Clinical Practice, 36*(1), 27–42. doi:10.1080/01609513.2012.698384

Greenberg, J. (2014). Significance of after-school programming for immigrant children during middle childhood: Opportunities for school social work. *Social Work, 59*(3), 243–251.

Greenberg, M. T. (1999). Attachment and psychopathology in childhood. In J. Cassidy & P. R. Shaver (Eds.), *Handbook of attachment: Theory, research, and clinical applications* (pp. 469–496). New York, NY: Guilford Press.

Greenberg, M. T., Weissberg, R. P., O'Brien, M. U., Zins, J. E., Fredericks, L., Resnik, H., & Elias, M. J. (2003). Enhancing school-based prevention and youth development through coordinated social, emotional, and academic learning. *American Psychologist, 58*, 466–474.

Greene, K. (2014). History Maker. *Instructor, 123*(4), 10–11.

Greenfield, P. M. (1998). The cultural evolution of IQ. In U. Neisser (Ed.), *The rising curve: Long-term gains in IQ and related measures* (pp. 81–123). Washington, DC: American Psychological Association.

Greenfield, P. M., & Quiroz, B. (2013). Context and culture in the socialization and development of personal achievement values: Comparing Latino immigrant families, European American families, and elementary school teachers. *Journal of Applied Developmental Psychology, 34*(2), 108–118. doi:10.1016/j.appdev.2012.11.002

Greenfield, P. M., DeWinstanley, P., Kilpatrick, H., & Kaye, D. (1996). Action video games and informal education: Effects on strategies for dividing visual attention. In P. M. Greenfield & R. R. Cocking (Eds.), *Advances in Applied Developmental Psychology: Vol. 11. Interacting with video* (pp. 187–205). Westport, CT: Ablex.

Greeno, J. G. (2007). Toward the development of intellective character. In E. W. Gordon & B. L. Bridglall (Eds.), *Affirmative development: Cultivating academic ability* (pp. 17–47). Lanham, MD: Rowman.

Greeno, J. G., Collins, A. M., & Resnick, L. B. (1996). Cognition and learning. In D. C. Berliner & R. C. Calfee (Eds.), *Handbook of educational psychology* (pp. 15–46). New York, NY: Macmillan.

Greenough, W. T., Black, J. E., & Wallace, C. S. (1987). Experience and brain development. *Child Development, 58*, 539–559.

Greenspan, D. A., Solomon, B., & Gardner, H. (2004). The development of talent in different domains. In L. V. Shavinina & M. Ferrari (Eds.), *Beyond knowledge: Extracognitive aspects of developing high ability* (pp. 119–135). Mahwah, NJ: Erlbaum.

Greenspan, S., & Granfield, J. M. (1992). Reconsidering the construct of mental retardation: Implications of a model of social competence. *American Journal of Mental Retardation, 96*, 442–453.

Greenwald, A. G., McGhee, D. E., & Schwartz, J. L. K. (1998). Measuring individual differences in implicit cognition: The implicit association test. *Journal of Personality and Social Psychology, 74*, 1464–1480. doi:10.1037/0022-3514.74.6.1464

Gregg, M., & Leinhardt, G. (1994a, April). *Constructing geography.* Paper presented at the annual meeting of the American Educational Research Association, New Orleans, LA.

Gregory, A., Cornell, D., Fan, X., Sheras, P., Shih, T., & Huang, F. (2010). Authoritative school discipline: High school practices associated with lower bullying and victimization. *Journal of Educational Psychology, 102*, 483–496. doi:10.1037/a0018562

Gremmen, M. C., Dijkstra, J. K., Steglich, C., & Veenstra, R. (2017). First selection, then influence: Developmental differences in friendship dynamics regarding academic achievement. *Developmental Psychology, 53*, 1356–1370. http://dx.doi.org.unco.idm.oclc.org/10.1037/dev0000314

Grenard, J. L., Dent, C. W., & Stacy, A. W. (2013). Exposure to alcohol advertisements and teenage alcohol-related problems. *Pediatrics, 131*, e369–e379. http://dx.doi.org/10.1542/peds.2012-1480

Griedler, M. E., & Shields, C. C. (2008). *Vygotsky's legacy: A foundation for research and practice.* New York, NY: Guilford Press.

Griffin, K., del Pilar, W., McIntosh, K., & Griffin, A. (2012). "Oh, of course I'm going to go to college": Understanding how habitus shapes the college choice process of black immigrant students. *Journal of Diversity in Higher Education, 5*, 96–111. doi:10.1037/a0028393

Griffin, S. (2009). Learning sequences in the acquisition of mathematical knowledge: Using cognitive developmental theory to inform curriculum design for pre-K–6 mathematics education. *Mind, Brain, and Education, 3*, 96–107.

Griffin, S. A., Case, R., & Siegler, R. S. (1994). Rightstart: Providing the central conceptual prerequisites for first formal learning of arithmetic to students at risk for school failure. In K. McGilly (Ed.), *Classroom lessons: Integrating cognitive theory and classroom practice* (pp. 25–49) . Cambridge, MA: MIT Press.

Griffin, S., & Case, R. (1997). Re-thinking the primary school math curriculum: An approach based on cognitive science. *Issues in Education, 3*(1), 1.

Griffin, S., & Green, R. (2012). Transforming high poverty, underperforming schools: Practices, processes, and procedures. *National Forum of Applied Educational Research Journal, 26*(1/2), 77–93.

Griffith, S., & Grolnick, W. (2014). Parenting in Caribbean families: A look at parental control, structure, and autonomy support. *Journal of Black Psychology, 40*, 166–190.

Griffiths, M. (2010). Online video gaming: What should educational psychologists know? *Educational Psychology in Practice, 26*(1), 35–40. doi:10.1080/02667360903522769

Griffiths, Y., & Stuart, M. (2013). Reviewing evidence-based practice for pupils with dyslexia and literacy difficulties. *Journal of Research in Reading, 36*(1), 96–116. doi:10.1111/j.1467-9817.2011.01495.x

Grigg-Damberger, M. M. (2017). Ontogeny of sleep and its functions in infancy, childhood, and adolescence. In S. Nevšímalová & O. Bruni (Eds.), *Sleep disorders in children* (pp. 3–29). doi:10.1007/978-3-319-28640-2_1

Gripshover, S. J., & Markman, E. M. (2013). Teaching young children a theory of nutrition: Conceptual change and the potential for increased vegetable consumption. *Psychological Science, 24*(8), 1541–1553.

Groh, A. M., Fearon, R., Bakermans-Kranenburg, M. J., van IJzendoorn, M. H., Steele, R. D., & Roisman, G. I. (2014). The significance of attachment security for children's social competence with peers: A meta-analytic study. *Attachment & Human Development, 16*, 103–136. doi:10.1080/14616734.2014.883636

Grolnick, W. S., & Pomerantz, E. M. (2009). Issues and challenges in studying parental control: Toward a new conceptualization. *Child Development Perspectives*, 3(3), 165–170.

Gromko, J. E., & Poorman, A. S. (1998). Developmental trends and relationships in children's aural perception and symbol use. *Journal of Research in Music Education, 46*, 16–23.

Gronlund, N. E., & Brookhart, S. M. (2009). *Gronlund's writing instructional objectives for teaching and assessment* (8th ed.). Upper Saddle River, NJ: Pearson Education.

Gross, R. H. (2004). Sports medicine in youth athletes. *Southern Medical Journal, 97*, 880.

Gross, T. (2010). Service learning builds bonds to school for young learners. *Phi Delta Kappan, 91*(5), 24–26.

Grossman, H. L. (1994). *Classroom behavior management in a diverse society.* Mountain View, CA: Mayfield.

Grossmann, K. E., Grossmann, K., Huber, F., & Wartner, U. (1981). German children's behavior toward their mothers at 12 months and their fathers at 18 months in Ainsworth's Strange Situation. *International Journal of Behavioral Development, 4*, 157–181.

Gruenenfelder-Steiger, A. E., Harris, M. A., & Fend, H. A. (2016). Subjective and objective peer approval evaluations and self-esteem development: A test of reciprocal, prospective, and long-term effects. *Developmental Psychology, 52*, 1563–1577.

Grumm, M., & Hein, S. (2013). Correlates of teachers' ways of handling bullying. *School Psychology International, 34*, 299–312.

Grünke, M., Wilbert, J., Tsiriotakis, I. K., & Agirregoikoa, A. L. (2017). Improving the length and quality of texts written by fourth graders with learning disabilities through a peer-tutoring graphic organizing strategy. *Insights on Learning Disabilities, 14*, 167–188.

Grusec, J. (2006). The development of moral behavior and conscience from a socialization perspective. In M. Killen & J. G. Smetana (Eds.), *Handbook of moral development* (pp. 243–265). Mahwah, NJ: Erlbaum.

Grusec, J. E., & Davidov, M. (2007). Socialization in the family: The roles of parents. In J. E. Grusec & P. D. Hastings (Eds.), *Handbook of socialization: Theory and research* (pp. 284–308). New York, NY: Guilford Press.

Grusec, J. E., & Redler, E. (1980). Attribution, reinforcement, and altruism. *Developmental Psychology, 16*, 525–534.

Guardino, C. M., & Dunkel Schetter, C. (2014). Coping during pregnancy: A systematic review and recommendations. *Health Psychology Review, 8*(1), 70–94. doi:10.1080/17437199.2012.752659

Guardino, C., & Cannon, J. E. (2016). Deafness and diversity: Reflections and directions. *American Annals of the Deaf, 161*(1), 104–112.

Guay, F., Boivin, M., & Hodges, E. V. E. (1999). Social comparison processes and academic achievement: The dependence of the development of self-evaluations on friends' performance. *Journal of Educational Psychology, 91*, 564–568.

Guilford, J. P. (1967). *The nature of human intelligence.* New York, NY: McGraw-Hill.

Guimarães, M. (2013). Does prosodic bootstrapping play any role in the acquisition of auxiliary fronting in English? *Syntax, 16*(2), 148–175. doi:10.1111/synt.12002

Gummerum, M., Keller, M., Takezawa, M., & Mata, J. (2008). To give or not to give: Children's and adolescents' sharing and moral negotiations in economic decision situations. *Child Development, 79*, 562–576.

Gunderson, E. A., Gripshover, S. J., Romero, C., Dweck, C. S., Goldin-Meadow, S., & Levine, S. C. (2013). Parent praise to 1- to 3-year-olds predicts children's motivational frameworks 5 years later. *Child Development, 84*, 1526–1541.

Gunderson, E. W., Kirkpatrick, M. G., Willing, L. M., & Holstege, C. P. (2013). Intranasal substituted cathinone "bath salts" psychosis potentially exacerbated by diphenhydramine. *Journal of Addiction Medicine, 7*, 163–168. doi:10.1097/ADM.0b013e31829084d5

Gunzburger, D. W. (1977). Moral judgment and distributive justice. *Human Development, 20*, 160–170.

Gupta, K. K., Gupta, V. K., & Shirasaka, T. (2016). An update on fetal alcohol syndrome—Pathogenesis, risks, and treatment. *Alcoholism: Clinical and Experimental Research, 40*, 1594–1602. doi:10.1111/acer.13135

Gurholt, K. P., & Sanderud, J. R. (2016). Curious play: Children's exploration of nature. *Journal of Adventure Education and Outdoor Learning, 16*, 318–329. doi:10.1080/14729679.2016.1162183

Gust, L. V. (2012). Can policy reduce the collateral damage caused by the criminal justice system? Strengthening social capital in families and communities. *American Journal of Orthopsychiatry, 82*(2), 174–180. doi:10.1111/j.1939-0025.2012.01156.x

Guszkowska, M. (2014). The effect of exercise and childbirth classes on fear of childbirth and locus of labor pain control. *Anxiety, Stress & Coping: An International Journal, 27*, 176–189. doi:10.1080/10615806.2013.830107

Gutiérrez, K. D., & Rogoff, B. (2003). Cultural ways of learning: Individual traits or repertoires of practice. *Educational Researcher, 32*(5), 19–25.

Guttman, N. (2013). "My son is reliable": Young drivers' parents' optimism and views on the norms of parental involvement in youth driving. *Journal of Adolescent Research, 28*, 241–268. doi:10.1177/0743558411435853

Guyer, A. E., & Jarcho, J. M. (2018). Neuroscience and peer relations. In W. M. Bukowski, B. Laursen, & K. H. Rubin (Eds.), *Handbook of peer interactions, relationships, and groups* (pp. 177–199). New York, NY: Guilford Press.

Guyll, M., Madon, S., Prieto, L., & Scherr, K. C. (2010). The potential roles of self-fulfilling prophecies, stigma consciousness, and stereotype threat in linking Latino ethnicity and educational outcomes. *Journal of Social Issues, 66*, 113–130.

Gygi, J. T., Hagmann-von Arx, P., Schweizer, F., & Grob, A. (2017). The predictive validity of four intelligence tests for school grades: A small sample longitudinal study. *Frontiers in Psychology, 8*, Article ID 375.

Ha, T., Dishion, T. J., Overbeek, G., Burk, W. J., & Engels, R. E. (2014). The blues of adolescent romance: Observed affective interactions in adolescent romantic relationships associated with depressive symptoms. *Journal of Abnormal Child Psychology, 42*, 551–562. doi:10.1007/s10802-013-9808-y

Haan, A. D., Deković, M., den Akker, A. L., Stoltz, S. J., & Prinzie, P. (2013). Developmental personality types from childhood to adolescence: Associations with parenting and adjustment. *Child Development, 84*, 2015–2030. doi:10.1111/cdev.12092

Haberlin, S. (2017). Using arts-based research to explore peak experiences in five gifted Children. *International Journal of Education & the Arts, 18*(23–25), 1–22.

Hack, M., Schluchter, M., Forrest, C. B., Taylor, H., Drotar, D., Holmbeck, G., . . . Andreias, L. (2012). Self-reported adolescent health status of extremely low birth weight children born 1992–1995. *Pediatrics, 130*(1), 46–53. doi:10.1542/peds.2011-3402

Hadjiachilleos, S., Valanides, N., & Angeli, C. (2013). The impact of cognitive and affective aspects of cognitive conflict on learners' conceptual change about floating and sinking. *Research in Science & Technological Education, 31*, 133–152. doi:10.1080/02635143.2013.811074

Hafford, C. (2010). Sibling caretaking in immigrant families: Understanding cultural practices to inform child welfare practice and evaluation. *Evaluation and Program Planning, 33*, 294–302. doi:10.1016/j.evalprogplan.2009.05.003

Hagay, G., & Baram-Tsabari, A. (2015). A strategy for incorporating students' interests into the high-school science classroom. *Journal of Research in Science Teaching, 52*, 949–978. doi:10.1002/tea.21228

Hagen, J. W., & Stanovich, K. G. (1977). Memory: Strategies of acquisition. In R. V. Kail, Jr., & J. W. Hagen (Eds.), *Perspectives on the development of memory and cognition* (pp. 89–111). Hillsdale, NJ: Erlbaum.

Hager, E. R., Rubio, D. S., Eidel, G. S., Penniston, E. S., Lopes, M., Saksvig, B. I., . . . Black, M. M. (2016). Implementation of local wellness policies in schools: Role of school systems, school health councils, and health disparities. *Journal of School Health, 86*, 742–750. doi:10.1111/josh.12430

Hagerman, R. J., & Lampe, M. E. (1999). Fragile X syndrome. In S. Goldstein & C. R. Reynolds (Eds.), *Handbook of neurodevelopmental and genetic disorders* (pp. 298–316). New York, NY: Guilford Press.

Hagger, M. S., Chatzisarantis, N. L. D., Barkoukis, V., Wang, C. K. J., & Baranowski, J. (2005). Perceived autonomy support in physical education and leisure-time physical activity: A cross-cultural evaluation of the trans-contextual model. *Journal of Educational Psychology, 97*, 376–390.

Haidt, J. (2008). Morality. *Perspectives on Psychological Science, 3*, 65–72.

Haith, M. M., Hazan, C., & Goodman, G. S. (1988). Expectation and anticipation of dynamic visual events by 3.5-month-old babies. *Child Development, 59*, 467–479.

Håkstad, R. B., Obstfelder, A., & Øberg, G. K. (2017). Let's play! An observational study of primary care physical therapy with preterm infants aged 3–14 months. *Infant Behavior & Development, 46*, 115–123. doi:10.1016/j.infbeh.2017.01.001

Hale-Benson, J. E. (1986). *Black children: Their roots, culture, and learning styles*. Baltimore, MD: Johns Hopkins University Press.

Hale, D. R., Fitzgerald-Yau, N., & Mark Viner, R. (2014). A systematic review of effective interventions for reducing multiple health risk behaviors in adolescence. *American Journal of Public Health, 104*(5), e19–e41. doi:10.2105/AJPH.2014.301874

Halford, G. S., & Andrews, G. (2006). Reasoning and problem solving. In W. Damon & R. M. Lerner (Series Eds.), & D. Kuhn & R. Siegler (Vol. Eds.), *Handbook of Child Psychology: Vol. 2. Cognition, perception, and language* (6th ed., pp. 557–608). New York, NY: Wiley.

Halim, M., Ruble, D. N., Tamis-LeMonda, C. S., Zosuls, K. M., Lurye, L. E., & Greulich, F. K. (2014). Pink frilly dresses and the avoidance of all things "girly": Children's appearance rigidity and cognitive theories of gender development. *Developmental Psychology, 50*, 1091–1101. doi:10.1037/a0034906

Halim, M., Ruble, D., & Tamis-Lemonda, C. (2013). Four-year-olds' beliefs about how others regard males and females. *British Journal of Developmental Psychology, 31*(1), 128–135. doi:10.1111/j.2044-835X.2012.02084.x

Hall, E. C., Kronborg, H., Aagaard, H., & Brinchmann, B. (2013). The journey towards motherhood after a very preterm birth: Mothers' experiences in hospital and after home-coming. *Journal of Neonatal Nursing, 19*, 109–113. doi:10.1016/j.jnn.2012.08.002

Hall, T. E., Meyer, A., & Rose, D. H. (2012). *Universal design for learning in the classroom: Practical applications*. New York, NY: Guilford.

Hall, W. A., Hauck, Y. L., Carty, E. M., Hutton, E. K., Fenwick, J., & Stoll, K. (2009). Childbirth fear, anxiety, fatigue, and sleep deprivation in pregnant women. *Journal of Obstetric, Gynecologic, and Neonatal Nursing, 38*, 567–576.

Hallenbeck, M. J. (1996). The cognitive strategy in writing: Welcome relief for adolescents with learning disabilities. *Learning Disabilities Research and Practice, 11*, 107–119.

Halliday, L. I., Tuomainen, O., & Rosen, S. (2017). Auditory processing deficits are sometimes necessary and sometimes sufficient for language difficulties in children: Evidence from mild to moderate sensorineural hearing loss. *Cognition, 166*, 139–151. doi:10.1016/j.cognition.2017.04.014

Halliday, M. A. K. (1975). *Learning how to mean: Explorations in the development of language*. London, UK: Edward Arnold.

Halpern, D. F. (1992). *Sex differences in cognitive abilities* (2nd ed.). Hillsdale, NJ: Erlbaum.

Halpern, D. F. (1998). Teaching critical thinking for transfer across domains. *American Psychologist, 53*, 449–455.

Halpern, D. F. (2004). A cognitive-process taxonomy for sex differences in cognitive abilities. *Current Directions in Psychological Science, 13*, 135–139.

Halpern, D. F. (2006). Assessing gender gaps in learning and academic achievement. In P. A. Alexander & P. H. Winne (Eds.), *Handbook of educational psychology* (2nd ed., pp. 635–653). Mahwah, NJ: Erlbaum.

Halpern, D. F., & LaMay, M. L. (2000). The smarter sex: A critical review of sex differences in intelligence. *Educational Psychology Review, 12*, 229–246.

Halpern, D. F., & LaMay, M. L. (2000). The smarter sex: A critical review of sex differences in intelligence. *Educational Psychology Review, 12*, 229–246.

Halpern, D. F., Bendow, C. P., Geary, D. C., Gur, R. C., Hyde, J. S., & Gernsbacher, M. A. (2007). The science of sex differences in science and mathematics. *Psychological Science in the Public Interest, 8*(1), 1–51.

Hamadani, J. D., Tofail, F., Huda, S. N., Alam, D. S., Ridout, D. A., Attanasio, O., & Grantham-McGregor, S. M. (2014). Cognitive deficit and poverty in the first 5 years of childhood in Bangladesh. *Pediatrics, 134*, e1001–e1008. http://dx.doi.org/10.1542/peds.2014-0694

Hamill, P. V., Drizd, T. A., Johnson, C. L., Reed, R. B., Roche, A. F., & Moore, W. M. (1979). Physical growth: National Center for Health Statistics percentiles. *American Journal of Clinical Nutrition, 32*, 607–629.

Hamilton, B. E., Martin, J. A, & Ventura, S. J. (2011). *Births: Preliminary data for 2010* (National Vital Statistics Reports, Vol. 60, No. 2). Retrieved from http://www.cdc.gov/nchs/data/nvsr/nvsr60/nvsr60_02.pdf

Hamilton, J. L., Stange, J. P., Kleiman, E. M., Hamlat, E. J., Abramson, L. Y., & Alloy, L. B. (2014). Cognitive vulnerabilities amplify the effect of early pubertal timing on interpersonal stress generation during adolescence. *Journal of*

Youth and Adolescence, 43, 824–833. doi:10.1007/s10964-013-0015

Hamlen, K. R. (2011). Children's choices and strategies in video games. *Computers in Human Behavior, 27*(1), 532–539. doi:10.1016/j.chb.2010.10.001

Hammond, L. (2001). Notes from California: An anthropological approach to urban science education for language minority families. *Journal of Research in Science Teaching, 38*, 983–999.

Hammond, S. I., Al-Jbouri, E., Edwards, V., & Feltham, L. E. (2017). Infant helping in the first year of life: Parents' recollection of infants' earliest prosocial behaviors. *Infant Behavior & Development, 47*, 54–57. http://dx.doi.org.unco.idm.oclc.org/10.1016/j.infbeh.2017.02.004

Hamre, B. K., & Pianta, R. C. (2005). Can instructional and emotional support in the first-grade classroom make a difference for children at risk for school failure? *Child Development, 76*, 949–967.

Hamre, B., Hatfield, B., Pianta, R., & Jamil, F. (2014). Evidence for general and Domain-specific elements of teacher-child interactions: Associations with preschool children's development. *Child Development, 85*, 1257–1274. doi:10.1111/cdev.12184

Hankin, B. L., Oppenheimer, C., Jenness, J., Barrocas, A., Shapero, B. G., & Goldband, J. (2009). Developmental origins of cognitive vulnerabilities to depression: Review of processes contributing to stability and change across time. *Journal of Clinical Psychology, 65*, 1327–1338.

Hanley, P., Bennett, J., & Ratcliffe, M. (2014). The inter-relationship of science and religion: A typology of engagement. *International Journal of Science Education, 36*, 1210–1229. doi:10.1080/09500693.2013.853897

Hanlon, T. E., Simon, B. D., O'Grady, K. E., Carswell, S. B., & Callaman, J. M. (2009). The effectiveness of an after-school program targeting urban African American youth. *Education and Urban Society, 42*(1), 96–118. doi:10.1177/0013124509343144

Hannon, E. E., Schachner, A., & Nave-Blodgett, J. E. (2017). Babies know bad dancing when they see it: Older but not younger infants discriminate between synchronous and asynchronous audiovisual musical displays. *Journal of Experimental Child Psychology, 159*, 159–174. doi:10.1016/j.jecp.2017.01.006

Hansen, D. M., & Jessop, N. (2017). A context for self-determination and agency: Adolescent developmental theories. In M. L. Wehmeyer, K. A. Shogren, T. D. Little, & S. J. Lopez (Eds.), *Development of self-determination through the life-course* (pp. 27–46). New York, NY, US: Springer Science + Business Media. http://dx.doi.org.unco.idm.oclc.org/10.1007/978-94-024-1042-6_3

Hansen, J., & Kissel, B. (2009). Writing instruction for adolescent learners. In K. D. Wood & W. E. Blanton (Eds.), *Literacy instruction for adolescents: Research-based practice* (pp. 392–419). New York, NY: Guilford Press.

Happé, F., & Frith, U. (2013). Annual research review: Towards a developmental neuroscience of atypical social cognition. *Journal of Child Psychology and Psychiatry*, 55(6), 553–577.

Happé, F., & Frith, U. (2014). Annual research review: Towards a developmental neuroscience of atypical social cognition. *Journal of Child Psychology and Psychiatry, 55*, 553–577. doi:10.1111/jcpp.12162

Harach, L., & Kuczynski, L. (2005). Construction and maintenance of parent–child relationships: Bidirectional contributions from the perspectives of parents. *Infant and Child Development, 14*, 327–343.

Harackiewicz, J. M., Barron, K. E., Pintrich, P. R., Elliot, A. J., & Thrash, T. M. (2002). Revision of achievement goal theory: Necessary and illuminating. *Journal of Educational Psychology*, 94, 638–645. http://dx.doi.org.unco.idm.oclc.org/10.1037/0022-0663.94.3.638

Harden, S. M., Beauchamp, M. R., Pitts, B. H., Nault, E. M., Davy, B. M., Wen, Y., . . . Estabrooks, P. A. (2014). Group-based lifestyle sessions for gestational weight gain management: A mixed method approach. *American Journal of Health Behavior, 38*, 560–569. doi:10.5993/AJHB.38.4.9

Hardy, I., Jonen, A., Möller, K., & Stern, E. (2006). Effects of instructional support within constructivist learning environments for elementary school students' understanding of "floating and sinking." *Journal of Educational Psychology, 98*, 307–326.

Hardy, S. A., Walker, L. J., Olsen, J. A., Woodbury, R. D., & Hickman, J. R. (2014). Moral identity as moral ideal self: Links to adolescent outcomes. *Developmental Psychology, 50*(1), 45–57. doi:10.1037/a0033598

Hareli, S., & Weiner, B. (2002). Social emotions and personality inferences: A scaffold for a new direction in the study of achievement motivation. *Educational Psychologist, 37*, 183–193.

Hargreaves, E. (2012). Teachers' classroom feedback: still trying to get it right. *Pedagogies, 7*(1), 1–15. doi:10.1080/1554480X.2012.630454

Härkönen, J. (2014). Birth order effects on educational attainment and educational transitions in West Germany. *European Sociological Review, 30*(2), 166–179.

Harlow, H. F., & Zimmerman, R. R. (1959). Affectional responses in the infant monkey. *Science, 130*, 421–432.

Harradine, C. C., Coleman, M. B., & Winn, D. C. (2014). Recognizing academic potential in students of color: Findings of U-STARS~PLUS. *Gifted Child Quarterly, 58*(1), 24–34. doi:10.1177/0016986213506040

Harris, B., & Sullivan, A. L. (2017). A framework for bilingual school consultation to facilitate multitier systems of support for English language learners. *Journal of Educational & Psychological Consultation, 27*, 367–392. doi:10.1080/10474412.2017.1307758

Harris, C. (2011). Oculomotor developmental pathology: An "evo-devo" perspective. In S. P. Liversedge, I. D. Gilchrist, & S. Everling (Eds.), *The Oxford handbook of eye movements* (pp. 663–686). New York, NY: Oxford University Press.

Harris, K. R., & Graham, S. (1992). Self-regulated strategy development: A part of the writing process. In M. Pressley, K. R. Harris, & J. T. Guthrie (Eds.), *Promoting academic competence and literacy in school* (pp. 277–309). San Diego, CA: Academic Press.

Harris, M. (1992). *Language experience and early language development: From input to uptake*. Hove, England: Erlbaum.

Harris, M. B. (1997). Preface: Images of the invisible minority. In M. B. Harris (Ed.), *School experiences of gay and lesbian youth: The invisible minority* (pp. xiv–xxii). Binghamton, NY: Harrington Park Press.

Harris, M. J., & Rosenthal, R. (1985). Mediation of interpersonal expectancy effects: 31 meta-analyses. *Psychological Bulletin, 97*, 363–386.

Harris, M., & Giannouli, V. (1999). Learning to read and spell in Greek: The importance of letter knowledge and morphological awareness. In M. Harris & G. Hatano (Eds.). *Learning to read and write: A cross-linguistic perspective* (pp. 51–70). Cambridge, England: Cambridge University Press.

Harris, P. L. (1989). *Children and emotion: The development of psychological understanding*. Oxford, England: Basil Blackwell.

Harris, P. L. (2006). Social cognition. In W. Damon & R. M. Lerner (Series Eds.), & D. Kuhn & R. Siegler (Vol. Eds.), *Handbook of Child Psychology: Vol. 2. Cognition, perception, and language* (6th ed., pp. 811–858). New York, NY: Wiley.

Harris, P. L., Bartz, D. T., & Rowe, M. L. (2017). Young children communicate their ignorance and ask questions. PNAS Proceedings of the National Academy of Sciences of the United States of America, 114, 7884–7891. http://dx.doi.org/10.1073/pnas.1620745114

Harris, Y. R., & Graham, J. A. (2007). *The African American child: Development and challenges*. New York, NY: Springer.

Harrison, A. O., Wilson, M. N., Pine, C. J., Chan, S. Q., & Buriel, R. (1990). Family ecologies of ethnic minority children. *Child Development, 61*, 347–362.

Hart, B., & Risley, T. R. (1995). *Meaningful differences in the everyday experiences of young American children*. Baltimore, MD: Paul H. Brookes.

Hart, B., & Risley, T. R. (1999). *The social world of children learning to talk*. Baltimore, MD: Paul H. Brookes.

Hart, D. (1988). The adolescent self-concept in social context. In D. K. Lapsley & F. C. Power (Eds.), *Self, ego, and identity: Integrative approaches* (pp. 71–90). New York, NY: Springer-Verlag.

Hart, D., & Fegley, S. (1995). Prosocial behavior and caring in adolescence: Relations to self-understanding and social judgment. *Child Development, 66*, 1346–1359.

Hart, D., Atkins, R., & Donnelly, T. M. (2006). Community service and moral development. In M. Killen & J. G. Smetana (Eds.), *Handbook of moral development* (pp. 633–656). Mahwah, NJ: Erlbaum.

Hart, J. E., Mourot, J. E., & Aros, M. (2012). Children of same-sex parents: In and out of the closet. *Educational Studies, 38*(3), 277–281. doi:10.1080/03055698.2011.598677

Hart, S. (2011). *The impact of attachment.* New York, NY: Norton.

Hart, S. A., Soden, B., Johnson, W., Schatschneider, C., & Taylor, J. (2013). Expanding the environment: gene × school-level SES interaction on reading comprehension. *Journal of Child Psychology & Psychiatry, 54*, 1047–1055. doi:10.1111/jcpp.12083

Harter, S. (1992). The relationship between perceived competence, affect, and motivational orientation within the classroom: Processes and patterns of change. In A. K. Boggiano & T. S. Pittman (Eds.), *Achievement and motivation: A social-developmental perspective (pp. 77–115).* Cambridge, England: Cambridge University Press.

Harter, S. (1996). Teacher and classmate influences on scholastic motivation, self-esteem, and level of voice in adolescents. In J. Juvonen & K. Wentzel (Eds.), *Social motivation: Understanding children's school adjustment* (pp. 11–42). New York, NY: Cambridge University Press.

Harter, S. (1999). *The construction of the self.* New York, NY: Guilford Press.

Harter, S. (2006). The self. In W. Damon & R. M. Lerner (Eds. in Chief) & N. Eisenberg (Vol. Ed.), *Handbook of Child Psychology, Vol. 3. Social, emotional, and personality development* (6th ed., pp. 505–570). Hoboken, NJ: Wiley.

Harter, S. (2012). *The construction of the self: developmental and sociocultural foundations.* New York, NY: Guilford Press.

Harter, S., & Whitesell, N. R. (1989). Developmental changes in children's understanding of single, multiple, and blended emotion concepts. In C. Saarni & P. Harris (Eds.), *Children's understanding of emotion* (pp. 81–116). Cambridge, England: Cambridge University Press.

Harter, S., Stocker, C., & Robinson, N. S. (1996). The perceived directionality of the link between approval and self-worth: The liabilities of a looking glass self-orientation among young adolescents. *Journal of Research on Adolescence, 6*, 285–308.

Harter, S., Whitesell, N. R., & Junkin, L. J. (1998). Similarities and differences in domain-specific and global self-evaluations of learning-disabled, behaviorally disordered, and normally achieving adolescents. *American Educational Research Journal, 35*, 653–680.

Hartman, S. C., Warash, B. G., Curtis, R., & Day Hirst, J. (2016). Level of structural quality and process quality in rural preschool classrooms. *Early Child Development & Care, 186*, 1952–1960. doi:10.1080/03004430.2015.1137563

Hartmann, A. S., Greenberg, J. L., & Wilhelm, S. (2013). The relationship between anorexia nervosa and body dysmorphic disorder. *Clinical Psychology Review, 33*, 675–685. doi:10.1016/j.cpr.2013.04.002

Hartmann, T., Krakowiak, K., & Tsay-Vogel, M. (2014). How violent video games communicate violence: A literature review and content analysis of moral disengagement factors. *Communication Monographs, 81*, 310–332. doi:10.1080/03637751.2014.922206

Hartup, W. W. (1983). Peer relations. In P. H. Mussen (Ed.), *Handbook of Child Psychology: Vol. IV. Socialization* (4th ed., pp. 91–152). New York, NY: Wiley.

Hartup, W. W. (1984). The peer context in middle childhood. In A. Collins (Ed.), *Development during middle childhood: The years from six to twelve.* Washington, DC: National Academy Press.

Hartup, W. W. (2009). Critical issues and theoretical viewpoints. In K. H. Rubin, W. M. Bukowski, & B. Laursen (Eds.) *Handbook of peer interactions, relationships, and groups* (pp. 3–19). New York, NY: Guilford Press.

Hartup, W. W., & Laursen, B. (1991). Relationships as developmental contexts. In R. Cohen & W. A. Siegel (Eds.), *Context and development* (pp. 253–279). Hillsdale, NJ: Erlbaum.

Harvey, S. (2011). Physical play with boys of all ages. In C. Haen (Ed.), *Engaging boys in treatment: Creative approaches to the therapy process* (pp. 91–113). New York, NY: Routledge/Taylor & Francis Group.

Haskill, A. M., & Corts, D. P. (2010). Acquiring language. In E. H. Sandberg & B. L. Spritz (Eds.), *A clinician's guide to normal cognitive development in childhood* (pp. 23–41). New York, NY: Routledge/Taylor & Francis.

Hastings, P. D., Miller, J. G., Kahle, S., & Zahn-Waxler, C. (2014). The neurobiological bases of empathic concern for others. In M. Killen & J. G. Smetana (Eds.), *Handbook of moral development* (pp. 411–434). New York, NY: Psychology Press.

Hatano, G., & Inagaki, K. (1996). Cognitive and cultural factors in the acquisition of intuitive biology. In D. R. Olson & N. Torrance (Eds.), *The handbook of education and human development: New models of learning, teaching, and schooling (pp.* 683–708). Cambridge, MA: Blackwell.

Hatfield, B. E., & Williford, A. P. (2017). Cortisol patterns for young children displaying disruptive behavior: Links to a techer-child, relationship-focused intervention. *Prevention Science, 18*(1), 40–49. doi:10.1007/s11121-016-0693-9

Hatfield, B. E., Burchinal, M. R., Pianta, R. C., & Sideris, J. (2016). Thresholds in the association between quality of teacher–child interactions and preschool children's school readiness skills. *Early Childhood Research Quarterly, 36*, 561–571. doi:10.1016/j.ecresq.2015.09.005

Hatfield, E., Cacioppo, J. T., & Rapson, R. L. (1994). *Emotional contagion.* Cambridge, England: Cambridge University Press.

Hatton, C. (1998). Pragmatic language skills in people with intellectual disabilities: A review. *Journal of Intellectual and Developmental Disability, 23*, 79–100. doi:10.1080/13668259800033601

Haviland, J. M., & Lelwica, M. (1987). The induced affect response: 10-week-old infants' responses to three emotional expressions. *Developmental Psychology, 23*, 97–104.

Havinga, P. J., Boschloo, L., Hartman, C. A., & Schoevers, R. A. (2018). Paternal and maternal depression and offspring risk: Additive effects or worse? *The Lancet Psychiatry, 5*, 107–108. http://dx.doi.org.unco.idm.oclc.org/10.1016/S2215-0366(18)30013-0

Hawes, D. J., Price, M. J., & Dadds, M. R. (2014). Callous-unemotional traits and the treatment of conduct problems in childhood and adolescence: A comprehensive review. *Clinical Child and Family Psychology Review, 17*, 248–267. http://dx.doi.org.unco.idm.oclc.org/10.1007/s10567-014-0167-1

Hawkins, B. L., Ryan, J. B., Cory, A., & Donaldson, M. C. (2014). Effects of equine-assisted therapy on gross motor skills of two children with autism spectrum disorder. *Therapeutic Recreation Journal, 48*, 135–149.

Hawkins, F. P. L. (1997). *Journey with children: The autobiography of a teacher.* Niwot: University Press of Colorado.

Hawthorne, N. (1892). *The scarlet letter: A romance.* Philadelphia, PA: H. Altemus Co.

Hay, D. F. (2017). The early development of human aggression. *Child Development Perspectives, 11*, 102–106. http://dx.doi.org.unco.idm.oclc.org/10.1111/cdep.12220

Hay, D. F., Caplan, M., & Nash, A. (2018). The beginnings of peer relations. In W. M. Bukowski, B. Laursen, & K. H. Rubin (Eds.), *Handbook of peer interactions, relationships, and groups* (pp. 200-221). New York, NY, US: Guilford Press.

Hay, D. F., Nash, A., Caplan, M., Swartzentruber, J. Ishikawa, F., & Vespo, J. (2011). The emergence of gender differences in physical aggression in the context of conflict between young peers. *British Journal of Developmental Psychology, 29*, 158–175. doi:10.1111/j.2044-835X.2011.02028.x

Hayashi, A., Karasawa, M., & Tobin, J. (2009). The Japanese preschool's pedagogy of feeling: Cultural strategies for supporting young children's emotional development. *Journal of the Society for Psychological Anthropology, 37*(1), 32–49.

Hayes, B., & Rehder, B. (2012). The development of causal categorization. *Cognitive Science, 36*, 1102–1128. doi:10.1111/j.1551-6709.2012.01244.x

Hayes, D. P., & Grether, J. (1983). The school year and vacations: When do students learn? *Cornell Journal of Social Relations, 17*(1), 56–71.

Hayes, J., & Stewart, I. (2016). Comparing the effects of derived relational training and computer coding on intellectual potential in school-age children. *British Journal of Educational Psychology, 86*, 397–411. doi:10.1111/bjep.12114

Hayne, H., & Simcock, G. (2009). Memory development in toddlers. In M. L. Courage & N. Cowan (Eds.), *The development of memory in infancy and childhood* (pp. 43–68). New York, NY: Psychology Press.

Haynes, J., & Zacarian, D. (2010). *Teaching English language learners across the content areas.* Alexandria, VA: ASCD.

Hayward, D. V., Annable, C. D., Fung, J. E., Williamson, R. D., Lovell-Johnston, M. A., & Phillips, L. M. (2017). Beyond the total score: A preliminary investigation into the types of phonological awareness errors made by first graders. *Early Childhood Education Journal, 45*, 809-820.

Haywood-Bird, E. (2017). Playing with power: An outdoor classroom exploration. Early *Child Development and Care, 187*(5–6), 1015–1027. doi:10.1080/03004430.2016.1223070

Haywood, H. C., & Lidz, C. S. (2007). *Dynamic assessment in practice: Clinical and educational applications*. Cambridge, England: Cambridge University Press.

Hazlett, H. C., Gaspar De Alba, M., & Hooper, S. R. (2011). Klinefelter syndrome. In S. Goldstein & C. R. Reynolds (Eds.), *Handbook of neurodevelopmental and genetic disorders in children* (2nd ed., pp. 382–397). New York, NY: Guilford Press.

Headden, S. (2013). The promise of personalized learning. *Education Next, 13*(4), 14–20.

Healy, K. L., Sanders, M. R., & Iyer, A. (2014). Facilitative parenting and children's social, emotional and behavioral adjustment. *Journal of Child and Family Studies*. doi:10.1007/s10826-014-9980-x

Healy, K. L., Sanders, M. R., & Iyer, A. (2015). Facilitative parenting and children's social, emotional and behavioral adjustment. *Journal of Child and Family Studies, 24*(6), 1762–1779. http://dx.doi.org.unco.idm.oclc.org/10.1007/s10826-014-9980-x

Heath, S. B. (1980). Questioning at home and at school: A comparative study. In G. Spindler (Ed.), *The ethnography of schooling: Educational anthropology in action* (pp. 20–47). New York, NY: Holt, Rinehart & Winston.

Heath, S. B. (1983). *Ways with words: Language, life, and work in communities and classrooms.* Cambridge, England: Cambridge University Press.

Heath, S. B. (1989). Oral and literate traditions among Black Americans living in poverty. *American Psychologist, 44*, 367–373.

Heatherton, T. F. (2011). Neuroscience of self and self-regulation. *Annual Review of Psychology, 62*, 363–390.

Hébert, T., & Pagnani, A. (2010). Engaging gifted boys in new literacies. *Gifted Child Today, 33*(3), 36–45.

Heck, A., Hock, A., White, H., Jubran, R., & Bhatt, R. S. (2016). The development of attention to dynamic facial emotions. *Journal of Experimental Child Psychology, 147*, 100–110.

Heckenhausen, H. (1984). Emergent achievement behavior: Some early developments. In J. Nicholls (Ed.), *Advances in achievement motivation (pp. 1–32)*. Greenwich, CT: JAI Press.

Heckman, J. J. (2011). Effective child development strategies. In E. Zigler, W. S. Gilliam, & W. S. Barnett (Eds.), *The pre-K debates: Current controversies and issues* (pp. 2–8). Baltimore, MD: Paul H. Brookes Publishing.

Hedegaard, M., & Fleer, M. (2013). *Play, learning, and children's development: Everyday life in families and transition to school*. New York, NY: Cambridge University Press.

Hedges, H. (2015). Sophia's funds of knowledge: Theoretical and pedagogical insights, possibilities and dilemmas. *International Journal of Early Years Education, 23*(1), 83–96. doi:10.1080/09669760.2014.976609

Hedges, K., & Korchmaros, J. D. (2016). Pubertal timing and substance abuse treatment outcomes: An analysis of early menarche on substance use patterns. *Journal of Child & Adolescent Substance Abuse, 25*, 598–605. doi:10.1080/1067828X.2016.1171186

Hedges, L. V., & Nowell, A. (1995). Sex differences in mental test scores, variability, and numbers of high-scoring individuals. *Science, 269*, 41–45.

Hedin, L. (2014). A sense of belonging in a changeable everyday life: A follow-up study of young people in kinship, network, and traditional foster families. *Child & Family Social Work*, 19(2), 165–173.

Heerboth, M. K., & Mason, K. (2012). Educational materials can induce stereotype threat in elementary school students: Evidence for impaired math performance following exposure to a token. *Psychology Journal, 9*, 120–128.

Heeren, A., & McNally, R. J. (2018). Social anxiety disorder as a densely interconnected network of fear and avoidance for social situations. *Cognitive Therapy and Research, 42*, 103–113. http://dx.doi.org.unco.idm.oclc.org/10.1007/s10608-017-9876-3

Hegarty, M., & Kozhevnikov, M. (1999). Types of visual-spatial representations and mathematical problem solving. *Journal of Educational Psychology, 91*, 684–689.

Hegde, A. V., Sugita, C., Crane-Mitchell, L., & Averett, P. (2014). Japanese nursery and kindergarten teachers' beliefs and practices regarding developmentally appropriate practices. *International Journal of Early Years Education, 22*, 301–314. doi:10.1080/09669760.2014.948390

Heilbronner, N. N. (2013). The STEM pathway for women: What has changed? *Gifted Child Quarterly, 57*(1), 39–55. doi:10.1177/0016986212460085

Heilig, J. (2011). Understanding the interaction between high-stakes graduation tests and English learners. *Teachers College Record, 113*(12), 2633–2669.

Heineman, K. R., Middelburg, K. J., & Hadders-Algra, M. (2010). Development of adaptive motor behaviour in typically developing infants. *Acta Paediatrica, 99*, 618–624.

Heiphetz, L., Strohminger, N., Gelman, S. A., & Young, L. L. (2018). Who am I? The role of m oral beliefs in children's and adults' understanding of identity. *Journal of Experimental Social Psychology*. Advance online publication. http://dx.doi.org.unco.idm.oclc.org/10.1016/j.jesp.2018.03.007

Helibronner, N. (2013). Creating and delivering differentiated science content through wikis. *Science Scope, 36*(5), 24–34.

Hellenga, K. (2002). Social space, the final frontier: Adolescents on the Internet. In J. T. Mortimer & R. W. Larson (Eds.), *The changing adolescent experience: Societal trends and the transition to adulthood* (pp. 208–249). Cambridge, England: Cambridge University Press.

Helth, T., & Jarden, M. (2013). Fathers' experiences with the skin-to-skin method in NICU: Competent parenthood and redefined gender roles. *Journal of Neonatal Nursing, 19*, 114–121. doi:10.1016/j.jnn.2012.06.001

Helwig, C. C., & Jasiobedzka, U. (2001). The relation between law and morality: Children's reasoning about socially beneficial and unjust laws. *Child Development, 72*, 1382–1393.

Helwig, C. C., Zelazo, P. D., & Wilson, M. (2001). Children's judgments of psychological harm in normal and noncanonical situations. *Child Development, 72*, 66–81.

Hemmer, I., Hemmer, M., Kruschel, K., Neidhardt, E., Obermaier, G., & Uphues, R. (2013). Which children can find a way through a strange town using a streetmap? Results of an empirical study on children's orientation competence. *International Research in Geographical Environmental Education, 22*(1), 23–40. doi:10.1080/10382046.2012.759436

Hemphill, L., & Snow, C. (1996). Language and literacy development: Discontinuities and differences. In D. R. Olson & N. Torrance (Eds.), *The handbook of education and human development: New models of learning, teaching, and schooling* (pp. 173–201). Cambridge, MA: Blackwell.

Hemphill, S. A., & Schneider, S. (2013). Excluding students from school: A re-examination from a children's rights perspective. *International Journal of Children's Rights, 21*(1), 88–96. doi:10.1163/15718182-55680008

Henderson, D., & Zipin, L. (2010). Bringing clay to life: Developing student literacy through clay animation artwork to tell life-based stories. In B. Prosser, B. Lucas, & A. Reid (Eds.), *Connecting lives and learning: Renewing pedagogy in the middle years* (pp. 20–39). Adelaide, Australia: Wakefield Press.

Henderson, J. (2009). Paying for performance: Giving students cash incentives for learning. *Education Update, 51*(3), 1, 6–7.

Henderson, N. D. (1982). Human behavior genetics. *Annual Review of Psychology, 33*, 403–440.

Hendry, A., Jones, E. J.H., & Charman, T. (2016). Executive function in the first three years of life: Precursors, predictors and patterns. *Developmental Review, 42*, 1–33.

Henkemans, O. A. B., Bierman, B. P. B., Janssen, J., Looije, R., Neerincx, M. A., van Dooren, M. M. M., . . . JanHuisman, S. D. (2017). Design and evaluation of a personal robot playing a self-management education game with children with diabetes type 1. *International Journal of Human-Computer Studies, 106*, 63–76. http://dx.doi.org.unco.idm.oclc.org/10.1016/j.ijhcs.2017.06.001

Hennessey, B. A. (1995). Social, environmental, and developmental issues and creativity. *Educational Psychology Review, 7*, 163–183.

Henriksen, R. C., Jr., & Paladino, D. A. (2009). Identity development in a multiple heritage world. In R. C. Henriksen & D. A. Paladino (Eds.), *Counseling multiple heritage individuals, couples, and families* (pp. 25–43). Alexandria, VA: American Counseling Association.

Henry, L. A., & Norman, T. (1996). The relationships between memory performance, use of simple memory strategies and metamemory in young children. *International Journal of Behavioral Development, 19*(1), 177–200. doi:10.1080/016502596386018

Hensley, L. (2013). To cheat or not to cheat: A review with implications for practice. *Community College Enterprise, 19*(2), 22–34

Hepper, P. (2015). Behavior during the prenatal period: Adaptive for development and survival. *Child Development Perspectives, 9*(1), 38–43. doi:10.1111/cdep.12104

Hernández Blasi, C., & Bjorklund, D. F. (2003). Evolutionary developmental psychology: A new tool for better understanding human ontogeny. *Human Development, 46*, 259–281. doi:10.1159/000071935

Hernandez, D. J. (2010). Internationally comparable indicators for children of immigrants. *Child Indicators Research, 3*, 409–411.

Hernandez, D. J., Denton, N. A., & Macartney, S. E. (2010). Children of immigrants and the future of America. In E. L. Grigorenko & R. Takanishi (Eds.), *Immigration, diversity, and education* (pp. 7–25). New York, NY: Routledge.

Herrell, A., & Jordan, M. (2004). *Fifty strategies for teaching English language learners* (2nd ed.). Upper Saddle River, NJ: Merrill/Prentice Hall.

Hersh, C. A., Stone, B. J., & Ford, L. (1996). Learning disabilities and learned helplessness: A heuristic approach. *International Journal of Neuroscience, 84*, 103–113.

Hess, R. D., & Azuma, M. (1991). Cultural support for learning: Contrasts between Japan and the United States. *Educational Researcher, 29*(9), 2–8.

Hess, R. D., & Holloway, S. D. (1984). Family and school as educational institutions. In R. D. Parke, R. N. Emde, H. P. McAdoo, & G. P. Sackett (Eds.), *Review of Child Development Research: Vol. 7. The family* (pp. 179–222). Chicago, IL: University of Chicago Press.

Hessels-Schlatter, C., Hessels, M. G. P., Godin, H., & Spillmann-Rojas, H. (2017). Fostering self-regulated learning: From clinical to whole class interventions. *Educational and Child Psychology, 34*, 110–125.

Hetherington, E. M., & Clingempeel, W. G. (1992). Coping with marital transitions: A family systems perspective. *Monographs of the Society for Research in Child Development, 57*(2–3, Serial No. 227).

Hetherington, E. M., Bridges, M., & Insabella, G. M. (1998). What matters? What does not? Five perspectives on the association between marital transitions and children's adjustment. *American Psychologist, 53*, 167–184.

Hetherington, E. M., Cox, M., & Cox, R. (1978). The aftermath of divorce. In J. H. Stevens, Jr., & M. Matthews (Eds.), *Mother–child, father–child relations* (pp. 110–155). Washington, DC: National Association for the Education of Young Children.

Hettinger, H. R., & Knapp, N. F. (2001). Potential, performance, and paradox: A case study of J.P., a verbally gifted, struggling reader. *Journal for the Education of the Gifted, 24*, 248–289.

Heyder, A., Kessels, U., & Steinmayr, R. (2017). Explaining academic-track boys' underachievement in language grades: Not a lack of aptitude but students' motivational beliefs and parents' perceptions? *British Journal of Educational Psychology, 87*, 205–223. doi:10.1111/bjep.12145

Hickendorff, M., van Putten, C. M., Verhelst, N. D., & Heiser, W. J. (2010). Individual differences in strategy use on division problems: Mental versus written computation. *Journal of Educational Psychology, 102*, 438–452. doi:10.1037/a0018177

Hickey, D. T. (1997). Motivation and contemporary socio-constructivist instructional perspectives. *Educational Psychologist, 32*, 175–193.

Hickey, D. T., & Granade, J. B. (2004). The influence of sociocultural theory on our theories of engagement and motivation. In D. M. McNerney & S. Van Etten (Eds.), *Big theories revisited* (pp. 223–247). Greenwich, CT: Information Age.

Hidi, S., & Renninger, K. A. (2006). The four-phase model of interest development. *Educational Psychologist, 41*, 111–127.

Hidi, S., Renninger, K. A., & Krapp, A. (2004). Interest, a motivational variable that combines affecting and cognitive functioning. In D. Y. Dai & R. J. Sternberg (Eds.), *Motivation, emotion, and cognition: Integrative perspectives on intellectual functioning and development* (pp. 89–115). Mahwah, NJ: Erlbaum.

Hiebert, E. H., & Raphael, T. E. (1996). Psychological perspectives on literacy and extensions to educational practice. In D. C. Berliner & R. C. Calfee (Eds.), *Handbook of educational psychology* (pp. 550–602). New York, NY: Macmillan.

Higgins, A. (1995). Educating for justice and community: Lawrence Kohlberg's vision of moral education. In W. M. Kurtines & J. L. Gewirtz (Eds.), *Moral development: An introduction* (pp. 49–81). Boston, MA: Allyn & Bacon.

Higgins, E., & Scholer, A. A. (2015). Goal pursuit functions: Working together. In M. Mikulincer, P. R. Shaver, E. Borgida, J. A. Bargh (Eds.), *APA Handbook of Personality and Social Psychology, Volume 1. Attitudes and social cognition* (pp. 843–889). Washington, DC: American Psychological Association. doi:10.1037/14341-02

Hill, D. (2013). Three mentor texts that support code-switching pedagogies. *Voices from the Middle, 20*(4), 10–15.

Hill, J. (2015). How useful is Dynamic Assessment as an approach to service delivery within educational psychology? *Educational Psychology in Practice, 31*, 127–136. doi:10.1080/02667363.2014.994737

Hill, P. L., & Lapsley, D. K. (2011). Adaptive and maladaptive narcissism in adolescent development. In C. T. Barry, P. K. Kerig, K. K. Stellwagen, & T. D. Barry (Eds.), *Narcissism and Machiavellianism in youth: Implications for the development of adaptive and maladaptive behavior* (pp. 89–105). Washington, DC: American Psychological Association.

Hilt, L. M., & Nolen-Hoeksema, S. (2009). The emergence of gender differences in depression in adolescence. In S. Nolen-Hoeksema, & L. M. Hilt (Eds.), *Handbook of depression in adolescents* (pp. 111–135). New York, NY: Routledge.

Hilt, L. M., Cha, C. B., & Nolen-Hoeksema, S. (2008). Nonsuicidal self-injury in young adolescent girls: Moderators of the distress-function relationship. *Journal of Consulting and Clinical Psychology, 76*, 63–71.

Hinduja, S., & Patchin, J. W. (2011, February). High-tech cruelty. *Educational Leadership, 68*(5), 48–52.

Hinkley, J. W., McInerney, D. M., & Marsh, H. W. (2001, April). *The multi-faceted structure of school achievement motivation: A case for social goals.* Paper presented at the annual meeting of the American Educational Research Association, Seattle, WA.

Hirschfield, P. (2009). Another way out: The impact of juvenile arrests on high school dropout. *Sociology of Education, 82*, 368–393. doi:10. 1177/003804070908200404

Hirsh-Pasek, K., & Golinkoff, R. M. (1996). *The origins of grammar: Evidence from early language comprehension.* Cambridge, MA: MIT Press.

Hirsh-Pasek, K., Golinkoff, R. M., Berk, L. E., & Singer, D. G. (2009). *A mandate for playful learning in preschool: Presenting the evidence.* New York, NY: Oxford University Press.

Ho, C. S., & Fuson, K. C. (1998). Children's knowledge of teen quantities as tens and ones: Comparisons of Chinese, British, and American kindergartners. *Journal of Educational Psychology, 90*, 536–544.

Ho, D. Y. F. (1994). Cognitive socialization in Confucian heritage cultures. In P. M. Greenfield & R. R. Cocking (Eds.), *Cross-cultural roots* of minority child development (pp. 285–313). Hillsdale, NJ: Erlbaum.

Hobson, P. (2004). *The cradle of thought: Exploring the origins of thinking*. Oxford, England: Oxford University Press.

Hobson, P. (2004). *The cradle of thought: Exploring the origins of thinking*. Oxford, England: Oxford University Press.

Hodgkinson, S., Beers, L., Southammakosane, C., & Lewin, A. (2014). Addressing the mental health needs of pregnant and parenting adolescents. *Pediatrics, 133*(1), 114–122. doi:10.1542/peds.2013-0927

Hoekstra, R. A., Bartels, M., & Boomsma, D. I. (2007). Longitudinal genetic study of verbal and nonverbal IQ from early childhood to young adulthood. *Learning and Individual Differences, 17*, 97–114.

Hoerr, T. R. (2003). Distributed intelligence and why schools need to foster it. *Independent School, 63*, 76–83.

Hoerr, T. T. (2015). Riding the technology wave. *Educational Leadership, 72*(8), 85–87.

Hoff, E., & Naigles, L. (2002). How children use input to acquire a lexicon. *Child Development, 73*, 418–433.

Hoffman, M. L. (1975). Altruistic behavior and the parent–child relationship. *Journal of Personality and Social Psychology, 31*, 937–943.

Hoffman, M. L. (1979). Development of moral thought, feeling, and behavior. *American Psychologist, 34*, 958–966. doi:10.1037/0003-066X.34.10.958

Hoffman, M. L. (1981). Is altruism part of human nature? *Journal of Personality and Social Psychology, 40*, 121–137.

Hoffman, M. L. (1988). Moral development. In M. H. Bornstein & M. E. Lamb (Eds.), *Developmental psychology: An advanced textbook* (2nd ed., pp. 497–548). Hillsdale, NJ: Erlbaum.

Hoffman, M. L. (1991). Empathy, social cognition, and moral action. In W. M. Kurtines & J. L. Gewirtz (Eds.), *Moral Behavior and Development: Vol. 1. Theory (pp. 275–301)*. Hillsdale, NJ: Erlbaum.

Hoffman, M. L. (1994). Discipline and internalization. *Developmental Psychology, 30*, 26–28.

Hoffman, M. L. (2000). *Empathy and moral development: Implications for caring and justice*. New York, NY: Cambridge University Press.

Hogg, L. (2011). Funds of knowledge: An investigation of coherence within the literature. *Teaching and Teacher Education, 27*, 666–677. doi:10.1016/j.tate.2010.11.005

Hoglund, W. G., & Chisholm, C. A. (2014). Reciprocating risks of peer problems and aggression for children's internalizing problems. *Developmental Psychology, 50*, 586–599. doi:10.1037/a0033617

Hokoda, A., & Fincham, F. D. (1995). Origins of children's helplessness and mastery achievement patterns in the family. *Journal of Educational Psychology, 87*, 375–385.

Holland, A. S., & McElwain, N. L. (2013). Maternal and paternal perceptions of coparenting as a link between marital quality and the parent–toddler relationship. *Journal of Family Psychology, 27*(1), 117–126. doi:10.1037/a0031427.

Holland, J. M. (2011). Career development planning: Getting students on the right track. *Techniques: Connecting Education & Careers, 86*(2), 8–9.

Hollenbaugh, E. E., & Ferris, A. L. (2014). Facebook self-disclosure: Examining the role of traits, social cohesion, and motives. *Computers In Human Behavior, 30*, 50–58. doi:10.1016/j.chb.2013.07.055

Holler, K. A., & Greene, S. M. (2010). Developmental changes in children's executive functioning. In E. J. Sandberg & B. L. Spritz (Eds.), *A clinician's guide to normal cognitive development in childhood* (pp. 215–238). New York, NY: Routledge.

Hollingsworth, H. L., & Buysse, V. (2009). Establishing friendships in early childhood inclusive settings: What roles do parents and teachers play? *Journal of Early Intervention, 31*, 287–307. doi:10.1177/1053815109352659

Holloway, S. D. (2000). *Contested childhood: Diversity and change in Japanese preschools*. New York, NY: Routledge.

Holm, S. M., Forbes, E. E., Ryan, N. D., Phillips, M. L., Tarr, J. A., & Dahl, R. E. (2009). Reward-related brain function and sleep in pre/early pubertal and mid/late pubertal adolescents. *Journal of Adolescent Health, 45*, 326–334.

Holt, N. L., Tink, L. N., Mandigo, J. L., & Fox, K. R. (2008). Do youth learn life skills through their involvement in high school sport? A case study. *Canadian Journal of Education, 31*, 281–304.

Holt, R. H., & Bent, T. (2017). Children's use of semantic context in perception of foreign-accented speech. *Journal of Speech, Language & Hearing Research, 60*, 223–230. doi:10.1044/2016_JSLHR-H-16-0014

Holt, S. (2016). 'Quality' contact post-separation/divorce: A review of the literature. *Children and Youth Services Review, 68*, 92–99. doi:10.1016/j.childyouth.2016.07.001

Holtz, P., & Appel, M. (2011). Internet use and video gaming predict problem behavior in early adolescence. *Journal of Adolescence, 34*(1), 49–58. doi:10.1016/j.adolescence.2010.02.004

Honig, A. S. (2009). Understanding and working with non-compliant and aggressive young children. *Early Child Development and Care, 179*, 1007–1023. doi:10.1080/03004430701726217

Hoover-Dempsey, K. V., & Sandler, H. M. (1997). Why do parents become involved in their children's education? *Review of Educational Research, 67*, 3–42.

Hopkins, S., & Bayliss, D. (2017). The prevalence and disadvantage of min-counting in seventh grade: Problems with confidence as well as accuracy? *Mathematical Thinking and Learning, 19*(1), 19–32. http://dx.doi.org.unco.idm.oclc.org/10.1080/10986065.2017.1258613

Hoppe, C., Fliessbach, K., Stausberg, S., Stojanovic, J., Trautner, P., Elger, C. E., & Weber, B. (2012). A key role for experimental task performance: Effects of math talent, gender and performance on the neural correlates of mental rotation. *Brain & Cognition, 78*(1), 14–27. doi:10.1016/j.bandc.2011.10.008

Horn, D. (2016). The effectiveness of apprenticeship training: A within-track comparison of workplace-based and school-based vocational training in Hungary. *Social Science Research, 55*, 139–154. doi:10.1016/j.ssresearch.2015.09.002

Horn, J. L. (2008). Spearman, *g*, expertise, and the nature of human cognitive capability. In P. C. Kyllonen, R. D. Roberts, & L. Stankov (Eds.), *Extending intelligence: Enhancement and new constructs* (pp. 185–230). New York, NY: Erlbaum/Taylor & Francis.

Horn, J. L., & Noll, J. (1997). Human cognitive capabilities: Gf-Gc theory. In D. P. Flanagan, J. L. Genshaft, & P. L. Harrison (Eds.), *Contemporary intellectual assessment: Theories, tests, and issues* (pp. 53–91). New York, NY: Guilford Press.

Horner, R. H., Todd, A. W., Lewis-Palmer, T., Irvin, L. K., Sugai, G., & Boland, J. B. (2004). The School-Wide Evaluation Tool (SET): A research instrument for assessing school-wide positive behavior support. *Journal of Positive Behavior Interventions, 6*(1), 3–12. http://dx.doi.org.unco.idm.oclc.org/10.1177/10983007040060010201

Horner, S. B., Fireman, G. D., & Wang, E. W. (2010). The relation of student behavior, peer status, race, and gender to decisions about school discipline using CHAID decision trees and regression modeling. *Journal of School Psychology, 48*, 135–161. doi:10.1016/j.jsp.2009.12.001

Hornstra, L., Majoor, M., & Peetsma, T. (2017). Achievement goal profiles and developments in effort and achievement in upper elementary school. *British Journal of Educational Psychology, 87*, 606–629.

Hornstra, L., van der Veen, I., Peetsma, T., & Volman, M. (2013). Developments in motivation and achievement during primary school: A longitudinal study on group-specific differences. *Learning and Individual Differences, 23*, 195–204. doi:10.1016/j.lindif.2012.09.004

Horowitz-Kraus, T., Schmitz, R., Hutton, J. S., & Schumacher, J. (2017). How to create a successful reader? Milestones in reading development from birth to adolescence. *Acta Paediatrica, 106*, 534–544.

Horowitz, F. D., Darling-Hammond, L., & Bransford, J. (with Comer, J., Rosebrock, K., Austin, K., & Rust, F.) (2005). Educating teachers for developmentally appropriate practice. In L. Darling-Hammond & J. Bransford (Eds.), *Preparing teachers for a changing world: What teachers should learn and be able to do* (pp. 88–125). San Francisco, CA: Jossey-Bass/Wiley.

Horst, J. S., Oakes, L. M., & Madole, K. L. (2005). What does it look like and what can it do? Category structure influences how infants categorize. *Child Development*, *76*, 614–631.

Hosokawa, R., & Katsura, T. (2017). A longitudinal study of socioeconomic status, family processes, and child adjustment from preschool until early elementary school: The role of social competence. *Child and Adolescent Psychiatry and Mental Health*, *11*, Article ID 62. http://dx.doi.org.unco.idm.oclc.org/10.1186/s13034-017-0206-z

Hou, Y., Kim, S. Y., Hazen, N., & Benner, A. D. (2016). Parents' perceived discrimination and adolescent adjustment in Chinese American families: Mediating family processes. *Child Development*. Advance online publication. doi:10.1111/cdev.12603

Howard, G. R. (2007). As diversity grows, so must we. *Educational Leadership*, *64*(6), 16–22.

Howe, C. (2009). Collaborative group work in middle childhood. *Human Development*, *52*, 215–239.

Howe, C. A., Freedson, P. S., Alhassan, S. S., Feldman, H. A., & Osganian, S. K. (2012). A recess intervention to promote moderate-to-vigorous physical activity. *Pediatric Obesity*, *7*(1), 82–88. doi:10.1111/j.2047-6310.2011.00007.x

Howe, C. C., Devine, A., & Taylor Tavares, J. (2013). Supporting Conceptual Change in School Science: A possible role for tacit understanding. *International Journal of Science Education*, *35*, 864–883. doi:10.1080/09500693.2011.585353

Howe, D. (2006). Disabled children, parent–child interaction and attachment. *Child and Family Social Work*, *11*, 95–106.

Howe, M. L., Courage, M. L., & Rooksby, M. (2009). The genesis and development of autobiographical memory. In M. L. Courage & N. Cowan (Eds.), *The development of memory in infancy and childhood* (pp. 177–196). New York, NY: Psychology Press.

Howe, N. N., Porta, S. D., Recchia, H., & Ross, H. (2016). "Because if you don't put the top on, it will spill": A longitudinal study of sibling teaching in early childhood. *Developmental Psychology*, *52*, 1832–1842. doi:10.1037/dev0000193

Howe, N., & Leach, J. (2018). Children's play and peer relations. In W. M. Bukowski, B. Laursen, & K. H. Rubin (Eds.), *Handbook of peer interactions, relationships, and groups* (pp. 222–242). New York, NY, US: Guilford Press.

Howe, N., Recchia, H., Della Porta, S., & Funamoto, A. (2012). "The driver doesn't sit, he stands up like the Flintstones!": Sibling teaching during teacher-directed and self-guided tasks. *Journal of Cognition & Development*, *13*, 208–231. doi:10.1080/15248372.2011.577703

Howe, T. R. (2014). *Is there hope for children who harm animals?* [Review of the book The Assessment and Treatment of Children Who Abuse Animals: The AniCare Child Approach. K. Shapiro, M. L. Randour, S. Krinsk & J. L. Wolf]. PsycCRITIQUES, 59(21). http://dx.doi.org.unco.idm.oclc.org/10.1037/a0035759

Howell, J. C., & Lynch, J. P. (2000, August). *Youth gangs in schools (Juvenile Justice Bulletin*, OJJDP Publication NCJ-183015). Washington, DC: U.S. Department of Justice, Office of Juvenile Justice and Delinquency Prevention.

Howes, C. (1988). The peer interactions of young children. *Monographs of the Society for Research in Child Development*, *53*(1, Serial No. 217).

Howes, C. (1999). Attachment relationships in the context of multiple caregivers. In J. Cassidy & P. R. Shaver (Eds.), *Handbook of attachment: Theory, research, and clinical applications* (pp. 671–687). New York, NY: Guilford Press.

Howes, C., & Matheson, C. C. (1992). Sequences in the development of competent play with peers: Social and social-pretend play. *Developmental Psychology*, *28*, 961–974.

Howes, C., Fuligni, A., Hong, S., Huang, Y., & Lara-Cinisomo, S. (2013). The preschool instructional context and child–teacher relationships. *Early Education & Development*, *24*, 273–291. doi:10.1080/10409289.2011.649664

Howes, C., Smith, E., & Galinsky, E. (1995). *The Florida child care quality improvement study*. New York, NY: Families and Work Institute.

Hoyte, F., Torr, J., & Degotardi, S. (2014). The language of friendship: Genre in the conversations of preschool children. *Journal of Early Childhood Research*, *12*(1), 20–34. doi:10.1177/1476718X13492941

Hrabok, M., & Kerns, K. A. (2010). The development of self-regulation: A neuropsychological perspective. In B. W. Sokol, U. Müeller, J. I. M. Carpendale, A. R. Young, & G. Iarocci (Eds.), *Self and social regulation: Social interaction and the development of social understanding and executive functions* (pp. 129–154). New York, NY: Oxford University Press.

Hromek, R., & Roffey, S. (2009). Promoting social and emotional learning with games: "It's fun and we learn things." *Simulation and Gaming*, *40*, 626–644.

Hsin, L. l., & Snow, C. (2017). Social perspective taking: A benefit of bilingualism in academic writing. *Reading & Writing*, *30*, 1193–1214. doi:10.1007/s11145-016-9718-9

Huang, B. (2014). The effects of age on second language grammar and speech production. *Journal of Psycholinguistic Research*, *43*, 397–420. doi:10.1007/s10936-013-9261-7

Huang, C. Y., Costeines, J., Ayala, C., & Kaufman, J. S. (2014). Parenting stress, social support, and depression for ethnic minority adolescent mothers: Impact on child development. *Journal of Child and Family Studies*, *23*, 255–262. doi:10.1007/s10826-013-9807-1

Huang, Y., Hsu, C., Su, Y., & Liu, C. (2014). Empowering classroom observation with an e-book reading behavior monitoring system using sensing technologies. *Interacting with Computers*, *26*, 372–387.

Hubbard, J. A., Morrow, M. T., Romano, L. J., & McAuliffe, M. D. (2010). The role of anger in children's reactive versus proactive aggression: Review of findings, issues of measurement, and implications for intervention. In W. F. Arsenio & E. A. Lemerise (Eds.), *Emotions, aggression, and morality in children: Bridging development and psychopathology* (pp. 201–217). Washington, DC: American Psychological Association. doi:10.1037/12129-01

Hubbard, T. L. (2013). Phenomenal causality II: Integration and implication. *Axiomathes: An International Journal in Ontology & Cognitive Systems*, *23*, 485–524. doi:10.1007/s10516-012-9200-5

Hubel, D., & Wiesel, T. (1965). Binocular interaction in striate cortex of kittens reared with artificial squint. *Journal of Neurophysiology*, *28*, 1041–1059.

Hudac, C. M., Stessman, H. A. F., DesChamps, T. D., Kresse, A., Faja, S., Neuhaus, E., . . . Bernier, R. A. (2017). Exploring the heterogeneity of neural social iVWndices for genetically distinct etiologies of autism. *Journal of Neurodevelopmental Disorders*, *9*, Article ID 24. http://dx.doi.org.unco.idm.oclc.org/10.1186/s11689-017-9199-4

Hudley, A. H. C. (2009). African American English. In H. A. Neville, B. M. Tynes, & S. O. Utsey (Eds.), *Handbook of African American psychology* (pp. 199–210). Thousand Oaks, CA: Sage.

Hudley, A. H. C., & Mallinson, C. (2011). *Understanding English language variation in U.S. schools*. New York, NY: Teachers College Press.

Hudson, J. A., & Mayhew, E. M. Y. (2009). The development of memory for recurring events. In M. L. Courage & N. Cowan (Eds.), *The development of memory in infancy and childhood* (pp. 69–91). New York, NY: Psychology Press.

Hudson, J., Lester, K., Lewis, C., Tropeano, M., Creswell, C., Collier, D., . . . Eley, T. C. (2013). Predicting outcomes following cognitive behaviour therapy in child anxiety disorders: the influence of genetic, demographic and clinical information. *Journal of Child Psychology & Psychiatry*, *54*, 1086–1094.

Huebner, A. J., & Mancini, J. A. (2005). *Adjustment among adolescents in military families when a parent is deployed: A final report submitted to the Military Family Research Institute and Department of Defense Quality of Life Office. Falls Church: Virginia Tech Department of Human Development.* Falls Church: Virginia Tech Department of Human Development.

Huebner, C. E., & Payne, K. (2010). Home support for emergent literacy: Follow-up of a community-based implementation of dialogic reading. *Journal of Applied Developmental Psychology*, *31*, 195–201.

Huennekens, M. E., & Xu, Y. (2010). Effects of a cross-linguistic storybook intervention on the second language development of two preschool English language learners. *Early Childhood Education Journal*, *38*(1), 19–26.

Huesmann, L. R., Dubow, E. F., & Boxer, P. (2011). The transmission of aggressiveness across generations: Biological, contextual, and social learning processes. In P. R. Shaver & M. Mikulincer

(Eds.), *Human aggression and violence: Causes, manifestations, and consequences. Herzilya series on personality and social psychology* (pp. 123–142). Washington, DC: American Psychological Association. doi:10.1037/12346-007

Huesmann, L. R., Dubow, E. F., Boxer, P., Landau, S. F., Gvirsman, S. D., & Shikaki, K. (2017). Children's exposure to violent political conflict stimulates aggression at peers by increasing emotional distress, aggressive script rehearsal, and normative beliefs favoring aggression. *Development and Psychopathology, 29*(1), 39–50. doi:10.1017/S0954579416001115

Hufton, N., Elliott, J., & Illushin, L. (2002). Achievement motivation across cultures: Some puzzles and their implications for future research. *New Directions for Child and Adolescent Development, 96*, 65–85.

Hughes, D. (2003). Correlates of African American and Latino parents' messages to children about ethnicity and race: A comparative study of racial socialization. *American Journal of Community Psychology, 31*, 15–33.

Hughes, F. P. (2010). *Children, play, and development* (4th ed.). Los Angeles, CA: Sage.

Hughes, J., & Kwok, O. (2007). Influence of student–teacher and parent–teacher relationships on lower achieving readers' engagement and achievement in the primary grades. *Journal of Educational Psychology, 99*, 39–51.

Hughes, S. O., Power, T. G., Beck, A., Betz, D., Calodich, S., Goodell, L. S., . . . Ullrich-French, S. (2016). Strategies for Effective Eating Development—SEEDS: Design of an obesity prevention program to promote healthy food preferences and eating self-regulation in children from low-income families. *Journal of Nutrition Education and Behavior, 48*, 405–418. doi:10.1016/j.jneb.2016.04.388

Hughes, T. L., Tansy, M. E., & Fallon, C. (2017). Evidence-based interventions for children and adolescents with emotional and behavioral disorders. In L. A. Theodore (Ed.), *Handbook of evidence-based interventions for children and adolescents*(pp. 205–216). New York, NY: Springer.

Huizink, A. C., Mulder, E. J. H., & Buitelaar, J. K. (2004). Prenatal stress and risk for psychopathology: Special effects or induction of general susceptibility? *Psychological Bulletin, 130*, 115–142.

Hulbert, A. (1999). The century of the child. *Wilson Quarterly, 23*(1), 14–29.

Hulit, L. M., & Howard, M. R. (2006). *Born to talk* (4th ed.). Boston, MA: Allyn & Bacon.

Hulme, C., & Snowling, M. J. (2013). Learning to read: What we know and what we need to understand better. *Child Development Perspectives, 7*(1), 1–5. doi:10.1111/cdep.12005

Humphreys, A. P., & Smith, P. K. (1987). Rough-and-tumble play, friendship, and dominance in school children: Evidence for continuity and change with age. *Child Development, 58*, 201–212.

Hunninus, S., & Bekkering, H. (2010). The early development of object knowledge: A study of infants' visual anticipations during action observation. *Developmental Psychology, 46*, 446–454.

Hunt, N. H., Too, L. K., Khaw, L. T., Guo, J., Hee, L., Mitchell, A. J., . . . Ball, H. J. (2017). The kynurenine pathway and parasitic infections that affect CNS function. *Neuropharmacology, 112*(Part B), 389–398. doi:10.1016/j.neuropharm.2016.02.029

Huotilainen, M. (2013). A new dimension on foetal language learning. *Acta Paediatrica, 102*, 102–103. doi:10.1111/apa.12122

Husman, J., & Freeman, B. (1999, April). *The effect of perceptions of instrumentality on intrinsic motivation.* Paper presented at the annual meeting of the American Educational Research Association, Montreal, Quebec, Canada.

Huston, A. C., Donnerstein, E., Fairchild, H., Feshbach, N. D., Katz, P. A., Murray, J. P., . . . Zuckerman, D. (1992). *Big world, small screen: The role of television in American society.* Lincoln: University of Nebraska Press.

Hutchins, D. J., Greenfield, M. D., Epstein, J. L., Sanders, G., & Galindo, C. L. (2012). *Multicultural partnerships: Involve all families.* Larchmont, NY: Eye on Education.

Hutman, T., & Dapretto, M. (2009). The emergence of empathy during infancy. *Cognition, Brain, Behavior, 13*, 367–390.

Huttenlocher, J., Jordan, N. C., & Levine, S. C. (1994). A mental model for early arithmetic. *Journal of Experimental Psychology: General, 123*, 284–296.

Huttenlocher, P. R. (1990). Morphometric study of human cerebral cortex development. *Neuropsychologia, 28*, 517–527.

Hwang, W.-C. (2006). Acculturative family distancing: Theory, research, and clinical practice. *Psychotherapy: Theory, Research, Practice, Training, 43*, 397–409.

Hyde, C., & Wilson, P. H. (2011). Dissecting online control in developmental coordination disorder: A kinematic analysis of double-step reaching. *Brain and Cognition, 75*, 232–241. doi:10.1016/j.bandc.2010.12.004

Hyde, J. S. (2005). The gender similarities hypothesis. *American Psychologist, 60*, 581–592. http://dx.doi.org.unco.idm.oclc.org/10.1037/0003-066X.60.6.581

Hyde, K. L., & Peretz, I. (2004). Brains that are out of tune but in time. *Psychological Science, 15*, 356–360.

Hye-Kyung, K. (2014). Influence of culture and community perceptions on birth and perinatal care of immigrant women: Doulas' perspective. *Journal of Perinatal Education, 23*(1), 25–32. doi:10.1891/1058-1243.23.1.25

Hygen, B. W., Belsky, J., Stenseng, F., Lydersen, S., Guzey, I. C., & Wichstrøm, L. (2015). Child exposure to serious life events, COMT, and aggression: Testing differential susceptibility theory. *Developmental Psychology, 51*, 1098–1104. doi:10.1037/dev0000020

Hyman, I., Kay, B., Tabori, A., Weber, M., Mahon, M., & Cohen, I. (2006). Bullying: Theory, research, and interventions. In C. M. Evertson & C. S. Weinstein (Eds.), *Handbook of classroom management: Research, practice, and contemporary issues*(pp. 855–884). Mahwah, NJ: Erlbaum.

Hynd, C. (1998). Conceptual change in a high school physics class. In B. Guzzetti & C. Hynd (Eds.), *Perspectives on conceptual change: Multiple ways to understand knowing and learning in a complex world* (pp. 27–36). Mahwah, NJ: Erlbaum.

Hyson, M. C., Hirsh-Pasek, K., Rescorla, L., Cone, J., & Martell-Boinske, L. (1991). Ingredients of parental "pressure" in early childhood. *Journal of Applied Developmental Psychology, 12*, 347–365.

Hyvönen, P., & Kangas, M. (2007). From bogey mountains to funny houses: Children's desires for play environment. *Australian Journal of Early Childhood, 32*(3), 39–47.

Igoa, C. (1995). *The inner world of the immigrant child.* Mahwah, NJ: Erlbaum.

Ilie, G., Boak, A., Mann, R. E., Adlaf, E. M., Hamilton, H., Asbridge, M., . . . Cusimano, M. D. (2015). Energy drinks, alcohol, sports and traumatic brain injuries among adolescents. *PLoS ONE, 10*(9). Article ID e0135860.

Imhof, M. (2001, March). *In the eye of the beholder: Children's perception of good and poor listening behavior.* Paper presented at the annual meeting of the International Listening Association, Chicago.

Immordino-Yang, M. H., & Damasio, A. (2007). We feel, therefore we learn: The relevance of affective and social neuroscience to education. *Mind, Brain, and Education, 1*, 3–10.

Inhelder, B., & Piaget, J. (1958). *The growth of logical thinking from childhood to adolescence* (A. Parsons & S. Milgram, Trans.). New York, NY: Basic Books.

Inkpen, C. (2014, September 2). *Seven facts about world migration.* Retrieved at http://www.pewresearch.org/fact-tank/2014/09/02/7-facts-about-world-migration/

Insana, S. P., Foley, K. P., Montgomery-Downs, H. E., Kolko, D. J., & McNeil, C. B. (2014). Children exposed to intimate partner violence demonstrate disturbed sleep and impaired functional outcomes. *Psychological Trauma: Theory, Research, Practice, and Policy, 6*(3), 290-298. http://dx.doi.org.unco.idm.oclc.org/10.1037/a0033108

Institute of Education Sciences. (2006). *Character education.* Retrieved from http://ies.ed.gov/ncee/wwc/reports/character_education/index.asp

International Bureau of Education (2011). *World data on education: Saudi Arabia. Geneva, Switzerland: United Nations Educational, Scientific, and Cultural Organization.* Retrieved January 4, 2017 from http://www.ibe.unesco.org/fileadmin/user_upload/Publications/WDE/2010/pdf-versions/Saudi_Arabia.pdf

Intrator, S. M., & Siegel, D. (2008). Project Coach: Youth development and academic achievement through sport. *Journal of Physical Education, Recreation, and Dance, 79*(7), 17–23.

Intrator, S. M., & Siegel, D. (2014). *The quest for mastery: Positive youth development through out-of-school programs*. Cambridge, MA: Harvard Education Press.

Intravia, J., Wolff, K. T., Stewart, E. A., & Simons, R. L. (2014). Neighborhood-level differences in police discrimination and subcultural violence: A multilevel examination of adopting the code of the street. *Journal of Crime & Justice, 37*(1), 42–60. doi:10.1080/0735648X.2013.832480

Irujo, S. (1988). An introduction to intercultural differences and similarities in nonverbal communication. In J. S. Wurzel (Ed.), *Toward multiculturalism: A reader in multicultural education*. Yarmouth, ME: Intercultural Press.

Isabella, R. A., & Belsky, J. (1991). Interactional synchrony and the origins of infant-mother attachment: A replication study. *Child Development, 62*, 373–384.

Iselin, A., Mulvey, E., Loughran, T., Chung, H., & Schubert, C. (2012). A longitudinal examination of serious adolescent offenders' perceptions of chances for success and engagement in behaviors accomplishing goals. *Journal of Abnormal Child Psychology, 40*, 237–249.

Ishizu, K. (2017). Contingent self-worth moderates the relationship between school stressors and psychological stress responses. *Journal of Adolescence, 56*, 113–117. http://dx.doi.org.unco.idm.oclc.org/10.1016/j.adolescence.2017.02.008

Isik-Ercan, Z., Zeynep Inan, H., Nowak, J. A., & Kim, B. (2014). "We put on the glasses and Moon comes closer!" Urban second graders exploring the earth, the sun and moon through 3D technologies in a science and literacy unit. *International Journal of Science Education, 36*(1), 129–156. doi:10.1080/09500693.2012.739718

Işıtan, S. S., & Doğan, Ö. O. (2015). An examination of 1st, 2nd and 3rd Grade elementary school students; story-telling skills based on narrative analysis. *Education & Science/Egitim Ve Bilim, 40*(177), 175–186. doi:10.15390/EB.2015.2167

Israel, M., Maynard, K., & Williamson, P. (2013). Promoting literacy—embedded, authentic STEM Instruction for students with disabilities and other struggling learners. *Teaching Exceptional Children, 45*(4), 18–25.

Iuculano, T., Rosenberg-Lee, M., Supekar, K., Lynch, C. J., Khouzam, A., Phillips, J., . . . Menon, V. (2014). Brain organization underlying superior mathematical abilities in children with autism. *Biological Psychiatry, 75*, 223–230. doi:10.1016/j.biopsych.2013.06.018

Iverson, J. M., & Goldin-Meadow, S. (2005). Gesture paves the way for language development. *Psychological Science, 16*, 367–371. doi:10.1111/j.0956-7976.2005.01542.x

Iyengar, S. S., & Lepper, M. R. (1999). Rethinking the value of choice: A cultural perspective on intrinsic motivation. *Journal of Personality and Social Psychology, 76*, 349–366.

Iyer, S., & Oiler, D. (2008). Prelinguistic vocal development in infants with typical hearing and infants with severe-to-profound hearing loss. *Volta Review, 108*, 115–138.

Jaber, L. Z., & Hammer, D. (2016). Learning to feel like a scientist. Science Education, 100, 189–220. http://dx.doi.org.unco.idm.oclc.org/10.1002/sce.21202

Jackson-Maldonado, D., & Maldonado, R. (2017). Grammaticality differences between Spanish-speaking children with specific language impairment and their typically developing peers. *International Journal of Language & Communication Disorders, 52*, 750–765. doi:10.1111/1460-6984.12312

Jackson, M. (2013). The special educational needs of adolescents living with chronic illness: A literature review. *International Journal of Inclusive Education, 17*, 543–554. doi:10.1080/13603116.2012.676085

Jacobs, J. E., Davis-Kean, P., Bleeker, M., Eccles, J. S., & Malanchuk, O. (2005). "I can, but I don't want to": The impact of parents, interests, and activities on gender differences in math. In A. M. Gallagher & J. C. Kaufman (Eds.), *Gender differences in mathematics: An integrative psychological approach* (pp. 246–263). Cambridge, England: Cambridge University Press.

Jacobs, J. E., Lanza, S., Osgood, D. W., Eccles, J. S., & Wigfield, A. (2002). Changes in children's self-competence and values: Gender and domain differences across grades one through twelve. *Child Development, 73*, 509–527.

Jacobs, K., & Sillars, A. (2012). Sibling support during post-divorce adjustment: An idiographic analysis of support forms, functions, and relationship types. *Journal of Family Communication, 12*, 167–187. doi:10.1080/15267431.2011.584056

Jacobsen, B., Lowery, B., & DuCette, J. (1986). Attributions of learning disabled children. *Journal of Educational Psychology, 78*, 59–64.

Jadcherla, S. R., Gupta, A., Stoner, E., Fernandez, S., & Shaker, R. (2007). Pharyngeal swallowing: Defining pharyngeal and supper esophageal sphincter relationships in human neonates. *Journal of Pediatrics, 151*, 597–603.

Jaddoe, V. W. V. (2009). Antenatal education programmes: Do they work? *Lancet, 374*(9693), 863–864.

Jäggi, L., & Kliewer, W. (2016). "Cause that's the only skills in school you need": A qualitative analysis of revenge goals in poor urban youth. *Journal of Adolescent Research, 31*(1), 32–58. doi:10.1177/0743558415569728

Jago, C. (2014). Writing Is TAUGHT Not CAUGHT. *Educational Leadership, 71*(7), 16–21.

Jahromi, L., Guimond, A., Umaña-Taylor, A., Updegraff, K., & Toomey, R. (2014). Family context, Mexican-origin adolescent mothers' parenting knowledge, and children's subsequent developmental outcomes. *Child Development, 85*, 593–609.

Jalongo, M. R. (2008). *Learning to listen, listening to learn: Building essential skills in young children*. Washington, DC: National Association for the Education of Young Children Press.

Jalongo, M. R., Isenberg, J. P., & Gerbracht, G. (1995). *Teachers' stories: From personal narrative to professional insight*. San Francisco, CA: Jossey-Bass.

Jambon, M., & Smetana, J. G. (2014). Moral complexity in middle childhood: Children's evaluations of necessary harm. *Developmental Psychology, 50*(1), 22–33. doi:10.1037/a0032992

Janssen, M., Bakker, J. A., Bosman, A. T., Rosenberg, K., & Leseman, P. M. (2012). Differential trust between parents and teachers of children from low-income and immigrant backgrounds. *Educational Studies, 38*, 383–396. doi:10.1080/03055698.2011.643103

Janssen, P. A., Saxell, L., Page, L. A., Klein, M. C., Liston, R. M., & Shoo, K. L. (2009). Outcomes of planned home birth with registered midwife versus planned hospital birth with midwife or physician. *Canadian Medical Association Journal, 181*(6–7), 377–383.

Jaramillo, J. M., Rendón, M. I., Muñoz, L., Weis, M., & Trommsdorff, G. (2017). Children's self-regulation in cultural contexts: The role of parental socialization theories, goals, and practices. *Frontiers in Psychology, 8*, Article ID 923. http://dx.doi.org.unco.idm.oclc.org/10.3389/fpsyg.2017.00923

Jarrett, R., Bahar, O. S., & Kersh, R. T. (2016). "When we do sit down together": Family meal times in low-income African American families. *Journal of Family Issues, 37*, 1483–1513.

Jarrold, C. (2017). Working out how working memory works: Evidence from typical and atypical development. *Quarterly Journal of Experimental Psychology, 70*, 1747–1767. doi:10.1080/17470218.2016.1213869

Jarrold, C., & Citroën, R. (2013). Reevaluating key evidence for the development of rehearsal: Phonological similarity effects in children are subject to proportional scaling artifacts. *Developmental Psychology, 49*, 837–847. doi:10.1037/a0028771

Järvelä, S., Järvenoja, H., & Malmberg, J. (2012). How elementary school students' motivation is connected to self-regulation. *Educational Research and Evaluation, 18*(1), 65–84. doi:10.1080/13803611.2011.641269

Jaswal, V. K., & Dodson, C. S. (2009). Metamemory development: Understanding the role of similarity in false memories. *Child Development, 80*, 629–635.

Jelalian, E., Wember, Y. M., Bungeroth, H., & Birmaher, V. (2007). Practitioner review: Bridging review: Bridging the gap between research and clinical practice in pediatric obesity. *Journal of Child Psychology and Psychiatry, 48*, 115–127.

Jenkins, J. M., Turrell, S. L., Kogushi, Y., Lollis, S., & Ross, H. S. (2003). A longitudinal investigation of the dynamics of mental state talk in families. *Child Development, 74*, 905–920.

Jenkins, S., Bax, M., & Hart, H. (1980). Behavior problems in preschool children. *Journal of Child Psychology and Psychiatry, 21*, 5–18.

Jenlink, C. L. (1994, April). *Music: A lifeline for the self-esteem of at-risk students.* Paper presented at the annual meeting of the American Educational Research Association, New Orleans, LA.

Jenny, S., & Armstrong, T. (2013). Distance running and the elementary-age child. *The Journal of Physical Education, Recreation & Dance, 84*(3), 17–25.

Jensen, A. R. (2007). Book review: *Howard Gardner under fire: The rebel psychologist faces his critics. Intelligence, 36*, 96–97.

Jensen, M. M. (2005). *Introduction to emotional and behavioral disorders: Recognizing and managing problems in the classroom.* Upper Saddle River, NJ: Merrill Prentice Hall.

Jeon, L., Buettner, C. K., & Hur, E. (2014). Examining pre-school classroom quality in a statewide quality rating and improvement system. *Child & Youth Care Forum, 43*, 469–487. doi:10.1007/s10566-014-9248-z

Jeong, Y., Levine, S. C., & Huttenlocher, J. (2007). The development of proportional reasoning: Effect of continuous versus discrete quantities. *Journal of Cognition and Development, 8*, 237–256.

Jerome, E. M., Hamre, B. K., & Pianta, R. C. (2009). Teacher–child relationships from kindergarten to sixth grade: Early childhood predictors of teacher-perceived conflict and closeness. *Social Development, 18*, 915–945. doi:10.1111/sode.2009.18.issue-410.1111/j.1467-9507.2008.00508.x

Jessor, R., & Jessor, S. L. (1977). *Problem behavior and psychosocial development: A longitudinal study of youth.* San Diego, CA: Academic Press.

Jeynes, W. H. (2016). Meta-analysis on the roles of fathers in parenting: Are they unique? *Marriage & Family Review, 52*, 665–688. doi:10.1080/01494929.2016.1157121

Jia, J., Chen, Y., Ding, Z., Bai, Y., Yang, B., Li, M., & Qi, J. (2013). Effects of an intelligent web-based English instruction system on students' academic performance. *Journal of Computer Assisted Learning, 29*, 556–568. doi:10.1111/jcal.12016

Jimenez, B., & Kemmery, M. (2013). Building the early numeracy skills of students with moderate intellectual disability. *Education & Training in Autism & Developmental Disabilities, 48*, 479–490.

Jimerson, S. R., Egeland, B., & Teo, A. (1999). A longitudinal study of achievement trajectories: factors associated with change. *Journal of Educational Psychology, 91*, 116–126. doi:10.1037/0022-0663.91.1.116

Jin, M., Jacobvitz, D., Hazen, N., & Jung, S. (2012). Maternal sensitivity and infant attachment security in Korea: Cross-cultural validation of the Strange Situation. *Attachment & Human Development, 14*(1), 33–44. doi:10.1080/14616734.2012.636656

Jing, J. (2013). Teaching English reading through MI theory in primary schools. *English Language Teaching, 6*(1), 132–140. doi:10.5539/elt.v6n1p132

Jing, X., Saether, L., & Sommerville, J. A. (2016). Experience facilitates the emergence of sharing behavior among 7.5-month-old infants. *Developmental Psychology, 52*, 1732–1743. doi:10.1037/dev0000174

Jipson, J. L., & Callanan, M. A. (2003). Mother-child conversation and children's understanding of biological and nonbiological changes in size. *Child Development, 74*, 629–644.

Joanisse, M. F. (2007). Phonological deficits and developmental language impairments: Evidence from connectionist models. In D. Mareschal, S. Sirois, G. Westermann, & M. H. Johnson (Eds.), *Neuro-Constructivism: Vol. 2. Perspectives and prospects* (pp. 205–229). Oxford, England: Oxford University Press.

John, O. P., Caspi, A., Robins, R. W., Moffitt, T. E., & Stouthamer-Loeber, M. (1994). The "Little Five": Exploring the five-factor model of personality in adolescent boys. *Child Development, 65*, 160–178.

Johnson, D. (2013). Technology skills every teacher needs. *Educational Leadership, 70*(6), 84–85.

Johnson, D. W., Johnson, R., Dudley, B., Ward, M., & Magnuson, D. (1995). The impact of peer mediation training on the management of school and home conflicts. *American Educational Research Journal, 32*, 829–844.

Johnson, K. E., Alexander, J. M., Spencer, S., Leibham, M. E., & Neitzel, C. (2004). Factors associated with the early emergence of intense interests within conceptual domains. *Cognitive Development, 19*, 325–343.

Johnson, L., Terry, N. P., Connor, C. M., & Thomas-Tate, S. (2017). The effects of dialect awareness instruction on nonmainstream American English speakers. *Reading and Writing.* Advance online publication. http://dx.doi.org.unco.idm.oclc.org/10.1007/s11145-017-9764-y

Johnson, S. B., Riley, A. W., Granger, D. A., & Riis, J. (2013). The science of early life toxic stress for pediatric practice and advocacy. *Pediatrics, 131*, 319–327. doi:10.1542/peds.2012-0469

Johnson, S. C., Dweck, C. S., Chen, F. S., Stern, H. L., Ok, S., & Barth, M. (2010). At the intersection of social and cognitive development: Internal working models of attachment in infancy. *Cognitive Science, 34*, 807–825.

Johnson, W., Deary, I. J., & Iacono, W. G. (2009). Genetic and environmental transactions underlying educational attainment. *Intelligence, 37*, 466–478.

Johnston, D. (1995). Jailed mothers. In K. Gabel & D. Johnston (Eds.), *Children of incarcerated parents* (pp. 41–55). New York, NY: Lexington Books.

Johnston, D. (2012). Services for children of incarcerated parents. *Family Court Review, 50*(1), 91–105. doi:10.1111/j.1744-1617.2011.01431.x

Johnston, J. R. (1997). Specific language impairment, cognition and the biological basis of language. In M. Gopnik (Ed.), *The inheritance and innateness of grammars* (pp. 161–180). New York, NY: Oxford University Press.

Johnston, L. D., O'Malley, P. M., Bachman, J. G., & Schulenberg, J. E. (2007). *Monitoring the Future national results on adolescent drug use: Overview of key findings, 2006* (NIH Publication No. 07-6202). Bethesda, MD: National Institute on Drug Abuse.

Johnston, P., & Afflerbach, P. (1985). The process of constructing main ideas from text. *Cognition and Instruction, 2*, 207–232.

Jones, A. M. (2017). When in Rome: Testing the moderating influence of neighborhood composition on the relationship between self-control and juvenile offending. *Crime & Delinquency, 63*, 759–785.

Jones, L. (2012). Measuring resiliency and its predictors in recently discharged foster youth. *Child & Adolescent Social Work Journal, 29*, 515–533. doi:10.1007/s10560-012-0275-z

Jones, S., Bub, K., & Raver, C. (2013). Unpacking the black box of the Chicago School Readiness Project Intervention: The mediating roles of teacher–child relationship quality and self-regulation. *Early Education & Development, 24*, 1043–1064. doi:10.1080/10409289.2013.825188

Jordan, A. B. (2005). Learning to use books and television. *American Behavioral Scientist, 48*, 523–538.

Jordan, N. C., Hanich, L. B., & Kaplan, D. (2003). A longitudinal study of mathematical competencies in children with specific mathematics difficulties versus children with comorbid mathematics and reading difficulties. *Child Development, 74*, 834–850.

Jorde, L. B., Carey, J. C., & Bamshad, M. J. (2010). *Medical genetics* (4th ed.). Philadelphia, PA: Mosby Elsevier.

Joseph-Salisbury, R. (2016). Mixed-race youth and schooling: The fifth minority. *Ethnic & Racial Studies, 39*, 2469–2471.

Joseph, N. (2010). Metacognition needed: Teaching middle and high school students to develop strategic learning skills. *Preventing School Failure, 54*(2), 99–103.

Josephson, A. M. (2013). Family intervention as a developmental psychodynamic therapy. *Child and Adolescent Psychiatric Clinics of North America, 22*, 241–260. doi:10.1016/j.chc.2012.12.006

Joshi, C., Torvaldsen, S., Hodgson, R., & Hayen, A. (2014). Factors associated with the use and quality of antenatal care in Nepal: A population-based study using the demographic and health survey data. *BMC Pregnancy & Childbirth, 14*(1), 1–21. doi:10.1186/1471-2393-14-94

Josselson, R. (1988). The embedded self: I and Thou revisited. In D. K. Lapsley & F. C. Power (Eds.), *Self, ego, and identity: Integrative approaches* (pp. 91–106). New York, NY: Springer-Verlag.

Jovanovic, J., & King, S. S. (1998). Boys and girls in the performance-based science classroom: Who's doing the performing? *American Educational Research Journal, 35*, 477–496.

Juel, C. (1991). Beginning reading. In R. Barr, M. L. Kamil, P. B. Mosenthal, & P. Pearson (Eds.), *Handbook of reading research* (Vol. 2, pp. 759–788). Hillsdale, NJ: Erlbaum.

Julian, M. M. (2013). Age at adoption from institutional care as a window into the lasting effects of early experiences. *Clinical Child and Family Psychology Review, 16(2), 101–145.* doi:10.1007/s10567-013-0130-6

Jung, J., & Recchia, S. (2013). Scaffolding infants' play through empowering and individualizing teaching practices. *Early Education and Development, 24*, 829–850. doi:10.1080/10409289.2013.744683

Jusczyk, P. W. (1995). Language acquisition: Speech sounds and phonological development. In J. L. Miller & P. D. Eimas (Eds.), *Handbook of Perception and Cognition: Vol. 11. Speech, language, and communication* (pp. 263-301). Orlando, FL: Academic Press.

Jusczyk, P. W. (1997). Finding and remembering words: Some beginnings by English-learning infants. *Current Directions in Psychological Science, 6*, 170–174.

Juster, N. (1961). *The phantom tollbooth.* New York, NY: Random House.

Justice, J. (1984). Can socio-cultural information improve health planning? A case study of Nepal's assistant nurse-midwife. *Social Science and Medicine, 19*, 193–198.

Juvonen, J. (1991). Deviance, perceived responsibility, and negative peer reactions. *Developmental Psychology, 27*, 672–681.

Juvonen, J. (2000). The social functions of attributional face-saving tactics among early adolescents. *Educational Psychology Review, 12*, 15–32.

Juvonen, J. (2006). Sense of belonging, social bonds, and school functioning. In P. A. Alexander & P. H. Winne (Eds.), *Handbook of educational psychology* (2nd ed., pp. 655–674). Mahwah, NJ: Erlbaum.

Juvonen, J., & Graham, S. (2014). Bullying in schools: The power of bullies and the plight of victims. *Annual Review of Psychology, 65*(1), 159 185.

Juvonen, J., Nishina, A., & Graham, S. (2000). Peer harassment, psychological adjustment, and school functioning in early adolescence. *Journal of Educational Psychology, 92*, 349–359.

Kabat-Zinn, J. (2005). *Wherever you go, there you are: Mindfulness meditation in everyday life.* New York, NY: Hyperion.

Kagan, J. (1981). *The second year: The emergence of self-awareness.* Cambridge, MA: Harvard University Press.

Kagan, J. (1984). *The nature of the child.* New York, NY: Basic Books.

Kagan, J. (2008). Reply to Fox and Killen and Whalen. In W. Sinnott-Armstrong (Ed.), *Moral Psychology, Vol. 3. The neuroscience of morality: Emotion, brain disorders, and development* (pp. 321–322). Cambridge, MA: MIT Press.

Kagan, J. (2010). Emotions and temperament. In M. H. Bornstein (Ed.), *Handbook of cultural developmental science* (pp. 175–194). New York, NY: Psychology Press.

Kagan, J. K., & Fox, N. A. (2006). Biology, culture, and temperamental biases. In W. Damon & R. M. Lerner (Eds. in Chief) & N. Eisenberg (Vol. Ed.), *Handbook of Child Psychology, Vol. 3. Social, emotional, and personality development* (6th ed.,pp. 167–225). Hoboken, NJ: Wiley.

Kagan, J. K., & Fox, N. A. (2006). Biology, culture, and temperamental biases. In W. Damon & R. M. Lerner (Eds. in Chief) & N. Eisenberg (Vol. Ed.), *Handbook of Child Psychology, Vol. 3. Social, emotional, and personality development* (6th ed., pp. 167–225). Hoboken, NJ: Wiley.

Kagan, J., Snidman, N., Vahn, V., & Towsley, S. (2007). The preservation of two infant temperaments into adolescence. *Monographs of the Society for Research in Child Development, 72*, 1–80.

Kağitçibaşi, Ç. (2007). *Family, self, and human development across cultures: Theory and applications* (2nd ed.). Mahwah, NJ: Erlbaum.

Kahlenberg, S. G., & Hein, M. M. (2010). Progression on Nickelodeon? Gender-role stereotypes in toy commercials. *Sex Roles, 62*, 830–847. doi.10.1007/s11199-009-9653-1

Kahneman, D. (2016). Heuristics and biases. In R. J. Sternberg, S. T. Fiske, & D. J. Foss (Eds.), *Scientists making a difference: One hundred eminent behavioral and brain scientists talk about their most important contributions* (pp. 171–174). New York, NY: Cambridge University Press.

Kail, R. (1990). *The development of memory in children* (3rd ed.). New York, NY: Freeman.

Kail, R. V. (2013). Influences of credibility of testimony and strength of statistical evidence on children's and adolescents' reasoning. *Journal of Experimental Child Psychology, 116*, 747–754. doi:10.1016/j.jecp.2013.04.004

Kail, R. V., McBride-Chang, C., Ferrer, E., Cho, J., & Shu, H. (2013). Cultural differences in the development of processing speed. *Developmental Science, 16*, 476–483. doi:10.1111/desc.12039

Kalashnikova, M., & Mattock, K. (2014). Maturation of executive functioning skills in early sequential bilingualism. *International Journal of Bilingual Education & Bilingualism, 17*(1), 111–123. doi:10.1080/13670050.2012.746284

Kalek, D. (2014). Community support for parents of young children with developmental disabilities. In L. Lo &D. B. Hiatt-Michael (Eds.), *Promising practices to empower culturally and linguistically diverse families of children with disabilities* (pp. 85–94). Charlotte, NC: Information Age.

Kam, J. A., Guntzviller, L. M., & Pines, R. (2017). Language brokering, prosocial capacities, and intercultural communication apprehension among Latina mothers and their adolescent children. *Journal of Cross-Cultural Psychology, 48*, 168–183. http://dx.doi.org.unco.idm.oclc.org/10.1177/0022022116680480

Kamps, D. M. (2002). Preventing problems by improving behavior. In B. Algozzine & P. Kay (Eds.), *Preventing problem behaviors: A handbook of successful prevention strategies* (pp. 11–36). Thousand Oaks, CA: Corwin.

Kanner, A. D., Feldman, S. S., Weinberger, D. A., & Ford, M. E. (1987). Uplifts, hassles, and adaptational outcomes in early adolescents. *Journal of Early Adolescence, 7*, 371–394.

Kapa, L. l., Plante, E., & Doubleday, K. (2017). Applying an integrative framework of executive function to preschoolers with Specific Language Impairment. *Journal of Speech, Language & Hearing Research, 60*, 2170–2184. doi:10.1044/2017_JSLHR-L-16-0027

Kapka, S. (2013). A hospital-based, healthy pregnancy promotion program to empower the socially at risk: The Healthy Beginnings Program. *Journal of Obstetric, Gynecologic & Neonatal Nursing, 42*(Suppl. 1), S4. doi:10.1111/1552-6909.12050

Kaplan, J. S. (2012). The effects of shared environment on adult intelligence: A critical review of adoption, twin, and MZA studies. *Developmental Psychology, 48*, 1292–1298. doi:10.1037/a0028133

Kaplan, J. T., & Iacoboni, M. (2006). Getting a grip on other minds: Mirror neurons, ntention understanding, and cognitive empathy. *Social Neuroscience, 1*(3–4), 175–183. http://dx.doi.org.unco.idm.oclc.org/10.1080/17470910600985605

Kaplan, U., & Tivnan, T. (2014). Moral motivational pluralism: Moral judgment as a function of the dynamic assembly of multiple developmental structures. *Journal of Adult Development, 21*, 193–206. http://dx.doi.org.unco.idm.oclc.org/10.1007/s10804-014-9191-0

Kapp-Simon, K., & Simon, D. J. (1991). Meeting the challenge: Social skills training for teens with special needs. *Connections: The Newsletter of the National Center for Youth and Disabilities*, 2(2), 1–5.

Kar, B., & Srinivasan, N. (2013). Development of selection and control. In B. Kar (Ed.), *Cognition and brain development: Converging evidence from various methodologies* (pp. 11–32). Washington, DC: American Psychological Association. doi:10.1037/14043-002

Karabenick, S. A., & Sharma, R. (1994). Seeking academic assistance as a strategic learning resource. In P. R. Pintrich, D. R. Brown, & C. E. Weinstein (Eds.), *Student motivation, cognition, and learning: Essays in honor of Wilbert J. McKeachie (pp. 189–211).* Hillsdale, NJ: Erlbaum.

Karabon, A. (2017). They're lovin' it: How preschool children mediated their funds of knowledge into dramatic play. *Early Child Development and Care, 187*, 896–909. http://dx.doi.org.unco.idm.oclc.org/10.1080/03004430.2016.1234467

Karcher, M. (2009). Increases in academic connectedness and self-esteem among high-school students who serve as cross-age peer mentors. *Professional School Counseling, 12*, 292–299.

Karmiloff-Smith, A. (1979). Language development after five. In P. Fletcher & M. Garman (Eds.), *Language acquisition: Studies in first language development (pp. 307-322)*. Cambridge, England: Cambridge University Press.

Karmiloff-Smith, A. (2012). From constructivism to neuroconstructivism: The activity-dependent structuring of the human brain. In E. Martí & C. Rodríguez (Eds.), *After Piaget* (pp. 1–14). Piscataway, NJ: Transaction Publishers.

Karmiloff-Smith, A. (2013). From constructivism to neuroconstructivism: Did we still fall into the foundationalism/encodingism trap? Commentary on "Stepping off the pendulum: Why only an action-based approach can transcend the nativist–empiricist debate" by J. Allen and M. Bickhard. *Cognitive Development, 28*, 154–158. doi:10.1016/j.cogdev.2013.01.007

Karniol, R. (2010). *Social development as preference management: How infants, children, and parents get what they want from one another*. New York, NY: Cambridge University Press.

Karpov, Y. V., & Haywood, H. C. (1998). Two ways to elaborate Vygotsky's concept of mediation: Implications for instruction. *American Psychologist, 53*, 27–36.

Kärtner, J., Keller, H., & Chaudhary, N. (2010). Cognitive and social influences on early prosocial behavior in two sociocultural contexts. *Developmental Psychology, 46*, 905–914. doi:10.1037/a0019718

Kaslow, F. W. (2000). Families experiencing divorce. In W. C. Nichols, M. A. Pace-Nichols, D. S. Becvar, & Y. A. Napier (Eds.), *Handbook of family development and intervention* (pp. 341–368). New York, NY: Wiley.

Katkovsky, W., Crandall, V. C., & Good, S. (1967). Parental antecedents of children's beliefs in internal-external control of reinforcements in intellectual achievement situations. *Child Development, 38*, 765–776.

Katz, E. W., & Brent, S. B. (1968). Understanding connectives. *Journal of Verbal Learning and Verbal Behavior, 7*, 501–509.

Katz, L. F., & Gottman, J. M. (1991). Marital discord and child outcomes: A social psychophysiological approach. In J. Garber & K. A. Dodge (Eds.), *The development of emotion regulation and dysregulation* (pp. 129–155). Cambridge, England: Cambridge University Press.

Katz, S. L., Selman, R. L., & Mason, J. R. (2008). A study of teasing in the real world through the eyes of a practice-inspired researcher. *Educational Action Research, 16*, 469–480.

Kaufmann, L. (2008). Discalculia: Neuroscience and education. *Educational Research, 50*, 163–175.

Kavšek, M. (2013). The comparator model of infant visual habituation and dishabituation: Recent insights. *Developmental Psychobiology, 55*, 793–808. doi:10.1002/dev.21081

Kawabata, Y., Alink, L. R., Tseng, W., van IJzendoorn, M. H., & Crick, N. R. (2011). Maternal and paternal parenting styles associated with relational aggression in children and adolescents: A conceptual analysis and meta-analytic review. *Developmental Review, 31*, 240–278. doi:10.1016/j.dr.2011.08.001

Kawabata, Y., Crick, N. R., & Hamaguchi, Y. (2010). The role of culture in relational aggression: Associations with social-psychological adjustment problems in Japanese and US school-aged children. *International Journal of Behavioral Development, 34*, 354–362. doi:10.1177/0165025409339151

Kaya, E., & Geban, Ö. (2012). Facilitating conceptual change in rate of reaction concepts using conceptual change oriented instruction. *Education & Science/Egitim Ve Bilim, 37*(163), 216–225.

Kaya, S., & Kablan, Z. (2013). Assessing the relationship between learning strategies and science achievement at the primary school level. *Journal of Baltic Science Education, 12*, 525–534.

Kayama, M., & Haight, W. (2013). The experiences of Japanese elementary-school children living with "developmental disabilities": Navigating peer relationships. *Qualitative Social Work: Research And Practice, 12*, 555–571. doi:10.1177/1473325012439321

Kazdin, A. E. (1997). Conduct disorder across the life-span. In S. S. Luthar, J. A. Burack, D. Cicchetti, & J. R. Weisz (Eds.), *Developmental psychopathology: Perspectives on adjustment, risk, and disorder* (pp. 248–272). Cambridge, England: Cambridge University Press.

Kazemi, A., & Noroozi, S. (2017). An investigation into the effectiveness of Dynamic Assessment: Interactionist and interventionist approaches. *International Journal of Assessment & Evaluation, 24*(1), 25–42.

Kearins, J. M. (1981). Visual spatial memory in Australian Aboriginal children of desert regions. *Cognitive Psychology, 13*, 434–460.

Kearns, L. (2016). The construction of 'illiterate' and 'literate' youth: The effects of high-stakes standardized literacy testing. *Race, Ethnicity & Education, 19*(1), 121–140. doi:10.1080/13613324.2013.843520

Keating, D. P. (2012). Cognitive and brain development in adolescence. *Enfance, 64*, 267–279. doi:10.4074/S0013754512003035

Keefer, K. V., Holden, R. R., & Parker, J. A. (2013). Longitudinal assessment of trait emotional intelligence: Measurement invariance and construct continuity from late childhood to adolescence. *Psychological Assessment, 25*, 1255–1272. doi:10.1037/a0033903

Keeley, P. (2012). Food for plants: A bridging concept. *Science & Children, 49*(8), 26–29.

Keenan, J. M., & Meenan, C. E. (2014). Test differences in diagnosing reading comprehension deficits. *Journal of Learning Disabilities, 47*, 125–135. doi:10.1177/0022219412439326

Kehoe, C. E., Havighurst, S. S., & Harley, A. E. (2014). Tuning in to teens: Improving parent emotion socialization to reduce youth internalizing difficulties. *Social Development, 23*(2), 413-431. doi:10.1111/sode.12060

Keil, F. C. (2010). The feasibility of folk science. *Cognitive Science, 34*, 826–862. doi:10.1111/j.1551-6709.2010.01108.x

Keil, F. C. (2012). Does folk science develop? In J. Shrager & S. Carver (Eds.), *The journey from child to scientist: Integrating cognitive development and the education sciences* (pp. 67–86). Washington, DC: American Psychological Association. doi:10.1037/13617-003

Keil, F. C., & Silberstein, C. S. (1996). Schooling and the acquisition of theoretical knowledge. In D. R. Olson & N. Torrance (Eds.), *The handbook of education and human development: New models of learning, teaching, and schooling* (pp. 621–645). Cambridge, MA: Blackwell.

Kelemen, D. (1999). Why are rocks pointy? Children's preference for teleological explanations of the natural world. *Developmental Psychology, 35*, 1440–1452.

Kelemen, D. (2004). Are children "intuitive theists"? Reasoning about purpose and design in nature. *Psychological Science, 15*, 295–301.

Keller, H. (2003). Socialization for competence: Cultural models of infancy. *Human Development, 46*, 288–311.

Keller, H. (2011). Culture and cognition: Developmental perspectives. *Journal of Cognitive Education & Psychology, 10*(1), 3–8. doi:10.1891/19458959.10.1.3

Keller, H. (2017). Cultural and historical diversity in early relationship formation. *European Journal of Developmental Psychology, 14*, 700–713. http://dx.doi.org.unco.idm.oclc.org/10.1080/17405629.2017.1323630

Keller, T. A., & Just, M. A. (2009). Altering cortical connectivity: Remediation-induced changes in the white matter of poor readers. *Neuron, 64*, 624–631.

Kelley, H. M., Siwatu, K. O., Tost, J. R., & Martinez, J. (2015). Culturally familiar tasks on reading performance and self-efficacy of culturally and linguistically diverse students. *Educational Psychology in Practice, 31*, 293–313. doi:10.1080/02667363.2015.1033616

Kellogg, R. (1967). *The psychology of children's art*. New York, NY: CRM–Random House.

Kelly, J. B. (2007). Children's living arrangements following separation and divorce: Insights from empirical and clinical research. *Family Process, 46*, 35–52.

Kelly, J. B., & Lamb, M. E. (2000). Using child development research to make appropriate custody and access decisions for young children. *Family and Conciliation Courts Review, 38*, 297–311.

Kelly, K., & Bailey, A. L. (2013). Dual development of conversational and narrative discourse: Mother and child interactions during narrative co-construction. *Merrill-Palmer Quarterly, 59*(4), 426–460. doi:10.1353/mpq.2013.0019

Keltikangas-Järvinen, L. L., Jokela, M. M., Hintsanen, M. M., Salo, J. J., Hintsa, T. T.,

Alatupa, S. S., & Lehtimäki, T. T. (2010). Does genetic background moderate the association between parental education and school achievement? *Genes, Brain & Behavior, 9*, 318–324.

Kemler Nelson, D. G., Egan, L. C., & Holt, M. B. (2004). When children ask, "What is it?" what do they want to know about artifacts? *Psychological Science, 15*, 384–389.

Kemper, S. (1984). The development of narrative skills: Explanations and entertainments. In S. Kuczaj (Ed.), *Discourse development: Progress in cognitive development research* (pp. 99–122). New York, NY: Springer-Verlag.

Kenneady, D., & Oswalt, S. B. (2014). Is Cass's model of homosexual identity formation relevant to today's society? *American Journal of Sexuality Education, 9*, 229–246. doi:10.1080/15546128.2014.900465

Kennedy Root, A. K., & Denham, S. A. (2010). The role of gender in the socialization of emotion: Key concepts and critical issues. In A. Kennedy Root & S. A. Denham (Eds.), *The role of gender in the socialization of emotion: Key concepts and critical issues (New Directions for Child and Adolescent Development, 128*, pp. 1–9). San Francisco, CA: Jossey-Bass.

Kennedy-Lewis, B. L., & Murphy, A. S. (2016). Listening to "frequent flyers": What persistently disciplined students have to say about being labeled as "bad." *Teachers College Record, 118*(1), 1–40.

Kennedy, K., & Romo, H. (2013). "All colors and hues": An autoethnography of a multiethnic family's strategies for bilingualism and multiculturalism. *Family Relations, 62*(1), 109–124. doi:10.1111/j.1741-3729.2012.00742.x

Kentoffio, K., Berkowitz, S. A., Atlas, S. J., Oo, S. A., & Percac-Lima, S. (2016). Use of maternal health services: Comparing refugee, immigrant and us-born populations. *Maternal and Child Health Journal*. Advance online publication. doi:10.1007/s10995-016-2072-3

Keogh, B. K. (2003). *Temperament in the classroom: Understanding individual differences.* Baltimore, MD: Paul H. Brookes.

Keogh, B. K., & MacMillan, D. L. (1996). Exceptionality. In D. C. Berliner & R. C. Calfee (Eds.), *Handbook of educational psychology (pp. 311–330).* New York, NY: Macmillan.

Kerewsky, W., & Lefstein, L. M. (1982). Young adolescents and their community: A shared responsibility. In L. M. Lefstein et al. (Eds.), *3:00 to 6:00 p.m.: Young adolescents at home and in the community.* Carrboro, NC: Center for Early Adolescence.

Kerns, L. L., & Lieberman, A. B. (1993). *Helping your depressed child.* Rocklin, CA: Prima.

Kersey, K. C., & Masterson, M. L. (2009). Teachers connecting with families: In the best interest of children. *Young Children, 64*(5), 34–38.

Kessels, U., Heyder, A., Latsch, M., & Hannover, B. (2014). How gender differences in academic engagement relate to students' gender identity. *Educational Research, 56*, 220–229. doi:10.1080/00131881.2014.898916

Khalid, T. (2010). An integrated inquiry activity in an elementary teaching methods classroom. *Science Activities, 47*(1), 29–34.

Khundrakpam, B. S., Lewis, J. D., Reid, A., Karama, S., Zhao, L., Chouinard-Decorte, F., & Evans, A. C. (2017). Imaging structural covariance in the development of intelligence. *NeuroImage, 144*(Part A), 227–240. doi:10.1016/j.neuroimage.2016.08.041

Kiang, L., & Fuligni, A. J. (2010). Meaning in life as a mediator of ethnic identity and adjustment among adolescents from Latin, Asian, and European American backgrounds. *Journal of Youth and Adolescence, 39*, 1253–1264.

Kienbaum, J., & Wilkening, F. (2009). Children's and adolescents' intuitive judgments about distributive justice: Integrating need, effort, and luck. *European Journal of Developmental Psychology, 6*, 481–498.

Killen, M., & Nucci, L. P. (1995). Morality, autonomy, and social conflict. In M. Killen & D. Hart (Eds.), *Morality in everyday life: Developmental perspectives* (pp. 52–86). Cambridge, England: Cambridge University Press.

Killen, M., & Smetana, J. G. (2010). Future directions: Social development in the context of social justice. *Social Development, 19*, 642–657. doi:10.1111/j.1467-9507.2009.00548.x

Killen, M., Margie, N. G., & Sinno, S. (2006). Morality in the context of intergroup relationships. In M. Killen & J. G. Smetana (Eds.), *Handbook of moral development* (pp. 155–183). Mahwah, NJ: Erlbaum.

Killen, M., Mulvey, K., & Hitti, A. (2013). Social exclusion in childhood: A developmental intergroup perspective. *Child Development, 84*, 772–790. doi:10.1111/cdev.12012

Killip, S., Bennett, J. M., & Chambers, M. D. (2007). Iron deficiency anemia. *American Family Physician, 75*, 671–678.

Kim-Cohen, J., Caspi, A., Taylor, A., Williams, B., Newcombe, R., Craig, I. W., & Moffitt, T. E. (2006). MAOA, maltreatment, and gene-environment interaction predicting children's mental health: New evidence and a meta-analysis. *Molecular Psychiatry, 11*, 903–913. doi:10.1038/sj.mp.4001851

Kim-Cohen, J., Moffitt, T. E., Caspi, A., & Taylor A. (2004). Genetic and environmental processes in young children's resilience and vulnerability to socioeconomic deprivation. *Child Development, 75*, 651–668.

Kim, C., O'Grady, W., Deen, K., & Kim, K. (2017). Syntactic fast mapping: The Korean extrinsic plural marker. *Language Acquisition, 24*(1), 70–79. doi:10.1080/10489223.2016.1187612

Kim, D., Solomon, D., & Roberts, W. (1995, April). *Classroom practices that enhance students' sense of community.* Paper presented at the annual meeting of the American Educational Research Association, San Francisco.

Kim, J., & Cicchetti, D. (2009). Mean-level change and intraindividual variability in self-esteem and depression among high-risk children. *International Journal of Behavioral Development, 33*, 202–214.

Kim, J., Schallert, D. L., & Kim, M. (2010). An integrative cultural view of achievement motivation: Parental and classroom predictors of children's goal orientations when learning mathematics in Korea. *Journal of Educational Psychology, 102*, 418–437. doi:10.1037/a0018676

Kim, S., Kim, S., & Kamphaus, R. W. (2010). Is aggression the same for boys and girls? Assessing measurement invariance with confirmatory factor analysis and item response theory. *School Psychology Quarterly, 25*(1), 45–61. doi:10.1037/a0018768

Kim, Y. (2016). Relationship-based developmentally supportive approach to infant childcare practice. *Early Child Development & Care, 186*(5), 734–749. doi:10.1080/03004430.2015.1057579

Kim, Y.-S., Apel, K., & Al Otaiba, S. (2013). The relation of linguistic awareness and vocabulary to word reading and spelling for first-grade students participating in response to intervention. *Language, Speech & Hearing Services in Schools, 44*, 337–347. doi:10.1044/0161-1461(2013/12-0013)

Kim, Y., Petscher, Y., Schatschneider, C., & Foorman, B. (2010). Does growth rate in oral reading fluency matter in predicting reading comprehension achievement? *Journal of Educational Psychology, 102*, 652–667.

King, P. E., & Benson, P. L. (2006). Spiritual development and adolescent well-being and thriving. In E. C. Roehlkepartain, P. E. King, L. Wagener, & P. L. Benson (Eds.), *The handbook of spiritual development in childhood and adolescence* (pp. 384–398). Thousand Oaks, CA: Sage.

King, R. B. (2016). Is a performance- avoidance achievement goal always maladaptive? Not necessarily for collectivists. *Personality and Individual Differences, 99*, 190–195.

King, R., McInerney, D., & Watkins, D. (2012). Studying for the sake of others: The role of social goals in academic engagement. *Educational Psychology, 32*, 749–776. doi:10.1080/01443410.2012.730479

King, V., Amato, P. R., & Lindstrom, R. (2015). Stepfather–adolescent relationship quality during the first year of transitioning to a stepfamily. *Journal of Marriage and Family, 77*(5), 1179–1189. doi:10.1111/jomf.12214

Kingery, J. N., Erdley, C. A., Marshall, K. C., Whitaker, K. G., & Reuter, T. R. (2010). Peer experiences of anxious and socially withdrawn youth: An integrative review of the developmental and clinical literature. *Clinical Child and Family Psychology Review, 13*(1), 91–128.

Kinney, H. C. (2009). Brainstem mechanisms underlying the sudden infant death syndrome: Evidence from human pathologic studies. *Developmental Psychobiology, 51*, 223–233.

Kirby, A., Edwards, L., & Hughes, A. (2008). Parents' concerns about children with specific learning difficulties: Insights gained from an online message centre. *Support for Learning, 23*(4), 193–200.

Kirby, D., & Laris, B. A. (2009). Effective curriculum-based sex and STD/HIV education programs for adolescents. *Child Development Perspectives, 3*(1), 21–29.

Kirby, J. R., Parrila, R. K., & Pfeiffer, S. L. (2003). Naming speed and phonological awareness as predictors of reading development. *Journal of Educational Psychology, 95*, 453–464.

Kirk, H. E., Gray, K. M., Ellis, K., Taffe, J., & Cornish, K. M. (2016). Computerised attention training for children with intellectual and developmental disabilities: A randomised controlled trial. *Journal of Child Psychology and Psychiatry, 57*, 1380–1389. doi:10.1111/jcpp.12615

Kirkorian, H. L., Wartella, E. A., & Anderson, D. R. (2008). Media and young children's learning. *Future of Children, 18*(1), 39–61.

Kirshner, B. (2008). Guided participation in three youth activism organizations: Facilitation, apprenticeship, and joint work. *Journal of the Learning Sciences, 17*, 60–101.

Kisilevsky, B. S., Hains, S. M. J., Brown, C. A., Lee, C. T., Cowperthwaite, B., Stutzman, S. S., . . . Wang, Z. (2009). Fetal sensitivity to properties of maternal speech and language. *Infant Behavior and Development, 32*(1), 59–71.

Kitayama, S., Duffy, S., & Uchida, Y. (2007). Self as cultural mode of being. In S. Kitayama & D. Cohen (Eds.), *Handbook of cultural psychology* (pp. 136–174). New York, NY: Guilford.

Kjellstrand, J. M., Cearley, J., Eddy, J., Foney, D., & Martinez, C. R. (2012). Characteristics of incarcerated fathers and mothers: Implications for preventive interventions targeting children and families. *Children and Youth Services Review, 34*, 2409–2415. doi:10.1016/j.childyouth.2012.08.008

Klaczynski, P. (2000). Motivated scientific reasoning biases, epistemological beliefs, and theory polarization: A two-process approach to adolescent cognition. *Child Development, 71*, 1347–1366.

Klahr, D. (1982). Non-monotone assessment of monotone development: An information processing analysis. In S. Strauss & R. Stavy (Eds.), *U-shaped behavioral growth* (pp. 63–86). New York, NY: Academic Press.

Klahr, D., & Robinson, M. (1981). Formal assessment of problem solving and planning processes in children. *Cognitive Psychology, 13*, 113–148.

Klapwijk, E. T., Goddings, A., Burnett Heyes, S., Bird, G., Viner, R. M., & Blakemore, S. (2013). Increased functional connectivity with puberty in the mentalising network involved in social emotion processing. *Hormones & Behavior, 64*, 314–322. doi:10.1016/j.yhbeh.2013.03.012

Klassen, T. P., MacKay, J. M., Moher, D., Walker, A., & Jones, A. L. (2000). Community-based injury prevention interventions. *The Future of Children, 10*(1), 83–110.

Klatzkin, A., Lieberman, A. F., & Van Horn, P. (2013). Child—Parent psychotherapy and historical trauma. In J. D. Ford, C. A. Courtois (Eds.), *Treating complex traumatic stress disorders in children and adolescents: Scientific foundations and therapeutic models* (pp. 295–314). New York, NY: Guilford Press.

Klausi, J. F., & Owen, M. T. (2009). Stable maternal cohabitation, couple relationship quality, and characteristics of the home environment in the child's first two years. *Journal of Family Psychology, 23*, 103–106.

Klein, M. R., Moran, L., Cortes, R., Zalewski, M., Ruberry, E. J., & Lengua, L. J. (2018). Temperament, mothers' reactions to children's emotional experiences, and emotion understanding predicting adjustment in preschool children. *Social Development*. Advance online publication. http://dx.doi.org.unco.idm.oclc.org/10.1111/sode.12282

Klevens, R. M., Jones, S. E., Ward, J. W., Holtzman, D., & Kann, L. (2016). Trends in injection drug use among high school students, U.S., 1995–2013. *American Journal of Preventive Medicine, 50*(1), 40–46. doi:10.1016/j.amepre.2015.05.026

Klibanoff, R. S., Levine, S. C., Huttenlocher, J., Vasilyeva, M., & Hedges, L. V. (2006). Preschool children's mathematical knowledge: The effect of teacher "math talk." *Developmental Psychology, 42*, 59–69.

Klimes-Dougan, B., Pearson, T. E., Jappe, L., Mathieson, L., Simard, M. R., Hastings, P., & Zahn-Waxler, C. (2014). Adolescent emotion socialization: A longitudinal study of friends' responses to negative emotions. *Social Development, 23*, 395–412. doi:10.1111/sode.12045

Klinnert, M. D. (1984). The regulation of infant behavior by maternal facial expression. *Infant Behavior and Development, 7*, 447–465.

Knafo-Noam, A., Uzefovsky, F., Israel, S., Davidov, M., & Zahn-Waxler, C. (2015). The prosocial personality and its facets: Genetic and environmental architecture of mother-reported behavior of 7-year-old twins. *Frontiers in Psychology, 6*, Article ID 112.

Knafo, A., & Plomin, R. (2006). Prosocial behavior from early to middle childhood: Genetic and environmental influences on stability and change. *Developmental Psychology, 42*, 771–786.

Knafo, A., Zahn-Waxler, C., Van Hulle, C., Robinson, J. L., & Rhee, S. H. (2008). The developmental origins of a disposition toward empathy: Genetic and environmental contributions. *Emotion, 8*, 737–752. doi:10.1037/a0014179

Knapp, M. S., Turnbull, B. J., & Shields, P. M. (1990). New directions for educating the children of poverty. *Educational Leadership, 48*(1), 4–9.

Knapp, N. F. (2002). Tom and Joshua: Perceptions, conceptions and progress in meaning-based reading instruction. *Journal of Literacy Research, 34*, 59–98.

Knerr, W., Gardner, F., & Cluver, L. (2013). Improving positive parenting skills and reducing harsh and abusive parenting in low- and middle-income countries: A systematic review. *Prevention Science, 14(4), 352–363*. doi:10.1007/s11121-012-0314-1

Knifsend, C. A., & Juvonen, J. (2014). Social identity complexity, cross-ethnic friendships, and intergroup attitudes in urban middle schools. *Child Development, 85*, 709–721. doi:10.1111/cdev.12157

Knight, Z. G. (2017). A proposed model of psychodynamic psychotherapy linked to Erik Erikson's eight stages of psychosocial development. *Clinical Psychology & Psychotherapy*. Advance online publication. http://dx.doi.org.unco.idm.oclc.org/10.1002/cpp.2066

Knowles, Z., Parnell, D., Stratton, G., & Ridgers, N. (2013). Learning from the experts: Exploring playground experience and activities using a write and draw technique. *Journal of Physical Activity & Health, 10*, 406–415.

Knudson, R. E. (1992). The development of written argumentation: An analysis and comparison of argumentative writing at four grade levels. *Child Study Journal, 22*, 167–181.

Kochanska, G. (1993). Toward a synthesis of parental socialization and child temperament in early development of conscience. *Child Development, 64*, 325–347.

Kochanska, G. (2002). Mutually responsive orientation between mothers and their young children: A context for the early development of conscience. *Current Directions in Psychological Science, 11*, 191–195. doi:10.1111/1467-8721.00198

Kochanska, G., & Kim, S. (2013). Early attachment organization with both parents and future behavior problems: from infancy to middle childhood. *Child Development, 84*(1), 283–296. doi:10.1111/j.1467-8624.2012.01852.x

Kochanska, G., & Kim, S. (2014). A complex interplay among the parent–child relationship, effortful control, and internalized, rule-compatible conduct in young children: Evidence from two studies. *Developmental Psychology, 50*(1), 8–21. doi:10.1037/a0032330

Kochanska, G., Casey, R. J., & Fukumoto, A. (1995). Toddlers' sensitivity to standard violations. *Child Development, 66*, 643–656.

Kochanska, G., Gross, J. N., Lin, M.-H., & Nichols, K. E. (2002). Guilt in young children: Development, determinants, and relations with a broader system of standards. *Child Development, 73*, 461–482.

Kodluboy, D. W. (2004). Gang-oriented interventions. In J. C. Conoley & A. P. Goldstein (Eds.), *School violence intervention* (2nd ed., pp. 194–232). New York, NY: Guilford Press.

Koekoek, J., Knoppers, A., & Stegeman, H. (2009). How do children think they learn skills in physical education? *Journal of Teaching in Physical Education, 28*, 310–332.

Koenig, M. A., Clément, F., & Harris, P. L. (2004). Trust in testimony: Children's use of true and false statements. *Psychological Science, 15*, 694–698.

Koeppel, J., & Mulrooney, M. (1992). The Sister Schools Program: A way for children to learn about cultural diversity—When there isn't any in their school. *Young Children, 48*(1), 44–47.

Kogan, S. M., Cho, J., Simons, L. G., Allen, K. A., Beach, S. R. H., Simons, R. L., & Gibbons, F. X. (2015). Pubertal timing and sexual risk behaviors among rural African American male youth: Testing a model based on Life History Theory. *Archives of Sexual Behavior, 44*(3), 609–618. doi:10.1007/s10508-014-0410-3

Kohlberg, L. (1963). Moral development and identification. In H. Stevenson (Ed.), *Child psychology: The sixty-second yearbook of the National Society for the Study of Education* (pp. 277–332). Chicago, IL: University of Chicago Press.

Kohlberg, L. (1964). Development of moral character and moral ideology. In M. L. Hoffman & L. W. Hoffman (Eds.), *Review of child development research: Vol. 1* (pp. 383–432). New York, NY: Russell Sage Foundation.

Kohlberg, L. (1966). A cognitive developmental analysis of children's sex-role concepts and attitudes. In E. E. Maccoby (Ed.), *The development of sex differences* (pp. 82–173). Stanford, CA: Stanford University Press.

Kohlberg, L. (1969). Stage and sequence: The cognitive-developmental approach to socialization. In D. A. Goslin (Ed.), *Handbook of socialization theory and research* (pp. 347–480). Chicago, IL: Rand McNally.

Kohlberg, L. (1975). The cognitive-developmental approach to moral education. *Phi Delta Kappan, 57*, 670–677.

Kohlberg, L. (1976). Moral stages and moralization: The cognitive-developmental approach. In T. Lickona (Ed.), *Moral development and behavior: Theory, research, and social issues (pp. 31–53)*. New York, NY: Holt, Rinehart & Winston.

Kohlberg, L. (1981). *The philosophy of moral development: Moral stages and the idea of justice*. San Francisco, CA: Harper & Row.

Kohlberg, L. (1984). *The psychology of moral development: The nature and validity of moral stages*. San Francisco, CA: Harper & Row.

Kohlberg, L. (1986). A current statement on some theoretical issues. In S. Modgil & C. Modgil (Eds.), *Lawrence Kohlberg: Consensus and controversy (pp. 485-546)*. Philadelphia, PA: Falmer Press.

Kohlberg, L., & Candee, D. (1984). The relationship of moral judgment to moral action. In W. M. Kurtines & J. L. Gewirtz (Eds.), *Morality, moral behavior, and moral development (pp. 52–73)*. New York, NY: Wiley.

Kohlberg, L., & Fein, G. G. (1987). Play and constructive work as contributors to development. In L. Kohlberg (Ed.), *Child psychology and childhood education: A cognitive-developmental view* (pp. 392–440). New York, NY: Longman.

Kohlberg, L., & Kramer, R. (1969). Continuities and discontinuities in childhood and adult moral development. *Human Development, 12*, 93–120.

Kohlberg, L., Levine, C., & Hewer, A. (1983). Moral stages: A current formulation and a response to critics. *Contributions to human development, 10*, 1–174.

Kohler, F. W., Greteman, C., Raschke, D., & Highnam, C. (2007). Using a buddy skills package to increase the social interactions between a preschooler with autism and her peers. *Topics in Early Childhood Education, 27*, 155–163.

Kokkinaki, T. S., Vasdekis, V. G. S., Koufaki, Z. E., & Trevarthen, C. B. (2017). Coordination of emotions in mother–infant dialogues. *Infant and Child Development, 26*(2), 1-25. doi:10.1002/icd.1973

Komolova, M., Wainryb, C., & Recchia, H. (2017). "She had a reason to be concerned": Youths making sense of their mothers' and friends' perspectives in their accounts of conflicts. *Cognitive Development, 43*, 201–213. http://dx.doi.org.unco.idm.oclc.org/10.1016/j.cogdev.2017.05.005

Kong, L., Cui, Y., Qiu, Y., Han, S., Yu, Z., & Guo, X. (2013). Anxiety and depression in parents of sick neonates: A hospital-based study. *Journal of Clinical Nursing, 22*, 1163–1172.

Koops, L. H. (2010). "Deñuy Jàngal seen bopp" (They teach themselves): Children's music learning in The Gambia. *Journal of Research in Music Education, 58*, 18–36.

Kopp, C. B. (1982). Antecedents of self-regulation: A developmental perspective. *Developmental Psychology, 18*, 199–214.

Kopp, C. B. (1982). Antecedents of self-regulation: A developmental perspective. *Developmental Psychology, 18*, 199–214.

Koppman, S. (2016). Different like me. *Administrative Science Quarterly, 61*, 291–331. doi:10.1177/0001839215616840

Koren-Karie, N., Oppenheim, D., Dolev, S., Sher, E., & Etzion-Carasso, A. (2002). Mothers' insightfulness regarding their infants' internal experience: Relations with maternal sensitivity and infant attachment. *Developmental Psychology, 38*, 534–542.

Korkman, M., Lahti-Nuuttila, P., Laasonen, M., Kemp, S. L., & Holdnack, J. (2013). Neurocognitive development in 5- to 16-year-old North American children: A cross-sectional study. *Child Neuropsychology, 19*(5), 516–539.

Korndewal, M. J., Oudesluys-Murphy, A. M., Kroes, A. C. M., Sande, M. A. B., Melker, H. E., & Vossen, A. C. T. M. (2017). Long-term impairment attributable to congenital cytomegalovirus infection: A retrospective cohort study. *Developmental Medicine & Child Neurology, 59*, 1261–1268. http://dx.doi.org.unco.idm.oclc.org/10.1111/dmcn.13556

Kosciw, J. G., Palmer, N. A., & Kull, R. M. (2015). Reflecting resiliency: Openness about sexual orientation and/or gender identity and its relationship to well-being and educational outcomes for LGBT students. *American Journal of Community Psychology, 55*, 167–178. doi:10.1007/s10464-014-9642-6

Koskinen, P. S., Blum, I. H., Bisson, S. A., Phillips, S. M., Creamer, T. S., & Baker, T. K. (2000). Book access, shared reading, and audio models: The effects of supporting the literacy learning of linguistically diverse students in school and at home. *Journal of Educational Psychology, 92*, 23–36.

Koss, K. J., George, M. W., Davies, P. T., Cicchetti, D., Cummings, E., & Sturge-Apple, M. L. (2013). Patterns of children's adrenocortical reactivity to interparental conflict and associations with child adjustment: A growth mixture modeling approach. *Developmental Psychology, 49*, 317–326. doi:10.1037/a0028246

Koss, M. D., Martinez, M., & Johnson, N. J. (2016). Meeting characters in Caldecotts: What does this mean for today's readers? *Reading Teacher, 70*(1), 19–28. doi:10.1002/trtr.1464

Kotila, L. E., & Kamp Dush, C. M. (2012). Another baby? Father involvement and childbearing in fragile families. *Journal of Family Psychology, 26*, 976–986. doi:10.1037/a0030715

Kotsopoulos, D., Zambrzycka, J., & Makosz, S. (2017). Gender differences in toddlers' visual-spatial skills. *Mathematical Thinking and Learning, 19*(3), 167-180 http://dx.doi.org/10.1080/10986065.2017.1328634

Kousholt, K. (2016). Testing as social practice: Analysing testing in classes of young children from the children's perspective. *Theory & Psychology, 26*(3), 377–392. doi:10.1177/0959354316641911

Koutsoftas, A., & Gray, S. (2013). A structural equation model of the writing process in typically-developing sixth grade children. *Reading & Writing, 26*, 941–966. doi:10.1007/s11145-012-9399-y

Kovack-Lesh, K. A., Horst, J. S., & Oakes, L. M. (2008). The cat is out of the bag: The joint influence of previous experience and looking behavior on infant categorization. *Infancy, 13*(4), 285–307.

Kovas, Y., Haworth, C. M. A., Dale, P. S., & Plomin, R. (2007). The genetic and environmental origins of learning abilities and disabilities in the early school years. *Monographs of the Society for Research in Child Development, 72*(3, Serial No. 288), 1–160.

Kovas, Y., Tikhomirova, T., Selita, F., Tosto, M. G., & Malykh, S. (2016). How genetics can help education. In Y. Lovas, S. Malykh, & D. Gaysina (Eds.), *Behavioural genetics for education* (pp. 1–23). New York, NY: Palgrave Macmillan.

Koziol , L. F., Budding, D. E., & Hale, J. B. (2013). Understanding neuropsychopathology in the 21st century: Current status, clinical application, and future directions. In L. A. Reddy, A. S. Weissman, & J. B. Hale (Eds.), *Neuropsychological assessment and intervention for youth: An evidence-based approach to emotional and behavioral disorders* (pp. 327-345). Washington, DC, US: American Psychological Association. http://dx.doi.org.unco.idm.oclc.org/10.1037/14091-014

Kozulin, A. (1986). Vygotsky in context. In L. S. Vygotsky, *Thought and language* (A. Kozulin, Ed. and Trans.; rev. ed.) Cambridge, MA: MIT Press.

Kozulin, A., Lebeer, J., Madella-Noja, A., Gonzalez, F., Jeffrey, I., Rosenthal, N., & Koslowsky, M. (2010). Cognitive modifiability of children with developmental disabilities: A multicentre study using Feuerstein's Instrumental Enrichment—Basic program. *Research in Developmental Disabilities, 31*, 551–559.

Krachman, S. B., LaRocca, R., & Gabrieli, C. (2018). Accounting for the whole child. *Educational Leadership, 55*(5), 28–34.

Kraljević, J., Cepanec, M., & Šimleša, S. (2014). Gestural development and its relation to a child's early vocabulary. *Infant Behavior & Development, 37*, 192–202. doi:10.1016/j.infbeh.2014.01.004

Kranzler, J. H., Benson, N., & Floyd, R. G. (2016). Intellectual assessment of children and youth in the United States of America: Past, present, and future. *International Journal of School & Educational Psychology, 4*, 276–282. http://dx.doi.org/10.1080/21683603.2016.1166759

Krasa, N., & Shunkwiler, S. (2009). *Number sense and number nonsense: Understanding the challenges of learning math*. Baltimore, MD: Paul H. Brookes.

Krashen, S. D. (1996). *Under attack: The case against bilingual education*. Culver City, CA: Language Education Associates.

Krauss Whitbourne, S. (2016). Updating your fable after the glory days pass. *Psychology Today, 49*(3), 56–57.

Krebs, D. L., & Van Hesteren, F. (1994). The development of altruism: Toward an integrative model. *Developmental Review, 14*, 103–158.

Kretsch, N. N., Mendle, J., Cance, J., & Harden, K. (2016). Peer group similarity in perceptions of pubertal timing. *Journal of Youth & Adolescence, 45*, 1696–1710. doi:10.1007/s10964-015-0275-3

Kreutzer, M. A., Leonard, C., & Flavell, J. H. (1975). An interview study of children's knowledge about memory. *Monographs of the Society for Research in Child Development, 40*(1, Serial No. 159).

Krikorian, R., & Bartok, J. A. (1998). Developmental data for the Porteus Maze Test. *Clinical Neuropsychologist, 12*, 305–310.

Krishnakumar, A., Narine, L., Roopnarine, J. L., & Logie, C. (2014). Multilevel and cross-level effects of neighborhood and family influences on children's behavioral outcomes in Trinidad and Tobago: The intervening role of parental control. *Journal of Abnormal Child Psychology, 42*, 1057–1068. doi:10.1007/s10802-014-9852-2

Krispin, O., Sternberg, K. J., & Lamb, M. E. (1992). The dimensions of peer evaluation in Israel: A cross-cultural perspective. *International Journal of Behavioral Development, 15*, 299–314.

Kristen-Antonow, S., Sodian, B., Perst, H., & Licata, M. (2015). A longitudinal study of the emerging self from 9 months to the age of 4 years. *Frontiers in Psychology, 6*, Article ID 789.

Kroger, J. (2003). What transits in an identity status transition? *Identity: An International Journal of Theory and Research, 3*, 197–220.

Kroger, J. (2004). Identity in formation. In K. Hoover (Ed.), *The future of identity: Centennial reflections on the legacy of Erik Erikson* (pp. 61–76). Lanham, MD: Lexington Books.

Kronholz, J. (2011). Truants: The challenges of keeping kids in school. *Education Next, 11*(1), 32–38.

Kufeldt, K., Simard, M., & Vachon, J. (2003). Improving outcomes for children in care: Giving youth a voice. *Adoptions and Fostering, 27*, 8–19.

Kuhl, P. K. (2007). Is speech learning "gated" by the social brain? *Developmental Science, 10*, 110–120.

Kuhl, P. K., Conboy, B. T., Padden, D., Nelson, T., & Pruitt, J. (2005). Early speech perception and later language development: Implications for the "critical period." *Language Learning and Development, 1*, 237–264.

Kuhn, D. (1997). Constraints or guideposts? Developmental psychology and science education. *Review of Educational Research, 67*, 141–150.

Kuhn, D. (2001a). How do people know? *Psychological Science, 12*, 1–8.

Kuhn, D. (2001b). Why development does (and does not) occur: Evidence from the domain of inductive reasoning. In J. L. McClelland & R. S. Siegler (Eds.), *Mechanisms of cognitive development: Behavioral and neural perspectives* (pp. 221–249). Mahwah, NJ: Erlbaum.

Kuhn, D. (2007). Is direct instruction an answer to the right question? *Educational Psychologist, 42*, 109–113.

Kuhn, D. (2009). Adolescent thinking. In R. M. Lerner, & L. Steinberg (Eds.), *Handbook of Adolescent Psychology, Vol. 1. Individual bases of adolescent development* (3rd ed., pp. 152–186). Hoboken, NJ: John Wiley & Sons.

Kuhn, D. (2011). What is scientific thinking and how does it develop? In U. Goswami (Ed.), *The Wiley-Blackwell handbook of childhood cognitive development* (2nd ed., pp. 497–523). Malden, MA: Wiley-Blackwell.

Kuhn, D., & Dean, D., Jr. (2005). Is developing scientific thinking all about learning to control variables? *Psychological Science, 16*, 866–870.

Kuhn, D., & Franklin, S. (2006). The second decade: What develops (and how)? In W. Damon & R. M. Lerner (Series Eds.), & D. Kuhn & R. Siegler (Vol. Eds.), *Handbook of Child Psychology: Vol. 1. Cognition, perception, and language* (6th ed., pp. 953–993). New York, NY: Wiley.

Kuhn, D., Garcia-Mila, M., Zohar, A., & Andersen, C. (1995). Strategies of knowledge acquisition. *Monographs of the Society for Research in Child Development, 60*(4, Whole No. 245).

Kuhn, D., & Park, S.-H. (2005). Epistemological understanding and the development of intellectual values. *International Journal of Educational Research, 43*, 111–124.

Kuhn, D., & Pearsall, S. (2000). Developmental origins of scientific thinking. *Journal of Cognition and Development, 1*, 113–129.

Kuhn, D., & Pease, M. (2010). The dual components of developing strategy use: Production and inhibition. In H. S. Waters & W. Schneider (Eds.), *Metacognition, strategy use, and instruction* (pp. 135–159). New York, NY: Guilford Press.

Kuhn, D., Amsel, E., & O'Loughlin, M. (1988). *The development of scientific thinking skills*. San Diego, CA: Academic Press.

Kuhn, D., Garcia-Mila, M., Zohar, A., & Andersen, C. (1995). Strategies of knowledge acquisition. *Monographs of the Society for Research in Child Development, 60*(4, Whole No. 245).

Kuhn, D., Pease, M., & Wirkala, C. (2009). Coordinating the effects of multiple variables: A skill fundamental to scientific thinking. *Journal of Experimental Child Psychology, 103*, 268–284.

Kuhn, M. A., Ahles, J. J., Aldrich, J. T., Wielgus, M. D., & Mezulis, A. H. (2017). Physiological self-regulation buffers the relationship between impulsivity and externalizing behaviors among nonclinical adolescents. *Journal of Youth and Adolescence*. Advance online publication. http://dx.doi.org.unco.idm.oclc.org/10.1007/s10964-017-0689-1

Kulberg, A. (1986). Substance abuse: Clinical identification and management. *Pediatrics Clinics of North America, 33*, 325–361.

Kulik, L., & Kasa, Y.-A. (2014). Adjustment to divorce: A comparison of Ethiopian immigrant and Israeli men. *Journal of Community Psychology, 42*, 191–208. doi:10.1002/jcop.21604

Kulkarni, B., Christian, P., LeClerq, S. C., & Khatry, S. K. (2009). Determinants of compliance to antenatal micronutrient supplementation and women's perceptions of supplement use in rural Nepal. *Public Health Nutrition, 13*(1), 82–90.

Kumar, U., Arya, A., & Agarwal, V. (2017). Neural alterations in ADHD children as indicated by voxel-based cortical thickness and morphometry analysis. *Brain & Development, 39*(5), 403-410. http://dx.doi.org.unco.idm.oclc.org/10.1016/j.braindev.2016.12.002

Kumasi, K. (2014). Connected Learning. *Teacher Librarian, 43*(3), 8–15.

Kunjufu, J. (2006). *An African centered response to Ruby Payne's poverty theory*. Chicago, IL: African American Images.

Kunzinger, E. L., III (1985). A short-term longitudinal study of memorial development during early grade school. *Developmental Psychology, 21*, 642–646.

Kuppen, S. E. A., & Bourke, E. (2017). Rhythmic rhymes for boosting phonological awareness in socially disadvantaged children. *Mind, Brain, and Education, 11*, 181–189.

Kurtines, W. M., Berman, S. L., Ittel, A., & Williamson, S. (1995). Moral development: A co-constructivist perspective. In W. M. Kurtines & J. L. Gewirtz (Eds.), *Moral development: An introduction*. Boston, MA: Allyn & Bacon.

Kutner, L. A., Olson, C. K., Warner, D. E., & Hertzog, S. M. (2008). Parents' and sons' perspectives on video game play: A qualitative study. *Journal of Adolescent Research, 23*(1), 76–96.

Kuzucu, Y., Bontempo, D. E., Hofer, S. M., Stallings, M. C., & Piccinin, A. M. (2014). Developmental change and time-specific variation in global and specific aspects of self-concept in adolescence and association with depressive symptoms. *The Journal of Early Adolescence, 34*, 638–666. doi :10.1177/0272431613507498

Kwisthout, J., Vogt, P., Haselager, P., & Dijkstra, T. (2008). Joint attention and language evolution. *Connection Science, 20*(2–3), 155–171.

Kwok, O.-M., Hughes, J. N., & Luo, W. (2007). Role of resilient personality on lower achieving first grade students' current and future achievement. *Journal of School Psychology, 45*, 61–82.

Kwon, K., & Lease, A. M. (2009). Children's social identification with a friendship group: A moderating effect on intent to conform to norms. *Small Group Research, 40*, 694–719. doi:10.1177/1046496409346578

Kwon, K., Lease, A., & Hoffman, L. (2012). The impact of clique membership on children's social behavior and status nominations. *Social Development, 21*(1), 150–169.

Kwon, S., Janz, K. F., Letuchy, E. M., Burns, T. L., & Levy, S. M. (2016). Parental characteristic patterns associated with maintaining healthy physical activity behavior during childhood and adolescence. *International Journal of Behavioral Nutrition and Physical Activity, 13*, Article ID 58.

Kwong, T. E., & Varnhagen, C. K. (2005). Strategy development and learning to spell new words: Generalization of a process. *Developmental Psychology, 41*, 148–159.

Kyratzis, A., & Tarım, Ş. (2010). Using directives to construct egalitarian or hierarchical social organization: Turkish middle-class preschool girls' socialization about gender, affect, and context in peer group conversations. *First Language, 30*, 473–492. doi:10.1177/0142723710370547

Kyza, E. A. (2009). Middle-school students' reasoning about alternative hypotheses in a scaffolded, software-based inquiry investigation. *Cognition and Instruction, 27*, 277–311.

La Paro, K. M., & Pianta, R. C. (2000). Predicting children's competence in the early school years: A meta-analytic review. *Review of Educational Research, 70*, 443–484.

Labella, M. H., & Masten, A. S. (2018). Family influences on the development of aggression and violence. *Current Opinion in Psychology, 19*, 11–16. http://dx.doi.org.unco.idm.oclc.org/10.1016/j.copsyc.2017.03.028

Laboratory of Comparative Human Cognition. (1982). Culture and intelligence. In R. J. Sternberg (Ed.), *Handbook of human intelligence* (pp. 642-719). Cambridge, England: Cambridge University Press.

Laborde, S., Lautenbach, F., Allen, M. S., Herbert, C., & Achtzehn, S. (2014). The role of trait emotional intelligence in emotion regulation and performance under pressure. *Personality & Individual Differences, 57*, 43–47. doi:10.1016/j.paid.2013.09.013

Lacourse, E. E., Boivin, M. M., Brendgen, M. M., Petitclerc, A. A., Girard, A. A., Vitaro, F. F., . . . Tremblay, R. E. (2014). A longitudinal twin study of physical aggression during early childhood: Evidence for a developmentally dynamic genome. *Psychological Medicine, 44*, 2617–2627. doi:10.1017/S0033291713003218

Ladd, G. W. (2005). *Children's peer relations and social competence: A century of progress.* New Haven, CT: Yale University Press.

Ladd, G. W., & Burgess, K. B. (1999). Charting the relationship trajectories of aggressive, withdrawn, and aggressive/withdrawn children during early grade school. *Child Development, 70*, 910–929.

Ladd, G. W., Herald-Brown, S. L., & Kochel, K. P. (2009). Peers and motivation. In K. R. Wentzel & A. Wigfield (Eds.), *Handbook of motivation at school* (pp. 323–348). New York, NY: Routledge.

Ladd, G., Ettekal, I., Kochenderfer-Ladd, B., Rudolph, K., & Andrews, R. (2014). Relations among chronic peer group rejection, maladaptive behavioral dispositions, and early adolescents' peer perceptions. *Child Development, 85*, 971–988. doi:10.1111/cdev.12214

Ladd, H. F., Muschkin, C. G., & Dodge, K. A. (2014). From birth to school: Early childhood initiatives and third-grade outcomes in North Carolina. *Journal of Policy Analysis and Management, 33*(1), 162–187. doi:10.1002/pam.21734

Ladegaard, H. J., & Bleses, D. (2003). Gender differences in young children's speech: The acquisition of sociolinguistic competence. *International Journal of Applied Linguistics, 13*, 222–233. doi:10.1111/1473-4192.00045

Ladson-Billings, G. (1994). *The dreamkeepers: Successful teachers of African American children.* San Francisco, CA: Jossey-Bass.

Ladson-Billings, G. (1995). But that's just good teaching! The case for culturally relevant pedagogy. *Theory into Practice, 34*, 159–165.

Lafay, A., Thevenot, C., Castel, C., & Fayol, M. (2013). The role of fingers in number processing in young children. *Frontiers in Psychology, 4*, Article ID 488..

Lafontana, K. M., & Cillessen, A. H. N. (1998). The nature of children's stereotypes of popularity. *Social Development, 7*, 301–320.

Lagattuta, K. (2014). Linking past, present, and future: Children's ability to connect mental states and emotions across time. *Child Development Perspectives, 8*, 90–95. doi:10.1111/cdep.12065

Lahat, A., Helwig, C. C., & Zelazo, P. (2013). An event-related potential study of adolescents' and young adults' judgments of moral and social conventional violations. *Child Development, 84*, 955–969. doi:10.1111/cdev.12001

Lahman, M. K. E. (2008). Always othered: Ethical research with children. *Early Childhood Research, 6*(3), 281–300.

Lai, D., Tseng, Y., Hou, Y., & Guo, H. (2012). Gender and geographic differences in the prevalence of intellectual disability in children: Analysis of data from the national disability registry of Taiwan. *Research in Developmental Disabilities, 33*, 2301–2307. doi:10.1016/j.ridd.2012.07.001

Lai, M. H., Graham, J. W., Caldwell, L. L., Smith, E. A., Bradley, S. A., Vergnani, T., . . . Wegner, L. (2013). Linking life skills and norms with adolescent substance use and delinquency in South Africa. *Journal of Research on Adolescence, 23*(1), 128–137. doi:10.1111/j.1532-7795.2012.00801.x

Laible, D. J., & Thompson, R. A. (2000). Mother–child discourse, attachment security, shared positive affect, and early conscience development. *Child Development, 71*, 1424–1440.

Laible, D. J., Murphy, T., & Augustine, M. (2014). Adolescents' aggressive and prosocial behaviors: Links with social information processing, negative emotionality, moral affect, and moral cognition. *The Journal of Genetic Psychology: Research and Theory on Human Development, 175*(3), 270–286. doi:10.1080/00221325.2014.885878

Lajoie, S. P., & Derry, S. J. (Eds.). (1993). *Computers as cognitive tools.* Mahwah, NJ: Erlbaum.

Laks, B. (2013). Why is there variation rather than nothing? *Language Sciences, 39*, 31–53. doi:10.1016/j.langsci.2013.02.009

Lalor, J., Begley, C., & Galavan, E. (2009). Recasting hope: A process of adaptation following fetal anomaly diagnosis. *Social Science and Medicine, 68*, 462–472.

Lam, S. S.-Y., & McBride, C. (2018). Learning to write: The role of handwriting for Chinese spelling in kindergarten children. *Journal of Educational Psychology*, Advance online publication.

Lamaze, F. (1958). *Painless childbirth.* London, England: Burke.

Lamb, M. E., & Ahnert, L. (2006). Nonparental child care: Context, concepts, correlates, and consequences. In W. Damon & R. M. Lerner (Series Eds.) & K. A. Renninger & I. E. Sigel (Vol. Eds.), *Handbook of Child Psychology: Vol. 3. Social, emotional, and personality development* (6th ed., pp. 950–1016). New York, NY: Wiley.

Lamb, M. E., & Lewis, C. (2004). The development and significance of father–child relationships in two-parent families. In M. E. Lamb (Ed.), *The role of the father in child development* (4th ed., pp. 272–306). Hoboken, NJ: John Wiley.

Lamb, M. E., Chuang, S. S., & Cabrera, N. (2005). Promoting child adjustment by fostering positive paternal involvement. In R. M. Lerner, F. Jacobs, & D. Wertlieb (Eds.), *Applied developmental science: An advanced textbook* (pp. 179–200). Thousand Oaks, CA: Sage.

Lamb, M. E., Frodi, A. M., Hwang, C. P., Frodi, M., & Steinberg, J. (1982). Mother– and father–infant interactions involving play and holding in traditional and non-traditional Swedish families. *Developmental Psychology, 18*, 215–221.

Lamb, S., & Feeny, N. C. (1995). Early moral sense and socialization. In W. M. Kurtines & J. L. Gewirtz (Eds.), *Moral development: An introduction (pp. 497–510).* Boston, MA: Allyn & Bacon.

Lamborn, S. D., Mounts, N. S., Steinberg, L., & Dornbusch, S. M. (1991). Patterns of competence and adjustment among adolescents from authoritative, authoritarian, indulgent, and neglectful families. *Child Development, 62*, 1049–1065.

Lamm, B., Keller, H., Teiser, J., Gudi, H., Yovsi, R. D., Freitag, C., . . . Lohaus, A. (2017). Waiting for the second treat: Developing culture-specific modes of self-regulation. *Child Development*. Advance online publication. http://dx.doi.org.unco.idm.oclc.org/10.1111/cdev.12847

Lancy, D. F. (2008). *The anthropology of childhood: Cherubs, chattel, and changelings*. Cambridge, England: Cambridge University Press.

Land, G., & Jarman, B. (1992). *Breakpoint and beyond: Mastering the future—today*. New York, NY: HarperBusiness.

Landau, B. (2017). Update on "what" and "where" in spatial language: A new division of labor for spatial terms. *Cognitive Science, 41*(Suppl 2), 321–350.

Landrum, T. J., & Kauffman, J. M. (2006). Behavioral approaches to classroom management. In C. M. Evertson & C. S. Weinstein (Eds.), *Handbook of classroom management: Research, practice, and contemporary issues* (pp. 47–71). Mahwah, NJ: Erlbaum.

Landry, S. H., & Smith, K. E. (2010). Early social and cognitive precursors and parental support for self-regulation and executive function: Relations from early childhood into adolescence. In B. W. Sokol, U. Müeller, J. I. M. Carpendale, A. R. Young, & G. Iarocci (Eds.), *Self and social regulation: Social interaction and the development of social understanding and executive functions* (pp. 386–417). New York, NY: Oxford University Press.

Landry, S. S., Zucker, T. A., Taylor, H. B., Swank, P. R., Williams, J. M., Assel, M., . . . Klein, A. (2014). Enhancing early child care quality and learning for toddlers at risk: The Responsive Early Childhood Program. *Developmental Psychology, 50*, 526–541. doi:10.1037/a0033494

Landsman, J. (2014). Overcoming the challenges of poverty. *Educational Leadership*, 71(9), 16-21.

Langacker, R. W. (2016). Working toward a synthesis. *Cognitive Linguistics, 27*, 465–477.

Langberg, J. M., Dvorsky, M. R., & Evans, S. W. (2013). What specific facets of executive function are associated with academic functioning in youth with attention-deficit/hyperactivity disorder? *Journal of Abnormal Child Psychology, 41*, 1145–1159. doi:10.1007/s10802-013-9750-z

Langdon, P. E., Clare, I. C. H., & Murphy, G. H. (2010). Developing an understanding of the literature relating to the moral development of people with intellectual disabilities. *Developmental Review, 30*(3), 273–293. doi:10.1016/j.dr.2010.01.001

Lange, G., & Pierce, S. H. (1992). Memory-strategy learning and maintenance in preschool children. *Developmental Psychology, 28*, 453–462.

Langfur, S. (2013). The You-I event: On the genesis of self-awareness. *Phenomenology and the Cognitive Sciences, 12*, 769–790. doi:10.1007/s11097-012-9282-y

Langhaug, L. F., Cheung, Y. B., Pascoe, S., Hayes, R., & Cowan, F. M. (2009). Differences in prevalence of common mental disorders as measured during four questionnaire delivery methods among young people in rural Zimbabwe. *Journal of Affective Disorders, 118*, 220–223.

Langley, H. A., Coffman, J. L., & Ornstein, P. A. (2017). The socialization of children's memory: Linking maternal conversational style to the development of children's autobiographical and deliberate memory skills. *Journal of Cognition and Development, 18*(1), 63–86. doi:10.1080/15248372.2015.1135800

Langwinska-Wosko, E., Skowronska, M., Kmiec, T., & Czlonkowska, A. (2016). Retinal and optic nerve abnormalities in neurodegeneration associated with mutations in C19orf12 (MPAN). *Journal of the Neurological Sciences, 370*, 237–240. doi:10.1016/j.jns.2016.09.046

Laninga-Wijnen, L., Harakeh, Z., Dijkstra, J. K., Veenstra, R., & Vollebergh, W. (2018). Aggressive and prosocial peer norms: Change, stability, and associations with adolescent aggressive and prosocial behavior development. *Journal of Early Adolescence, 38*, 178–203. http://dx.doi.org.unco.idm.oclc.org/10.1177/0272431616665211

Lansford, J. E. (2009). Parental divorce and children's adjustment. *Perspectives on Psychological Science, 4*, 140–152.

Lapan, R. T., Tucker, B., Kim, S.-K., & Kosciulek, J. F. (2003). Preparing rural adolescents for post-high school transitions. *Journal of Counseling and Development, 81*, 329–342.

Lapsley, D. K. (1993). Toward an integrated theory of adolescent ego development: The "new look" at adolescent egocentrism. *American Journal of Orthopsychiatry, 63*, 562–571.

Lapsley, D., & Carlo, G. (2014). Moral development at the crossroads: New trends and possible futures. *Developmental Psychology, 50*(1), 1–7. doi:10.1037/a0035225

Laranjo, J., Bernier, A., Meins, E., & Carlson, S. M. (2014). The roles of maternal mind-mindedness and infant security of attachment in predicting preschoolers' understanding of visual perspective taking and false belief. *Journal of Experimental Child Psychology, 125*, 48–62. doi:10.1016/j.jecp.2014.02.005

Lareau, A. (2003). *Unequal childhoods: Class, race, and family life*. Berkeley: University of California Press.

Larkina, M., Merrill, N. A., & Bauer, P. J. (2017). Developmental changes in consistency of autobiographical memories: Adolescents' and young adults' repeated recall of recent and distance events. *Memory, 25*, 1036–1051.

Larner, M. B., Stevenson, C. S., & Behrman, R. E. (1998). Protecting children from abuse and neglect: Analysis and recommendations. *The Future of Children: Protecting Children from Abuse and Neglect, 8*(1), 4–22.

Larrain, A., Freire, P., & Howe, C. (2014). Science Teaching and Argumentation: One-sided versus dialectical argumentation in Chilean middle-school science lessons. *International Journal of Science Education, 36*, 1017–1036. doi:10.1080/09500693.2013.832005

Larson, R. W., Clore, G. L., & Wood, G. A (1999). The emotions of romantic relationships: Do they wreak havoc on adolescents? In W. Furman, B. B. Brown, & C. Feiring (Eds.), *The development of romantic relationships in adolescence* (pp. 19–49). Cambridge, England: Cambridge University Press.

Larson, R., & Richards, M. H. (1994). *Divergent realities: The emotional lives of mothers, fathers, and adolescents*. New York, NY: Basic Books.

Laski, E. V., & Siegler, R. S. (2014). Learning from number board games: You learn what you encode. *Developmental Psychology, 50*, 853–864. doi:10.1037/a0034321

Last, C. G., Hersen, M., Kazdin, A. E., Francis, G., & Grubb, H. J. (1987). Psychiatric illness in the mothers of anxious children. *American Journal of Psychiatry, 144*, 1580–1583.

Latham, R. M., Mark, K. M., & Oliver, B. R. (2018). Coparenting and children's disruptive behavior: Interacting processes for parenting sense of competence. *Journal of Family Psychology, 32*, 151–156. http://dx.doi.org.unco.idm.oclc.org/10.1037/fam0000362

Laupa, M., & Turiel, E. (1995). Social domain theory. In W. M. Kurtines & J. L. Gewirtz (Eds.), *Moral development: An introduction (pp. 455–474)*. Boston, MA: Allyn & Bacon.

Laurent, H. K. (2014). Clarifying the contours of emotion regulation: Insights from parent–child stress research. *Child Development Perspectives, 8*(1), 30–35. doi:10.1111/cdep.12058

Lave, J., & Wenger, E. (1991). *Situated learning: Legitimate peripheral participation*. Cambridge, England: Cambridge University Press.

Lavenex, P., & Banta Lavenex, P. (2013). Building hippocampal circuits to learn and remember: Insights into the development of human memory. *Behavioural Brain Research, 254*, 8–21. doi:10.1016/j.bbr.2013.02.007

Law, A., & Fung, A. (2013). Different forms of online and face-to-face victimization among schoolchildren with pure and co-occurring dimensions of reactive and proactive aggression. *Computers In Human Behavior, 29*, 1224–1233

Law, Y. (2014). The role of structured cooperative learning groups for enhancing Chinese primary students' reading comprehension. *Educational Psychology, 34*, 470–494. doi:10.1080/01443410.2013.860216

Lazard, D. S., Innes-Brown, H., & Barone, P. (2014). Adaptation of the communicative brain to post-lingual deafness. Evidence from functional imaging. *Hearing Research, 307*, 136–143. doi:10.1016/j.heares.2013.08.006

Lazonder, A. W., & Kamp, E. (2012). Bit by bit or all at once? Splitting up the inquiry task to promote children's scientific reasoning. *Learning & Instruction, 22*, 458–464. doi:10.1016/j.learninstruc.2012.05.005

Leander, E.-M. B., Larsen, P. L., & Munk, K. P. (2018). Children's doctor games and nudity at danish childcare institutions. *Archives of Sexual Behavior*. Advance online publication. http://dx.doi.org.unco.idm.oclc.org/10.1007/s10508-017-1144-9

Leaper, C., & Friedman, C. K. (2007). The socialization of gender. In J. E. Grusec & P. D. Hastings (Eds.), *Handbook of socialization: Theory and research* (pp. 561–587). New York, NY: Guilford Press.

Leaper, C., & Smith, T. E. (2004). A meta-analytic review of gender variations in children's language use: Talkativeness, affiliative speech, and assertive speech. *Developmental Psychology, 40*, 993–1027. doi:10.1037/0012-1649.40.6.993

Learning First Alliance. (2001). *Every child learning: Safe and supportive schools*. Washington, DC: Learning First Alliance and Association for Supervision and Curriculum Development.

Lebrun, M., Moreau, P., McNally-Gagnon, A., Goulet, G., & Peretz, I. (2012). Congenital amusia in childhood: A case study. *Cortex: A Journal Devoted to the Study of the Nervous System and Behavior, 48*, 683–688. doi:10.1016/j.cortex.2011.02.018

Lederberg, A. R., Schick, B., & Spencer, P. E. (2013). Language and literacy development of deaf and hard-of-hearing children: Successes and challenges. *Developmental Psychology, 49*(1), 15–30. doi:10.1037/a0029558

Lee Smith, M., Gilmer, M. H., Salge, L. E., Dickerson, J. B., & Wilson, K. L. (2013). Who enrolls in teen parent education programs? An emphasis on personal and familial characteristics and services received. *Child & Adolescent Social Work Journal, 30*(1), 21–36. doi:10.1007/s10560-012-0276-y

Lee-Pearce, M. L., Plowman, T. S., & Touchstone, D. (1998). Starbase-Atlantis, a school without walls: A comparative study of an innovative science program for at-risk urban elementary students. *Journal of Education for Students Placed at Risk, 3*, 223–235.

Lee, C. C., & Picanco, K. E. (2013). Accommodating diversity by analyzing practices of teaching (ADAPT). *Teacher Education & Special Education, 36*, 132–144. doi:10.1177/0888406413483327

Lee, C. D., & Slaughter-Defoe, D. T. (1995). Historical and sociocultural influences on African and American education. In J. A. Banks & C. A. M. Banks (Eds.), *Handbook of research on multicultural education* (pp. 348–371). New York, NY: Macmillan.

Lee, C. S., & Therriault, D. (2013). The cognitive underpinnings of creative thought: A latent variable analysis exploring the roles of intelligence and working memory in three creative thinking processes. *Intelligence, 41*, 306–320. doi:10.1016/j.intell.2013.04.008

Lee, D. H., & Anderson, A. K. (2017). Emotions as information-processing functions in behavior and experience. *Psychological Inquiry, 28*(1), 39–44. doi:10.1080/1047840X.2017.1256129

Lee, E. J., & Lee, S. H. (2009). Effects of instructional rubrics on class engagement behaviors and the achievement of lesson objectives by students with mild mental retardation and their typical peers. *Education and Training in Developmental Disabilities, 44*, 396–408.

Lee, I. (2013). The application of speech recognition technology for remediating the writing difficulties of students with learning disabilities. *Dissertation Abstracts International Section A, 73*.

Lee, J. (2009). Escaping embarrassment: Face-work in the rap cipher. *Social Psychology Quarterly, 72*, 306–324.

Lee, J. (2014). Universal factors of student achievement in high-performing Eastern and Western countries. *Journal of Educational Psychology, 106*, 364–374. doi:10.1037/a0035609

Lee, K. K., Lewis, R. W., Kataoka, S., Schenke, K., & Vandell, D. L. (2018). Out-of-school time and behaviors during adolescence. *Journal of Research on Adolescence, 28*, 284–293. doi:10.1111/jora.12389

Lee, K., & Ludington, B. (2016). Head start's impact on socio-emotional outcomes for children who have experienced violence or neighborhood crime. *Journal of Family Violence, 31*, 499–513. doi:10.1007/s10896-015-9790-y

Lee, K., Cameron, C. A., Doucette, J., & Talwar, V. (2002). Phantoms and fabrications: Young children's detection of implausible lies. *Child Development, 73*, 1688–1702.

Lee, N. R., Adeyemi, E. I., Lin, A., Clasen, L. S., Lalonde, F. M., Condon, E., . . . Giedd, J. N. (2016). Dissociations in cortical morphometry in youth with Down syndrome: Evidence for reduced surface area but increased thickness. *Cerebral Cortex, 26*, 2982–2990. doi:10.1093/cercor/bhv107

Lee, O. (1999). Science knowledge, world views, and information sources in social and cultural contexts: Making sense after a natural disaster. *American Educational Research Journal, 36*, 187–219.

Lee, R., Zhai, F., Brooks-Gunn, J., Han, W., & Waldfogel, J. (2013). Head Start participation and school readiness: Evidence from the Early Childhood Longitudinal Study–Birth Cohort. *Developmental Psychology, 50, 202–215*. doi:10.1037/a0032280

Lee, S., & Tsai, S. S. (2017). Experimental intervention research on students with specific poor comprehension: A systematic review of treatment outcomes. *Reading & Writing, 30*, 917–943. doi:10.1007/s11145-016-9697-x

Leech, K., Wei, R., Harring, J. R., & Rowe, M. L. (2017). A brief parent-focused intervention to improve preschoolers' conversational skills and school readiness. *Developmental Psychology*. Advance online publication. http://dx.doi.org/10.1037/dev0000411

Lefever, J. B., Nicholson, J. S., & Noria, C. W. (2007). Children's uncertain futures: Problems in school. In J. G. Borkowski, J. R. Farris, T. L. Whitman, S. S. Carothers, K. Weed, & D. A. Keogh (Eds.), *Risk and resilience: Adolescent mothers and their children grow up* (pp. 259–278). Mahwah, NJ: Erlbaum.

Lefmann, T., & Combs-Orme, T. (2013). Early brain development for social work practice: Integrating neuroscience with Piaget's theory of cognitive development. *Journal of Human Behavior in the Social Environment, 23*, 640–647. doi:10.1080/10911359.2013.775936

Lefstein, L. M., & Lipsitz, J. (1995). *3:00 to 6:00 p.m.: Programs for young adolescents*. Minneapolis, MN: Search Institute.

Legare, C. H. (2014). The contributions of explanation and exploration to children's scientific reasoning. *Child Development Perspectives, 8*(2), 101–106. doi:10.1111/cdep.12070

Legare, C. H., Evans, E., Rosengren, K. S., & Harris, P. L. (2012). The coexistence of natural and supernatural explanations across cultures and development. *Child Development, 83*, 779–793. doi:10.1111/j.1467-8624.2012.01743.x

Legare, C. H., Gelman, S. A., & Wellman, H. M. (2010). Inconsistency with prior knowledge triggers children's causal explanatory reasoning. *Child Development, 81*, 929–944.

Legaspi, B., & Straits, W. (2011). Living or nonliving? *Science and Children, 48*(8), 27–31.

Legault, L., Green-Demers, I., & Pelletier, L. G. (2006). Why do high school students lack motivation in the classroom? Toward an understanding of academic amotivation and the role of social support. *Journal of Educational Psychology, 98*, 567–582. doi:10.1037/0022-0663.98.3.567

Legerstee, M. (2013). The developing social brain: Social connections and social bonds, social loss, and jealousy in infancy. In M. Legerstee, D. W. Haley, & M. H. Bornstein (Eds.), *The infant mind: Origins of the social brain* (pp. 223–247). New York, NY: Guilford Press.

Lehman, D. R., & Nisbett, R. E. (1990). A longitudinal study of the effects of undergraduate training on reasoning. *Developmental Psychology, 26*, 952–960.

Lehmann, M., & Hasselhorn, M. (2012). Rehearsal dynamics in elementary school children. *Journal of Experimental Child Psychology, 111*, 552–560. doi:10.1016/j.jecp.2011.10.013

Lehrer, J., & Petrakos, H. (2011). Parent and child perceptions of grade one children's out of school play. *Exceptionality Education International, 21*(2–3), 74–92.

Lei, M.-K., Beach, S. R. H., & Simons, R. L. (2018). Childhood trauma, pubertal timing, and cardiovascular risk in adulthood. *Health*

Psychology, 37(7), 613-617.http://dx.doi.org.unco.idm.oclc.org/10.1037/hea0000609

Leichtman, M. D., & Ceci, S. J. (1995). The effects of stereotypes and suggestions on preschoolers' reports. *Developmental Psychology, 31*, 568–578.

Lein, L. (1975). Black American immigrant children: Their speech at home and school. *Council on Anthropology and Education Quarterly, 6*, 1–11.

Leman, P. J., & Björnberg, M. (2010). Conversation, development, and gender: A study of changes in children's concepts of punishment. *Child Development, 81*, 958–971. doi:10.1111/j.1467-8624.2010.01445.x

Lemery-Chalfant, K., Kao, K., Swann, G., & Goldsmith, H. (2013). Childhood temperament: Passive gene–environment correlation, gene–environment interaction, and the hidden importance of the family environment. *Development and Psychopathology, 25*(1), 51–63.

Leming, J. S. (2000). Tell me a story: An evaluation of a literature-based character education programme. *Journal of Moral Education, 29*, 413–427.

Lemmens, J. S., Valkenburg, P. M., & Peter, J. (2011). The effects of pathological gaming on aggressive behavior. *Journal of Youth and Adolescence, 40*(1), 38–47. doi:10.1007/s10964-010-9558-x

Lennox, C., & Siegel, L. S. (1998). Phonological and orthographic processes in good and poor spellers. In C. Hulme & R. Joshi (Eds.), *Reading and spelling: Development and disorders* (pp. 395–404). Mahwah, NJ: Erlbaum.

Lens, W. (2001). How to combine intrinsic task motivation with the motivational effects of the instrumentality of present tasks for future goals. In A. Efklides, J. Kuhl, & R. Sorrentino (Eds.), *Trends and prospects in motivation research* (pp. 37–52). Dordrecht, the Netherlands: Kluwer.

Leonard, J., & Martin, D. B. (2013). *The brilliance of Black children in mathematics: Beyond the numbers and toward new discourse*. Charlotte, NC: Information Age Publishing.

Leong, D., & Bodrova, E. (2012). Assessing and scaffolding make-believe play. *YC: Young Children, 67*(1), 28–34.

Leont'ev, A. N. (1959). *Problemy razvitiia psikhiki* [Problems of mental development]. Oxford, England: Rsfsr Academy Pedagogical Sciences.

Lepage, J., Dunkin, B., Hong, D. S., & Reiss, A. L. (2013). Impact of cognitive profile on social functioning in prepubescent females with Turner syndrome. *Child Neuropsychology, 19*, 161–172. doi:10.1080/09297049.2011.647900

Lepola, J., Lynch, J., Laakkonen, E., Silvén, M., & Niemi, P. (2012). The role of inference making and other language skills in the development of narrative listening comprehension in 4-6-Year-Old Children. *Reading Research Quarterly, 47*, 259–282. doi:10.1002/rrq.020

Lessard, A., Fortin, L., Marcotte, D., Potvin, P., & Royer, É. (2009). Why did they not drop out? Narratives from resilient students. *The Prevention Researcher, 16*(3), 21–24.

Lester, N., Garcia, D., Lundström, S., Brändström, S., Råstam, M., Kerekes, N., . . . Anckarsäter, H. (2016). The genetic and environmental structure of the character sub-scales of the temperament and character inventory in adolescence. *Annals of General Psychiatry, 15*, Article ID 10. doi:10.1186/s12991-016-0094-2

Lester, P., Aralis, H., Sinclair, M., Kiff, C., Lee, K.-H., Mustillo, S., & Wadsworth, S. M. (2016). The impact of deployment on parental, family and child adjustment in military families. *Child Psychiatry and Human Development, 47*, 938–949. doi:10.1007/s10578-016-0624-9

Letiecq, B. L., Bailey, S. J., & Dahlen, P. (2008). Ambivalence and coping among custodial grandparents. In B. Hayslip & P. L. Kaminski (Eds.), *Parenting the custodial grandchild* (pp. 3–16). New York, NY: Springer.

Leung, A., & McBride-Chang, C. (2013). Game on? Online friendship, cyberbullying, and psychosocial adjustment in Hong Kong Chinese Children. *Journal of Social & Clinical Psychology, 32*, 159–185. doi:10.1521/jscp.2013.32.2.159

LeVay, S. (2011). *Gay, straight, and the reason why: The science of sexual orientation*. New York, NY: Oxford University Press.

Leve, L. D., DeGarmo, D. S., Bridgett, D. J., Neiderhiser, J. M., Shaw, D. S., Harold, G. T., . . . Reiss, D. (2013). Using an adoption design to separate genetic, prenatal, and temperament influences on toddler executive function. *Developmental Psychology, 49*, 1045–1057. doi:10.1037/a0029390

Leventhal, T., Dupéré, V., & Brooks-Gunn, J. (2009). Neighborhood influences on adolescent development. In R. M. Lerner & L. Steinberg (Eds.), *Handbook of Adolescent Psychology, Vol. 2: Contextual influences on adolescent development* (3rd ed., pp. 411–443). Hoboken, NJ: Wiley.

Levine, L. (1983). Mine: Self-definition in 2-year-old boys. *Developmental Psychology, 19*, 544–549.

Levine, M. (2006). *The price of privilege: How parental pressure and material advantage are creating a generation of disconnected and unhappy kids*. New York, NY: HarperCollins.

LeVine, R. A. (2004). Challenging expert knowledge: Findings from an African study of infant care and development. In U. P. Gielen & J. P. Roopnarine (Eds.), *Childhood and adolescence: Cross-cultural perspectives and applications* (pp. 149–165). Westport, CT: Praeger.

LeVine, R. A., & Norman, K. (2008). Attachment in anthropological perspective. In R. A. LeVine & R. S. New (Eds.), *Anthropology and child development: A cross-cultural reader* (pp. 127–142). Malden, MA: Blackwell Publishing.

Levitt, M. J., Guacci-Franco, N., & Levitt, J. L. (1993). Convoys of social support in childhood and early adolescence: Structure and function. *Developmental Psychology, 29*, 811–818.

Levstik, L. S. (2008). Building a sense of history in a first-grade classroom. In L. S. Levstik & K. C. Barton (Eds.), *Researching history education: Theory, method, and context* (pp. 30–60). New York, NY: Routledge.

Levy, E., & McNeill, D. (2013). Narrative development as symbol formation: Gestures, imagery and the emergence of cohesion. *Culture & Psychology, 19*, 548–569. doi:10.1177/1354067X13500328

Lewandowski, L. J., & Rieger, B. (2009). The role of a school psychologist in concussion. *Journal of Applied School Psychology, 25*(1), 95–110.

Lewandowski, R., Verdeli, H., Wickramaratne, P., Warner, V., Mancini, A., & Weissman, M. (2014). Predictors of positive outcomes in offspring of depressed parents and non-depressed parents across 20 years. *Journal of Child & Family Studies, 23*, 800–811.

Lewin, A., Hodgkinson, S., Waters, D. M., Prempeh, H. A., Beers, L. S., & Feinberg, M. E. (2015). Strengthening positive coparenting in teen parents: A cultural adaptation of an evidence-based intervention. *Journal of Primary Prevention, 36*(3), 139–154. doi:10.1007/s10935-015-0388-1

Lewin, T. (2000, June 25). Growing up, growing apart: Fast friends try to resist the pressure to divide by race. *The New York Times*, pp. 1, 18–20.

Lewis, F. C., Reeve, R. A., Kelly, S. P., & Johnson, K. A. (2017). "Evidence of substantial development of inhibitory control and sustained attention between 6 and 8years of age on an unpredictable go/no-go task": Corrigendum. *Journal of Experimental Child Psychology, 159*, 327–328. doi:10.1016/j.jecp.2017.04.001

Lewis, M. (1993). Self-conscious emotions: Embarrassment, pride, shame, and guilt. In M. Lewis & J. Haviland (Eds.), *The handbook of emotions* (pp. 563–573). New York, NY: Guilford Press.

Lewis, M. (2005). The child and its family: The social network model. *Human Development, 48*, 8–27.

Lewis, M. (2014). *The rise of consciousness and the development of emotional life*. New York, NY: Guilford Press.

Lewis, M., & Brooks-Gunn, J. (1979). *Social cognition and the acquisition of self*. New York, NY: Plenum.

Lewis, M., Feiring, C., & Rosenthal, S. (2000). Attachment over time. *Child Development, 71*, 707–720.

Lewis, P., Abbeduto, L., Murphy, M., Richmond, E., Giles, N., Bruno, L., & Schroeder, S. (2006). Cognitive, language and social-cognitive skills of individuals with fragile X with and without autism. *Journal of Intellectual Disability Research, 50*, 532–545.

Li, J. (2004). High abilities and excellence: A cultural perspective. In L. V. Shavinina & M. Ferrari (Eds.), *Beyond knowledge: Extracognitive aspects of developing high ability* (pp. 187–208). Mahwah, NJ: Erlbaum.

Li, J. (2006). Self in learning: Chinese adolescents' goals and sense of agency. *Child Development, 77*, 482–501.

Li, J., & Fischer, K. W. (2004). Thought and affect in American and Chinese learners' beliefs about learning. In D. Y. Dai & R. J. Sternberg (Eds.), *Motivation, emotion, and cognition: "Integrative perspectives on intellectual functioning and development* (pp. 385–418). Mahwah, NJ: Erlbaum.

Li, J. J., & Lee, S. S. (2014). Negative emotionality mediates the association of 5-HTTLPR genotype and depression in children with and without ADHD. *Psychiatry Research, 215*, 163–169. doi:10.1016/j.psychres.2013.10.026

Li, S.-C. (2007). Biocultural co-construction of developmental plasticity across the lifespan. In S. Kitayama & D. Cohen (Eds.), *Handbook of cultural psychology* (pp. 528–544). New York, NY: Guilford Press.

Li, S., Jin, X., Yan, C., Wu, S., Jiang, F., & Shen, X. (2009). Factors associated with bed and room sharing in Chinese school-age children. *Child: Care, Health, and Development, 35*, 171–177.

Liben, L. S. (2009). The road to understanding maps. *Current Directions in Psychological Science, 18*(6), 310–315.

Liben, L. S., & Myers, L. J. (2007). Developmental changes in children's understanding of maps: What, when, and how? In J. M. Plumert & J. P. Spencer (Eds.), *The emerging spatial mind* (pp. 193–218). New York, NY: Oxford University Press.

Lickona, T. (1991). Moral development in the elementary school classroom. In W. M. Kurtines & J. L. Gewirtz (Eds.), *Moral Behavior and Development: Vol. 3. Application.* Hillsdale, NJ: Erlbaum.

Licona, M. (2013). Mexican and Mexican-American children's funds of knowledge as interventions into deficit thinking: opportunities for praxis in science education. *Cultural Studies of Science Education, 8*(4), 859–872. doi:10.1007/s11422-013-9515-6

Liddell, G. A., & Rasmussen, C. (2005). Memory profile of children with Nonverbal Learning Disability. *Learning Disabilities Research & Practice, 20*, 137–141. http://dx.doi.org.unco.idm.oclc.org/10.1111/j.1540-5826.2005.00128.x

Lidz, C. S. (1991). Issues in the assessment of preschool children. In B. A. Bracken (Ed.), *The psychoeducational assessment of preschool children* (2nd ed., pp. 18–31). Boston, MA: Allyn & Bacon.

Lieberman, A. F., & Van Horn, P. (2013). Infants and young children in military families: A conceptual model for intervention. *Clinical Child and Family Psychology Review, 16*, 282–293. doi:10.1007/s10567-013-0140-4

Lieberman, D. A. (1997). Interactive video games for health promotion: Effects on knowledge, self-efficacy, social support, and health. In R. L. Street, Jr., W. R. Gold, & T. R. Manning (Eds.), *Health promotion and interactive technology: Theoretical applications and future directions* (pp. 103–120). Mahwah, NJ: Erlbaum.

Liechty, J. M., Clarke, S., Birky, J. P., Harrison, K., & STRONG Kids Team. (2016). Perceptions of early body image socialization in families: Exploring knowledge, beliefs, and strategies among mothers of preschoolers. *Body Image, 19*, 68–78. doi:10.1016/j.bodyim.2016.08.010

Lieven, E., & Stoll, S. (2010). Language. In M. H. Bornstein (Ed.), *Handbook of cultural developmental science* (pp. 143–160). New York, NY: Psychology Press.

Lightfoot, C. (1992). Constructing self and peer culture: A narrative perspective on adolescent risk taking. In L. T. Winegar & J. Valsiner (Eds.), *Children's Development within Social Context: Vol. 2. Research and methodology* (pp. 229–245). Hillsdale, NJ: Erlbaum.

Lightfoot, D. (1999). *The development of language: Acquisition, change, and evolution.* Malden, MA: Blackwell.

Lillard, A. S. (1993). Pretend play skills and the child's theory of mind. *Child Development, 64*, 348–371.

Lillard, A. S. (1997). Other folks' theories of mind and behavior. *Psychological Science, 8*, 268–274.

Lillard, A. S. (1998). Playing with a theory of mind. In O. N. Saracho & B. Spodek (Eds.), *Multiple perspectives on play in early childhood education.* Albany: State University of New York Press.

Lillard, A. S. (1999). Developing a cultural theory of mind: The CIAO approach. *Current Directions in Psychological Science, 8*, 57–61.

Lillard, A. S., Lerner, M. D., Hopkins, E. J., Dore, R. A., Smith, E. D., & Palmquist, C. M. (2013). The impact of pretend play on children's development: A review of the evidence. *Psychological Bulletin, 139*(1), 1–34. doi:10.1037/a0029321

Lin, Y., Xu, J., Huang, J., Jia, Y., Zhang, J., Yan, C., & Zhang, J. (2017). Effects of prenatal and postnatal maternal emotional stress on toddlers' cognitive and temperamental development. *Journal of Affective Disorders, 207*, 9–17. doi:10.1016/j.jad.2016.09.010

Lin, Z. (2010). Interactive dynamic assessment with children learning EFL in kindergarten. *Early Childhood Education Journal, 37*, 279–287.

Lindberg, L. D., & Maddow-Zimet, I. (2012). Consequences of sex education on teen and young adult sexual behaviors and outcomes, *Journal of Adolescent Health, 51*, 332–333.

Lindberg, L., Santelli, J., & Desai, S. (2016). Understanding the decline in adolescent fertility in the united states, 2007–2012. *Journal of Adolescent Health.* Advance online publication. doi:10.1016/j.jadohealth.2016.06.024

Lindberg, M. A., & Zeid, D. (2017). Interactive pathways to substance abuse. *Addictive Behaviors, 66*, 76–82. doi:10.1016/j.addbeh.2016.11.016

Lindberg, S., Linkersdörfer, J., Ehm, J., Hasselhorn, M., & Lonnemann, J. (2013). Gender differences in children's math self-concept in the first years of elementary school. *Journal of Education & Learning, 2*(3), 1–8. doi:10.5539/jel.v2n3p1

Linder, J. R., & Gentile, D. A. (2009). Is the television rating system valid? Indirect, verbal, and physical aggression in programs viewed by fifth grade girls and associations with behavior. *Journal of Applied Developmental Psychology, 30*, 286–297.

Lindfors, K., Elovainio, M., Wickman, S., Vuorinen, R., Sinkkonen, J., Dunkel, L., & Raappana, A. (2007). Brief report: The role of ego development in psychosocial adjustment among boys with delayed puberty. *Journal of Research on Adolescence, 17*, 601–612.

Linn, M. C., & Muilenburg, L. (1996). Creating lifelong science learners: What models form a firm foundation? *Educational Researcher, 25*(5), 18–24.

Linn, M. C., Songer, N. B., & Eylon, B. (1996). Shifts and convergences in science learning and instruction. In D. C. Berliner & R. C. Calfee (Eds.), *Handbook of educational psychology* (pp. 438–490). New York, NY: Macmillan.

Linn, R. L., & Miller, M.D. (2005). *Measurement and assessment in teaching* (9th ed.). Upper Saddle River, NJ: Merrill/Prentice Hall.

Linnemeier, E. (2012). School-based conflict resolution education and peer mediation programs: The Western Justice Center Experience. *Dispute Resolution, 18*(4), 14–19.

Linnenbrink, E. A. (2005). The dilemma of performance-approach goals: The use of multiple goal contexts to promote students' motivation and learning. *Journal of Educational Psychology, 97*, 197–213.

Linnenbrink, E. A., & Pintrich, P. R. (2004). Role of affect in cognitive processing in academic contexts. In D. Y. Dia & R. J. Sternberg (Eds.), *Motivation, emotion, and cognition: Integrative perspectives on intellectual functioning and development* (pp. 57–87). Mahwah, NJ: Erlbaum.

Linver, M. R., Brooks-Gunn, J., & Kohen, D. E. (2002). Family processes as pathways from income to young children's development. *Developmental Psychology, 38*, 719–734.

Lippa, R. A. (2002). *Gender, nature, and nurture.* Mahwah, NJ: Erlbaum.

Lipson, M. Y. (1983). The influence of religious affiliation on children's memory for text information. *Reading Research Quarterly, 18*, 448–457.

Lipton, J. S., & Spelke, E. S. (2005). Preschool children's mapping of number words to nonsymbolic numerosities. *Child Development, 76*, 978–988.

Little, C. W., Hart, S. A., Quinn, J. M., Tucker-Drob, E. M., Taylor, J., & Schatschneider, C. (2017). Exploring the co-development of reading fluency and reading comprehension: A twin study. *Child Development, 88*, 934–945. doi:10.1111/cdev.12670

Liu, Y. (2017). Fraction magnitude understanding and its unique role in predicting general mathematics achievement at two early stages of fraction instruction. *British Journal of Educational Psychology*. Advance online publication. http://dx.doi.org.unco.idm.oclc.org/10.1111/bjep.12182

Liu, D., Wellman, H. M., Tardif, T., & Sabbagh, M. A. (2008). Theory of mind development in Chinese children: A meta-analysis of false-belief understanding across cultures and languages. *Developmental Psychology, 44*, 523–531.

Liu, R. T., Kraines, M. A., Massing-Schaffer, M., & Alloy, L. B. (2014). Rejection sensitivity and depression: Mediation by stress generation. *Psychiatry: Interpersonal & Biological Processes, 77*(1), 86–97. doi:10.1521/psyc.2014.77.1.86

Livingston, B. A. (2014). Bargaining behind the scenes: Spousal negotiation, labor, and work–family burnout. *Journal of Management, 40*, 949–977. doi:10.1177/0149206311428355

Lloyd, M. E., & Newcombe, N. S. (2009). Implicit memory in childhood: Reassessing developmental invariance. In M. L. Courage & N. Cowan (Eds.), *The development of memory in infancy and childhood* (pp. 93–113). New York, NY: Psychology Press.

Lo, Y.-Y., Correa, V. I., Anderson, A. L., & Swart, K. (2014). Family involvement in culturally responsive social skills instruction for Latino students with disabilities. In L. Lo & D. B. Hiatt-Michael (Eds.), *Promising practices to empower culturally and linguistically diverse families of children with disabilities* (pp. 15–32). Charlotte, NC: Information Age.

Lobel, A. (1979). *Frog and Toad are friends*. New York, NY: HarperCollins.

Lochman, J. E., Wayland, K. K., & White, K. J. (1993). Social goals: Relationship to adolescent adjustment and to social problem solving. *Journal of Abnormal Child Psychology, 21*, 1993.

Lochrie, A. S., Wysocki, T., Hossain, J., Milkes, A., Antal, H., Buckloh, L., Canas J. A., . . . Lang, J. (2013). The effects of a family-based intervention (FBI) for overweight/obese children on health and psychological functioning. *Clinical Practice in Pediatric Psychology, 1*(2), 159–170. doi:10.1037/cpp0000020

Locke, J. L. (1993). *The child's path to spoken language*. Cambridge, MA: Harvard University Press.

Lockhart, K. L., Chang, B., & Story, T. (2002). Young children's beliefs about the stability of traits: Protective optimism? *Child Development, 73*, 1408–1430.

Lodewyk, K. R., & Winne, P. H. (2005). Relations among the structure of learning tasks, achievement, and changes in self-efficacy in secondary students. *Journal of Educational Psychology, 97*, 3–12.

Loeb, S., Fuller, B., Kagan, S. L., & Carrol, B. (2004). Child care in poor communities: Early learning effects of type, quality, and stability. *Child Development, 75*, 47–65.

Löffler, E., von der Linden, N., & Schneider, W. (2016). Influence of domain knowledge on monitoring performance across the life span. *Journal of Cognition and Development, 17*, 765–785. doi:10.1080/15248372.2016.1208204

Logan, J. (2013). Contemporary adoptive kinship: A contribution to new kinship studies. *Child & Family Social Work, 18*(1), 35–45. doi:10.1111/cfs.12042

Logan, J. R., Hart, S. A., Cutting, L., Deater-Deckard, K., Schatschneider, C., & Petrill, S. (2013). Reading development in young children: Genetic and environmental influences. *Child Development, 84*, 2131–2144. doi:10.1111/cdev.12104

Logsdon, B. J., Alleman, L. M., Straits, S. A., Belka, D. E., & Clark, D. (1997). *Physical education unit plans for Grades 5–6* (2nd ed.). Champaign, IL: Human Kinetics.

Lohvansuu, K., Hämäläinen, J. A., Ervast, L., Lyytinen, H., & Leppänen, P. H. T. (2018). Longitudinal interactions between brain and cognitive measures on reading development from 6 months to 14 years. *Neuropsychologia, 108*, 6–12. http://dx.doi.org.unco.idm.oclc.org/10.1016/j.neuropsychologia.2017.11.018

London, M. L., Ladewig, P. A. W., Ball, J. W., Bindler, R. C., & Cowen, K. J. (2011). *Maternal and child nursing care* (3rd ed.). Upper Saddle River, NJ: Pearson.

London, M. L., Ladewig, P. W., Ball, J. W., & Bindler, R. C. (2007). *Maternal and child nursing care* (2nd ed.). Upper Saddle River, NJ: Pearson Prentice Hall.

Lonigan, C. J., Burgess, S. R., Anthony, J. L., & Barker, T. A. (1998). Development of phonological sensitivity in 2- to 5-year-old children. *Journal of Educational Psychology, 90*, 294–311.

Lonigro, A., Laghi, F., Baiocco, R., & Baumgartner, E. (2014). Mind reading skills and empathy: Evidence for nice and nasty ToM behaviours in school-aged children. *Journal of Child and Family Studies, 23*, 581–590. doi:10.1007/s10826-013-9722-5

Loper, A., Phillips, V., Nichols, E., & Dallaire, D. H. (2013). Characteristics and effects of the co-parenting alliance between incarcerated parents and child caregivers. *Journal of Child and Family Studies, 23(2), 225–241*. doi:10.1007/s10826-012-9709-7

Lopez Boo, F. (2016). Socio-economic status and early childhood cognitive skills: A mediation analysis using the Young Lives panel. *International Journal of Behavioral Development, 40*, 500–508. doi:10.1177/0165025416644689

Lopez, A. M. (2003). Mixed-race school-age children: A summary of census 2000 data. *Educational Researcher, 32*(6), 25–37.

Lopez, E. C. (1997). The cognitive assessment of limited English proficient and bilingual children. In D. P. Flanagan, J. L. Genshaft, & P. L. Harrison (Eds.), *Contemporary intellectual assessment: Theories, tests, and issues* (pp. 503–516). New York, NY: Guilford Press.

Lopez, V. A., & Emmer, E. T. (2002). Influences of beliefs and values on male adolescents' decision to commit violent offenses. *Psychology of Men and Masculinity, 3*, 28–40.

Lorber, M. F., Del Vecchio, T., & Smith Slep, A. M. (2014). Infant externalizing behavior as a self-organizing construct. *Developmental Psychology, 50*, 1854–1861. doi:10.1037/a0036985

Lorch, R. R., Lorch, E. P., Freer, B., Dunlap, E. E., Hodell, E. C., & Calderhead, W. J. (2014). Using valid and invalid experimental designs to teach the control of variables strategy in higher and lower achieving classrooms. *Journal of Educational Psychology, 106*, 18–35. doi:10.1037/a0034375

Lorenz, R. C., Gleich, T., Beck, A., Pöhland, L., Raufelder, D., Sommer, W., . . . Gallinat, J. (2014). Reward anticipation in the adolescent and aging brain. *Human Brain Mapping, 35*(10), 5153-5165. http://dx.doi.org.unco.idm.oclc.org/10.1002/hbm.22540

Losey, K. M. (1995). Mexican American students and classroom interaction: An overview and critique. *Review of Educational Research, 65*, 283–318.

Losh, M., Martin, G. E., Klusek, J., Hogan-Brown, A. L., & Sideris, J. (2012). Social communication and theory of mind in boys with autism and fragile X syndrome. *Frontiers in Psychology, 3*, Article ID 266. doi:10.3389/fpsyg.2012.00266

Lotan, R. A. (2006). Managing groupwork in the heterogeneous classroom. In C. M. Evertson & C. S. Weinstein (Eds.), *Handbook of classroom management: Research, practice, and contemporary issues* (pp. 525–539). Mahwah, NJ: Erlbaum.

Louie, J. Y., Wang, S.-W., Fung, J., & Lau, A. (2015). Children's emotional expressivity and teacher perceptions of social competence: A cross-cultural comparison. *International Journal of Behavioral Development, 39*, 497–507. doi:10.1177/0165025414548775

Loukas, A., Roalson, L. A., & Herrera, D. E. (2010). School connectedness buffers the effects of negative family relations and poor effortful control on early adolescent conduct problems. *Journal of Research on Adolescence, 20*(1), 13–22. doi:10.1111/j.1532-7795.2009.00632.x

Lovett, B. J., & Sparks, R. L. (2013). The identification and performance of gifted students with learning disability diagnoses: A quantitative synthesis. *Journal of Learning Disabilities, 46*, 304–316. doi:10.1177/0022219411421810

Lovett, M. W., Wolf, M., Frijters, J. C., Steinbach, K. A., Sevcik, R. A., & Morris, R. D. (2017). Early intervention for children at risk for reading sisabilities: The impact of grade at intervention and individual differences on intervention outcomes. *Journal of Educational Psychology, 109*, 889–914. doi:10.1037/edu0000181

Lovett, S. B., & Flavell, J. H. (1990). Understanding and remembering: Children's knowledge about the differential effects of strategy and task variables on comprehension and memorization. *Child Development, 61*, 1842–1858.

Luby, J. L. (2010). Preschool depression: The importance of identification of depression early in development. *Current Directions in Psychological Science, 19*, 91–95.

Luby, J., Belden, A., Sullivan, J., Hayen, R., McCadney, A., & Spitznagel, E. (2009). Shame and guilt in preschool depression: Evidence for elevations in self-conscious emotions in depression as early as age 3. *Journal of Child Psychology and Psychiatry, 50*, 1156–1166. doi:10.1111/j.1469-7610.2009.02077.x

Lucariello, J., Kyratzis, A., & Nelson, K. (1992). Taxonomic knowledge: What kind and when? *Child Development, 63*, 978–998.

Lucion, M. K., Oliveira, V., Bizarro, L., Bischoff, A. R., Silveira, P. P., & Kauer-Sant'Anna, M. (2017). Attentional bias toward infant faces—Review of the adaptive and clinical relevance. *International Journal of Psychophysiology, 114*, 1–8. doi:10.1016/j.ijpsycho.2017.01.008

Luckner, A. A., & Pianta, R. R. (2011). Teacher–student interactions in fifth grade classrooms: Relations with children's peer behavior. *Journal of Applied Developmental Psychology, 32*, 257–266. doi:10.1016/j.appdev.2011.02.010

Luckner, J., & Sebald, A. (2013). Promoting self-determination of students who are eaf or hard of hearing. *American Annals of the Deaf, 158*(3), 377–386.

Ludwig-Körner, C. (2012). Anna Freud and her collaborators in the early post-war period. In N. T. Malberg & J. Raphael-Leff (Eds.), *The Anna Freud tradition: Lines of development—Evolution of theory and practice over the decades* (pp. 17–29). London, England: Karnac Books.

Ludwig, J., & Miller, D. L. (2007). Does Head Start improve children's life chances? Evidence from a regression discontinuity design. *Quarterly Journal of Economics, 122*, 159–208.

Luehrman, M., & Unrath, K. (2006). Making theories of children's artistic development meaningful for preservice teachers. *Art Education, 59*(3), 6–12.

Lueptow, L. B. (1984). *Adolescent sex roles and social change.* New York, NY: Columbia University Press.

Lüftenegger, M., van de Schoot, R., Schober, B., Finsterwald, M., & Spiel, C. (2014). Promotion of students' mastery goal orientations: Does TARGET work? *Educational Psychology, 34*, 451–469. doi:10.1080/01443410.2013.814189

Lugo-Neris, M. J., Jackson, C., & Goldstein, H. (2010). Effects of a conversation facilitating Vocabulary acquisition of young English language learners. *Language, Speech & Hearing Services in Schools, 41*, 314–327. doi:10.1044/0161-1461(2009/07-0082)

Luijk, M. M., Mileva-Seitz, V. R., Jansen, P. W., van IJzendoorn, M. H., Jaddoe, V. V., Raat, H., . . . Tiemeier, H. (2013). Ethnic differences in prevalence and determinants of mother–child bed-sharing in early childhood. *Sleep Medicine, 14*, 1092–1099. doi:10.1016/j.sleep.2013.04.019

Luijk, M. P. C. M., Saridjan, N., Tharner, A., van IJzendoorn, M. H., Bakermans-Kranenburg, M. J., Jaddoe, V. W. V., . . . Tiemeier, H. (2010). Attachment, depression, and cortisol: Deviant patterns in insecure-resistant and disorganized infants. *Developmental Psychobiology, 52*, 441–452.

Luiselli, J. K. (2009). Aggression and noncompliance. In J. L. Matson (Ed.), *Applied behavior analysis for children with autism spectrum disorders* (pp. 175–187). New York, NY: Springer Science + Business Media. doi:10.1007/978-1-4419-0088-3_10

Luke, N., & Banerjee, R. (2012). Maltreated children's social understanding and empathy: A preliminary exploration of foster carers' perspectives. *Journal of Child and Family Studies, 21*, 237–246. doi:10.1007/s10826-011-9468-x

Lumeng, J. (2006). Childhood obesity prevention: Responsibilities of the family, schools, and community. In K. Freeark & W. S. Davidson II (Vol. Eds.), & H. E. Fitzgerald, R. Zucker, & K. Freeark (Eds. in Chief), *The Crisis in Mental Health: Critical Issues and Effective Programs. Vol. 3. Issues for families, schools, and communities* (pp. 55–77). Westport, CT: Praeger.

Luna, B. (2009). The maturation of cognitive control and the adolescent brain. In F. Aboitiz & D. Cosmelli (Eds.), *From attention to goal-directed behavior: Neurodynamical, methodological, clinical trends* (pp. 249–274). Berlin, Germany: Springer.

Lundahl, B., Bettmann, J., Hurtado, M., & Goldsmith, D. (2014). Different histories, different stories: Using a narrative tool to assess children's internal worlds. *Child & Adolescent Social Work Journal, 31*, 143–161. doi:10.1007/s10560-013-0312-6

Lunkenheimer, E., Lichtwarck-Aschoff, A., Hollenstein, T., Kemp, C. J., & Granic, I. (2016). Breaking down the coercive cycle: How parent and child risk factors influence real-time variability in parental responses to child misbehavior. *Parenting: Science and Practice, 16*, 237–256. doi:10.1080/15295192.2016.1184925

Lupo, S. M., Strong, J. Z., Lewis, W., Walpole, S., & McKenna, M. C. (2018). Building background knowledge through reading: Rethinking text sets. *Journal of Adolescent & Adult Literacy, 61*, 433–444. doi:10.1002/jaal.701

Luthar, S. S., & Eisenberg, N. (2017). Resilient adaptation among at-risk children: Harnessing science toward maximizing salutary environments. *Child Development, 88*, 337–349. http://dx.doi.org.unco.idm.oclc.org/10.1111/cdev.12737

Luthar, S. S., & Latendresse, S. J. (2005). Children of the affluent: Challenges to well-being. *Current Directions in Psychological Science, 14*, 49–53.

Lutter, C., & Lutter, R. (2012). Fetal and early childhood undernutrition, mortality, and lifelong health. *Science, 337*(6101), 1495–1499. doi:10.1126/science.1224616

Luykx, A., Lee, O., Mahotiere, M., Lester, B., Hart, J., & Deaktor, R. (2007). Cultural and home influences on children's responses to science assessments. *Teachers College Record, 109*, 897–926.

Lyman, E. T. (1981). The responsive classroom discussion: The inclusion of all students. In A. Anderson (Ed.), *Mainstreaming digest* (pp. 109–113). College Park: University of Maryland Press.

Lynch, A., Lerner, R., & Leventhal, T. (2013). Adolescent academic achievement and school engagement: An examination of the role of school-wide peer culture. *Journal of Youth & Adolescence, 42*(1), 6–19.

Lyon, T. D., & Flavell, J. H. (1994). Young children's understanding of "remember" and "forget." *Child Development, 65*, 1357–1371.

Lyons-Ruth, K., Pechtel, P., Yoon, S. A., Anderson, C. M., & Teicher, M. H. (2016). Disorganized attachment in infancy predicts greater amygdala vol. in adulthood. *Behavioural Brain Research, 308*, 83–93. doi:10.1016/j.bbr.2016.03.050

Lyons, K. E., & Ghetti, S. (2013). I don't want to pick! Introspection on uncertainty supports early strategic behavior. *Child Development, 84*, 726–736. doi:10.1111/cdev.12004

Lyons, K. E., & Zelazo, P. D. (2011). Monitoring, metacognition, and executive function: Elucidating the role of self-reflection in the development of self-regulation. *Advances in Child Development and Behavior, 40*, 379–412. doi:10.1016/B978-0-12-386491-8.00010-4

Mac Iver, M. M., Epstein, J. J., Sheldon, S. S., & Fonseca, E. E. (2015). Engaging Families to Support Students' Transition to High School: Evidence from the Field. *High School Journal, 99*(1), 27–45.

MacArthur, C., & Graham, S. (1987). Learning disabled students' composing with three methods: Handwriting, dictation, and word processing. *Journal of Special Education, 21*, 22–42.

Maccoby, E. E. (1984). Middle childhood in the context of the family. In W. A. Collins (Ed.), *Development during middle childhood* (pp. 184–239). Washington, DC: National Academy Press.

Maccoby, E. E. (2007). Historical overview of socialization research and theory. In J. E. Grusec & P. D. Hastings (Eds.), *Handbook of socialization: Theory and research* (pp. 13–41). New York, NY: Guilford.

Maccoby, E. E., & Jacklin, C. N. (1974). *The psychology of sex differences.* Stanford, CA: Stanford University Press.

MacDermott, S. T., Gullone, E., Allen, J. S., King, N. J., & Tonge, B. (2010). The emotion regulation index for children and adolescents (ERICA): A psychometric investigation. *Journal of Psychopathology and Behavioral Assessment, 32*, 301–314. doi:10.1007/s10862-009-9154-0

MacDonald, S., Uesiliana, K., & Hayne, H. (2000). Cross-cultural and gender differences in childhood amnesia. *Memory, 8*, 365–376.

Mackey, W. C. (2001). Support for the existence of an independent man-to-child affiliative bond: Fatherhood as a biocultural invention. *Psychology of Men and Masculinity, 2*, 51–66.

Mackintosh, V. H., Myers, B. J., & Kennon, S. S. (2006). Children of incarcerated mothers and their caregivers: Factors affecting the quality of their relationship. *Journal of Child and Family Studies, 15*, 581–596. doi:10.1007/s10826-006-9030-4

Macklem, G. L. (2008). *Practitioner's guide to emotion regulation in school-aged children*. New York, NY: Springer Science + Business Media.

Macklem G. L. (2011). *Evidence-based school mental health services: Affect education, emotion regulation training, and cognitive behavioral therapy*. New York, NY: Springer.

MacWhinney, B., & Chang, F. (1995). Connectionism and language learning. In C. Nelson (Ed.), *Basic and applied perspectives on learning, cognition, and development: The Minnesota Symposia on Child Psychology* (Vol. 28, pp. 33–57). Mahwah, NJ: Erlbaum.

Madden, K. L., Turnbull, D., Cyna, A. M., Adelson, P., & Wilkinson, C. (2013). Pain relief for childbirth: The preferences of pregnant women, midwives and obstetricians. *Women & Birth, 26*(1), 33–40. doi:10.1016/j.wombi.2011.12.002

Madden, N. A., & Slavin, R. E. (1983). Mainstreaming students with mild handicaps: Academic and social outcomes. *Review of Educational Research, 53*, 519–569.

Madsen, H. B., & Kim, J. H. (2016). Ontogeny of memory: An update on 40 years of work on infantile amnesia. *Behavioural Brain Research, 298*(Part A), 4–14. doi:10.1016/j.bbr.2015.07.030

Maehr, M. L., & Zusho, A. (2009). Achievement goal theory: The past, present, and future. In K. R. Wenzel & A. Wigfield (Eds.), *Handbook of motivation at school (Educational Psychology Handbook Series*, pp. 77–104). New York, NY: Routledge/Taylor & Francis Group.

Magnuson, K., & Berger, L. M. (2009). Family structure states and transitions: Associations with children's well-being during middle childhood. *Journal of Marriage and Family, 71*, 575–591.

Maguth, B. B., Boit, R., Muenz, L., & Smith, F. R. (2015). Grappling with death and loss through children's literature in the social studies. *Social Studies Research & Practice* (Board of Trustees of the University of Alabama), *10*(3), 80–87.

Mahaffy, K. A., & Ward, S. K. (2002). The gendering of adolescents' childbearing and educational plans: Reciprocal effects and the influence of social context. *Sex Roles, 46*, 403–417.

Mahn, H., & John-Steiner, V. (2013). Vygotsky and sociocultural approaches to teaching and learning. In W. M. Reynolds, G. E. Miller, & I. B. Weiner (Eds.), *Handbook of Psychology, Vol. 7. Educational psychology* (2nd ed., pp. 117–145). Hoboken, NJ: John Wiley & Sons Inc.

Mahoney J. L., & Parente, M. E. (2009). Should we care about adolescents who care for themselves? What we have learned and what we need to know about youth in self-care. *Child Development Perspectives*, 3, 189–195.

Mahony, L., Walsh, K., Lunn, J., & Petriwskyj, A. (2015). Teachers facilitating support for young children experiencing parental separation and divorce. *Journal of Child and Family Studies, 24*, 2841–2852. doi:10.1007/s10826-014-0088-0

Maier, M. A., Bernier, A., Pekrun, R., Zimmermann, P., & Grossmann, K. E. (2004). Attachment working models as unconscious structures: An experimental test. *International Journal of Behavioral Development, 28*, 180–189.

Maier, M., Vitiello, V., & Greenfield, D. (2012). A multilevel model of child- and classroom-level psychosocial factors that support language and literacy resilience of children in Head Start. *Early Childhood Research Quarterly, 27*(1), 104–114. doi:10.1016/j.ecresq.2011.06.002

Main, M., & Cassidy, J. (1988). Categories of response to reunion with the parent at age 6: Predictable from infant attachment classification and stable over a 1-month period. *Developmental Psychology, 24*, 415–426.

Main, M., & Solomon, J. (1986). Discovery of an insecure-disorganized/disoriented attachment pattern. In T. B. Brazelton & M. W. Yogman (Eds.), *Affective development in infancy* (pp. 95–124). Norwood, NJ: Ablex.

Main, M., & Solomon, J. (1990). Procedures for identifying infants as disorganized/disoriented during the Ainsworth Strange Situation. In M. T. Greenberg, D. Cicchetti, & E. M. Cummings (Eds.), *Attachment in the preschool years* (pp. 121–160). Chicago, IL: University of Chicago.

Main, M., Kaplan, N., & Cassidy, J. (1985). Security in infancy, childhood, and adulthood: A move to the level of representation. *Monographs of the Society for Research in Child Development, 50*, 66–104.

Majorano, M., Brondino, M., Morelli, M., & Maes, M. (2017). Quality of relationship with parents and emotional autonomy as predictors of self concept and loneliness in adolescents with learning disabilities: The moderating role of the relationship with teachers. *Journal of Child and Family Studies, 26*(3), 690-700. doi:10.1007/s10826-016-0591-6

Makarova, E., & Herzog, W. (2013). Hidden school dropout among immigrant students: a cross-sectional study. *Intercultural Education, 24*, 559–572. doi:10.1080/14675986.2013.867603

Maker, C. J. (1993). Creativity, intelligence, and problem solving: A definition and design for cross-cultural research and measurement related to giftedness. *Gifted Education International, 9*(2), 68–77.

Malatesta, C. Z., & Haviland, J. M. (1982). Learning display rules: The socialization of emotion expression in infancy. *Child Development, 53*, 991–1003.

Malboeuf-Hurtubise, C., Joussemet, M., Taylor, G., & Lacourse, E. (2018). Effects of a mindfulness-based intervention on the perception of basic psychological need satisfaction among special education students. *International Journal of Disability, Development and Education, 65*(1), 33–44.

Maldonado-Molina, M. M., Reingle, J. M., Tobler, A. L., Jennings, W. G., & Komro, K. A. (2010). Trajectories of physical aggression among Hispanic urban adolescents and young adults: An application of latent trajectory modeling from ages 12 to 18. *American Journal of Criminal Justice, 35*, 121–133. doi:10.1007/s12103-010-9074-2

Malinsky, K. P. (1997). Learning to be invisible: Female sexual minority students in America's public high schools. In M. B. Harris (Ed.), *School experiences of gay and lesbian youth: The invisible minority* (pp. 35–50). Binghamton, NY: Harrington Park Press.

Mallick, S. K., & McCandless, B. R. (1966). A study of catharsis of aggression. *Journal of Personality and Social Psychology, 4*, 591–596.

Malmberg, J., Järvenoja, H., & Järvelä, S. (2013). Patterns in elementary school students? strategic actions in varying learning situations. *Instructional Science, 41*, 933–954. doi:10.1007/s11251-012-9262-1

Malmberg, L. E., Stein, A., West, A., Simon, L., Barnes, J., Leach, P., . . . FCCC (2007). Parent–infant interaction: A growth model approach. *Infant Behavior and Development, 30*, 615–630.

Malone, A. A., & Fuchs, L. S. (2017). Error patterns in ordering fractions among at-risk fourth-grade students. *Journal of Learning Disabilities, 50*, 337–352. doi:10.1177/0022219416629647

Malone, D. M., Stoneham, Z., & Langone, J. (1995). Contextual variation of correspondences among measures of play and developmental level of preschool children. *Journal of Early Intervention, 18*, 199–215.

Malti, T., Chaparro, M. P., Zuffianò, A., & Colasante, T. (2016). School-based interventions to promote empathy-related responding in children and adolescents: A developmental analysis. *Journal of Clinical Child & Adolescent Psychology, 45*, 718–731. doi:10.1080/15374416.2015.1121822

Malti, T., Eisenberg, N., Kim, H., & Buchmann, M. (2013). Developmental trajectories of sympathy, moral emotion attributions, and moral reasoning: The role of parental support. *Social Development, 22*, 773–793. doi:10.1111/sode.12031

Mana, A., Orr, E., & Mana, Y. (2009). An integrated acculturation model of immigrants' social identity. *Journal of Social Psychology, 149*, 450–473.

Mandel, D. R., Jusczyk, P. W., & Pisoni, D. B. (1995). Infants' recognition of the sound patterns of their own names. *Psychological Science, 6*, 314–317.

Mandel, E., Osana, H., & Venkatesh, V. (2013). Addressing the effects of reciprocal teaching on the receptive and expressive vocabulary of 1st-grade students. *Journal of Research in Childhood Education, 27*, 407–426. doi:10.1080/02568543.2013.824526

Mandler, J. M. (2007a). The conceptual foundations of animals and artifacts. In E. Margolis & S. Laurence (Eds.), *Creations of the mind: Theories of artifacts and their representation* (pp. 191–211). New York, NY: Oxford University Press.

Mandler, J. M., Fivush, R., & Reznick, J. S. (1987). The development of contextual categories. *Cognitive Development, 2*, 339–354.

Manfra, L., Dinehart, L., & Sembiante, S. (2014). Associations between counting ability in preschool and mathematic performance in first grade among a sample of ethnically diverse, low-income children. *Journal of Research in Childhood Education, 28*(1), 101–114. doi:10.1080/02568543.2013.850129

Mangelsdorf, S. C., Shapiro, J. R., & Marzolf, D. (1995). Developmental and temperamental differences in emotion regulation in infancy. *Child Development, 66*, 1817–1828.

Manning, W. D. (2015). Cohabitation and child wellbeing. *Future of Children, 25*(2), 51–66.

Mannion, A., Leader, G., & Healy, O. (2013). An investigation of comorbid psychological disorders, sleep problems, gastrointestinal symptoms and epilepsy in children and adolescents with autism spectrum disorder. *Research in Autism Spectrum Disorders, 7*(1), 35–42. doi:10.1016/j.rasd.2012.05.002

Manolitsis, G., Georgiou, G. K., & Parrila, R. (2011). Revisiting the home literacy model of reading development in an orthographically consistent language. *Learning & Instruction, 21*, 496–505. doi:10.1016/j.learninstruc.2010.06.005

Manuel, A., & Wade, T. D. (2013). Emotion regulation in broadly defined anorexia nervosa: Association with negative affective memory bias. *Behaviour Research and Therapy, 51*, 417–424. doi:10.1016/j.brat.2013.04.005

Manzi, C., Ferrari, L., Rosnati, R., & Benet-Martinez, V. (2014). Bicultural identity integration of transracial adolescent adoptees: Antecedents and outcomes. *Journal of Cross-Cultural Psychology, 45*, 888–904.

Maoz, H., Tsviban, L., Gvirts, H., Shamay-Tsoory, S., Levkovitz, Y., Watemberg, N., & Bloch, Y. (2014). Stimulants improve theory of mind in children with attention deficit/hyperactivity disorder. *Journal of Psychopharmacology, 28*, 212–219. doi:10.1177/0269881113492030

Mar, R. A., & Oatley, K. (2008). The function of fiction is the abstraction and simulation of social experience. *Perspectives on Psychological Science, 3*, 173–192.

Maraj, B. K. V., & Bonertz, C. M. (2007). Verbal-motor learning in children with Down syndrome. *Journal of Sport and Exercise Psychology, 29* (Suppl.), 108.

March of Dimes. (2013). *Chromosomal abnormalities. Healthy babies, Healthy business quick references and fact sheets.* Retrieved from http://www.marchofdimes.com/hbhb_syndication/15530_1209.asp

Marchand, G. C., & Taasoobshirazi, G. (2013). Stereotype threat and women's performance in physics. *International Journal of Science Education, 35*, 3050–3061. doi:10.1080/09500693.2012.683461

Marchand, G., & Skinner, E. A. (2007). Motivational dynamics of children's help-seeking and concealment. *Journal of Educational Psychology, 99*, 65–82.

Marcia, J. (1991). Identity and self-development. In R. M. Lerner, A. C. Petersen, & J. Brooks-Gunn (Eds.), *Encyclopedia of adolescence* (Vol. 1, pp. 529–533). New York, NY: Garland.

Marcia, J. E. (1980). Identity in adolescence. In J. Adelson (Ed.), *Handbook of adolescent psychology* (pp. 159–177). New York, NY: Wiley.

Marcia, J. E. (1988). Common processes underlying ego identity, cognitive/moral development, and individuation. In D. K. Lapsley & F. C. Power (Eds.), *Self, ego, and identity: Integrative approaches* (pp. 211–225). New York, NY: Springer-Verlag.

Marcia, J., & Josselson, R. (2013). Eriksonian personality research and its implications for psychotherapy. *Journal of Personality, 81*, 617–629. doi:10.1111/jopy.12014

Marcovitch, S., Goldberg, S., Gold, A., Washington, J., Wasson, C., Krekewich, K., & Handley-Derry, M. (1997). Determinants of behavioral problems in Romanian children adopted in Ontario. *International Journal of Behavioral Development, 20*, 17–31.

Marcus, G. F. (1996). Why do children say "breaked"? *Current Directions in Psychological Science, 5*, 81–85.

Marcus, G. F., Vijayan, S., Bandi Rao, S., & Vishton, P. M. (1999). Rule learning by seven-month-old infants. *Science, 283*, 77–80.

Mares, M., Palmer, E., & Sullivan, T. (2008). Prosocial effects of media exposure. In S. L. Calvert, & B. J. Wilson (Eds.), *The handbook of children, media, and development. Handbooks in communication and media* (pp. 268–289). Malden, MA: Blackwell. doi:10.1002/9781444302752.ch12

Mares, S. H. W., de Leeuw, R. N. H., Scholte, R. H. J., & Engels, R. C. M. E. (2010). Facial attractiveness and self-esteem in adolescence. *Journal of Clinical Child and Adolescent Psychology, 39*, 627–637.

Marin, S. E., & Saneto, R. P. (2016). Neuropsychiatric features in primary mitochondrial disease. *Neurologic Clinics, 34*, 247–294. doi:10.1016/j.ncl.2015.08.011

Marinak, B. A., & Gambrell, L. B. (2010). Reading motivation: Exploring the elementary gender gap. *Literacy Research and Instruction, 49*, 129–141.

Markman, E. M. (1979). Realizing that you don't understand: Elementary school children's awareness of inconsistencies. *Child Development, 50*, 643–655.

Markman, E. M. (1989). *Categorization and naming in children: Problems of induction.* Cambridge, MA: MIT Press.

Markova, G., & Legerstee, M. (2012). Social pretence with mothers and peers at 15 months. *European Journal of Developmental Psychology, 9*, 711–722. doi:10.1080/17405629.2012.671714

Markovits, H., Brisson, J., de Chantal, P.-L., & St-Onge, C. M. (2016). Elementary school-children know a logical argument when they see one. *Journal of Cognitive Psychology, 28*, 877–883. doi:10.1080/20445911.2016.1189918

Marks, D. F. (2011). IQ variations across time, race, and nationality: An artifact of differences in literacy skills. *Counselor Education and Supervision, 50*, 643–664.

Markstrom, C. A., Huey, E., Stiles, B. M., & Krause, A. L. (2010). Frameworks of caring and helping in adolescence: Are empathy, religiosity, and spirituality related constructs? *Youth & Society, 42*(1), 59–80. doi:10.1177/0044118X09333644

Markus, H. R., & Hamedani, M. G. (2007). Sociocultural psychology: The dynamic interdependence among self systems and social systems. In S. Kitayama & D. Cohen (Eds.), *Handbook of cultural psychology* (pp. 3–39). New York, NY: Guilford Press.

Marquez, B., Marquez, J., Vincent, C. G., Pennefather, J., Sprague, J. R., Smolkowski, K., & Yeaton, P. (2014). The iterative development and initial evaluation of We Have Skills! An innovative approach to teaching social skills to elementary students. *Education & Treatment of Children, 37*(1), 137–161.

Marques, S. C. F., Oliveira, C. R., Pereira, C. M. F., & Outeiro, T. F. (2011). Epigenetics in neurodegeneration: A new layer of complexity. Progress in Neuro *Psychopharmacology & Biological Psychiatry, 35*(2), 348–355. doi:10.1016/j.pnpbp.2010.08.008

Marsh, H. W. (1990a). Causal ordering of academic self-concept and academic achievement: A multiwave, longitudinal panel analysis. *Journal of Educational Psychology, 82*, 646–656.

Marsh, H. W. (1990b). A multidimensional, hierarchical model of self-concept: Theoretical and empirical justification. *Educational Psychology Review, 2*, 77–172.

Marsh, H. W., & Craven, R. (1997). Academic self-concept: Beyond the dustbowl. In G. D. Phye (Ed.), *Handbook of classroom assessment: Learning, achievement, and adjustment* (pp. 131–198). San Diego, CA: Academic Press.

Marsh, H. W., & Hau, K.-T. (2003). Big-fish–little-pond effect on academic self-concept: A cross-cultural (26-country) test of the negative effects of academically selective schools. *American Psychologist, 58*, 364–376.

Marsh, H. W., Parada, R. H., Yeung, A. S., & Healey, J. (2001). Aggressive school trouble-makers and victims: A longitudinal model examining the pivotal role of self-concept. *Journal of Educational Psychology, 93*, 411–419.

Marsh, H. W., Pekrun, R., Murayama, K., Arens, A. K., Parker, P. D., Guo, J., & Dicke, T. (2018). An integrated model of academic self-concept development: Academic self-concept, grades, test scores, and tracking over 6 years. *Developmental Psychology, 54*, 263–280. http://dx.doi.org.unco.idm.oclc.org/10.1037/dev0000393

Marshall, E., & Toohey, K. (2010). Representing family: Community funds of knowledge, bilingualism, and multimodality. *Harvard Educational Review, 80*, 221–241.

Marshall, N. A., Marusak, H. A., Sala-Hamrick, K. J., Crespo, L. M., Rabinak, C. A., & Thomason, M. E. (2018). Socioeconomic disadvantage and altered corticostriatal circuitry in urban youth. *Human Brain Mapping*. Advance online publication.

Marshall, N. L. (2004). The quality of early child care and children's development. *Current Directions in Psychological Science, 13*, 165–168.

Marshall, S. L., Parker, P. D., Ciarrochi, J., & Heaven, P. L. (2014). Is self-esteem a cause or consequence of social support? A 4-year longitudinal study. *Child Development, 85*, 1275–1291. doi:10.1111/cdev.12176

Martens, R., de Brabander, C., Rozendaal, J., Boekaerts, M., & van der Leeden, R. (2010). Inducing mind sets in self-regulated learning with motivational information. *Educational Studies, 36*, 311–327. doi:10.1080/03055690903424915

Martin, C. L., & Ruble, D. N. (2010). Patterns of gender development. *Annual Review of Psychology, 61*, 353–381. doi:10.1146/annurev.psych.093008.100511

Martin, J. L. (2009). Formation and stabilization of vertical hierarchies among adolescents: Towards a quantitative ethology of dominance among humans. *Social Psychology Quarterly, 72*, 241–264. doi:10.1177/019027250907200307

Martin, J., & Sokol, B. (2011). Generalized others and imaginary audiences: A neo-Meadian approach to adolescent egocentrism. *New Ideas in Psychology, 29*, 364–375. doi:10.1016/j.newideapsych.2010.03.006

Martin, K. A., & Torres, J. C. (2014). Where did I come from? US parents' and preschool children's participation in sexual socialisation. *Sex Education, 14*, 174–190. doi:10.1080/14681811.2013.856291

Martin, L., & Smolen, L. (2010). Using citizenship education, adolescent literature, and service learning to promote social justice. *International Journal of Learning, 17*, 425–432.

Martínez-Álvarez, P., & Ghiso, M. P. (2017). On languaging and communities: Latino/a emergent bilinguals' expansive learning and critical inquiries into global childhoods. *International Journal of Bilingual Education & Bilingualism, 20*, 667–687. doi:10.1080/13670050.2015.1068270

Martinez, C. R., & Forgatch, M. S. (2001). Preventing problems with boys' noncompliance: Effects of a parent-training intervention for divorcing mothers. *Journal of Consulting and Clinical Psychology, 69*, 416–428.

Martino, S. C., Ellickson, P. L., Klein, D. J., McCaffrey, D., & Edelen, M. O. (2008). Multiple trajectories of physical aggression among adolescent boys and girls. *Aggressive Behavior, 34*, 61–75.

Maruši, ć. M., & Sliško, J. (2012). Influence of three different methods of teaching physics on the gain in students' development of reasoning. *International Journal of Science Education, 34*, 301–326. doi:10.1080/09500693.2011.582522

Marzecová, A., Bukowski, M., Correa, Á., Boros, M., Lupiáñez, J., & Wodniecka, Z. (2013). Tracing the bilingual advantage in cognitive control: The role of flexibility in temporal preparation and category switching. *Journal of Cognitive Psychology, 25*, 586–604. doi:10.1080/20445911.2013.809348

Masataka, N. (1992). Pitch characteristics of Japanese maternal speech to infants. *Journal of Child Language, 19*, 213–224.

Maschinot, B. (2008). *The changing face of the United States: The influence of culture on early child development*. Washington, DC: Zero to Three.

Mascolo, M. F., & Fischer, K. W. (2015). Dynamic development of thinking, feeling, and acting. In W. F. Overton, P. C. M. Molenaar, & R. M. Lerner (Eds.), *Handbook of child psychology and developmental science: Theory and method* (pp. 113–161). Hoboken, NJ: Wiley. doi:10.1002/9781118963418.childpsy104

Mascolo, M. F., van Geert, P., Steenbeek, H., & Fischer, K. W. (2016). What can dynamic systems models of development offer to the study of developmental psychopathology? In D. Cicchetti (Ed.), *Developmental psychopathology: Theory and method* (pp. 665–716). Hoboken, NJ: Wiley.

Mash, C., Bornstein, M. H., & Banerjee, A. (2014). Development of object control in the first year: Emerging category discrimination and generalization in infants' adaptive selection of action. *Developmental Psychology, 50*, 325–335. doi:10.1037/a0033234

Mason, L. (2003). Personal epistemologies and intentional conceptual change. In G. M. Sinatra & P. R. Pintrich (Eds.), *Intentional conceptual change* (pp. 199–236). Mahwah, NJ: Erlbaum.

Massey, C. M., & Gelman, R. (1988). Preschoolers' ability to decide whether a photographed unfamiliar object can move itself. *Developmental Psychology, 24*, 307–317.

Massey, S. L. (2013). From the reading rug to the play center: Enhancing vocabulary and comprehensive language skills by connecting storybook reading and guided play. *Early Childhood Education Journal, 41*, 125–131. doi:10.1007/s10643-012-0524-y

Massimini, K. (2000). *Genetic disorders sourcebook* (2nd ed.). Detroit, MI: Omnigraphics.

Masur, E. F., McIntyre, C. W., & Flavell, J. H. (1973). Developmental changes in apportionment of study time among items in a multitrial free recall task. *Journal of Experimental Child Psychology, 15*, 237–246.

Mather, N. (2009). The intelligent testing of children with specific learning disabilities. In J. C. Kaufman (Ed.), *Intelligent testing: Integrating psychological theory and clinical practice* (pp. 30–52). New York, NY: Cambridge University Press.

Matheson, C., Olsen, R. J., & Weisner, T. (2007). A good friend is hard to find: Friendship among adolescents with disabilities. *American Journal on Mental Retardation, 112*, 319–329.

Mathieson, K., & Banerjee, R. (2010). Pre-school peer play: The beginnings of social competence. *Educational and Child Psychology. Special Issue: In-School Relationships and their Outcomes, 27*(1), 9–20.

Matjasko, J. L., Needham, B. L., Grunden, L. N., & Farb, A. F. (2010). Violent victimization and perpetration during adolescence: Developmental stage dependent ecological models. *Journal of Youth and Adolescence, 39*, 1053–1066. doi:10.1007/s10964-010-9508-7

Matson, J. L., & Fodstad, J. C. (2010). Teaching social skills to developmentally delayed preschoolers. In C. E. Schaefer (Ed.), *Play therapy for preschool children* (pp. 301–322). Washington, DC: American Psychological Association.

Matsuyama, A., & Moji, K. (2008). Perception of bleeding as a danger sign during pregnancy, delivery, and the postpartum period in rural Nepal. *Qualitative Health Research, 18*, 196–208.

Matthews, D. J. (2009). Developmental transitions in giftedness and talent: Childhood into adolescence. In F. D. Horowitz, R. F. Subotnik, & D. J. Matthews (Eds.), *The development of giftedness and talent across the life span* (pp. 89–107). Washington, DC: American Psychological Association.

Matthews, D., Lieven, E., & Tomasello, M. (2007). How toddlers and preschoolers learn to uniquely identify referents for others: A training study. *Child Development, 78*, 1744–1759.

Matvienko-Sikar, K., Lee, L., Murphy, G., & Murphy, L. (2016). The effects of mindfulness interventions on prenatal well-being: A systematic review. *Psychology & Health, 31*, 1415–1434. doi:10.1080/08870446.2016.1220557

Maulana, R., Opdenakker, M., & Bosker, R. (2014). Teacher-student interpersonal relationships do change and affect academic motivation: A multilevel growth curve modelling. *British Journal of Educational Psychology, 84*, 459–482. doi:10.1111/bjep.12031

Mavilidi, M.-F., Okely, A. D., Chandler, P., & Paas, F. (2016). Infusing physical activities into the classroom: Effects on preschool children's geography learning. *Mind, Brain, and Education, 10*, 256–263. doi:10.1111/mbe.12131

Mayer, D. L., & Dobson, V. (1982). Visual acuity development in infants and young children, as assessed by operant preferential looking. *Vision Research, 22*, 1141–1151.

Mayer, D., Sodian, B., Koerber, S., & Schwippert, K. (2014). Scientific reasoning in elementary school children: Assessment and relations with cognitive abilities. *Learning & Instruction, 29*, 43–55. doi:10.1016/j.learninstruc.2013.07.005

Mayer, R. E. (2004). Should there be a three-strikes rule against pure discovery learning? *American Psychologist, 59*, 14–19.

Mayer, R. E. (2010). Fostering scientific reasoning with multimedia instruction. In H. S. Waters & W. Schneider (Eds.), *Metacognition, strategy use, and instruction* (pp. 160–175). New York, NY: Guilford Press.

Mayer, R. E. (2012). Information processing. In K. R. Harris, S. Graham, T. Urdan, C. B. McCormick, G. M. Sinatra, & J. Sweller (Eds.), *APA Educational Psychology Handbook, Vol. 1. Theories, constructs, and critical issues* (pp. 85–99). Washington, DC: American Psychological Association. doi:10.1037/13273-004

Mayer, S. J. (2005). The early evolution of Jean Piaget's clinical method. *History of Psychology, 8*, 362–382. doi:10.1037/1093-4510.8.4.362

Mayes, L. C., & Bornstein, M. H. (1997). The development of children exposed to cocaine. In S. S. Luthar, J. A. Burack, D. Cicchetti, & J. R. Weisz (Eds.), *Developmental psychopathology: Perspectives on adjustment, risk, and disorder* (pp. 166–188). Cambridge, England: Cambridge University Press.

Maynard, A. E. (2002). Cultural teaching: The development of teaching skills in Maya sibling interactions. *Child Development, 73*, 969–982.

Maynard, A. E. (2008). What we thought we knew and how we came to know it: Four decades of cross-cultural research from a Piagetian point of view. *Human Development, 51*, 56–65.

Mayseless, O. (2005). Ontogeny of attachment in middle childhood: Conceptualization of normative changes. In K. A. Kerns & R. A. Richardson (Eds.), *Attachment in middle childhood* (pp. 1–23). New York, NY: Guilford Press.

Mayworm, A. M., & Sharkey, J. D. (2014). Ethical considerations in a three-tiered approach to school discipline policy and practice. *Psychology in the Schools, 51*(7), 693-704. doi:10.1002/pits.21782

Mazzone, A., Camodeca, M., & Salmivalli, C. (2018). Stability and change of outsider behavior in school bullying: The role of shame and guilt in a longitudinal perspective. *The Journal of Early Adolescence, 38*, 164–177. http://dx.doi.org.unco.idm.oclc.org/10.1177/0272431616659560

McAdams, D. P., & McLean, K. C. (2013). Narrative identity. *Current Directions in Psychological Science, 22*, 233–238.

McAlister, A., & Peterson, C. (2013). Siblings, theory of mind, and executive functioning in children aged 3-6 years: New longitudinal evidence. *Child Development, 84*, 1442–1458. doi:10.1111/cdev.12043

McAlpine, L., & Taylor, D. M. (1993). Instructional preferences of Cree, Inuit, and Mohawk teachers. *Journal of American Indian Education, 33*(1), 1–20.

McBride-Chang, C., & Treiman, R. (2003). Hong Kong Chinese kindergartners learn to read English analytically. *Psychological Science, 14*, 138–143.

McBrien, J. L. (2005a). *Discrimination and academic motivation in adolescent refugee girls* (Unpublished doctoral dissertation). Emory University, Atlanta, GA. *Dissertation Abstracts International Section A: Humanities and Social Sciences, 66*(5-A), 2055, 1602.

McBrien, J. L. (2005b). Educational needs and barriers for refugee students in the United States: A review of the literature. *Review of Educational Research, 75*, 329–364.

McCabe, A., Tamis-Lemonda, C. S., Bornstein, M. H., Cates, C. B., Golinkoff, R., Guerra, A. W., . . . Song, L. (2013). Multilingual children: Beyond myths and toward best practices. *Social Policy Support, 27*(4).

McCall, R. B. (1993). Developmental functions for general mental performance. In D. K. Detterman (Ed.), *Current topics in human intelligence* (Vol. 3, pp. 3–29). Norwood, NJ: Ablex.

McCall, R. B., Kennedy, C. B., & Applebaum, M. I. (1977). Magnitude of discrepancy and the distribution of attention in infants. *Child Development, 48*, 772–786.

McCallum, R., & Bracken, B. A. (2012). The Universal Nonverbal Intelligence Test: A multidimensional nonverbal alternative for cognitive assessment. In D. P. Flanagan & P. L. Harrison (Eds.), *Contemporary intellectual assessment: Theories, tests, and issues* (3rd ed., pp. 357–375). New York, NY: Guilford Press.

McCann, T. M. (1989). Student argumentative writing knowledge and ability at three grade levels. *Research in the Teaching of English, 23*, 62–72.

McCarney, D., Peters, L., Jackson, S., Thomas, M., & Kirby, A. (2013). Does poor handwriting conceal literacy potential in primary school children? *International Journal of Disability, Development & Education, 60*, 105–118. doi:10.1080/1034912X.2013.786561

McCarthy, M., & Kuh, G. D. (2005, September 9). Student engagement: A missing link in improving high schools. *Teachers College Record, 87*, 664–669.

McCaslin, M., & Good, T. L. (1996). The informal curriculum. In D. C. Berliner & R. C. Calfee (Eds.), *Handbook of educational psychology* (pp. 622–670). New York, NY: Macmillan.

McClain, D., Schmertzing, L., & Schmertzing, R. (2012). Priming the pump: Implementing Response to Intervention in preschool. *Rural Special Education Quarterly, 31*(1), 33–45.

McClelland, J. L. (2001). Failures to learn and their remediation: A Hebbian account. In J. L. McClelland & R. S. Siegler (Eds.), *Mechanisms of cognitive development: Behavioral and neural perspectives* (pp. 97–121). Mahwah, NJ: Erlbaum.

McClelland, J. L., Fiez, J. A., & McCandliss, B. D. (2002). Teaching the /r/–/l/ discrimination to Japanese adults: Behavioral and neural aspects. *Physiology and Behavior, 77*, 657–662.

McClelland, M. M., Geldhof, G. J., Cameron, C. E., & Wanless, S. B. (2015). Development and self-regulation. In W. F. Overton, P. C. M. Molenaar, & R. M. Lerner (Eds.), *Handbook of child psychology and developmental science: Theory and method* (pp. 523–565). Hoboken, NJ: Wiley.

McCloskey, M. (1983). Naïve theories of motion. In D. Genter & A. L. Stevens (Eds.), *Mental models* (pp. 299–324). Hillsdale, NJ: Erlbaum.

McCloskey, R. (1948). *Blueberries for Sal*. New York, NY: Viking Press.

McClowry, S., Rodriguez, E., Tamis-LeMonda, C., Spellmann, M., Carlson, A., & Snow, D. (2013). Teacher/student interactions and classroom behavior: The role of student temperament and gender. *Journal of Research in Childhood Education, 27*, 283–301. doi:10.1080/02568543.2013.796330

McCombs, B. L., & Vakili, D. (2005). A learner-centered framework for e-learning. *Teachers College Record, 107*, 1582–1600.

McConney, M., & Perry, M. (2011). A change in questioning tactics: prompting student autonomy. *Investigations in Mathematics Learning, 3*(3), 26–45.

McCormick, M. M., O'Connor, E. E., & Parham Horn, E. (2017). Can teacher-child relationships alter the effects of early socioeconomic status on achievement in middle childhood? *Journal of School Psychology, 64*, 76–92. doi:10.1016/j.jsp.2017.05.001

McCormick, M. M., O'Connor, E. E., Cappella, E., & McClowry, S. G. (2013). Teacher–child relationships and academic achievement: A multilevel propensity score model approach. *Journal of School Psychology, 51*(5), 611-624. doi:10.1016/j.jsp.2013.05.001

McCoy, K. (1994). *Understanding your teenager's depression*. New York, NY: Perigee.

McCrink, K., & Wynn, K. (2004). Large-number addition and subtraction by 9-month-old infants. *Psychological Science, 15*, 776–781.

McCrink, K., & Wynn, K. (2007). Ratio abstraction by 6-month-old infants. *Psychological Science, 18*, 740–745.

McCullough, M. E., Kurzban, R., & Tabak, B. A. (2011). Evolved mechanisms for revenge and forgiveness. In P. R. Shaver & M. Mikulincer (Eds.), *Human aggression and violence: Causes, manifestations, and consequences (Herzilya Series on Personality and Social Psychology*, pp. 221–239). Washington, DC: American Psychological Association. doi:10.1037/12346-012

McCutchen, D. (1987). Children's discourse skill: Form and modality requirements of schooled writing. *Discourse Processes, 10*, 267–286.

McDevitt, M., & Kiousis, S. (2015). Active political parenting: Youth contributions during election campaigns. *Social Science Quarterly*, 96(1), 19–33.

McDevitt, M., & Ostrowski, A. (2009). The adolescent unbound: Unintentional influence of curricula and ideological conflict seeking. *Political Communication, 26*(1), 11–29. doi:10.1080/10584600802622811

McDevitt, T. M. (1990). Encouraging young children's listening skills. *Academic Therapy, 25*, 569–577.

McDevitt, T. M., & Ford, M. E. (1987). Processes in young children's communicative functioning and development. In M. E. Ford & D. H. Ford (Eds.), *Humans as self-constructing systems: Putting the framework to work* (pp. 145–175). Hillsdale, NJ: Erlbaum.

McDevitt, T. M., Jobes, R. D., Sheehan, E. P., & Cochran, K. (2010). Is it nature of nurture? Beliefs about child development held by students in psychology courses. *College Student Journal, 44*, 533–550.

McDevitt, T. M., Spivey, N., Sheehan, E. P., Lennon, R., & Story, R. (1990). Children's beliefs about listening: Is it enough to be still and quiet? *Child Development, 61*, 713–721.

McDonald, K. L., Baden, R. E., & Lochman, J. E. (2013). Parenting influences on the social goals of aggressive children. *Applied Developmental Science, 17*(1), 29–38. doi:10.1080/10888691.2013.748423

McDonald, K. L., Malti, T., Killen, M., & Rubin, K. H. (2014). Best friends' discussions of social dilemmas. *Journal of Youth and Adolescence, 43*, 233–244. doi:10.1007/s10964-013-9961-1

McDonald, K. L., Malti, T., Killen, M., & Rubin, K. H. (2014). Best friends' discussions of social dilemmas. *Journal of Youth and Adolescence, 43*(2), 233–244. doi:10.1007/s10964-013-9961-1

McDonald, S. E., Dmitrieva, J., Shin, S., Hitti, S. A., Graham-Bermann, S. A., Ascione, F. R., & Williams, J. H. (2017). The role of callous/unemotional traits in mediating the association between animal abuse exposure and behavior problems among children exposed to intimate partner violence. *Child Abuse & Neglect, 72*, 421–432. http://dx.doi.org.unco.idm.oclc.org/10.1016/j.chiabu.2017.09.004

McDougall, P., & Hymel, S. (2007). Same-gender versus cross-gender friendship conceptions: Similar or different? *Merrill-Palmer Quarterly, 53*, 347–380. doi:10.1353/mpq.2007.0018

McDuffie, A., Thurman, A. J., Channell, M. M., & Abbeduto, L. (2017). Learning words in a social world: Impairments associated with ASD and fragile X syndrome. In L. R. Naigles (Ed.), *Language and the human lifespan series. Innovative investigations of language in autism spectrum disorder* (pp. 71-87). Washington, DC, US: American Psychological Association; Berlin, Germany: Walter de Gruyter GmbH.

McGee, E., & Spencer, M. (2014). The development of coping skills for science, technology, engineering, and mathematics students: Transitioning from minority to majority environments. In C. Camp Yeakey, V. L. Sanders Thompson, & A. Wells (Eds.), *Urban ills: Twenty-first-century complexities of urban living in global contexts* (Vol. 1, pp. 351–378). Lanham, MD: Lexington Books/Rowman & Littlefield.

McGee, E., & Spencer, M. B. (2015). Black parents as advocates, motivators, and teachers of mathematics. *Journal of Negro Education, 84*, 473–490. doi:10.7709/jnegroeducation.84.3.0473

McGeown, S., & Medford, E. (2014). Using method of instruction to predict the skills supporting initial reading development: insight from a synthetic phonics approach. *Reading & Writing, 27*, 591–608. doi:10.1007/s11145-013-9460-5

McGill, R. J. (2015). Review of Cognitive Assessment System—second edition (2nd ed.). [Review of the software Cognitive Assessment System—Second Edition (2nd ed.). J. A. Naglieri, J. P. Das & S. Goldstein]. *Journal of Psychoeducational Assessment, 33*, 375–380. http://dx.doi.org/10.1177/0734282914566123

McGillicuddy, D. d., & Devine, D. (2018). "Turned off" or "ready to fly" – Ability grouping as an act of symbolic violence in primary school. *Teaching & Teacher Education, 70* 88–99. doi:10.1016/j.tate.2017.11.008

McGillion, M., Pine, J. M., Herbert, J. S., & Matthews, D. (2017). A randomised controlled trial to test the effect of promoting caregiver contingent talk on language development in infants from diverse socioeconomic status backgrounds. *Journal of Child Psychology and Psychiatry, 58*, 1122–1131.http://dx.doi.org/10.1111/jcpp.12725

McGowan, D. (2007). *Parenting beyond belief: On raising ethical, caring kids without religion.* New York, NY: AMACOM.

McGrady, P. B., & Reynolds, J. R. (2013). Racial mismatch in the classroom: Beyond black-white differences. *Sociology of Education, 86*(1), 3–17. doi:10.1177/0038040712444857

McGregor, H. R., & Gribble, P. L. (2015). Changes in visual and sensory-motor resting-state functional connectivity support motor learning by observing. *Journal of Neurophysiology, 114*, 677–688. http://dx.doi.org.unco.idm.oclc.org/10.1152/jn.00286.2015

McGrew, K. S. (2005). The Cattell-Horn-Carroll theory of cognitive abilities: Past, present, and future. In D. P. Flanagan & P. L. Harrison (Eds.), *Contemporary intellectual assessment: Theories, tests, and issues* (2nd ed., pp. 136–181). New York, NY: Guilford Press.

McGue, M., Bouchard, T. J., Jr., Iacono, W. G., & Lykken, D. T. (1993). Behavioral genetics of cognitive ability: A life-span perspective. In R. Plomin & G. E. McClearn (Eds.), *Nature, nurture, and psychology* (pp. 59–76). Washington, DC: American Psychological Association.

McGuire, J. K., Anderson, C. R., Toomey, R. B., & Russell, S. T. (2010). School climate for transgender youth: A mixed method investigation of student experiences and school responses. *Journal of Youth and Adolescence, 39*, 1175–1188. doi:10.1007/s10964-010-9540-7

McHale, J. P., & Rasmussen, J. L. (1998). Coparental and family group-level dynamics during infancy: Early family precursors of child and family functioning during preschool. *Development and Psychopathology, 10*, 39–59.

McHugh, M. T., Kvernland, A., & Palusci, V. J. (2015). An adolescent parents' programme to reduce child abuse. *Child Abuse Review.* Advance online publication. doi:10.1002/car.2426

McKenzie, J. K. (1993). Adoption of children with special needs. *The Future of Children, 3*(1), 26–42.

McKeough, A. (1995). Teaching narrative knowledge for transfer in the early school years. In A. McKeough, J. Lupart, & A. Marini (Eds.), *Teaching for transfer: Fostering generalization in learning* (pp. 156–176). Mahwah, NJ: Erlbaum.

McKie, B. K., Butty, J., & Green, R. D. (2012). Reading, reasoning, and literacy: Strategies for early childhood education from the analysis of classroom observations. *Early Childhood Education Journal, 40*(1), 55–61. doi:10.1007/s10643-011-0489-2

McKinlay, A., Grace, R. C., Horwood, L. J., Fergusson, D. M., Ridder, E. M., & MacFarlane, M. R. (2008). Prevalence of traumatic brain injury among children, adolescents and young adults: Prospective evidence from a birth cohort. *Brain Injury, 22*, 175–181.

McKown, C., & Weinstein, R. S. (2002). Modeling the role of child ethnicity and gender in children's differential response to teacher expectations. *Journal of Applied Social Psychology, 32*, 159–184.

McLachlan, C., & Arrow, A. (2013). Promoting alphabet knowledge and phonological awareness in low socioeconomic child care settings: A quasi experimental study in five New Zealand centers. *Reading and Writing, 27*, 819–839. doi:10.1007/s11145-013-9467-y

McLane, J. B., & McNamee, G. D. (1990). *Early literacy.* Cambridge, MA: Harvard University Press.

McLoyd, V. C. (1998a). Children in poverty: Development, public policy, and practice. In W. Damon (Series Ed.), & I. E. Sigel, & K. A. Renninger (Vol. Eds.), *Handbook of Child Psychology: Vol. 4. Child psychology in practice* (5th ed., pp. 135–208). New York, NY: Wiley.

McLoyd, V. C. (1998b). Socioeconomic disadvantage and child development. *American Psychologist, 53*, 185–204.

McLoyd, V. C., Kaplan, R., Purtell, K. M., Bagley, E., Hardaway, C. R., & Smalls, C. (2009). Poverty and socioeconomic disadvantage in adolescence. In R. M. Lerner & L. Steinberg (Eds.), *Handbook of Adolescent Psychology. Vol. 2. Contextual influences on adolescent development* (3rd ed., pp. 444–491). Hoboken, NJ: Wiley.

McMahon, S. (1992). Book club: A case study of a group of fifth graders as they participate in a literature-based reading program. *Reading Research Quarterly, 27*, 292–294.

McMillan, B. (2013). Inuit legends, oral histories, art, and science in the collaborative development of lessons that foster two-way learning: The return of the sun in Nunavut. *Interchange, 43*, 129–145. doi: 10.1007/s10780-013-9189-8

McMillan, J., & Jarvis, J. (2013). Mental health and students with disabilities: A review of literature. *Australian Journal of Guidance & Counselling, 23*, 236–251. doi:10.1017/jgc.2013.14

McMurray, B., Horst, J. S., & Samuelson, L. K. (2012). Word learning emerges from the interaction of online referent selection and slow associative learning. *Psychological Review, 119*, 831–877. doi:10.1037/a0029872

McMurray, B., Kovack-Lesh, K., Goodwin, D., & McEchron, W. (2013). Infant directed speech and the development of speech perception: Enhancing development or an unintended consequence? *Cognition, 129*, 362–378. doi:10.1016/j.cognition.2013.07.015

McNally, S. S., & Slutsky, R. (2018). Teacher–child relationships make all the difference: constructing quality interactions in early childhood settings. *Early Child Development & Care, 188*, 508–523. doi:10.1080/03004430.2017.1417854

McNeill, B., & Kirk, C. (2014). Theoretical beliefs and instructional practices used for teaching spelling in elementary classrooms. *Reading & Writing, 27*, 535–554. doi:10.1007/s11145-013-9457-0

McNeill, D. (1966). Developmental psycholinguistics. In F. Smith & G. A. Miller (Eds.), *The genesis of language* (pp. 15–84). Cambridge, MA: MIT Press.

McNeill, D. (1970). *The acquisition of language: The study of developmental psycholinguistics.* NewYork, New York: Harper & Row.

Meadan, H., Angell, M. E., Stoner, J. B., & Daczewitz, M. E. (2014). Parent-implemented social-pragmatic communication intervention: A pilot study. *Focus on Autism & Other Developmental Disabilities, 29*, 95–110. doi:10.1177/1088357613517504

Meadows, S. (2010). *The child as a social person.* London, England: Routledge.

Mears, A. (2013). Ethnography as precarious work. *The Sociological Quarterly, 54*(1), 20–34. doi:10.1111/tsq.12005

Medrich, E. A. (1981). *The serious business of growing up: A study of children's lives outside the school.* Berkeley: University of California Press.

Medwell, J., & Wray, D. (2014). Handwriting automaticity: the search for performance thresholds. *Language & Education: An International Journal, 28*(1), 34–51. doi:10.1080/09500782.2013.763819

Meece, J. L., & Holt, K. (1993). A pattern analysis of students' achievement goals. *Journal of Educational Psychology, 85*, 582–590.

Meehan, C. L., & Hawks, S. (2013). Cooperative breeding and attachment among the Aka foragers. In N. Quinn & J. Mageo (Eds.), *Attachment reconsidered: Cultural perspectives on a Western theory* (pp. 85–113). New York, NY: Palgrave.

Meeusen, C. (2014). The parent–child similarity in cross-group friendship and anti-immigrant prejudice: A study among 15-year old adolescents and both their parents in Belgium. *Journal of Research in Personality, 50*, 46–55. doi:10.1016/j.jrp.2014.03.001

Mega, C., Ronconi, L., & De Beni, R. (2014). What makes a good student? How emotions, self-regulated learning, and motivation contribute to academic achievement. *Journal of Educational Psychology, 106*, 121–131. doi:10.1037/a0033546

Megalakaki, O. (2008). Pupils' conceptions of force in inanimates and animates. *European Journal of Psychology of Education, 23*, 339–353.

Megalakaki, O., & Yazbek, H. (2013). Categorization activities performed by children with intellectual disability and typically developing children. *International Journal of Child Health and Human Development, 6*, 355–366.

Mehan, H. (1979). *Social organization in the classroom.* Cambridge, MA: Harvard University Press.

Mehl, N. M., Bergmann, S., Klein, A. M., Daum, M., von Klitzing, K., & Horstmann, A. (2017). Cause or consequence? Investigating attention bias and self-regulation skills in children at risk for obesity. *Journal of Experimental Child Psychology, 155*, 113–127. doi:10.1016/j.jecp.2016.11.003

Mehler, J., Jusczyk, P., Lambertz, G., Halsted, N., Bertoncini, J., & Amiel-Tison, C. (1988). A precursor of language acquisition in young infants. *Cognition, 29*, 143–178.

Mehnert, J., Akhrif, A., Telkemeyer, S., Rossi, S., Schmitz, C. H., Steinbrink, J., . . . Neufang, S. (2013). Developmental changes in brain activation and functional connectivity during response inhibition in the early childhood brain. *Brain & Development, 35*, 894–904. doi:10.1016/j.braindev.2012.11.006

Mehta, D., Klengel, T., Conneely, K. N., Smith, A. K., Altmann, A., Pace, T. W., . . . Binder, E. B. (2013). Childhood maltreatment is associated with distinct genomic and epigenetic profiles in posttraumatic stress disorder. *PNAS Proceedings of the National Academy of Sciences of the United States of America, 110*, 8302–8307. doi:10.1073/pnas.1217750110

Mehta, N., Baker, A. L., & Chong, J. (2013). Training foster parents in loyalty conflict: A training evaluation. *Children and Youth Services Review, 35*(1), 75–81. doi:10.1016/j.childyouth.2012.10.006

Meichenbaum, D. (1977). *Cognitive-behavior modification: An integrative approach.* New York, NY: Plenum Press.

Meichenbaum, D. (1985). Teaching thinking: A cognitive-behavioral perspective. In S. F. Chipman, J. W. Segal, & R. Glaser (Eds.), *Thinking and Learning Skills: Vol. 2. Research and open questions* (pp. 407–426). Hillsdale, NJ: Erlbaum.

Meisels, S. J., Wen, X., & Beachy-Quick, K. (2010). Authentic assessment for infants and toddlers: Exploring the reliability and validity of the ounce scale. *Applied Developmental Science, 14*(2), 55–71. doi:10.1080/1088691003697911

Meisgeier, C., & Kellow, J. T. (2015). Type, temperament, and teacher perceptions of ideal and problem students. *Journal of Psychological Type, 75*, 39–49.

Melde, C., Taylor, T. J., & Esbensen, F. (2009). "I got your back": An examination of the protective function of gang membership in adolescence. *Criminology: An Interdisciplinary Journal, 47*, 565–594. doi:10.1111/j.1745-9125.2009.00148.x

Mello, Z., Mallett, R., Andretta, J., & Worrell, F. (2012). Stereotype threat and school belonging in adolescents from diverse racial/ethnic backgrounds. *Journal of At-Risk Issues, 17*(1), 9–14.

Meloni, M. (2013). Moralizing biology: The appeal and limits of the new compassionate view of nature. *History of the Human Sciences, 26*, 82–106. doi:10.1177/0952695113492163

Meltzer, L. (2010). *Promoting executive function in the classroom.* New York, NY: Guilford Press.

Meltzer, L. (Ed.). (2007). *Executive function in education: From theory to practice.* New York, NY: Guilford Press.

Meltzer, L., & Krishnan, K. (2007). Executive function difficulties and learning disabilities: Understandings and misunderstandings. In L. Meltzer (Ed.), *Executive function in education: From theory to practice* (pp. 77–105). New York, NY: Guilford Press.

Meltzer, L., Pollica, L. S., & Barzillai, M. (2007). Executive function in the classroom: Embedding strategy instruction into daily teaching practices. In L. Meltzer (Ed.), *Executive function in education: From theory to practice* (pp. 165–193). New York, NY: Guilford Press.

Meltzoff, A. N. (2007). "Like me": A foundation for social cognition. *Developmental Science, 10*, 126–134.

Menard, S., & Grotpeter, J. K. (2014). Evaluation of bully-proofing your school as an elementary school antibullying intervention. *Journal of School Violence, 13*, 188–209. doi:10.1080/15388220.2013.840641

Mendez, L., Ogg, J., Loker, T., & Fefer, S. (2013). Including parents in the continuum of school-based mental health services: A review of intervention program research from 1995 to 2010. *Journal of Applied School Psychology, 29*(1), 1–36. doi:10.1080/15377903.2012.725580

Menghini, D., Finzi, A., Benassi, M., Bolzani, R., Facoetti, A., Giovagnoli, S., . . . Vicari, S. (2010). Different underlying neurocognitive deficits in developmental dyslexia: A comparative study. *Neuropsychologia, 48*, 863–872.

Mennella, J. A., Jagnow, C. P., & Beauchamp, G. K. (2001). Prenatal and postnatal flavor learning by human infants. *Pediatrics, 107*, 88.

Menyuk, P., & Menyuk, D. (1988). Communicative competence: A historical and cultural perspective. In J. S. Wurzel (Ed.), *Toward multiculturalism: A reader in multicultural education* (pp. 151–161). Yarmouth, ME: Intercultural Press.

Mercer, J. (2006). *Understanding attachment: Parenting, child care, and emotional development.* Westport, CT: Praeger.

Mermelshtine, R., & Barnes, J. (2016). Maternal responsive–didactic caregiving in play interactions with 10-month-olds and cognitive development at 18 months. *Infant and Child Development, 25*, 296–316. http://dx.doi.org/10.1002/icd.1961

Mero, D., & Hartzman, M. (2012). Breaking ranks in action: Collaboration is the foundation. *Principal Leadership, 12*(9), 18–19.

Merrill, E. C., & Conners, F. A. (2013). Age-related interference from irrelevant distracters in visual feature search among heterogeneous distracters. *Journal of Experimental Child Psychology, 115*, 640–654. doi:10.1016/j.jecp.2013.03.013

Merrill, N. N., & Fivush, R. (2016). Intergenerational narratives and identity across development. *Developmental Review, 40*, 72–92. doi:10.1016/j.dr.2016.03.001

Merrin, G. J., Haye, K. D. L., Espelage, D. L., Ewing, B., Tucker, J. S., Hoover, M., & Green, H. D., Jr. (2018). The co-evolution of bullying perpetration, homophobic teasing, and a school friendship network. *Journal of Youth and Adolescence, 47*, 601–618. http://dx.doi.org.unco.idm.oclc.org/10.1007/s10964-017-0783-4

Merritt, D. H., & Klein, S. (2015). Do early care and education services improve language development for maltreated children? Evidence from a national child welfare sample. *Child Abuse & Neglect, 39*, 185–196. http://dx.doi.org/10.1016/j.chiabu.2014.10.011

Merritt, E., Wanless, S., Rimm-Kaufman, S., Cameron, C., & Peugh, J. (2012). The contribution of teachers' emotional support to children's social behaviors and self-regulatory skills in first grade. *School Psychology Review, 41*, 141–159.

Mervis, C. B., & Becerra, A. M. (2007). Language and communicative development in Williams syndrome. *Mental Retardation & Developmental Disabilities Research Reviews, 13*(1), 3–15. doi:10.1002/mrdd.20140

Mesman, J., van IJzendoorn, M., Behrens, K., Carbonell, O. A., Cárcamo, R., Cohen-Paraira, I., . . . Zreik, G. (2016). Is the ideal mother a sensitive mother? Beliefs about early childhood parenting in mothers across the globe. *International Journal of Behavioral Development, 40*, 385–397. doi:10.1177/0165025415594030

Mestre, M. V., Samper, P., Frías, M. D., & Tur, A. M. (2009). Are women more empathetic than men? A longitudinal study in adolescence. *The Spanish Journal of Psychology, 12*(1), 76–83.

Metcalfe, J., & Finn, B. (2013). Metacognition and control of study choice in children. *Metacognition & Learning, 8*(1), 19–46. doi:10.1007/s11409-013-9094-7

Meteyer, K. B., & Perry-Jenkins, M. (2009). Dyadic parenting and children's externalizing symptoms. *Family Relations, 58*, 289–302.

Metsala, J. L., & David, M. D. (2017). The effects of age and sublexical automaticity on reading outcomes for students with reading disabilities. *Journal of Research in Reading, 40*, S209–S227. doi:10.1111/1467-9817.12097

Metz, K. E. (2004). Children's understanding of scientific inquiry: Their conceptualizations of uncertainty in investigations of their own design. *Cognition and Instruction, 22*, 219–290.

Mevel, K., Fransson, P., & Bölte, S. (2015). Multimodal brain imaging in autism spectrum disorder and the promise of twin research. *Autism: The International Journal of Research & Practice, 19*, 527–541. doi:10.1177/1362361314535510

Meyer, A., Rose, D., & Gordon, D. (2014). *Universal design for learning: Theory and practice*. Wakefield, MA: Cast Professional Publishing.

Meyer, D. K., Turner, J. C., & Spencer, C. A. (1994, April). *Academic risk taking and motivation in an elementary mathematics classroom*. Paper presented at the annual meeting of the American Educational Research Association, New Orleans, LA.

Meyer, D. K., Turner, J. C., & Spencer, C. A. (1997). Challenge in a mathematics classroom: Students' motivation and strategies in project-based learning. *Elementary School Journal, 97*, 501–521.

Meyer, S., Raikes, H., Virmani, E. A., Waters, S., & Thompson, R. A. (2014). Parent emotion representations and the socialization of emotion regulation in the family. *International Journal of Behavioral Development, 38*, 164–173. doi:10.1177/0165025413519014

Meyers, D. T. (1987). The socialized individual and individual autonomy: An intersection between philosophy and psychology. In E. F. Kittay & D. T. Meyers (Eds.), *Women and moral theory* (pp. 139–153). Totowa, NJ: Rowman & Littlefield.

Meylan, S. C., Frank, M. C., Roy, B. C., & Levy, R. (2017). The emergence of an abstract grammatical category in children's early speech. *Psychological Science, 28*, 181–192. http://dx.doi.org/10.1177/0956797616677753

Micheli, L. J. (1995). Sports injuries in children and adolescents: Questions and controversies. *Clinics in Sports Medicine, 14*, 727–745.

Middleton, J. (2013). More than motivation: The combined effects of critical motivational variables on middle school mathematics achievement. *Middle Grades Research Journal, 8*(1), 77–95.

Midgley, C. (Ed.). (2002). *Goals, goal structures, and patterns of adaptive learning*. Mahwah, NJ: Erlbaum.

Miele, D., Son, L., & Metcalfe, J. (2013). Children's naive theories of intelligence influence their metacognitive judgments. *Child Development, 84*, 1879–1886. doi:10.1111/cdev.12101

Miksza, P., & Gault, B. M. (2014). Classroom music experiences of U.S. elementary school children: An analysis of the early childhood longitudinal study of 1998–1999. *Journal of Research in Music Education, 62*, 4–17. doi:10.1177/0022429413519822

Mikulincer, M., & Shaver, P. R. (2007). *Attachment in adulthood: Structure, dynamics, and change*. New York, NY: Guilford Press.

Mikulincer, M., & Shaver, P. R. (2013). Attachment orientations and meaning in life. In J. A. Hicks, & C. Routledge (Eds.), *The experience of meaning in life: Classical perspectives, emerging themes, and controversies* (pp. 287–304). New York, NY: Springer Science + Business Media. doi:10.1007/978-94-007-6527-6_22

Milanowicz, A., & Bokus, B. (2013). Gender and moral judgments: The role of who is speaking to whom. *Journal of Gender Studies, 22*, 423–443. doi:10.1080/09589236.2012.719314

Milardo, R. M. (2010). *The forgotten kin: Aunts and uncles*. New York, NY: Cambridge University Press.

Military Child Education Coalition. (2013). *A military parent's guide to school policies and transitions*. Harker Heights, TX: Author. Retrieved from http://www.militarychild.org/parents-and-students/resources

Miljkovitch, R., Danet, M., & Bernier, A. (2012). Intergenerational transmission of attachment representations in the context of single parenthood in France. *Journal of Family Psychology, 26*, 784–792. doi:10.1037/a0029627

Miller, A. B., Sheridan, M. A., Hanson, J. L., McLaughlin, K. A., Bates, J. E., Lansford, J. E., . . . Dodge, K. A. (2018). Dimensions of deprivation and threat, psychopathology, and potential mediators: A multi-year longitudinal analysis. *Journal of Abnormal Psychology*, 127(2), 160–170. http://dx.doi.org.unco.idm.oclc.org/10.1037/abn0000331

Miller, A., Franzen-Castle, L., Aguirre, T., Krehbiel, M., Colby, S., Kattelmann, K., . . . White, A. (2016). Food-related behavior and intake of adult main meal preparers of 9–10-year-old children participating in iCook 4-H: A five-state childhood obesity prevention pilot study. *Appetite, 101*, 163–170. doi:10.1016/j.appet.2016.03.006

Miller, G. E. (1987). School interventions for dishonest behavior. *Special Services in the Schools*, 3(3–4), 21–36. doi:10.1300/J008v03n03_03

Miller, J. (2013). Resilience, violent extremism and religious education. *British Journal of Religious Education, 35*, 188–200. doi:10.1080/01416200.2012.740444

Miller, J. G. (1987). Cultural influences on the development of conceptual differentiation in person description. *British Journal of Developmental Psychology, 5*, 309–319.

Miller, J. G. (2007). Cultural psychology of moral development. In S. Kitayama & D. Cohen (Eds.), *Handbook of cultural psychology* (pp. 477–499). New York, NY: Guilford Press.

Miller, J. L., & Lossia, A. K. (2013). Prelinguistic infants' communicative system: Role of caregiver social feedback. *First Language, 33*, 524–544. doi:10.1177/0142723713503147

Miller, J. L., Lynn, C. H., Shuster, J. J., & Driscoll, D. J. (2013). A reduced-energy intake, well-balanced diet improves weight control in children with Prader-Willi syndrome. *Journal of Human Nutrition and Dietetics, 26*(1), 2–9. doi:10.1111/j.1365-277X.2012.01275.x

Miller, K. (1989). Measurement as a tool for thought: The role of measuring procedures in children's understanding of quantitative invariance. *Developmental Psychology, 25*, 589–600.

Miller, K. (2013). Variable input: What Sarah reveals about nonagreeing don't and theories of root infinitives. *Language Acquisition, 20*, 305–324. doi:10.1080/10489223.2013.828061

Miller, K. F., Smith, C. M., Zhu, J., & Zhang, H. (1995). Preschool origins of cross-national differences in mathematical competence: The role of number-naming systems. *Psychological Science, 6*, 56–60.

Miller, L. S. (1995). *An American imperative: Accelerating minority educational advancement*. New Haven, CT: Yale University Press.

Miller, N., & Maruyama, G. (1976). Ordinal position and peer popularity. *Journal of Personality and Social Psychology, 33*, 123–131.

Miller, P. M., Danaher, D. L., & Forbes, D. (1986). Sex-related strategies of coping with interpersonal conflict in children aged five to seven. *Developmental Psychology, 22*, 543–548.

Miller, R. B., & Brickman, S. J. (2004). A model of future-oriented motivation and self-regulation. *Educational Psychology Review, 16*, 9–33.

Mills, G. E. (2007). *Action research: A guide for the teacher researcher* (3rd ed.). Upper Saddle River, NJ: Pearson Merrill/Prentice Hall.

Mills, K. K. (2010). Shrek meets Vygotsky: Rethinking adolescents' multimodal literacy practices in schools. *Journal of Adolescent & Adult Literacy, 54*(1), 35–45. doi:10.1598/JAAL.54.1.4

Mills, M., Watkins, R., Washington, J., Nippold, M., & Schneider, P. (2013). Structural and dialectal characteristics of the fictional and personal narratives of school-age African American children. *Language, Speech & Hearing Services in Schools, 44*, 211–223. doi:10.1044/0161-1461(2012/12-0021)

Mills, R. S. L., & Grusec, J. E. (1989). Cognitive, affective, and behavioral consequences of praising altruism. *Merrill-Palmer Quarterly, 35*, 299–326.

Mills, S., & Black, L. (2014). Ensuring children with Down's syndrome reach their full potential. *British Journal of School Nursing, 9*, 97–99.

Milner, H. R. (2006). Classroom management in urban classrooms. In C. M. Evertson & C. S. Weinstein (Eds.), *Handbook of classroom management: Research, practice, and contemporary issues* (pp. 491–522). Mahwah, NJ: Erlbaum.

Milner, H. R., & Ford, D. Y. (2007). Cultural considerations of culturally diverse elementary students in gifted education. *Roeper Review, 29*, 166–173.

Mingroni, M. A. (2007). Resolving the IQ paradox: Heterosis as a cause of the Flynn effect and other trends. *Psychological Review, 114*, 806–829.

Minnameier, G., & Schmidt, S. (2013). Situational moral adjustment and the happy victimizer. *European Journal of Developmental Psychology, 10*, 253–268. doi:10.1080/17405629.2013.765797

Minshawi, N. F., Hurwitz, S., Fodstad, J. C., Biebl, S., Morriss, D. H., & McDougle, C. J. (2014). The association between self-injurious behaviors and autism spectrum disorders. *Psychology Research & Behavior Management, 7*, 125–136. doi:10.2147/PRBM.S44635

Minshew, N. J., & Williams, D. L. (2007). The new neurobiology of autism: Cortex, connectivity, and neuronal organization. *Archives of Neurology, 64*, 945–950. doi:10.1001/archneur.64.7.945

Minskoff, E. H. (1980). Teaching approach for developing nonverbal communication skills in students with social perception deficits: II. Proxemic, vocalic, and artifactual cues. *Journal of Learning Disabilities, 13*, 203–208.

Minstrell, J., & Stimpson, V. (1996). A classroom environment for learning: Guiding students' reconstruction of understanding and reasoning. In L. Schauble & R. Glaser (Eds.), *Innovations in learning: New environments for education* (pp. 175–202). Mahwah, NJ: Erlbaum.

Mireault, G. C., Crockenberg, S. C., Heilman, K., Sparrow, J. E., Cousineau, K., & Rainville, B. (2017). Social, cognitive, and physiological aspects of humour perception from 4 to 8 months: Two longitudinal studies. *British Journal of Developmental Psychology*. Advance online publication. http://dx.doi.org.unco.idm.oclc.org/10.1111/bjdp.12216

Mischel, W. (1974). Processes in delay of gratification. In L. Berkowitz (Ed.), *Advances in experimental social psychology* (Vol. 7, pp. 249–292). New York, NY: Academic Press.

Mischel, W., & Ebbesen, E. B. (1970). Attention in delay of gratification. *Journal of Personality and Social Psychology, 6*, 329–337. https://doi.org/10.1037/h0029815

Mischel, W., Shoda, Y., & Rodriguez, M. L. (1989). Delay of gratification in children. *Science, 244*(4907), 933–938. doi:10.1126/science.2658056

Missana, M., Grigutsch, M., & Grossmann, T. (2014). Developmental and individual differences in the neural processing of dynamic expressions of pain and anger. *Plos ONE, 9*(4), 1–13. doi:10.1371/journal.pone.0093728

Mistry, J., Easterbrooks, M. A., Fauth, R. C., Raskin, M., Jacobs, F., & Goldberg, J. (2016). Heterogeneity among adolescent mothers and home visiting program outcomes. *Children and Youth Services Review, 65*, 86–93. doi:10.1016/j.childyouth.2016.04.002

Mitchell, M. L., & Brendtro, L. K. (2013). Victories over violence: The quest for safe schools and communities. *Reclaiming Children & Youth*, pp. 5–11.

Mitchell, S., Foulger, T. S., & Wetzel, K. (2009). Ten tips for involving families through internet-based communication. *Young Children, 64*(5), 46–49.

Mittal, R., Russell, B., Britner, P., & Peake, P. (2013). Delay of gratification in two- and three-year-olds: Associations with attachment, personality, and temperament. *Journal of Child & Family Studies, 22*, 479–489. doi:10.1007/s10826-012-9600-6

Miura, I. T., & Okamoto, Y. (2003). Language supports for mathematics understanding and performance. In A. J. Baroody, A. Dowker (Eds.), *The development of arithmetic concepts and skills: Constructing adaptive expertise* (pp. 229–242). Mahwah, NJ: Erlbaum.

Miyake, K., Chen, S.-J., & Campos, J. J. (1985). Infant temperament, mother's mode of interaction, and attachment in Japan: An interim report. In I. Bretherton & E. Waters (Eds.), Growing points of attachment theory and research. *Monographs of the Society for Research in Child Development, 50*(1–2, Serial No. 209), 276–297.

Miyauchi, A., Osaka, H., Nagashima, M., Kuwajima, M., Monden, Y., Kohda, M., . . . Yamagata, T. (2018). Leigh syndrome with spinal cord involvement due to a hemizygous NDUFA1 mutation. *Brain & Development, 40*(6), 498-502. http://dx.doi.org.unco.idm.oclc.org/10.1016/j.braindev.2018.02.007

Miyazaki, K., Makomaska, S., & Rakowski, A. (2012). Prevalence of absolute pitch: A comparison between Japanese and Polish music students. *Journal of the Acoustical Society of America, 132*, 3484–3493. doi:10.1121/1.4756956

Modestou, M., & Gagatsis, A. (2010). Cognitive and metacognitive aspects of proportional reasoning. *Mathematical Thinking and Learning, 12*(1), 36–53.

Moely, B. E., Santulli, K. A., & Obach, M. S. (1995). Strategy instruction, metacognition, and motivation in the elementary school classroom. In F. E. Weinert & W. Schneider (Eds.), *Memory performance and competencies: Issues in growth and development* (pp. 301–321). Hillsdale, NJ: Erlbaum.

Moksnes, U. K., Espnes, G. A., & Haugan, G. (2014). Stress, sense of coherence and emotional symptoms in adolescents. *Psychology & Health, 29*(1), 32–49. doi:10.1080/08870446.2013.822868

Moksnes, U. K., Moljord, I. E. O., Espnes, G. A., & Byrne, D. G. (2010). The association between stress and emotional states in adolescents: The role of gender and self-esteem. *Personality and Individual Differences, 49*(5), 430–435.

Moll, L., Amanti, C., Neff, D., & González, N. (2005). Funds of knowledge for teaching: Using a qualitative approach to connect homes and classrooms. In N. González, L. C. Moll, & C. Amanti (Eds.), *Funds of knowledge: Theorizing practices in households, communities, and classrooms* (pp. 71–87). Mahwah, NJ: Erlbaum.

Monei, T., & Pedro, A. (2017). A systematic review of interventions for children presenting with dyscalculia in primary schools. *Educational Psychology in Practice, 33*, 277–293. doi:10.1080/02667363.2017.1289076

Montagu, A. (1999). Introduction. In A. Montagu (Ed.), *Race and IQ* (expanded ed., pp. 1–18). New York, NY: Oxford University Press.

Montague, M., Enders, C., & Dietz, S. (2011). Effects of cognitive strategy instruction on math problem solving of middle school students with learning disabilities. *Learning Disability Quarterly, 34,* 262–272.

Montemayor, R. (1982). The relationship between parent–adolescent conflict and the amount of time adolescents spend with parents, peers, and alone. *Child Development, 53,* 1512–1519.

Montessori, M. (1949). *The absorbent mind* (M. J. Costelloe, Trans.). New York, NY: Holt, Rinehart & Winston.

Montessori, M. (1966). *The secret of childhood* (M. J. Costelloe, Trans.). New York, NY: Ballantine Books. (Original work published 1936)

Montgomery, H. (2009). *An introduction to childhood: Anthropological perspectives on children's lives.* Chichester, England: Wiley.

Montgomery, K. S., Mackey, J., Thuett, K., Ginestra, S., Bizon, J. L., & Abbott, L. C. (2008). Chronic, low-dose prenatal exposure to methylmercury impairs motor and mnemonic function in adult C57/B6 mice. *Behavioural Brain Research, 191,* 55–61.

Montroy, J., Bowles, R., Skibbe, L., & Foster, T. (2014). Social skills and problem behaviors as mediators of the relationship between behavioral self-regulation and academic achievement. *Early Childhood Research Quarterly, 29,* 298–309. doi:10.1016/j.ecresq.2014.03.002

Moomaw, S. M. (2014). Don't forget to play. *School Science & Mathematics, 114*(2), 51–52. doi:10.1111/ssm.12056

Moon, C., Lagercrantz, H., & Kuhl, P. (2013). Language experienced in utero affects vowel perception after birth: A two-country study. *Acta Paediatrica, 102,* 156–160. doi:10.1111/apa.12098

Moon, S. M., Feldhusen, J. F., & Dillon, D. R. (1994). Long term effects of an enrichment program based on the Purdue three-stage model. *Gifted Child Quarterly, 38,* 38–47.

Mooney, R. (2014). The preschool playground: A young child's experience of entering the emotional field. *Infant Observation, 17*(1), 35–49. doi:10.1080/13698036.2014.895220

Moore, A. F., McCallum, R. S., & Bracken, B. A. (2017). The Universal Nonverbal Intelligence Test: Second Edition. In R. S. McCallum (Ed.), *Handbook of nonverbal assessment* (pp. 105–125). Cham, Switzerland: Springer Nature. http://dx.doi.org/10.1007/978-3-319-50604-3_7

Moore, C. (2010). The development of future-oriented decision-making. In B. W. Sokol, U. Müeller, J. I. M. Carpendale, A. R. Young, & G. Iarocci (Eds.), *Self and social regulation: Social interaction and the development of social understanding and executive functions* (pp. 270–286). New York, NY: Oxford University Press.

Moore, D. A., Russell, A. E., Arnell, S., & Ford, T. J. (2017). Educators' experiences of managing students with ADHD: A qualitative study. *Child: Care, Health and Development, 43,* 489–498. doi:10.1111/cch.12448

Moore, K. L., & Persaud, T. V. N. (2008). *Before we are born: Essentials of embryology and birth defects* (7th ed.). Philadelphia, PA: Saunders/Elsevier.

Moore, K. L., Persaud, T. V. N., & Torchia, M. G. (2013). *Before we are born: Essentials of embryology and birth defects* (9th ed.). Philadelphia, PA: Saunders/Elsevier.

Moore, L. C. (2006). Learning by heart in Qur'anic and public schools in northern Cameroon. *Social Analysis, 50,* 109–126.

Moore, L. C. (2010). Learning in schools. In D. F. Lancy, J. Bock, & S. Gaskins (Eds.), *The anthropology of learning in childhood* (pp. 207–232). Lanham, MD: AltaMira Press/Rowman & Littlefield.

Moore, L. C. (2013). Qur'anic school sermons as a site for sacred and second language socialisation. *Journal of Multilingual & Multicultural Development, 34,* 445–458. doi:10.1080/01434632.2013.783036

Moore, P. S., Whaley, S. E., & Sigman, M. (2004). Interactions between mothers and children: Impacts of maternal and child anxiety. *Journal of Abnormal Psychology, 113,* 471–476.

Moore, R. (2013). Imitation and conventional communication. *Biology & Philosophy, 28,* 481–500. doi:10.1007/s10539-012-9349-8

Morales, D. D. (2017). Writing for real. *Reading Teacher, 71*(1), 109. doi:10.1002/trtr.1585

Moran, S., & Gardner, H. (2006). Extraordinary achievements: A developmental and systems analysis. In W. Damon & R. M. Lerner (Series Eds.), & D. Kuhn & R. Siegler (Vol. Eds.), *Handbook of Child Psychology: Vol. 2. Cognition, perception, and language* (6th ed., pp. 905–949). New York, NY: Wiley.

Morawska, A., Laws, R., Moretto, N., & Daniels, L. (2014). Observing the mother–infant feeding interaction. *Early Child Development & Care, 184,* 522–536. doi:10.1080/03004430.2013.800051

Morelli, G. A., & Rothbaum, F. (2007). Situating the child in context: Attachment relationships and self-regulation in different cultures. In S. Kitayama & D. Cohen (Eds.), *Handbook of cultural psychology* (pp. 500–527). New York, NY: Guilford Press.

Morelli, G. A., & Rothbaum, F. (2007). Situating the child in context: Attachment relationships and self-regulation in different cultures. In S. Kitayama & D. Cohen (Eds.), *Handbook of cultural psychology* (pp. 500–527). New York, NY: Guilford Press.

Moreno, A. J., Shwayder, I., & Friedman, I. D. (2017). The function of executive function: Everyday manifestations of regulated thinking in preschool settings. *Early Childhood Education Journal, 45,* 143–153. doi:10.1007/s10643-016-0777-y

Moreno, M. A., Jelenchick, L. A., & Christakis, D. A. (2013). Problematic internet use among older adolescents: A conceptual framework. *Computers in Human Behavior, 29,* 1879–1887. doi:10.1016/j.chb.2013.01.053

Morgan, H. (2012). What teachers and schools can do to control the growing problem of school bullying. *Clearing House, 85,* 174–178. doi:10.1080/00098655.2012.677075

Morimoto, S., & Friedland, L. (2013). Cultivating success: Youth achievement, capital and civic engagement in the contemporary United States. *Sociological Perspectives, 56,* 523–546.

Morin, A. S., Maïano, C., Marsh, H. W., Nagengast, B., & Janosz, M. (2013). School life and adolescents' self-esteem trajectories. *Child Development, 84,* 1967–1988. doi:10.1111/cdev.12089

Moroney, S. K. (2006). Higher stages? Some cautions for Christian integration with Kohlberg's Theory. *Journal of Psychology and Theology, 34,* 361–371.

Moroni, S., Dumont, H., Trautwein, U., Niggli, A., & Baeriswyl, F. (2015). The need to distinguish between quantity and quality in research on parental involvement: The example of parental help with homework. *Journal of Educational Research, 108,* 417–431. doi:10.1080/00220671.2014.901283

Morra, S. (2015). How do subvocal rehearsal and general attentional resources contribute to verbal short-term memory span? *Frontiers in Psychology, 6,* Article ID 145.

Morra, S., Gobbo, C., Marini, Z., & Sheese, R. (2008). *Cognitive development: Neo-Piagetian perspectives.* New York, NY: Erlbaum.

Morris, A. S., Criss, M. M., Silk, J. S., & Houltberg, B. J. (2017). The impact of parenting on emotion regulation during childhood and adolescence. *Child Development Perspectives, 11,* 233–238. http://dx.doi.org.unco.idm.oclc.org/10.1111/cdep.12238

Morris, A. S., Cui, L., & Steinberg, L. (2013). Parenting research and themes: What we have learned and where to go next. In R. E. Larzelere, A. Morris, & A. W. Harrist (Eds.), *Authoritative parenting: Synthesizing nurturance and discipline for optimal child development* (pp. 35–58). Washington, DC: American Psychological Association. doi:10.1037/13948-003

Morris, D. (1977). *Manwatching: A field guide to human behaviour.* New York, NY: Harry N. Abrams.

Morris, H. (2014). Socioscientific issues and multidisciplinarity in school science textbooks. *International Journal of Science Education, 36,* 1137–1158. doi:10.1080/09500693.2013.848493

Morrison, G. M., Furlong, M. J., D'Incau, B., & Morrison, R. L. (2004). The safe school: Integrating the school reform agenda to prevent disruption and violence at school. In J. C. Conoley & A. P. Goldstein (Ed.), *School violence intervention* (2nd ed., pp. 256–296). New York, NY: Guilford Press.

Morrongiello, B. A., Fenwick, K. D., Hillier, L., & Chance, G. (1994). Sound localization in newborn human infants. *Developmental Psychobiology, 27,* 519–538.

Mortimer, J. T., Shanahan, M., & Ryu, S. (1994). The effects of adolescent employment on school-related orientation and behavior. In R. K. Silbereisen & E. Todt (Eds.), *Adolescence in context: The interplay of family, school, peers and work in adjustment (pp. 304–326)*. New York, NY: Springer-Verlag.

Mortimer, J. T., Shanahan, M., & Ryu, S. (1994). The effects of adolescent employment on school-related orientation and behavior. In R. K. Silbereisen & E. Todt (Eds.), *Adolescence in context: The interplay of family, school, peers and work in adjustment (pp. 304–326)*. New York, NY: Springer-Verlag.

Morton, A. (1980). *Frames of mind: Constraints on the common-sense conception of the mental*. Oxford, England: Clarendon Press.

Moser, G. P., Morrison, T. G., & Wilcox, B. (2017). Supporting fourth-grade students' word identification using application software. *Reading Psychology, 38*, 349–368.

Mosier, K. L. (2013). Judgment and prediction. In J. D. Lee, A. Kirlik (Eds.), *The Oxford handbook of cognitive engineering* (pp. 68–87). New York, NY: Oxford University Press.

Mou, Y., & vanMarle, K. (2014). Two core systems of numerical representation in infants. *Developmental Review, 34*(1), 1–25. doi:10.1016/j.dr.2013.11.001

Moul, C., Hawes, D., & Dadds, M. (2015). The moral brain: Psychopathology. In J. Decety & T. Wheatley (Eds.), *The moral brain: A multidisciplinary perspective* (pp. 253–264). Cambridge, MA, US: MIT Press.

Moyse, R., & Porter, J. (2015). The experience of the hidden curriculum for autistic girls at mainstream primary schools. *European Journal of Special Needs Education, 30*, 187–201. doi:10.1080/08856257.2014.986915

Mueller, T. G. (2014). Learning to navigate the special education maze: A 3-tiered model CLD family empowerment. In L. Lo & D. B. Hiatt-Michael (Eds.), *Promising practices to empower culturally and linguistically diverse families of children with disabilities* (pp. 3–14). Charlotte, NC: Information Age Publishers.

Müeller, U., & Overton, W. F. (2010). Thinking about thinking—Thinking about measurement: A Rasch analysis of recursive thinking. *Journal of Applied Measurement, 11*(1), 78–90.

Muennig, P., Schweinhart, L., Montie, J., & Neidell, M. (2009). Effect of a prekindergarten educational intervention on adult health: 37-year follow-up results of a randomized control trial. *American Journal of Public Health, 99*, 1431–1437.

Muftuler, L. T., Davis, E. P., Buss, C., Solodkin, A., Su, M. Y., Head, K. M., . . . Sandman, C. A. (2012). Development of white matter pathways in typically developing preadolescent children. *Brain Research, 1466*, 33–43. http://dx.doi.org.unco.idm.oclc.org/10.1016/j.brainres.2012.05.035

Muijselaar, M. L., Swart, N. M., Steenbeek-Planting, E. G., Droop, M., Verhoeven, L., & de Jong, P. F. (2017). Developmental relations between reading comprehension and reading strategies. *Scientific Studies of Reading, 21*, 194–209. doi:10.1080/10888438.2017.1278763

Muis, K. R. (2007). The role of epistemic beliefs in self-regulated learning. *Educational Psychologist, 42*, 173–190.

Mukherjee, A., Datta, S., Sanyal, A., Dogra, A. K., & Das, S. (2016). Personality of children with emotional disorders: A psychodynamic study. *SIS Journal of Projective Psychology & Mental Health, 23*(1), 22–26.

Mullins, D., & Tisak, M. S. (2006). Moral, conventional, and personal rules: The perspective of foster youth. *Journal of Applied Developmental Psychology, 27*, 310–325.

Mullis, R. L., Graf, S. C., & Mullis, A. K. (2009). Parental relationships, autonomy, and identity processes of high school students. *The Journal of Genetic Psychology: Research and Theory on Human Development, 170*, 326–338.

Mundy, P., & Newell, L. (2007). Attention, joint attention, and social cognition. *Current Directions in Psychological Science, 16*, 269–274.

Muñoz-García, A., & Aviles-Herrera, M. (2014). Effects of academic dishonesty on dimensions of spiritual well-being and satisfaction: A comparative study of secondary school and university students. *Assessment & Evaluation in Higher Education, 39*, 349–363. doi:10.1080/02602938.2013.832729

Munroe, R. L., & Munroe, P. J. (1992). Fathers in children's environments: A four culture study. In B. S. Hewlett (Ed.), *Father–child relations: Cultural and biosocial contexts* (pp. 213–230). New York, NY: Aldine de Gruyter.

Muramoto, Y., Yamaguchi, S., & Kim, U. (2009). Perception of achievement attribution in individual and group contexts: Comparative analysis of Japanese, Korean, and Asian-American results. *Asian Journal of Social Psychology, 12*, 199–210. doi:10.1111/j.1467-839X.2009.01285.x

Murdock, T. B. (1999). The social context of risk: Status and motivational predictors of alienation in middle school. *Journal of Educational Psychology, 91*, 62–75.

Muris, P., & Meesters, C. (2014). Small or big in the eyes of the other: On the developmental psychopathology of self-conscious emotions as shame, guilt, and pride. *Clinical Child and Family Psychology Review, 17*(1), 19–40. doi:10.1007/s10567-013-0137-z

Muris, P., Meesters, C., & Rompelberg, L. (2006). Attention control in middle childhood: Relations to psychopathological symptoms and threat perception distortions. *Behaviour Research and Therapy, 45*, 997–1010.

Murnane, R. J. (2007, Fall). Improving the education of children living in poverty. *Future of Children, 17*(2), 161–182.

Murphy, P. K. (2007). The eye of the beholder: The interplay of social and cognitive components in change. *Educational Psychologist, 42*, 41–53.

Murphy, P. K., & Alexander, P. A. (2008). Examining the influence of knowledge, beliefs, and motivation in conceptual change. In S. Vosniadou (Ed.), *International handbook of research on conceptual change* (pp. 583–616). New York, NY: Taylor & Francis.

Murphy, P. K., & Mason, L. (2006). Changing knowledge and beliefs. In P. A. Alexander & P. H. Winne (Eds.), *Handbook of educational psychology* (2nd ed., pp. 305–324). Mahwah, NJ: Erlbaum.

Murray, T. J. (2016). Public or private? The influence of immigration on native schooling choices in the United States. *Economics of Education Review, 53*, 268–283. doi:10.1016/j.econedurev.2016.04.003

Musholt, K. (2017). The personal and the subpersonal in the theory of mind debate. *Phenomenology and the Cognitive Sciences*. Advance online publication. doi:10.1007/s11097-017-9504-4

Musick, K. M., Meier, A., & Flood, S. (2016). How parents fare. *American Sociological Review, 81*, 1069–1095.

Mustanski, B. S., Viken, R. J., Kaprio, J., Pulkkinen, L., & Rose, R. (2004). Genetic and environmental influences on pubertal influences on pubertal development: Longitudinal data from Finnish twins at ages 11 and 14. *Developmental Psychology, 40*, 1188–1198.

Muter, V. (1998). Phonological awareness: Its nature and its influence over early literacy development. In C. Hulme & R. M. Joshi (Eds.), *Reading and spelling: Development and disorders* (pp. 113–125). Mahwah, NJ: Erlbaum.

Mweru, M., & Murungi, C. (2013). What can schools learn from children about use of culturally relevant methods and materials? *Journal of Emerging Trends in Educational Research & Policy Studies, 4*, 491–498.

Myatchin, I., & Lagae, L. (2013). Developmental changes in visuo-spatial working memory in normally developing children: Event-related potentials study. *Brain & Development, 35*, 853–864. doi:10.1016/j.braindev.2012.11.005

Myers, B. J., Smarsh, T. M., Amlund-Hagen, K., & Kennon, S. (1999). Children of incarcerated mothers. *Journal of Child and Family Studies, 8*(1), 11–25. doi:10.1023/A:1022990410036

Myers, L. L. (2013). Substance use among rural African American adolescents: Identifying risk and protective factors. *Child & Adolescent Social Work Journal, 30*(1), 79–93. doi:10.1007/s10560-012-0280-2

Myles, B. M., & Simpson, R. L. (2001). Understanding the hidden curriculum: An essential social skill for children and youth with Asperger syndrome. *Intervention in School and Clinic, 36*, 279–286.

Myrberg, E., & Rosén, M. (2009). Direct and indirect effects of parents' education on reading achievement among third graders in Sweden. *British Journal of Educational Psychology, 79*, 695–711.

Nabors, L. A., Little, S. G., Akin-Little, A., & Iobst, E. A. (2008). Teacher knowledge of and confidence in meeting the needs of children with chronic medical conditions: Pediatric psychology's contribution to education. *Psychology in the Schools, 45*, 217–226.

Naegele, J. R., & Lombroso, P. J. (2001). Genetics of central nervous system developmental disorders. *Child and Adolescent Psychiatric Clinics of North America, 10*, 225–239.

Nærde, A., Ogden, T., Janson, H., & Daae Zachrisson, H. (2014). Normative development of physical aggression from 8 to 26 months. *Developmental Psychology, 50*, 1710–1720. doi:10.1037/a0036324

Naglieri, J. A., & Conway, C. (2009). The Cognitive Assessment System. In J. A. Naglieri & S. Goldstein (Eds.), *Practitioner's guide to assessing intelligence and achievement* (pp. 27–59). Hoboken, NJ: Wiley.

Naglieri, J. A., & Otero, T. M. (2012). The Cognitive Assessment System: From theory to practice. In D. P. Flanagan, P. L. Harrison (Eds.), *Contemporary intellectual assessment: Theories, tests, and issues* (3rd ed., pp. 376–399). New York, NY: Guilford Press.

Naglieri, J. A., De Lauder, B. Y., Goldstein, S., & Schwebech, A. (2006). WISC-III and CAS: Which correlates higher with achievement for a clinical sample? *School Psychology Quarterly, 21*(1), 62–76.

Nail, M. H. (2007). Reaching out to families with student-created newsletters. *Kappa Delta Pi Record, 44*(1), 39–41.

Nakayasu, C. (2016). School curriculum in Japan. *Curriculum Journal, 27*(1), 134-150. doi:10.1080/09585176.2016.1144518

Nalkur, P. G. (2009). A cultural comparison of Tanzanian street children, former street children, and school-going children. *Journal of Cross-Cultural Psychology, 40*, 1012–1027. doi:10.1177/0022022109346954

Nanu, C., Tăut, D., & Băban, A. (2013). Appearance esteem and weight esteem in adolescence. Are they different across age and gender? *Cognition, Brain, Behavior: An Interdisciplinary Journal, 17*, 189–200.

Narayanan, U., & Warren, S. T. (2006). Neurobiology of related disorders: Fragile X syndrome. In S. O. Moldin & J. L. R. Rubenstein (Eds.), *Understanding autism: From basic neuroscience to treatment* (pp. 113–131). Boca Raton, FL: CRC Press.

Narváez, D. (1998). The influence of moral schemas on the reconstruction of moral narratives in eighth graders and college students. *Journal of Educational Psychology, 90*, 13–24.

Narváez, D., & Rest, J. (1995). The four components of acting morally. In W. M. Kurtines & J. L. Gewirtz (Eds.), *Moral development: An introduction (pp. 385–399)*. Boston, MA: Allyn & Bacon.

Nash, P. (2017). Disruptive behavior and unsolved problems. (D. Colley & P. Cooper Eds.). (2017). *Attachment and emotional development in the classroom: Theory and practice* (pp. 265–278). London, England: Jessica Kinglsey.

Natarajan, G., Shankaran, S., Laptook, A. R., Pappas, A., Bann, C. M., McDonald, S. A., . . . Vohr, B. R. (2013). Apgar scores at 10 min and outcomes at 6–7 years following hypoxic-ischaemic encephalopathy. *Archives of Disease in Childhood—Fetal & Neonatal Edition, 98*(6), F473–F479. doi:10.1136/archdischild-2013-303692

Nathanson, L., Rivers, S. E., Flynn, L. M., & Brackett, M. A. (2016). Creating emotionally intelligent schools with RULER. *Emotion Review, 8*, 305–310.

Nation, K., & Hulme, C. (1998). The role of analogy in early spelling development. In C. Hulme & R. Joshi (Eds.), *Reading and spelling: Development and disorders* (pp. 433–445). Mahwah, NJ: Erlbaum.

National Association for the Education of Young Children. (1997). *Developmentally appropriate practice in early childhood programs serving children from birth through age 8*. Washington, DC: Author.

National Association for the Education of Young Children. (2009). *Developmentally appropriate practice in early childhood programs serving children birth through age 8*. Retrieved from http://208.118.177.216/about/positions/pdf/PSDAP.pdf

National Association of Secondary School Principals. (2004). *Breaking ranks II: Strategies for leading high school reform*. Reston, VA: Author.

National Board for Professional Teaching Standards. (2001). *NBTS middle childhood generalist standards* (2nd ed.). Retrieved from http://www.nbpts.org/the_standards/standards_by_cert?ID=27&x=57&y=9

National Center for Education Statistics. (2017). *Fact facts: English language learners*. Retrieved on from https://nces.ed.gov/fastfacts/display.asp?id=96

National Center for Missing and Exploited Children. (2004). HDOP: *Help delete online predators*. Retrieved from http://www.missingkids.com/adcouncil

National Center on Linguistic and Cultural Responsiveness. (2014). *Gathering information on language that families share*. Retrieved from http://eclkc.ohs.acf.hhs.gov/hslc/tta-system/cultural-linguistic/docs/dll_background_info.pdf

National Council for the Social Studies (2016). *NCSS position statement: A vision of powerful teaching and learning in the social studies*. Retrieved from https://www.socialstudies.org/publications/socialeducation/may-june2016/vision-of-powerful-teaching-and-learning-in-social-studies

National Dissemination Center for Children with Disabilities. (2013). *Intellectual disability*. Retrieved from http://nichcy.org/disability/specific/intellectual#causes

National Drug Intelligence Center. (2008). *Attorney General's report to Congress on the growth of violent street gangs in suburban areas*. Retrieved from http://www.usdoj.gov/ndic/pubs27/27612/estimate.htm

National Eating Disorder Toolkit (2017). *Educator toolkit*. Retrieved from https://www.nationaleatingdisorders.org/sites/default/files/Toolkits/EducatorToolkit.pdf

National Governors Association and Council of Chief State School Officers. (2014). *Common Core State Standards Initiative: Preparing America's students for college and career*. Retrieved from http://www.corestandards.org

National Institute of Mental Health. (2008b). *Suicide in the U.S.: Statistics and prevention*. Retrieved from http://www.nimh.nih.gov/health/publications/suicide-in-the-us-statistics-and-prevention.shtml#races

National Institute on Drug Abuse (2015). *Synthetic cannabinoids*. Retrieved from https://www.drugabuse.gov/publications/drugfacts/synthetic-cannabinoids

National Institute on Drug Abuse (2017). *Prescription drugs*. Retrieved from https://teens.drugabuse.gov/drug-facts/prescription-drugs

National Institute on Drug Abuse. (2003). *Preventing drug use among children and adolescents: A research-based guide for parents, educators, and community leaders*. Bethesda, MD: U.S. Department of Health and Human Services, National Institutes of Health, National Institute on Drug Abuse.

National Institute on Drug Abuse. (2010a). *Alcohol*. Retrieved from http://www.drugabuse.gov/drugpages/alcohol.html

National Institute on Drug Abuse. (2010b). *Cocaine*. Retrieved from http://www.drugabuse.gov/drugpages/cocaine.html

National Institute on Drug Abuse. (2010c). *Inhalants*. Retrieved from http://www.drugabuse.gov/drugpages/inhalants.html

National Institute on Drug Abuse. (2010d). *Marijuana*. Retrieved from http://www.drugabuse.gov/drugpages/marijuana.html

National Institute on Drug Abuse. (2010e). *MDMA (ecstasy)*. Retrieved from http://www.drugabuse.gov/drugpages/mdma.html

National Institute on Drug Abuse. (2010f). *Methamphetamines*. Retrieved from http://www.drugabuse.gov/drugpages/methamphetamine.html

National Institute on Drug Abuse. (2010g). *Prescription drugs*. Retrieved from http://www.drugabuse.gov/drugpages/prescription.html

National Institute on Drug Abuse. (2010h). *Steroids (anabolic)*. Retrieved from http://www.drugabuse.gov/drugpages/steroids.html

National Institute on Drug Abuse. (2014). *Principles of adolescent substance use disorder treatment: A research-based guide*. Retrieved from https://www.drugabuse.gov/publications/principles-adolescent-substance-use-disorder-treatment-research-based-guide/evidence-based-approaches-to-treating-adolescent-substance-use-disorders

National Research Council. (1999). *How people learn: Brain, mind, experience, and school*. Washington, DC: Author.

National Science Teachers Association. (2014). NSTA position statement: Early childhood science education. *Science & Children, 51*(7), 10–12.

National Technical Assistance Center on Positive Behavioral Interventions and Supports. (2018). *About us*. Retrieved March 2, 2018, from https://www.pbis.org/about-us

National Technical Assistance Center on Positive Behavioral Interventions and Supports. (2018). School. Retrieved on February 27, 2018, from https://www.pbis.org/school

Naumova, O. Y., Hein, S., Suderman, M., Barbot, B., Lee, M., Raefski, A., . . . Grigorenko, E. L. (2016). Epigenetic patterns modulate the connection between developmental dynamics of parenting and offspring psychosocial adjustment. *Child Development, 87*(1), 98–110. doi:10.1111/cdev.12485

NCSS Task Force on Ethnic Studies Curriculum Guidelines. (1992). Curriculum guidelines for multicultural education. *Social Education, 56*, 274–294.

Neal, J., Neal, Z. P., & Cappella, E. (2014). I know who my friends are, but do you? Predictors of self-reported and peer-inferred relationships. *Child Development, 85*, 1366–1372. doi:10.1111/cdev.12194

Needham-Penrose, J., & Friedman, H. L. (2012). Moral identity versus moral reasoning in religious conservatives: Do Christian evangelical leaders really lack moral maturity? *The Humanistic Psychologist, 40*, 343–363. doi:10.1080/08873267.2012.724256

Needham, B. L., & Austin, E. L. (2010). Sexual orientation, parental support, and health during the transition to young adulthood. *Journal of Youth and Adolescence, 39*, 1189–1198. doi:10.1007/s10964-010-9533-6

Neiheiser, L. L. (2015). Students in foster care: Individualized school-based supports for successful lives. *School Psychology Forum, 9*(1), 21–31.

Neinstein, L. S. (2004). *Substance abuse—Stimulants/ inhalants/opioids/anabolic steroids/ designer and club drugs. Adolescent health curriculum*. Retrieved from http://www.usc.edu/student-affairs/Health_Center/adolhealth/content/b8subs3.html

Neisser, U. (1976). *Cognition and reality*. San Francisco, CA: Freeman.

Neisser, U. (1998a). Introduction: Rising test scores and what they mean. In U. Neisser (Ed.), *The rising curve: Long-term gains in IQ and related measures* (pp. 3–22). Washington, DC: American Psychological Association.

Neisser, U. (Ed.). (1998b). *The rising curve: Long-term gains in IQ and related measures*. Washington, DC: American Psychological Association.

Neisser, U., Boodoo, G., Bouchard, T. J., Boykin, A. W., Brody, N., Ceci, S. J., . . . Urbina, S. (1996). Intelligence: Knowns and unknowns. *American Psychologist, 51*, 77–101.

Nelson, B. B., Chung, P. J., Forness, S. R., Pillado, O., Savage, S., Duplessis, H. M., . . . Hataoka, S. H. (2013). Developmental and health services in Head Start preschools: A tiered approach to early intervention. *Academic Pediatrics, 13*(2), 145–151.

Nelson, C. A., III, Thomas, K. M., & de Haan, M. (2006). Neural bases of cognitive development. In D. Kuhn & R. Siegler (Vol. Eds.), & W. Damon, & R. M. Lerner (Series Eds.), *Handbook of Child Psychology, Vol. 2. Cognition, perception, and language* (6th ed., pp. 3–57). New York, NY: Wiley.

Nelson, K. (1973). Structure and strategy in learning to talk. *Monographs of the Society for Research in Child Development, 38*(1–2, Serial No. 149). http://dx.doi.org.unco.idm.oclc.org/10.2307/1165788

Nelson, K. (1996a). *Language in cognitive development: The emergence of the mediated mind*. Cambridge, England: Cambridge University Press.

Nelson, K. (1996b). Memory development from 4 to 7 years. In A. J. Sameroff & M. M. Haith (Eds.), *The 5 to 7 shift* (pp. 141–160). Chicago, IL: University of Chicago Press.

Nelson, K. (1997). Event representations then, now, and next. In P. van den Broek, P. J. Bauer, & T. Bourg (Eds.), *Developmental spans in event representation and comprehension: Bridging fictional and actual events* (pp. 1–26). Mahwah, NJ: Erlbaum.

Nelson, K. (2005). Evolution and development of human memory systems. In B. J. Ellis & D. F. Bjorklund (Eds.), *Origins of the social mind: Evolutionary psychology and child development* (pp. 354–382). New York, NY: Guilford Press.

Nelson, S. W., & Guerra, P. L. (2009). For diverse families, parent involvement takes on a new meaning. *Journal of Staff Development, 30*(4), 65–66.

Nesteruk, O., Marks, L., & Garrison, M. E. B. (2009). Immigrant parents' concerns regarding their children's education in the United States. *Family and Consumer Sciences Research Journal, 37*, 422–441.

Nettelbeck, T., & Wilson, C. (2005). Intelligence and IQ: What teachers should know. *Educational Psychology, 25*, 609–630.

Neumann, M. M. (2018). Using tablets and apps to enhance emergent literacy skills in young children. *Early Childhood Research Quarterly, 42*, 239–246. http://dx.doi.org.unco.idm.oclc.org/10.1016/j.ecresq.2017.10.006

Neumann, M. M., & Neumann, D. L. (2017). The use of touch-screen tablets at home and pre-school to foster emergent literacy. *Journal of Early Childhood Literacy, 17*, 203–220. doi:10.1177/1468798415619773

Neumann, M. M., Finger, G., & Neumann, D. L. (2017). A conceptual framework for emergent digital literacy. *Early Childhood Education Journal, 45*, 471–479. http://dx.doi.org.unco.idm.oclc.org/10.1007/s10643-016-0792-z

Neville, H. J., & Bavelier, D. (2001). Variability of developmental plasticity. In J. L. McClelland & R. S. Siegler (Eds.), *Mechanisms of cognitive development: Behavioral and neural perspectives* (pp. 271–287). Mahwah, NJ: Erlbaum.

Newcomb, A. F., & Bagwell, C. L. (1995). Children's friendship relations: A meta-analysis review. *Psychological Bulletin, 117*, 306–347.

Newcomb, A. F., & Brady, J. E. (1982). Mutuality in boys' friendship relations. *Child Development, 53*, 392–395.

Newcombe, N. N., & Frick, A. (2010). Early education for spatial intelligence: Why, what, and how. *Mind, Brain & Education, 4*(3), 102–111. doi:10.1111/j.1751-228X.2010.01089.x

Newcombe, N. S. (2013). Cognitive development: Changing views of cognitive change. WIREs *Cognitive Science, 4*, 479–491. doi:10.1002/wcs.1245

Newcombe, N. S., Sluzenski, J., & Huttenlocher, J. (2005). Preexisting knowledge versus on-line learning: What do young infants really know about spatial location? *Psychological Science, 16*, 222–227.

Newell, D. A. (2012). Risk and protective factors for secondary girls of incarcerated parents. *Family Court Review, 50*(1), 106–112. doi:10.1111/j.1744-1617.2011.01432.x

Newkirk, T. (2002). *Misreading masculinity: Boys, literacy, and popular culture*. Portsmouth, NH: Heinemann.

Newland, L. A. (2015). Family well-being, parenting, and child well-being: Pathways to healthy adjustment. *Clinical Psychologist, 19*(1), 3–14. doi:10.1111/cp.12059

Newman, A. J., Supalla, T., Hauser, P. C., Newport, E. L., & Bavelier, D. (2010). Prosodic and narrative processing in American Sign Language: An fMRI study. *NeuroImage, 52*, 669–676.

Newman, J., & Hubner, J. (2012). Designing challenging science experiences for high-ability learners through partnerships with university professors. *Gifted Child Today, 35*, 102–115. doi:10.1177/1076217511436093

Newman, L. S. (1990). Intentional and unintentional memory in young children: Remembering vs. playing. *Journal of Experimental Child Psychology, 50*, 243–258.

Newman, R. S., & Schwager, M. T. (1992). Student perceptions and academic help seeking. In D. Schunk & J. Meece (Eds.), *Student perceptions in the classroom (pp. 123–146)*. Hillsdale, NJ: Erlbaum.

Newport, E. L. (1990). Maturational constraints on language learning. *Cognitive Science, 14*, 11–28.

Newson, J., & Newson, E. (1975). Intersubjectivity and the transmission of culture: On the origins of symbolic functioning. *Bulletin of the British Psychological Society, 28*, 437–446.

Nguyen, H. N., Laski, E. I., Thomson, D. T., Bronson, M. M., & Casey, B. C. (2017). More than counting: Learning to label quantities in preschool. *Young Children, 72*(3), 22–29.

Nguyen, L., & Gu, Y. (2013). Strategy-based instruction: A learner-focused approach to developing learner autonomy. *Language Teaching Research, 17*(1), 9–30. doi:10.1177/1362168812457528

Ni, Y., & Zhou, Y.-D. (2005). Teaching and learning fraction and rational numbers: The origins and implications of whole number bias. *Educational Psychologist, 40*, 27–52.

NICHD Early Child Care Research Network. (2002). Early child care and children's development prior to school entry: Results from the NICHD study of early child care. *American Educational Research Journal, 39*, 133–164.

NICHD Early Child Care Research Network. (2006a). Child-care effect sizes for the NICHD Study of Early Child Care and Youth Development. *American Psychologist, 61*, 99–116.

NICHD Early Child Care Research Network. (2006b). Infant–mother attachment classification: Risk and protection in relation to changing maternal caregiving quality. *Developmental Psychology, 42*, 38–58.

Nicholls, J. G. (1984). Conceptions of ability and achievement motivation. In R. Ames & C. Ames (Eds.), *Research on Motivation in Education: Vol. 1. Student motivation* (pp. 39–73). San Diego, CA: Academic Press.

Nicholls, J. G. (1990). What is ability and why are we mindful of it? A developmental perspective. In R. J. Sternberg & J. Kolligian (Eds.), *Competence considered (pp. 11–40)*. New Haven, CT: Yale University Press.

Nicholls, J. G., Cobb, P., Yackel, E., Wood, T., & Wheatley, G. (1990). Students' theories of mathematics and their mathematical knowledge: Multiple dimensions of assessment. In G. Kulm (Ed.), *Assessing higher order thinking in mathematics (pp. 137–154)*. Washington, DC: American Association for the Advancement of Science.

Nichols, E. B., Loper, A. B., & Meyer, J. P. (2016). Promoting educational resiliency in youth with incarcerated parents: The impact of parental incarceration, school characteristics, and connectedness on school outcomes. *Journal of Youth and Adolescence, 45*, 1090–1109. doi:10.1007/s10964-015-0337-6

Nichols, M. L., & Ganschow, L. (1992). Has there been a paradigm shift in gifted education? In N. Colangelo, S. G. Assouline, & D. L. Ambroson (Eds.), *Talent development: Proceedings from the 1991 Henry B. and Jocelyn Wallace National Research Symposium on Talent Development*. New York, NY: Trillium.

Nichter, M., Nichter, M., Muramoto, M., Adrian, S., Goldade, K., Tesler, L., Tesler, L., & Thompson, J. (2007). Smoking among low-income pregnant women: An ethnographic analysis. *Health Education and Behavior, 34*, 748–764.

Nickerson, R. S. (2010). *Mathematical reasoning: Patterns, problems, conjectures, and proofs*. New York, NY: Psychology Press.

Nicolaidou, I. (2013). E-portfolios supporting primary students' writing performance and peer feedback. *Computers & Education, 68*, 404–415. doi:10.1016/j.compedu.2013.06.004

Nicolas, G. (2016). Overview of historical and political factors affecting parenting practices. In G. Nicolas, A. Bejarano, & D. L. Lee (Eds.), *Contemporary parenting: A global perspective* (pp. 3–8). New York: Routledge/Taylor & Francis Group.

Nicolopoulou, A., & Richner, E. S. (2007). From actors to agents to persons: The development of character representation in young children's narratives. *Child Development, 78*, 412–429.

Nicolson, S., & Shipstead, S. G. (2002). *Through the looking glass: Observations in the early childhood classroom* (3rd ed.). Upper Saddle River, NJ: Merrill/Prentice Hall.

Niechwiej-Szwedo, E., Chin, J., Wolfe, P. J., Popovich, C., & Staines, W. R. (2016). Abnormal visual experience during development alters the early stages of visual-tactile integration. *Behavioural Brain Research, 304*, 111–119. doi:10.1016/j.bbr.2016.02.018

Nieto, S. (1995). *Affirming diversity* (2nd ed.). White Plains, NY: Longman.

Nigg, J. T. (2017). Annual research review: On the relations among self-regulation, self-control, executive functioning, effortful control, cognitive control, impulsivity, risk-taking, and inhibition for developmental psychopathology. *Journal of Child Psychology and Psychiatry, 58*, 361–383. doi:10.1111/jcpp.12675

Nihiser, A. J., Lee, S. M., Wechsler, H., McKenna, M., Odom, E., Reinold, C., & ... Grummer-Strawn, L. (2009). BMI Measurement in Schools. *Pediatrics, 124*, S89-S97. doi:10.1542/peds.2008-3586L

Nijnatten, C. H.C.J., Matarese, M. T., & Noordegraaf, M. (2017). Accomplishing irony: Socializing foster children into peer culture. *Child & Family Social Work*. Advance online publication. http://dx.doi.org.unco.idm.oclc.org/10.1111/cfs.12372

Nilsen, E. S., Huyder, V., McAuley, T., & Liebermann, D. (2017). Ratings of Everyday Executive Functioning (REEF): A parent-report measure of preschoolers' executive functioning skills. *Psychological Assessment, 29*(1), 50–64.

Nilsson, D. E., & Bradford, L. W. (1999). Neurofibromatosis. In S. Goldstein & C. R. Reynolds (Eds.), *Handbook of neurodevelopmental and genetic disorders* (pp. 350–367). New York, NY: Guilford Press.

Nisbett, R. (2013). Schooling makes you smarter. *American Educator, 37*(1), 10–39.

Nisbett, R. E. (2003). *The geography of thought: How Asians and Westerners think differently—and why*. New York, NY: Free Press.

Nisbett, R. E. (2009). *Intelligence and how to get it: Why schools and cultures count*. New York, NY: W. W. Norton.

Nisbett, R. E., Aronson, J., Blair, C., Dickens, W., Flynn, J., Halpern, D. F., & Turkheimer, E. (2012). Group differences in IQ are best understood as environmental in origin. *American Psychologist, 67*, 503–504. doi:10.1037/a0029772

Noam, G. G., & Bernstein-Yamashiro, B. (2013). Youth development practitioners and their relationships in schools and after-school programs. *New Directions for Youth Development, 2013*(137), 57–68. doi:10.1002/yd.20048

Noffke, S. (1997). Professional, personal, and political dimensions of action research. *Review of Research in Education, 22*, 305–343.

Nokes, J. D., Dole, J. A., & Hacker, D. J. (2007). Teaching high school students to use heuristics while reading historical texts. *Journal of Educational Psychology, 99*, 492–504.

Nolen-Hoeksema, S., Morrow, J., & Fredrickson, B. L. (1993). Response styles and the duration of episodes of depressed moods. *Journal of Abnormal Psychology, 102*, 20–28.

Nolte, K., Krüger, P. E., Els, P., & Nolte, H. (2013). Three dimensional musculoskeletal modelling of the abdominal crunch resistance training exercise. *Journal of Sports Sciences, 31*(3), 264–275.

Nomura, Y., Fifer, W., & Brooks-Gunn, J. (2005). *The role of perinatal factors for risk of co-occurring psychiatric and medical disorders in adulthood*. Paper presented at the biennial meeting of the Society for Research in Child Development, Atlanta, GA.

Noonan, R. J., Boddy, L. M., Fairclough, S. J., & Knowles, Z. R. (2016). Write, draw, show, and tell: a child-centred dual methodology to explore perceptions of out-of-school physical activity. *BMC Public Health, 16*(1), 19. doi:10.1186/s12889-016-3005-1

Nordahl, K., Janson, H., Manger, T., & Zachrisson, H. (2014). Family concordance and gender differences in parent-child structured interaction at 12 months. *Journal of Family Psychology, 28*, 253–259. doi:10.1037/a0035977

Norenzayan, A. (2014). Does religion make people moral? *Behaviour, 151*, 365–384. doi:10.1163/1568539X-00003139

Norton, N. L. (2014). Young children manifest spiritualities in their hip-hop writing. Education & Urban Society, 46(3), 329–351. doi:10.1177/0013124512446216.

Nucci, L. P. (2001). *Education in the moral domain*. Cambridge, England: Cambridge University Press.

Nucci, L. P. (2006). Education for moral development. In M. Killen & J. G. Smetana (Eds.), *Handbook of moral development* (pp. 657–681). Mahwah, NJ: Erlbaum.

Nucci, L. P. (2009). *Nice is not enough: Facilitating moral development*. Upper Saddle River, NJ: Pearson Education.

Nucci, L. P., & Weber, E. K. (1991). The domain approach to values education: From theory to practice. In W. M. Kurtines & J. L. Gewirtz (Eds.), *Handbook of Moral Behavior and Development: Vol. 3. Application* (pp. 251–266). Hillsdale, NJ: Erlbaum.

Nucci, L., Creane, M. W., & Powers, D. W. (2015). Integrating moral and social development within middle school social studies: A social cognitive domain approach. *Journal of Moral Education, 44*, 480–497. http://dx.doi.org.

unco.idm.oclc.org/10.1080/03057240.2015.1087391

Nugent, J. (2013). The competent newborn and the Neonatal Behavioral Assessment Scale: T. Berry Brazelton's legacy. *Journal of Child and Adolescent Psychiatric Nursing, 26*, 173–179. doi:10.1111/jcap.12043

Nuijens, K. L., Teglasi, H., & Hancock, G. R. (2009). Self-perceptions, discrepancies between self- and other-perceptions, and children's self-reported emotions. *Journal of Psychoeducational Assessment, 27*, 477–493.

Núñez, J., Suárez, N., Rosário, P., Vallejo, G., Valle, A., & Epstein, J. (2015). Relationships between perceived parental involvement in homework, student homework behaviors, and academic achievement: differences among elementary, junior high, and high school students. *Metacognition & Learning, 10*, 375–406. doi:10.1007/s11409-015-9135-5

Nunner-Winkler, G. (2007). Development of moral motivation from childhood to early adulthood. *Journal of Moral Education, 36*(4), 399–414. doi:10.1080/03057240701687970

Nuttall, R. L., Casey, M. B., & Pezaris, E. (2005). Spatial ability as mediator of gender differences on mathematics tests. In A. M. Gallagher & J. C. Kaufman (Eds.), *Gender differences in mathematics: An integrative psychological approach* (pp. 121–142). Cambridge, England: Cambridge University Press.

Nwokah, E. E., Burnette, S. E., & Graves, K. N. (2013). Joke telling, humor creation, and humor recall in children with and without hearing loss. *Humor: International Journal of Humor Research, 26*(1), 69–96. doi:10.1515/humor-2013-0005

O'Brennan, L. M., & Furlong, M. J. (2010). Relations between students' perceptions of school connectedness and peer victimization. *Journal of School Violence, 9*, 375–391. doi:10.1080/15388220.2010.509009

O'Connor, E., & McCartney, K. (2006). Testing associations between young children's relationships with mothers and teachers. *Journal of Educational Psychology, 98*, 87–98.

O'Connor, J. (2012). Is it good to be gifted? The social construction of the gifted child. *Children & Society, 26*, 293–303. doi:10.1111/j.1099-0860.2010.00341.x

O'Connor, T. G., & Hirsch, N. (1999). Intra-individual differences and relationship-specificity of mentalising in early adolescence. *Social Development, 8*, 256–274. doi:10.1111/1467 9507.00094

O'Flaherty, J. Liddy, M.,Tansey, L., Roche, C. (2011). Educating engaged citizens: Four projects from Ireland. *Education + Training, 53*, 267–283.

O'Grady, W. (1997). *Syntactic development.* Chicago, IL: University of Chicago Press.

O'Keefe, P. A. (2013). Mindsets and self-evaluation: How beliefs about intelligence can create a preference for growth over defensiveness. In S. Kaufman (Ed.), *The complexity of greatness: Beyond talent or practice* (pp. 119–134). New York, NY: Oxford University Press.

O'Leary, K. D., & O'Leary, S. G. (Eds.). (1972). *Classroom management: The successful use of behavior modification.* New York, NY: Pergamon Press.

O'Leary, S. G., & Vidair, H. B. (2005). Marital adjustment, child-rearing disagreements, and overreactive parenting: Predicting child behavior problems. *Journal of Family Psychology, 19*, 208–216.

O'Malley, P. M., & Bachman, J. G. (1983). Self-esteem: Change and stability between ages 13 and 23. *Developmental Psychology, 19*, 257–268.

O'Neill, G., & Miller, P. (2013). A show of hands: Relations between young children's gesturing and executive function. *Developmental Psychology, 49*, 1517–1528. doi:10.1037/a0030241

O'Neill, S., Fleer, M., Agbenyega, J., Ozanne-Smith, J., & Urlichs, M. (2013). A cultural-historical construction of safety education programs for preschool children: Findings from SeeMore Safety, the pilot study. *Australasian Journal of Early Childhood, 38*(2), 74–84.

O'Reilly, F., & Matt, J. (2012). The selection of gifted students: Did Malcolm Gladwell overstate the role of relative age in the gifted program selection process? *Gifted Child Today, 35*, 122–127. doi:10.1177/1076217512437733

O'Sullivan-Lago, R., & de Abreu, G. (2010). The dialogical self in a cultural contact zone: Exploring the perceived 'cultural correction' function of schooling. *Journal of Community and Applied Social Psychology, 20*, 275 287.

O'Toole, M. E. (2000). *The school shooter: A threat assessment perspective.* Quantico, VA: Federal Bureau of Investigation. Retrieved from http://www.fbi.gov/publications/school/school2.pdf

Oakes, J., & Guiton, G. (1995). Matchmaking: The dynamics of high school tracking decisions. *American Educational Research Journal, 32*, 3–33.

Øberg, G., Blanchard, Y., & Obstfelder, A. (2014). Therapeutic encounters with preterm infants: interaction, posture and movement. *Physiotherapy Theory & Practice, 30*(1), 1–5. doi:10.3109/09593985.2013.806621

Oberman, L. M., & Ramachandran, V. S. (2015). The role of the mirror neuron system in the pathophysiology of autism spectrum disorder. In P. F. Ferrari & G. Rizzolatti (Eds.), *New frontiers in mirror neurons research* (pp. 380–396). New York, NY: Oxford University Press. http://dx.doi.org.unco.idm.oclc.org/10.1093/acprof:oso/9780199686155.003.0021

Obradović, J., Long, J. D., Cutuli, J. J., Chan, C., Hinz, E., Heistad, D., & Masten, A. S. (2009). Academic achievement of homeless and highly mobile children in an urban school district: Longitudinal evidence on risk, growth, and resilience. *Development and Psychopathology, 21*, 493–518.

Ochs, E. (2002). Becoming a speaker of culture. In C. Kramsch (Ed.), *Language acquisition and language socialization* (pp. 99–120). London, England: Continuum.

Ochs, E., & Schieffelin, B. (1995). The impact of language socialization on grammatical development. In P. Fletcher & B. MacWhinney (Eds.), *The handbook of child language* (pp. 73–94). Cambridge, MA: Blackwell.

Ogbu, J. U. (1994). From cultural differences to differences in cultural frames of reference. In P. M. Greenfield & R. R. Cocking (Eds.), *Cross-cultural roots of minority child development* (pp. 365–391). Hillsdale, NJ: Erlbaum.

Ogbu, J. U. (1999). Beyond language: Ebonics, proper English, and identity in a Black-American speech community. *American Educational Research Journal, 36*, 147–184.

Ogbu, J. U. (2003). *Black American students in an affluent suburb: A study of academic disengagement.* Mahwah, NJ: Erlbaum.

Ogden, E. H., & Germinario, V. (1988). *The at-risk student: Answers for educators.* Lancaster, PA: Technomic.

Ogliari, A., Spatola, C. A., Pesenti Gritti, P., Medda, E., Penna, L., Stazi, M. A., . . . Fagnani, C. (2010). The role of genes and environment in shaping co-occurrence of DSM IV defined anxiety dimensions among Italian twins aged 8–17. *Journal of Anxiety Disorders, 24*, 433–439.

Oguntoyinbo, L. (2009). Disappearing act. *Diverse Issues in Higher Education, 26*(16), 14–15.

Ohye, B., Rauch, P., & Bostic, J. (2012). *Educator toolkit to increase awareness and support to military children in schools.* Red Sox Foundation and Massachusetts General Hospital. Retrieved from http://www.homebaseprogram.org/community-education/tool-kits.aspx

Okagaki, L. (2001). Triarchic model of minority children's school achievement. *Educational Psychologist, 36*, 9–20.

Okoza, J., Aluede, O., & Owens-Sogolo, O. (2013). Assessing students' metacognitive awareness of learning strategies among secondary school students in Edo State, Nigeria. *Research in Education, 90*, 82–97. doi:10.7227/RIE.90.1.6

Oktay-Gür, N., Schulz, A., & Rakoczy, H. (2018). Children exhibit different performance patterns in explicit and implicit theory of mind tasks. *Cognition, 173*, 60–74.

Olinghouse, N. G., Graham, S., & Gillespie, A. (2015). The relationship of discourse and topic knowledge to fifth graders' writing performance. *Journal of Educational Psychology, 107*, 391–406. http://dx.doi.org.unco.idm.oclc.org/10.1037/a0037549

Olive, T., Favart, M., Beauvais, C., & Beauvais, L. (2009). Children's cognitive effort and fluency in writing: Effects of genre and of handwriting automatisation. *Learning and Instruction, 19*, 299–308.

Ollendick, T. H., Costa, N. M., & Benoit, K. E. (2010). Interpersonal processes and the anxiety disorders of childhood. In J. G. Beck (Ed.), *Interpersonal processes in the anxiety disorders: Implications for understanding psychopathology and treatment* (pp. 71–95). Washington, DC: American Psychological Association.

Oller, J. R., Oller, S. D., & Oller, S. N. (2014). *Milestones: Normal speech and language development across the life span* (2nd ed.). San Diego, CA: Plural Publishing.

Olmedo, I. M. (2009). Blending borders of language and culture: Schooling in La Villita. *Journal of Latinos and Education, 8*(1), 22–37.

Olowokere, A. E., & Okanlawon, F. A. (2014). The effects of a school-based psychosocial intervention on resilience and health outcomes among vulnerable children. *The Journal of School Nursing, 30*, 206–215. doi:10.1177/1059840513501557

Olson, C. B., Kim, J., Scarcella, R., Kramer, J., Pearson, M., van Dyk, D., . . . Land, R. E. (2012). Enhancing the interpretive reading and analytical writing of mainstreamed English learners in secondary school: Results from a randomized field trim using a cognitive strategies approach. *American Educational Research Journal, 49*, 323–355. doi:10.3102/0002831212439434

Olson, C. K. (2010). Children's motivations for video game play in the context of normal development. *Review of General Psychology, 14*, 180–187. doi:10.1037/a0018984

Olson, R. R., Keenan, J. M., Byrne, B., & Samuelsson, S. (2014). Why do children differ in their development of reading and related skills? *Scientific Studies of Reading, 18*(1), 38–54. doi:10.1080/10888438.2013.800521

Olszewski-Kubilius, P., Lee, S., & Thomson, D. (2014). Family environment and social development in gifted students. *Gifted Child Quarterly, 58*, 199–216. doi:10.1177/0016986214526430

Olszewski-Kubilius, P., Subotnik, R. F., & Worrell, F. C. (2017). Response to ACCEL: Emphasize development, domains, and application. *Roeper Review, 39*(3), 199–202. doi:10.1080/02783193.2017.1318995

Oltmanns, T. F., & Emery, R. E. (2007). *Abnormal psychology* (5th ed.). Upper Saddle River, NJ: Pearson Prentice Hall.

Ongley, S. F., & Malti, T. (2014). The role of moral emotions in the development of children's sharing behavior. *Developmental Psychology, 50*, 1148–1159. doi:10.1037/a0035191

Onyekuru, B. U., & Njoku, J. (2015). Metacognition, intelligence, motivation and students' academic achievement: A theoretical review. *Journal of Educational Review, 8*, 195–204.

Oortwijn, M. B., Boekaerts, M., Vedder, P., & Fortuin, J. (2008). The impact of a cooperative learning experience on pupils' popularity, non-cooperativeness, and interethnic bias in multiethnic elementary schools. *Educational Psychology, 28*, 211–221.

Opfer, J. E., & Siegler, R. S. (2004). Revisiting preschoolers' living things concept: A microgenetic analysis of conceptual change in basic biology. *Cognitive Psychology, 49*, 301–332. doi:10.1016/j.cogpsych.2004.01.002

Ordaz, S. J., Goyer, M. S., Ho, T. C., Singh, M. K., & Gotlib, I. H. (2018). Network basis of suicidal ideation in depressed adolescents. Journal of Affective Disorders, 226, 92–99. http://dx.doi.org.unco.idm.oclc.org/10.1016/j.jad.2017.09.021

Organization of Teratology Information Specialists. (2013a). *Isotretinoin (Accutane®) and pregnancy*. Retrieved from http://www.mothertobaby.org/files/isotretinoin.pdf

Organization of Teratology Information Specialists. (2013b). *Marijuana and pregnancy*. Retrieved from http://www.mothertobaby.org/files/marijuana.pdf

Organization of Teratology Information Specialists. (2013c). *Methamphetamine/Dextroamphetamine and pregnancy*. Retrieved from http://www.mothertobaby.org/files/methamphetamine.pdf

Organization of Teratology Information Specialists. (2013d). *Toxoplasmosis and pregnancy*. Retrieved from http://www.mothertobaby.org/files/toxoplasmosis.pdf

Orkibi, H., Hamama, L., Gavriel-Fried, B., & Ronen, T. (2018). Pathways to adolescents' flourishing: Linking self-control skills and positivity ratio through social support. *Youth & Society, 50*(1), 3–25.

Orme, J. G., & Buehler, C. (2001). Foster family characteristics and behavioral and emotional problems of foster children: A narrative review. *Family Relations, 50*, 3–15.

Ormrod, J. E. (2008). *Human learning* (5th ed.). Upper Saddle River, NJ: Merrill/Prentice Hall.

Ormrod, J. E. (2011). *Educational psychology: Developing learners* (7th ed.). Boston: Pearson/Allyn & Bacon.

Ormrod, J. E. (2014). *Human learning* (7th ed.). Boston, MA: Pearson.

Ormrod, J. E., & McGuire, D. J. (2007). *Case studies: Applying educational psychology* (2nd ed.). Upper Saddle River, NJ: Merrill/Prentice Hall.

Ormrod, J. E., & McGuire, D. J. (2007). *Case studies: Applying educational psychology* (2nd ed.). Upper Saddle River, NJ: Merrill/Prentice Hall.

Ormrod, J. E., Jackson, D. L., Kirby, B., Davis, J., & Benson, C. (1999, April). *Cognitive development as reflected in children's conceptions of early American history*. Paper presented at the annual meeting of the American Educational Research Association, Montreal, Quebec, Canada.

Ornstein, P. A., Grammer, J. K., & Coffman, J. L. (2010). Teachers' "mnemonic style" and the development of skilled memory. In H. S. Waters & W. Schneider (Eds.), *Metacognition, strategy use, and instruction*. (pp. 23–53). New York, NY: Guilford Press.

Ornstein, R. (1997). *The right mind: Making sense of the hemispheres*. San Diego, CA: Harcourt Brace.

Ortiz-Mantilla, S., Hämäläinen, J. A., Realpe-Bonilla, T., & Benasich, A. A. (2016). Oscillatory dynamics underlying perceptual narrowing of native phoneme mapping from 6 to 12 months of age. *Journal of Neuroscience, 36*, 12095–12105. http://dx.doi.org/10.1523/JNEUROSCI.1162-16.2016

Ortlieb, E. (2013). Using anticipatory reading guides to improve elementary students' comprehension. *International Journal of Instruction, 6*, 145–162.

Ortony, A., Turner, T. J., & Larson-Shapiro, N. (1985). Cultural and instructional influences on figurative comprehension by inner city children. *Research in the Teaching of English, 19*(1), 25–36.

Oser, F. K., Althof, W., & Higgins-D'Alessandro, A. (2008). The Just Community approach to moral education: System change or individual change? *Journal of Moral Education, 37*, 395–415. doi:10.1080/03057240802227551

Osório, A., Meins, E., Martins, C., Martins, E., & Soares, I. (2012). Child and mother mental-state talk in shared pretense as predictors of children's social symbolic play abilities at age 3. *Infant Behavior & Development, 35*, 719–726. doi:10.1016/j.infbeh.2012.07.012

Ostad, S. (2013). Private speech use in arithmetical calculation: Contributory role of phonological awareness in children with and without mathematical difficulties. *Journal of Learning Disabilities, 46*, 291–303. doi:10.1177/0022219411419013

Ostenson, J. U. (2014). Reconsidering the checklist in teaching internet source evaluation. *Portal: Libraries & The Academy, 14*(1), 33–50.

Osterhaus, C., Koerber, S., & Sodian, B. (2017). Scientific thinking in elementary school: Children's social cognition and their epistemological understanding promote experimentation skills. *Developmental Psychology, 53*, 450–462. doi:10.1037/dev0000260

Osterman, K. F. (2000). Students' need for belonging in the school community. *Review of Educational Research, 70*, 323–367.

Ota, C. L., & Austin, A. (2013). Training and mentoring: Family child care providers' use of linguistic inputs in conversations with children. *Early Childhood Research Quarterly, 28*, 972–983. doi:10.1016/j.ecresq.2013.04.001

Otake, S., Treiman, R., & Yin, L. (2017). Differentiation of writing and drawing by U.S. two- to five-year-olds. *Cognitive Development, 43*, 119–128. doi:10.1016/j.cogdev.2017.03.004

Otgaar, H., Verschuere, B., Meijer, E. H., & van Oorsouw, K. (2012). The origin of children's implanted false memories: Memory traces or compliance? *Acta Psychologica, 139*, 397–403. doi:10.1016/j.actpsy.2012.01.002

Otis, N., Grouzet, F. M. E., & Pelletier, L. G. (2005). Latent motivational change in an academic setting: A 3-year longitudinal study. *Journal of Educational Psychology, 97*, 170–183.

Otto, B. (2010). *Language development in early childhood* (3rd ed.). Upper Saddle River, NJ: Merrill Pearson.

Oudeyer, P.-Y., & Smith, L. B. (2016). How evolution may work through curiosity-driven developmental process. *Topics in Cognitive Science, 8*, 492–502.

Õun, T., Tuul, M., Tera, S., Sagen, K., & Mägi, H. (2018). The relationship between quality of pre-school child care institutions and teachers' teaching approach. *Early Child Development & Care, 188*, 542–556. doi:10.1080/03004430.2018.1445729

Overton, W. F., & Molenaar, P. C. M. (2015). Concepts, theory, and methods in developmental science: A view of the issues. In R. M. Lerner, W. F. Overton, & P. M. Molenaar (Eds.), *Handbook of child psychology and developmental science: Theory and method* (7th ed., Vol. 1, pp. 1–8) Hoboken, NJ: Wiley.

Owens, R. E., Jr. (2008). *Language development* (7th ed.). Boston, MA: Allyn & Bacon.

Owens, R. E., Jr. (2012). *Language development* (8th ed.). Boston, MA: Pearson.

Owens, R. E., Jr. (2015). *Language development* (9th ed.). Boston, MA: Pearson.

Oyserman, D., & Lee, S. W.-S. (2007). Priming "culture": Culture as situated cognition. In S. Kitayama & D. Cohen (Eds.), *Handbook of cultural psychology* (pp. 255–279). New York, NY: Guilford Press.

Oyserman, D., & Markus, H. R. (1993). The sociocultural self. In J. Suls (Ed.), *Psychological perspectives on the self* (Vol. 7, pp. 187–220). Mahwah, NJ: Erlbaum.

Ozdemir, A. (2008). Shopping malls: Measuring interpersonal distance under changing conditions and across cultures. *Field Methods, 20*, 226–248.

Ozonoff, S. (2010). Autism spectrum disorders. In K. O. Yeates, M. D. Ris, H. G. Taylor, & B. F. Pennington (Eds.), *Pediatric neuropsychology: Research, theory, and practice* (pp. 418–446). New York, NY: Guilford Press.

Paciello, M., Masi, G., Clemente, M. G., Milone, A., & Muratori, P. (2017). Moral disengagement and callous unemotional traits configurations in adolescents with disruptive behavior disorder: A person-oriented approach. *Psychiatry Research, 258*, 591–593. http://dx.doi.org.unco.idm.oclc.org/10.1016/j.psychres.2017.08.043

Padilla-Walker, L. M., & Carlo, G. (2007). Personal values as a mediator between parent and peer expectations and adolescent behaviors. *Journal of Family Psychology, 21*, 538–541.

Padilla-Walker, L. M., Carlo, G., Christensen, K. J., & Yorgason, J. B. (2012). Bidirectional relations between authoritative parenting and adolescents' prosocial behaviors. *Journal of Research on Adolescence, 22*, 400–408. doi:10.1111/j.1532-7795.2012.00807.x

Padilla, A. M. (2006). Second language learning: Issues in research and teaching. In P. A. Alexander & P. H. Winne (Eds.), *Handbook of educational psychology* (2nd ed., pp. 571–591). Mahwah, NJ: Erlbaum.

Padilla, A. M. (2006). Second language learning: Issues in research and teaching. In P. A. Alexander & P. H. Winne (Eds.), *Handbook of educational psychology* (2nd ed., pp. 571–591). Mahwah, NJ: Erlbaum.

Paget, K. F., Kritt, D., & Bergemann, L. (1984). Understanding strategic interactions in television commercials: A developmental study. *Journal of Applied Developmental Psychology, 5*, 145–161.

Pahl, K., & Way, N. (2006). Longitudinal trajectories of ethnic identity among urban Black and Latino adolescents. *Child Development, 77*, 1403–1415.

Paik, A., Sanchagrin, K. J., & Heimer, K. (2016). Broken promises: Abstinence pledging and sexual and reproductive health. *Journal of Marriage and Family, 78*, 546–561. doi:10.1111/jomf.12279

Paikoff, R. L., & Brooks-Gunn, J. (1991). Do parent–child relationships change during puberty? *Psychological Bulletin, 110*, 47–66.

Palacios, J., & Sánchez-Sandoval, Y. (2005). Beyond adopted/nonadopted comparisons. In D. M. Brodzinsky & J. Palacios (Eds.), *Psychological issues in adoption: Research and practice* (pp. 117–144). Westport, CT: Praeger/Greenwood.

Palacios, N. N., Kibler, A. K., Yoder, M., Baird, A. S., & Bergey, R. (2016). Older sibling support of younger siblings' socio-emotional development. *Hispanic Journal of Behavioral Sciences, 38*, 395–419. doi:10.1177/0739986316658865

Palermo, D. S. (1974). Still more about the comprehension of "less." *Developmental Psychology, 10*, 827–829.

Paley, V. G. (1984). *Boys and girls: Superheroes in the doll corner.* Chicago, IL: University of Chicago Press.

Paley, V. G. (2007). Goldilocks and her sister: An anecdotal guide to the doll corner. *Harvard Educational Review, 77*(2), 144–151.

Palincsar, A. S., & Brown, A. L. (1984). Reciprocal teaching of comprehension-fostering and comprehension-monitoring activities. *Cognition and Instruction, 1*, 117–175.

Palincsar, A. S., & Brown, A. L. (1989). Classroom dialogues to promote self-regulated comprehension. In J. Brophy (Ed.), *Advances in research on teaching* (Vol. 1, pp. 36–67). Greenwich, CT: JAI Press.

Pallante, D. H., & Kim, Y. (2013). The effect of a multicomponent literacy instruction model on literacy growth for kindergartners and first-grade students in Chile. *International Journal of Psychology, 48*, 747–761. doi:10.1080/00207594.2012.719628

Pallini, S., Chirumbolo, A., Morelli, M., Baiocco, R., Laghi, F., & Eisenberg, N. (2018). The relation of attachment security status to effortful self-regulation: A meta-analysis. *Psychological Bulletin.* Advance online publication.

Pallotta, J., & Mazzola, F., Jr. (Illustrator). (1986). *The ocean alphabet book.* Watertown, MA: Charlesbridge.

Palmer, E. L. (1965). Accelerating the child's cognitive attainments through the inducement of cognitive conflict: An interpretation of the Piagetian position. *Journal of Research in Science Teaching, 3*, 324.

Palmer, R. C., Knopik, V. S., Rhee, S., Hopfer, C. J., Corley, R. C., Young, S. E., . . . Hewitt, J. K. (2013). Prospective effects of adolescent indicators of behavioral disinhibition on DSM-IV alcohol, tobacco, and illicit drug dependence in young adulthood. *Addictive Behaviors, 38*, 2415–2421. doi:10.1016/j.addbeh.2013.03.021

Palsbo, S. E., Marr, D., Streng, T., Bay, B. K., & Norblad, A. W. (2011). Towards a modified consumer haptic device for robotic-assisted fine-motor repetitive motion training. *Disability and Rehabilitation: Assistive Technology, 6*, 546–551. doi:10.3109/17483107.2010.532287

Pan, B. A., Rowe, M. L., Singer, J. D., & Snow, C. E. (2005). Maternal correlates of growth in toddler vocabulary production in low-income families. *Child Development, 76*, 763–782.

Panadero, E., Tapia, J., & Huertas, J. (2012). Rubrics and self-assessment scripts effects on self-regulation, learning and self-efficacy in secondary education. *Learning & Individual Differences, 22*(6), 806–813. doi:10.1016/j.lindif.2012.04.007

Panahon, C. J., & Martens, B. K. (2013). A comparison of noncontingent plus contingent reinforcement to contingent reinforcement alone on students' academic performance. *Journal of Behavioral Education, 22*, 37–49. doi:10.1007/s10864-012-9157-x

Pang, V. (2007). Asian Pacific American cultural capital: Understanding diverse parents and students. In S. J. Paik & H. J. Walberg (Eds.), *Narrowing the achievement gap strategies for educating Latino, Black, and Asian students* (pp. 49–64). New York, NY: Springer Science + Business Media.

Pangrazi, R. P., & Beighle, A. (2010). *Dynamic physical education for elementary school children* (16th ed.). San Francisco, CA: Pearson Benjamin Cummings.

Panksepp, J. (1998). Attention deficit hyperactivity disorders, psychostimulants, and intolerance of childhood playfulness: A tragedy in the making? *Current Directions in Psychological Science, 7*, 91–98.

Panter, J. E., & Bracken, B. A. (2013). Preschool assessment. In K. F. Geisinger, B. A. Bracken, J. F. Carlson, J. C. Hansen, N. R. Kuncel, S. P. Reise, & M. C. Rodriguez (Eds.), *APA Handbook of Testing and Assessment in Psychology, Vol. 3. Testing and assessment in school psychology and education* (pp. 21–37). Washington, DC: American Psychological Association. doi:10.1037/14049-002

Papandreou, M. (2014). Communicating and thinking through drawing activity in early childhood. *Journal of Research in Childhood Education, 28*, 85–100. doi:10.1080/02568543.2013.851131

Papathomas, L., & Kuhn, D. (2017). Learning to argue via apprenticeship. *Journal of Experimental Child Psychology, 159*, 129–139. doi:10.1016/j.jecp.2017.01.013

Paradise, R., & Robles, A. (2016). Two Mazahua (Mexican) communities: introducing a collective orientation into everyday school life. *European Journal of Psychology of Education - EJPE (Springer Science & Business Media B.V.), 31*(1), 61–77. doi:10.1007/s10212-015-0262-9

Paradise, R., & Rogoff, B. (2009). Side by side: Learning by observing and pitching in. *Ethos, 37*(1), 102–138.

Parent, A.-S., Franssen, D., Fudvoye, J., Gérard, A., & Bourguignon, J.-P. (2015). Developmental variations in environmental influences including endocrine disruptors on pubertal timing and neuroendocrine control: Revision of human observations and mechanistic insight from rodents. *Frontiers in Neuroendocrinology, 38*, 12–36. doi:10.1016/j.yfrne.2014.12.004

Parent, J., Jones, D. J., Forehand, R., Cuellar, J., & Shoulberg, E. K. (2013). The role of coparents in African American single-mother families: The indirect effect of coparent identity on youth psychosocial adjustment. *Journal of Family Psychology, 27*, 252–262. doi:10.1037/a0031477

Paris, D. (2009). "They're in my culture, they speak the same way": African American language in multiethnic high schools. *Harvard Educational Review, 79*, 428–447.

Paris, S. G., & Ayres, L. R. (1994). *Becoming reflective students and teachers with portfolios and authentic assessment*. Washington, DC: American Psychological Association.

Paris, S. G., & Byrnes, J. P. (1989). The constructivist approach to self-regulation and learning in the classroom. In B. J. Zimmerman & D. H. Schunk (Eds.), *Self-regulated learning and academic achievement: Theory, research, and practice* (pp. 168–200). New York, NY: Springer-Verlag.

Paris, S. G., & Cunningham, A. E. (1996). Children becoming students. In D. C. Berliner & R. C. Calfee (Eds.), *Handbook of educational psychology* (pp. 117–146). New York, NY: Macmillan.

Paris, S. G., & Turner, J. C. (1994). Situated motivation. In P. R. Pintrich, D. R. Brown, & C. E. Weinstein (Eds.), *Student motivation, cognition, and learning: Essays in honor of Wilbert J. McKeachie (pp. 213–238)*. Mahwah, NJ: Erlbaum.

Paris, S. G., & Upton, L. R. (1976). Children's memory for inferential relationships in prose. *Child Development, 47*, 660–668.

Paris, S. G., Morrison, F. J., & Miller, K. F. (2006). Academic pathways from preschool through elementary school. In P. A. Alexander & P. H. Winne (Eds.), *Handbook of educational psychology* (2nd ed., pp. 61–85). Mahwah, NJ: Erlbaum.

Paris, S. G., Yeung, A., Wong, H., & Luo, S. (2012). Global perspectives on education during middle childhood. In K. R. Harris, S. Graham, T. Urdan, A. G. Bus, S. Major, & H. L. Swanson (Eds.), *APA Educational Psychology Handbook, Vol. 3. Application to teaching and learning* (pp. 23–41). Washington, DC: American Psychological Association. doi:10.1037/13275-002

Parisette-Sparks, A., Bufferd, S. J., & Klein, D. N. (2017). Parental predictors of children's shame and guilt at age 6 in a multimethod, longitudinal study. *Journal of Clinical Child and Adolescent Psychology, 46*, 721–731.

Park, L. E., Crocker, J., & Vohs, K. D. (2006). Contingencies of self-worth and self-validation goals: Implications for close relationships. In K. D. Vohs & E. J. Finkel (Eds.), *Self and relationships: Connecting intrapersonal and interpersonal processes* (pp. 84–103). New York, NY: Guilford Press.

Park, S. S., Stone, S. I., & Holloway, S. D. (2017). School-based parental involvement as a predictor of achievement and school learning environment: An elementary school-level analysis. *Children & Youth Services Review, 82*, 195–206. doi:10.1016/j.childyouth.2017.09.012

Parke, R. D., & Buriel, R. (2006). Socialization in the family: Ethnic and ecological perspectives. In W. Damon & R. M. Lerner (Eds. in Chief) & N. Eisenberg (Vol. Ed.), *Handbook of Child Psychology: Vol. 3. Social, emotional, and personality development* (6th ed., pp. 429–504). Hoboken, NJ: Wiley.

Parke, R. D., & Clarke-Stewart, A. (2011). *Social development*. Hoboken, NJ: Wiley.

Parke, R. D., Ornstein, P. A., Rieser, J. J., & Zahn-Waxler, C. (1994). The past as prologue: An overview of a century of developmental psychology. In R. D. Parke, P. A. Ornstein, J. J. Rieser, & C. Zahn-Waxler (Eds.), *A century of developmental psychology* (pp. 1–70). Washington, DC: American Psychological Association.

Parker, J. G. (1986). Becoming friends: Conversational skills for friendship formation in young children. In J. M. Gottman & J. G. Parker (Eds.), *Conversations of friends: Speculations on affective development* (pp. 103–138). Cambridge, England: Cambridge University Press.

Parker, J. G., & Gottman, J. M. (1989). Social and emotional development in a relational context: Friendship interaction from early childhood to adolescence. In T. J. Berndt & G. W. Ladd (Eds.), *Peer relations in child development* (pp. 95–131). New York: Wiley.

Parker, J. G., Kruse, S. A., & Aikins, J. W. (2010). When friends have other friends: Friendship jealousy in childhood and early adolescence. In S. L. Hart & M. Legerstee (Eds.), *Handbook of jealousy: Theory, research, and multidisciplinary approaches* (pp. 516–546). Chichester, England, and Malden, MA: Wiley-Blackwell. doi:10.1002/9781444323542.ch22

Parker, W. D. (1997). An empirical typology of perfectionism in academically talented children. *American Educational Research Journal, 34*, 545–562.

Parkhurst, J. T., & Hopmeyer, A. (1998). Sociometric popularity and peer-perceived popularity: Two distinct dimensions of peer status. *Journal of Early Adolescence, 18*, 125–144.

Parkhurst, J., & Gottman, J. M. (1986). How young children get what they want. In J. M. Gottman & J. G. Parker (Eds.), *Conversations of friends: Speculations on affective development* (pp. 315–345). Cambridge, England: Cambridge University Press.

Parks, C. P. (1995). Gang behavior in the schools: Reality or myth? *Educational Psychology Review, 7*, 41–68.

Partanen, E., Kujala, T., Näätänen, R., Liitola, A., Sambeth, A., & Huotilainen, M. (2013). Learning-induced neural plasticity of speech processing before birth. *PNAS Proceedings of the National Academy of Sciences of the United States of America, 110*, 15145–15150. doi:10.1073/pnas.1302159110

Partanen, E., Pakarinen, S., Kujala, T., & Huotilainen, M. (2013). Infants' brain responses for speech sound changes in fast multifeature MMN paradigm. *Clinical Neurophysiology, 124*, 1578–1585. doi:10.1016/j.clinph.2013.02.014

Parten, M. B. (1932). Social participation among preschool children. *Journal of Abnormal and Social Psychology, 27*, 243–269.

Pascarella, E. T., & Terenzini, P. T. (1991). *How college affects students: Findings and insights from twenty years of research*. San Francisco, CA: Jossey-Bass.

Pascual-Leone, J. (1970). A mathematical model for the transition rule in Piaget's developmental stages. *Acta Psychologica, 32*, 301–345.

Pascual-Leone, J. (2013). Can we model organismic causes of working memory, efficiency and fluid intelligence? A meta-subjective perspective. *Intelligence, 41*, 738–743. doi:10.1016/j.intell.2013.06.001

Pasta, T., Mendola, M., Longobardi, C., Prino, L., & Gastaldi, F. (2013). Attributional style of children with and without specific learning disability. *Electronic Journal of Research in Educational Psychology, 11*, 649–664. doi:10.14204/ejrep.31.13064'

Patall, E. A., Cooper, H., & Wynn, S. (2008, March). *The importance of providing choices in the classroom*. Paper presented at the annual meeting of the American Educational Research Association, New York, NY.

Patall, E. A., Cooper, H., & Wynn, S. R. (2010). The effectiveness and relative importance of choice in the classroom. *Journal of Educational Psychology, 102*(4), 896–915. doi:10.1037/a0019545

Patall, E. A., Steingut, R. R., Vasquez, A. C., Trimble, S. S., Pituch, K. A., & Freeman, J. L. (2017). Daily autonomy supporting or thwarting and students' motivation and engagement in the high school science classroom. *Journal of Educational Psychology*. Advance online publication. http://dx.doi.org.unco.idm.oclc.org/10.1037/edu0000214

Patel, F. V. (2014). Advisory programs in middle and high schools. *Dissertation Abstracts International Section A, 74*.

Patnode, C. D., O'Connor, E., Rowland, M., Burda, B. U., Perdue, L. A., & Whitlock, E. P. (2014). Primary care behavioral interventions to prevent or reduce illicit drug use and nonmedical pharmaceutical use in children and adolescents: A systematic evidence review for the U.S. Preventive Services Task Force. *Annals of Internal Medicine, 160*, 612–620.

Patrick, M. E., O'Malley, P. M., Kloska, D. D., Schulenberg, J. E., Johnston, L. D., Miech, R. A., & Bachman, J. G. (2016). Novel psychoactive substance use by US adolescents: Characteristics associated with use of synthetic cannabinoids and synthetic cathinones. *Drug and Alcohol Review, 35*, 586–590. doi:10.1111/dar.12372

Patrick, R. B., & Gibbs, J. C. (2012). Inductive discipline, parental expression of disappointed expectations, and moral identity in adolescence. *Journal of Youth and Adolescence, 41*(8), 973–983. doi:10.1007/s10964-011-9698-7

Patterson, C. J. (1995). Sexual orientation and human development: An overview. *Developmental Psychology, 31*, 3–11.

Patterson, C. J. (2009). Children of lesbian and gay parents: Psychology, law, and policy. *American Psychologist*, 64, 727–736.

Patterson, C. J., & Hastings, P. D. (2007). Socialization in the context of family diversity. In J. E. Grusec & P. D. Hastings (Eds.), *Handbook of socialization: Theory and research* (pp. 328–351). New York, NY: Guilford.

Patterson, G. R., & Reid, J. B. (1970). Reciprocity and coercion: Two facets of social systems. In C. Neuringer & J. Michael (Eds.), *Behavior modification in clinical psychology*. New York, NY: Appleton-Century-Crofts.

Patterson, G. R., DeBaryshe, B. D., & Ramsey, E. (1989). A developmental perspective on antisocial behavior. *American Psychologist, 44*, 329–335.

Patterson, J., & Vakili, S. (2014). Relationships, environment, and the brain: How emerging research is changing what we know about the impact of families on human development. *Family Process, 53*(1), 22–32. doi:10.1111/famp.12057

Patton, J. R., Blackbourn, J. M., & Fad, K. (1996). *Exceptional individuals in focus* (6th ed.). Upper Saddle River, NJ: Merrill/Prentice Hall.

Paulus, M. (2014). The emergence of prosocial behavior: Why do infants and toddlers help, comfort, and share? *Child Development Perspectives, 8*, 77–81. doi:10.1111/cdep.12066

Paunesku, D., Walton, G. M., Romero, C., Smith, E. N., Yeager, D. S., & Dweck, C. S. (2015). Mind-set interventions are a scalable treatment for academic underachievement. *Psychological Science, 26*, 784–793. doi:10.1177/0956797615571017

Pawlas, G. E. (1994). Homeless students at the school door. *Educational Leadership, 51*(8), 79–82.

Payne, R. K., DeVol, P., & Smith, R. D. (2006). *Bridges out of poverty: Strategies for professionals and communities*. Highlands, TX: aha! Process.

Pea, R. D. (1993). Practices of distributed intelligence and designs for education. In G. Salomon (Ed.), *Distributed cognitions: Psychological and educational considerations* (pp. 47–87). Cambridge, England: Cambridge University Press.

Peak, L. (2001). Learning to become part of the group: The Japanese child's transition to preschool. In H. Shimizu & R. A. Levine (Eds.), *Japanese frames of mind: Cultural perspectives on human development* (pp. 143–169). New York, NY: Cambridge University Press.

Pears, K. C., Fisher, P. A., Kim, H. K., Bruce, J., Healey, C. V., & Yoerger, K. (2013). Immediate effects of a school readiness intervention for children in foster care. *Early Education and Development, 24*, 771–791. doi:10.1080/10409289.2013.736037

Pearson, B. Z., Conner, T., & Jackson, J. E. (2013). Removing obstacles for African American English-speaking children through greater understanding of language difference. *Developmental Psychology, 49*, 31–44. doi:10.1037/a0028248

Pearson, B. Z., Velleman, S. L., Bryant, T. J., & Charko, T. (2009). Phonological milestones for African American English-speaking children learning Mainstream American English as a second dialect. *Language, Speech, and Hearing Services in Schools, 40*, 229–244.

Pearson, P. D., Hansen, J., & Gordon, C. (1979). The effect of background knowledge on young children's comprehension of explicit and implicit information. *Journal of Reading Behavior, 11*, 201–209.

Peck, S. C., Roeser, R. W., Zarrett, N., & Eccles, J. S. (2008). Exploring the roles of extracurricular activity quantity and quality in the educational resilience of vulnerable adolescents: Variable- and pattern-centered approaches. *Journal of Social Issues, 64*, 135–156. doi:10.1111/j.1540-4560.2008.00552.x

Pederson, D. R., Rook-Green, A., & Elder, J. L. (1981). The role of action in the development of pretend play in young children. *Developmental Psychology, 17*, 756–759.

Pedro-Carroll, J. L. (2005). Fostering resilience in the aftermath of divorce: The role of evidence-based programs for children. *Family Court Review, 43*, 52–64.

Pedro-Carroll, J., & Velderman, M. K. (2016). Extending the global reach of a play-based intervention for children dealing with separation and divorce. In L. A. Reddy, T. M. Files-Hall, & C. E. Schaefer (Eds.), *Empirically based play interventions for children* (2nd ed., pp. 35–53). Washington, DC: American Psychological Association. doi:10.1037/14730-003

Pekrun, R., Lichtenfeld, S., Marsh, H. W., Murayama, K., & Goetz, T. (2017). Achievement emotions and academic performance: longitudinal models of reciprocal effects. *Child Development, 88*, 1653–1670. doi:10.1111/cdev.12704

Pelatti, C. C., Dynia, J., Logan, J., Justice, L., & Kaderavek, J. (2016). Examining quality in two preschool settings: Publicly funded early childhood education and inclusive early childhood education classrooms. *Child & Youth Care Forum, 45*, 829–849. doi:10.1007/s10566-016-9359-9

Pellegrini, A. D. (1996). *Observing children in their natural worlds: A methodological primer*. Mahwah, NJ: Erlbaum.

Pellegrini, A. D. (2002). Bullying, victimization, and sexual harassment during the transition to middle school. *Educational Psychologist, 37*, 151–163.

Pellegrini, A. D. (2006). The development and function of rough-and-tumble play in childhood and adolescence: A sexual selection theory perspective. In A. Göncü & S. Gaskins (Eds.), *Play and development: Evolutionary, sociocultural, and functional perspectives* (pp. 77–98) Mahwah, NJ: Erlbaum.

Pellegrini, A. D. (2013). Object use in childhood: development and possible functions. *Behaviour, 150*, 813–843. doi:10.1163/1568539X-00003086

Pellegrini, A. D., & Bjorklund, D. F. (1997). The role of recess in children's cognitive performance. *Educational Psychologist, 32*, 35–40.

Pellegrini, A. D., & Bohn, C. M. (2005). The role of recess in children's cognitive performance and school adjustment. *Educational Researcher, 34*(1), 13–19.

Pellegrini, A. D., & Horvat, M. (1995). A developmental contextualist critique of attention deficit hyperactivity disorder. *Educational Researcher, 24*(1), 13–19.

Pellegrini, A. D., Bartini, M., & Brooks, F. (1999). School bullies, victims, and aggressive victims: Factors relating to group affiliation and victimization in early adolescence. *Journal of Educational Psychology, 91*, 216–224.

Peltzer, K. (2010). Early sexual debut and associated factors among in-school adolescents in eight African countries. *Acta Paediatrica, 99*, 1242–1247. doi:10.1111/j.1651-2227.2010.01874 xdoi:10.1177/0165025410368943

Pence, K. L., & Justice, L. M. (2008). *Language development from theory to practice*. Upper Saddle River, NJ: Merrill/Prentice Hall.

Pener-Tessler, R., Avinun, R., Uzefovsky, F., Edelman, S., Ebstein, R. P., & Knafo, A. (2013). Boys' serotonin transporter genotype affects maternal behavior through self-control: A case of evocative gene–environment correlation. *Development and Psychopathology, 25*, 151–162.

Pennington, B. F., & Bennetto, L. (1993). Main effects of transactions in the neuropsychology of conduct disorder. Commentary on "The neuropsychology of conduct disorder." *Development and Psychopathology, 5*, 153–164.

Pennington, R. R., & Koehler, M. (2017). Effects of modeling, story templates, and self-graphing in the use of story elements by students with moderate intellectual disability. *Education & Training in Autism & Developmental Disabilities, 52*, 280–290.

Pennisi, E. (2012, September). *How genome is much more than genes*. Retrieved from http://news.sciencemag.org/sciencenow/2012/09/human-genome-is-much-more-than-j.html

Pentimonti, J. M., & Justice, L. M. (2010). Teachers' use of scaffolding strategies during read alouds in the preschool classroom. *Early Childhood Education, 37*, 241–248.

Peper, J. S., & Dahl, R. E. (2013). The teenage brain: Surging hormones—Brain-behavior interactions during puberty. *Current*

Directions in Psychological Science, 22, 134–139. doi:10.1177/0963721412473755

Peregoy, S. F., & Boyle, O. F. (2008). *Reading, writing, and learning in ESL: A resource book for teaching K–12 English learners*. Boston, MA: Pearson Education/Allyn & Bacon.

Perels, F., Merget-Kullmann, M., Wende, M., Schmitz, B., & Buchbinder, C. (2009). Improving self-regulated learning of preschool children: Evaluation of training for kindergarten teachers. *British Journal of Educational Psychology, 79*, 311–327.

Pérez, B. (Ed.). (1998). *Sociocultural contexts of language and literacy*. Mahwah, NJ: Erlbaum.

Perez, S. M., & Gauvain, M. (2009). Mother-child planning, child emotional functioning, and children's transition to first grade. *Child Development, 80*, 776–791.

Perfetti, C. A. (1985). Reading ability. In R. J. Sternberg (Ed.), *Human abilities: An information-processing approach* (pp. 59–81). New York, NY: Freeman.

Perfetti, C. A., & McCutchen, D. (1987). Schooled language competence: Linguistic abilities in reading and writing. In S. Rosenberg (Ed.), *Advances in applied psycholinguistics* (pp. 105 -141). Cambridge, England: Cambridge University Press.

Perkins, D. F., Syvertsen, A. K., Mincemoyer, C., Chilenski, S. M., Olson, J. R., Berrena, E., . . . Spoth, R. (2016). Thriving in school: The role of sixth-grade adolescent–parent–school relationships in predicting eighth-grade academic outcomes. *Youth & Society, 48*, 739–762. doi:10.1177/0044118X13512858

Perkins, D. N. (1992). *Smart schools: From training memories to educating minds*. New York, NY: Free Press/Macmillan.

Perkins, D. N. (1995). *Outsmarting IQ: The emerging science of learnable intelligence*. New York, NY: Free Press.

Perkinson-Gloor, N., Lemola, S., & Grob, A. (2013). Sleep duration, positive attitude toward life, and academic achievement: The role of daytime tiredness, behavioral persistence, and school start times. *Journal of Adolescence, 36*, 311–318. doi:10.1016/j.adolescence.2012.11.008

Perner, J., & Wimmer, H. (1985). "John *thinks* that Mary *thinks* that??" Attribution of second-order beliefs by 5- to 10-year-old children. *Journal of Experimental Child Psychology, 39*, 437–471.

Perone, S., & Spencer, J. P. (2014). The co-development of looking dynamics and discrimination performance. *Developmental Psychology, 50*, 837–852. doi:10.1037/a0034137

Perovic, A., Vuksanović, J., Petrović, B., & Avramović-Ilić, I. (2014). The acquisition of passives in Serbian. *Applied Psycholinguistics, 35*(1), 1–26. doi:10.1017/S0142716412000240

Perreira, K. M., Kiang, L., & Potochnick, S. (2013). Ethnic discrimination: Identifying and intervening in its effects on the education of immigrant children. In E. L. Grigorenko (Ed.), *U.S. immigration and education: Cultural and policy issues across the lifespan* (pp. 137–161). New York, NY: Springer Publishing Co.

Perren, J., Grove, N., & Thornton, J. (2013). Three empowering curricular innovations for service-learning in ESL programs. *TESOL Journal, 4*, 463–486. doi:10.1002/tesj.95

Perry, E., & Flood, A. (2016). Autism spectrum disorder and attachment: A clinician's perspective. In H. K. Fletcher, A. Flood, & D. J. Hare (Eds.), *Attachment in intellectual and developmental disability: A clinician's guide to practice and research* (pp. 79–103). Chichester, UK: Wiley.

Perry, N. E. (1998). Young children's self-regulated learning and contexts that support it. *Journal of Educational Psychology, 90*, 715–729.

Perry, N. E., Vande Cooper, H., Robinson, J. C., & Patall, E. A. (2006). Does homework improve academic achievement? A synthesis of research, 1987–2003. *Review of Educational Research, 76*, 1–62.

Perry, N. E., VandeKamp, K. O., Mercer, L. K., & Nordby, C. J. (2002). Investigating teacher–student interactions that foster self-regulated learning. *Educational Psychologist, 37*, 5–15.

Persellin, D., & Bateman, L. (2009). A comparative study on the effectiveness of two song-teaching methods: Holistic vs. phrase-by-phrase. *Early Child Development and Care, 179*, 799–806.

Pescarmona, I. (2014). Learning to participate through Complex Instruction. *Intercultural Education, 25*, 187–196. doi:10.1080/14675986.2014.905360

Peskin, J., Prusky, C., & Comay, J. (2014). Keeping the reader's mind in mind: Development of perspective-taking in children's dictations. *Journal of Applied Developmental Psychology, 35*, 35–43. http://dx.doi.org.unco.idm.oclc.org/10.1016/j.appdev.2013.11.001

Pessanha, M., Peixoto, C., Barros, S., Cadima, J., Pinto, A. I., Coelho, V., & Bryant, D. M. (2017). Stability and change in teacher-infant interaction quality over time. *Early Childhood Research Quarterly, 40*, 87–97. http://dx.doi.org.unco.idm.oclc.org/10.1016/j.ecresq.2016.10.003

Petering, R. P., Rhoades, H., Winetrobe, H., Dent, D., & Rice, E. (2017). Violence, trauma, mental health, and substance use among homeless youth Juggalos. *Child Psychiatry & Human Development, 48*, 642–650. doi:10.1007/s10578-016-0689-5

Peterson, B. (2017). The struggle for bilingual education. *Rethinking Schools, 32*(1), 44-49.

Peterson, B. E., & Stewart, A. J. (1996). The antecedents and contexts of generativity motivation at midlife. *Psychology and Aging, 11*(1), 21–33.

Peterson, C. C. (2002). Drawing insight from pictures: The development of concepts of false drawing and false belief in children with deafness, normal hearing, and autism. *Child Development, 73*, 1442–1459.

Peterson, C., Maier, S. F., & Seligman, M. E. P. (1993). *Learned helplessness: A theory for the age of personal control*. New York, NY: Oxford University Press.

Peterson, J., Puhl, R. M., & Luedicke, J. (2012). An experimental assessment of physical educators' expectations and attitudes: The importance of student weight and gender. *Journal of School Health, 82*, 432–440. doi:10.1111/j.1746-1561.2012.00719.x

Peterson, L. (1980). Developmental changes in verbal and behavioral sensitivity to cues of social norms of altruism. *Child Development, 51*, 830–838.

Peterson, S. (2014). Award-winning authors and illustrators talk about writing and teaching writing. *Reading Teacher, 67*, 498–506. doi:10.1002/trtr.1249

Petitto, A. L. (1985). Division of labor: Procedural learning in teacher-led small groups. *Cognition and Instruction, 2*, 233–270.

Petitto, L. A. (1997). In the beginning: On the genetic and environmental factors that make early language acquisition possible. In M. Gopnik (Ed.), *The inheritance and innateness of grammars* (pp. 45–69). New York, NY: Oxford University Press.

Petrill, S. A., & Wilkerson, B. (2000). Intelligence and achievement: A behavioral genetic perspective. *Educational Psychology Review, 12*, 185–199.

Petrill, S. A., Lipton, P. A., Hewitt, J. K., Plomin, R., Cherny, S. S., Corley, R., & DeFries, J. C. (2004). Genetic and environmental contributions to general cognitive ability through the first 16 years of life. *Developmental Psychology, 40*, 805–812.

Pettigrew, J. (2013). "I'll take what I can get": Identity development in the case of a stepfather. *Journal of Divorce & Remarriage, 54*(1), 25–42. doi:10.1080/10502556.2012.725360

Pfeifer, J. H., Brown, C. S., & Juvonen, J. (2007). Prejudice reduction in schools. Teaching tolerance in schools: Lessons learned since *Brown v. Board of Education* about the development and reduction of children's prejudice. *Social Policy Report, 21*(2), 1, 3–13, 20–23.

Pham, Y. Y., & Murray, C. (2016). Social relationships among adolescents with disabilities: Unique and cumulative associations with adjustment. *Exceptional Children, 82*, 234–250. doi:10.1177/0014402915585491

Phares, V., Fields, S., & Kamboukos, D. (2009). Fathers' and mothers' involvement with their adolescents. *Journal of Child and Family Studies, 28*, 1–9.

Perry, N. E., VandeKamp, K. O., Mercer, L. K., & Nordby, C. J. (2002). Investigating teacher–student interactions that foster self-regulated learning. *Educational Psychologist, 37*, 5–15.

Phelan, P., Yu, H. C., & Davidson, A. L. (1994). Navigating the psychosocial pressures of adolescence: The voices and experiences of high school youth. *American Educational Research Journal, 31*, 415–447.

Phillips, D., & Zimmerman, M. (1990). The developmental course of perceived competence and incompetence among competent children. In R. Sternberg & J. Kolligian (Eds.), *Competence considered* (pp. 41–66). New Haven, CT: Yale University Press.

Phillips, K. T., Phillips, M., Lalonde, T. L., & Prince, M. A. (2018). Does social context matter? An ecological momentary assessment study of marijuana use among college students. *Addictive Behaviors, 83*, 154-159. doi:10.1016/j.addbeh.2018.01.004

Phinney, J. S. (1989). Stages of ethnic identity development in minority group adolescents. *Journal of Early Adolescence, 9*, 34–49.

Phinney, J. S., & Tarver, S. (1988). Ethnic identity search and commitment in Black and White eighth graders. *Journal of Early Adolescence, 8*, 265–277.

Phinney, J. S., Cantu, C. L., & Kurtz, D. A. (1997). Ethnic and American identity as predictors of self-esteem among African American, Latino, and White adolescents. *Journal of Youth and Adolescence, 26*, 165–185.

Piaget, J. (1928). *Judgment and reasoning in the child* (M. Warden, Trans.). New York, NY: Harcourt, Brace.

Piaget, J. (1929). *The child's conception of the world*. New York, NY: Harcourt, Brace.

Piaget, J. (1941). Le mécanisme du développement mental et les lois du groupement des operations [The mechanism of mental development and the laws of grouping of operations]. *Archives de Psychologie, 28*, 215–285.

Piaget, J. (1952a). *The child's conception of number* (C. Gattegno & F. M. Hodgson, Trans.). London, England: Routledge & Kegan Paul.

Piaget, J. (1952b). *The origins of intelligence in children*. New York, NY: International Universities Press.

Piaget, J. (1954). *The construction of reality in the child*. New York, NY: Basic Books.

Piaget, J. (1959). *The language and thought of the child* (3rd ed.; M. Gabain, Trans.). London, England: Routledge & Kegan Paul.

Piaget, J. (1960a). *The child's conception of physical causality* (M. Gabain, Trans.). Paterson, NJ: Littlefield, Adams.

Piaget, J. (1960b). The definition of stages of development. In J. M. Tanner & B. Inhelder (Eds.), *Discussions on child development: A consideration of the biological, psychological and cultural approaches to the understanding of human development and behavior: Vol. 4. The proceedings of the fourth meeting of the World Health Organization Study Group on the Psychobiological Development of the Child, Geneva, 1956* (pp. 116–135). New York, NY: International Universities Press.

Piaget, J. (1962). *Play, dreams, and imitation in childhood*. New York, NY: W. W. Norton.

Piaget, J. (1970). *Genetic epistemology*. Trans. E. Duckworth. New York, NY, US: Columbia University Press.

Piaget, J. (1971). The theory of stages in cognitive development. In D. R. Green (Ed.), *Measurement and Piaget* (pp. 1–11). New York, NY: McGraw-Hill.

Piaget, J. (1972). Intellectual evolution from adolescence to adulthood. *Human Development, 15*, 1–12.

Piaget, J. (1985). *The equilibration of cognitive structures: The central problem of intellectual development*. Chicago: University of Chicago Press.

Pianta, R. C., Hamre, B., & Stuhlman, M. (2003). Relationships between teachers and children. In W. M. Reynolds & G. E. Miller (Eds.), *Handbook of psychology: Educational psychology* (Vol. 7, pp. 199–234). New York, NY: Wiley.

Piasta, S., Pelatti, C., & Miller, H. (2014). Mathematics and science learning opportunities in preschool classrooms. *Early Education & Development, 25*, 445–468. doi:10.1080/10409289.2013.817753

Piekarski, D. J., Johnson, C. M., Boivin, J. R., Thomas, A. W., Lin, W. C., Delevich, K., . . . Wilbrecht, L. (2017). Does puberty mark a transition in sensitive periods for plasticity in the associative neocortex? *Brain Research, 1654*(Part B), 123–144. doi:10.1016/j.brainres.2016.08.042

Pieloch, K. A., McCullough, M. B., & Marks, A. K. (2016). Resilience of children with refugee statuses: A research review. *Canadian Psychology/Psychologie canadienne, 57*, 330–339. doi:10.1037/cap0000073

Piirto, J. (1999). *Talented children and adults: Their development and education* (2nd ed.). Upper Saddle River, NJ: Merrill/Prentice Hall.

Pike, A., & Oliver, B. R. (2016). Child behavior and sibling relationship quality: A cross-lagged analysis. *Journal of Family Psychology*. Advance online publication. doi:10.1037/fam0000248

Pilegard, C., & Fiorella, L. (2016). Helping students help themselves: Generative learning strategies improve middle school students' self regulation in a cognitive tutor. *Computers in Human Behavior, 65*, 121–126. doi:10.1016/j.chb.2016.08.020

Pillow, B. H. (2002). Children's and adults' evaluation of the certainty of deductive inferences, inductive inferences, and guesses. *Child Development, 73*, 779–792.

Pilyoung, K., Evans, G. W., Angstadt, M., Shaun Ho, S. S., Sripada, C. S., Swain, J. E., . . . Luan Phan, K. K. (2013). Effects of childhood poverty and chronic stress on emotion regulatory brain function in adulthood. *Proceedings of the National Academy of Sciences of the United States of America, 110*, 18442–18447. doi:10.1073/pnas.1308240110

Pine, K. J., Lufkin, N., Kirk, E., & Messer, D. (2007). A microgenetic analysis of the relationship between speech and gesture in children: Evidence for semantic and temporal asynchrony. *Language and Cognitive Processes, 22*, 234–246.

Pinel, P., & Dehaene, S. (2009). Beyond hemispheric dominance: Brain regions underlying the joint lateralization of language and arithmetic to the left hemisphere. *Journal of Cognitive Neuroscience, 22*(1), 48–66.

Pinkard, N., Erete, S., Martin, C. K., & de Royston, M. M. (2017). Digital youth divas: Exploring narrative-driven curriculum to spark middle school girls' interest in computational activities. *Journal of the Learning Sciences, 26*, 477–516. http://dx.doi.org.unco.idm.oclc.org/10.1080/10508406.2017.1307199

Pinker, S. (1984). *Language learnability and language development*. Cambridge, MA: Harvard University Press.

Pinker, S. (1987). The bootstrapping problem in language acquisition. In B. MacWhinney (Ed.), *Mechanisms of language acquisition* (pp. 399–441). Hillsdale, NJ: Erlbaum.

Pinquart, M. (2016). Associations of parenting styles and dimensions with academic achievement in children and adolescents: A meta-analysis. *Educational Psychology Review, 28*, 475–493. doi:10.1007/s10648-015-9338-y

Pinquart, M., Feußner, C., & Ahnert, L. (2013). Meta-analytic evidence for stability in attachments from infancy to early adulthood. *Attachment & Human Development, 15*, 189–218. doi:10.1080/14616734.2013.746257

Pintrich, P. R. (2003). Motivation and classroom learning. In W. M. Reynolds & G. E. Miller (Eds.), *Handbook of psychology: Educational psychology* (Vol. 7, pp. 103–122). Hoboken, NJ: Wiley.

Pintrich, P. R., & Schunk, D. H. (2002). *Motivation in education: Theory, research, and applications* (2nd ed.). Upper Saddle River, NJ: Merrill/Prentice Hall.

Pipher, M. (1994). *Reviving Ophelia: Saving the selves of adolescent girls*. New York, NY: Putnam.

Plante, C. N., Gentile, D. A., Groves, C. L., Modlin, A., & Blanco-Herrera, J. (2018). Video games as coping mechanisms in the etiology of video game addiction. *Psychology of Popular Media Culture*. Advance online publication. http://dx.doi.org.unco.idm.oclc.org/10.1037/ppm0000186

Płatos, M., & Wojaczek, K. (2018). Broadening the scope of peer-mediated intervention for individuals with autism spectrum disorders. *Journal of Autism and Developmental Disorders, 48*, 747–750. http://dx.doi.org.unco.idm.oclc.org/10.1007/s10803-017-3429-1

Plomin, R., & Deary, I. J. (2015). Genetics and intelligence differences: Five special findings. *Molecular Psychiatry, 20*(1), 98–108. doi:10.1038/mp.2014.105

Plomin, R., & Petrill, S. A. (1997). Genetics and intelligence: What's new? *Intelligence, 24*, 53–77.

Plomin, R., DeFries, J. C., & Loehlin, J. C. (1977). Genotype-environment interaction and correlation in the analysis of human behavior. *Psychological Bulletin, 84*, 309–322. doi:10.1037/0033-2909.84.2.309

Plomin, R., DeFries, J. C., Knopik, V. S., & Neiderhiser, J. M. (2016). Top 10 replicated findings from behavioral genetics. *Perspectives on Psychological Science, 11*, 3–23. doi:10.1177/1745691615617439

Plomin, R., Fulker, D. W., Corley, R., & DeFries, J. C. (1997). Nature, nurture, and cognitive development from 1 to 16 years: A parent–offspring adoption study. *Psychological Science, 8*, 442–447.

Plomin, R., Owen, M. J., & McGuffin, P. (1994). The genetic basis of complex human behaviors. *Science, 24*, 1733–1739.

Plucker, J. A., Guo, J., & Dilley, A. (2018). Research-guided programs and strategies for nurturing creativity. In S. I. Pfeiffer, E. Shaunessy-Dedrick, & M. Foley-Nicpon (Eds.), *APA handbook of giftedness and talent* (APA Handbooks in Psychology, pp. 387–397). Washington, DC: American Psychological Association.

Poehner, M. E., & Infante, P. (2017). Mediated development: A Vygotskian approach to transforming second language learner abilities. *TESOL Quarterly, 51*, 332–357. doi:10.1002/tesq.308

Poel, E. W. (2007). Enhancing what students can do. *Educational Leadership, 64*(5), 64–66.

Pokhrel, P., Herzog, T. A., Black, D. S., Zaman, A., Riggs, N. R., & Sussman, S. (2013). Adolescent neurocognitive development, self-regulation, and school-based drug use prevention. *Prevention Science, 14*(3), 218–228. http://dx.doi.org.unco.idm.oclc.org/10.1007/s11121-012-0345-7

Polat, N., & Mahalingappa, L. (2013). Pre- and in-service teachers' beliefs about ELLs in content area classes: a case for inclusion, responsibility, and instructional support. *Teaching Education, 24*(1), 58–83. doi:10.1080/10476210.2012.71393

Pollack, W. S. (2010). Gender issues: Modern models of young male resilient mental health. In J. E. Grant & M. N. Potenza (Eds.), *Young adult mental health* (pp. 96–109). New York, NY: Oxford University Press.

Pomerantz, E. M., Altermatt, E. R., & Saxon, J. L. (2002). Making the grade but feeling distressed: Gender differences in academic performance and internal distress. *Journal of Educational Psychology, 94*, 396–404.

Pontes, H. M. (2017). Investigating the differential effects of social networking site addiction and Internet gaming disorder on psychological health. *Journal of Behavioral Addictions, 6*, 601–610. http://dx.doi.org.unco.idm.oclc.org/10.1556/2006.6.2017.075

Portes, P. R. (1996). Ethnicity and culture in educational psychology. In D. C. Berliner & R. C. Calfee (Eds.), *Handbook of educational psychology* (pp. 331–357). New York, NY: Macmillan.

Posada, G. (2013). Piecing together the sensitivity construct: Ethology and cross-cultural research. *Attachment & Human Development, 15*(5–6), 637–656. doi:10.1080/14616734.2013.842753

Posner, M. I. (Ed.). (2004). *Cognitive neuroscience of attention*. New York, NY: Guilford Press.

Posner, M. I., & Rothbart, M. K. (2007). *Educating the human brain*. Washington, DC: American Psychological Association.

Posner, M. I., & Rothbart, M. K. (2013). Development of attention networks. In B. Kar (Ed.), *Cognition and brain development: Converging evidence from various methodologies* (pp. 61–83). Washington, DC: American Psychological Association. doi:10.1037/14043-004

Potocki, A., Sanchez, M., Ecalle, J., & Magnan, A. (2017). Linguistic and cognitive profiles of 8- to 15-year-old children with specific reading comprehension difficulties: The role of executive functions. *Journal of Learning Disabilities, 50*, 128–142. doi:10.1177/0022219415613080

Potvin, M., Snider, L., Prelock, P., Kehayia, E., & Wood-Dauphinee, S. (2013). Recreational participation of children with high functioning autism. *Journal of Autism and Developmental Disorders, 43*, 445–457. doi:10.1007/s10803-012-1589-6

Poulin-Dubois, D., & Pauen, S. (2017). The development of object categories: What, when, and how? In H. Cohen & C. Lefebvre (Eds.), *Handbook of categorization in cognitive science* (pp. 653–671). San Diego, CA, US: Elsevier Academic Press http://dx.doi.org.unco.idm.oclc.org/10.1016/B978-0-08-101107-2.00027-0

Poulin-Dubois, D., Frenkiel-Fishman, S., Nayer, S., & Johnson, S. (2006). Infants' inductive generalization of bodily, motion, and sensory properties to animals and people. *Journal of Cognition and Development, 7*, 431–453.

Poulin, F., & Boivin, M. (1999). Proactive and reactive aggression and boys' friendship quality in mainstream classrooms. *Journal of Emotional and Behavioral Disorders, 7*, 168–177.

Powell, M. P., & Schulte, T. (1999). Turner syndrome. In S. Goldstein & C. R. Reynolds (Eds.), *Handbook of neurodevelopmental and genetic disorders* (pp. 277–297). New York, NY: Guilford Press.

Power, F. C., & Scott, S. E. (2014). Democratic citizenship: Responsible life in a free society. *School Psychology International, 35*(1), 50–66. doi:10.1177/0143034313515985

Power, F. C., Higgins, A., & Kohlberg, L. (1989). *Lawrence Kohlberg's approach to moral education*. New York, NY: Columbia University Press.

Power, F., & Power, A. R. (2006). Cheating. In G. G. Bear, K. M. Minke (Eds.), *Children's needs III: Development, prevention, and intervention* (pp. 185–197). Washington, DC, US: National Association of School Psychologists.

Powers, N., & Trevarthen, C. (2009). Voices of shared emotion and meaning: Young infants and their mothers in Scotland and Japan. In S. Malloch & C. Trevarthen (Eds.), *Communicative musicality: Exploring the basis of human companionship* (pp. 209–240). New York, NY: Oxford University Press.

Pozzoli, T., Gini, G., & Thornberg, R. (2017). Getting angry matters: Going beyond perspective taking and empathic concern to understand bystanders' behavior in bullying. *Journal of Adolescence, 61*, 87–95. http://dx.doi.org.unco.idm.oclc.org/10.1016/j.adolescence.2017.09.011

Pratt, S., & Urbanowski, M. (2016). Teaching early readers to self-monitor and self-correct. *Reading Teacher, 69*, 559–567. doi:10.1002/trtr.1443

Pressley, M. (1982). Elaboration and memory development. *Child Development, 53*, 296–309.

Pressley, M., & Hilden, K. (2006). Cognitive strategies: Production deficiencies and successful strategy instruction everywhere. In W. Damon & R. M. Lerner (Series Eds.), & D. Kuhn & R. Siegler (Vol. Eds.), *Handbook of Child Psychology: Vol. 2. Cognition, perception, and language* (6th ed., pp. 511–556). New York, NY: Wiley.

Pressley, M., Almasi, J., Schuder, T., Bergman, J., Hite, S., El-Dinary, P. B., & Brown, R. (1994). Transactional instruction of comprehension strategies: The Montgomery County Maryland SAIL program. *Reading and Writing Quarterly, 10*, 5–19.

Pressley, M., Borkowski, J. G., & Schneider, W. (1987). Cognitive strategies: Good strategy users coordinate metacognition and knowledge. In R. Vasta (Ed.), *Annals of child development* (Vol. 4, pp. 89–129). Greenwich, CT: JAI Press.

Pressley, M., El-Dinary, P. B., Marks, M. B., Brown, R., & Stein, S. (1992). Good strategy instruction is motivating and interesting. In K. A. Renninger, S. Hidi, & A. Krapp (Eds.), *The role of interest in learning and development*. Hillsdale, NJ: Erlbaum .

Pretti-Frontczak, K., Harjusola-Webb, S., Chin, M., Grisham-Brown, J., Acar, S., Heo, K., . . . Zeng, S. (2016). Three mistakes made worldwide in "getting children ready" for school. *Young Exceptional Children, 19*(1), 48–51. doi:10.1177/1096250616629591

Preus, B., Payne, R., Wick, C., & Glomski, E. (2016). Listening to the voices of civically engaged high school students. *High School Journal, 100*(1), 66–84.

Price-Williams, D. R., Gordon, W., & Ramirez, M. (1969). Skill and conservation. *Developmental Psychology, 1*, 769.

Price, J. R., Roberts, J. E., & Jackson, S. C. (2006). Structural development of the fictional narratives of African American preschoolers. *Language, Speech, and Hearing Services in Schools, 37*, 178–190.

Priddis, L., Landy, S., Moroney, D., & Kane, R. (2014). An exploratory study of aggression in school-age children: Underlying factors and implications for treatment. *Australian Journal of Guidance & Counselling, 24*(1), 18–35. doi:10.1017/jgc.2013.12

Priebe, S., Keenan, J., & Miller, A. (2012). How prior knowledge affects word identification and comprehension. *Reading & Writing, 25*, 131–149. doi:10.1007/s11145-010-9260-0

Prinstein, M. J., Rancourt, D., Guerry, J. D., & Browne, C. B. (2009). Peer reputations and psychological adjustment. In K. H. Rubin, W. M. Bukowski, & B. Laursen (Eds.), *Handbook* of peer interactions, relationships, and groups (pp. 548–567). New York, NY: Guilford Press.

Proctor, C. P., August, D., Carlo, M. S., & Snow, C. (2006). The intriguing role of Spanish language vocabulary knowledge in predicting English reading comprehension. *Journal of Educational Psychology, 98*, 159–169.

Proctor, R. W., & Dutta, A. (1995). *Skill acquisition and human performance.* Thousand Oaks, CA: Sage.

Protzko, J., Aronson, J., & Blair, C. (2013). How to make a young child smarter: Evidence from the database of raising intelligence. *Perspectives on Psychological Science, 8*(1), 25–40. doi:10.1177/1745691612462585

Provost, B., Lopez, B. R., & Heimerl, S. (2007). A comparison of motor delays in young children: Autism spectrum disorder, developmental delay, and developmental concerns. *Journal of Autism and Developmental Disorders, 37*, 321–328.

Prows, C. A., Hopkin, R. J., Barnoy, S., & Van Riper, M. (2013). An update of childhood genetic disorders. *Journal of Nursing Scholarship, 45*(1), 34–42. doi:10.1111/jnu.12003

Pruett, K., & Pruett, M. K. (2009). *Partnership parenting: How men and women parent differently—Why it helps your kids and can strengthen your marriage.* Cambridge, MA: Da Capo Press.

Pulkkinen, L. (1982). Self-control and continuity from childhood to adolescence. In P. B. Baltes & O. G. Brim (Eds.), *Life span development and behavior* (Vol. 4, pp. 63–105). Orlando, FL: Academic Press.

Pulos, S. (1997). Adolescents' implicit theories of physical phenomena: A matter of gravity. *International Journal of Behavioral Development, 20*, 493–507.

Pulos, S., & Linn, M. C. (1981). Generality of the controlling variables scheme in early adolescence. *Journal of Early Adolescence, 1*, 26–37.

Pulverman, R., Song, L., Hirsh-Pasek, K., Pruden, S. M., & Golinkoff, R. M. (2013). Preverbal infants' attention to manner and path: Foundations for learning relational terms. *Child Development, 84*, 241–252. doi:10.1111/cdev.12030

Puranik, C. S., Phillips, B. M., Lonigan, C. J., & Gibson, E. (2018). Home literacy practices and preschool children's emergent writing skills: An initial investigation. *Early Childhood Research Quarterly, 42*, 228–238. http://dx.doi.org.unco.idm.oclc.org/10.1016/j.ecresq.2017.10.004

Puranik, C., Petscher, Y., & Lonigan, C. (2013). Dimensionality and reliability of letter writing in 3- to 5-year-old preschool children. *Learning & Individual Differences, 28*, 133–141. doi:10.1016/j.lindif.2012.06.011

Purcell-Gates, V. (1995). *Other people's words: The cycle of low literacy.* Cambridge, MA: Harvard University Press.

Purdie, N., & Hattie, J. (1996). Cultural differences in the use of strategies for self-regulated learning. *American Educational Research Journal, 33*, 845–871.

Purpura, D. J., Baroody, A. J., Eiland, M. D., & Reid, E. E. (2016). Fostering first graders' reasoning strategies with basic sums. *Elementary School Journal, 117*(1), 72–100.

Puskás, T., & Andersson, A. (2017). "Why do we celebrate . . . ?" Filling traditions with meaning in an ethnically diverse Swedish preschool. *International Journal of Early Childhood, 49*(1), 21–37.

Putallaz, M., & Gottman, J. M. (1981). Social skills and group acceptance. In S. R. Asher & J. M. Gottman (Eds.), *The development of children's friendships* (pp. 116–149). New York, NY: Cambridge University Press.

Putallaz, M., & Heflin, A. H. (1986). Toward a model of peer acceptance. In J. M. Gottman & J. G. Parker (Eds.), *Conversations of friends: Speculations on affective development* (pp. 292–314). Cambridge, England: Cambridge University Press.

Puustinen, M., Lyyra, A., Metsäpelto, R., & Pulkkinen, L. (2008). Children's help seeking: The role of parenting. *Learning and Instruction, 18*, 160–171.

Qian, G., & Pan, J. (2002). A comparison of epistemological beliefs and learning from science text between American and Chinese high school students. In B. K. Hofer & P. R. Pintrich (Eds.), *Personal epistemology: The psychology of beliefs about knowledge and knowing* (pp. 365–385). Mahwah, NJ: Erlbaum.

Qu, Y., & Pomerantz, E. M. (2015). Divergent school trajectories in early adolescence in the United States and China: An examination of underlying mechanisms. *Journal of Youth and Adolescence, 44*, 2095–2109.

Quinn, P. C. (2002). Category representation in young infants. *Current Directions in Psychological Science, 11*, 66–70.

Quinn, P. C. (2007). On the infant's prelinguistic conception of spatial relations: Three developmental trends and their implications for spatial language learning. In J. M. Plumert & J. P. Spencer (Eds.), *The emerging spatial mind* (pp. 117–141). New York, NY: Oxford University.

Quinn, S., & Oldmeadow, J. (2013). Is the igeneration a "we" generation? Social networking use among 9- to 13-year-olds and belonging. *British Journal of Developmental Psychology, 31*(1), 136–142. doi:10.1111/bjdp.12007

Raccanello, D., Brondino, M., & Bernardi, B. (2013). Achievement emotions in elementary, middle, and high school: How do students feel about specific contexts in terms of settings and subject-domains? *Scandinavian Journal of Psychology, 54*, 477–484. doi:10.1111/sjop.12079

Raevuori, A., Dick, D. M., Keski-Rahkonen, A., Pulkkinen, L., Rose, R. J., Rissanen, A., . . . Silventoinen, K. (2007). Genetic and environmental factors affecting self-esteem from age 14 to 17: A longitudinal study of Finnish twins. *Psychological Medicine, 37*, 1625–1633.

Raghupathy, S., Klein, C., & Card, J. (2013). Online activities for enhancing sex education curricula: Preliminary evidence on the effectiveness of the abstinence and contraception education storehouse. *Journal of HIV/AIDS & Social Services, 12*, 160–171. doi:10.1080/15381501.2013.790749

Rague, L., Caravella, K., Tonnsen, B., Klusek, J., & Roberts, J. (2018). Early gesture use in fragile x syndrome. *Journal of Intellectual Disability Research.* Advance online publication.http://dx.doi.org.unco.idm.oclc.org/10.1111/jir.12498

Rahman, K. (2013). Belonging and learning to belong in school: the implications of the hidden curriculum for indigenous students. *Discourse: Studies in the Cultural Politics of Education, 34*, 660–672. doi:10.1080/01596306.2013.728362

Rahman, Q., & Wilson, G. D. (2003). Sexual orientation and the 2nd to 4th finger length ratio: Evidence for organising effects of sex hormones or developmental instability? *Psychoneuroendocrinology, 28*, 288–303.

Raikes, H., Virmani, E. A., Thompson, R. A., & Hatton, H. (2013). Declines in peer conflict from preschool through first grade: Influences from early attachment and social information processing. *Attachment & Human Development, 15*(1), 65–82. doi:10.1080/14616734.2012.728381

Raine, A., & Scerbo, A. (1991). Biological theories of violence. In J. S. Milner (Ed.), *Neuropsychology of aggression* (pp. 1–25). Boston, MA: Kluwer Academic Press.

Rakic, P. (1995). Corticogenesis in human and nonhuman primates. In M. S. Gazzaniga (Ed.), *The cognitive neurosciences* (pp. 127–145). Cambridge, MA: MIT Press.

Rakoczy, H., Kaufmann, M., & Lohse, K. (2016). Young children understand the normative force of standards of equal resource distribution. *Journal of Experimental Child Psychology, 150*, 396–403. doi:10.1016/j.jecp.2016.05.015

Rakow, S. (2012). Helping gifted learners SOAR. *Educational Leadership, 69*(5), 34–40.

Ramaswamy, V., & Bergin, C. (2009). Do reinforcement and induction increase prosocial behavior? Results of a teacher-based intervention in preschools. *Journal of Research in Childhood Education, 23*, 527–538.

Ramey, K. E., & Uttal, D. H. (2017). Making sense of space: Distributed spatial sensemaking in a middle school summer engineering camp. *Journal of the Learning Sciences, 26*, 277–319.

Ramirez, A. Y. F., & Soto-Hinman, I. (2009). A place for all families. *Educational Leadership, 66*(7), 79–82.

Ramírez, E., Ortega, A., Chamorro, A., & Colmenero, J. (2014). A program of positive intervention in the elderly: Memories, gratitude and forgiveness. *Aging & Mental Health, 18*, 463–470. doi:10.1080/13607863.2013.856858

Ramos Olazagasti, M. A., Klein, R. G., Mannuzza, S., Belsky, E., Hutchison, J. A., Lashua-Shriftman, E. C., & Castellanos, F. (2013). Does childhood attention-deficit/hyperactivity disorder predict risk-taking and medical illnesses in adulthood? *Journal of the American Academy of*

Child & Adolescent Psychiatry, 52, 153–162. doi:10.1016/j.jaac.2012.11.012

Randell, A. C., & Peterson, C. C. (2009). Affective qualities of sibling disputes, mothers' conflict attitudes, and children's theory of mind development. *Social Development, 18,* 857–874.

Ranzini, G., & Hoek, E. (2017). To you who (I think) are listening: Imaginary audience and impression management on Facebook. *Computers in Human Behavior, 75,* 228–235. http://dx.doi.org.unco.idm.oclc.org/10.1016/j.chb.2017.04.047

Rao, K. K., Smith, S. J., & Lowrey, K. A. (2017). UDL and intellectual disability: What do we know and where do we go? *Intellectual & Developmental Disabilities, 55*(1), 37–47. doi:10.1352/1934-9556-55.1.37

Rapport, M. D., Orban, S. A., Kofler, M. J., & Friedman, L. M. (2013). Do programs designed to train working memory, other executive functions, and attention benefit children with ADHD? A meta-analytic review of cognitive, academic, and behavioral outcomes. *Clinical Psychology Review, 33,* 1237–1252 . doi:10.1016/j.cpr.2013.08.005

Rasmussen, M., & Laumann, K. (2013). The academic and psychological benefits of exercise in healthy children and adolescents. *European Journal of Psychology of Education, 28,* 945–962. doi:10.1007/s10212-012-0148-z

Rassin, M., Klug, E., Nathanzon, H., Kan, A., & Silner, D. (2009). Cultural differences in child delivery: Comparisons between Jewish and Arab women. *International Nursing Review, 56,* 123–130.

Rattan, A., Good, C., & Dweck, C. S. (2012). "It's ok—Not everyone can be good at math": Instructors with an entity theory comfort (and demotivate) students. *Journal of Experimental Social Psychology, 48,* 731–737. doi:10.1016/j.jesp.2011.12.012

Rattanavich, S. (2013). Comparison of effects of teaching English to Thai undergraduate teacher-students through cross-curricular thematic instruction program based on multiple intelligence theory and conventional instruction. *English Language Teaching, 6*(9), 1–18. doi:10.5539/elt.v6n9p1

Ratz, C. (2013). Do students with Down syndrome have a specific learning profile for reading? *Research in Developmental Disabilities, 34,* 4504–4514. doi:10.1016/j.ridd.2013.09.031

Rauer, A. J., Pettit, G. S., Lansford, J. E., Bates, J. E., & Dodge, K. A. (2013). Romantic relationship patterns in young adulthood and their developmental antecedents. *Developmental Psychology, 49,* 2159–2171. doi:10.1037/a0031845

Raustorp, A., & Lindwall, M. (2015). Physical self-esteem—A ten-year follow-up study from early adolescence to early adulthood. *International Journal of Adolescent Medicine and Health, 27*(1), 31–39.

Raval, V. (2013). Fight or flight? Competing discourses of individualism and collectivism in runaway boys' interpersonal relationships in India. *Journal of Social & Personal Relationships, 30,* 410–429. doi:10.1177/0265407512458655

Raver, C. (2012). Low-income children's self-regulation in the classroom: Scientific inquiry for social change. *American Psychologist, 67,* 681–689. doi:10.1037/a0030085

Ravid, D., & Geiger, V. (2009). Promoting morphological awareness in Hebrew-speaking grade-schoolers: An intervention study using linguistic humor. *First Language, 29*(1), 81–112.

Ravid, D., & Zilberbuch, S. (2003). Morphosyntactic constructs in the development of spoken and written Hebrew text production. *Journal of Child Language, 30,* 395–418.

Ray, J. A., Prewitt-Kinder, J., & George, S. (2009). Partnering with families of children with special needs. *Young Children, 64*(5), 16–22.

Rayner, K., Foorman, B. R., Perfetti, C. A., Pesetsky, D., & Seidenberg, M. S. (2001). How psychological science informs the teaching of reading. *Psychological Science in the Public Interest, 2,* 31–74.

Recchia, H. E., & Howe, N. (2009). Associations between social understanding, sibling relationship quality, and siblings' conflict strategies and outcomes. *Child Development, 80,* 1564–1578.

Recchia, H. E., Wainryb, C., Bourne, S., & Pasupathi, M. (2014). The construction of moral agency in mother–child conversations about helping and hurting across childhood and adolescence. *Developmental Psychology, 50*(1), 34–44. doi:10.1037/a0033492

Recchia, S. L., & Dvorakova, K. (2012). How three young toddlers transition from an infant to a toddler child care classroom: Exploring the influence of peer relationships, teacher expectations, and changing social contexts. *Early Education and Development, 23,* 181–201. doi:10.1080/10409289.2012.630824

Recchia, S. L., & Shin, M. (2012). In and out of synch: Infant childcare teachers' adaptations to infants' developmental changes. *Early Child Development and Care, 182,* 1545–1562.

Recker, N., Clark, L., & Foote, R. A. (2008, June). About my families and me. *Journal of Extension, 46*(3).

Reemst, K., Noctor, S. C., Lucassen, P. J., & Hol, E. M. (2016). The indispensable roles of microglia and astrocytes during brain development. *Frontiers in Human Neuroscience, 10,* Article ID 566.

Rees, S., Harding, R., & Inder, T. (2006). The developmental environment and the origins of neurological disorders. In P. Gluckman & M. Hanson (Eds.), *Developmental origins of health and disease* (pp. 379–391). New York, NY: Cambridge University Press.

Reese, E., Hayne, H., & MacDonald, S. (2008). Looking back to the future: Māori and Pakeha mother–child birth stories. *Child Development, 79*(1), 114–125.

Reese, E., Myftari, E., McAnally, H. M., Chen, Y., Neha, T., Wang, Q., . . . Robertson, S.-J. (2017). Telling the tale and living well: Adolescent narrative identity, personality traits, and well-being across cultures. *Child Development, 88,* 612–628. doi:10.1111/cdev.12618

Reese, E., Sparks, A., & Leyva, D. (2010). A review of parent interventions for preschool children's language and emergent literacy. *Journal of Early Childhood Literacy, 10*(1), 97–117.

Reese, E., Yan, C., Jack, F., & Hayne, H. (2010). Emerging identities: Narrative and self from early childhood to early adolescence. In K. C. McLean, & M. Pasupathi (Eds.), *Narrative development in adolescence: Creating the storied self. Advancing responsible adolescent development* (pp. 23–43). New York, NY: Springer Science + Business Media.

Reese, L., Garnier, H., Gallimore, R., & Goldenberg, C. (2000). Longitudinal analysis of the antecedents of emergent Spanish literacy and middle-school English reading achievement of Spanish-speaking students. *American Educational Research Journal, 37,* 633–662.

Reese, S. (1996). KIDMONEY: Children as big business. *Technos Quarterly, 5*(4), 1–7. Retrieved from http://www.ait.net/technos/tq_05/4reesephp

Reeve, J., Deci, E. L., & Ryan, R. M. (2004). Self-determination theory: A dialectical framework for understanding sociocultural influences on student motivation. In D. M. McInerney & S. Van Etten (Eds.), *Big theories revisited* (pp. 31–60). Greenwich, CT: Information Age.

Regev, R., & Ehrenberg, M. F. (2012). A pilot study of a support group for children in divorcing families: Aiding community program development and marking pathways to resilience. *Journal of Divorce & Remarriage, 53,* 220–230. doi:10.1080/10502556.2012.663271

Regmi, K., & Madison, J. (2009). Contemporary childbirth practices in Nepal: Improving outcomes. *British Journal of Midwifery, 17,* 382–387.

Reich, P. A. (1986). *Language development.* Englewood Cliffs, NJ: Prentice Hall.

Reid Chassiakos, Y., Radesky, J., Christakis, D., Moreno, M. A., & Cross, C. (2016). Children and adolescents and the media. *Pediatrics, 138*(5), e1–e18. doi:10.1542/peds.2016-2593

Reid, N. (1989). Contemporary Polynesian conceptions of giftedness. *Gifted Education International, 6*(1), 30–38.

Reid, S. E., & Listwan, S. S. (2018). Managing the threat of violence: Coping strategies among juvenile inmates. *Journal of Interpersonal Violence, 33,* 1306–1326. doi:10.1177/0886260515615143

Reidy, D. E., Krusemark, E., Kosson, D. S., Kearns, M. C., Smith-Darden, J., & Kiehl, K. A. (2017). The development of severe and chronic violence among youth: The role of psychopathic traits and reward processing. *Child Psychiatry and Human Development, 48,* 967–982. http://dx.doi.org.unco.idm.oclc.org/10.1007/s10578-017-0720-5

Reigosa-Crespo, V., Valdés-Sosa, M., Butterworth, B., Estévez, N., Rodríguez, M.,

Santos, E., . . . Lage, A. (2012). Basic numerical capacities and prevalence of developmental dyscalculia: The Havana Survey. *Developmental Psychology, 48*, 123–135. doi:10.1037/a0025356

Reilly, C. (2012). Behavioural phenotypes and special educational needs: Is aetiology important in the classroom? *Journal of Intellectual Disability Research, 56*, 929–946. doi:10.1111/j.1365-2788.2012.01542.x

Reilly, D., & Neumann, D. (2013). Gender-role differences in spatial ability: A meta-analytic review. *Sex Roles, 68*(9/10), 521–535. doi:10.1007/s11199-013-0269-0

Reimer, J., Paolitto, D. P., & Hersh, R. H. (1983). *Promoting moral growth: From Piaget to Kohlberg* (2nd ed.). White Plains, NY: Longman.

Reiner, M., Slotta, J. D., Chi, M. T. H., & Resnick, L. B. (2000). Naïve physics reasoning: A commitment to substance-based conceptions. *Cognition and Instruction, 18*, 1–34.

Reinke, W., Herman, K., & Stormont, M. (2013). Classroom-level positive behavior supports in schools implementing SW-PBIS: Identifying areas for enhancement. *Journal of Positive Behavior Interventions, 15*(1), 39–50. doi:10.1177/1098300712459079

Reis, S. M. (2011). Self-regulated learning and academically talented students. In J. L. Jolly, D. J. Treffinger, T. F. Inman, & J. F. Smutny (Eds.), *Parenting gifted children: The authoritative guide from the National Association for Gifted Children* (pp. 42–52). Waco, TX: Prufrock Press.

Reiss, D. (2005). The interplay between genotypes and family relationships: Reframing concepts of development and prevention. *Current Directions in Psychological Science, 14*, 139–143.

Reissland, N. (2006). Teaching a baby the language of emotions: A father's experience. *Zero to Three, 27*(1), 42–47.

Ren, L., & Pope Edwards, C. (2016). Contemporary Chinese parents' socialization priorities for preschoolers: A mixed methods study. *Early Child Development & Care, 186*, 1779–1791. doi:10.1080/03004430.2015.1132418

Rendle-Short, J., & Moses, K. (2010). Taking an interactional perspective: Examining children's talk in the Australian Aboriginal community of Yakanarra. *Australian Journal of Linguistics, 30*, 397–421. doi:10.1080/07268602.2010.518553

Renk, K., White, R. W., Scott, S., & Middleton, M. (2009). Evidence-based methods of dealing with social deficits in conduct disorder. In J. L. Matson (Ed.), *Social behavior and skills in children* (pp. 187–218). New York, NY: Springer Science + Business Media.

Repacholi, B. M., & Gopnik, A. (1997). Early reasoning about desires: Evidence from 14- and 18-month-olds. *Developmental Psychology, 33*, 12–21.

Repaskey, L. L., Schumm, J., & Johnson, J. (2017). First and fourth grade boys' and girls' preferences for and perceptions about narrative and expository text. *Reading Psychology, 38*, 808–847. doi:10.1080/02702711.2017.1344165

Rest, J. R., Narváez, D., Bebeau, M., & Thoma, S. (1999). A neo-Kohlbergian approach: The DIT and schema theory. *Educational Psychology Review, 11*, 291–324.

Reston, J. (2007). Reflecting on admission criteria. In G. E. Mills, *Action research: A guide for the teacher researcher* (3rd ed., pp. 141–142). Upper Saddle River, NJ: Pearson Merrill/Prentice Hall.

Reutzel, D., Child, A., Jones, C. D., & Clark, S. K. (2014). Explicit instruction in core reading programs. *Elementary School Journal, 114*, 406–430.

Revelle, G. (2013). Applying developmental theory and research to the creation of educational games. *New Directions for Child & Adolescent Development, 2013*(139), 31–40. doi:10.1002/cad.20029

Reyes, I., & Azuara, P. (2008). Emergent biliteracy in young Mexican immigrant children. *Reading Research Quarterly, 43*, 374–398.

Reyna, C. (2000). Lazy, dumb, or industrious: When stereotypes convey attribution information in the classroom. *Educational Psychology Review, 12*, 85–110.

Reyna, V. F., & Farley, F. (2006). Risk and rationality in adolescent decision making: Implications for theory, practice, and public policy. *Psychological Science in the Public Interest, 7*, 1–44.

Reynolds, A. J., Englund, M. M., Ou, S., Schweinhart, L. J., & Campbell, F. A. (2010). Paths of effects of preschool participation to educational attainment at age 21: A three study analysis. In A. J. Reynolds, A. J. Rolnick, M. M. Englund, & J. A. Temple (Eds.), *Childhood programs and practices in the first decade of life: A human capital integration* (pp. 415–452). New York, NY: Cambridge University Press. doi:10.1017/CBO9780511762666.022

Reznick, J. S. (2009). Working memory in infants and toddlers. In M. L. Courage & N. Cowan (Eds.), *The development of memory in infancy and childhood* (pp. 343–365). New York, NY: Psychology Press.

Reznick, J. S., & Goldfield, B. A. (1992). Rapid change in lexical development in comprehension and production. *Developmental Psychology, 28*, 408–414.

Rhoads, D. (1956). *The corn grows ripe*. New York, NY: Viking Press.

Rhodes, M., & Wellman, H. (2013). Constructing a new theory from old ideas and new evidence. *Cognitive Science, 37*, 592–604. doi:10.1111/cogs.12031

Ribeaud, D., & Eisner, M. (2015). The nature of the association between moral neutralization and aggression: A systematic test of causality in early adolescence. *Merrill-Palmer Quarterly, 61*(1), 68–84. http://dx.doi.org.unco.idm.oclc.org/10.13110/merrpalmquar1982.61.1.0068

Ricci, D., Romeo, D. M., Serrao, F., Gallini, F., Leone, D., Longo, M., . . . Mercuri, E. (2010). Early assessment of visual function in preterm infants: How early is early? *Early Human Development, 86*(1), 29–33. doi:10.1016/j.earlhumdev.2009.11.004

Ricciuti, H. N. (1993). Nutrition and mental development. *Current Directions in Psychological Science, 2*, 43–46.

Rice, M. L. (2013). Language growth and genetics of specific language impairment. *International Journal of Speech-Language Pathology, 15*, 223–233.

Rice, M. M. (2016). Specific Language Impairment, Nonverbal IQ, Attention-Deficit/Hyperactivity Disorder, Autism Spectrum Disorder, Cochlear Implants, Bilingualism, and Dialectal Variants: Defining the boundaries, clarifying clinical conditions, and sorting out causes. *Journal of Speech, Language & Hearing Research, 59*, 122–132. doi:10.1044/2015_JSLHR-L-15-0255

Richard, J. F., & Schneider, B. H. (2005). Assessing friendship motivation during preadolescence and early adolescence. *Journal of Early Adolescence, 25*, 367–385.

Richards, J. E., & Turner, E. D. (2001). Extended visual fixation and distractibility in children from six to twenty-four months of age. *Child Development, 72*, 963–972.

Richards, K., & Levesque-Bristol, C. (2014). Student learning and motivation in physical education. *Strategies, 27*(2), 43–45.

Richardson, W. (2011, February). Publishers, participants all. *Educational Leadership, 68*(5), 22–26.

Riches, N. G. (2013). Treating the passive in children with specific language impairment: A usage-based approach. *Child Language Teaching & Therapy, 29*(2), 155–169. doi:10.1177/0265659012466667

Richman, G., Hope, T., & Mihalas, S. (2010). Assessment and treatment of self-esteem in adolescents with ADHD. In M. H. Guindon (Ed.), *Self-esteem across the lifespan: Issues and interventions* (pp. 111–123). New York, NY: Routledge/Taylor & Francis Group.

Richman, S. B., & Mandara, J. (2013). Do socialization goals explain differences in parental control between Black and White parents? *Family Relations: An Interdisciplinary Journal of Applied Family Studies, 62*, 625–636. doi:10.1111/fare.12022

Richmond, K., Carroll, K., & Denboske, K. (2010). Gender identity disorder: Concerns and controversies. In J. C. Chrisler & D. R. McCreary (Eds.), *Handbook of Gender Research in Psychology, Vol. 2. Gender research in social and applied psychology* (pp. 111–131). New York, NY: Springer Science / Business Media. doi:10.1007/978-1-4419-1467-5_6

Ricketts, H., & Anderson, P. (2008). The impact of poverty and stress on the interaction of Jamaican caregivers with young children. *International Journal of Early Years Education, 16*(1), 61–74.

Ridenour, T. A., Clark, D. B., & Cottler, L. B. (2009). The illustration-based assessment of liability and exposure to substance use and antisocial behavior for children. *The American Journal of Drug and Alcohol Abuse, 35*, 242–252.

Rieffe, C., & Wiefferink, C. H. (2017). Happy faces, sad faces: Emotion understanding in toddlers and preschoolers with language impairments. *Research in Developmental Disabilities, 62*, 40–49. http://dx.doi.org.unco.idm.oclc.org/10.1016/j.ridd.2016.12.018

Riehle-Colarusso, T., & Oster, M. E. (2016). Down Syndrome: Changing Cardiac Phenotype? *Pediatrics, 138*(1), 1–2. doi:10.1542/peds.2016-1223

Riemer, F. J., & Blasi, M. (2008). Rethinking relationships, reconfiguring teacher research: Teachers as ethnographers of culture, childhood, and classrooms. *Action in Teacher Education, 29*(4), 53–65.

Rihtman, T., Tekuzener, E., Parush, S., Tenenbaum, A., Bachrach, S. J., & Ornoy, A. (2010). Are the cognitive functions of children with Down syndrome related to their participation? *Developmental Medicine & Child Neurology, 52*(1), 72–78.

Rimm-Kaufman, S. E., Early, D. M., Cox, M. J., Saluja, G., Pianta, R. C., Bradley, R. H., & Payne, C. (2002). Early behavioral attributes and teachers' sensitivity as predictors of competent behavior in the kindergarten classroom. *Journal of Applied Developmental Psychology, 23*, 451–470.

Rindermann, H., & Baumeister, A. E. E. (2015). Parents' SES vs. parental educational behavior and children's development: A reanalysis of the Hart and Risley study. *Learning and Individual Differences, 37*, 133–138. http://dx.doi.org/10.1016/j.lindif.2014.12.005

Rine, R., & Wiener-Vacher, S. (2013). Evaluation and treatment of vestibular dysfunction in children. *Neurorehabilitation, 32*, 507–518.

Rinehart, S. D., Stahl, S. A., & Erickson, L. G. (1986). Some effects of summarization training on reading and studying. *Reading Research Quarterly, 21*, 422–438.

Riojas-Cortez, M., Huerta, M. E., Flores, B. B., Perez, B., & Clark, E. R. (2008). Using cultural tools to develop scientific literacy of young Mexican American preschoolers. *Early Child Development and Care, 178*, 527–536.

Riordan, D., Morris, C., Hattie, J., & Stark, C. (2012). Family size and perinatal circumstances, as mental health risk factors in a Scottish birth cohort. *Social Psychiatry and Psychiatric Epidemiology, 47*, 975–983. doi:10.1007/s00127-011-040

Rios-Aguilar, C. González-Canche, M., Moll, L. C. (2010). *The study of Arizona's teachers of English Language learners*. Retrieved from http://civilrightsproject.ucla.edu/research/k-12-education/language-minority-students/a-study-of-arizonas-teachers-of-english-language-learners

Rissman, B. (2011). Nonverbal learning disability explained: The link to shunted hydrocephalus. *British Journal of Learning Disabilities, 39*, 209–215. http://dx.doi.org.unco.idm.oclc.org/10.1111/j.1468-3156.2010.00652.x

Rittle-Johnson, B. (2006). Promoting transfer: Effects of self-explanation and direct instruction. *Child Development, 77*, 1–15.

Rittle-Johnson, B. (2017). Developing mathematics knowledge. *Child Development Perspectives, 11*, 184–190. doi:10.1111/cdep.12229

Rittle-Johnson, B., & Siegler, R. S. (1999). Learning to spell: Variability, choice, and change in children's strategy use. *Child Development, 70*, 332–348.

Ritts, V., Patterson, M. L., & Tubbs, M. E. (1992). Expectations, impressions, and judgments of physically attractive students: A review. *Review of Educational Research, 62*, 413–426.

Rizzo, K., & Bosacki, S. (2013). Social cognitive theory and practice of moral development in educational settings. In B. J. Irby, G. Brown, R. Lara-Alecio, & S. Jackson (Eds.), *The handbook of educational theories* (pp. 595–606). Charlotte, NC: Information Age Publishing.

Rizzo, V. (2009). The Howard Gardner School for Discovery. In J.-Q. Chen, S. Moran, & H. Gardner, (Eds.), *Multiple intelligences around the world* (pp. 3–16). San Francisco, CA: Jossey-Bass.

Rizzolatti, G., & Fabbri-Destro, M. (2010). Mirror neurons: From discovery to autism. *Experimental Brain Research, 200*(3–4), 223–237. doi:10.1007/s00221-009-2002-3

Robb, L. (2018). The myth of learn to read/read to learn. *Scholastic Teacher Magazine*. Retrieved from http://teacher.scholastic.com/professional/readexpert/mythread.htm

Robbers, M. L. P. (2008). The caring equation: An intervention program for teenage mothers and their male partners. *Children and Schools, 30*(1), 37–47.

Robbins, W. J., Brody, S., Hogan, A. G., Jackson, C. M., & Green, C. W. (Eds.). (1928). *Growth*. New Haven, CT: Yale University Press.

Roberts, D. F., & Foehr, U. G. (2008). Trends in media use. *Future of Children, 18*(1), 11–37.

Roberts, D. F., Christenson, P., Gibson, W. A., Mooser, L., & Goldberg, M. E. (1980). Developing discriminating consumers. *Journal of Communication, 30*, 94–105.

Roberts, K. L. (2013). Comprehension strategy instruction during parent–child shared reading: An intervention study. *Literacy Research and Instruction, 52*, 106–129. doi:10.1080/19388071.2012.754521

Roberts, M. C., Brown, K. J., Boles, R. E., & Mashunkashey, J. O. (2004). Prevention of injuries: Concepts and interventions for pediatric psychology in the schools. In R. T. Brown (Ed.), *Handbook of pediatric psychology in school settings* (pp. 65–80). Mahwah, NJ: Erlbaum.

Roberts, T. A. (2005). Articulation accuracy and vocabulary size contributions to phonemic awareness and word reading in English language learners. *Journal of Educational Psychology, 97*, 601–616.

Roberts, W., Strayer, J., & Denham, S. (2014). Empathy, anger, guilt: Emotions and prosocial behaviour. *Canadian Journal of Behavioural Science/Revue Canadienne Des Sciences Du Comportement*, doi:10.1037/a0035057

Robertson, S., von Hapsburg, D., Hay, J. S., Champlin, C., & Werner, L. (2013). The effect of hearing loss on the perception of infant- and adult-directed speech. *Journal of Speech, Language & Hearing Research, 56*, 1108–1119. doi:10.1044/1092-4388(2012/12-0110)

Robins, R. W., & Trzesniewski, K. H. (2005). Self-esteem development across the lifespan. *Current Directions in Psychological Science, 14*, 158–162.

Robinson-Cimpian, J. P., Lubienski, S., Ganley, C. M., & Copur-Gencturk, Y. (2014). Teachers' perceptions of students' mathematics proficiency may exacerbate early gender gaps in achievement. *Developmental Psychology, 50*, 1262–1281. doi:10.1037/a0035073

Robinson, T. N., & Borzekowski, D. L. G. (2006). Effects of the SMART classroom curriculum to reduce child and family screen time. *Journal of Communication, 56*(1), 1–26.

Rochat, P., & Bullinger, A. (1994). Posture and functional action in infancy. In A. Vyt, H. Bloch, & M. H. Bornstein (Eds.), *Early child development in the French tradition: Contributions from current research* (pp. 15-34). Hillsdale, NJ: Erlbaum.

Roche, K. M., Ghazarian, S. R., & Fernandez-Esquer, M. (2012). Unpacking acculturation: Cultural orientations and educational attainment among Mexican-origin youth. *Journal of Youth and Adolescence, 41*, 920–931. doi:10.1007/s10964-011-9725-8

Roderick, M., & Camburn, E. (1999). Risk and recovery from course failure in the early years of high school. *American Educational Research Journal, 36*, 303–343.

Rodkin, P. C., Ryan, A. M., Jamison, R., & Wilson, T. (2013). Social goals, social behavior, and social status in middle childhood. *Developmental Psychology, 49*, 1139–1150. doi:10.1037/a0029389

Rodriguez, G. (2013). Power and agency in education: Exploring the pedagogical dimensions of funds of knowledge. *Review of Research in Education, 37*, 87–120. doi:10.3102/0091732X12462686

Roebers, C. M., Krebs, S. S., & Roderer, T. (2014). Metacognitive monitoring and control in elementary school children: Their interrelations and their role for test performance. *Learning & Individual Differences, 29*, 141–149. doi:10.1016/j.lindif.2012.12.003

Roediger, H., McDermott, K. B., & McDaniel, M. A. (2011). Using testing to improve learning and memory. In M. Gernsbacher, R. W. Pew, L. M. Hough, & J. R. Pomerantz (Eds.), *Psychology and the real world: Essays illustrating fundamental contributions to society* (pp. 65–74). New York, NY: Worth Publishers.

Roeper, T. (2012). Minimalism and bilingualism: How and why bilingualism could benefit children with SLI. *Bilingualism: Language & Cognition, 15*, 88–101. doi:10.1017/S1366728911000605

Roeser, R. W., Midgley, C., & Urdan, T. C. (1996). Perceptions of school psychological environment and early adolescents' psychological and behavioral functioning in school: The mediating role of goals and belonging. *Journal of Educational Psychology, 88*, 408–422.

Roffey, S. (2016). Building a case for whole-child, whole-school wellbeing in challenging contexts. *Educational & Child Psychology, 33*(2), 30–42.

Rogoff, B. (1990). *Apprenticeship in thinking: Cognitive development in social context.* New York, NY: Oxford University Press.

Rogoff, B. (1991). Social interaction as apprenticeship in thinking: Guidance and participation in spatial planning. In L. B. Resnick, J. M. Levine, & S. D. Teasley (Eds.), *Perspectives on socially shared cognition* (pp. 349–364). Washington, DC: American Psychological Association.

Rogoff, B. (1994, April). *Developing understanding of the idea of communities of learners.* Paper presented at the annual meeting of the American Educational Research Association, New Orleans, LA.

Rogoff, B. (2003). *The cultural nature of human development.* New York, NY: Oxford University Press.

Rogoff, B., & Morelli, G. (1989). Perspectives on children's development from cultural psychology. *American Psychologist, 44*, 343–348.

Rogoff, B., Mistry, J., Göncü, A., & Mosier, C. (1993). Guided participation in cultural activity by toddlers and caregivers. *Monographs of the Society for Research in Child Development, 58*(8, Serial No. 236).

Rogoff, B., Moore, L., Najafi, B., Dexter, A., Correa-Chávez, M., & Solís, J. (2007). Children's development of cultural repertoires through participation in everyday routines and practices. In J. E. Grusec & P. D. Hastings (Eds.), *Handbook of socialization: Theory and research* (pp. 490–515). New York, NY: Guilford Press.

Rogoff, B., Topping, K., Baker-Sennett, J., & Lacasa, P. (2002). Mutual contributions of individuals, partners, and institutions: Planning to remember in Girl Scout cookie sales. *Social Development, 11*, 266–289. doi:10.1111/1467-9507.00198.

Rohde, M. C., Corydon, T. J., Hansen, J., Bak Pedersen, C., Schmidt, S., Gregersen, N., & Banner, J. (2013). Heat stress and sudden infant death syndrome–Stress gene expression after exposure to moderate heat stress. *Forensic Science International, 232*(1–3), 16–24.

Rohner, R. P., & Rohner, E. C. (1981). Parental acceptance-rejection and parental control: Cross-cultural codes. *Ethnology, 20*, 245–260.

Roid, G. (2003). *Stanford-Binet Intelligence Scales* (5th ed.). Itasca, IL: Riverside.

Roid, G. H., & Pomplun, M. (2012). The Stanford-Binet Intelligence Scales, fifth edition. In D. P. Flanagan & P. L. Harrison (Eds.), *Contemporary intellectual assessment: Theories, tests, and issues* (3rd ed., pp. 249–268). New York, NY: Guilford Press.

Roid, G. H., & Tippin, S. M. (2009). Assessment of intellectual strengths and weaknesses with the Stanford-Binet Intelligence Scales–Fifth Edition (SB5). In J. A. Naglieri & S. Goldstein (Eds.), *Practitioner's guide to assessing intelligence and achievement* (pp. 127–152). Hoboken, NJ: Wiley.

Rojek, J., Petrocelli, M., & Oberweis, T. (2010). Recent patterns in gang prevalence: A two state comparison. *Journal of Gang Research, 18*(1), 1–18.

Rollison, J., Banks, D., Martin, A. J., Owens, C., Thomas, N., Dressler, K. J., & Wells, M. (2013). Improving school-justice partnerships: Lessons learned from the Safe Schools/Healthy Students Initiative. *Family Court Review, 51*, 445–451. doi:10.1111/fcre.12041

Rolls, C., & Chamberlain, M. (2004). From east to west: Nepalese women's experiences. *International Council of Nurses, 51*, 176–184.

Rolon-Arroyo, B., Arnold, D. H., Breaux, R. P., & Harvey, E. A. (2018). Reciprocal relations between parenting behaviors and conduct disorder symptoms in preschool children. *Child Psychiatry and Human Development.* Advance online publication. http://dx.doi.org.unco.idm.oclc.org/10.1007/s10578-018-0794-8

Romens, S. E., McDonald, J., Svaren, J., & Pollak, S. D. (2015). Associations between early life stress and gene methylation in children. *Child Development, 86*, 303–309. doi:10.1111/cdev.12270

Romero-Little, M. (2011). Learning the community's curriculum: The linguistic, social, and cultural resources of American Indian and Alaska Native children. In M. C. Sarche, P. Spicer, P. Farrell, & H. E. Fitzgerald (Eds.), *American Indian and Alaska Native children and mental health: Development, context, prevention, and treatment* (pp. 89–99). Santa Barbara, CA: Praeger/ABC-CLIO.

Romero, A. J., & Roberts, R. E. (2003). The impact of multiple dimensions of ethnic identity on discrimination and adolescents' self-esteem. *Journal of Applied Social Psychology, 33*, 2288–2305.

Romero, A., Edwards, L., Fryberg, S., & Orduña, M. (2014). Resilience to discrimination stress across ethnic identity stages of development. *Journal of Applied Social Psychology, 44*(1), 1–11.

Rönnau-Böse, M., & Fröhlich-Gildhoff, K. (2009). The promotion of resilience: A person-centered perspective of prevention in early childhood institutions. *Person-Centered and Experiential Psychotherapies, 8*, 299–318.

Roos, S., Hodges, E. E., & Salmivalli, C. (2014). Do guilt- and shame-proneness differentially predict prosocial, aggressive, and withdrawn behaviors during early adolescence? *Developmental Psychology, 50*, 941–946. doi:10.1037/a0033904

Roosa, M. W., Weaver, S. R., White, R. M. B., Tein, J.-Y., Knight, G. P., Gonzales, N., & Saenz, D. (2009). Family and neighborhood fit or misfit and the adaptation of Mexican Americans. *American Journal of Community Psychology, 44*, 15–27.

Roque, I. P., Lemos, M., & Gonçalves, T. (2014). A longitudinal developmental analysis of students' causality beliefs about school performance. *European Journal Of Psychology Of Education—EJPE, 29*, 159–173. doi:10.1007/s10212-013-0192-3

Rose, A. J., & Smith, R. L. (2009). Sex differences in peer relationships. In K. H. Rubin, W. M. Bukowski, & B. Laursen (Eds.), *Handbook of peer interactions, relationships, and groups* (pp. 379–393). New York, NY: Guilford Press.

Roseboom, T., de Rooij, S., & Painter, R. (2006). The Dutch famine and its long-term consequences for adult health. *Early Human Development, 82*(8), 485–491.

Rosen, L., Mark Carrier, L., & Cheever, N. (2013). Facebook and texting made me do it: Media-induced task-switching while studying. *Computers in Human Behavior, 29*, 948–958. doi:10.1016/j.chb.2012.12.001

Rosenberg, E. E., Burt, K., Forehand, R., & Paysnick, A. (2016). Youth self-views, coping with stress, and behavioral/emotional problems: The role of Incremental Self-Theory. *Journal of Child & Family Studies, 25*, 1713–1723. doi:10.1007/s10826-015-0346-9

Rosenblum, K. L., & Muzik, M. (2014). STRoNG intervention for military families with young children. *Psychiatric Services, 65*, 399.

Rosende-Vázquez, M., & Vieiro-Iglesias, P. (2013). Inferential processes in children with Down syndrome. *RELIEVE—Revista Electrónica De Investigación Y Evaluación Educativa, 19*(1), 1–12. doi:10.7203/relieve.19.1.2612

Rosenkoetter, L. I., Rosenkoetter, S. E., Ozretich, R. A., & Acock, A. C. (2004). Mitigating the harmful effects of violent television. *Applied Developmental Psychology, 25*, 25–47.

Rosenshine, B., & Meister, C. (1992). The use of scaffolds for teaching higher-level cognitive strategies. *Educational Leadership, 49*(7), 26–33.

Rosenshine, B., Meister, C., & Chapman, S. (1996). Teaching students to generate questions: A review of the intervention studies. *Review of Educational Research, 66*, 181–221.

Rosenthal, R. (1994). Interpersonal expectancy effects: A 30-year perspective. *Current Directions in Psychological Science, 3*, 176–179.

Roseth, C. J., Lee, Y.-k., & Saltarelli, W. A. (2018). Reconsidering jigsaw social psychology: Longitudinal effects on social interdependence, sociocognitive conflict regulation, motivation, and achievement. *Journal of Educational Psychology.* Advance online publication. http://dx.doi.org.unco.idm.oclc.org/10.1037/edu0000257

Ross, J. (2017). You and me: Investigating the role of self-evaluative emotion in preschool prosociality. *Journal of Experimental Child Psychology, 155*, 67–83.

Rostad, K., & Pexman, P. M. (2014). Developing appreciation for ambivalence: The understanding of concurrent conflicting desires in 4- to 7-year-old children. *Canadian Journal of Experimental Psychology/Revue Canadienne De Psychologie Expérimentale, 68*, 122–132. doi:10.1037/cep0000016

Rotenberg, K. J., & Boulton, M. (2013). Interpersonal trust consistency and the quality of peer relationships during childhood. *Social Development, 22*, 225–241. doi:10.1111/sode.12005

Rothbart, M. K. (2007). Temperament, development, and personality. *Current Directions in Psychological Science, 16*, 207–212.

Rothbart, M. K. (2012). Advances in temperament: History, concepts, and measures. In M. Zentner & R. L. Shiner (Eds.), *Handbook of temperament* (pp. 3–20). New York, NY: Guilford Press.

Rothbart, M. K., & Bates, J. E. (2006). Temperament. In W. Damon & R. M. Lerner (Eds. in Chief) & N. Eisenberg (Vol. Ed.), *Handbook of Child Psychology, Vol. 3. Social, emotional, and personality development* (6th ed., pp. 99–225). Hoboken, NJ: Wiley.

Rothbart, M. K., & Posner, M. I. (2015). The developing brain in a multitasking world. *Developmental Review, 35*, 42–63. http://dx.doi.org.unco.idm.oclc.org/10.1016/j.dr.2014.12.006

Rothbart, M. K., Hanley, D., & Albert, M. (1986). Gender differences in moral reasoning. *Sex Roles, 15*, 645–653.

Rothbart, M. K., Posner, M. I., & Kieras, J. (2006). Temperament, attention, and the development of self-regulation. In K. McCartney & D. Phillips (Eds.), *Blackwell handbook of early childhood development* (pp. 338–357). Malden, MA: Blackwell.

Rothbart, M. K., Sheese, B. E., & Conradt, E. D. (2009). Childhood temperament. In P. J. Corr, & G. Matthews (Eds.), *The Cambridge handbook of personality psychology* (pp. 177–190). New York, NY: Cambridge University Press.

Rothbaum, F., Nagaoka, R., & Ponte, I. C. (2006). Caregiver sensitivity in cultural context: Japanese and U.S. teachers' beliefs about anticipating and responding to children's needs. *Journal of Research in Childhood Education, 21*(1), 23–40.

Rothbaum, F., Pott, M., Azuma, H., Miyake, K., & Weisz, J. (2000). The development of close relationships in Japan and the United States: Paths of symbiotic harmony and generative tension. *Child Development, 71*, 1121–1142. doi:10.1111/1467-8624.00214

Rothenberg, C., & Fisher, D. (2007). *Teaching English language learners: A differentiated approach.* Upper Saddle River, NJ: Pearson Merrill.

Rothrauff, T. C., Cooney, T. M., & An, J. S. (2009). Remembered parenting styles and adjustment in middle and late adulthood. *Journal of Gerontology, 64B*(1), 137–146.

Rothstein-Fisch, C., & Trumbull, E. (2008). *Managing diverse classrooms: How to build on students' strengths*. Alexandria, VA: Association for Supervision and Curriculum Development.

Rothstein-Fisch, C., Trumbull, E., & Garcia, S. G. (2009). Making the implicit explicit: Supporting teachers to bridge cultures. *Early Childhood Research Quarterly, 24*, 474–486. doi:10.1016/j.ecresq.2009.08.006

Roussotte, F. F., Bramen, J. E., Nunez, S. C., Quandt, L. C., Smith, L., O'Connor, M. J., . . . Sowell, E. R. (2011). Abnormal brain activation during working memory in children with prenatal exposure to drugs of abuse: The effects of methamphetamine, alcohol, and polydrug exposure. *NeuroImage, 54*, 3067–3075 http://dx.doi.org/10.1016/j.neuroimage.2010.10.072

Roux, C., Dion, E., Barrette, A., Dupéré, V., & Fuchs, D. (2015). Efficacy of an intervention to enhance reading comprehension of students with high-functioning Autism Spectrum Disorder. *Remedial & Special Education, 36*, 131–142. doi:10.1177/0741932514533998

Rovee-Collier, C. (1999). The development of infant memory. *Current Directions in Psychological Science, 8*, 80–85.

Rovee-Collier, C., & Cuevas, K. (2009). Multiple memory systems are unnecessary to account for infant memory development: An ecological model. *Developmental Psychology, 45*, 160–174. doi:10.1037/a0014538

Rowe, D. C., Almeida, D. M., & Jacobson, K. C. (1999). School context and genetic influences on aggression in adolescence. *Psychological Science, 10*, 277–280.

Rowe, D. W., & Harste, J. C. (1986). Metalinguistic awareness in writing and reading: The young child as curricular informant. In D. B. Yaden, Jr., & S. Templeton (Eds.), *Metalinguistic awareness and beginning literacy: Conceptualizing what it means to read and write* (pp. 235–256). Portsmouth, NH: Heinemann.

Rowe, E., Miller, C., Ebenstein, L., & Thompson, D. (2012). Cognitive predictors of reading and math achievement among gifted referrals. *School Psychology Quarterly, 27*, 144–153. doi:10.1037/a0029941

Rowe, M. B. (1974). Wait-time and rewards as instructional variables, their influence on language, logic, and fate control: Part one—wait time. *Journal of Research in Science Teaching, 11*, 81–94.

Rowe, M. B. (1978). *Teaching science as continuous inquiry*. New York, NY: McGraw-Hill.

Rowe, M. B. (1987). Wait-time: Slowing down may be a way of speeding up. *American Educator, 11*, 38–43, 47.

Rowe, M. L. (2017). Understanding socioeconomic differences in parents' speech to children. *Child Development Perspectives*. Advance online publication http://dx.doi.org.unco.idm.oclc.org/10.1111/cdep.12271

Rowland, T. W. (1990). *Exercise and children's health*. Champaign, IL: Human Kinetics.

Roy, A. L., & Raver, C. (2014). Are all risks equal? Early experiences of poverty-related risk and children's functioning. *Journal of Family Psychology, 28*, 391–400. doi:10.1037/a0036683

Rozalski, M. E., & Yell, M. L. (2004). Law and school safety. In J. C. Conoley & A. P. Goldstein (Eds.), *School violence intervention* (2nd ed., pp. 507–523). New York, NY: Guilford Press.

Rozendaal, E., Buijzen, M., & Valkenburg, P. M. (2012). Think-aloud process superior to thought-listing in increasing children's critical processing of advertising. *Human Communication Research, 38*, 199–221. doi:10.1111/j.1468-2958.2011.01425.x

Rozendaal, M., & Baker, A. (2010). The acquisition of reference: Pragmatic aspects and the influence of language input. *Journal of Pragmatics, 42*, 1866–1879. doi:10.1016/j.pragma.2009.05.013

Rubie-Davies, C. M. (2007). Classroom interactions: Exploring the practices of high- and low- expectation teachers. *British Journal of Educational Psychology, 77*, 289–306.

Rubin, K. H., Bowker, J. C., & Kennedy, A. E. (2009). Avoiding and withdrawing from the peer group. In K. H. Rubin, W. M. Bukowski, & B. Laursen (Eds.), *Handbook of peer interactions, relationships, and groups* (pp. 303–321). New York, NY: Guilford Press.

Rubin, K. H., Bukowski, W. M., & Parker, J. G. (2006). Peer interactions, relationships, and groups. In W. Damon & R. M. Lerner (Series Eds.) & N. Eisenberg (Vol. Ed.), *Handbook of Child Psychology: Vol. 3. Social, emotional, and personality development* (6th ed., pp. 571–645). New York, NY: Wiley.

Rubin, K. H., Lynch, D., Coplan, R., Rose-Krasnor, L., & Booth, C. L. (1994). "Birds of a feather": Behavioral concordances and preferential personal attraction in children. *Child Development, 65*, 1778–1785.

Ruble, D. N., Martin, C. L., & Berenbaum, S. A. (2006). Gender development. In W. Damon & R. M. Lerner (Eds. in Chief) & N. Eisenberg (Vol. Ed.), *Handbook of Child Psychology, Vol. 3. Social, emotional, and personality development* (6th ed., pp. 858–932). Hoboken, NJ: Wiley.

Ruble, D. N., Taylor, L. J., Cyphers, L., Greulich, F. K., Lurye, L. E., & Shrout, P. E. (2007). The role of gender constancy in early gender development. *Child Development, 78*, 1121–1136.

Rudasill, K. M., Gallagher, K. C., & White, J. M. (2010). Temperamental attention and activity, classroom emotional support, and academic achievement in third grade. *Journal of School Psychology, 48*, 113–134.

Rudasill, K., Pössel, P., Winkeljohn Black, S., & Niehaus, K. (2014). Teacher support mediates concurrent and longitudinal associations between temperament and mild depressive symptoms in sixth grade. *Early Child Development & Care, 184*, 803–818.

Rudlin, C. R. (1993). Growth and sexual development: What is normal, and what is not? *Journal of the American Academy of Physician Assistants, 6*, 25–35.

Rudolph, J. M. (2017). Case history risk factors for specific language impairment: A systematic review and meta-analysis. *American Journal of Speech-Language Pathology, 26*, 991–1010. http://dx.doi.org.unco.idm.oclc.org/10.1044/2016_AJSLP-15-0181

Rudolph, K. D., Caldwell, M. S., & Conley, C. S. (2005). Need for approval and children's wellbeing. *Child Development, 76*, 309–323.

Rudolph, K. D., Davis, M. M., & Monti, J. D. (2017). Cognition–emotion interaction as a predictor of adolescent depressive symptoms. *Developmental Psychology, 53*, 2377–2383.

Rudy, D., & Grusec, J. E. (2006). Authoritarian parenting in individualistic and collectivist groups: Associations with maternal emotion and cognition and children's self-esteem. *Journal of Family Psychology, 20*, 68–78.

Rudy, D., Carlo, G., Lambert, M., & Awong, T. (2014). Undergraduates' perceptions of parental relationship-oriented guilt induction versus harsh psychological control: Does cultural group status moderate their associations with self-esteem? *Journal of Cross-Cultural Psychology, 45*, 905–920.

Rueger, S., Chen, P., Jenkins, L., & Choe, H. (2014). Effects of perceived support from mothers, fathers, and teachers on depressive symptoms during the transition to middle school. *Journal of Youth & Adolescence, 43*, 655–670.

Ruff, H. A., & Lawson, K. R. (1990). Development of sustained, focused attention in young children during free play. *Developmental Psychology, 26*, 85–93.

Ruhe, K. M., Badarau, D. O., Brazzola, P., Hengartner, H., Elger, B. S., & Wangmo, T. (2016). Participation in pediatric oncology: views of child and adolescent patients. *Psycho-Oncology, 25*, 1036–1042.

Ruhland, E. L., Hardman, A. M., Becher, E. H., & Marczak, M. S. (2016). Co-parent court: A problem-solving, community-based model for serving low-income unmarried co-parents. *Family Court Review, 54*, 336–348. doi:10.1111/fcre.12235

Ruitenberg, M. L., Abrahamse, E. L., & Verwey, W. B. (2013). Sequential motor skill in preadolescent children: The development of automaticity. *Journal of Experimental Child Psychology, 115*, 607–623. doi:10.1016/j.jecp.2013.04.005

Ruiz-Gallardo, J., Verde, A., & Valdés, A. (2013). Garden-based learning: An experience with "at risk" secondary education students. *Journal of Environmental Education, 44*, 252–270. doi:10.1080/00958964.2013.786669

Rule, A. C. (2007). Mystery boxes: Helping children improve their reasoning. *Early Childhood Education Journal, 35*(1), 13–18.

Rumberger, R. W. (1995). Dropping out of middle school: A multilevel analysis of students and schools. *American Educational Research Journal, 32*, 583–625.

Rumi, H., Toshihiro, K., & Kenryu, N. (2013). Development of handwriting patterns in elementary school children using digital. *Japanese Journal of Developmental Psychology, 24*(1), 13–21.

Rusby, J. C., Jones, L., Crowley, R., & Smolkowski, K. (2013). The child care ecology inventory: A domain-specific measure of home-based child care quality to promote social competence for school readiness. *Early Childhood Research Quarterly, 28*, 947–959. doi:10.1016/j.ecresq.2013.02.003

Rushton, J. P., Fulkner, D. W., Neal, M. C., Nias, D. K. B., & Eysenck, H. J. (1986). Altruism and aggression: The heritability of individual differences. *Journal of Personality and Social Psychology, 50*, 1192–1198.

Russell, A., & Finnie, V. (1990). Preschool children's social status and maternal instructions to assist group entry. *Developmental Psychology, 26*, 603–611. doi:10.1037/0012-1649.26.4.603

Rutgers, D., & Evans, M. (2017). Bilingual education and L3 learning: metalinguistic advantage or not? *International Journal of Bilingual Education & Bilingualism, 20*, 788–806. doi:10.1080/13670050.2015.1103698

Rutland, A., Cameron, L., Jugert, P., Nigbur, D., Brown, R., Watters, C., . . . Le Touze, D. (2012). Group identity and peer relations: A longitudinal study of group identity, perceived peer acceptance, and friendships amongst ethnic minority English children. *British Journal of Developmental Psychology, 30*, 283–302. doi:10.1111/j.2044-835X.2011.02040.x

Rutland, A., Killen, M., & Abrams, D. (2010). A new social-cognitive developmental perspective on prejudice: The interplay between morality and group identity. *Perspectives on Psychological Science, 5*, 279–291. doi:10.1177/1745691610369468

Rutledge, C. M., Rimer, D., & Scott, M. (2008). Vulnerable goth teens: The role of schools in this psychosocial high-risk culture. *Journal of School Health, 78*, 459–464. doi:10.1111/j.1746-1561.2008.00331.x

Rutledge, S. A., & Cannata, M. (2016). Identifying and understanding effective high school practices. *Phi Delta Kappan, 97*(6), 60–64. doi:10.1177/0031721716636876

Rutter, M. (2005). Adverse preadoption experiences and psychological outcomes. In D. M. Brodzinsky & J. Palacios (Eds.), *Psychological issues in adoption: Research and practice* (pp. 67–92). Westport, CT: Praeger/Greenwood.

Rutter, M. (2014). Nature-nurture integration. In M. Lewis & K. D. Rudolph (Eds.), *Handbook of developmental psychopathology* (pp. 45–65). doi:10.1007/978-1-4614-9608-3_3

Rutter, M. L. (1997). Nature–nurture integration: The example of antisocial behavior. *American Psychologist, 52*, 390–398.

Ruzek, E. E., Hafen, C. A., Allen, J. P., Gregory, A., Mikami, A. Y., & Pianta, R. C. (2016). How teacher emotional support motivates students: The mediating roles of perceived peer relatedness, autonomy support, and competence. *Learning & Instruction, 42*, 95–103. doi:10.1016/j.learninstruc.2016.01.004

Ryan, R. M., & Deci, E. L. (2000). Self-determination theory and the facilitation of intrinsic motivation, social development, and well-being. *American Psychologist, 55*, 68–78.

Ryan, R. M., & Deci, E. L. (2009). Promoting self-determined school engagement. In K. R. Wentzel & A. Wigfield (Eds.), *Handbook of motivation at school* (pp. 171–195). New York, NY: Routledge.

Ryan, R. M., & Kuczkowski, R. (1994). The imaginary audience, self-consciousness, and public individuation in adolescence. *Journal of Personality, 62*, 219–237.

Ryan, R. M., & Lynch, J. H. (1989). Emotional autonomy versus detachment: Revisiting the vicissitudes of adolescence and young adulthood. *Child Development, 60*, 340–356.

Ryan, R. M., Connell, J. P., & Grolnick, W. S. (1992). When achievement is *not* intrinsically motivated: A theory of internalization and self-regulation in school. In A. K. Boggiano & T. S. Pittman (Eds.), *Achievement and motivation: A social-developmental perspective* (pp. 167–188). Cambridge, England: Cambridge University Press.

Ryan, R. M., Stiller, J. D., & Lynch, J. H. (1994). Representations of relationships to teachers, parents, and friends as predictors of academic motivation and self-esteem. *Journal of Early Adolescence, 14*, 226–249.

Saarni, C., Campos, J. J., Camras, L. A., & Witherington, D. (2006). Emotional development: Action, communication, and understanding. In W. Damon & R. M. Lerner (Eds. in Chief) & N. Eisenberg (Vol. Ed.), *Handbook of Child Psychology, Vol. 3. Social, emotional, and personality development* (6th ed., pp. 226–299). Hoboken, NJ: Wiley.

Sabbagh, M. A., Koenig, M. A., & Kuhlmeier, V. A. (2016). Conceptual constraints and mechanisms in children's selective learning. *Developmental Science*. Advance online publication. doi:10.1111/desc.12415

Sabol, T. J., & Pianta, R. C. (2012). Recent trends in research on teacher–child relationships. *Attachment & Human Development, 14*, 213–231. doi:10.1080/14616734.2012.672262

Sadler, T. W. (2010). *Langman's medical embryology* (11th ed.). Baltimore, MD: Lippincott Williams & Wilkins.

Safe Motherhood Network Federation. (2010). *Safe motherhood in Nepal*. Retrieved from http://www.safemotherhood.org.np/index.php

Saffran, J. R., & Griepentrog, G. J. (2001). Absolute pitch in infant auditory learning: Evidence for developmental reorganization. *Developmental Psychology, 37*, 74–85.

Saine, N. L., Lerkkanen, M., Ahonen, T., Tolvanen, A., & Lyytinen, H. (2013). Long-term intervention effects of spelling development for children with compromised preliteracy skills. *Reading & Writing Quarterly*, *29*, 333–357. doi:10.1080/10573569.2013.741962

Sala, G., & Gobet, F. (2017). Working memory training in typically developing children: A meta-analysis of the available evidence. *Developmental Psychology*, *53*, 671–685. doi:10.1037/dev0000265

Salley, B., Panneton, R. K., & Colombo, J. (2013). Separable attentional predictors of language outcome. *Infancy*, *18*, 462–489. doi:10.1111/j.1532-7078.2012.00138.x

Salley, B., Sheinkopf, S. J., Neal-Beevers, A. R., Tenenbaum, E. J., Miller-Loncar, C. L., Tronick, E., . . . Lester, B. M. (2016). Infants' early visual attention and social engagement as developmental precursors to joint attention. *Developmental Psychology*, *52*, 1721–1731. doi:10.1037/dev0000205

Salley, C. G., Vannatta, K., Gerhardt, C. A., & Noll, R. B. (2010). Social self-perception accuracy: Variations as a function of child age and gender. *Self and Identity*, *9*, 209–223.

Sallquist, J., Didonato, M., Hanish, L., Martin, C., & Fabes, R. (2012). The importance of mutual positive expressivity in social adjustment: Understanding the role of peers and gender. *Emotion*, *12*, 304–313.

Salmani Nodoushan, M. (2009). The Shaffer-Gee perspective: Can epistemic games serve education? *Teaching and Teacher Education*, *25*, 897–901. doi:10.1016/j.tate.2009.01.013

Salmon, A. K., & Lucas, T. (2011). Exploring young children's conceptions about thinking. *Journal of Research in Childhood Education*, *25*, 364–375. doi:10.1080/02568543.2011.605206

Salmon, K., & Reese, E. (2016). The benefits of reminiscing with young children. *Current Directions in Psychological Science*, *25*, 233–238. doi:10.1177/0963721416655100

Salomo, D., & Liszkowski, U. (2013). Sociocultural settings influence the emergence of prelinguistic deictic gestures. *Child Development*, *84*, 1296–1307. doi:10.1111/cdev.12026

Salti, N., & Ghattas, H. (2016). Food insufficiency and food insecurity as risk factors for physical disability among Palestinian refugees in Lebanon: Evidence from an observational study. *Disability and Health Journal*, *9*, 655–662. doi:10.1016/j.dhjo.2016.03.003

Saltz, E. (1971). *The cognitive bases of human learning*. Homewood, IL: Dorsey.

Saltz, J. B., & Nuzhdin, S. V. (2014). Genetic variation in niche construction: Implications for development and evolutionary genetics. *Trends in Ecology & Evolution*, *29*(1), 8–14. doi:10.1016/j.tree.2013.09.011

Salvas, M., Vitaro, F., Brendgen, M., Dionne, G., Tremblay, R. E., & Boivin, M. (2014). Friendship conflict and the development of generalized physical aggression in the early school years: A genetically informed study of potential moderators. *Developmental Psychology*, *50*, 1794–1807. doi:10.1037/a0036419

Samad, A., Reaburn, P., & Di Milia, L. (2015). The contribution of job strain, social support and working hours in explaining work–family conflict. *Asia Pacific Journal of Human Resources*, *53*, 281–295. doi:10.1111/1744-7941.12058

Sampson, V., Enderle, P., Grooms, J., & Witte, S. (2013). Writing to learn by learning to write during the school science laboratory: Helping middle and high school students develop argumentative writing skills as they learn core ideas. *Science Education*, *97*, 643–670. doi:10.1002/sce.21069

Samson, A., Phillips, J., Parker, K., Shah, S., Gross, J., & Hardan, A. (2014). Emotion dysregulation and the core features of autism spectrum disorder. *Journal of Autism & Developmental Disorders*, *44*, 1766–1772. doi:10.1007/s10803-013-2022-5

Samuels, B., & Blitz, C. (2014). A call to action promoting effective interventions for children in child welfare using neuroscience. *Social Policy Report*, *28*(1), 28–31.

Samuels, G. M. (2009). Ambiguous loss of home: The experience of familial (im)permanence among young adults with foster care backgrounds. *Children and Youth Services Review*, *31*, 1229–1239.

Samuelson, L. K., & McMurray, B. (2017). What does it take to learn a word? *WIREs Cognitive Science*, *8*(1–2). http://dx.doi.org/10.1002/wcs.1421

Sanchez, C. E., Richards, J. E., & Almli, C. R. (2012), Neurodevelopmental MRI brain templates for children from 2 weeks to 4 years of age. *Developmental Psychobiology*, *54*, 77–91. doi: 10.1002/dev.20579

Sanchez, F., & Anderson, M. L. (1990). Gang mediation: A process that works. *Principal*, *69*(4), 54–56.

Sandamas, G., Foreman, N., & Coulson, M. (2009). Interface familiarity restores active advantage in a virtual exploration and reconstruction task in children. *Spatial Cognition and Computation*, *9*, 96–108.

Sanden, S. (2012). Independent reading: Perspectives and practices of highly effective teachers. *Reading Teacher*, *66*, 222–231. doi:10.1002/TRTR.01120

Sanders, A. (2016). Emotional response to gaming producing Rosenblatt's Transaction. In S. Y. Tettegah & W. D. Huang (Eds.). (2016). *Emotions, technology, and digital games* (pp. 115–136). San Diego, CA: Elsevier Academic Press.

Sanders, M. R. & Mazzucchelli, T. (2013). The promotion of self-regulation through parenting interventions. *Clinical Child & Family Psychology Review*, *16*(1), 1–17. doi:10.1007/s10567-013-0129-z

Sanders, W. H. (2010). Walking alongside children as they form compassion. *Exchange*, *32*(3), 50–53.

Sands, D. J., & Wehmeyer, M. L. (Eds.). (1996). *Self-determination across the life span: Independence and choice for people with disabilities.* Baltimore, MD: Paul H. Brookes.

Santo, J., Bukowski, W. M., Stella-Lopez, L., Carmago, G., Mayman, S. B., & Adams, R. E. (2013). Factors underlying contextual variations in the structure of the self: Differences related to SES, gender, culture, and "majority/nonmajority" status during early adolescence. *Journal of Research on Adolescence*, *23*(1), 69–80. doi:10.1111/j.1532-7795.2012.00793.x

Santoli, S., Vitulli, P., & Giles, R. (2015). Picturing equality: Exploring civil rights' marches through photographs. *Social Studies*, *106*(2), 72–76. doi:10.1080/00377996.2014.988866

Santos, A. J., Vaughn, B. E., Peceguina, I., & Daniel, J. R. (2014). Longitudinal stability of social competence indicators in a Portuguese sample: Q-sort profiles of social competence, measures of social engagement, and peer sociometric acceptance. *Developmental Psychology*, 50(3), 968-978. http://dx.doi.org.unco.idm.oclc.org/10.1037/a0034344

Saracho, O. N. (2014). Theory of mind: Understanding young children's pretence and mental states. *Early Child Development and Care*, *184*, 1281–1294. doi:10.1080/03004430.2013.865617

Saracho, O. N. (2017). Parents' shared storybook reading – learning to read. *Early Child Development & Care*, *187*, 554–567. doi:10.1080/03004430.2016.1261514

Sarahan, N., & Copas, R. (2014). Autism assets. *Reclaiming Children & Youth*, *22*(4), 34–37.

Sarnecka, B. W., & Wright, C. E. (2013). The idea of an exact number: Children's understanding of cardinality and equinumerosity. *Cognitive Science*, *37*, 1493–1506. doi:10.1111/cogs.12043

Satcher, D. (2010). Taking charge of school wellness. *Educational Leadership*, *67*(4), 38–43.

Sattler, J. M. (2001). *Assessment of children: Cognitive applications* (4th ed.). San Diego, CA: Author.

Savin-Williams, R. C. (1989). Gay and lesbian adolescents. *Marriage and Family Review*, *14*, 197–216.

Savin-Williams, R. C. (2005). *The new gay teenager*. Cambridge, MA: Harvard University Press.

Savin-Williams, R. C., & Diamond, L. M. (1997). Sexual orientation as a developmental context for lesbians, gays, and bisexuals: Biological perspectives. In N. L. Segal, G. E. Weisfeld, & C. C. Weisfeld (Eds.), *Uniting psychology and biology: Integrative perspectives on human development* (pp. 217–238). Washington, DC: American Psychological Association.

Sawyer, J. (2017). I think I can: Preschoolers' private speech and motivation in playful versus non-playful contexts. *Early Childhood Research Quarterly*, *38*, 84–96. doi:10.1016/j.ecresq.2016.09.004

Sawyer, M. G., Pfeiffer, S., Spence, S. H., Bond, L., Graetz, B., Kay, D., . . . Sheffield, J. (2010). School-based prevention of depression: A randomised controlled study of the *beyond blue* schools research initiative. *Journal of Child Psychology and Psychiatry*, *51*, 199–209.

Sawyer, R. J., Graham, S., & Harris, K. R. (1992). Direct teaching, strategy instruction, and strategy instruction with explicit self-regulation: Effects on the composition skills and self-efficacy of students with learning disabilities. *Journal of Educational Psychology, 84*, 340–352.

Saxe, G. B. (1988). The mathematics of child street vendors. *Child Development, 59*, 1415–1425.

Sayer, E., Beaven, A., Stringer, P., & Hermena, E. (2013). Investigating sense of community in primary schools. *Educational & Child Psychology, 30*(1), 9–25.

Scardamalia, M., & Bereiter, C. (1986). Writing. In R. F. Dillon & R. J. Sternberg (Eds.), *Cognition and instruction* (pp. 59–81). San Diego, CA: Academic Press.

Scarr, S. (1992). Developmental theories for the 1990s: Development and individual differences. *Child Development, 63*, 1–19.

Scarr, S., & McCartney, K. (1983). How people make their own environments: A theory of genotype environment effects. *Child Development, 54*, 424–435.

Schaan, V. K., & Vögele, C. (2016). Resilience and rejection sensitivity mediate long-term outcomes of parental divorce. *European Child & Adolescent Psychiatry*. Advance online publication. doi:10.1007/s00787-016-0893-7

Schaffer, H. R. (1996). *Social development*. Cambridge, MA: Blackwell.

Scharf, M. (2014). Children's social competence within close friendship: The role of self-perception and attachment orientations. *School Psychology International, 35*, 206–220. doi:10.1177/0143034312474377

Schauble, L. (1990). Belief revision in children: The role of prior knowledge and strategies for generating evidence. *Journal of Experimental Child Psychology, 49*, 31–57.

Scherer, M. (2011, February). Transforming education with technology. *Educational Leadership, 68*(5), 17–21.

Scherer, N., & Olswang, L. (1984). Role of mothers' expansions in stimulating children's language production. *Journal of Speech and Hearing Research, 27*, 387–396.

Schibli, K., Wong, K., Hedayati, N., & D'Angiulli, A. (2017). Attending, learning, and socioeconomic disadvantage: Developmental cognitive and social neuroscience of resilience and vulnerability. *Annals of the New York Academy of Sciences, 1396*(1), 19–38. doi:10.1111/nyas.13369

Schiefele, U. (2009). Situational and individual interest. In K. R. Wentzel & A. Wigfield (Eds.), *Handbook of motivation at school* (pp. 197–222). New York, NY: Routledge.

Schieffelin, B. B. (1985). The acquisition of Kaluli. In D. I Slobin (Ed.), *The crosslinguistic study of language acquisition* (pp. 525–593). Hillsdale, NJ: Erlbaum.

Schieffelin, B. B. (1990). *The give and take of everyday life: Language socialization of Kaluli children*. New York, NY: Cambridge University Press.

Schilling, T. A. (2008). An examination of resilience processes in context: The case of Tasha. *Urban Review, 40*, 296–316.

Schinke, S. P., Moncher, M. S., & Singer, B. R. (1994). Native American youths and cancer risk prevention. *Journal of Adolescent Health, 15*, 105–110.

Schlaefli, A., Rest, J. R., & Thoma, S. J. (1985). Does moral education improve moral judgment? A meta-analysis of intervention studies using the defining issues test. *Review of Educational Research, 55*, 319–352.

Schlam, T. R., Wilson, N. L., Shoda, Y., Mischel, W., & Ayduk, O. (2013). Preschoolers' delay of gratification predicts their body mass 30 years later. *The Journal of Pediatrics, 162*(1), 90–93.

Schlegel, A., & Barry, H. L., III. (1980). The evolutionary significance of adolescent initiation ceremonies. *American Ethnologist, 7*(4), 696–715.

Schleppenbach, M., Perry, M., Miller, K. F., Sims, L., & Fang, G. (2007). The answer is only the beginning: Extended discourse in Chinese and U.S. mathematics classrooms. *Journal of Educational Psychology, 99*, 380–396.

Schlottmann, A., Ray, E. D., & Surian, L. (2012). Emerging perception of causality in action-and-reaction sequences from 4 to 6 months of age: Is it domain-specific? *Journal of Experimental Child Psychology, 112*, 208–230. doi:10.1016/j.jecp.2011.10.011

Schmeer, K. K., & Yoon, A. J. (2016). Home sweet home? Home physical environment and inflammation in children. *Social Science Research, 60*, 236–248. doi:10.1016/j.ssresearch.2016.04.001

Schmelzkopf, J., Greer, R. D., Singer-Dudek, J., & Du, L. (2017). Experiences that establish preschoolers' interest in speaking and listening to others. *Behavioral Development Bulletin, 22*(1), 44–66.

Schmitow, C., & Stenberg, G. (2013). Social referencing in 10-month-old infants. *European Journal of Developmental Psychology, 10*(5), 533-545. http://dx.doi.org.unco.idm.oclc.org/10.1080/17405629.2013.763473

Schneider, M., & Hardy, I. (2013). Profiles of inconsistent knowledge in children's pathways of conceptual change. *Developmental Psychology, 49*, 1639–1649. doi:10.1037/a0030976

Schneider, W., & Lockl, K. (2002). The development of metacognitive knowledge in children and adolescents. In T. J. Perfect & B. L. Schwartz (Eds.), *Applied metacognition* (pp. 224–257). Cambridge, England: Cambridge University Press.

Schneider, W., & Pressley, M. (1989). *Memory development between 2 and 20*. New York, NY: Springer-Verlag.

Schneider, W., & Shiffrin, R. M. (1977). Controlled and automatic human information processing: I. Detection, search, and attention. *Psychological Review, 84*, 1–66.

Schoenfeld, A. H. (1988). When good teaching leads to bad results: The disasters of "well-taught" mathematics courses. *Educational Psychologist, 23*, 145–166.

Schofield, G., & Beek, M. (2009). Growing up in foster care: Providing a secure base through adolescence. *Child and Family Social Work, 14*, 255–266.

Schonert-Reichl, K. A. (1993). Empathy and social relationships in adolescents with behavioral disorders. *Behavioral Disorders, 18*, 189–204.

Schramm, D. G., Harris, S. M., Whiting, J. B., Hawkins, A. J., Brown, M., & Porter, R. (2013). Economic costs and policy implications associated with divorce: Texas as a case study. *Journal of Divorce & Remarriage, 54*(1), 1–24. doi:10.1080/10502556.2012.725354

Schraw, G., Flowerday, T., & Lehman, S. (2001). Increasing situational interest in the classroom. *Educational Psychology Review, 13*, 211–224.

Schraw, G., Potenza, M. T., & Nebelsick-Gullet, L. (1993). Constraints on the calibration of performance. *Contemporary Educational Psychology, 18*, 455–463.

Schreibman, L. (2008). Treatment controversies in autism. *Zero to Three, 28*(4), 38–45.

Schröder, L., Kärtner, J., & Keller, H. (2015). Telling a "baby story": Mothers narrating their pre-schoolers' past across two cultural contexts. *Memory, 23*(1), 39–54. http://dx.doi.org.unco.idm.oclc.org/10.1080/09658211.2014.931974

Schrodt, P. (2016). Coparental communication with nonresidential parents as a predictor of children's feelings of being caught in stepfamilies. *Communication Reports, 29*(2), 63–74. doi:10.1080/08934215.2015.1020562

Schubert, A.-L., Hagemann, D., & Frischkorn, G. T. (2017). Is general intelligence little more than the speed of higher-order processing? *Journal of Experimental Psychology: General, 146*(10), 1498-1512. http://dx.doi.org.unco.idm.oclc.org/10.1037/xge0000325

Schuchardt, K., Gebhardt, M., & Mäehler, C. (2010). Working memory functions in children with different degrees of intellectua disability. *Journal of Intellectual Disability Research, 54*, 346–353.

Schuengel, C., de Schipper, J., Sterkenburg, P. S., & Kef, S. (2013). Attachment, intellectual disabilities and mental health: Research, assessment and intervention. *Journal of Applied Research in Intellectual Disabilities, 26*(1), 34–46. doi:10.1111/jar.12010

Schuitema, J., Peetsma, T., & van der Veen, I. (2014). Enhancing student motivation: A longitudinal intervention study based on future time perspective theory. *The Journal of Educational Research, 107*, 467–481.

Schultz, G. F., & Switzky, H. N. (1990). The development of intrinsic motivation in students with learning problems: Suggestions for more effective instructional practice. *Preventing School Failure, 34*(2), 14–20.

Schulz, L. E., Goodman, N. D., Tenenbaum, J. B., & Jenkins, A. C. (2008). Going beyond the evidence: Abstract laws and preschoolers' responses to anomalous data. *Cognition, 109*, 211–223.

Schunk, D. H. (1996). Goal and self-evaluative influences during children's cognitive skill learning. *American Educational Research Journal, 33*, 359–382.

Schunk, D. H. (2012). Social cognitive theory. In K. R. Harris, S. Graham, T. Urdan, C. B. McCormick, G. M. Sinatra, & J. Sweller (Eds.), *APA Educational Psychology Handbook, Vol. 1. Theories, constructs, and critical issues* (pp. 101–123). Washington, DC: American Psychological Association. doi:10.1037/13273-005

Schunk, D. H., & Hanson, A. R. (1985). Peer models: Influence on children's self-efficacy and achievement. *Journal of Educational Psychology, 77*, 313–322.

Schunk, D. H., & Pajares, F. (2004). Self-efficacy in education revisited: Empirical and applied evidence. In D. M. McNerney & S. Van Etten (Eds.), *Big theories revisited* (pp. 115–138). Greenwich, CT: Information Age.

Schunk, D. H., & Pajares, F. (2009). Self-efficacy theory. In K. R. Wentzel & A. Wigfield (Eds.), *Handbook of motivation at school* (pp. 35–53). New York, NY: Routledge.

Schunk, D. H., & Rice, J. (1989). Learning goals and children's reading comprehension. *Journal of Reading Behavior, 21*, 279–293.

Schunk, D. H., & Zimmerman, B. J. (2013). Self-regulation and learning. In W. M. Reynolds, G. E. Miller, & I. B. Weiner (Eds.), *Handbook of psychology: Educational psychology* (pp. 45–68). Hoboken, NJ: John Wiley.

Schutz, P. A. (1994). Goals as the transactive point between motivation and cognition. In P. R. Pintrich, D. R. Brown, & C. E. Weinstein (Eds.), *Student motivation, cognition, and learning: Essays in honor of Wilbert J. McKeachie (pp. 113–133)*. Hillsdale, NJ: Erlbaum.

Schwab, J. F., & Lew-Williams, C. (2016). Repetition across successive sentences facilitates young children's word learning. *Developmental Psychology, 52*, 879–886. http://dx.doi.org.unco.idm.oclc.org/10.1037/dev0000125

Schwartz, J. L., Yarushalmy, M., & Wilson, B. (Eds.) (1993). *The geometric supposer: What is it a case of?* Hillsdale, NJ: Erlbaum.

Schwartz, M., & Shaul, Y. (2013). Narrative development among language-minority children: The role of bilingual versus monolingual preschool education. *Language, Culture and Curriculum, 26*(1), 36–51. doi:10.1080/07908318.2012.760568

Schwartz, P. D., Maynard, A. M., & Uzelac, S. M. (2008). Adolescent egocentrism: A contemporary view. *Adolescence, 43*(171), 441–448.

Schwartz, S. J., Syed, M., Yip, T., Knight, G. P., Umaña-Taylor, A. J., Rivas-Drake, D., & Lee, R. M. (2014). Methodological issues in ethnic and racial identity research with ethnic minority populations: Theoretical precision, measurement issues, and research designs. *Child Development, 85*(1), 58–76. doi:10.1111/cdev.12201

Schwarz, C. V., & White, B. Y. (2005). Metamodeling knowledge: Developing students' understanding of scientific modeling. *Cognition and Instruction, 23*, 165–205.

Schweinhart, L. J. (2006). The High/Scope approach: Evidence that participatory learning in early childhood contributes to human development. In N. F. Watt, C. Ayoub, R. H. Bradley, J. E. Puma, & W. A. LeBoeuf (Eds.), *The Crisis in Youth Mental Health: Critical Issues and Effective Programs, Vol. 4. Early intervention programs and policies* (pp. 207–227). Westport, CT: Praeger Publishers/Greenwood Publishing Group.

Schweinhart, L. J., & Weikart, D. P. (1993, November). Success by empowerment: The High/Scope Perry Preschool Study through age 27. *Young Children, 48*, 54–58.

Schweinle, A., Berg, P., & Sorenson, A. (2013). Preadolescent perceptions of challenging and difficult course activities and their motivational distinctions. *Educational Psychology, 33*, 797–816. doi:10.1080/01443410.2013.785049

Schwenck, C., Göhle, B., Hauf, J., Warnke, A., Freitag, C. M., & Schneider, W. (2014). Cognitive and emotional empathy in typically developing children: The influence of age, gender, and intelligence. *European Journal of Developmental Psychology, 11*(1), 63–76. doi:10.1080/17405629.2013.808994

Sciaraffa, M. A., Zeanah, P. D., & Zeanah, C. H. (2018). Understanding and promoting resilience in the context of adverse childhood experiences. *Early Childhood Education Journal, 46*(3), 343-353. http://dx.doi.org.unco.idm.oclc.org/10.1007/s10643-017-0869-3

Scott-Little, M., & Holloway, S. (1992). Child care providers' reasoning about misbehaviors: Relation to classroom control strategies and professional training. *Early Childhood Research Quarterly, 7*, 595–606.

Scott, K. E., & Graham, J. J. (2015). Service-Learning. *Journal of Experiential Education, 38*, 354–372. doi:10.1177/1053825915592889

Scrimin, S., Moscardino, U., & Natour, M. (2014). Socio-ecological correlates of mental health among ethnic minorities in areas of political conflict: A study of Druze adolescents in Israel. *Transcultural Psychiatry, 51*, 209–227. doi:10.1177/1363461513520342

Sear, R., & Mace, R. (2008). Who keeps children alive? A review of the effects of kin on child survival. *Evolution and Human Behavior, 29*, 1–18.

Searle, A. K., Miller-Lewis, L. R., Sawyer, M. G., & Baghurst, P. A. (2013). Predictors of children's kindergarten classroom engagement: Preschool adult–child relationships, self-concept, and hyperactivity/inattention. *Early Education and Development, 24*, 1112–1136. http://dx.doi.org/10.1080/10409289.2013.764223

Seaton, E., Yip, T., Morgan-Lopez, A., & Sellers, R. (2012). Racial discrimination and racial socialization as predictors of African American adolescents' racial identity development using latent transition analysis. *Developmental Psychology, 48*, 448–458.

Seaton, M., Parker, P., Marsh, H., Craven, R., & Yeung, A. (2014). The reciprocal relations between self-concept, motivation and achievement: Juxtaposing academic self-concept and achievement goal orientations for mathematics success. *Educational Psychology, 34*(1), 49–72. doi:10.1080/01443410.2013.825232

Sebire, S. J., Jago, R., Fox, K. R., Edwards, M. J., & Thompson, J. (2013). Testing a self-determination theory model of children's physical activity motivation: A cross-sectional study. *The International Journal of Behavioral Nutrition and Physical Activity, 10*. doi:10.1186/1479-5868-10-111

Sedaghatjou, M., & Campbell, S. R. (2017). Exploring cardinality in the era of touch-screen-based technology. *International Journal of Mathematical Education in Science & Technology, 48*, 1225–1239. doi:10.1080/0020739X.2017.1327089

Segal, N. L. (2012). *Born together—reared apart: The landmark Minnesota Twin Study*. Cambridge, MA: Harvard University Press. doi:10.4159/harvard.9780674065154

Seibert, A. C., & Kerns, K. A. (2009). Attachment figures in middle childhood. *International Journal of Behavioral Development, 33*, 347–355.

Seidel, M., Petermann, J., Diestel, S., Ritschel, F., Boehm, I., King, J. A., . . . Ehrlich, S. (2016). A naturalistic examination of negative affect and disorder-related rumination in anorexia nervosa. *European Child & Adolescent Psychiatry, 25*, 1207–1216. doi:10.1007/s00787-016-0844-3

Seiffge-Krenke, I. (2016). Leaving home: Antecedents, consequences, and cultural patterns. In J. J. Arnett (Ed.), *Oxford library of psychology. The Oxford handbook of emerging adulthood* (pp. 177–189). New York, NY: Oxford University Press.

Seiver, E., Gopnik, A., & Goodman, N. D. (2013). Did she jump because she was the big sister or because the trampoline was safe? Causal inference and the development of social attribution. *Child Development, 84*, 443–454. doi:10.1111/j.1467-8624.2012.01865.x

Sejnost, R. L., & Thiese, S. M. (2010). *Building content literacy: Strategies for the adolescent learner*. Thousand Oaks, CA: Corwin.

Sela, T., Panzer, M.-S., & Lavidor, M. (2017). Divergent and convergent hemispheric processes in idiom comprehension: The role of idioms predictability. *Journal of Neurolinguistics, 44*, 134–146. http://dx.doi.org/10.1016/j.jneuroling.2017.05.002

Selfe, L. (1977). *Nadia: A case of extraordinary drawing ability in an autistic child*. London, England: Academic Press.

Selfe, L. (1995). Nadia reconsidered. In C. Golomb (Ed.), *The development of artistically gifted children: Selected case studies* (pp. 197–236). Hillsdale, NJ: Erlbaum.

Seligman, M. E. P. (1991). *Learned optimism.* New York, NY: Knopf.

Selman, R. L. (1980). *The growth of interpersonal understanding: Developmental and clinical analysis.* New York, NY: Academic Press.

Selman, R. L. (2003). *The promotion of social awareness: Powerful lessons from the partnership of developmental theory and classroom practice.* New York, NY: Russell Sage Foundation.

Selman, R. L., & Byrne, D. F. (1974). A structural-developmental analysis of levels of role taking in middle childhood. *Child Development, 45,* 803–806.

Selman, R. L., & Schultz, L. J. (1990. *Making a friend in youth: Developmental theory and pair therapy.* Chicago, IL: University of Chicago Press.

Semrud-Clikeman, M., Fine, J., & Bledsoe, J. (2013). Comparison among children with children with autism spectrum disorder, nonverbal learning disorder and typically developing children on measures of executive functioning. *Journal of Autism and Developmental Disorders, 44,* 331–342. doi:10.1007/s10803-013-1871-2

Sénéchal, M., & LeFevre, J.-A. (2002). Parental involvement in the development of children's reading skill: A five-year longitudinal study. *Child Development, 73,* 445–460.

Senn, N. (2012). Effective approaches to motivate and engage reluctant boys in literacy. *Reading Teacher, 66,* 211–220. doi:10.1002/TRTR.01107

Seo, H. (2014). Promoting the self-determination of elementary and secondary students with disabilities: Perspectives of general and special educators in Korea. *Education & Training in Autism & Developmental Disabilities, 49,* 277–289.

Serpell, R. (2017). How the study of cognitive growth can benefit from a cultural lens. *Perspectives on Psychological Science, 12,* 889–899. http://dx.doi.org.unco.idm.oclc.org/10.1177/1745691617704419

Serpell, R., Baker, L., & Sonnenschein, S. (2005). *Becoming literate in the city: The Baltimore Early Childhood Project.* Cambridge, England: Cambridge University Press.

Seuss, Dr. (1968). *The foot book.* New York, NY: Random House.

Sewell, A. (2011). Exploring the development of a community of learners in four primary classrooms. *New Zealand Journal of Educational Studies, 46*(2), 61–74.

Sewell, A., St George, A., & Cullen, J. (2013). The distinctive features of joint participation in a community of learners. *Teaching & Teacher Education, 31,* 46–55. doi:10.1016/j.tate.2012.11.00

Shackman, A. J., Fox, A. S., Oler, J. A., Shelton, S. E., Oakes, T. R., Davidson, R. J., & Kalin, N. H. (2017). Heightened extended amygdala metabolism following threat characterizes the early phenotypic risk to develop anxiety-related psychopathology. *Molecular Psychiatry, 22*(5), 724–732. http://dx.doi.org.unco.idm.oclc.org/10.1038/mp.2016.132

Shahaeian, A., Nielsen, M., Peterson, C., & Slaughter, V. (2014). Cultural and family influences on children's theory of mind development: A comparison of Australian and Iranian school-age children. *Journal of Cross-Cultural Psychology, 45,* 555–568.

Shahinfar, A., Kupersmidt, J. B., & Matza, L. S. (2001). The relation between exposure to violence and social information processing among incarcerated adolescents. *Journal of Abnormal Psychology, 110,* 136–141.

Shanahan, T., & Tierney, R. J. (1990). Reading-writing connection: The relations among three perspectives. In J. Zutell & S. McCormick (Eds.), *Literacy theory and research: Analyses from multiple paradigms. Thirty-ninth yearbook of the National Reading Conference.* Chicago, IL: National Reading Conference.

Shapiro, E. S., & Manz, P. H. (2004). Collaborating with schools in the provision of pediatric psychological services. In R. T. Brown (Ed.), *Handbook of pediatric psychology in school settings* (pp. 49–64). Mahwah, NJ: Erlbaum.

Shapiro, S. L., Lyons, K. E., Miller, R. C., Butler, B., Vieten, C., & Zelazo, P. D. (2015). Contemplation in the classroom: A new direction for improving childhood education. *Educational Psychology Review, 27*(1), 1–30. http://dx.doi.org/10.1007/s10648-014-9265-3

Share, D. L., & Gur, T. (1999). How reading begins: A study of preschoolers' print identification strategies. *Cognition and Instruction, 17,* 177–213.

Sharkey, J. J., Shekhtmeyster, Z. Z, Chavez-Lopez, L. C., Norris, E. E., & Sass, L. I. (2011). The protective influence of gangs: Can schools compensate?. *Aggression & Violent Behavior, 16*(1), 45-54. doi:10.1016/j.avb.2010.11.001

Sharnoff, M. (2014). How to boost parent-teacher communication. *Eschool News, 17*(9), 1–23.

Shatz, M., & Gelman, R. (1973). The development of communication skills: Modifications in the speech of young children as a function of listener. *Monographs of the Society for Research in Child Development, 38*(5, Serial No. 152), 1–37. doi:10.2307/1165783

Shavinina, L. V., & Ferrari, M. (2004). Extracognitive facets of developing high ability: Introduction to some important issues. In L. V. Shavinina & M. Ferrari (Eds.), *Beyond knowledge: Extracognitive aspects of developing high ability* (pp. 3–13). Mahwah, NJ: Erlbaum.

Shaw, D. (2013). Future directions for research on the development and prevention of early conduct problems. *Journal of Clinical Child & Adolescent Psychology, 42,* 418–428.

Shaw, G. B. (1916). *Androcles and the lion; Overruled; Pygmalion.* New York, NY: Brentano.

Shayne, R., & Miltenberger, R. G. (2013). Evaluation of behavioral skills training for teaching functional assessment and treatment selection skills to parents. *Behavioral Interventions, 28*(1), 4–21. doi:10.1002/bin.1350

Shear, K., & Shair, H. (2005). Attachment, loss, and complicated grief. *Developmental Psychobiology, 47,* 253–267. doi:10.1002/dev.20091

Shechtman, Z., & Ifargan, M. (2009). School-based integrated and segregated interventions to reduce aggression. *Aggressive Behavior, 35,* 342–356.

Sheehan, E. P., & Smith, H. V. (1986). Cerebral lateralization and handedness and their effects on verbal and spatial reasoning. *Neuropsychologia, 24,* 531–540.

Sheets, R. H. (1999). Human development and ethnic identity. In R. H. Sheets & E. R. Hollins (Eds.), *Racial and ethnic identity in school practices: Aspects of human development* (pp. 91–101). Mahwah, NJ: Erlbaum.

Sheffield, E., Stromswold, K., & Molnar, D. (2005, April). *Do prematurely born infants catch up?* Paper presented at the biennial meeting of the Society for Research in Child Development, Atlanta, GA.

Sheffield, L. S. (2017). Dangerous myths about 'gifted' mathematics students. *Zdm, 49*(1), 13-23. doi:10.1007/s11858-016-0814-8

Sheldon, K. M. (2013). Motivation: Internalized motivation in the classroom. In J. J. Froh & A. C. Parks (Eds.), *Activities for teaching positive psychology: A guide for instructors* (pp. 155–160). Washington, DC: American Psychological Association. doi:10.1037/14042-025

Shellenberg, E. G., & Trehub, S. E. (2003). Good pitch memory is widespread. *Psychological Science, 14,* 262–266.

Shelton, A., Smith, A., Wiebe, E., Behrle, C., Sirkin, R., & Lester, J. (2016). Drawing and writing in digital science notebooks: Sources of formative assessment data. *Journal of Science Education and Technology, 25*(3), 474–488. doi:10.1007/s10956-016-9607-7

Shen, M., & Troia, G. A. (2018). Teaching children with language-learning disabilities to plan and revise Compare–Contrast Texts. *Learning Disability Quarterly, 41,* 44–61. doi:10.1177/0731948717701260

Shen, Y., Kim, S. Y., & Wang, Y. (2016). Intergenerational transmission of educational attitudes in Chinese American families: Interplay of socioeconomic status and acculturation. *Child Development, 87,* 1601–1616. doi:10.1111/cdev.12545

Shen, Z. (2009). Multiple intelligences theory on the mainland of China. In J.-Q. Chen, S. Moran, & H. Gardner (Eds.), *Multiple intelligences around the world* (pp. 55–65). San Francisco, CA: Jossey-Bass.

Shenfield, T., Trehub, S. E., & Nakata, T. (2003). Maternal singing modulates infant arousal. *Psychology of Music, 31,* 365–375.

Shenkin, S. D., Starr, J. M., & Deary, I. J. (2004). Birth weight and cognitive ability in childhood:

A systematic review. *Psychological Bulletin, 130,* 989–1013.

Shepard, R. N., & Metzler, J. (1971). Mental rotation of three-dimensional objects. *Science, 171,* 701–703.

Sheras, P. L., & Bradshaw, C. P. (2016). Fostering policies that enhance positive school environment. *Theory into Practice, 55,* 129–135. doi:10.1080/00405841.2016.1156990

Sheridan, M. D. (1975). *Children's developmental progress from birth to five years: The Stycar Sequences.* Windsor, England: NFER.

Sherif, M., Harvey, O. J., White, B. J., Hood, W. R., & Sherif, C. (1961). *Inter-group conflict and cooperation: The Robbers Cave experiment.* Norman: University of Oklahoma Press.

Sherman, L. J., Rice, K., & Cassidy, J. (2015). Infant capacities related to building internal working models of attachment figures: A theoretical and empirical review. *Developmental Review, 37,* 109–141. http://dx.doi.org.unco.idm.oclc.org/10.1016/j.dr.2015.06.001

Sherry, J. L. (2013). Formative research for STEM educational games: Lessons from the Children's Television Workshop. *Zeitschrift Für Psychologie, 221*(2), 90–97. doi:10.1027/2151-2604/a000134

Sherry, J. L. (2016). Debating how to learn from video games. In R. Kowert & T. Quandt (Eds.), *The video game debate: Unravelling the physical, social, and psychological effects of digital games* (pp. 116–130). New York, NY: Routledge/Taylor & Francis Group.

Sherwen, L. N., Scoloveno, M. A., & Weingarten, C. T. (1999). *Maternity nursing: Care of the childbearing family* (3rd ed.). Stamford, CT: Appleton & Lange.

Shevell, M. (2009). The tripartite origins of the tonic neck reflex. *Neurology, 72,* 850–853.

Shi, B., & Xie, H. (2014). Moderating effects of group status, cohesion, and ethnic composition on socialization of aggression in children's peer groups. *Developmental Psychology, 50, 2188–2198.* doi:10.1037/a0037177

Shi, R., & Werker, J. F. (2001). Six-month-old infants' preference for lexical words. *Psychological Science, 12,* 70–75.

Shields, M. K., & Behrman, R. E. (2004). Children of immigrant families: Analysis and recommendations. *The Future of Children, 14*(2), 4–15.

Shih, S. (2009). An examination of factors related to Taiwanese adolescents' reports of avoidance strategies. *Journal of Educational Research, 102,* 377–388.

Shilubane, H., Ruiter, R., Bos, A., den Borne, B., James, S., & Reddy, P. (2014). Psychosocial correlates of suicidal ideation in rural South African Adolescents. *Child Psychiatry & Human Development, 45,* 153–162.

Shing, R. (2013). Relationships between early language skills and future literacy development in Hong Kong. *Early Child Development & Care, 183,* 1397–1406. doi:10.1080/03004430.2013.788820

Shoda, Y., Mischel, W., & Peake, P. K. (1990). Predicting adolescent cognitive and self-regulatory competencies from preschool delay of gratification: Identifying diagnostic conditions. *Developmental Psychology, 26,* 978–986. doi:10.1037/0012-1649.26.6.978

Shogren, K. A., Kennedy, W., Dowsett, C., & Little, T. D. (2014). Autonomy, psychological empowerment, and self-realization: Exploring data on self-determination from NLTS2. *Exceptional Children, 80,* 221–235.

Shonkoff, J. P. & Phillips, D. A. (Eds.). (2000). *From neurons to neighborhoods: The science of early childhood development.* Washington, DC: National Academy of Sciences.

Shore, K. (1998). *Special kids problem solver.* Paramus, NJ: Prentice Hall.

Short, E. J., & Ryan, E. B. (1984). Metacognitive differences between skilled and less skilled readers: Remediating deficits through story grammar and attribution training. *Journal of Educational Psychology, 76,* 225–235.

Short, K., Eadie, P., Descallar, J., Comino, E., & Kemp, L. (2017). Longitudinal vocabulary development in Australian Urban aboriginal children: Protective and risk factors. *Child: Care, Health and Development, 43,* 906–917. http://dx.doi.org.unco.idm.oclc.org/10.1111/cch.12492

Short, M., Gradisar, M., Lack, L., Wright, H., Dewald, J., Wolfson, A., & Carskadon, M. (2013). A cross-cultural comparison of sleep duration between U.S. and Australian adolescents: The effect of school start time, parent-set bedtimes, and extracurricular load. *Health Education & Behavior, 40,* 323–330. doi:10.1177/1090198112451266

Shoshani, A., & Steinmetz, S. (2014). Positive psychology at school: A school-based intervention to promote adolescents' mental health and well-being. *Journal of Happiness Studies* 15(6), 1289-1311 doi:10.1007/s10902-013-9476-1

Shrum, W., & Cheek, N. H. (1987). Social structure during the school years: Onset of the degrouping process. *American Sociological Review, 52,* 218–223.

Shultz, T. R. (1974). Development of the appreciation of riddles. *Child Development, 45,* 100–105.

Shultz, T. R., & Horibe, F. (1974). Development of the appreciation of verbal jokes. *Developmental Psychology, 10,* 13–20.

Shweder, R. A., Goodnow, J., Hatano, G., LeVine, R. A., Markus, H., & Miller, P. (1998). The cultural psychology of development: One mind, many mentalities. In W. Damon (Series Ed.) & R. M. Lerner (Vol. Ed.), *Handbook of Child Psychology: Vol. 1. Theoretical models of human development* (5th ed., pp. 865–937). New York, NY: Wiley.

Shweder, R. A., Mahapatra, M., & Miller, J. G. (1987). Culture and moral development. In J. Kagan & S. Lamb (Eds.), *The emergence of morality in young children* (pp. 1–83). Chicago, IL: University of Chicago Press.

Sieber, J. E., O'Neil, H. F., & Tobias, S. (1977). *Anxiety, learning, and instruction.* Oxford England: Lawrence Erlbaum Associates.

Siegel, D. J. (2001). Toward an interpersonal neurobiology of the developing mind: Attachment relationships, "mindsight," and neural integration. *Infant Mental Health Journal, 22,* 67–94.

Siegler, R. S. (1989). Mechanisms of cognitive growth. *Annual Review of Psychology, 40,* 353–379.

Siegler, R. S. (2006). Microgenetic analyses of learning. In W. Damon & R. M. Lerner (Eds. in Chief) & D. Kuhn & R. S. Siegler (Vol. Eds.), *Handbook of Child Psychology: Vol. 2. Cognition, perception, and language* (6th ed., pp. 464–510). Hoboken, NJ: Wiley.

Siegler, R. S. (2016). Continuity and change in the field of cognitive development and in the perspectives of one cognitive developmentalist. *Child Development Perspectives, 10*(2), 128–133. doi:10.1111/cdep.12173

Siegler, R. S., & Alibali, M. W. (2005). *Children's thinking* (4th ed.). Upper Saddle River, NJ: Prentice Hall.

Siegler, R. S., & Jenkins, E. (1989). *How children discover new strategies.* Hillsdale, NJ: Erlbaum.

Siegler, R. S., & Lortie-Forgues, H. (2014). An integrative theory of numerical development. *Child Development Perspectives, 8,* 144–150. doi:10.1111/cdep.12077

Sigman, M., & Whaley, S. E. (1998). The role of nutrition in the development of intelligence. In U. Neisser (Ed.), *The rising curve: Long-term gains in IQ and related measures* (pp. 155–182). Washington, DC: American Psychological Association.

Sigurdson, J. F., Wallander, J., & Sund, A. M. (2014). Is involvement in school bullying associated with general health and psychosocial adjustment outcomes in adulthood? *Child Abuse & Neglect, 38*(10), 1607-1617.http://dx.doi.org.unco.idm.oclc.org/10.1016/j.chiabu.2014.06.001

Sikder, S. (2017). Relations of dynamic aspects of motives in infant-toddler's play: Enhance small science learning experience. In L. Li, G. Quiñones, & A. Ridgway (Eds.), *International perspectives on earlychildhood education and development: Vol. 20. Studying babies and toddlers: Relationships in cultural contexts* (pp. 193-206). New York, NY, US: Springer Science + Business Media.

Silcock, P. (2013). Should the Cambridge Primary Review be wedded to Vygotsky? *Education 3-13, 41,* 316–329. doi:10.1080/03004279.2011.586641

Silinskas, G., Niemi, P., Lerkkanen, M., & Nurmi, J. (2013). Children's poor academic performance evokes parental homework assistance—but does it help? *International Journal of Behavioral Development, 37*(1), 44–56. doi:10.1177/0165025412456146

Silva, M., Lopes, J., & Silva, A. (2013). Using senses and sensors in the environment to develop abstract thinking: A theoretical and instrumental framework. *Problems of Education in the 21st Century*, *53*, 99–119.

Silverman, L. K. (1994). The moral sensitivity of gifted children and the evolution of society. *Roeper Review*, *17*, 110–116.

Silvestri, R., & Aricò, I. (2017). Sleep in children with psychiatric and behavioral problems. In S. Nevšímalová & O. Bruni (Eds.), *Sleep disorders in children* (pp. 389–404). doi:10.1007/978-3-319-28640-2_17

Silvetti, M., Wiersema, J. R., Sonuga-Barke, E., & Verguts, T. (2013). Deficient reinforcement learning in medial frontal cortex as a model of dopamine-related motivational deficits in ADHD. *Neural Networks*, *46*, 199–209. doi:10.1016/j.neunet.2013.05.008

Simmons, C. (2014). Playing with popular culture – an ethnography of children's sociodramatic play in the classroom. *Ethnography & Education*, *9*, 270–283. doi:10.1080/17457823.2014.904753

Simmons, D. C., Taylor, A. B., Oslund, E. L., Simmons, L. E., Coyne, M. D., Little, M. E., . . . Kim, M. (2013). Predictors of at-risk kindergarteners' later reading difficulty: Examining learner-by-intervention interactions. *Reading and Writing*, *27*(3), 451–479 . doi:10.1007/s11145-013-9452-5

Simons-Morton, B., & Chen, R. (2009). Peer and parent influences on school engagement among early adolescents. *Youth and Society*, *41(1)*, 3–25.

Simons, L., Schrager, S. M., Clark, L. F., Belzer, M., & Olson, J. (2013). Parental support and mental health among transgender adolescents. *Journal of Adolescent Health*, *53*, 791–793. http://dx.doi.org/10.1016/j.jadohealth.2013.07.019

Simons, R. L., Robertson, J. F., & Downs, W. R. (1989). The nature of the association between parental rejection and delinquent behavior. *Journal of Youth and Adolescence*, *18*, 297–310.

Simos, P. G., Fletcher, J. M., Sarkari, S., Billingsley, R. L., Denton, C., & Papanicolaou, A. C. (2007). Altering the brain circuits for reading through intervention: A magnetic source imaging study. *Neuropsychology*, *21*, 485–496.

Simpkins, S. D., Delgado, M. Y., Price, C. D., Quach, A., & Starbuck, E. (2013). Socioeconomic status, ethnicity, culture, and immigration: Examining the potential mechanisms underlying Mexican-origin adolescents' organized activity participation. *Developmental Psychology*, *49*, 706–721. doi:10.1037/a0028399

Simpson, C. (2017). Language, relationships and skills in mixed-nationality Active Learning classrooms. *Studies in Higher Education*, *42*, 611–622. doi:10.1080/03075079.2015.1049141

Simpson, J. S., & Parsons, E. C. (2009). African American perspectives and informal science educational experiences. *Science Education*, *93*, 293–321.

Sims, M. (1993). How my question keeps evolving. In M. Cochran-Smith & S. L. Lytle (Eds.), *Inside/outside: Teacher research and knowledge* (pp. 283–289). New York, NY: Teachers College Press.

Sinclaire-Harding, L., Miserez, C., Arcidiacono, F., & Perret-Clermont, A.-N. (2013). Argumentation in the Piagetian clinical interview: A step further in dialogism. In M. B. Ligorio & M. César (Eds.), *Advances in cultural psychology. Interplays between dialogical learning and dialogical self* (pp. 53–82). Charlotte, NC: IAP Information Age Publishing.

Singer, E., & Doornenbal, J. (2006). Learning morality in peer conflict: A study of schoolchildren's narratives about being betrayed by a friend. *Childhood*, *13*, 225–245.

Singer, J., Marx, R. W., Krajcik, J., & Chambers, J. C. (2000). Constructing extended inquiry projects: Curriculum materials for science education reform. *Educational Psychologist*, *35*, 165–178.

Singh, A. A., Meng, S. E., & Hansen, A. W. (2014). "I am my own gender": Resilience strategies of trans youth. *Journal of Counseling & Development*, *92*, 208–218. doi:10.1002/j.1556-6676.2014.00150.x

Sinnott, J., Hilton, S., Wood, M., Spanos, E., & Topel, R. (2016). Does motivation affect emerging adults' intelligence and complex postformal problem solving? *Journal of Adult Development*, *23*(2), 69–78. doi:10.1007/s10804-015-9222-5

Sirois, S., Buckingham, D., & Shultz, T. R. (2000). Artificial grammar learning by infants: An auto-associator perspective. *Developmental Science*, *3*, 442–456.

Siry, C., & Max, C. (2013). The collective construction of a science unit: Framing curricula as emergent from kindergarteners' wonderings. *Science Education*, *97*, 878–902. doi:10.1002/sce.21076

Sitko, B. M. (1998). Knowing how to write: Metacognition and writing instruction. In D. J. Hacker, J. Dunlosky, & A. C. Graesser (Eds.), *Metacognition in educational theory and practice* (pp. 93–115). Mahwah, NJ: Erlbaum.

Sitnick, S. L., Masyn, K., Ontai, L. L., & Conger, K. J. (2016). Mothers' physical illness in one- and two-parent families. *Journal of Family Issues*, *37*, 902–920. doi:10.1177/0192513X14536563

Sittichai, R., & Smith, P. P. (2018). Bullying and cyberbullying in Thailand: Coping strategies and relation to age, gender, religion and victim status. *Journal of New Approaches in Educational Research*, *7*(1), 24–30. doi:10.7821/naer.2018.1.254

Sjostrom, L., & Stein, N. (1996). *Bully proof: A teacher's guide on teasing and bullying for use with fourth and fifth grade students.* Wellesley, MA: Wellesley College Center for Women.

Skarakis-Doyle, E., & Dempsey, L. (2008). The detection and monitoring of comprehension errors by preschool children with and without language impairment. *Journal of Speech, Language, and Hearing Research*, *51*, 1227–1243.

Skinner, B. F. (1953). *Science and human behavior.* New York, NY: Macmillan.

Skinner, B. F. (1957). *Verbal behavior.* New York, NY: Appleton-Century-Crofts.

Skinner, B. F. (1968). *The technology of teaching.* New York, NY: Appleton-Century-Crofts.

Slater, A. M., Bremner, J., Johnson, S. P., & Hayes, R. A. (2011). The role of perceptual processes in infant addition/subtraction experiments. In L. M. Oakes, C. H. Cashon, M. Casasola, & D. H. Rakison (Eds.), *Infant perception and cognition: Recent advances, emerging theories, and future directions* (pp. 85–110). New York, NY: Oxford University Press.

Slavin, R. E. (1990). *Cooperative learning: Theory, research, and practice.* Upper Saddle River, NJ: Prentice Hall.

Slavin, R. E., & Cheung, A. (2005). A synthesis of research on language of reading instruction for English language learners. *Review of Educational Research*, *75*, 247–284.

Slavin, R., Lake, C., & Groff, C. (2009). Effective programs in middle and high school mathematics: A best-evidence synthesis. *Review of Educational Research*, *79*, 839–911. doi:10.3102/0034654308330968

Sleeter, C. E., & Grant, C. A. (1999). *Making choices for multicultural education: Five approaches to race, class, and gender* (3rd ed.). Upper Saddle River, NJ: Merrill/Prentice Hall.

Slesnick, N., Feng, X., Brakenhoff, B., & Brigham, G. (2014). Parenting under the influence: The effects of opioids, alcohol and cocaine on mother–child interaction. *Addictive Behaviors*, *39*(5), 897–900.

Slopen, N., McLaughlin, K. A., & Shonkoff, J. P. (2014). Interventions to improve cortisol regulation in children: A systematic review. *Pediatrics*, *133*, 312–326.

Slotkin, T. A. (2008). If nicotine is a developmental neurotoxicant in animal studies, dare we recommend nicotine replacement therapy in pregnant women and adolescents? *Neurotoxicology and Teratology*, *20*, 1–19.

Smart, C., Neale, B., & Wade, A. (2001). *The changing experience of childhood: Families and divorce.* Cambridge, England: Polity.

Smetana, J. G. (1981). Preschool children's conceptions of moral and social rules. *Child Development*, *52*, 1333–1336.

Smetana, J. G. (2006). Social-cognitive domain theory: Consistencies and variations in children's moral and social judgments. In M. Killen & J. G. Smetana (Eds.), *Handbook of moral development* (pp. 119–153). Mahwah, NJ: Lawrence.

Smetana, J. G., & Braeges, J. L. (1990). The development of toddlers' moral and conventional judgments. *Merrill-Palmer Quarterly*, *36*, 329–346.

Smetana, J. G., & Killen, M. (2008). Moral cognitions, emotions, and neuroscience: An integrative developmental view. *European Journal of Developmental Science*, *2*, 324–339.

Smetana, J. G., & Villalobos, M. (2009). Social cognitive development in adolescence. In R. M. Lerner & L. Steinberg (Eds.), *Handbook of Adolescent Psychology, Vol. 1. Individual bases of adolescent development* (3rd ed., pp. 187–228). Hoboken, NJ: Wiley.

Smetana, J. G., Killen, M., & Turiel, E. (1991). Children's reasoning about interpersonal and moral conflicts. *Child Development, 62*, 629–644.

Smetana, J. G., Metzger, A., Gettman, D. C., & Campione-Barr, N. (2006). Disclosure and secrecy in adolescent–parent relationships. *Child Development, 77*, 201–217.

Smilansky, S. (1968). *The effects of sociodramatic play on disadvantaged preschool children*. Oxford, England: Wiley.

Smit, J., van Eerde, H. A., & Bakker, A. (2013). A conceptualisation of whole-class scaffolding. *British Educational Research Journal, 39*, 817-834. doi:10.1002/berj.3007

Smith College Jandon Center for Community Engagement. (2018). *Project Coach & the Urban Education Initiative Impact Report 2016-2017*. Retrieved July 1, 2018 from https://docs.wixstatic.com/ugd/ce0d52_50445664199e4861992041f63ef6b94e.pdf

Smith-Lock, K. M., Leitao, S., Lambert, L., & Nickels, L. (2013). Effective intervention for expressive grammar in children with specific language impairment. *International Journal of Language & Communication Disorders, 48*, 265–282. doi:10.1111/1460-6984.12003

Smith, A., & Thomson, M. (2014). Alternative education programmes: Synthesis and psychological perspectives. *Educational Psychology in Practice, 30*, 111–119. doi:10.1080/02667363.2014.891101

Smith, A., & Weber, C. (2016). Childhood stuttering: Where are we and where are we going? *Seminars in Speech and Language, 37*, 291–297. doi:10.1055/s-0036-1587703

Smith, A., Andrews, J., Ausbrooks, M., Gentry, M., & Jacobowitz, E. (2013). A metalinguistic awareness test for ASL/English bilingual deaf children: The TASLA-R. *Journal of Language Teaching & Research, 4*, 885–899. doi:10.4304/jltr.4.5.885-899

Smith, C. B., Battin, M. P., Francis, L. P., & Jacobson, J. A. (2007). Should rapid tests for HIV infection now be mandatory during pregnancy? Global differences in scarcity and a dilemma of technological advance. *Developing World Bioethics, 7*(2), 86–103.

Smith, C.E., Fischer, K.W., & Watson, Malcolm W.. Toward a refined view of aggressive fantasy as a risk factor for aggression: Interaction effects involving cognitive and situational variables.. Aggressive Behavior *35*. (2009): 313–323.

Smith, C. E., & Warneken, F. (2016). Children's reasoning about distributive and retributive justice across development. *Developmental Psychology, 52*, 613–628. http://dx.doi.org.unco.idm.oclc.org/10.1037/a0040069

Smith, C. E., Fischer, K. W., & Watson, M. W. (2009). Toward a refined view of aggressive fantasy as a risk factor for aggression: Interaction effects involving cognitive and situational variables. *Aggressive Behavior, 35*(4), 313–323.

Smith, C. L. (2007). Bootstrapping processes in the development of students' commonsense matter theories: Using analogical mappings, thought experiments, and learning to measure to promote conceptual restructuring. *Cognition and Instruction, 25*, 337–398.

Smith, E. P., & Bradshaw, C. P. (2017). Promoting nurturing environments in afterschool settings. *Clinical Child and Family Psychology Review, 20*, 117–126. http://dx.doi.org.unco.idm.oclc.org/10.1007/s10567-017-0239-0

Smith, E. P., Boutte, G. S., Zigler, E., & Finn-Stevenson, M. (2004). Opportunities for schools to promote resilience in children and youth. In K. I. Maton, C. J. Schellenbach, B. J. Leadbeater, & A. L. Solarz (Eds.), *Investing in children, youth, families, and communities: Strengths-based research and policy* (pp. 213–231). Washington, DC: American Psychological Association.

Smith, J. T. (1999). Sickle cell disease. In S. Goldstein & C. R. Reynolds (Eds.), *Handbook of neurodevelopmental and genetic disorders* (pp. 368–384). New York, NY: Guilford Press.

Smith, J., Boone, A., Gourdine, R. M., & Brown, A. W. (2013). Fictions and facts about parents and parenting older first-time entrants to foster care. *Journal of Human Behavior in the Social Environment, 23*, 211–219. doi:10.1080/10911359.2013.747400

Smith, K. A., Shepley, S. B., Alexander, J. L., & Ayres, K. M. (2015). The independent use of self-instructions for the acquisition of untrained multi-step tasks for individuals with an intellectual disability: A review of the literature. *Research in Developmental Disabilities, 40*, 19–30.

Smith, M. J., & Perkins, K. (2008). Attending to the voice of adolescents who are overweight to promote mental health. *Archives of Psychiatric Nursing, 22*, 391–393.

Smith, M., Roediger III, H., & Karpicke, J. (2013). Covert retrieval practice benefits retention as much as overt retrieval practice. *Journal of Experimental Psychology. Learning, Memory & Cognition, 39*, 1712–1725. doi:10.1037/a0033569

Smith, N. R., Cicchetti, L., Clark, M. C., Fucigna, C., Gordon-O'Connor, B., Halley, B. A., & Kennedy, M. (1998). *Observation drawing with children: A framework for teachers*. New York, NY: Teachers College Press.

Smith, R. E., & Smoll, F. L. (1997). Coaching the coaches: Youth sports as a scientific and applied behavioral setting. *Current Directions in Psychological Science, 6*, 16–21.

Smith, S. (2013). Would you step through my door? *Educational Leadership, 70*(8), 76–78.

Smitherman, G. (1994). "The blacker the berry the sweeter the juice": African American student writers. In A. H. Dyson & C. Genishi (Eds.), *The need for story: Cultural diversity in classroom and community* (pp. 80-101). Urbana, IL: National Council of Teachers of English.

Smitherman, G. (2007). The power of the rap: The Black idiom and the new Black poetry. In H. S. Alim & J. Baugh (Eds.), *Talkin Black talk: Language, education, and social change* (pp. 77–91). New York, NY: Teachers College Press.

Smithsonian National Museum of Natural History. (2010). *Volcanoes and hot spots*. Retrieved from http://www.mnh.si.edu/earth/main_frames.html

Smutny, J. F., & von Fremd, S. E. (2009). *Igniting creativity in gifted learners, K–6: Strategies for every teacher*. Thousand Oaks, CA: Corwin.

Smutny, J. F., von Fremd, S. E., & Artabasy, J. (2009). Creativity: A gift for the gifted. In J. F. Smutny & S. E. von Fremd (Eds.), *Igniting creativity in gifted learners, K–6: Strategies for every teacher* (pp. 5–17). Thousand Oaks, CA: Corwin.

Snow, C. E., & Van Hemel, S. B. (Eds.) (2008). *Early childhood assessment: Why, what, and how/ Committee on Developmental Outcomes and Assessment of Young Children*. Washington, DC: National Research Council.

Snow, C. W., & McGaha, C. G. (2003). *Infant development* (3rd ed.). Upper Saddle River, NJ: Prentice Hall.

Snow, K., & Mann-Feder, V. (2013). Peer-centered practice: A theoretical framework for intervention with young people in and from care. *Child Welfare, 92*(4), 75–93.

Snyder, K. E., Nietfeld, J. L., & Linnenbrink-Garcia, L. (2011). Giftedness and metacognition: A short-term longitudinal investigation of metacognitive monitoring in the classroom. *Gifted Child Quarterly, 55*, 181–193. doi:10.1177/0016986211412769

Snyder, K., Malin, J., Dent, A., & Linnenbrink-Garcia, L. (2014). The message matters: The role of implicit beliefs about and failure experiences in academic self-handicapping. *Journal of Educational Psychology, 106*(1), 230–241. doi:10.1037/a0034553

Snyder, L., & Caccamise, D. (2010). Comprehension processes for expository text: Building meaning and making sense. In M. A. Nippold & C. M. Scott (Eds.), *Expository discourse in children, adolescents, and adults: Development and disorders* (pp. 13–39). New York, NY: Psychology Press.

Society for Research in Child Development. (2007). *Ethical standards for research with children*. First published in the 1990–91 Directory and Fall 1991 Newsletter. Retrieved from http://www.srcd.org/ethicalstandards.html

Soet, J. E., Brack, G. A., & Dilorio, C. (2003). Prevalence and predictors of women's experience of psychological trauma during childbirth. *Birth, 30*(1), 36–46.

Sokol, S. (1978). Measurement of infant visual acuity from pattern reversal evoked potentials. *Vision Research, 18*(1), 33–39. doi:10.1016/0042-6989(78)90074-3

Solé-Padullés, C., Castro-Fornieles, J., de la Serna, E., Calvo, R., Baeza, I., Moya, . . . Sugranyes,

G. (2016). Intrinsic connectivity networks from childhood to late adolescence: Effects of age and sex. *Developmental Cognitive Neuroscience, 17*, 35–44. doi:10.1016/j.dcn.2015.11.004

Solem, M. (2013). Understanding parenting as situated in the larger sociocultural context in clinical social work. *Child & Adolescent Social Work Journal, 30*(1), 61–78. doi:10.1007/s10560-012-0278-9

Solity, J., & Vousden, J. (2009). Real books vs reading schemes: A new perspective from instructional psychology. *Educational Psychology, 29*, 469–511.

Solomon, D., Watson, M. S., Delucchi, K. L., Schaps, E., & Battistich, V. (1988). Enhancing children's prosocial behavior in the classroom. *American Educational Research Journal, 25*, 527–554.

Solomon, D., Watson, M., Battistich, E., Schaps, E., & Delucchi, K. (1992). Creating a caring community: Educational practices that promote children's prosocial development. In F. K. Oser, A. Dick, & J. L. Patry (Eds.), *Effective and responsible teaching: The new synthesis* (pp. 383–395). San Francisco, CA: Jossey-Bass.

Solomontos-Kountouri, O., Tsagkaridis, K., Gradinger, P., & Strohmeier, D. (2017). Academic, socio-emotional and demographic characteristics of adolescents involved in traditional bullying, cyberbullying, or both: Looking at variables and persons. International *Journal of Developmental Science, 11*, 19–30. http://dx.doi.org.unco.idm.oclc.org/10.3233/DEV-17219

Somerville, L. H., Jones, R. M., & Casey, B. J. (2010). A time of change: Behavioral and neural correlates of adolescent sensitivity to appetitive and aversive environmental cues. *Brain and Cognition, 72*, 124–133.

Sommerville, J. A. (2018). Infants' understanding of distributive fairness as a test case for identifying the extents and limits of infants' sociomoral cognition and behavior. *Child Development Perspectives*. Advance online publication. http://dx.doi.org.unco.idm.oclc.org/10.1111/cdep.12283

Sommerville, J. A., & Ziv, T. (2018). The developmental origins of infants' distributive fairness concerns. In K. Gray & J. Graham (Eds.), *Atlas of moral psychology* (pp. 420–429). New York, NY: Guilford Press.

Sonnenschein, S. (1988). The development of referential communication: Speaking to different listeners. *Child Development, 59*, 694–702.

Sophian, C. (2013). Vicissitudes of children's mathematical knowledge: Implications of developmental research for early childhood mathematics education. *Early Education and Development, 24*, 436–442. doi:10.1080/10409289.2013.773255

Sophian, C., & Vong, K. I. (1995). The parts and wholes of arithmetic story problems: Developing knowledge in the preschool years. *Cognition and Instruction, 13*, 469–477.

Sorenson, R., & Goldsmith, L. (2012). The pressure of high stakes testing. *Principal Matters, 91*, 48–52.

Sorsana, C., Guizard, N., & Trognon, A. (2013). Preschool children's conversational skills for explaining game rules: Communicative guidance strategies as a function of type of relationship and gender. *European Journal of Psychology of Education, 28*, 1453–1475. doi:10.1007/s10212-013-0175-4

Sotelo-Dynega, M., Flanagan, D. P., & Alfonso, V. C. (2011). Overview of specific learning disabilities. In D. P. Flanagan & V. C. Alfonso (Eds.), *Essentials of specific learning disability identification* (pp. 1–19). Hoboken, NJ: Wiley.

Souchal, C., Toczek, M., Darnon, C., Smeding, A., Butera, F., & Martinot, D. (2014). Assessing does not mean threatening: The purpose of assessment as a key determinant of girls' and boys' performance in a science class. *British Journal of Educational Psychology, 84*(1), 125–136. doi:10.1111/bjep.12012

Sousa, D. A. (2009). *How the gifted brain works* (2nd ed.). Thousand Oaks, CA: Corwin.

South, D. (2007). What motivates unmotivated students? In G. E. Mills (Ed.), *Action research: A guide for the teacher researcher* (3rd ed., pp. 1–2). Upper Saddle River, NJ: Pearson Merrill/Prentice Hall.

Soutullo, O. R., Smith-Bonahue, T. M., Sanders-Smith, S. C., & Navia, L. E. (2016). Discouraging partnerships? Teachers' perspectives on immigration-related barriers to family-school collaboration. *School Psychology Quarterly, 31*, 226–240. doi:10.1037/spq0000148

Sowell, E. R., Delis, D., Stiles, J., & Jernigan, T. L. (2001). Improved memory functioning and frontal lobe maturation between childhood and adolescence: A structural MRI study. *Journal of the International Neuropsychological Society, 7*, 312–322.

Spangler, G. (2013). Individual dispositions as precursors of differences in attachment quality: Why maternal sensitivity is nevertheless important. *Attachment & Human Development, 15*, 657–672. doi:10.1080/14616734.2013.842065

Sparks, A., Lee, M., & Spjeldnes, S. (2012). Evaluation of the high school relationship curriculum connections: Dating and emotions. *Child & Adolescent Social Work Journal, 29*(1), 21–40. doi:10.1007/s10560-011-0244-y

Spearman, C. (1904). General intelligence, objectively determined and measured. *American Journal of Psychology, 15*, 201–293.

Spearman, C. (1927). *The abilities of man: Their -nature and measurement*. New York, NY: Macmillan.

Spector, R. E. (2004). *Cultural diversity in health and illness* (6th ed.). Upper Saddle River, NJ: Prentice Hall.

Spelke, E. S. (1994). Initial knowledge: Six suggestions. *Cognition, 50*, 431–445.

Spelke, E. S. (2000). Core knowledge. *American Psychologist, 55*, 1233–1243.

Spelke, E. S. (2005). Sex differences in intrinsic aptitude for mathematics and science? A critical review. *American Psychologist, 60*, 950–958.

Spelke, E. S., & Kinzler, K. D. (2007). Core knowledge. *Developmental Science, 10*(1), 89–96.

Spencer, M. B. (2006). Phenomenology and ecological systems theory: Development of diverse groups. In W. Damon & R. M. Lerner (Eds. in Chief) & R. M. Lerner (Vol. Ed.), *Handbook of Child Psychology, Vol. 1. Theoretical models of human development* (6th ed., pp. 829–893). Hoboken, NJ: Wiley.

Spencer, M. B. (2014). Pursuing identity-focused resiliency research post-Brown v. Board of Education 1954. In R. M. Lerner, A. C. Petersen, R. K. Silbereisen, & J. Brooks-Gunn (Eds.), *The developmental science of adolescence: History through autobiography* (pp. 482–493). New York, NY: Psychology Press.

Spencer, M. B., & Markstrom-Adams, C. (1990). Identity processes among racial and ethnic minority children in America. *Child Development, 61*, 290–310.

Spencer, M. B., & Spencer, T. R. (2014). Invited commentary: Exploring the promises, intricacies, and challenges to positive youth development. *Journal of Youth and Adolescence*, doi:10.1007/s10964-014-0125-8

Spencer, M. B., Dupree, D., Tinsley, B., McGee, E. O., Hall, J., Fegley, S. G., & Elmore, T. (2012). Resistance and resiliency in a color conscious society: Implications for learning and teaching. In K. R. Harris, S. Graham, T. Urdan, C. B. McCormick, G. M. Sinatra, & J. Sweller (Eds.), *APA Educational Psychology Handbook, Vol. 1. Theories, constructs, and critical issues* (pp. 461–494). Washington, DC: American Psychological Association. doi:10.1037/13273-016

Spencer, M., & Swanson, D. (2013). Opportunities and challenges to the development of healthy children and youth living in diverse communities. *Development and Psychopathology, 25*(4, Pt. 2), 1551–1566. doi:10.1017/S095457941300076X

Spengler, M. M., Damian, R. I., Martin, R., Brunner, M., Lüdtke, O., & Roberts, B. W. (2015). Student characteristics and behaviors at age 12 predict occupational success 40 years later over and above childhood IQ and parental socioeconomic status. *Developmental Psychology, 51*, 1329–1340. doi:10.1037/dev0000025

Sperling, M. (1996). Revisiting the writing-speaking connection: Challenges for research on writing and writing instruction. *Review of Educational Research, 66*, 53–86.

Speybroeck, S., Kuppens, S., Damme, J., Petegem, P., Lamote, C., Boonen, T., & Bilde, J. (2012). The role of teachers' expectations in the association between children's SES and performance in kindergarten: A moderated mediation analysis. *PLoS ONE, 7*(4), 1–8. doi:10.1371/journal.pone.0034502

Spicker, H. H. (1992). Identifying and enriching: Rural gifted children. *Educational Horizons, 70*(2), 60–65.

Spiegel, C., & Halberda, J. (2011). Rapid fast-mapping abilities in 2-year-olds. *Journal of*

Experimental Child Psychology, 109, 132–140. doi:10.1016/j.jecp.2010.10.013

Spilt, J. L., Leflot, G., & Colpin, H. (2018). Teacher involvement prevents increases in children's depressive symptoms: Bidirectional associations in elementary school. *Journal of Abnormal Child Psychology*. Advance online publication. http://dx.doi.org.unco.idm.oclc.org/10.1007/s10802-018-0441-7

Spinath, B., & Steinmayr, R. (2012). The roles of competence beliefs and goal orientations for change in intrinsic motivation. *Journal of Educational Psychology, 104*, 1135–1148. doi:10.1037/a0028115

Spirito, A., Valeri, S., Boergers, J., & Donaldson, D. (2003). Predictors of continued suicidal behaviors in adolescents following a suicide attempt. *Journal of Clinical Child and Adolescent Psychology, 32*, 284–289.

Spivey, N. N. (1997). *The constructivist metaphor: Reading, writing, and the making of meaning*. San Diego, CA: Academic Press.

Sprafkin, C., Serbin, L. A., Denier, C., & Connor, J. M. (1983). Sex-differentiated play: Cognitive consequences and early interventions. In M. B. Liss (Ed.), *Social and cognitive skills: Sex roles and children's play* (pp. 167–192). San Diego, CA: Academic Press.

Sprague, J. J., Nishioka, V. V., & Smith, S. S. (2007). Safe schools, positive behavior supports, and mental health supports: Lessons learned from three Safe Schools/Healthy Students Communities. *Journal of School Violence, 6*, 93–115.

Sprague, J. R., & Horner, R. H. (2012). School-wide positive behavioral interventions and supports: Proven practices and future directions. In S. R. Jimerson, A. B. Nickerson, M. J. Mayer, & M. J. Furlong (Eds.), *Handbook of school violence and school safety: International research and practice* (pp. 447–462). New York, NY: Routledge/Taylor & Francis Group.

Springen, K. (2014). Occupy summer. *School Library Journal, 60*(3), 32.

Sroufe, L. A. (1983). Infant-caregiver attachment and patterns of adaptation in preschool: The roots of maladaptation and competence. In M. Perlmutter (Ed.), *Development and policy concerning children with special needs* (Minnesota Symposium on Child Psychology, Vol. 16, pp. 41–83). Hillsdale, NJ: Erlbaum.

Sroufe, L. A., Egeland, B., Carlson, E., & Collins, W. (2005). *Minnesota study of risk and adaptation from birth to maturity: The development of the person*. New York, NY: Guilford Press.

St. James-Roberts, I., & Plewis, I. (1996). Individual differences, daily fluctuations, and developmental changes in amounts of infant waking, fussiness, crying, feeding, and sleeping. *Child Development, 67*, 2527–2540.

Staats, C. (2016). Understanding Implicit Bias. *Education Digest, 82*(1), 29–38.

Staff, J., Messersmith, E. E., & Schulenberg, J. E. (2009). Adolescents and the world of work. In R. M. Lerner & L. Steinberg (Eds.), *Handbook of Adolescent Psychology, Vol. 2: Contextual influences on adolescent development* (pp. 270–313). Hoboken, NJ: Wiley.

Stainthorp, R., Stuart, M., Powell, D., Quinlan, P., & Garwood, H. (2010). Visual processing deficits in children with slow RAN performance. *Scientific Studies of Reading, 14*, 266–292.

Standage, M., Cumming, S. P., & Gillison, F. B. (2013). A cluster randomized controlled trial of the be the best you can be intervention: Effects on the psychological and physical well-being of school children. *BMC Public Health, 13*(1), 1–10. doi:10.1186/1471-2458-13-666

Stanovich, K. E. (1999). The sociopsychometrics of learning disabilities. *Journal of Learning Disabilities, 32*, 350–361.

Stanovich, K. E. (2000). *Progress in understanding reading: Scientific foundations and new frontiers*. New York, NY: Guilford Press.

Stanovich, K. E., West, R. F., & Toplak, M. E. (2012). Judgment and decision making in adolescence: Separating intelligence from rationality. In V. F. Reyna, S. B. Chapman, M. R. Dougherty, & J. Confrey (Eds.), *The adolescent brain: Learning, reasoning, and decision making* (pp. 337–378). Washington, DC: American Psychological Association. doi:10.1037/13493-012

Stanton-Chapman, T. L. (2014). Promoting positive peer interactions in the preschool classroom: The role and the responsibility of the teacher in supporting children's sociodramatic play. *Early Childhood Education Journal, 43*(2), 99-107. doi:10.1007/s10643-014-0635-8

Stanton-Chapman, T. L., & Brown, T. (2015). Facilitating commenting and requesting skills in 3-year-old children with disabilities. *Journal of Early Intervention 37*(2). doi: 10.1177/1053815115598005

Stanton-Chapman, T. L., Walker, V. L., Voorhees, M. D., Snell, M. E. (2016). The evaluation of a three-tier model of positive behavior interventions and supports for preschoolers in Head Start. *Remedial and Special Education, 37*(6), 333–344.

Stanutz, S., Wapnick, J., & Burack, J. (2014). Pitch discrimination and melodic memory in children with autism spectrum disorders. *Autism: The International Journal of Research & Practice, 18*, 137–147. doi:10.1177/1362361312462905

Starke, M., Wikland, K. A., & Möller, A. (2003). Parents' descriptions of development and problems associated with infants with Turner syndrome: A retrospective study. *Journal of Paediatrics and Child Health, 39*, 293–298.

Stathi, S., Cameron, L., Hartley, B., & Bradford, S. (2014). Imagined contact as a prejudice-reduction intervention in schools: The underlying role of similarity and attitudes. *Journal of Applied Social Psychology, 44*(8), 536-546. doi:10.1111/jasp.12245

Staub, D. (1998). *Delicate threads: Friendships between children with* Bethesda, *and without special needs in inclusive settings.* MD: Woodbine House.

Steegen, S., & De Neys, W. (2012). Belief inhibition in children's reasoning: Memory-based evidence. *Journal of Experimental Child Psychology, 112*, 231–242. doi:10.1016/j.jecp.2012.01.006

Steele, C. M. (1997). A threat in the air: How stereotypes shape intellectual identity and performance. *American Psychologist, 52*, 613–629.

Steenpaß, A., & Steinbring, H. (2014). Young students' subjective interpretations of mathematical diagrams: elements of the theoretical construct "frame-based interpreting competence." *Zdm, 46*(1), 3–14. doi:10.1007/s11858-013-0544-0

Steensma, T. D., Kreukels, B. C., de Vries, A. C., & Cohen-Kettenis, P. T. (2013). Gender identity development in adolescence. *Hormones and Behavior, 64*, 288–297. doi:10.1016/j.yhbeh.2013.02.020

Stein, N. L. (1982). What's in a story: Interpreting the interpretations of story grammars. *Discourse Processes, 5*, 319–335.

Steinberg, L. (1986). Latchkey children and susceptibility to peer pressure: An ecological analysis. *Developmental Psychology, 22*, 433–439.

Steinberg, L. (2007). Risk taking in adolescence: New perspectives from brain and behavioral science. *Current Directions in Psychological Science, 16*, 55–59.

Steinberg, L. (2015). How to improve the health of American adolescents. *Perspectives on Psychological Science, 10*(6), 711–715. doi:10.1177/1745691615598510

Steinberg, L., Blinde, P. L., & Chan, K. S. (1984). Dropping out among language minority youth. *Review of Educational Research, 54*, 113–132.

Steinberg, L., Brown, B. B., Cider, M., Kaczmarek, N., & Lazzaro, C. (1988). *Noninstructional influences on high school student achievement: The contributions of parents, peers, extracurricular activities, and part-time work.* Madison, WI: National Center on Effective Secondary Schools. (ERIC Document Reproduction Service No. ED 307 509)

Steinberg, L., Lamborn, S., Darling, N., Mounts, S., & Dornbusch, S. (1994). Over time change in adjustment and competence among adolescents from authoritative, authoritarian, indulgent, and neglectful families. *Child Development, 65*, 754–770.

Steiner, K. L., & Pillemer, D. B. (2018). Development of the life story in early adolescence. *The Journal of Early Adolescence, 38*, 125–138.

Steinka-Fry, K. T., Wilson, S. J., & Tanner-Smith, E. E. (2013). Effects of school dropout prevention programs for pregnant and parenting adolescents: A meta-analytic review. *Journal of the Society for Social Work and Research, 4*, 373–389.

Stenberg, C. R., & Campos, J. J. (1990). The development of anger expressions in infancy. In N. L. Stein, B. Leventhal, & T. Trabasso (Eds.), *Psychological and biological approaches to emotion* (pp. 247–282). Hillsdale, NJ: Erlbaum.

Stenberg, G. (2017). Does contingency in adults' responding influence 12-month-old infants' social referencing? *Infant Behavior & Development, 46*, 67–79. doi:10.1016/j.infbeh.2016.11.013

Stephan, K. E., Fink, G. R., & Marshall, J. C. (2007). Mechanisms of hemispheric specialization: Insights from analyses of connectivity. *Neuropsychologia, 45*, 209–228.

Stephens, A. A., Knuth, E. K., Blanton, M. M., Isler, I. I., Gardiner, A. A., & Marum, T. T. (2013). Equation structure and the meaning of the equal sign: The impact of task selection in eliciting elementary students' understandings. *Journal of Mathematical Behavior, 32*, 173–182. doi:10.1016/j.jmathb.2013.02.001

Stern, D. N. (1977). *The first relationship: Mother and infant*. Cambridge, MA: Harvard University Press.

Stern, W. (1949). The Intelligence Quotient. In W. Dennis (Ed.), *Readings in general psychology* (pp. 338–341). New York, NY: Prentice-Hall, Inc. http://dx.doi.org.unco.idm.oclc.org/10.1037/11352-048

Sternberg, R. J. (1985). *Beyond IQ: A triarchic theory of human intelligence*. Cambridge, England: Cambridge University Press.

Sternberg, R. J. (1996). Myths, countermyths, and truths about intelligence. *Educational Researcher, 25*(2), 11–16.

Sternberg, R. J. (1997). The concept of intelligence and its role in lifelong learning and success. *American Psychologist, 52*, 1030–1037.

Sternberg, R. J. (2002). Raising the achievement of all students: Teaching for successful intelligence. *Educational Psychology Review, 14*, 383–393.

Sternberg, R. J. (2003a). "My house is a very very very fine house"—But it is not the only house. In H. Nyborg (Ed.), *The scientific study of general intelligence: Tribute to Arthur Jensen* (pp. 373–395). Oxford, England: Elsevier.

Sternberg, R. J. (2003b). *Wisdom, intelligence, and creativity synthesized*. Cambridge, England: Cambridge University Press.

Sternberg, R. J. (2005). The triarchic theory of successful intelligence. In D. P. Flanagan & P. L. Harrison (Eds.), *Contemporary intellectual assessment: Theories, tests, and issues* (2nd ed., pp. 103–119). New York, NY: Guilford Press.

Sternberg, R. J. (2009). The theory of successful intelligence as a basis for new forms of ability testing at the high school, college, and graduate school levels. In J. C. Kaufman (Ed.), *Intelligent testing: Integrating psychological theory and clinical practice* (pp. 113–147). New York, NY: Cambridge University Press.

Sternberg, R. J. (2012). Intelligence in its cultural context. In M. J. Gelfand, C. Ciu, & Y. Hong (Eds.), *Advances in culture and psychology* (Vol 2, pp. 205–248). New York, NY: Oxford University Press.

Sternberg, R. J. (2013). Contemporary theories of intelligence. In W. M. Reynolds, G. E. Miller, I. B. Weiner (Eds.), *Handbook of Psychology, Vol. 7. Educational psychology* (2nd ed., pp. 23–44). Hoboken, NJ: John Wiley & Sons Inc.

Sternberg, R. J. (2018). Theories of intelligence. In S. I. Pfeiffer, E. Shaunessy-Dedrick, & M. Foley-Nicpon (Eds.), *APA handbook of giftedness and talent* (APA Handbooks in Psychology, pp. 145–161). Washington, DC: American Psychological Association.

Sternberg, R. J., & Grigorenko, E. L. (2000). Theme-park psychology: A case study regarding human intelligence and its implications for education. *Educational Psychology Review, 12*, 247–268.

Sternberg, R. J., Forsythe, G. B., Hedlund, J., Horvath, J. A., Wagner, R. K., Williams, W. M., . . . Grigorenko, E. (2000). *Practical intelligence in everyday life*. Cambridge, England: Cambridge University Press.

Sternberg, R. J., Grigorenko, E. L., & Bridglall, B. L. (2007). Intelligence as a socialized phenomenon. In E. W. Gordon & B. L. Bridglall (Eds.), *Affirmative development: Cultivating academic ability* (pp. 49–72). Lanham, MD: Rowman.

Sternberg, R. J., Jarvin, L., & Grigorenko, E. L. (2009). *Teaching for wisdom, intelligence, creativity, and success*. Thousand Oaks, CA: Corwin.

Sternberg, R. J., Torff, B., & Grigorenko, E. L. (1998). Teaching for successful intelligence raises school achievement. *Phi Delta Kappa, 79*, 667–669.

Sterponi, L. (2010). Learning communicative competence. In D. F. Lancy, J. Bock, & S. Gaskins (Eds.), *The anthropology of learning in childhood* (pp. 235–259). Lanham, MD: AltaMira Press/Rowman & Littlefield.

Stevens, P., & Smith, R. L. (2013). *Substance abuse counseling: Theory and practice* (5th ed.). Boston, MA: Pearson.

Stevens, R. J., & Slavin, R. E. (1995). The cooperative elementary school: Effects of students' achievement, attitudes, and social relations. *American Educational Research Journal, 32*, 321–351.

Stevenson, M. M., Braver, S. L., Ellman, I. M., & Votruba, A. M. (2013). Fathers, divorce, and child custody. In N. J. Cabrera & C. S. Tamis-LeMonda (Eds.), *Handbook of father involvement: Multidisciplinary perspectives* (2nd ed., pp. 379–396). New York, NY: Routledge/Taylor & Francis Group.

Stevick, R. A. (2014). *Growing up Amish: The Rumspringa years* (2nd ed.). Baltimore, MD: Johns Hopkins University Press.

Stewart, L., & Pascual-Leone, J. (1992). Mental capacity constraints and the development of moral reasoning. *Journal of Experimental Child Psychology, 54*, 251–287.

Stewart, M. (2013). Giving voice to Valeria's story: Support, value, and agency for immigrant adolescents. *Journal of Adolescent & Adult Literacy, 57*(1), 42–50. doi:10.1002/jaal.217

Stice, E., Gau, J. M., Rohde, P., & Shaw, H. (2017). Risk factors that predict future onset of each DSM–5 eating disorder: Predictive specificity in high-risk adolescent females. *Journal of Abnormal Psychology, 126*, 38–51. doi:10.1037/abn0000219

Stice, E., Marti, C., & Rohde, P. (2013). Prevalence, incidence, impairment, and course of the proposed DSM-5 eating disorder diagnoses in an 8-year prospective community study of young women. *Journal of Abnormal Psychology, 122*, 445–457. doi:10.1037/a0030679

Stichter, J. P., Herzog, M. J., Kilgus, S. P., & Schoemann, A. M. (2018). Exploring the moderating effects of cognitive abilities on social competence intervention outcomes. *Behavior Modification, 42*(1), 84–107. http://dx.doi.org.unco.idm.oclc.org/10.1177/0145445517698654

Stiggins, R. (2007). Assessment through students' eyes. *Educational Leadership, 64*(8), 22–26.

Stiles, J. (2008). *The fundamentals of brain development: Integrating nature and nurture*. Cambridge, MA: Harvard University Press.

Stipek, D. (2002). At what age should children enter kindergarten? A question for policy makers and parents. *Social Policy Report, 16*(1), 3–16.

Stipek, D. J. (1993). *Motivation to learn: From theory to practice* (2nd ed.). Needham Heights, MA: Allyn & Bacon.

Stipek, D. J. (1996). Motivation and instruction. In D. C. Berliner & R. C. Calfee (Eds.), *Handbook of educational psychology* (pp. 85-113). New York, NY: Macmillan.

Stipek, D. J., & Kowalski, P. S. (1989). Learned helplessness in task-orienting versus performance-orienting testing conditions. *Journal of Educational Psychology, 81*, 384–391.

Stipek, D. J., Recchia, S., & McClintic, S. M. (1992). Self-evaluation in young children. *Monographs of the Society for Research in Child Development, 57*(2, Serial No. 226).

Stocco, A., Yamasaki, B., Natalenko, R., & Prat, C. S. (2014). Bilingual brain training: A neurobiological framework of how bilingual experience improves executive function. *International Journal of Bilingualism, 18*(1), 67–92. doi:10.1177/1367006912456617

Stoicovy, C., Fee, R., & Fee, J. (2012). Culturally responsive instruction Leaves No Child Behind: The Story of Juan, a Pacific Island special needs student. *International Journal of Multicultural Education, 14*(1), 1–19.

Stoll, G., Rieger, S., Lüdtke, O., Nagengast, B., Trautwein, U., & Roberts, B. W. (2017). Vocational interests assessed at the end of high school predict life outcomes assessed 10 years later over and above IQ and Big Five personality traits. *Journal of Personality and Social Psychology, 113*, 167–184. http://dx.doi.org.unco.idm.oclc.org/10.1037/pspp0000117

Stormont, M. (2001). Social outcomes of children with AD/HD: Contributing factors and implications for practice. *Psychology in the Schools, 38*, 521–531.

Stover, K., Yearta, L., & Harris, C. (2016). Formative assessment in the digital age. *Reading Teacher, 69*, 377–381. doi:10.1002/trtr.1420

Straehler-Pohl, H., Fernández, S., Gellert, U., & Figueiras, L. (2014). School mathematics registers in a context of low academic expectations. *Educational Studies in Mathematics, 85*, 175–199. doi:10.1007/s10649-013-9503-5

Strand-Cary, M., & Klahr, D. (2008). Developing elementary science skills: Instructional effectiveness and path independence. *Cognitive Development, 23*, 488–511.

Straus, M. A. (2000). The benefits of never spanking: New and more definitive evidence. In M. A. Straus (Ed.), *Beating the devil out of them: Corporal punishment by American families and its effects on children.* New Brunswick, NJ: Transaction Publications.

Strayer, F. F. (1991). The development of agonistic and affiliative structures in preschool play groups. In J. Silverberg & P. Gray (Eds.), *To fight or not to fight: Violence and peacefulness in humans and other primates.* Oxford, England: Oxford University Press.

Streissguth, A. P., Barr, H. M., Sampson, P. D., & Bookstein, F. L. (1994). Prenatal alcohol and offspring development: The first fourteen years. *Drug and Alcohol Dependence, 36*, 89–99.

Streri, A., Coulon, M., & Guellaï, B. (2013). The foundations of social cognition: Studies on face/voice integration in newborn infants. *International Journal of Behavioral Development*, 37(2), 79–83. doi:10.1177/0165025412465361

Stricklin, K. (2011). Hands-on reciprocal teaching: A comprehension technique. *The Reading Teacher, 64*, 620–625. doi:10.1598/RT.64.8.8

Strolin-Goltzman, J. J., Woodhouse, V., Suter, J., & Werrbach, M. (2016). A mixed method study on educational well-being and resilience among youth in foster care. *Children & Youth Services Review, 70*, 30–36. doi:10.1016/j.childyouth.2016.08.014

Strozer, J. R. (1994). *Language acquisition after puberty.* Washington, DC: Georgetown University Press.

Strzelecka, J. (2014). Electroencephalographic studies in children with autism spectrum disorders. *Research in Autism Spectrum Disorders, 8*, 317–323. doi:10.1016/j.rasd.2013.11.010

Styne, D. M. (2003). The regulation of pubertal growth. *Hormone Research, 60*(Suppl.1), 22–26.

Su, W., Mrug, S., & Windle, M. (2010). Social cognitive and emotional mediators link violence exposure and parental nurturance to adolescent aggression. *Journal of Clinical Child and Adolescent Psychology, 39*, 814–824. doi:10.1080/15374416.2010.517163

Subrahmanyam, K., & Greenfield, P. (2012). Digital media and youth: Games, Internet, and development. In D. G. Singer & J. L. Singer (Eds.), *Handbook of children and the media* (2nd ed., pp. 75–96). Thousand Oaks, CA: Sage.

Sudhalter, V., & Braine, M. D. (1985). How does comprehension of passives develop? A comparison of actional and experiential verbs. *Journal of Child Language, 12*, 455–470.

Suh, S., Suh, J., & Houston, I. (2007). Predictors of categorical at-risk high school dropouts. *Journal of Counseling & Development, 85*, 196–203.

Suhr, D. D. (1999). *An investigation of mathematics and reading achievement of 5- through 14-year-olds using latent growth curve methodology* (Unpublished doctoral dissertation). University of Northern Colorado, Greeley.

Suina, J. H., & Smolkin, L. B. (1994). From natal culture to school culture to dominant society culture: Supporting transitions for Pueblo Indian students. In P. M. Greenfield & R. R. Cocking (Eds.), *Cross-cultural roots of minority child development* (pp. 115–130). Mahwah, NJ: Erlbaum.

Sukhram, D., & Hsu, A. (2012). Developing reading partnerships between parents and children: A reflection on the reading together program. *Early Childhood Education Journal, 40*, 115–121. doi:10.1007/s10643-011-0500-y

Sullivan-DeCarlo, C., DeFalco, K., & Roberts, V. (1998). Helping students avoid risky behavior. *Educational Leadership, 56*(1), 80–82.

Sullivan, F. M., & Barlow, S. M. (2001). Review of risk factors for sudden infant death syndrome. *Paediatric and Perinatal Epidemiology, 15*, 144–200.

Sullivan, H. S. (1953). *The interpersonal theory of psychiatry.* New York, NY: Norton.

Sullivan, J. R., & Conoley, J. C. (2004). Academic and instructional interventions with aggressive students. In J. C. Conoley & A. P. Goldstein (Eds.), *School violence intervention* (2nd ed., pp. 235–255). New York, NY: Guilford Press.

Sullivan, M. W., & Lewis, M. (2003). Contextual determinants of anger and other negative expressions in young infants. *Developmental Psychology, 39*, 693–705.

Sullivan, R. C. (1994). Autism: Definitions past and present. *Journal of Vocational Rehabilitation, 4*, 4–9.

Sulzby, E. (1985). Children's emergent reading of favorite storybooks: A developmental study. *Reading Research Quarterly, 20*, 458–481.

Sulzby, E. (1986). Children's elicitation and use of metalinguistic knowledge about word during literacy interactions. In D. Yaden & S. Templeton (Eds.), *Metalinguistic awareness and beginning literacy: Conceptualizing what it means to read and write* (pp. 219–233). Portsmouth, NH: Heinemann Educational Books.

Summers, A., Gatowski, S., & Dobbin, S. (2012). Terminating parental rights: The relation of judicial experience and expectancy-related factors to risk perceptions in child protection cases. *Psychology, Crime & Law, 18*(1), 95–112. doi:10.1080/1068316X.2011.589388

Sun, L., & Nippold, M. A. (2012). Narrative writing in children and adolescents: Examining the literate lexicon. *Language, Speech & Hearing Services in Schools, 43*(1), 2–13. doi:10.1044/0161-1461(2011/10-0099)

Sundqvist, A., Lyxell, B., Jönsson, R., & Heimann, M. (2014). Understanding minds: Early cochlear implantation and the development of theory of mind in children with profound hearing impairment. *International Journal of Pediatric Otorhinolaryngology, 78*, 538–544. doi:10.1016/j.ijporl.2013.12.039

Sunni, M. S., Farah, M., Hardie, C., Dhunkal, A., Abuzzahab, M., Kyllo, J., . . . Moran, A. (2015). Understanding cultural beliefs in families of Somali children with diabetes in the Twin Cities, Minnesota. *Journal of Community Health, 40*, 827–833. doi:10.1007/s10900-015-0006-4

Suor, J. H., Sturge-Apple, M. L., & Jones-Gordils, H. R. (2018). Parsing profiles of temperamental reactivity and differential routes to delay of gratification: A person-based approach. *Development and Psychopathology.* Advance online publication.

Suskind, R. (1998). *A hope in the unseen: An American odyssey from the inner city to the Ivy League.* New York, NY: Broadway Books.

Susman, E. J., Inoff-Germain, G., Nottelmann, E. D., Loriaux, D. L., Cutler, G. B. Jr., & Chrousos, G. P. (1987). Hormones, emotional dispositions, and aggressive attributes in young adolescents. *Child Development, 58*, 1114–1134.

Sutherland, S. L., & Friedman, O. (2013). Just pretending can be really learning: Children use pretend play as a source for acquiring generic knowledge. *Developmental Psychology, 49*, 1660–1668. doi:10.1037/a0030788

Suttles, G. D. (1970). Friendship as a social institution. In G. J. McCall, M. McCall, N. K. Denzin, G. D. Scuttles, & S. Kurth (Eds.), *Social relationships* (pp. 95–135). Chicago, IL: Aldine de Gruyter.

Sutton-Smith, B. (1986). The development of fictional narrative performances. *Topics in Language Disorders, 7*(1), 1–10.

Sutton-Smith, B. (Ed.). (1979). *Play and learning.* New York, NY: Gardner Press.

Suzuki, L. A., Onoue, M., & Hill, J. S. (2013). Clinical assessment: A multicultural perspective. In K. F. Geisinger, B. A. Bracken, J. F. Carlson, J. C. Hansen, N. R. Kuncel, S. P. Reise, & M. C. Rodriguez (Eds.), *APA Handbook of Testing and Assessment in Psychology, Vol. 2. Testing and assessment in clinical and counseling psychology* (pp. 193–212). Washington, DC: American Psychological Association. doi:10.1037/14048-012

Svanberg, P. O., Mennet, L., & Spieker, S. (2010). Promoting a secure attachment: A primary prevention practice model. *Clinical Child Psychology and Psychiatry, 15*, 363–378.

Svirsky, M. A., Robbins, A. M., Kirk, K. I., Pisoni, D. B., & Miyamoto, R. T. (2000). Language development in profoundly deaf children with cochlear implants. *Psychological Science, 11*, 153–158.

Swan, K., Karb, J., & Hofer, M. (2017). Students as modern muckrakers: Creating films for social change. *Social Education, 81*, 166–168.

Swanborn, M. S. L., & de Glopper, K. (1999). Incidental word learning while reading: A meta-analysis. *Review of Educational Research, 69*, 261–285.

Swanson, H. (2011). Working memory, attention, and mathematical problem solving: A longitudinal study of elementary school children. *Journal of Educational Psychology, 103*(4), 821–837. doi:10.1037/a0025114

Swanson, H. L. (2001). Research on interventions with learning disabilities: a meta-analysis of outcomes related to higher-order processing. *Elementary School Journal, 101*, 331–348. doi:10.1086/499671

Swanson, H. L., & Jerman, O. (2006). Math disabilities: A selective meta-analysis of the literature. *Review of Educational Research, 76*, 249–274.

Swanson, H. L., & Lussier, C. M. (2001). A selective synthesis of the experimental literature on dynamic assessment. *Review of Educational Research, 71*, 321–363.

Swanson, H. L., Jerman, O., & Zheng, X. (2008). Growth in working memory and mathematical problem solving in children at risk and not at risk for serious math difficulties. *Journal of Educational Psychology, 100*, 343–379.

Swanson, H. L., Mink, J., & Bocian, K. M. (1999). Cognitive processing deficits in poor readers with symptoms of reading disabilities and ADHD: More alike than different? *Journal of Educational Psychology, 91*, 321–333.

Swart, N. M., Muijselaar, M. M. L., Steenbeek-Planting, E. G., Droop, M., de Jong, P. F., & Verhoeven, L. (2017). Cognitive precursors of the developmental relation between lexical quality and reading comprehension in the intermediate elementary grades. *Learning and Individual Differences, 59*, 43–54. http://dx.doi.org.unco.idm.oclc.org/10.1016/j.lindif.2017.08.009

Swenson, L. P., & Rose, A. J. (2009). Friends' knowledge of youth internalizing and externalizing adjustment: Accuracy, bias, and the influences of gender, grade, positive friendship quality, and self-disclosure. *Journal of Abnormal Child Psychology, 37*, 887–901. doi:10.1007/s10802-009-9319-z

Swiatek, M. A. (1998). Helping gifted adolescents cope with social stigma. *Gifted Child Today Magazine, 21*(1), 42–46.

Swim, J. K., & Stangor, C. (Eds.). (1998). *Prejudice: The target's perspective*. San Diego, CA: Academic Press.

Sylva, K., Melhuish, E., Sammons, P., Siraj-Blatchford, I., & Taggart, B. (2004). *Effective preschool education*. London, England: Institute of Education, University of London.

Symon, A., Winter, C., Inkster, M. & Donnan, P. T. (2009). Outcomes for births booked under an independent midwife and births in NHS maternity units: Matched comparison study. *British Medical Journal, 338*, 1–9.

Symonds, J., & Hargreaves, L. (2016). Emotional and motivational engagement at school transition: A qualitative stage-environment fit study. *Journal of Early Adolescence, 36*(1), 54-85. http://dx.doi.org.unco.idm.oclc.org/10.1177/0272431614556348

Szynal-Brown, C., & Morgan, R. R. (1983). The effects of reward on tutor's behaviors in a cross-age tutoring context. *Journal of Experimental Child Psychology, 36*, 196–208.

Taffoni, F., Tamilia, E., Focaroli, V., Formica, D., Ricci, L., Di Pino, G., . . . Keller, F. (2014). Development of goal-directed action selection guided by intrinsic motivations: An experiment with children. *Experimental Brain Research, 232*, 2167–2177. doi:10.1007/s00221-014-3907-z

Tajfel, H. (2010). Social categorization, social identity and social comparison. In T. Postmes & N. R. Branscombe (Eds.), *Key readings in social psychology. Rediscovering social identity* (pp. 119–128). New York, NY: Psychology Press.

Takahashi, K. (1990). Are the key assumptions of the "Strange Situation" procedure universal? A view from Japanese research. *Human Development, 33*, 23–30.

Taki, Y., Thyreau, B., Hashizume, H., Sassa, Y., Takeuchi, H., Wu, K., . . . Kawashima, R. (2013). Linear and curvilinear correlations of brain white matter volume, fractional anisotropy, and mean diffusivity with age using voxel-based and region-of-interest analyses in 246 healthy children. *Human Brain Mapping, 34*, 1842–1856.

Talamas, S. N., Mavor, K. I., Axelsson, J., Sundelin, T., & Perrett, D. I. (2016). Eyelid-openness and mouth curvature influence perceived intelligence beyond attractiveness. *Journal of Experimental Psychology: General, 145*, 603–620. http://dx.doi.org.unco.idm.oclc.org/10.1037/xge0000152

Taliaferro, L. A., & Muehlenkamp, J. J. (2014). Risk and protective factors that distinguish adolescents who attempt suicide from those who only consider suicide in the past year. *Suicide & Life-Threatening Behavior, 44*(1), 6–22. doi:10.1111/sltb.12046

Tamburrini, J. (1982). Some educational implications of Piaget's theory. In S. Modgil & C. Modgil (Eds.), *Jean Piaget: Consensus and controversy*. New York, NY: Praeger.

Tamis-LeMonda, C. S., & Song, L. (2013). Parent–infant communicative interactions in cultural context. In R. M. Lerner, M. Easterbrooks, J. Mistry, & I. B. Weiner (Eds.), *Handbook of Psychology, Vol. 6. Developmental psychology* (2nd ed., pp. 143–170). Hoboken, NJ: Wiley.

Tan, E. T., & Goldberg, W. A. (2009). Parental school involvement in relation to children's grades and adaptation to school. *Journal of Applied Developmental Psychology, 30*, 442–453.

Tangney, J. P., & Dearing, R. L. (2002). *Shame and guilt*. New York, NY: Guilford Press.

Tannen, D. (1990). *You just don't understand: Talk between the sexes*. New York, NY: Ballantine.

Tanner, J. M. (1990). *Foetus into man: Physical growth from conception to maturity* (Rev. ed.). Cambridge, MA: Harvard University Press.

Tas, Y., & Cakir, B. (2014). An investigation of science active learning strategy use in relation to motivational beliefs. *Mevlana International Journal of Education, 4*(1), 55–66. doi:10.13054/mije.13.55.4.1

Tasca, M., Mulvey, P., & Rodriguez, N. (2016). Families coming together in prison: An examination of visitation encounters. *Punishment & Society, 18*(4), 459–478. doi:10.1177/1462474516642856

Task Force on Sudden Infant Death Syndrome. (2011). SIDS and other sleep-related infant deaths: Expansions of recommendations for a safe infant sleeping environment. *Pediatrics, 128*, 1341–1367. doi:10.1542/peds.2011-2285.

Tassoni, P. (2013). Side by side. *Nursery World, 112*(4312), 20–22.

Tatlow-Golden, M., & Guerin, S. (2017). Who I am: The meaning of early adolescents' most valued activities and relationships, and implications for self-concept research. *The Journal of Early Adolescence, 37*, 236–266.

Tatum, A. W. (2008). Toward a more anatomically complete model of literacy instruction: A focus on African American male adolescents and teens. *Harvard Educational Review, 78*(1), 155–180.

Tatum, B. D. (1997). *Why are all the Black kids sitting together in the cafeteria? and other conversations about race*. New York, NY: Basic Books.

Taumoepeau, M., & Ruffman, T. (2008). Stepping stones to others' minds: Maternal talk relates to child mental state language and emotion understandings at 15, 24, and 33 months. *Child Development, 79*, 284–302.

Tavassolie, T., Dudding, S., Madigan, A., Thorvardarson, E., & Winsler, A. (2016). Differences in perceived parenting style between mothers and fathers: Implications for child outcomes and marital conflict. *Journal of Child & Family Studies, 25*, 2055–2068. doi:10.1007/s10826-016-0376-y

Taylor, L. K., Merrilees, C. E., Goeke-Morey, M. C., Shirlow, P., Cairns, E., & Cummings, E. (2014). Political violence and adolescent out-group attitudes and prosocial behaviors: Implications for positive inter-group relations. *Social Development, 23*(4), 840-859.

Taylor, J. M. (1994). *MDMA frequently asked questions list*. Retrieved from http://ibbserver.ibb.uu.nl/jboschma/ecstasy/xtc01

Taylor, M., Esbensen, B. M., & Bennett, R. T. (1994). Children's understanding of knowledge acquisition: The tendency for children to report that they have always known what they have just learned. *Child Development, 65*, 1581–1604.

Taylor, R. D., Oberle, E., Durlak, J. A., & Weissberg, R. P. (2017). Promoting positive youth development through school-based social and emotional learning interventions: A meta-analysis of follow-up effects. *Child*

Development, 88, 1156–1171. doi:10.1111/cdev.12864

Taylor, S. J., Barker, L. A., Heavey, L., & McHale, S. (2013). The typical developmental trajectory of social and executive functions in late adolescence and early adulthood. *Developmental Psychology, 49*, 1253–1265. http://dx.doi.org.unco.idm.oclc.org/10.1037/a0029871

Taylor, W. C., Beech, B. M., & Cummings, S. S. (1998). Increasing physical activity levels among youth: A public health challenge. In D. K. Wilson, J. R. Rodrigue, & W. C. Taylor (Eds.), *Health-promoting and health-compromising behaviors among minority adolescents* (pp. 107–128). Washington, DC: American Psychological Association.

Telingator, C. (2013). Clinical work with children and adolescents growing up with lesbian, gay, and bisexual parents. In A. E. Goldberg & K. R. Allen (Eds.), *LGBT-parent families: Innovations in research and implications for practice [E-book]* (pp. 261–274). New York, NY: Springer Science + Business Media.

Téllez, K., & Waxman, H. (2010). A review of research on effective community programs for English Language Learners. *School Community Journal, 20*(1), 103–119.

Temple, J., Reynolds, A., & Arteaga, I. (2010). Low birth weight, preschool education, and school remediation. *Education and Urban Society, 42*, 705–729. doi:10.1177/0013124510370946

Tennenbaum, H. R., & Leaper, C. (2002). Are parents' gender schemas related to their children's gender-related cognitions? A meta-analysis. *Developmental Psychology, 38*, 615–630.

Tennyson, R. D., & Cocchiarella, M. J. (1986). An empirically based instructional design theory for teaching concepts. *Review of Educational Research, 56*, 40–71.

Terman, L. M. (1916). *The measurement of intelligence.* Boston, MA: Houghton Mifflin.

Terman, L. M., & Merrill, M. A. (1972). *Stanford-Binet Intelligence Scale* (3rd ed.). Boston, MA: Houghton Mifflin.

Terry, A. W. (2000). An early glimpse: Service learning from an adolescent perspective. *Journal of Secondary Gifted Education, 11*, 115–134.

Terry, A. W. (2001). *A case study of community action service learning on young, gifted adolescents and their community* (Doctoral dissertation, University of Georgia, 2000). *Dissertation Abstracts International, 61*(08), 3058.

Terry, A. W. (2003). Effects of service learning on young, gifted adolescents and their community. *Gifted Child Quarterly, 47*, 295–308.

Terry, A. W. (2008). Student voices, global echoes: Service-learning and the gifted. *Roeper Review, 30*, 45–51.

Terry, A., & Panter, T. (2010). Students make sure the Cherokees are not removed . . . again: A study of service-learning and artful learning in teaching history. *Journal for the Education of the Gifted, 34*, 156–176.

Terry, J., Smith, B., & McQuillin, S. (2014). Teaching evidence-based practice in service-learning: A model for education and service. *Journal on Excellence in College Teaching, 25*(1), 55–69.

Teti, D. M., Gelfand, D., Messinger, D. S., & Isabella, R. (1995). Maternal depression and the quality of early attachment: An examination of infants, preschoolers and their mothers. *Developmental Psychology, 31*, 364–376.

Tharp, R. G. (1989). Psychocultural variables and constants: Effects on teaching and learning in schools. *American Psychologist, 44*, 349–359.

Tharp, R. G. (1994). Intergroup differences among Native Americans in socialization and child cognition: An ethnogenetic analysis. In P. M. Greenfield & R. R. Cocking (Eds.), *Cross-cultural roots of minority child development* (pp. 87–105). Hillsdale, NJ: Erlbaum.

Thatch, L V. L. (2008). *A case study of an elementary science teacher's efforts to transform students' scientific communication from "informal science talk" to "formal science talk"* (PhD dissertation). The University of Texas at Austin. Retrieved from Dissertations & Theses: A&I. (Publication No. AAT 3315081)

Thatcher, K. L. (2010). The development of phonological awareness with specific language-impaired and typical children. *Psychology in the Schools, 47*, 467–480.

The Freedom Writers (with Gruwell, E.). (1999). *The Freedom Writers diary: How a teacher and 150 teens used writing to change themselves and the world around them.* New York, NY: Broadway Books.

Thelen, E., & Smith, L. B. (2006). Dynamic systems theories. In W. Damon & R. M. Lerner (Eds. in Chief) & R. M. Lerner (Vol. Ed.), *Handbook of Child Psychology: Vol. 1. Theoretical models of human development* (6th ed., pp. 258–312). Hoboken, NJ: Wiley.

Thomas, A., & Chess, S. (1977). *Temperament and development.* New York, NY: Brunner/Mazel.

Thomas, H. (2006). Obesity prevention programs for children and youth: Why are their results so modest? *Health Education Research, 21*, 783–795.

Thomas, J. (2012). Language play for infants: Man in the moon for male caregivers. *Aplis, 25*(2), 71–75.

Thomas, M. C., Forrester, N. A., & Ronald, A. (2013). Modeling socioeconomic status effects on language development. *Developmental Psychology, 49*, 2325–2343. doi:10.1037/a0032301

Thomas, S., & Oldfather, P. (1997). Intrinsic motivations, literacy, and assessment practices: "That's my grade. That's me." *Educational Psychologist, 32*, 107–123.

Thompson, E. C., Woodruff Carr, K., White-Schwoch, T., Otto-Meyer, S., & Kraus, N. (2017). Individual differences in speech-in-noise perception parallel neural speech processing and attention in preschoolers. *Hearing Research, 344*, 148–157. doi:10.1016/j.heares.2016.11.007

Thompson, M., & Grace, C. O. (with L. J. Cohen). (2001). *Best friends, worst enemies: Understanding the social lives of children.* New York, NY: Ballantine.

Thompson, R. (2014). Stress and child development. *Future of Children, 24*(1), 41–59.

Thompson, R. A. (1994). The role of the father after divorce. *Future of Children: Children and Divorce, 4*(1), 210–235.

Thompson, R. A. (2006). The development of the person: Social understanding, relationships, conscience, self. In W. Damon & R. M. Lerner (Eds. in Chief) & N. Eisenberg (Vol. Ed.), *Handbook of Child Psychology, Vol. 3. Social, emotional, and personality development* (6th ed., pp. 24–98). Hoboken, NJ: Wiley.

Thompson, R. A. (2012). Whither the preconventional child? Toward a life-span moral development theory. *Child Development Perspectives, 6*, 423–429.

Thompson, R. A. (2014). Conscience development in early childhood. In M. Killen & J. G. Smetana (Eds.), *Handbook of moral development* (pp. 73–92). New York, NY: Psychology Press.

Thompson, R. A., & Newton, E. K. (2010). Emotions in early conscience. In W. F. Arsenio & E. A. Lemerise (Eds.), *Emotions, aggression, and morality in children: Bridging development and psychopathology* (pp. 13–31). Washington, DC: American Psychological Association.

Thompson, R. A., & Virmani, E. A. (2010). Self and personality. In M. H. Bornstein (Ed.), *Handbook of cultural developmental science* (pp. 195–207). New York, NY: Psychology Press.

Thompson, R. A., Easterbrooks, M. A., & Padilla-Walker, L. M. (2003). Social and emotional development in infancy. In R. M. Lerner, M. A. Easterbrooks, & J. Mistry (Vol. Eds.), & I. B. Weiner (Editor-in-Chief), *Handbook of Psychology, Vol. 6. Developmental psychology* (pp. 91–112). Hoboken, NJ: Wiley.

Thompson, S., Noblin, S. J., Lemons, J., Peterson, S. K., Carreno, C., & Harbison, A. (2015). Perceptions of Latinas on the traditional prenatal genetic counseling model. *Journal of Genetic Counseling, 24*, 675–682. doi:http://dx.doi.org/10.1007/s10897-014-9797-1

Thomson, D. M. (2010). Marshmallow power and frooty treasures: Disciplining the child consumer through online cereal advergaming. *Critical Studies in Media Communication, 27*, 438–454. doi:10.1080/15295030903583648

Thorkildsen, T. A. (1995). Conceptions of social justice. In W. M. Kurtines & J. L. Gewirtz (Eds.), *Moral development: An introduction.* Boston, MA: Allyn & Bacon.

Thornberg, R. (2008). "It's not fair!"—Voicing pupils' criticisms of school rules. *Children & Society, 22*, 418–428. doi:10.1111/j.1099-0860.2007.00121.x

Thornberg, R. (2010). A study of children's conceptions of school rules by investigating their judgments of transgressions in the absence of rules. *Educational Psychology, 30*, 583–603. doi:10.1080/01443410.2010.492348

Thorndike, R., Hagen, E., & Sattler, J. (1986). *Stanford-Binet Intelligence Scale* (4th ed.). Chicago, IL: Riverside.

Throndsen, I. (2011). Self-regulated learning of basic arithmetic skills: A longitudinal study. *British Journal of Educational Psychology, 81*, 558–578. doi:10.1348/2044-8279.002008

Thys, S. S., & Van Houtte, M. (2016). Ethnic composition of the primary school and educational choice: Does the culture of teacher expectations matter? *Teaching & Teacher Education, 59*, 383–391. doi:10.1016/j.tate.2016.06.011

Tiedemann, J. (2000). Parents' gender stereotypes and teachers' beliefs as predictors of children's concept of their mathematical ability in elementary school. *Journal of Educational Psychology, 92*, 144–151.

Tierney, A. L., & Nelson, C. A. III. (2009). Brain development and the role of experience in the early years. *Zero to Three, 30*(2), 9–13.

Tilley, S., & Taylor, L. (2013). Understanding curriculum as lived: Teaching for social justice and equity goals. *Race, Ethnicity & Education, 16*, 406–429. doi:10.1080/13613324.2011.645565

Timler, G. R., Olswang, L. B., & Coggins, L. E. (2005). "Do I know what I need to do?" A social communication intervention for children with complex clinical profiles. *Language, Speech, and Hearing Services in Schools, 36*, 73–85.

Tiruchittampalam, S., Nicholson, T., Levin, J. R., & Ferron, J. M. (2018). The effects of preliteracy knowledge, schooling, and summer vacation on literacy acquisition. *Journal of Educational Research, 111*, 28–42. doi:10.1080/00220671.2016.1190911

Tisak, M. S. (1993). Preschool children's judgments of moral and personal events involving physical harm and property damage. *Merrill-Palmer Quarterly: Journal of Developmental Psychology, 39*, 375–390.

Tisak, M. S., & Turiel, E. (1984). Children's conceptions of moral and prudential rules. *Child Development, 55*, 1030–1039. doi:10.2307/1130154

Tobias, J. W., & Andreasen, J. B. (2013). Developing multiplicative thinking from additive reasoning. *Teaching Children Mathematics, 20*, 102–109.

Tobin, J. J., Wu, D. Y. H., & Davidson, D. H. (1989). *Preschool in three cultures: Japan, China, and the United States*. New Haven, CT, US: Yale University Press.

Tobin, M., & Hill, E. W. (2012). The development of reading skills in young partially sighted readers. *British Journal of Special Education, 39*(2), 80–86. doi:10.1111/j.1467-8578.2012.00540.x

Toffalini, E., Giofrè, D., & Cornoldi, C. (2017). Strengths and weaknesses in the intellectual profile of different subtypes of specific learning disorder: A study on 1,049 diagnosed children. *Clinical Psychological Science, 5*, 402–409. doi:10.1177/2167702616672038'

Toga, A. W., & Thompson, P. M. (2003). Mapping brain asymmetry. *Nature Review Neuroscience, 4*, 37–48.

Tolani, N., & Brooks-Gunn, J. (2006). Are there socio-economic disparities in children's mental health? In H. E. Fitzgerald, B. M. Lester, & B. Zuckerman (Vol. Eds.), & H. E. Fitzgerald, R. Zucker, & K. Freeark (Eds. in Chief), *The crisis in youth mental health: Critical issues and effective programs* (Vol. 1, pp. 277–303). Westport, CT: Praeger.

Toldson, I., & Lemmons, B. (2013). Social demographics, the school environment, and parenting practices associated with parents' participation in schools and academic success among black, Hispanic, and white Students. *Journal of Human Behavior in the Social Environment, 23*, 237–255. doi:10.1080/10911359.2013.747407

Tomasello, M. (1999). *The cultural origins of human cognition*. Cambridge, MA: Harvard University Press.

Tomasello, M., & Gonzalez-Cabrera, I. (2017). The role of ontogeny in the evolution of human cooperation. *Human Nature, 28*, 274–288.

Tomasello, M., Carpenter, M., & Liszkowski, U. (2007). A new look at infant pointing. *Child Development, 78*, 705–722.

Tomlinson, R. M., Keyfitz, L., Rawana, J. S., & Lumley, M. N. (2017). Unique contributions of positive schemas for understanding child and adolescent life satisfaction and happiness. *Journal of Happiness Studies, 18*, 1255–1274.

Tompkins, G. E., & McGee, L. M. (1986). Visually impaired and sighted children's emerging concepts about written language. In D. B. Yaden, Jr., & S. Templeton (Eds.), *Metalinguistic awareness and beginning literacy: Conceptualizing what it means to read and write* (pp. 259–275). Portsmouth, NH: Heinemann.

Tompkins, V., Guo, Y., & Justice, L. (2013). Inference generation, story comprehension, and language skills in the preschool years. *Reading & Writing, 26*, 403–429. doi:10.1007/s11145-012-9374-7

Tong, S., Baghurst, P., Vimpani, G., & McMichael, A. (2007). Socioeconomic position, maternal IQ, home environment, and cognitive development. *Journal of Pediatrics, 151*, 284–288.e1.

Tong, X., Shigetomi, E., Looger, L. L., & Khakh, B. S. (2013). Genetically encoded calcium indicators and astrocyte calcium microdomains. *The Neuroscientist, 19*, 274–291. doi:10.1177/1073858412468794

Tooley, U. A., Makhoul, Z., & Fisher, P. A. (2016). Nutritional status of foster children in the U.S.: Implications for cognitive and behavioral development. *Children and Youth Services Review, 70*, 369–374. doi:10.1016/j.childyouth.2016.10.027

Toplak, M. E., West, R. F., & Stanovich, K. E. (2017). Real-world correlates of performance on heuristics and biases tasks in a community sample. *Journal of Behavioral Decision Making, 30*, 541–554. doi:10.1002/bdm.1973

Torges, C., Stewart, A., & Duncan, L. (2009). Appreciating life's complexities: Assessing narrative ego integrity in late midlife. *Journal of Research in Personality, 43*, 66–74.

Torrance, E. (1981). Empirical validation of criterion-referenced indicators of creative ability through a longitudinal study. *Creative Child & Adult Quarterly, 6*, 136–140.

Torrance, E. P. (1995). Insights about creativity: Questioned, rejected, ridiculed, ignored. *Educational Psychology Review, 7*, 313–322.

Torres-Guzmán, M. E. (1998). Language, culture, and literacy in Puerto Rican communities. In B. Pérez (Ed.), *Sociocultural contexts of language and literacy* (pp. 91–121). Mahwah, NJ: Erlbaum.

Torres-Guzmán, M. E. (2011). Methodologies and teacher stances: How do they interact in classrooms? *International Journal of Bilingual Education and Bilingualism, 14*, 225–241. doi:10.1080/13670050.2010.539675

Torres, M. E., Smithwick, J., Luchok, K. J., & Rodman-Rice, G. (2012). Reducing maternal and child health disparities among Latino immigrants in South Carolina through a tailored, culturally appropriate and participant-driven initiative. *Californian Journal of Health Promotion, 10*(2), 1–14.

Tourniaire, F., & Pulos, S. (1985). Proportional reasoning: A review of the literature. *Educational Studies in Mathematics, 16*, 181–204.

Towne, J. (2009). A dropout's guide to education reform. *Education Week, 29*(8), 25.

Trach, J., Lee, M., & Hymel, S. (2018). A social-ecological approach to addressing emotional and behavioral problems in schools: Focusing on group processes and social dynamics. *Journal of Emotional & Behavioral Disorders, 26*, 11–20. doi:10.1177/1063426617742346

Tracy, B., Reid, R., & Graham, S. (2009). Teaching young students strategies for planning and drafting stories: The impact of self-regulated strategy development. *Journal of Educational Research, 102*, 323–331.

Trawick-Smith, J. (2010). *Early childhood development: A multicultural perspective* (5th ed.). Upper Saddle River, NJ: Merrill/Pearson.

Trawick-Smith, J. (2014). *Early childhood development: A multicultural perspective* (6th ed.). Boston, MA: Pearson.

Trawick-Smith, J., Swaminathan, S., Baton, B., Danieluk, C., Marsh, S., & Szarwacki, M. (2017). Block play and mathematics learning in preschool: The effects of building complexity, peer and teacher interactions in the block area, and replica play materials. *Journal of Early Childhood Research, 15*, 433–448. doi:10.1177/1476718X16664557

Traylor, A. C., Williams, J. D., Kenney, J. L., & Hopson, L. M. (2016). Relationships between adolescent well-being and friend support and behavior. *Children & Schools, 38*, 179–186. http://dx.doi.org.unco.idm.oclc.org/10.1093/cs/cdw021

Treffert, D. A. (2014). Savant syndrome: Realities, myths and misconceptions. *Journal of*

Autism and Developmental Disorders, 44, 564–571. doi:10.1007/s10803-013-1906-8

Treffert, D. A., & Wallace, G. L. (2002). Islands of genius. *Scientific American, 286*(6), 76–85.

Treiman, R. (1998). Beginning to spell in English. In C. Hulme & R. M. Joshi (Eds.), *Reading and spelling: Development and disorders.* Mahwah, NJ: Erlbaum.

Treiman, R., & Kessler, B. (2013). Learning to use an alphabetic writing system. *Language Learning and Development, 9,* 317–330. doi:10.1080/15475441.2013.812016

Treiman, R., Cohen, J., Mulqueeny, K., Kessler, B., & Schechtman, S. (2007). Young children's knowledge about printed names. *Child Development, 78,* 1458–1471.

Trelease, J. (1982). *The read-aloud handbook.* New York, NY: Penguin Books.

Tremblay, R. E., Nagin, D. S, Seguin, J. R., Zoccolillo, M., Zelazo, P. D., Boivin, M., . . . Japel, C. (2004). Physical aggression during early childhood: Trajectories and predictors. *Pediatrics, 114,* E43–E50.

Trevarthen, C., & Hubley, P. (1978). Secondary intersubjectivity: Confidence, confiding and acts of meaning in the first year. In A. Lock (Ed.), *Action, gesture, and symbol: The emergence of language* (pp. 183–230). London, England: Academic Press.

Triandis, H. C. (1995). *Individualism and collectivism.* Boulder, CO: Westview Press.

Trommsdorff, G. (2012). Development of "agentic" regulation in cultural context: The role of self and world views. *Child Development Perspectives, 6*(1), 19–26. doi:10.1111/j.1750-8606.2011.00224.x

Trommsdorff, G., & Heikamp, T. (2013). Socialization of emotions and emotion regulation in cultural context. In S. Barnow & N. Balkir (Eds.), *Cultural variations in psychopathology: From research to practice* (pp. 67–92). Cambridge, MA: Hogrefe Publishing.

Tron, R. (2013). How students respond to a jury of their peers. *TES: Times Educational Supplement* (5063), 40–41.

Tronick, E. Z., Cohn, J., & Shea, E. (1986). The transfer of affect between mother and infant. In T. B. Brazelton & M. W. Yogman (Eds.), *Affective development in infancy* (pp. 11–25). Norwood, NJ: Ablex.

Trzaskowski, M., Yang, J., Visscher, P., & Plomin, R. (2014). DNA evidence for strong genetic stability and increasing heritability of intelligence from age 7 to 12. *Molecular Psychiatry, 19*(3), 380–384. doi:10.1038/mp.2012.191

Tsai, P.-Y., Chen, S., Chang, H.-P., & Chang, W.-H. (2013). Effects of prompting critical reading of science news on seventh graders' cognitive achievement. *International Journal of Environmental and Science Education, 8,* 85–107.

Tsantefski, M., Parkes, A., Tidyman, A., & Campion, M. (2013). An extended family for life for children affected by parental substance dependence. *Family Matters,* No. 93, 74–83.

Tsethlikai, M., & Rogoff, B. (2013). Involvement in traditional cultural practices and American Indian children's incidental recall of a folktale. *Developmental Psychology, 49,* 568–578. doi:10.1037/a0031308

Tsubota, Y., & Chen, Z. (2012). How do young children's spatio-symbolic skills change over short time scales? *Journal of Experimental Child Psychology, 111*(1), 1–21. doi:10.1016/j.jecp.2011.06.005

Tsui, J. M., & Mazzocco, M. M. M. (2007). Effects of math anxiety and perfectionism on timed versus untimed math testing in mathematically gifted sixth graders. *Roeper Review, 29,* 132–139.

Tucker-Drob, E. M., & Harden, K. (2012). Early childhood cognitive development and parental cognitive stimulation: Evidence for reciprocal gene–environment transactions. *Developmental Science, 15,* 250–259. doi:10.1111/j.1467-7687.2011.01121.x

Tucker, C.J., Kazura, K. (2013). Parental responses to school-aged children's sibling conflict. *Journal of Child and Family Studies, 22*(5), pp. 737–745.

Tucker, J. S., Ellickson, P. L., & Klein, D. J. (2008). Growing up in a permissive household: What deters at-risk adolescents from heavy drinking. *Journal of Studies on Alcohol and Drugs, 69,* 528–534.

Tucker, V., & Schwartz, I. (2013). Parents' perspectives of collaboration with school professionals: Barriers and facilitators to successful partnerships in planning for students with ASD. *School Mental Health, 5*(1), 3–14. doi:10.1007/s12310-012-9102-0

Tully, E. C., & Donohue, M. R. (2017). Empathic responses to mother's emotions predict internalizing problems in children of depressed mothers. *Child Psychiatry and Human Development, 48*(1), 94–106. http://dx.doi.org.unco.idm.oclc.org/10.1007/s10578-016-0656-1

Turati, C., Gava, L., Valenza, E., & Ghirardi, V. (2013). Number versus extent in newborns' spontaneous preference for collections of dots. *Cognitive Development, 28*(1), 10–20. doi:10.1016/j.cogdev.2012.06.002

Turiel, E. (1983). *The development of social knowledge: Morality and convention.* Cambridge, England: Cambridge University Press.

Turiel, E. (1998). The development of morality. In W. Damon (Series Ed.) & N. Eisenberg (Vol. Ed.), *Handbook of Child Psychology: Vol. 3. Social, emotional, and personality development* (pp. 863–932). New York, NY: Wiley.

Turiel, E. (2002). *The culture of morality: Social development, context, and conflict.* Cambridge, England: Cambridge University Press.

Turiel, E. (2006a). The development of morality. In W. Damon & R. M. Lerner (Eds. in Chief) & N. Eisenberg (Vol. Ed.), *Handbook of Child Psychology, Vol. 3. Social, emotional, and personality development* (6th ed., pp. 789–857). Hoboken, NJ: Wiley.

Turiel, E. (2006b). Thought, emotions, and social interactional processes in moral development. In M. Killen & J. G. Smetana (Eds.), *Handbook of moral development* (pp. 7–35). Mahwah, NJ: Erlbaum.

Turiel, E. (2008a). The development of children's orientations toward moral, social, and personal orders: More than a sequence in development. *Human Development, 51,* 21–39.

Turiel, E. (2008b). Thought about actions in social domains: Morality, social conventions, and social interactions. *Cognitive Development, 23*(1), 136–154. doi:10.1016/j.cogdev.2007.04.001

Turiel, E. (2018). Reasoning at the root of morality. In K. Gray & J. Graham (Eds.), *Atlas of moral psychology* (pp. 9–19). New York, NY: Guilford Press.

Turiel, E., & Killen, M. (2010). Taking emotions seriously: The role of emotions in moral development. In W. F. Arsenio & E. A. Lemerise (Eds.), *Emotions, aggression, and morality in children: Bridging development and psychopathology* (pp. 33–52). Washington, DC: American Psychological Association.

Turiel, E., Killen, M., & Helwig, C. C. (1987). Morality: Its structure, function, and vagaries. In J. Kagan & S. Lamb (Eds.), *The emergence of morality in young children* (pp. 155–243). Chicago, IL: University of Chicago Press.

Turiel, E., Smetana, J. G., & Killen, M. (1991). Social contexts in social cognitive development. In W. M. Kurtines & J. L. Gewirtz (Eds.), *Moral behavior and development: Vol. 2. Research* (pp. 307–332). Hillsdale, NJ: Erlbaum.

Turkanis, C. G. (2001). Creating curriculum with children. In B. Rogoff, C. G. Turkanis, & L. Bartlett (Eds.), *Learning together: Children and adults in a school community* (pp. 91–102). New York, NY: Oxford University Press.

Turkheimer, E. (2000). Three laws of behavior genetics and what they mean. *Current Directions in Psychological Science, 9,* 160–164.

Turkheimer, E., Haley, A., Waldron, M., D'Onofrio, B., & Gottesman, I. I. (2003). Socioeconomic status modifies heritability of IQ in young children. *Psychological Science, 14,* 623–628.

Turnbull, A. P., Pereira, L., & Blue-Banning, M. (2000). Teachers as friendship facilitators: Young children's trust beliefs in peers: Relations to social competence and interactive behaviors in a peer group. *Early Education and Development, 25,* 601–618. doi:10.1080/10409289.2013.836698

Turnbull, A. P., Turnbull, R., & Wehmeyer, M. L. (2010). *Exceptional lives: Special education in today's schools* (6th ed.). Upper Saddle River, NJ: Merrill Pearson.

Turner, K. L., & Brown, C. S. (2007). The centrality of gender and ethnic identities across individuals and contexts. *Social Development, 16,* 700–719.

Tuvblad, C., Bezdjian, S., Raine, A., & Baker, L. (2013). Psychopathic personality and negative parent-to-child affect: A longitudinal cross-lag twin study. *Journal of Criminal Justice, 41*, 331–341.

Tversky, A., & Kahneman, D. (1990). Judgment under uncertainty: Heuristics and biases. In P. K. Moser (Ed.), *Rationality in action: Contemporary approaches* (pp. 171–188). New York, NY: Cambridge University Press.

Tynes, B. M. (2007). Role taking in online "classrooms": What adolescents are learning about race and ethnicity. *Developmental Psychology, 43*, 1312–1320.

Tzilos, G., Hess, L., Kao, J. C.-W., & Zlotnick, C. (2013). Characteristics of perinatal women seeking treatment for marijuana abuse in a community-based clinic. *Archives of Women's Mental Health, 16*(4), 333-337. http://dx.doi.org.unco.idm.oclc.org/10.1007/s00737-013-0358-7

Tzuriel, D. (2000). Dynamic assessment of young children: Educational and intervention perspectives. *Educational Psychology Review, 12*, 385–435.

U.S. Bureau of Consular Affairs. (2018). U.S. Department of State. *Intercountry adoption*. FY 2017 Annual Report on Intercountry Adoption (March 23, 2018). Retrieved June 26, 2018 from https://travel.state.gov/content/dam/NEWadoptionassets/pdfs/Annual%20Report%20on%20Intercountry%20Adoptions%20FY2017%20(release%20date%20March%2023%2020.._.pdf

U.S. Census Bureau. (2013a). *Table C3. Living arrangements of children under 18 years and marital status of parents, by age, sex, race, and Hispanic origin and selected characteristics of the child for all children: 2012*. Retrieved from http://www.census.gov/hhes/families/data/cps2012.html

U.S. Census Bureau. (2013b). *Table C4. Children with grandparents by presence of parents, sex, race, and Hispanic origin for selected characteristics: 2012*. Retrieved from http://www.census.gov/hhes/families/data/cps2012.html

U.S. Department of Agriculture. (2012). *The school day just got healthier (USDA Center for Nutrition Policy and Promotion 10 Tips Education Series)*. Retrieved from http://www.choosemyplate.gov/food-groups/downloads/TenTips/DGTipsheet21SchoolDayJustGotHealthier.pdf

U.S. Department of Agriculture. (2013). *Diet Quality of Children Age 2-17 Years as Measured by the Healthy Eating Index-2010*. Retrieved from https://www.cnpp.usda.gov/sites/default/files/nutrition_insights_uploads/Insight52.pdf

U.S. Department of Agriculture Center for Nutrition Policy and Promotion. (2013). *Getting started with MyPlate*. Retrieved from http://www.choosemyplate.gov/downloads/GettingStartedWithMyPlate.pdf

U.S. Department of Education. (1993). *National excellence: A case for developing America's talent*. Washington, DC: Office of Educational Research and Improvement.

U.S. Department of Education. (2004). *Individuals with Disabilities Education Act. Sec. 300.8* (c) (4) (i). Retrieved from https://sites.ed.gov/idea/regs/b/a/300.8/c/4/i

U.S. Department of Energy Office of Science. (2008). *Genomics and its impact on science and society*. Retrieved from http://www.ornl.gov/sci/techresources/Human_Genome/publicat/primer/

U.S. Department of Education Office of Civil Rights. (2013). *Supporting the academic success of pregnant and parenting students*. Retrieved from http://www2.ed.gov/about/offices/list/ocr/docs/pregnancy.pdf.

U.S. Department of Health and Human Services. (2007). *The AFCARS Report: Preliminary FY 2005 estimates as of September 2006*. Retrieved from http://www.acf.hhs.gov/programs/cb/stats_research/afcars/tar/report13.htm

U.S. Department of Health and Human Services. (2015). *How do you get HIV or AIDS?* Retrieved from https://www.aids.gov/hiv-aids-basics/hiv-aids-101/how-you-get-hiv-aids/

U.S. Department of Health and Human Services Administration for Children and Families (2018). *Trends in U.S. adoptions: 2008 2012*. Retrieved June 26, 2018 from Child Welfare Information Gateway https://www.childwelfare.gov/pubPDFs/adopted0812.pdf

U.S. Department of Justice and U.S. Department of Education. (2016). *Guidance on transgender students and civil rights*. Retrieved from https://www2.ed.gov/about/offices/list/ocr/letters/colleague-201605-title-ix-transgender.pdf

U.S. Department of Justice, Drug Enforcement Administration. (2011). *Drugs of abuse*. Retrieved from http://www.justice.gov/dea/pr/multimedia-library/publications/drug_of_abuse.pdf http://www.justice.gov/dea/druginfo/factsheets.shtml

U.S. Department of Labor. (2013). *Employment characteristics of families summary*. Retrieved from http://www.bls.gov/news.release/famee.nr0.htm

U.S. Drug Enforcement Administration. (2002). *Team up: A drug prevention manual for high school athletic coaches*. Washington, DC: U.S. Department of Justice Drug Enforcement Administration.

Uji, M., Sakamoto, A., Adachi, K., & Kitamura, T. (2014). The impact of authoritative, authoritarian, and permissive parenting styles on children's later mental health in Japan: Focusing on parent and child gender. *Journal of Child and Family Studies, 23*(2), 293–302. doi:10.1007/s10826-013-9740-3

Ullman, E. (2010a). Closing the STEM gender gap. *Education Update, 52*(3), 1, 6–7.

Ullrich-French, S., & Smith, A. L. (2006). Perceptions of relationships with parents and peers in youth sport: Independent and combined prediction of motivational outcome. *Psychology of Sport and Exercise, 7*, 193–214.

Ulusoy, Y., & Duy, B. (2013). Effectiveness of a psycho-education program on learned helplessness and irrational beliefs. *Educational Sciences: Theory & Practice, 13*, 1440–1446. doi:10.12738/estp.2013.3.1469

Umaña-Taylor, A. J., & Alfaro, E. C. (2006). Ethnic identity among U.S. Latino adolescents: Theory, measurement, and implications for well-being. In K. Freeark & W. S. Davidson II (Vol. Eds.), & H. E. Fitzgerald, R. Zucker, & K. Freeark (Eds. in Chief), *The Crisis in Youth Mental Health: Vol. 3: Critical issues and effective programs* (pp. 195–211). Westport, CT: Praeger.

United Nations. (1990). *Conventions on the Rights of the Child*. Retrieved July 24, 2018 from https://www.ohchr.org/EN/ProfessionalInterest/Pages/CRC.aspx.

Upegui-Hernández, D. (2012). "Because I'm neither Gringa nor Latina": Conceptualizing multiple identities within transnational social fields. In R. Josselson, M. Harway (Eds.), *Navigating multiple identities: Race, gender, culture, nationality, and roles* (pp. 227–253). New York, NY: Oxford.

Urban, J., Carlson, E., Egeland, B., & Sroufe, L. A. (1991). Patterns of individual adaptation across childhood. *Development and Psychopathology, 3*, 445–460.

Urdan, T. (1997). Achievement goal theory: Past results, future directions. In M. L. Maehr & P. R. Pintrich (Eds.), *Advances in motivation and achievement* (Vol. 10, pp. 99–141). Greenwich, CT: JAI Press.

Urdan, T. (2004). Predicators of academic self-handicapping and achievement: Examining achievement goals, classroom goal structures, and culture. *Journal of Educational Psychology, 96*, 251–264.

Urdan, T. (2012). Factors affecting the motivation and achievement of immigrant students. In K. R. Harris, S. Graham, T. Urdan, S. Graham, J. M. Royer, & M. Zeidner (Eds.), *APA Educational Psychology Handbook, Vol. 2. Individual differences and cultural and contextual factors* (pp. 293–313). Washington, DC: American Psychological Association. doi:10.1037/13274-012

Urdan, T., Ryan, A. M., Anderman, E. M., & Gheen, M. H. (2002). Goals, goal structures, and avoidance behaviors. In C. Midgley (Ed.), *Goals, goal structures, and patterns of adaptive learning* (pp. 55–83). Mahwah, NJ: Erlbaum.

Ursache, A., & Raver, C. (2014). Trait and state anxiety: Relations to executive functioning in an at-risk sample. *Cognition & Emotion, 28*, 845–855. doi:10.1080/02699931.2013.855173

Ursache, A., Blair, C., & Raver, C. (2012). The promotion of self-regulation as a means of enhancing school readiness and early achievement in children at risk for school failure. *Child Development Perspectives, 6*, 122–128. doi:10.1111/j.1750-8606.2011.00209.x

Usinger, J., & Smith, M. (2010). Career development in the context of self-construction during adolescence. *Journal of Vocational Behavior, 76*, 580–591. doi:10.1016/j.jvb.2010.01.010

Uvaas, T. (2010). *Improving transitions to high school: Examining the effectiveness of a school connectedness program* (ProQuest Information & Learning, 3344249).

Vacca, D. M. (2001). Confronting the puzzle of nonverbal learning disabilities. *Educational Leadership, 59*(3), 26–31.

Valdés, G., Bunch, G., Snow, C., & Lee, C. (with Matos, L.). (2005). Enhancing the development of students' language(s). In L. Darling-Hammond & J. Bransford (Eds.), *Preparing teachers for a changing world: What teachers should learn and be able to do* (pp. 126–168). San Francisco, CA: Jossey-Bass/Wiley.

Valiente, C., Lemery-Chalfant, K., Swanson, J., & Reiser, M. (2008). Prediction of children's academic competence from their effortful control, relationships, and classroom participation. *Journal of Educational Psychology, 100*, 67–77.

Vallotton, C. D., & Ayoub, C. C. (2010). Symbols build communication and thought: The role of gestures and words in the development of engagement skills and social-emotional concepts during toddlerhood. *Social Development, 19*, 601–626. doi:10.1111/j.1467-9507.2009.00549.x

Van de Vondervoort, J. W., & Hamlin, J. K. (2018). The infantile roots of sociomoral evaluations. In K. Gray & J. Graham (Eds., *Atlas of moral psychology* (pp. 402–412)). New York, NY: Guilford Press.

van de Weijer-Bergsma, E., Langenberg, G., Brandsma, R., Oort, F. J., Bögels, S. M. (2014). The effectiveness of a school-based mindfulness training as a program to prevent stress in elementary school children. *Mindfulness, 5*, 238–248. http://dx.doi.org/10.1007/s12671-012-0171-9

van den Berg, M., Harskamp, E. G., & Suhre, C. M. (2016). Developing classroom formative assessment in Dutch primary mathematics education. *Educational Studies, 42*(4), 305–322. doi:10.1080/03055698.2016.1193475

van den Bos, E., van Duijvenvoorde, A. C. K., & Westenberg, P. M. (2016). Effects of adolescent sociocognitive development on the cortisol response to social evaluation. *Developmental Psychology, 52*, 1151–1163.

van den Broek, P., Bauer, P. J., & Bourg, T. (Eds.). (1997). *Developmental spans in event comprehension and representation: Bridging fictional and actual events.* Mahwah, NJ: Erlbaum.

van den Broek, P., Lynch, J. S., Naslund, J., Ievers-Landis, C. E., & Verduin, K. (2003). The development of comprehension of main ideas in narratives: Evidence from the selection of titles. *Journal of Educational Psychology, 95*, 707–718.

van den Heuvel, M. P., Stam, C. J., Kahn, R. S., & Hulshoff Pol, H. E. (2009). Efficiency of functional brain networks and intellectual performance. *Journal of Neuroscience, 29*, 7619–7624.

van der Schoot, M., Reijntjes, A., & Lieshout, E. (2012). How do children deal with inconsistencies in text? An eye fixation and self-paced reading study in good and poor reading comprehenders. *Reading & Writing, 25*, 1665–1690. doi:10.1007/s11145-011-9337-4

van der Ven, S. G., Boom, J., Kroesbergen, E. H., & Leseman, P. M. (2012). Microgenetic patterns of children's multiplication learning: Confirming the overlapping waves model by latent growth modeling. *Journal of Experimental Child Psychology, 113*(1), 1–19. doi:10.1016/j.jecp.2012.02.001

Van Dooren, W., De Bock, D., Hessels, A., Janssens, D., & Verschaffel, L. (2005). Not everything is proportional: Effects of age and problem type on propensities for overgeneralization. *Cognition and Instruction, 23*, 57–86.

van Hof-van Duin, J., & Mohn, G. (1986). The development of visual acuity in normal full-term and preterm infants. *Vision Research, 26*, 909–916.

Van Hulle, C. A., Moore, M. N., Lemery-Chalfant, K., Goldsmith, H. H., & Brooker, R. J. (2017). Infant stranger fear trajectories predict anxious behaviors and diurnal cortisol rhythm during childhood. *Development and Psychopathology, 29*, 1119–1130.http://dx.doi.org.unco.idm.oclc.org/10.1017/S0954579417000311

van Hulst, B. M., de Zeeuw, P., Bos, D. J., Rijks, Y., Neggers, S. F. W., & Durston, S. (2017). Children with ADHD symptoms show decreased activity in ventral striatum during the anticipation of reward, irrespective of ADHD diagnosis. *Journal of Child Psychology and Psychiatry, 58*, 206–214. doi:10.1111/jcpp.12643

van IJzendoorn, M. H., Goldberg, S., Kroonenberg, P. M., & Frenkel, O. J. (1992). The relative effects of maternal and child problems on the quality of attachment: A meta-analysis of attachment in clinical samples. *Child Development, 63*, 840–858.

van Kraayenoord, C. E., & Paris, S. G. (1997). Children's self-appraisal of their work samples and academic progress. *Elementary School Journal, 97*, 523–537.

Van Leijenhorst, L., & Crone, E. A. (2010). Paradoxes in adolescent risk taking. In P. D. Zelazo, M. Chandler, & E. Crone (Eds.), *Developmental social cognitive neuroscience. The Jean Piaget symposium series* (pp. 209–225). New York, NY: Psychology Press.

Van Lissa, C. J., Hawk, S. T., & Meeus, W. H. J. (2017). The effects of affective and cognitive empathy on adolescents' behavior and outcomes in conflicts with mothers. *Journal of Experimental Child Psychology, 158*, 32–45. http://dx.doi.org.unco.idm.oclc.org/10.1016/j.jecp.2017.01.002

Van Ouytsel, J., Walrave, M., & Ponnet, K. (2014). How schools can help their students to strengthen their online reputations. *Clearing House, 87*, 180–185. doi:10.1080/00098655.2014.909380

van Soelen, I. C., Brouwer, R. M., van Leeuwen, M., Kahn, R. S., Pol, H., & Boomsma, D. I. (2011). Heritability of verbal and performance intelligence in a pediatric longitudinal sample. *Twin Research and Human Genetics, 14*, 119–128. doi:10.1375/twin.14.2.119

van Staden, A. (2013). An evaluation of an intervention using sign language and multi-sensory coding to support word learning and reading comprehension of deaf signing children. *Child Language Teaching & Therapy, 29*, 305–318. doi:10.1177/0265659013479961

van Tuijl, L. A., de Jong, P. J., Sportel, B., de Hullu, E., & Nauta, M. H. (2014). Implicit and explicit self-esteem and their reciprocal relationship with symptoms of depression and social anxiety: A longitudinal study in adolescents. *Journal of Behavior Therapy & Experimental Psychiatry, 45*(1), 113–121. doi:10.1016/j.jbtep.2013.09.007

VanderLaan, D. P., Blanchard, R., Wood, H., & Zucker, K. J. (2014). Birth order and sibling sex ratio of children and adolescents referred to a gender identity service. *PLoS ONE, 9*(3), 1–9. doi:10.1371/journal.pone.0090257

Vandermaas-Peeler, M., Nelson, J., Bumpass, C., & Sassine, B. (2009). Social contexts of development: Parent-child interactions during reading and play. *Journal of Early Childhood Literacy, 9*, 295–317.

Vanderwert, R. E., & Nelson, C. A. (2014). The use of near-infrared spectroscopy in the study of typical and atypical development. *NeuroImage, 85*(Pt. 1), 264–271. doi:10.1016/j.neuroimage.2013.10.009

Vansteenkiste, M., Lens, W., & Deci, E. L. (2006). Intrinsic versus extrinsic goal contents in self-determination theory: Another look at the quality of academic motivation. *Educational Psychologist, 41*, 19–31.

VanTassel-Baska, J., & Hubbard, G. F. (2016). Classroom-based strategies for advanced learners in rural settings. *Journal of Advanced Academics, 27*, 285–310. doi:10.1177/1932202X16657645

Vaughan, D., Cleary, B., & Murphy, D. (2014). Delivery outcomes for nulliparous women at the extremes of maternal age—a cohort study. *BJOG: An International Journal of Obstetrics & Gynaecology, 121*, 261–268. doi:10.1111/1471-0528.12311

Vaughan, M. D., & Rodriguez, E. M. (2013). The influence of Erik Erikson on positive psychology theory and research. In J. D. Sinnott (Ed.), *Positive psychology: Advances in understanding adult motivation* (pp. 231–245). New York, NY: Springer Science + Business Media. doi:10.1007/978-1-4614-7282-7_15

Vaughn, B. E., Egeland, B., Sroufe, L. A., & Waters, E. (1979). Individual differences in infant-mother attachment at twelve and eighteen months: Stability and change in families under stress. *Child Development, 50*, 971–975.

Vaughn, B. E., Kopp, C. B., & Krakow, J. B. (1984). The emergence and consolidation of self-control from eighteen to thirty months of age: Normative trends and individual differences. *Child Development, 55*, 990–1004.

Vaughn, B. E., Shin, N., Kim, M., Coppola, G., Krzysik, L., Santos, A. J., . . . Korth, B. (2009). Hierarchical models of social competence in preschool children: A multisite, multinational study. *Child Development, 80*, 1775–1796. doi:10.1111/j.1467-8624.2009.01367.x

Vedder-Weiss, D. (2016). Serendipitous science engagement: A family self-ethnography. *Journal of Research in Science Teaching*. Advance online publication. doi:10.1002/tea.21369

Veiga, G., de Leng, W., Cachucho, R., Ketelaar, L., Kok, J. N., Knobbe, A., . . . Rieffe, C. (2017). Social competence at the playground: Preschoolers during recess. *Infant and Child Development, 26*(1), 1–15. http://dx.doi.org.unco.idm.oclc.org/10.1002/icd.1957

Vella, S. A., Gardner, L. A., & Liddle, S. K. (2016). Coaching, positive youth development, and mental health. In N. L. Holt (Ed.), *Positive youth development through sport* (pp. 205–215). New York, NY: Routledge/Taylor & Francis Group

Venables, P. H., & Raine, A. (2016). The impact of malnutrition on intelligence at 3 and 11 years of age: The mediating role of temperament. *Developmental Psychology, 52*(2), 205–220. http://dx.doi.org.unco.idm.oclc.org/10.1037/dev0000046

Venta, A., Shmueli-Goetz, Y., & Sharp, C. (2014). Assessing attachment in adolescence: A psychometric study of the Child Attachment Interview. *Psychological Assessment, 26*(1), 238–255. doi:10.1037/a0034712

Venter, E., & Rambau, E. (2011). The effect of a latchkey situation on a child's educational success. *South African Journal of Education, 31*, 345–356.

Vereen, L. G., Hill, N. R., & Butler, S. (2013). The use of humor and storytelling with African American men: Innovative therapeutic strategies for success in counseling. *International Journal for the Advancement of Counselling, 35*(1), 57–63. doi:10.1007/s10447-012-9165-5

Vermeer, H. J., Boekaerts, M., & Seegers, G. (2000). Motivational and gender differences: Sixth-grade students' mathematical problem-solving behavior. *Journal of Educational Psychology, 92*, 308–315.

Véronneau, M., & Dishion, T. J. (2011). Middle school friendships and academic achievement in early adolescence: A longitudinal analysis. *The Journal of Early Adolescence, 31*(1), 99–124. doi:10.1177/0272431610384485

Vickery, J. (2014). The role of after-school digital media clubs in closing participation gaps and expanding social networks. *Equity & Excellence in Education, 47*(1), 78–95. doi:10.1080/10665684.2013.866870

Victor, E. (2012). Mental health and hooking up: A self-discrepancy perspective. *New School Psychology Bulletin, 9*(2), 24–34.

Villalobos Solís, M., Smetana, J. G., Tasopoulos-Chan, M. (2017). Evaluations of conflicts between Latino values and autonomy desires among Puerto Rican adolescents. *Child Development, 88*, 1581–1597. doi:10.1111/cdev.12687

Villegas, A. M., & Lucas, T. (2007). The culturally responsive teacher. *Educational Leadership, 64*(6), 28–33.

Vlachou, A., Eleftheriadou, D., & Metallidou, P. (2014). Do learning difficulties differentiate elementary teachers' attributional patterns for students' academic failure? A comparison between Greek regular and special education teachers. *European Journal of Special Needs Education, 29*(1), 1–15. doi:10.1080/08856257.2013.830440

Vohr, B., Topol, D., Watson, V., St Pierre, L., & Tucker, R. (2014). The importance of language in the home for school-age children with permanent hearing loss. *Acta Paediatrica, 103*(1), 62–69. doi:10.1111/apa.12441

Volker, M. A., Lopata, C., & Cook-Cottone, C. (2006). Assessment of children with intellectual giftedness and reading disabilities. *Psychology in the Schools, 43*, 855–869.

Volling, B. L. (2001). Early attachment relationships as predictors of preschool children's emotion regulation with a distressed sibling. *Early Education and Development, 12*, 185–207.

Vollmer, T. R., & Hackenberg, T. D. (2001). Reinforcement contingencies and social reinforcement: Some reciprocal relations between basic and applied research. *Journal of Applied Behavior Analysis, 34*, 241–253.

Volterra, A., Liaudet, N., & Savtchouk, I. (2014). Astrocyte Ca2+ signalling: an unexpected complexity. *Nature Reviews Neuroscience, 15*, 327–335. doi:10.1038/nrn3725

Volterra, V., Caselli, M. C., Capirci, O., & Pizzuto, E. (2005). Gesture and the emergence and development of language. In M. Tomasello & D. I. Slobin (Eds.), *Beyond nature–nurture: Essays in honor of Elizabeth Bates* (pp. 3–40). Mahwah, NH: Erlbaum.

Vollmer, K., & von Salisch, M. (2017). Three meta-analyses of children's emotion knowledge and their school success. *Learning & Individual Differences, 59*, 107–118. doi:10.1016/j.lindif.2017.08.006

von Károlyi, C. (2013). From Tesla to Tetris: Mental rotation, vocation, and gifted education. *Roeper Review, 35*, 231–240. doi:10.1080/02783193.2013.829547

Vorrath, H. (1985). *Positive peer culture*. New York, NY: Aldine de Gruyter.

Vorstius, C., Radach, R., Mayer, M. B., & Lonigan, C. J. (2013). Monitoring local comprehension monitoring in sentence reading. *School Psychology Review, 42*, 191–206.

Vosniadou, S. (1991). Conceptual development in astronomy. In S. M. Glynn, R. H. Yeany, & B. K. Britton (Eds.), *The psychology of learning science* (pp. 149–177). Hillsdale, NJ: Erlbaum.

Vosniadou, S. (2009). Science education for young children: A conceptual-change point of view. In O. A. Barbarin & B. H. Wasik (Eds.), *Handbook of child development and early education: Research to practice* (pp. 544–557). New York, NY: Guilford Press.

Vosniadou, S. (2009). Science education for young children: A conceptual-change point of view. In O. A. Barbarin & B. H. Wasik (Eds.), *Handbook of child development and early education: Research to practice* (pp. 544–557). New York, NY: Guilford Press.

Vosniadou, S., & Brewer, W. F. (1992). Mental models of the earth: A study of conceptual change in childhood. *Cognitive Psychology, 24*, 535–585. doi:10.1016/0010-0285(92)90018-W

Vosniadou, S., & Mason, L. (2012). Conceptual change induced by instruction: A complex interplay of multiple factors. In K. R. Harris, S. Graham, T. Urdan, S. Graham, J. M. Royer, & M. Zeidner (Eds.), *APA Educational Psychology Handbook, Vol. 2. Individual differences and cultural and contextual factors* (pp. 221–246). Washington, DC: American Psychological Association. doi:10.1037/13274-009

Vossekuil, B., Fein, R., Reddy, M., Borum, R., & Modzeleski, W. (2004). The Final Report and Findings of the Safe School Initiative: Implications for the Prevention of School Attacks in the United States. U.S. Department of Education, Office of Elementary and Secondary Education, Safe and Drug-Free Schools Program and U.S. than Kohlberg proposed vice, National Threat Assessment Center, Washington, D.C., 2002. Retrieved August 9, 2018 from https://www2.ed.gov/admins/lead/safety/preventingattacksreport.pdf

Voyer, A.-P., Tessier, R., & Nadeau, L. (2017). Sociometric status and the attribution of intentions in a sample of adolescents with cerebral palsy. *Disability and Rehabilitation: An International, Multidisciplinary Journal, 39*, 477–482. http://dx.doi.org.unco.idm.oclc.org/10.3109/09638288.2016.1147618

Vozzola, E. C. (2014). *Moral development: Theory and applications*. New York, NY: Routledge/Taylor & Francis Group.

Vrijsen, J. N., Becker, E. S., Arias-Vásquez, A., van Dijk, M. K., Speckens, A., & Oostrom, I. (2014). What is the contribution of different cognitive biases and stressful childhood events to the presence and number of previous depressive episodes? *Psychiatry Research, 217*, 134–142. doi:10.1016/j.psychres.2014.02.033

Vu, J. A. (2015). Children's representations of relationships with mothers, teachers, and friends, and associations with social competence. *Early Child Development and Care, 185*, 1695–1713. http://dx.doi.org.unco.idm.oclc.org/10.1080/03004430.2015.1022538

Vugs, B. B., Hendriks, M., Cuperus, J., Knoors, H., & Verhoeven, L. (2017). Developmental associations between working memory and language in children with specific language impairment: a longitudinal study. *Journal of Speech, Language & Hearing Research, 60*, 3284–3294. doi:10.1044/2017_JSLHR-L-17-0042

Vuksanovic, J., & Bjekic, J. (2013). Developmental relationship between language and joint attention in late talkers. *Research in Developmental Disabilities, 34*, 2360–2368. doi:10.1016/j.ridd.2013.04.017

Vygotsky, L. S. (1962). *Thought and language* (E. Haufmann & G. Vakar, Eds. and Trans.). Cambridge, MA: MIT Press.

Vygotsky, L. S. (1966). [Imaginary] play and its role in the mental development of the child. *Soviet Psychology, 5*(3), 6–18. (Original work published 1931)

Vygotsky, L. S. (1978). *Mind in society: The development of higher psychological processes* (M. Cole, V. John-Steiner, S. Scribner, & E. Souberman, Eds.). Cambridge, MA: Harvard University Press.

Vygotsky, L. S. (1986). *Thought and language* (rev. ed.; A. Kozulin, Ed. and Trans.). Cambridge, MA: MIT Press. (Original work published 1934)

Vygotsky, L. S. (1987a). The problem and the method of investigation. In R. W. Rieber & A. S. Carton (Eds.), *Collected Works of L. S. Vygotsky: Vol. 1. Problems of general psychology* (pp. 167–241). New York, NY: Plenum Press.

Vygotsky, L. S. (1987b). *The Collected Works of L.S. Vygotsky: Vol 2. The fundamentals of defectology* (R. W. Rieber and A. S. Carton, Eds., & N. Minick, Trans.). New York, NY: Plenum Press.

Vygotsky, L. S. (1997a). Analysis of higher mental functions. In R. W. Rieber (Ed.), *Collected Works of L. S. Vygotsky: Vol. 4. The history of the development of higher mental functions* (pp. 65–82). New York, NY: Plenum Press.

Vygotsky, L. S. (1997b). *Educational psychology*. Boca Raton, FL: St. Lucie Press.

Vygotsky, L. S. (1997c). The development of mnemonic and mnemotechnical functions. In R. W. Rieber (Ed.), *Collected Works of L. S. Vygotsky: Vol. 4. The history of the development of higher mental functions* (pp. 179–190). New York, NY: Plenum (Originally published 1982–1984).

Vygotsky, L. S. (1997d). The historical meaning of the crisis in psychology: A methodological investigation. In R. W. Rieber & J. Wollock (Eds.), *Collected Works of L. S. Vygotsky: Vol. 3. Problem of the theory and history of psychology* (pp. 233–343). New York, NY: Plenum Press.

Vygotsky, L. S. (1997e). Research method. In R. W. Rieber (Ed.), *Collected Works of L. S. Vygotsky: Vol. 4. The history of the development of higher mental functions* (pp. 27–63). New York, NY: Plenum. (Originally published 1982–1984)

Vygotsky, L. S. (1997f). Genesis of higher mental functions. In R. W. Rieber (Ed.), *Collected Works of L. S. Vygotsky: Vol. 4. The history of the development of higher mental functions* (pp. 97–119). New York, NY: Plenum Press.

Wagener, U. (2013). Young children's self-regulated learning: A reflection on Pintrich's model from a microanalytic perspective. *Journal of Cognitive Education and Psychology, 12*, 306–322. doi:10.1891/1945-8959.12.3.306

Wagley, C. (1977). *Welcome of tears: The Tapirapé Indians of central Brazil*. New York, NY: Oxford University Press.

Wagner, L., Greene-Havas, M., & Gillespie, R. (2010). Development in children's comprehension of linguistic register. *Child Development, 81*, 1678–1686. doi:10.1111/j.1467-8624.2010.01502.x

Wagner, S., Forer, B., Cepeda, I., Goelman, H., Maggi, S., D'angiulli, A., . . . Grunau, R. E. (2013). Perceived stress and Canadian early childcare educators. *Child & Youth Care Forum, 42*(1), 53–70. doi:10.1007/s10566-012-9187-5

Wahlsten, D., & Gottlieb, G. (1997). The invalid separation of effects of nature and nurture: Lessons from animal experimentation. In R. J. Sternberg & E. L. Grigorenko (Eds.), *Intelligence, heredity, and environment* (pp. 163–192). Cambridge, England: Cambridge University Press.

Wainryb, C. (2006). Moral development in culture: Diversity, tolerance, and justice. In M. Killen & J. G. Smetana (Eds.), *Handbook of moral development* (pp. 211–240). Mahwah, NJ: Erlbaum.

Waisbren, S. E., & Antshel, K. M. (2013). Phenylketonuria. In I. Baron & C. Rey-Casserly (Eds.), *Pediatric neuropsychology: Medical advances and lifespan outcomes* (pp. 219–236). New York, NY: Oxford University Press.

Wakeel, F., Wisk, L. E., Gee, R., Chao, S. M., & Witt, W. P. (2013). The balance between stress and personal capital during pregnancy and the relationship with adverse obstetric outcomes: Findings from the 2007 Los Angeles Mommy and Baby (LAMB) study. *Archives of Women's Mental Health, 16*(6), 435-451. http://dx.doi.org.unco.idm.oclc.org/10.1007/s00737-013-0367-6

Walker, C. M., & Lombrozo, T. (2016). Explaining the moral of the story. *Cognition*. Advance online publication. doi:10.1016/j.cognition.2016.11.007

Walker, C. M., Bridgers, S., & Gopnik, A. (2016). The early emergence and puzzling decline of relational reasoning: Effects of knowledge and search on inferring abstract concepts. *Cognition, 156*, 30–40. doi:10.1016/j.cognition.2016.07.008

Walker, C. M., Lombrozo, T., Williams, J. J., Rafferty, A. N., & Gopnik, A. (2017). Explaining constrains causal learning in childhood. *Child Development, 88*(1), 229–246. doi:10.1111/cdev.12590

Walker, E. A., McGregor, K. K., Bacon, S., & Tobey, E. (2013). Word learning processes in children with cochlear implants. *Journal of Speech, Language & Hearing Research, 56*, 375–387. doi:10.1044/1092-4388(2012/11-0343)

Walker, H. M., Horner, R. H., Sugai, G., Bullis, M., Sprague, J. R., Bicker, D., & Kaufman, M. J. (1996). Integrated approaches to preventing antisocial behavior patterns among school-age children and youth. *Journal of Emotional and Behavioral Disorders, 4*, 194–209.

Walker, L. J. (1991). Sex differences in moral reasoning. In W. M. Kurtines & J. L. Gewirtz (Eds.), *Handbook of Moral Behavior and Development: Vol. 2. Research* (pp. 333–364). Hillsdale, NJ: Erlbaum.

Walker, L. J. (1995). Sexism in Kohlberg's moral psychology? In W. M. Kurtines & J. L. Gewirtz (Eds.), *Moral development: An introduction (pp. 83–107)*. Boston, MA: Allyn & Bacon.

Walker, L. J. (2006). Gender and morality. In M. Killen & J. G. Smetana (Eds.), *Handbook of moral development* (pp. 93–115). Mahwah, NJ: Erlbaum.

Walker, L. J., & Reimer, K. S. (2006). The relationship between moral and spiritual development. In E. C. Roehlkepartain, P. E. King, L. Wagener, & P. L. Benson (Eds.), *The handbook of spiritual development in childhood and adolescence* (pp. 224–238). Thousand Oaks, CA: Sage.

Walker, S. (2009). Sociometric stability and the behavioral correlates of peer acceptance in early childhood. *The Journal of Genetic Psychology: Research and Theory on Human Development, 170*, 339–358. doi:10.1080/00221320903218364

Walker, S. P., Wachs, T. D., Gardner, J. M., Lozoff, B., Wasserman, G. A., Pollitt, . . . International Development Steering Group. (2007). Child development: Risks factors for adverse outcomes in developing countries. *Lancet, 369*(9556), 145–157.

Walkley, M., & Cox, T. L. (2013). Building trauma-informed schools and communities. *Children & Schools, 35*, 123–126.

Wallace, N. E. (2006). *The kindness quilt*. New York, NY: Marshall Cavendish.

Wallach, G. P., & Ocampo, A. (2017). Comprehending comprehension: Selected possibilities for clinical practice within a multidimensional model. *Language, Speech, and Hearing Services in Schools, 48*, 98–103. http://dx.doi.org.unco.idm.oclc.org/10.1044/2017_LSHSS-16-0035

Wallerstein, J. S., & Kelly, J. B. (1980). *Surviving the break-up: How children and parents cope with divorce*. New York, NY: Basic Books.

Wallerstein, J., & Lewis, J. M. (2007). Sibling outcomes and disparate parenting and stepparenting after divorce: Report from a 10-year longitudinal study. *Psychoanalytic Psychology, 24*(3), 445–458.

Wallingford, J., Niswander, L., Shaw, G., & Finnell, R. (2013). The continuing challenge of understanding, preventing, and treating neural tube defects. *Science, 339*(6123), 1047. doi:10.1002/bdra.20676

Walters, G. C., & Grusec, J. E. (1977). *Punishment*. San Francisco, CA: Freeman.

Wang, D., & Fletcher, A. C. (2017). The role of interactions with teachers and conflict with friends in shaping school adjustment. *Social Development, 26*, 545–559. http://dx.doi.org.unco.idm.oclc.org/10.1111/sode.12218

Wang, H., & Olson, N. (2009). *A journey to unlearn and learn in multicultural education*. New York, NY: Peter Lang.

Wang, J., & Lin, E. (2005). Comparative studies on U.S. and Chinese mathematics learning and the implications for standards-based mathematics teaching reform. *Educational Researcher, 34*(5), 3–13.

Wang, M., & Eccles, J. (2013). School context, achievement motivation, and academic engagement: A longitudinal study of school engagement using a multidimensional perspective. *Learning & Instruction, 28,* 12–23. doi:10.1016/j.learninstruc.2013.04.002

Wang, P. P., & Baron, M. A. (1997). Language and communication: Development and disorders. In M. L. Batshaw (Ed.), *Children with disabilities* (4th ed.). Baltimore, MD: Paul H. Brookes.

Wang, Q. (2006). Culture and the development of self-knowledge. *Current Directions in Psychological Science, 15,* 182–187.

Wang, Q. (2013). *The autobiographical self in time and culture.* New York, NY: Oxford University Press. doi:10.1093/acprof:oso/9780199737833.001.0001

Wang, Q., & Pomerantz, E. M. (2009). The motivational landscape of early adolescence in the United States and China: A longitudinal investigation. *Child Development, 80,* 1272–1287.

Wang, T.-H. (2010). Web-based dynamic assessment: Taking assessment as teaching and learning strategy for improving students' e-learning effectiveness. *Computers and Education, 5,* 1157–1166.

Wang, Y., & Lim, H. (2012). The global childhood obesity epidemic and the association between socio-economic status and childhood obesity. *International Review of Psychiatry, 24,* 176–188. doi:10.3109/09540261.2012.688195

Wang, Z., & Deater-Deckard, K. (2013). Resilience in gene–environment transactions. In S. Goldstein & R. B. Brooks (Eds.), *Handbook of resilience in children* (2nd ed., pp. 57–72). New York, NY: Springer Science+Business Media. doi:10.1007/978-1-4614-3661-4_4

Ward, B. A. (2017). Pregnancy-related sleep disturbances and sleep disorders. In H. P. Attarian (Ed.), Current clinical neurology. *Clinical handbook of insomnia* (pp. 159-180). Totowa, NJ, US: Humana Press. http://dx.doi.org.unco.idm.oclc.org/10.1007/978-3-319-41400-3_9

Ward, R. A., & Spitze, G. (1998). Sandwiched marriages: The implications of child and parent relations for marital quality in midlife. *Social Forces, 77,* 647–666.

Ward, S., & Parker, M. (2013). The voice of youth: atmosphere in positive youth development program. *Physical Education & Sport Pedagogy, 18,* 534–548. doi:10.1080/17408989.2012.726974

Ward, T. C. S., & Balfour, G. M. (2016). Infant safe sleep interventions, 1990–2015: A review. *Journal of Community Health: The Publication for Health Promotion and Disease Prevention, 41*(1), 180–196. doi:10.1007/s10900-015-0060-y

Ward, T., & Durrant, R. (2011). Evolutionary psychology and the rehabilitation of offenders: Constraints and consequences. *Aggression & Violent Behavior,* 16(5), 444-452. doi:10.1016/j.avb.2011.02.011

Ware, E. A. (2017). Individual and developmental differences in preschoolers' categorization biases and vocabulary across tasks. *Journal of Experimental Child Psychology, 153,* 35–56. doi:10.1016/j.jecp.2016.08.009

Warton, P. M., & Goodnow, J. J. (1991). The nature of responsibility: Children's understanding of "your job." *Child Development, 62,* 156–165.

Wasik, B. A., & Bond, M. A. (2001). Beyond the pages of a book: Interactive book reading and language development in preschool classrooms. *Journal of Educational Psychology, 93,* 243–250.

Wasik, B. A., Karweit, N., Burns, L., & Brodsky, E. (1998, April). *Once upon a time: The role of rereading and retelling in storybook reading.* Paper presented at the annual meeting of the American Educational Research Association, San Diego, CA.

Wasserberg, M. J. (2014). Stereotype threat effects on African American children in an urban elementary school. *Journal of Experimental Education, 82,* 502–517. doi:10.1080/00220973.2013.876224

Wasserberg, M. J., & Rottman, A. (2016). Urban High School Students' Perspectives on Test-Centered Curriculum. *American Secondary Education, 44*(3), 56–71.

Water Educational Training Science Project. (2010). *Wet science lesson #6: There is acid in my rain!* Retrieved from http://www.cloudnet.com/~edrbsass/edsci.htm#wetlands

Waterhouse, L. (2006). Multiple intelligences, the Mozart Effect, and emotional intelligence: A critical review. *Educational Psychologist, 41,* 207–225. doi:10.1207/s15326985ep4104_1

Waterhouse, L., & Gillberg, C. (2014). Why autism must be taken apart. *Journal of Autism & Developmental Disorders, 44,* 1788–1792. doi:10.1007/s10803-013-2030-5

Waters, E., Merrick, S., Treboux, D., Crowell, J., & Albersheim, L. (2000). Attachment security in infancy and early adulthood: A twenty-year longitudinal study. *Child Development, 71,* 684–689.

Waters, H. S. (1982). Memory development in adolescence: Relationships between metamemory, strategy use, and performance. *Journal of Experimental Child Psychology, 33,* 183–195.

Waters, H., & Waters, T. A. (2010). Bird experts: A study of child and adult knowledge utilization. In H. Waters & W. Schneider (Eds.), *Metacognition, strategy use, and instruction* (pp. 113–134). New York, NY: Guilford Press.

Waters, N. (2013). What goes up must come down! A primary care approach to preventing injuries amongst highflying cheerleaders. *Journal of the American Academy of Nurse Practitioners, 25*(2), 55–64. doi:10.1111/1745-7599.12000

Waters, S. F., Virmani, E. A., Thompson, R. A., Meyer, S., Raikes, H. A., & Jochem, R. (2010). Emotion regulation and attachment: Unpacking two constructs and their association. *Journal of Psychopathology and Behavioral Assessment, 32,* 37–47.

Watkins, M. W., & Beaujean, A. (2013). Bifactor structure of the Wechsler Preschool and Primary Scale of Intelligence—Fourth Edition. *School Psychology Quarterly.* doi:10.1037/spq0000038

Watson, M., & Battistich, V. (2006). Building and sustaining caring communities. In C. M. Evertson & C. S. Weinstein (Eds.), *Handbook of classroom management: Research, practice, and contemporary issues* (pp. 253–279). Mahwah, NJ: Erlbaum.

Waxman, S., Fu, X., Arunachalam, S., Leddon, E., Geraghty, K., & Song, H. (2013). Are nouns learned before verbs? Infants provide insight into a long-standing debate. *Child Development Perspectives, 7,* 155–159. doi:10.1111/cdep.12032

Way, N. (1998). *Everyday courage: The lives and stories of urban teenagers.* New York, NY: New York University Press.

Weaver-Hightower, M. (2003). The "boy turn" in research on gender and education. *Review of Educational Research, 73,* 471–498.

Weaver, J. M., & Schofield, T. J. (2015). Mediation and moderation of divorce effects on children's behavior problems. *Journal of Family Psychology, 29*(1), 39–48. doi:10.1037/fam0000043

Webb, N. M., & Farivar, S. (1994). Promoting helping behavior in cooperative small groups in middle school mathematics. *American Educational Research Journal, 31,* 369–395.

Webb, N. M., & Palincsar, A. S. (1996). Group processes in the classroom. In D. C. Berliner & R. C. Calfee (Eds.), *Handbook of educational psychology* (pp. 841–873). New York, NY: Macmillan.

Webb, T. L., Gallo, I. S., Miles, E., Gollwitzer, P. M., & Sheeran, P. (2012). Effective regulation of affect: An action control perspective on emotion regulation. *European Review of Social Psychology, 23,* 143–186. http://dx.doi.org.unco.idm.oclc.org/10.1080/10463283.2012.718134

Webber, J., Scheuermann, B., McCall, C., & Coleman, M. (1993). Research on self-monitoring as a behavior management technique in special education classrooms: A descriptive review. *Remedial and Special Education, 14*(2), 38–56.

Weber, S., Appel, M. A., & Kronberger, N. (2015). Stereotype threat and the cognitive performance of adolescent immigrants: The role of cultural identity strength. *Contemporary Educational Psychology, 42,* 71–81. doi:10.1016/j.cedpsych.2015.05.001

Wechsler, D. (2002). *Wechsler Preschool and Primary Scale of Intelligence–Third Edition.* San Antonio, TX: Psychological Corporation.

Wechsler, D. (2003). *Wechsler Intelligence Scale for Children* (4th ed.). San Antonio, TX: Psychological Corporation.

Wechsler, D. (2012). *Wechsler Preschool and Primary Scale of Intelligence—fourth edition technical manual and interpretive manual*. San Antonio, TX: Psychological Corporation.

Wechsler, D. (2014). *Wechsler Intelligence Scale for Children–Fifth Edition*. Bloomington, MN: Pearson.

Weeks, T. L., & Pasupathi, M. (2010). Autonomy, identity, and narrative construction with parents and friends. In K. C. McLean, & M. Pasupathi (Eds.), *Narrative development in adolescence: Creating the storied self. Advancing responsible adolescent development* (pp. 65–91). New York, NY: Springer Science/Business Media. doi:10.1007/978-0-387-89825-4_4

Weinberg, R. A. (1989). Intelligence and IQ: Landmark issues and great debates. *American Psychologist, 44*, 98–104.

Weiner, B. (1984). Principles for a theory of student motivation and their application within an attributional framework. In R. Ames & C. Ames (Eds.), *Research on Motivation in Education: Vol. 1. Student motivation (pp. 15–38)*. San Diego, CA: Academic Press.

Weiner, B. (1986). *An attributional theory of motivation and emotion*. New York, NY: Springer-Verlag.

Weiner, B. (2000). Intrapersonal and interpersonal theories of motivation from an attributional perspective. *Educational Psychology Review, 12*, 1–14.

Weiner, B. (2004). Attribution theory revisited: Transforming cultural plurality into theoretical unity. In D. M. McNerney & S. Van Etten (Eds.), *Big theories revisited* (pp. 13–29). Greenwich, CT: Information Age.

Weinert, S. (2009). Implicit and explicit modes of learning: Similarities and differences from a developmental perspective. *Linguistics, 47*, 241–271.

Weinstein, C. E., Ridley, D., & Dahl, T. (1988). Helping students develop strategies for effective learning. *Educational Leadership, 46*, 17–19.

Weinstein, J. J., Chohan, M. O., Slifstein, M., Kegeles, L. S., Moore, H., & Abi-Dargham, A. (2017). Pathway-specific dopamine abnormalities in schizophrenia. *Biological Psychiatry, 81*(1), 31–42. doi:10.1016/j.biopsych.2016.03.2104

Weinstein, R. S. (1993). Children's knowledge of differential treatment in school: Implications for motivation. In T. M. Tomlinson (Ed.), *Motivating students to learn: Overcoming barriers to high achievement* (pp. 197–224). Berkeley, CA: McCutchan.

Weinstein, R. S., Madison, S. M., & Kuklinski, M. R. (1995). Raising expectations in schooling: Obstacles and opportunities for change. *American Educational Research Journal, 32*, 121–159.

Weisberg, D., Hirsh-Pasek. K. & Golinkoff, R.M. (2013). Guided play: Where curricular goals meet a playful pedagogy. Mind, Brain and Education, 7, 2, 104–112.

Weisberg, D. S., Hirsh-Pasek, K., Golinkoff, R. M., Kittredge, A. K., & Klahr, D. (2016). Guided play: Principles and practices. *Current Directions in Psychological Science, 25*, 177–182. doi:10.1177/0963721416645512

Weisgram, E. S., Bigler, R. S., & Liben, L. S. (2010). Gender, values, and occupational interests among children, adolescents, and adults. *Child Development, 81*, 778–796. doi:10.1111/j.1467-8624.2010.01433.x

Weisleder, A., & Fernald, A. (2013). Talking to children matters: Early language experience strengthens processing and builds vocabulary. *Psychological Science, 24*, 2143–2152. doi:10.1177/0956797613488145

Weisner, T. S., & Gallimore, R. (1977). My brother's keeper: Child and sibling caregiving. *Current Anthropology, 18*, 169–190.

Weissbourd, R. (2011). The overpressured student. *Educational Leadership, 68*(5), 22–27.

Wellman, H. M. (1990). *The child's theory of mind*. Cambridge, MA: MIT Press.

Wellman, H. M., & Estes, D. (1986). Early understanding of mental entities: A reexamination of childhood realism. *Child Development, 57*, 910–923.

Wellman, H. M., & Hickling, A. K. (1994). The mind's "I": Children's conception of the mind as an active agent. *Child Development, 65*, 1564–1580.

Wellman, H. M., Fang, F., Liu, D., Zhu, L., & Zhu, G. (2006). Scaling of theory-of-mind understandings in Chinese children. *Psychological Science, 17*, 1075–1081.

Wellman, H. M., Phillips, A. T., & Rodriguez, T. (2000). Young children's understanding of perception, desire, and emotion. *Child Development, 71*, 895–912.

Welsh, M. C. (1991). Rule-guided behavior and self-monitoring on the tower of Hanoi disk-transfer task. *Cognitive Development, 4*, 59–76.

Welsh, M. G. (2011). Growing up in a same-sex parented family: The adolescent voice of experience. *Journal of GLBT Family Studies, 7*(1–2), 49–71. doi:10.1080/1550428X.2010.537241

Wen, M. (2008). Family structure and children's health and behavior. *Journal of Family Issues, 29*, 1492–1519.

Wentzel, K. R. (1999). Social-motivational processes and interpersonal relationships: Implications for understanding motivation at school. *Journal of Educational Psychology, 91*, 76–97.

Wentzel, K. R. (2000). What is it that I'm trying to achieve? Classroom goals from a content perspective. *Contemporary Educational Psychology, 25*, 105–115.

Wentzel, K. R. (2009). Peers and academic functioning at school. In K. H. Rubin, W. M. Bukowski, & B. Laursen (Eds.), *Handbook of peer interactions, relationships, and groups. Social, emotional, and personality development in context* (pp. 531–547). New York, NY: Guilford Press.

Wentzel, K. R. (2014). Prosocial behavior and peer relations in adolescence. In L. M. Padilla-Walker, G. Carlo (Eds.), *Prosocial development: A multidimensional approach* (pp. 178–200). New York, NY: Oxford University Press.

Wentzel, K. R., & Wigfield, A. (1998). Academic and social motivational influences on students' academic performance. *Educational Psychology Review, 10*, 155–175.

Werbner, P. (2009). The hidden lion: Tswapong girls' puberty rituals and the problem of history. *American Ethnologist, 36*, 441–458.

Werker, J. F., & Lalonde, C. E. (1988). Cross-language speech perception: Initial capabilities and developmental change. *Developmental Psychology, 24*, 672–683.

Werker, J. F., Maurer, D. M., & Yoshida, K. A. (2010). Perception. In M. H. Bornstein (Ed.), *Handbook of cultural developmental science* (pp. 89–125). New York, NY: Psychology Press.

Werner, E. E., & Smith, R. S. (2001). *Journeys from childhood to midlife: Risk, resilience, and recovery*. Ithaca, NY: Cornell University Press.

Wernholm, M., & Vigmo, S. (2015). Capturing children's knowledge-making dialogues in Minecraft. *International Journal of Research & Method in Education, 38*, 230–246. doi:10.1080/1743727X.2015.1033392

Wery, J., & Thomson, M. (2013). Motivational strategies to enhance effective learning in teaching struggling students. *Support for Learning, 28*(3), 103–108. doi:10.1111/1467-9604.12027

Wesley, M. J., & Bickel, W. K. (2013). Remember the future ii: Meta-analyses and functional overlap of working memory and delay discounting. *Biological Psychiatry, 75*, 435–448. doi:10.1016/j.biopsych.2013.08.008

West, A. E., & Weinstein, S. M. (2012). Bipolar disorder: School-based cognitive-behavioral interventions. In R. B. Mennuti, R. W. Christner, & A. Freeman (Eds.), *Cognitive-behavioral interventions in educational settings: A handbook for practice* (2nd ed., pp. 239–274). New York, NY: Routledge/Taylor & Francis Group.

Wheeler, S. (2014). Organized activities, educational activities and family activities: How do they feature in the middle-class family's weekend? *Leisure Studies, 33*, 215–232. doi:10.1080/02614367.2013.833972

Wheeler, S. R., & Austin, J. K. (2001). The impact of early pregnancy loss. *MCN: The American Journal of Maternal/Child Nursing, 26*, 154–159. doi:10.1097/00005721-200105000-00014

White, B. A., Jarrett, M. A., & Ollendick, T. H. (2013). Self-regulation deficits explain the link between reactive aggression and internalizing and externalizing behavior problems in children. *Journal of Psychopathology and Behavioral Assessment*, *35*(1), 1–9. doi:10.1007/s10862-012-9310-9

White, B. Y., & Frederiksen, J. R. (1998). Inquiry, modeling, and metacognition: Making science accessible to all students. *Cognition and Instruction*, *16*, 3–118.

White, K. M. (2016). "My teacher helps me": Assessing teacher–child relationships from the child's perspective. *Journal of Research in Childhood Education*, *30*(1), 29–41. doi:10.1080/02568543.2015.1105333

White, L. l., Alexander, A., & Greenfield, D. B. (2017). The relationship between executive functioning and language: Examining vocabulary, syntax, and language learning in preschoolers attending Head Start. *Journal of Experimental Child Psychology*, *164*, 16–31. doi:10.1016/j.jecp.2017.06.010

White, R. (1959). Motivation reconsidered: The concept of competence. *Psychological Review*, *66*, 297–333.

White, S. F., VanTieghem, M., Brislin, S. J., Sypher, I., Sinclair, S., Pine, D. S., . . . Blair, R. J. R. (2016). Neural correlates of the propensity for retaliatory behavior in youths with disruptive behavior disorders. *The American Journal of Psychiatry*, *173*, 282–290. http://dx.doi.org.unco.idm.oclc.org/10.1176/appi.ajp.2015.15020250

White, S. H. (1994). G. Stanley Hall: From philosophy to developmental psychology. In R. D. Parke, P. A. Ornstein, J. R. Rieser, & C. Zahn-Waxler, *A century of developmental psychology* (pp. 103–125). Washington, DC: American Psychological Association.

White, S., Brislin, S., Sinclair, S., Fowler, K., Pope, K., & Blair, R. (2013). The relationship between large cavum septum pellucidum and antisocial behavior, callous-unemotional traits and psychopathy in adolescents. *Journal of Child Psychology & Psychiatry*, *54*, 575–581.

Whitehead, D., & Murphy, F. (2014). Mind Your Language. *Journal of Adolescent & Adult Literacy*, *57*(6), 492–502. doi:10.1002/jaal.272

Whitehurst, G. J., Arnold, D. S., Epstein, J. N., Angell, A. L., Smith, M., & Fischel, J. E. (1994). A picture book reading intervention in day care and home for children from low-income families. *Developmental Psychology*, *30*, 679–689.

Whiting, B. B., & Edwards, C. P. (1988). *Children of different worlds*. Cambridge, MA: Harvard University Press.

Whiting, B. B., & Whiting, J. W. M. (1975). *Children of six cultures: A psycho-cultural analysis*. Cambridge, MA: Harvard University Press.

Whitley, B. E., Jr., & Frieze, I. H. (1985). Children's causal attributions for success and failure in achievement settings: A meta-analysis. *Journal of Educational Psychology*, *77*, 608–616.

Whitney, R. V., & Whitney, R. V. (2008). *Nonverbal learning disorder: Understanding and coping with NLD and Asperger's—What parents and teachers need to know*. New York, NY: Penguin.

Whyte, K. L., & Karabon, A. (2016). Transforming teacher–family relationships: shifting roles and perceptions of home visits through the Funds of Knowledge approach. *Early Years: Journal of International Research & Development*, *36*, 207–221. doi:10.1080/09575146.2016.1139546

Wieder, S., Greenspan, S., & Kalmanson, B. (2008). Autism assessment and intervention: The developmental individual-difference, relationship-based DIR®/Floortime™ model. *Zero to Three*, *28*(4), 31–37.

Wiesel, T. N., & Hubel, D. H. (1965). Comparison of the effects of unilateral and bilateral eye closure on cortical unit responses in kittens. *Journal of Neurophysiology*, *28*, 1029–1040.

Wigfield, A. (1994). Expectancy-value theory of achievement motivation: A developmental perspective. *Educational Psychology Review*, *6*, 49–78.

Wigfield, A., & Eccles, J. (2000). Expectancy-value theory of achievement motivation. *Contemporary Educational Psychology*, *25*, 68–81.

Wigfield, A., Byrnes, J. P., & Eccles, J. S. (2006). Development during early and middle adolescence. In P. A. Alexander & P. H. Winne (Eds.), *Handbook of educational psychology* (2nd ed., pp. 87–113). Mahwah, NJ: Erlbaum.

Wigfield, A., Eccles, J. S., & Pintrich, P. R. (1996). Development between the ages of 11 and 25. In D. C. Berliner & R. C. Calfee (Eds.), *Handbook of educational psychology* (pp. 148–185) . New York, NY: Macmillan.

Wigfield, A., Eccles, J., Mac Iver, D., Reuman, D., & Midgley, C. (1991). Transitions at early adolescence: Changes in children's domain-specific self-perceptions and general self-esteem across the transition to junior high school. *Developmental Psychology*, *27*, 552–565.

Wigfield, A., Tonks, S., & Eccles, J. S. (2004). Expectancy value theory in cross-cultural perspective. In D. M. McNerney & S. Van Etten (Eds.), *Big theories revisited* (pp. 165–198). Greenwich, CT: Information Age.

Wiig, E. H., Gilbert, M. F., & Christian, S. H. (1978). Developmental sequences in perception and interpretation of ambiguous sentences. *Perceptual and Motor Skills*, *46*, 959–969.

Wilhelm, J., Jackson, C., Sullivan, A., & Wilhelm, R. (2013). Examining differences between preteen groups' spatial-scientific understandings: A quasi-experimental study. *Journal of Educational Research*, *106*, 337–351. doi:10.1080/00220671.2012.753

Will, G.-J., Crone, E. A., Lier, P. A. C., & Güroğlu, B. (2018). Longitudinal links between childhood peer acceptance and the neural correlates of sharing. *Developmental Science*, *21*(1), 1–13. http://dx.doi.org.unco.idm.oclc.org/10.1111/desc.12489

Willard, N. E. (2007). *Cyberbullying and cyberthreats: Responding to the challenge of online social aggression, threats, and distress*. Champaign, IL: Research Press.

Willats, J. (1995). An information-processing approach to drawing development. In C. Lange-Kuttner & G. V. Thomas (Eds.), *Drawing and looking: Theoretical approaches to pictorial representation in children* (pp. 27–43). New York, NY: Harvester Wheatsheaf.

Willatts, P. (1990). Development of problem solving strategies in infancy. In D. F. Bjorklund (Ed.), *Children's strategies* (pp. 23–66). Hillsdale, NJ: Erlbaum.

Willcock, E., Imuta, K., & Hayne, H. (2011). Children's human figure drawings do not measure intellectual ability. *Journal of Experimental Child Psychology*, *110*, 444–452. doi:10.1016/j.jecp.2011.04.013

Willemse, T. M., Vloeberghs, L., de Bruïne, E. J., & Van Eynde, S. (2016). Preparing teachers for family–school partnerships: A Dutch and Belgian perspective. *Teaching Education*, *27*(2), 212-228. doi:10.1080/10476210.2015.1069264

Williams, A. (2012). Boys into books. *IS: International School*, *14*(3), 17–18.

Williams, H. L., & Conway, M. A. (2009). Networks of autobiographical memories. In P. Boyer & J. V. Wertsch (Eds.), *Memory in mind and culture* (pp. 33–61). New York, NY: Cambridge University Press.

Williams, J. L., & Smalls-Glover, C. (2014). Content and attributions of caregiver racial socialization as predictors of African American adolescents' private racial regard. *Journal of Black Psychology*, *40*, 69–80. doi:10.1177/0095798412471681

Williams, J., & Williamson, K. (1992). "I wouldn't want to shoot nobody": The out-of-school curriculum as described by urban students. *Action in Teacher Education*, *14*(2), 9–15.

Williams, K. E., Ciarrochi, J., & Heaven, P. L. (2012). Inflexible parents, inflexible kids. A 6-year longitudinal study of parenting style and the development of psychological flexibility in adolescents. *Journal of Youth and Adolescence*, *41*, 1053–1066. doi:10.1007/s10964-012-9744-0

Williams, K. K., & Berthelsen, D. D. (2017). The development of prosocial behaviour in early childhood: Contributions of early parenting and self-regulation. *International Journal of Early Childhood, 49*(1), 73–94. doi:10.1007/s13158-017-0185-5

Williams, K. M. (2001). What derails peer mediation? In J. N. Burstyn, G. Bender, R. Casella, H. W. Gordon, D. P. Guerra, K. V. Luschen, Stevens, R., & Williams, K. M. (Eds.), *Preventing violence in schools: A challenge to American democracy* (pp. 199–208). Mahwah, NJ: Erlbaum.

Williams, R. L. (2013). Overview of the Flynn effect. *Intelligence, 41*, 753–764. doi:10.1016/j.intell.2013.04.010

Williams, R. W., & Herrup, K. (1998). The control of neuron number. *Annual Review of Neuroscience, 11*, 423–453.

Williams, T. T., & Sánchez, B. (2013). Identifying and decreasing barriers to parent involvement for inner-city parents. *Youth & Society, 45*(1), 54–74. doi:10.1177/0044118X11409066

Williams, T. T., Mance, G., Caldwell, C., & Antonucci, T. C. (2012). The role of prenatal stress and maternal emotional support on the postpartum depressive symptoms of African American adolescent fathers. *Journal of Black Psychology, 38*, 455–470. doi:10.1177/0095798411433842

Williford, A. P., Whittaker, J., Vitiello, V. E., & Downer, J. T. (2013). Children's engagement within the preschool classroom and their development of self-regulation. *Early Education and Development, 24*, 162–187. doi:10.1080/10409289.2011.628270

Willingham, D. (2012). Why does family wealth affect learning? *American Educator, 36*(1), 33–39.

Wilson, B. (1997). Types of child art and alternative developmental accounts: Interpreting the interpreters. *Human Development, 40*, 155–168.

Wilson, B. J. (2008). Media and children's aggression, fear, and altruism. *Future of Children, 18*(1), 87–118.

Wilson, B. L., & Corbett, H. D. (2001). *Listening to urban kids: School reform and the teachers they want*. Albany: State University of New York Press.

Wilson, C., Robertson, S. J., Herlong, L. H., & Haynes, S. N. (1979). Vicarious effects of time-out in the modification of aggression in the classroom. *Behavior Modification, 3*(1), 97–111. doi:10.1177/014544557931006

Wilson, H. K., Pianta, R. C., & Stuhlman, M. (2007). Typical classroom experiences in first grade: The role of classroom climate and functional risk in the development of social competencies. *Elementary School Journal, 108*(2), 81–96.

Wilson, L. (2007). Great American schools: The power of culture and passion. *Educational Horizons, 86*(1), 33–44.

Wimmer, H., & Perner, J. (1983). Beliefs about beliefs: Representation and constraining function of wrong beliefs in young children's understanding of deception. *Cognition, 13*, 103–128.

Wimmer, L., Bellingrath, S., & von Stockhausen, L. (2016). Cognitive effects of mindfulness training: Results of a pilot study based on a theory driven approach. *Frontiers in Psychology, 7*, Article ID 1037.

Wimmer, M. C., & Howe, M. L. (2009). The development of automatic associative processes and children's false memories. *Journal of Experimental Child Psychology, 104*, 447–465.

Winberg, J. (2005). Mother and newborn baby: Mutual regulation of physiology and behavior—A selective review. *Developmental Psychobiology, 47*, 219–229.

Winkler-Rhoades, N., Carey, S. C., & Spelke, E. S. (2013). Two-year-old children interpret abstract, purely geometric maps. *Developmental Science, 16*, 365–376. doi:10.1111/desc.12038

Winne, P. H. (1995a). Inherent details in self-regulated learning. *Educational Psychologist, 30*, 173–187.

Winne, P. H. (1995b). Self-regulation is ubiquitous but its forms vary with knowledge. *Educational Psychologist, 30*, 223–228.

Winner, E. (1997). Exceptionally high intelligence and schooling. *American Psychologist, 52*, 1070–1081.

Winner, E. (2000). The origins and ends of giftedness. *American Psychologist, 55*, 159–169.

Winner, E. (2006). Development in the arts: Drawing and music. In D. Kuhn, R. S. Siegler, W. Damon, & R. M. Lerner (Eds.), *Handbook of Child Psychology: Vol. 2. Cognition, perception, and language* (6th ed., pp. 859–904). Hoboken, NJ: Wiley.

Winsler, A., & Naglieri, J. (2003). Overt and covert verbal problem-solving strategies: Developmental trends in use, awareness, and relations with task performance in children aged 5 to 17. *Child Development, 74*, 659–678.

Winsler, A., Díaz, R. M., Espinosa, L., & Rodriguez, J. L. (1999). When learning a second language does not mean losing the first: Bilingual language development in low-income, Spanish-speaking children attending bilingual preschool. *Child Development, 70*, 349–362.

Winston, P. (1973). Learning to identify toy block structures. In R. L. Solso (Ed.), *Contemporary issues in cognitive psychology: The Loyola Symposium*. New York, NY: Halsted/Wiley.

Witkow, M. R., & Fuligni, A. J. (2007). Achievement goals and daily school experiences among adolescents with Asian, Latino, and European American backgrounds. *Journal of Educational Psychology, 99*, 584–596.

Witt, A., & Vinter, A. (2013). Children with intellectual disabilities may be impaired in encoding and recollecting incidental information. *Research in Developmental Disabilities, 34*, 864–871. doi:10.1016/j.ridd.2012.11.003

Wittmer, D. (2012). The wonder and complexity of infant and toddler peer relationships. *Young Children, 67*(4), 16–25.

Wittmer, D. S., & Honig, A. S. (1994). Encouraging positive social development in young children. *Young Children, 49*(5), 4–12.

Witvliet, M., van Lier, P. A. C., Cuijpers, P., & Koot, H. M. (2010). Change and stability in childhood clique membership, isolation from cliques, and associated child characteristics. *Journal of Clinical Child and Adolescent Psychology, 39*(1), 12–24. doi:10.1080/15374410903401161

Wodrich, D. L., Tarbox, J., Balles, J., & Gorin, J. (2010). Medical diagnostic consultation concerning mental retardation: An analogue study of school psychologists' attitudes. *Psychology in the Schools, 47*, 246–256.

Wolak, J., Finkelhor, D., Mitchell, K. J., & Ybarra, M. L. (2010). Online "predators" and their victims: Myths, realities, and implications for prevention and treatment. *Psychology of Violence, 1*(S), 13–35. http://dx.doi.org.unco.idm.oclc.org/10.1037/2152-0828.1.S.13

Wolcott, H. F. (1999). *Ethnography: A way of seeing*. Walnut Creek, CA: AltaMira.

Wolf, M., & Bowers, P. G. (1999). The double-deficit hypothesis for the developmental dyslexias. *Journal of Educational Psychology, 91*, 415–438.

Wolfe, D. A., & Wekerle, C. (1997). Pathways to violence in teen dating relationships. In D. Cicchetti & S. L. Toth (Eds.), *Rochester Symposium on Developmental Psychology, Vol. 8. Developmental perspectives on trauma: Theory, research, and intervention* (pp. 315–341). Rochester, NY: University of Rochester Press.

Wolfe, M. B. W., & Goldman, S. R. (2005). Relations between adolescents' text processing and reasoning. *Cognition and Instruction, 23*, 467–502.

Wölfer, R., & Scheithauer, H. (2014). Social influence and bullying behavior: Intervention-based network dynamics of the fairplayer.manual bullying prevention program. *Aggressive Behavior, 40*, 309–319. doi:10.1002/ab.21524

Wolff, P. G. (1966). The causes, controls, and organization of behavior in the neonate. *Psychological Issues, 5*(1, Serial No. 17).

Wolfson, A. R., & Carskadon, M. A. (2005). A survey of factors influencing high school start times. *NASSP Bulletin, 89*(642), 47–66.

Wolke, D. D., Lereya, S. T., Fisher, H. L., Lewis, G. G., & Zammit, S. S. (2014). Bullying in elementary school and psychotic experiences at 18 years: A longitudinal, population-based cohort study. *Psychological Medicine, 44*, 2199–2211. doi:10.1017/S0033291713002912

Wolock, I., Sherman, P., Feldman, L. H., & Metzger, B. (2001). Child abuse and neglect referral patterns: A longitudinal study. *Children and Youth Services Review, 23*, 21–47.

Wong-Lo, M., & Bai, H. (2013). Recommended practices: Cultivating a culturally responsive learning environment for Chinese immigrants and Chinese American students. *Preventing School Failure, 57*(1), 17–21. doi:10.1080/1045988X.2013.731272

Wong, A. M.-Y., Ho, C. S.-H., Au, T. K.-F., McBride, C., Ng, A. K.-H., Yip, L. P.-W., & Lam, C. C.-C. (2017). Reading comprehension, working memory and higher-level language skills in children with SLI and/or dyslexia. *Reading and Writing, 30*, 337–361. http://dx.doi.org.unco.idm.oclc.org/10.1007/s11145-016-9678-0

Wong, H., & Edwards, P. (2013). Nature or nurture: A systematic review of the effect of socioeconomic status on the developmental and cognitive outcomes of children born preterm. *Maternal & Child Health Journal, 17*, 1689–1700. doi:10.1007/s10995-012-1183-8

Wong, S. C. (1993). Promises, pitfalls, and principles of text selection in curricular diversification: The Asian-American case. In T. Perry & J. W. Fraser (Eds.), *Freedom's plow: Teaching in the multicultural classroom* (pp. 109-120). New York, NY: Routledge.

Wood, A., & Wood, B. (2001). *Alphabet adventure.* New York, NY: Scholastic Books.

Wood, C. (2007). *Yardsticks: Children in the classroom ages 4–14.* Turner Falls, MA: Northeast Foundation for Children, Inc.

Wood, D., Bruner, J. S., & Ross, G. (1976). The role of tutoring in problem-solving. *Journal of Child Psychology and Psychiatry, 17*, 89–100.

Wood, J. W. (1998). *Adapting instruction to accommodate students in inclusive settings* (3rd ed.). Upper Saddle River, NJ: Merrill/Prentice Hall.

Wood, M. B., Olson, A. M., Freiberg, E. J., & Vega, R. I. (2013). Fractions as subtraction: An activity-oriented perspective from elementary children. *School Science & Mathematics, 113*, 390–399. doi:10.1111/ssm.12040

Woodlawn Middle School. (n.d.). *Woodlawn Middle School Beavers Code of Conduct.* Retrieved March 2, 2018 from https://www.pbis.org/training/staff/student

Woods, A., Graber, K., & Daum, D. (2012). Children's recess physical activity: Movement patterns and preferences. *Journal of Teaching in Physical Education, 31*, 146–162.

Woodward, L. J., Lu, Z., Morris, A. R., & Healey, D. M. (2017). Preschool self-regulation predicts later mental health and educational achievement in very preterm and typically developing children. *The Clinical Neuropsychologist, 31*, 404–422.

Woody, J. D., D'Souza, H. J., & Russel, R. (2003). Emotions and motivations in first adolescent intercourse: An exploratory study based on object relations theory. *Canadian Journal of Human Sexuality, 12*(1), 35–51.

Woolley, J. D. (1995). The fictional mind: Young children's understanding of pretense, imagination, and dreams. *Developmental Review, 15*, 172–211.

World Health Organization. (2000). *Obesity: Preventing and managing the global epidemic* (WHO Report No. 894). Geneva: Author.

Worley, J. (2012). To speak in a clear voice. *Tribal College Journal, 23*(3), 60–61.

Wouters, S., Doumen, S., Germeijs, V., Colpin, H., & Verschueren, K. (2013). Contingencies of self-worth in early adolescence: The antecedent role of perceived parenting. *Social Development, 22*, 242–258. doi:10.1111/sode.12010

Wright, B. C., & Mahfoud, J. (2012). A child-centred exploration of the relevance of family and friends to theory of mind development. *Scandinavian Journal of Psychology, 53*(1), 32–40. doi:10.1111/j.1467-9450.2011.00920.x

Wright, R. (2009). Methods for improving test scores: The good, the bad, and the ugly. *Kappa Delta Pi Record, 45*, 116–121.

WritersCorps. (2003). *Paint me like I am: Teen poems from WritersCorps.* New York, NY: HarperTempest.

Wu, H., & Chu, S. (2012). Self-determination of young children with special needs from culturally and linguistically diverse backgrounds. *Preventing School Failure, 56*, 149–156. doi:10.1080/1045988X.2011.619221

Wu, P., Liu, X., & Fan, B. (2010). Factors associated with initiation of ecstasy use among US adolescents: Findings from a national survey. *Drug and Alcohol Dependence, 106*(2–3), 193–198.

Wu, R., Gopnik, A., Richardson, D. C., & Kirkham, N. Z. (2011). Infants learn about objects from statistics and people. *Developmental Psychology, 47*, 1220–1229. doi:10.1037/a0024023

Wu, W., West, S. G., & Hughes, J. N. (2010). Effect of grade retention in first grade on psychosocial outcomes. *Journal of Educational Psychology, 102*, 135–152.

Wu, Y., & Schulz, L. E. (2017). Inferring beliefs and desires from emotional reactions to anticipated and observed events. *Child Development, 89*, 649–662.

Wynbrandt, J., & Ludman, M. D. (2000). *The encyclopedia of genetic disorders and birth defects* (2nd ed.). New York, NY: Facts on File.

Wynn, C. T. (2015). A cognitive rationale for a problem-based U.S. history survey. *Teaching History: A Journal of Methods, 40*(1), 28–42.

Wynn, K. (1990). Children's understanding of counting. *Cognition, 36*, 155–193.

Wynn, K. (1992). Addition and subtraction by human infants. *Nature, 358*, 749–750.

Wynn, K. (1995). Infants possess a system of numerical knowledge. *Current Directions in Psychological Science, 4*, 172–177.

Xia, Z., Hancock, R., & Hoeft, F. (2017). Neurobiological bases of reading disorder Part 1: Etiological investigations. *Language and Linguistics Compass, 11*(4), 1–18. doi:10.1111/lnc3.12239

Xiang, P., Ağbuğa, B., Liu, J., & McBride, R. E. (2017). Relatedness need satisfaction, intrinsic motivation, and engagement in secondary school physical education. *Journal of Teaching in Physical Education, 36*, 340–352. http://dx.doi.org.unco.idm.oclc.org/10.1123/jtpe.2017-0034

Xiao, S. X., Cook, R. E., Martin, C. L., Nielson, M. G., & Field, R. D. (2018). Will they listen to me? An examination of in-group gender bias in children's communication beliefs. *Sex Roles. Advance online publication.* http://dx.doi.org.unco.idm.oclc.org/10.1007/s11199-018-0924-6

Xu, F., & Kushnir, T. (2013). Infants are rational constructivist learners. *Current Directions in Psychological Science, 22*(1), 28–32.

Xu, F., & Spelke, E. S. (2000). Large number discrimination in 6-month-old infants. *Cognition, 74*, B1–B11.

Xu, J., Saether, L., & Sommerville, J. A. (2016). Experience facilitates the emergence of sharing behavior among 7.5-month-old infants. *Developmental Psychology, 52*, 1732–1743. http://dx.doi.org.unco.idm.oclc.org/10.1037/dev0000174

Xu, L., & Clarke, D. (2012). What does distributed cognition tell us about student learning of science? *Research in Science Education, 42*, 491–510. doi:10.1007/s11165-011-9207-8

Xu, M.-Q., Sun, W.-S., Liu, B. X., Feng, G.-Y., Yu, L., Yang, L., . . . Lin, H. (2009). Prenatal malnutrition and adult schizophrenia: Further evidence from the 1959–1961 Chinese famine. *Schizophrenia Bulletin, 35*, 568–576.

Xu, Y., Farver, J. A. M., Chang, L., Zhang, Z., & Yu, L. (2007). Moving away or fitting in? Understanding shyness in Chinese children. *Merrill-Palmer Quarterly: Journal of Developmental Psychology, 53*, 527–556.

Xue, J. J., Ooh, J. J., & Magiati, I. I. (2014). Family functioning in Asian families raising children with autism spectrum disorders: The role of capabilities and positive meanings. *Journal of Intellectual Disability Research, 58*, 406–420. doi:10.1111/jir.12034

Yaden, D. B., Jr., & Templeton, S. (Eds.). (1986). *Metalinguistic awareness and beginning literacy: Conceptualizing what it means to read and write.* Portsmouth, NH: Heinemann.

Yakovlev, P. I., & Lecours, A. R. (1967). The myelogenetic cycles of regional maturation of the brain. In A. Minkowski (Ed.), *Regional development of the brain in early life* (pp. 3–70). Oxford, England: Blackwell Scientific.

Yamamoto, Y., & Sonnenschein, S. (2016). Family contexts of academic socialization: The role of culture, ethnicity, and socioeconomic status. *Research in Human Development*, *13*(3), 183–190. doi:10.1080/15427609.2016.1194711

Yang, F., & Tsai, C. (2010). Reasoning about science-related uncertain issues and epistemological perspectives among children. *Instructional Science*, *38*, 325–354.

Yang, T.-C., & Chen, D. (2018). A multi-group path analysis of the relationship between perceived racial discrimination and self-rated stress: How does it vary across racial/ethnic groups? *Ethnicity & Health*, *23*, 249–275. http://dx.doi.org.unco.idm.oclc.org/10.1080/13557858.2016.1258042

Yardley, A. (2014). Children describing the world: Mixed-method research by child practitioners developing an intergenerational dialogue. *Educational & Child Psychology*, *31*(1), 48–62.

Yasri, P., & Mancy, R. (2010, June–July). *Perceptions of the relationship between evolutionary theory and biblical explanations of the origins of life and their effects on the learning of evolution among high school students.* Paper presented at the International Conference of the Learning Sciences, Conference Proceedings. Chicago, IL.

Yates, M., & Youniss, J. (1996). A developmental perspective on community service in adolescence. *Social Development*, *5*, 85–111.

Yau, J., & Smetana, J. G. (2003). Conceptions of moral, social-conventional, and personal events among Chinese preschoolers in Hong Kong. *Child Development*, *74*, 647–658.

Yeager, E. A., Foster, S. J., Maley, S. D., Anderson, T., Morris, J. W., III, & Davis, O. L., Jr. (1997, March). *The role of empathy in the development of historical understanding.* Paper presented at the annual meeting of the American Educational Research Association, Chicago.

Yermolayeva, Y., & Rakison, D. H. (2014). Connectionist modeling of developmental changes in infancy: Approaches, challenges, and contributions. *Psychological Bulletin*, *140*(1), 224–255. http://dx.doi.org.unco.idm.oclc.org/10.1037/a0032150

Yiallourou, S. R., Wallace, E. M., Miller, S. L., & Horne, R. S. C. (2016). Effects of intrauterine growth restriction on sleep and the cardiovascular system: The use of melatonin as a potential therapy? *Sleep Medicine Reviews*, *26*, 64–73. doi:10.1016/j.smrv.2015.04.001

Yildirim, K., Rasinski, T., Ates, S., Fitzgerald, S., Zimmerman, B., & Yildiz, M. (2014). The relationship between reading fluency and vocabulary in fifth grade Turkish students. *Literacy Research & Instruction*, *53*, 72–89. doi:10.1080/19388071.2013.812166

Yim, D., & Rudoy, J. (2013). Implicit statistical learning and language skills in bilingual children. *Journal of Speech, Language, and Hearing Research*, *56*(1), 310–322.

Ying, Y.-W., & Han, M. (2007). The longitudinal effect of intergenerational gap in acculturation on conflict and mental health in Southeast Asian American adolescents. *American Journal of Orthopsychiatry*, *77*, 61–66.

Yoo, Y. S., Popp, J., & Robinson, J. (2014). Maternal distress influences young children's family representations through maternal view of child behavior and parent–child interactions. *Child Psychiatry and Human Development*, *45*(1), 52–64. http://dx.doi.org.unco.idm.oclc.org/10.1007/s10578-013-0377-7

Yoon, C. (2009). Self-regulated learning and instructional factors in the scientific inquiry of scientifically gifted Korean middle school students. *Gifted Child Quarterly*, *53*, 203–216.

Yoon, E., Chang, C., Kim, S., Clawson, A., Cleary, S., Hansen, M., . . . Gomes, A. M. (2013). A meta-analysis of acculturation/enculturation and mental health. *Journal of Counseling Psychology*, *60*(1), 15–30. doi:10.1037/a0030652

Youn, M. (2016). Inequality from the first day of school: The role of teachers' academic intensity and sense of responsibility in moderating the learning growth gap. *Journal of Educational Research*, *109*(1), 50–67. doi:10.1080/00220671.2014.918529

Young-Suk, K., Al Otaiba, S., Folsom, J. S., Greulich, L., & Puranik, C. (2014). Evaluating the dimensionality of first-grade written composition. *Journal of Speech, Language & Hearing Research*, *57*, 199–211. doi:10.1044/1092-4388(2013/12-0152)

Young-Suk, K., Apel, K., Al Otaiba, S., Nippold, M., & Joffe, V. (2013). The relation of linguistic awareness and vocabulary to word reading and spelling for first-grade students participating in response to intervention. *Language, Speech & Hearing Services in Schools*, *44*, 337–347. doi:10.1044/0161-1461(2013/12-0013)

Young, A. G., Alibali, M. W., & Kalish, C. W. (2012). Disagreement and causal learning: Others' hypotheses affect children's evaluations of evidence. *Developmental Psychology*, *48*(5), 1242-1253. doi:10.1037/a0027540

Young, G. (2012). A unitary Neo-Piagetian/Neo-Eriksonian model of development: Fundamental assumptions and meta-issues. *New Ideas in Psychology*, *30*, 241–249. doi:10.1016/j.newideapsych.2011.11.002

Young, J. M., Howell, A. N., & Hauser-Cram, P. (2005, April). *Predictors of mastery motivation in children with disabilities born prematurely.* Paper presented at the biennial meeting of the Society for Research in Child Development, Atlanta, GA.

Young, R., Sproeber, N., Groschwitz, R. C., Preiss, M., & Plener, P. L. (2014). Why alternative teenagers self-harm: Exploring the link between non-suicidal self-injury, attempted suicide and adolescent identity. *BMC Psychiatry*, *14*, Article ID 137.

Youngblood, J., II, & Spencer, M. B. (2002). Integrating normative identity processes and academic support requirements for special needs adolescents: The application of an identity-focused cultural ecological (ICE) perspective. *Applied Developmental Science*, *6*, 95–108.

Youniss, J. (1983). Social construction of adolescence by adolescents and their parents. In H. D. Grotevant & C. R. Cooper (Eds.), *Adolescent development in the family: New directions for child development* (No. 22; pp. 27-42). San Francisco, CA: Jossey-Bass.

Youniss, J., & Yates, M. (1999). Youth service and moral-civic identity: A case of everyday morality. *Educational Psychology Review*, *11*, 361–376.

Ysseldyke, J. E., & Algozzine, B. (1984). *Introduction to special education.* Boston, MA: Houghton Mifflin.

Yu, J., Cheah, C. S. L., & Calvin, G. (2016). Acculturation, psychological adjustment, and parenting styles of Chinese immigrant mothers in the United States. *Cultural Diversity and Ethnic Minority Psychology*, *22*, 504–516. doi:10.1037/cdp0000091

Yuan, L., Uttal, D., & Gentner, D. (2017). Analogical processes in children's understanding of spatial representations. *Developmental Psychology*. Advance online publication. doi:10.1037/dev0000302

Yuill, N. (2009). The relation between ambiguity understanding and metalinguistic discussion of joking riddles in good and poor comprehenders: Potential for intervention and possible processes of change. *First Language*, *29*(1), 65–79.

Zaff, J. F., Donlan, A. E., Pufall Jones, E. E., & Lin, E. S. (2015). Supportive developmental systems for children and youth: A theoretical framework for comprehensive community initiatives. *Journal of Applied Developmental Psychology*, *40*, 1–7. doi:10.1016/j.appdev.2015.03.004

Zahn-Waxler, C. (1991). The case for empathy: A developmental perspective. *Psychological Inquiry*, *2*, 155–158. doi:10.1207/s15327965pli0202_16

Zahn-Waxler, C., & Kochanska, G. (1990). The origins of guilt. In R. A. Dientsbier (Series Ed.), & R. A. Thompson (Vol. Ed.), *The 36th Annual Nebraska Symposium on Motivation: Socioemotional development. Current theory and research in motivation* (Vol. 36, pp. 183–258). Lincoln: University of Nebraska Press.

Zahn-Waxler, C., & Robinson, J. (1995). Empathy and guilt: Early origins of feelings of responsibility. In J. P. Tangney & K. W. Fischer (Eds.), *Self-conscious emotions: The psychology of shame, guilt, embarrassment, and pride* (pp. 143–173). New York, NY: Guilford Press.

Zahn-Waxler, C., Radke-Yarrow, M., Wagner, E., & Chapman, M. (1992). Development of concern for others. *Developmental Psychology, 28*, 126–136.

Zajdel, R. T., Bloom, J., Fireman, G., & Larsen, J. T. (2013). Children's understanding and experience of mixed emotions: The roles of age, gender, and empathy. *The Journal of Genetic Psychology: Research and Theory on Human Development, 174*, 582–603. doi:10.1080/00221325.2012.732125

Zajicek-Farber, M. L., Mayer, L. M., & Daughtery, L. G. (2012). Connections among parental mental health, stress, child routines, and early emotional behavioral regulation of preschool children in low-income families. *Journal of the Society for Social Work and Research, 3*(1). doi:10.5243/jsswr.2012.3

Zajonc, R. B., & Mullally, P. R. (1997). Birth order: Reconciling conflicting effects. *American Psychologist, 52*, 685–699.

Zakar, T., & Mesiano, S. (2011). How does progesterone relax the uterus in pregnancy? *New England Journal of Medicine, 364*, 972–973. doi:http://dx.doi.org/10.1056/NEJMcibr1100071

Zalewski, B M., Patro, B., Veldhorst, M., Kouwenhoven, S., Crespo Escobar, P., Calvo Lerma, J., . . . Szajewska, H. (2017). Nutrition of infants and young children (one to three years) and its effect on later health: A systematic review of current recommendations (EarlyNutrition project). *Critical Reviews in Food Science and Nutrition, 57*, 489–500.

Zalewski, M., Lengua, L. J., Thompson, S. F., & Kiff, C. J. (2016). Income, cumulative risk, and longitudinal profiles of hypothalamic–pituitary–adrenal axis activity in preschool-age children. *Development and Psychopathology, 28*(2), 341–353. doi:10.1017/S0954579415000474

Zamarian, L., Ischebeck, A., & Delazer, M. (2009). Neuroscience of learning arithmetic—Evidence from brain imaging studies. *Neuroscience and Biobehavioral Reviews, 33*, 909–925.

Zambo, D. (2003, April). *Thinking about reading: Talking to children with learning disabilities.* Paper presented at the annual meeting of the American Educational Research Association, Chicago, IL.

Zambo, D., & Brem, S. K. (2004). Emotion and cognition in students who struggle to read: New insights and ideas. *Reading Psychology, 25*, 1–16.

Zampini, L., Suttora, C., D'Odorico, L., & Zanchi, P. (2013). Sequential reasoning and listening text comprehension in preschool children. *European Journal of Developmental Psychology, 10*, 563–579. doi:10.1080/17405629.2013.766130

Zeanah, C. H. (2000). Disturbances of attachment in young children adopted from institutions. *Journal of Developmental and Behavioral Pediatrics, 21*, 230–236.

Zee, M., & Koomen, H. M. Y. (2017). Similarities and dissimilarities between teachers' and students' relationship views in upper elementary school: The role of personal teacher and student attributes. *Journal of School Psychology, 64*, 43–60. http://dx.doi.org.unco.idm.oclc.org/10.1016/j.jsp.2017.04.007

Zehr, J. L., Culbert, K. M., Sisk, C. L., & Klump, K. L. (2007). An association of early puberty with disordered eating and anxiety in a population of undergraduate women and men. *Hormones and Behavior, 52*, 427–435.

Zelazo, P. D., Müller, U., Frye, D., & Marcovitch, S. (2003). The development of executive function in early childhood. *Monographs of the Society for Research in Child Development, 68*(3, Serial No. 274).

Zentner, M., & Eerola, T. (2010). Rhythmic engagement with music in infancy. *Proceedings of the National Academy of Sciences of the United States of America, 107*, 5768–5773.

Zero to Three: National Center for Infants, Toddlers, and Families. (2002). Temperament. Retrieved from http://www.zerotothree.org/Archive/TEMPERAM.HTM

Zero to Three: National Center for Infants, Toddlers, and Families. (2010). *It's too mushy! It's too spicy! The peas are touching the chicken! (Or, how to handle your picky eater).* Retrieved from http://www.zerotothree.org/site/PageServer?pagename?ter_key_health_picky

Zhang, C. C., Bingham, G. G., & Quinn, M. M. (2017). The associations among preschool children's growth in early reading, executive function, and invented spelling skills. *Reading & Writing, 30*, 1705–1728. doi:10.1007/s11145-017-9746-0

Zhang, D., Chin, C., & Li, L. (2017). Metalinguistic awareness in bilingual children's word reading: A cross-lagged panel study on cross-linguistic transfer facilitation. *Applied Psycholinguistics, 38*, 395–426. doi:10.1017/S0142716416000278

Zhang, M., & Kong, L. (2012). An exploration of reasons for Shanghai's success in the OECD Program for International Student Assessment (PISA) 2009. *Frontiers of Education in China, 7*, 124–162. doi:10.3868/s110-001-012-0007-3

Zhang, W. Z., Cao, C. C., Wang, M. M., Ji, L. S., & Cao, Y. C. (2016). Monoamine oxidase A (MAOA) and catechol-o-methyltransferase (COMT) gene polymorphisms interact with maternal parenting in association with adolescent reactive aggression but not proactive aggression: Evidence of differential susceptibility. *Journal of Youth & Adolescence, 45*, 812–829. doi:10.1007/s10964-016-0442-1

Zhang, W., Rajendran, K., Ham, J., Finik, J., Buthmann, J., Davey, K., . . . Nomura, Y. (2018). Prenatalexposure to disaster-related traumatic stress and developmental trajectories of temperament in early childhood: Superstorm Sandy pregnancy study. *Journal of Affective Disorders, 234*, 335–345. http://dx.doi.org.unco.idm.oclc.org/10.1016/j.jad.2018.02.067

Zhou, N., Lam, S., & Chan, K. (2012). The Chinese classroom paradox: A cross-cultural comparison of teacher controlling behaviors. *Journal of Educational Psychology, 104*, 1162–1174. doi:10.1037/a0027609

Zhou, Q., Eisenberg, N., Losoya, S. H., Fabes, R. A., Reiser, M., Guthrie, I. K., . . . Shepard, S. A. (2002). The relations of parental warmth and positive expressiveness to children's empathy-related responding and social functioning: A longitudinal study. *Child Development, 73*, 893–915.

Zhu, M. I., Urhahne, D., & Rubie-Davies, C. M. (2018). The longitudinal effects of teacher judgement and different teacher treatment on students' academic outcomes. *Educational Psychology, 38*, 648–668. doi:10.1080/01443410.2017.1412399

Zhu, X., Sun, H., Chen, A., & Ennis, C. (2012). Measurement invariance of expectancy-value questionnaire in physical education. *Measurement in Physical Education & Exercise Science, 16*(1), 41–54. doi:10.1080/1091367X.2012.639629

Ziegert, D. I., Kistner, J. A., Castro, R., & Robertson, B. (2001). Longitudinal study of young children's responses to challenging achievement situations. *Child Development, 72*, 609–624.

Ziegler, S. G. (1987). Effects of stimulus cueing on the acquisition of groundstrokes by beginning tennis players. *Journal of Applied Behavior Analysis, 20*, 405–411.

Zigler, E. (2003). Forty years of believing in magic is enough. *Social Policy Report, 17*(1), 10.

Zigler, E. F., & Finn-Stevenson, M. (1992). Applied developmental psychology. In M. H. Bornstein & M. E. Lamb (Eds.), *Developmental psychology: An advanced textbook* (pp. 677–729). Hillsdale, NJ: Erlbaum.

Zigler, E., & Styfco, S. J. (2010). *The hidden history of Head Start.* New York, NY: Oxford University Press.

Zilberstein, K., & Messer, E. A. (2010). Building a secure base: Treatment of a child with disorganized attachment. *Clinical Social Work Journal, 38*(1), 85–97.

Zimmer-Gembeck, M., & Skinner, E. (2008). Adolescents coping with stress: development and diversity. *Prevention Researcher, 15*(4), 3–7.

Zimmerman, B. J. (2004). Sociocultural influence and students' development of academic self-regulation: A social-cognitive perspective. In D. M. McNerney & S. Van Etten (Eds.), *Big theories revisited* (pp. 139–164). Greenwich, CT: Information Age.

Zimmerman, B. J., & Cleary, T. J. (2009). Motives to self-regulate learning. In K. R. Wentzel & A. Wigfield (Eds.), *Handbook of motivation at school* (pp. 247–264). New York, NY: Routledge.

Zimmerman, B. J., & Risemberg, R. (1997). Self-regulatory dimensions of academic learning and motivation. In G. D. Phye (Ed.), *Handbook of academic learning: Construction of knowledge* (pp. 105–125). San Diego, CA: Academic Press.

Zimmerman, B. J., & Schunk, D. H. (2004). Self-regulating intellectual processes and outcomes; A social cognitive perspective. In D. Y. Dai & R. J. Sternberg (Eds.), *Motivation, emotion, and cognition: Integrative perspectives on intellectual functioning and development* (pp. 323–349). Mahwah, NJ: Erlbaum.

Zimmerman, C. (2007). The development of scientific thinking skills in elementary and middle school. *Developmental Review, 27,* 172–223.

Zimmerman, H. T., & McClain, L. R. (2016). Family learning outdoors: Guided participation on a nature walk. *Journal of Research in Science Teaching, 53,* 919–942. doi:10.1002/tea.21254

Ziv, M., Smadja, M., & Aram, D. (2013). Mothers' mental-state discourse with preschoolers during storybook reading and wordless storybook telling. *Early Childhood Research Quarterly, 28*(1), 177–186. doi:10.1016/j.ecresq.2012.05.005

Zosuls, K. M., Field, R. D., Martin, C., Andrews, N. Z., & England, D. E. (2014). Gender-based relationship efficacy: Children's self-perceptions in intergroup contexts. *Child Development, 85,* 1663–1676. doi:10.1111/cdev.12209

Zucker, T. A., Cabell, S. Q., Justice, L. M., Pentimonti, J. M., & Kaderavek, J. N. (2013). The role of frequent, interactive prekindergarten shared reading in the longitudinal development of language and literacy skills. *Developmental Psychology, 49,* 1425–1439. doi:10.1037/a0030347

Zumbrunn, S., & Bruning, R. (2013). Improving the writing and knowledge of emergent writers: The effects of self-regulated strategy development. *Reading & Writing, 26,* 91–110. doi:10.1 bv007/s11145-012-9384-5

Name Index

Subject Index